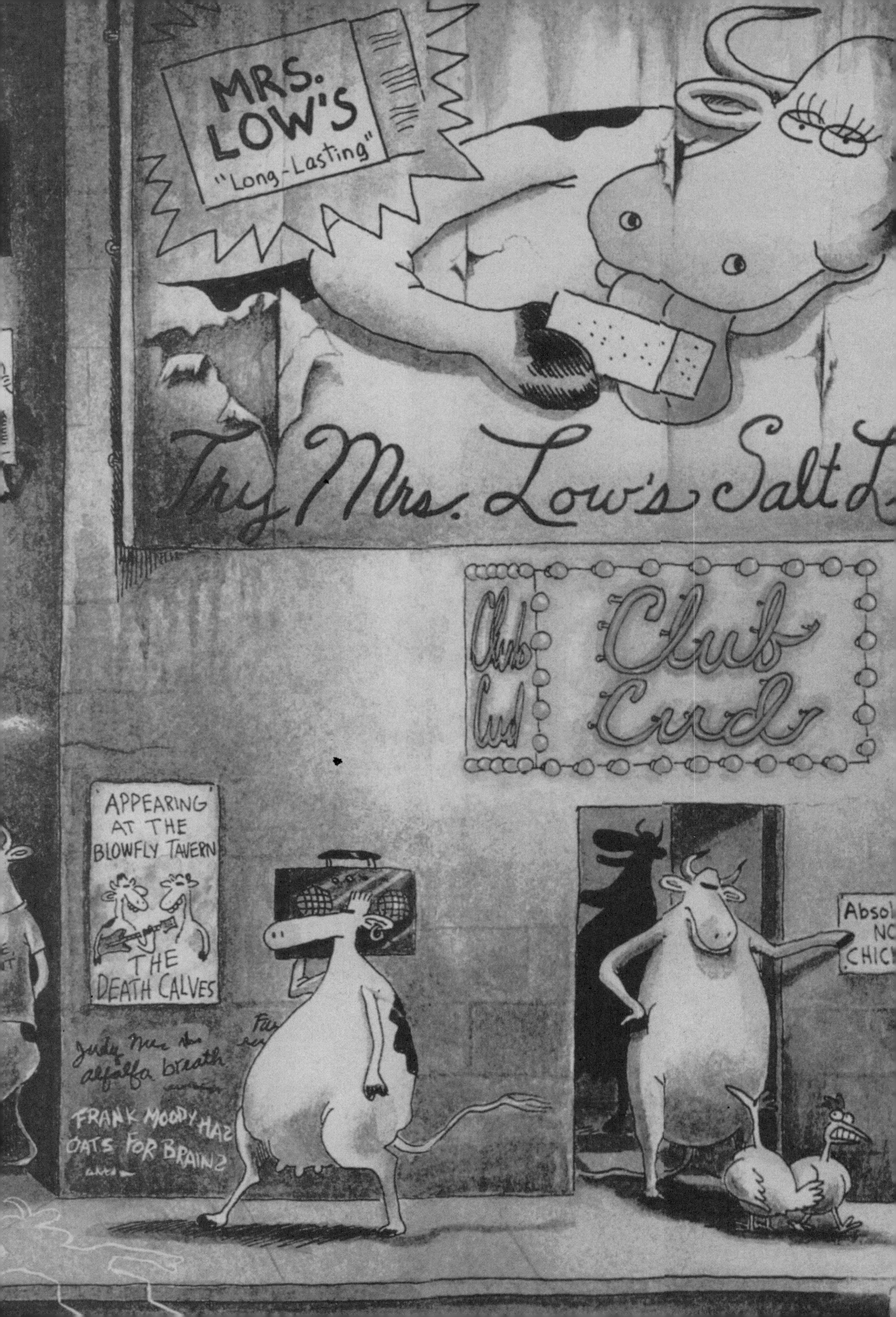
MRS. LOW'S
"Long-Lasting"
Try Mrs. Low's Salt L
Club Cud
Club Cud
APPEARING AT THE BLOWFLY TAVERN
THE DEATH CALVES
Judy ... alfalfa breath
FRANK MOODY HAS OATS FOR BRAINS
Absol
NO
CHICK

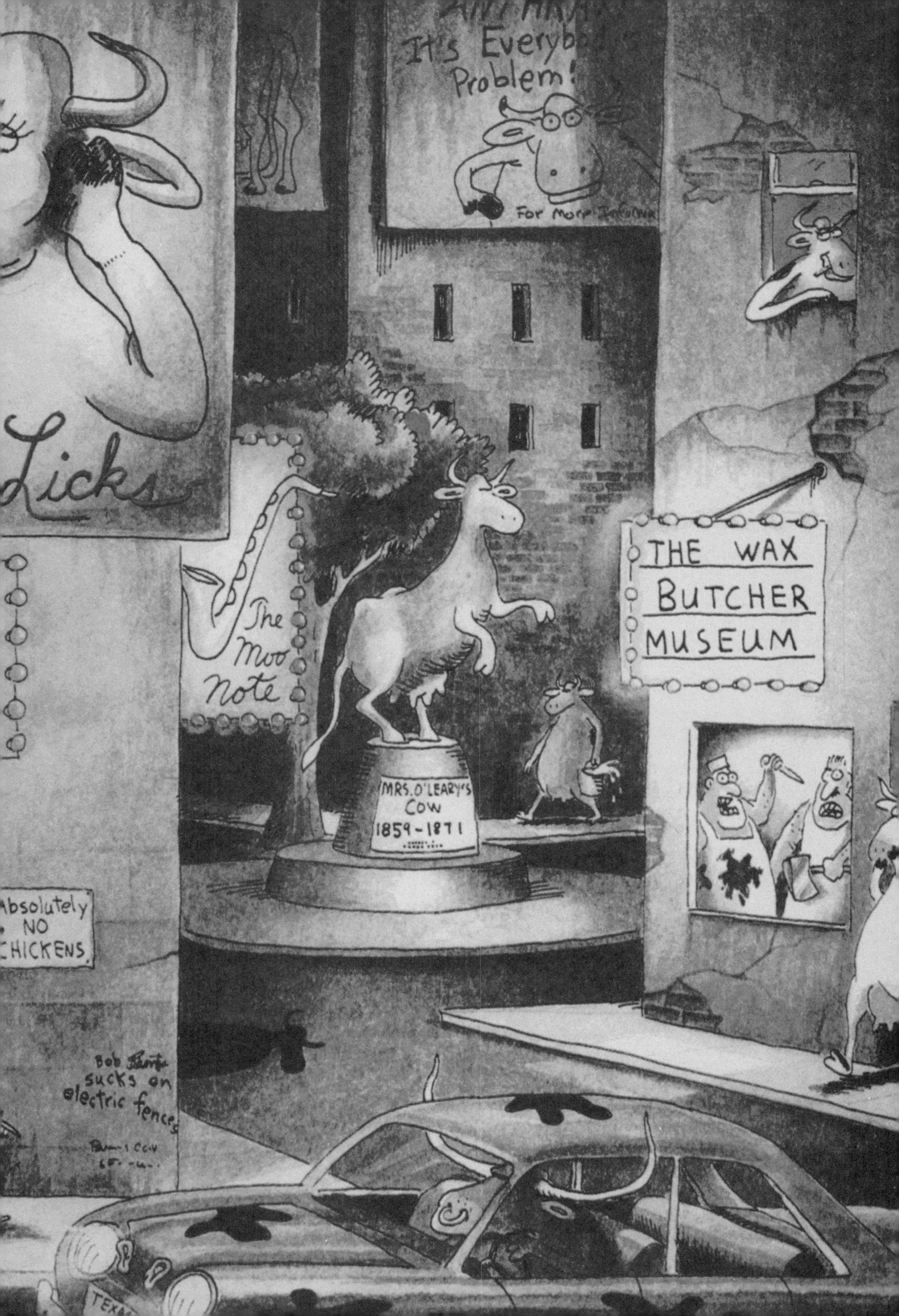

It's Everyb
Problem!
For More Informa
Licks
The Moo Note
THE WAX BUTCHER MUSEUM
MRS. O'LEARY'S COW 1859-1871
Absolutely NO CHICKENS
Bob sucks on electric fences

P9-DUC-880

THE COMPLETE FAR SIDE

VOLUME TWO
1987-1994

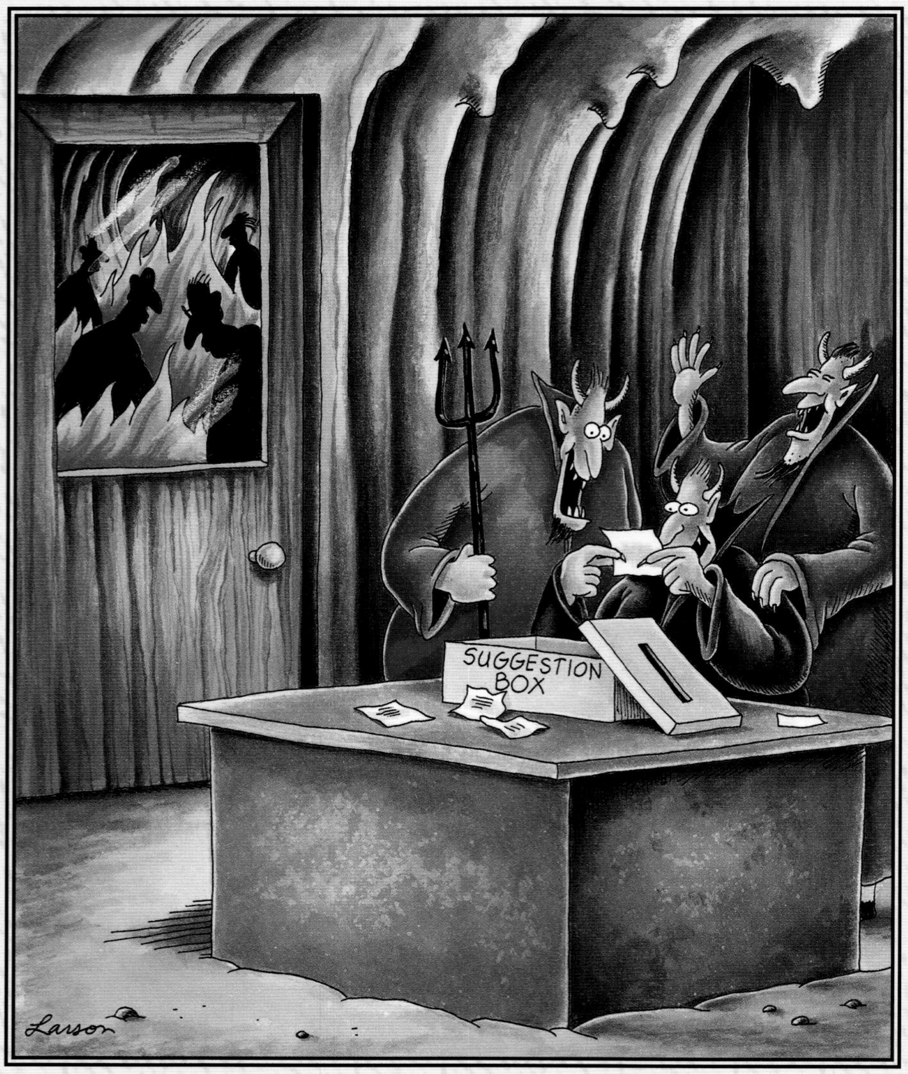
SUGGESTION BOX
Larson

THE COMPLETE FAR SIDE

VOLUME TWO
1987–1994

Gary Larson

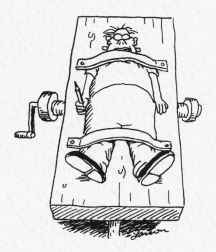

Andrews McMeel Publishing
an Andrews McMeel Universal company
Kansas City

The Complete Far Side copyright © 2003 by FarWorks, Inc.;
The Far Side® cartoons copyright © 1979,
1980, 1981, 1982, 1983, 1984, 1985, 1986, 1987, 1988, 1990,
1991, 1992, 1993, 1994, 1995, 1996, 1998, 1999, 2002, 2003
by FarWorks, Inc. All Rights Reserved.
The Far Side® is a registered trademark of FarWorks, Inc.

Printed in Hong Kong and bound in China. No part of this
publication may be reproduced, stored in a retrieval system,
transmitted in any form or by any means, or otherwise
circulated in any form, binding, or cover, other than
the form, binding, and cover in which it was
published, without the prior written
permission of the copyright owner.

For information, write Andrews McMeel Publishing,
an Andrews McMeel Universal company,
4520 Main Street, Kansas City, Missouri 64111.

First Edition
First Printing, July 2003
Sixth Printing, October 2007

Library of Congress Cataloging-in-Publication Data
Larson, Gary.
  [Far side]
  The Complete Far Side / Gary Larson.
      p. cm.
"Presents every Far side cartoon ever syndicated. More than 4,000 cartoons,
1,100 which have never been published in a book, are included in this
two-volume, slipcased treasure trove"--CIP text.
  ISBN 0-7407-2113-5
  1. American wit and humor, Pictorial. 2. Caricatures and
cartoons--United States--History--20th century. I. Title.

NC1429.L32A4 2003
741.5'973--dc21

                             2003045301

Produced by Lionheart Books, Ltd.
5200 Peachtree Rd. #2103,
Atlanta, Georgia 30341
Designed by Michael Reagan
Printed and bound through Asia Pacific Offset
Cover, slipcase, and page xxi paintings by Jerry Tiritilli

CONTENTS

Volume Two

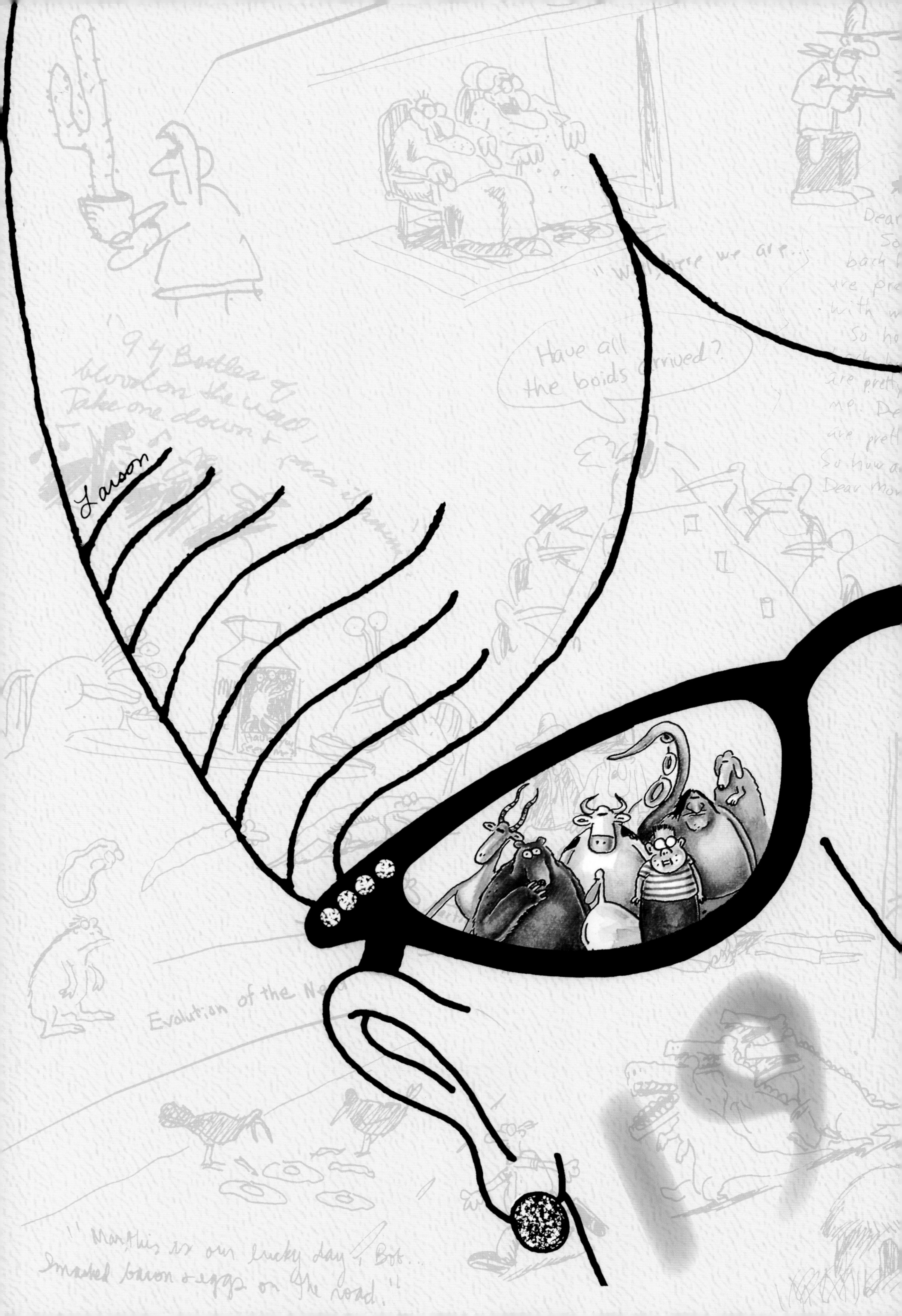
Larson
Have all the boids arrived?

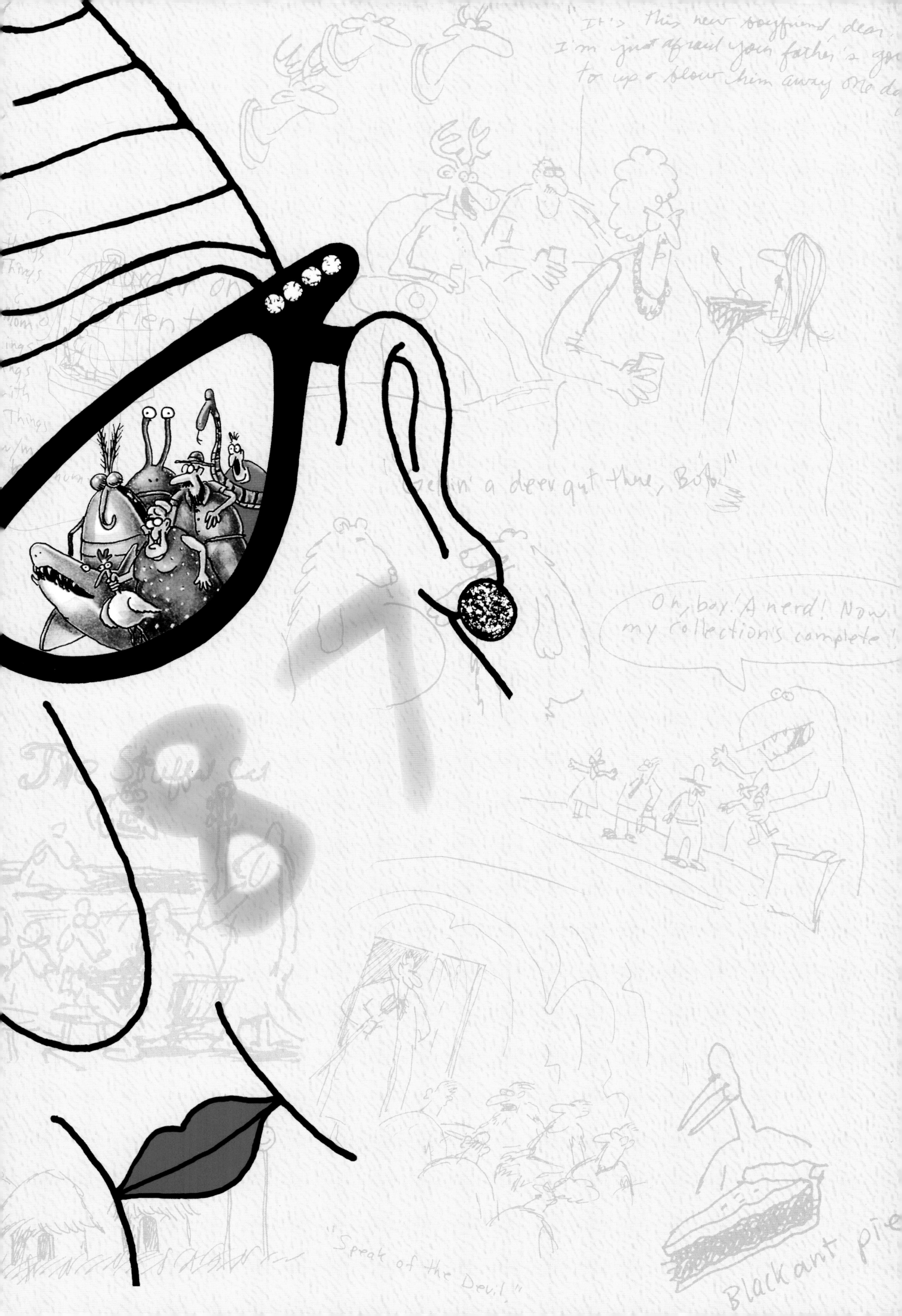

Oh, boy! A nerd! Now my collection's complete!
"Speak of the Devil"
Black ant pie

The Jungle in My Room

When I was growing up, Saturday mornings were paradise. As soon as I got my 25¢ allowance, I'd jump on my bike and head for the local drugstore. I had just two things on my mind: a Big Hunk candy bar and a *Tarzan* comic book.

If *Tarzan* wasn't available, I only had one backup choice: *Turok, Son of Stone. Turok* was about a couple of Indian braves trapped in this prehistoric valley, and they were constantly fighting off dinosaurs with their poison arrows. (Worked for me.)

That was it: *Tarzan* or *Turok*. (Candy bar-wise, I was more flexible.) Everything else was just taking up valuable shelf space. I mean, what was the deal with *Archie*? Give me a break! I never could figure out who could get their heart racing when they read about Archie and Jughead getting into "hot water" at Riverdale High School and—Oh, my God!—being sent to Mr. Weatherbee's office. (Although, I admit, Betty was sort of cute.)

There was this one issue of *Tarzan* that had a great impact on me—even more than the one where he battled the crocodile men. (That was pretty exciting, though; Archie, for the record, would have gotten his ass kicked by the crocodile men.) The *Tarzan* issue that I coveted was this one that had a dictionary in the back containing the *entire vocabulary* of the great apes!

This was a gold mine. Edgar Rice Burroughs, for those of you who haven't read the books, had created an actual language for the great apes. If you really wanted to be "inside" this world when you read about Tarzan's various adventures, you had to know Ape. Oddly enough, the apes themselves always mixed a little English in with their own language, but I never thought about that a whole lot.

I memorized that entire dictionary. (Well, it was only one or two pages long; they *were* apes, you know.) But today there are just a few words I still recall, especially *kreegah* and *bundolo*. English translation: "beware" and "kill," respectively. *Kreegah* and *bundolo* seemed to come up a lot in the jungle.

Note: Tarzan, for the record, never uttered "cowabunga" or "oongowa." They're Hollywood inventions, as far as I know. And the same goes for "Cheetah." Tarzan never had a sidekick chimpanzee named Cheetah. *Sheetah*, on the other hand, was the Ape word for leopard. So, theoretically, if a leopard ever got inside his treehouse, Tarzan might say something like, "Jane! Kreegah! ... Sheetah! ... Tarzan bundolo!" Now you're talking Ape.

However, if there was ever a reason to cry "foul" on the subject of Tarzan, it was what the movie makers did to his famous Tarzan yell. What in the hell was that? Were we all supposed to recoil in fear at the sound of someone yodeling in a tree? Even as a little kid, I never could believe that someone had done that to Tarzan's "victory cry," a sound that Burroughs described as "shrill and horrible ... an awful cry ... a roaring shriek ... fearsome ... blood-curdling ... inhuman." He did *not* say "a sort of yodeling sound ... like someone being goosed while singing. ..."

But my growing interest in Nature began to conflict with my zeal for Tarzan. I remember being especially troubled by the countless varieties of tropical insects and parasites he would have been exposed to. Raised by apes, maybe, but still basically a half-naked Brit. And Tarzan, equipped with two standard-issue opposable thumbs, was described as being able to "fly" through the forest canopy like a monkey. This was getting tough to take, but I was still hanging in there. (As Judy Tenuta might say, "It could happen.")

And then there was this: Where did Tarzan get his hair cut? And his shave? Did you ever see any image of him with a beard? It seems to me, if you were (1) raised by apes, and (2) lived in the jungle, you'd sort of look like this:

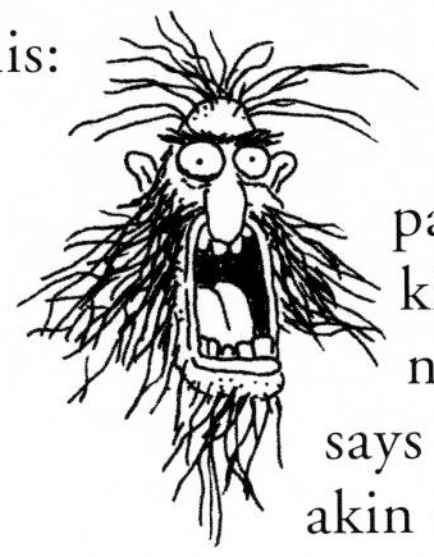

My final problem, which perhaps made me have to part ways with The Lord of the Jungle, was this: What kind of apes did Tarzan get raised by? Mr. Burroughs never comes right out and says "chimpanzees"—he just says "apes." Their physical description is something more akin to a gorilla, but they weren't gorillas, because the author distinguishes them from Tarzan's apes. In Africa, ape-wise, there's nothing left. (Yes, I know about bonobos; he wasn't Tarzan of the bonobos.) So he was Tarzan of *what* apes? This has driven me crazy all my life. (I had to share.)

I have no clear idea why I've written this essay on the subject of Tarzan. (You may be wondering the same thing.) I guess this ape-man has been such a frequent subject of mine, and such an enduring, pop-cultural icon, that I just had to go back. In particular, I recognize today, the artistic style of those comic books had an influence on the way I drew vines, ferns, trees, lions, buffaloes, spears, huts, and a lot of other jungle "stuff"—especially gorillas. The eyes of gorillas were almost never revealed in those early comics; they were only implied by the dark shadow created from an overhanging browridge. I loved that. I stole that.

Still, *Tarzan* was a great yarn for a kid like me, who could spend hours in his room and yet be somewhere far, far away. I suppose if I had built more model airplanes and cars, I would be a little more mechanically inclined than I am today. Edgar Rice Burroughs, however, stoked my imagination. His ape-man creation fed my interests in wild animals, Africa, and Nature as a whole—even if Tarzan eventually posed a few problems in logic for me.

Now Mowgli: There's a jungle character that makes perfect sense.

1/3/87

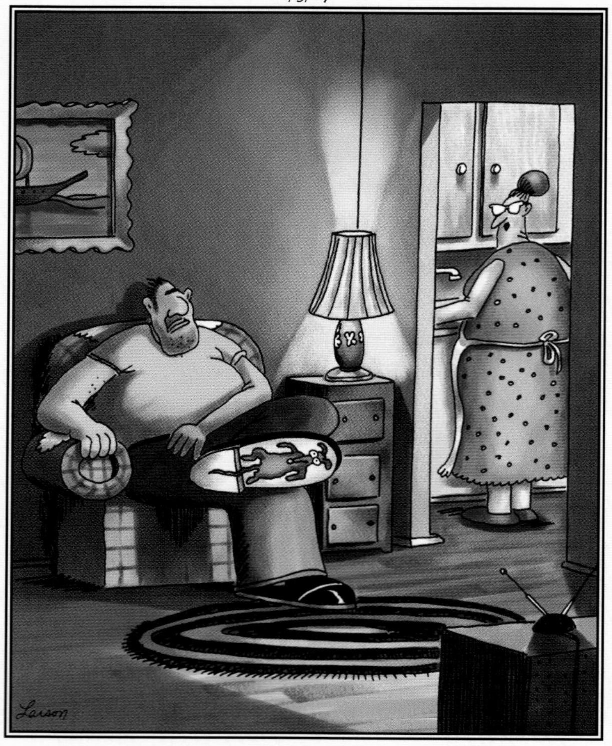
Larson

Helen paused. With an audible "wumph," Muffy's familiar yipping had ended, and only the sounds of Ed's football game now emanated from the living room.

1/2/87

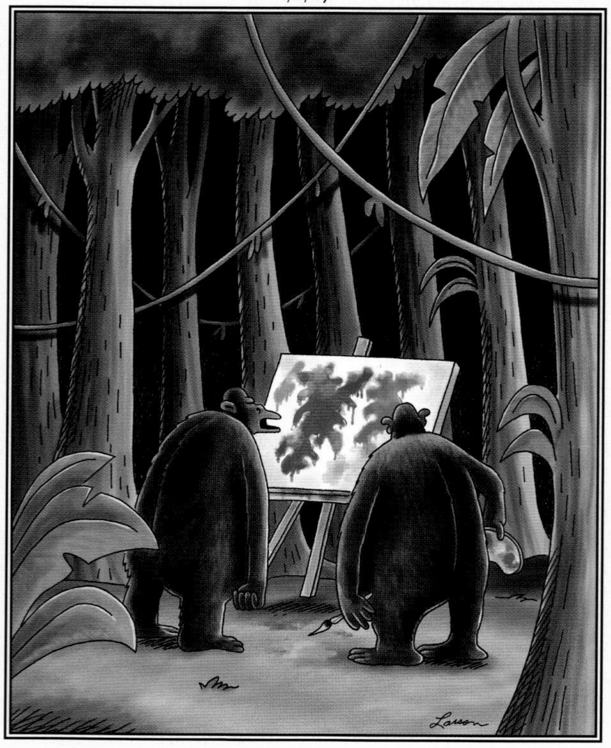
Larson

"I'll *tell* you what it looks like—it looks like it was done by a chimpanzee."

1/1/87

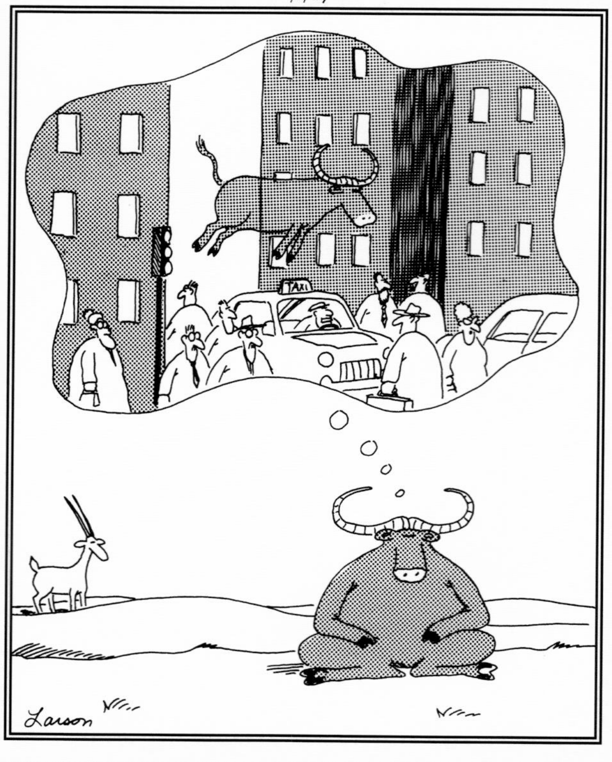
TAXI
Larson

Astral traveling in water buffaloes

1/7/87

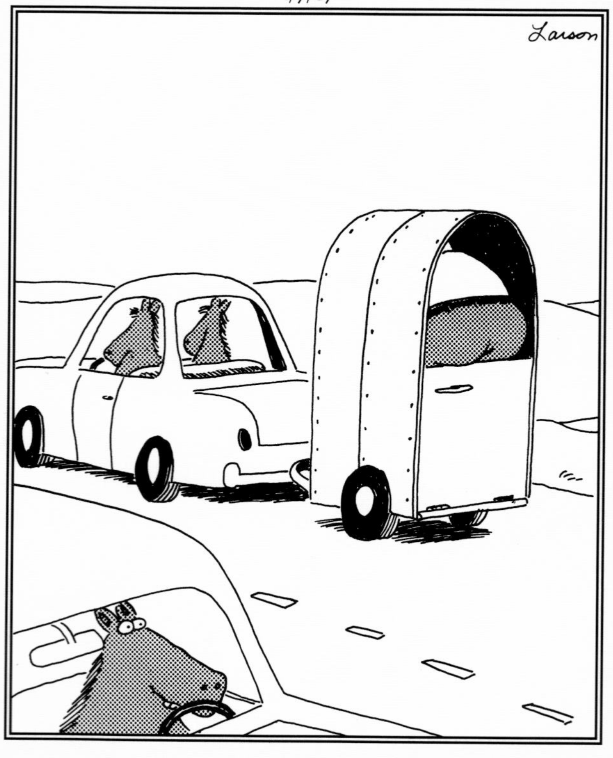
Larson

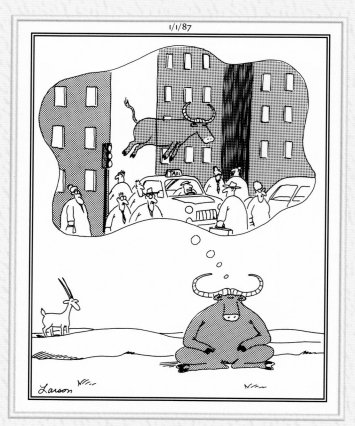

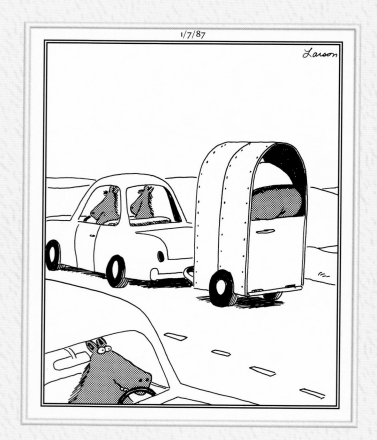

1/12/87

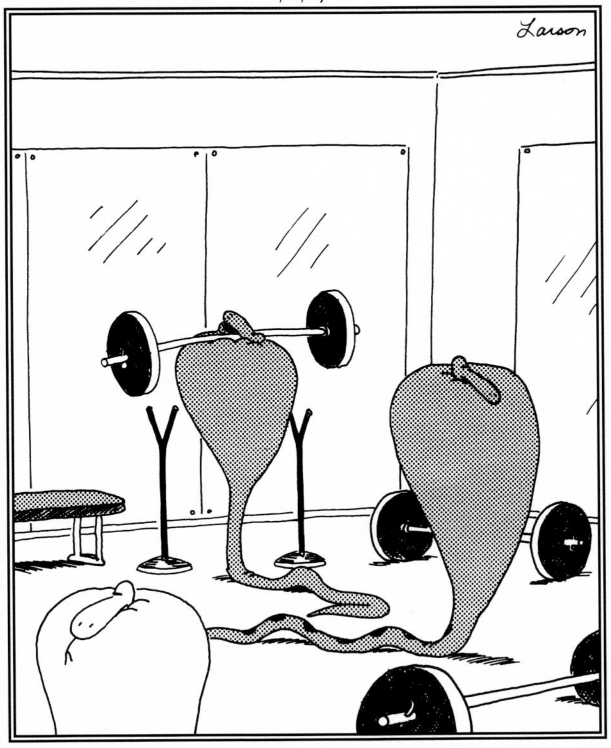
Larson

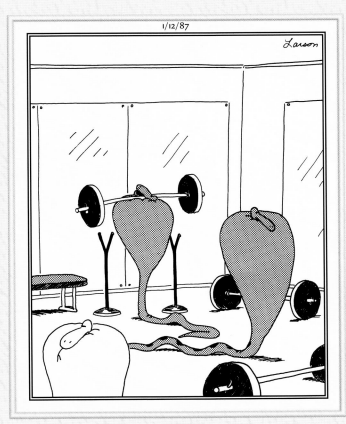

Snake weight rooms

1/17/87

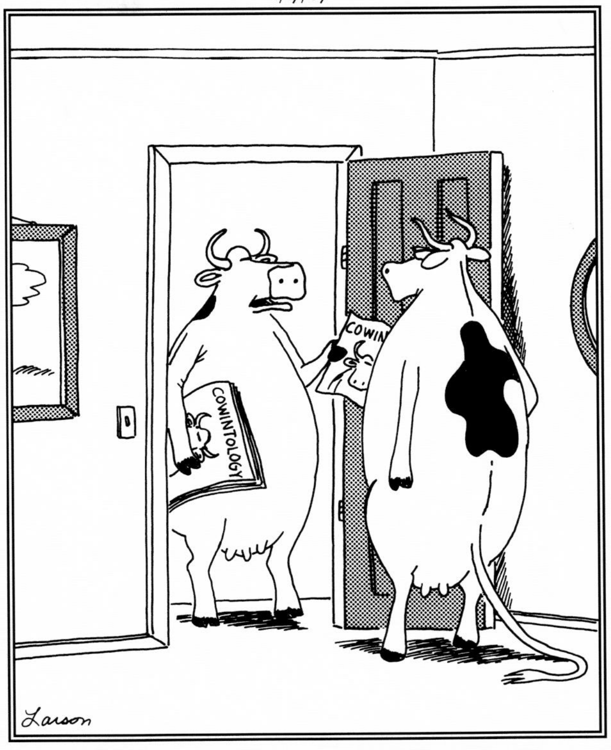
COWIN
COWINTOLOGY
Larson

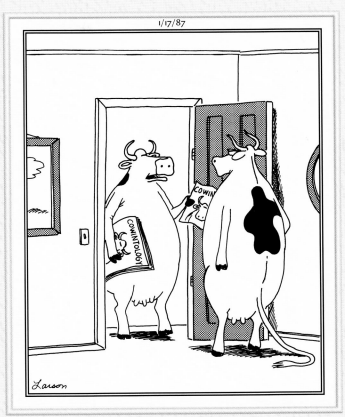

"Listen—just take one of our brochures and see what we're all about. ... In the meantime, you may wish to ask yourself, 'Am I a happy cow?'"

1/6/87

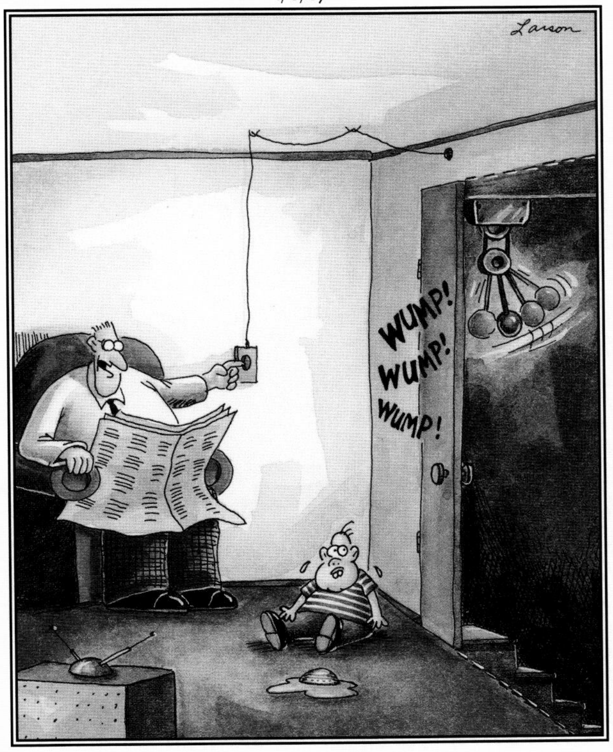
Larson
WUMP!
WUMP!
WUMP!

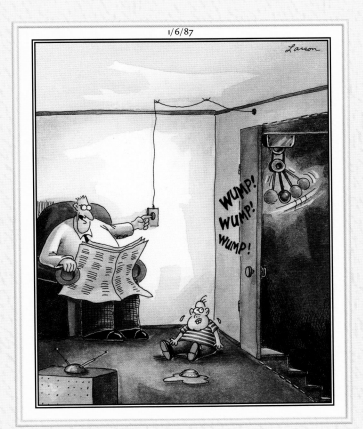

"Uh-oh, Donny. Sounds like the monster in the basement has heard you crying again. ... Let's be reeeeal quiet and hope he goes away."

1/5/87

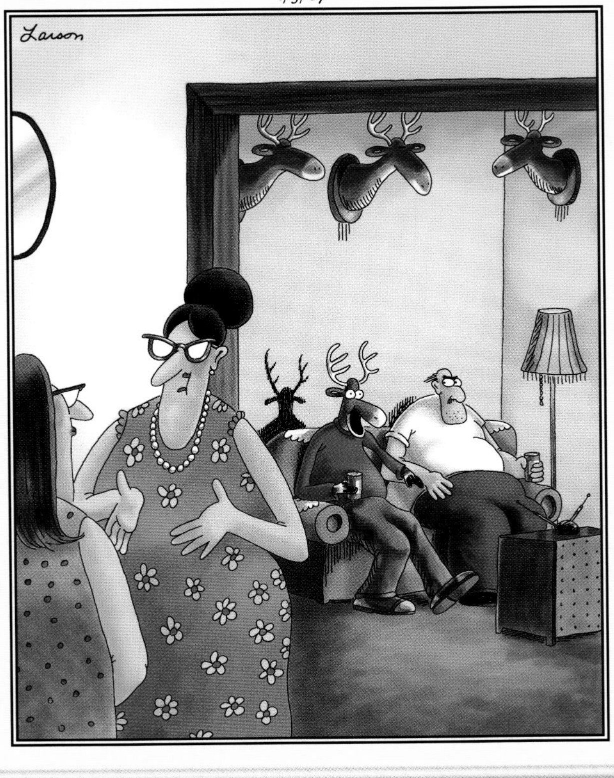
Larson

"It's this new boyfriend, dear. ... I'm just afraid one day your father's going to up and blow him away."

"Yeah. My boss don't appreciate me either. To him, I'm just a gofer. 'Igor! Go for brains! ... Igor! Go for dead bodies! ... Igor! Go for sandwiches!' ... I dunno—give me another beer."

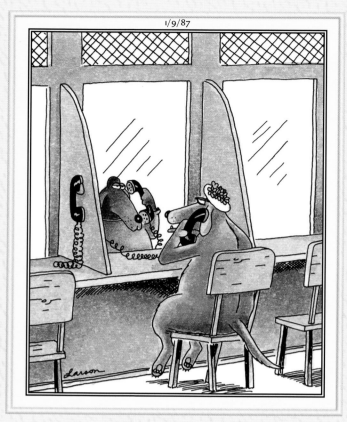

"Why'd you do it, Biff? I mean, I always knew car chasing was in your blood— but the president's limo?"

A young Genghis Khan and his Mongol hordette

Onward they pushed, through the thick, steamy jungle, separately ruing the witch doctor's parting words: "Before you leave this valley, each of you will be wearing a duck."

"For heaven's sake, Henry, tell the kids a *pleasant* story for once—they don't always have to hear the one about your head."

1/18/87

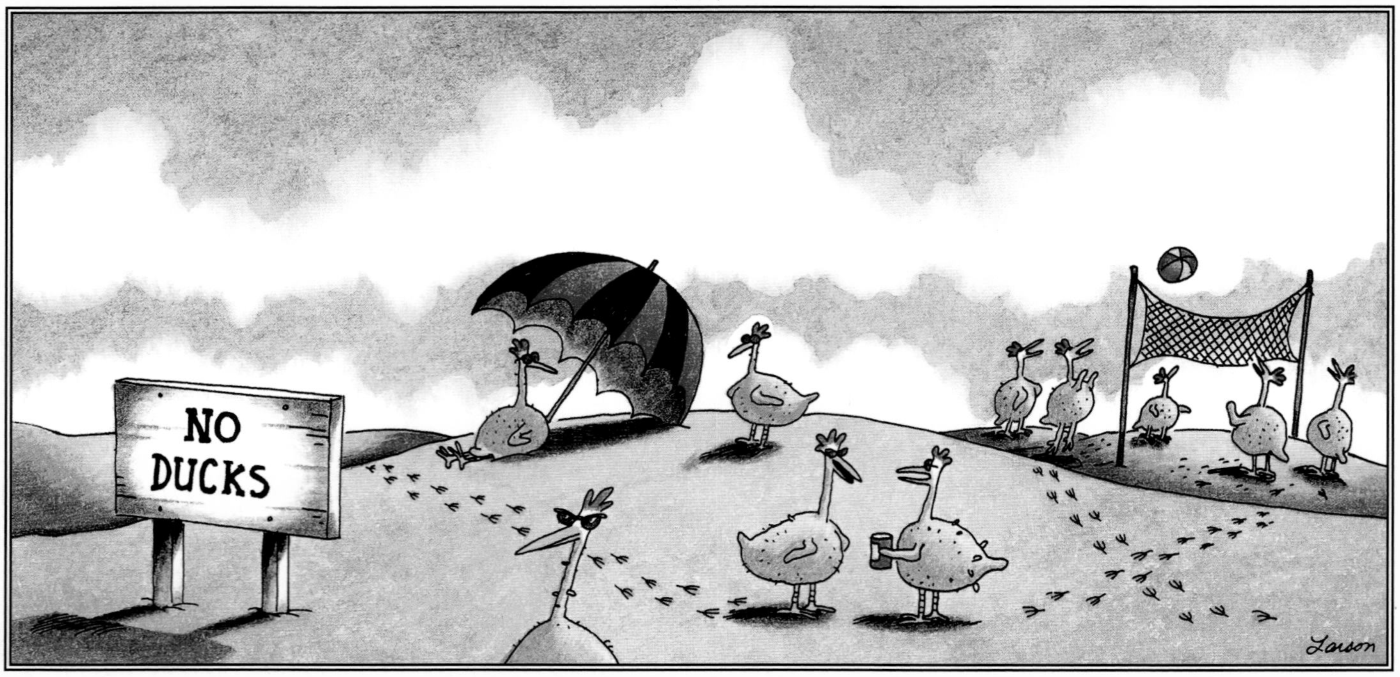
NO
DUCKS
Larson

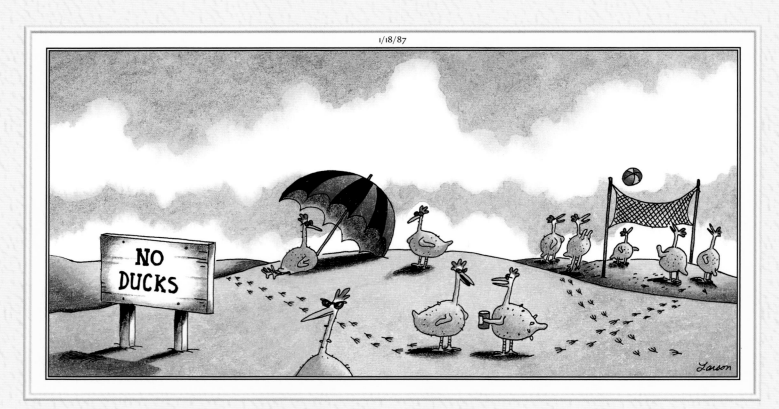

Chicken nudist colonies

1/14/87

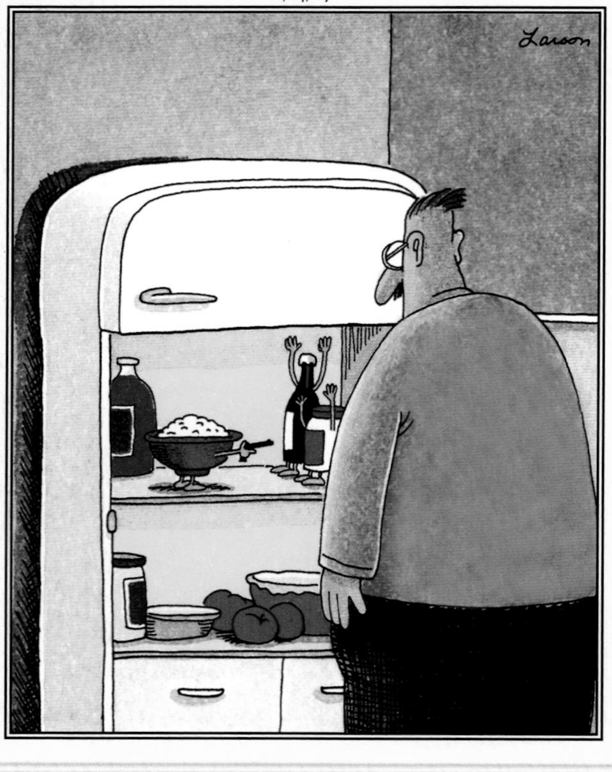
Larson

When potato salad goes bad

1/20/87

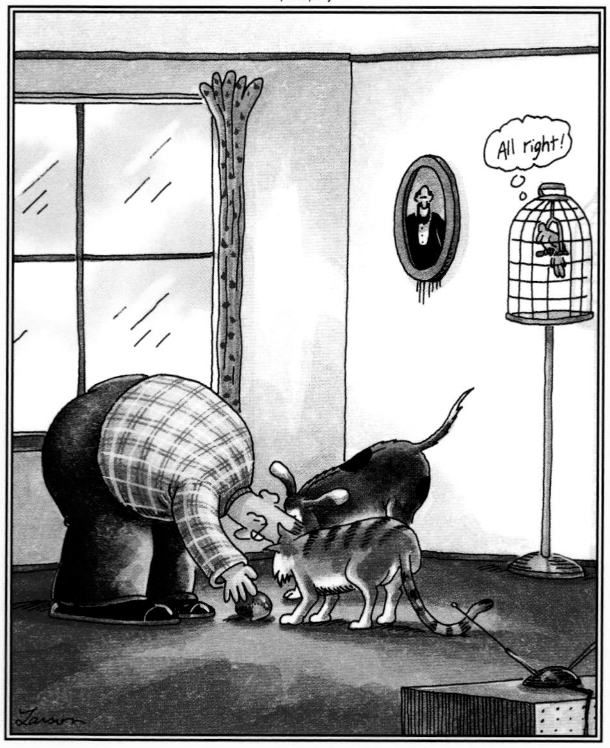
All right!
Larson

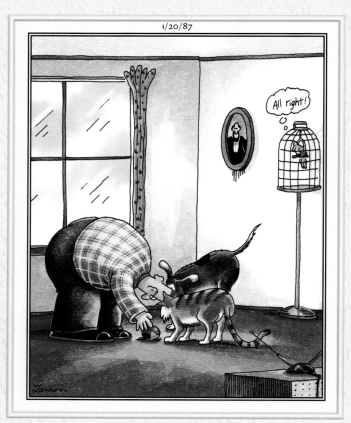

Simultaneously all three went for the ball,
and the coconut-like sound of their heads
colliding secretly delighted the bird.

1/15/87

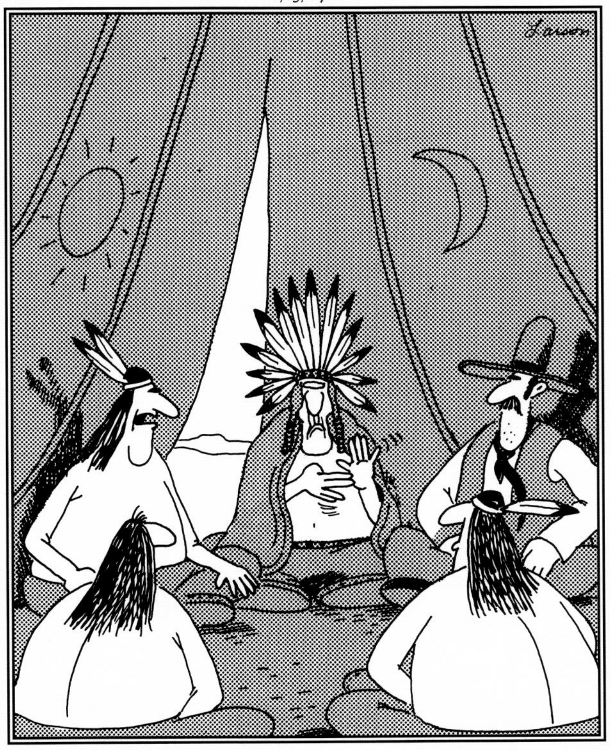

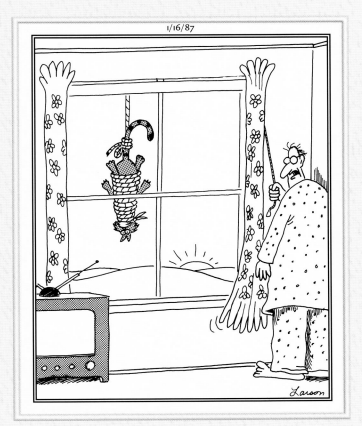

"Chief say, 'Someone ... here ... walk ... through ... buffalo ... field.'"

1/16/87

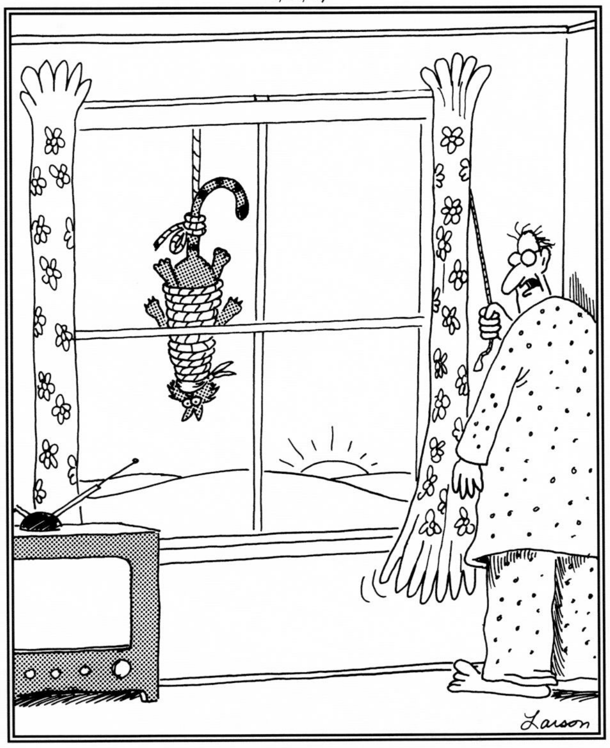

"Emma ... the dog ain't goin' for the new cat."

To whom it may concern:
I have tried throughout this book to hold fast to my own rule of not attaching explanations or apologies to any particular cartoons. Once I started that, I realized, it might never end. But here, I need to "make my case" regarding a cartoon that was almost universally misunderstood upon its initial publication. (And it especially stirred up my most dreaded enemy, the Cat People.) Therefore, let it be known, it is the dog—in a mafia-like gesture—who has done this to the cat. The humans here are innocent. This time.

—Gary Larson

1/25/87

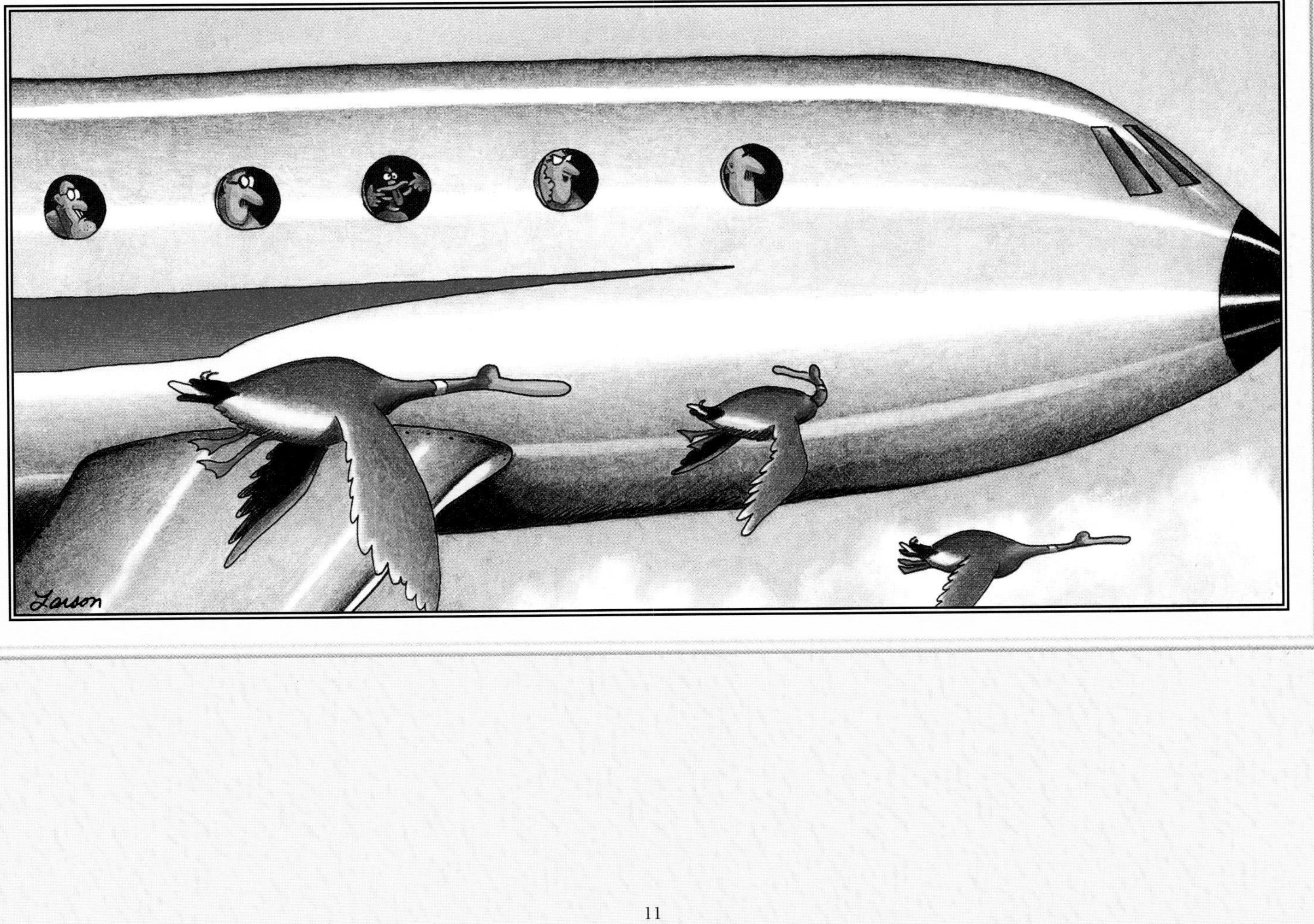

1/19/87

Larson

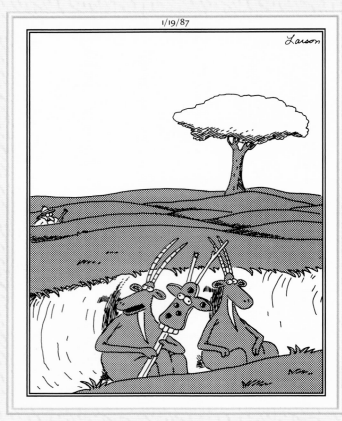

"He's got one shot left, Murray—and then he's *ours!*"

1/24/87

Larson

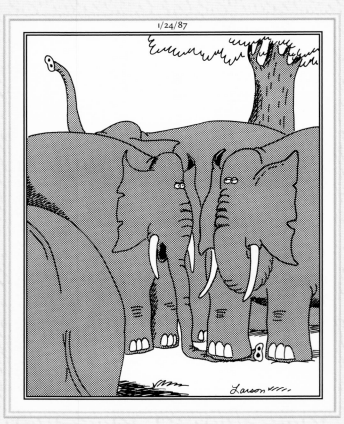

"Two questions, Mitch: How much do you weigh, and what's the most sensitive part of any elephant's anatomy?"

1/21/87

Larson
8
33
12
27
35

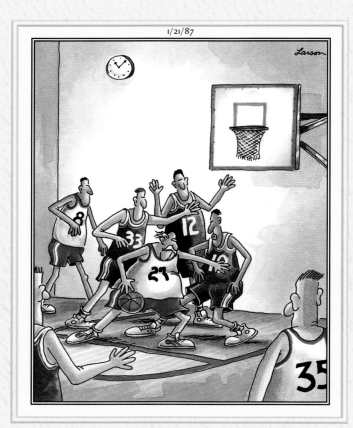

Unbeknownst to most historians, Einstein started down the road of professional basketball before an ankle injury diverted him into science.

1/23/87

GENERAL
STORE
Larson

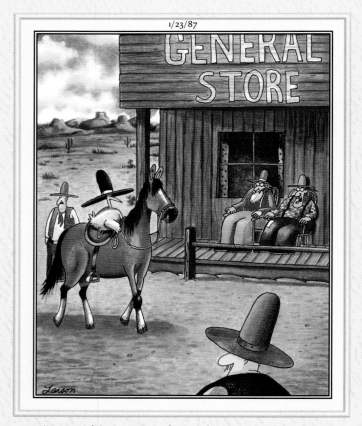

"Somethin's up, Jed. ... That's Ben Potter's horse, all right, but ain't that Henry Morgan's chicken ridin' him?"

1/27/87

Larson

"Maybe it's *not* me, y'know? ... Maybe it's the *rest* of the herd that's gone insane."

1/29/87

Larson
Put 'er there, Rob... Ha ha ha ha ha ha!..

Snake inventors

1/22/87

Larson

Non-singing canaries have to take wood shop.

1/26/87

Larson
Cuckoo!
SEND HELP!

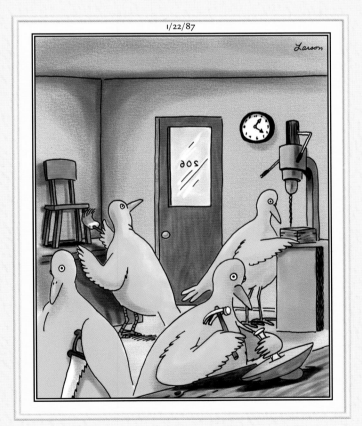

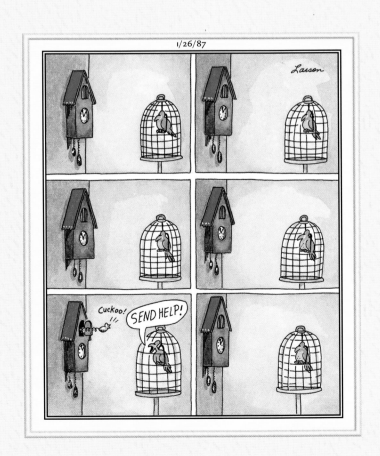

Night of the Living Dead Chipmunks

The embarrassment of riding off into a
fake sunset

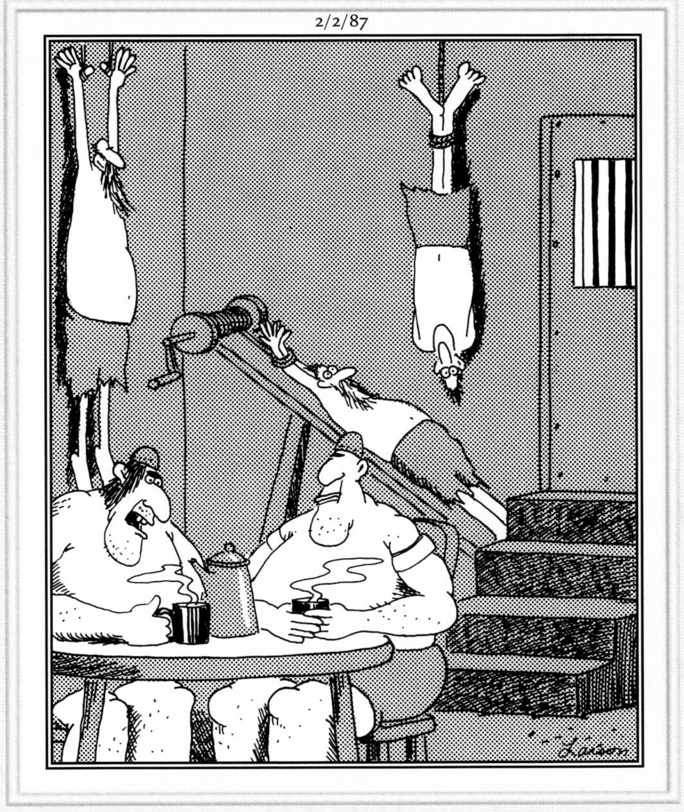
2/2/87
Larson

"You know, Russell, you're a great torturer. I mean, you can make a man scream for mercy in nothing flat ... but boy, you sure can't make a good cup of coffee."

The Herald Statesman, Yonkers, N.Y., 2/19/87

Beyond the bounds of decency? or simply humor out of this world?

NANCY Q. KEEFE

Dear Mrs. Keefe:

I was so upset after seeing the enclosed comic page? cartoon that appeared Monday (Feb. 2) in The Herald Statesman. It was the ugliest, (most) obnoxious and sadistic cartoon I have ever seen in a family paper. The so-called artist, Gary Larson, must be sick. I hope you agree.

I believe that you, being in touch with the various branches of your editorial staff, have more "clout" than I could have and would see that never again such a vile cartoon would be printed. It certainly is not fit for exposure to children.

Very truly yours, etc.

Here is my reply, which I have already mailed to him:

Dear Mr. Vail:

One of the first ideas that my father taught me as a child was that there are no wrong opinions and no really wrong tastes. He even taught me two foreign language phrases to express this. In Latin: *De gustibus non est disputandum,* and in French: *Chacun a son gout.* Further, he said, these applied more to humor than even to food.

As it happens, Gary Larson's strip is one of my favorites. We haven't carried it long in these newspapers, but my first newspaper, the highly regarded Berkshire Eagle (of Pittsfield, Mass.) has been carrying Larson for years. One of my oldest friends gave me a 1987 calendar of Larson cartoons, about which I guffaw every day.

So I am not a good candidate to carry your message of disenchantment. But I will say this: Don't worry about the children. They don't get it. And when they do, they will not be as much affected, on infected, as they are now, daily, by the offerings of television or the hypocrisy of fundamentalists.

Satire is an ancient tradition, as old as Dean Swift in "Gulliver's Travels" (or in "A Modest Proposal for Preventing the Children of Ireland from being a Burden to their Parents or Country" — by stewing or roasting them to eat), and as old as Horace of the first century before Christ (who wrote a whole series of Satires, and, I should add, Aristophanes, the Greek playwright of the fifth century B.C., who wrote entire plays of satire).

To many, "Satire is what closes Saturday night," as George S. Kaufman, put it. To a few of us, satire is what makes it possible to deal with the outrages of daily life.

To each his own.

Peace, etc.

Nancy Q. Keefe is editorial page editor.

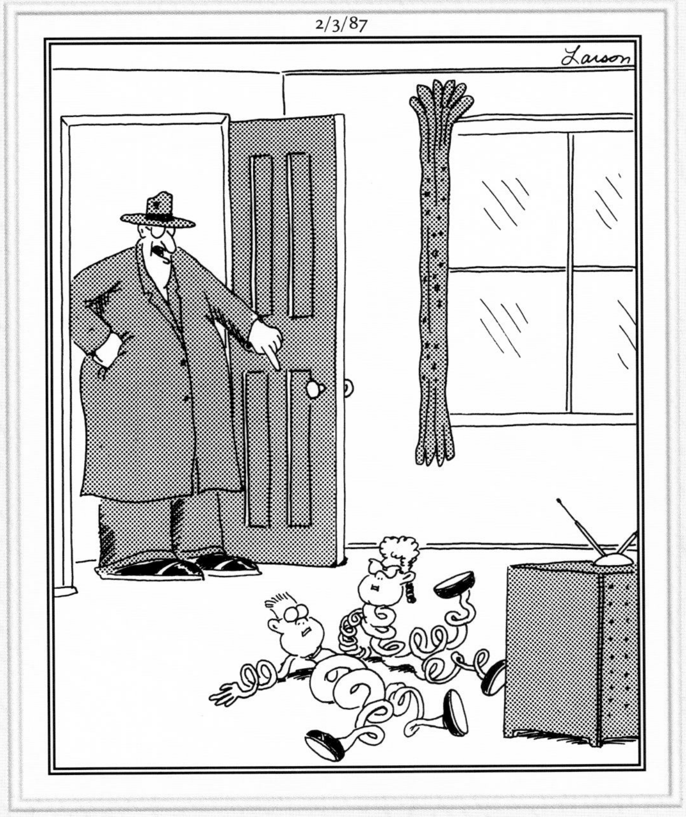
2/3/87
Larson

"I've warned you kids about this—now I'm gonna straighten you out once and for all."

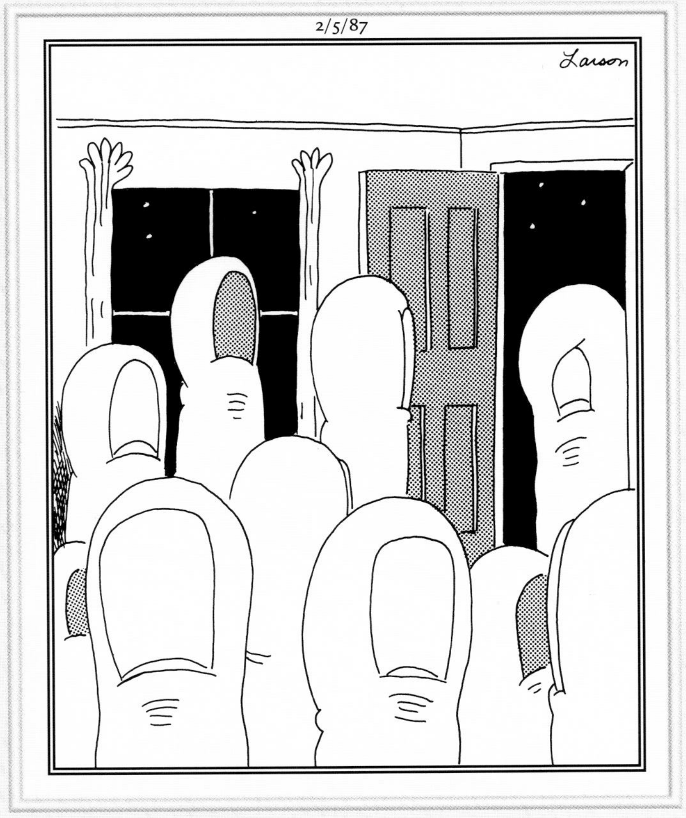
2/5/87
Larson

Suddenly, everyone turned and looked—there, standing in the doorway, was one wretched, mean-looking ingrown.

2/1/87

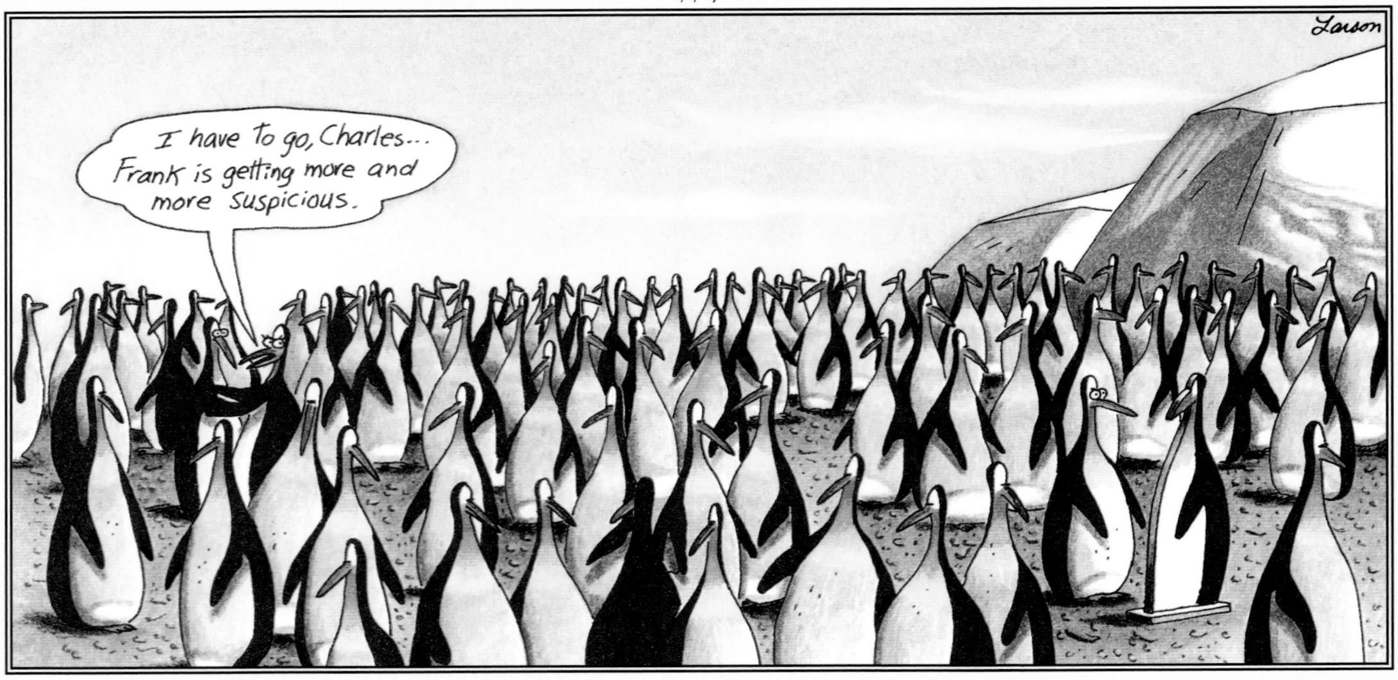
Larson
I have to go, Charles... Frank is getting more and more suspicious.

2/4/87

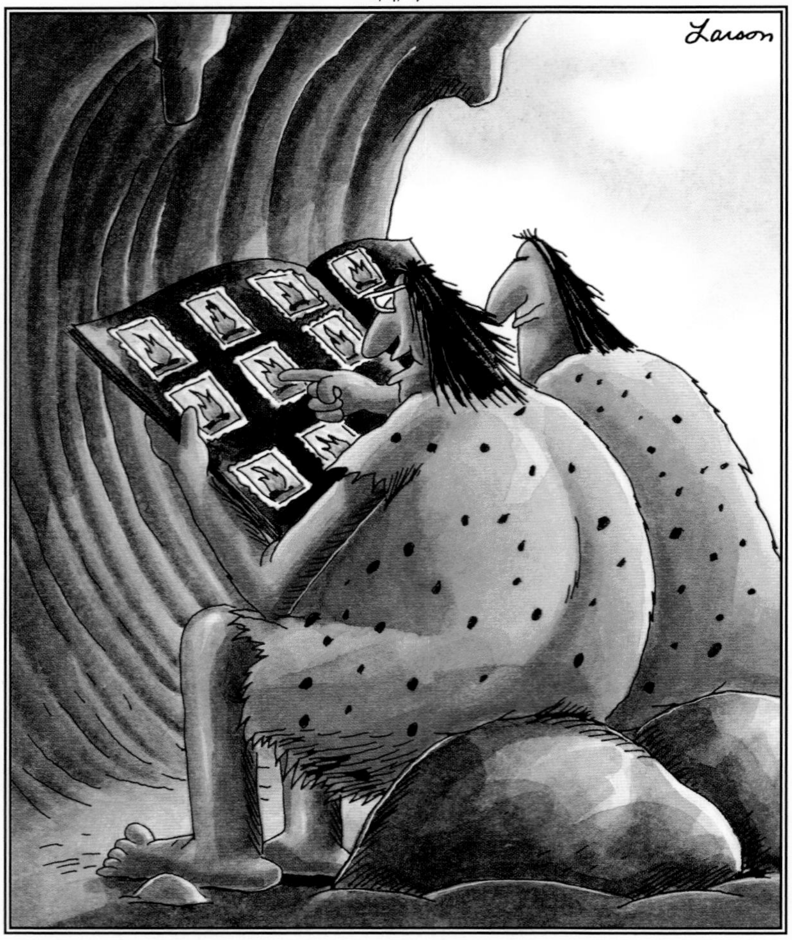
Larson

"Ooo! Now here's a nice one we built last fall."

2/14/87

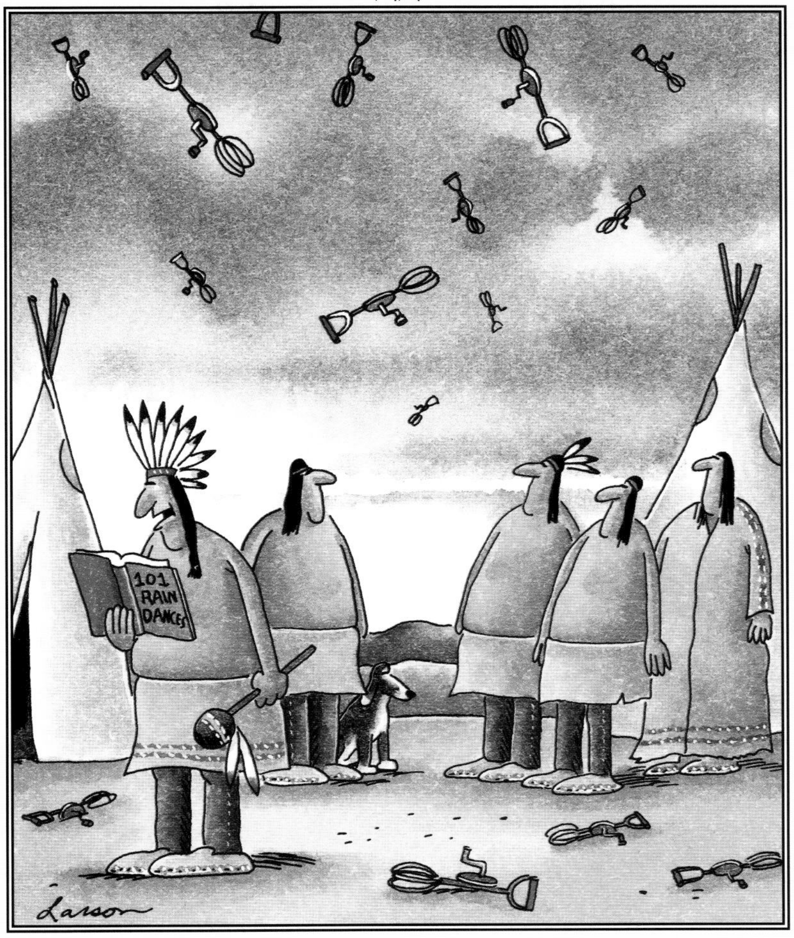
101
RAIN
DANCES
Larson

"Oh! *Four* steps to the left and *then* three to the right! ... What kind of a dance was *I* doing?"

2/8/87

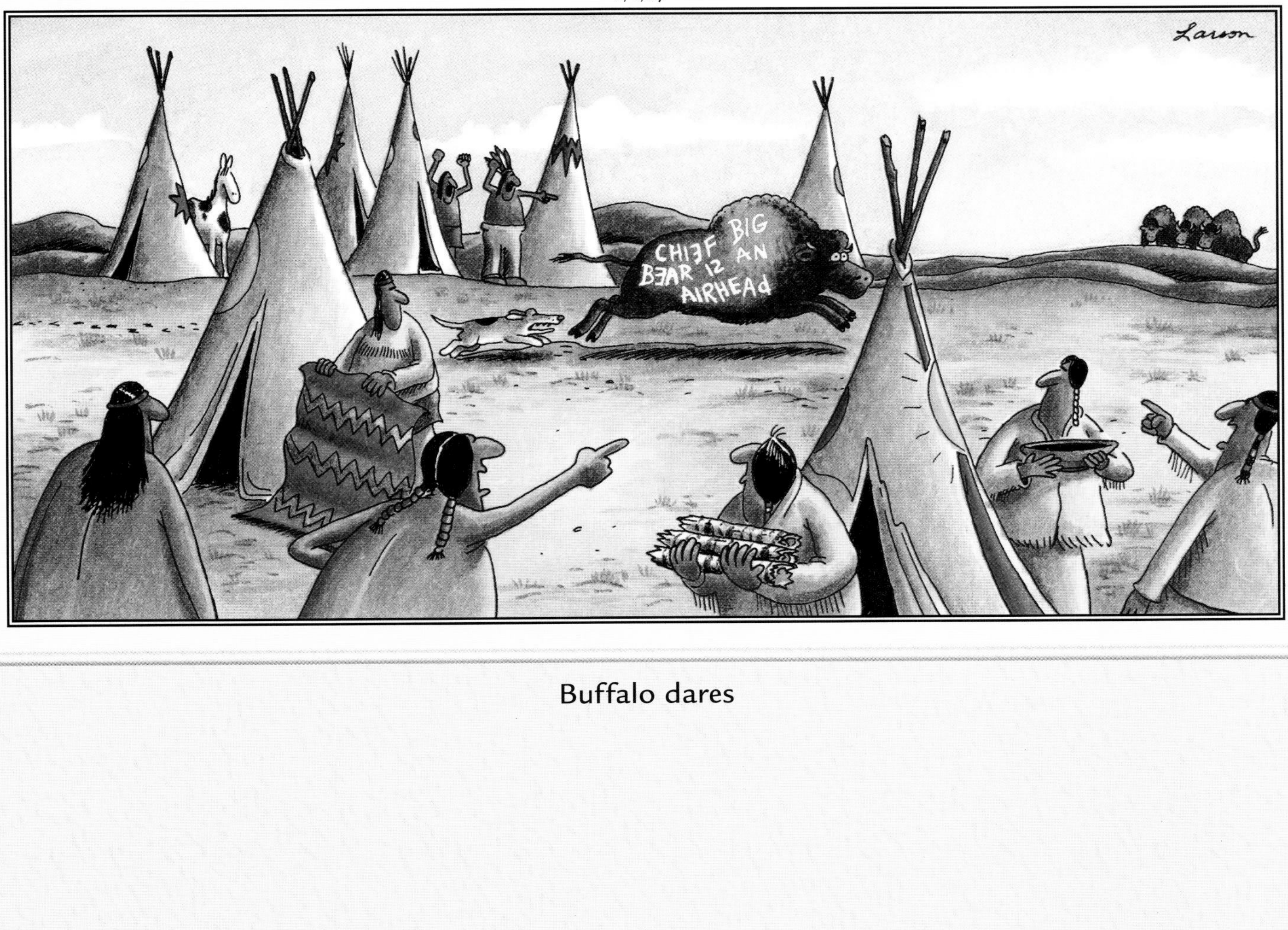
Larson
CHIEF BIG
BEAR IS AN
AIRHEAD

Buffalo dares

2/12/87

SPIDER PERSONALS
BLACK WIDOW seeks male for fun weekends.
BLACK WIDOW looking for nice male, same species
BLACK WIDOW; attractive; large red hourglass, out-going. Call Susan
BLACK WIDOW, fun-loving attractive, long legs, wants to meet any male
BLACK WIDOW, non-smoker, seeks male to share indoor web. 555-0617
BLACK WIDOW, young, likes dark places
WIDOW wants to meet male with no strings attach
BLACK WIDO
SPIDER PE
Larson

2/16/87

Larson

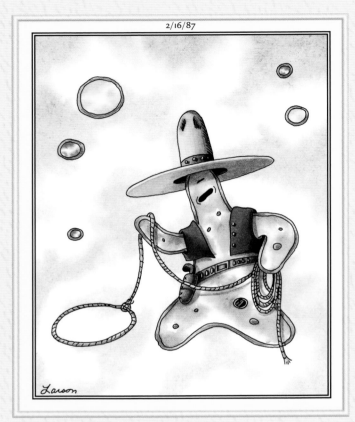

"So, until next week—adios, amoebas."

2/6/87

Larson

2/7/87

Larson

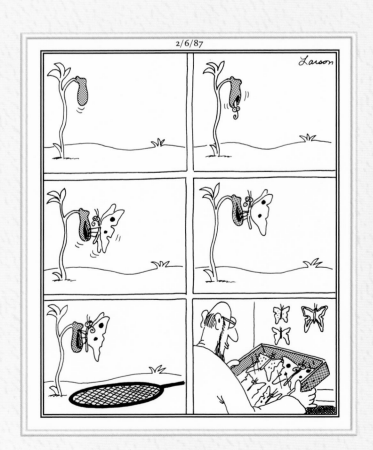

"You idiot! Don't write that down—his name ain't Puddin' Tame!"

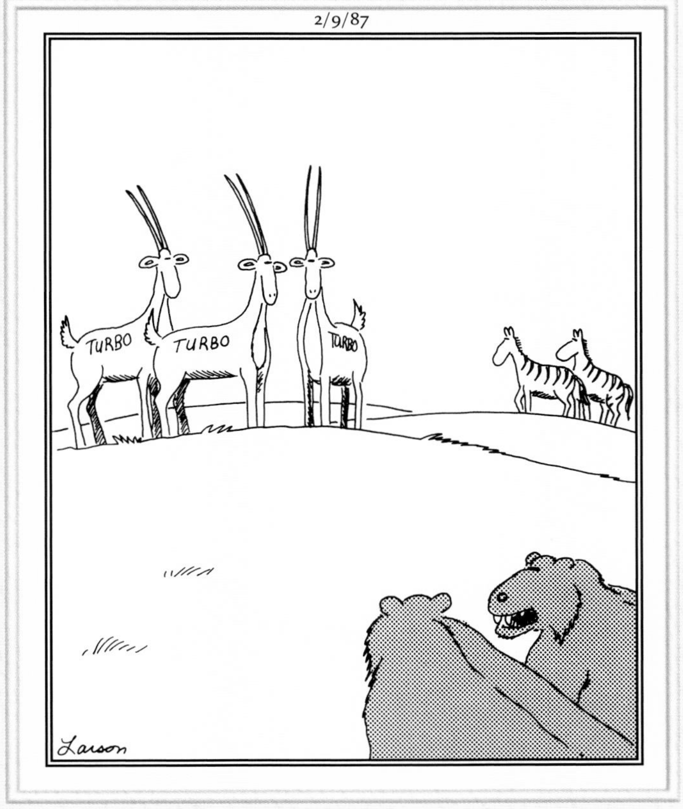
2/9/87
TURBO
TURBO
TURBO
Larson

"Forget these guys."

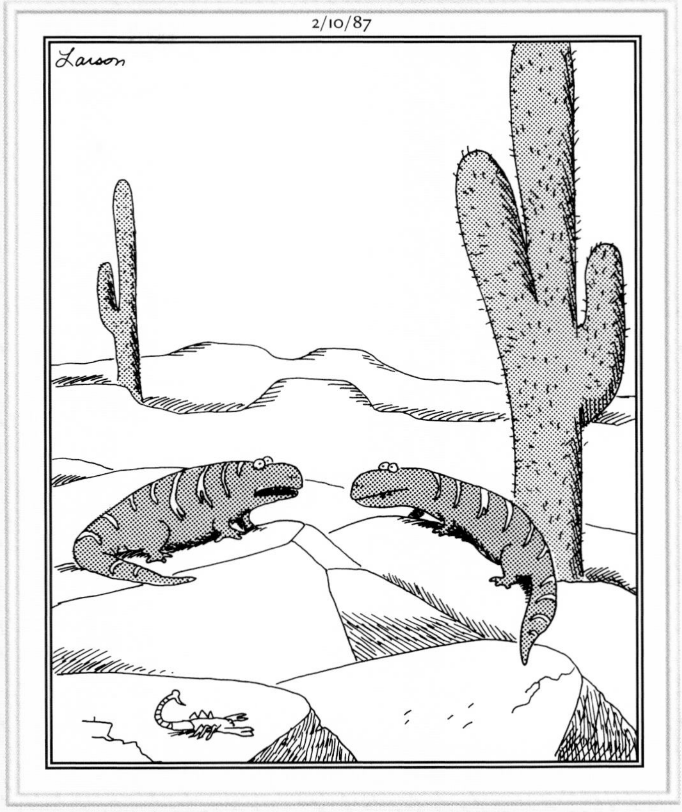
2/10/87
Larson

"There it is again ... a feeling that in a past life I was someone named Shirley MacLaine."

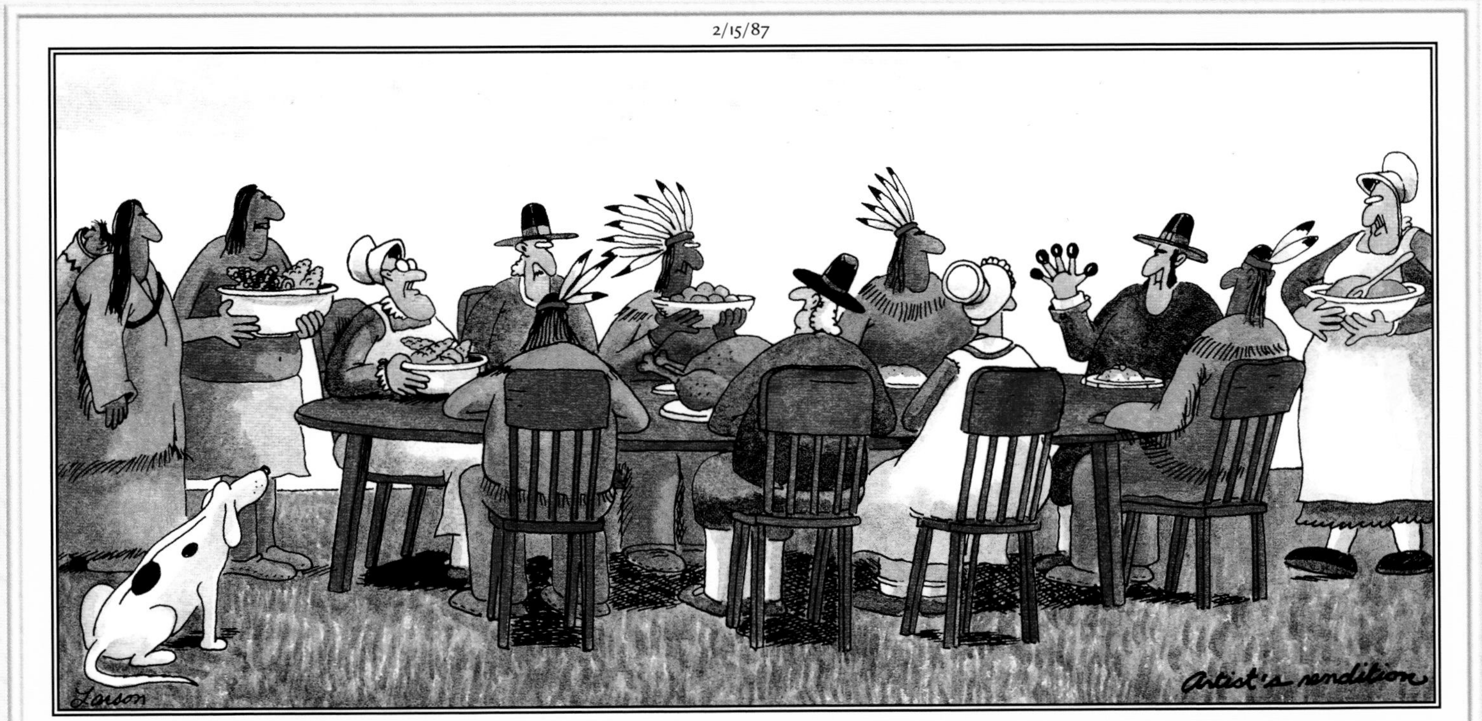
2/15/87
Larson
Artist's rendition

Thomas Sullivan, a blacksmith who attended the original Thanksgiving dinner, is generally credited as being the first person to stick olives on all his fingers.

2/11/87

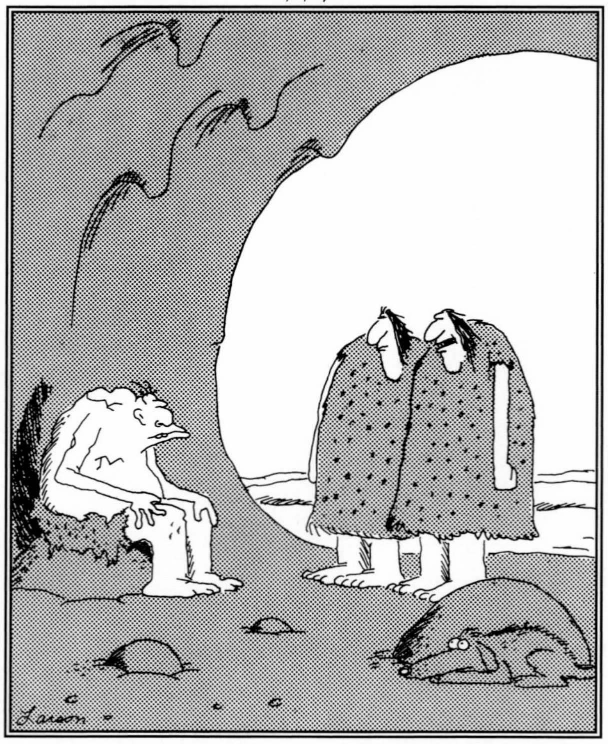
Larson

"Seems like Gramp's been there forever—
fossilized right there on his favorite rock. ...
Scares the hell out of the dog."

2/13/87

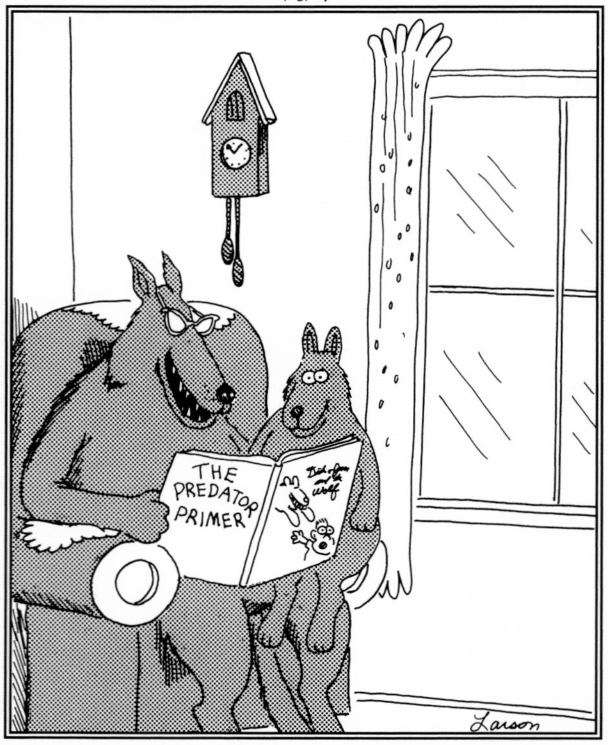
THE PREDATOR PRIMER
Larson

"See Dick run. See Jane run. Run run run.
See the wolves chase Dick and Jane.
Chase chase chase. ..."

2/20/87

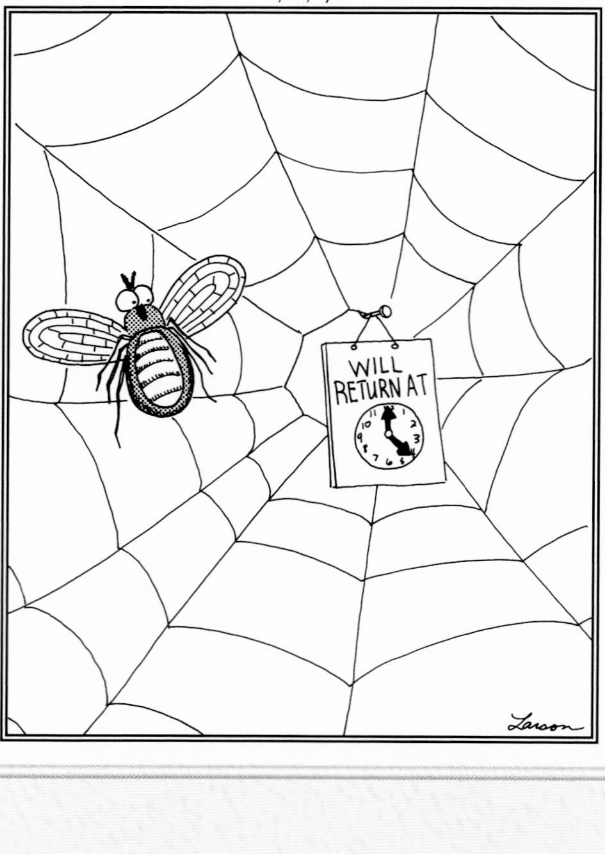
WILL RETURN AT
Larson

2/21/87

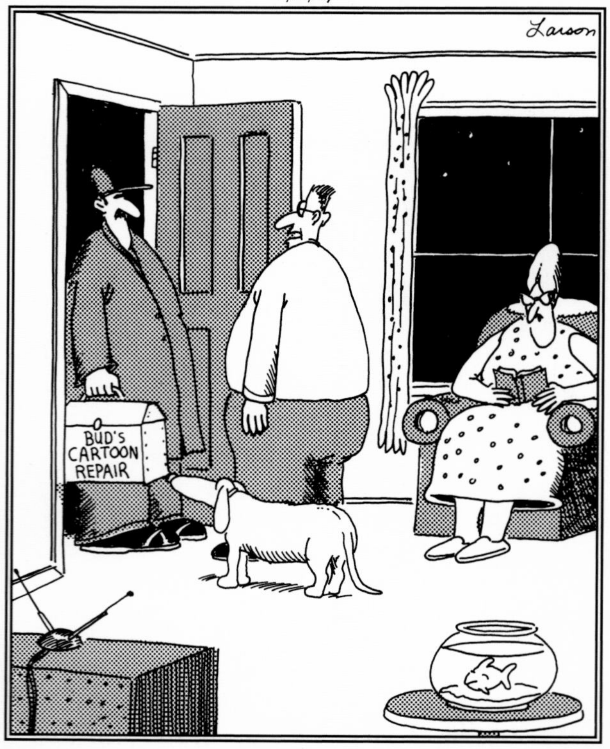
Larson
BUD'S CARTOON REPAIR

"Thanks for coming. Something's wrong—
everything just seems a little too quiet
and normal today."

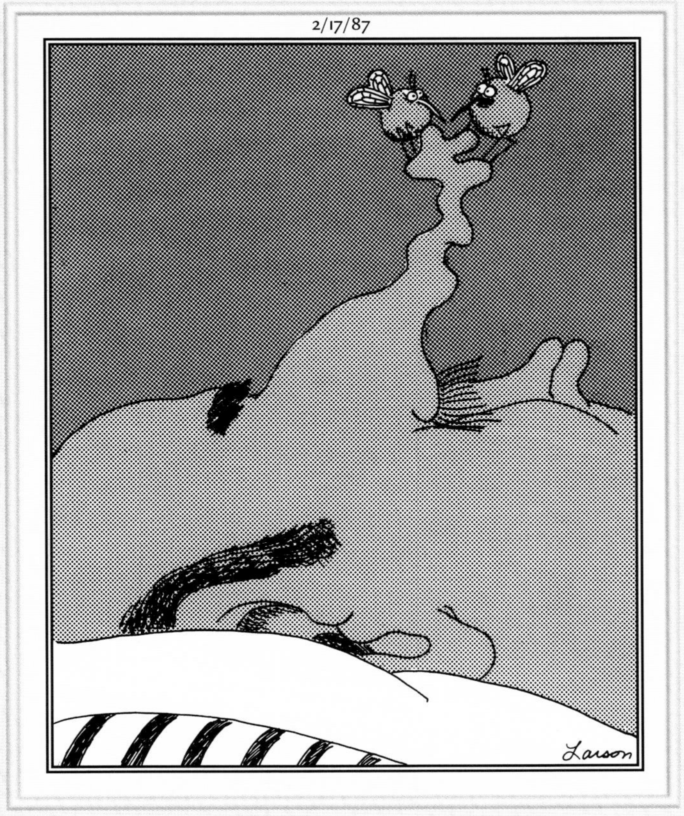
2/17/87
Larson

"Well, that about does it for the nose—I'm starting to hit cartilage."

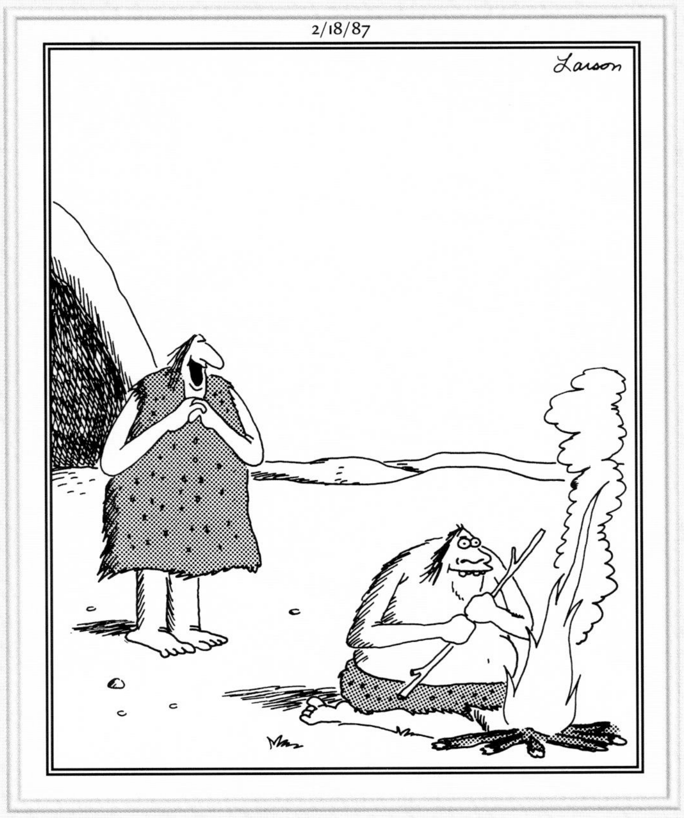
2/18/87
Larson

"Oh, Thak! You've done it! ... If only we had a camera—but, of course, I'm getting ahead of myself."

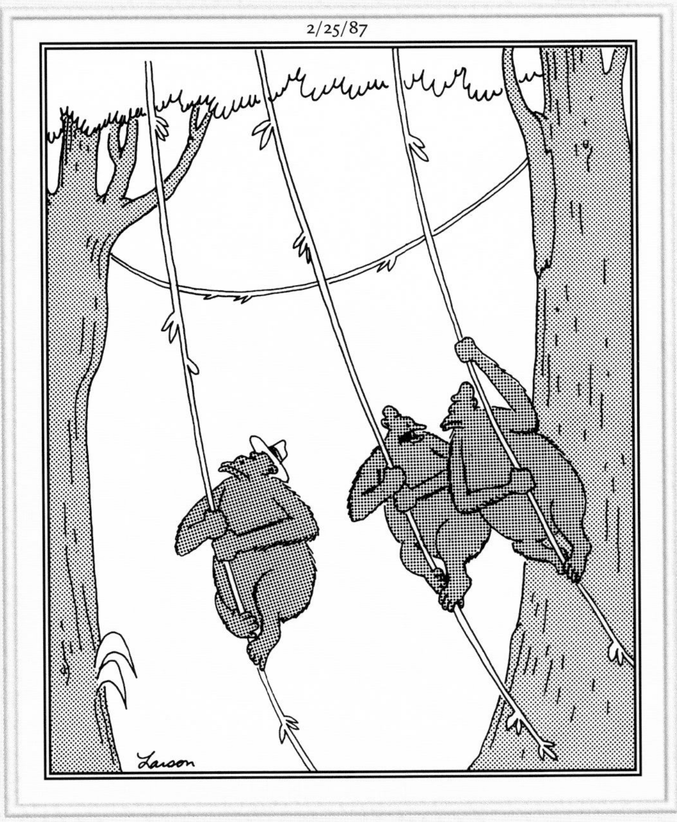
2/25/87
Larson

"Have you noticed that? ... You get stuck swinging behind some guy who's just lollygagging along, and sure enough he'll be wearin' a hat on the back of his head."

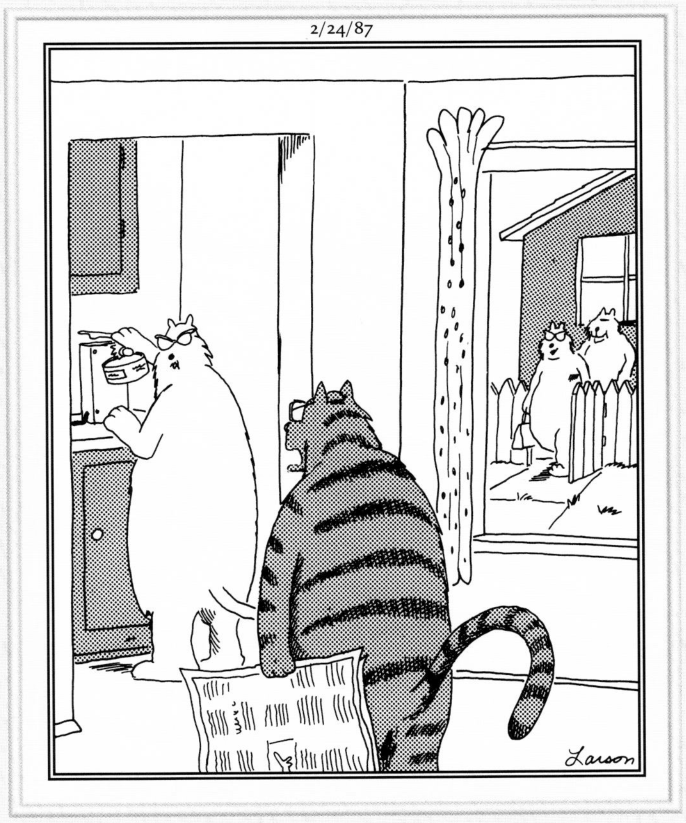
2/24/87
Larson

"Zelda! Cool it! ... The Rothenbergs hear the can opener!"

2/19/87

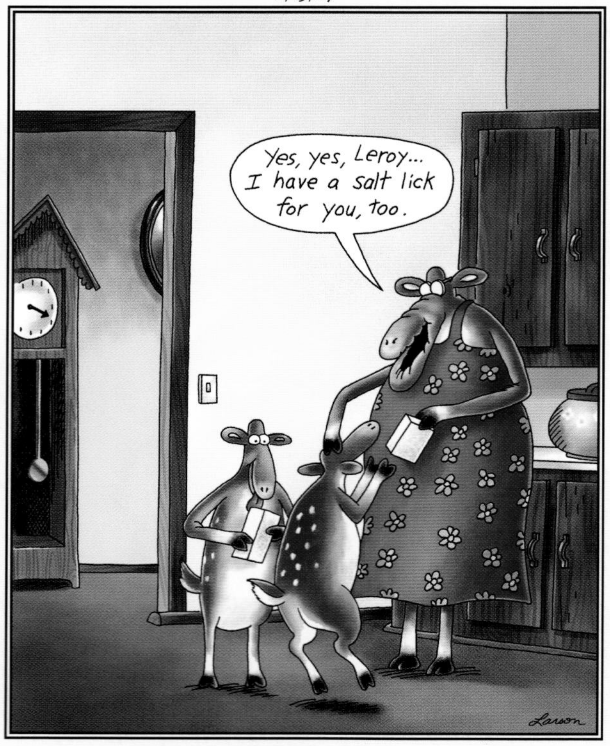
Yes, yes, Leroy...
I have a salt lick
for you, too.

Deer grandmothers

2/26/87

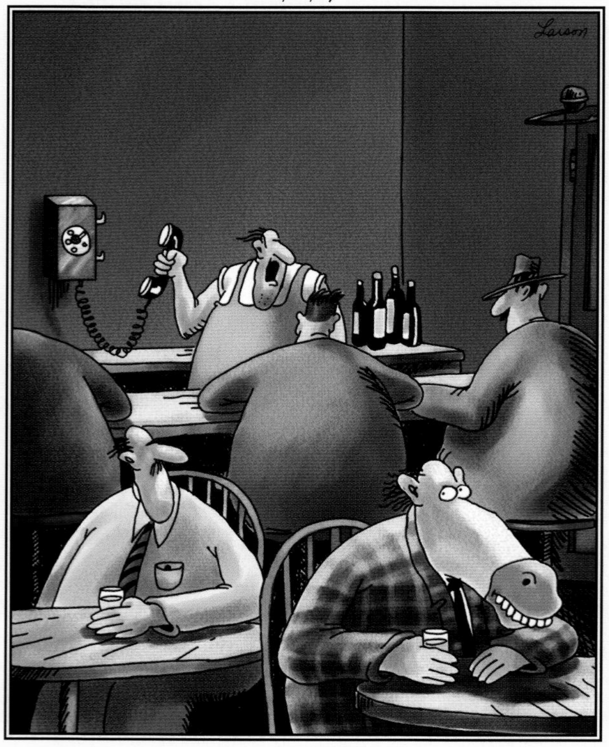

"Horse! ... Is there a man called 'Horse' in here?"

2/22/87

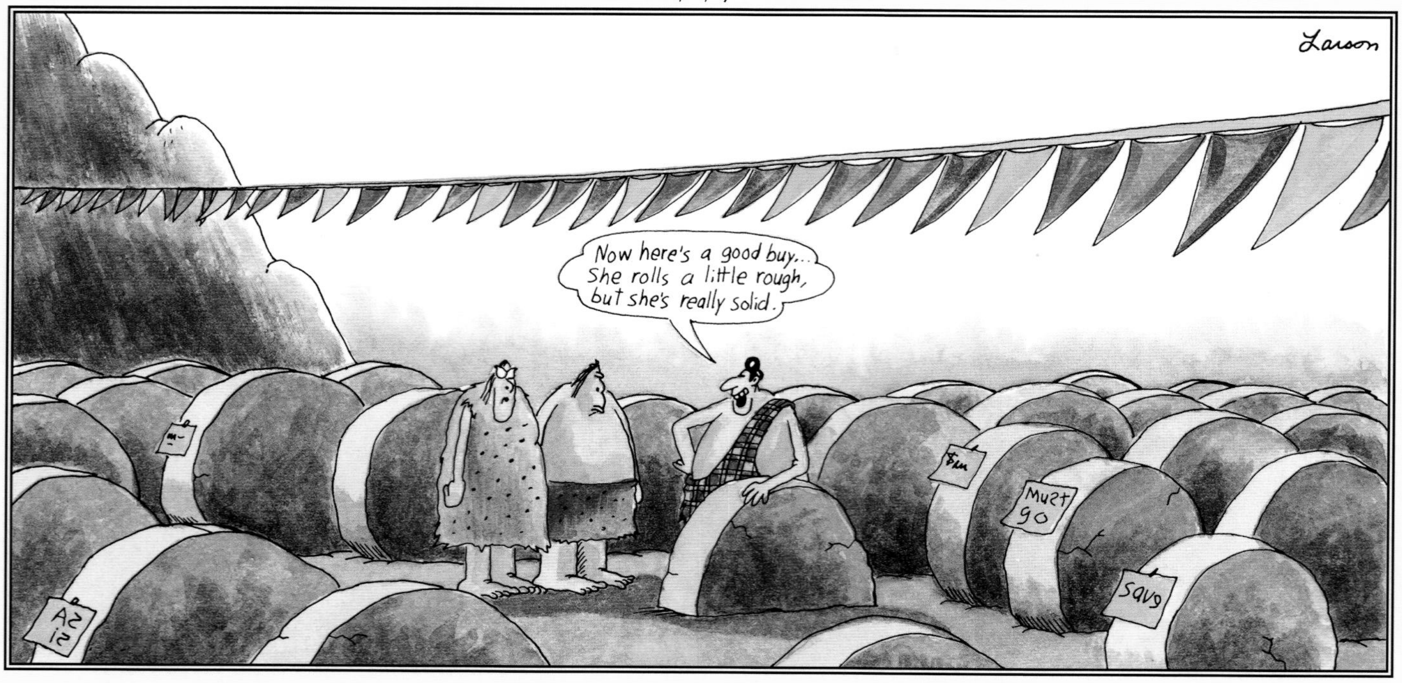
Now here's a good buy...
She rolls a little rough,
but she's really solid.
Must go

Early wheeler-dealers

2/23/87

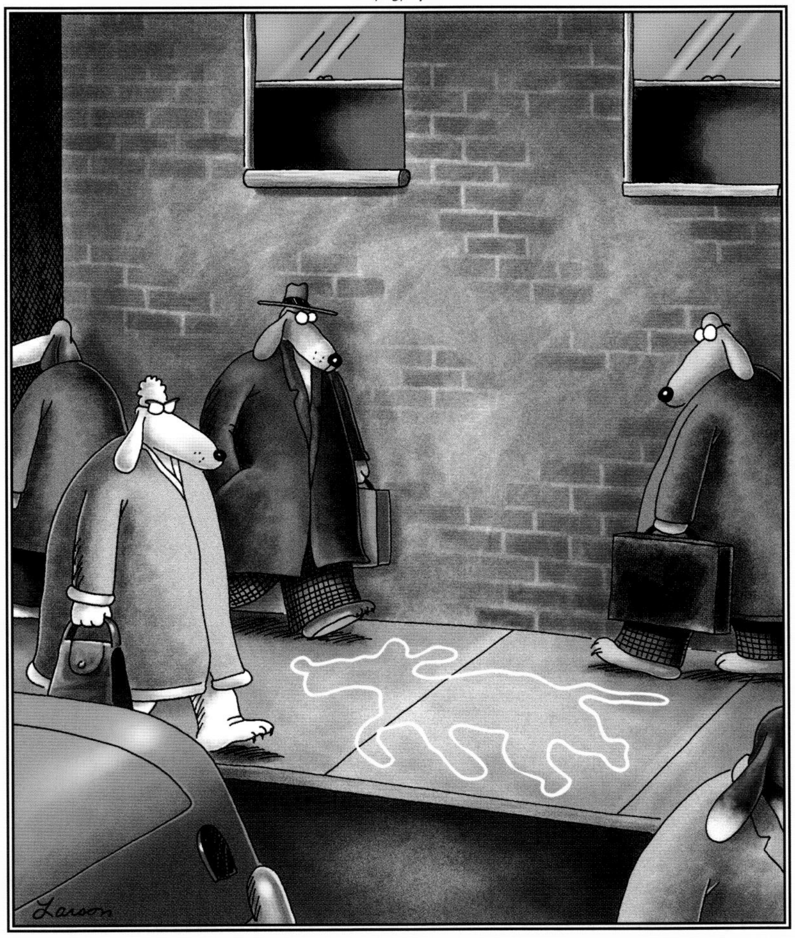
Larson

2/28/87

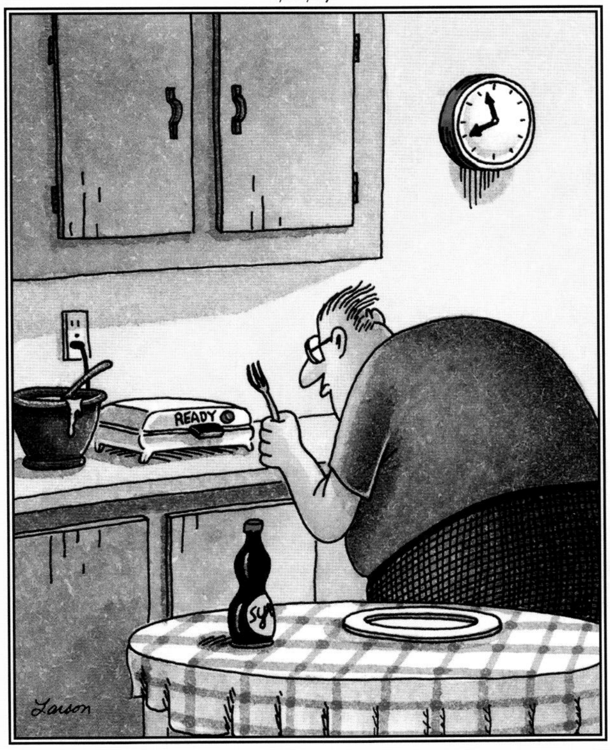
READY
Larson

Wendall Zurkowitz: slave to the waffle light

2/27/87

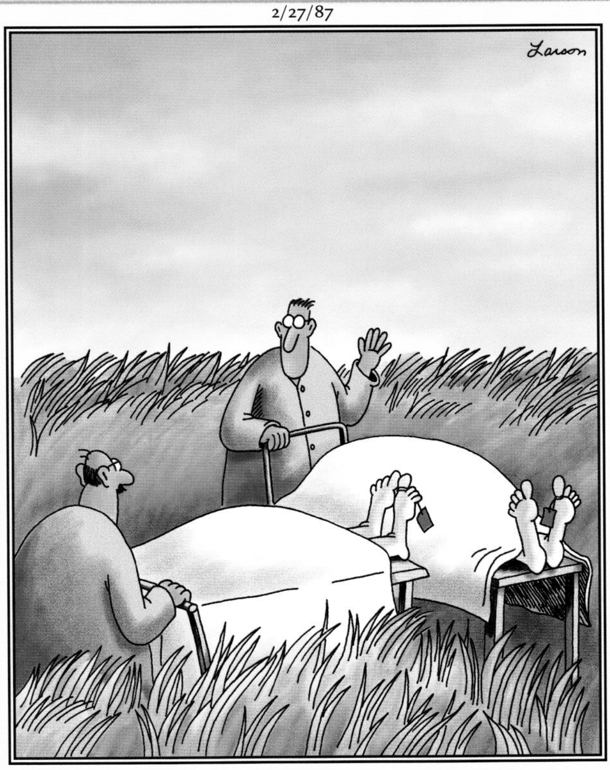
Larson

When a body meets a body comin'
through the rye

3/4/87

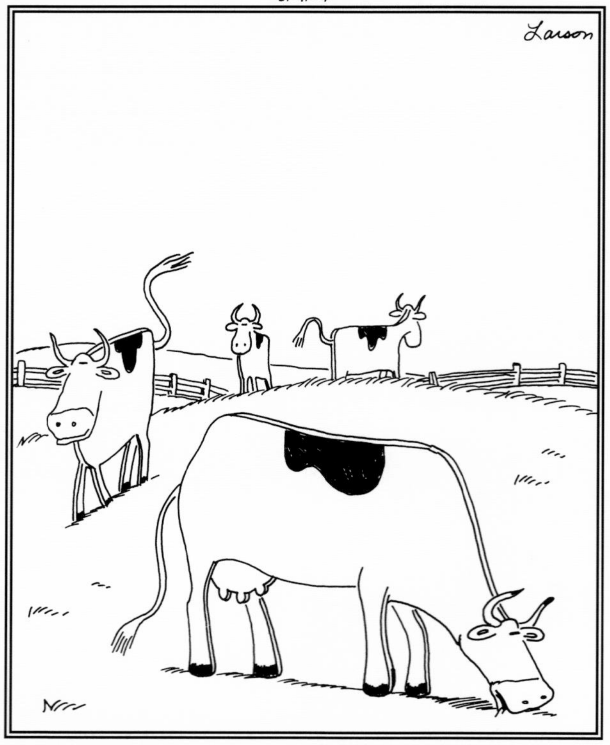
Larson

Where "minute" steaks come from

3/6/87

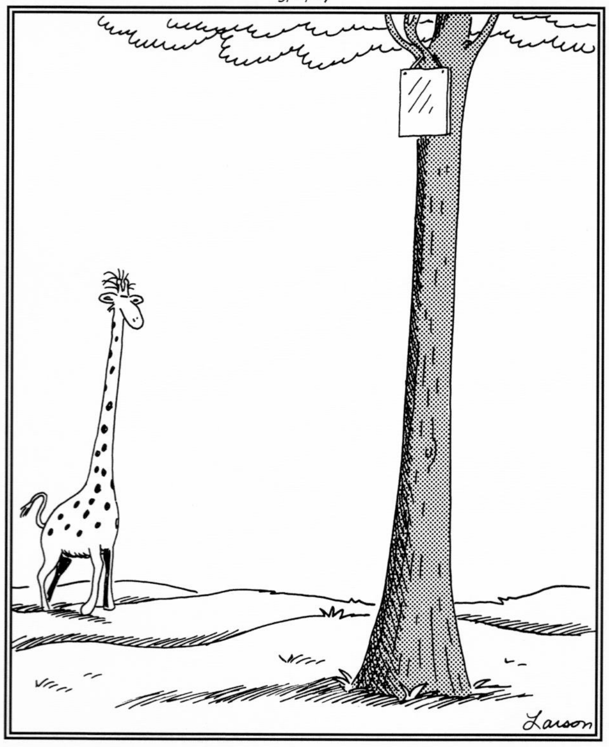
Larson

Where giraffes go to comb their hair

3/1/87

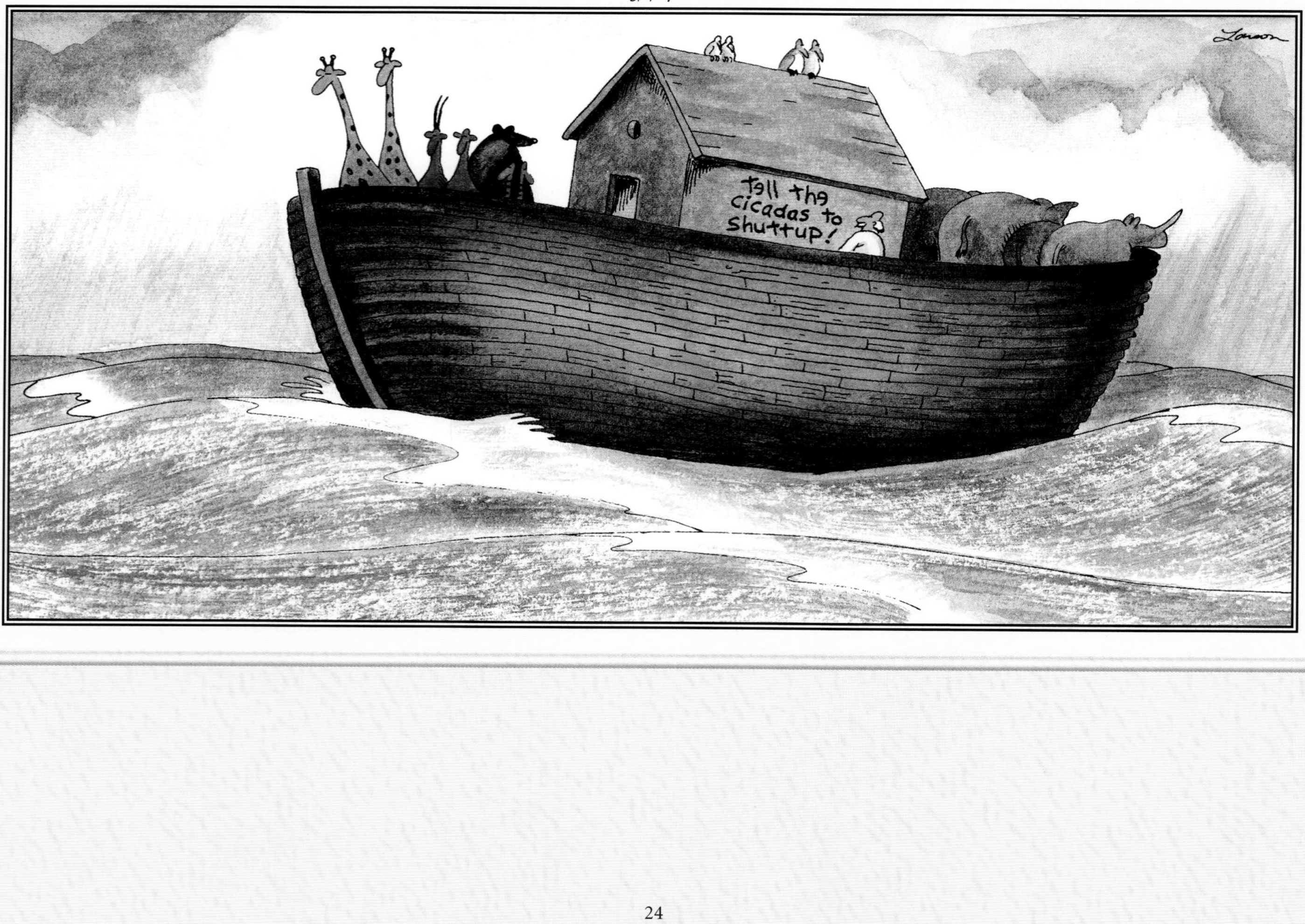
Larson
Tell the cicadas to shuttup!

3/2/87

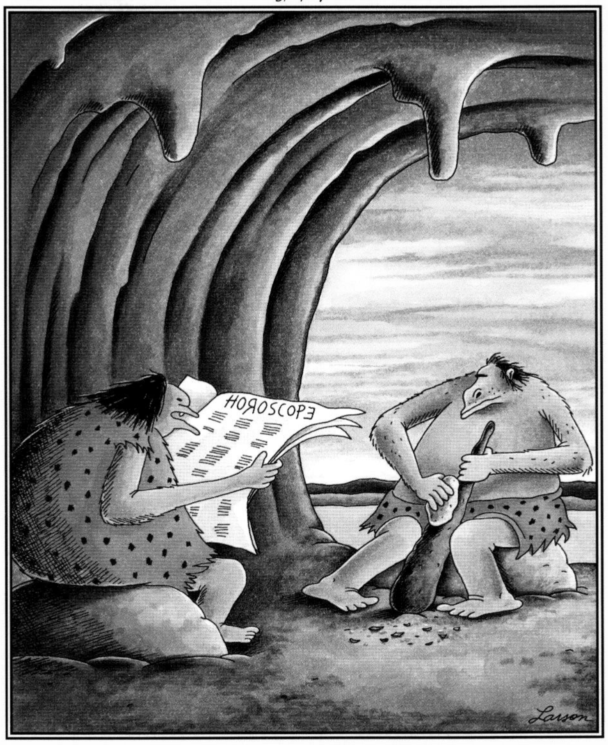
HOROSCOPE

"'You have a small capacity for reason, some basic tool-making skills, and the use of a few simple words.'... Yep. That's you."

3/3/87

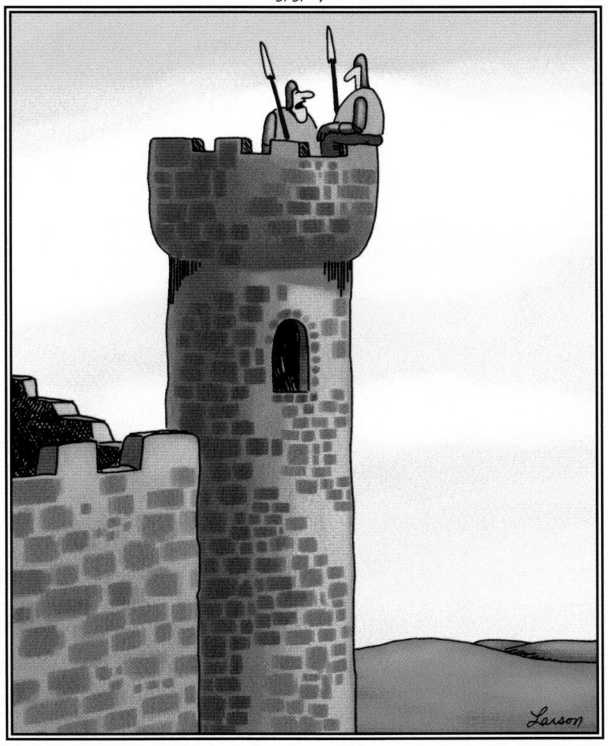

"Mom said no sitting on the edge, Wayne."

3/9/87

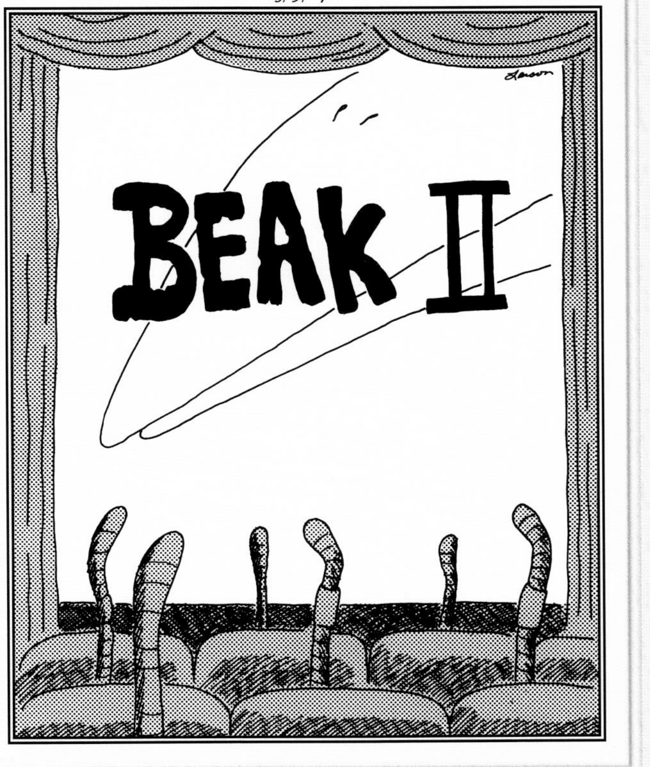
BEAK II

Just when you thought it was safe to go back into the topsoil ...

3/10/87

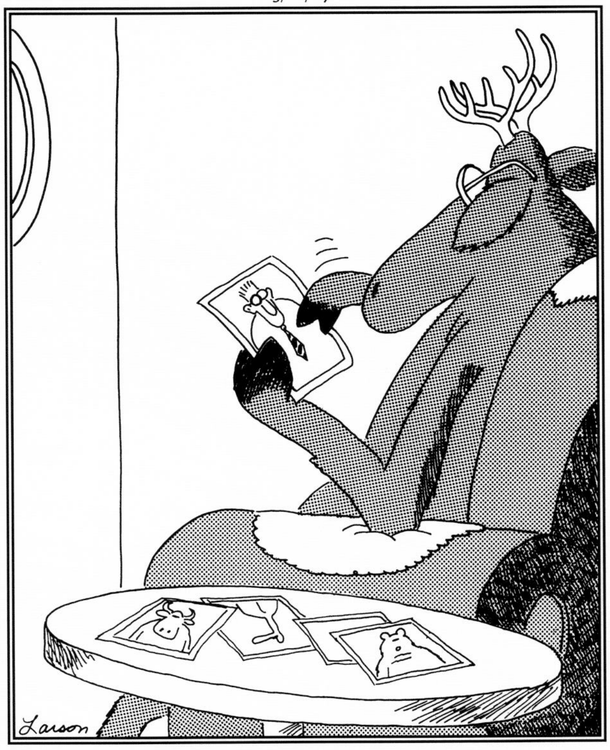

Animal scratch 'n' sniffs

3/5/87

"I'm sorry, Roger... but I've met someone else with brighter plumage."
Larson

3/12/87

Larson
"She's Life-size!"
A-1 NOVELTY INC.
Inflatable Cow!

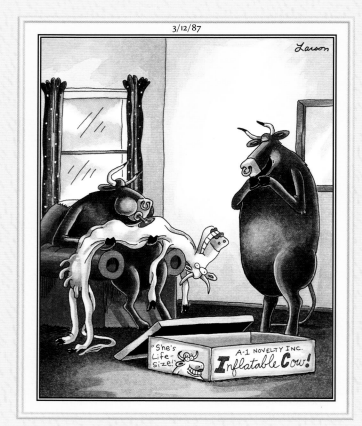

"She's lookin' good, Vern!"

3/7/87

OONEOS
HAVE YOU SEEN ME?
Larson

Breakfast on other planets

3/8/87

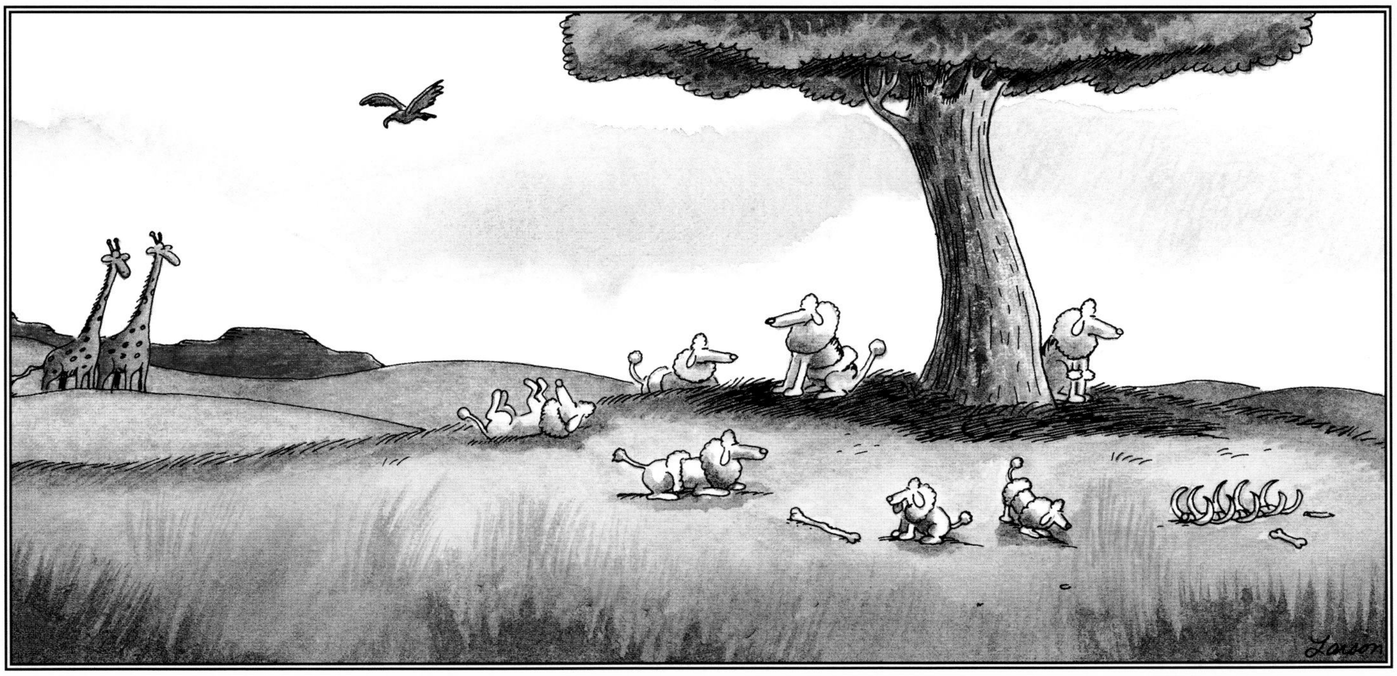
Larson

Poodles of the Serengeti

3/16/87

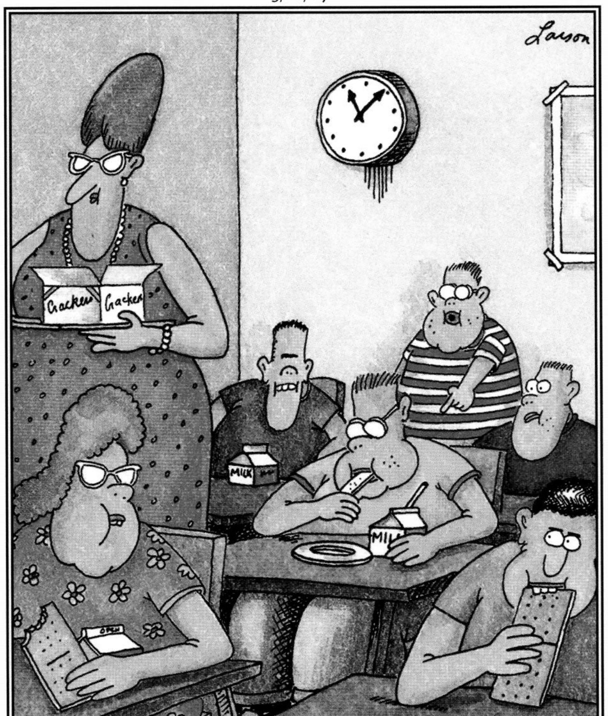
Larson
Crackers
Crackers
MILK

Nov. 12, 1957: Kevin Wakefield, during snack time, makes kindergarten history by selecting the soda cracker over the graham.

3/17/87

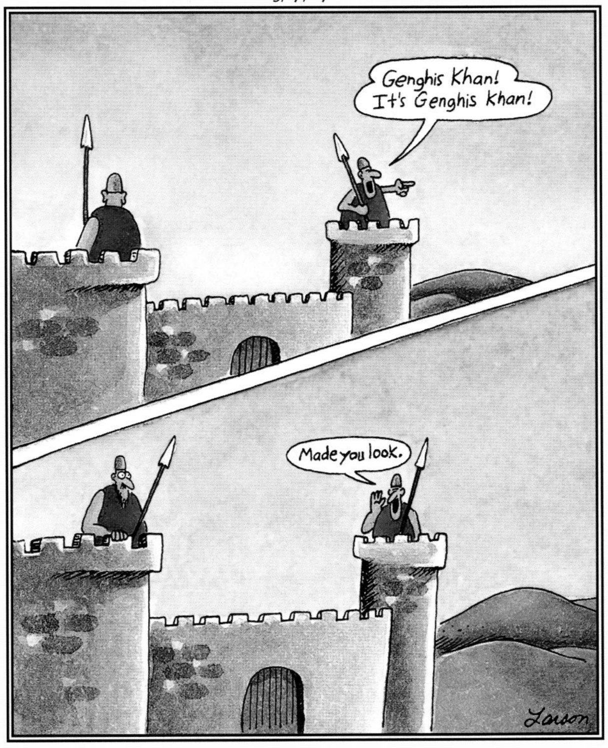
Genghis Khan! It's Genghis Khan!
Made you look.
Larson

3/15/87

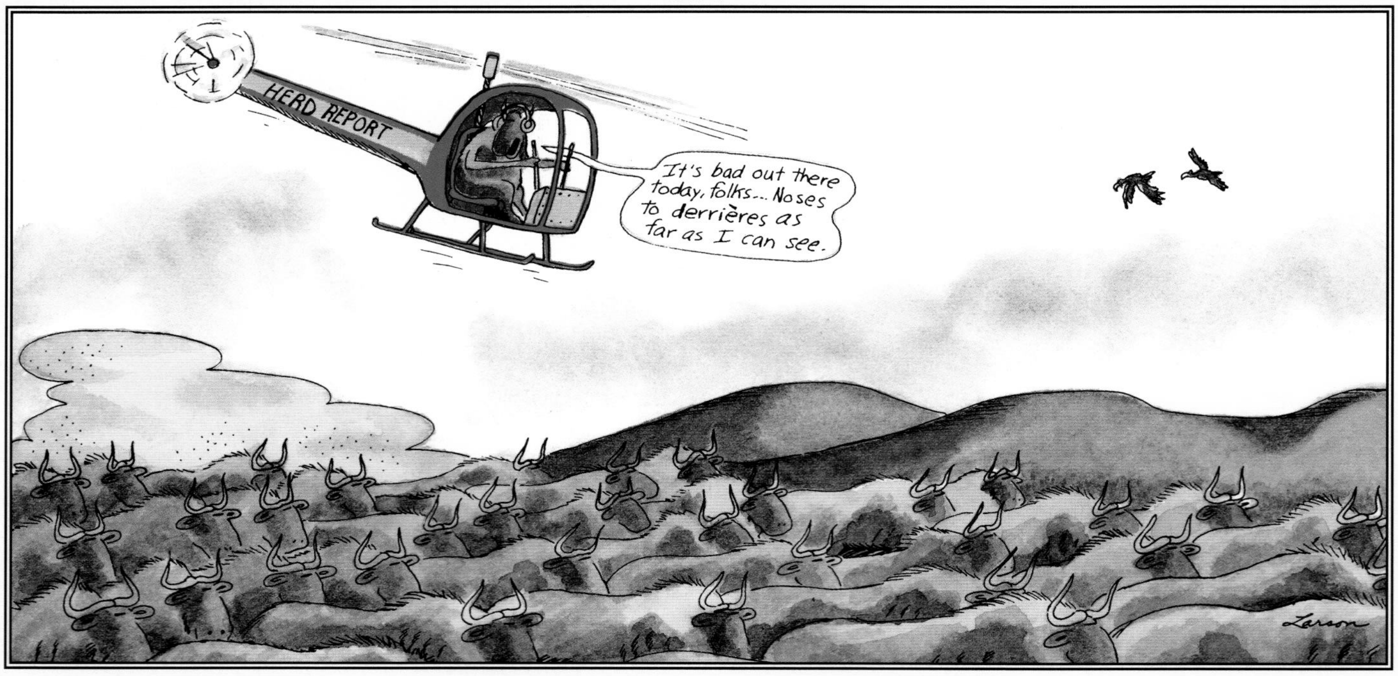
HEAD REPORT
It's bad out there today, folks... Noses to derrières as far as I can see.
Larson

3/11/87

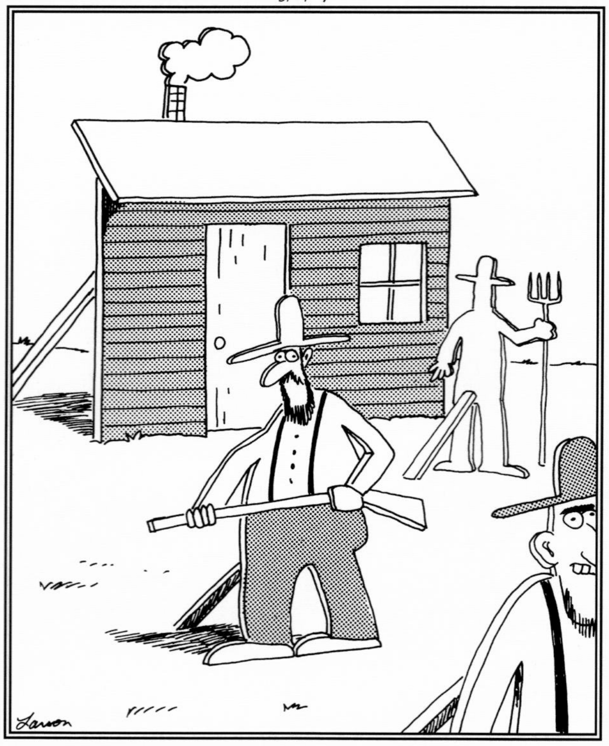
Larson

The fake McCoys

3/13/87

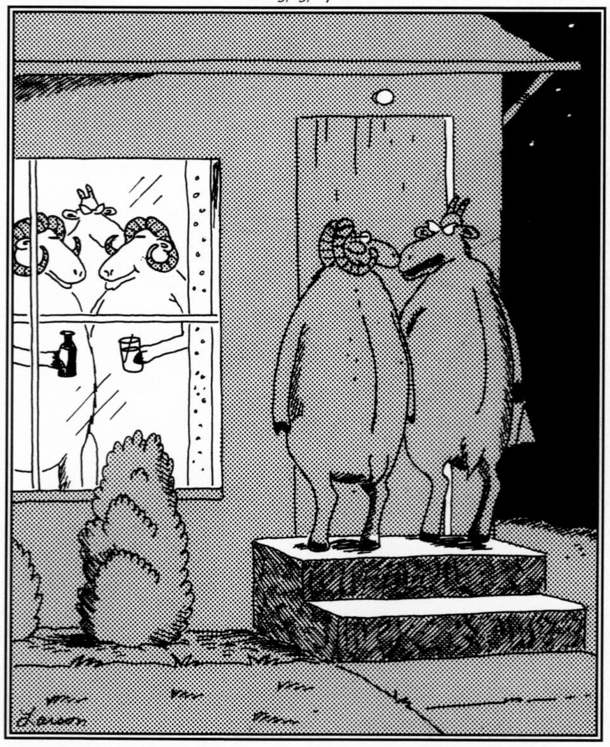
Larson

"Now listen—will you *please* try to control yourself tonight? ... I don't want to see you goading some guy into crashing heads with you."

3/14/87

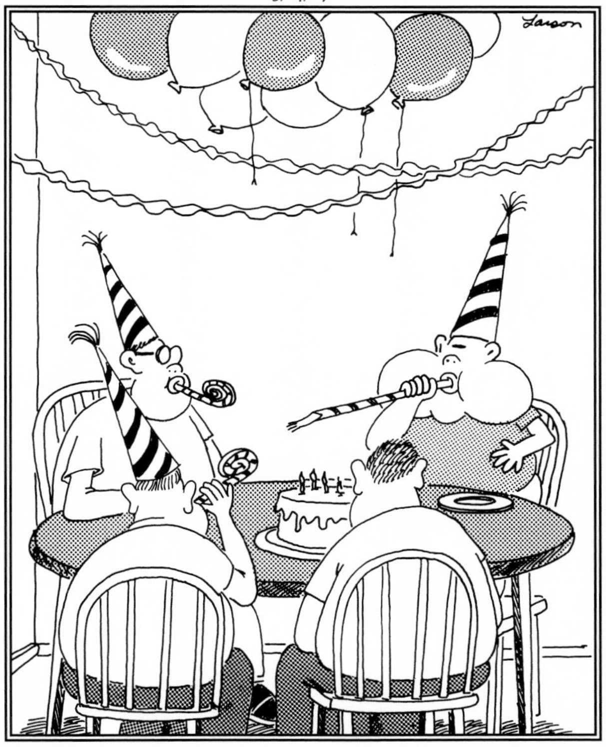

Dizzy Gillespie's seventh birthday party

3/19/87

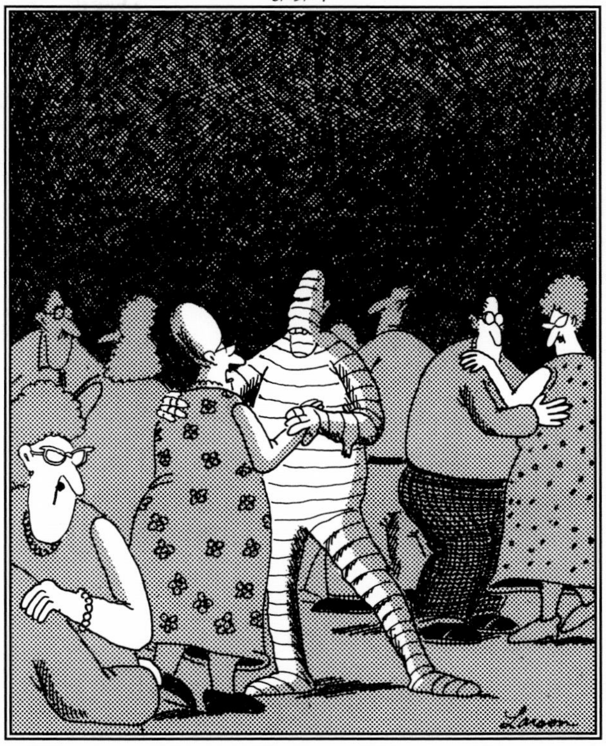

"For heaven's sake, Roger—stop dragging that one leg."

3/20/87

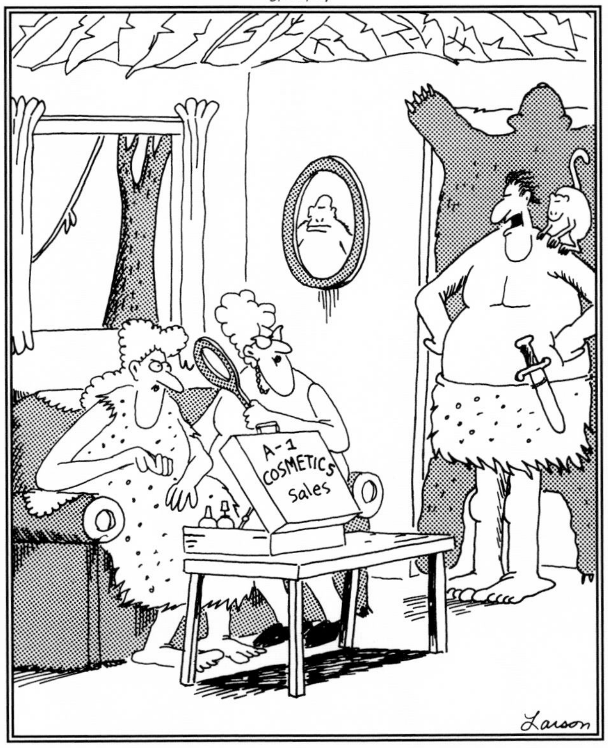
A-1 COSMETICS Sales

"Whoa! Smells like a French primate house in here."

3/25/87

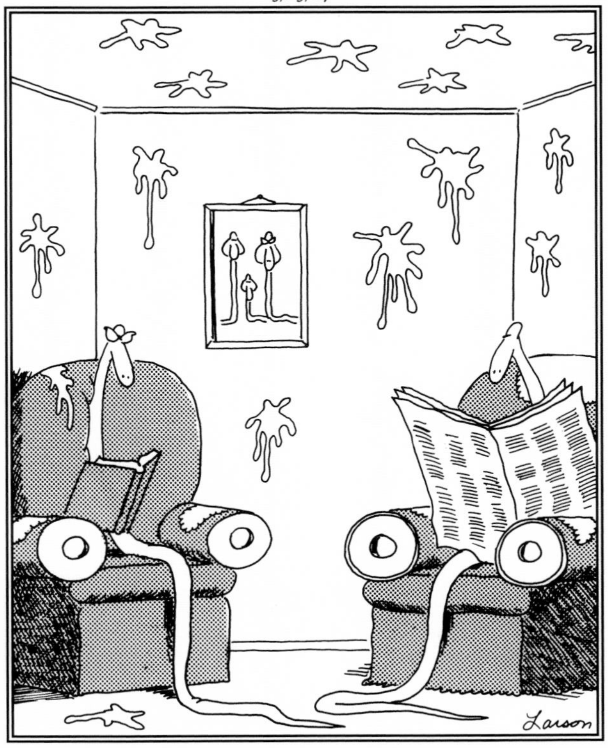

The spitting cobras at home

3/26/87

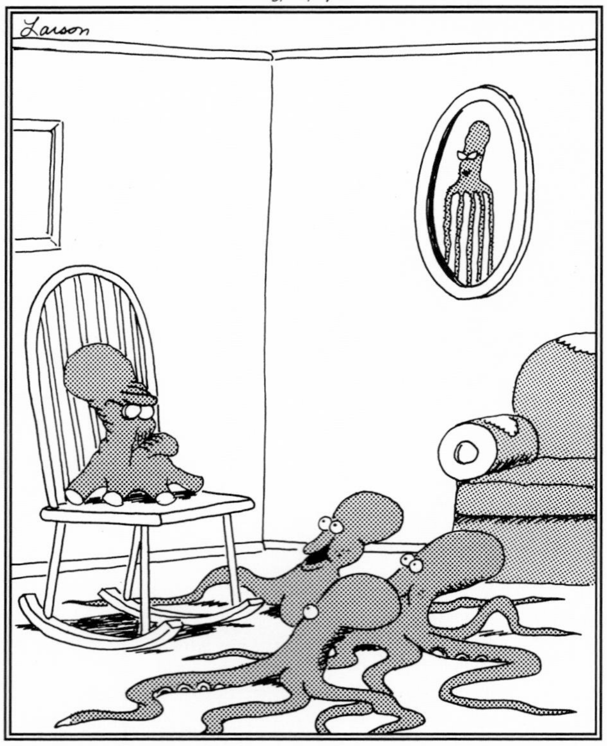
Larson

"Tell it again, Gramps! The one about being caught in the shark frenzy off the Great Barrier Reef!"

3/27/87

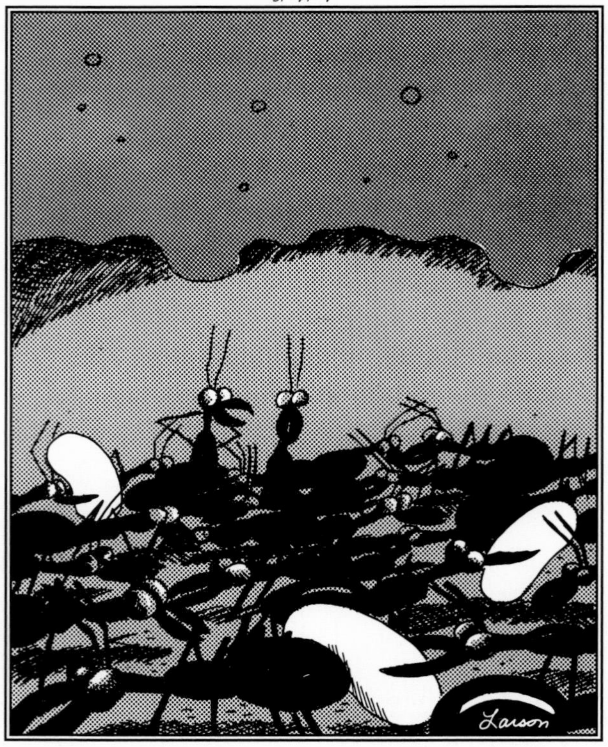
Larson

"You ever do this? ... Just sit in a place like this and antwatch?"

3/18/87

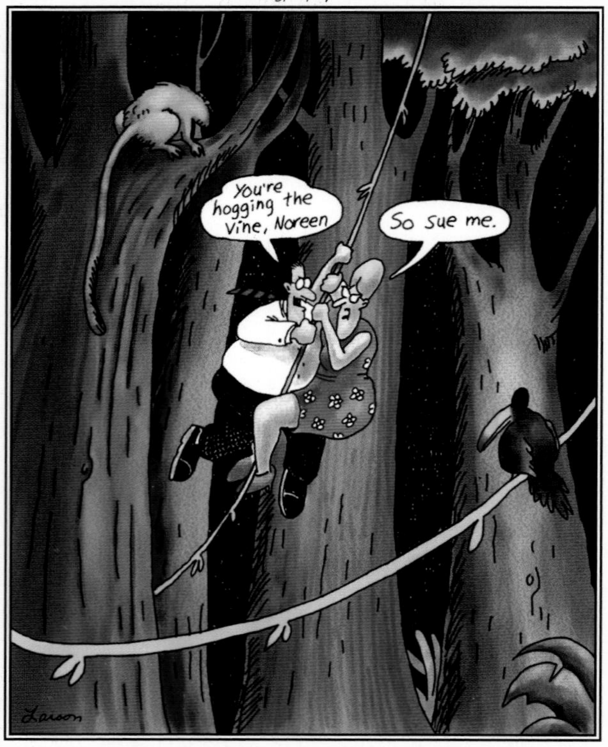
You're hogging the vine, Noreen.
So sue me.
Larson

The Hendersons of the Jungle

3/23/87

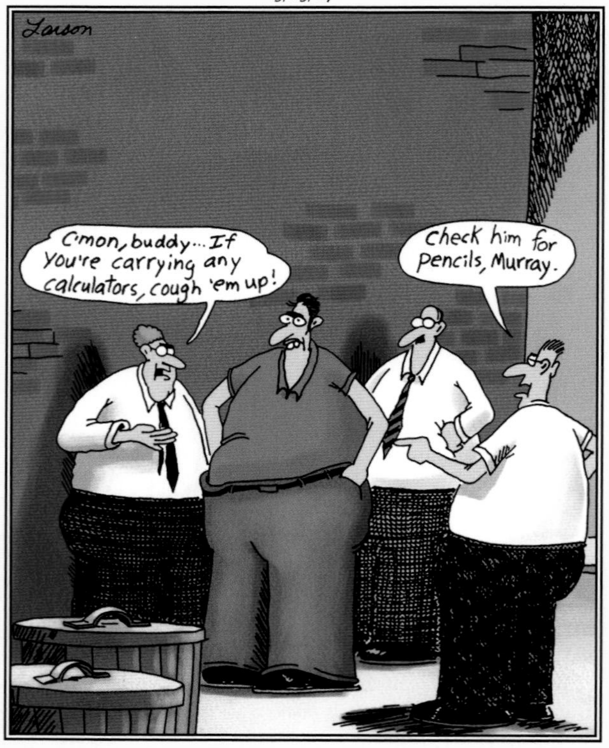
Larson
C'mon, buddy... If you're carrying any calculators, cough 'em up!
Check him for pencils, Murray.

Accountant street gangs

3/21/87

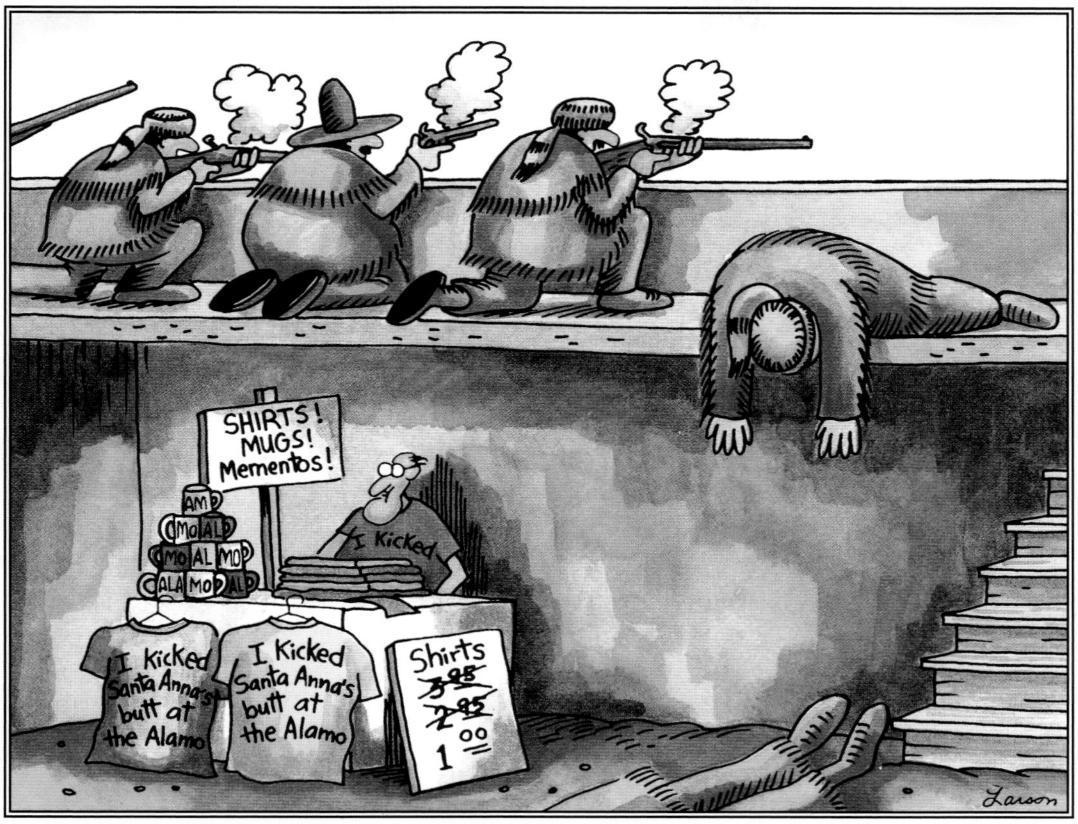
SHIRTS! MUGS! Mementos!
I Kicked
I Kicked Santa Anna's butt at the Alamo
I Kicked Santa Anna's butt at the Alamo
Shirts
~~3.95~~
~~2.95~~
1.00

3/30/87

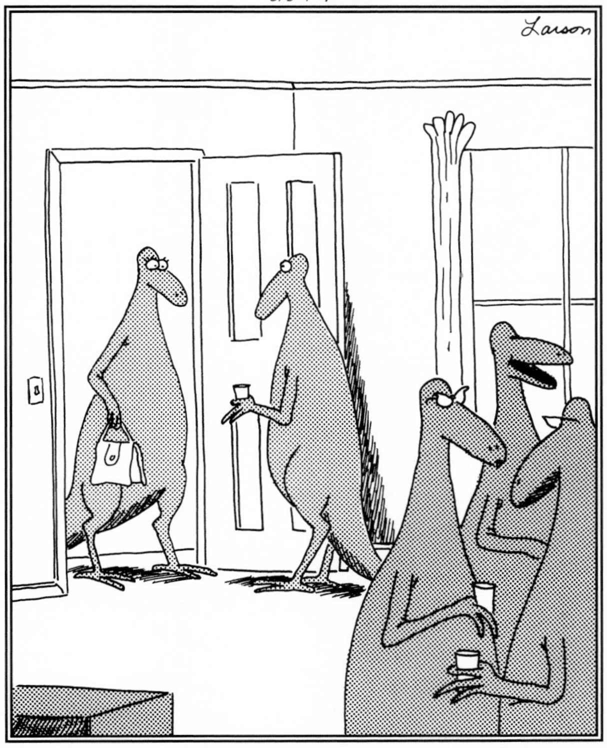

Chameleon faux pas: Arriving at a party in the same color as the host.

3/28/87

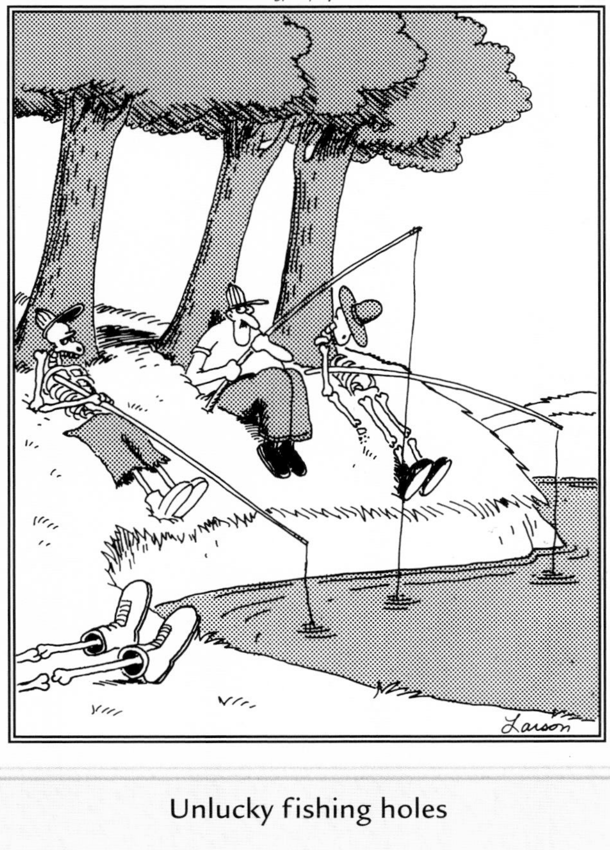

Unlucky fishing holes

3/22/87

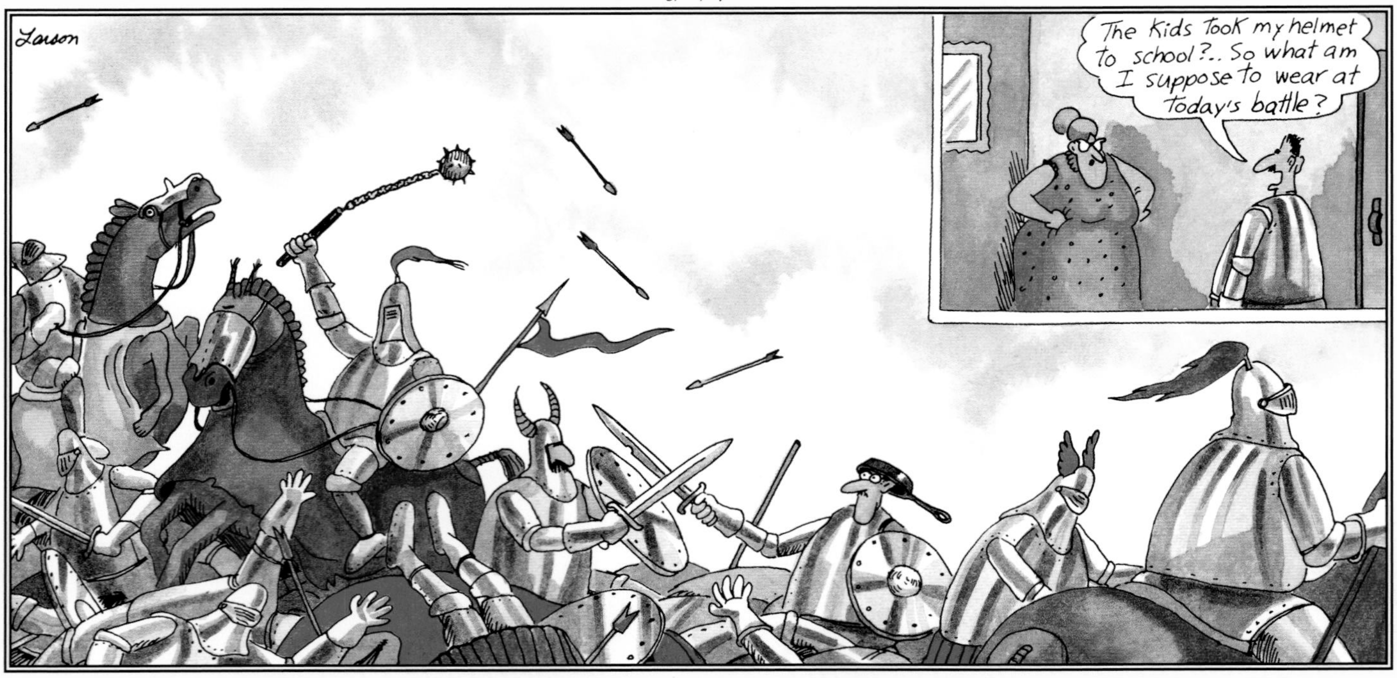
Larson
The kids took my helmet to school?.. So what am I suppose to wear at today's battle?

3/24/87

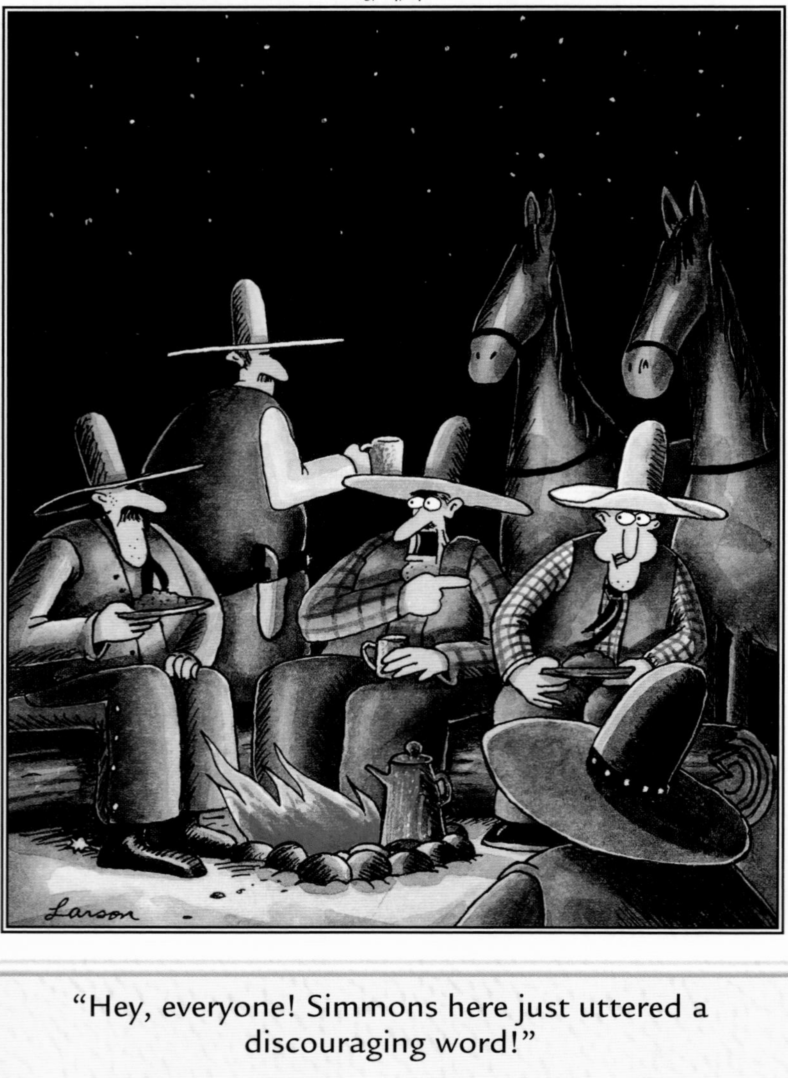
Larson

"Hey, everyone! Simmons here just uttered a discouraging word!"

3/31/87

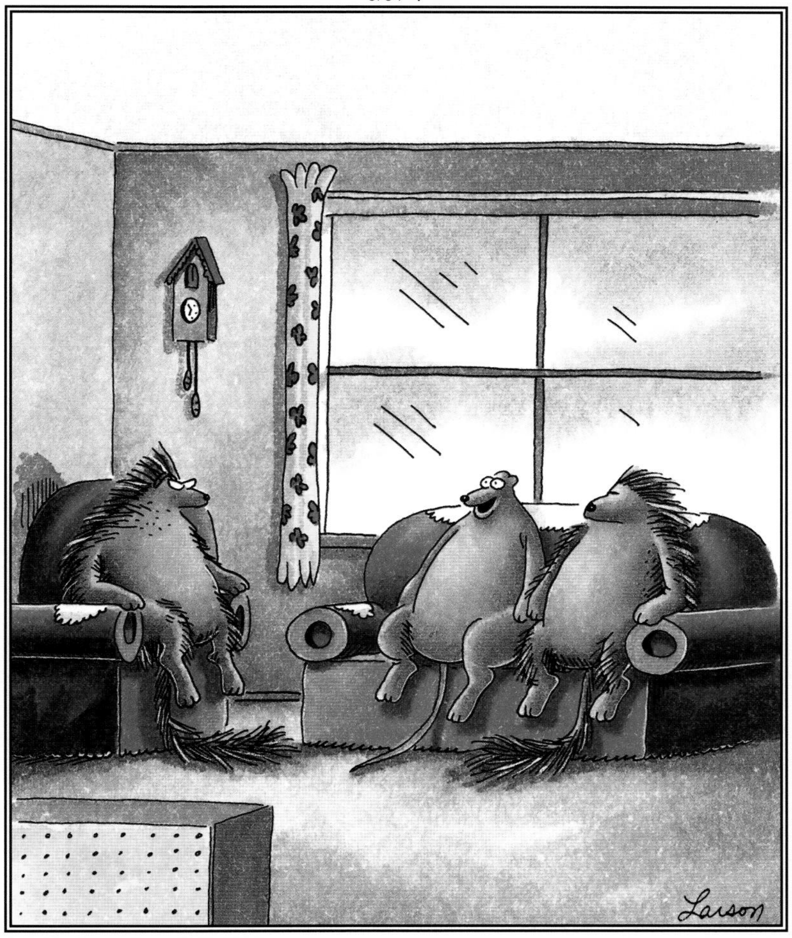

"I had them all removed last week and boy, do I feel great!"

3/29/87

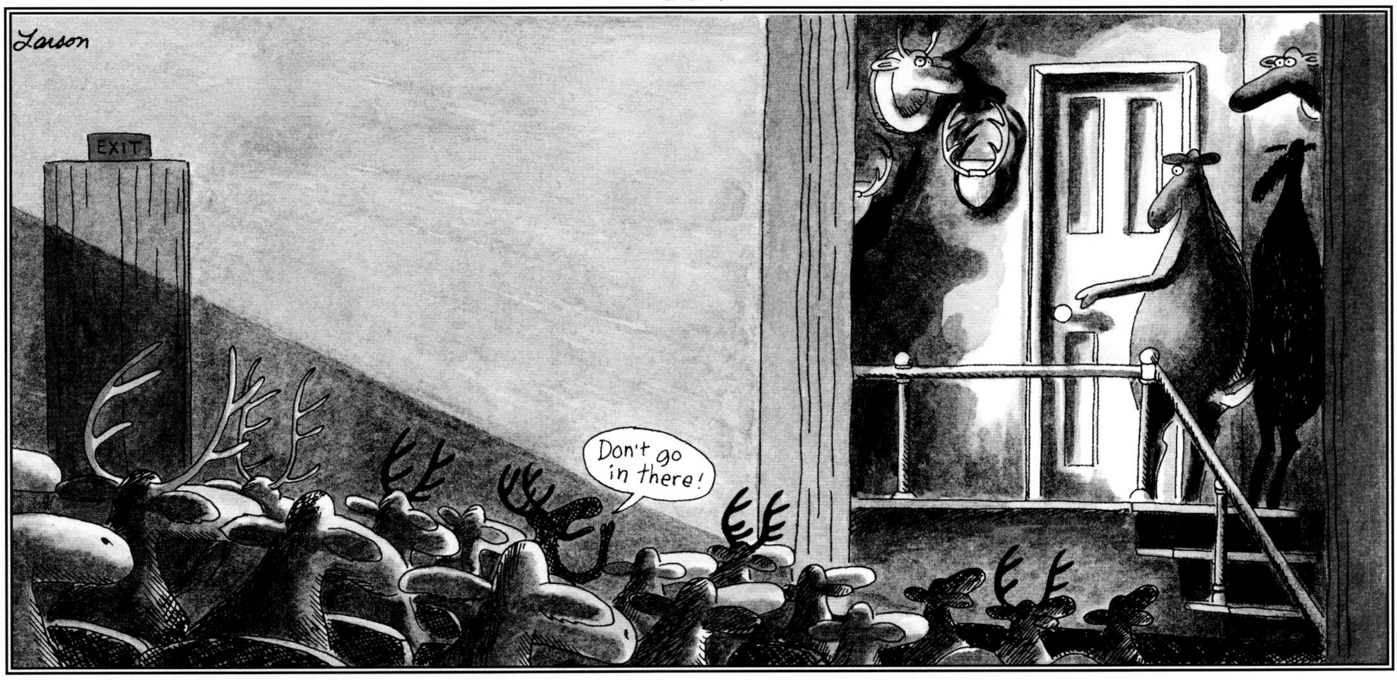
EXIT
Don't go in there!

Horror films of the Wild

4/1/87

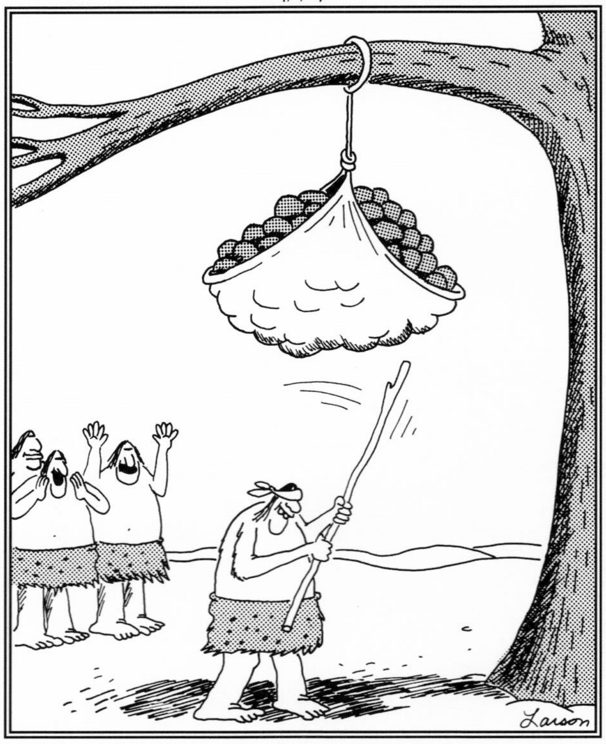
Larson

Early piñatas

4/2/87

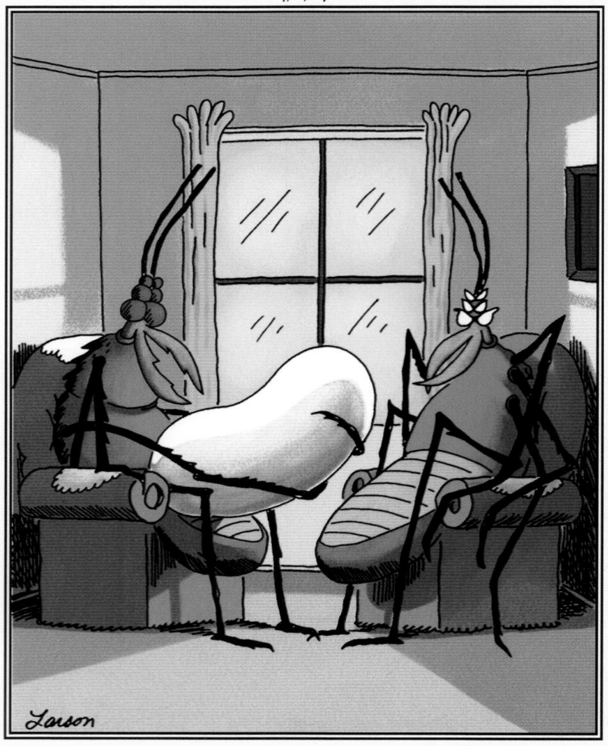
Larson

"Well, Frank's hoping for a male and I'd like a little female. ... But, really, we'll both be happy if it just has six eyes and eight legs."

4/3/87

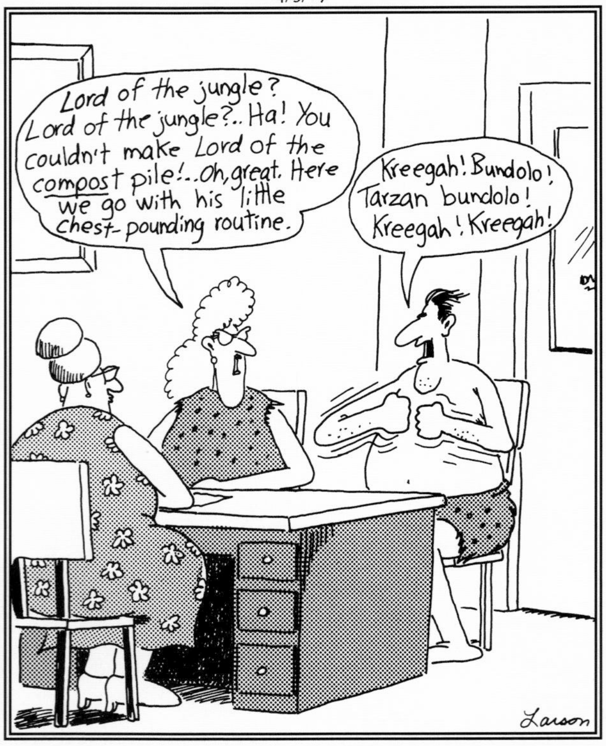
Lord of the jungle? Lord of the jungle?.. Ha! You couldn't make Lord of the compost pile!..Oh, great. Here we go with his little chest-pounding routine.
Kreegah! Bundolo! Tarzan bundolo! Kreegah! Kreegah!
Larson

The Greystokes at marriage counseling

4/4/87

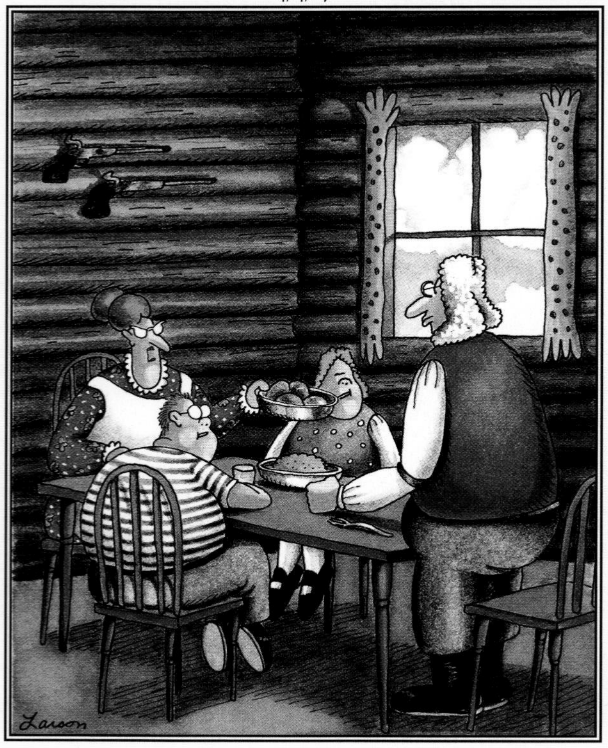
Larson

"For crying out loud, Patrick—sit down. ... And enough with the 'give me the potatoes or give me death' nonsense."

4/9/87

...and then I see Wilbur go around to the back of the barn carrying this shovel and he's got this wild look in his eyes and he's like real nervous and then I notice he's trying to bury this big plastic bag which at first I figure is just full of manure but then I start to wonder what the hey is going on and then...
Larson

Mr. Ed spills his guts.

4/11/87

Larson

"And we're eating soon, so stay out of the kitty jar."

4/7/87

I don't believe you heard me right, stranger... I said I'd like to buy you a chicken leg!
Larson

In the Old West, vegetarians were often shot with little provocation.

4/6/87

Larson

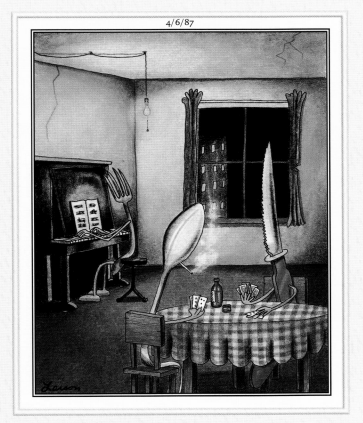

In the early days, living in their squalid apartment, all three shared dreams of success. In the end, however, Bob the Spoon and Ernie the Fork wound up in an old silverware drawer, and only Mack went on to fame and fortune.

4/5/87

Here he comes!
SURPRISE!

4/8/87

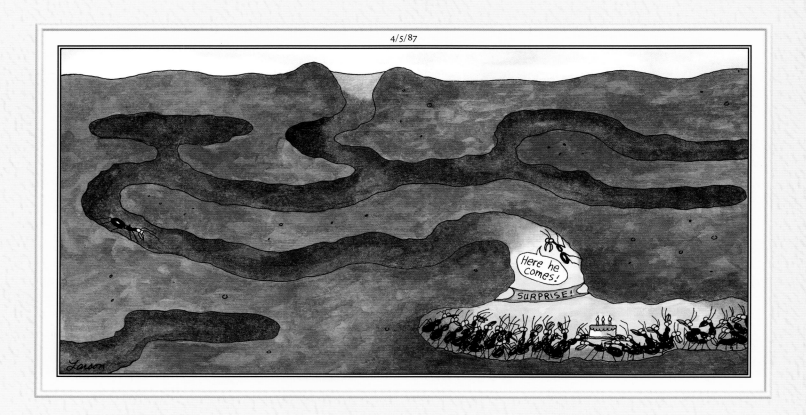

"Again? You just had a glass of water twelve days ago."

4/10/87

SALT
SALT
SALT
SALT
SALT

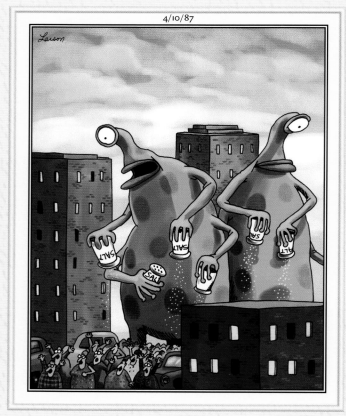

"Well, this is getting nowhere fast."

Thor's hammer, screwdriver, and
crescent wrench

"Won't talk, huh? ... Frankie! Hand me
that scaler."

4/17/87

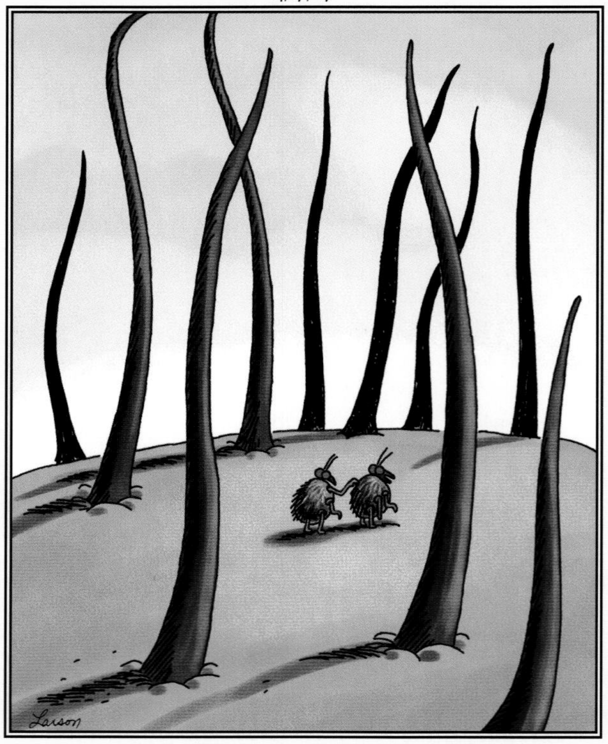

"Yes! Yes! That's it! Just a little higher. ... Ahhhhhhhhh ..."

4/13/87

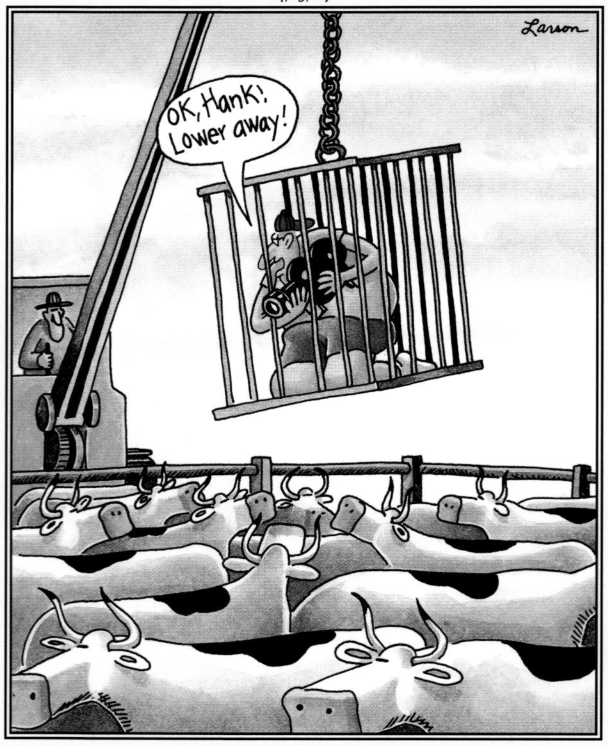
OK, Hank! Lower away!

How cow documentaries are made

4/16/87

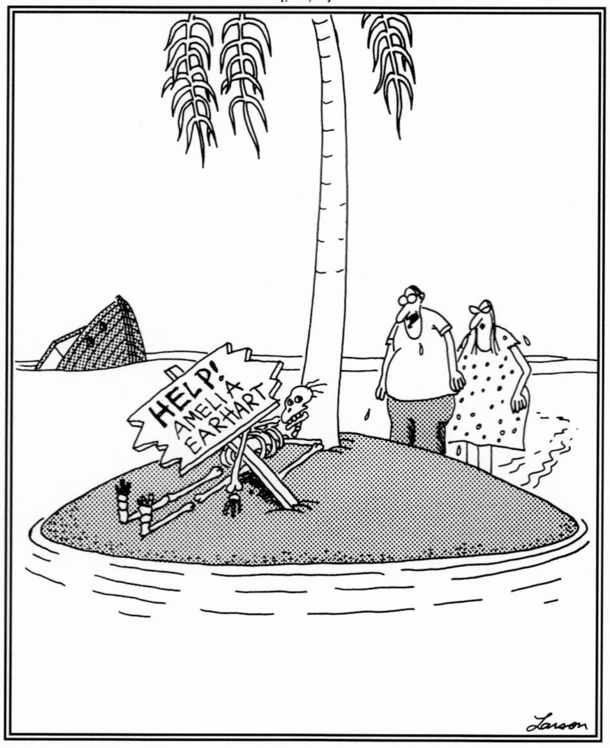
HELP! AMELIA EARHART

"Well, *this* isn't very promising."

4/18/87

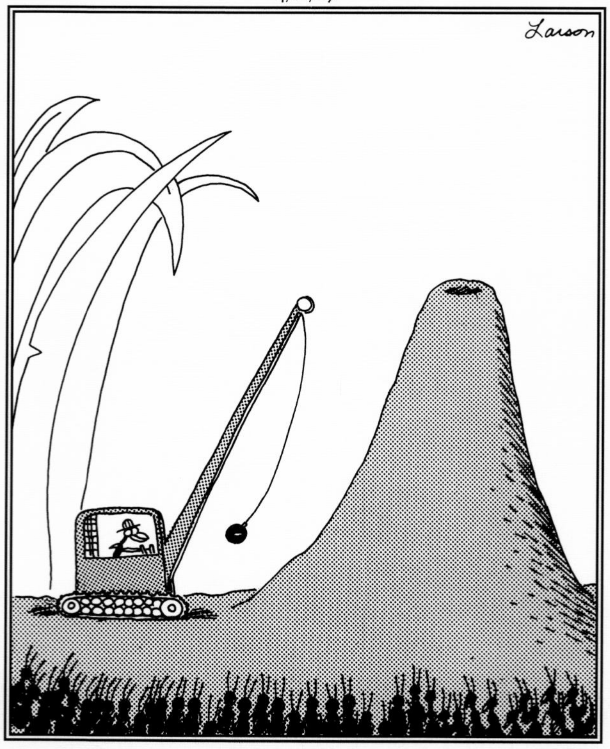

4/20/87

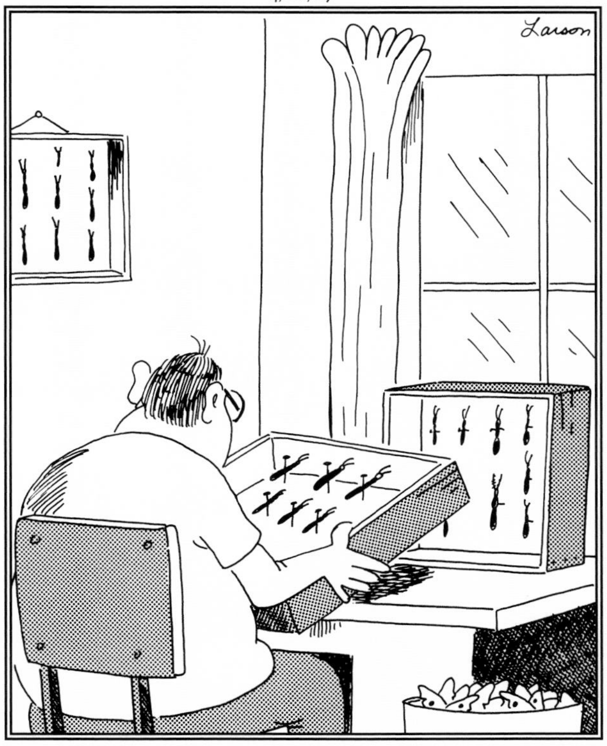
Larson

Randy Schueler's wingless butterfly collection

4/21/87

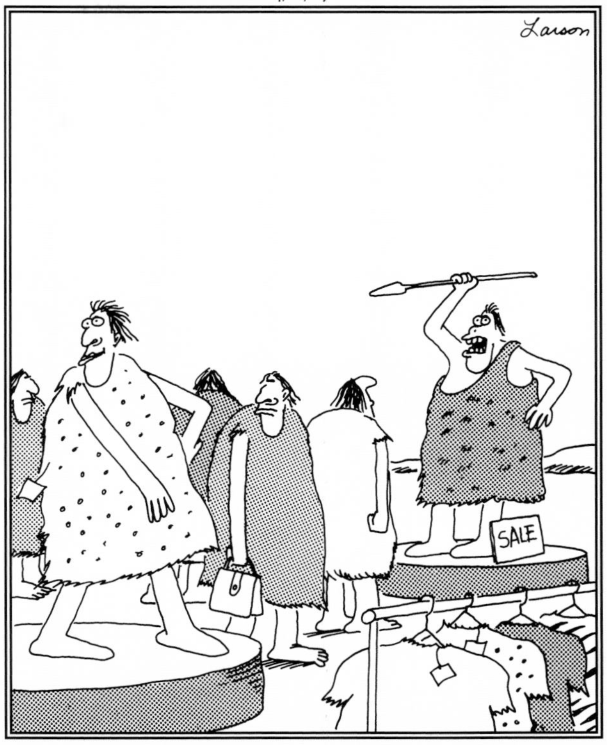
Larson
SALE

Early department stores

4/19/87

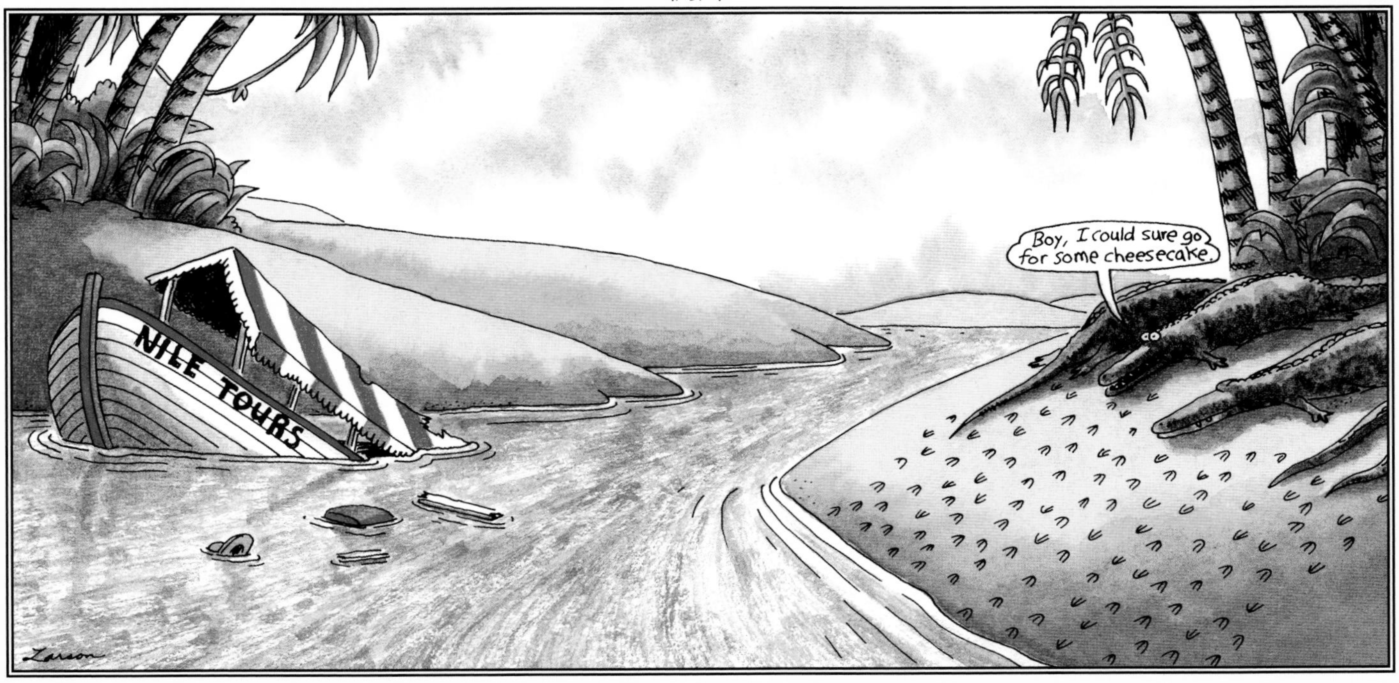
NILE TOURS
Boy, I could sure go for some cheesecake.
Larson

4/27/87

Man, Bernie, you're a mess!... You ain't itchin' anywhere, are you? Man, I had a cast on my leg years ago and boy did it itch!...Drove me crazy! Y'know what I'm sayin'?... 'Cause you can't scratch it, y'know... Don't think about itching anywhere, Bernie, 'cause it'll drive you nuts!

4/30/87

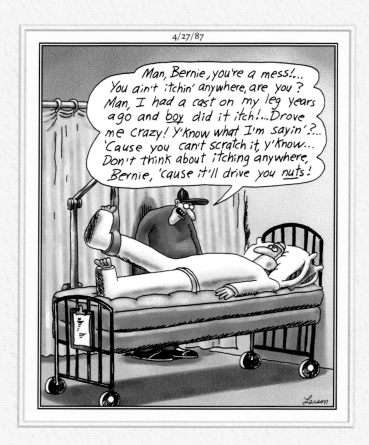

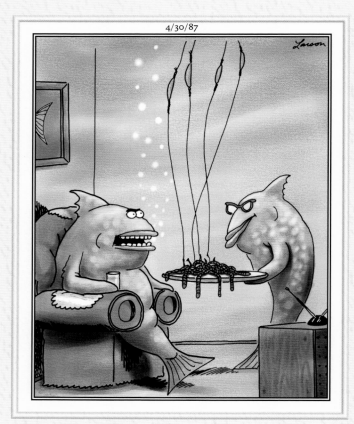

"More worms? ... Saaaaaaaaay—why are you being so nice to me all of a sudden?"

4/22/87

Now listen up! We're going to do this alphabetically!
damn

4/29/87

"Well, if I'm lucky, I should be able to get off this thing in about six more weeks."

4/24/87

Larson
BONUS QUESTION:
(50 points)
What's the name
of that thing that
hangs down in the
back of our throats?

Final page of the medical boards

4/26/87

Larson
Whoa! That's plenty.

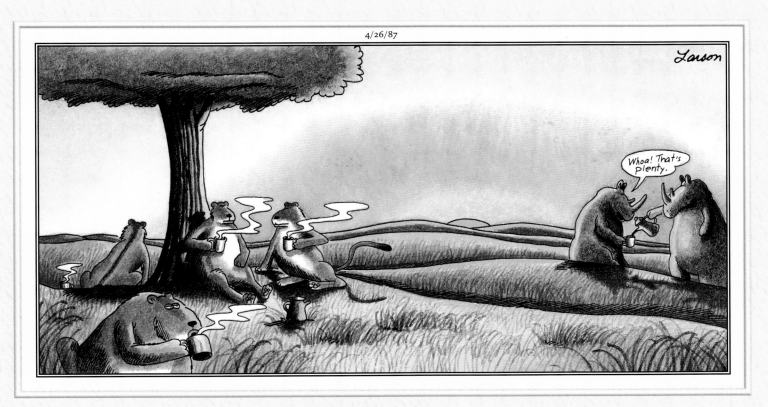

The African dawn

4/25/87

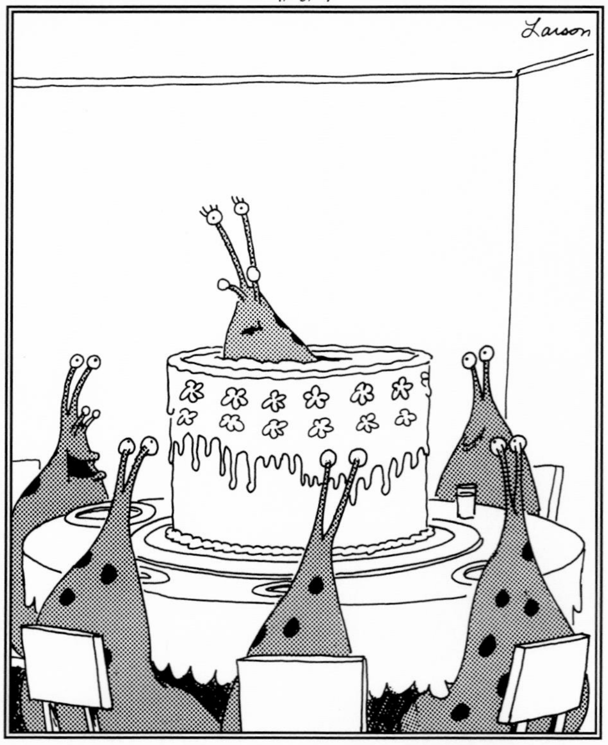
Larson

"Hey! *Now* her whole head is out! ...
This is getting better every minute!"

4/28/87

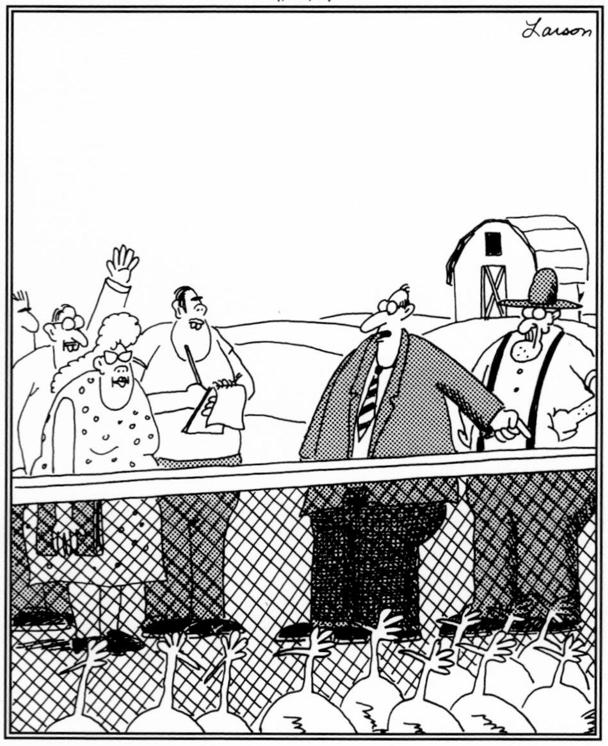
Larson

Ornithology 101 field trips

4/23/87

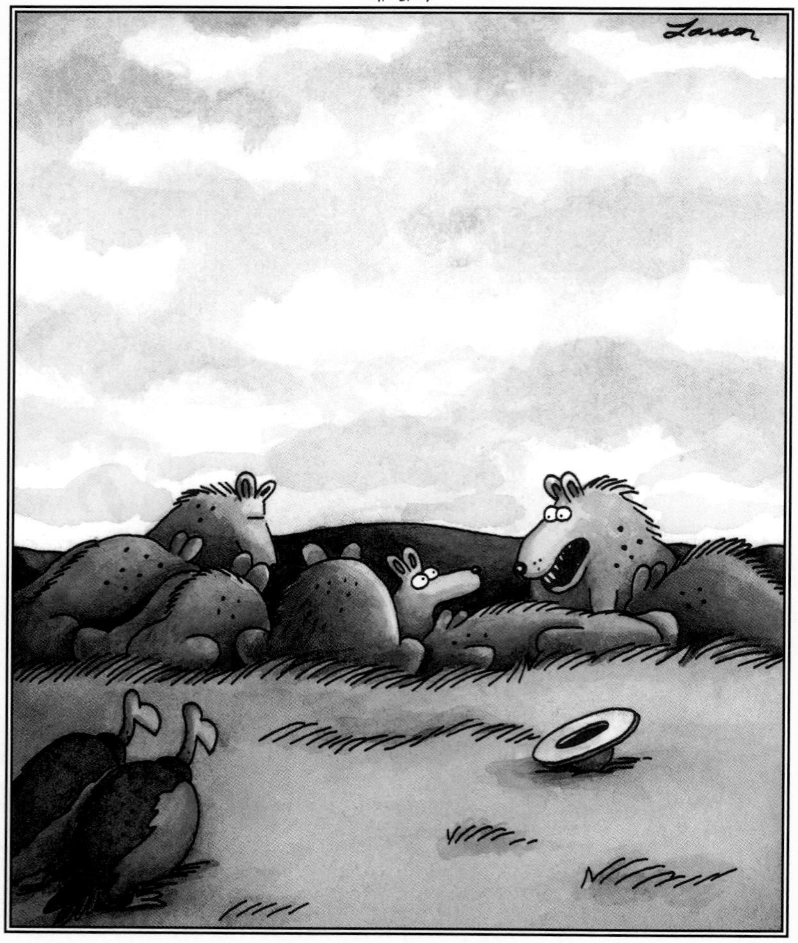
Larson

"You're not fooling anyone, Mitchell. ... You're not eating, you're just spreading it around."

5/6/87

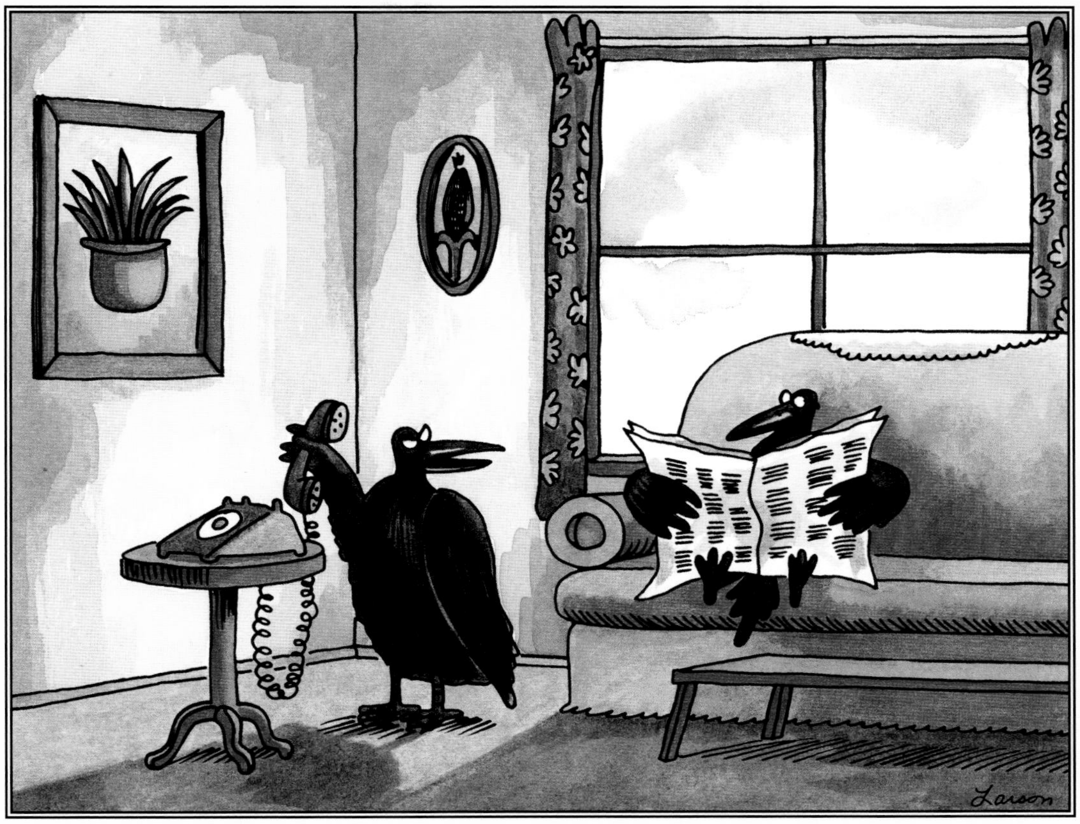
Larson

"Louis ... phonecaw."

5/1/87

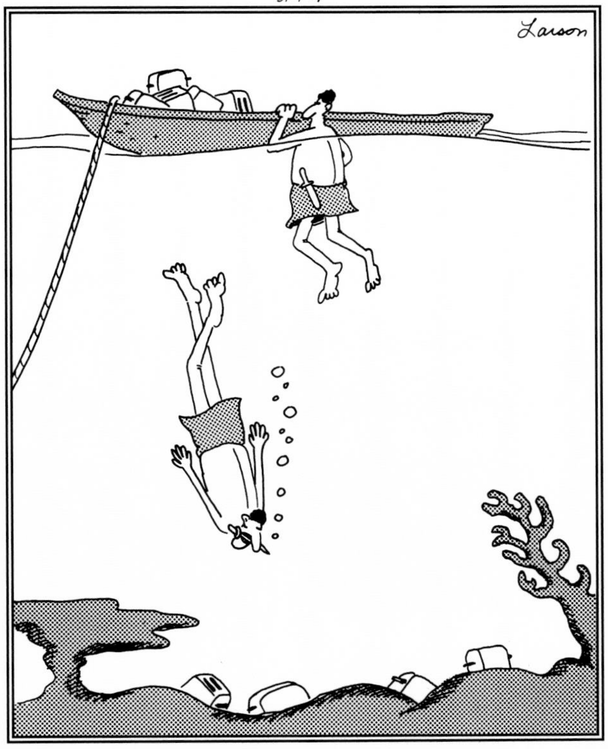
Larson

The toaster divers of Pago Pago

5/4/87

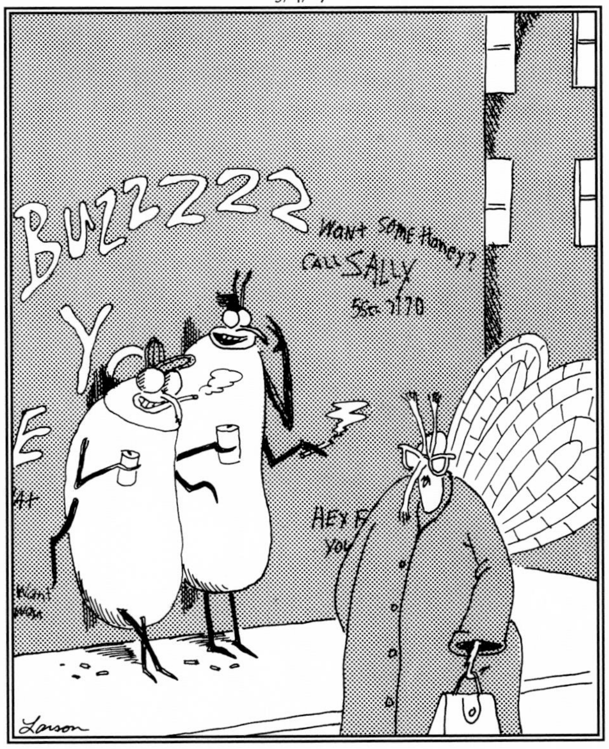
BUZZZZZ
Want Some Honey?
CALL SALLY
555-7170
HEY F
YOU
Larson

Killer bees are generally described as starting out as larvae delinquents.

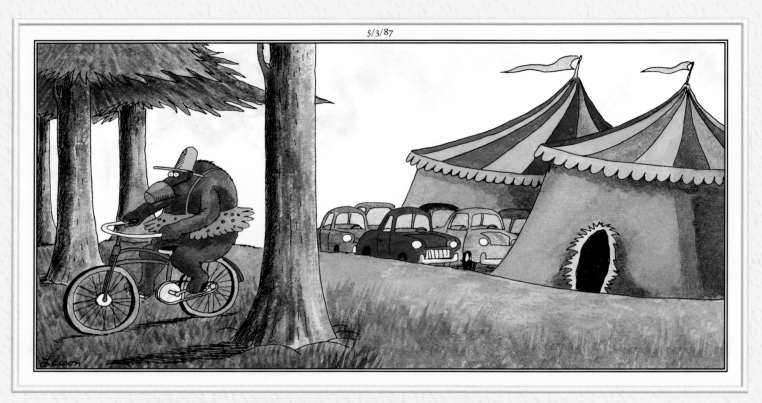

5/3/87

Bobo remained free the rest of his life, although he did find it necessary to seek counseling.

5/2/87

Inexplicably, Bob's porcupine goes flat.

5/7/87

Mutants on the *Bounty*

5/14/87

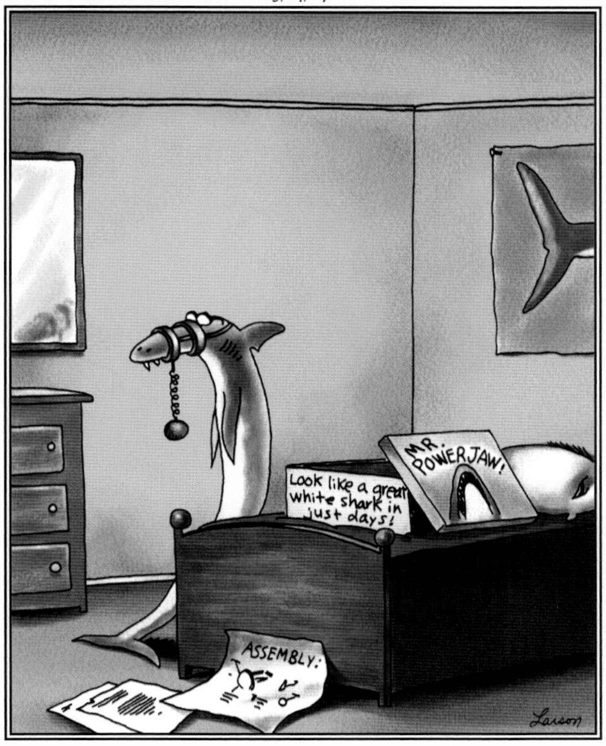
Look like a great white shark in just days!
MR POWER JAW!
ASSEMBLY:
Larson

Products that prey on shark wimps

5/21/87

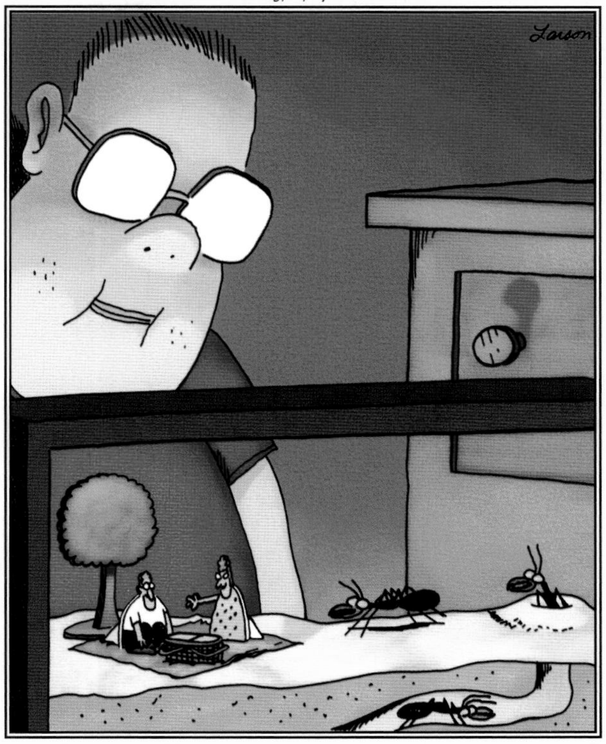
Larson

Stephen King's childhood ant farm

5/10/87

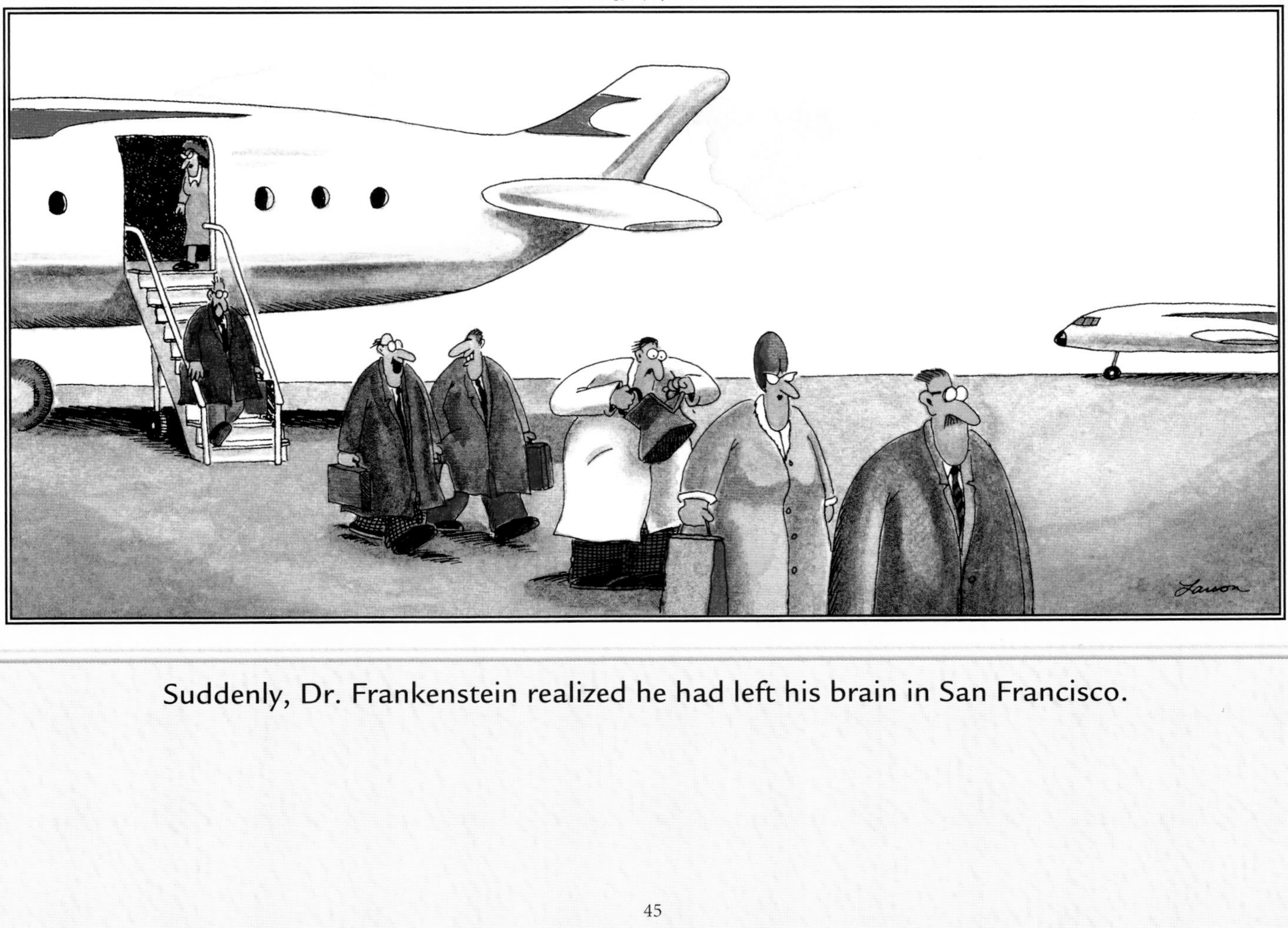
Larson

Suddenly, Dr. Frankenstein realized he had left his brain in San Francisco.

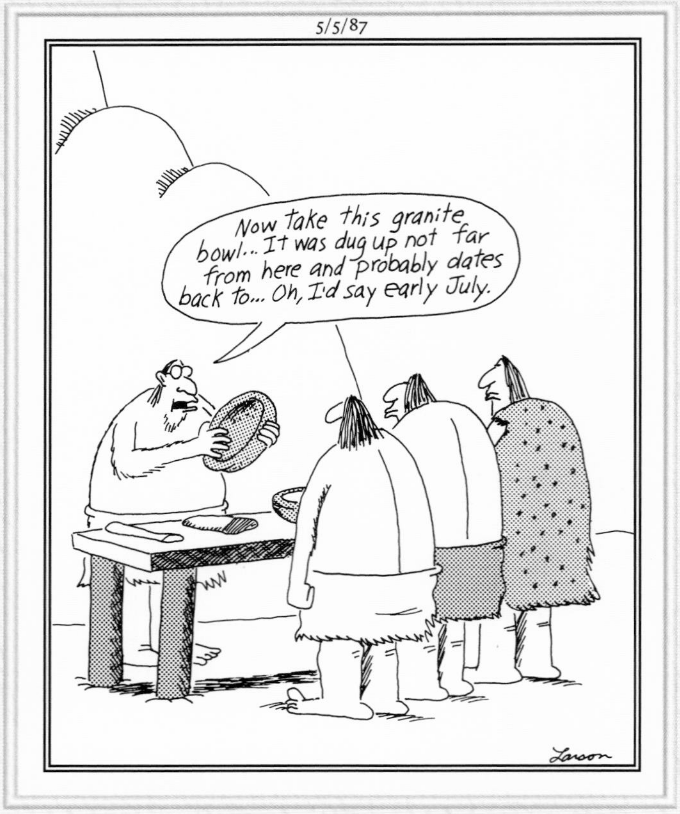
5/5/87
Now take this granite bowl... It was dug up not far from here and probably dates back to... Oh, I'd say early July.
Larson

Early archaeologists

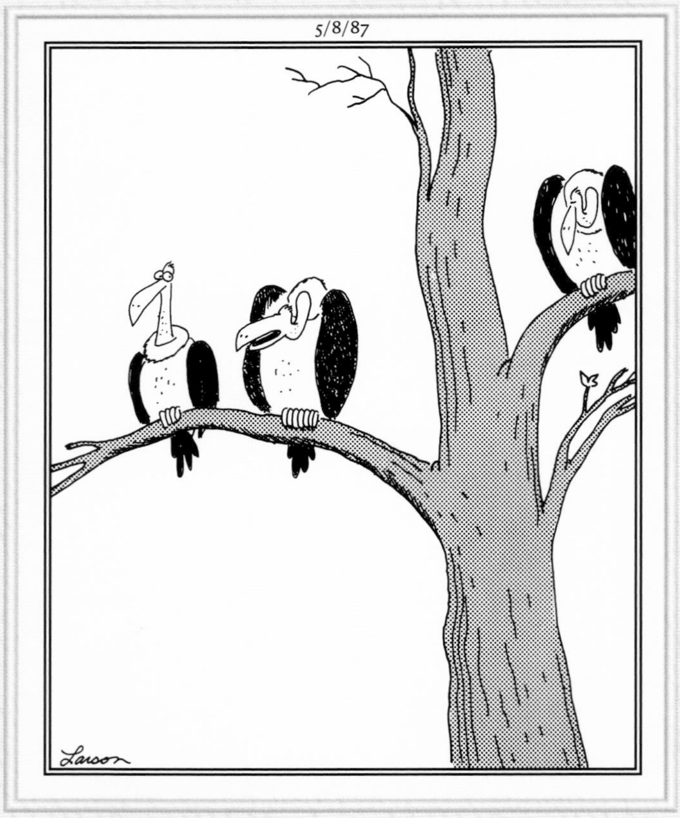
5/8/87
Larson

"Douglas! ... Hunch your shoulders!"

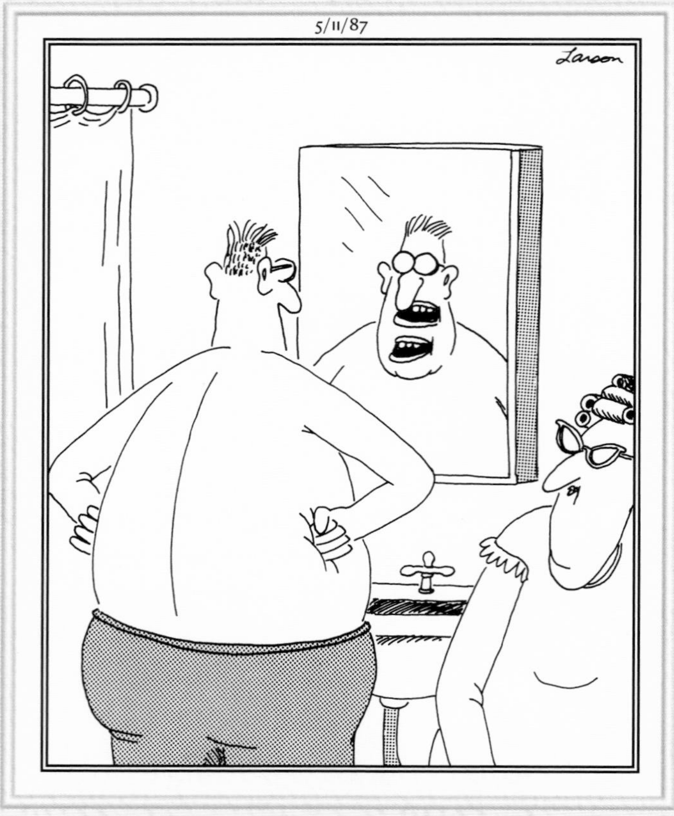
5/11/87
Larson

"Oh, wonderful! Look at this, Etta—another mouth to feed."

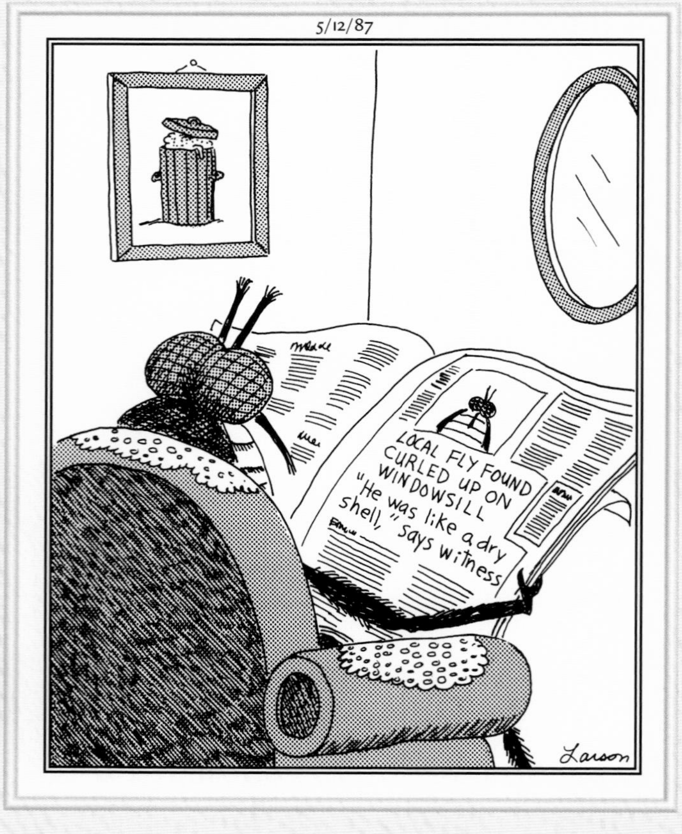
5/12/87
LOCAL FLY FOUND CURLED UP ON WINDOWSILL
"He was like a dry shell," says witness
Larson

5/13/87

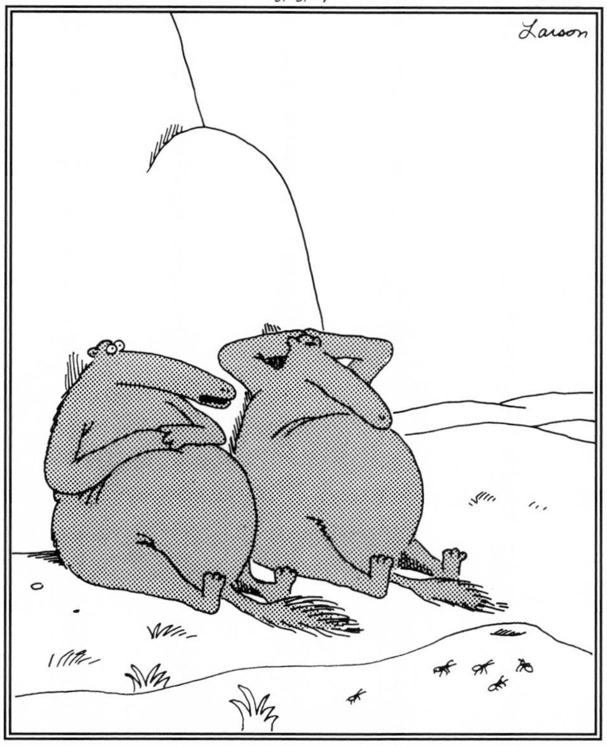

"You know, I don't feel so good, Dale. ... I think some of those red ants were still on the pink side."

5/16/87

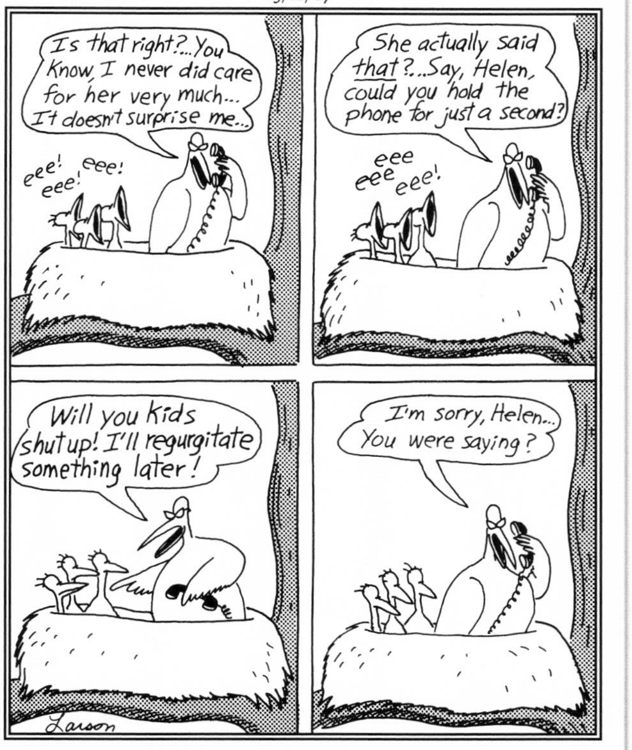
Is that right?...You know, I never did care for her very much... It doesn't surprise me...
eee! eee! eee!
She actually said that?...Say, Helen, could you hold the phone for just a second?
eee eee eee!
Will you kids shut up! I'll regurgitate something later!
I'm sorry, Helen... You were saying?

5/18/87

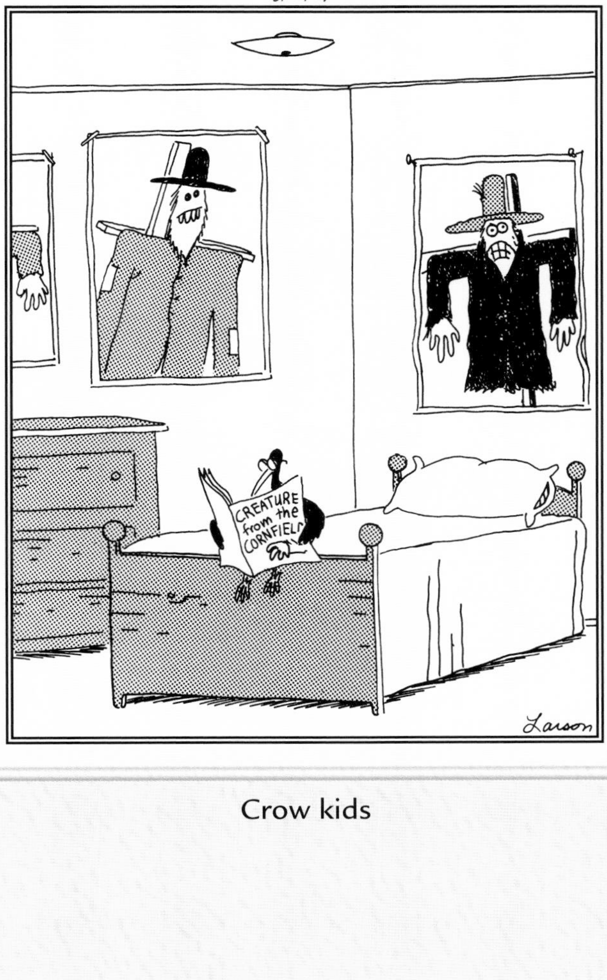
CREATURE from the CORNFIELD

Crow kids

5/22/87

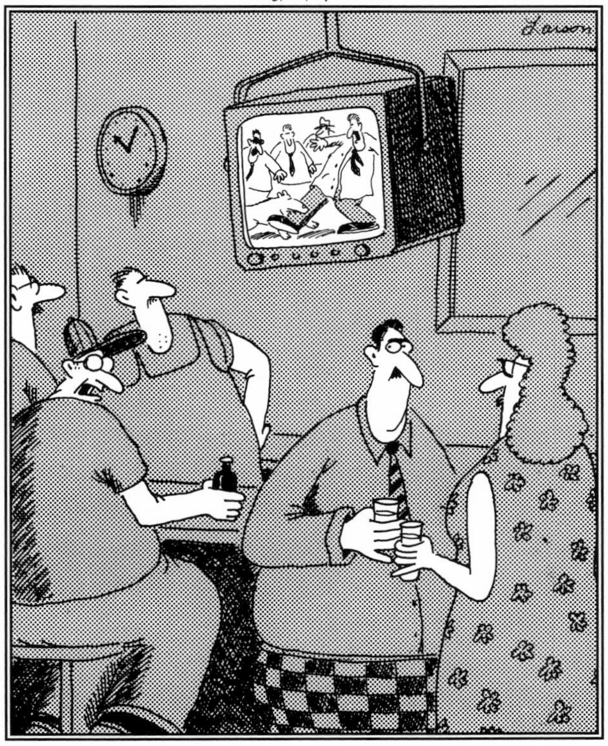

"Hey, Norton! ... Ain't that your dog attackin' the president?"

5/9/87

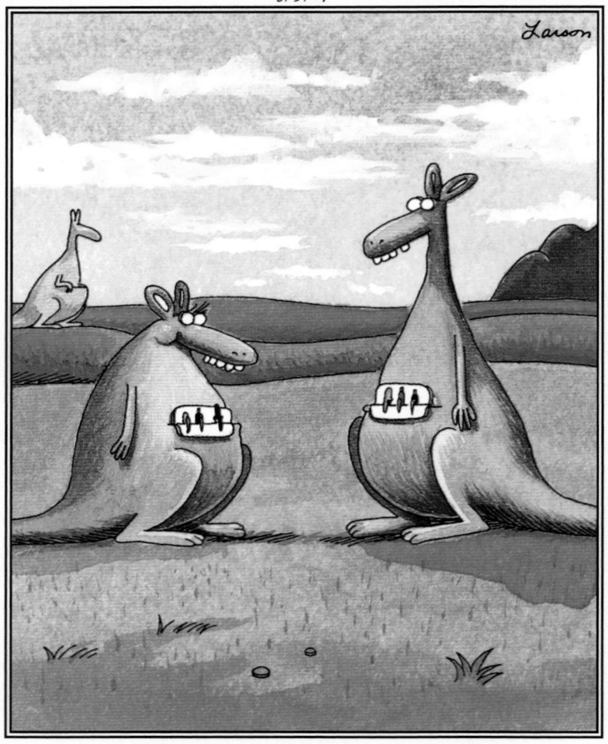
Larson

Kangaroo nerds

5/15/87

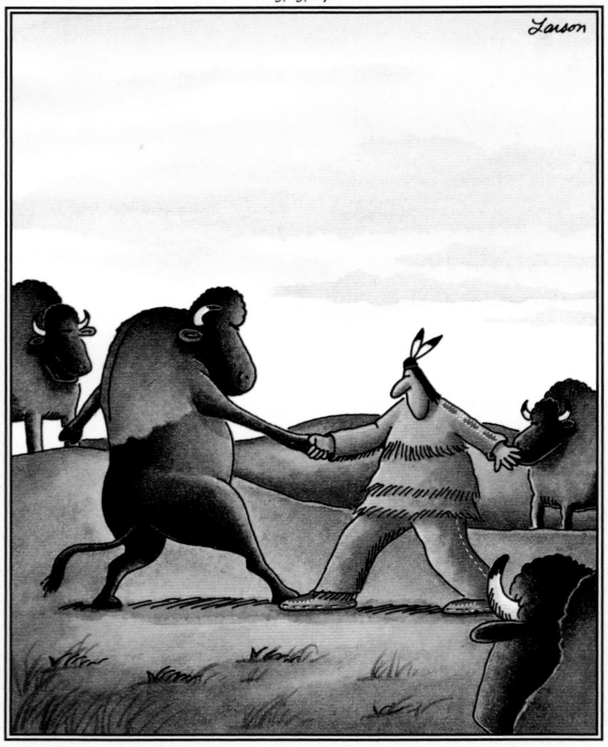
Larson

"Vince! Just trample him! ... He's drawing you into his kind of fight!"

5/17/87

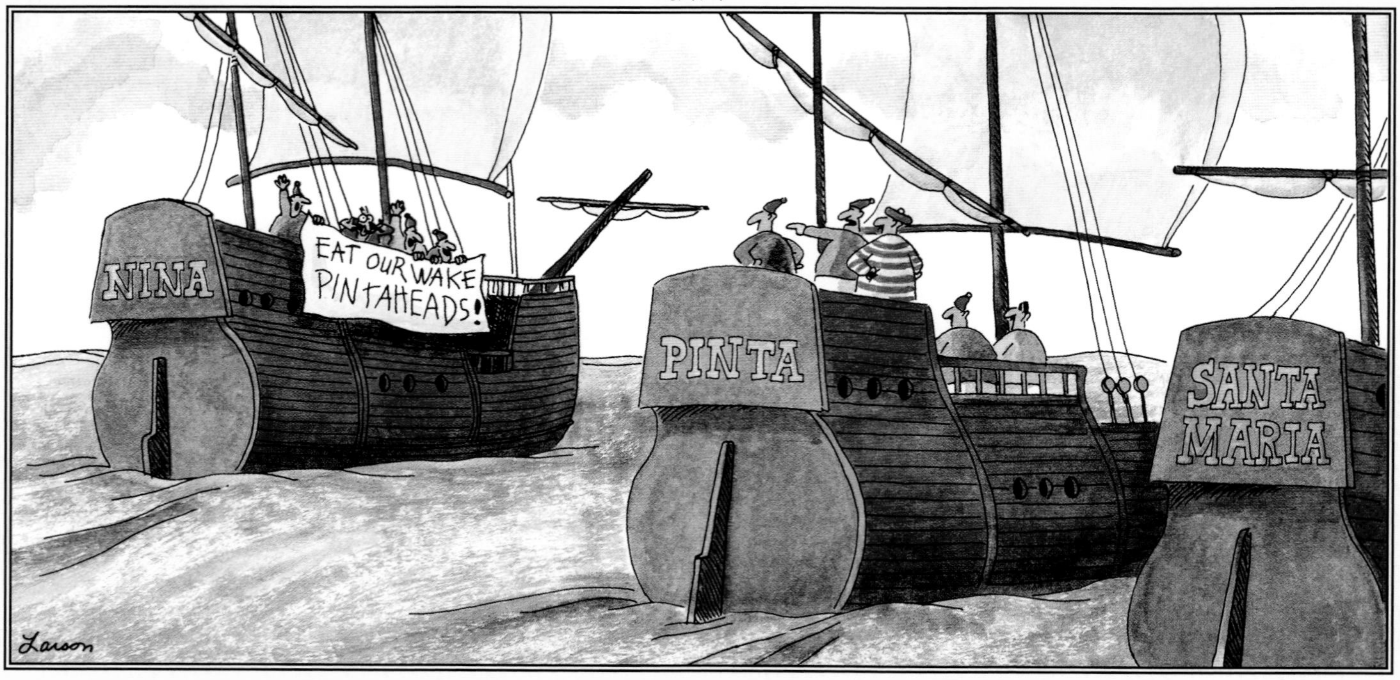
NINA
EAT OUR WAKE PINTAHEADS!
PINTA
SANTA MARIA
Larson

5/19/87

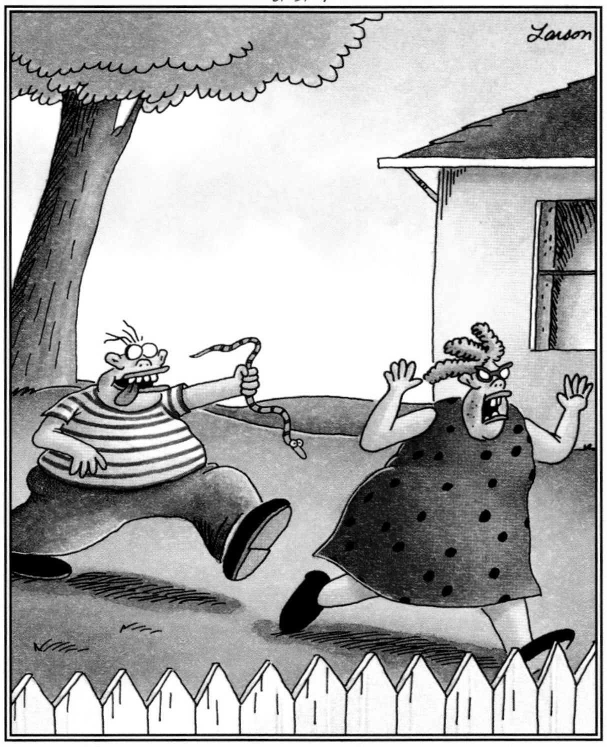
Larson

And for the rest of his life, the young reptile suffered deep emotional scars.

5/20/87

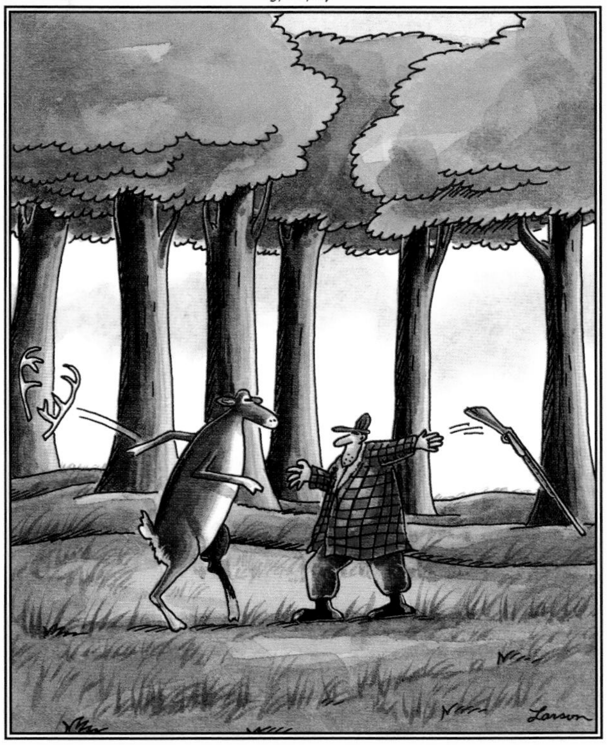
Larson

And there, deep in the forest, both of them decided they would settle this the old-fashioned way.

5/24/87

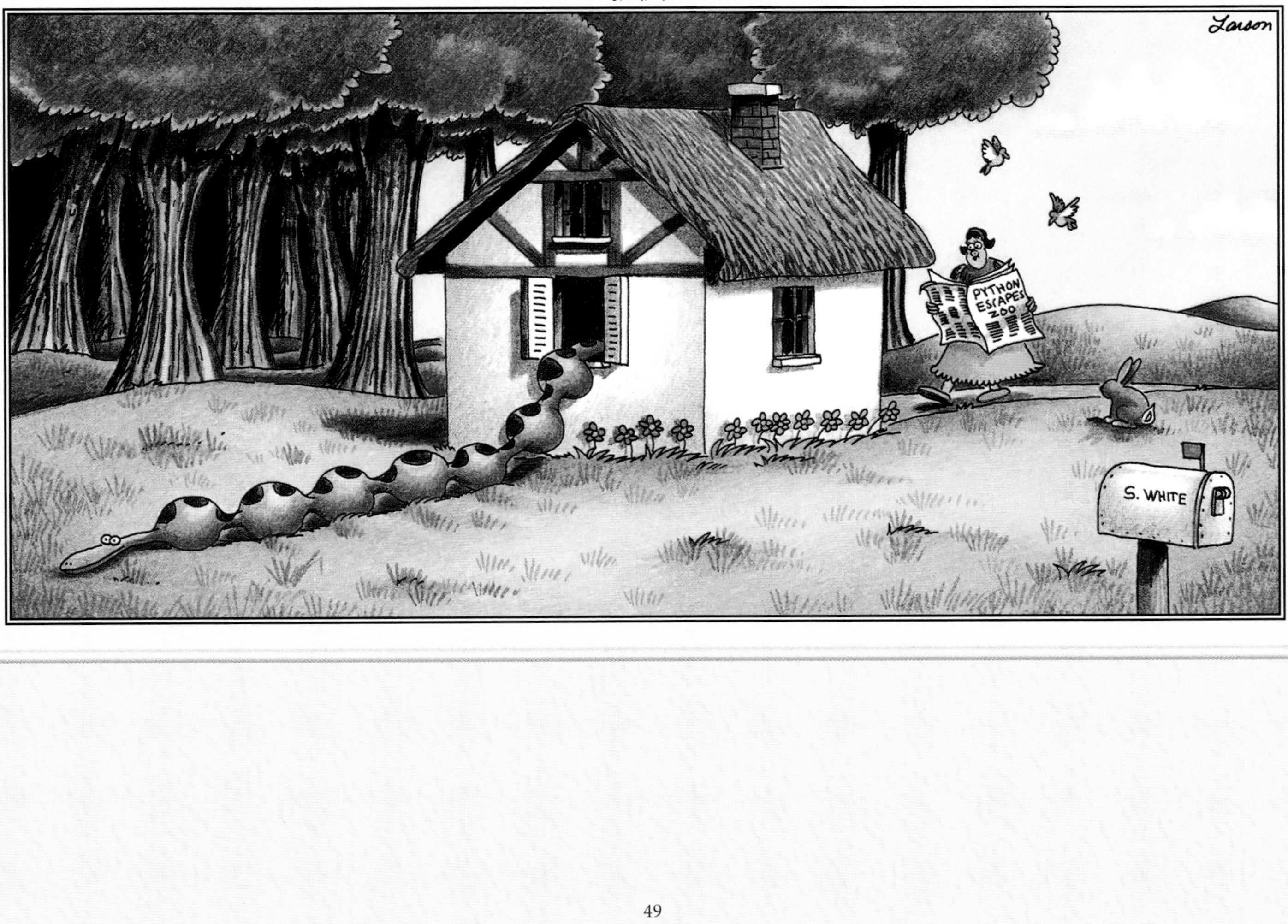
Larson
PYTHON ESCAPES ZOO
S. WHITE

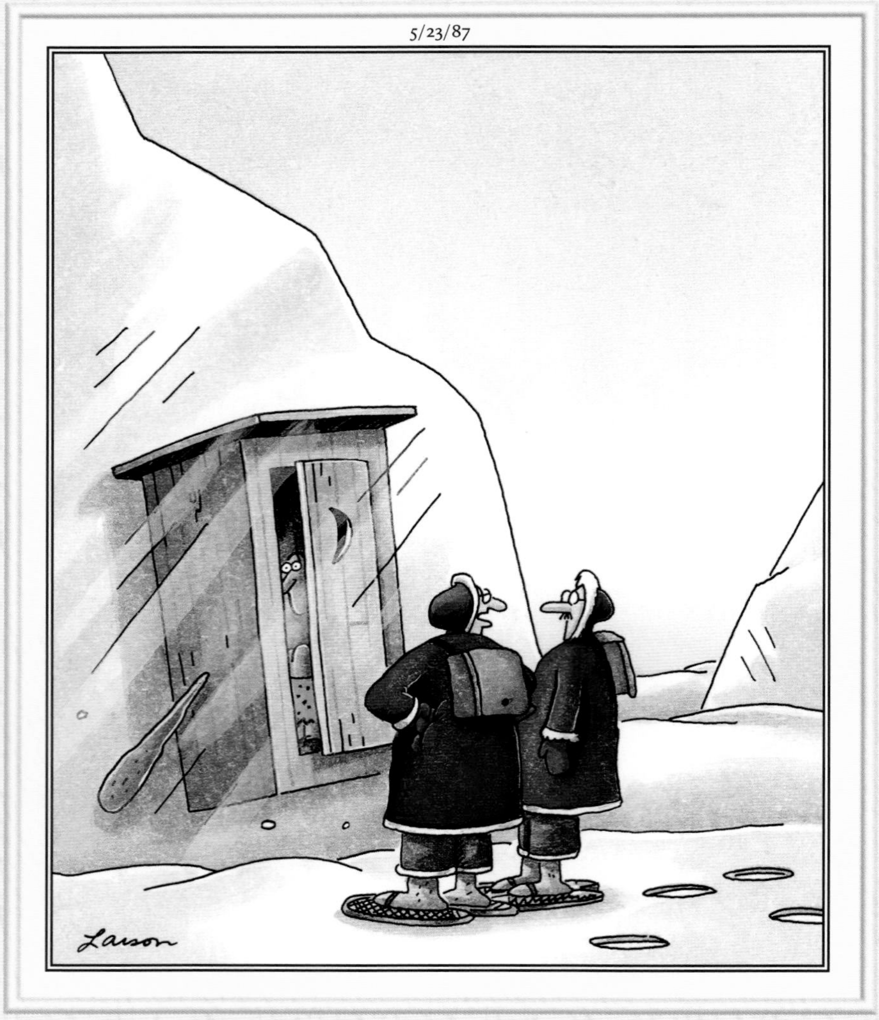
5/23/87
Larson

"This is it, Jenkins—indisputable proof that the Ice Age caught these people completely off guard."

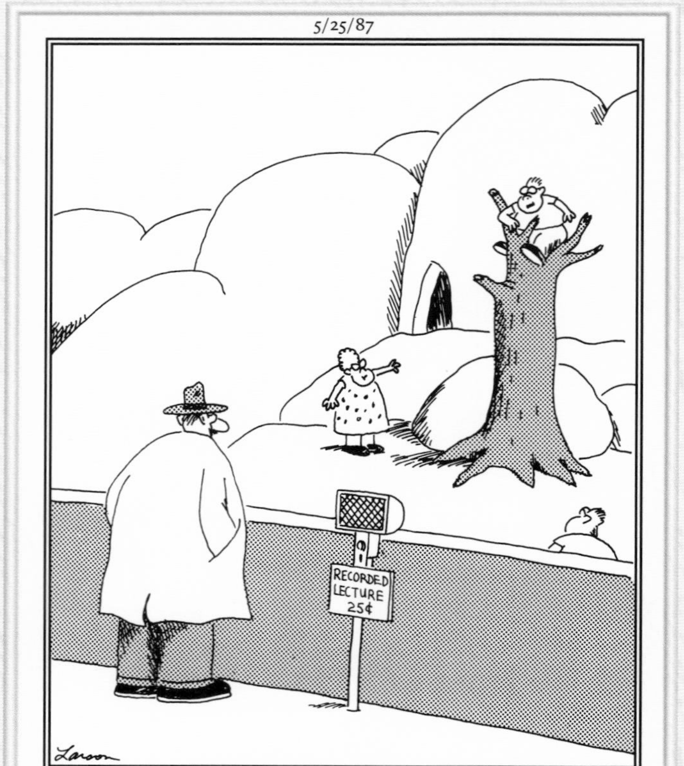
5/25/87
RECORDED LECTURE 25¢
Larson

At the Children's Zoo

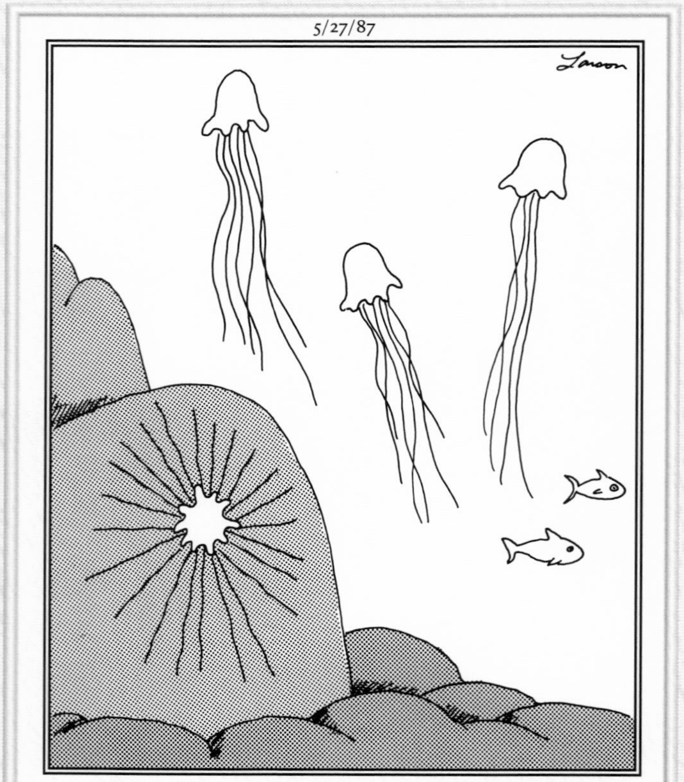
5/27/87
Larson

When jellyfish travel at unsafe speeds

5/29/87

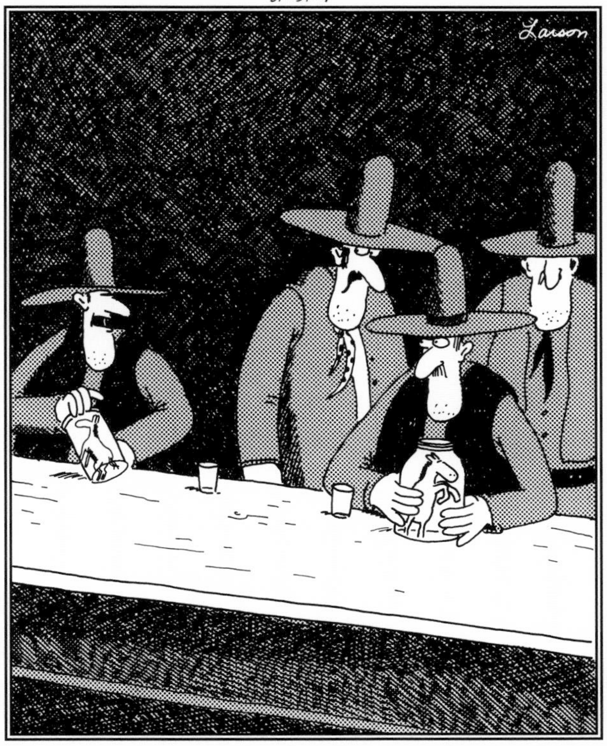
Larson

"Not bad, but you guys wanna see a *really* small horse?"

5/30/87

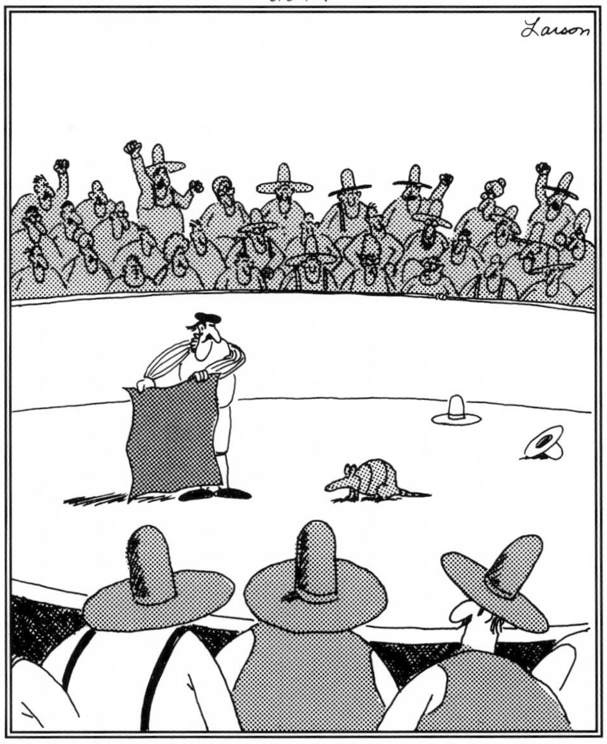
Larson

The armadillo ring of Belize

5/26/87

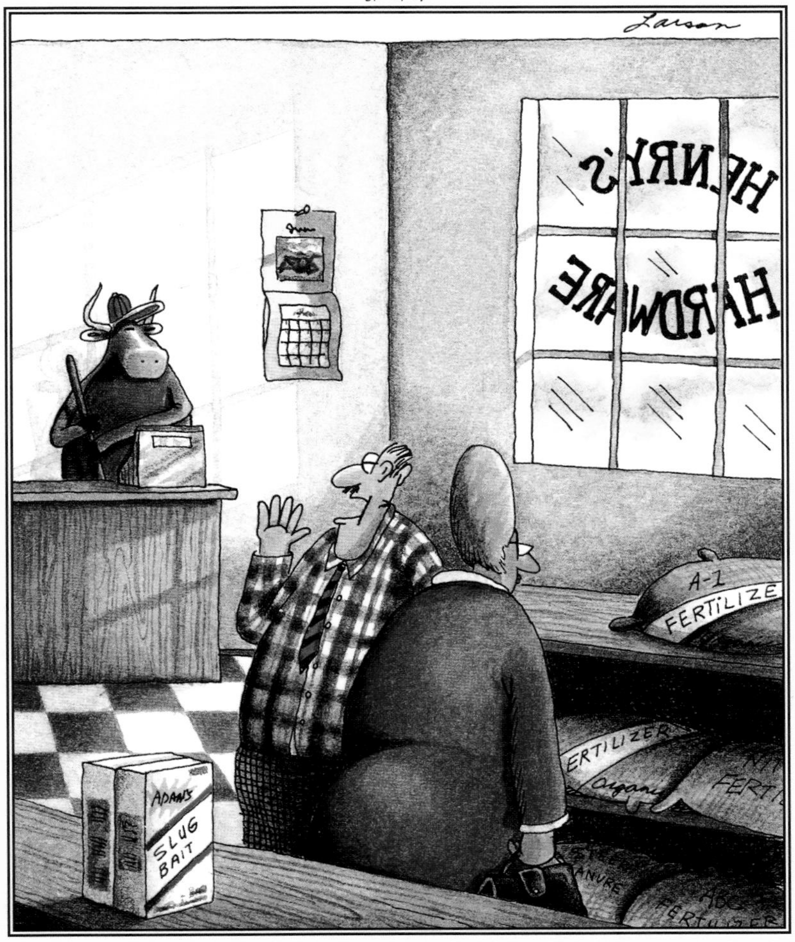
Larson
HENRY'S
HARDWARE
A-1
FERTILIZE
FERTILIZER
ADAMS
SLUG
BAIT

"Actually, Johnny knows this stuff better than me. ... Hey, Johnny! This lady wants to know the difference in all these fertilizers!"

5/31/87

Larson
My story? Well, it's pretty simple, actually... I guess you could just call me the "late" bird.

5/28/87

Larson

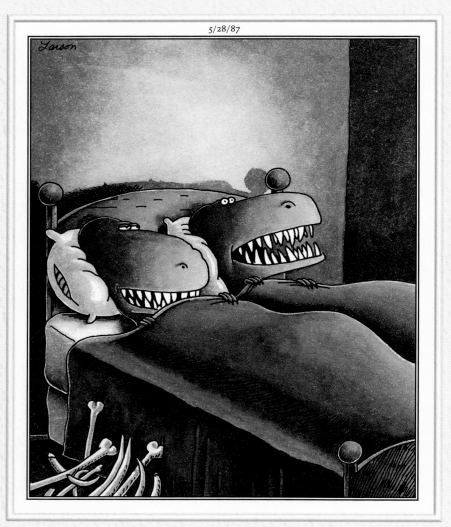

"Wait a minute here. ... Did I floss?"

6/1/87

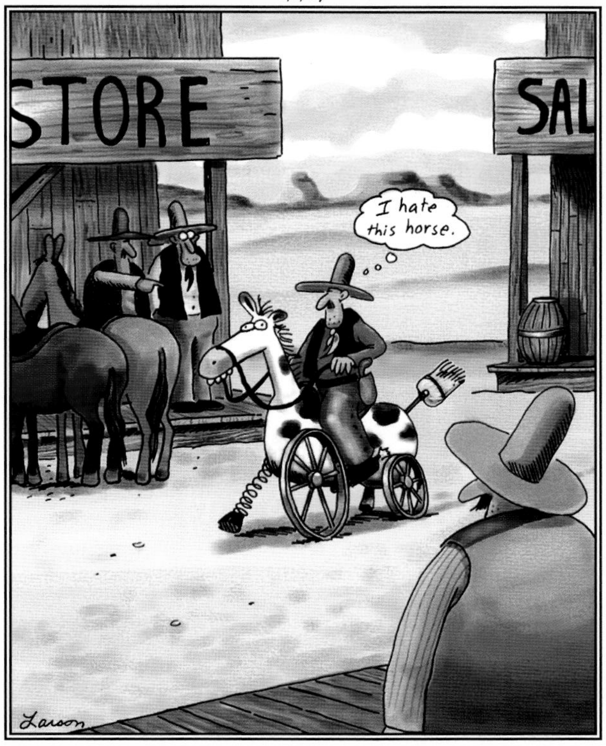
STORE
SAL
I hate this horse.
Larson

6/2/87

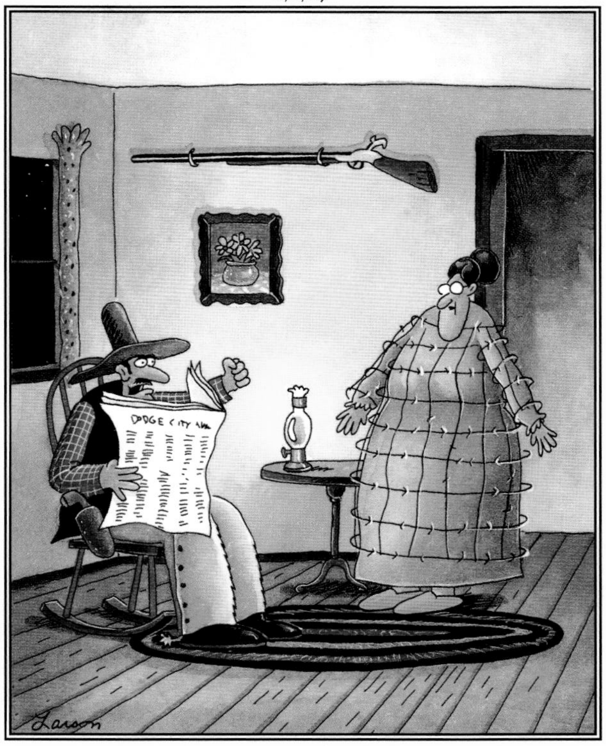
DODGE CITY
Larson

"Do I like it? Do I *like* it? ... Dang it, Thelma, you *know* my feelings on barbed wire!"

6/3/87

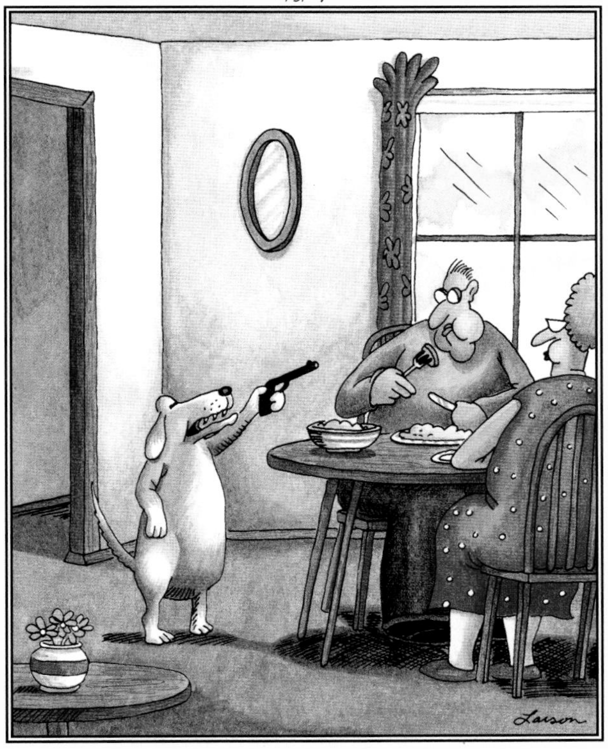
Larson

"Hey, bucko ... I'm *through* begging."

6/8/87

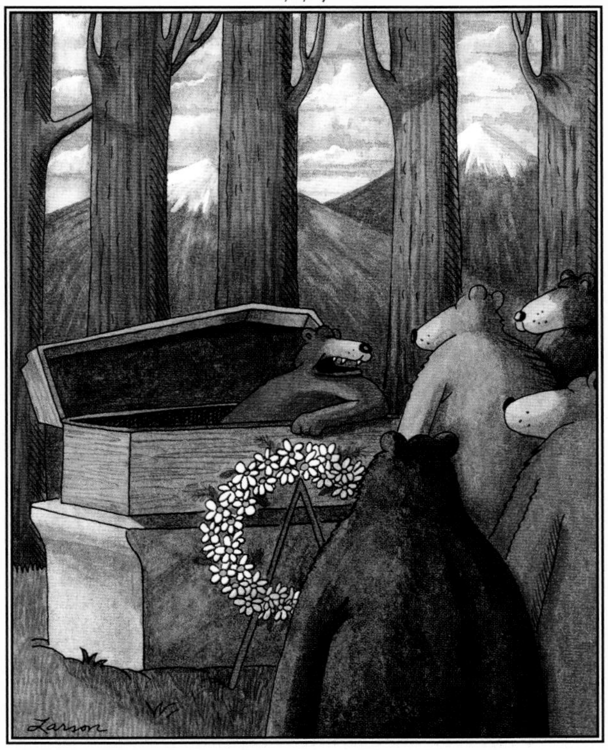
Larson

"For crying out loud, I was *hibernating!* ... Don't you guys ever take a pulse?"

6/7/87

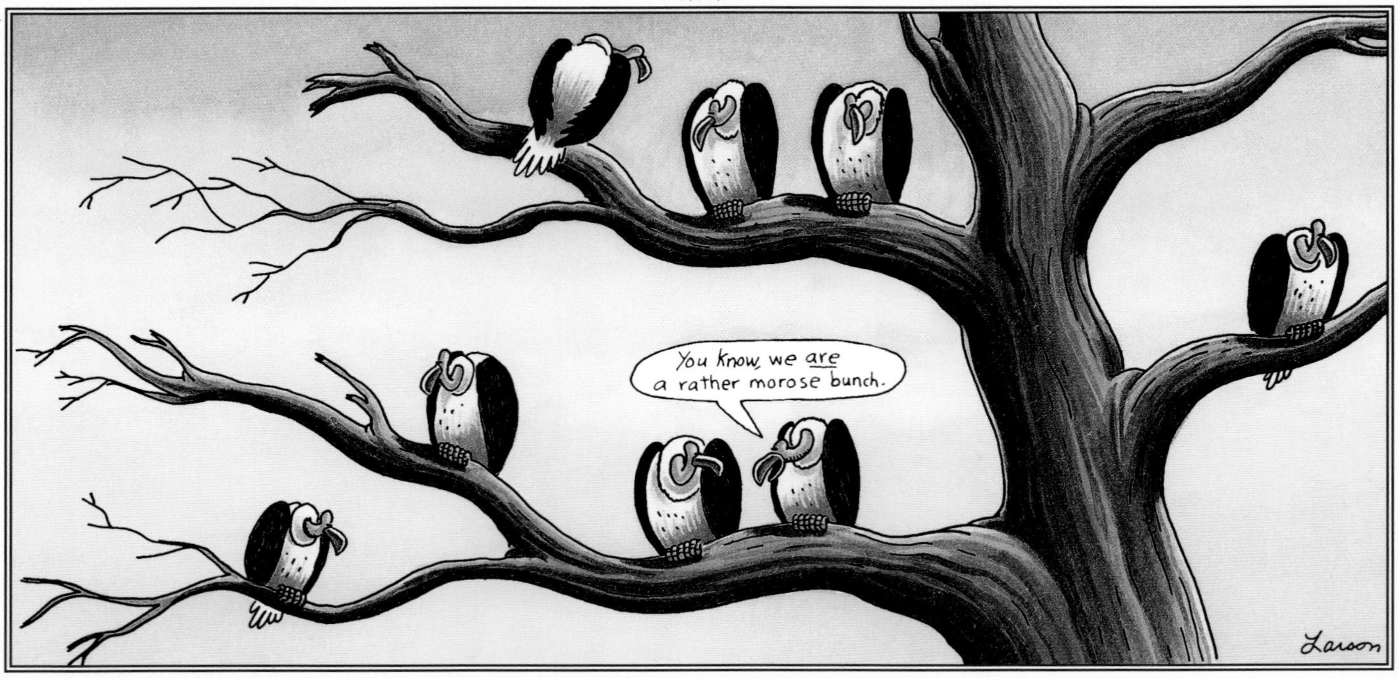
You know, we are
a rather morose bunch.

6/4/87

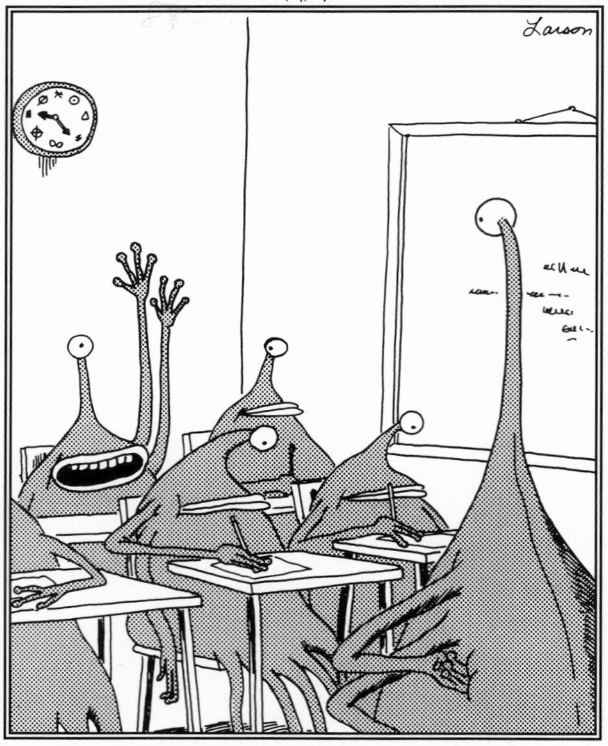

"Mrs. Xxgzhr, may I be excused? I have to go Number √(17.003)(n-2)."

6/5/87

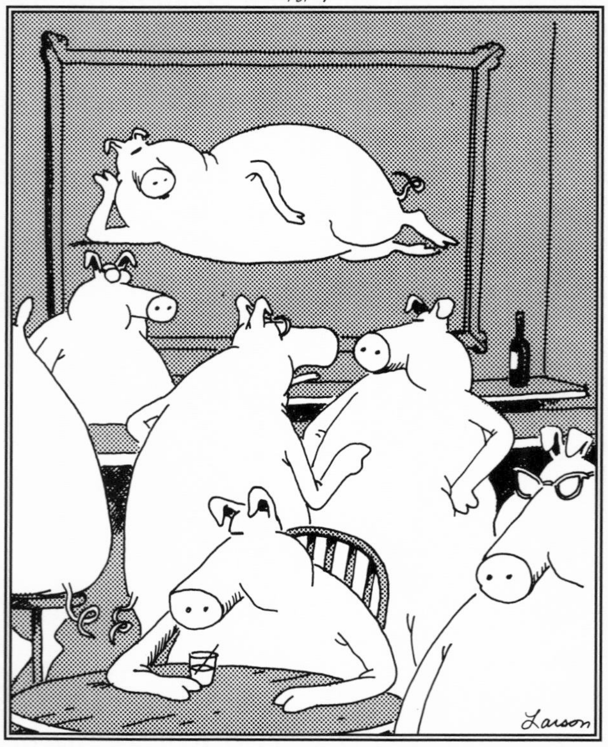

"Oh, yeah? ... How'd you like your nose unflattened?"

6/6/87

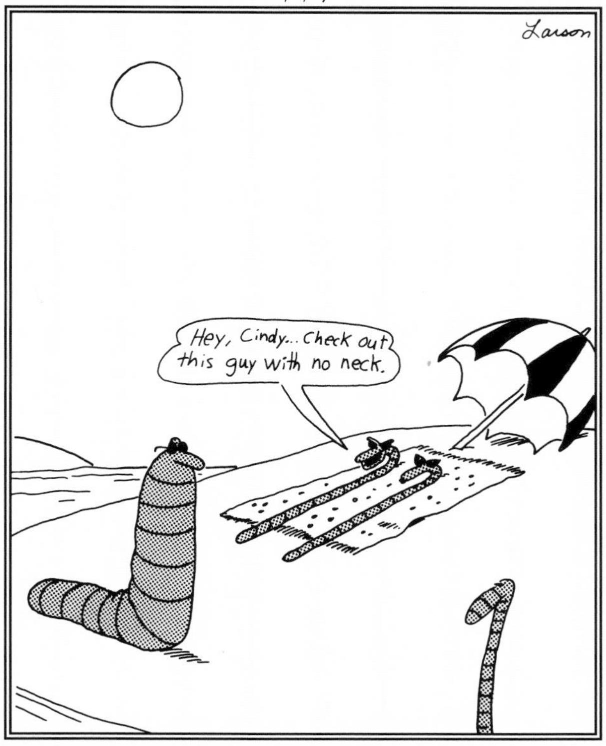
Larson
Hey, Cindy... Check out this guy with no neck.

At the worm beach

6/10/87

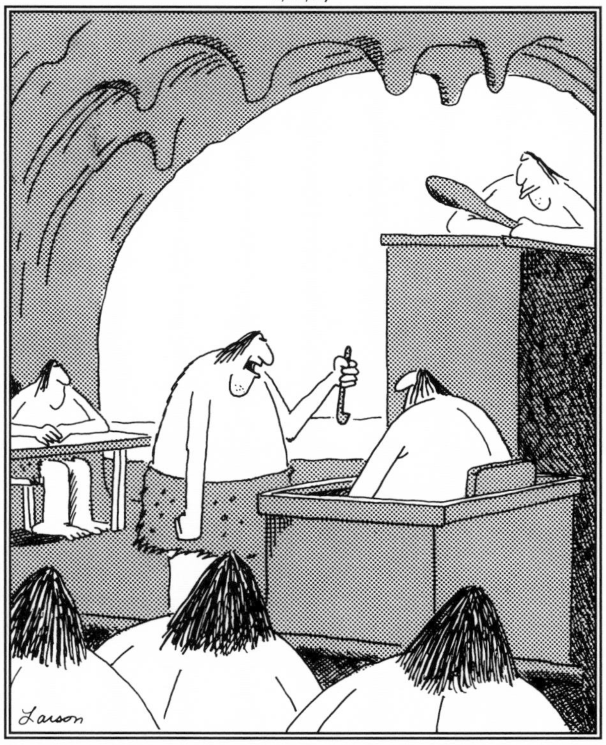
Larson

"You recognize this, Mr. Grok? ... We found it in the bushes near the victim's cave. Isn't this your atlatl, Mr. Grok?"

6/9/87

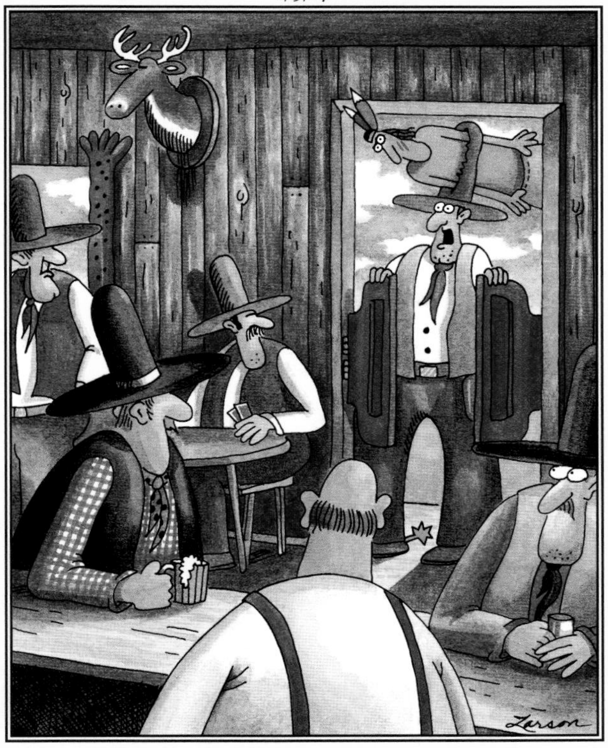
Larson

"INDIANS!"

6/15/87

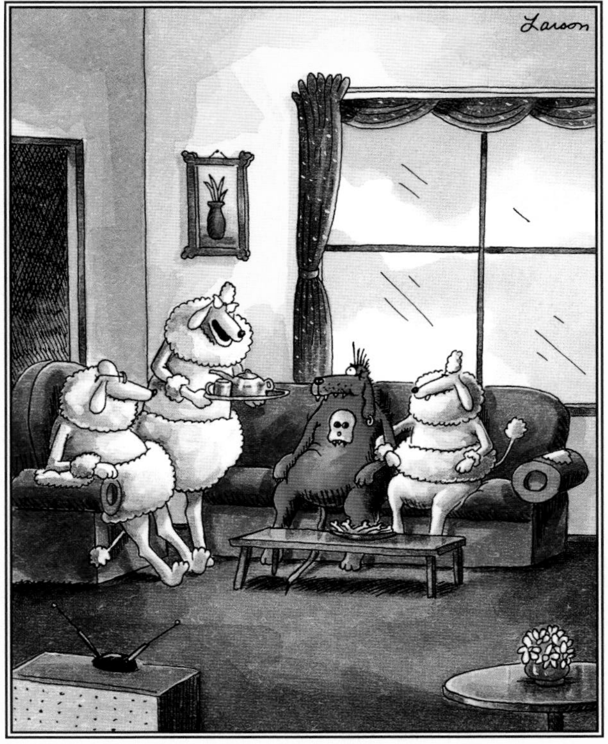
Larson

"So, Raymond ... Linda tells us you work in the security division of an automobile wreckage site."

6/11/87

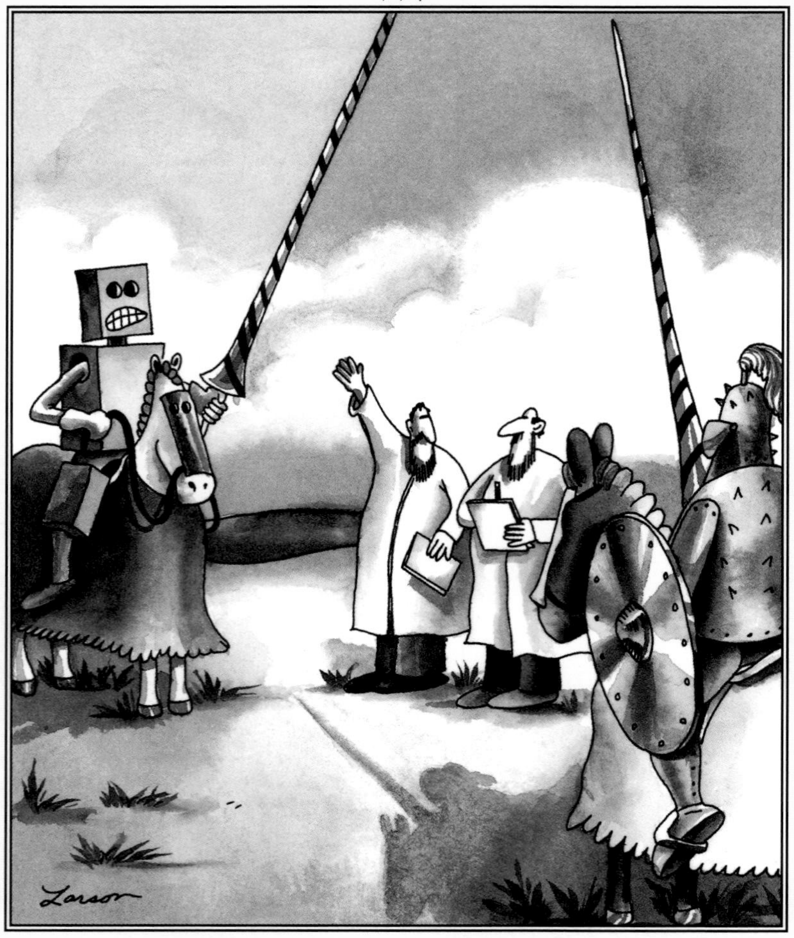
Larson

For a very brief period, medieval scientists were known to have dabbled in the merits of cardboard armor.

6/12/87

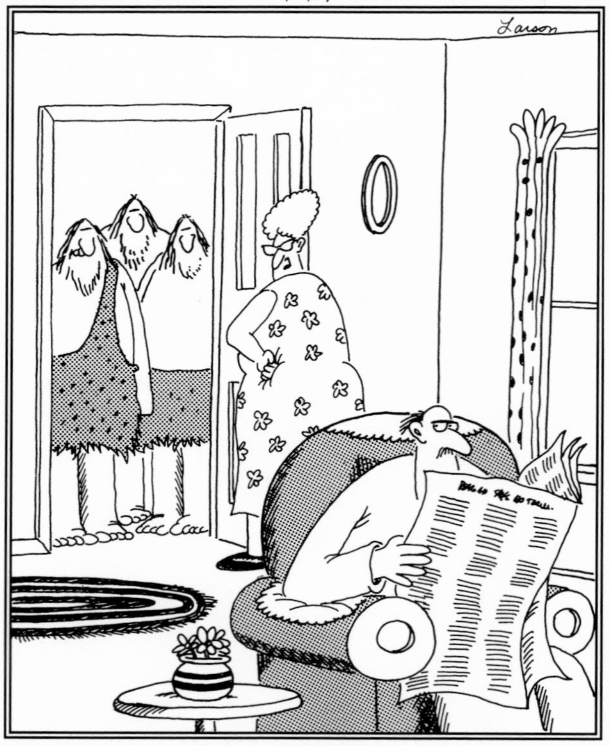
Larson

"Wendell ... it's a quest for fire."

6/13/87

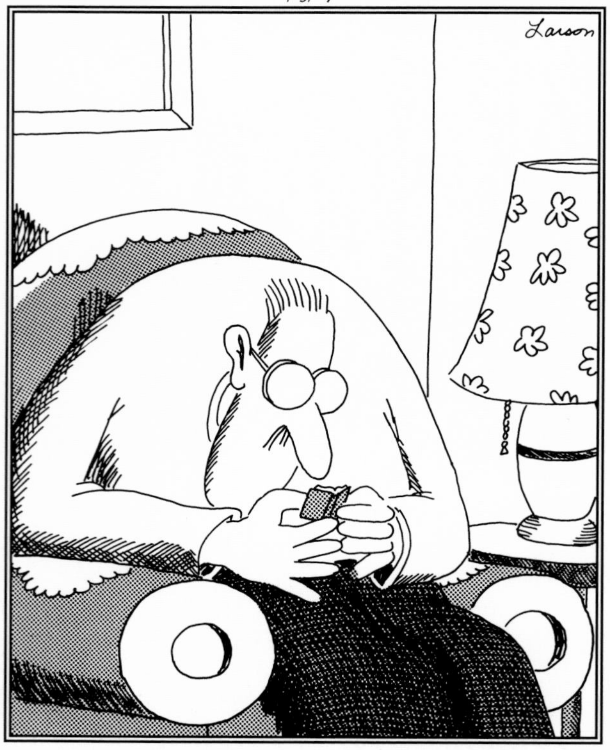
Larson

Roger crams for his microbiology midterm.

6/17/87

Larson

"Shoot! Drain's clogged. ... Man, I hate to think what might be down there."

6/18/87

Larson

Early attempts at the milkshake

6/20/87

Larson

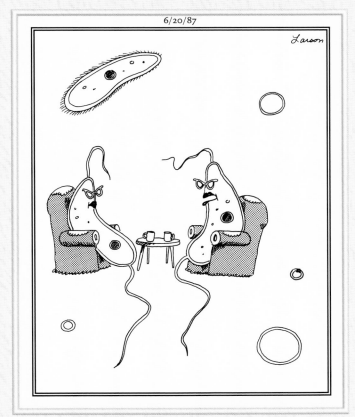

"He told you *that?* Well, he's pulling your flagellum, Nancy."

6/23/87

Larson

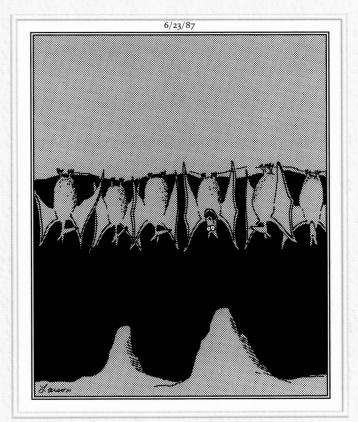

"AAAAAA! ... I CAN SEE! I CAN SEE! AAAAAAAAAAAAA!"

6/14/87

Larson

When chickens dream

6/16/87

Larson

"That does it, Sid! ... You yell 'tarantula' one more time and you're gonna be wearin' this thing!"

6/19/87

Larson
CARTOON DEPT.

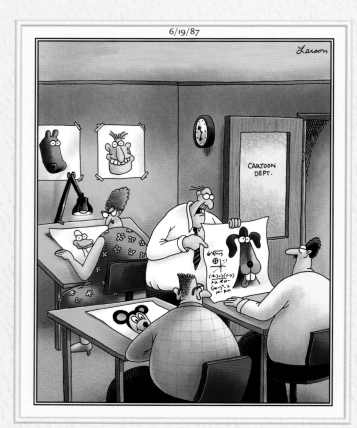

"Hey! What's this, Higgins? Physics equations? ... Do you enjoy your job here as a cartoonist, Higgins?"

6/24/87

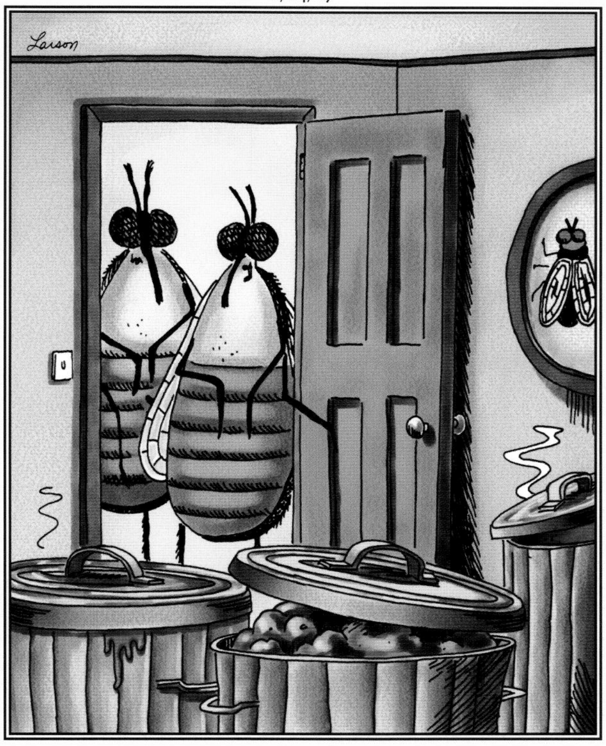
Larson

"And when the big moment comes, here's the nursery Robert and I have fixed up."

6/22/87

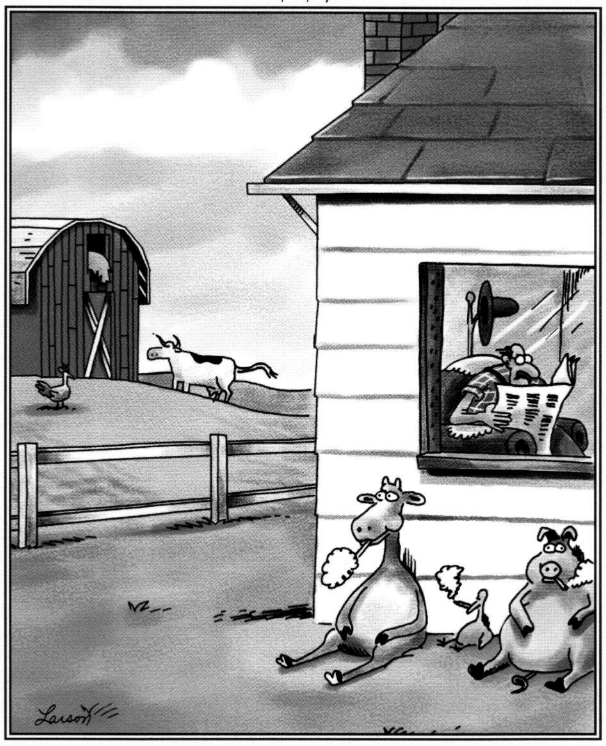
Larson

Where all the young farm animals go to smoke

6/21/87

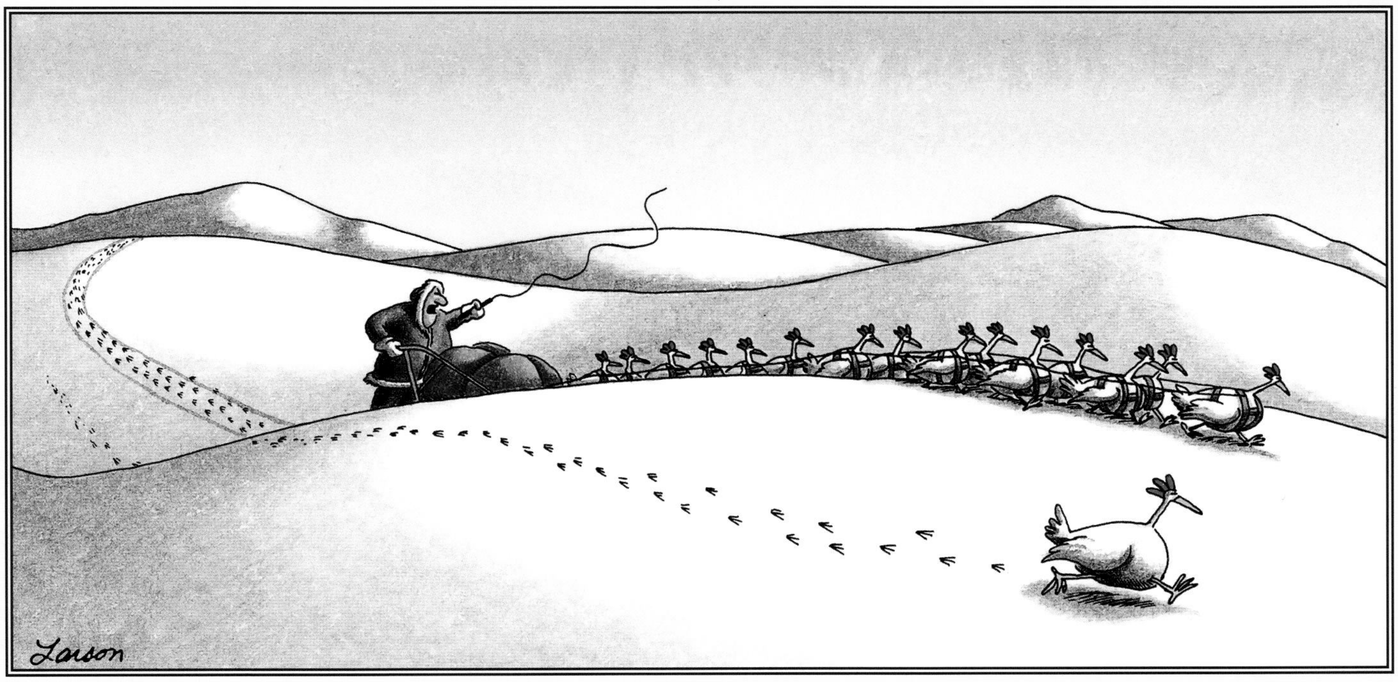
Larson

Sled chickens of the North

6/25/87

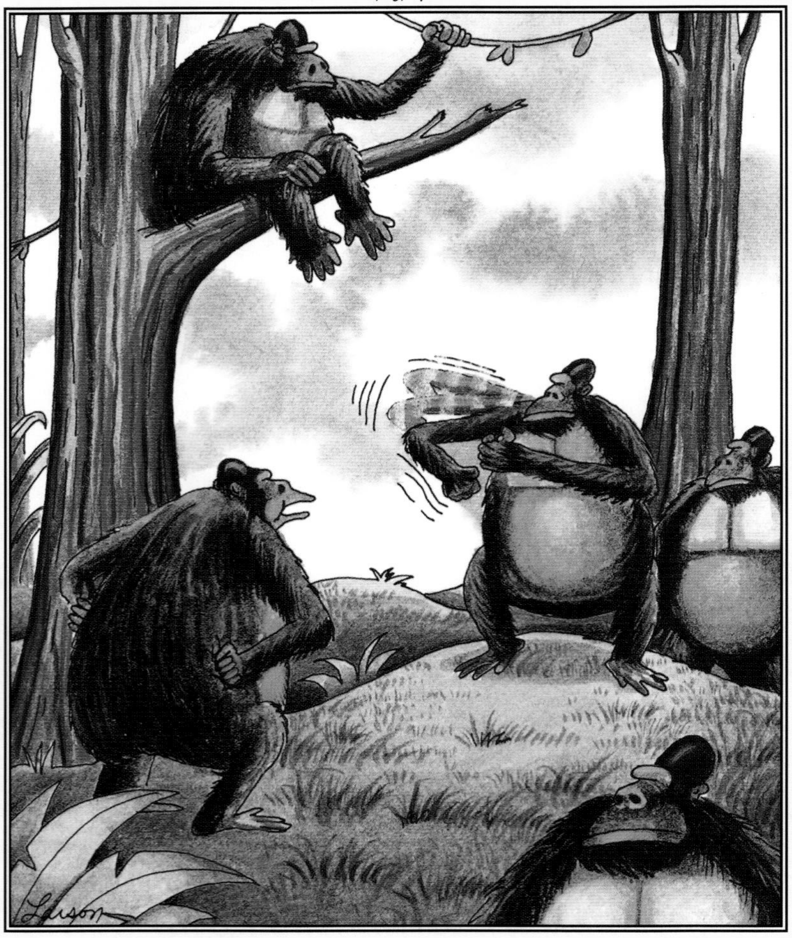

"For crying out loud, Warren ... can't you just beat your chest like everyone else?"

6/26/87

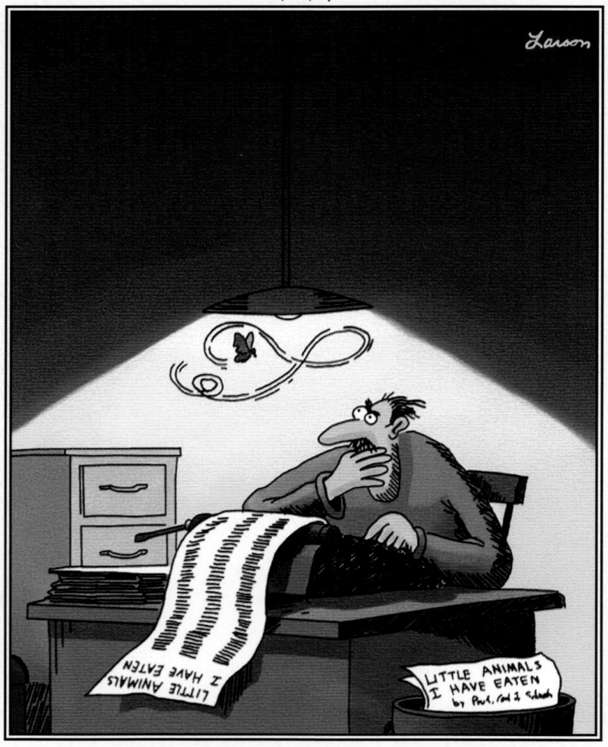
LITTLE ANIMALS
I HAVE EATEN

And by a lucky coincidence, Carl had just reached the "m's."

6/27/87

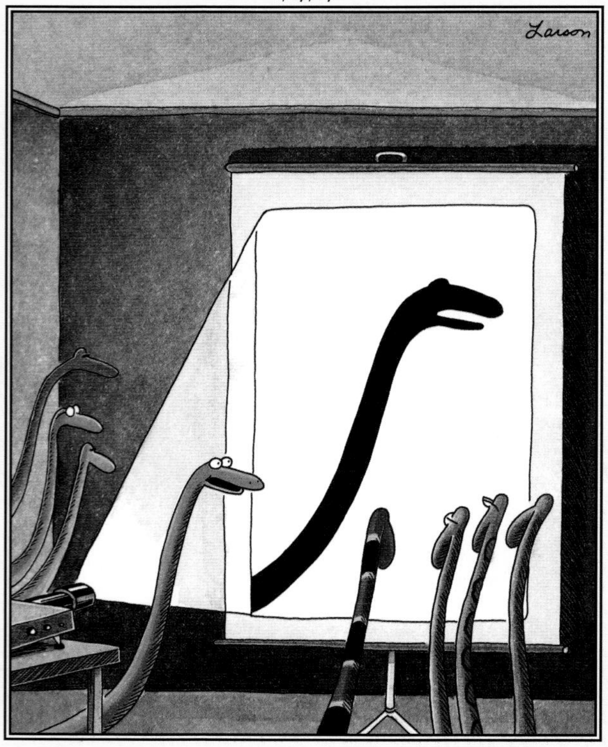

"Now this is ... this is ... well, I guess it's another snake."

6/29/87

MUSIC
STUDIO

"No, no, no! What are you doing? ...
Fifth leg! Fifth leg!"

6/30/87

HOME VISITOR
14 20
9:41

"And *you,* Johnson! You stick with your man
and *keep that hand in his face!*"

6/28/87

That can't be right... What's your radar sayin', Ed?

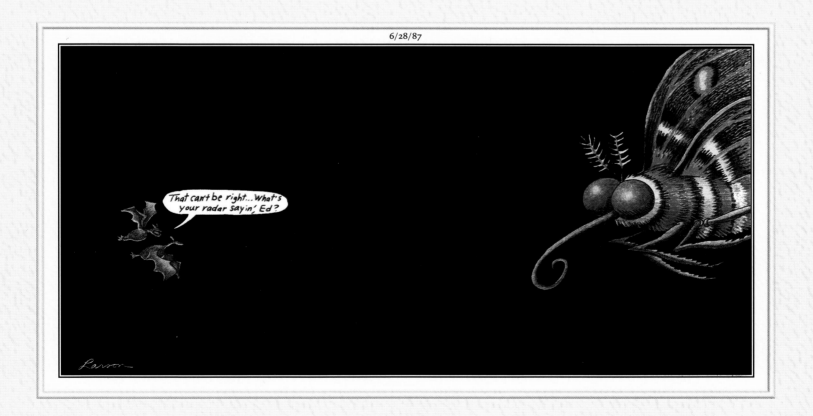

7/1/87

Larson

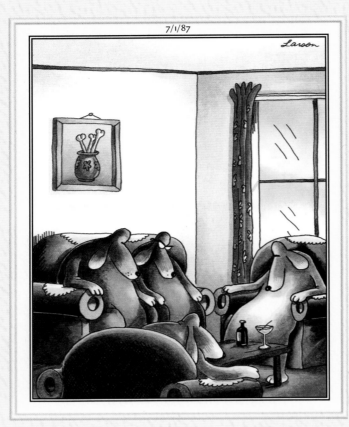

The conversation had been brisk and pleasant when, suddenly and simultaneously, everyone just got dog tired.

7/2/87

Larson

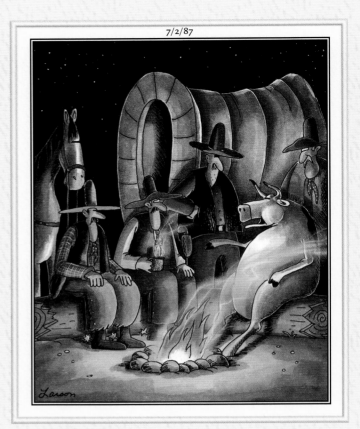

"A few cattle are going to stray off in the morning, and tomorrow night a stampede is planned around midnight. Look, I gotta get back. ... Remember, when we reach Santa Fe, I ain't slaughtered."

7/5/87

LOST IN THE DESERT?
DYING OF THIRST?
Next time, bring along a...
JONES BROS. CANTEEN
SEEMS LIKE THEY'RE ALWAYS FULL!
JONES BROS.
Larson

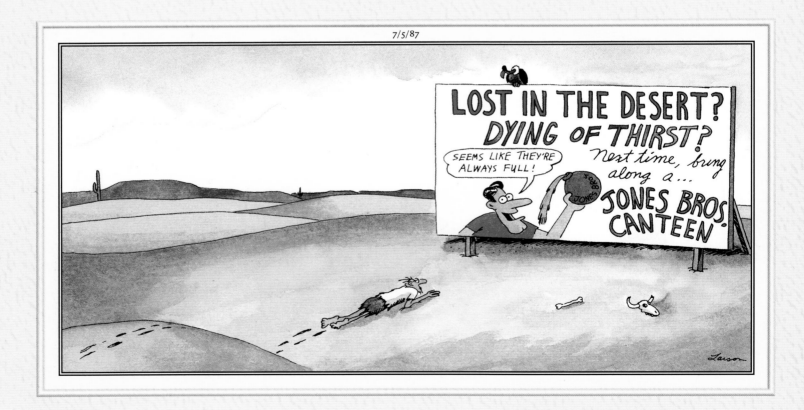

7/8/87

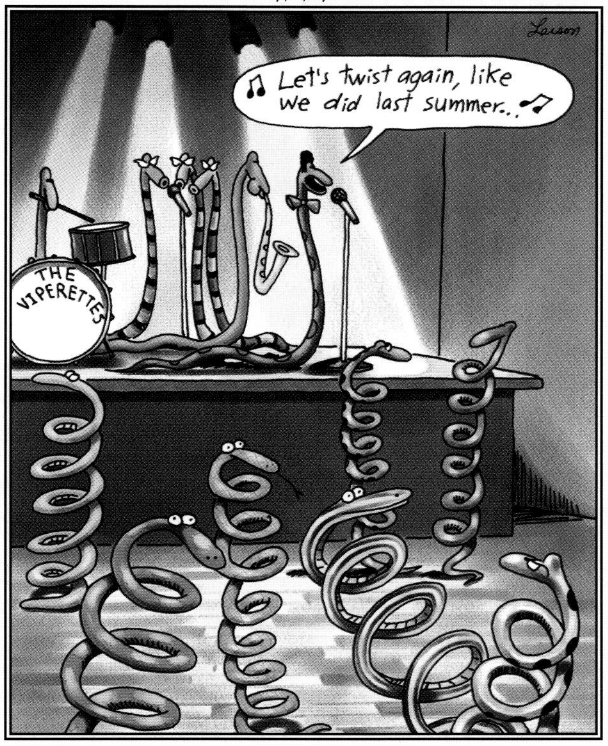
Larson
Let's twist again, like we did last summer...
THE VIPERETTES

7/14/87

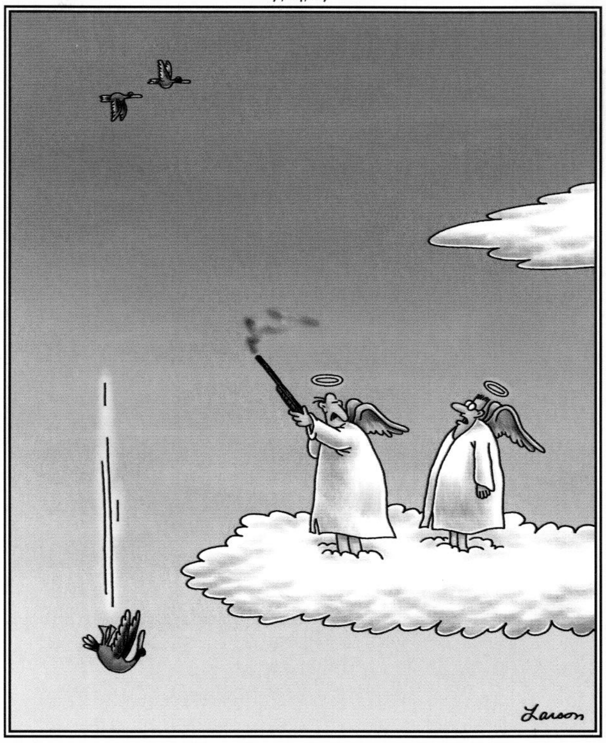
Larson

"You sure you're supposed to be doin' that, Mitch?"

7/12/87

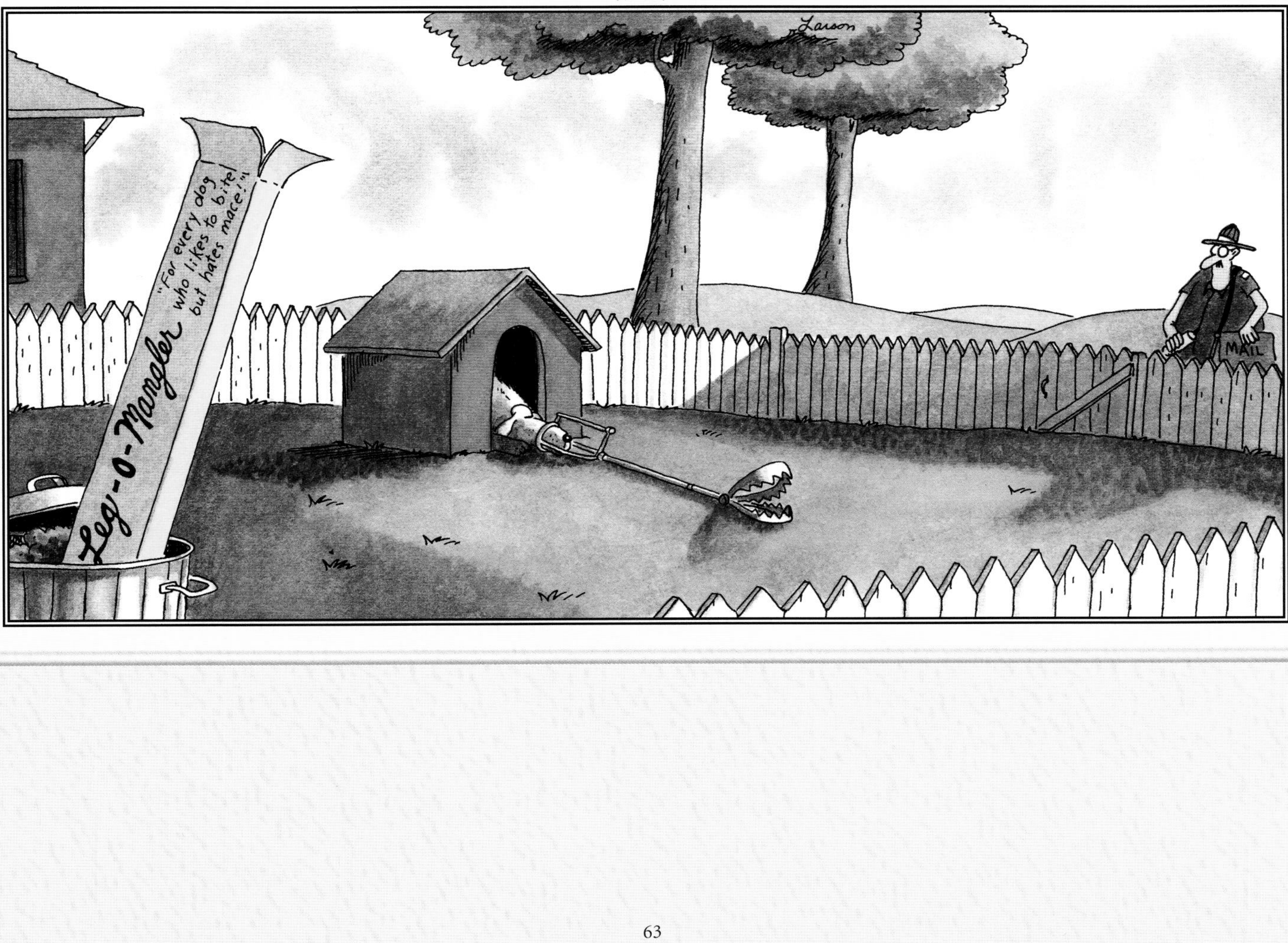
Larson
Leg-O-Mangler
"For every dog who likes to bite! but hates mace!"™
MAIL

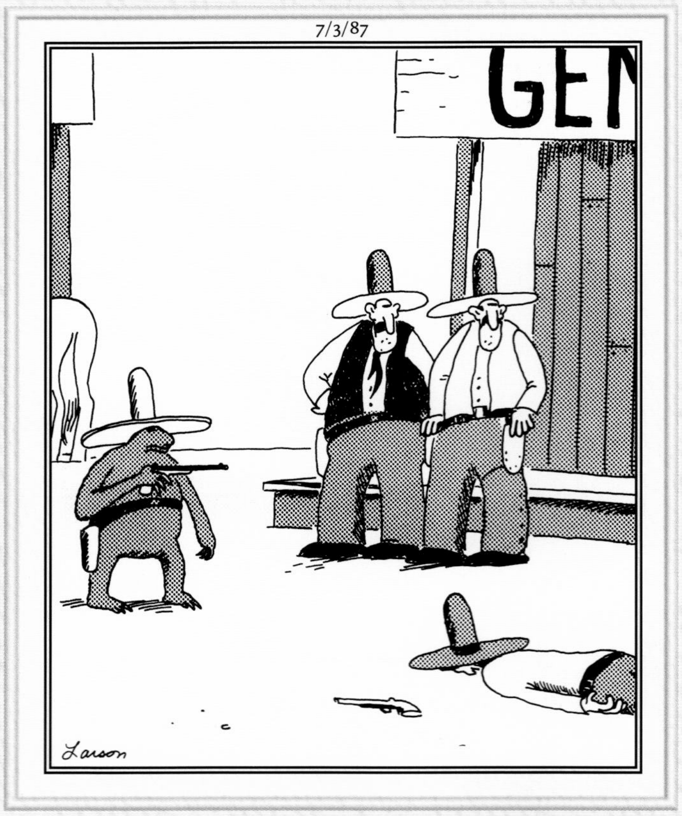
7/3/87
GEN
Larson

"Well, the sloth nailed him. ... Y'know, ol' Hank never was exactly a 'quick draw.'"

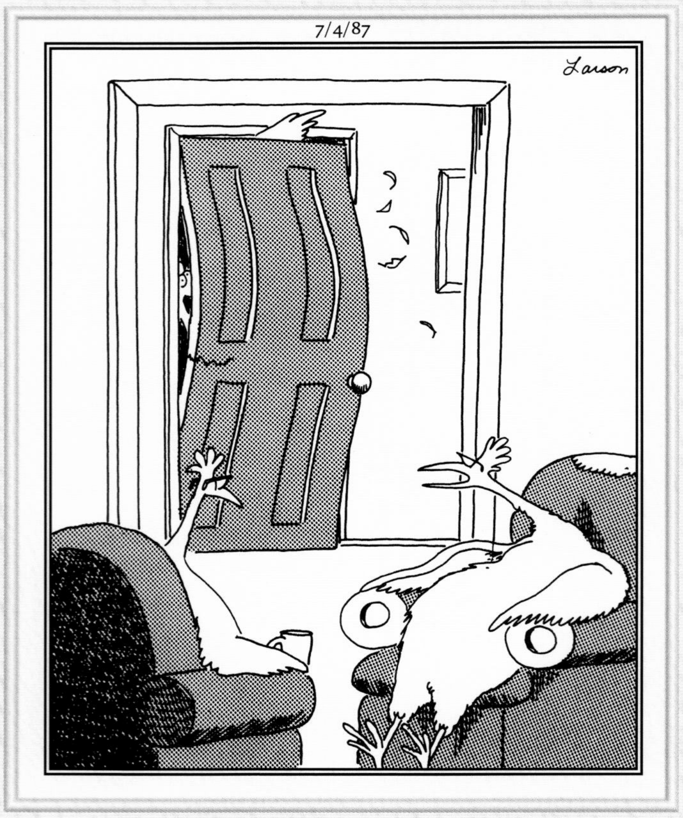
7/4/87
Larson

"Oh my God! Murray's attacking the bathroom mirror!"

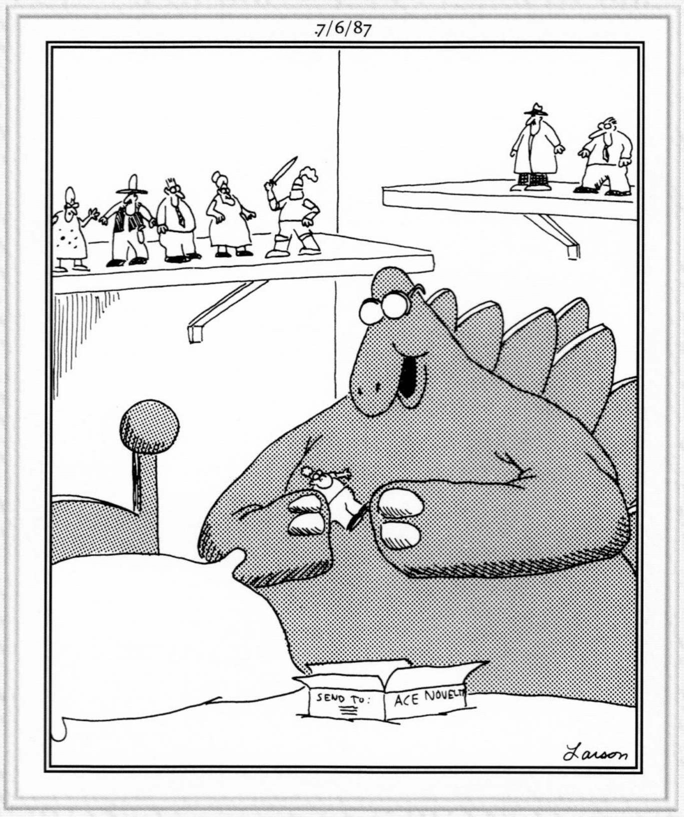
7/6/87
SEND TO:
Larson

"Oh, boy! The 'Nerd'! ... Now my collection's complete!"

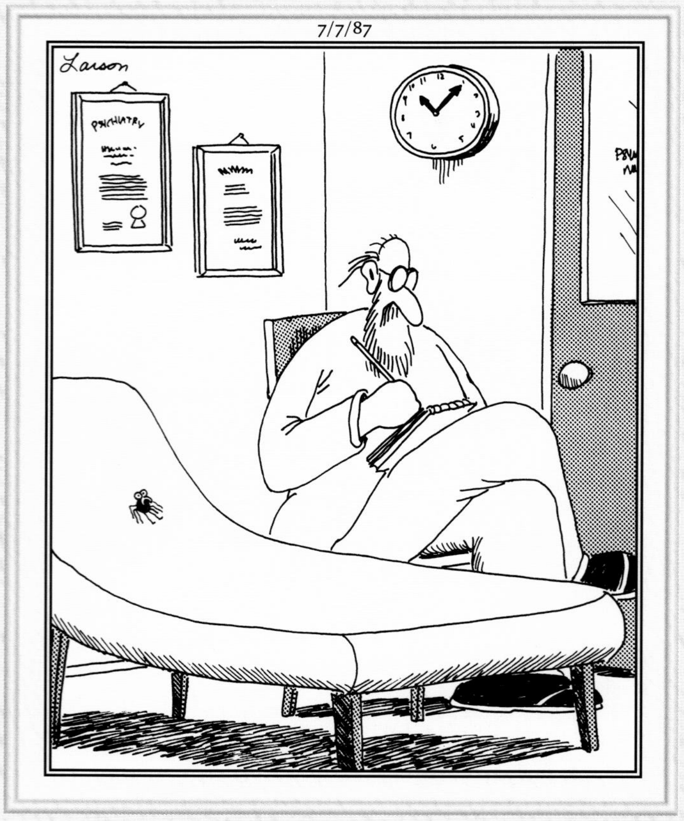
7/7/87
Larson

"It's the same dream night after night ... I walk out on my web, and suddenly a foot sticks—and then another foot sticks, and another, and another, and another ..."

7/9/87

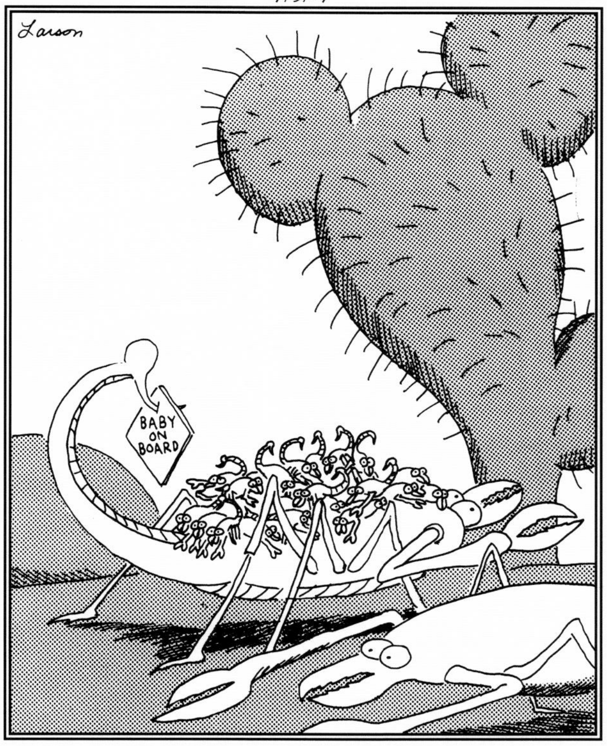
Larson
BABY ON BOARD

7/10/87

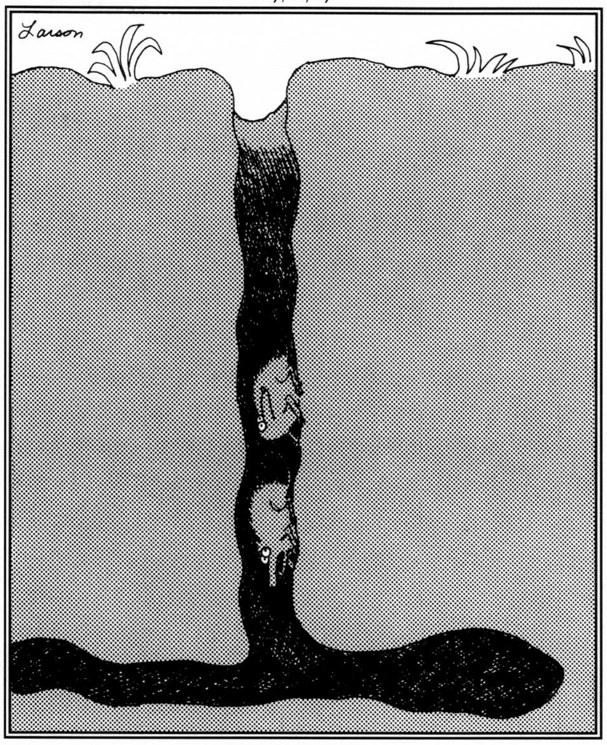
Larson

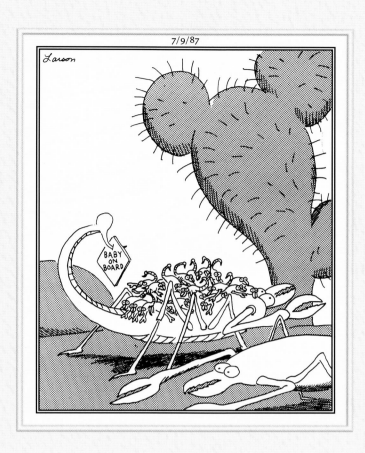

"Arnold, you fool! Don't look up!"

7/11/87

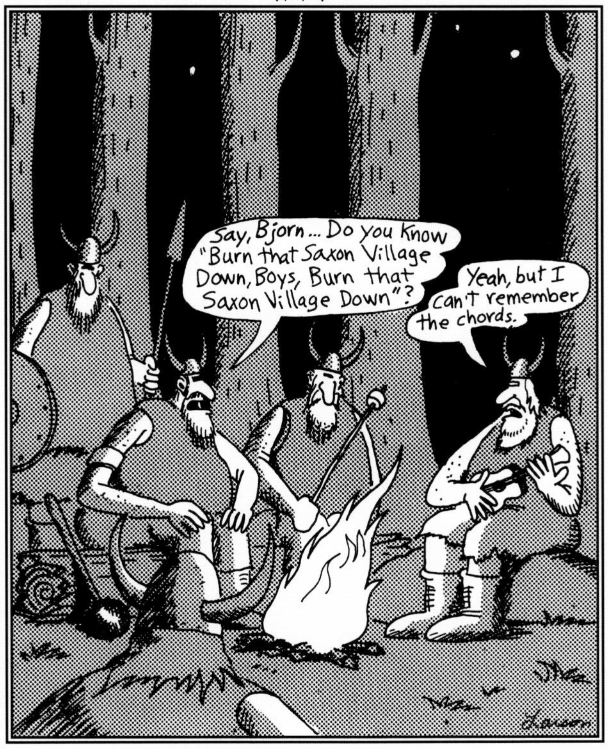
Say, Bjorn... Do you know "Burn that Saxon Village Down, Boys, Burn that Saxon Village Down"?
Yeah, but I can't remember the chords.
Larson

Viking campfires

7/17/87

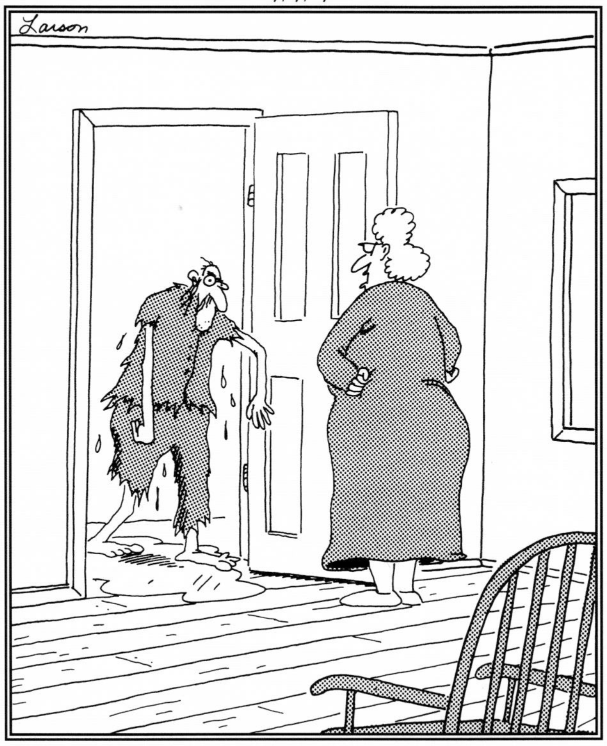
Larson

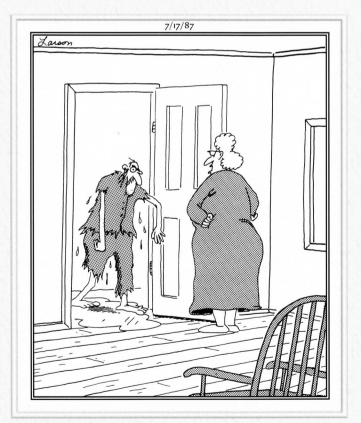

"For crying out loud, Jonah! Three days late, covered with slime, and smelling like fish! ... And what story have I got to swallow this time?"

Although impolite, the other bears could never help
staring at Larry's enormous deer gut.

"You eat your dirt, Billy. You want to grow up
as big and slimy as your dad, don't you?"

"What the hey? ... Someone's short-sheeted
my bed again!"

7/25/87

IT CAME FROM OLDUVAI

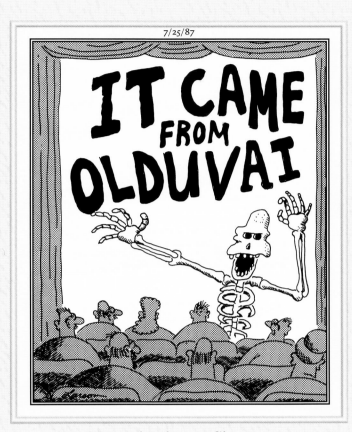

Anthro horror films

7/28/87

JOHN DENVER SONG BOOK

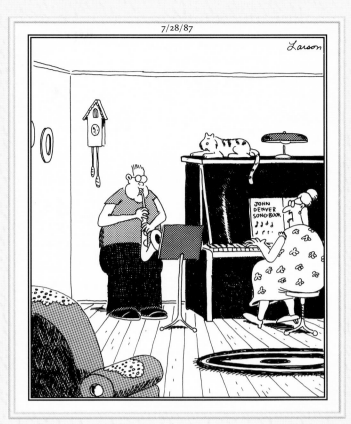

"Blow, Howie, blow! ... Yeah, yeah, yeah! You're cookin' now, Howie! ... All right! ... Charlie Parker, move over! ... Yeah!"

7/13/87

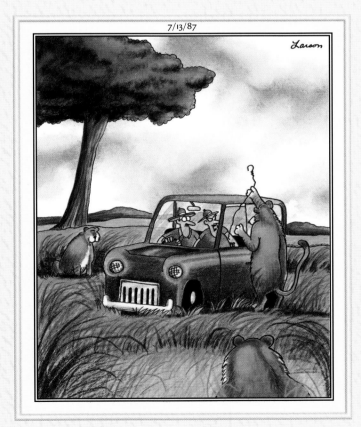

"Drive, George, drive! This one's got a coat hanger!"

7/15/87

HERIFF
SA

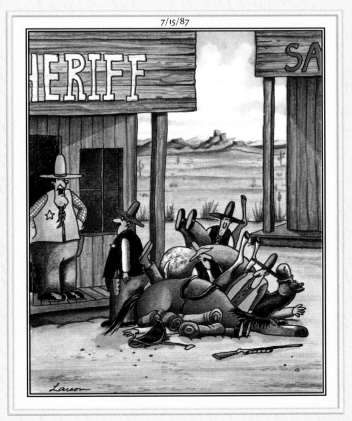

"And so you just threw everything together? Matthews, a posse is something you have to *organize*."

7/19/87

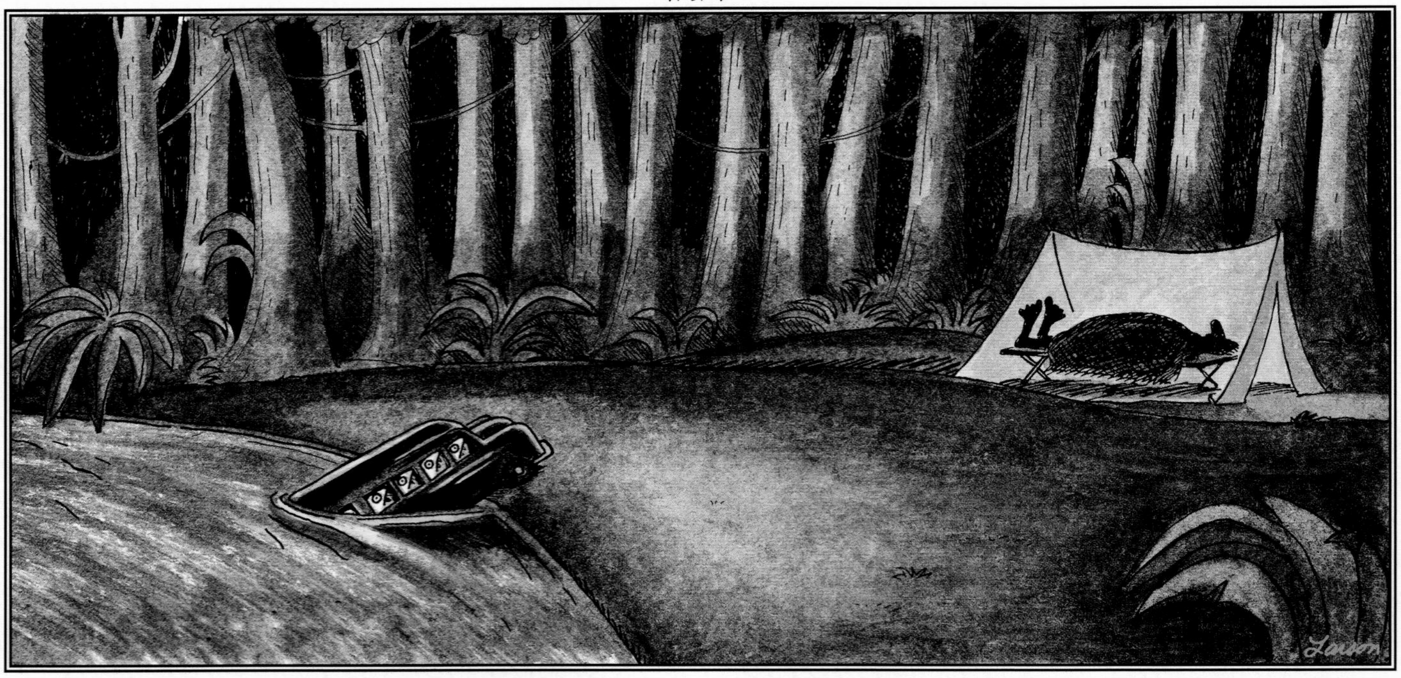

When piranha dine out

7/18/87

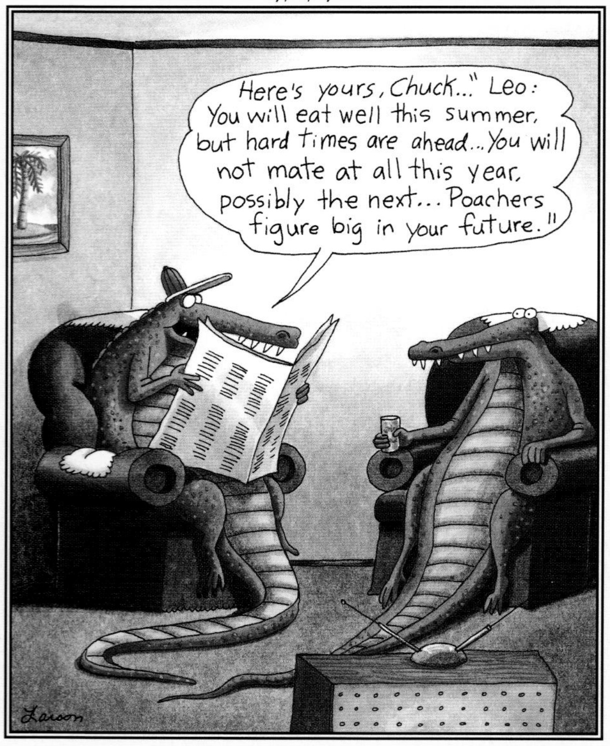
"Here's yours, Chuck..." Leo: You will eat well this summer, but hard times are ahead...You will not mate at all this year, possibly the next... Poachers figure big in your future."

Animal horoscopes

7/22/87

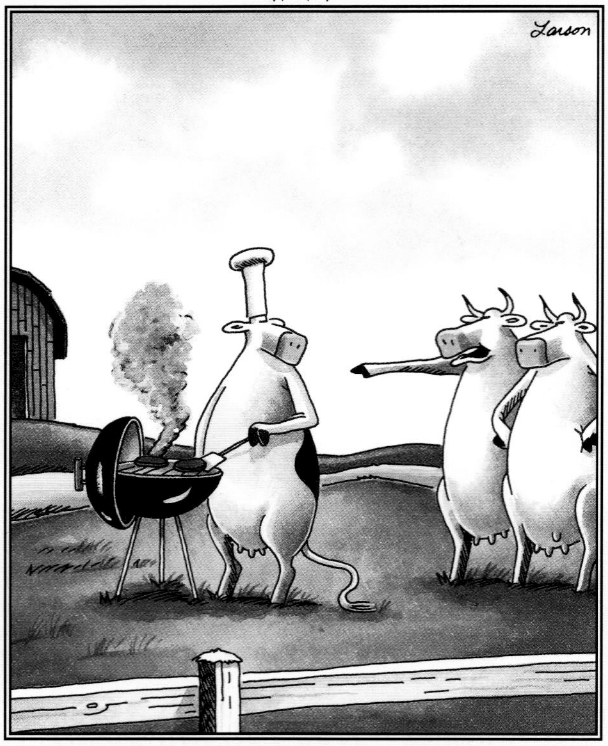

"You're sick, Jessy! ... Sick, sick, sick!"

7/23/87

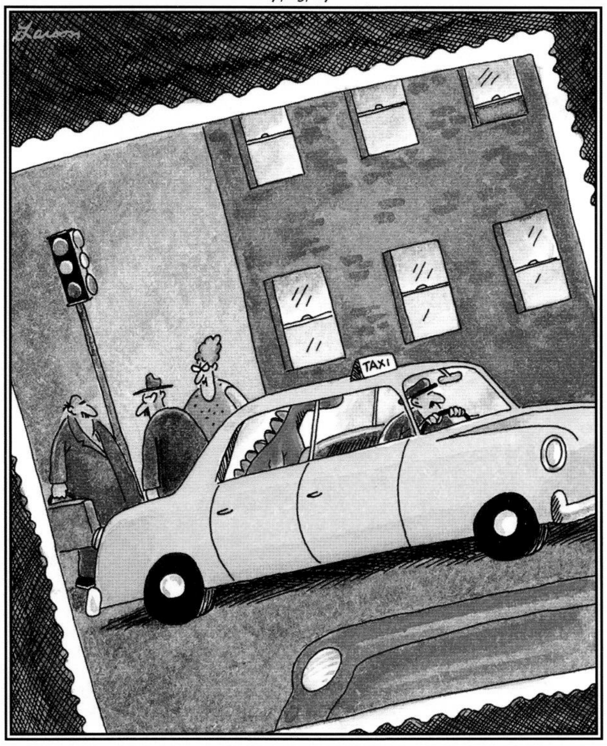
TAXI

Another unsubstantiated photograph of the Loch Ness monster (taken by Reuben Hicks, 5/24/84, Chicago).

7/24/87

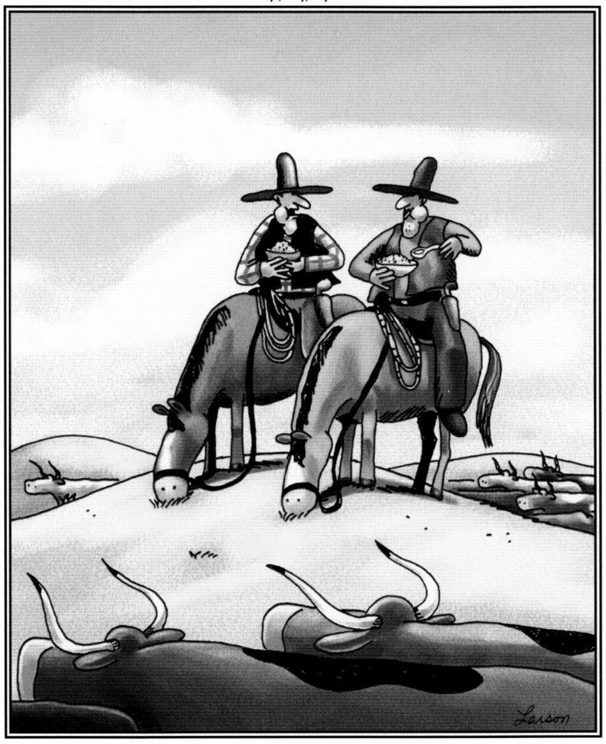

"Man, Ben, I'm gettin' tired of this. ... How many days now we've been eatin' this trail dust?"

7/26/87

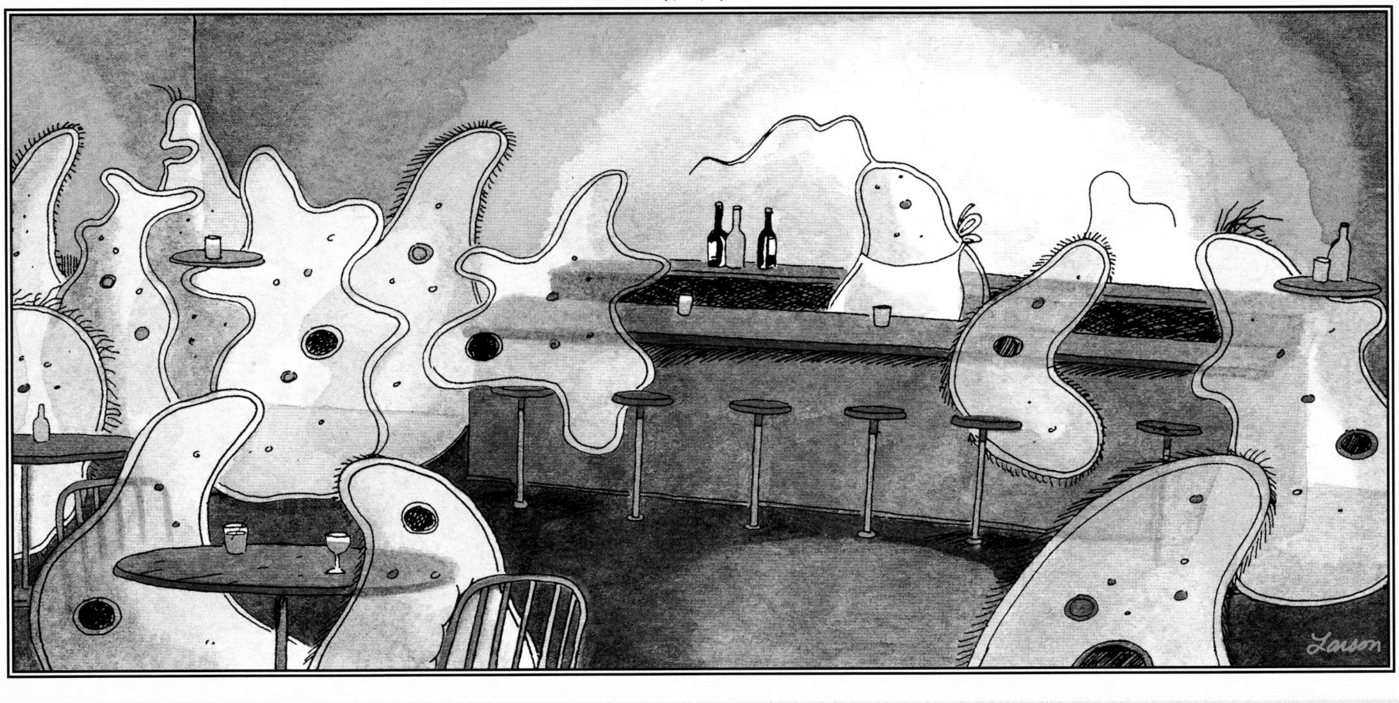

Single-cell bars

7/27/87

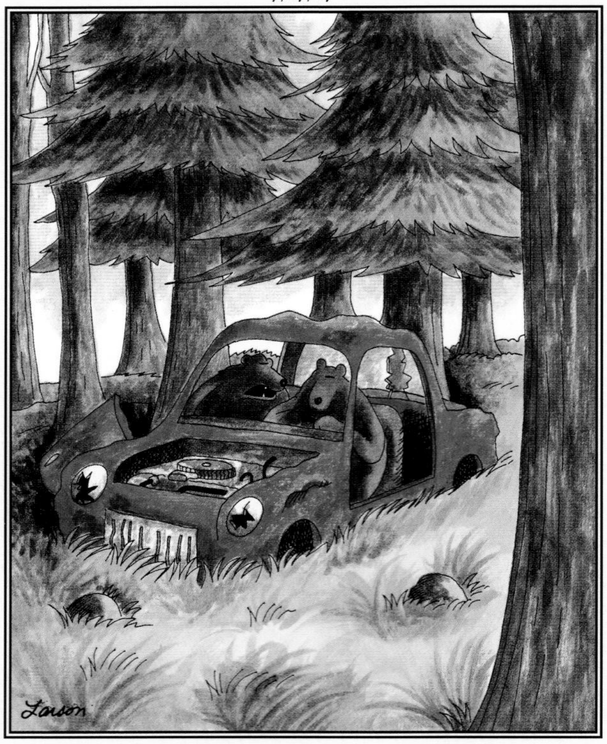

“Think about it, Murray. ... If we could get this baby runnin’, we could run over hikers, pick up females, chase down mule deer—man, we’d be the grizzlies from hell.”

7/30/87

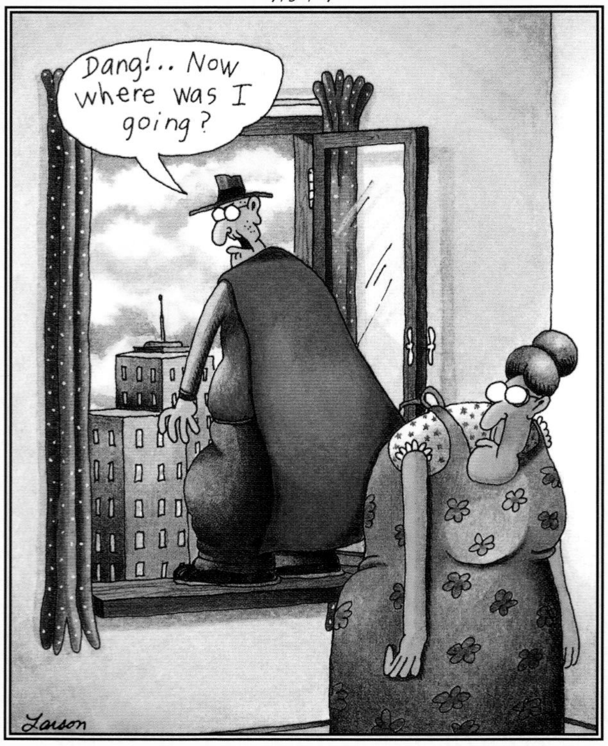
Dang!.. Now where was I going?

Superman in his later years

7/29/87

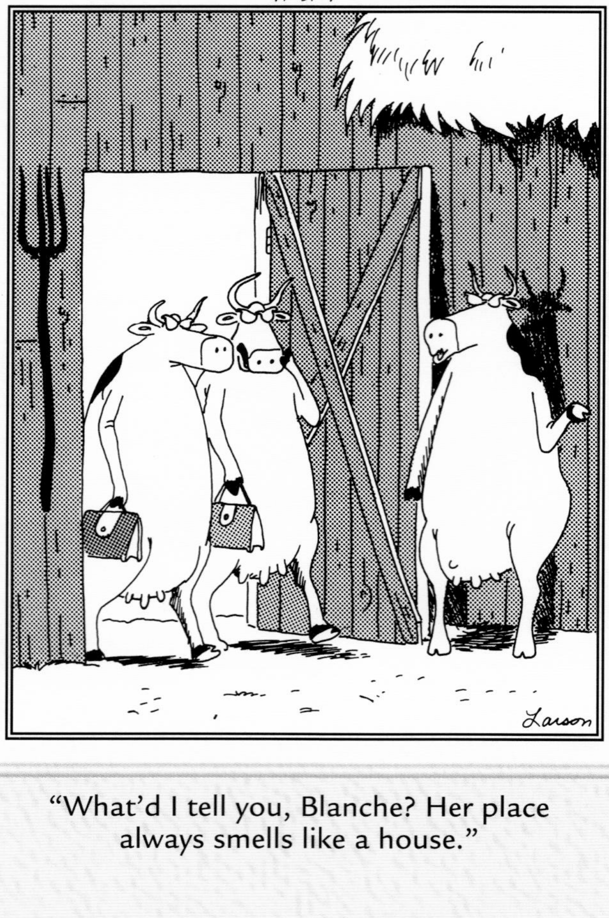

“What’d I tell you, Blanche? Her place always smells like a house.”

7/31/87

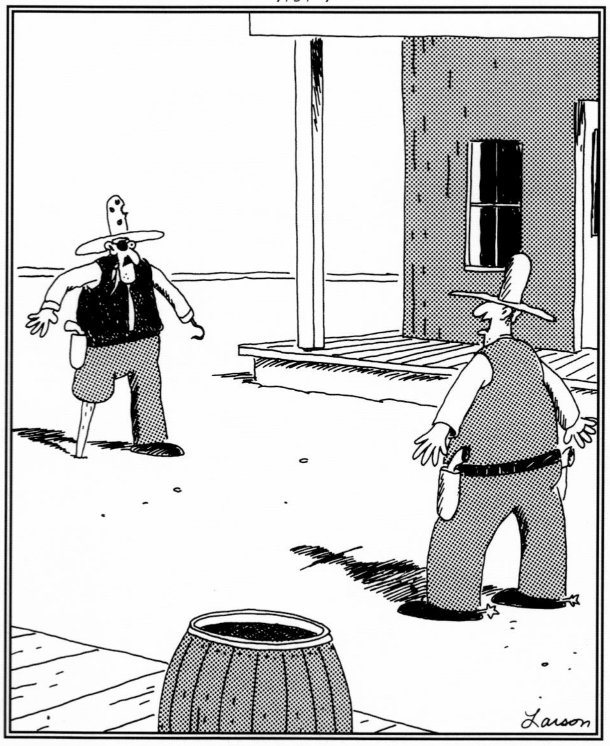

“Make your move, Bart—if you’re feelin’ lucky, that is.”

"It's a letter from Julio in America. ... His banana bunch arrived safely and he's living in the back room of some grocery store."

"Bummer, Rusty. ... Seven years bad luck—of course, in your case, that works out to be 49 years."

8/2/87

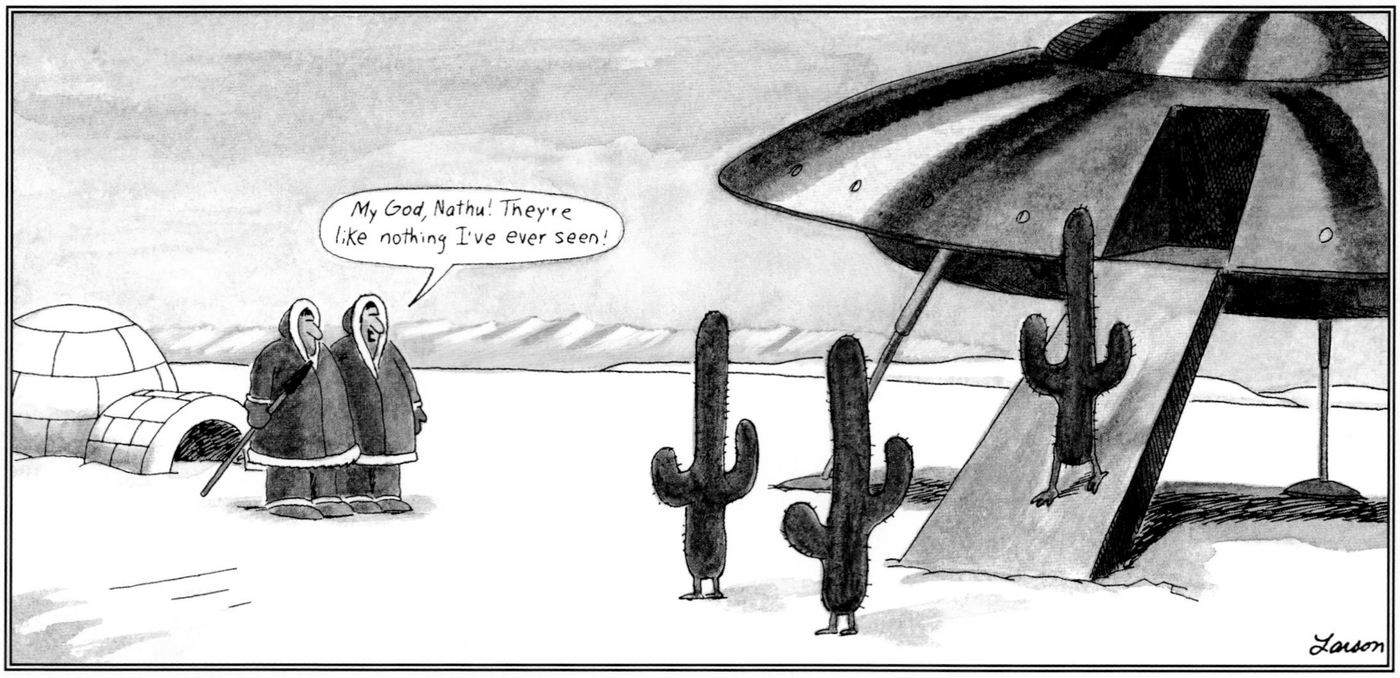
My God, Nathu! They're like nothing I've ever seen!
Larson

8/4/87

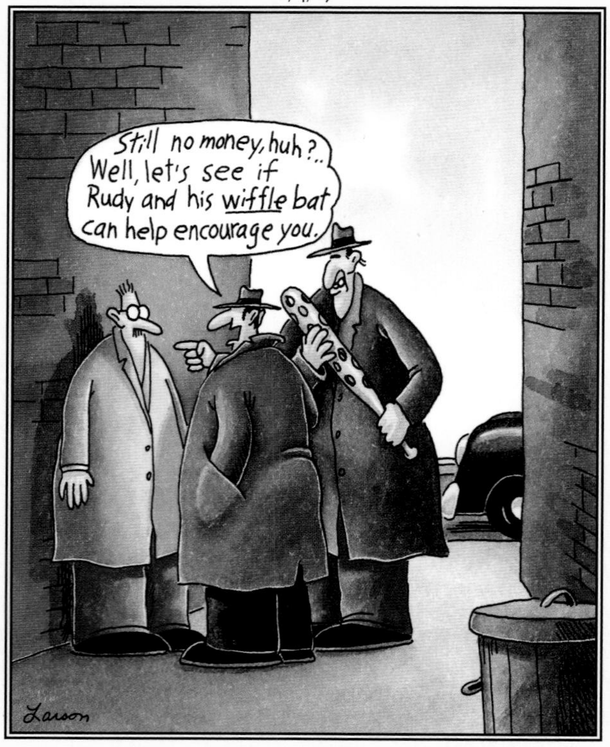
Still no money, huh?.. Well, let's see if Rudy and his wiffle bat can help encourage you.
Larson

Ineffective tools of persuasion

August 10, 1987

Universal Press Syndicate
4900 Main Street
Kansas City, Missouri 64112

Re: Our Reference No. 1185/General

Dear Sirs:

We represent The Wiffle Ball, Inc. in trademark matters. It has come to our attention that the trademark WIFFLE was referred to in the comic strip "The Far Side" by Gary Larson. A copy of the comic strip is enclosed.

In the comic strip you refer to a "...wiffle bat" and then show a man holding a bat with perforations. Please be advised that WIFFLE does not make a bat with perforations, and therefore the use of the brand name WIFFLE to a product that is not a product of The Wiffle Ball, Inc. is an inappropriate use of our client's valuable trademark WIFFLE.

In the future, when you use the brand name WIFFLE, the entire brand should be capitalized, and it should only be used in reference to a product currently manufactured by The Wiffle Ball, Inc.

Please forward a copy of this letter to Mr. Gary Larson.

Thank you for your attention to this matter.

Very truly yours,

Gene S. Winter

GSW:led
Enclosure
cc: David A. Mullany

8/5/87

Just as Dale entered the clearing and discovered, standing together, the Loch Ness monster, Bigfoot, and Jackie Onassis, his camera jammed.

8/13/87

Parakeet furniture

8/9/87

Well, this isn't a cheerful sign.

8/8/87

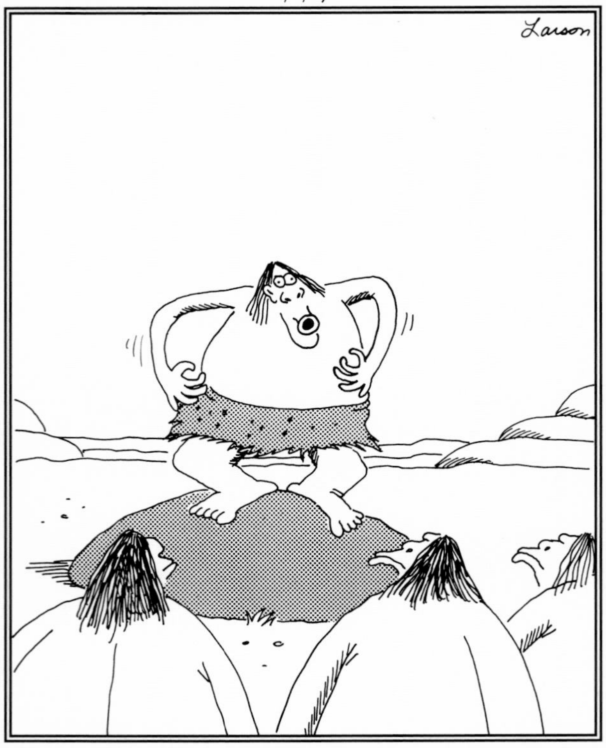

And then, just as he predicted, Thag became the spiritual channeler for a two-million-year-old gibbon named Gus.

8/7/87

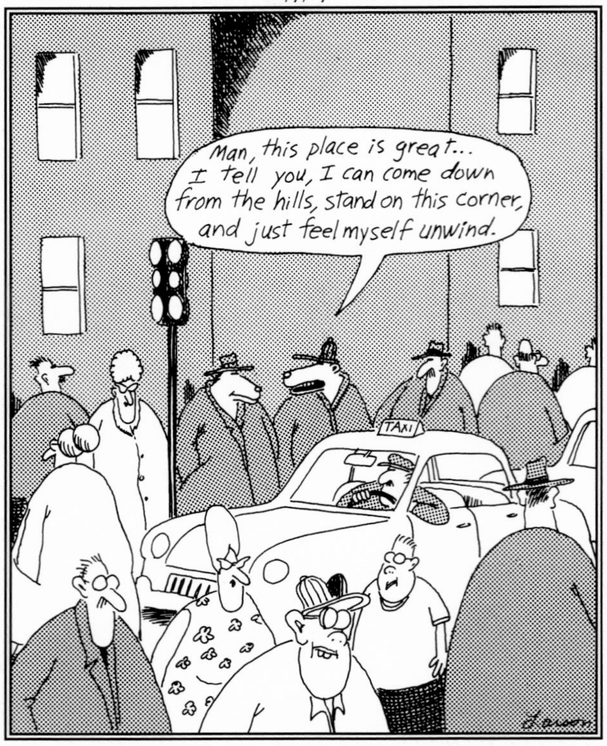
Man, this place is great... I tell you, I can come down from the hills, stand on this corner, and just feel myself unwind.
TAXI

How bears relax

8/10/87

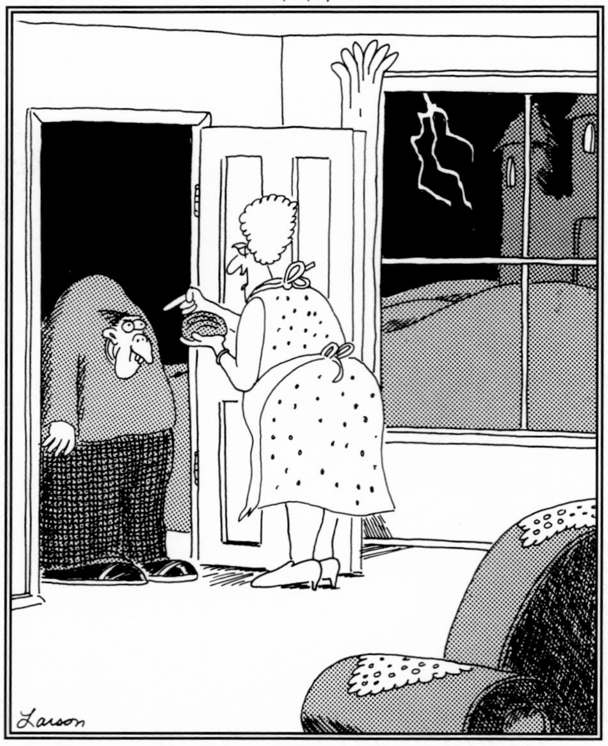

"Oh, don't be silly! No thanks needed. Just take the brain—but tell that doctor you work for not to be such a stranger."

8/11/87

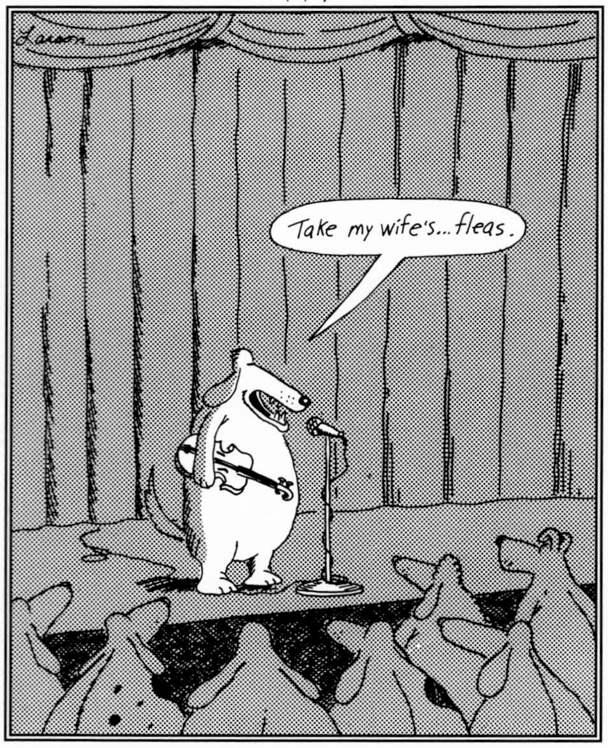
Take my wife's... fleas.

Canine comedians

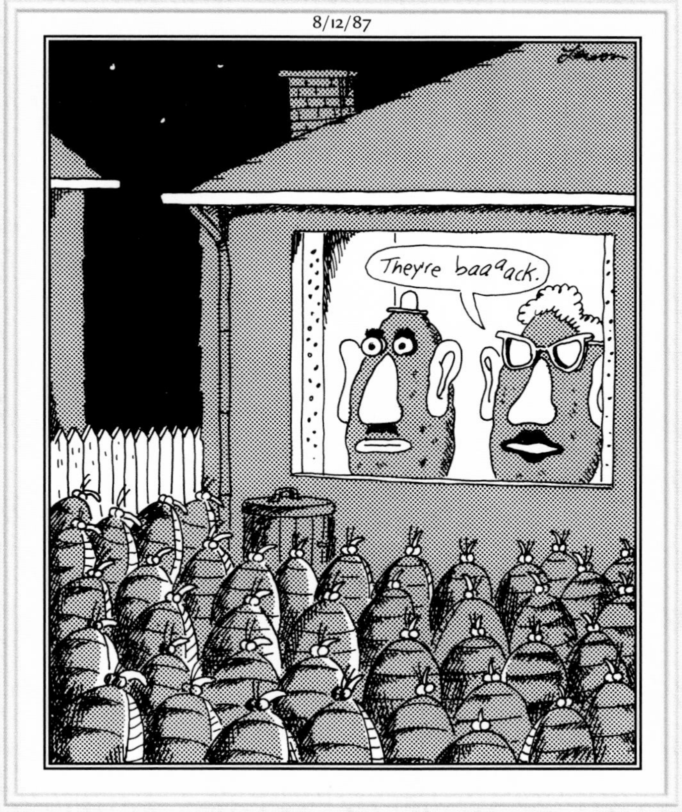
8/12/87
Larson
They're baaaack.

Night of the Potato Bugs

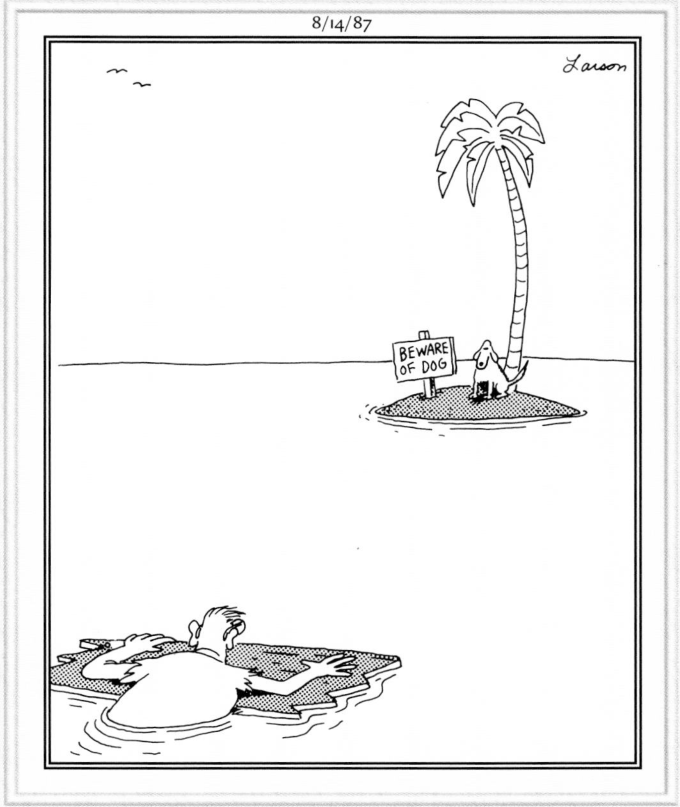
8/14/87
Larson
BEWARE OF DOG

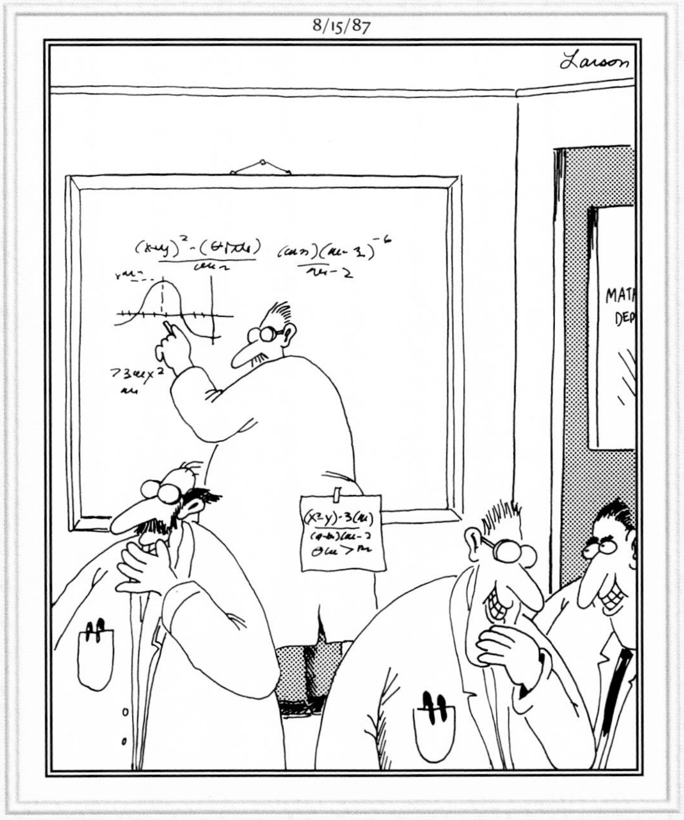
8/15/87
Larson

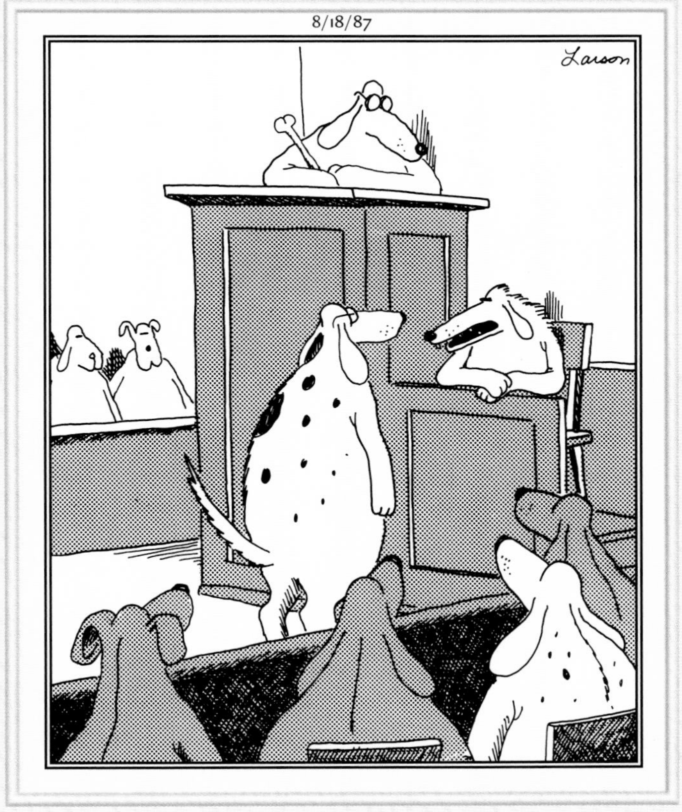
8/18/87
Larson

"Well, the defendant and I had made this deal in which we both prospered. ... You know, one of those 'you-scratch-me-behind-my-ears-I'll-scratch-you-behind-yours' arrangements."

8/16/87

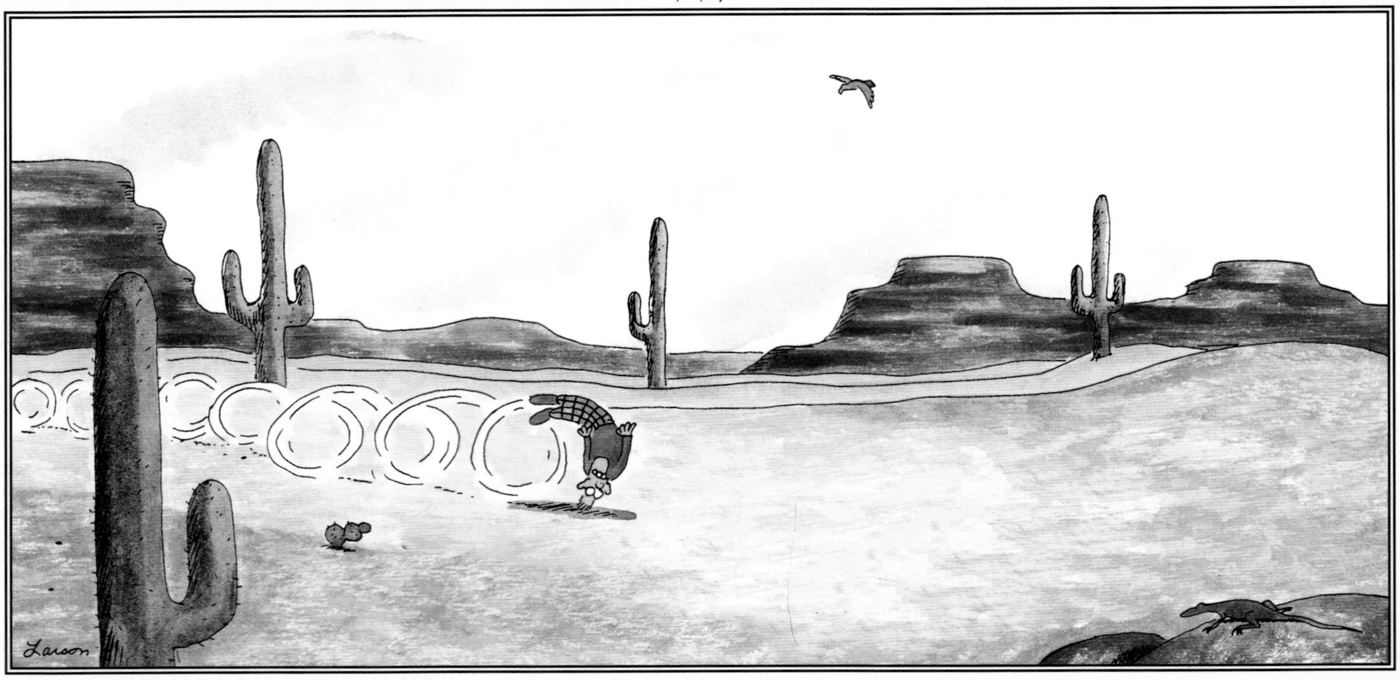
Larson

As the cactus stood watch over the sun-drenched land, a red-tailed hawk hung motionless in the desert sky. Little stirred, except an occasional lizard scurrying for shade or a tumblenerd drifting by.

8/20/87

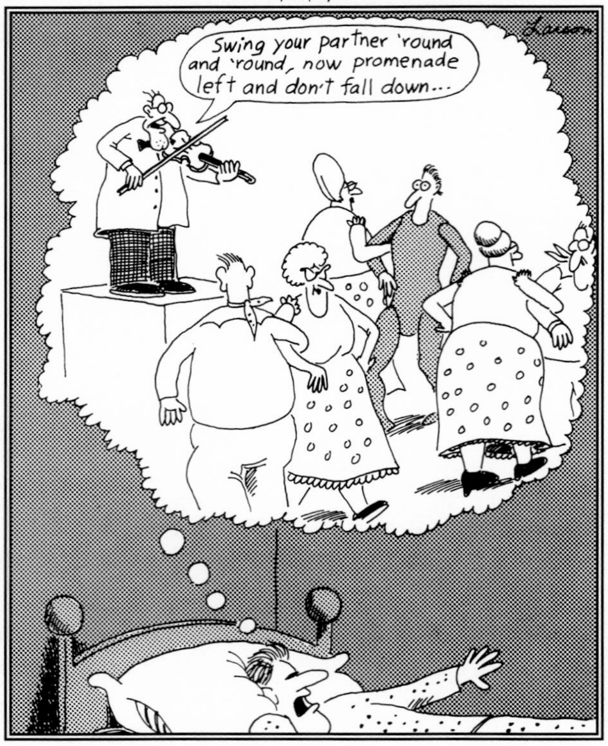
Swing your partner 'round and 'round, now promenade left and don't fall down...
Larson

Baryshnikov's ultimate nightmare

8/21/87

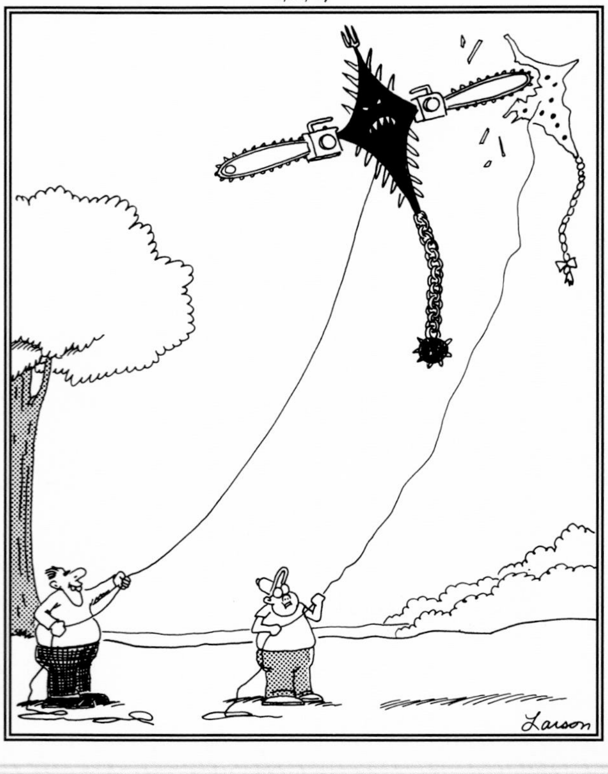
Larson

Eddie Nordquist and his "Death Kite"

8/22/87

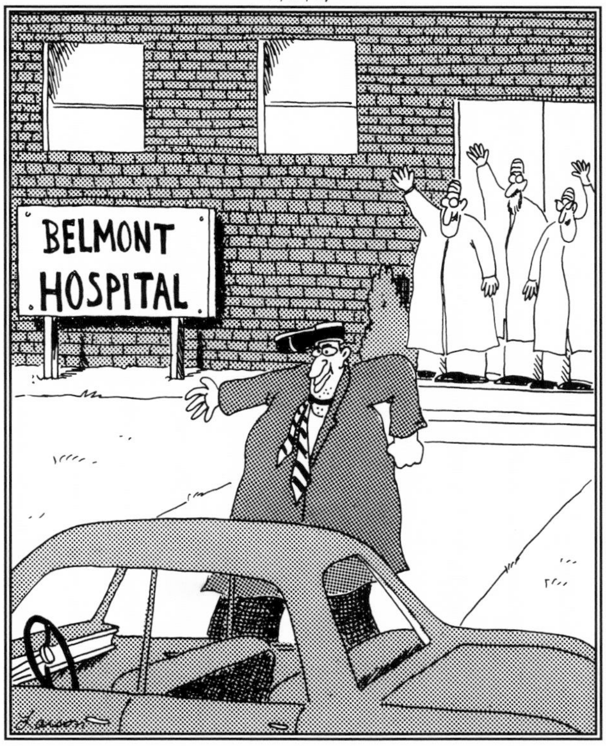
BELMONT
HOSPITAL
Larson

Gus Ferguson: recipient of the first brain bypass operation.

8/24/87

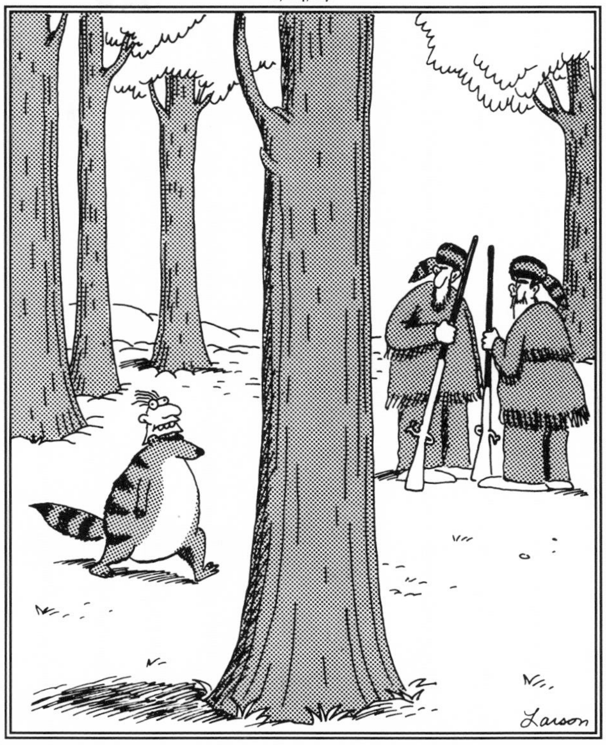
Larson

8/23/87

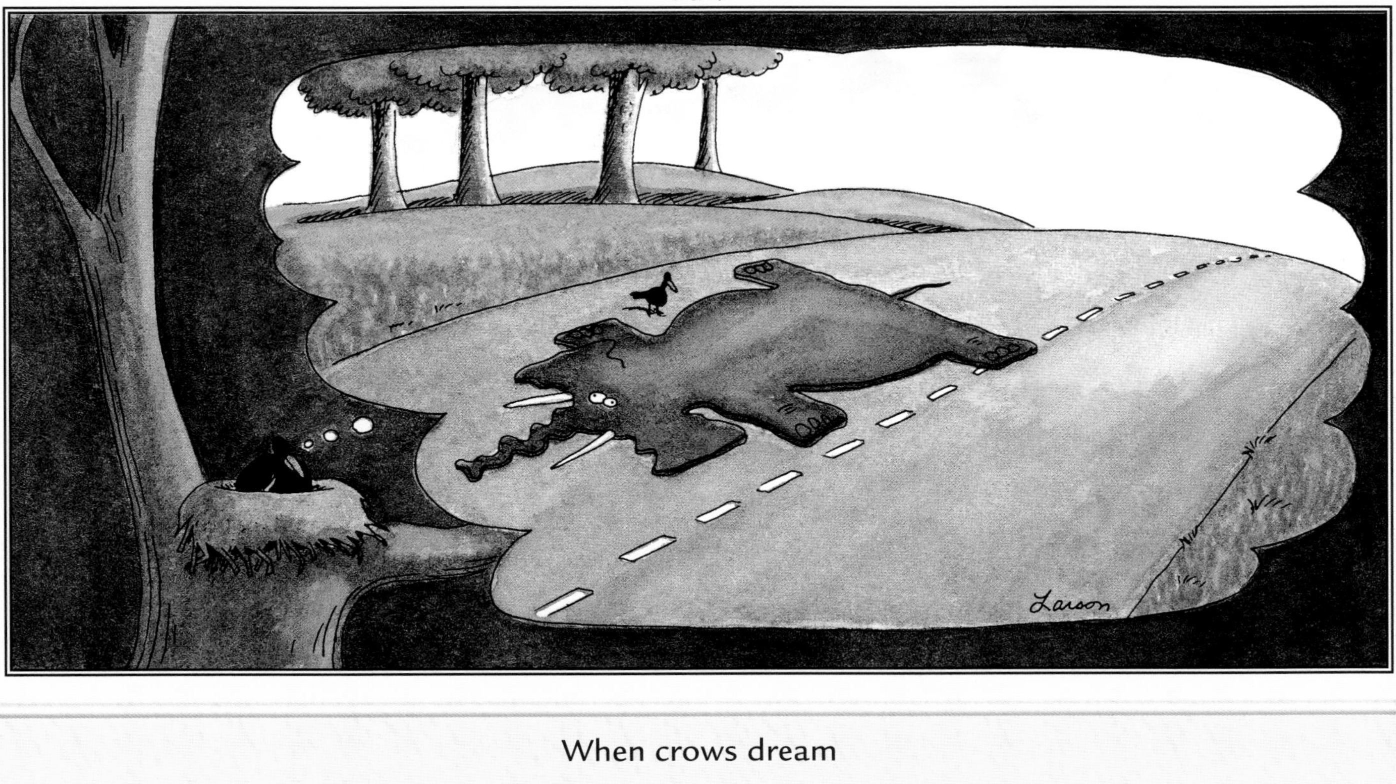
Larson

When crows dream

8/19/87

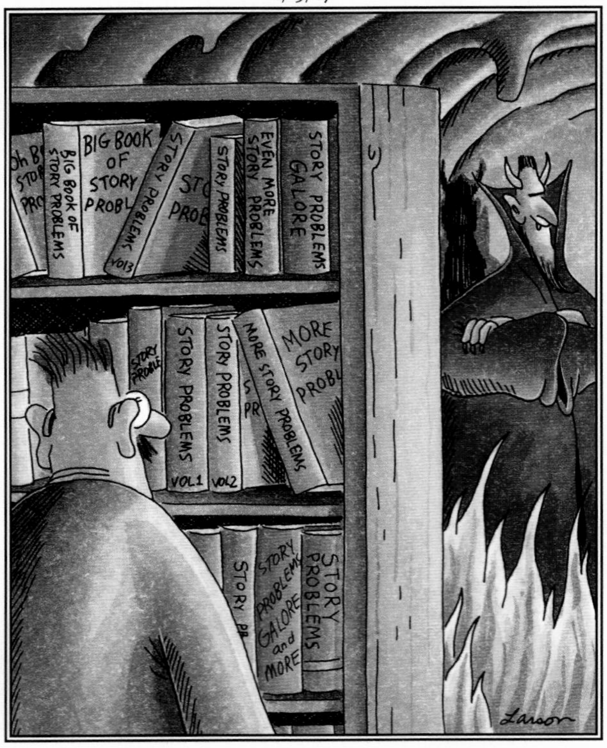
BIG BOOK OF STORY PROBL
BIG BOOK OF STORY PROBLEMS
STORY PROBLEMS
EVEN MORE STORY PROBLEMS
STORY PROBLEMS GALORE
STORY PROBLEMS VOL1
STORY PROBLEMS VOL2
MORE STORY PROBLEMS
MORE STORY PROBL
STORY PROBLEMS GALORE and MORE
STORY PROBLEMS
Larson

Hell's library

8/17/87

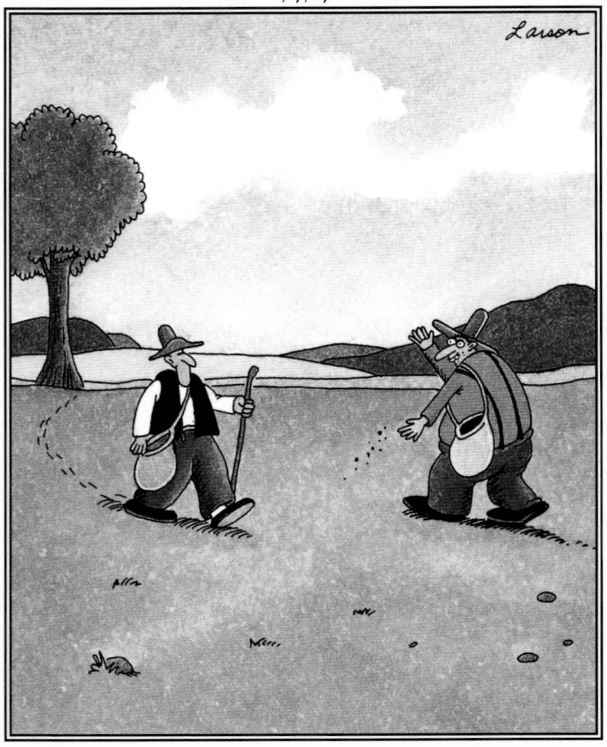
Larson

Crossing paths on their respective journeys of destiny, Johnny Appleseed and Irving Ragweed nod "hello."

8/25/87

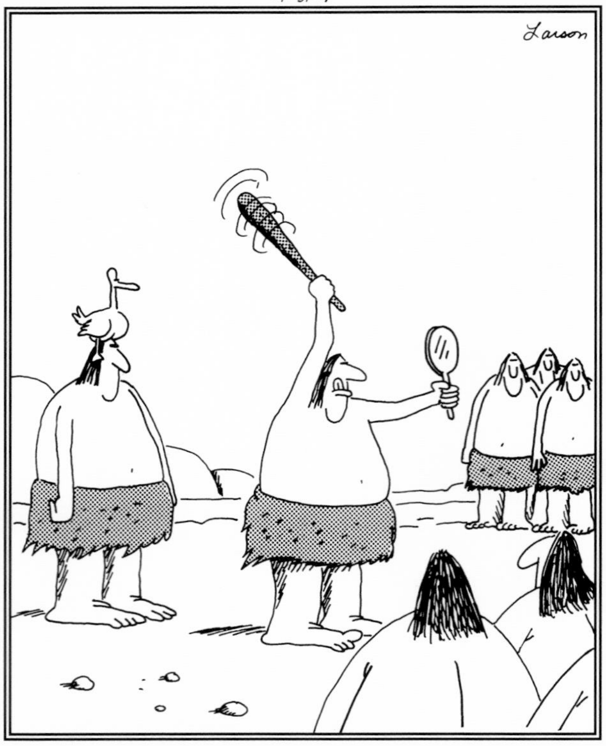
Larson

Trick clubbing exhibitions

8/27/87

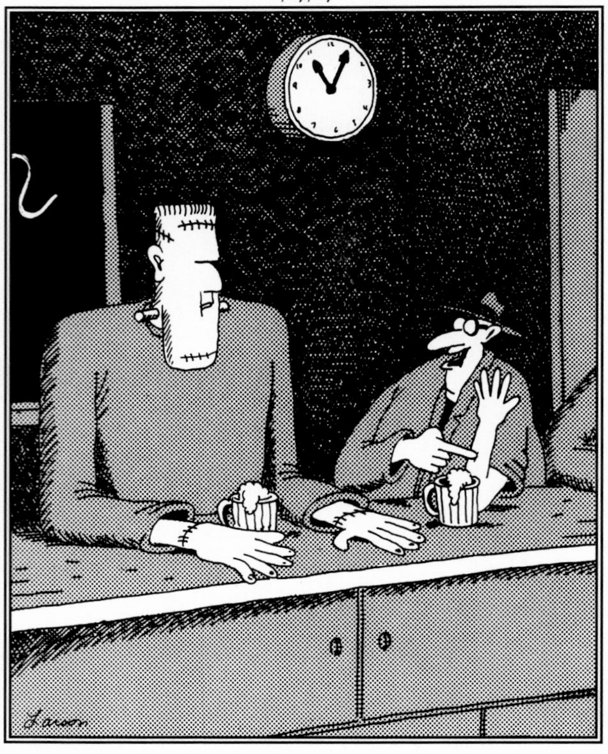
Larson

"Hey, you wanna see a *real* scar? Check *this* baby out!"

8/29/87

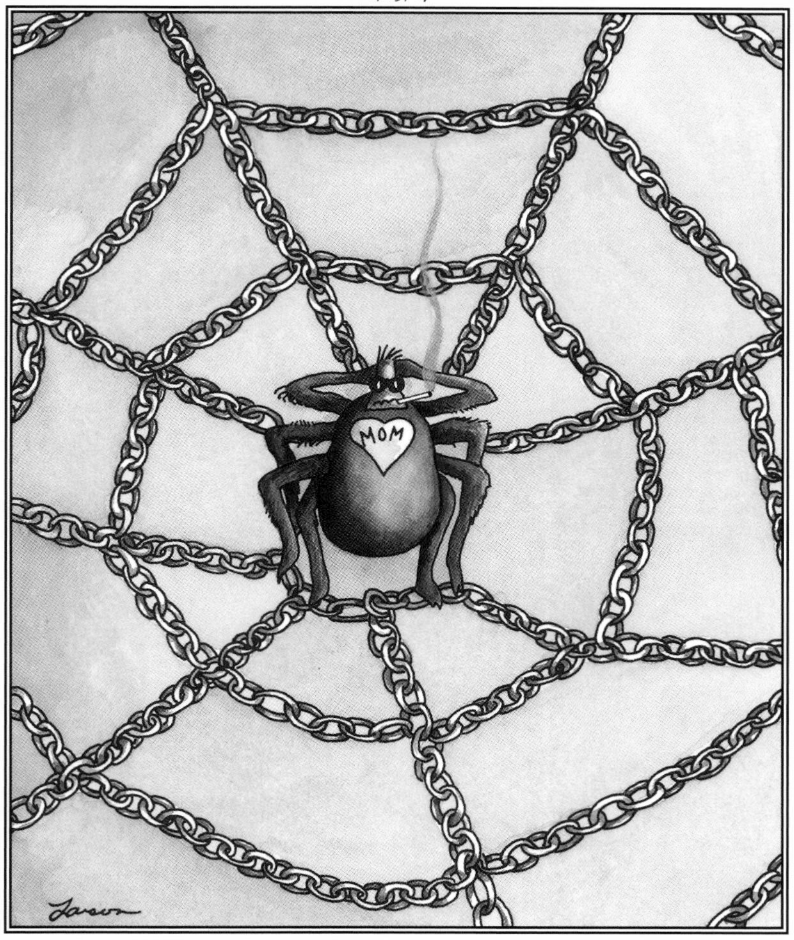
MOM

Tough spiders

8/28/87

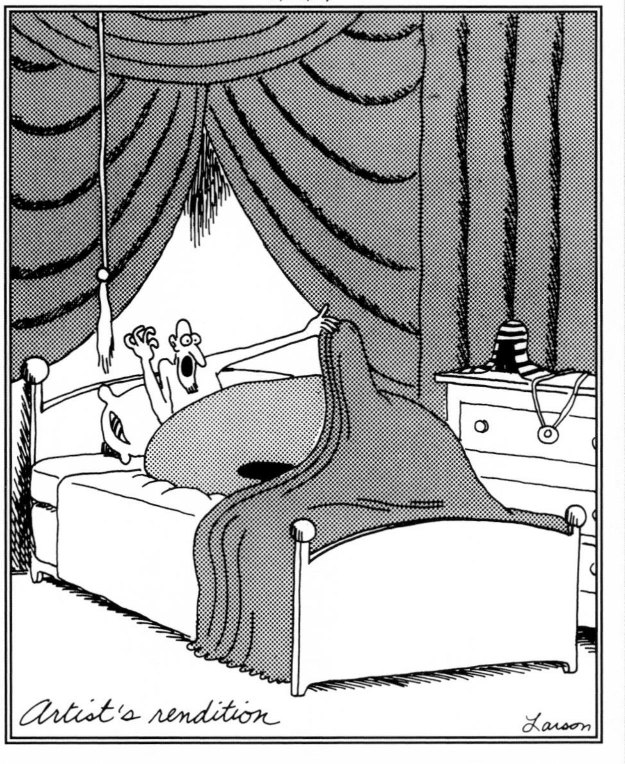
Artist's rendition

Some historians theorize that the Sphinx's nose was actually severed by Egyptian mobsters and, in an act of defiance, "delivered" to an unpopular pharaoh.

8/31/87

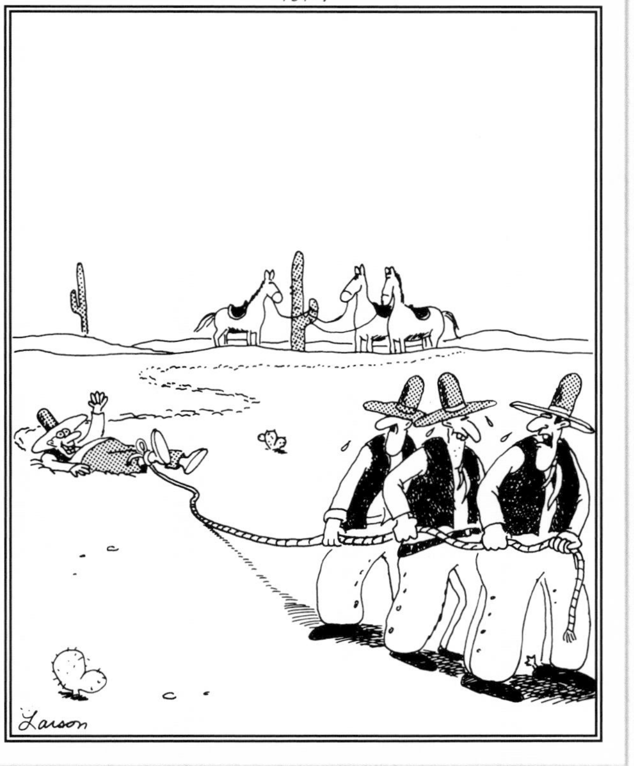

"Man, this is havin' no effect. ... But if the boss wants this varmint dragged through the desert, I ain't gonna argue."

Arizona Daily Star, Tucson, Ariz., 9/1/87

Offensive 'Far Side'

To the editor:

I was appalled when I saw Gary Larson's "The Far Side" cartoon in the Star Aug. 26. This was of two Larson animals — presumably chimpanzees — in a tree. One, which was evidently supposed to be the female, was picking a long hair from the other's shoulder. The caption read: "Well, well — another blond hair . . . Conducting a little more 'research' with that Jane Goodall tramp?"

To refer to Dr. Goodall as a tramp is inexcusable — even by a self-described "loony" as Larson. The cartoon was incredibly offensive and in such poor taste that readers might well question the editorial judgment of running such an atrocity in a newspaper that reputes to be supplying the news to persons with a better than average intelligence. The cartoon and its message were absolutely stupid.

Dr. Goodall is a world-renowned scientist who has devoted 28 years of her life to studying chimpanzees in the wild. Her findings have caused the scientific world to redefine the meaning of the word "mankind" with her discoveries that include the erroneous assumption that man was the only primate to make and use tools, a distinction that had — until her findings disproved it — been a measure of superiority of human beings over other primates.

With no alignment to any animal welfare group, Dr. Goodall is working very hard to instigate better treatment of chimpanzees in biomedical laboratories. Dr. Goodall has vowed to speak out for these animals that cannot speak for themselves.

"Tramp?" Hardly.

The irresponsibility of the Star in choosing to run such an obscenity is disgusting. In fact, any woman should be insulted by the reference that the female — in this case, a typical Larson eyeglass wearing animal — would be unaware of what Dr. Goodall's research really is, its seriousness and the assumption that a female only would have the mentality to look for sexual implications.

Sue Engel
Executive director
The Jane Goodall Institute

Editor's note: Jane Goodall was out of the country when this cartoon appeared in newspapers and had not seen it when this letter was written. Unbeknownst to her then executive director, Dr. Goodall was a big fan of The Far Side. *Her reaction upon seeing the cartoon was to guffaw (her word) and say, "Wow! Fantastic! Real fame at last! Fancy being in a Gary Larson cartoon!" She intended to write Gary an apology herself but got sidetracked. A year or so later, the National Geographic Society requested permission from Gary's syndicate to reprint the cartoon and was denied, because of this letter. They responded, "That doesn't sound like the Jane Goodall we know." They checked around and discovered that Dr. Goodall loved the cartoon; permission was granted. Jane and Gary eventually met at her research facility in Gombe, and she went on to write the introduction to* The Far Side Gallery 5 *(1995).*

8/26/87

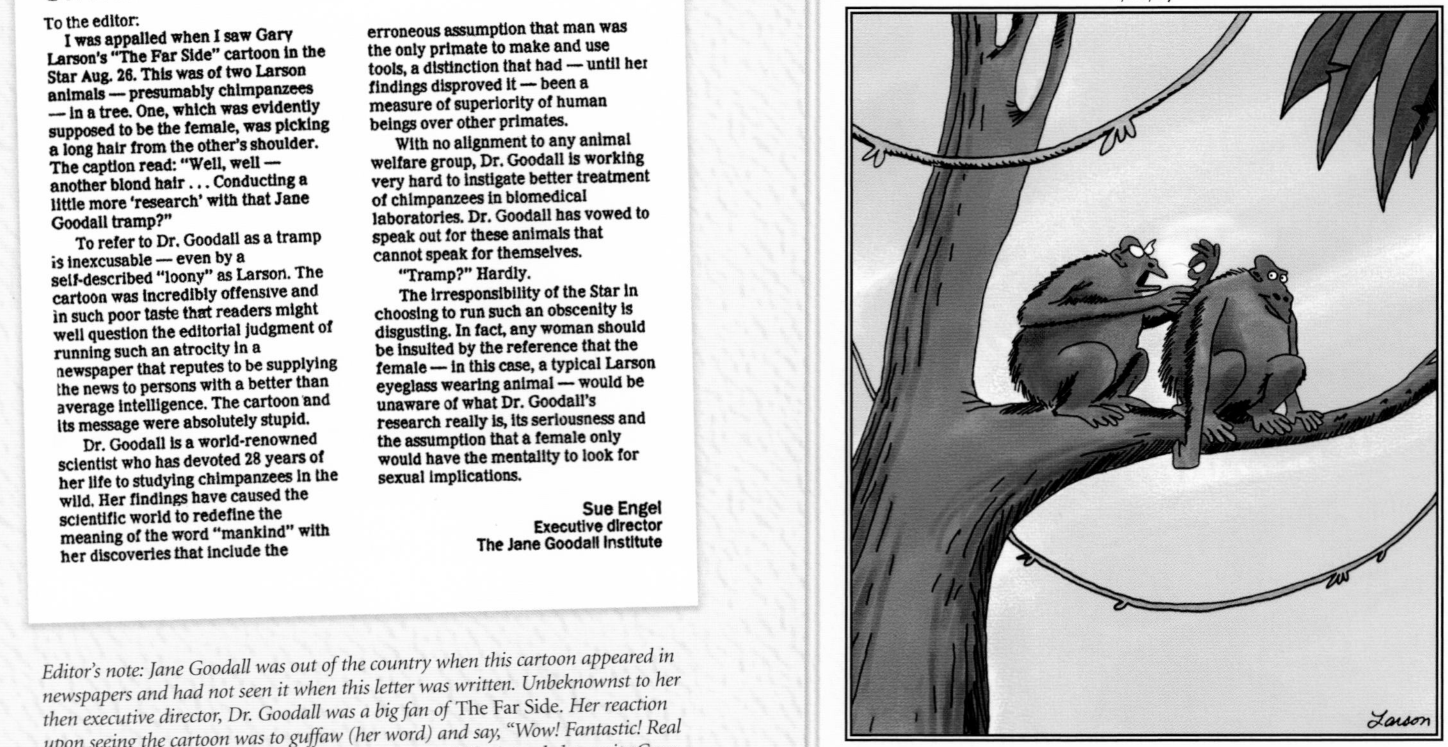
Larson

"Well, well—another blonde hair. ... Conducting a little more 'research' with that Jane Goodall tramp?"

8/30/87

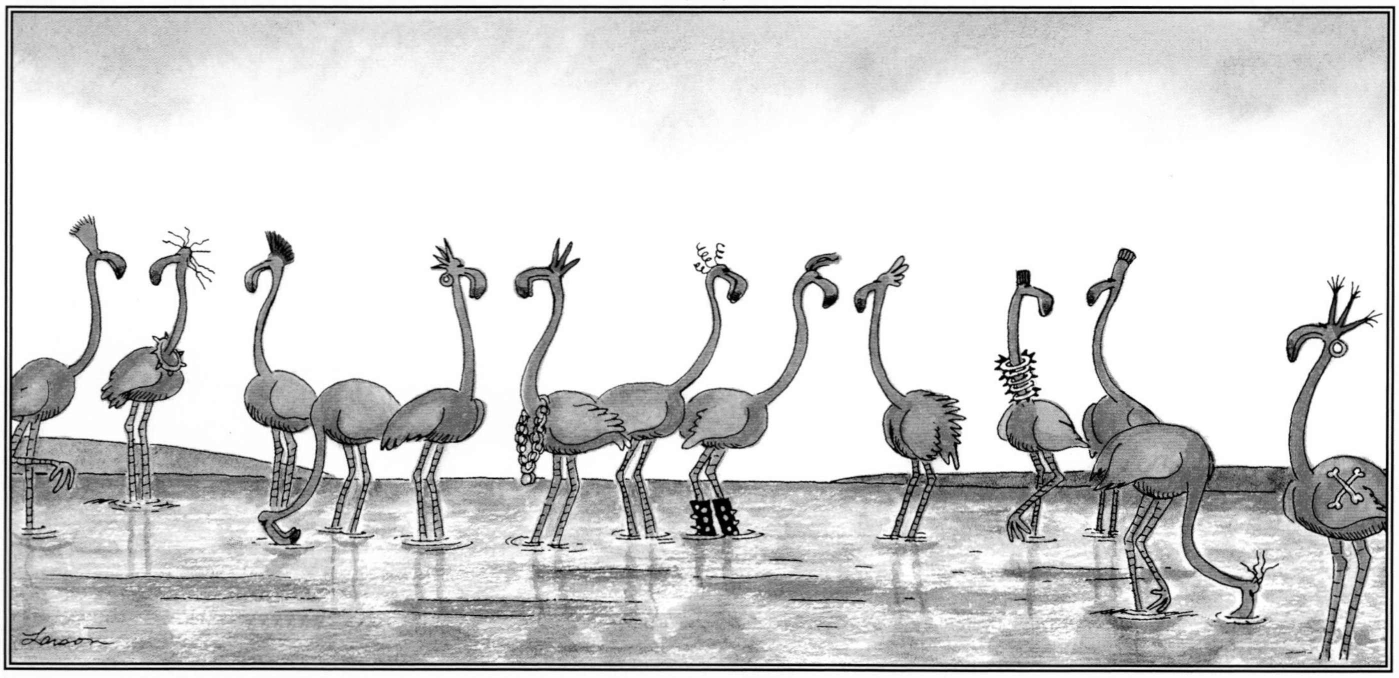
Larson

Punk flamingoes

9/6/87

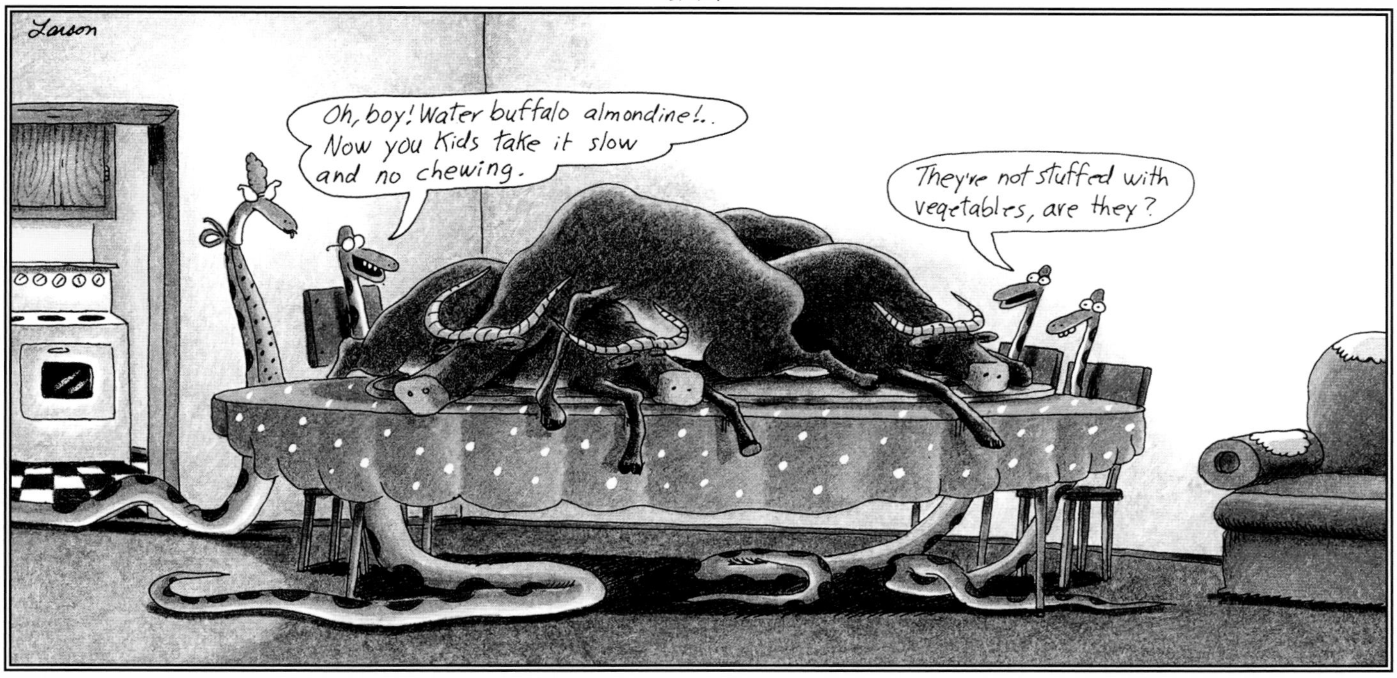
Larson
Oh, boy! Water buffalo almondine!.. Now you kids take it slow and no chewing.
They're not stuffed with vegetables, are they?

Python dinners

9/2/87

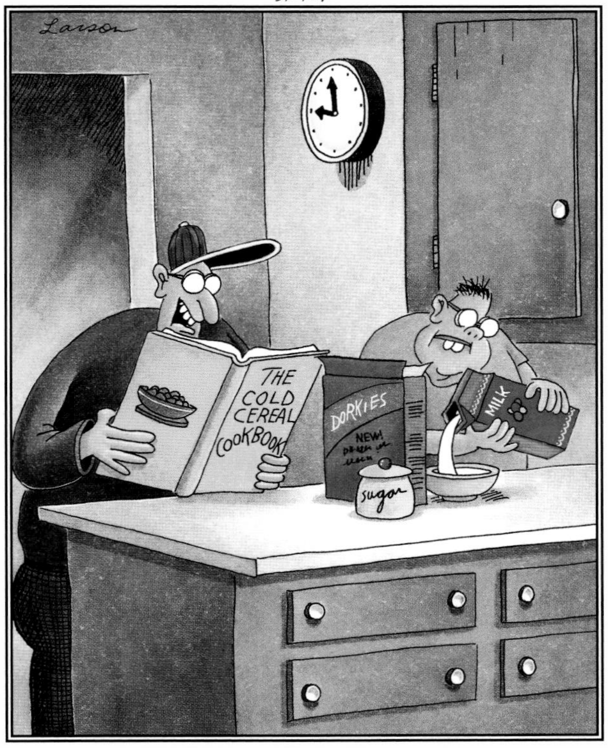
Larson
THE COLD CEREAL COOKBOOK
DORKIES
MILK
sugar

"Oh, wait! Wait, Cory! ... Add the cereal *first* and *then* the milk!"

9/1/87

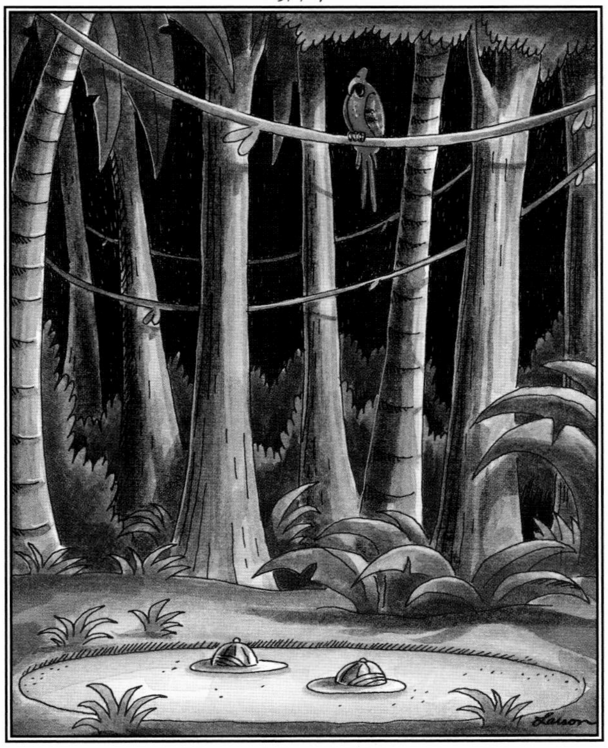
Larson

"Let go, Morty! Let go, Morty! You're pulling me in! ... Let go, Morty! You're pulling me in!"

9/3/87

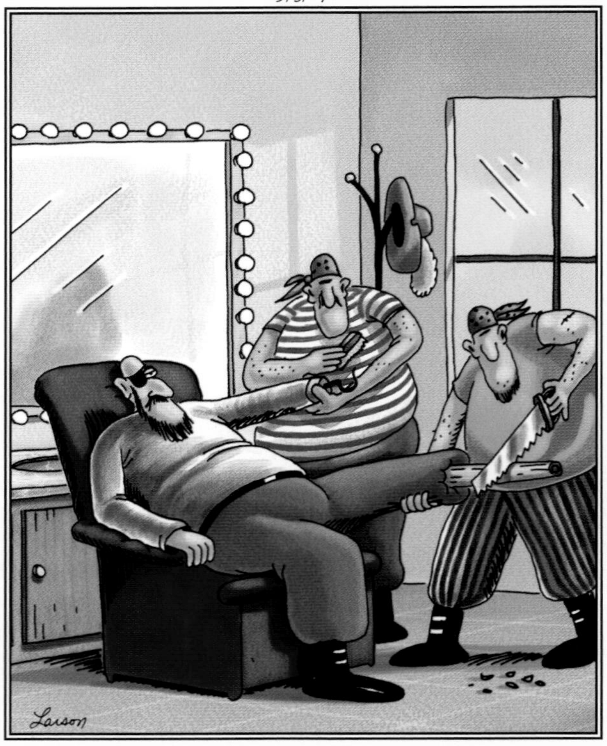
Larson

Pirate manicures

9/12/87

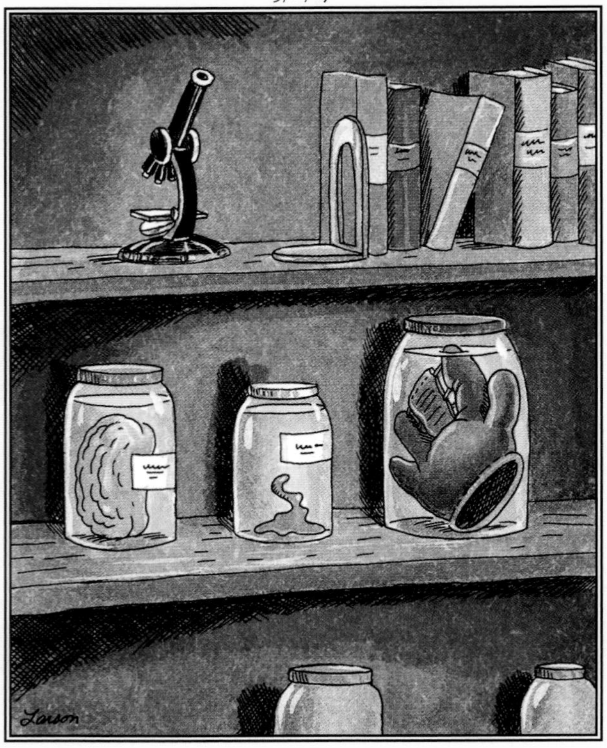
Larson

Broca's brain, appendix, and baseball glove

9/5/87

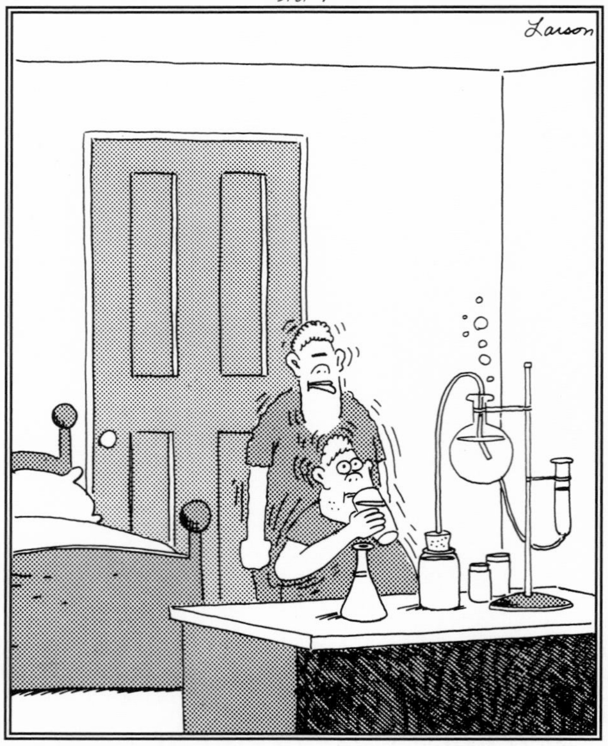
Larson

As a child, little Henry Jekyll would often change himself into a big, red-haired delinquent that parents in the neighborhood simply dubbed "that Hyde kid."

9/4/87

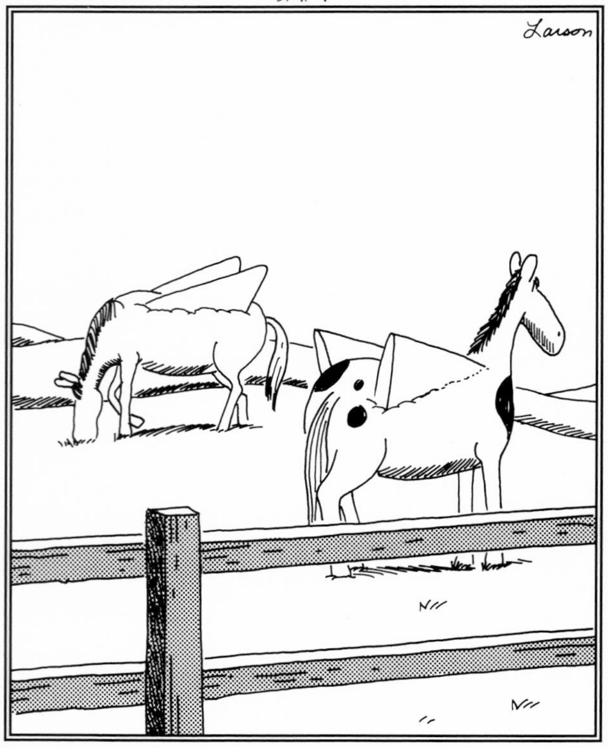
Larson

Horse styles of the '50s

9/10/87

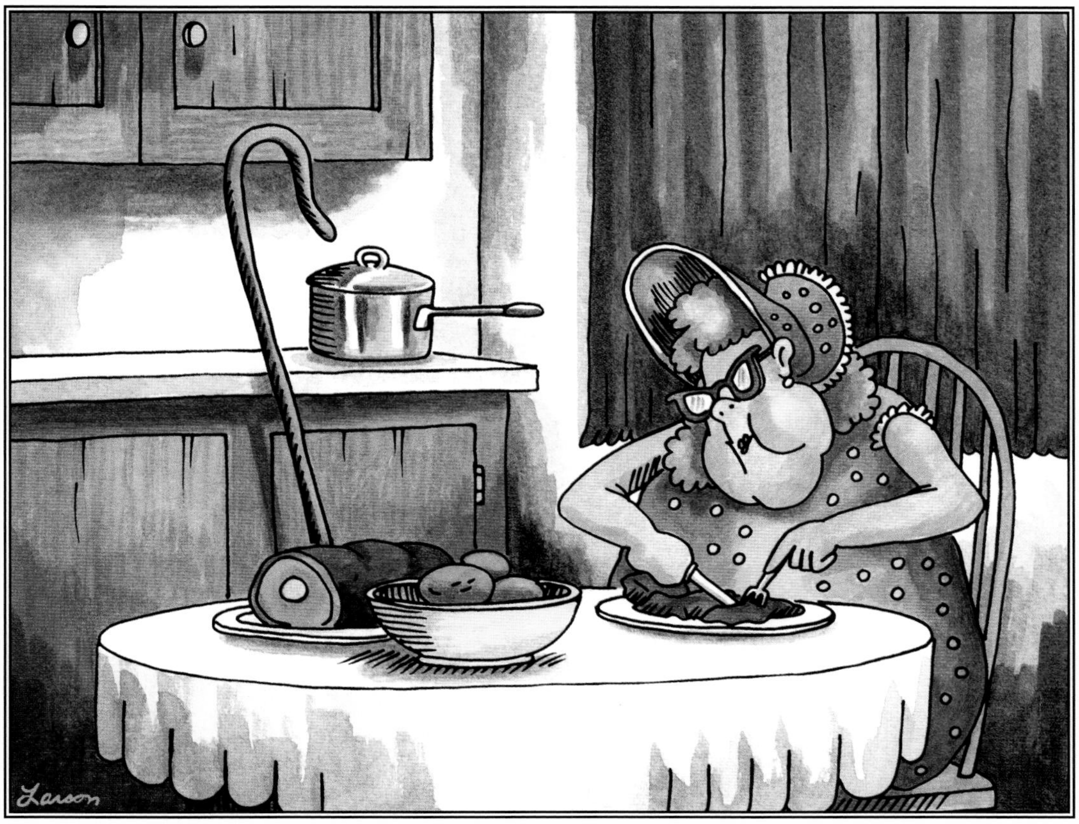

That evening, with her blinds pulled, Mary had three helpings of corn, two baked potatoes, extra bread, and a little lamb.

9/9/87

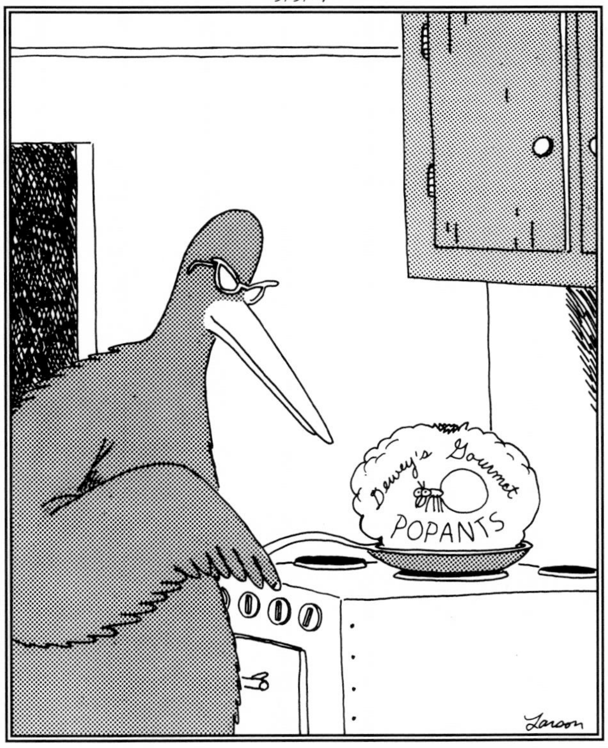
Dewey's Gourmet
POPANTS

9/8/87

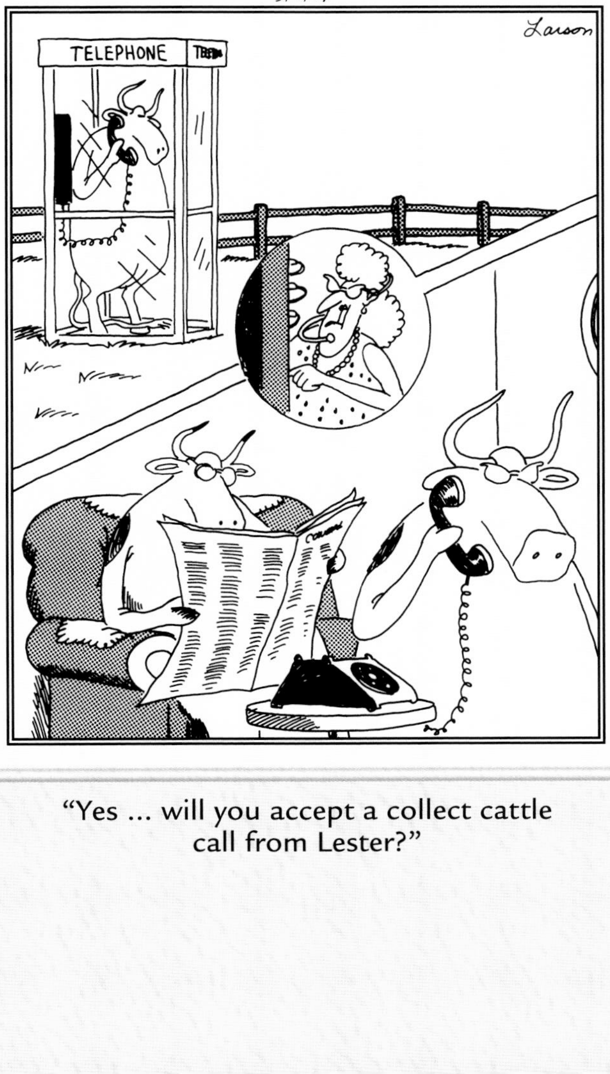
TELEPHONE

"Yes ... will you accept a collect cattle call from Lester?"

9/7/87

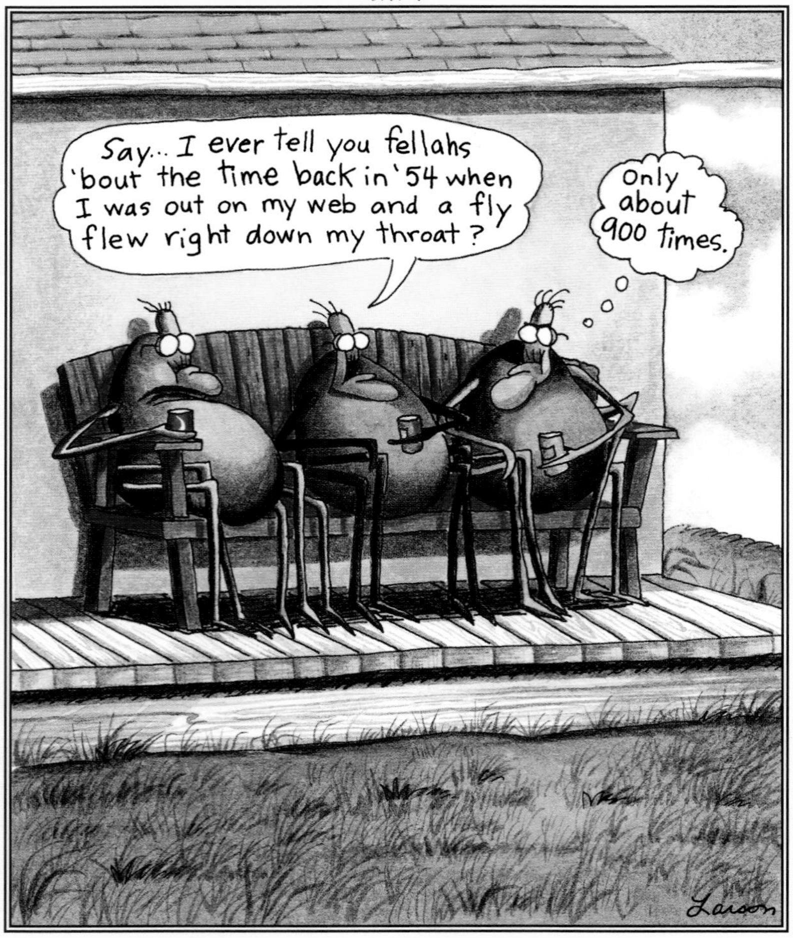
Say... I ever tell you fellahs 'bout the time back in '54 when I was out on my web and a fly flew right down my throat?
Only about 900 times.
Larson

At the Old Spiders' Home

9/13/87

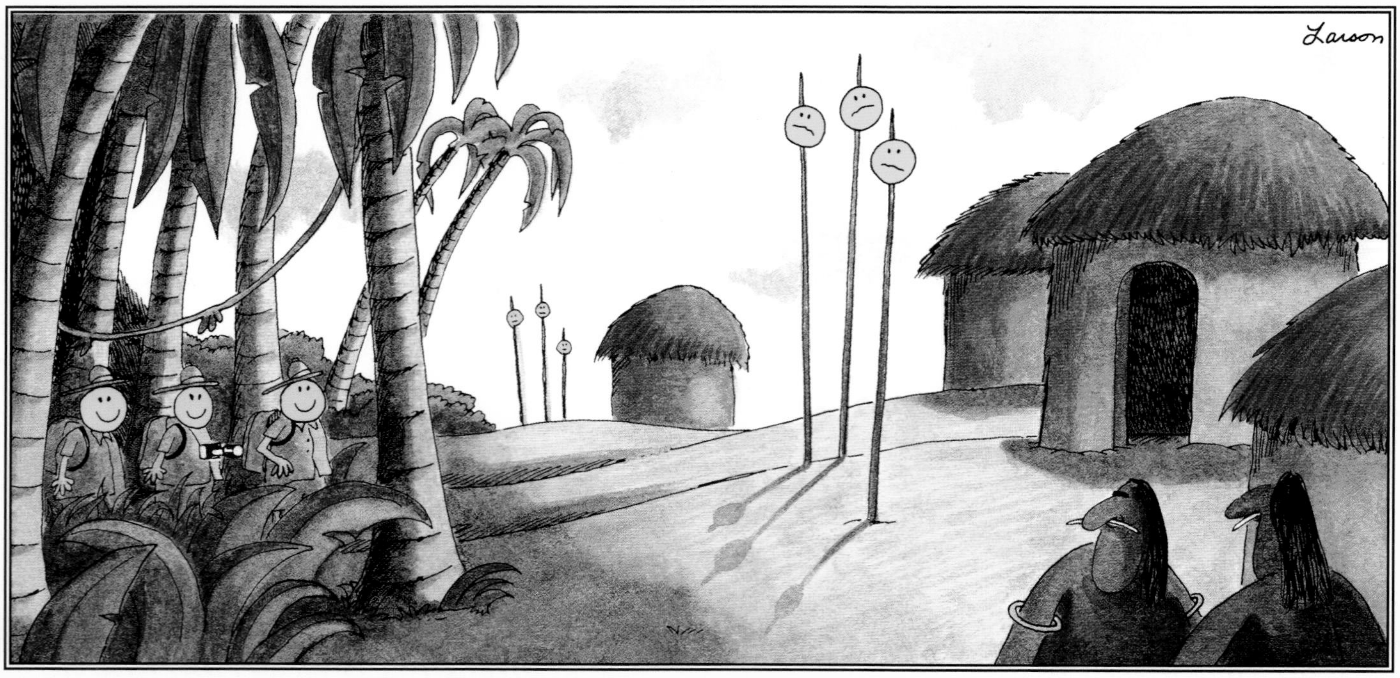
Larson

9/20/87

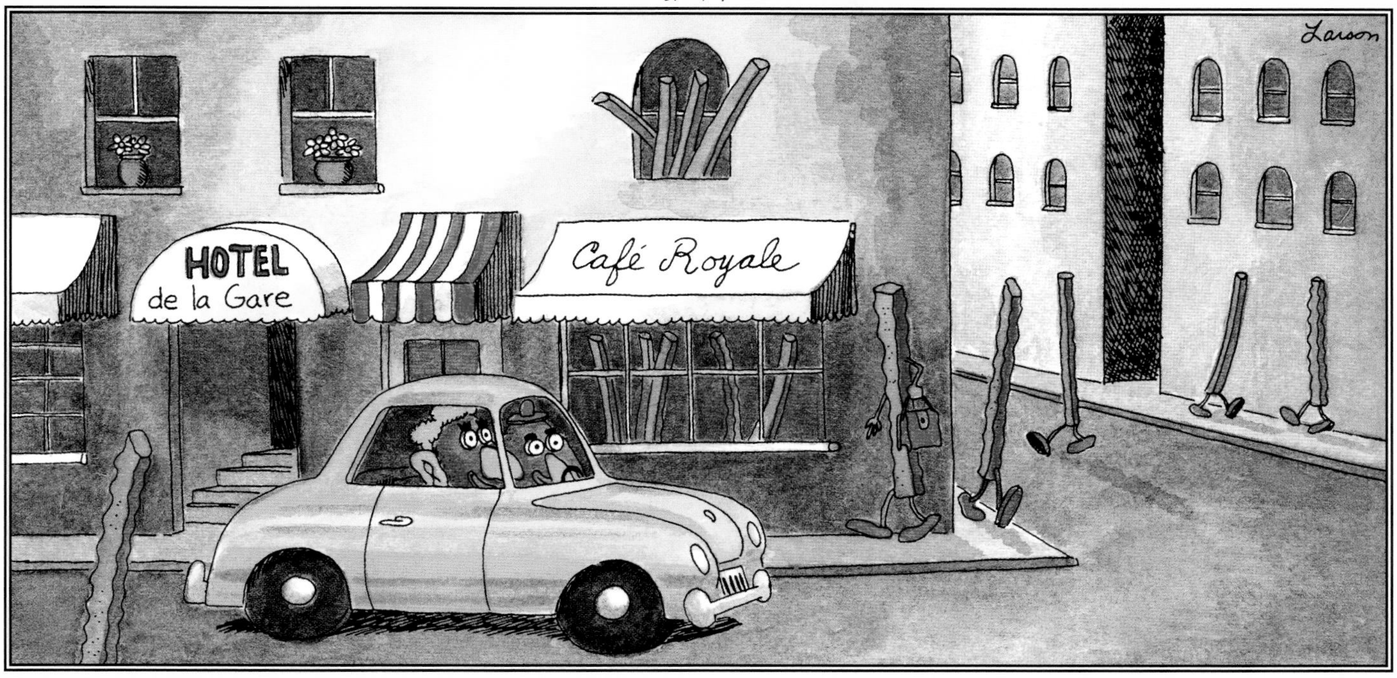
HOTEL
de la Gare
Café Royale
Larson

The Potatoheads in Paris

9/18/87

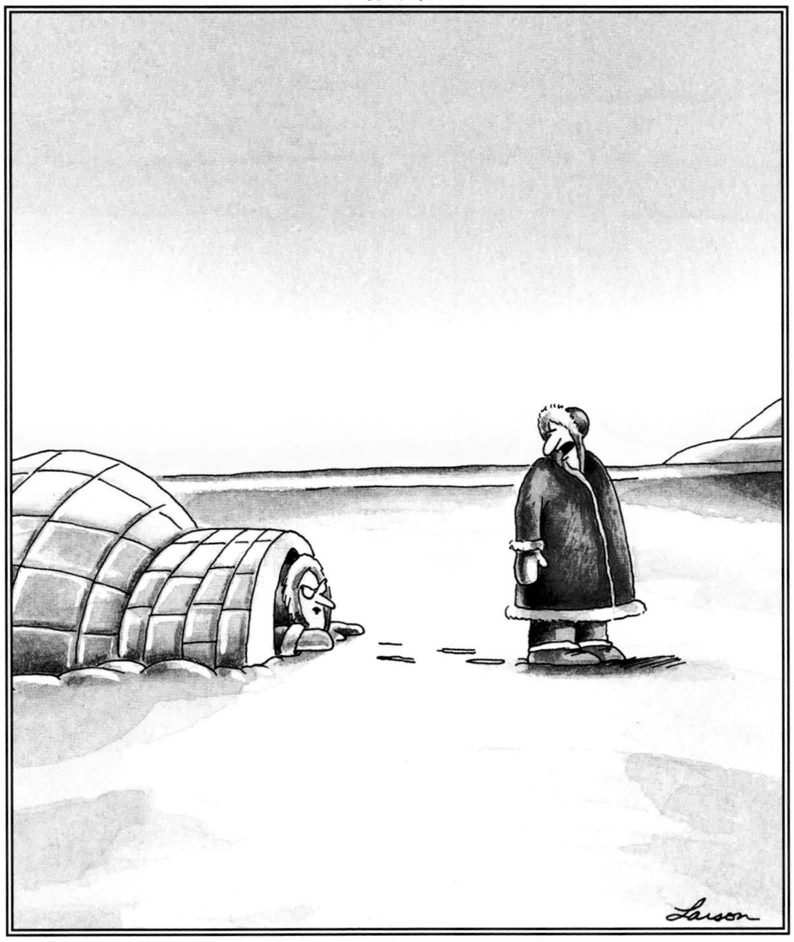
Larson

"Well, it's cold again."

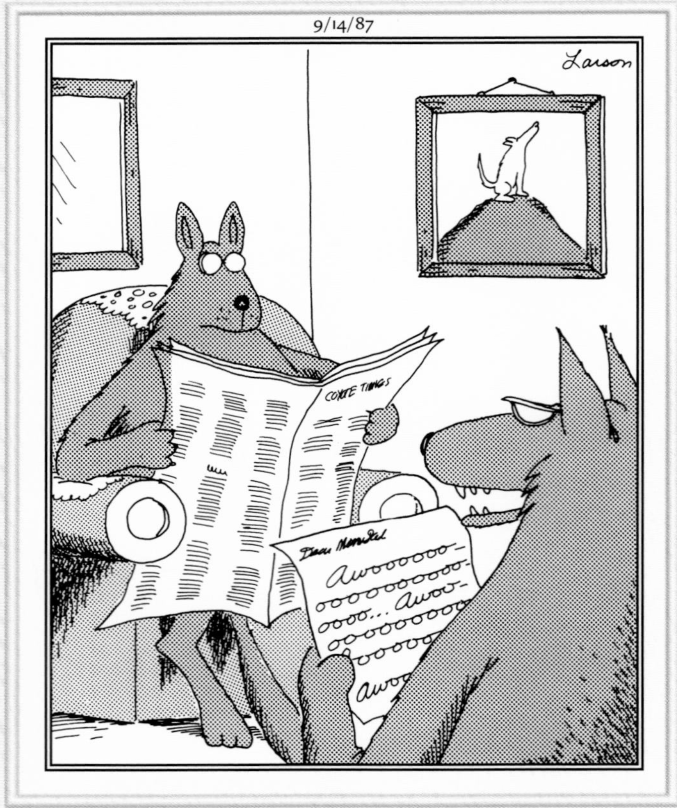
9/14/87
Larson

"Letter from Lonso ... and he sounds pretty lonely."

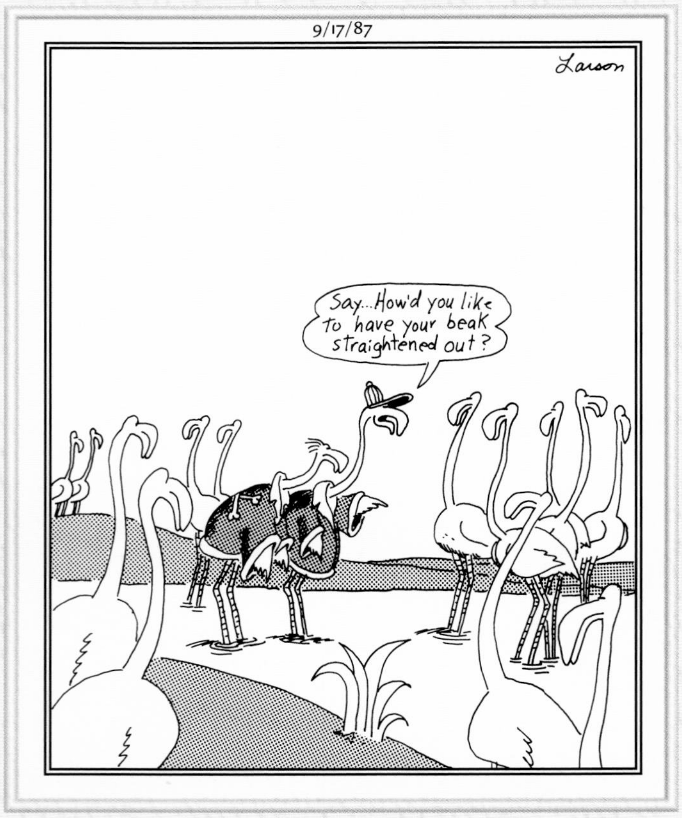
9/17/87
Larson
Say...How'd you like to have your beak straightened out?

Flamingo toughs

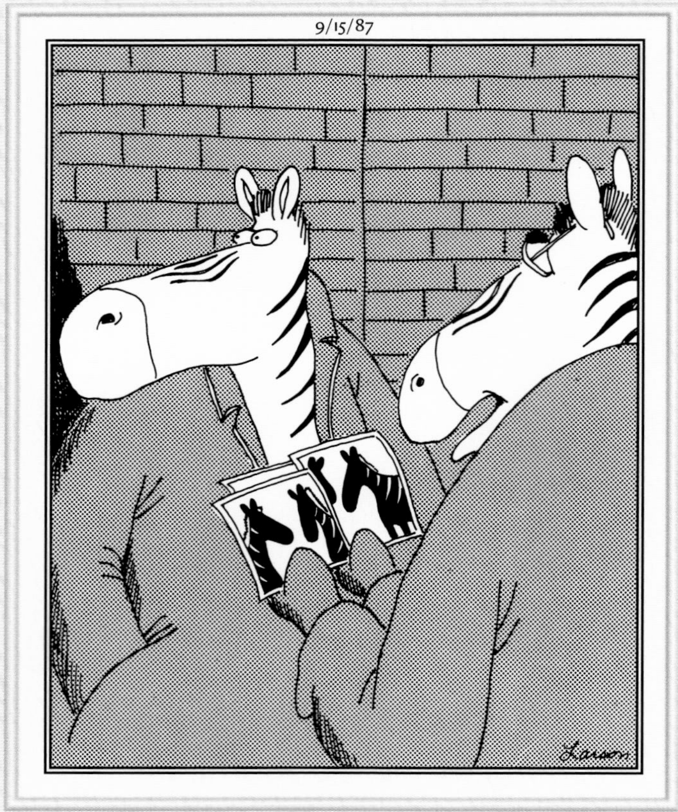
9/15/87
Larson

"Okay, you've got me over a barrel ... but how do I know these are *all* the negatives?"

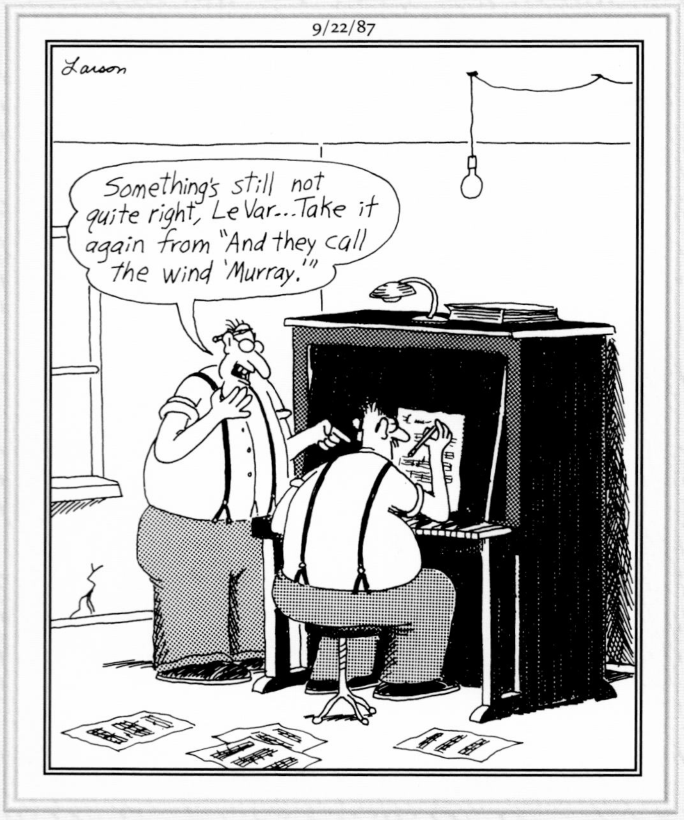
9/22/87
Larson
Something's still not quite right, LeVar...Take it again from "And they call the wind 'Murray.'"

Songwriters of the Old West

9/24/87

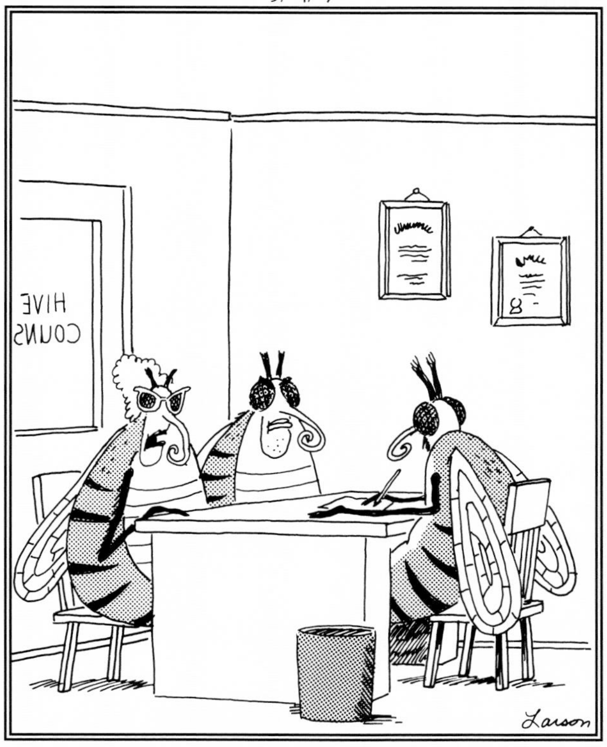
HIVE
COUNS

"Listen. I've *tried* to communicate with him, but he's like a broken record: 'None of your beeswax, none of your beeswax.'"

9/26/87

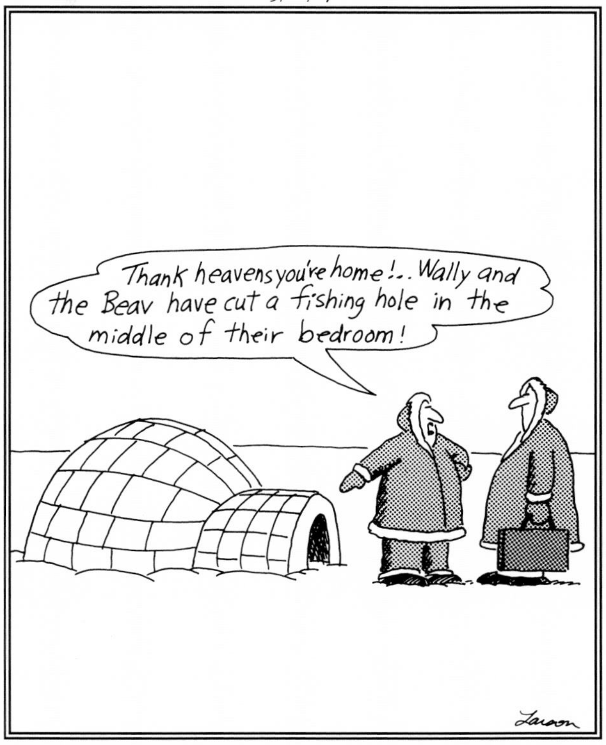
Thank heavens you're home!.. Wally and the Beav have cut a fishing hole in the middle of their bedroom!

If the Cleavers had been Eskimos

9/28/87

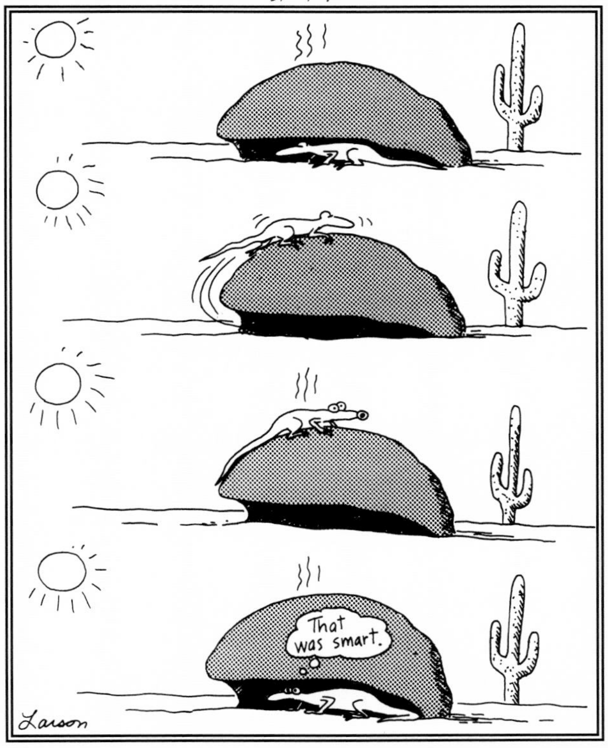
That was smart.

9/29/87

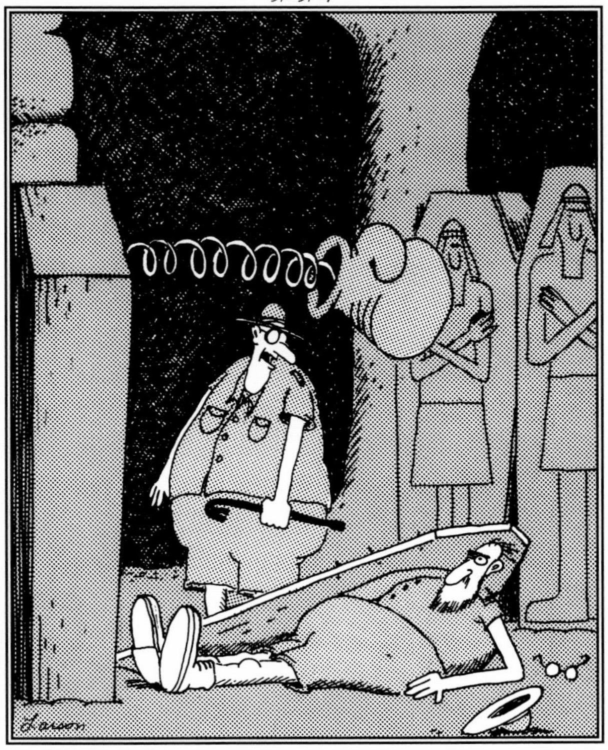

"Consider yourself fortunate, Belsky. ... As curses go, that sure beats having your descendants strangled in the night by a walking corpse."

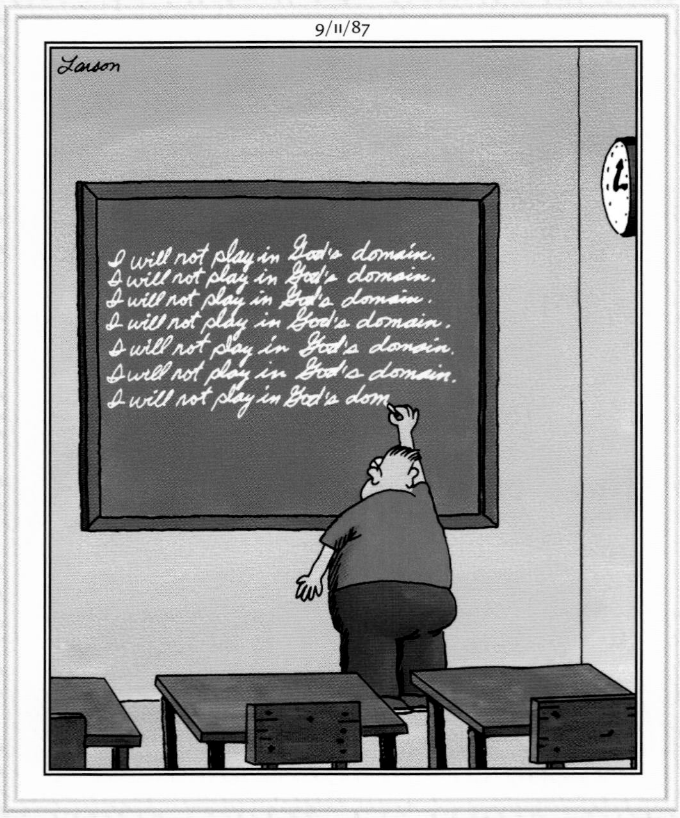
9/11/87
Larson
I will not play in God's domain.
I will not play in God's domain.
I will not play in God's domain.
I will not play in God's domain.
I will not play in God's domain.
I will not play in God's domain.
I will not play in God's dom

Young Victor Frankenstein stays after school.

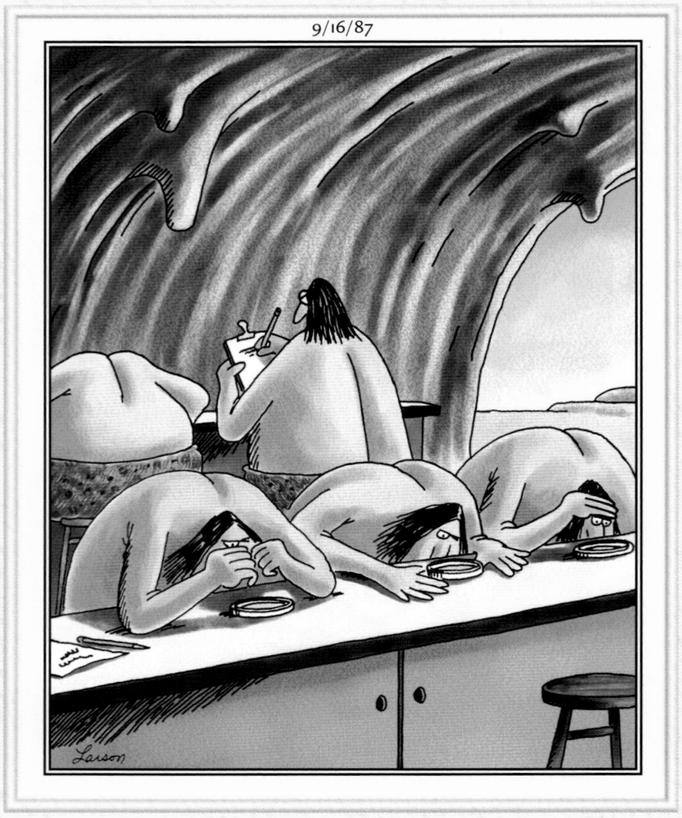
9/16/87
Larson

Early microbiologists

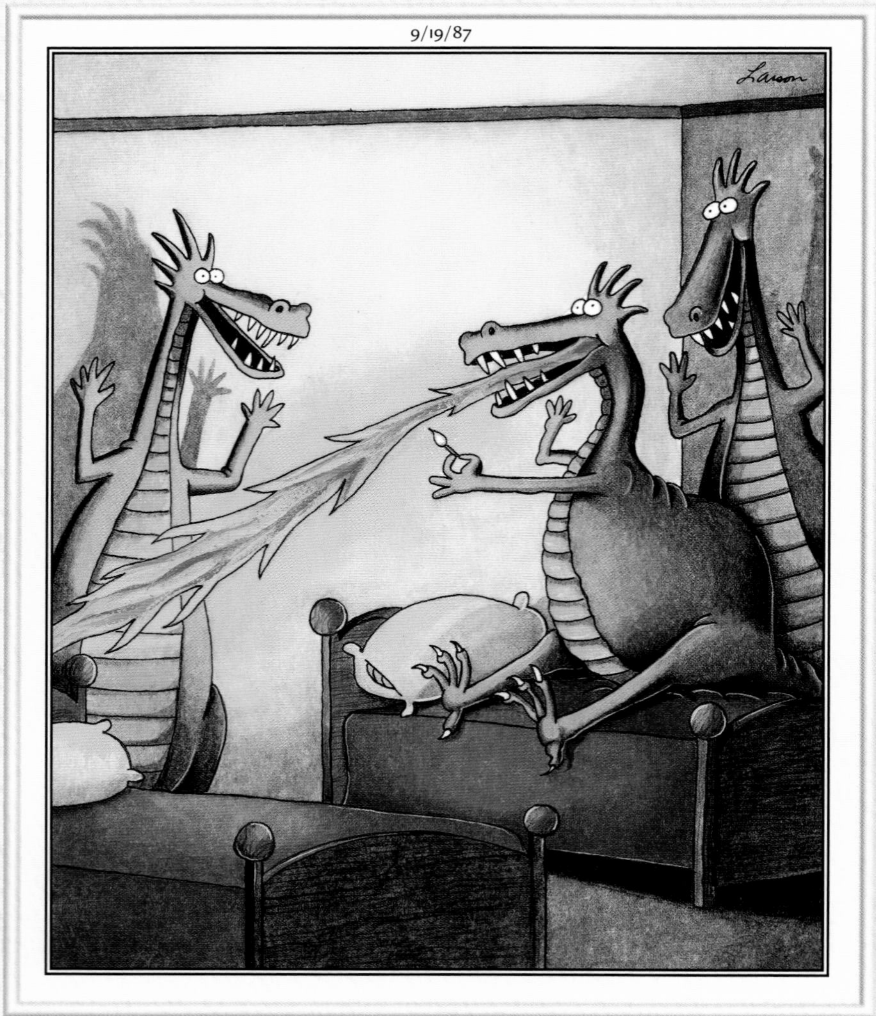
9/19/87
Larson

With their parents away, the young dragons would stay up late lighting their sneezes.

9/23/87

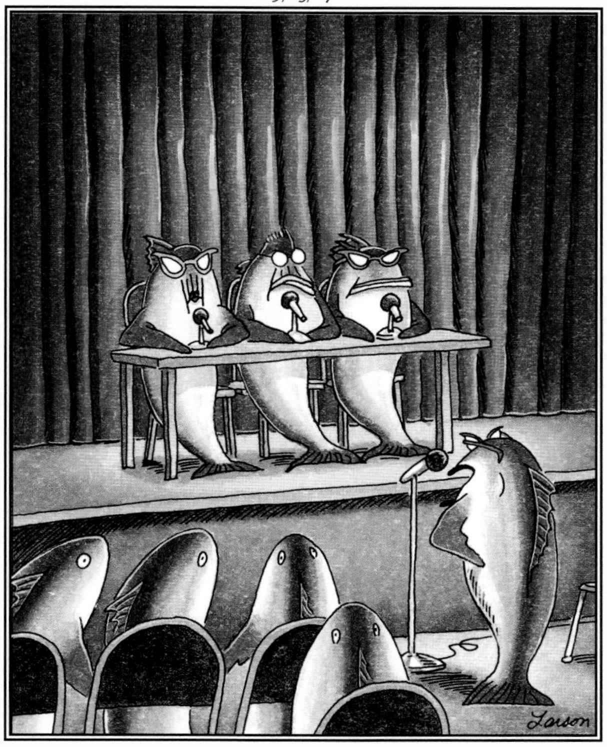
Larson

The committee to decide whether spawning should be taught in school.

9/21/87

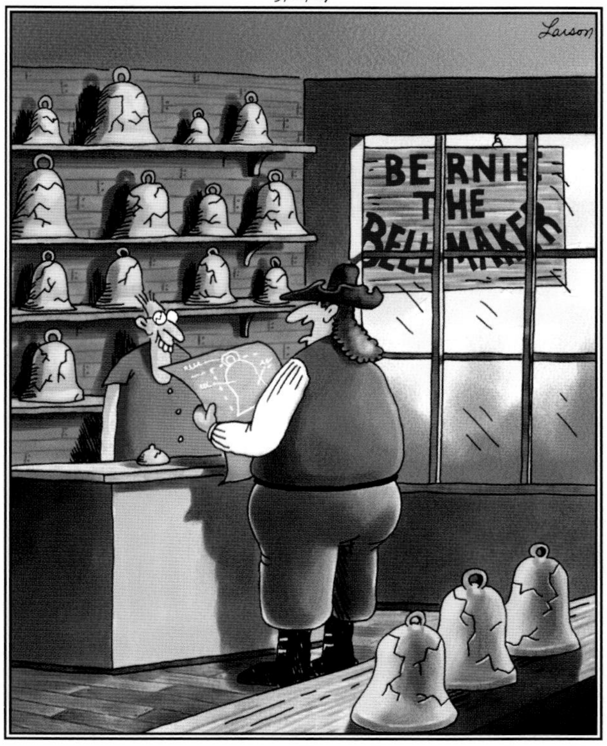
Larson
BERNIE
THE
BELLMAKER

"Here are the blueprints. Now look: This is going to be the *Liberty* Bell, so we obviously expect that it be forged with great diligence and skill."

9/25/87

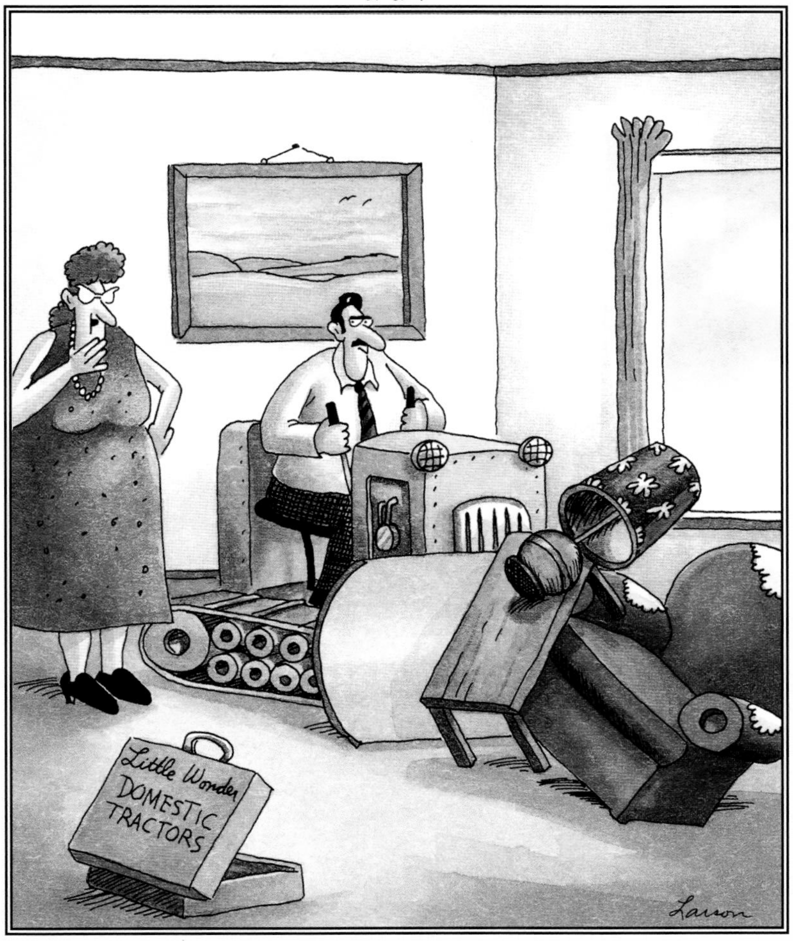
Little Wonder
DOMESTIC
TRACTORS
Larson

Darren's heart quickened: Once inside the home, and once the demonstration was in full swing, a sale was inevitable.

"Yes, yes, I *know* that, Sidney—*every*body knows *that!* ... But look: Four wrongs *squared,* minus two wrongs to the fourth power, divided by this formula, *do* make a right."

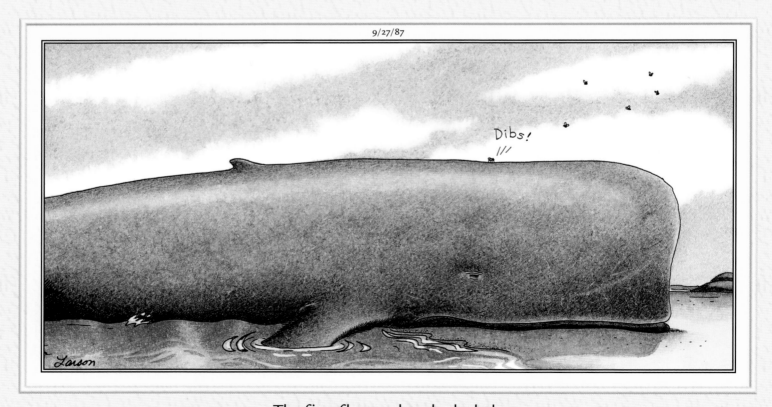

The first fly on a beached whale

10/4/87

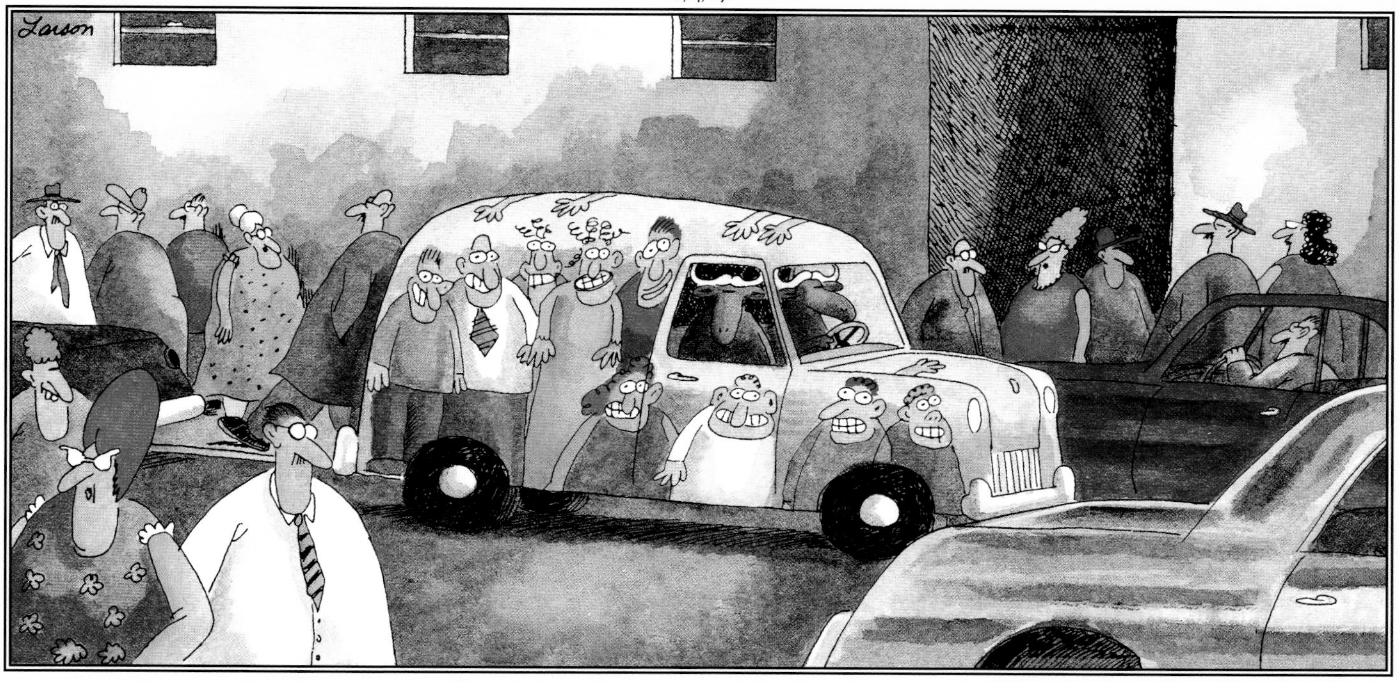
Larson

Animal camouflage

10/1/87

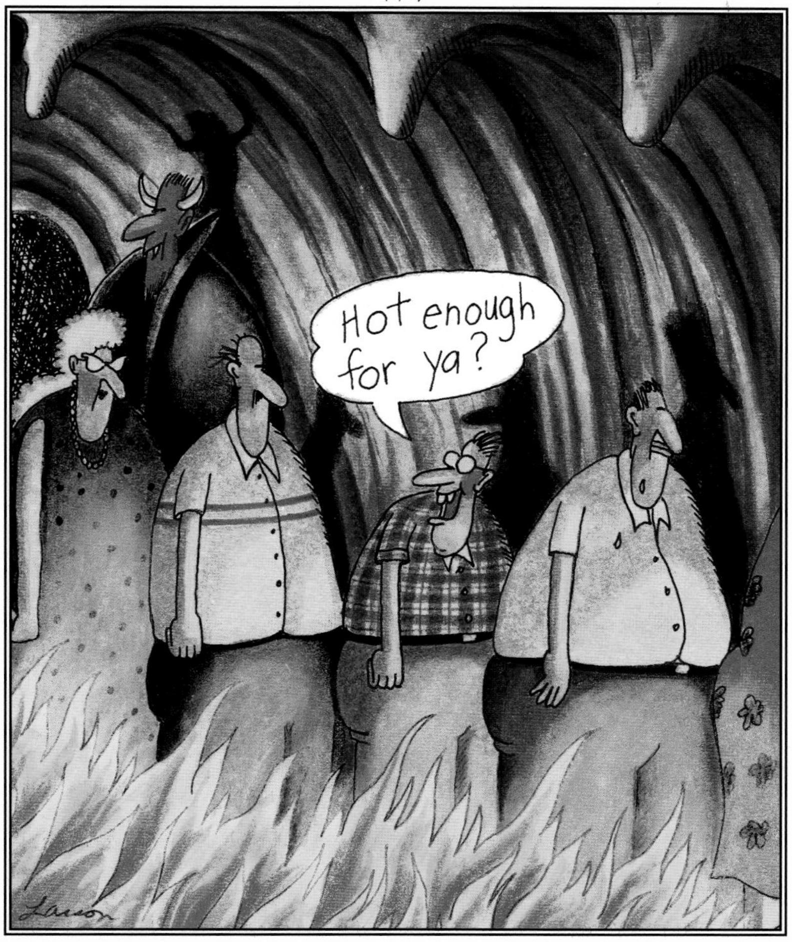
Hot enough for ya?
Larson

Nerds in hell

10/3/87

Larson
The market has fluctuated a little since last... Aaaaaaa!...The wolf!

Scene from a corporate fairy tale

10/2/87

Larson

"And always—*always*—remember this: A swimmer in the water is worth two on the beach."

10/6/87

Larson

Although of some scientific debate, Neanderthal mobsters are frequently linked with the anthropological treasures of Olduvai Gorge.

10/7/87

Larson
You idiot! "You're getting too close to the rocks," I said. "Turn the boat," I said, "Turn the boat!" "I'll do the steering," you said. "Quit worrying," you said...You stupid pinhead!
Sorry, Bob... Once a year I just have to say that.

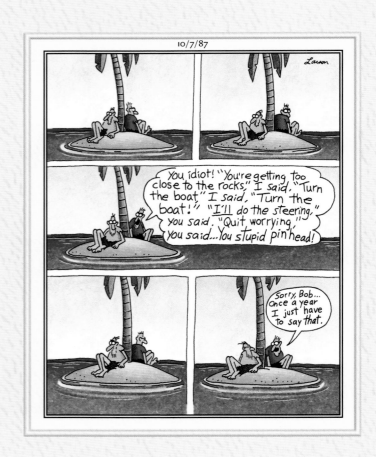

10/9/87

BA
Larson

"Okay. The bank's open. ... Now, I know you're scared, Ramone. ... Obviously, we're *all* a little yellow."

10/5/87

Larson

"Julian ... you're cheating."

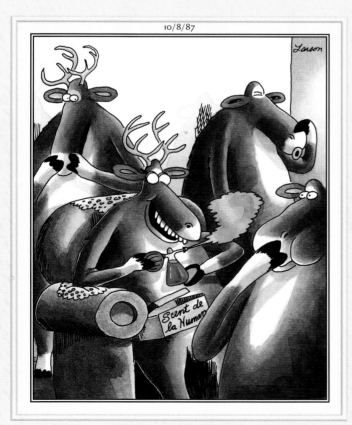

10/8/87

Larson
Scent de la Human

Animal joke gifts

10/12/87

THE TREE
THE DOOR
THE HOUSE
SHIRT
PANTS
THE CAT
THE DOG
Larson

"Now! ... *That* should clear up a few things around here!"

10/11/87

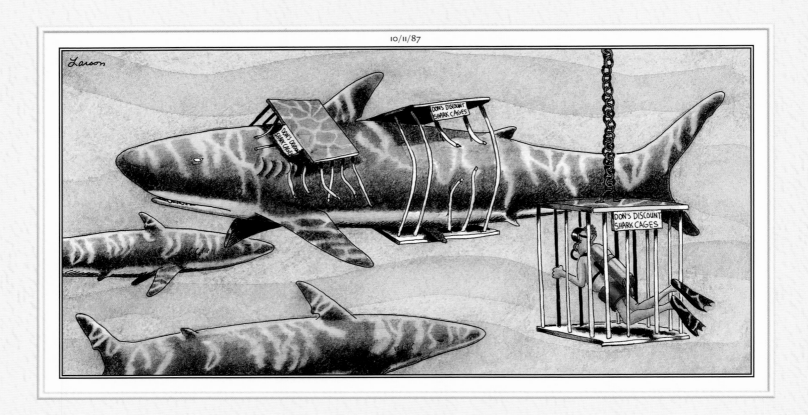

Larson
DON'S DISCOUNT SHARK CAGES
DON'S DISCOUNT SHARK CAGES
DON'S DISCOUNT SHARK CAGES

10/17/87

Larson
THE VACCINATION MAN

Slowly he would cruise the neighborhood, waiting for that occasional careless child who confused him with another vendor.

10/14/87

Larson

Cat showers

10/10/87

"No doubt about it, boys. ... See these markings on the bottom? This is an *Apache* pie pan!"

10/13/87

"Well, he's done it *again!* ... Curse that paper chimp!"

10/16/87

Giraffe beach parties

10/15/87

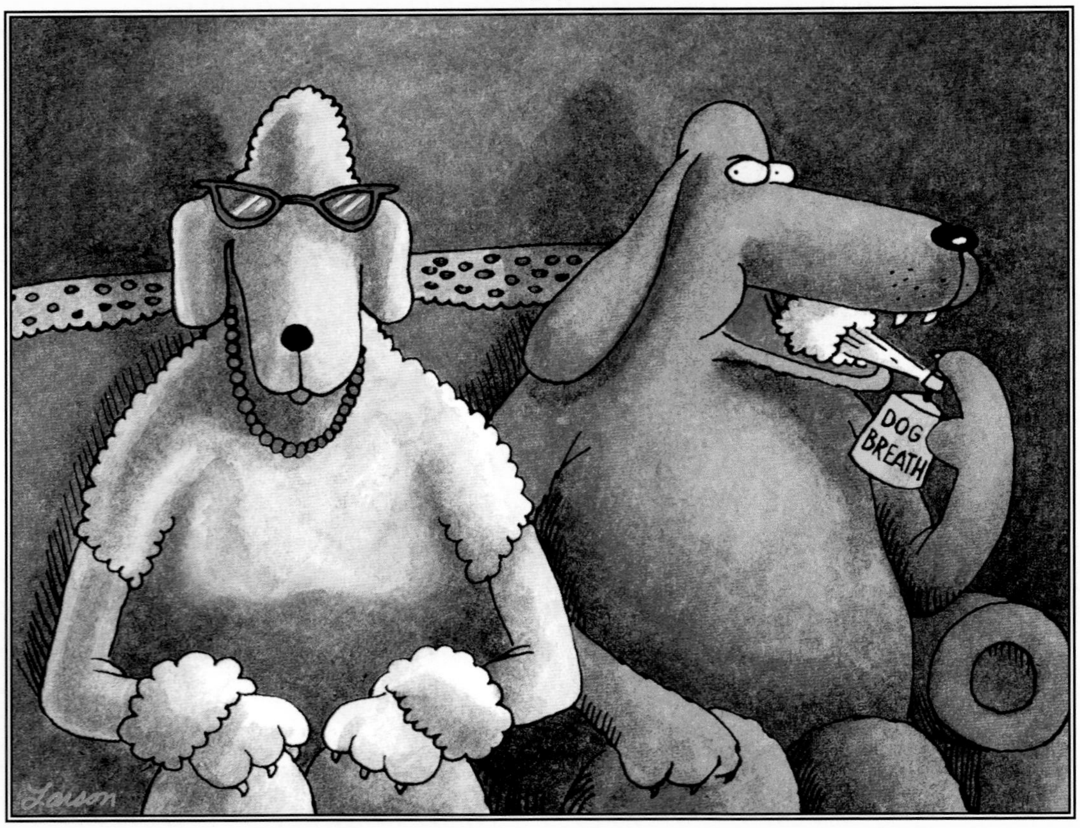
DOG BREATH

Rusty makes his move.

10/19/87

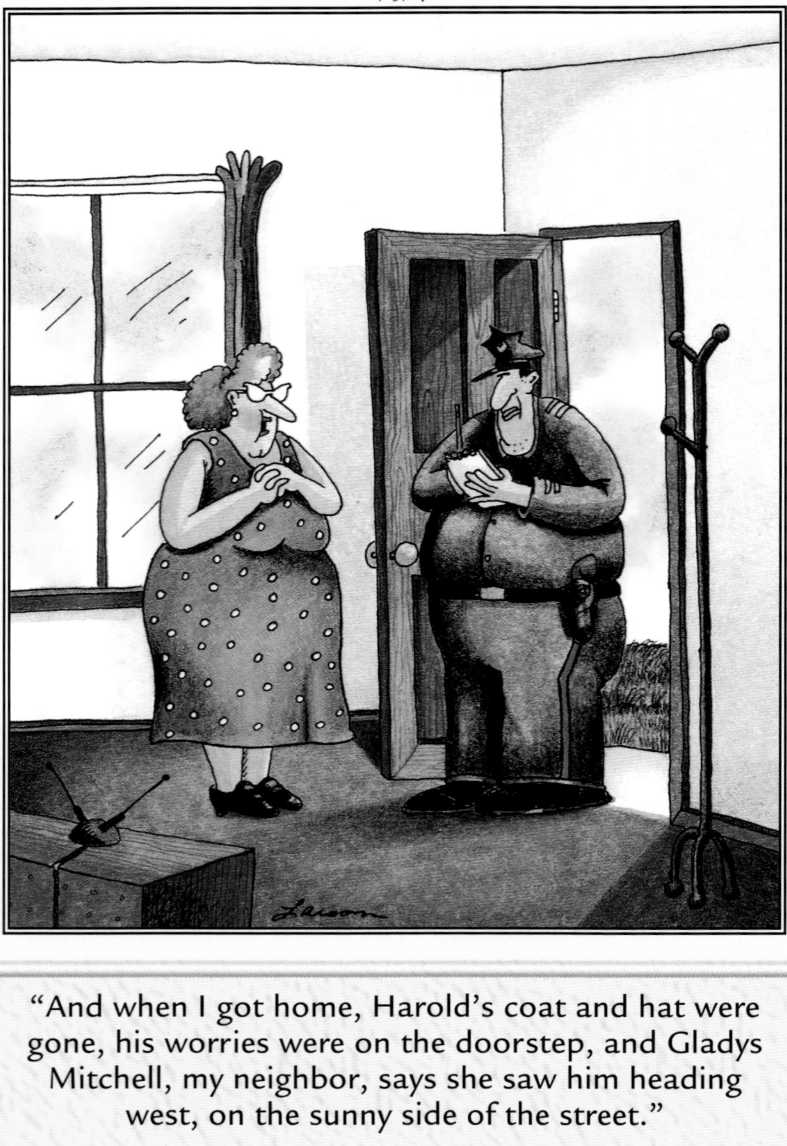

"And when I got home, Harold's coat and hat were gone, his worries were on the doorstep, and Gladys Mitchell, my neighbor, says she saw him heading west, on the sunny side of the street."

10/18/87

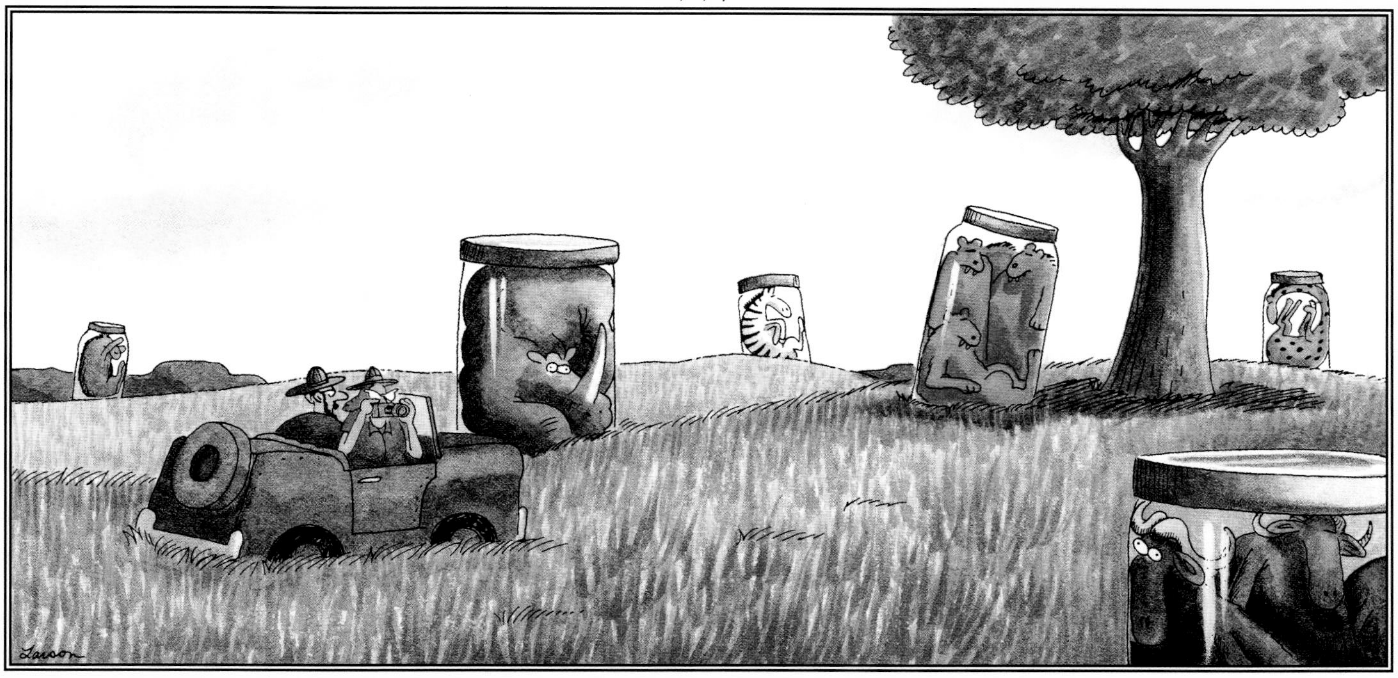
Larson

Wildlife preserves

10/29/87

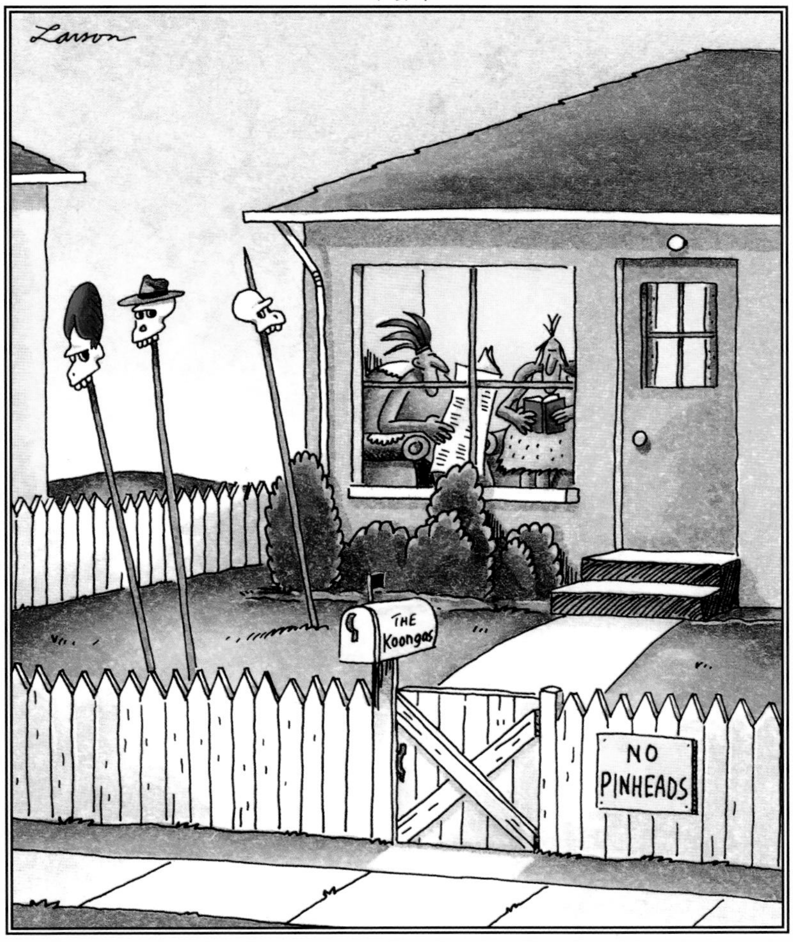
Larson
THE Koongas
NO PINHEADS

Suburban headhunters

10/21/87
Larson

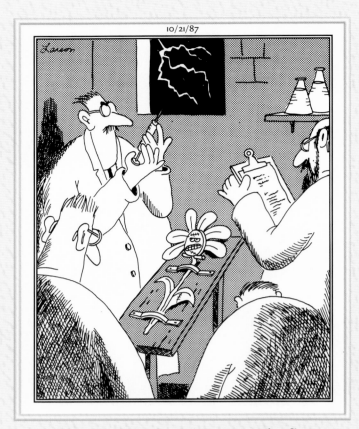

Feb. 22, 1946: Botanists create the first artificial flower.

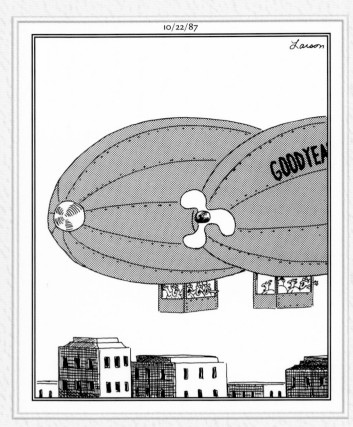

10/22/87
Larson
GOODYEA

Blimp near-misses

10/23/87
Larson

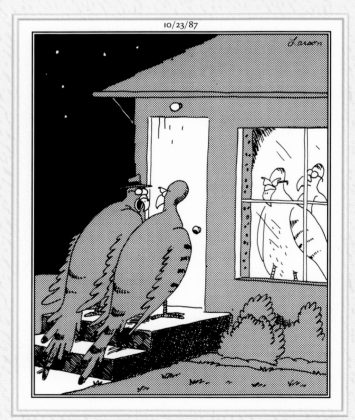

"Well, here we go, another exciting evening at the neighbors', with all of us sitting around going, 'Hello, my name is so-and-so. ... What's your name? ... I wanna cracker. ... Hello, my name is so-and-so.'"

10/20/87
Larson

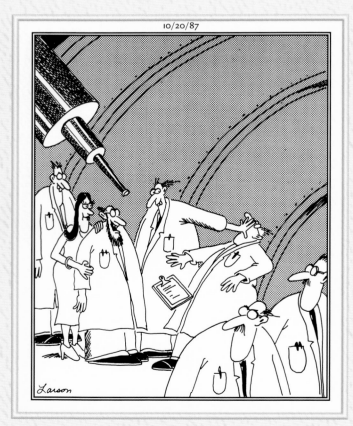

All day long, a tough gang of astrophysicists would monopolize the telescope and intimidate the other researchers.

10/24/87

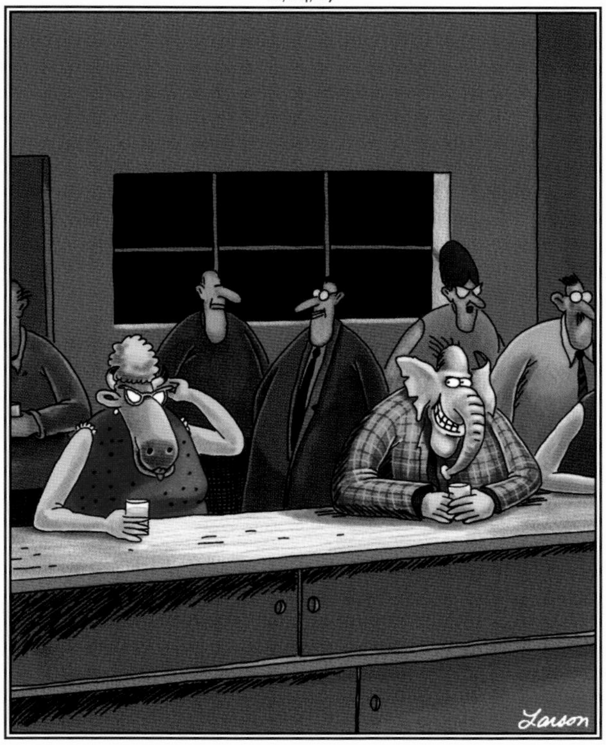

The elephant man meets a buffalo gal.

10/30/87

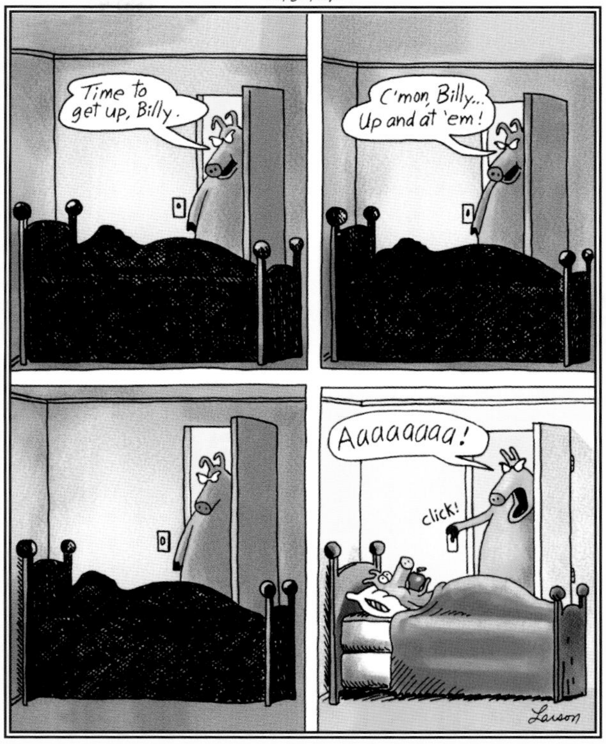
Time to get up, Billy.
C'mon, Billy... Up and at 'em!
Aaaaaaaa!
click!

Piglet practical jokes

10/25/87

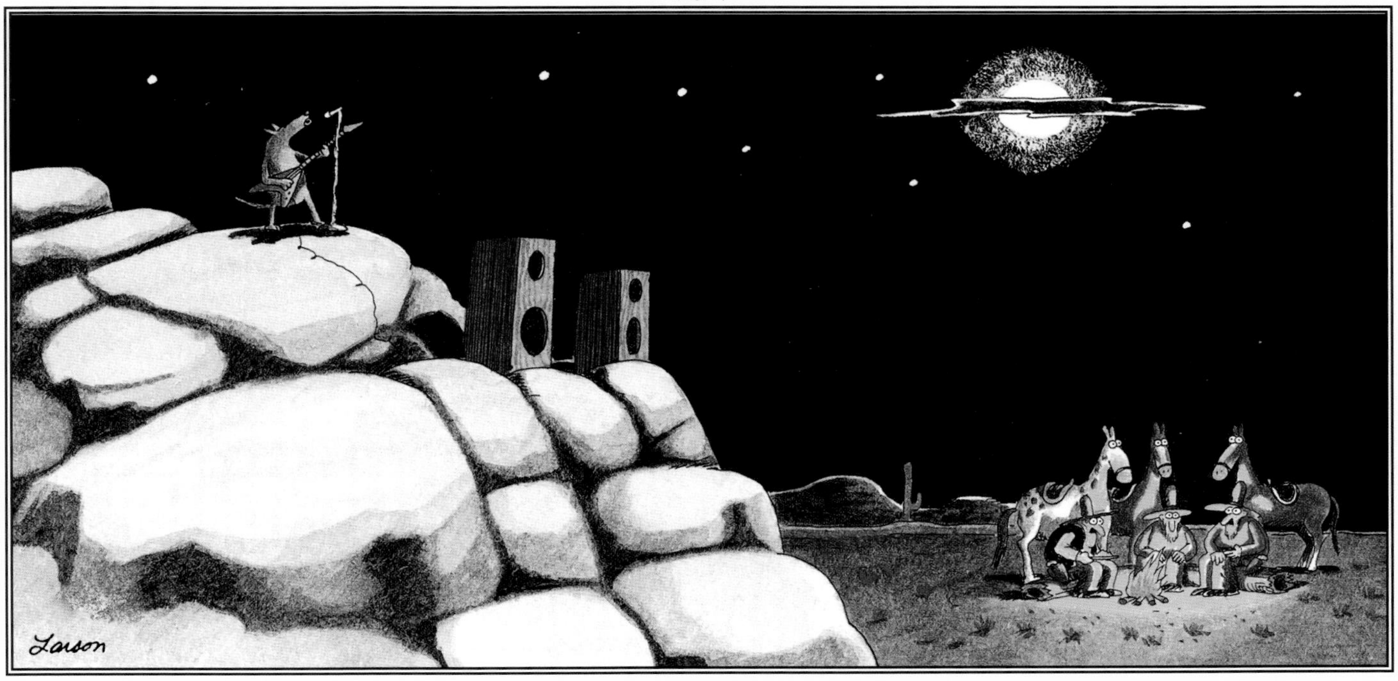

The birth of acid howl

10/27/87

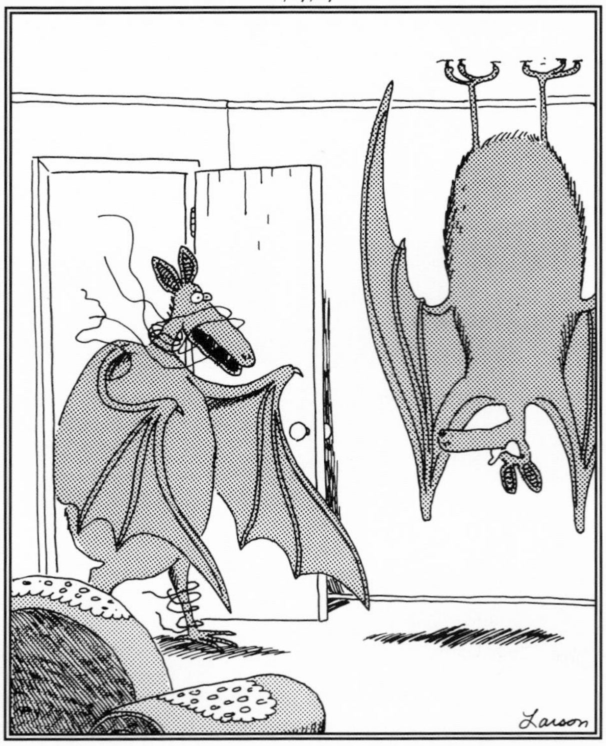
Larson

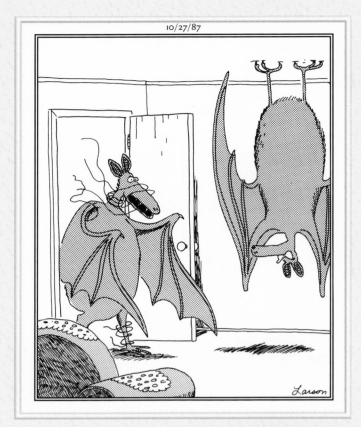

"Crimony! ... I must've been tangled in some bimbo's hair for more than two hours!"

10/26/87

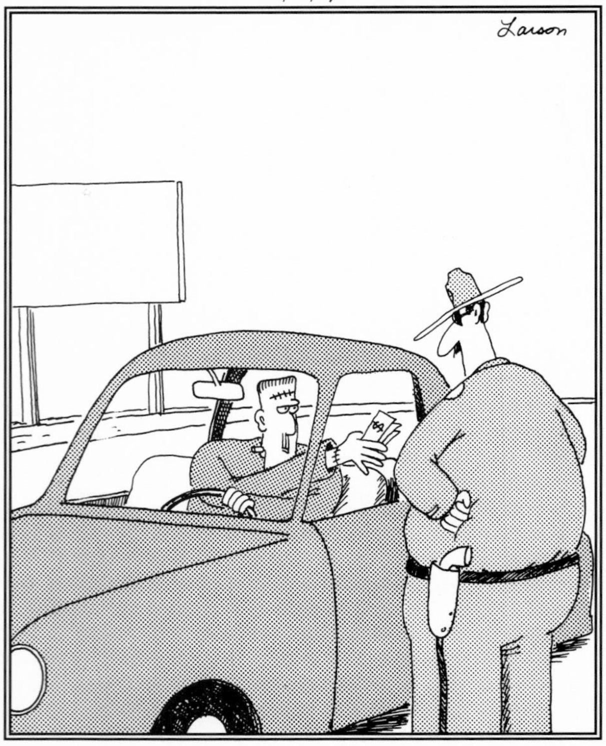
Larson

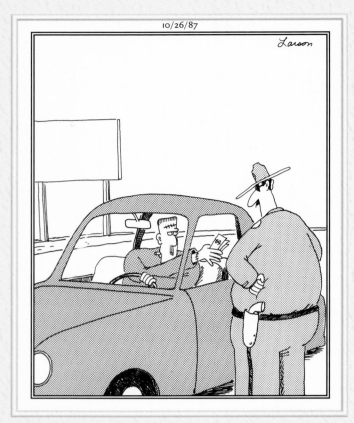

The bribe of Frankenstein

10/28/87

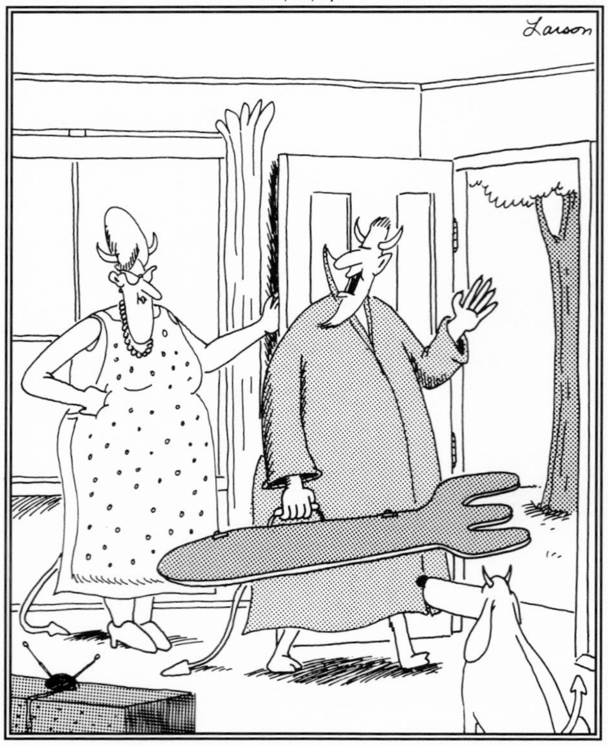
Larson

"Well, down I go."

10/31/87

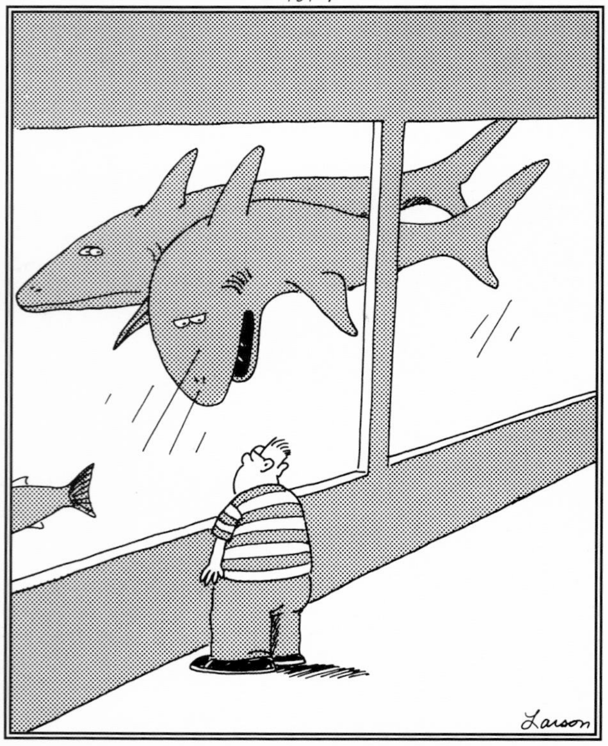
Larson

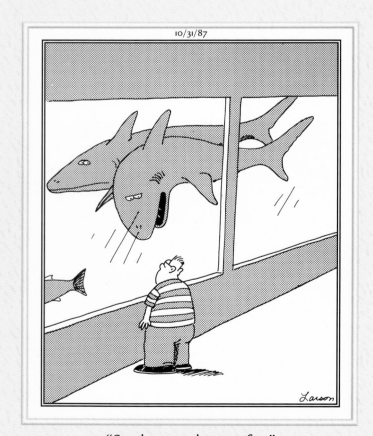

"So close, and yet so far."

11/4/87

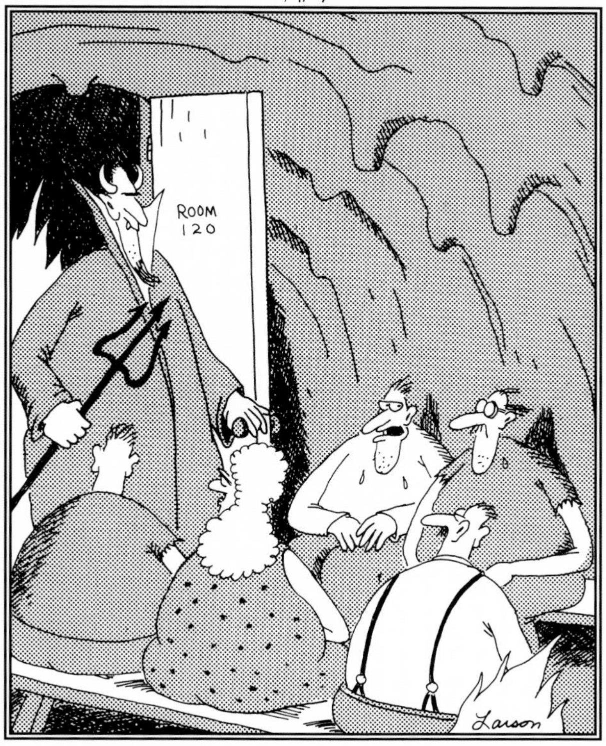
ROOM 120
Larson

"Speak of the devil."

11/5/87

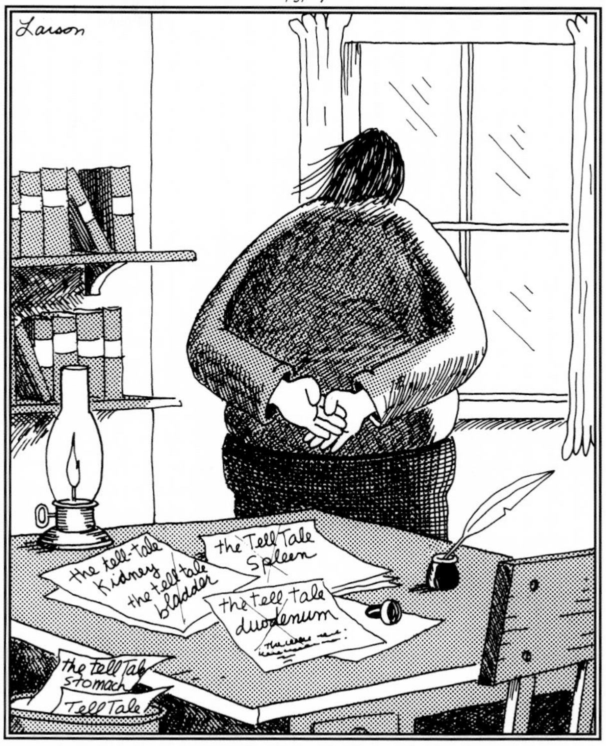
Larson
the tell-tale kidney
the tell tale bladder
the Tell Tale Spleen
the tell tale duodenum
the tell tale stomach
Tell Tale

Edgar Allan Poe in a moment of writer's block

11/6/87

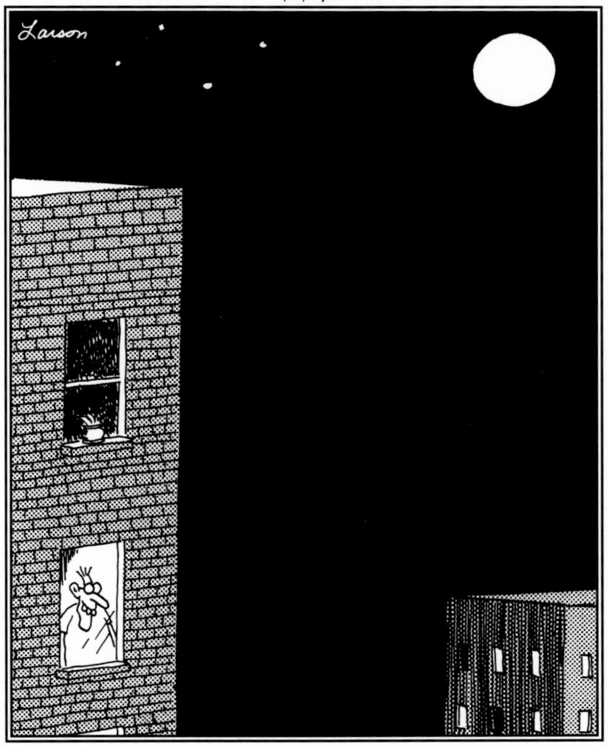
Larson

A full moon and an empty head

11/7/87

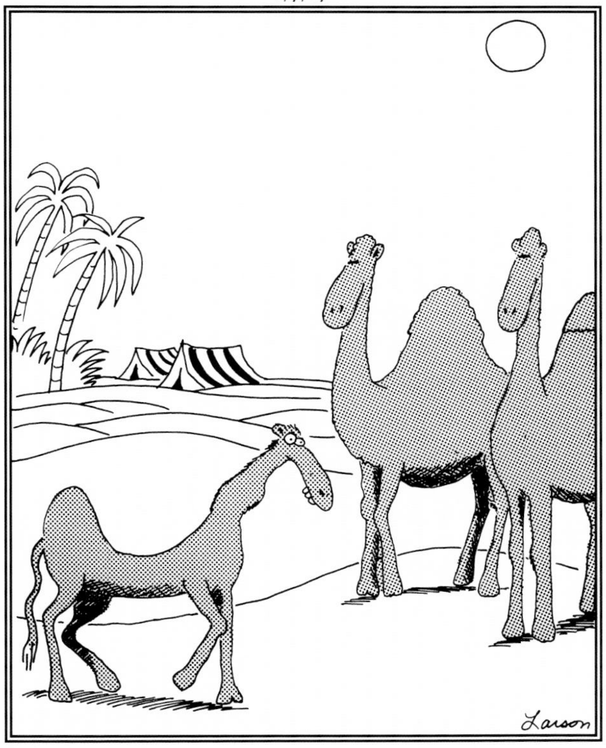
Larson

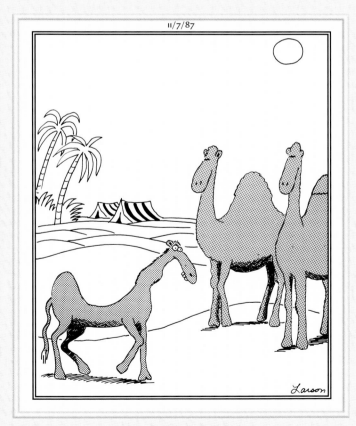

A camel named Igor

11/1/87

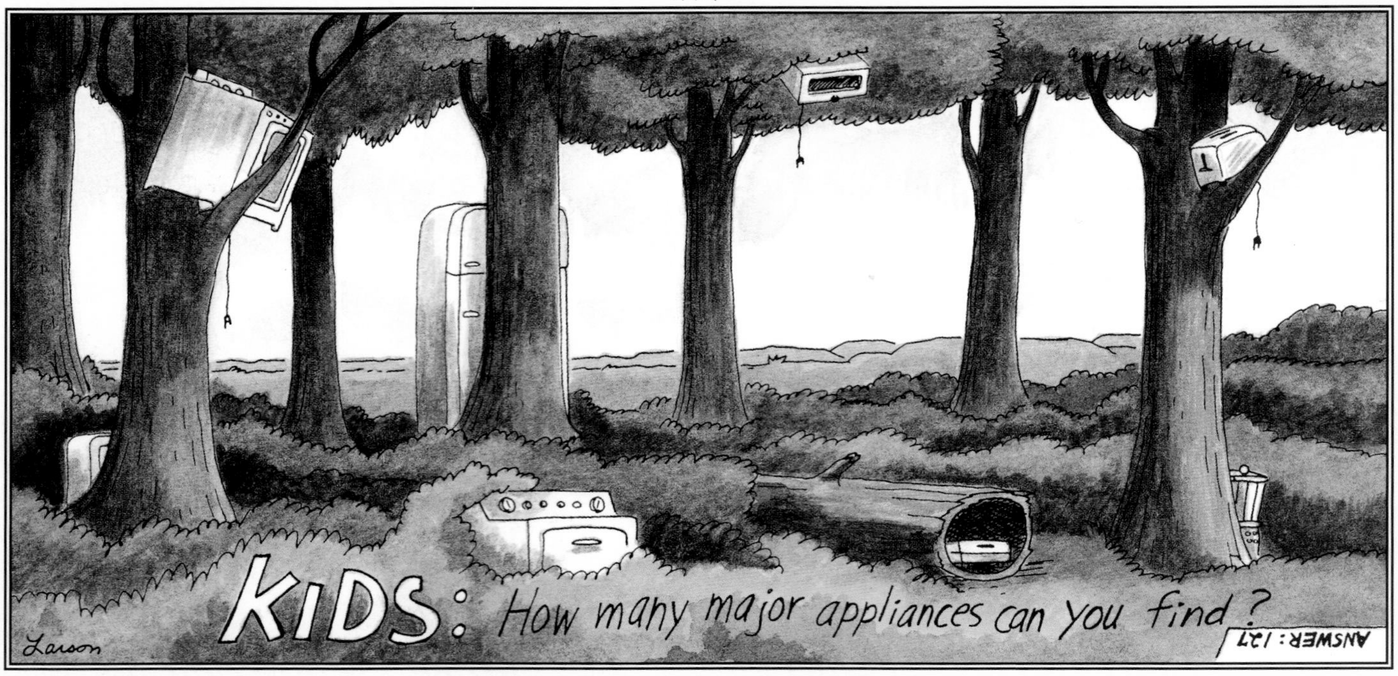
KIDS: How many major appliances can you find?
ANSWER: 127

November 11,1987

Gary Larsen
c/o Springfield Newspaper

851 Boonville
Spfld,MO. 65806

Halltown Elem.School
Miller R-2
5-6 grade/Beth Hurst
300 East Elm
Halltown, MO. 65664

Dear Mr. Larsen,

Our class has been looking at your comic strip the Far Side. We would like to know how you got the answer 127 major appliances in the November 1,1987 newspaper.

We would appreciate it if you could let us in on the puzzle. Thank you for your time.

Thank you,
Mrs.Beth Hurst
5-6 grade

Jenny Holman
Joanna
Coi Lawlers
Michael Perusse
Troy Chappell
Ricky Pendergrass
Melissa Williams
Craig Hodgson
Mrs. Beth Hurst
Shawnda Owens
Summer Steadman
Dana Erickson

UNIVERSAL
PRESS
SYNDICATE

Dear Mrs. Hurst and Class:

We are in receipt of your recent letter to Gary Larson asking about his cartoon for Sunday, Nov. 1.

Gary's cartoon was a parody of those puzzles that are full of hidden pictures. His cartoon had such clumsily hidden objects (kitchen appliances) in it, and such an outrageous answer (127), that it was not meant to be taken seriously.

I hope this explanation is of some use to you.

Sincerely,

Jake Morrissey
Associate Editor

4900 Main Street • Kansas City, Missouri 64112 • Phone 816/932-6600

11/2/87

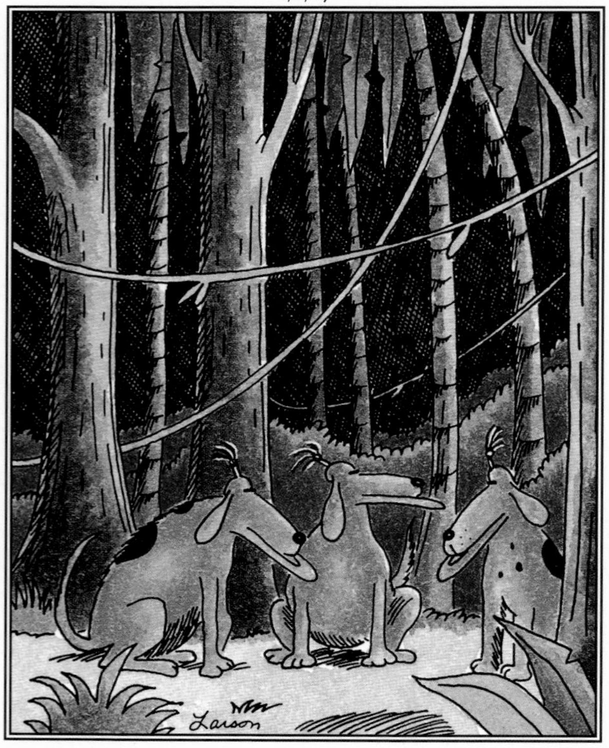

The big-lipped dogs of the equatorial rain forest

11/3/87

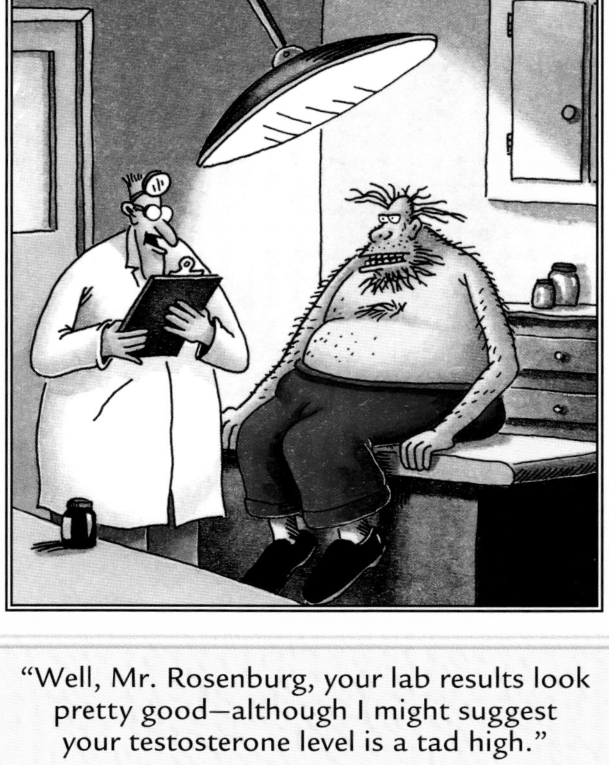
Larson

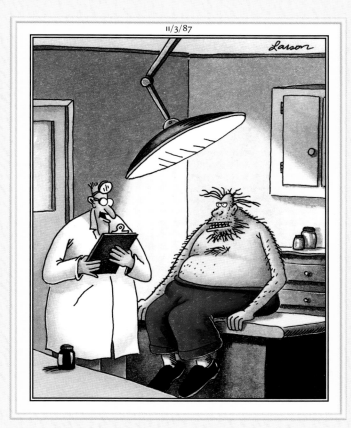

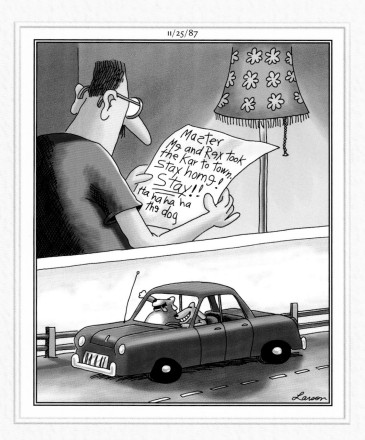

"Well, Mr. Rosenburg, your lab results look pretty good—although I might suggest your testosterone level is a tad high."

11/25/87

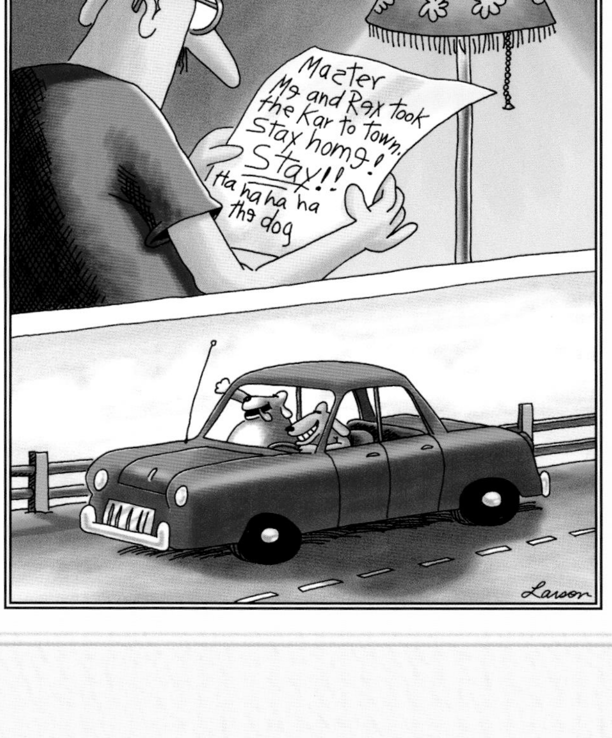
Mazter
Me and Rex took
the Kar to town.
Stay home!
Stay!!
Ha ha ha ha
the dog
Larson

11/8/87

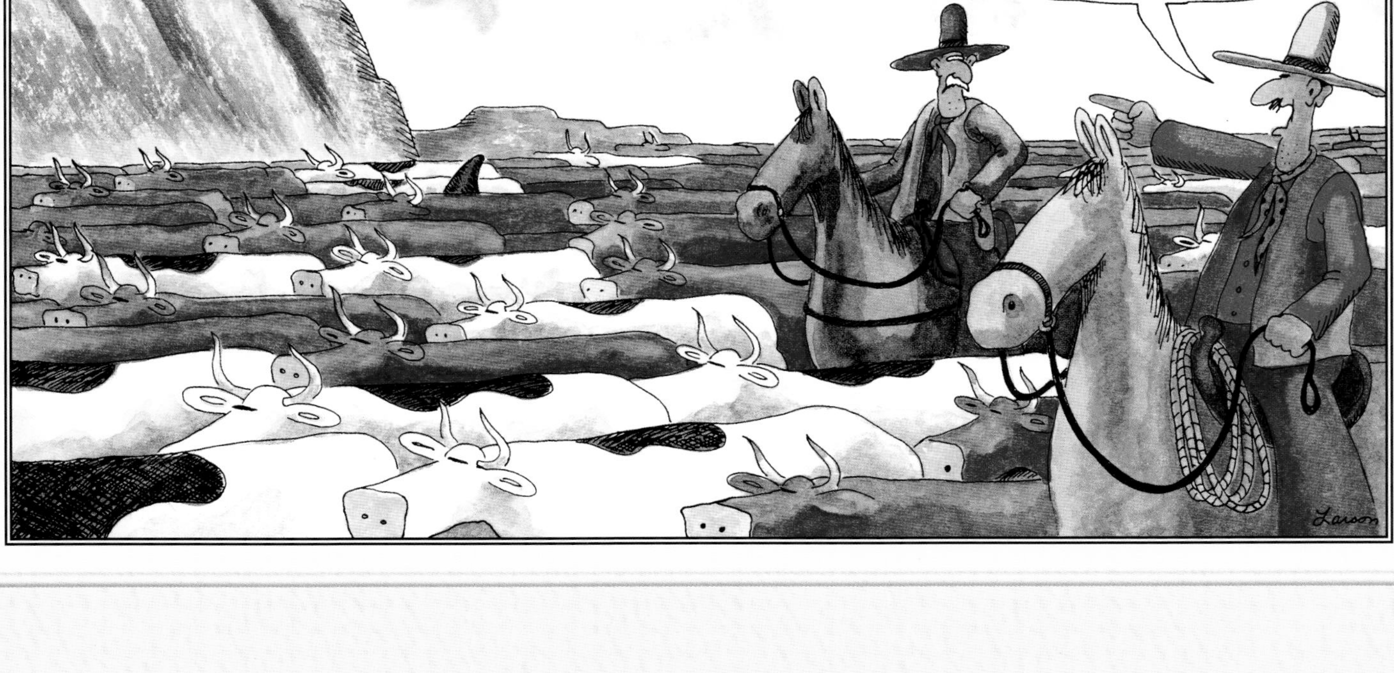
Luke! On your right!
Cattle shark!
Larson

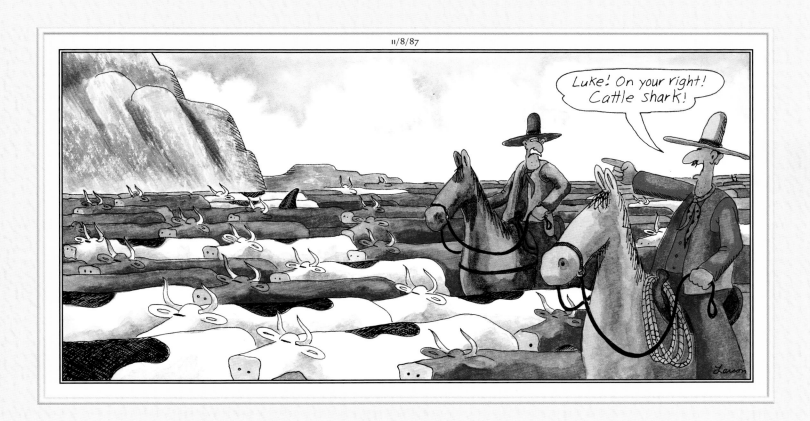

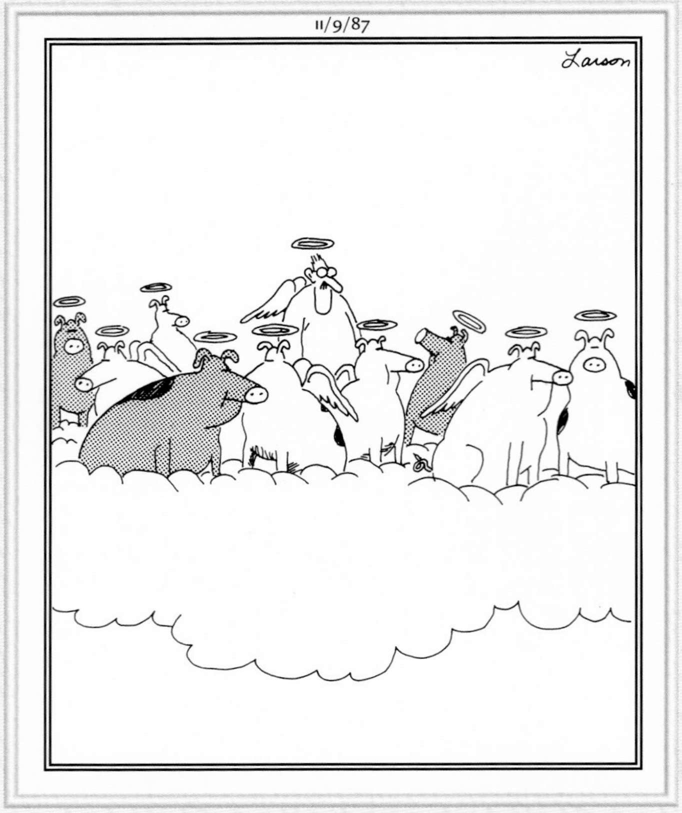

Through some unfortunate celestial error, Ernie is sent to Hog Heaven.

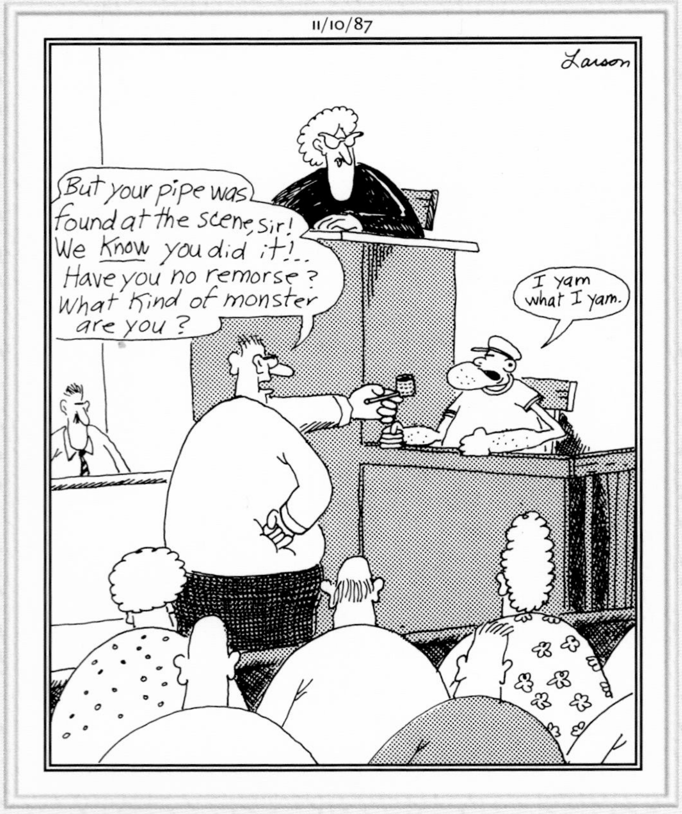
But your pipe was found at the scene, sir! We Know you did it!... Have you no remorse? What kind of monster are you?
I yam what I yam.

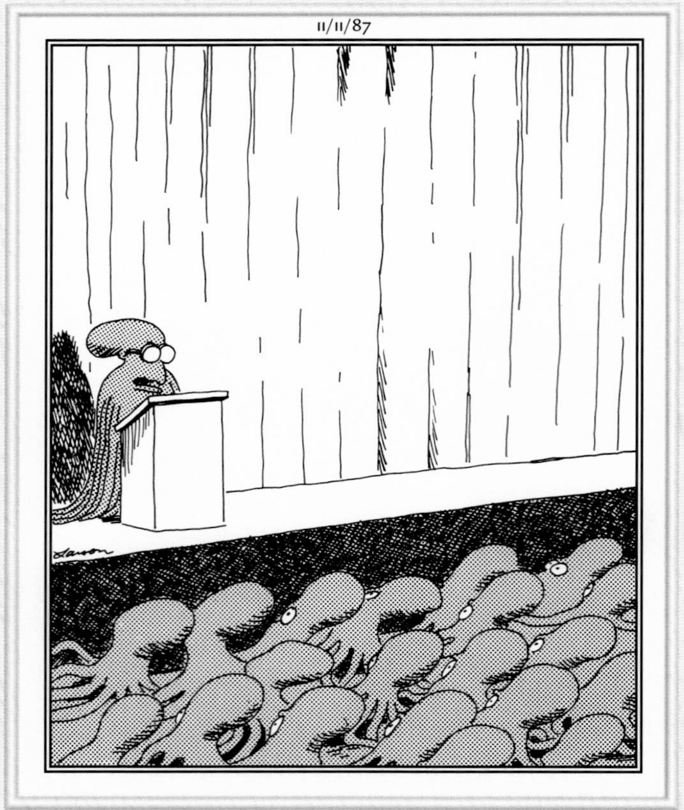

"Fellow octopi, or octopuses ... octopi? ... Dang, it's hard to start a speech with this crowd."

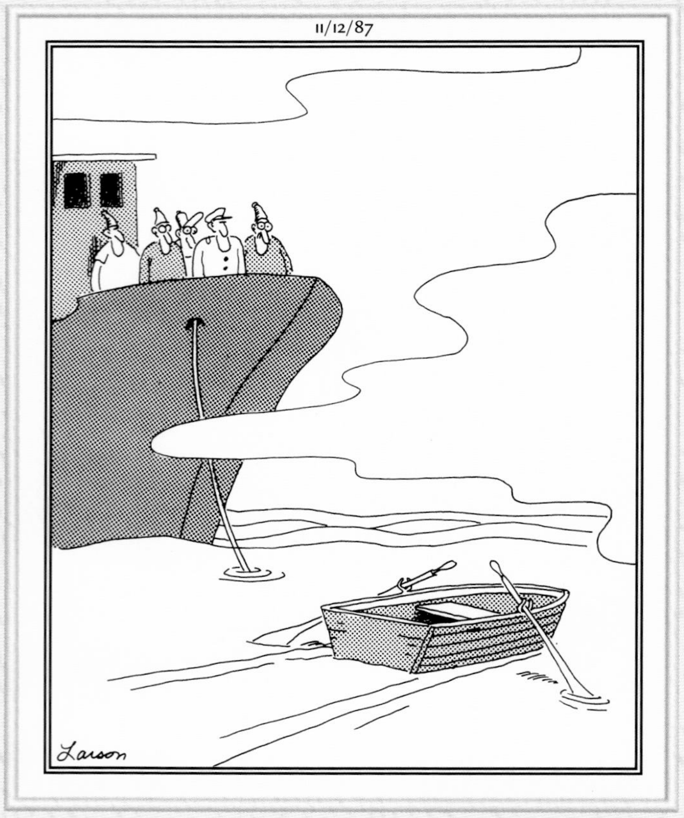

At first, the crew could hear only the creaking of oars. And then, out of the fog, the terrifying ghost dinghy appeared.

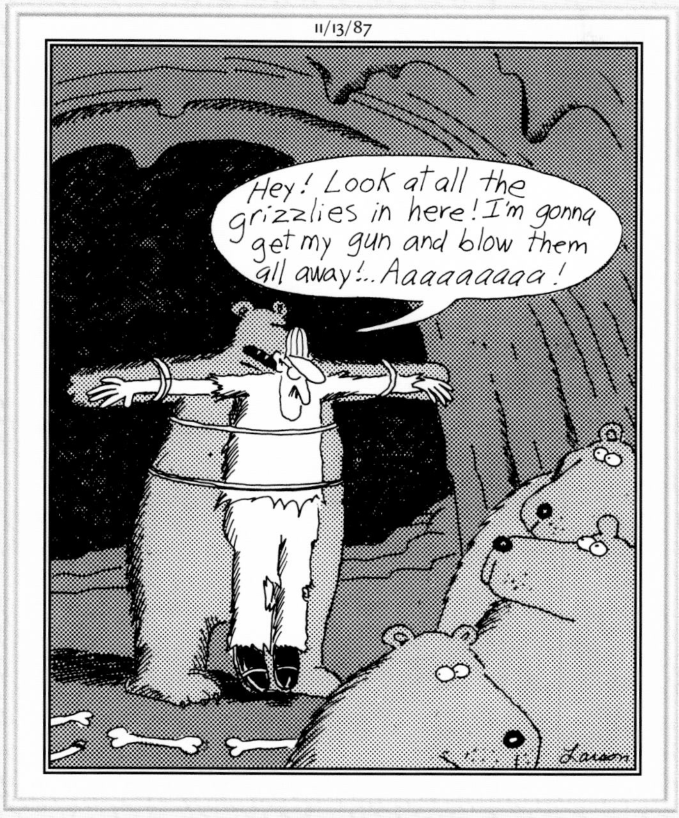
11/13/87
Hey! Look at all the grizzlies in here! I'm gonna get my gun and blow them all away!.. Aaaaaaaaa!
Larson

Bernie's sense of humor was seldom appreciated among the other bears.

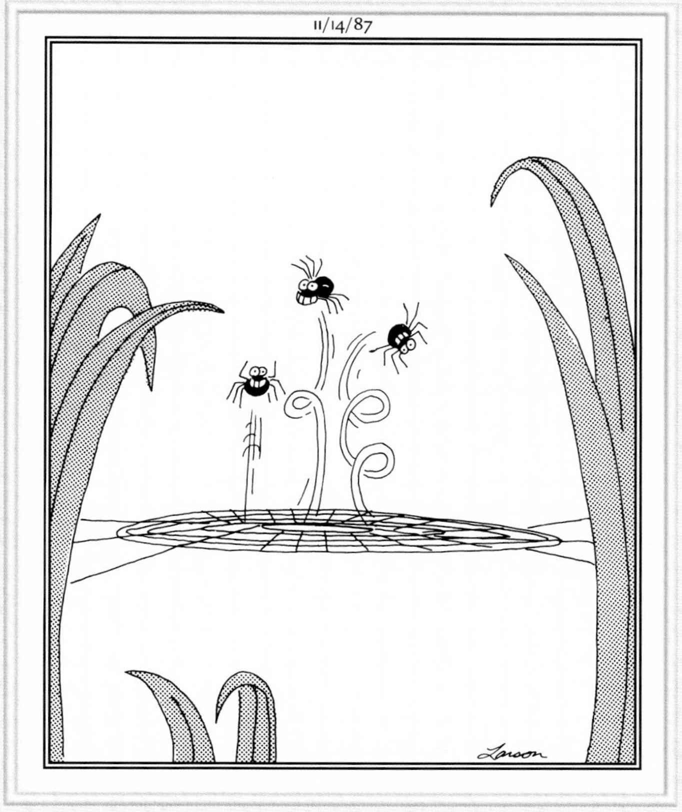
11/14/87
Larson

On the weboline

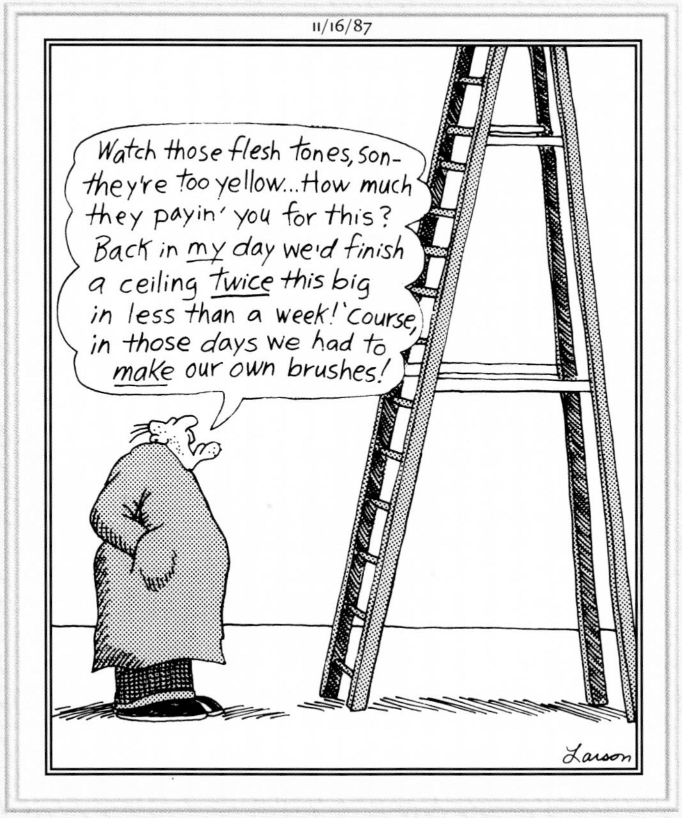
11/16/87
Watch those flesh tones, son- they're too yellow... How much they payin' you for this? Back in my day we'd finish a ceiling twice this big in less than a week! 'Course, in those days we had to make our own brushes!
Larson

Michelangelo's father

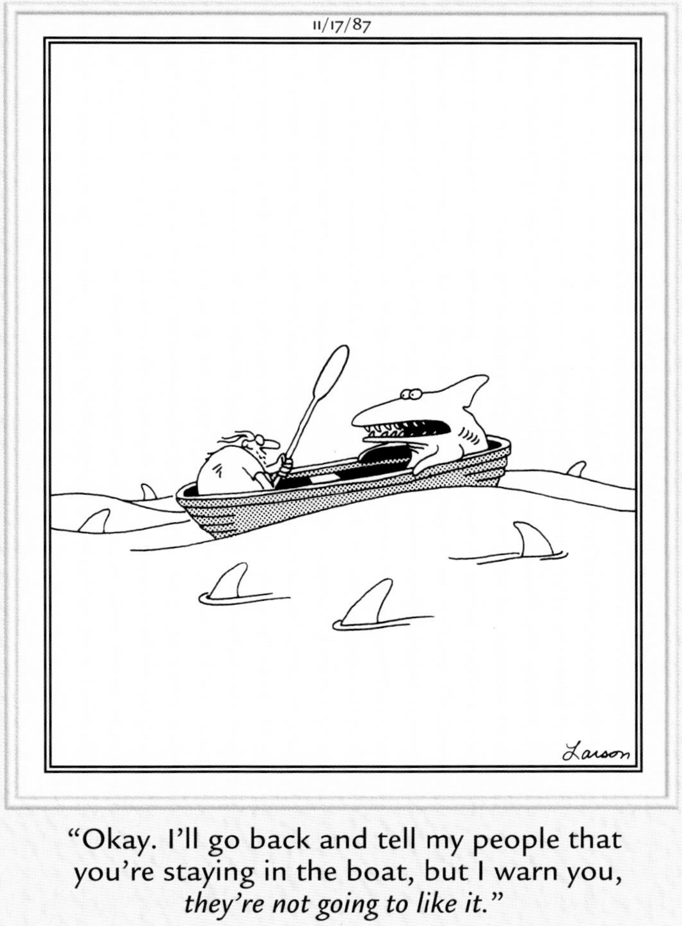
11/17/87
Larson

"Okay. I'll go back and tell my people that you're staying in the boat, but I warn you, *they're not going to like it.*"

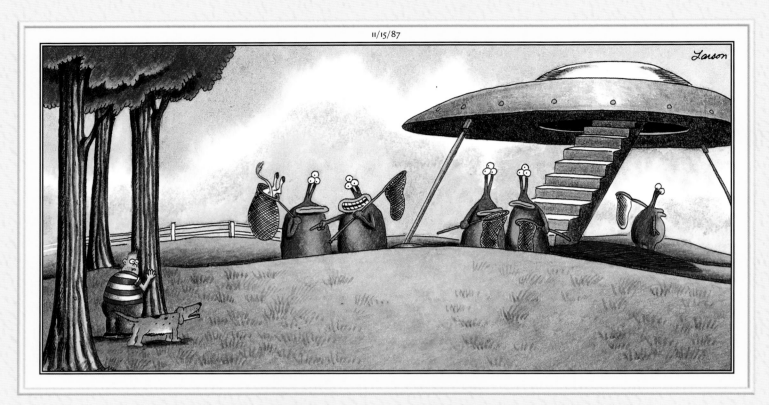

Suddenly, Jake started barking and, as a result, both he and Billy ended up sharing a small but interesting diorama in the Venutian Natural History Museum.

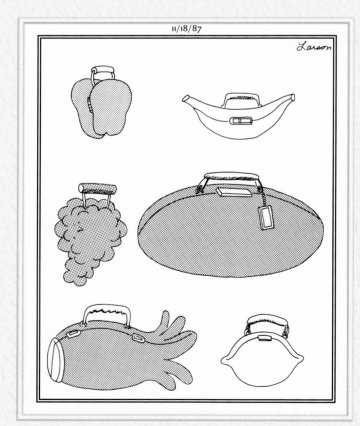

Fruitcases

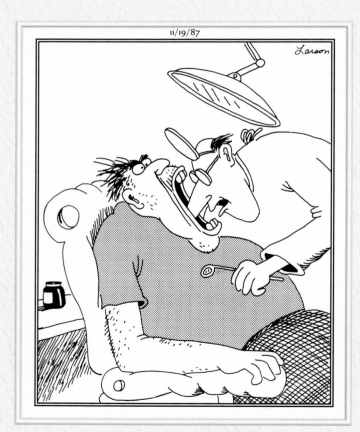

"Good heavens, Mr. Farley, is that the end of someone's nose I see down there?"

11/20/87

TOY
RESEARCH &
DEVELOPMENT
Larson

The Etch A Sketch division at work

11/21/87

Larson

Houdini escapes from a black hole.

11/22/87

Larson

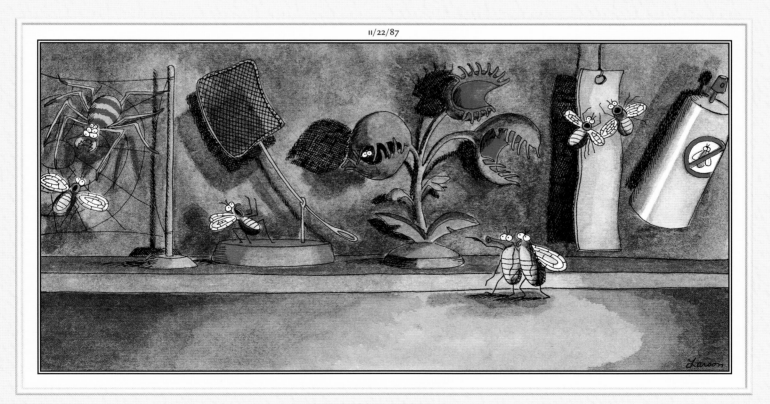

In the Fly House of Horrors

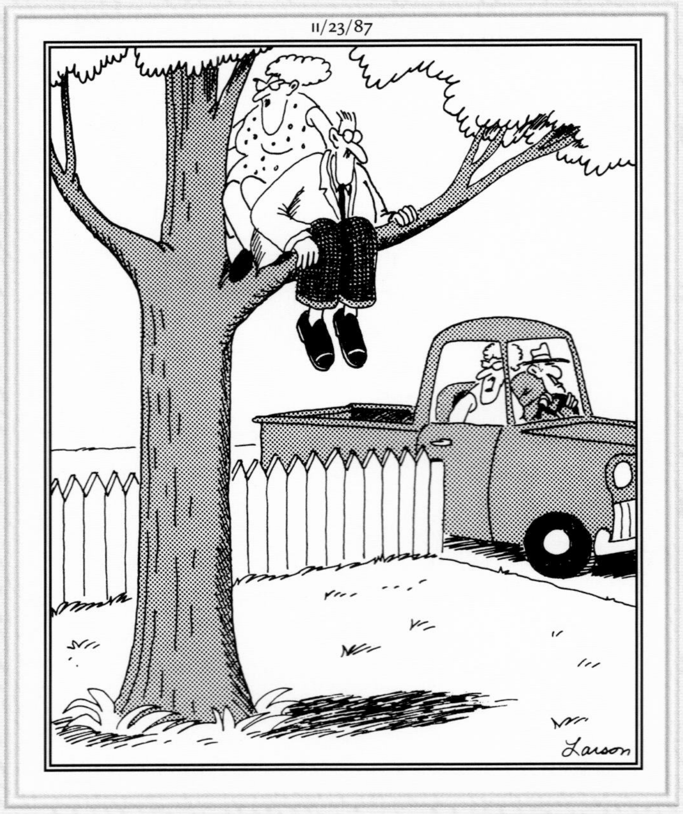
11/23/87
Larson

"Uh-oh, Vern! The Schumachers are in the tree again. We'll have to spray."

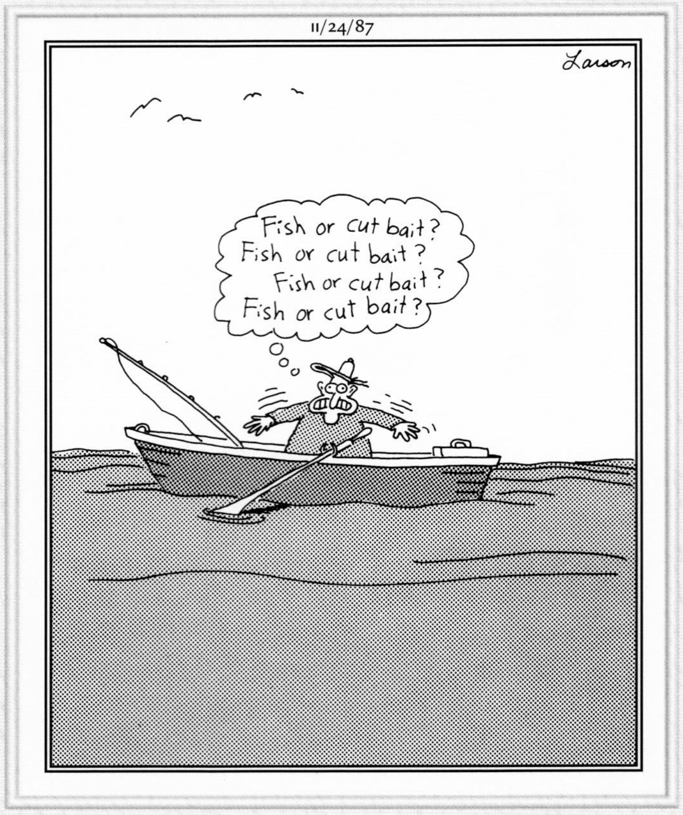
11/24/87
Larson
Fish or cut bait?
Fish or cut bait?
Fish or cut bait?
Fish or cut bait?

How fishermen blow their minds

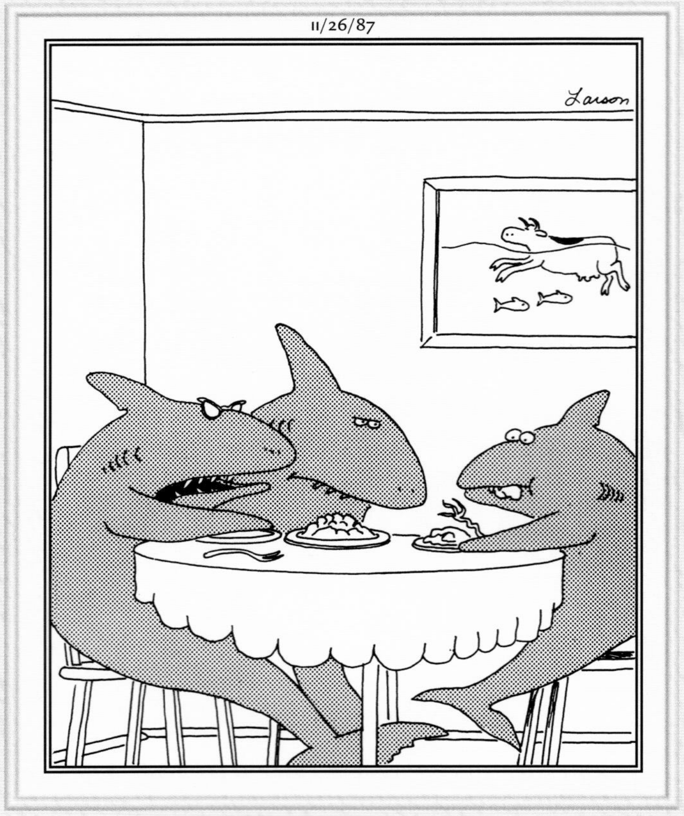
11/26/87
Larson

"Andy! Look what you're doing to your fork! ... Tuna salad doesn't require seven tons of pressure per square inch!"

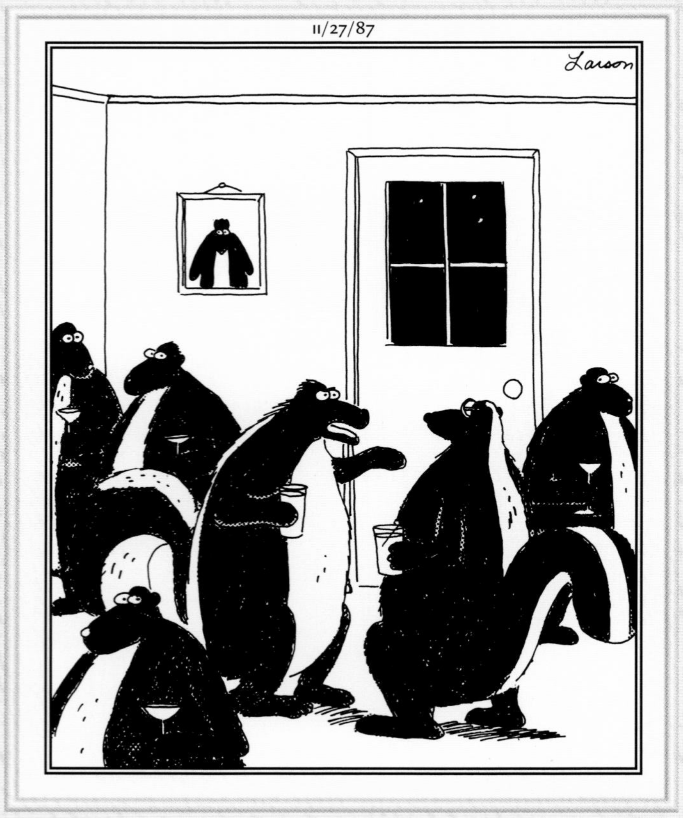
11/27/87
Larson

"Oh, yeah? Well you don't *stink!* You never did and you never will, you mama's little rose!"

11/28/87

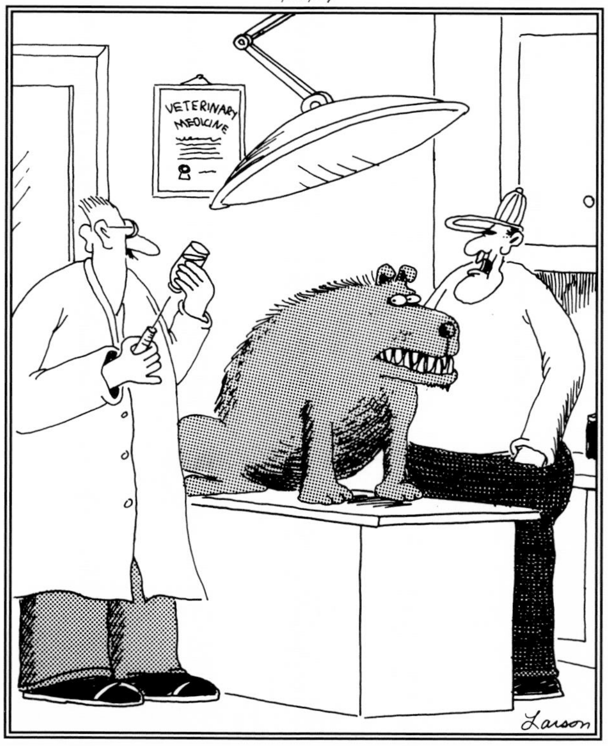
VETERINARY MEDICINE

"Whoa! Is that a needle, Doc? 'Cause Zack don't *like* needles."

11/30/87

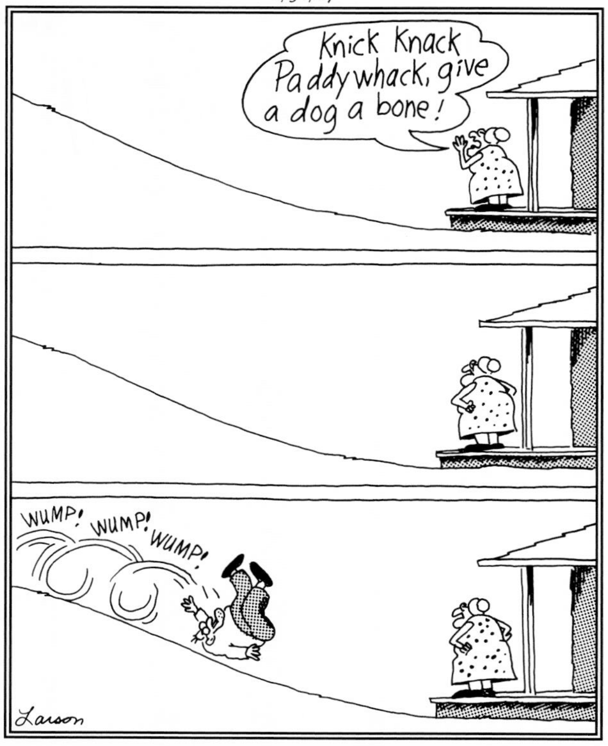
Knick Knack Paddywhack, give a dog a bone!
WUMP! WUMP! WUMP!

11/29/87

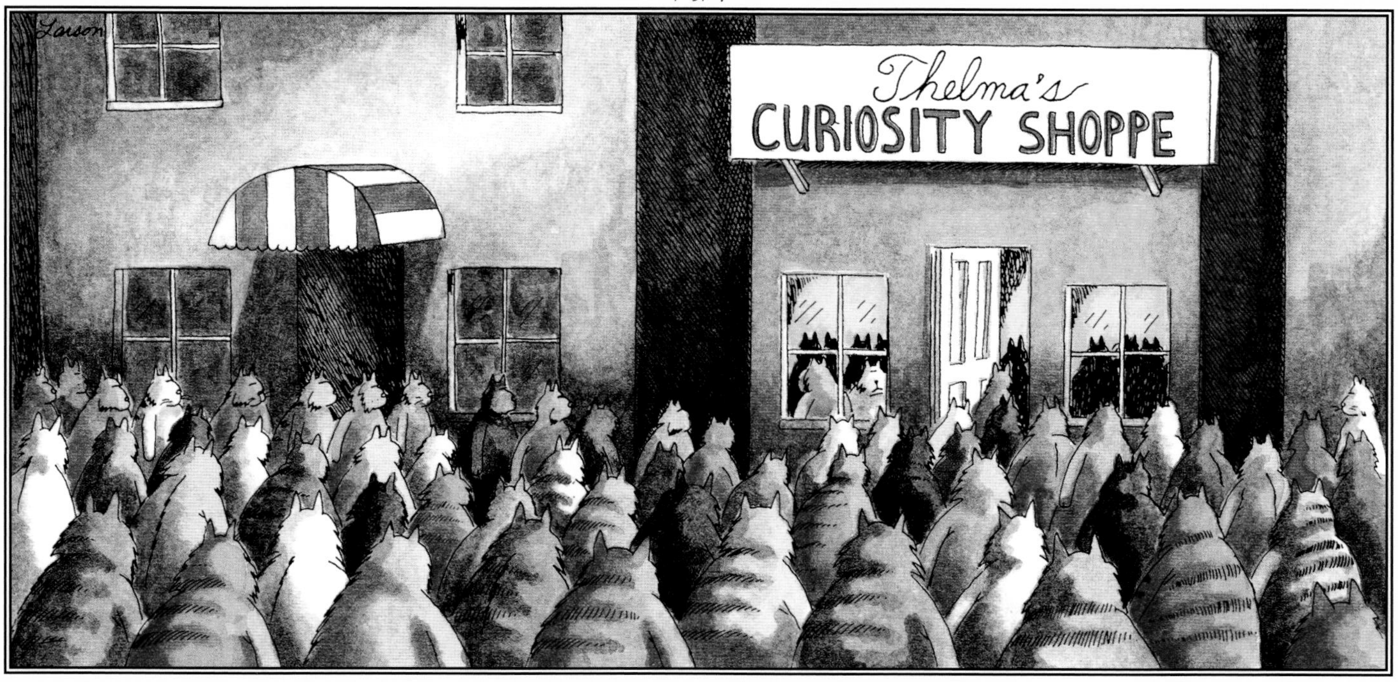
Thelma's CURIOSITY SHOPPE

12/2/87

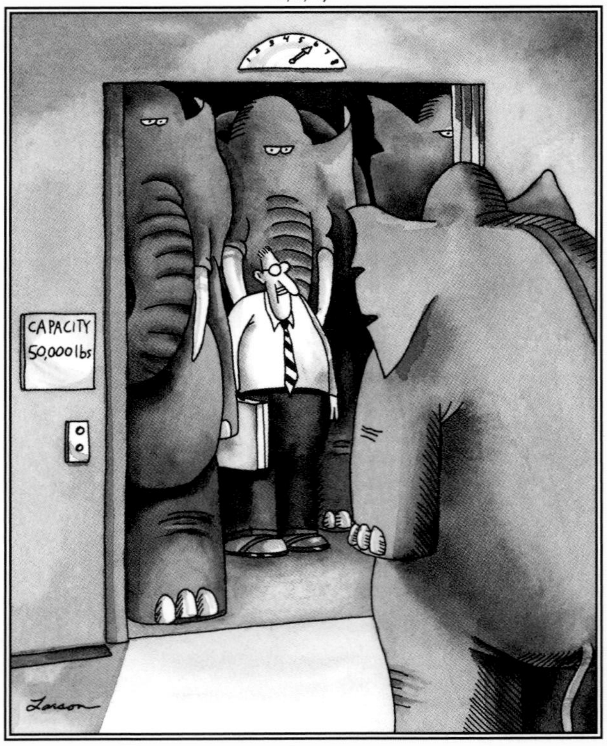
CAPACITY
50,000 lbs

To Ernie's horror, and the ultimate disaster of all, one more elephant tried to squeeze on.

12/1/87

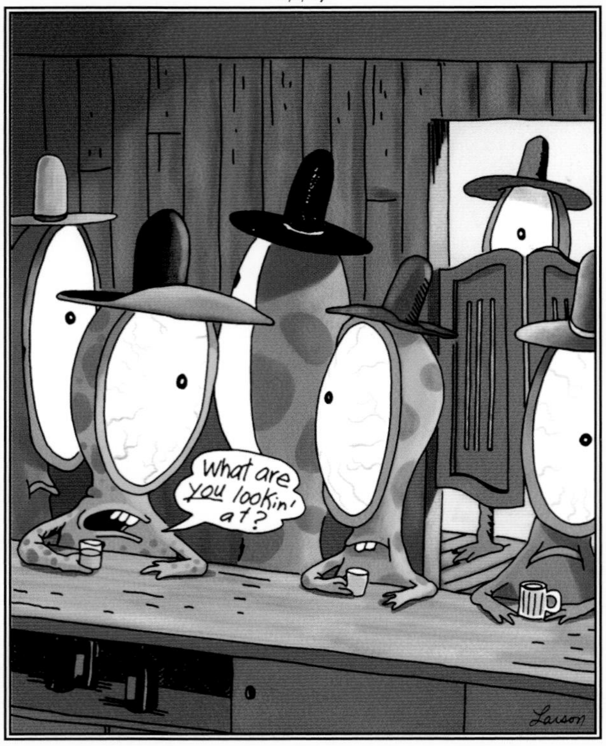
What are you lookin' at?

Saloon scenes on other planets

12/4/87

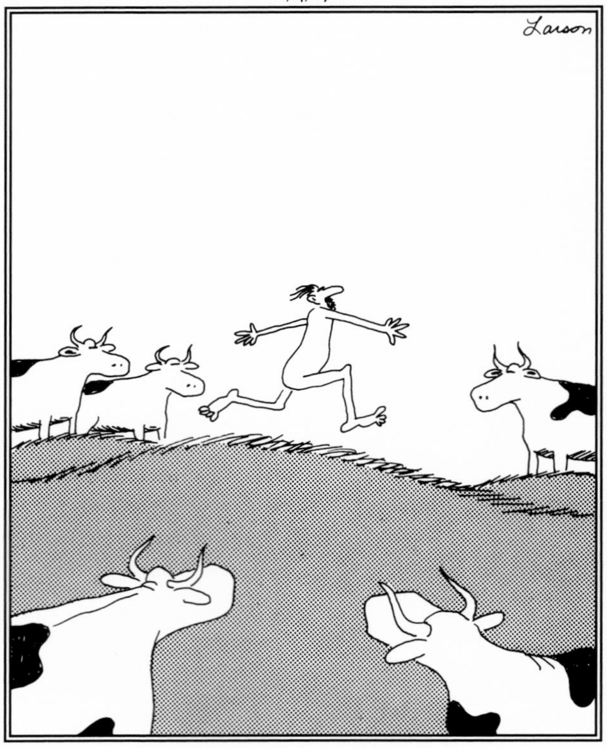

Scene from *Never Cry Cow*

12/7/87

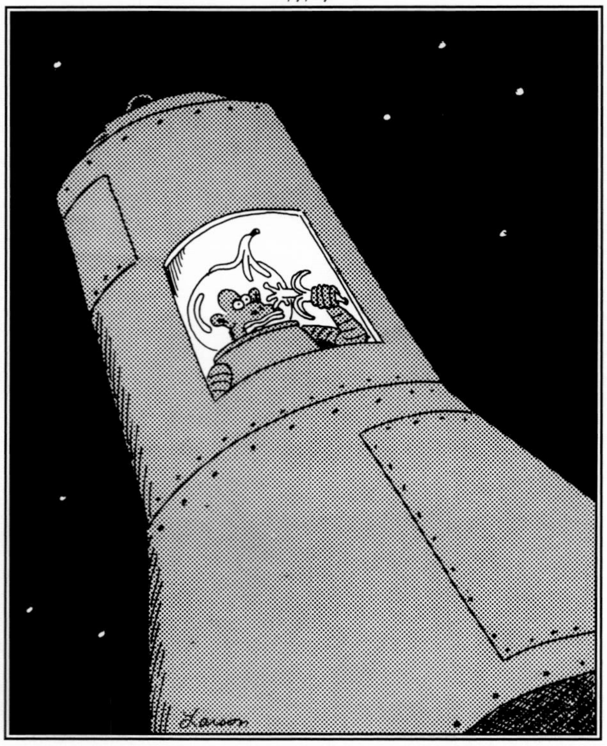

12/9/87

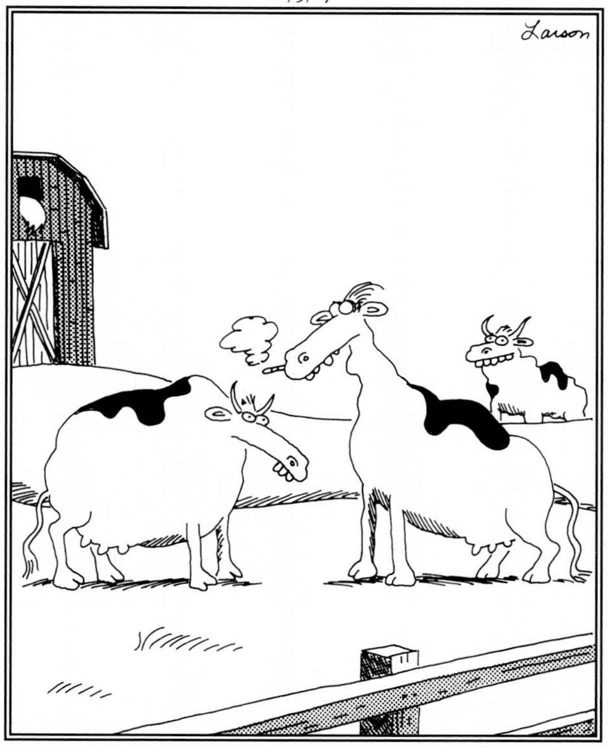
Larson

Where beef jerky comes from

12/11/87

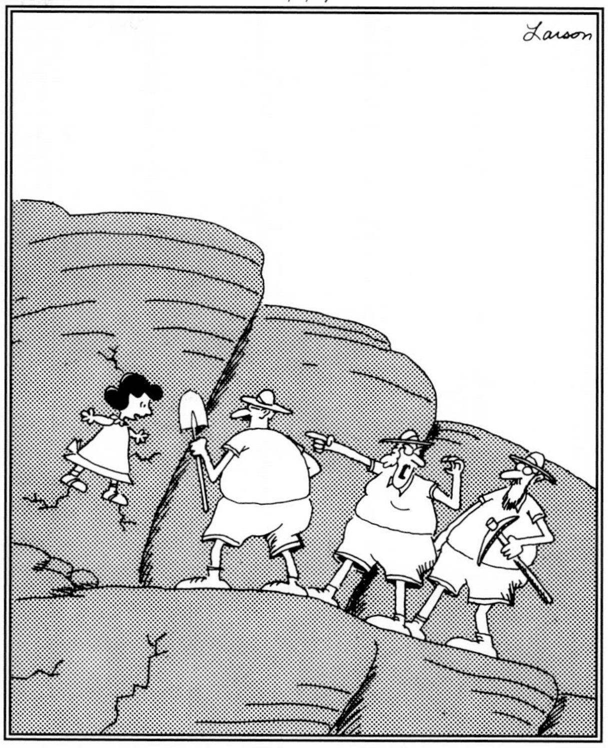
Larson

Rocking the anthropological world, a second "Lucy" is discovered in southern Uganda.

12/3/87

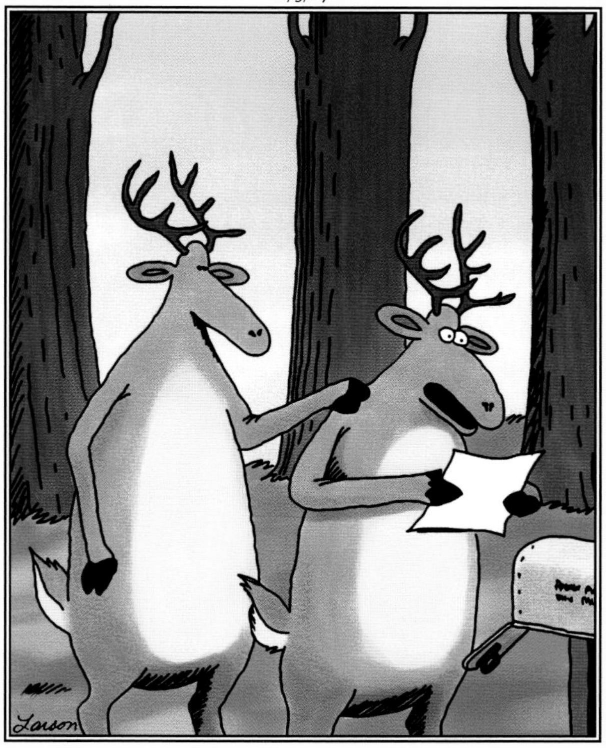
Larson

"Oh my God! It's from Connie! She's written me a 'John deer' letter!"

12/5/87

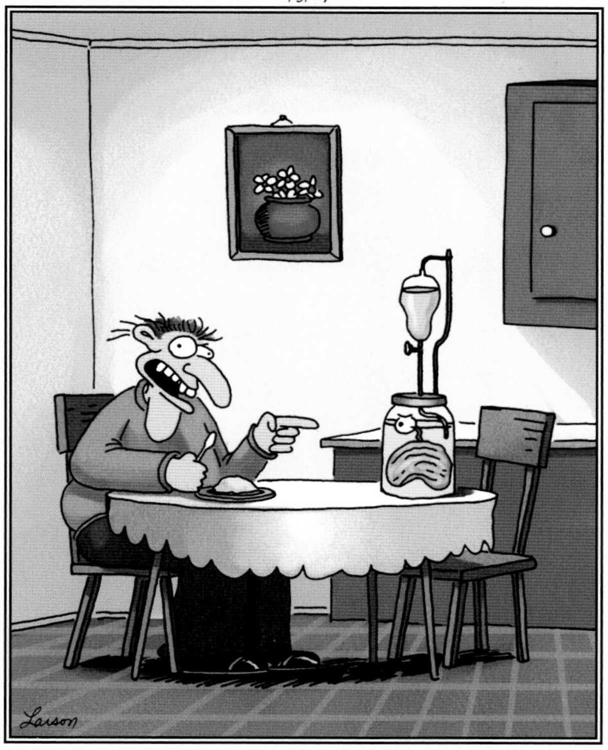
Larson

"That's a lie, Morty! ... Mom says you might have got the brains in the family, but *I* got the looks!"

12/6/87

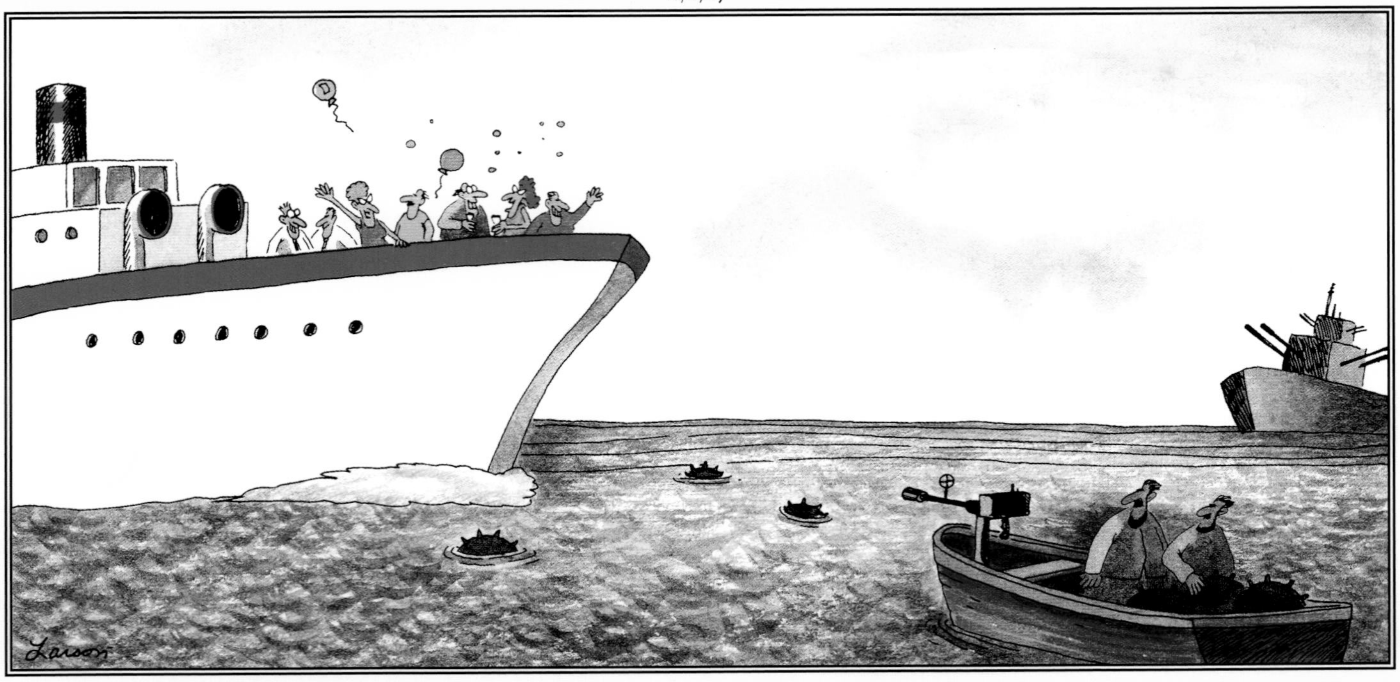
Larson

Through a gross navigational error, the *Love Boat* steams into the Strait of Hormuz.

12/12/87

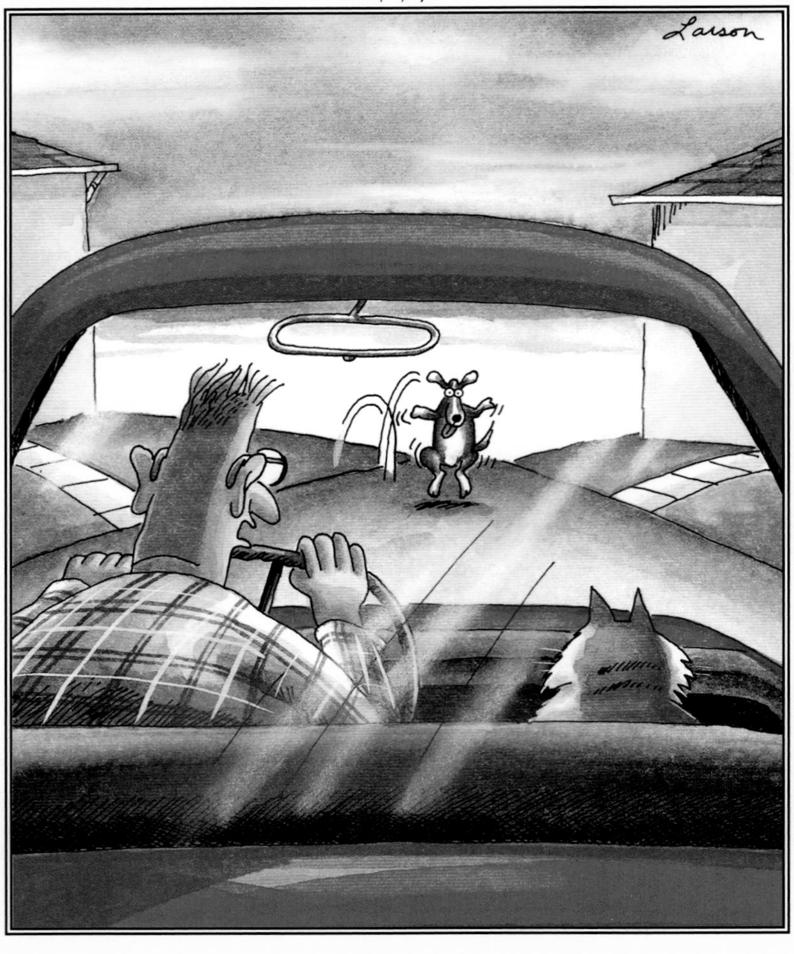
Larson

"Well, look who's excited to see you back from being declawed."

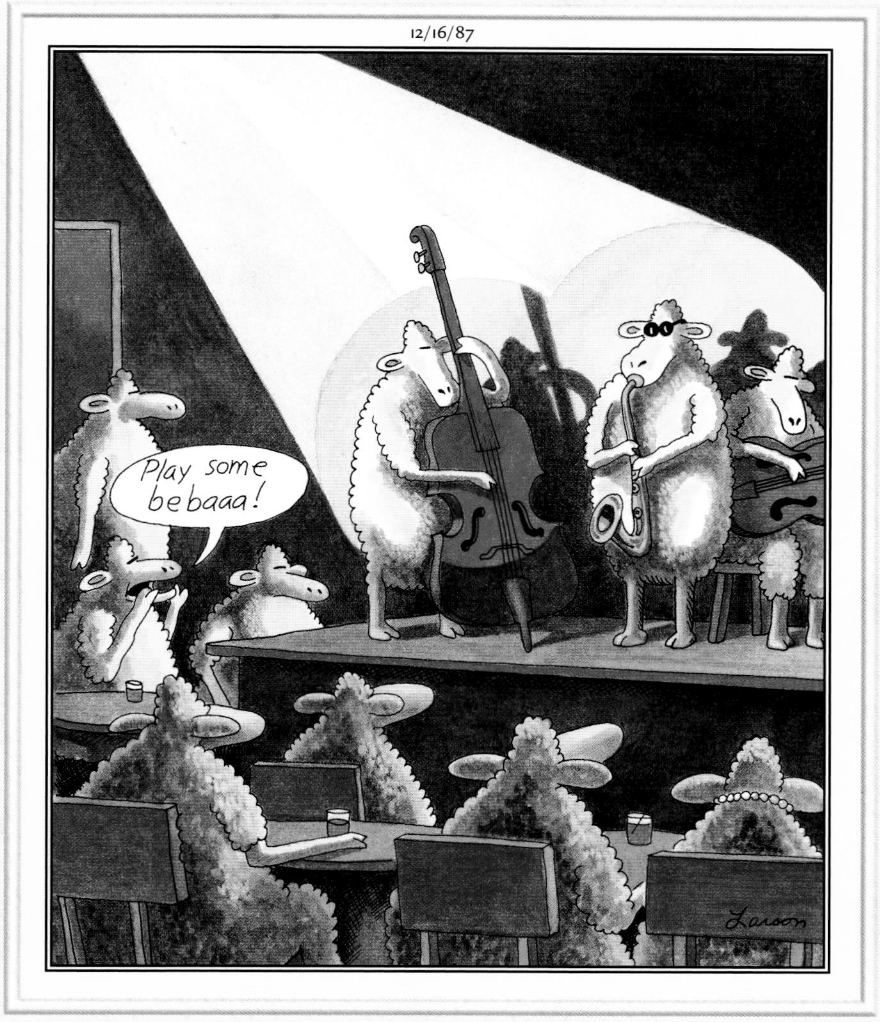
12/16/87
Play some bebaaa!
Larson

Jazz at the Wool Club

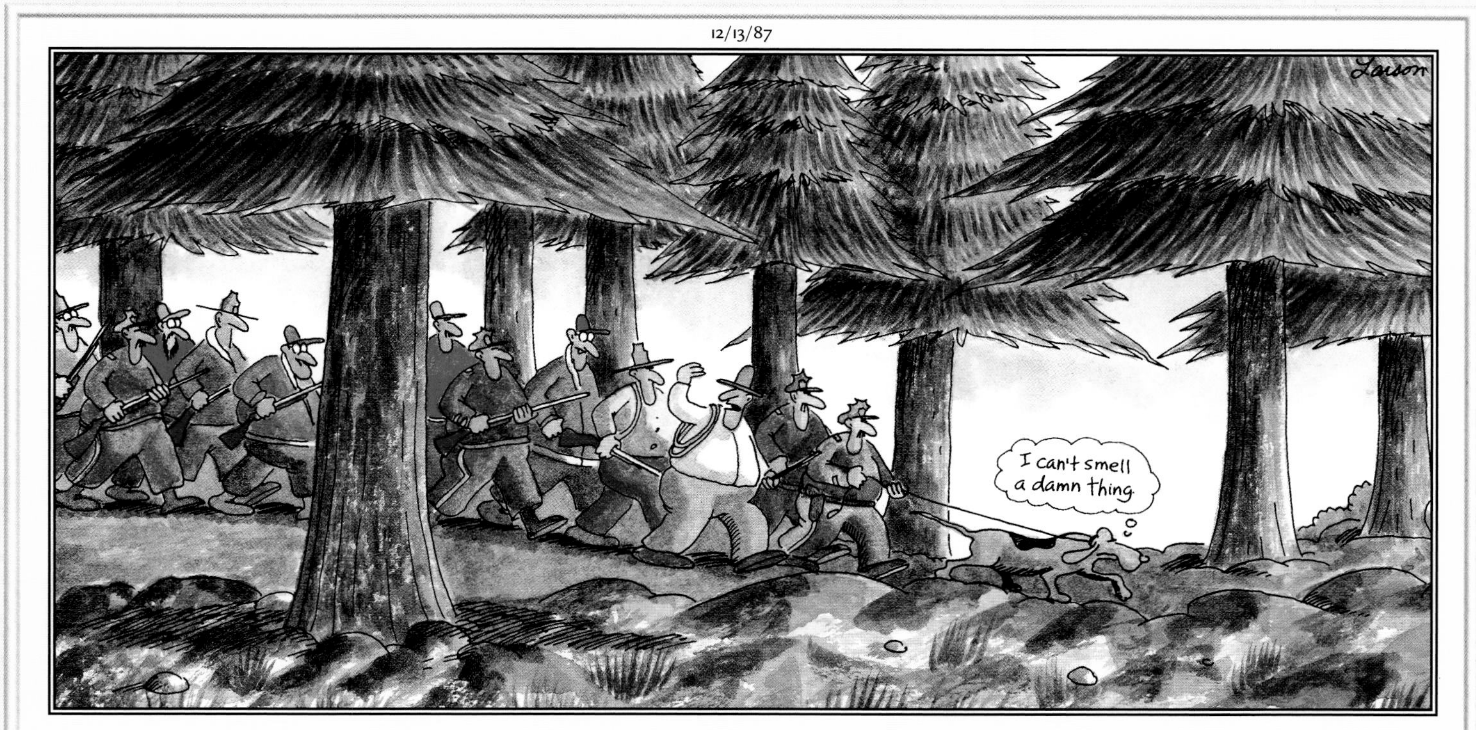
12/13/87
Larson
I can't smell a damn thing

12/14/87

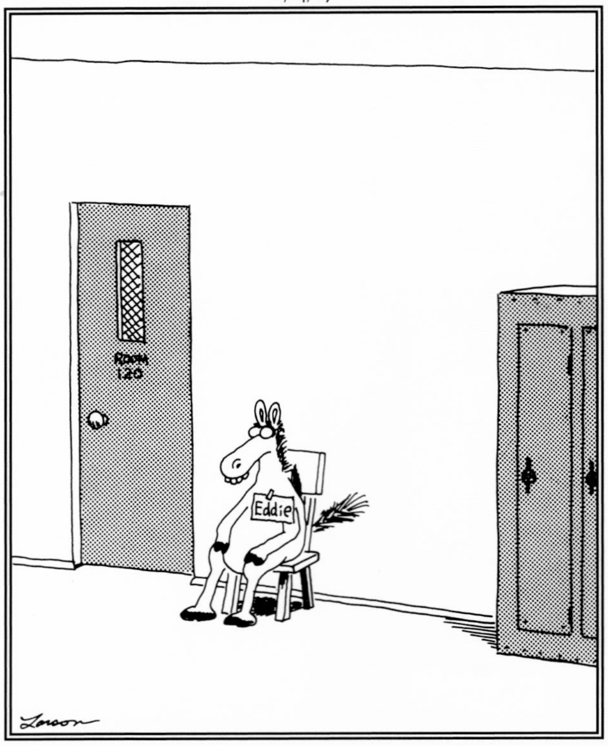
ROOM
120
Eddie

As a young colt, Mr. Ed was often sent to the hall for speaking out of turn.

12/15/87

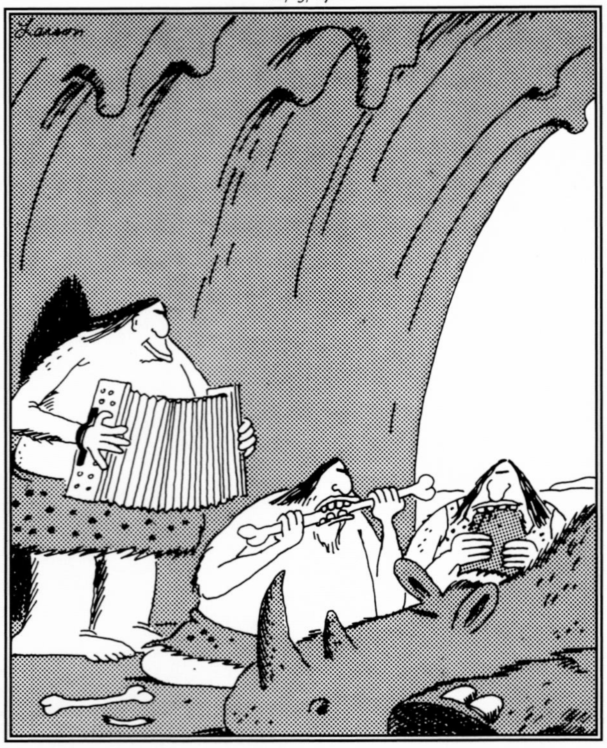

Primitive mood music

12/10/87

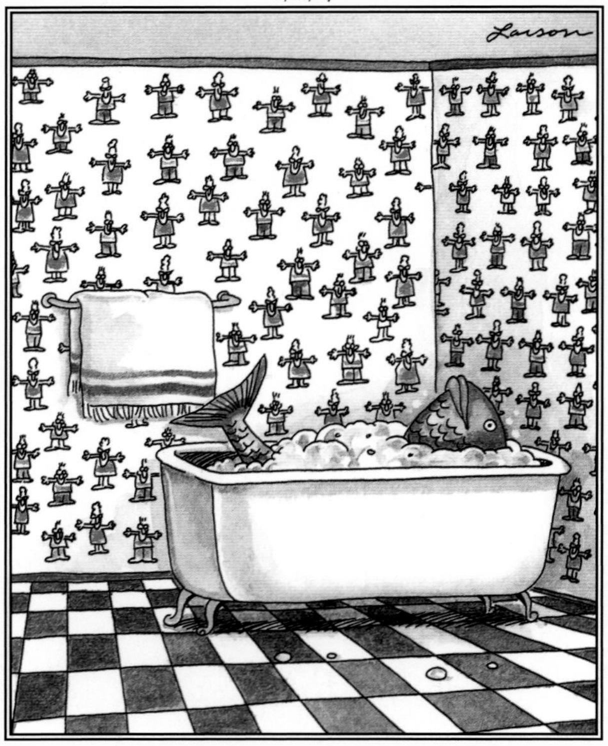

12/8/87

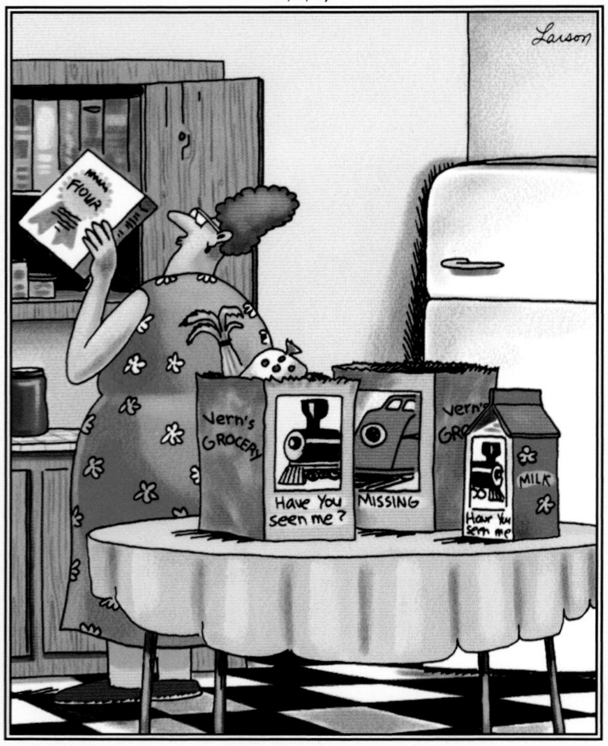
FLOUR
Vern's GROCERY
Have You seen me?
MISSING
MILK
Have You seen me

Runaway trains

"I don't know what to tell you, Mr. Miller, but something has definitely gone awry with your workout program."

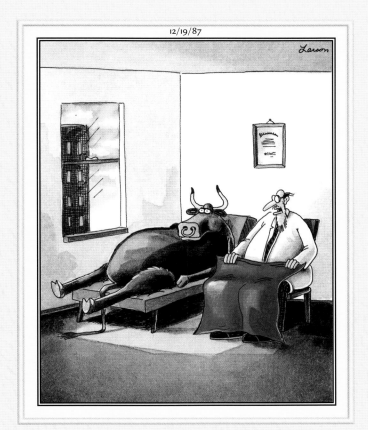

"Now relax. ... Just like last week, I'm going to hold the red cape up for the count of 10. ... When you start getting angry, I'll put it down."

"Oh my God! It's Leonard! ... He stuffed himself!"

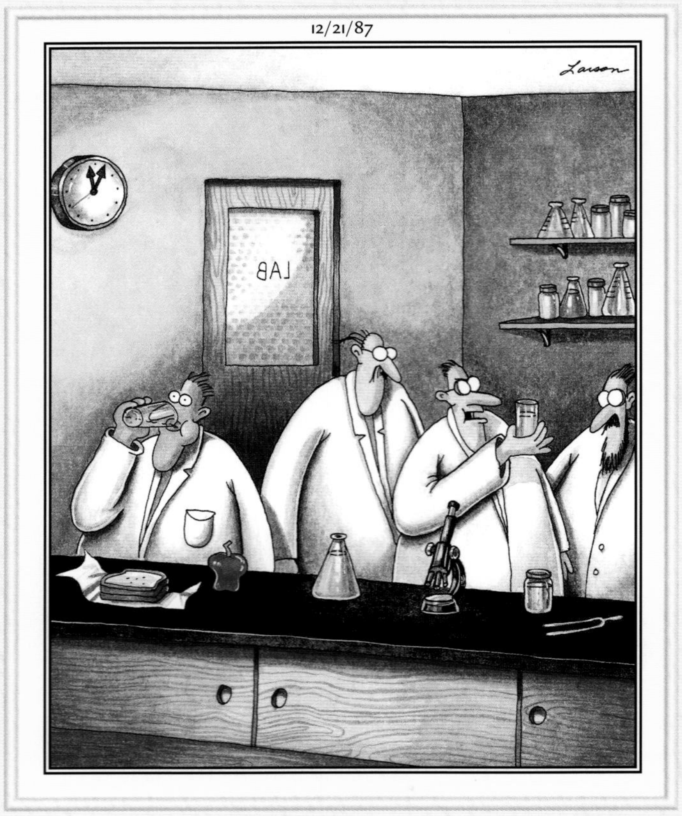
12/21/87
Larson

"What the? ... This is lemonade! Where's my culture of amoebic dysentery?"

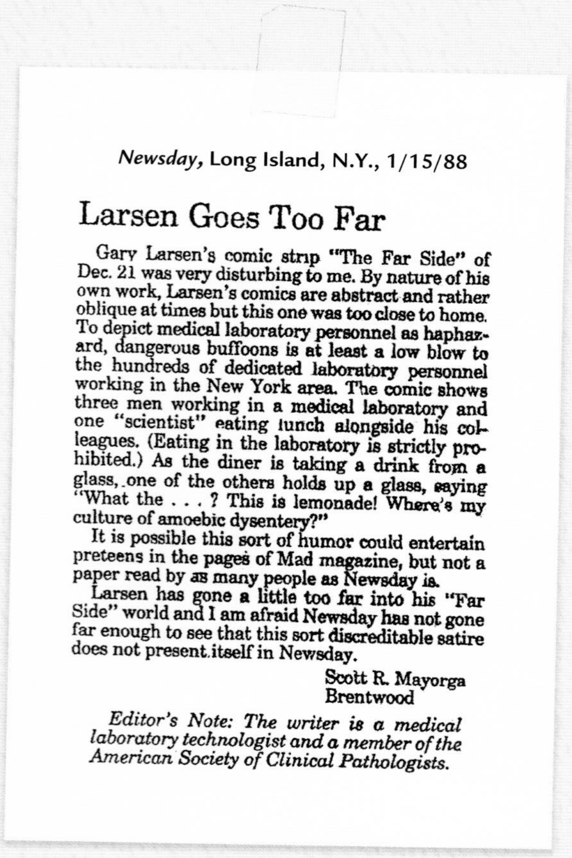

Newsday, Long Island, N.Y., 1/15/88

Larsen Goes Too Far

Gary Larsen's comic strip "The Far Side" of Dec. 21 was very disturbing to me. By nature of his own work, Larsen's comics are abstract and rather oblique at times but this one was too close to home. To depict medical laboratory personnel as haphazard, dangerous buffoons is at least a low blow to the hundreds of dedicated laboratory personnel working in the New York area. The comic shows three men working in a medical laboratory and one "scientist" eating lunch alongside his colleagues. (Eating in the laboratory is strictly prohibited.) As the diner is taking a drink from a glass, one of the others holds up a glass, saying "What the . . . ? This is lemonade! Where's my culture of amoebic dysentery?"

It is possible this sort of humor could entertain preteens in the pages of Mad magazine, but not a paper read by as many people as Newsday is.

Larsen has gone a little too far into his "Far Side" world and I am afraid Newsday has not gone far enough to see that this sort discreditable satire does not present itself in Newsday.

Scott R. Mayorga
Brentwood

Editor's Note: The writer is a medical laboratory technologist and a member of the American Society of Clinical Pathologists.

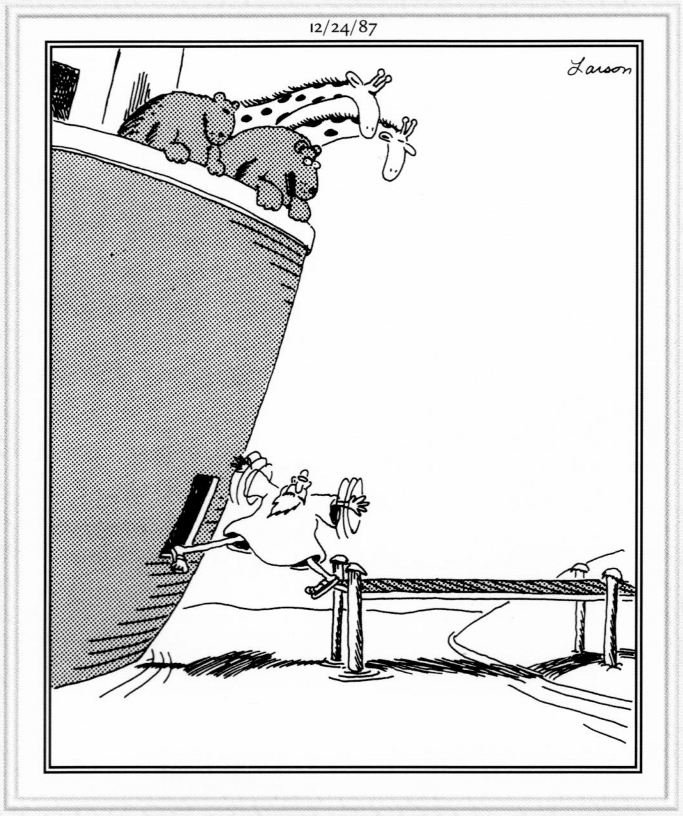
12/24/87
Larson

"We're in trouble."

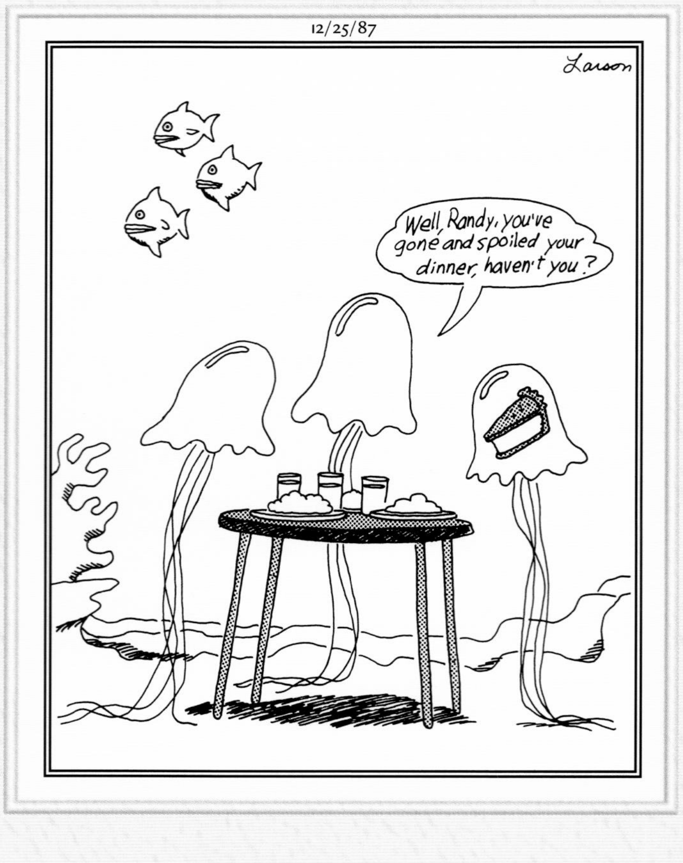
12/25/87
Larson
Well, Randy, you've gone and spoiled your dinner, haven't you?

12/23/87

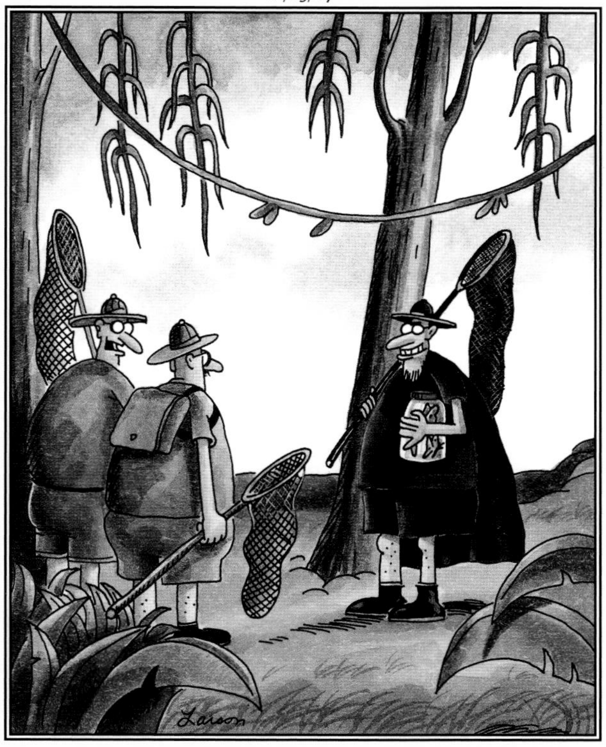

"Egad! It's Professor DeArmond—the epitome of evil amongst butterfly collectors!"

12/29/87

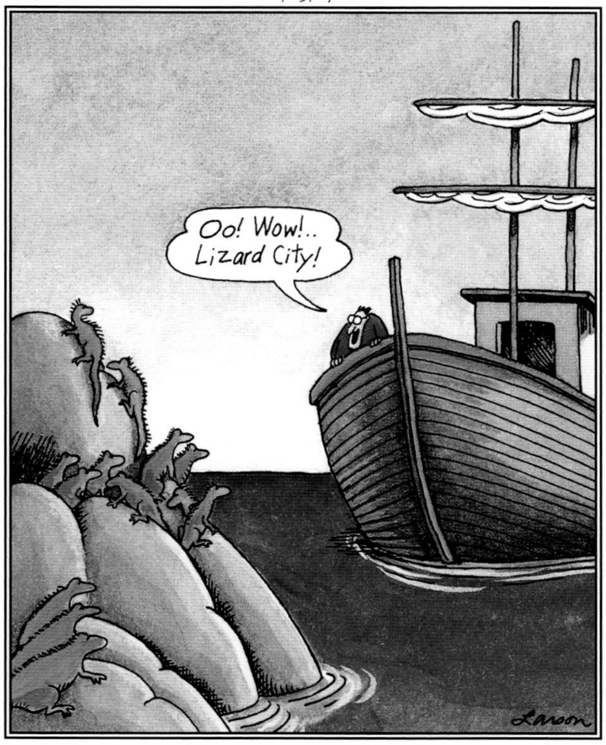
Oo! Wow!.. Lizard City!

Darwin reaches the Galápagos

12/28/87

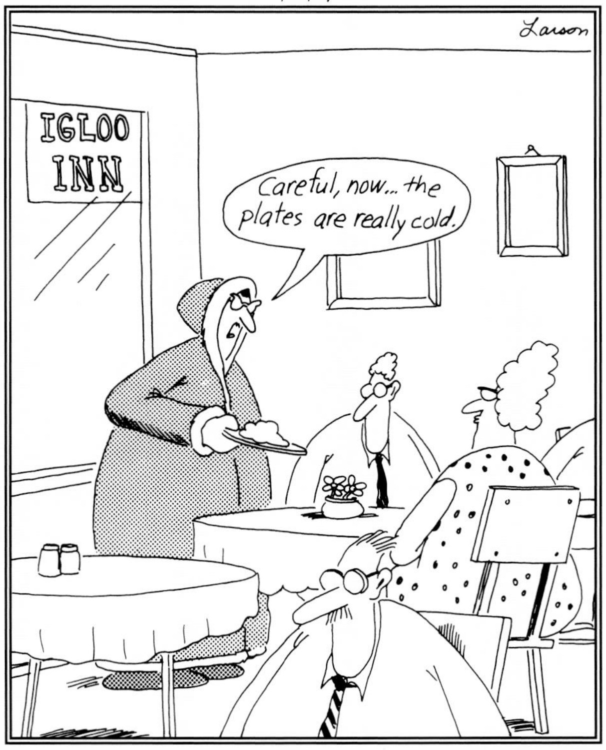
IGLOO INN
Careful, now... the plates are really cold.

Eskimo restaurants

12/31/87

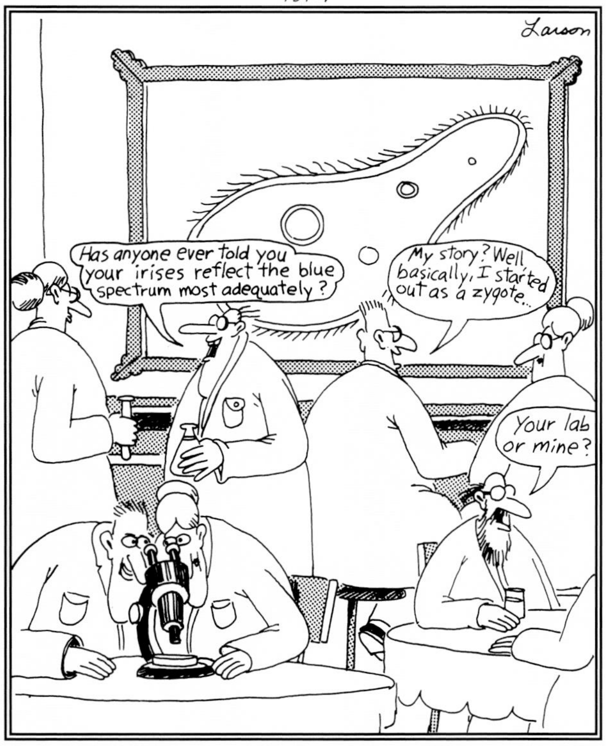
Has anyone ever told you your irises reflect the blue spectrum most adequately?
My story? Well basically, I started out as a zygote..
Your lab or mine?

Scientific meat markets

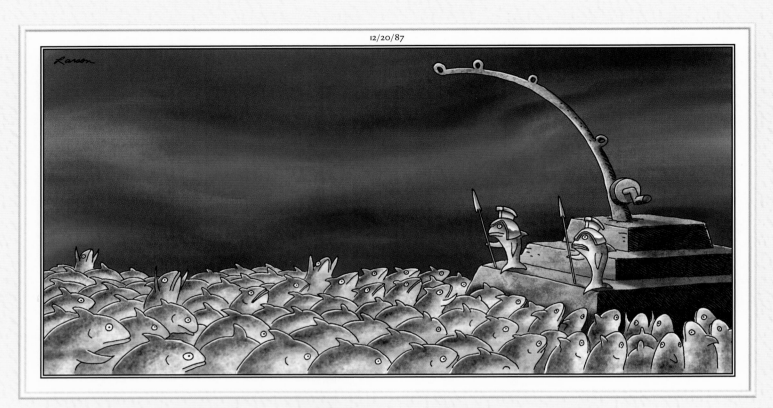

Temple of the Cods

An instant later, both Professor Waxman and his time machine are obliterated, leaving the cold-blooded/warm-blooded dinosaur debate still unresolved.

12/30/87

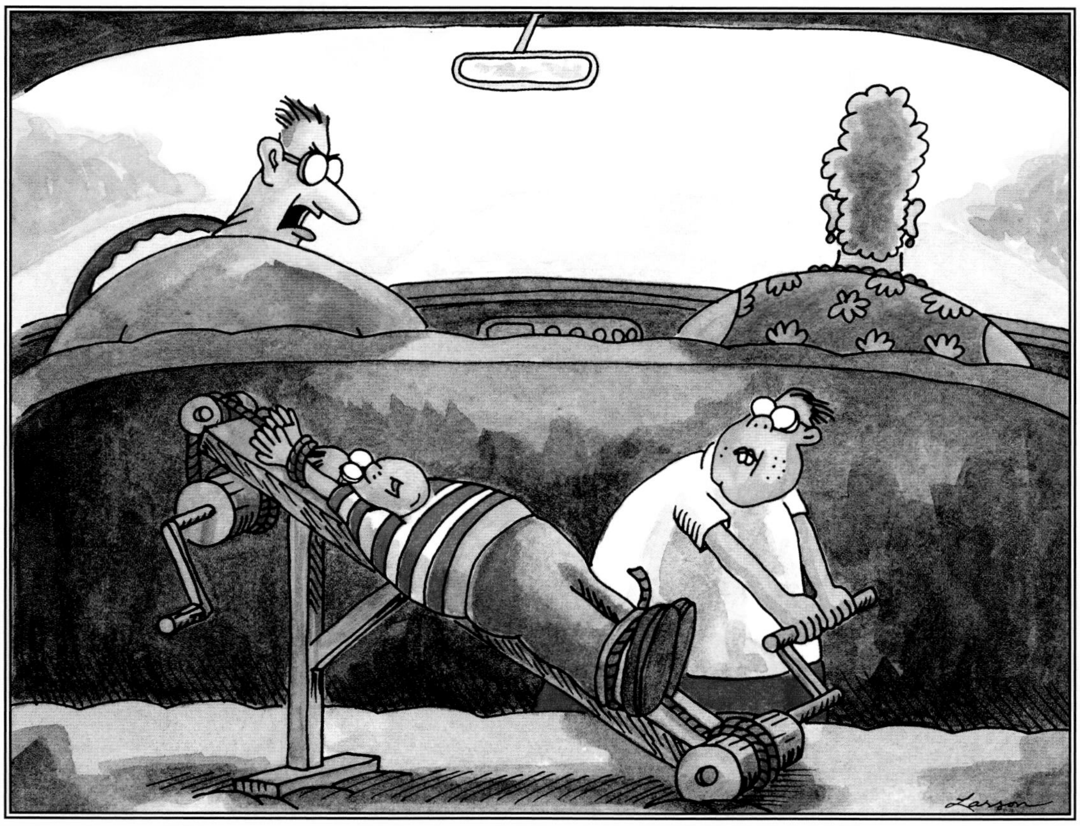
Larson

"You want me to stop the car, Larry, or do you want to take your brother off the rack this instant?"

12/27/87

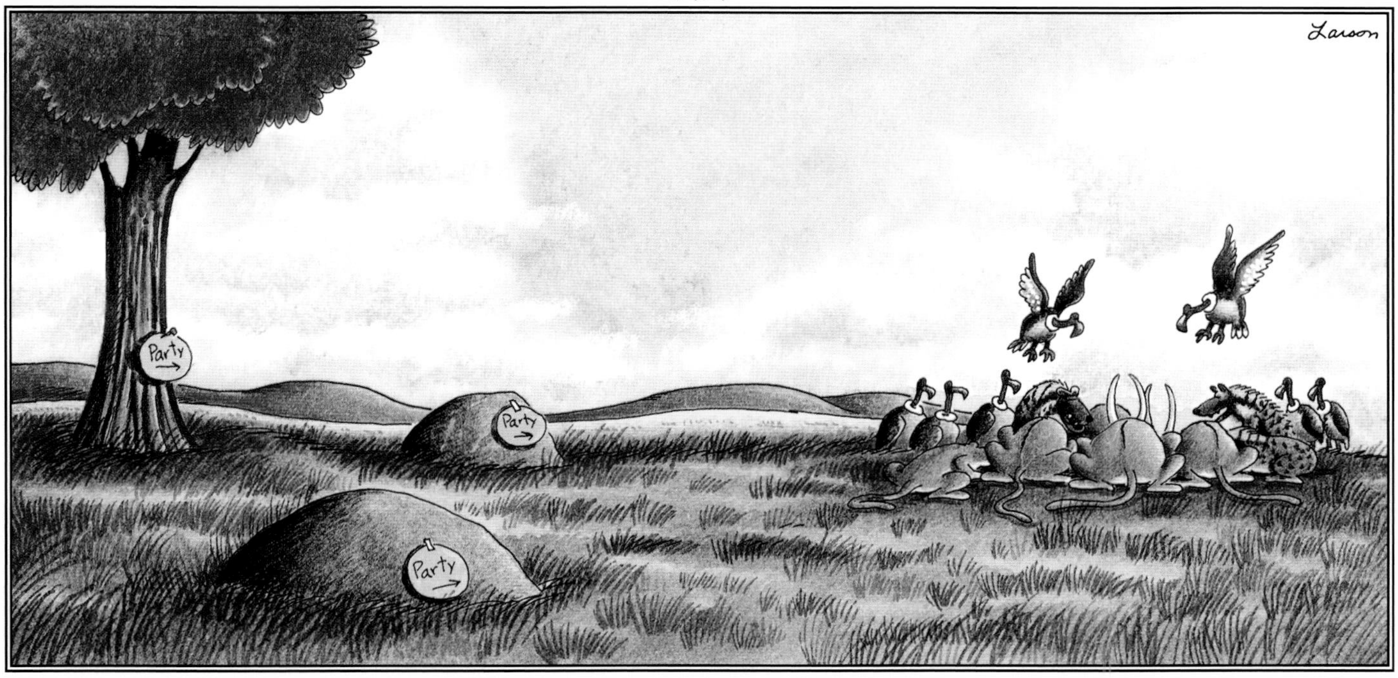
Larson
Party
Party
Party

Flatten the creep, Jack!
TODAY'S SPECIAL
19
When ornithologists of the opposite sex meet in singles bars.
Larson

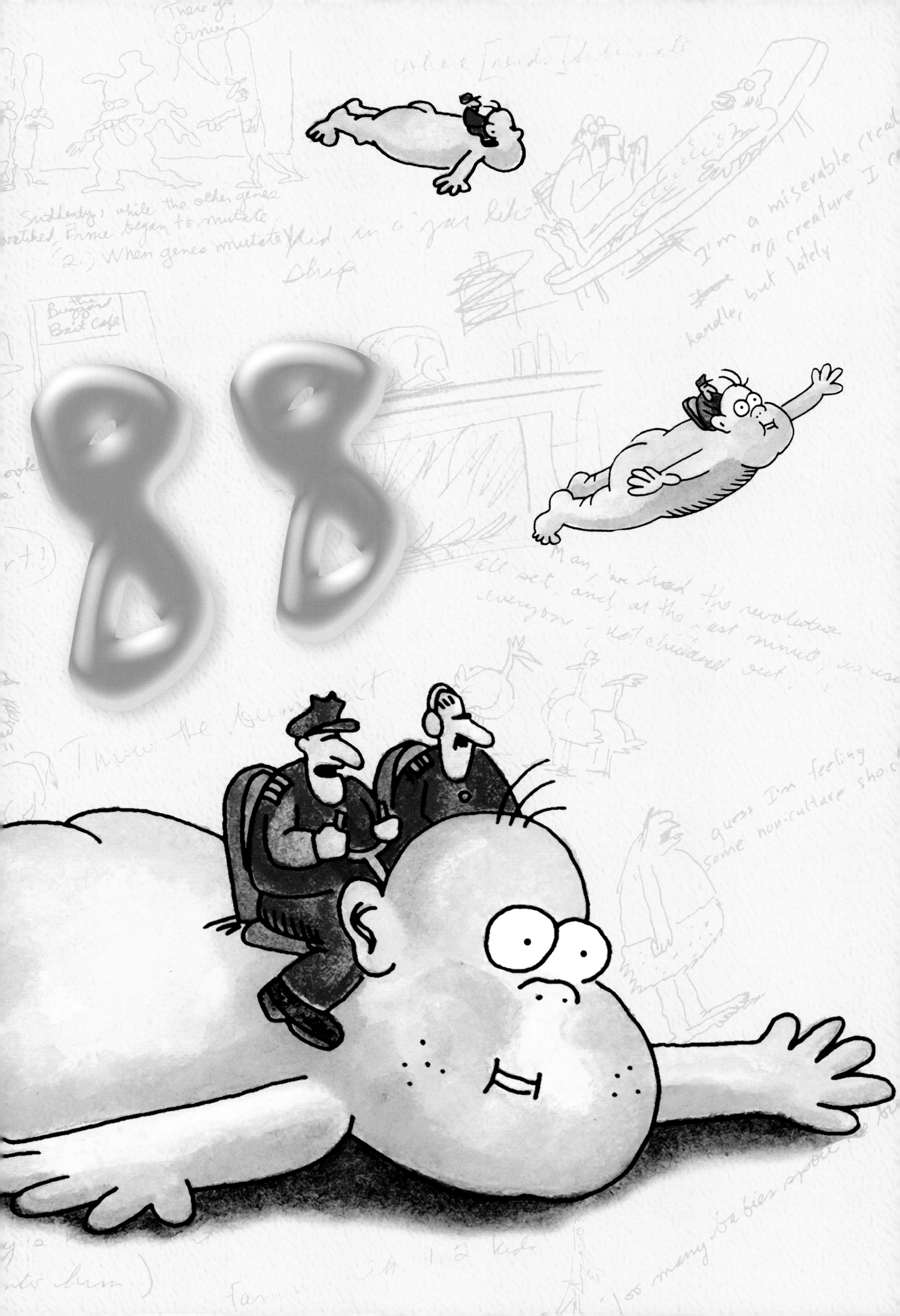
88
Suddenly, while the other genes
watched, Ernie began to mutate
(2.) When genes mutate

The Good Wetch

Gladys Wetch was a neighbor of ours when I was a kid. (Does everyone have a neighbor named Gladys?) She was an older woman, short and stout, with a foreign accent whose origin eludes me now. She and her husband lived in a small gray house, kitty-corner to our own. If they had kids, the kids must have been older or something because I don't remember them. In fact, I was never once in the Wetches' house. The place just always seemed "apart" from everything else. But Gladys Wetch, herself, made a big impression on me when I was very young.

Mrs. Wetch was a frequent baby-sitter for my brother and me. (My parents both worked.) We had other baby-sitters over the years, but over time my brother, Dan, drove most of them away. (He was quite professional in that area.) The other sitters were all rather normal women, sort of like variations on Opie's Aunt Bee. They'd make us lunch, sometimes bake cookies, maybe clean the house, and essentially try to keep both themselves and the Larson boys alive for the few hours until my parents got home.

But Gladys Wetch was different. Gladys Wetch had a handle on Dan and me. She didn't bake cookies or clean the house. What she did was tell us stories. And I'm not talking about Mother Goose-type stories. Mrs. Wetch's specialty was the horror story. More specifically, her stories were the detailed retellings of the movies she had seen on *Nightmare Theater,* the local scare-the-hell-out-of-you show that aired on channel 13 every Friday night—exactly at midnight, of course.

So here's how it played out for some time: On weekends, I learned about Brer Rabbit, the Little Engine Who Could, and Mr. Toad from my mom. On weekdays, from Gladys Wetch, I learned all about Dracula, Frankenstein, werewolves, the Mummy, and the Creature from the Black Lagoon. I think it was a pretty balanced childhood. I especially remember Mrs. Wetch telling us about Rodan, this giant flying lizard creature. (A pterodactyl, I surmised years later.)

I used to think about Rodan a lot. Maybe it's because nothing could be more scary in my mind than a giant lizard-creature whose name sort of sounded like my brother's. And the story of Rodan is being told to me by a woman whose name, as you may have noticed, is one letter removed from "witch." Lots of buttons being pushed here.

But I also remember her vivid description of Dracula, and how he could change into a fog, flow under a bedroom door, and then re-form into his usual, undead body. I stuffed clothes under my door for a while after that, oblivious to the flaw that my door had no lock; Dracula could've just walked in, sucked my blood, and left. But if he *had* decided to go fog on me, my clothes barricade was in place, and I had Mrs. Wetch to thank for that.

The thing is, Gladys Wetch was our favorite baby-sitter.

And then one day something happened. I think my mom somehow found out about Mrs. Wetch and the things she was telling us, and I believe she and my mom must have had a "conversation." Anyway, I don't remember Mrs. Wetch coming around anymore. More recently, in writing this little essay, I asked my mom what she remembered about the woman. My mom suddenly seemed a little anxious. "Oh, she told you boys very strange stories! And once she even threatened to throw you both in the fireplace!" There was a pause, and then she quickly added, "But she meant it in a nice way, I'm sure."

I honestly don't remember the fireplace episode. But boy, do I remember those stories.

Yeah, Gladys Wetch was cool. She's passed on, no doubt, but believe me, she still haunts these pages. In a nice way, I'm sure.

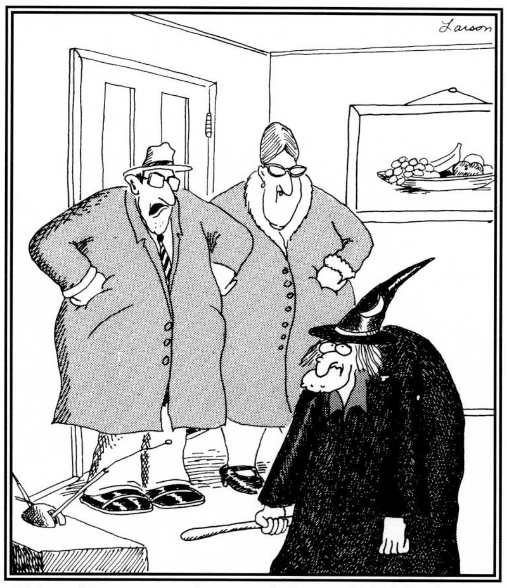
Larson

"Now let me get this straight. ... We hired you to babysit the kids, and instead you cooked and ate them *both?*"

1/1/88

Hey, baby! Do those legs go all the way up?
Larson

Daddy long-leg jerks

1/5/88

Larson

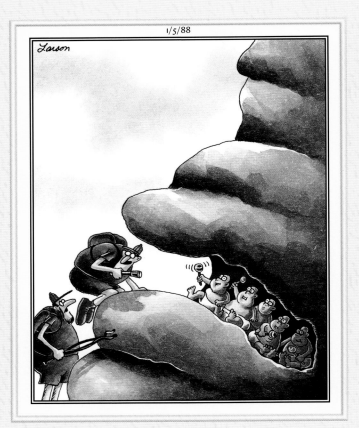

"All right! Hand me the tongs, Frank. ... We got us a big den of rattlers here."

1/3/88

WUMP!
My! What was that?
Larson

1/4/88

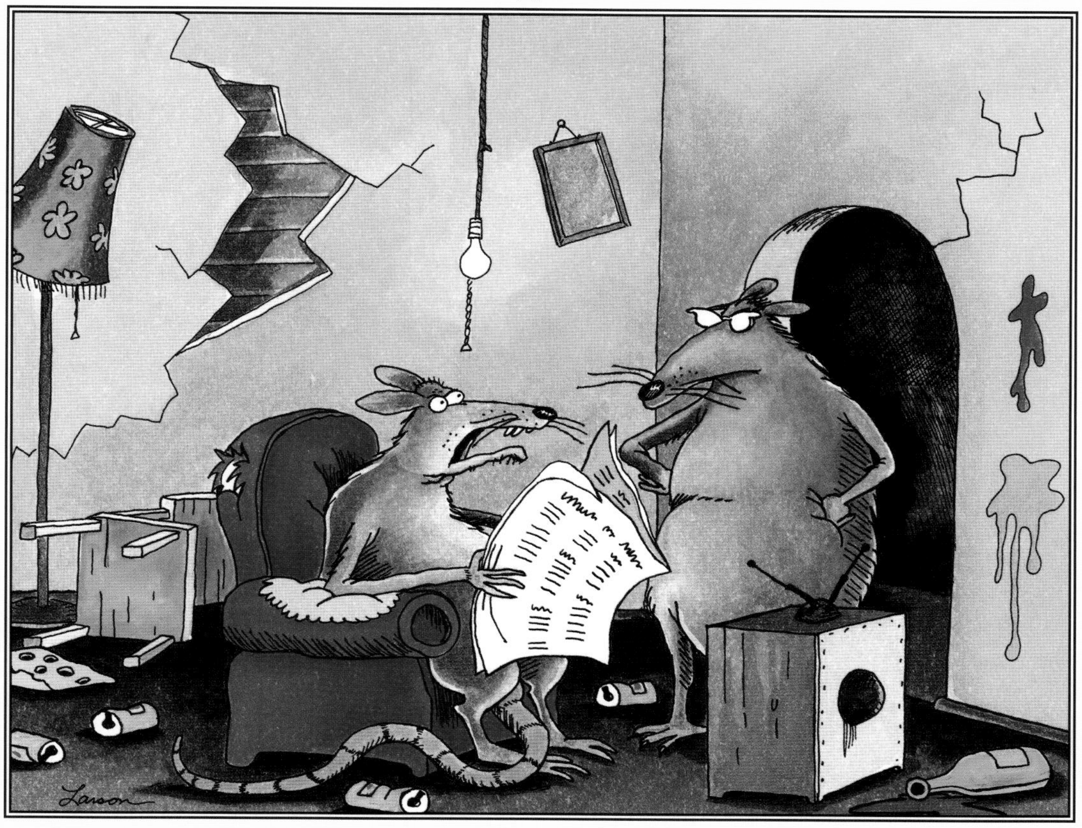
Larson

"Clean it up? Clean it up? Crimony, it's *supposed* to be a rathole!"

1/7/88

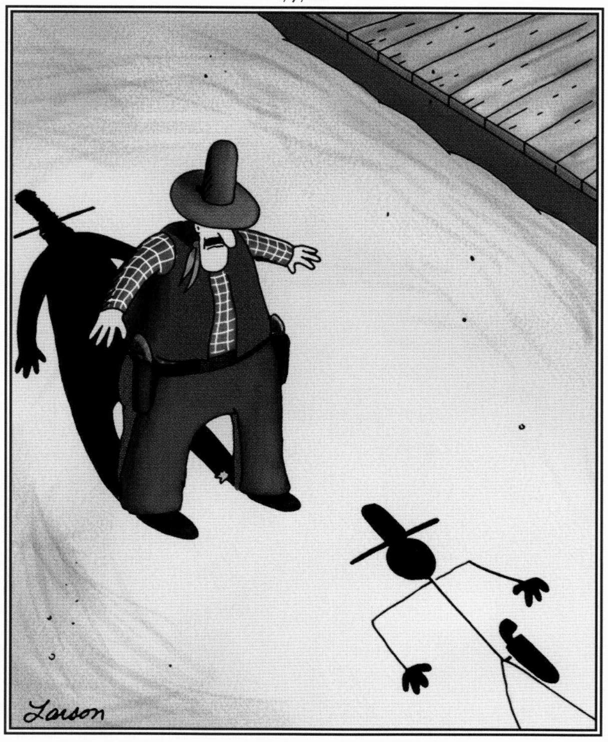
Larson

"Anytime, Slim."

1/6/88

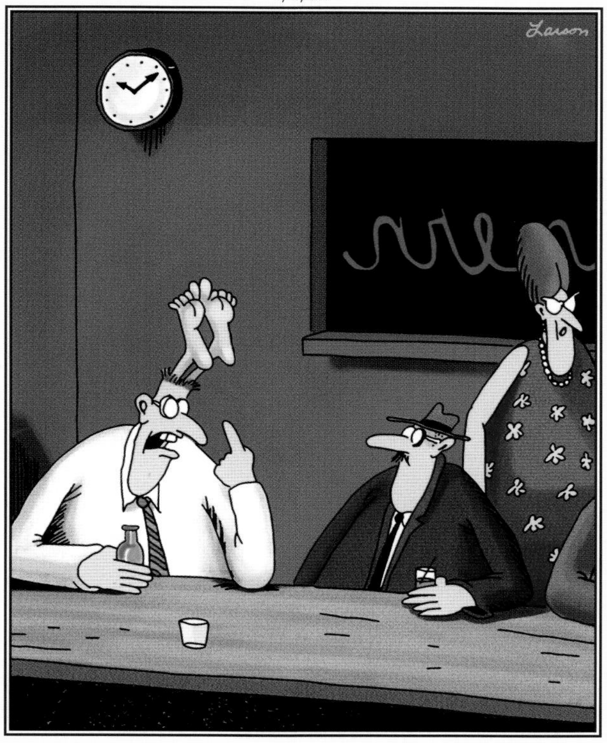
Larson

"Mind? Hey, buddy, these flat feet kept me out of the Army!"

1/2/88

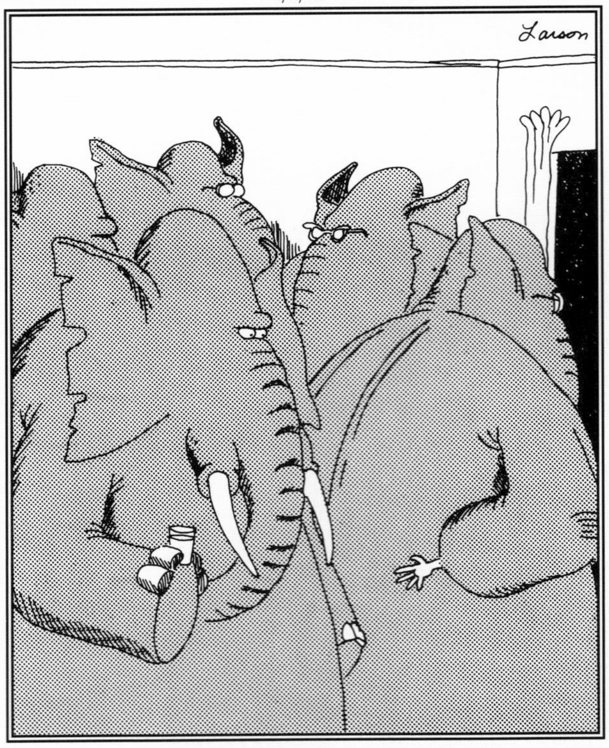

Although Edgar discreetly tried to hide his ailment, his friends still noticed his humantiasis.

1/9/88

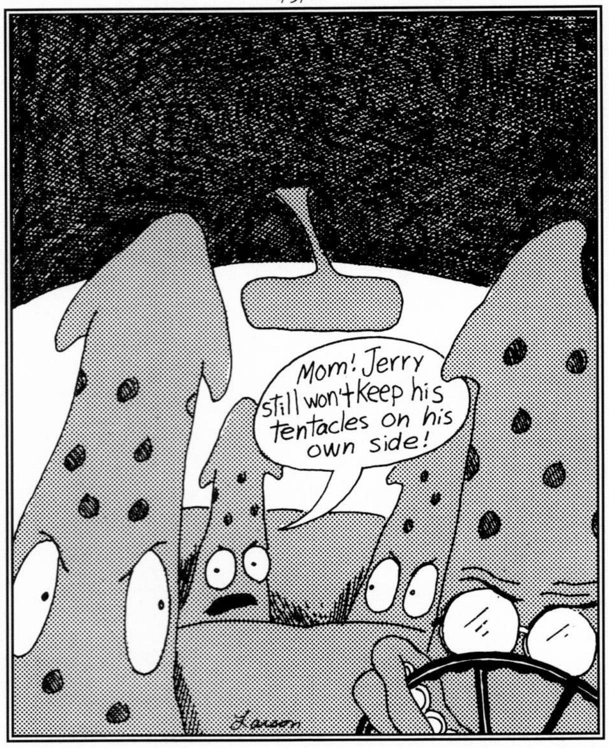
Mom! Jerry still won't keep his tentacles on his own side!

The Squid family on vacation

1/11/88

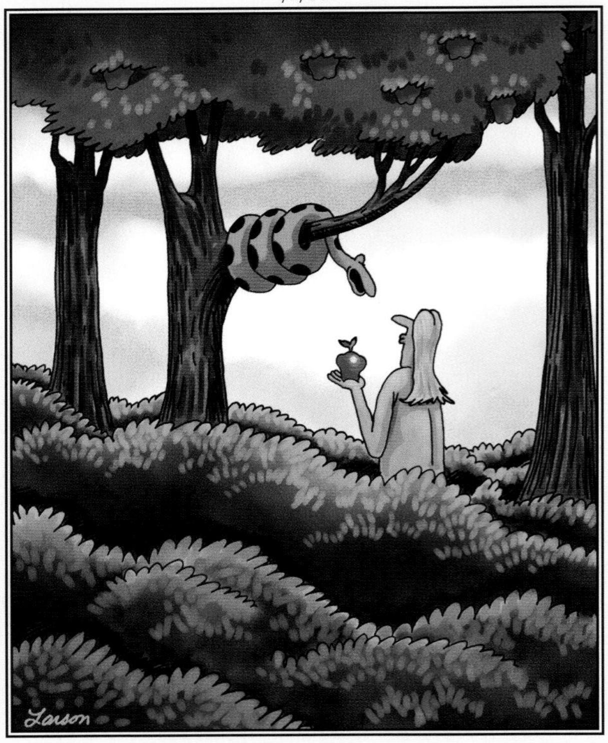

"Well, I'm not sure. ... I guess it's been washed."

1/16/88

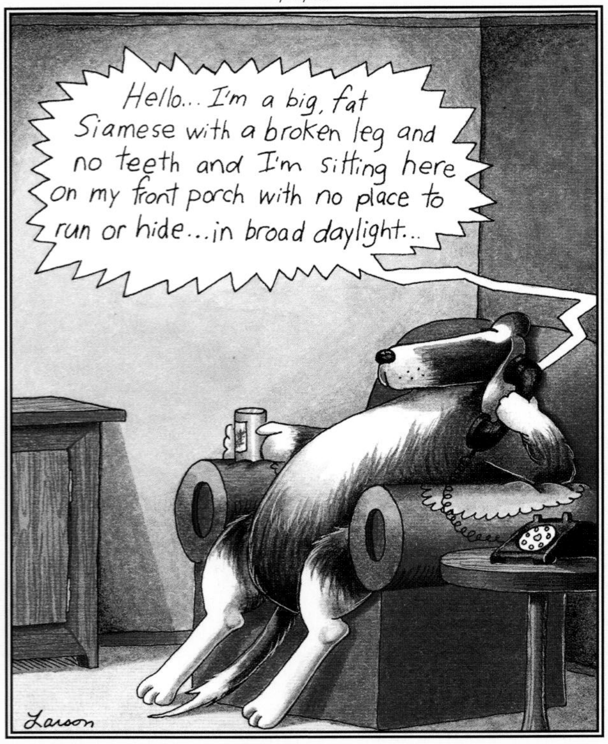
Hello... I'm a big, fat Siamese with a broken leg and no teeth and I'm sitting here on my front porch with no place to run or hide... in broad daylight...

Dial-a-Cat

1/13/88

Larson
CONGRATULATIONS
BOB
TORTURER
OF THE MONTH

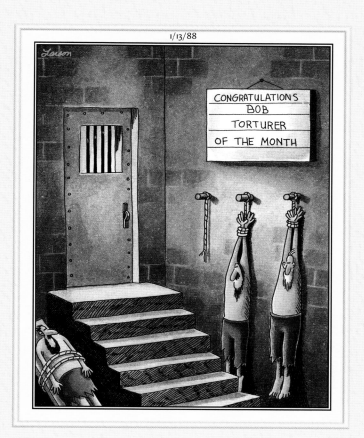

The Des Moines Register, Des Moines, Iowa, 2/9/88

A blot on the conscience of mankind

I AM WRITING to express my revulsion at the "Far Side" cartoon that offers congratulations to Bob, the "Torturer of the Month."

Using torture as the subject of humor is, to say the least, offensive to me. Perhaps the author of the cartoon believes that torture is something so far removed from today's world that we can afford to laugh at it. If the author or the editor believes that, you are ill-informed.

Torture is practiced today, according to Amnesty International, by one out of every three governments. As I write this letter, I am aware that in numerous places, people are being beaten, burned, having limbs amputated, put through mock execution, sexually abused, and, as depicted in the cartoon, hung by their wrists for long periods of time. How can this be presented as the subject of humor?

Torture is not a laughing matter. It is a blot on the conscience of mankind that must be eradicated, not laughed at. The cartoon has done nothing to educate people about this evil, or to arouse people to work to stop torture and other violations of human rights.

The torturers of the world would like people to believe that the torture cells do not exist and that their crimes are so far removed from reality that the very concept can be the subject of funny little cartoons. In the meantime, their victims suffer in darkness and isolation.

Ignorance and silence are the torturers' best friends. . . . — Michael L. Messina

1/12/88

Larson

"Okay, you've passed the fire test, the riding test, and the combat test ... but now, paleface, *now* you must say 'toy boat' three times real fast!"

1/8/88

Larson

"Mom! The kids at school say we're a family of Nerdenthals! ... Is that true?"

1/10/88

Larson
SURVEILLANCE
CAT
1400 NAP

1/14/88

Larson

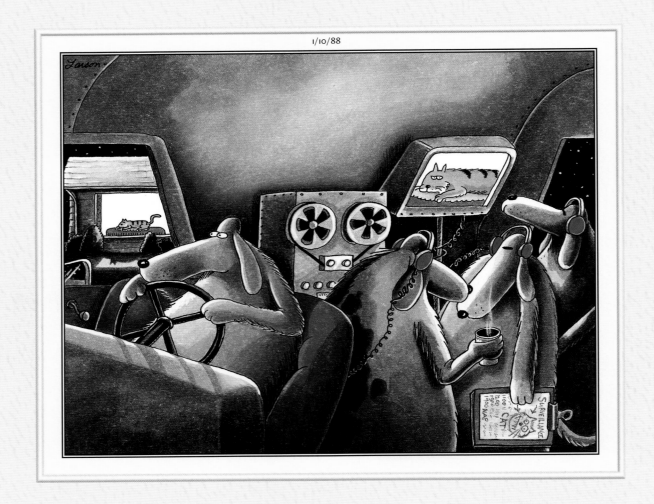

Suddenly, in the middle of the flock, the cook is goosed.

1/15/88

Mastodon Mothers
THE Mastodon Mothers
Mastodon
THE Mastodon Mothers
Larson

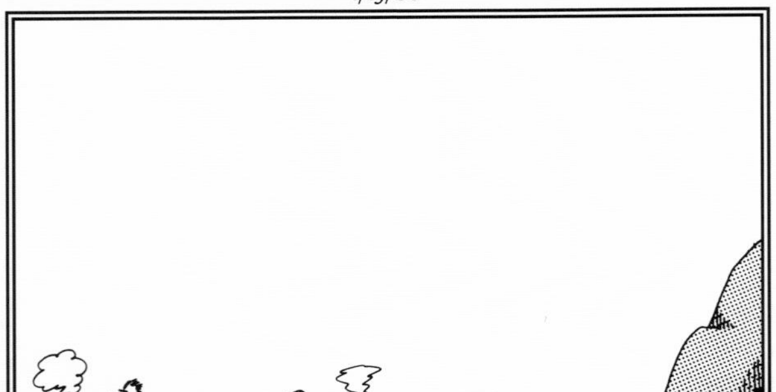

Early wheel gangs

1/20/88

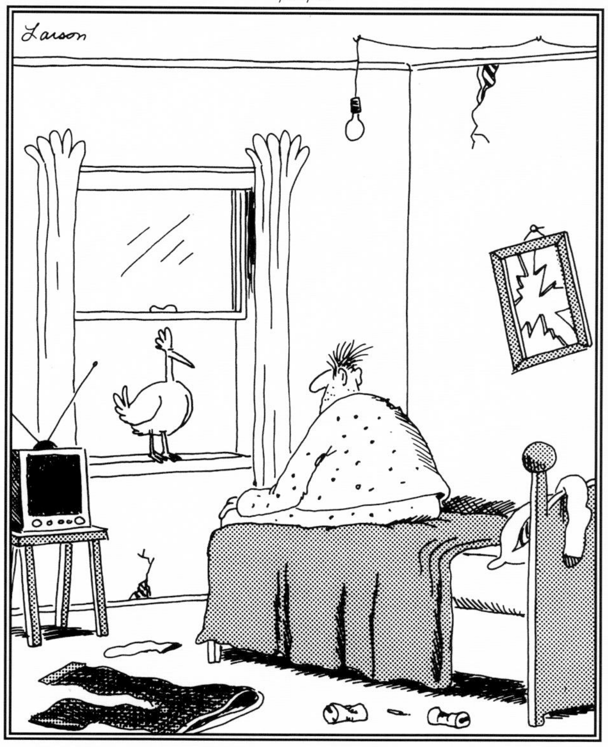
Larson

The Bluebird of Happiness long absent from his life, Ned is visited by the Chicken of Depression.

1/27/88

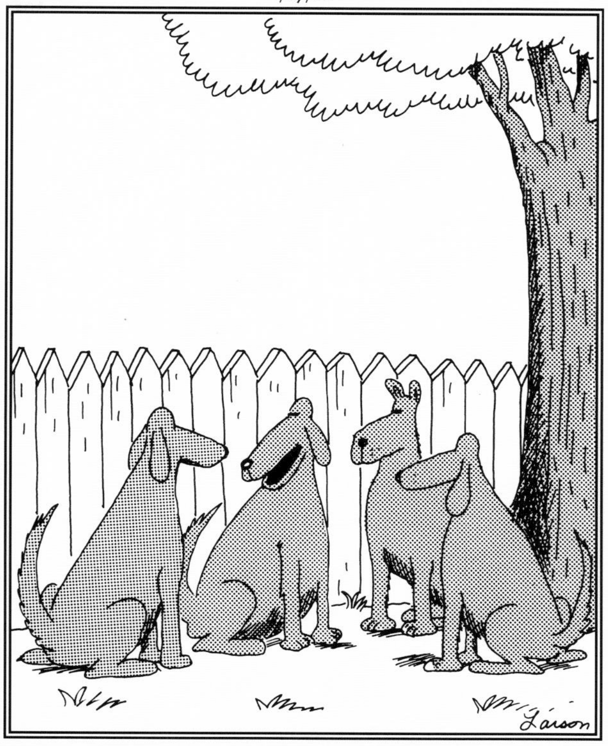
Larson

"Nope, I can't do it either. ... Dusty! Can you make an 'O' with your lips?"

1/19/88

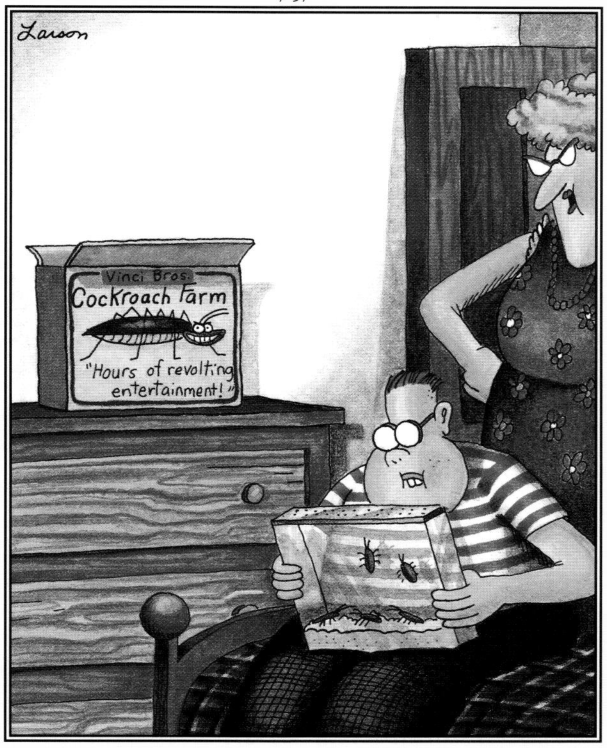
Larson
Vinci Bros.
Cockroach Farm
"Hours of revolting entertainment!"

"Now remember, Cory, show us that you can take good care of these little fellows and maybe next year we'll get you that puppy."

1/18/88

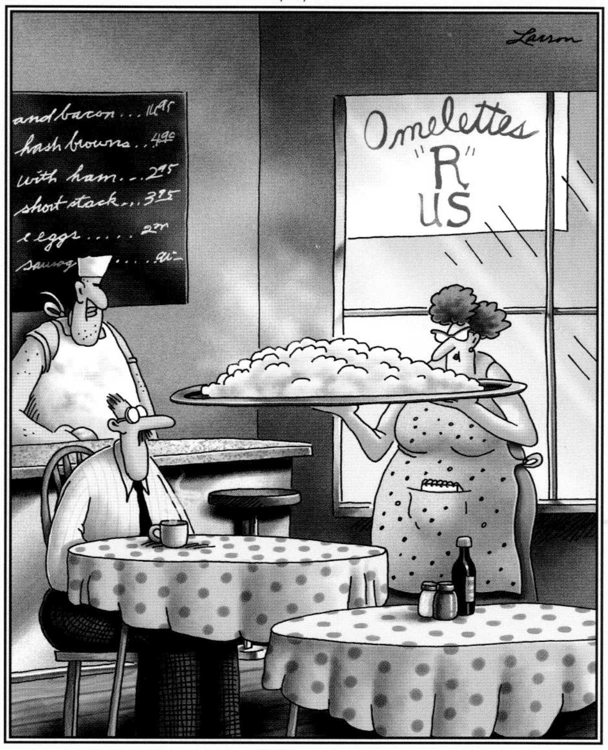
Larson
Omelettes "R" US

Humpty Dumpty's final days

1/21/88

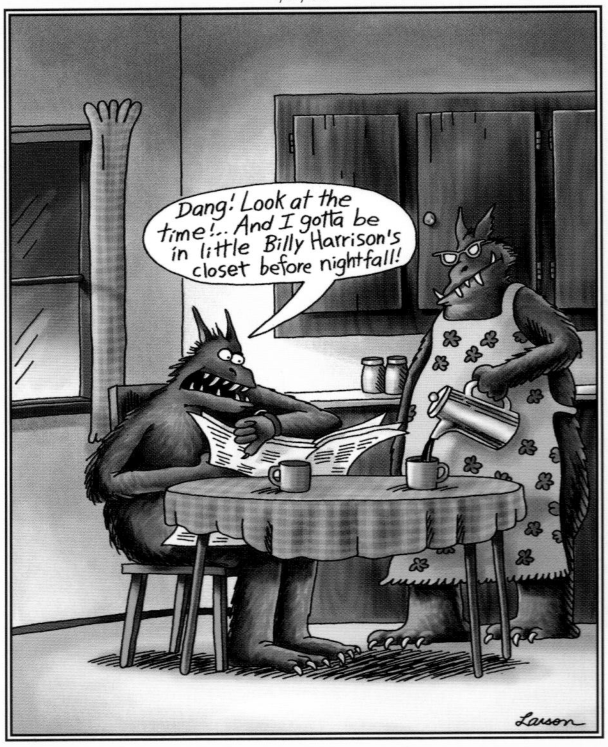
Dang! Look at the time!.. And I gotta be in little Billy Harrison's closet before nightfall!
Larson

Monster jobs

1/22/88

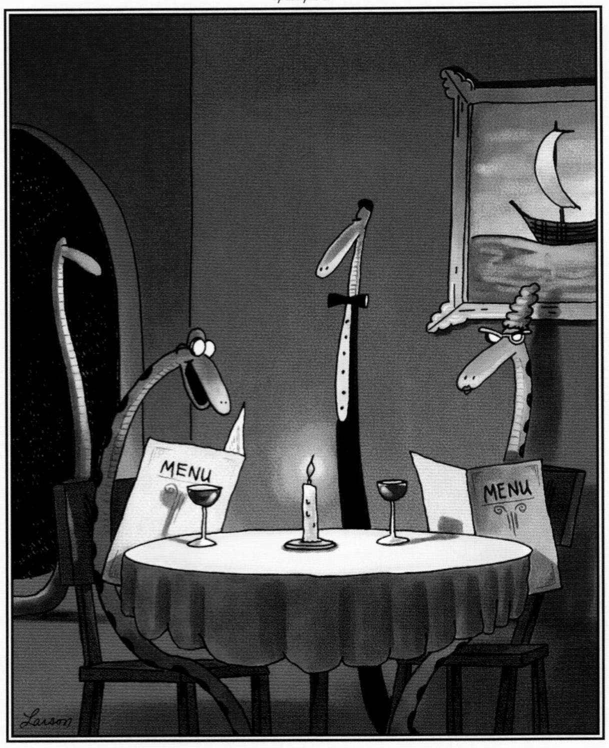
MENU
MENU
Larson

"Well, this may not be wise on a first date, but I just gotta try your garlic wharf rats."

1/17/88

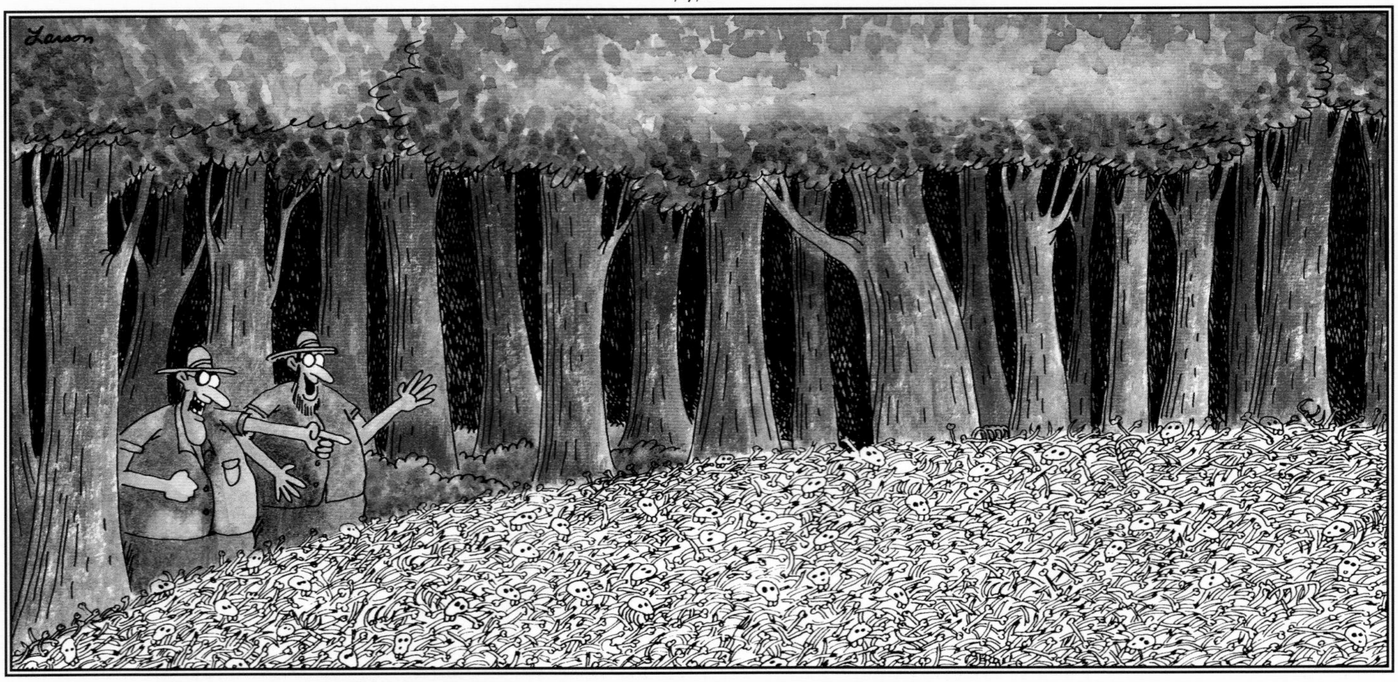
Larson

June 2, 1952: Naturalists discover the Secret Chipmunk Burial Grounds.

1/23/88

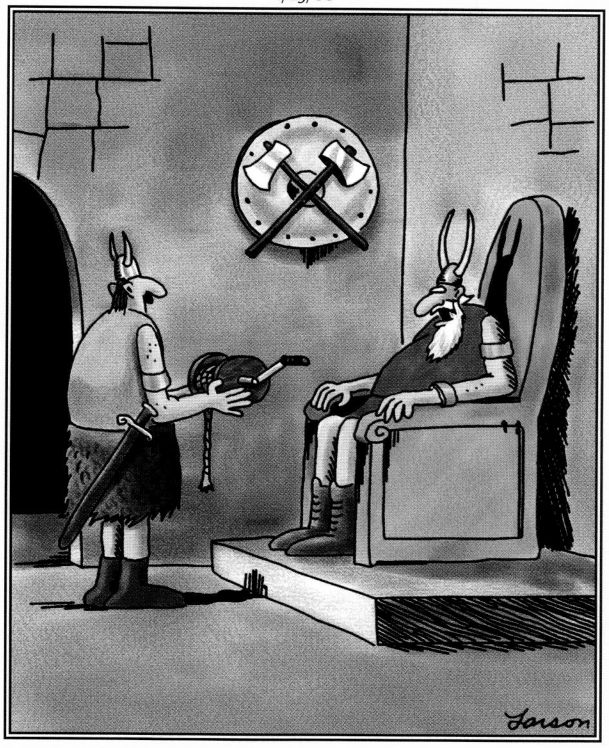

"The wench, you idiot! Bring me the *wench!*"

1/26/88

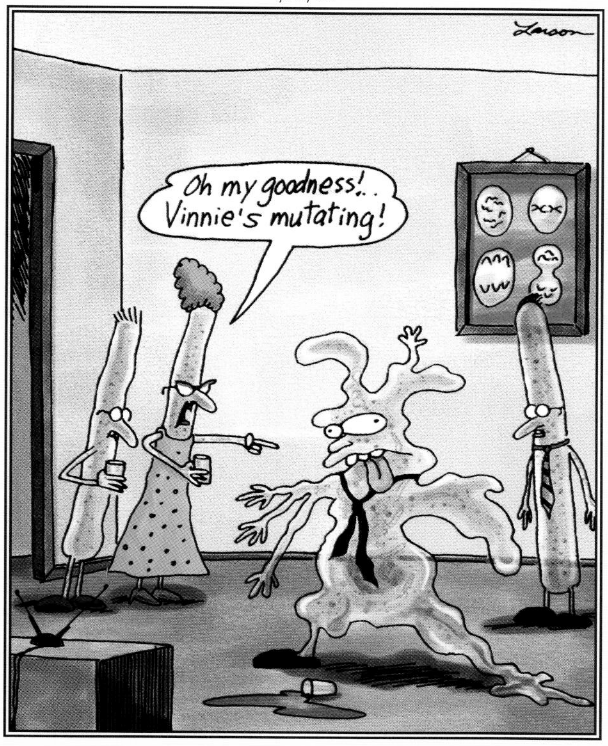
Oh my goodness!.. Vinnie's mutating!

Embarrassing moments at gene parties

1/24/88

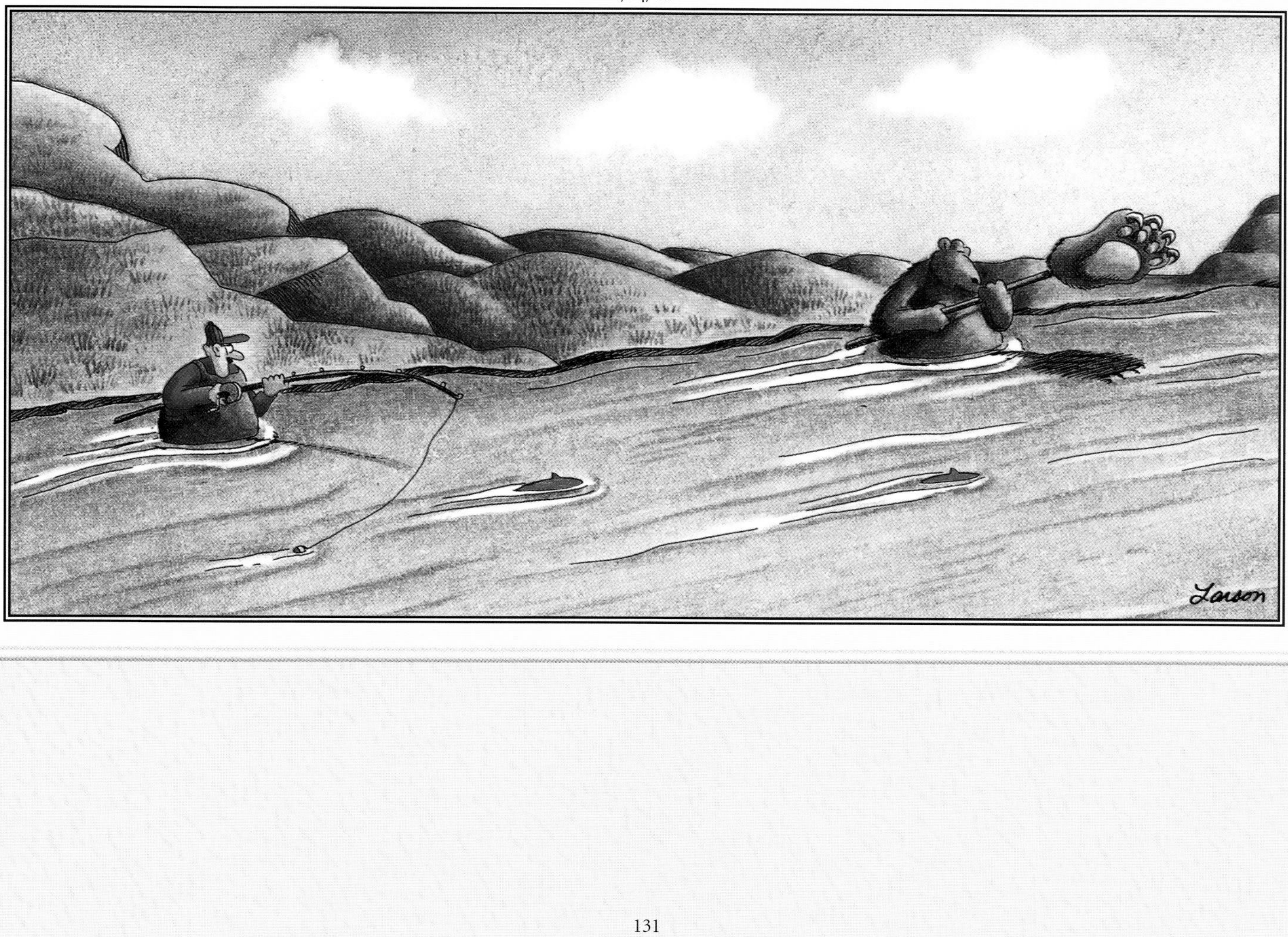

1/25/88

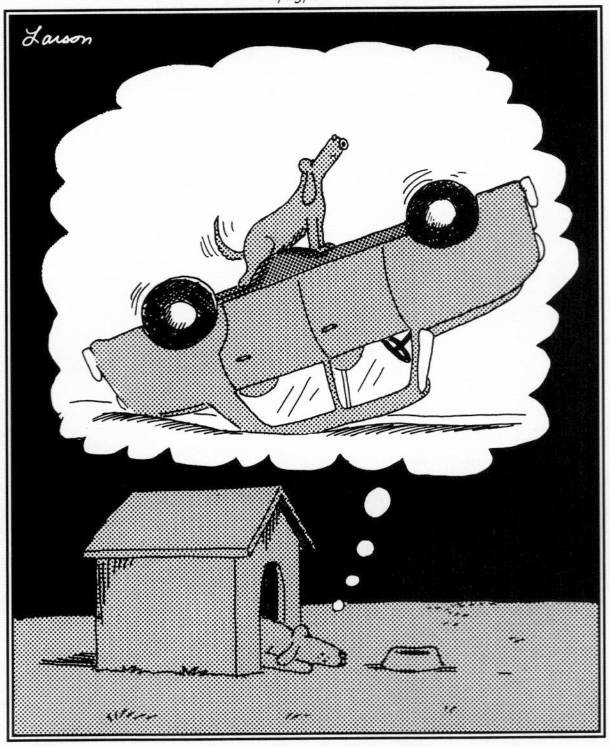
Larson

When car chasers dream

Established 1837

The Pantagraph

Bill Wills
Managing Editor

Feb. 12, 1988

Robert Duffy
Vice President/
National Sales Director
Universal Press Syndicate
4900 Main St.
Kansas City, Mo. 64112

Dear Bob:

Today, for the second time in less than a month, I feel like I got blind-sided by a comic, specifically Gary Larson's Far Side.

Comics are something that we have routinely handled through a clerical person.

We can no longer do that with Larson. Effective today, all Far Side cartoons will be run through an editor. What a waste of time and talent because Larson seems to have forgotten that good taste is just as important as good artwork and witty remarks in a family newspaper.

We caught the first comic because an editor happened to be going by the comics page and saw the dog on the overturned car with sexual overtones. We had our artists take care of that and shrugged it off as one of those things open to interpretation. However, today's cartoon of a child in a bottle is too close on the heals of the first incident to ignore.

We're not talking censorship of interpretation, we're talking about not purposely offending readers.

The next such comic may be considered our 30-day t.f. cancelation notice.

I am not going to waste valuable time checking on comics and spending time on the telephone with irate readers.

I am a fan of Larson's work, but I don't need any more headaches!

Sincerely,

Bill Wills
Managing Editor

301 West Washington Street • P.O. Box 2907 • Bloomington, Illinois 61702-2907 • 309/829-9411 • Toll-free in Illinois 800/233-6397

UNIVERSAL PRESS SYNDICATE

Dear Bill:

In retrospect, we should have altered the art on the January 25 release of "The Far Side." Neither Gary Larson, nor two editors here, read any sexual overtures into that cartoon. Blame it on naivete, or a lack of a prurient mind, but not on any desire to "purposely" offend readers.

As for the baby-in-the-bottle, we thought it was funny, and I still can't figure out why anyone was offended. Larson's humor is strange and serendipitous, but not perverted.

In either case, if we had thought readers would become irate, we would not have distributed the cartoons in question.

Best regards.

Sincerely,

Lee Salem
Editorial Director

4900 Main Street • Kansas City, Missouri 64112 • Phone 816/932-6600

1/28/88

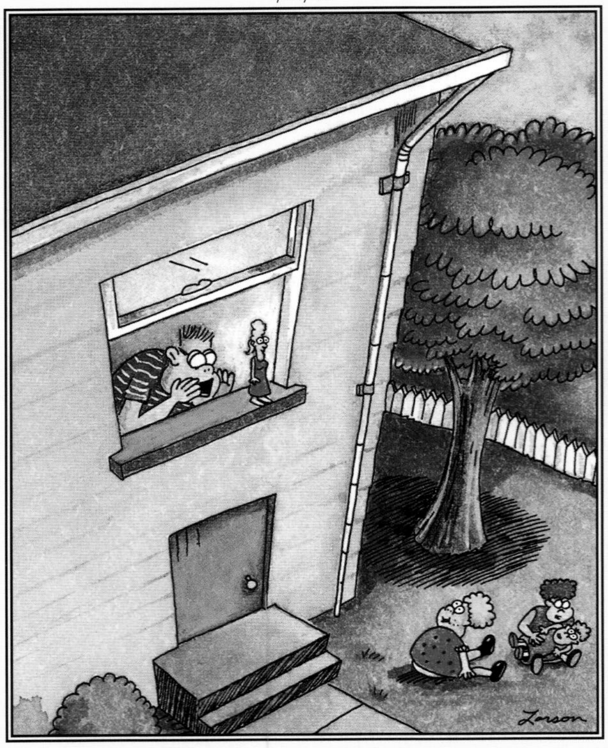
Larson

"Oh, my gosh! Linda! Linda! ... I think your Barbie's contemplating suicide!"

1/30/88

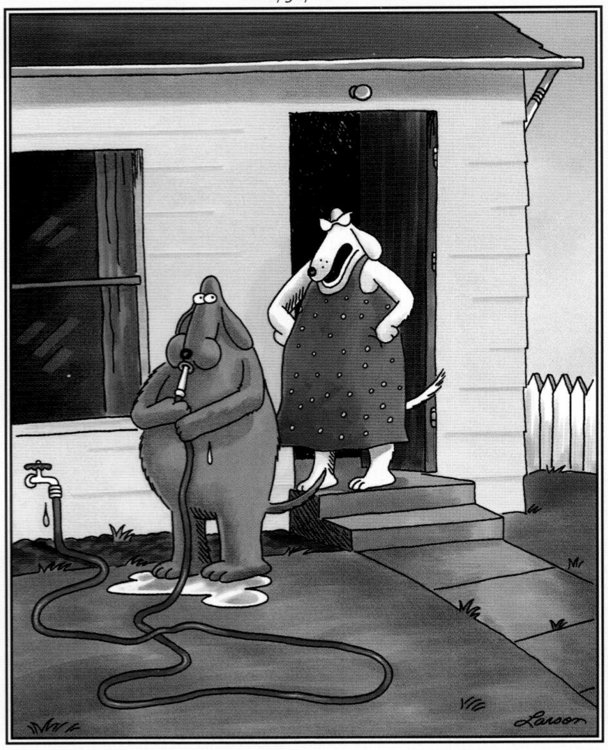
Larson

"So! Planning on roaming the neighborhood with some of your buddies today?"

1/29/88

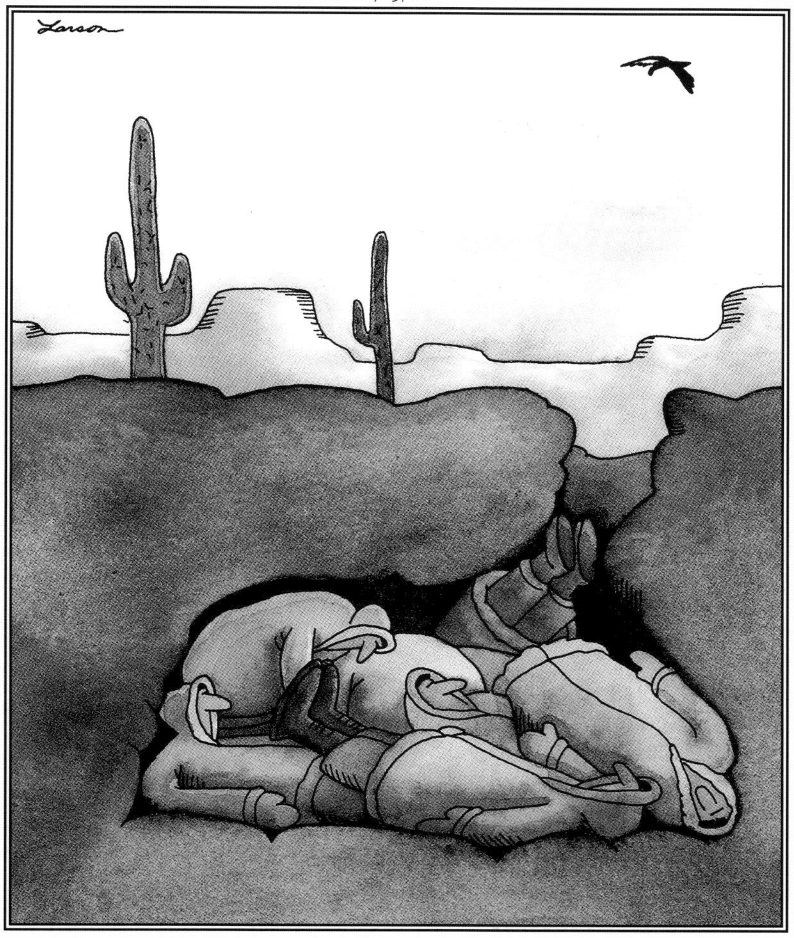
Larson

Hibernating Eskimos

1/31/88

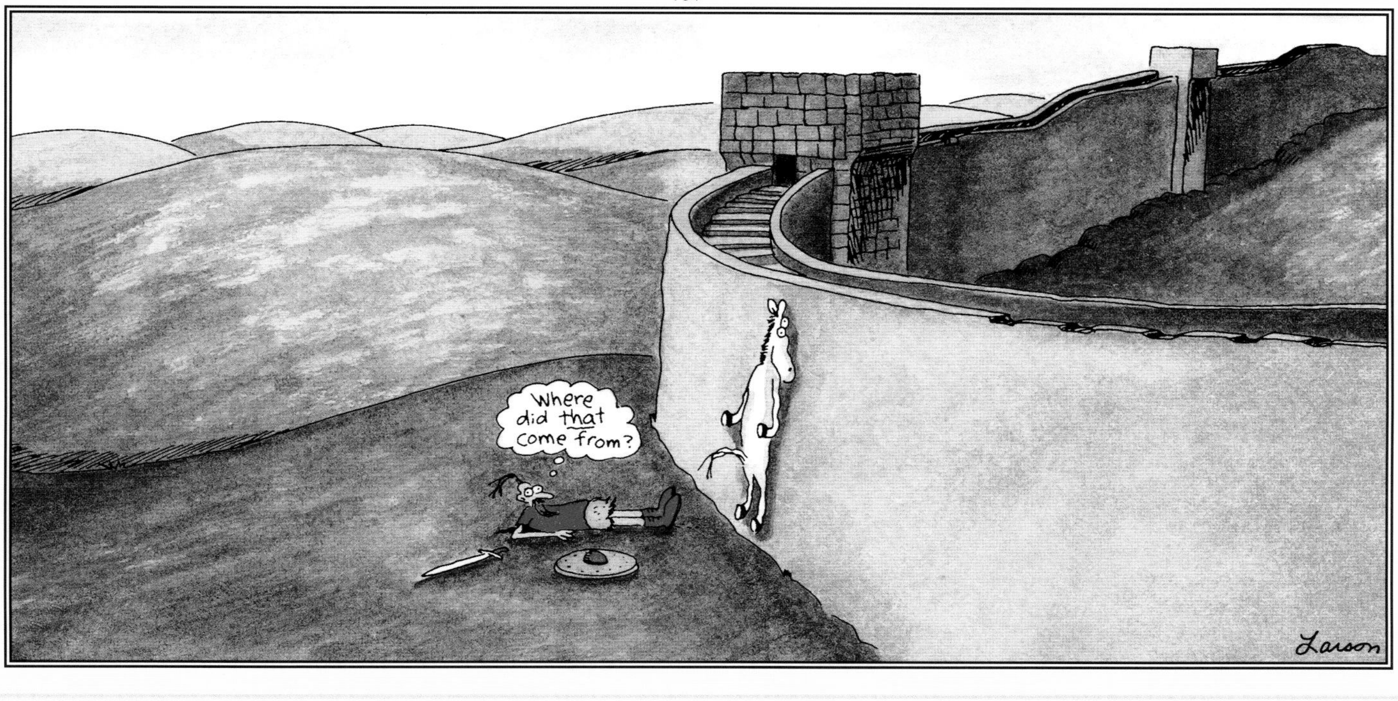
Where did that come from?
Larson

Circa 300 B.C.: The first barbarian invader reaches the Great Wall of China.

2/2/88

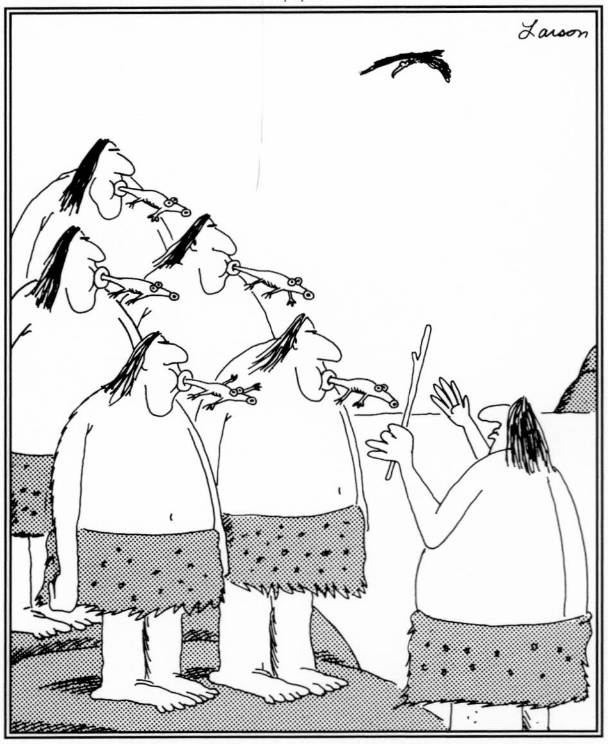
Larson

Early kazoo bands

2/3/88

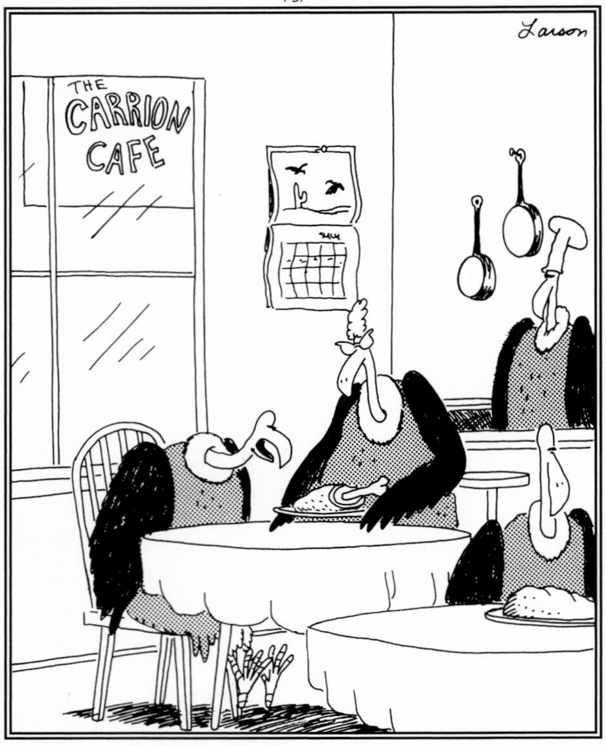
Larson
THE
CARRION
CAFE

"Saaaaaaay ... *this* doesn't look spoiled."

2/1/88

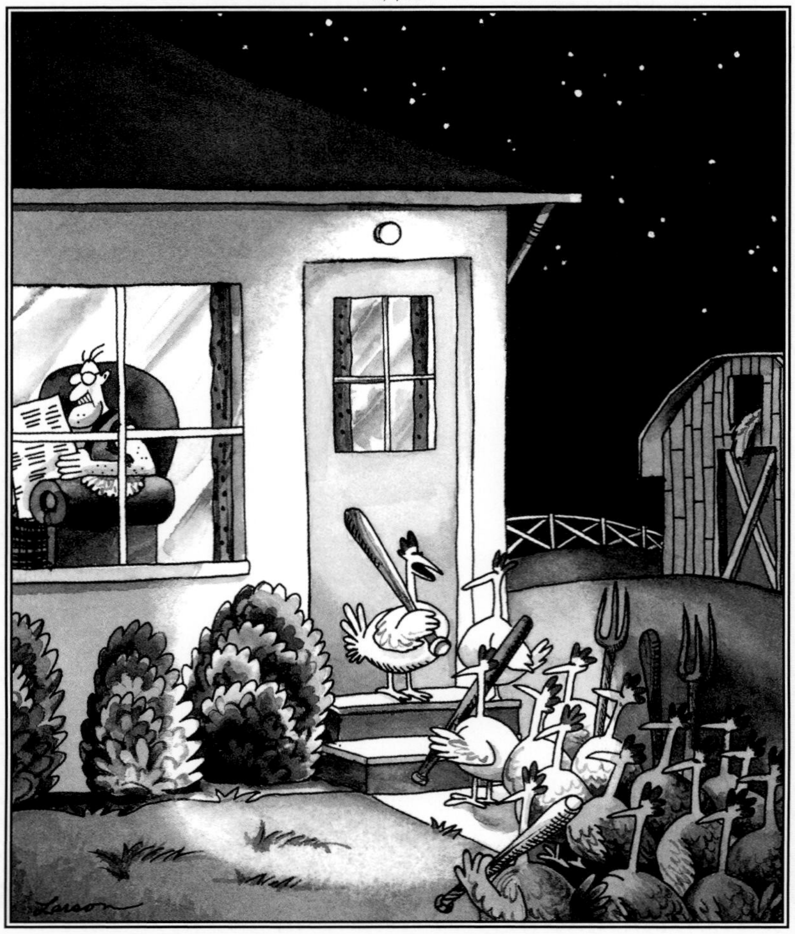
Larson

"Again? Why is it that the revolution always gets this far and then everyone just chickens out?"

2/5/88

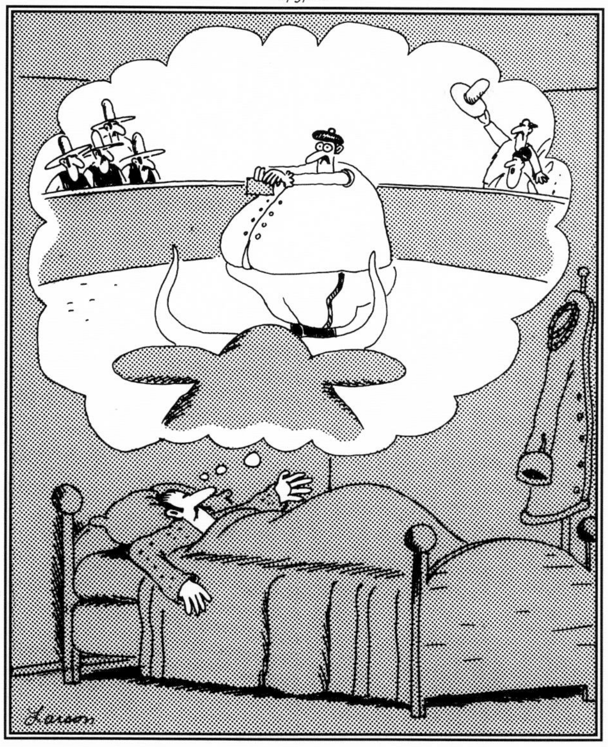

The matador's nightmare

2/8/88

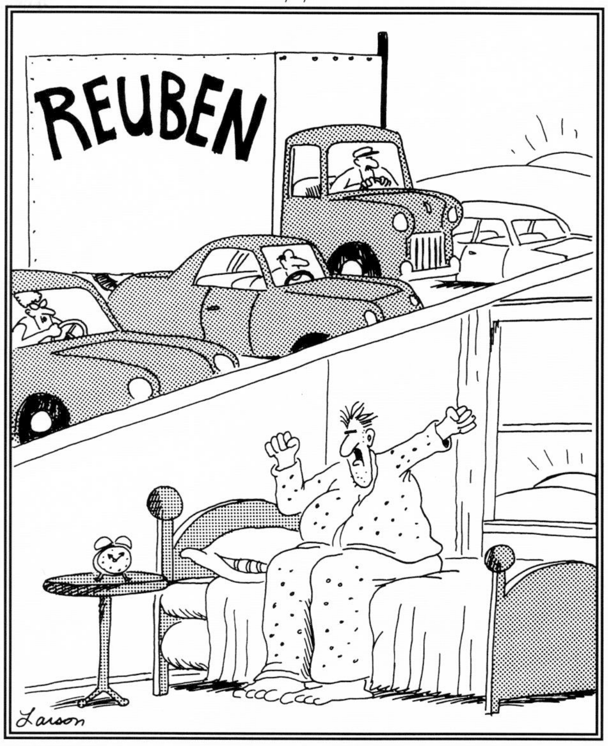
REUBEN

Out there, ominously moving toward its destiny, was a truck with Reuben's name on it.

2/11/88

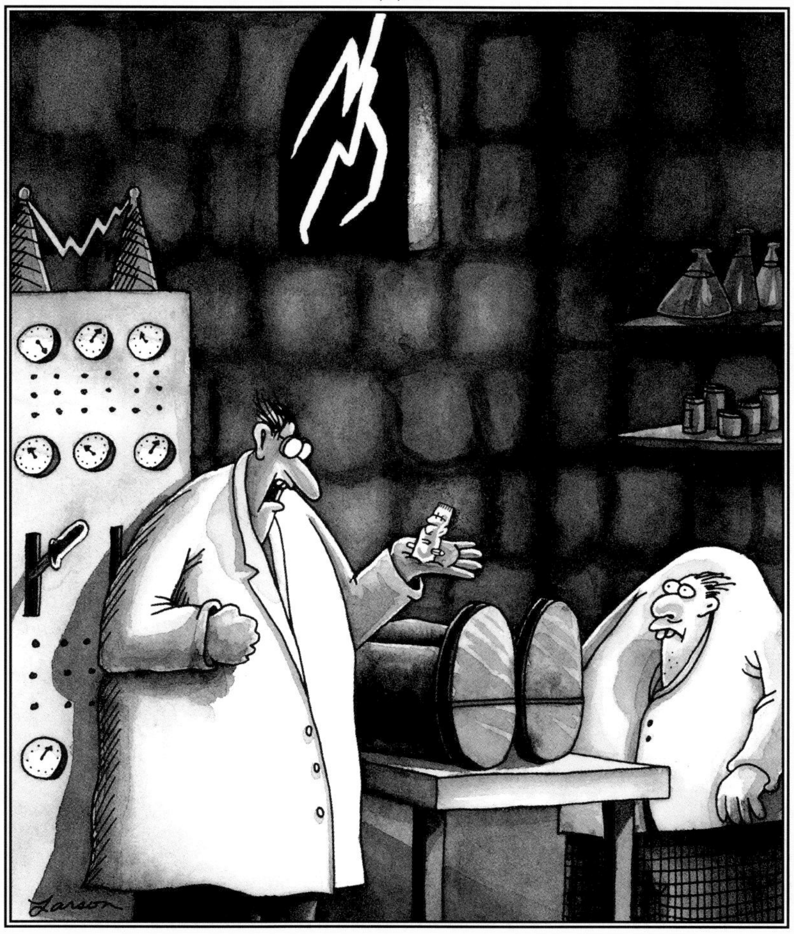

"For crying out loud, Igor! First there's that screw-up with the wrong brain business, and *now* you've let his head go through the wash in your pants pocket!"

2/7/88

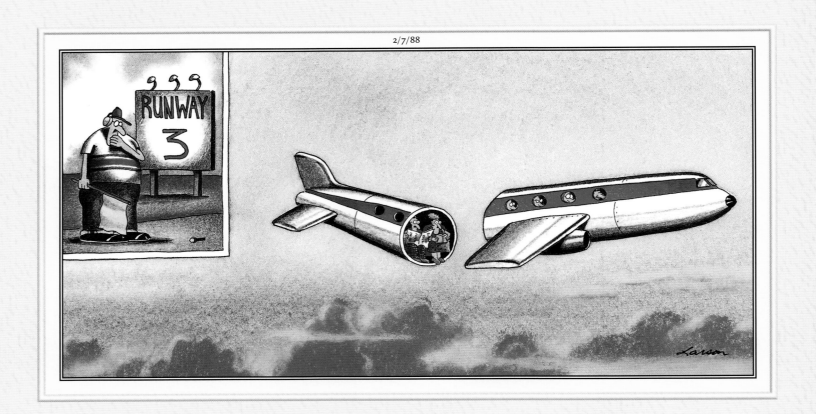

RUNWAY
3
Larson

2/4/88

Larson

When ornithologists are mutually attracted

2/10/88

Larson

"Ah, yes, Mr. Frischberg, I thought you'd come ... but which of us is the *real* duck, Mr. Frischberg, and not just an illusion?"

2/12/88

"Beats me how they did it ... I got the whole thing at a garage sale for five bucks—and that included the stand."

The Florida Times-Union, Jacksonville, Fla., 2/21/88

Gary Larson's Far Side goes too far this time

The Times-Union is a better newspaper than to be associated with Gary Larson and his Far Side smut! I've had enough! This is a letter of protest!

I read the Times-Union every morning and ignore the Far Side because I find it very distasteful and unedifying. However, on Feb. 12, it caught my eye and it totally disgusted me.

Larson, in his sick art, depicted a "pickled" or "preserved" child in a bottle on display on a fireplace mantel as a conversation piece! How utterly revolting! Larson's expressions of himself are dehumanizing, demoralizing and insulting. I am offended, not only for myself and children, but for all the other decent folks out there who patronize the Times-Union and don't have the time to let the newspaper know how they feel

Unfortunately, there are too many sick minds in this world. None of us are perfect for we all fall short of the glory of God. But Larson is showing us all the inside of his mind by communicating to the world his Far Side material.

If Larson must earn a living by selling his material, I suggest that he peddle it elsewhere. There are plenty of junk publications that his material would appeal to. Does the Times-Union really need it? It is a quality publication. I hope it is kept that way for everyone's sake.

DENNIS HARNISCH
Jacksonville Beach

Herald-Dispatch, Huntington, W.V.
2/22/88

Insensitive comic

To the editor:

"The Far Side" cartoon in The Herald-Dispatch on Friday, Feb. 12, was a perfect example of today's growing insensitivity to human life.

The cartoon depicted a man boasting to his friend about his "five bucks" garage sale find. The garage sale purchase happened to be an infant in a corked bottle which the man had placed conspicuously on his mantel in his living room. This cartoon was most abusive to children and most distasteful to those who view human life in all forms as sacred and priceless.

Children are naturally attracted to the comics. Morally sound lessons should be taught there.

Mary Meehan

2/14/88

Metamorphosis nightclubs

2/9/88

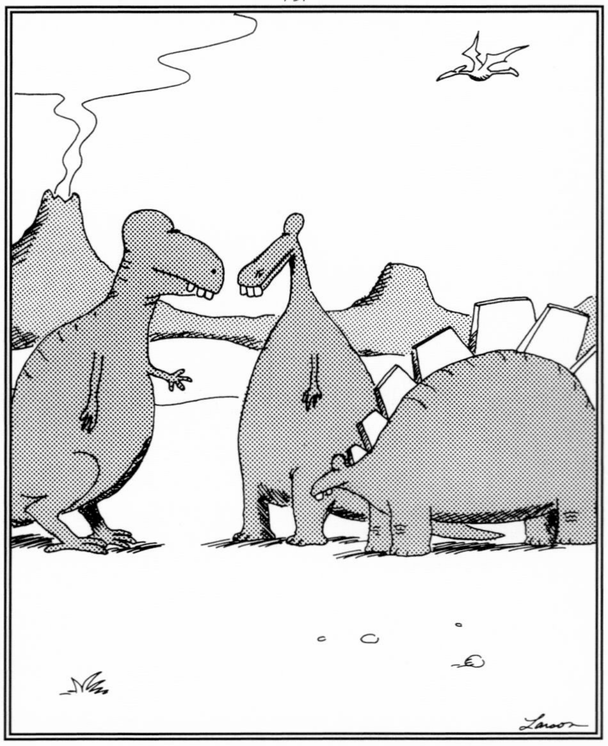

Dinosaur nerds

2/13/88

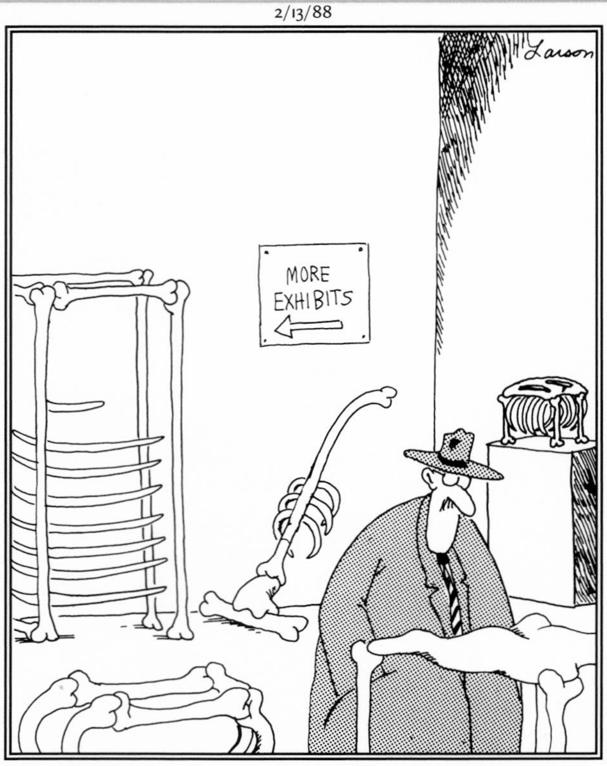
MORE EXHIBITS

In the Hall of Fossil Appliances

2/6/88

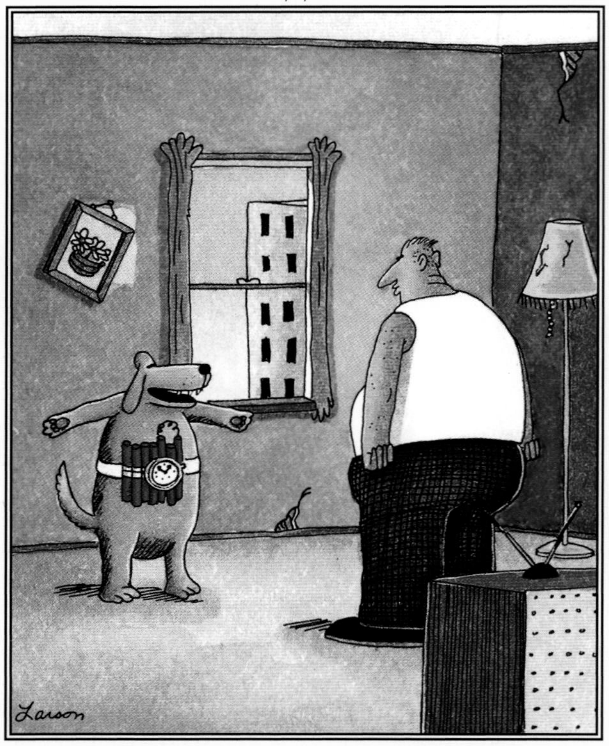

"Hey! You wanna kick me? Go ahead! C'mon, tough guy! Cat got your tongue? Maybe he took your whole *brain!* ... C'mon! KICK ME!"

2/16/88

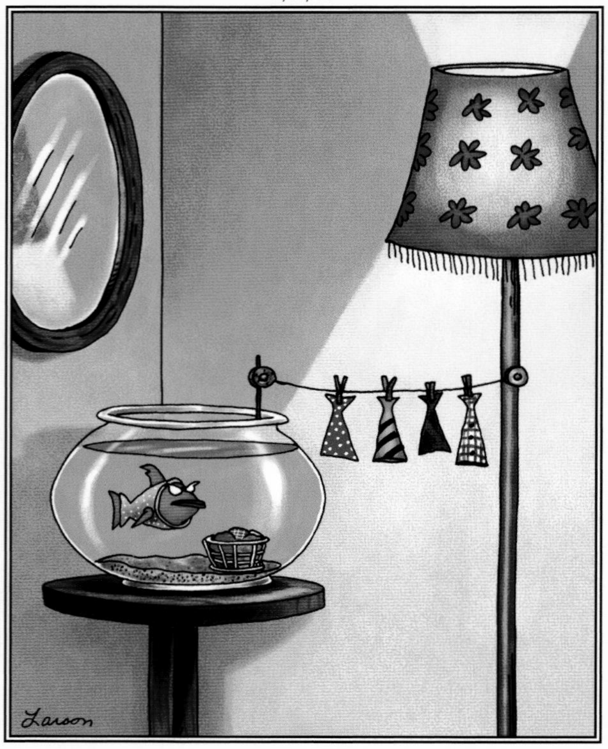

2/15/88

Gargoyle socks

2/17/88

Miserable little monsters.

2/18/88

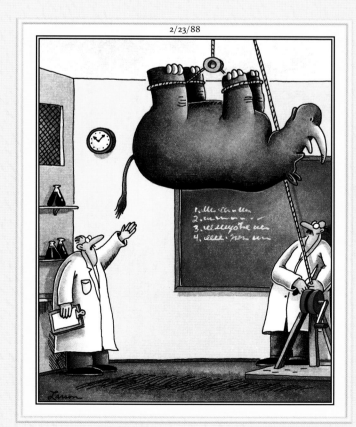

"Well, let's see—so far, I've got rhythm and I've got music. ... Actually, who could ask for anything more?"

2/23/88

Testing whether or not rhinos land on their feet.

2/19/88

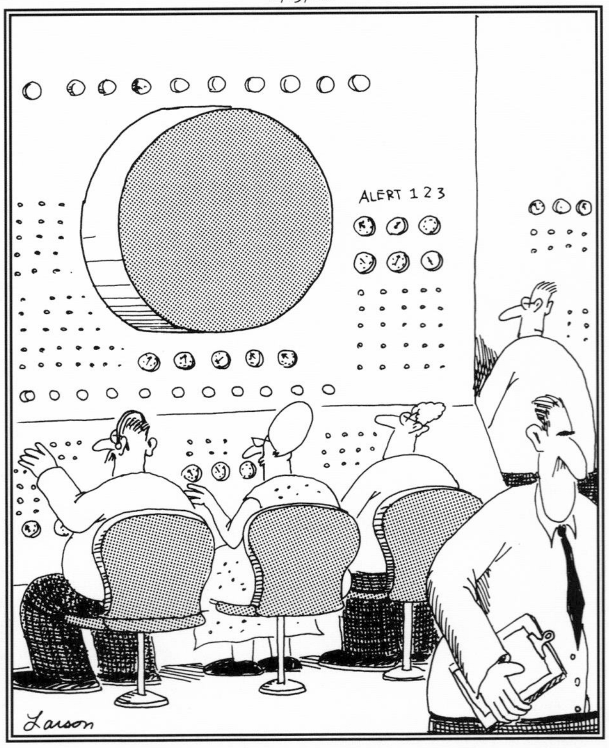
ALERT 1 2 3
Larson

One day, Irwin knew, he was just going to have to push that big button.

2/20/88

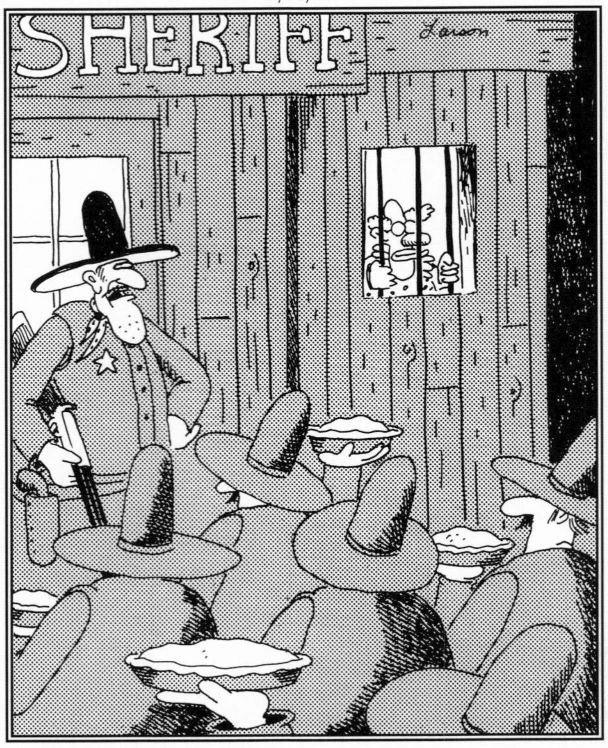
SHERIFF
Larson

"Look, I know you folks are lookin' for revenge—but there'll be no 'pie-for-a-pie' justice in *my* town!"

2/22/88

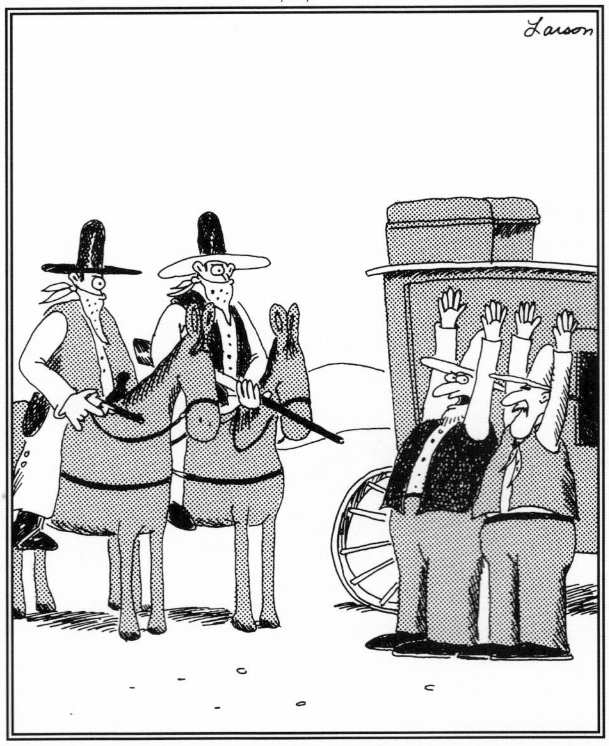
Larson

"Dollar to a doughnut it's them Cyclops brothers again."

2/24/88

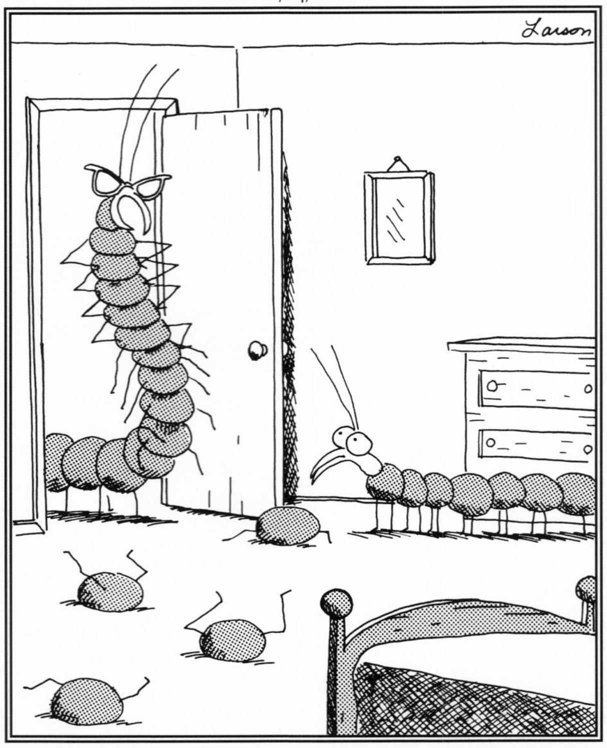
Larson

"Just look at this room—body segments everywhere!"

2/21/88

In the quiet of the early dawn, before the village had awakened, Frank and Vern removed the fire god's emerald eye and fled the island—not calculating how soon the inhabitants would notice their defiled temple.

2/25/88

"Wow! Now Ed and Carl are gone. ... Seems like lately we've been dropping like ourselves."

2/27/88

"I'm serious this time, Norton. ... Get the theme from *Mr. Ed* out of your system or I'll kill you as you sleep!"

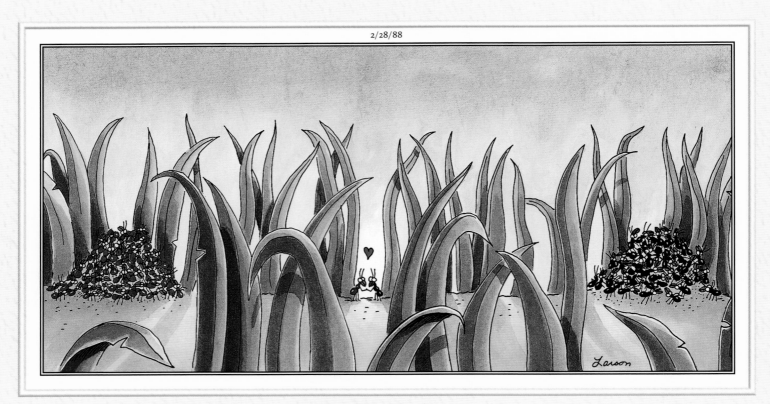

2/28/88

Larson

Romeo and Juliant

2/26/88

Larson
Java man
Peking man
Cro-Magnon man
Jazz man

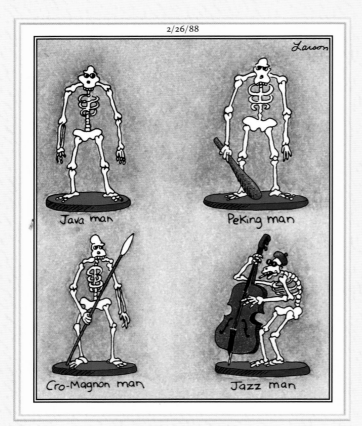

Hominid reconstructions

2/29/88

Larson

"Green blood? I *hate* green blood."

3/2/88

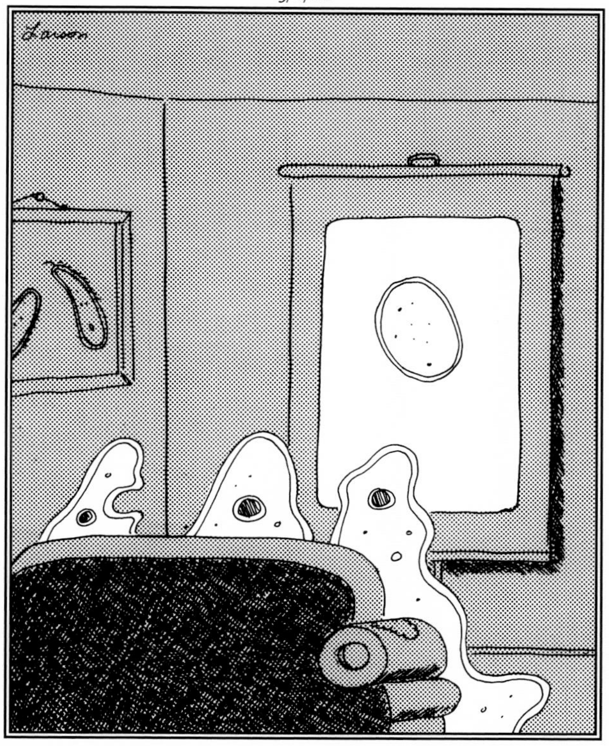

"No, wait! *That's* not Uncle Floyd! Who is that? ... Crimony, I think it's just an air bubble!"

3/3/88

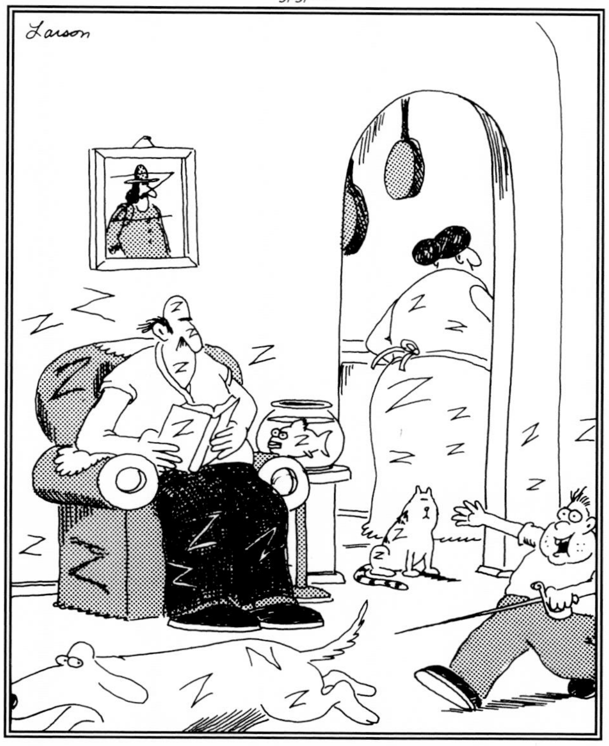

Although troubled as a child, Zorro, as is well known, ultimately found his niche in history.

3/6/88

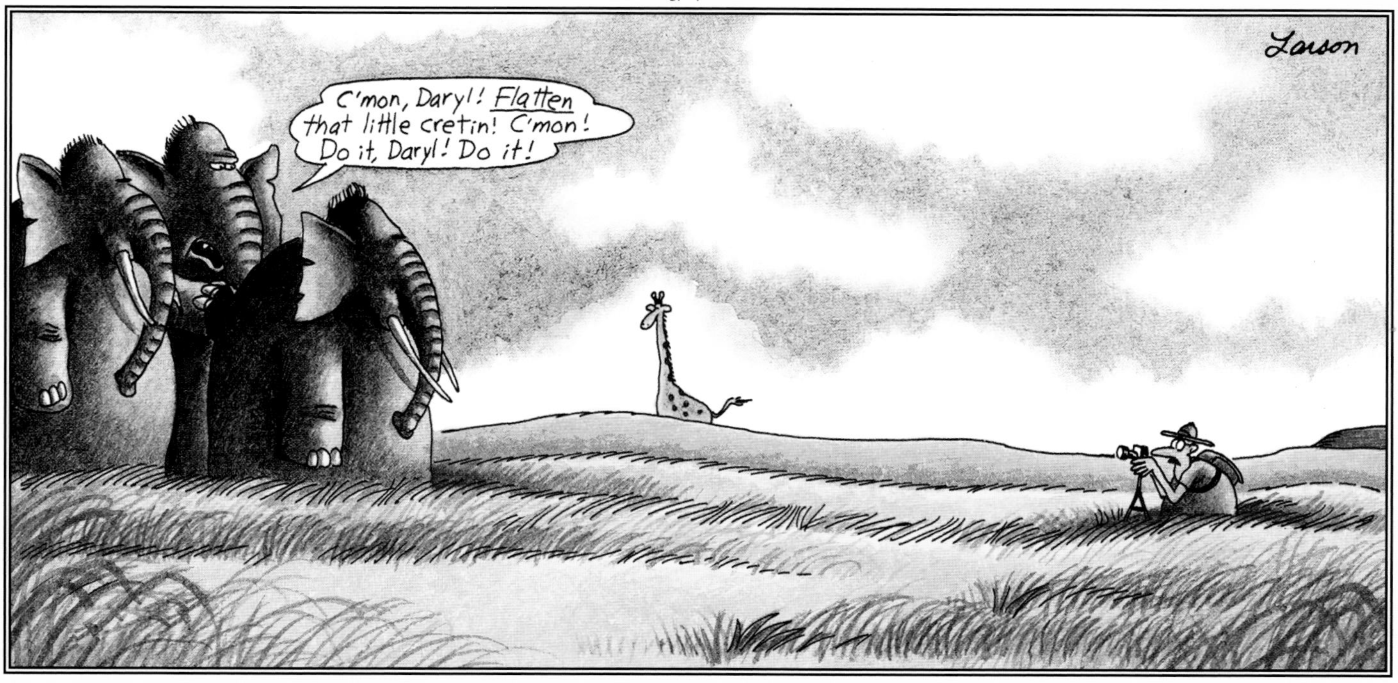
C'mon, Daryl! Flatten that little cretin! C'mon! Do it, Daryl! Do it!

Elephant peer pressure

3/1/88

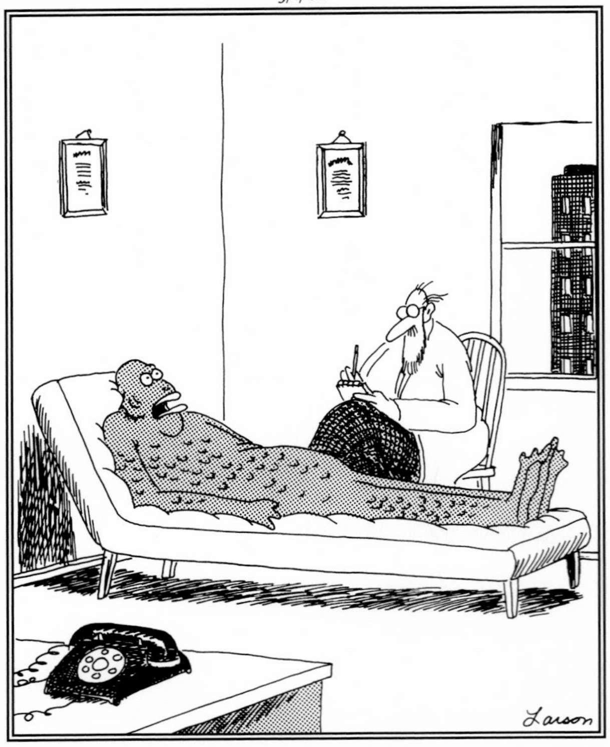

"Sure, I'm a creature—and I can accept that ... but lately it seems I've been turning into a miserable creature."

3/4/88

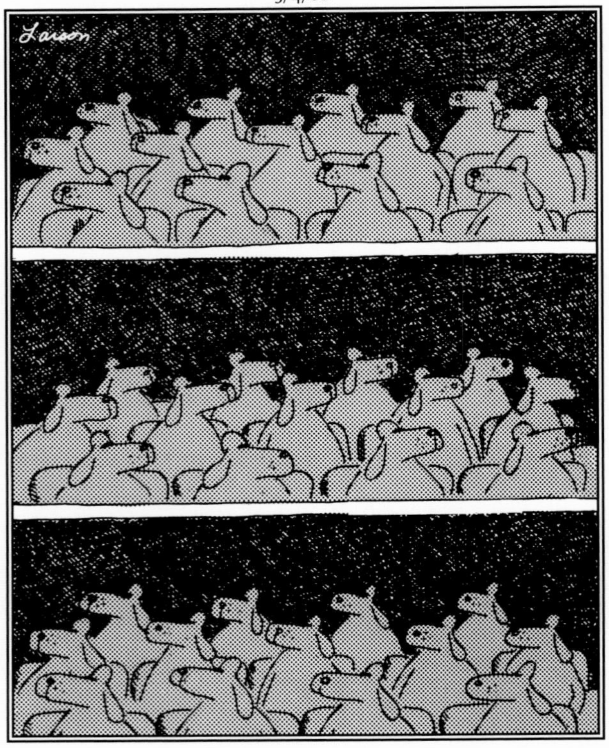

At the popular dog film *Man Throwing Sticks*

3/7/88

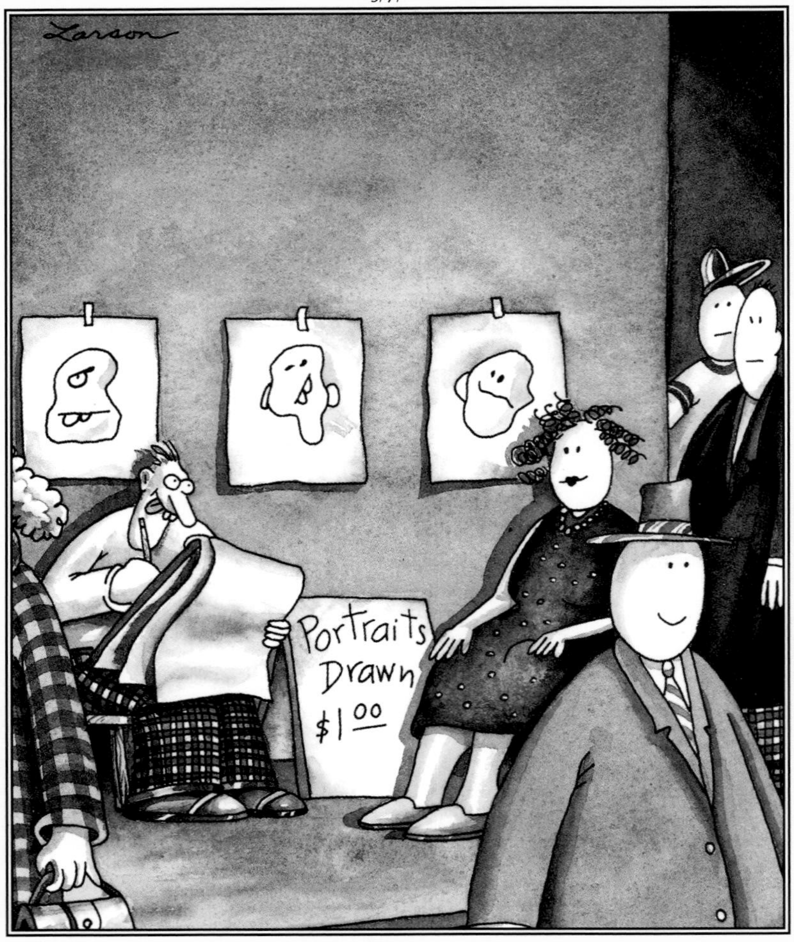
Portraits
Drawn
$1.00

3/10/88

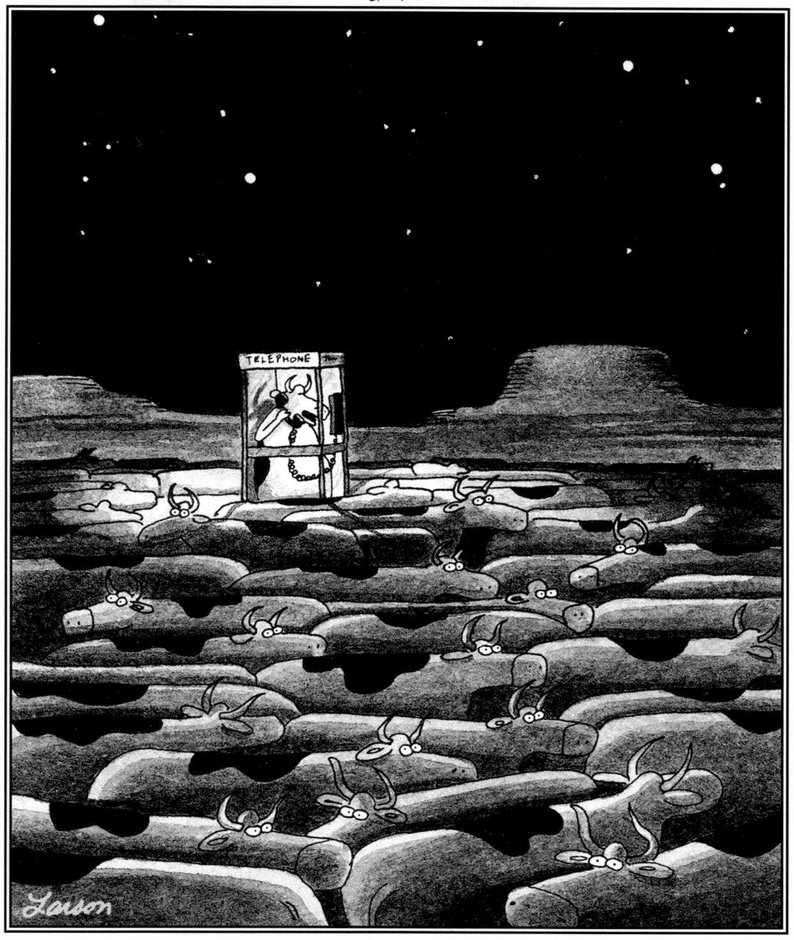
TELEPHONE
Larson

"Listen, Mom ... I just wanted you to know I'm okay. The stampede seems about over—although everyone's still a little spooked. Yeah, I know ... I miss the corral."

3/5/88

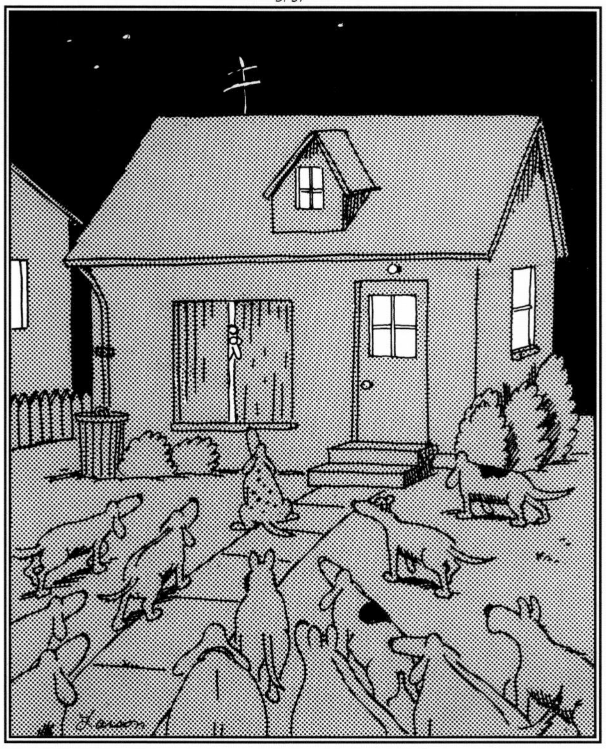
Larson

Like moths to a light, the neighborhood dogs were all drawn by Emile's uncontrollable fear.

3/9/88

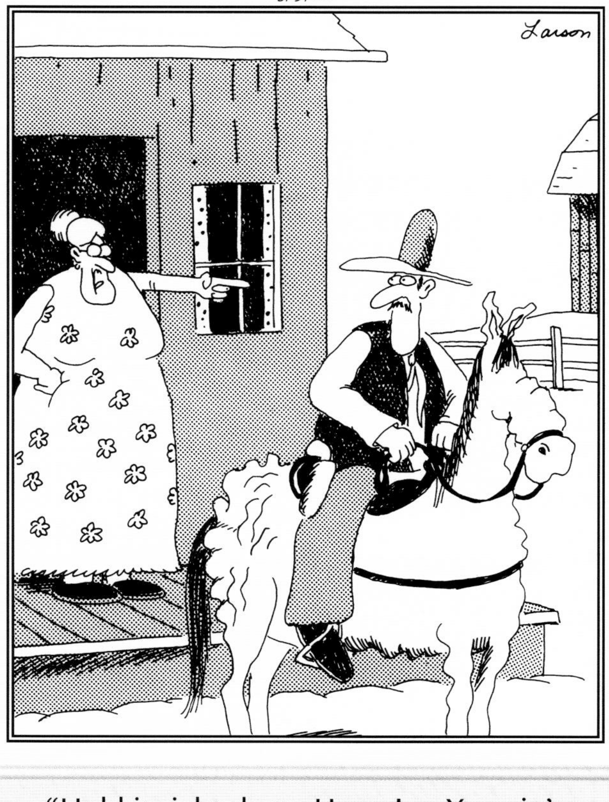
Larson

"Hold it right there, Henry! ... You ain't plannin' on takin' that wrinkled horse into town, are you?"

3/8/88

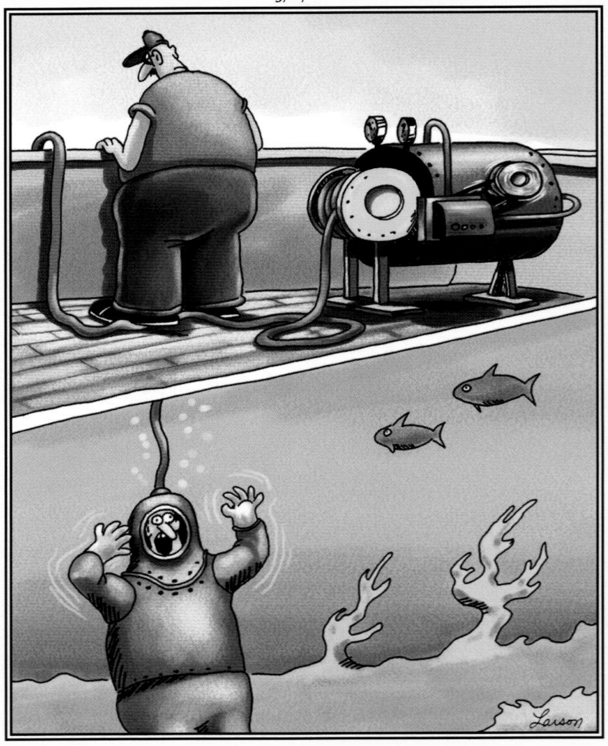
Larson

3/14/88

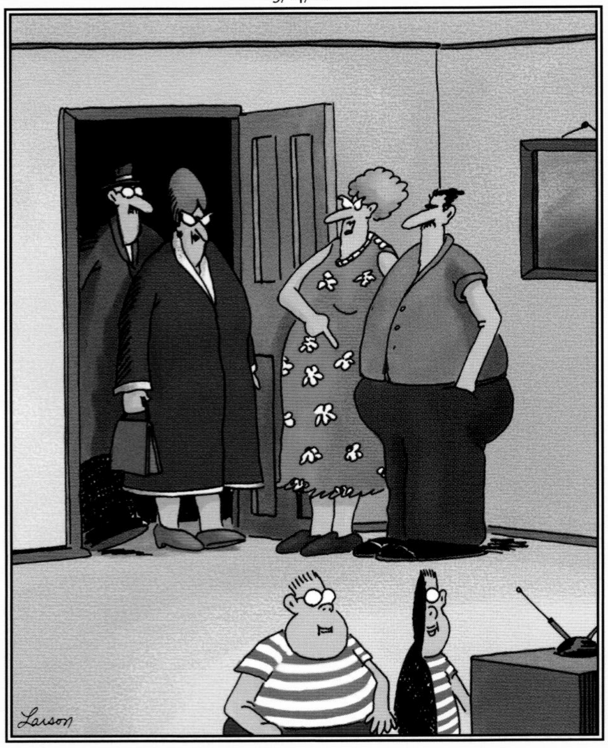
Larson

"Bob and Ruth! Come on in. ... Have you met Russell and Bill, our 1.5 children?"

3/11/88

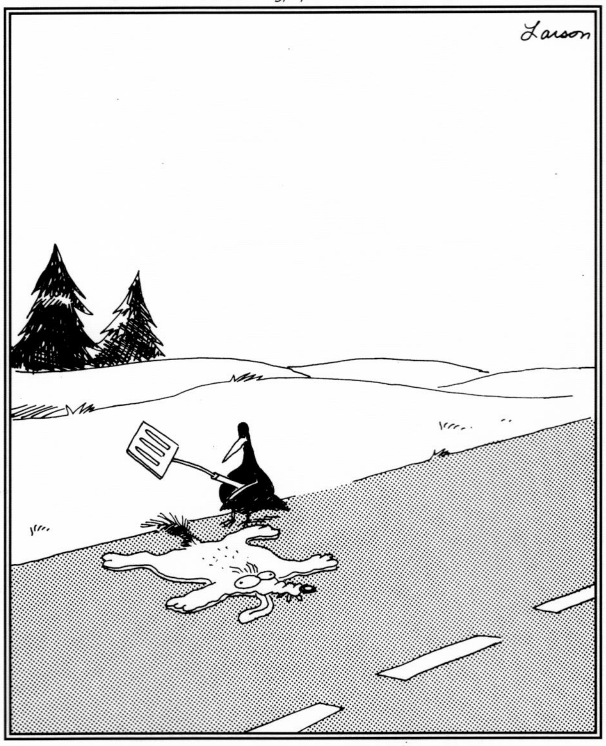
Larson

Secret tools of the common crow

3/12/88

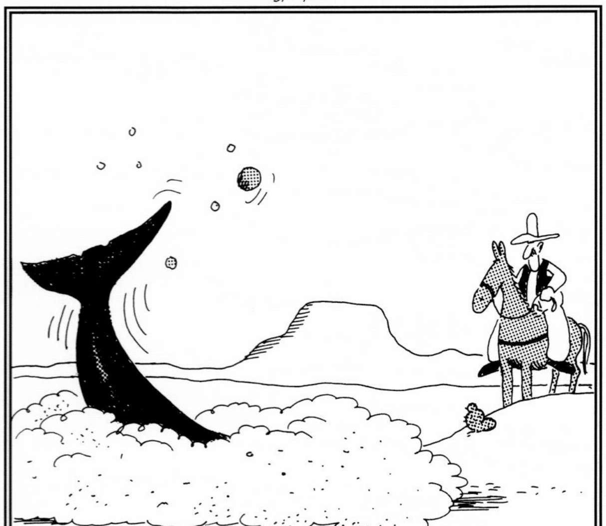
Larson

Whale dust baths

3/13/88

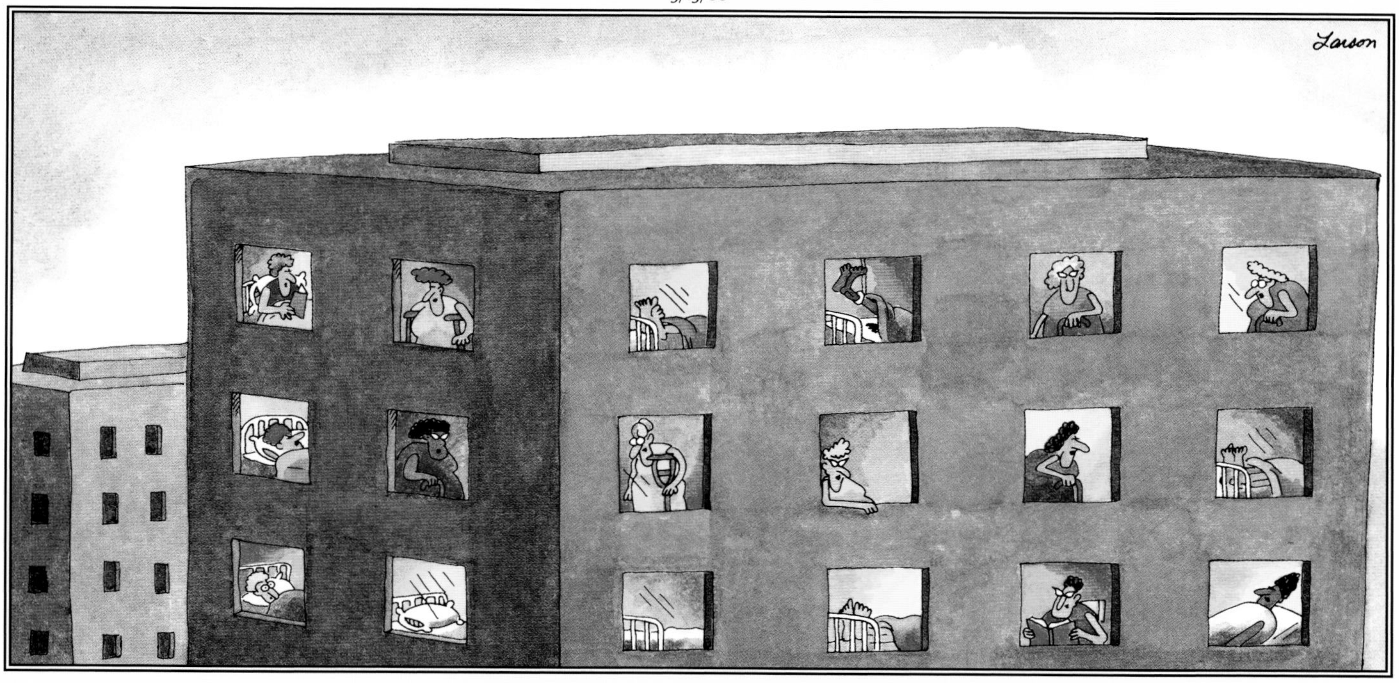
Larson

At the hospital for mothers whose children stepped on sidewalk cracks

3/16/88

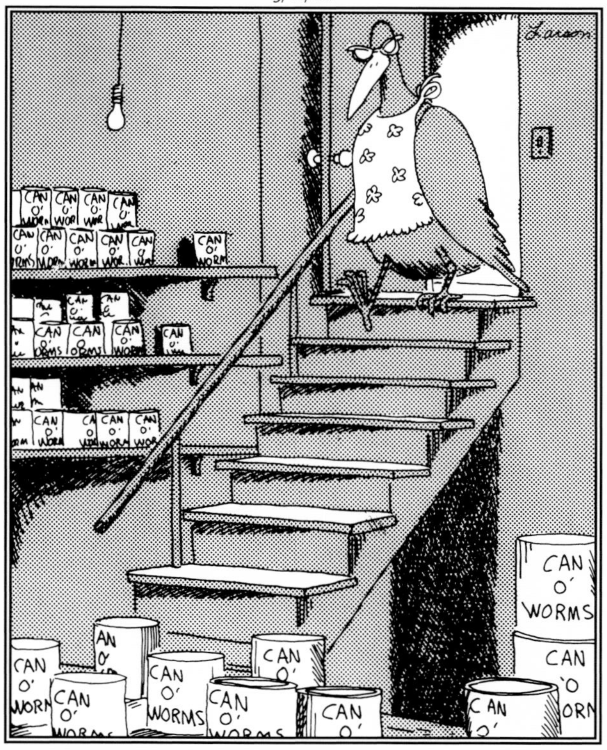
Larson
CAN O' WORMS

Bird cellars

3/19/88

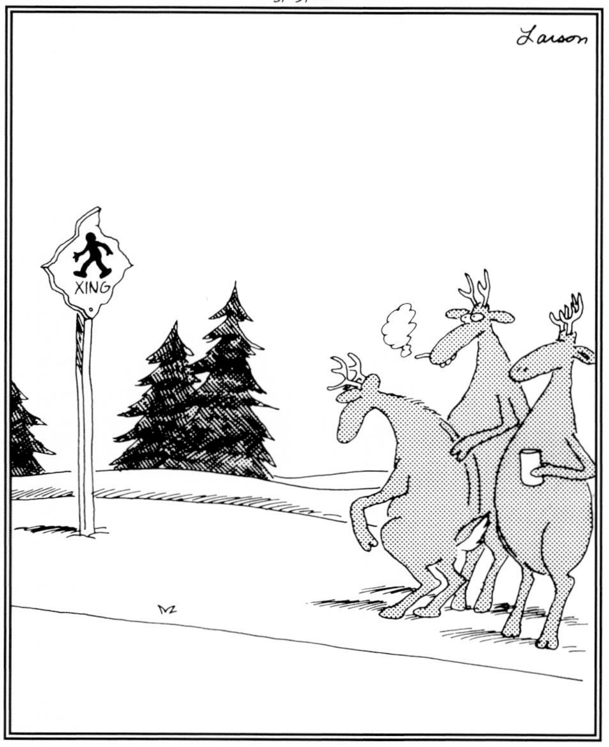
Larson
XING

Deer vandals

3/15/88

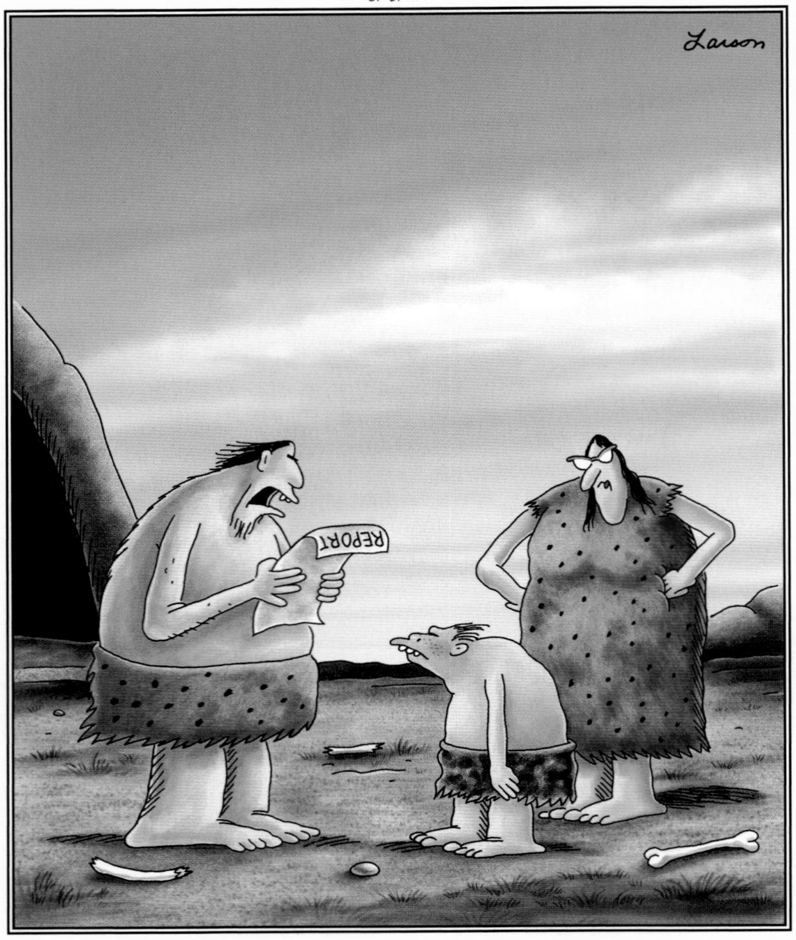
REPORT
Larson

"Oh, look, this get better ...'F' in history!
You even flunk something not happen yet?"

3/18/88

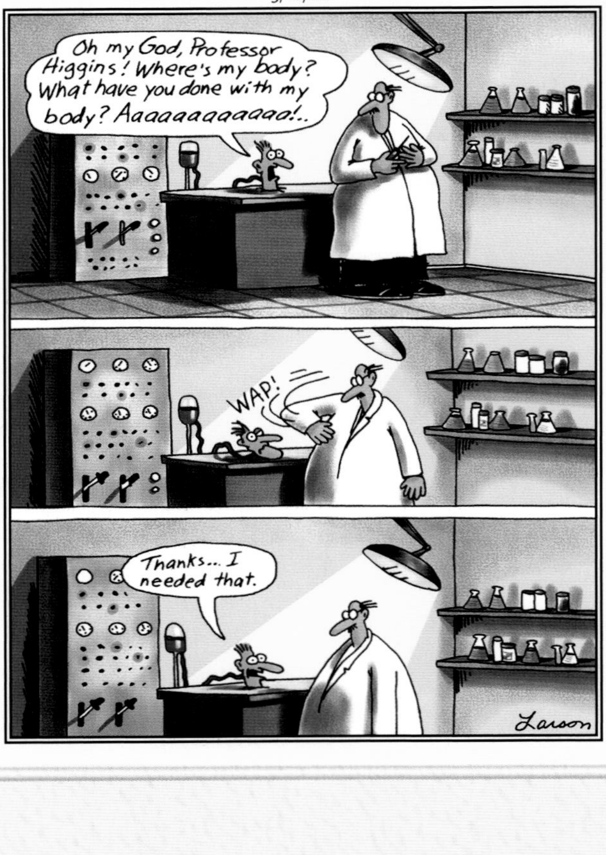
Oh my God, Professor Higgins! Where's my body? What have you done with my body? Aaaaaaaaaaaa!..
WAP!
Thanks... I needed that.
Larson

3/21/88

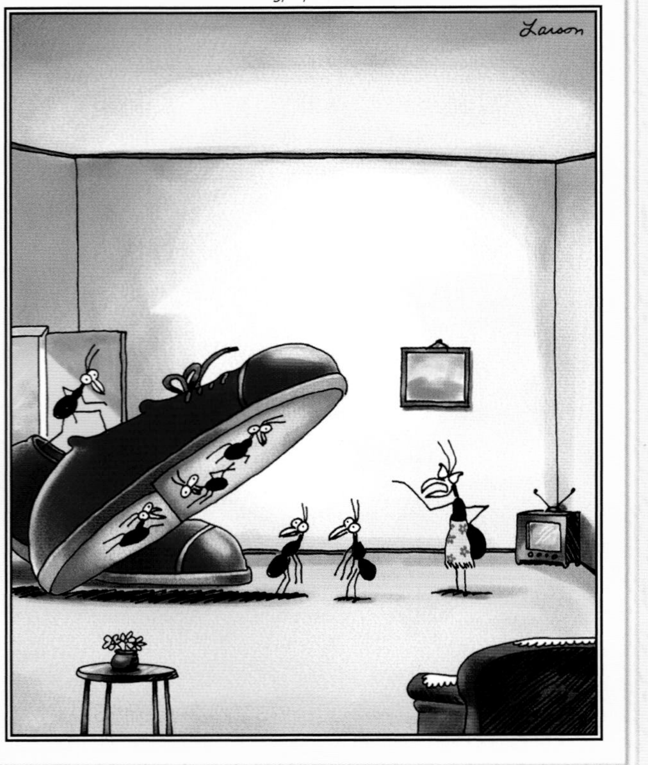
Larson

"Ernie! Look what you're doing—take those shoes off this instant!"

3/17/88

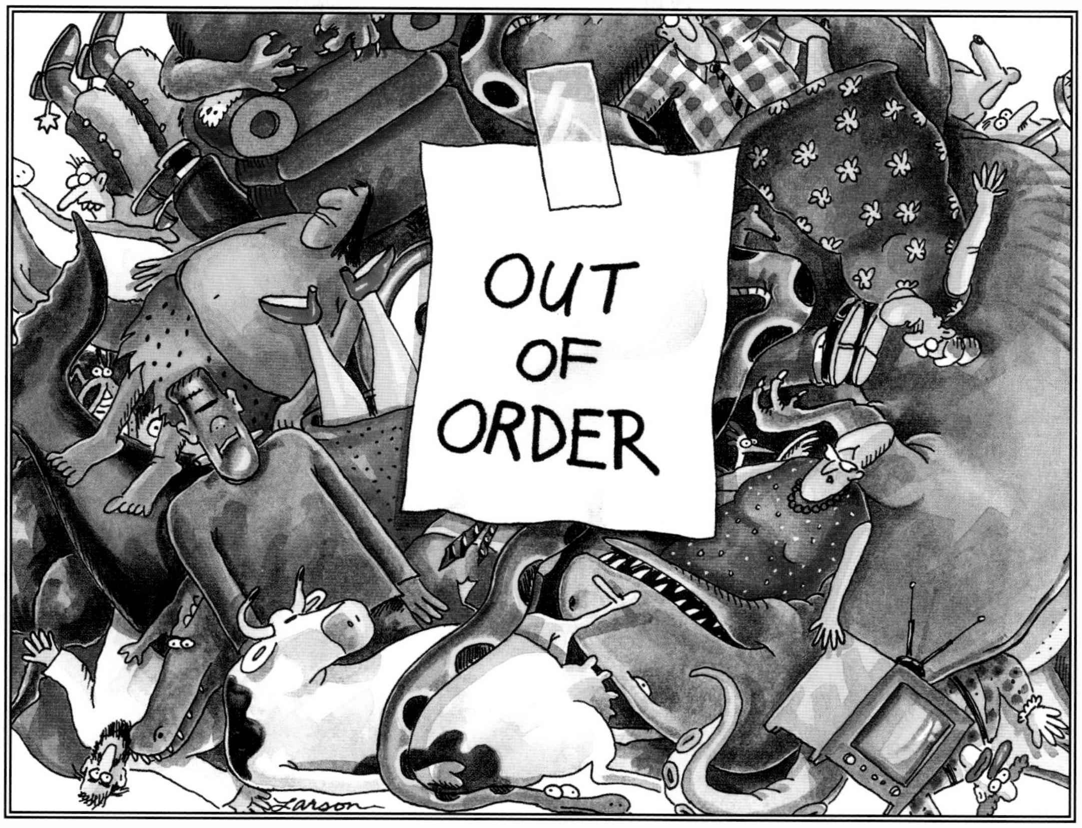
OUT
OF
ORDER
Larson

3/23/88

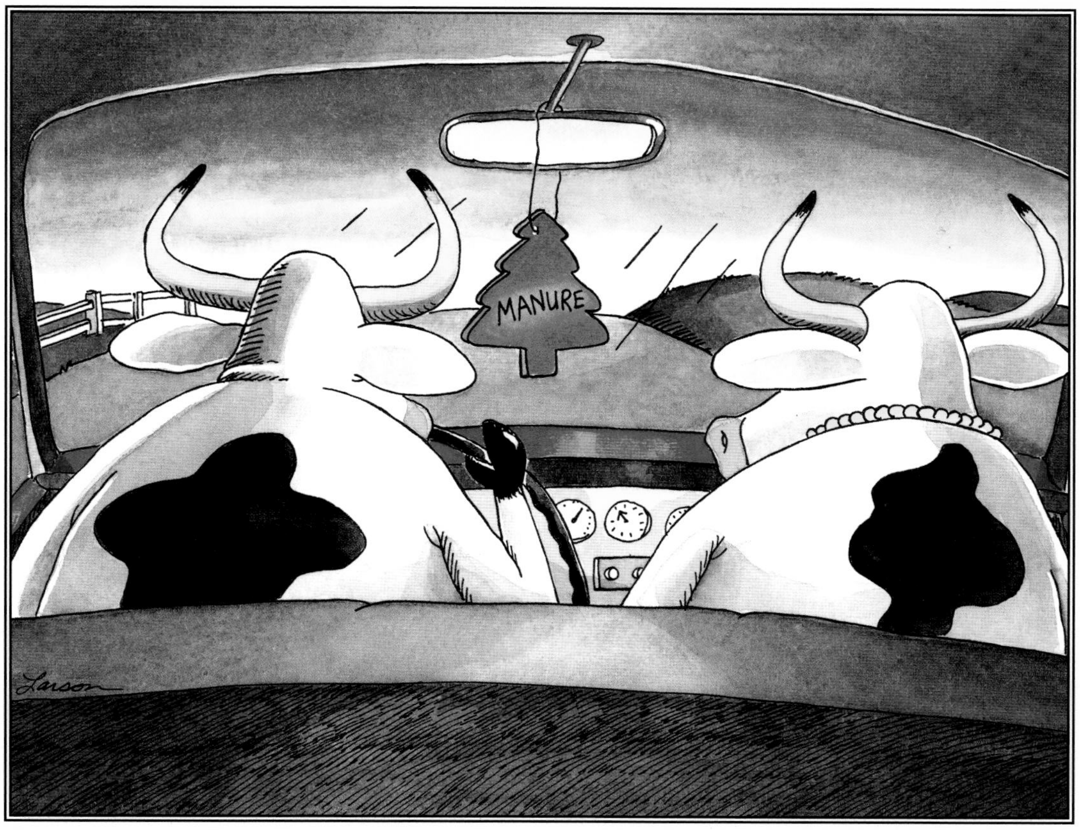
MANURE
Larson

3/20/88

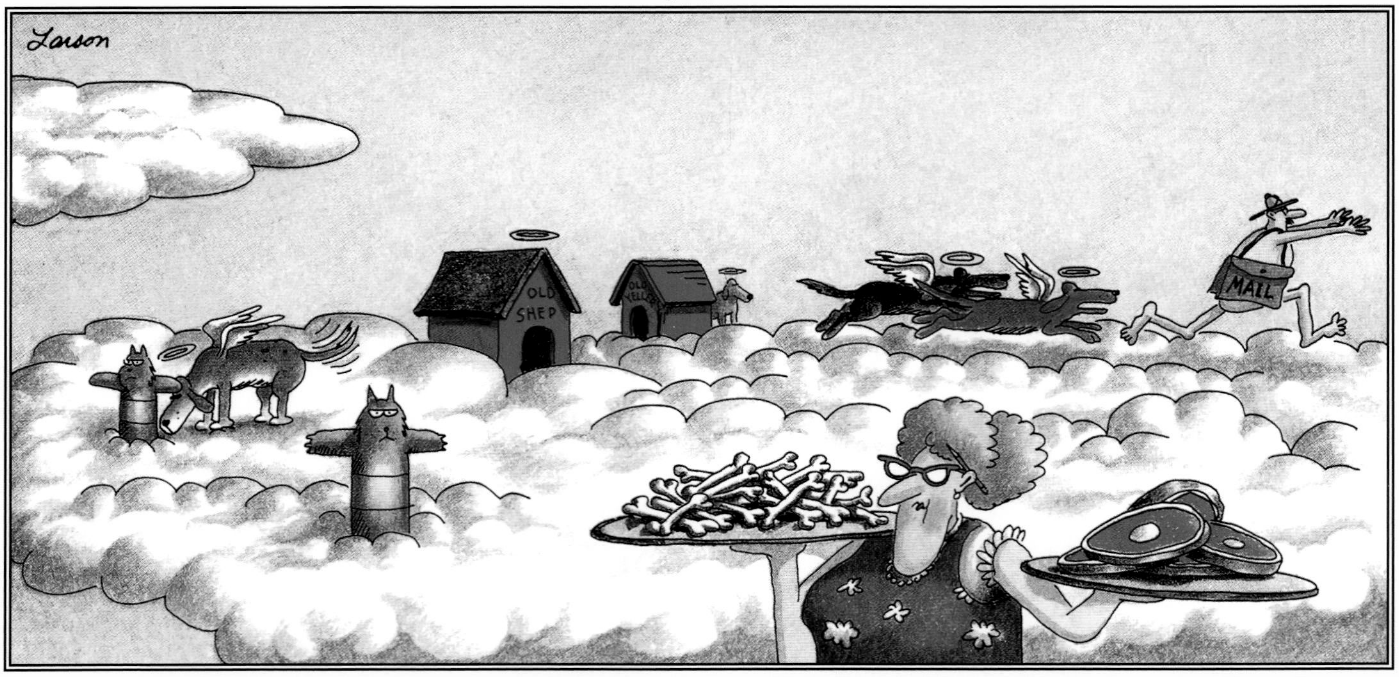
Larson
OLD SHEP
MAIL

Dog heaven

3/25/88

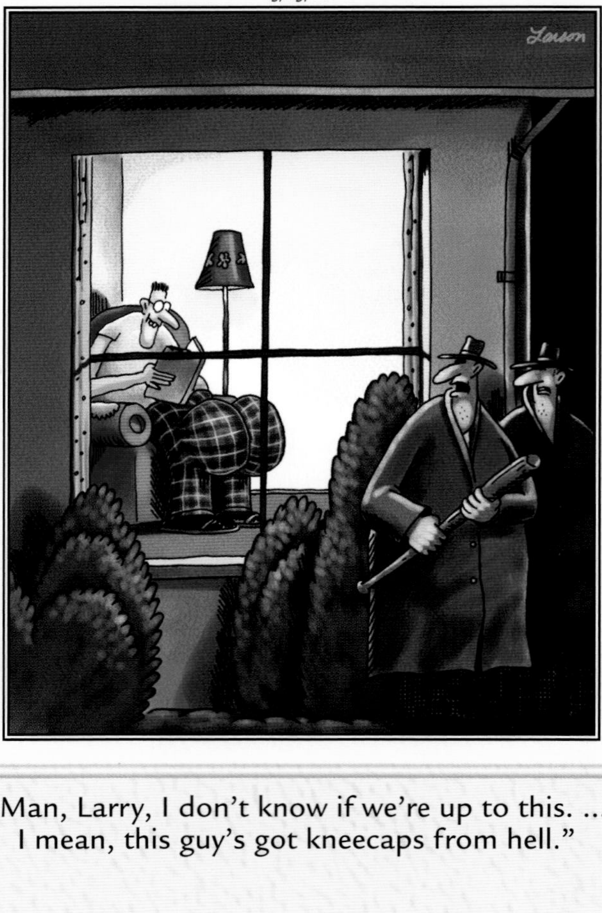
Larson

"Man, Larry, I don't know if we're up to this. ... I mean, this guy's got kneecaps from hell."

3/26/88

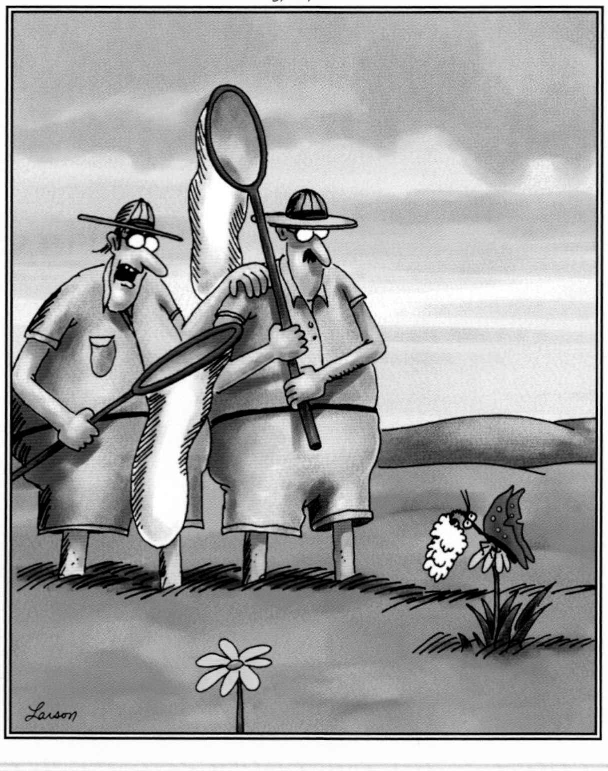
Larson

"Johnson, back off! It's an *Armandia lidderdalii*, all right—but it's rabid!"

3/30/88

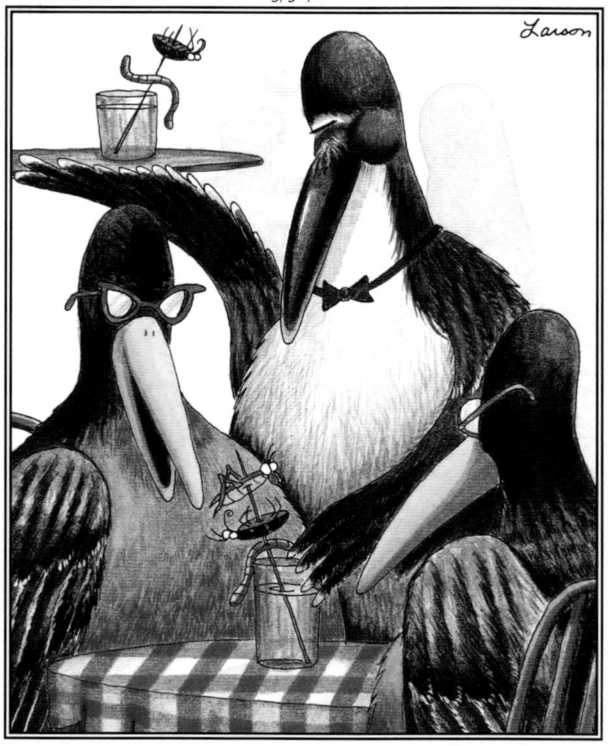

"Oh, my! Aren't *these* fancy drinks!"

3/28/88

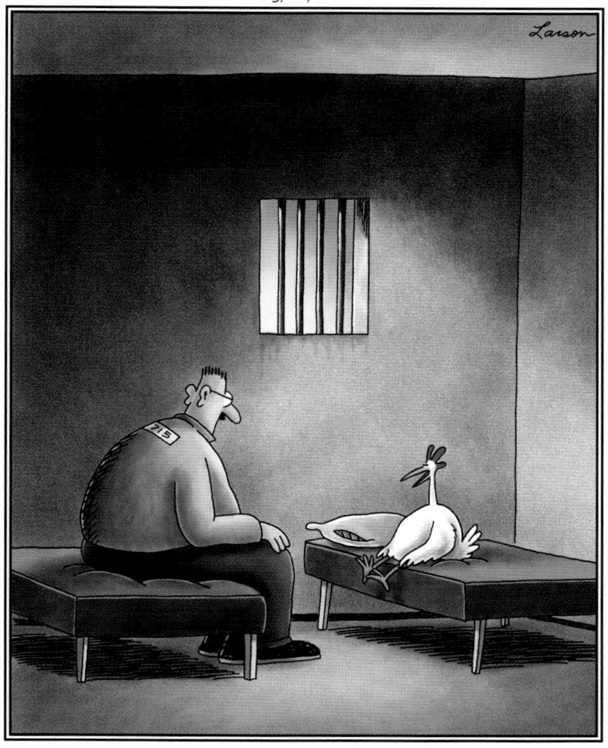

"So then, when Old MacDonald turned his back, I took that ax and with a whack whack here and a whack whack there, I finished him off."

3/27/88

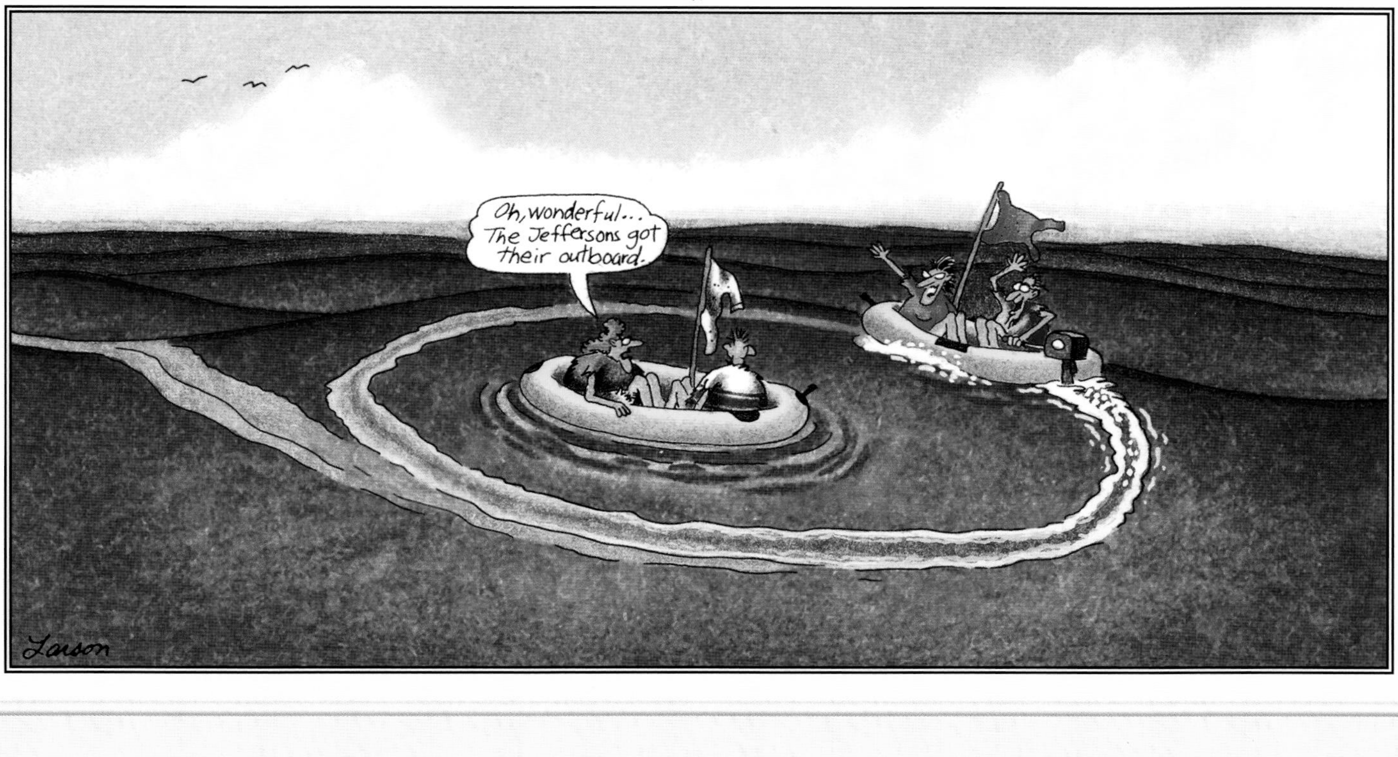
Oh, wonderful... The Jeffersons got their outboard.

3/22/88

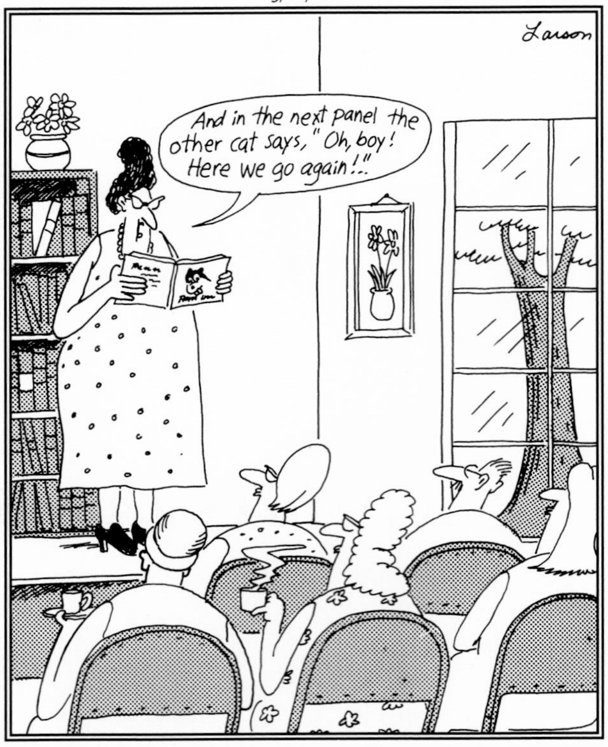
Larson
And in the next panel the other cat says, "Oh, boy! Here we go again!"

Cartoon readings

3/24/88

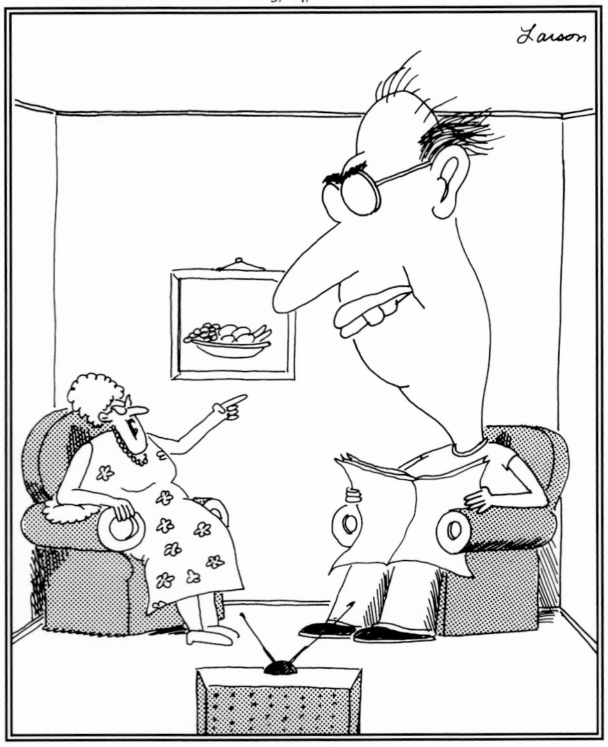
Larson

"Okay, here it is—I'm sick of your face, Ned."

3/29/88

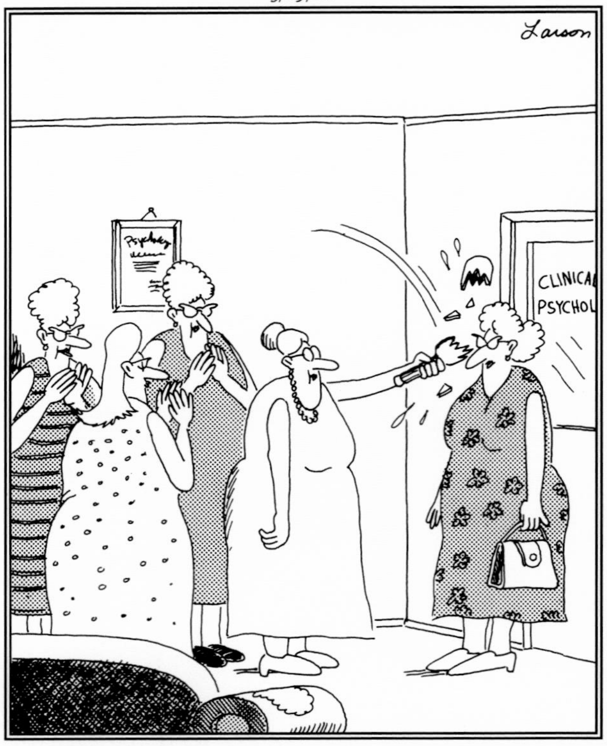
Larson
CLINICAL
PSYCHOL

Amidst congratulatory applause, Cindy leaves the group.

3/31/88

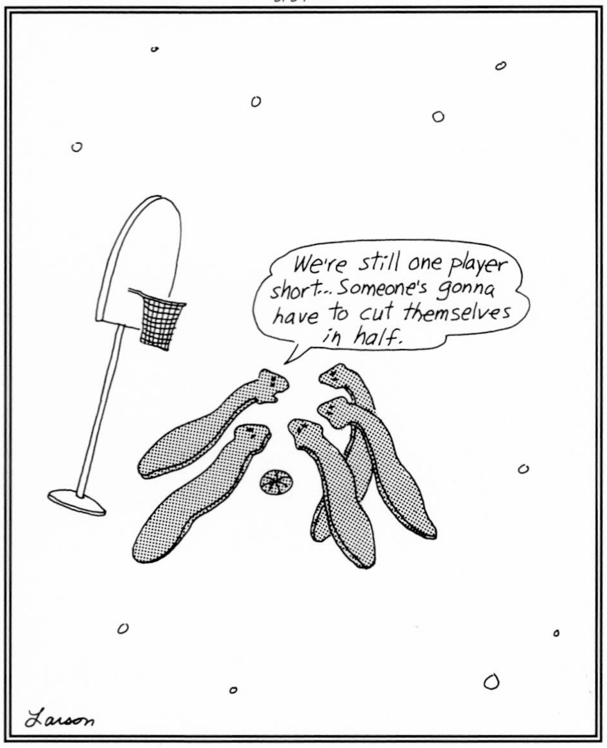
We're still one player short... Someone's gonna have to cut themselves in half.
Larson

Planaria sports

4/2/88

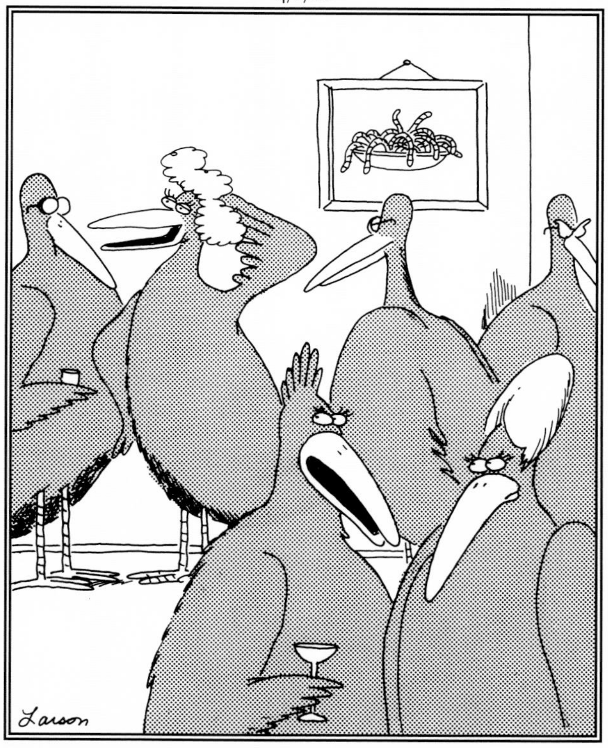
Larson

"Well, she's at it again ... that no-good nestwrecker."

4/4/88

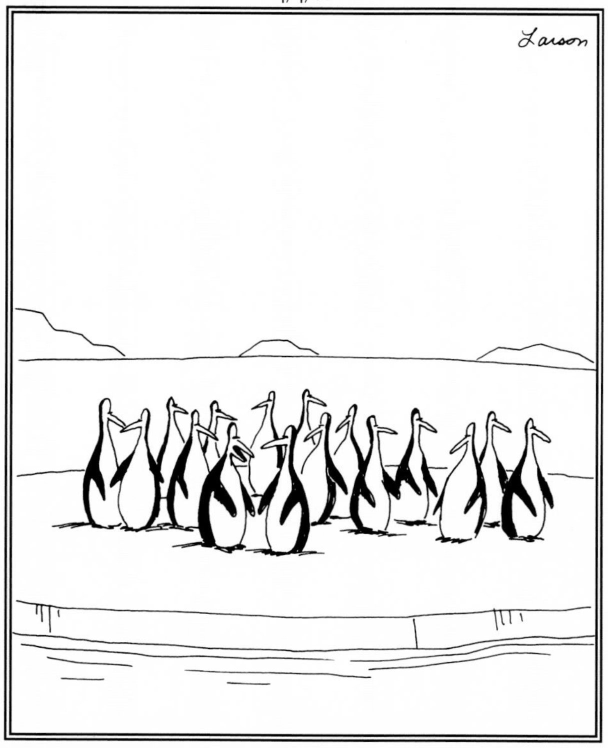
Larson

"Well, that's an interesting bit of trivia—I guess I do only dream in black and white."

4/5/88

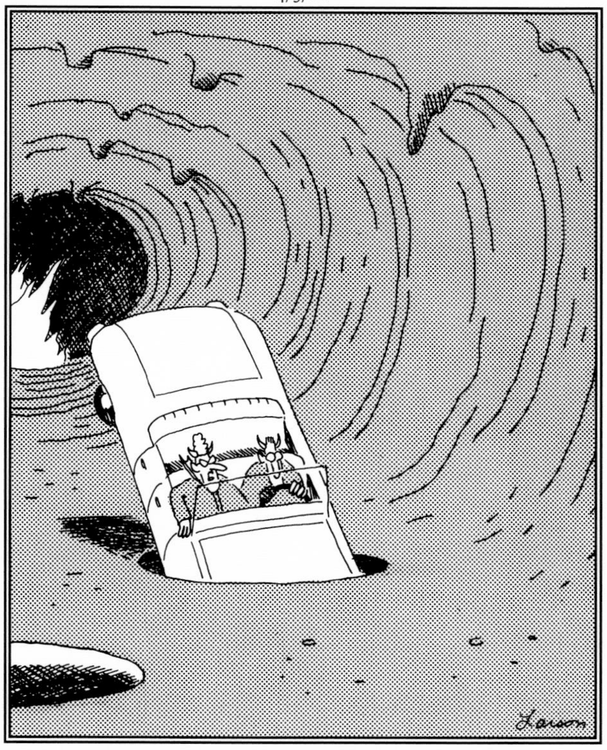
Larson

"You moron! From a hundred yards back I was screaming, 'Hellhole! Hellhole!'"

4/7/88

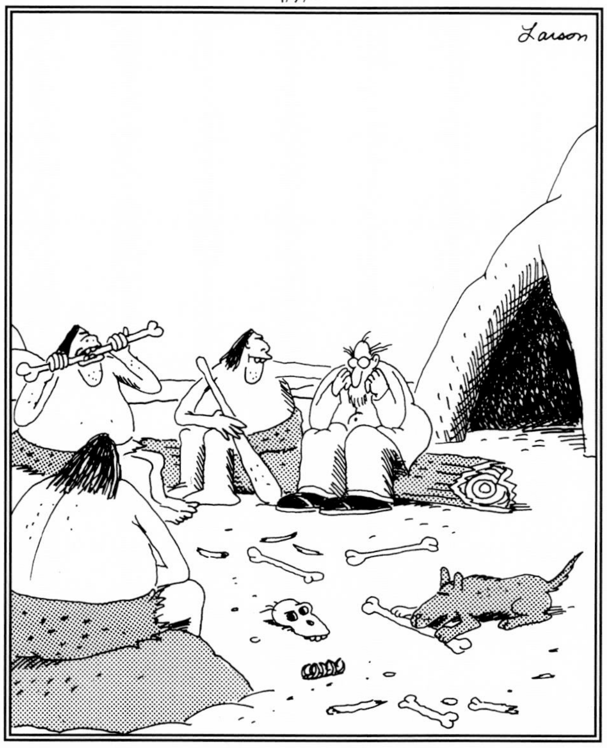
Larson

Professor Feldman, traveling back in time, gradually succumbs to the early stages of nonculture shock.

4/1/88

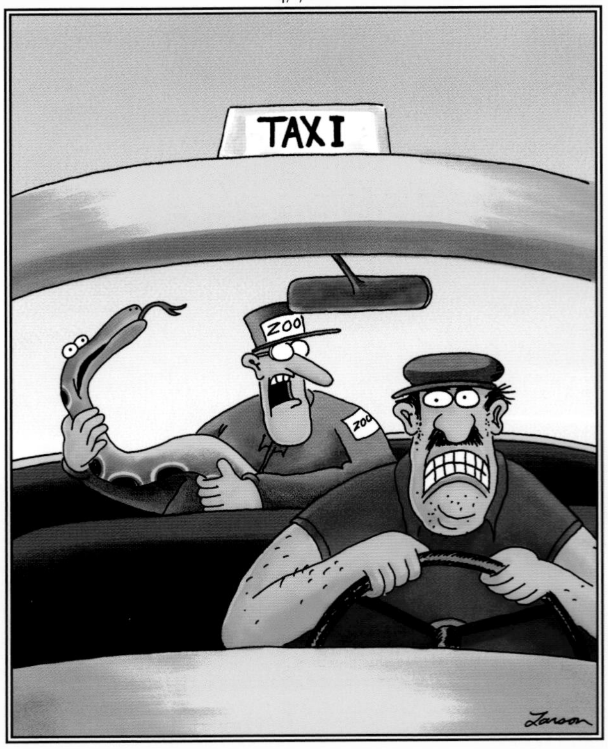
TAXI
ZOO
ZOO

"For God's sake, hurry, driver! ... She's dropping babies all over the place!"

4/6/88

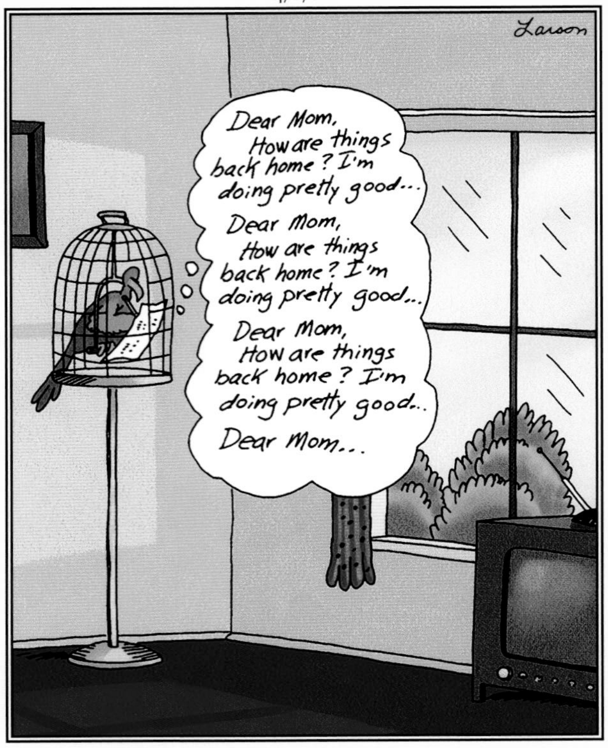
Dear Mom,
How are things back home? I'm doing pretty good...
Dear Mom,
How are things back home? I'm doing pretty good...
Dear Mom,
How are things back home? I'm doing pretty good...
Dear Mom...

4/3/88

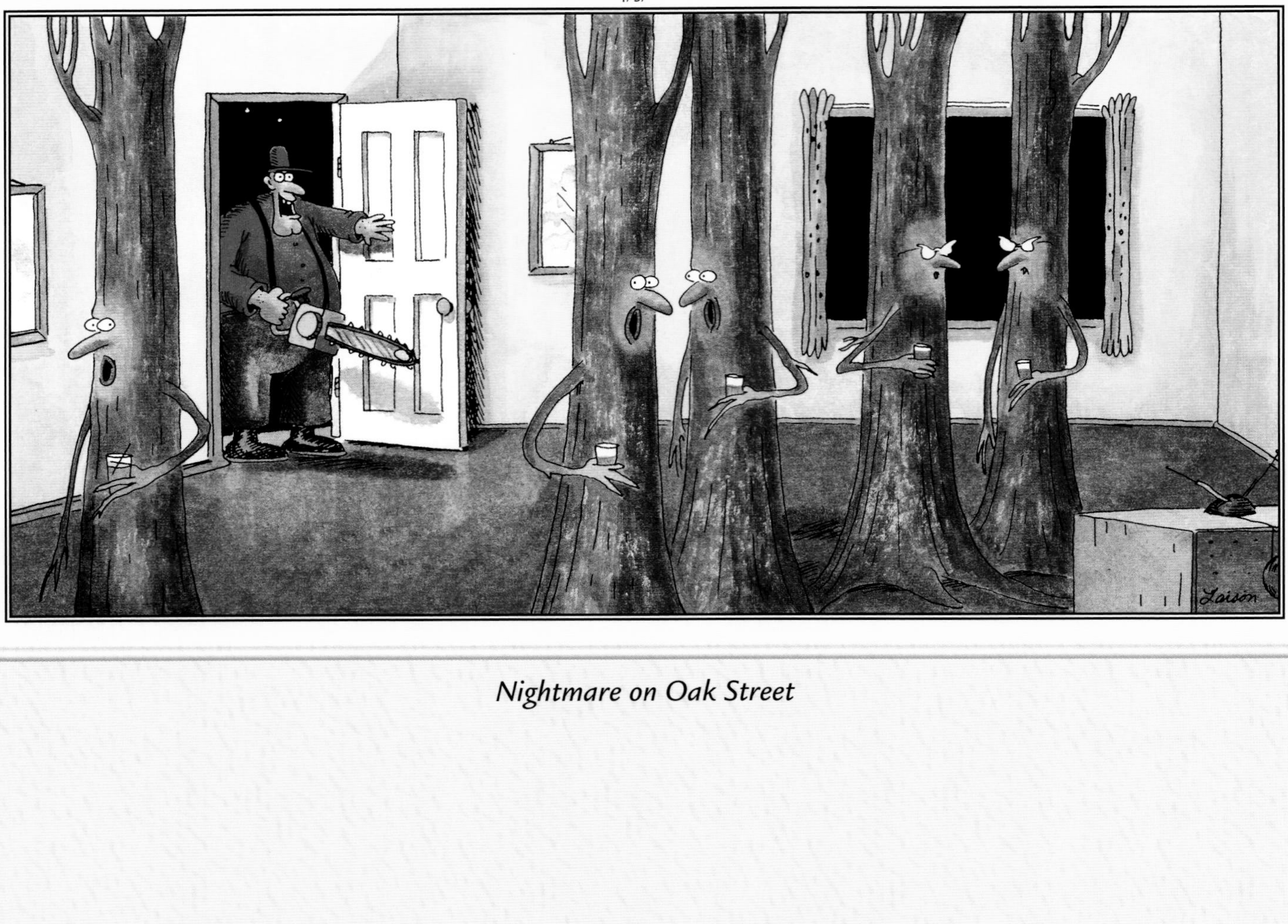

Nightmare on Oak Street

4/8/88

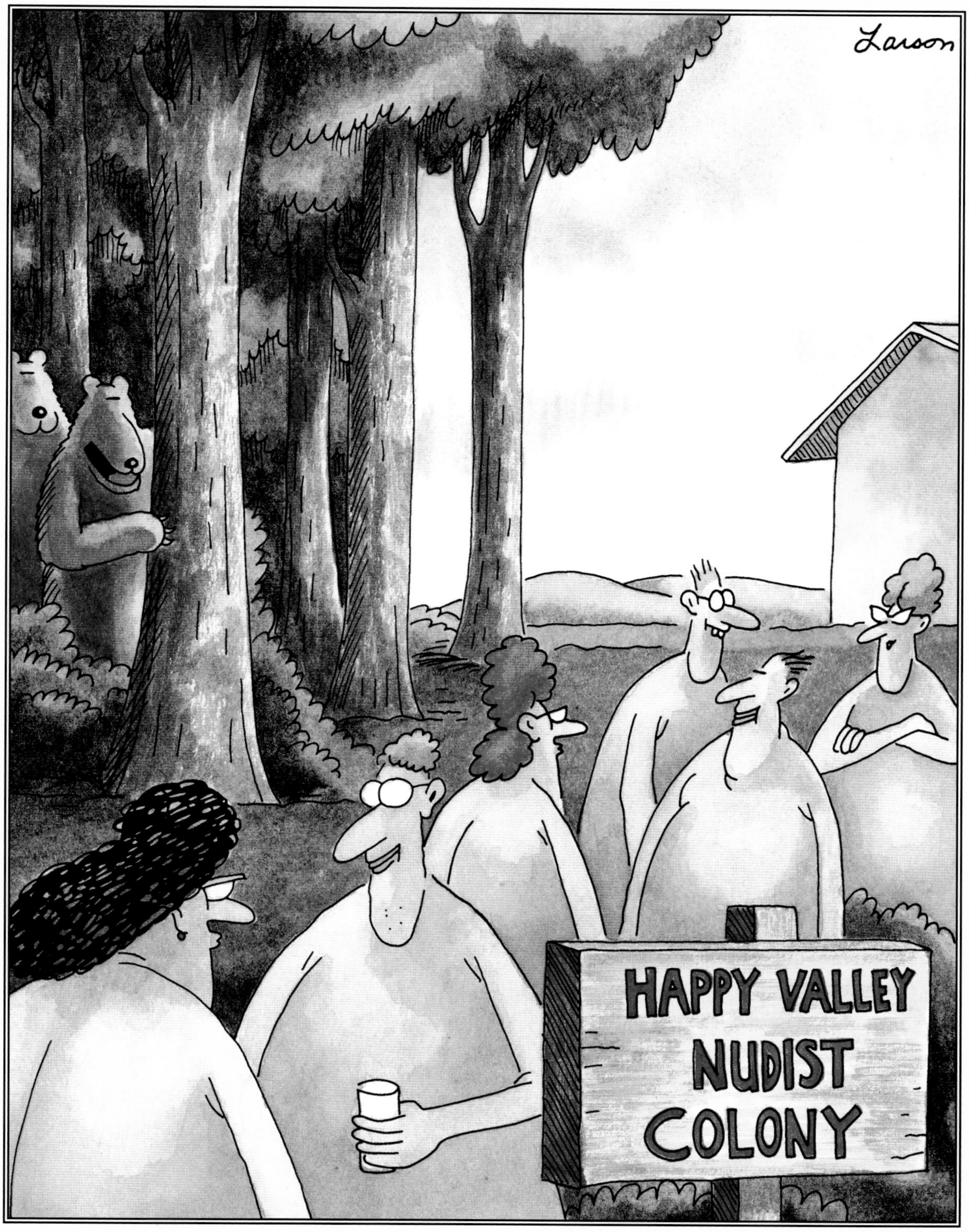
Larson
HAPPY VALLEY
NUDIST
COLONY

"Well, there goes *my* appetite."

4/10/88

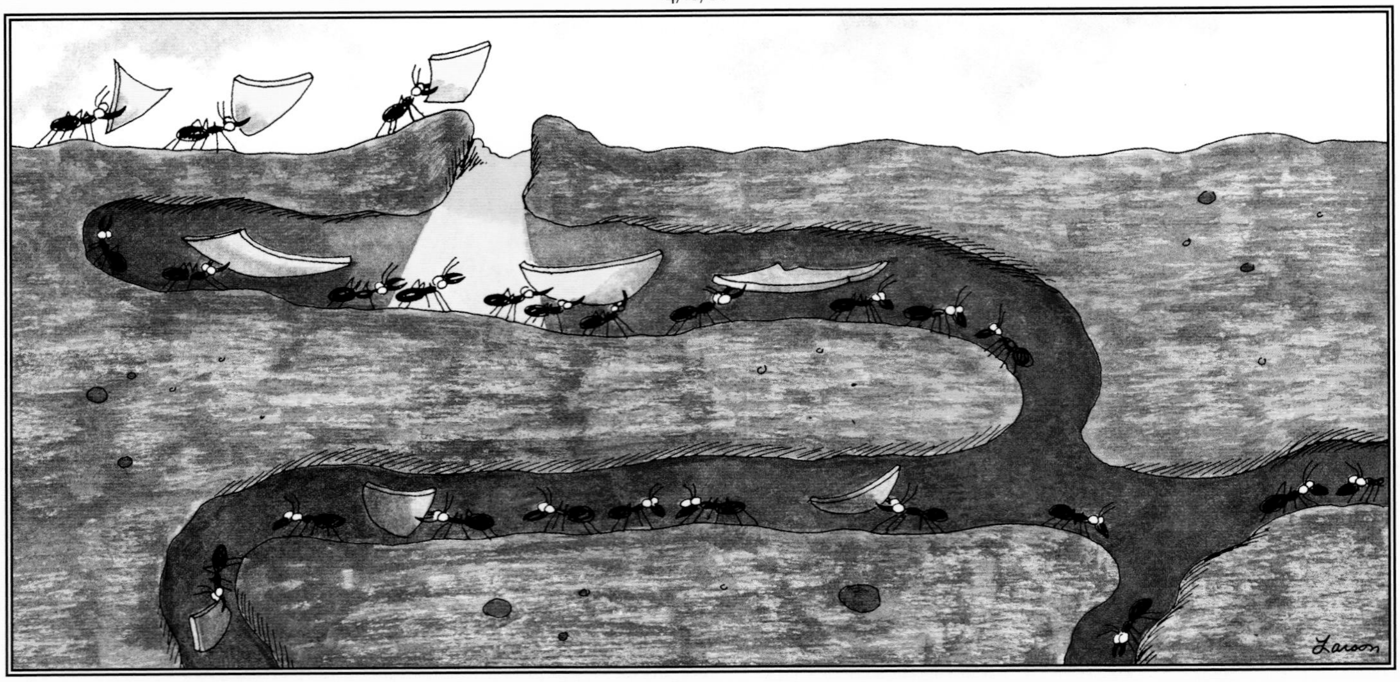

Humpty's final resting place

4/9/88

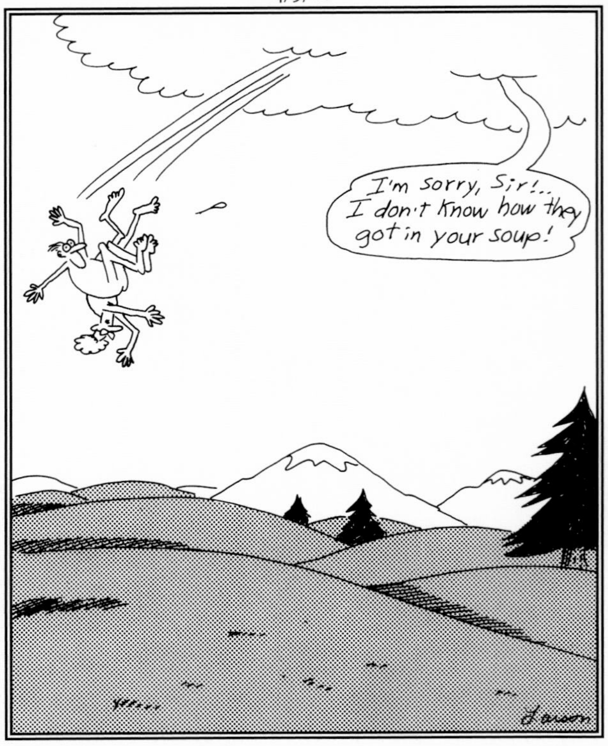
I'm sorry, Sir!... I don't know how they got in your soup!

Mankind arrives on Earth

4/12/88

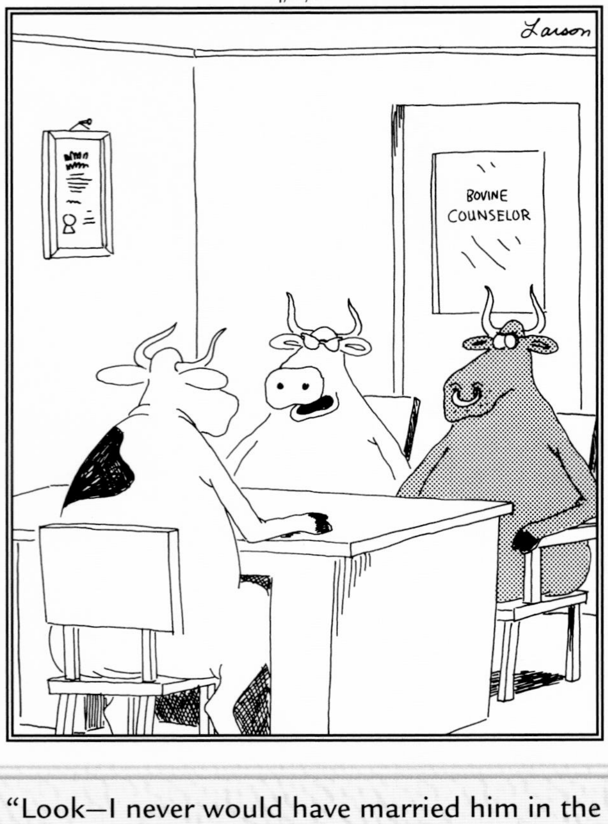
BOVINE COUNSELOR

"Look—I never would have married him in the first place, but the jerk used a cattle prod."

4/17/88

Larson
No way, Fenwick... Your kids got the last box... This one's mine!
Yes! It's a...
Polaris Missile
Easy Assembly

4/19/88

...but the Secretary of State declined to comment on the latest round of talks... ...And today the A-1 Life Raft Co. issued a statement recalling 50,000 of its small rubber boats due to defective glue used in their manufacture, causing the boats to lose air and gradually sink over a matter of a few days...
And now let's go to Lou Jackson for what's happening in sports...
A-1
Larson

4/15/88

Larson

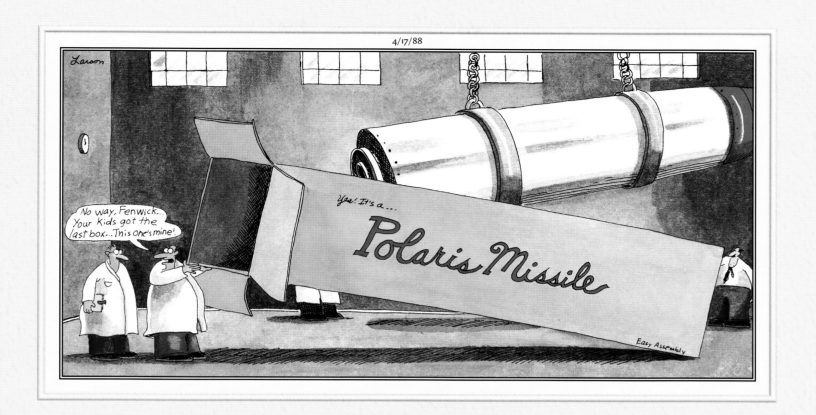

Seconds before his ax fell, Farmer Dale suddenly noticed the chicken's tattoo—the tattoo that marked them both as brothers of an ancient Tibetan order sworn to loyalty and mutual aid.

4/14/88

WANTED
DEAD OR
ALIVE
$5,000
Larson

The townsfolk all stopped and stared; they didn't know the tall stranger who rode calmly through their midst, but they did know the reign of terror had ended.

4/16/88

Larson

Moses as a kid

4/13/88

Larson
DANGER
AVALANCHE
AREA

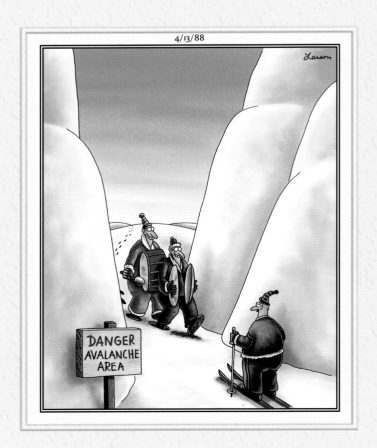

April 1988

4/11/88

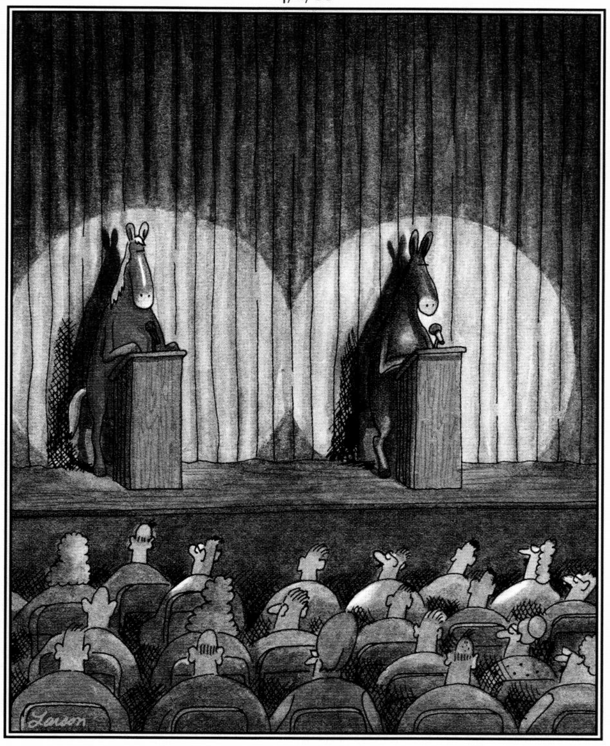
Larson

The famous "Mr. Ed vs. Francis the Talking Mule" debates

4/27/88

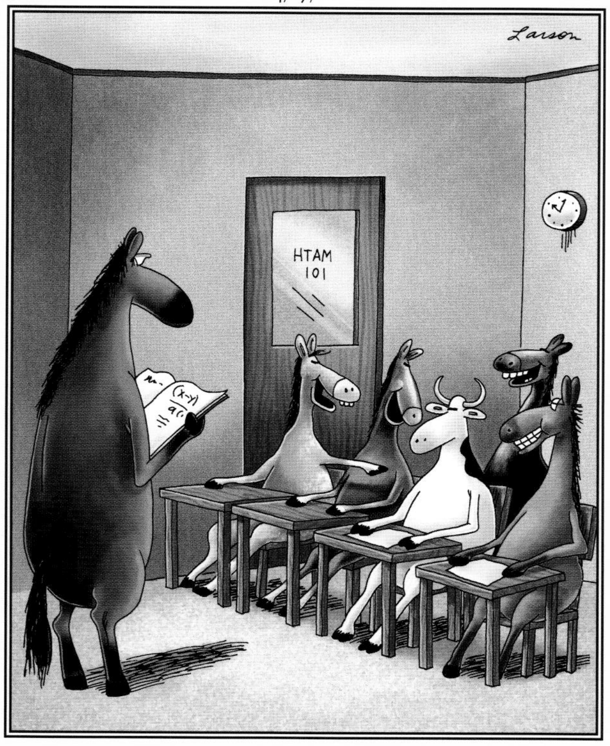
Larson
HTAM
101

Her answer off by miles, Sheila's "cow sense" was always a target of ridicule.

4/21/88

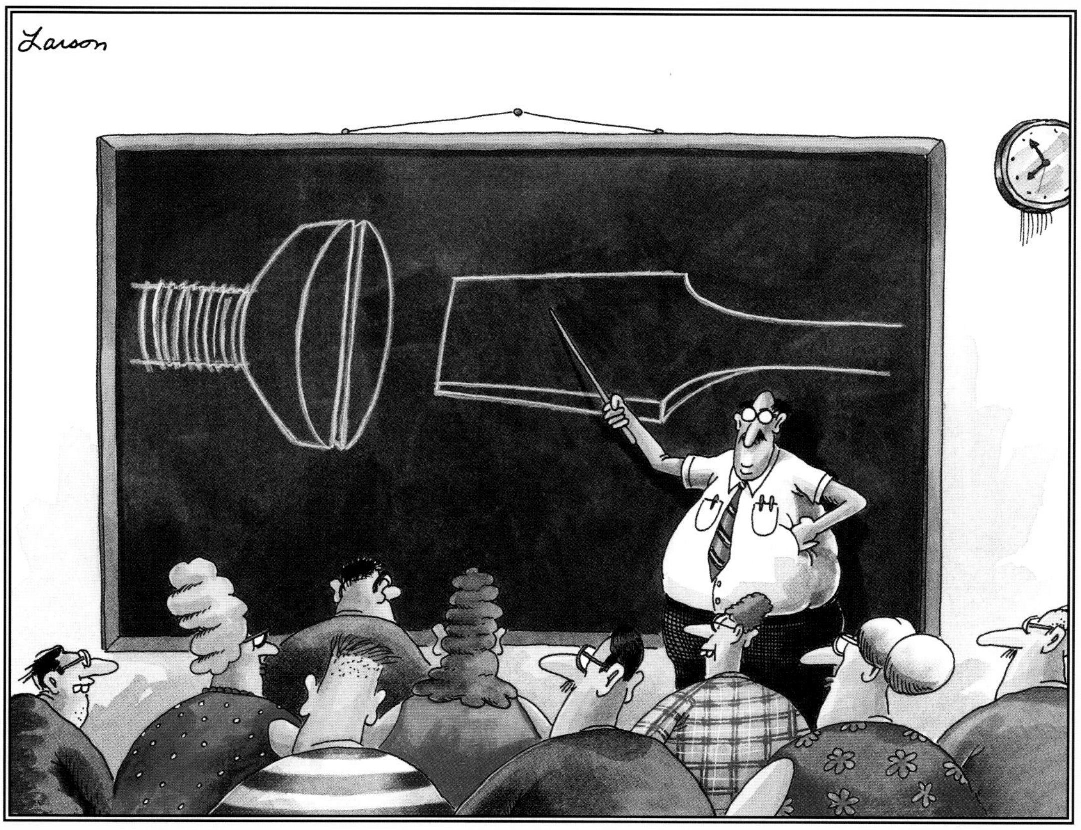
Larson

School for the mechanically declined

4/18/88

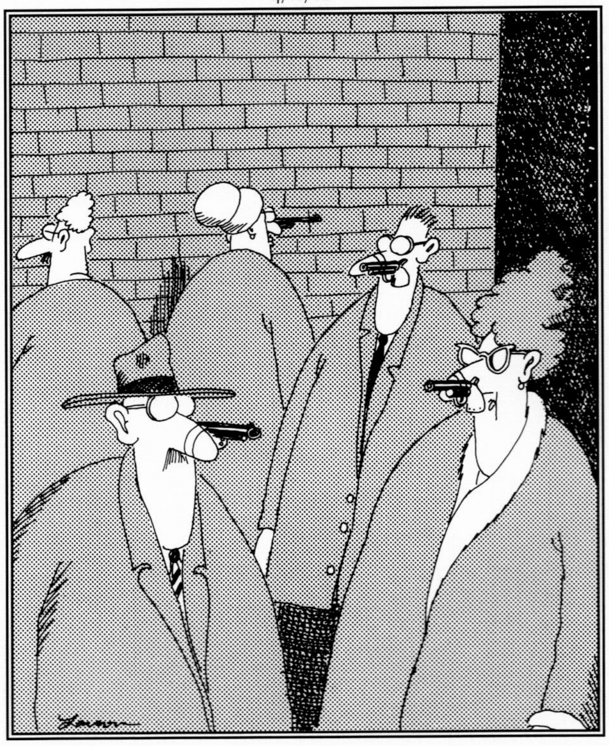

The tragic proliferation of noseguns

4/20/88

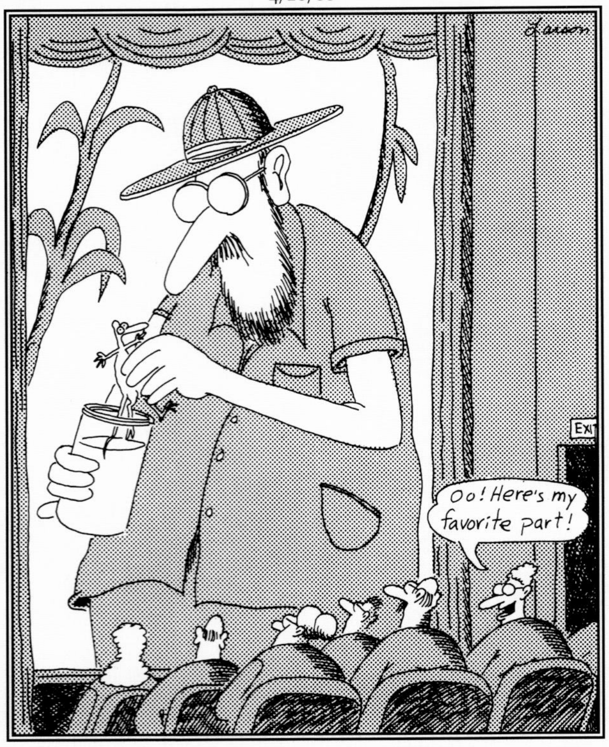
Oo! Here's my favorite part!

Scene from *Bring 'Em Back Preserved*

4/22/88

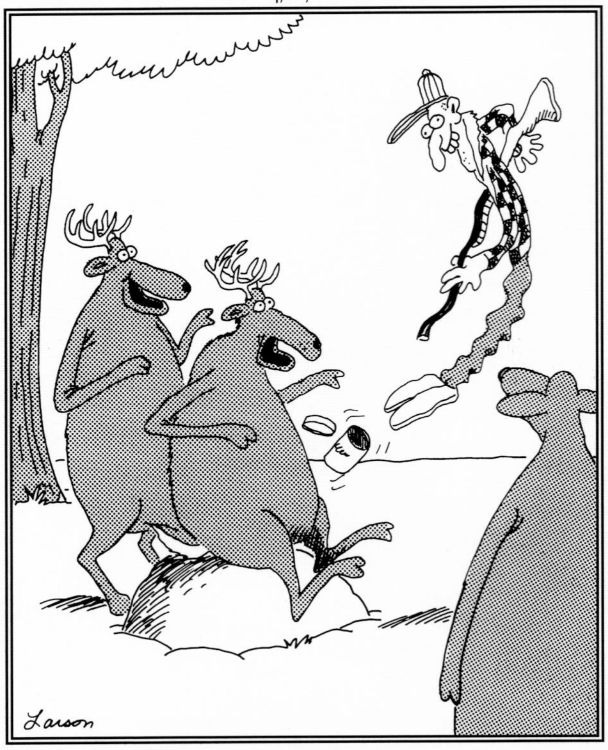

Animal joke gifts

4/23/88

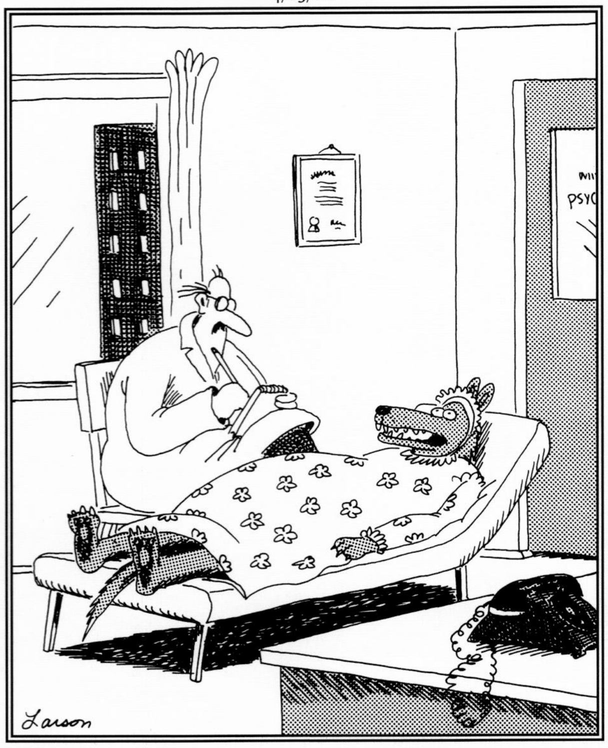

"You know, it was just supposed to be a way to trick this little girl ... but off and on, I've been dressing up as a grandmother ever since."

4/24/88

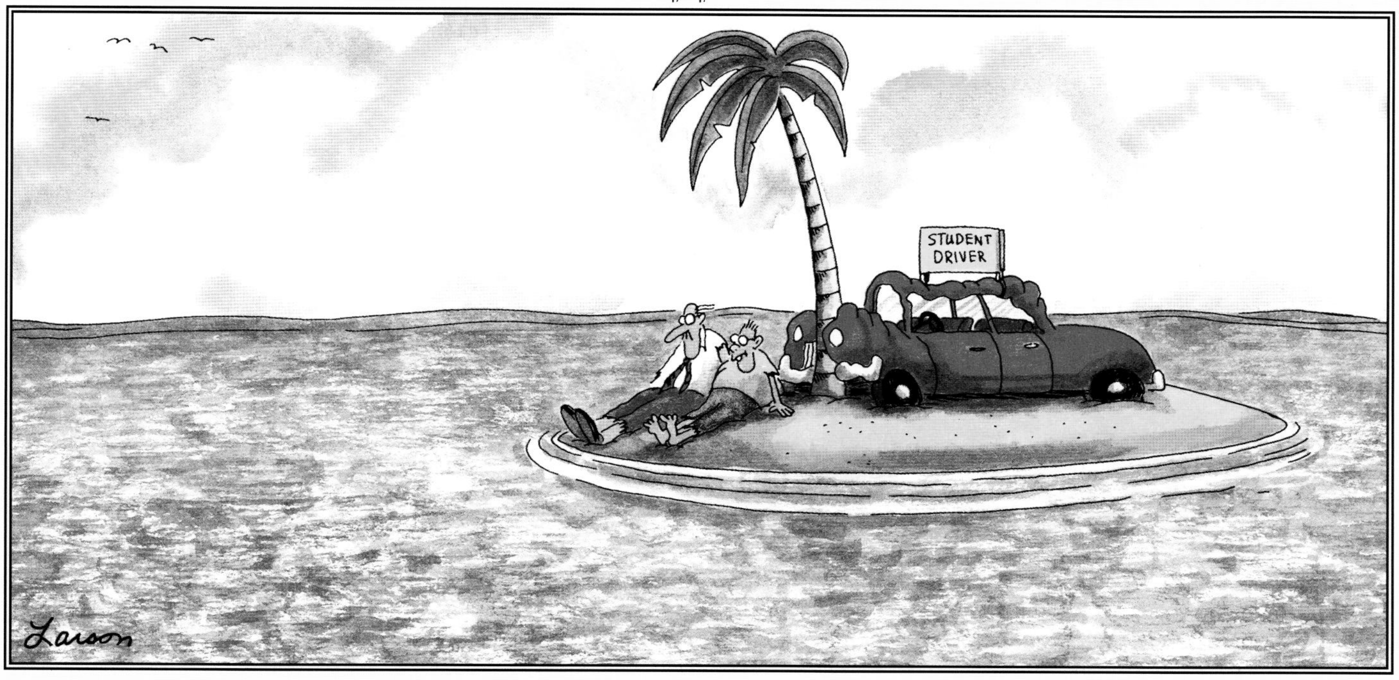
STUDENT DRIVER
Larson

4/25/88

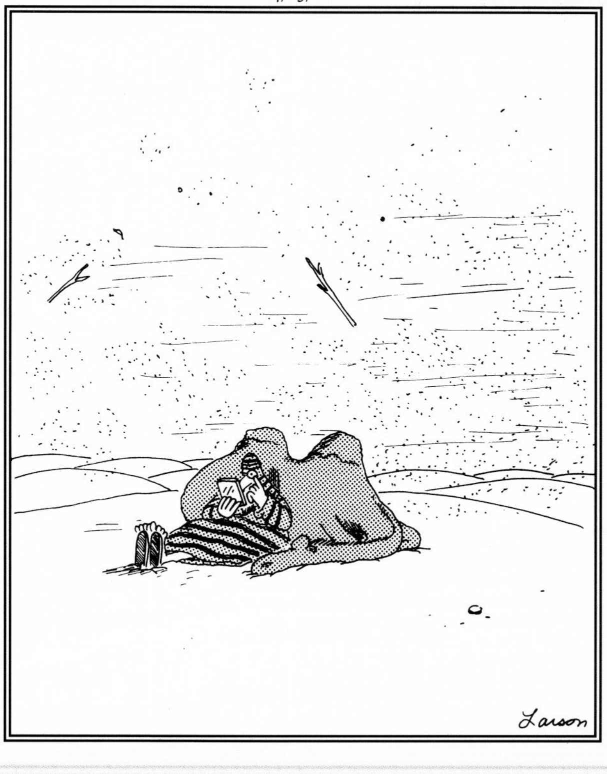
Larson

Times and places never to insert your contact lens

4/30/88

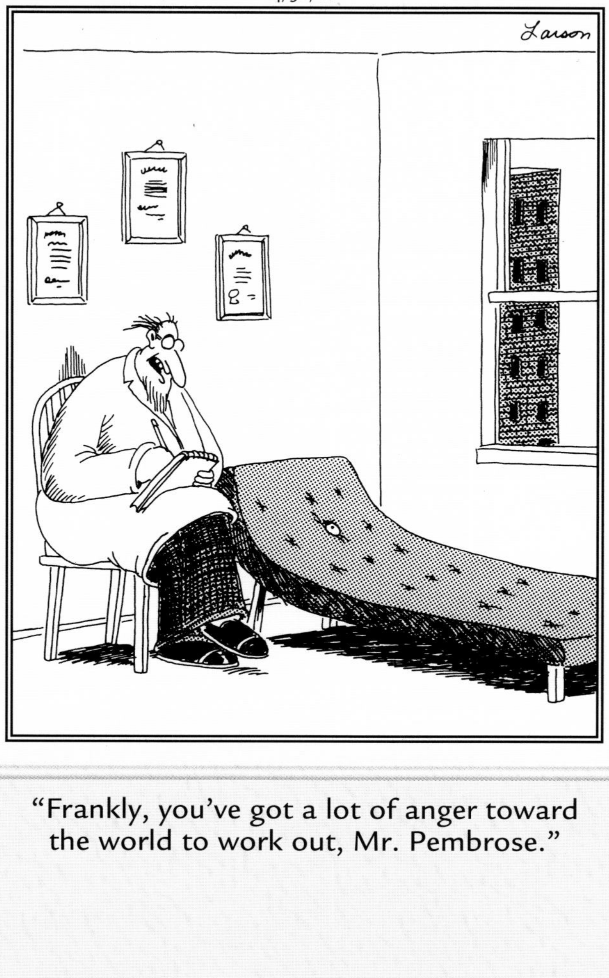
Larson

"Frankly, you've got a lot of anger toward the world to work out, Mr. Pembrose."

Suddenly, throwing the festivities into utter confusion, Ujang begins to play "Stardust."

"Say, Will—why don't you pull that thing out and play us a tune?"

At the Vincent van Gogh School of Art

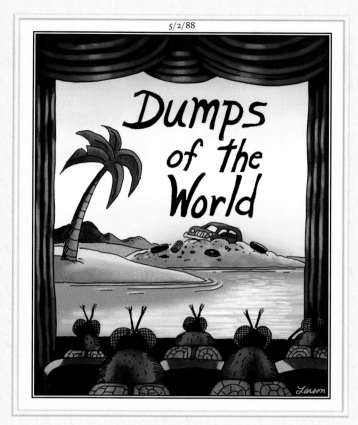

5/2/88

Dumps of the World
Larson

Fly travelogues

5/6/88

Larson
Oh, here it is..."Kemosabe: Apache expression for a horse's rear end!"... What the hey?..
INDIAN DICTIONARY

The Lone Ranger, long since retired, makes an unpleasant discovery.

5/1/88

AL's MEATS
Noreen's Vegetarian Cafe
OPEN
Larson

5/3/88

BEN & VERA'S
ROTTWEILER
FARM

The untold ending of D. B. Cooper

5/4/88

COMICS REPORTEDLY
GETTING SMALLER

5/7/88

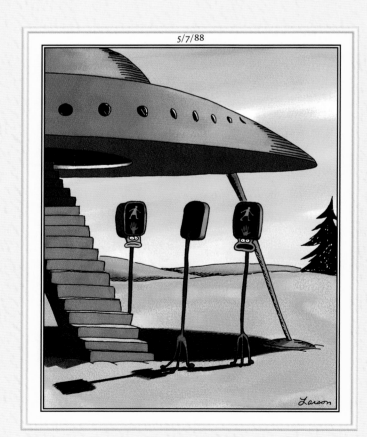

"Our people are positioned on every street corner, commander. ... Shall we commence with our plan to gradually eliminate these creatures?"

5/10/88

Aladdin's lamp, end table, and sofa

5/11/88

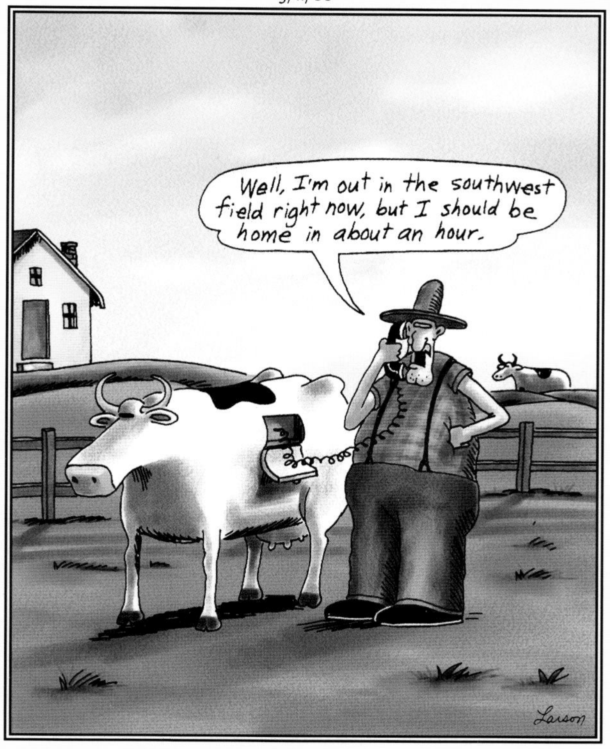
Well, I'm out in the southwest field right now, but I should be home in about an hour.

The rural professional and his cowphone

5/16/88

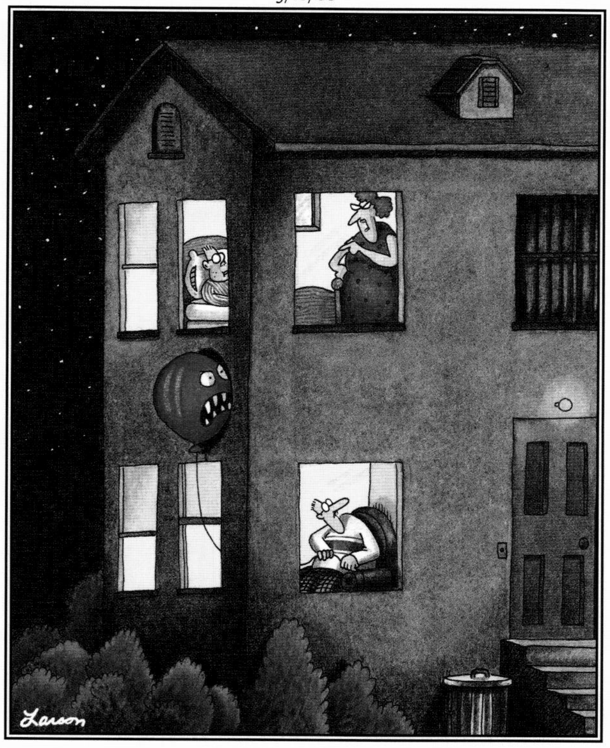

"Now go to sleep, Kevin—or once again I'll have to knock three times and summon the Floating Head of Death."

5/5/88

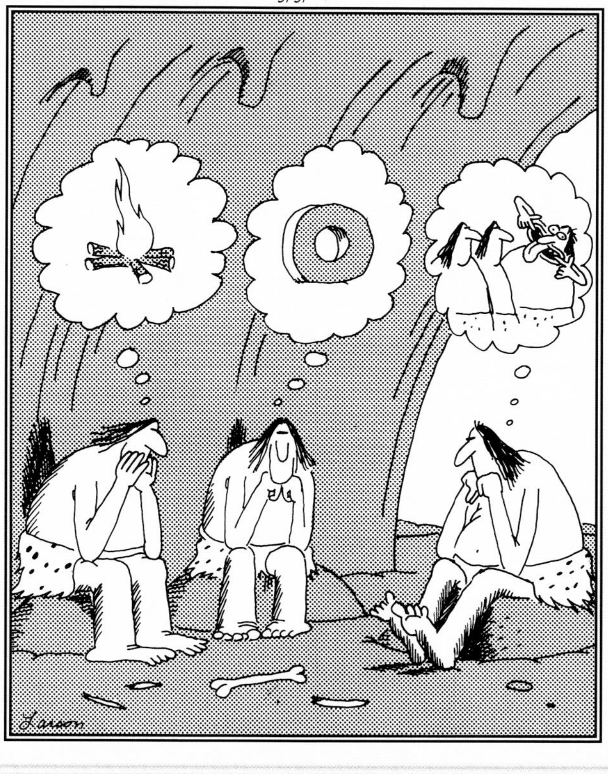

Primitive think tanks

5/9/88

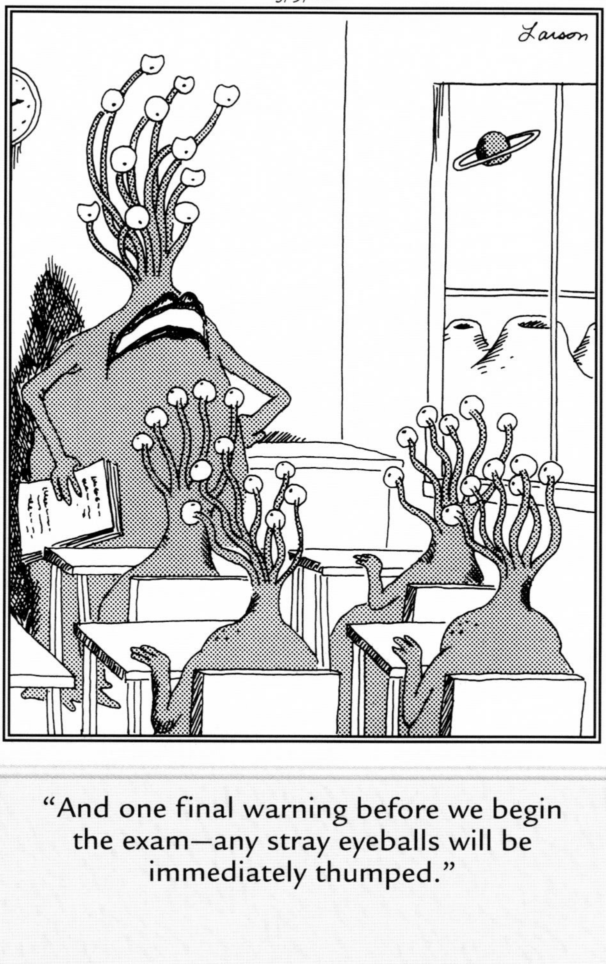

"And one final warning before we begin the exam—any stray eyeballs will be immediately thumped."

5/8/88

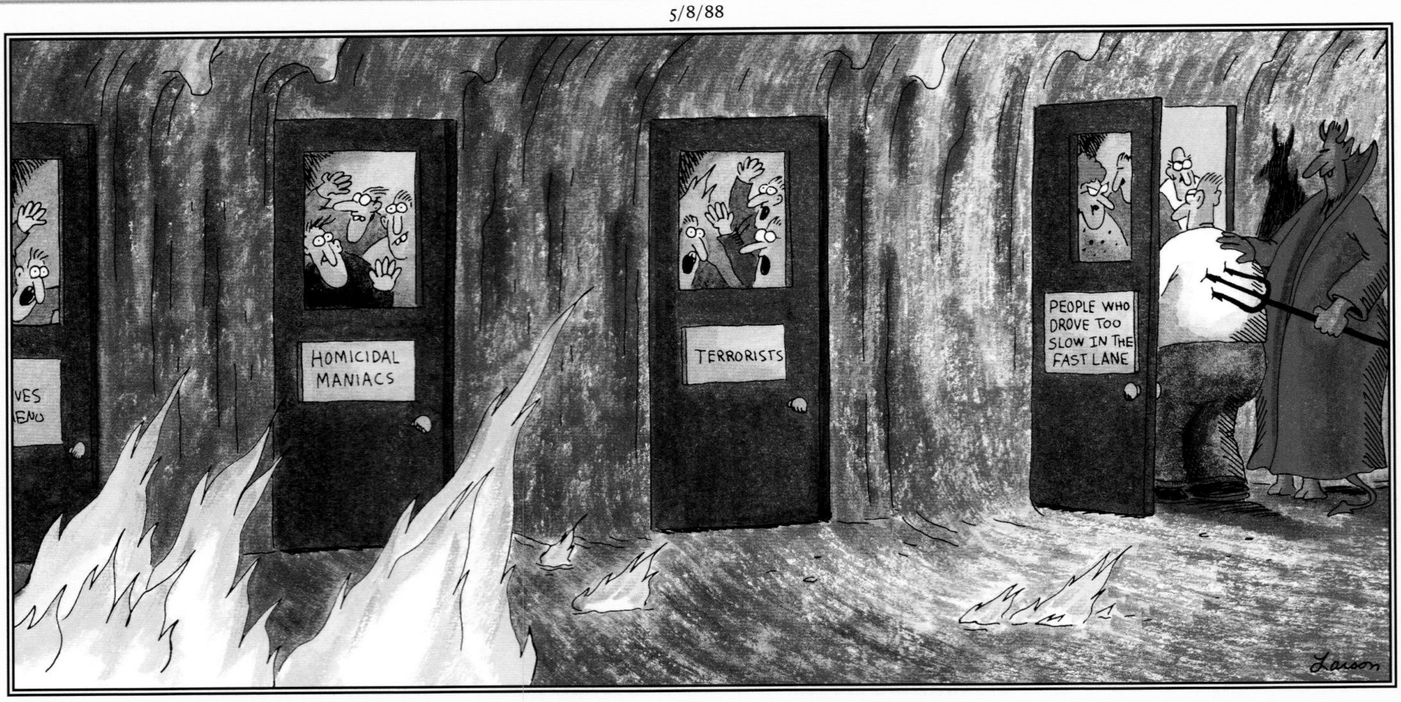
HOMICIDAL MANIACS
TERRORISTS
PEOPLE WHO DROVE TOO SLOW IN THE FAST LANE

5/12/88

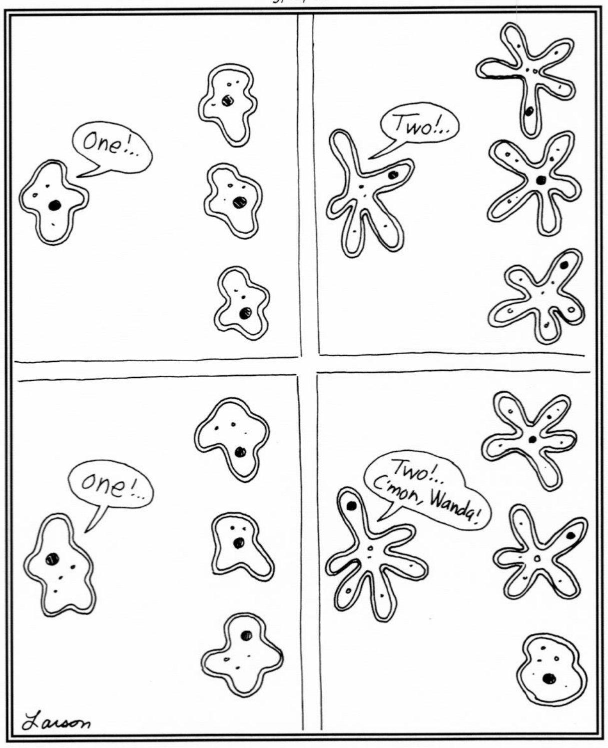
One!..
Two!..
One!..
Two!.. C'mon, Wanda!

Amoeba aerobics

5/13/88

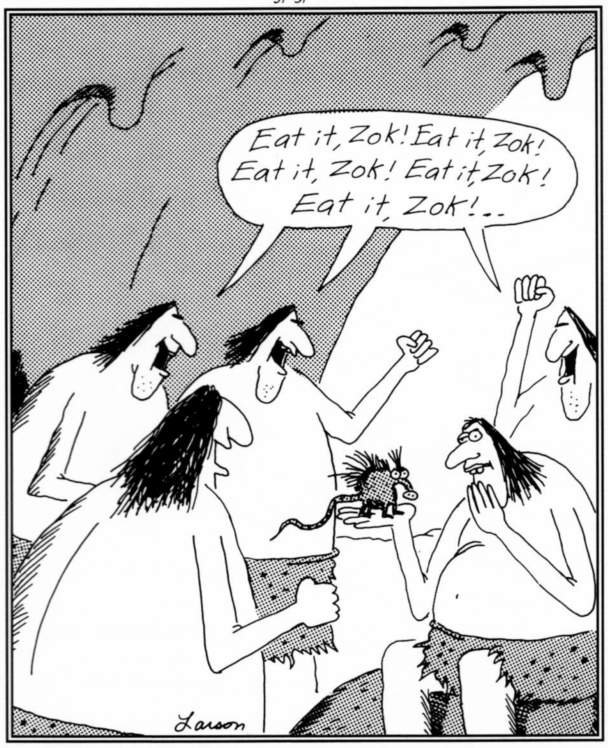
Eat it, Zok! Eat it, Zok! Eat it, Zok! Eat it, Zok! Eat it, Zok!..

Primitive fraternities

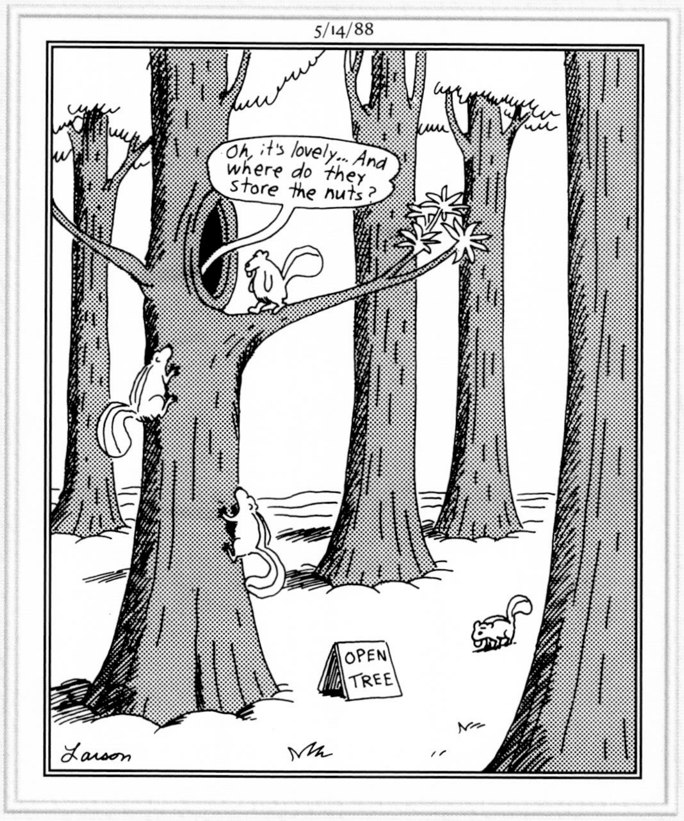
5/14/88
Oh, it's lovely... And where do they store the nuts?
OPEN TREE
Larson

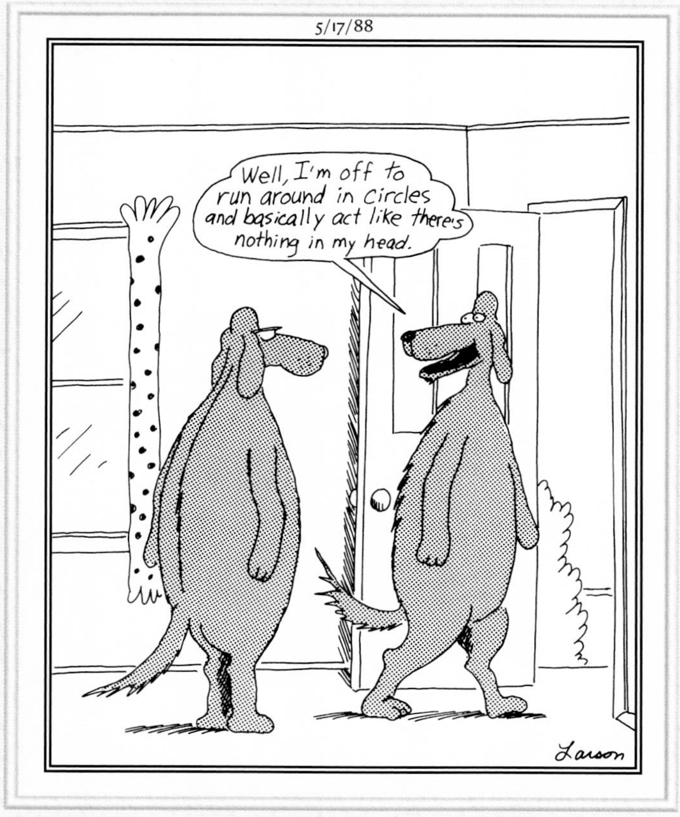
5/17/88
Well, I'm off to run around in circles and basically act like there's nothing in my head.
Larson

When Irish setters go to work

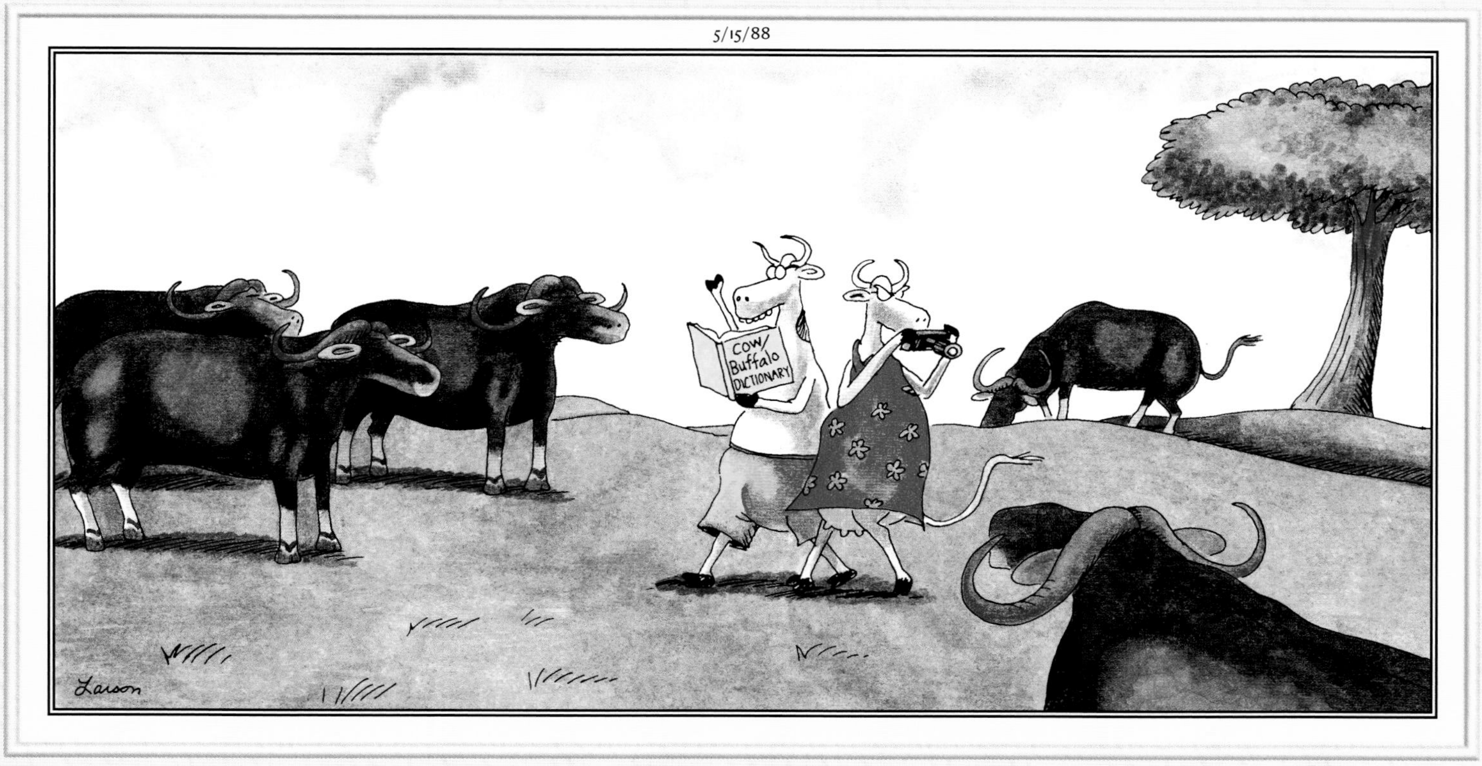
5/15/88
COW/Buffalo DICTIONARY
Larson

Cow tourists

5/19/88

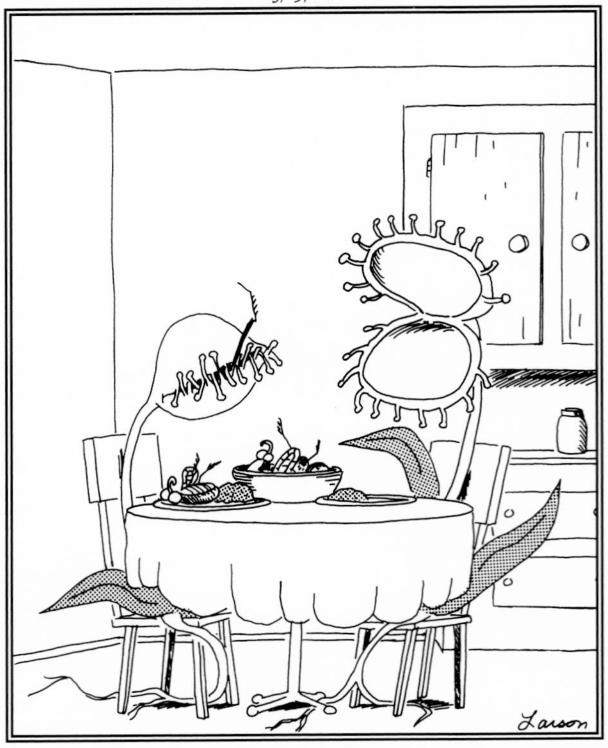
Larson

"No more flies, Arnold, until you've eaten some of your fertilizer."

5/21/88

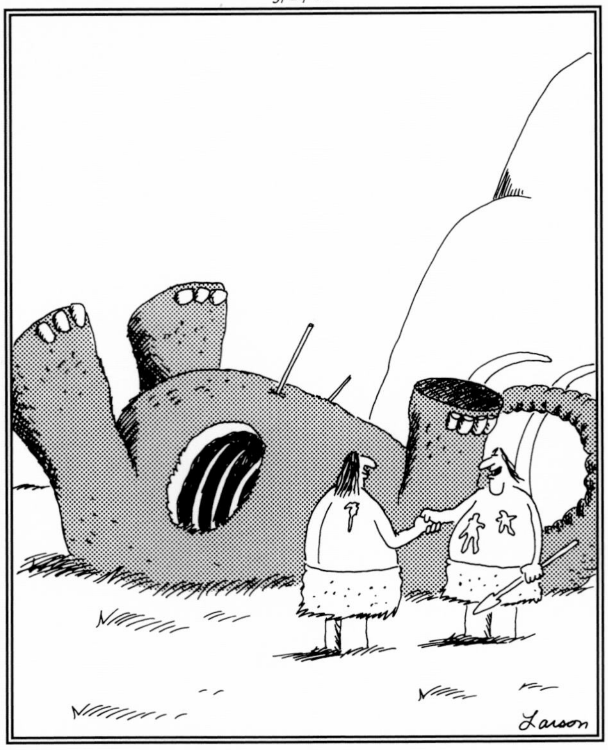
Larson

"So! ... Let's do this again real soon."

5/23/88

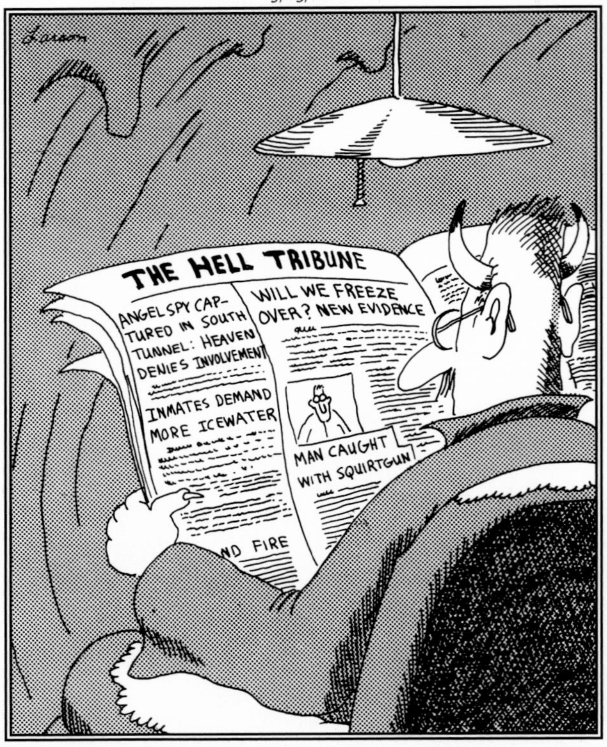
Larson
THE HELL TRIBUNE
ANGEL SPY CAPTURED IN SOUTH TUNNEL: HEAVEN DENIES INVOLVEMENT
WILL WE FREEZE OVER? NEW EVIDENCE
INMATES DEMAND MORE ICEWATER
MAN CAUGHT WITH SQUIRTGUN
ND FIRE

5/24/88

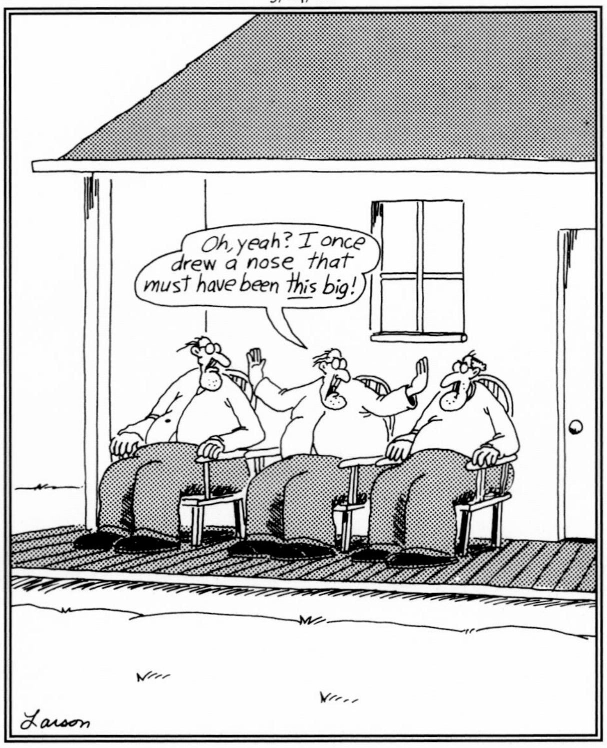
Oh, yeah? I once drew a nose that must have been this big!
Larson

At the Old Cartoonists' Home

5/25/88

Larson

"Mom! Randy sneezed poison all over my rat!"

5/26/88

ACME
CAKE
Zelda's
Fruitcake
AKERY
AKE
"Lasts forever"
Mrs. Millers
Shirley
Larson

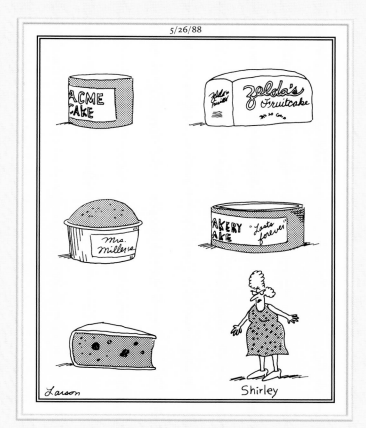

Fruitcakes of the World

5/27/88

Why
EVERY DOG
SHOULD BE
EUTHANIZED
The Author
1001 Ways
to Skin
A Cat
Larson

5/28/88

Larson

"Look, Sid! Another snowball! ... I tell you, this place is slipping."

5/18/88

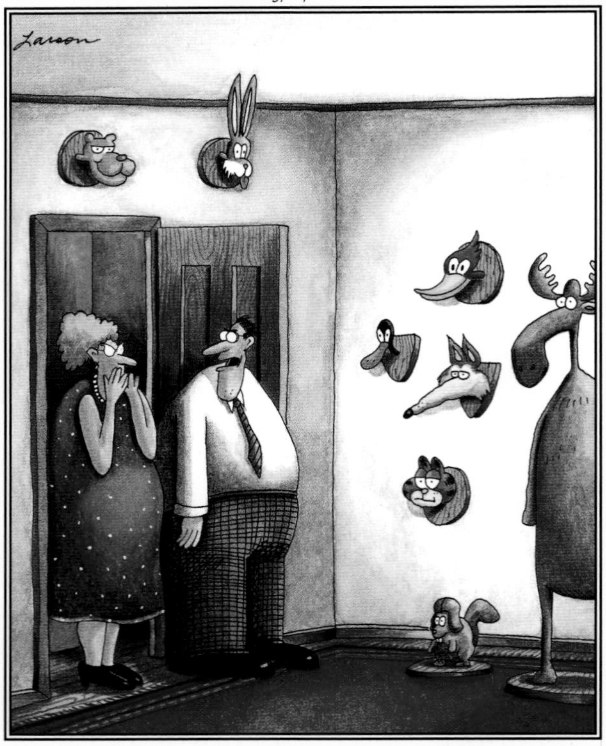

"Oh, for heaven's sake, Miss Carlisle! ...
They're only cartoon animals!"

5/20/88

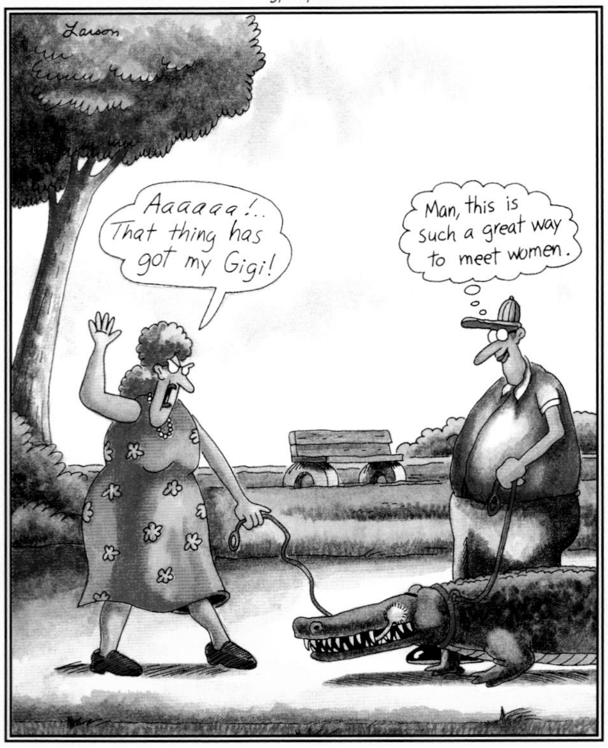
Aaaaaa!.. That thing has got my Gigi!
Man, this is such a great way to meet women.

5/22/88

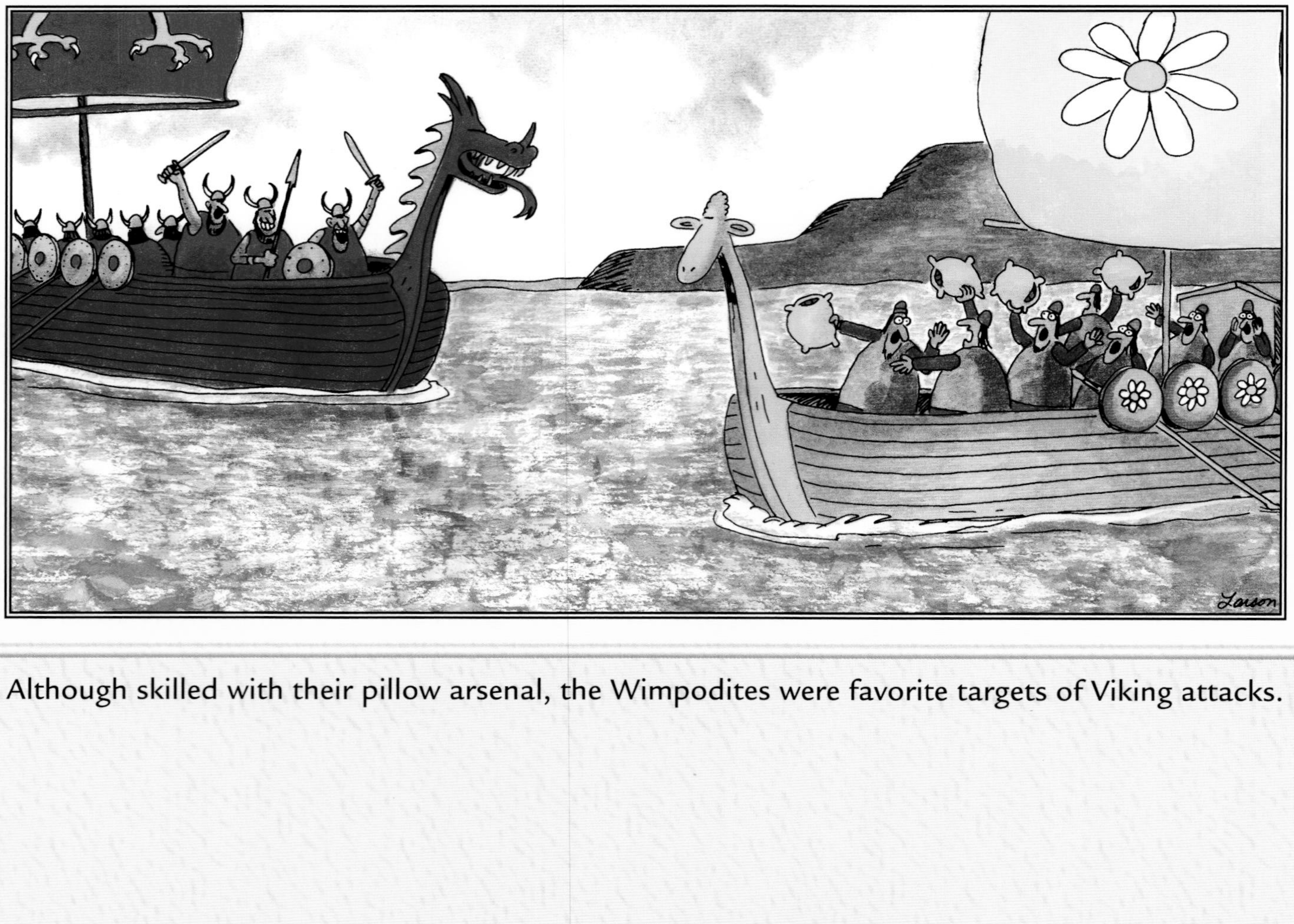

Although skilled with their pillow arsenal, the Wimpodites were favorite targets of Viking attacks.

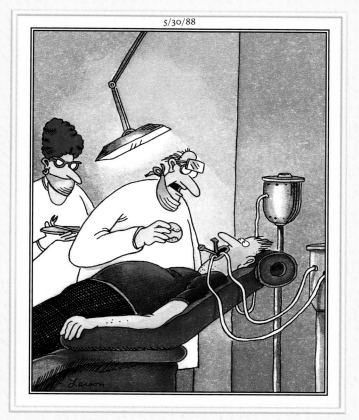

"Now open even wider, Mr. Stevens. ... Just out of curiosity, we're going to see if we can also cram in this tennis ball."

Cowmen Miranda

6/2/88

823
Larson

Suddenly, through forces not yet fully understood, Darren Belsky's apartment became the center of a new black hole.

6/4/88

Larson

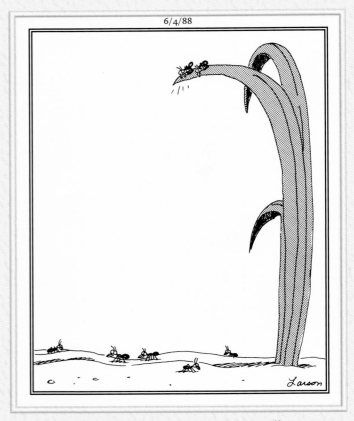

"Man, from way up here, we *really* look like ants."

6/8/88

Shoot...If only I had a red five.
Larson

The last cilium on a smoker's lung

6/10/88

Larson

Babette's Botulism: The Sequel

6/1/88

When the monster came, Lola, like the peppered moth and the arctic hare,
remained motionless and undetected. Harold, of course,
was immediately devoured.

6/5/88

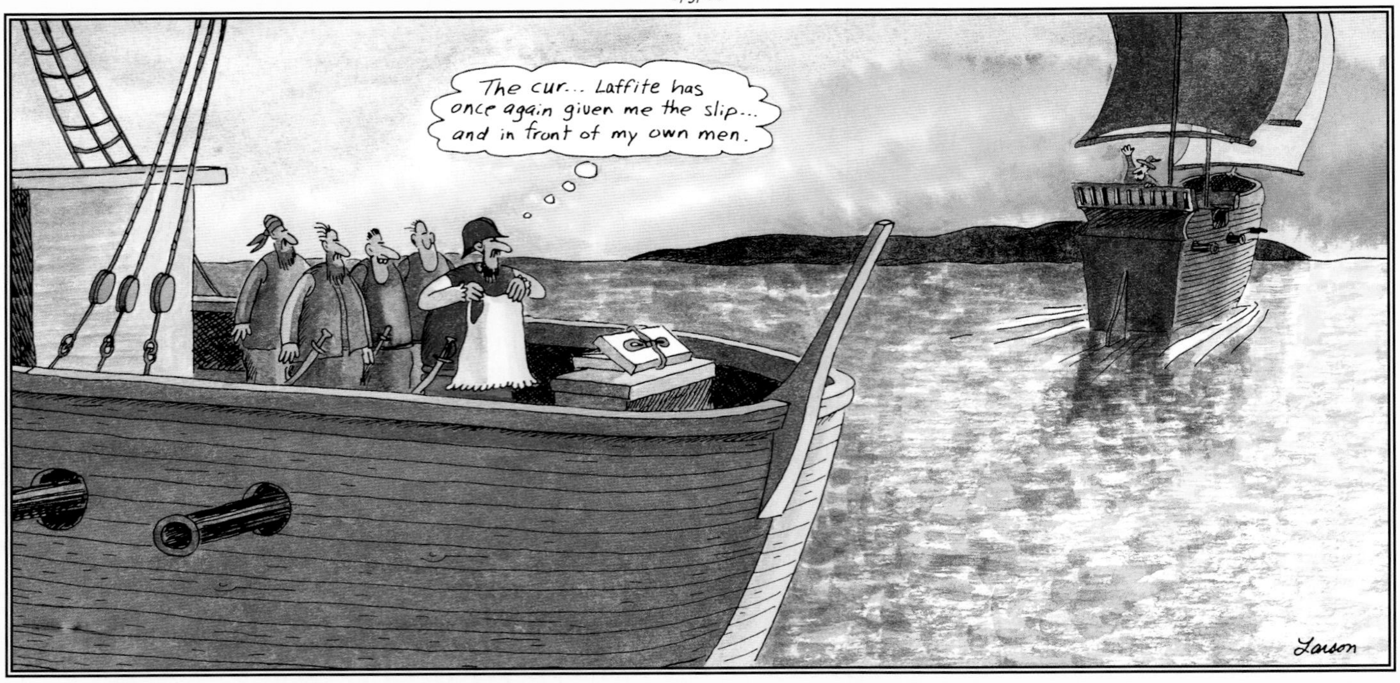
The cur... Laffite has once again given me the slip... and in front of my own men.
Larson

6/3/88

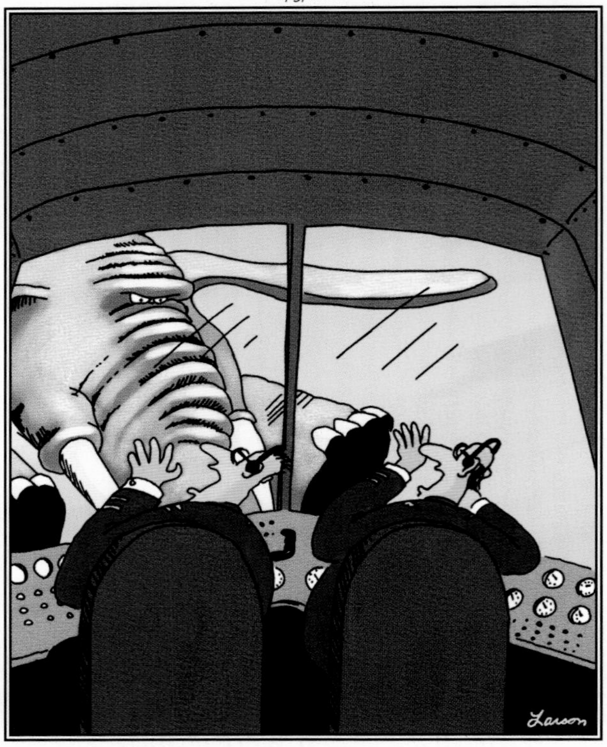
Larson

Becoming a rogue in his later years,
Dumbo terrorized the world's flyways.

6/6/88

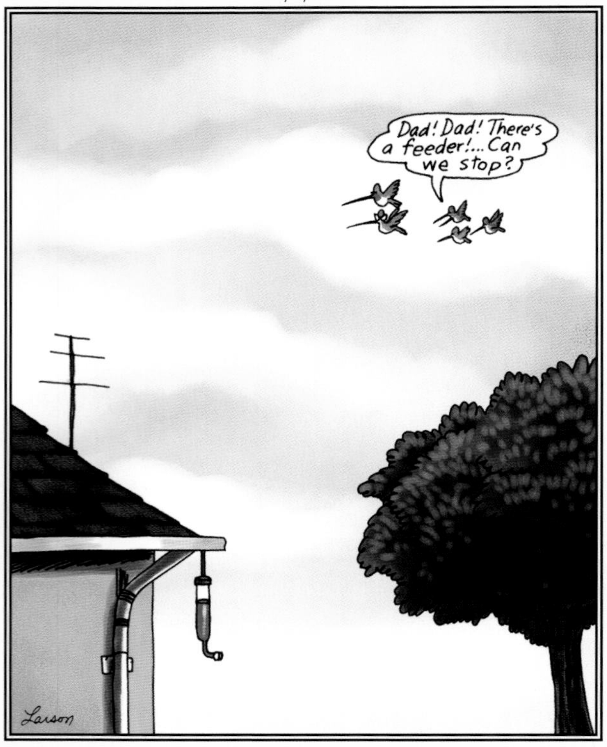
Dad! Dad! There's a feeder!... Can we stop?
Larson

Hummingbirds on vacation

6/7/88

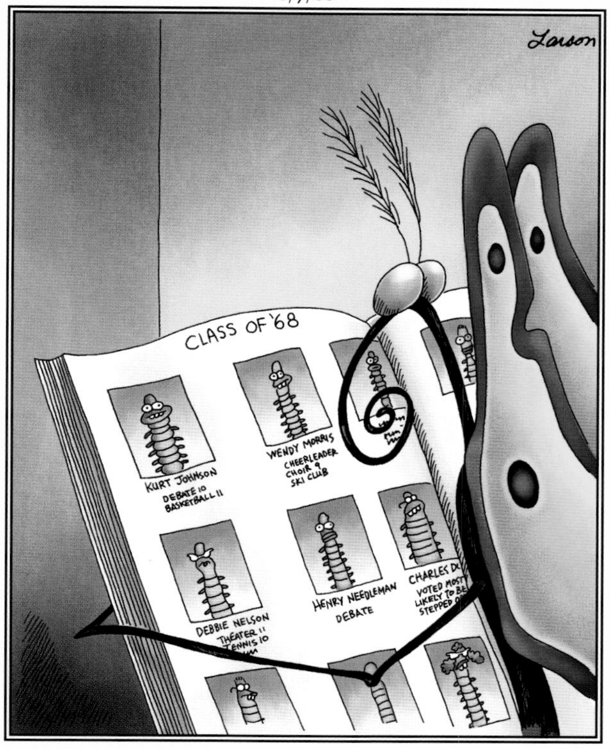
Larson
CLASS OF '68
KURT JOHNSON
DEBATE 10
BASKETBALL 11
WENDY MORRIS
CHEERLEADER
CHOIR 9
SKI CLUB
DEBBIE NELSON
HENRY NEEDLEMAN
DEBATE

Butterfly yearbooks

6/9/88

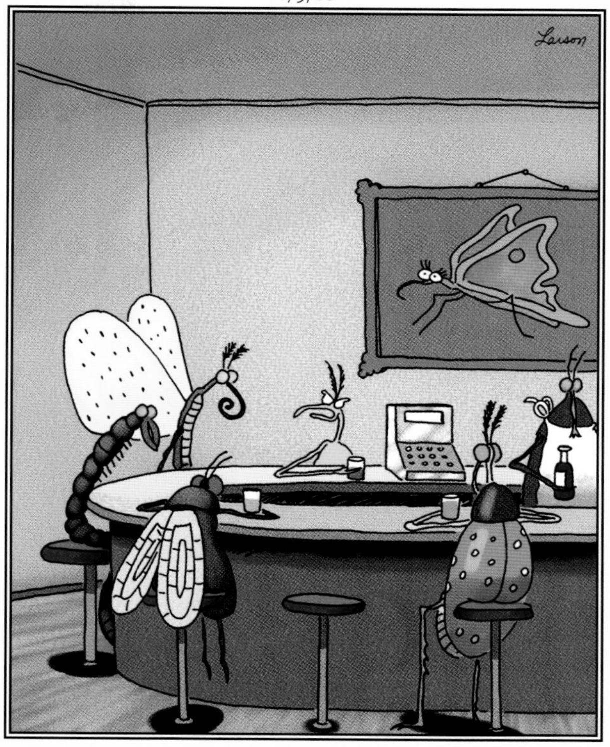
Larson

"Yeah, yeah, buddy, I've heard it all before: You've just metamorphosed and you've got 24 hours to find a mate and breed before you die. ... Well, buzz off!"

6/12/88

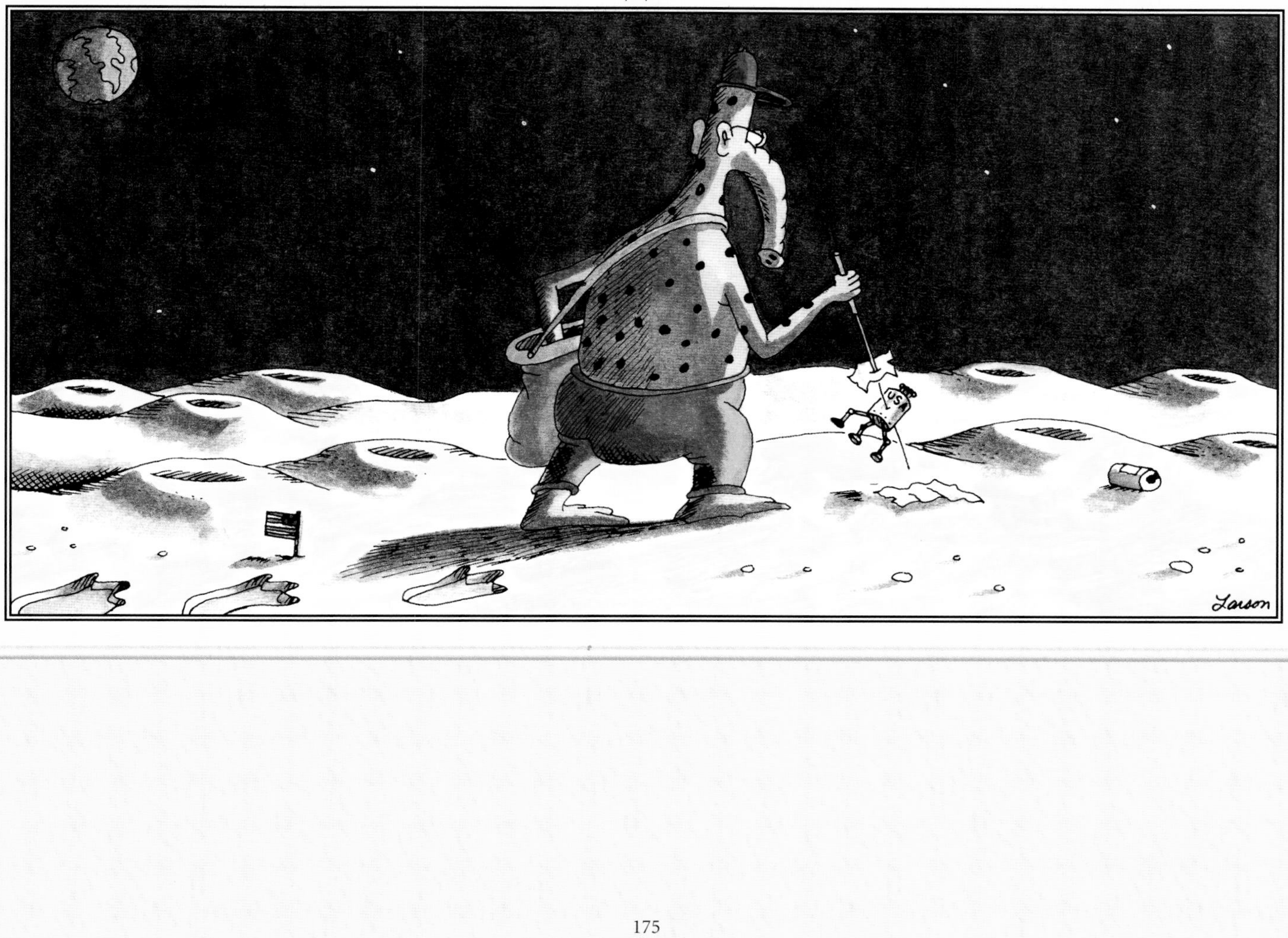
Larson

6/13/88

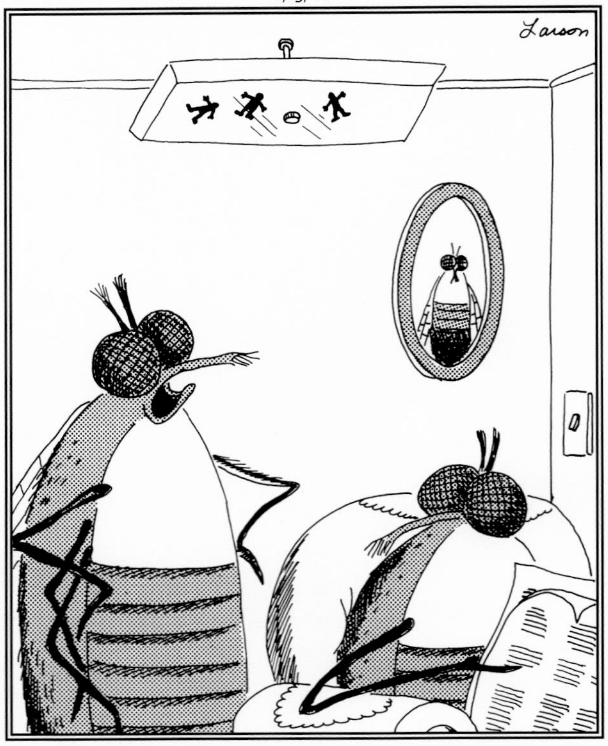

"Crimony! ... Seems like I just cleaned out that fixture last week."

6/14/88

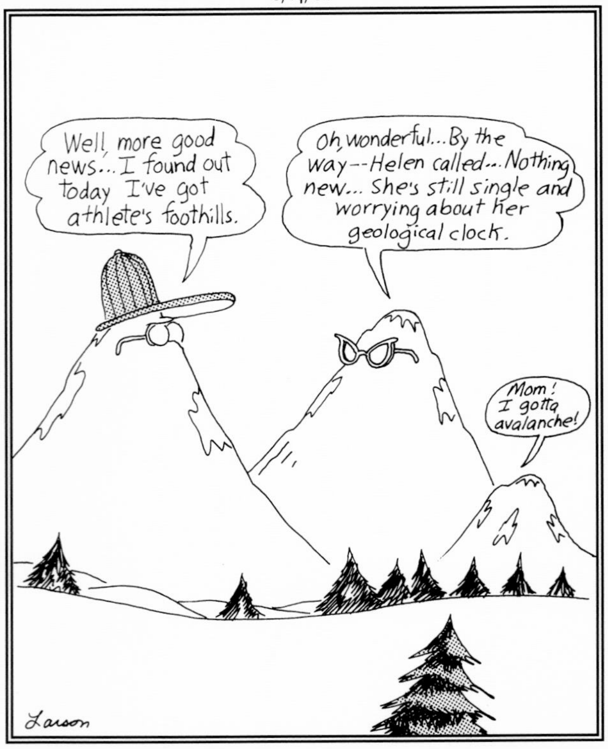
Well, more good news...I found out today I've got athlete's foothills.
Oh, wonderful...By the way--Helen called...Nothing new... She's still single and worrying about her geological clock.
Mom! I gotta avalanche!

Mountain families

6/15/88

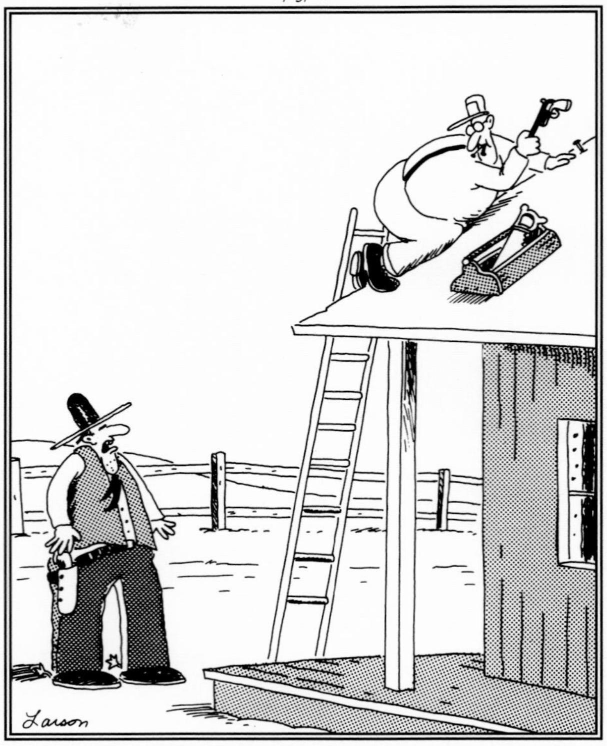

"So ... they tell me you're pretty handy with a gun."

6/16/88

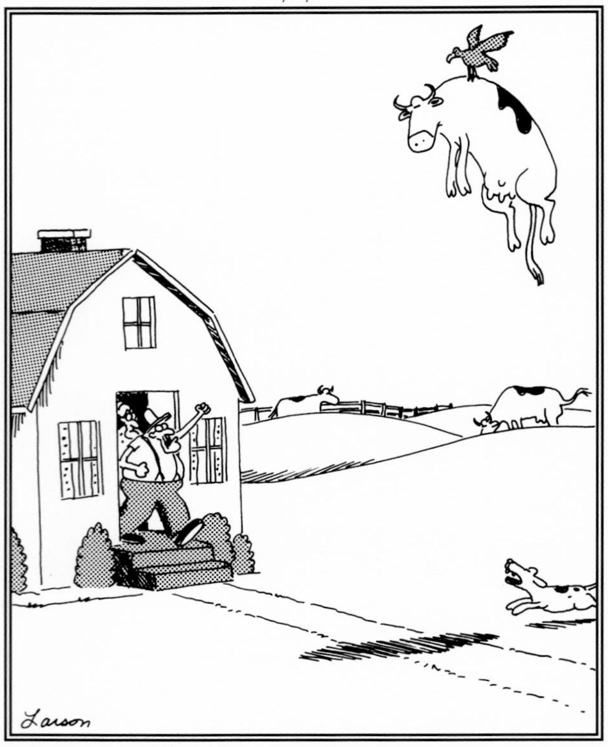

"Dang! ... That cowhawk's back."

6/17/88

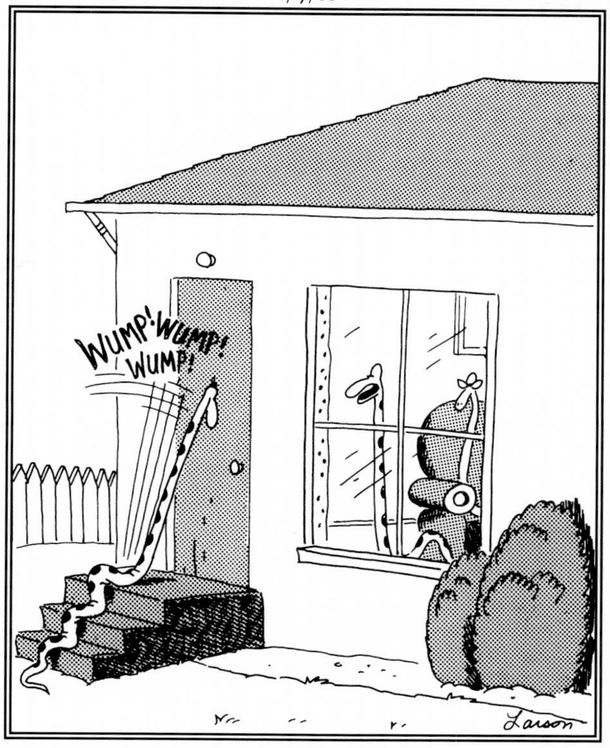
WUMP! WUMP!
WUMP!
Larson

"I'm coming! I'm coming! ... Keep your skin on!"

6/23/88

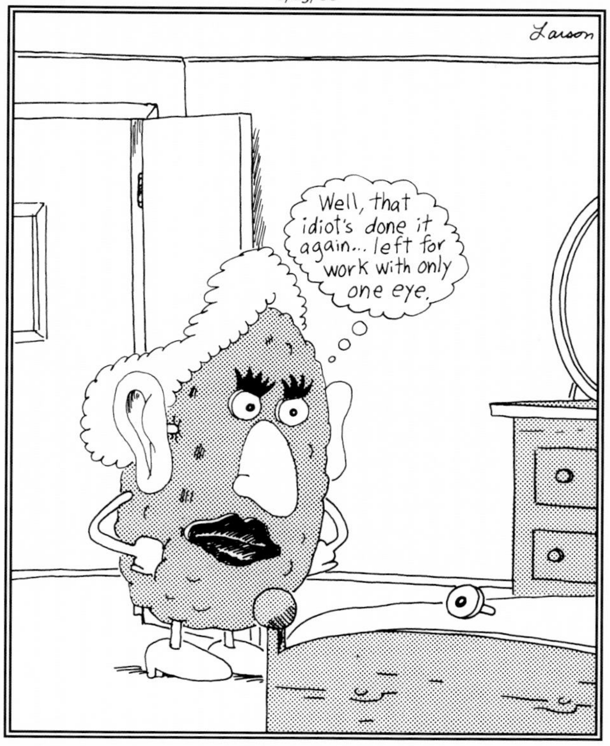
Larson
Well, that idiot's done it again... left for work with only one eye.

6/11/88

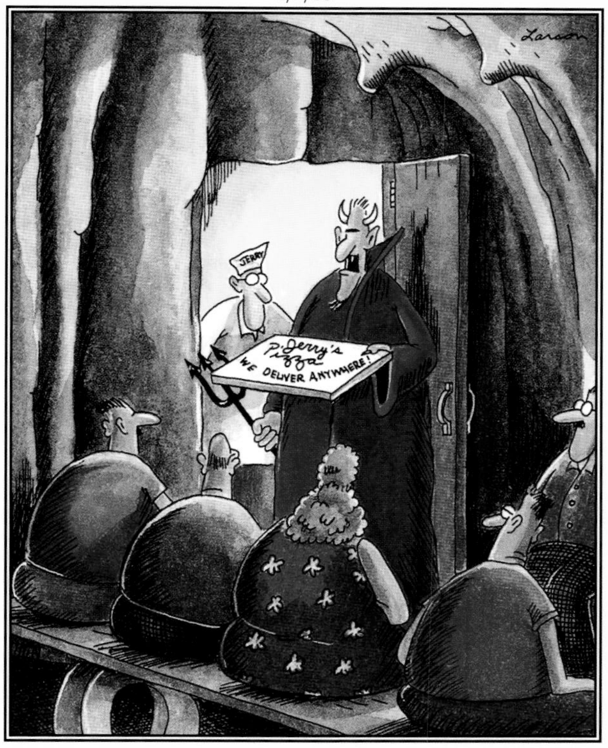
Larson
Jerry's Pizza
WE DELIVER ANYWHERE!

"First of all, this is going straight back—and I'll just have a little chat with whoever placed the order."

6/20/88

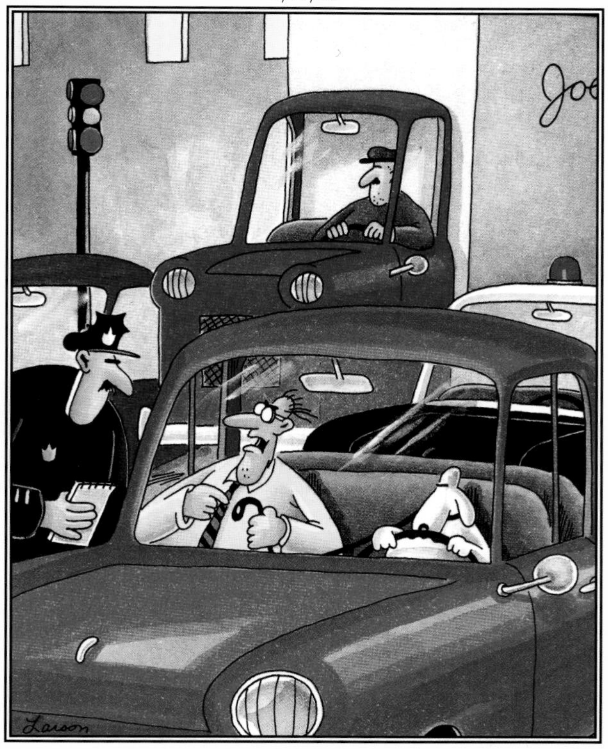
Larson

"Hey, I'm not *crazy*. ... Sure, I let him drive once in a while, but he's never, *never* off this leash for even a second."

6/19/88

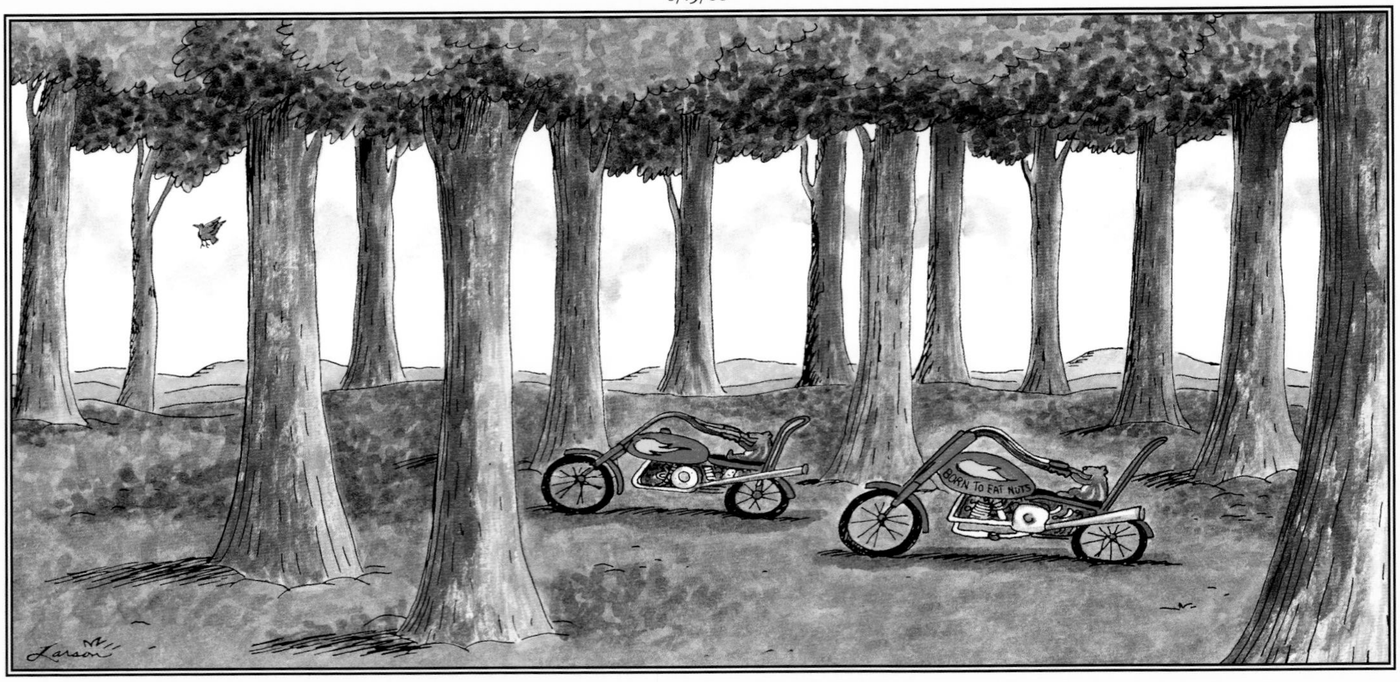
BORN TO EAT NUTS
Larson

Hell's Chipmunks

6/22/88

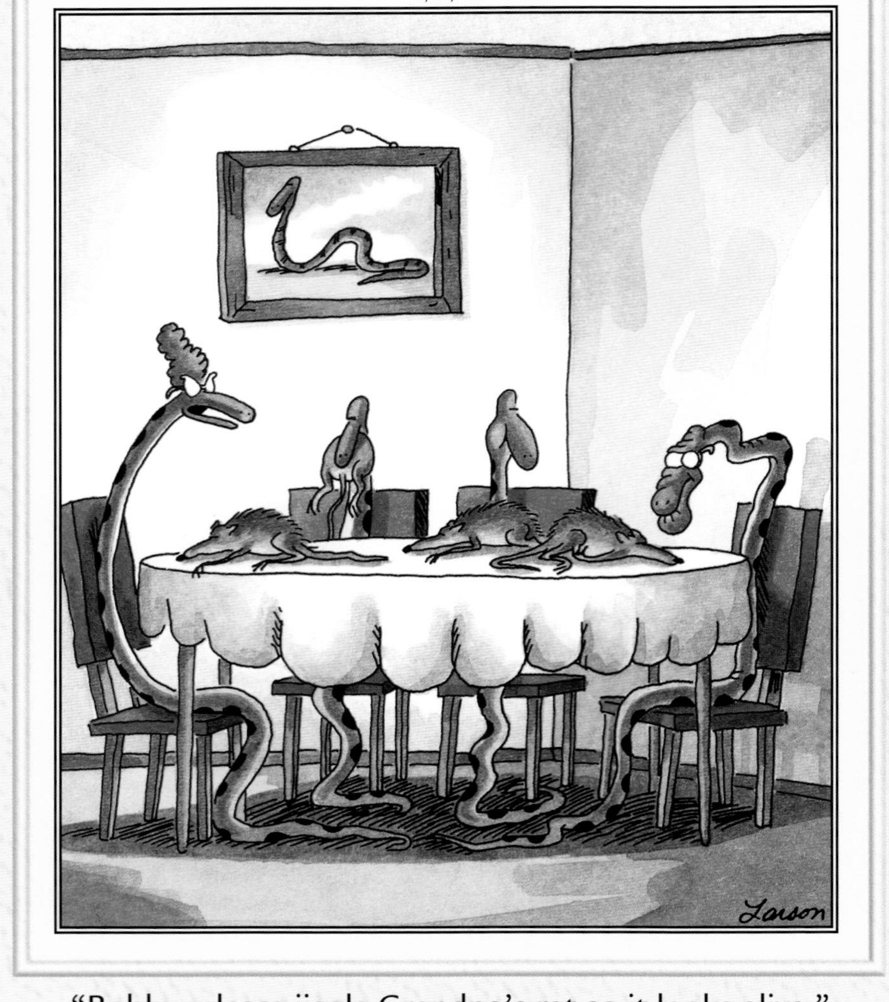
Larson

"Bobby, please jiggle Grandpa's rat so it looks alive."

6/27/88

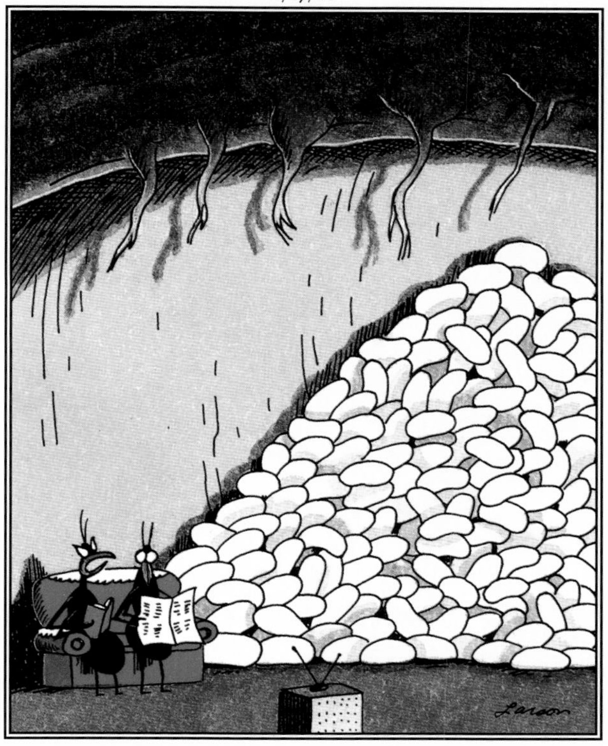

"You know, Vern ... the thought of what this place is gonna look like in about a week just creeps me out."

6/28/88

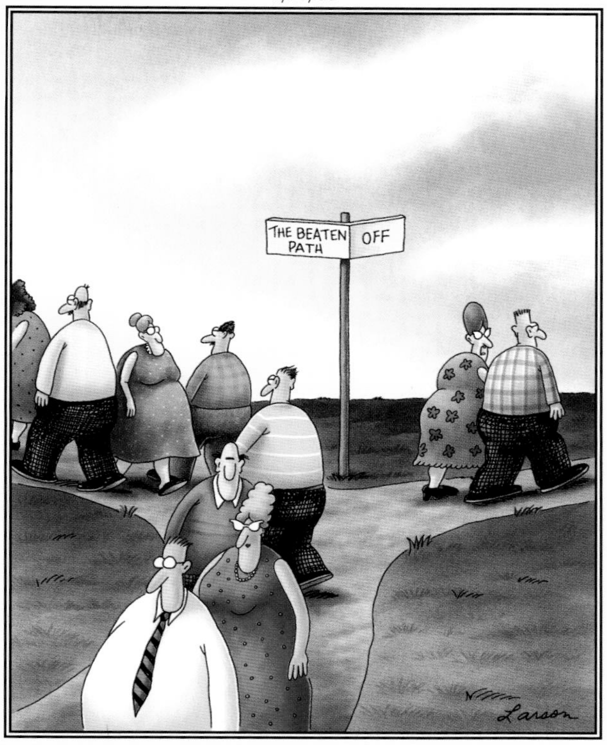
THE BEATEN PATH
OFF

"I don't know if this is such a wise thing to do, George."

6/26/88

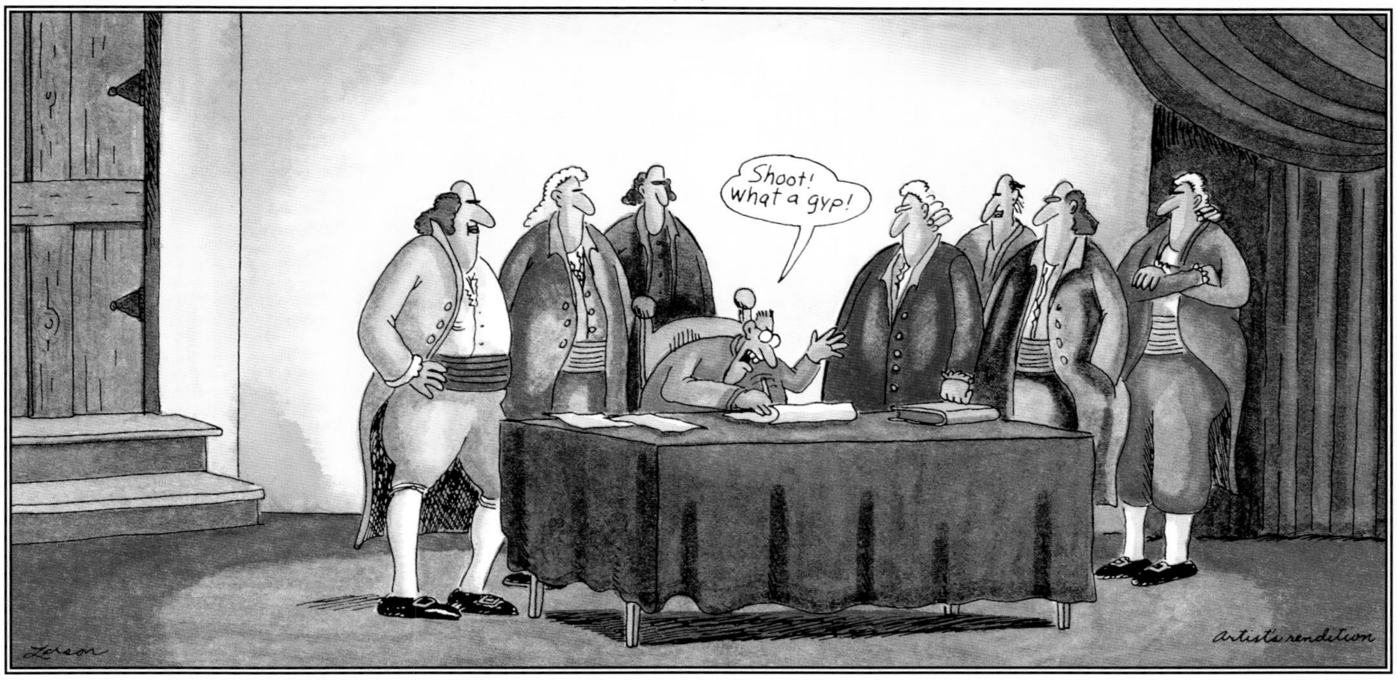
Shoot! what a gyp!
Artist's rendition

Historical note: According to some researchers, the final signer of the Declaration of Independence would have been Iggy Fenton if the pen hadn't suddenly gone dry.

6/21/88

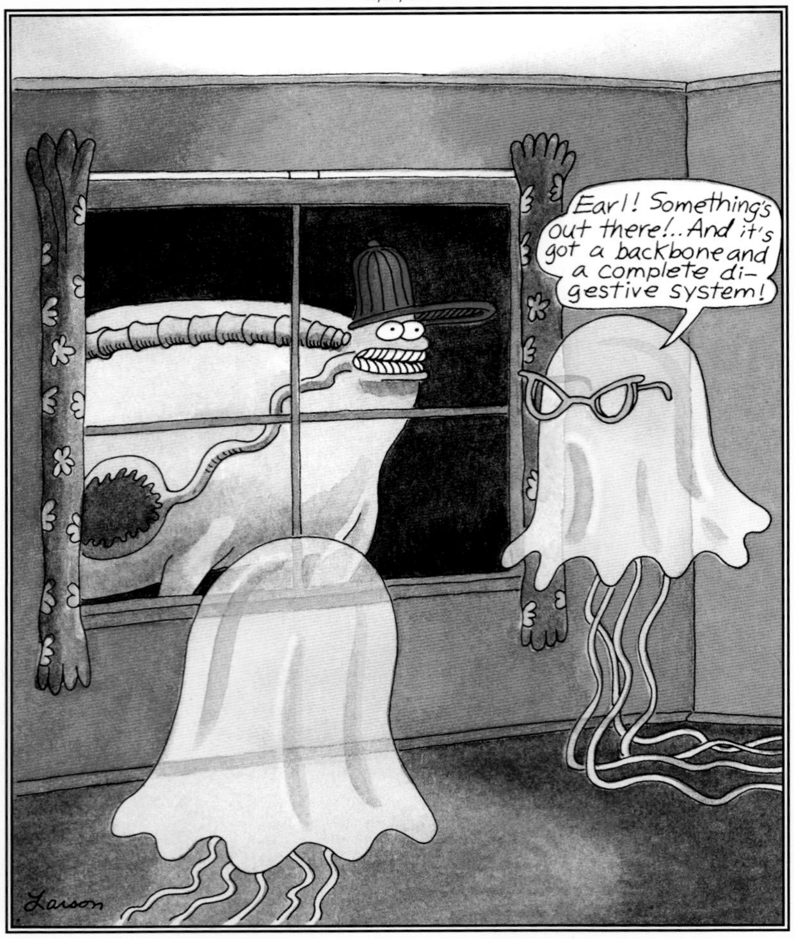
Earl! Something's out there!.. And it's got a backbone and a complete digestive system!
Larson

Life in the primordial soup

6/18/88

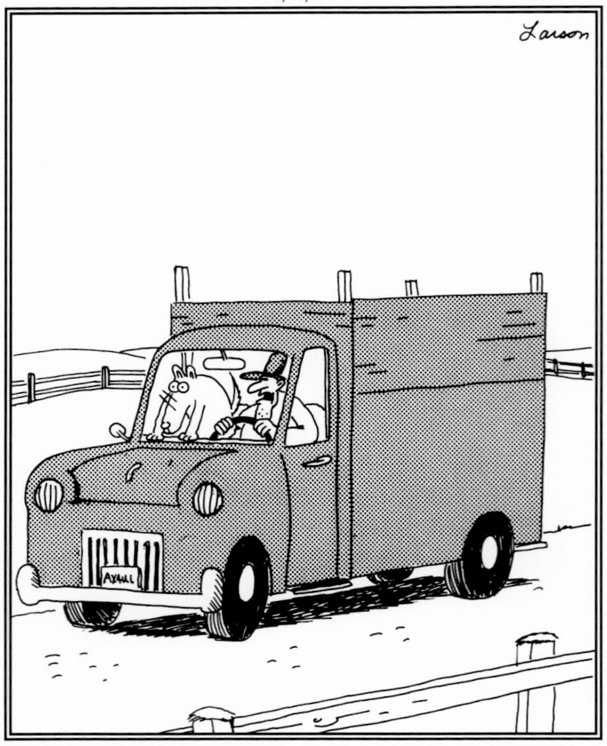
Larson

"Somethin' dead in the road up ahead. ... Is that a cat? Too dang big for a cat. ... Calf, maybe. ... Sure do look like a cat, though."

6/24/88

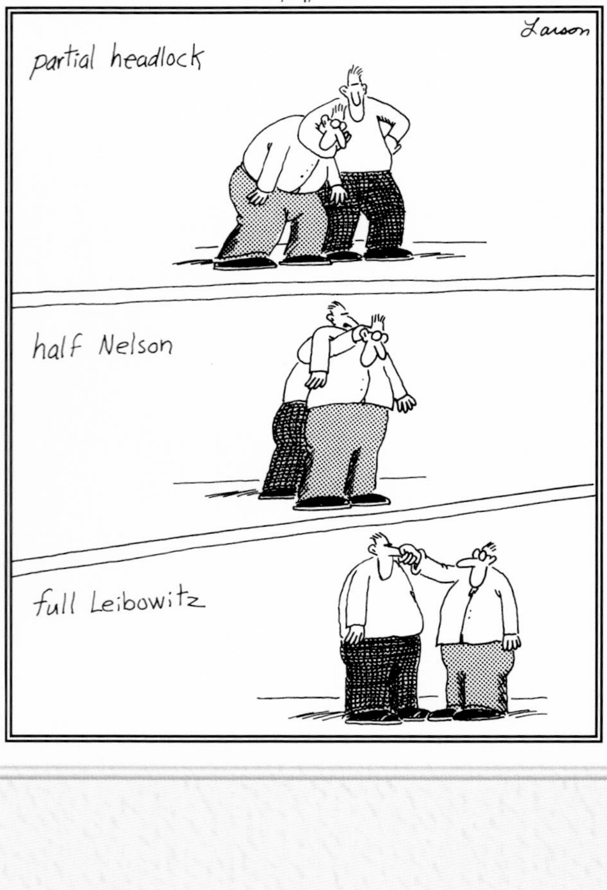
Larson
partial headlock
half Nelson
full Leibowitz

6/30/88

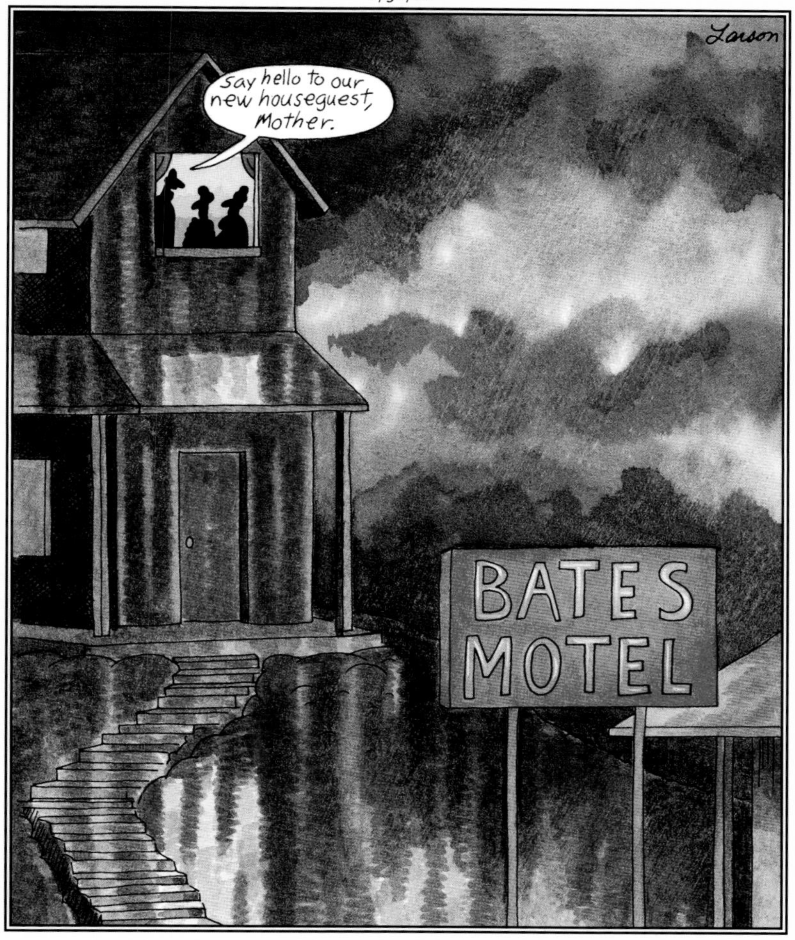
Larson
Say hello to our new houseguest, Mother.
BATES MOTEL

What really happened to Elvis

6/25/88

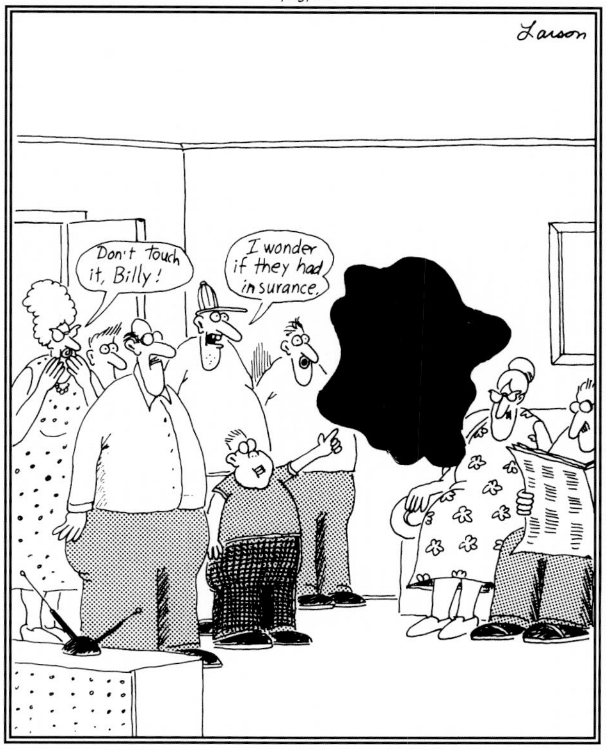
Larson
Don't touch it, Billy!
I wonder if they had insurance.

Folks came from miles around to see the Herringtons' ink smudge.

6/29/88

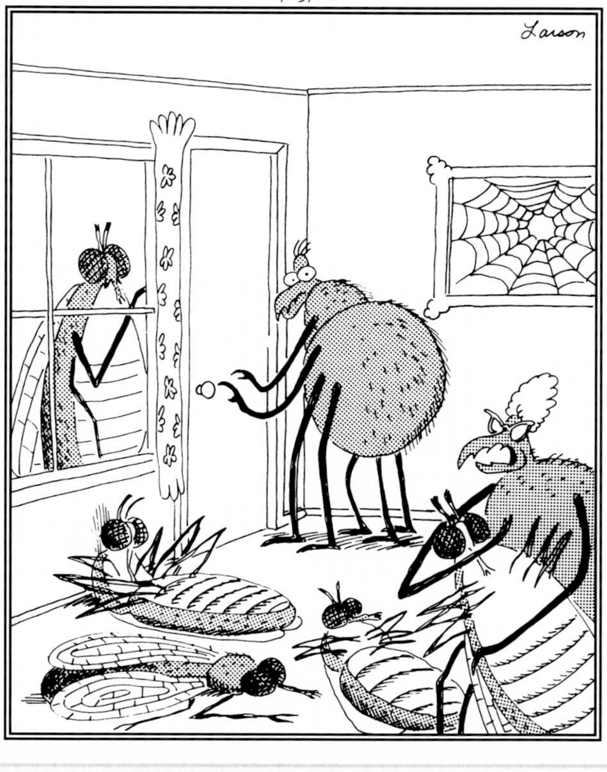
Larson

"Wait, you idiot! Let me first get rid of these exoskeletons!"

7/2/88
Larson
Dear Lola,
This is farewell.
Tonight I'm going to
fly right smack into
the middle of a
roaring bonfire.
(Of course, I plan to
circle a few times first.)
Your mate,
Donald

7/4/88
Larson

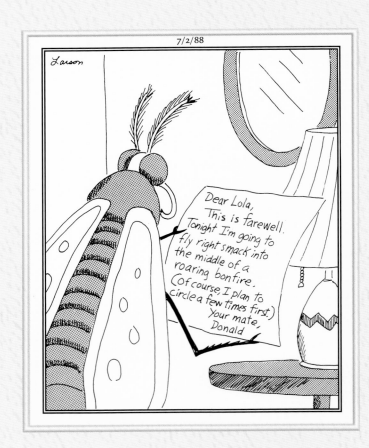

"*Sure* it's true! ... Cross my heart and hope to die, stick a sharp chunk of obsidian in my eye."

7/1/88
Larson

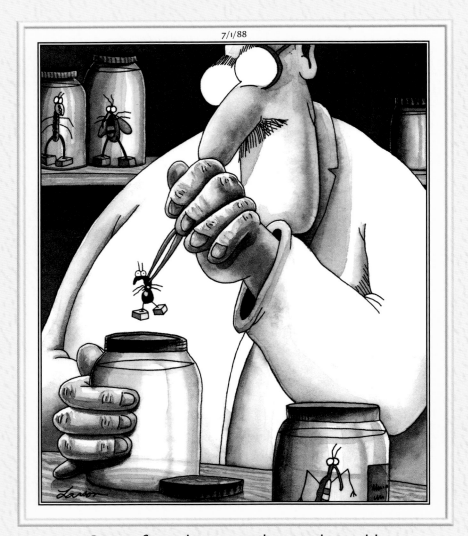

Scenes from the entomology underworld

7/5/88

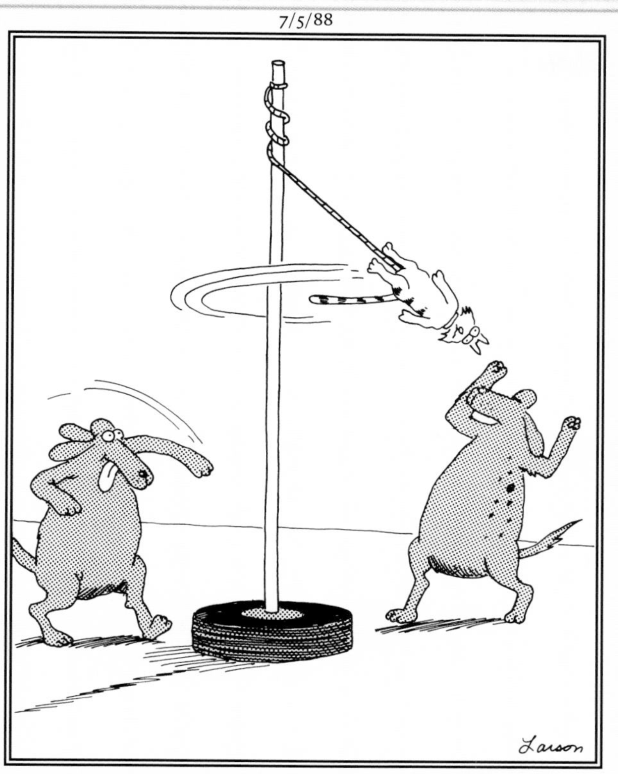
Larson

Tethercat

7/8/88

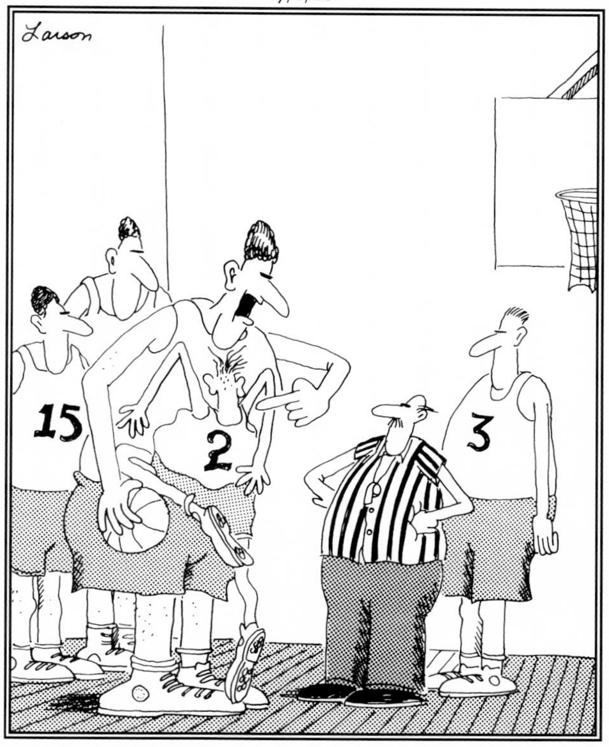
Larson
15
2
3

"Offensive foul? *Offensive* foul? Are you crazy? ... He was *moving!*"

7/9/88

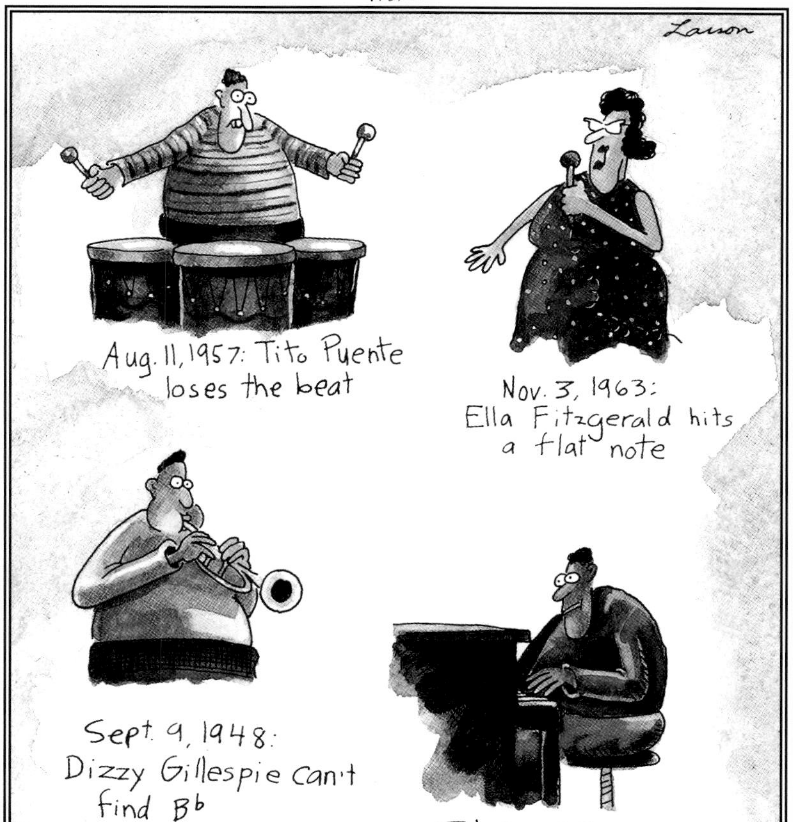
Larson
Aug. 11, 1957: Tito Puente loses the beat
Nov. 3, 1963: Ella Fitzgerald hits a flat note
Sept. 9, 1948: Dizzy Gillespie can't find B♭
July 14, 1974: Oscar Peterson forgets the chords to "Heart and Soul."

Infamous moments in jazz

7/3/88

When dogs go to work

7/6/88

Embedded in Styrofoam "shoes," Carl is sent
to "sleep with the humans."

7/11/88

"No, they're not real exciting pets—mostly they
just lie around and wait to be fed—although a
couple years ago Charles tried teachin' him to
take a cookie from his mouth."

7/12/88

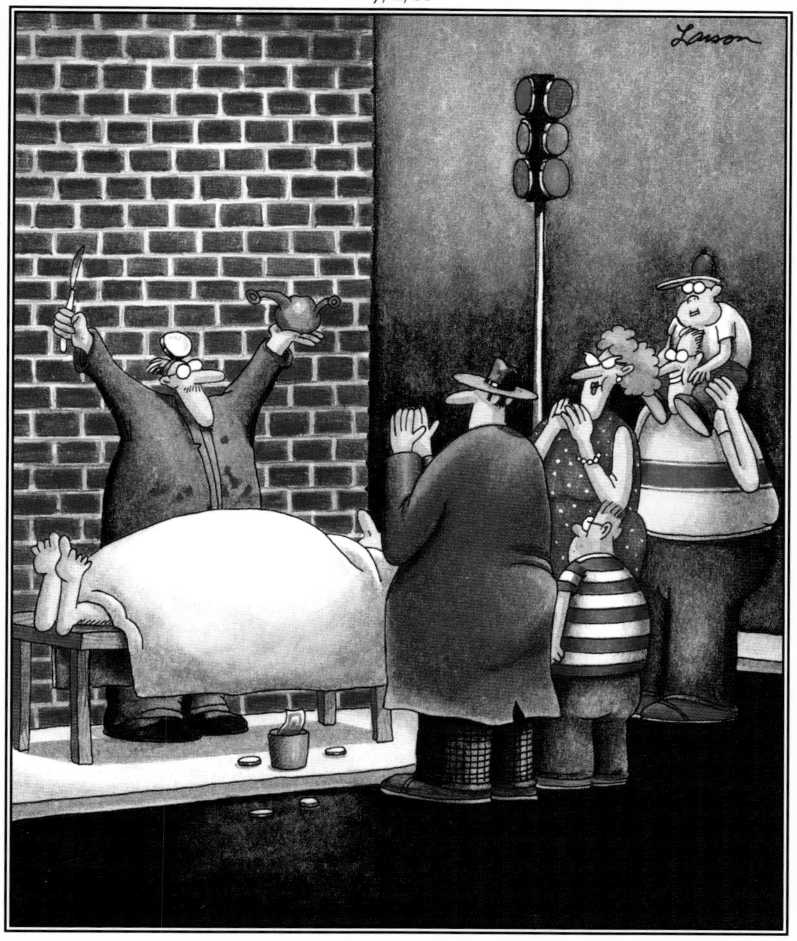

Street physicians

7/10/88

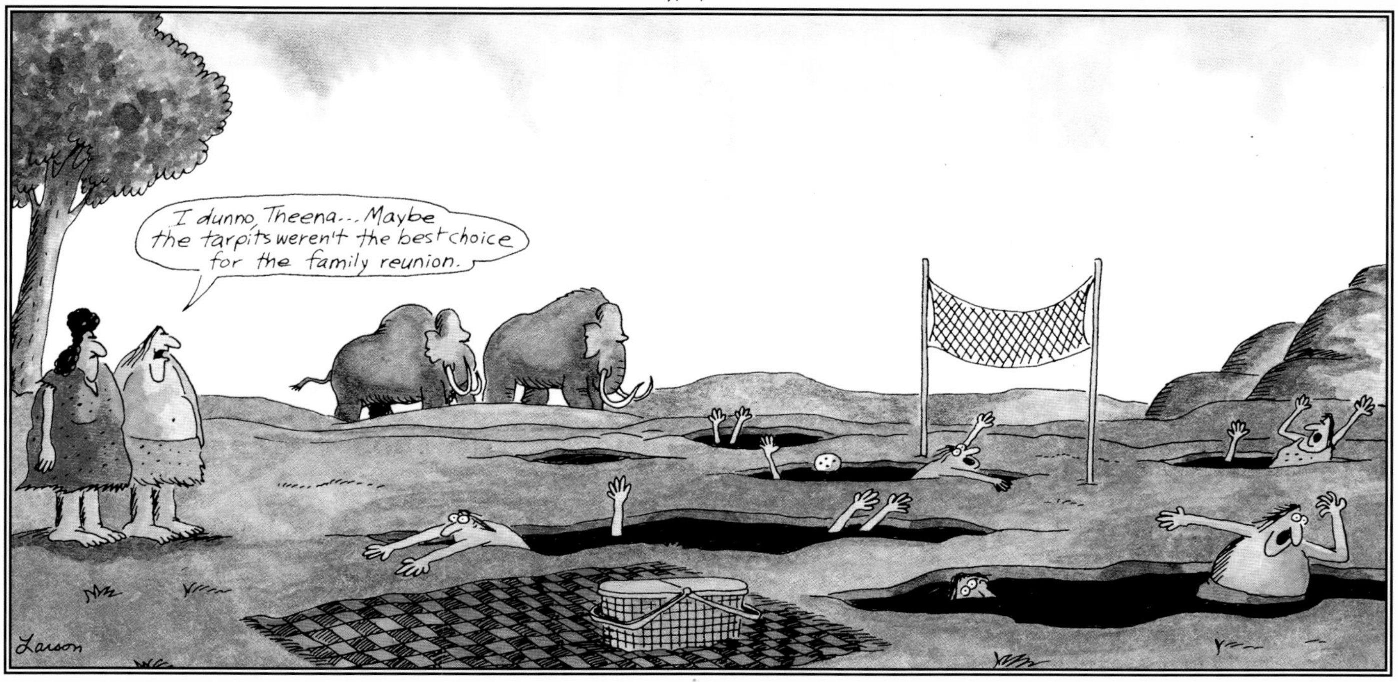
I dunno, Theena... Maybe the tarpits weren't the best choice for the family reunion.

7/7/88

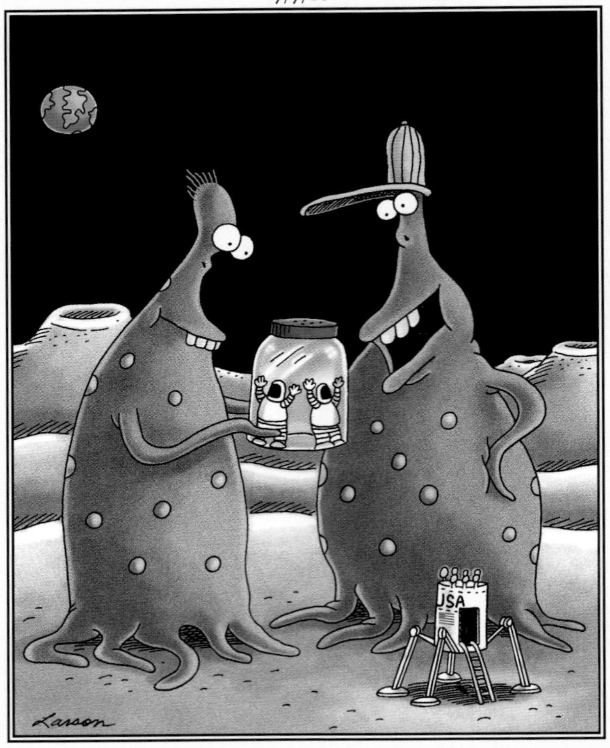
JSA
Larson

"Pretty cool, Dewey. ... Hey! Shake the jar and see if they'll fight!"

7/14/88

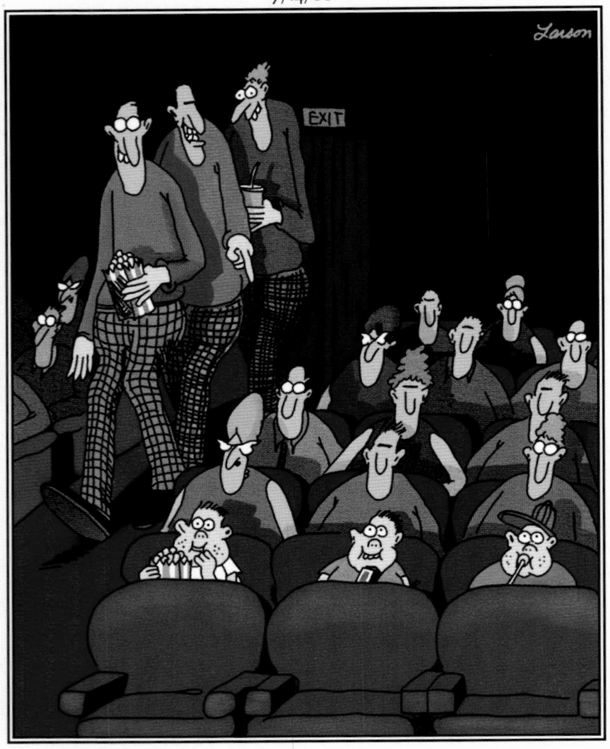
Larson
EXIT

7/13/88

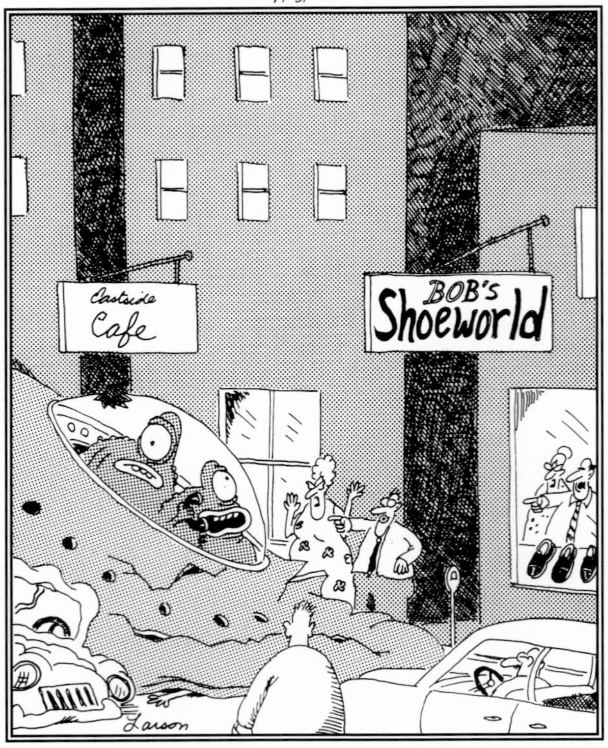
Eastside Cafe
BOB's Shoeworld
Larson

"Listen! Just follow our distress beacon and send some help! ... We're in quadrant 57 of the Milky Way—on a planet called 'Bob's Shoeworld.'"

7/15/88

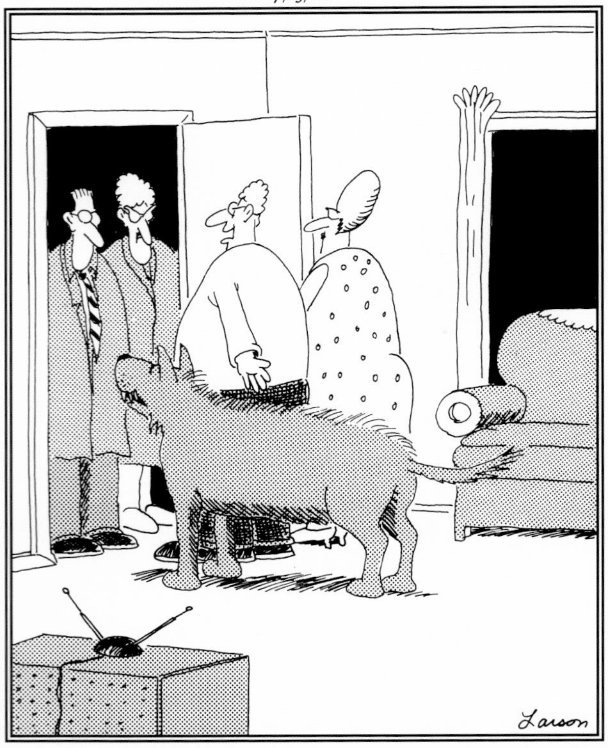
Larson

"Hey! Jack and Paula! You made it! ... Now, quickly: Keep one hand across your throat and put the other one confidently down on Bruno's head—stupid dog's going to get Agnes and me into a giant lawsuit one day."

"Yeah? Well, I'll tell you who your friend saw me with—a decoy! That's who!"

"I built the forms around him just yesterday afternoon when he fell asleep, and by early evening I was able to mix and pour."

7/17/88

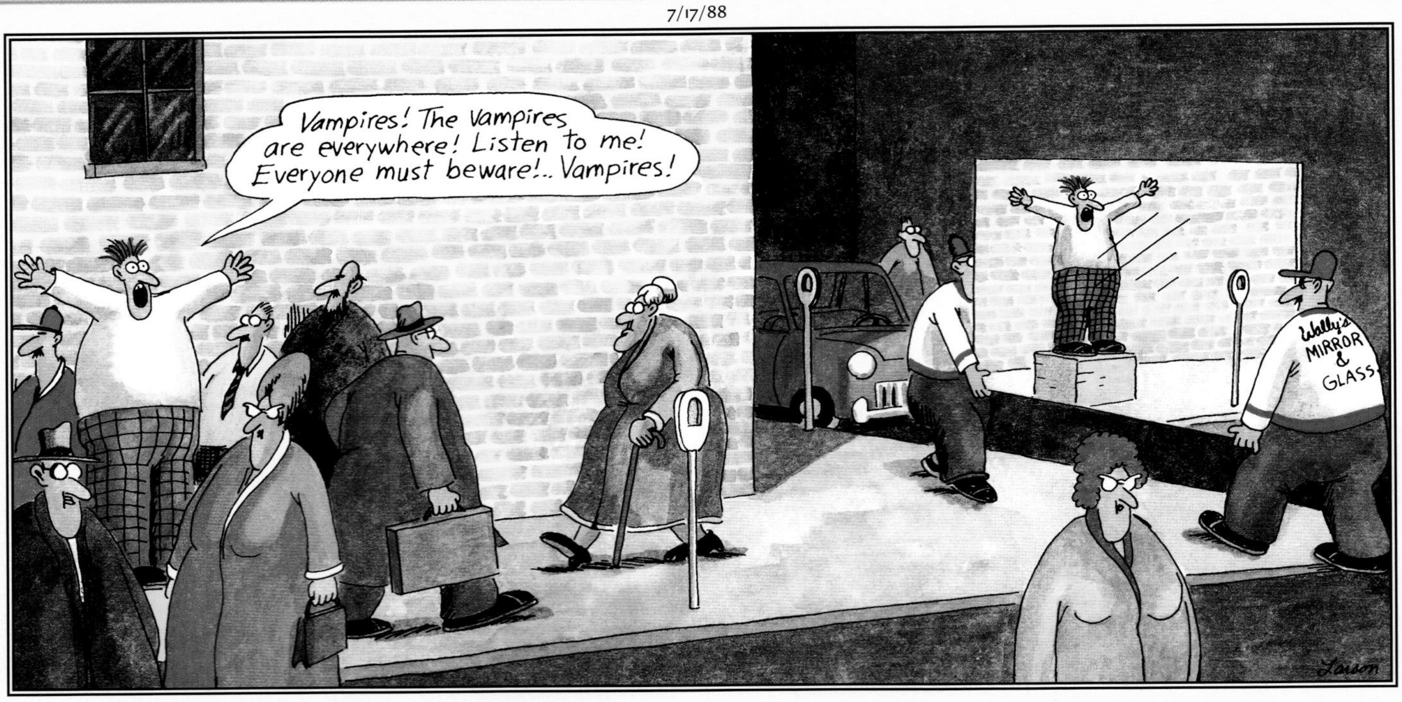
Vampires! The vampires are everywhere! Listen to me! Everyone must beware!.. Vampires!
Wally's MIRROR & GLASS
Larson

7/20/88

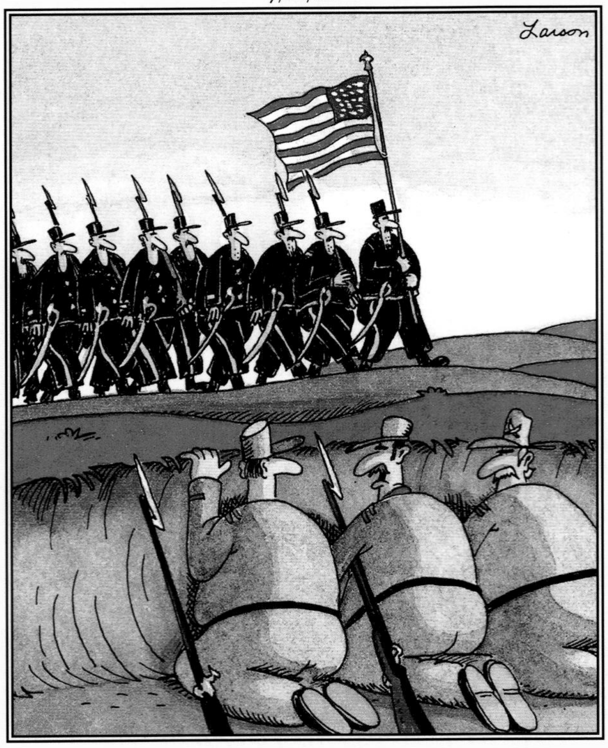
Larson

"*I* wasn't just whistling 'Dixie'! ... Sam, were *you* just whistling 'Dixie'?"

7/22/88

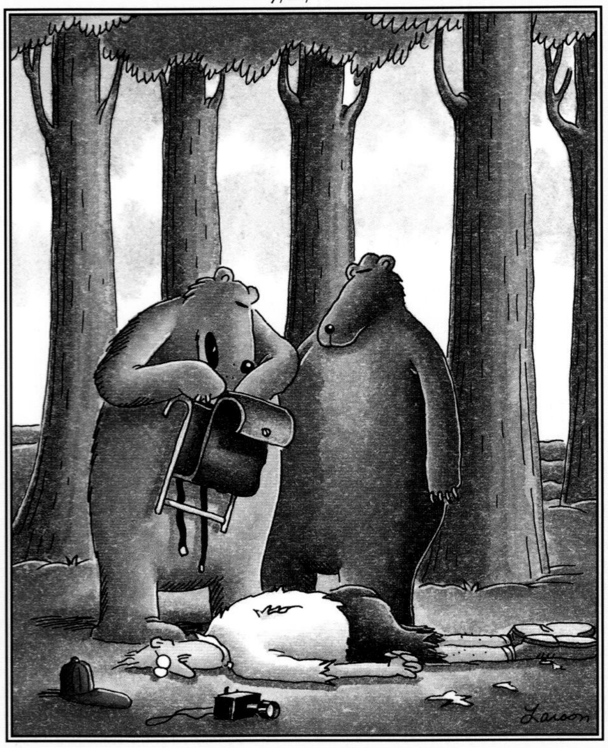
Larson

"I can't believe it! This is impossible! Nothing here but—wait! Wait! I see something! ... Yes! There they are—granola bars!"

7/27/88

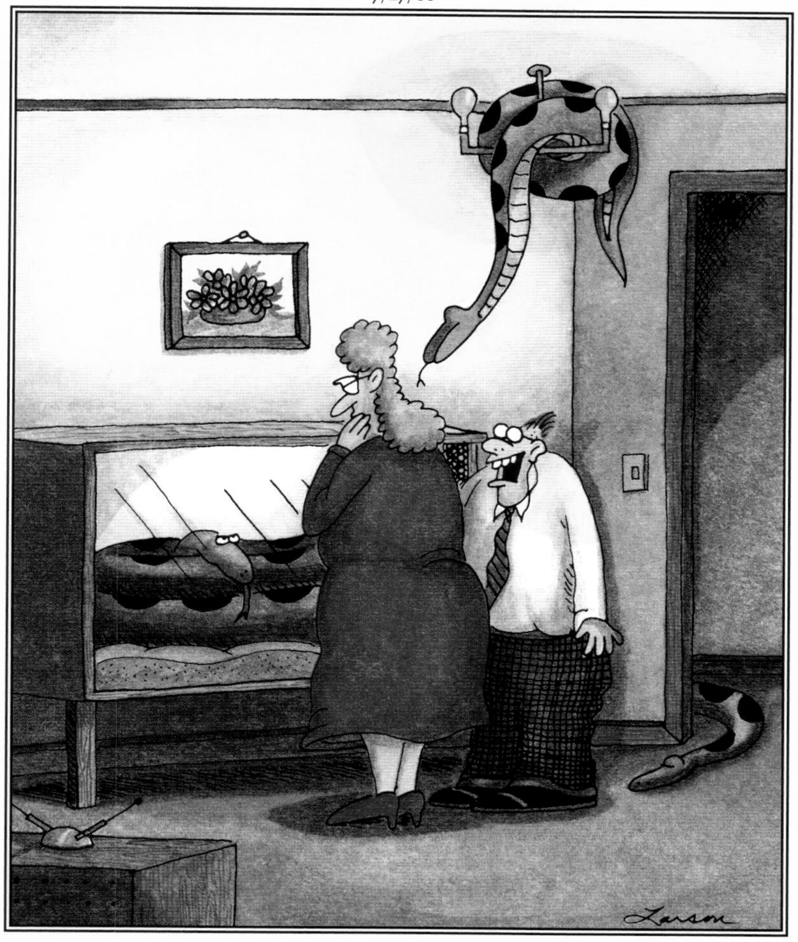

"Oh, no! I have several others—Oggy here is just a tad aggressive, so he has to stay in a cage."

7/24/88

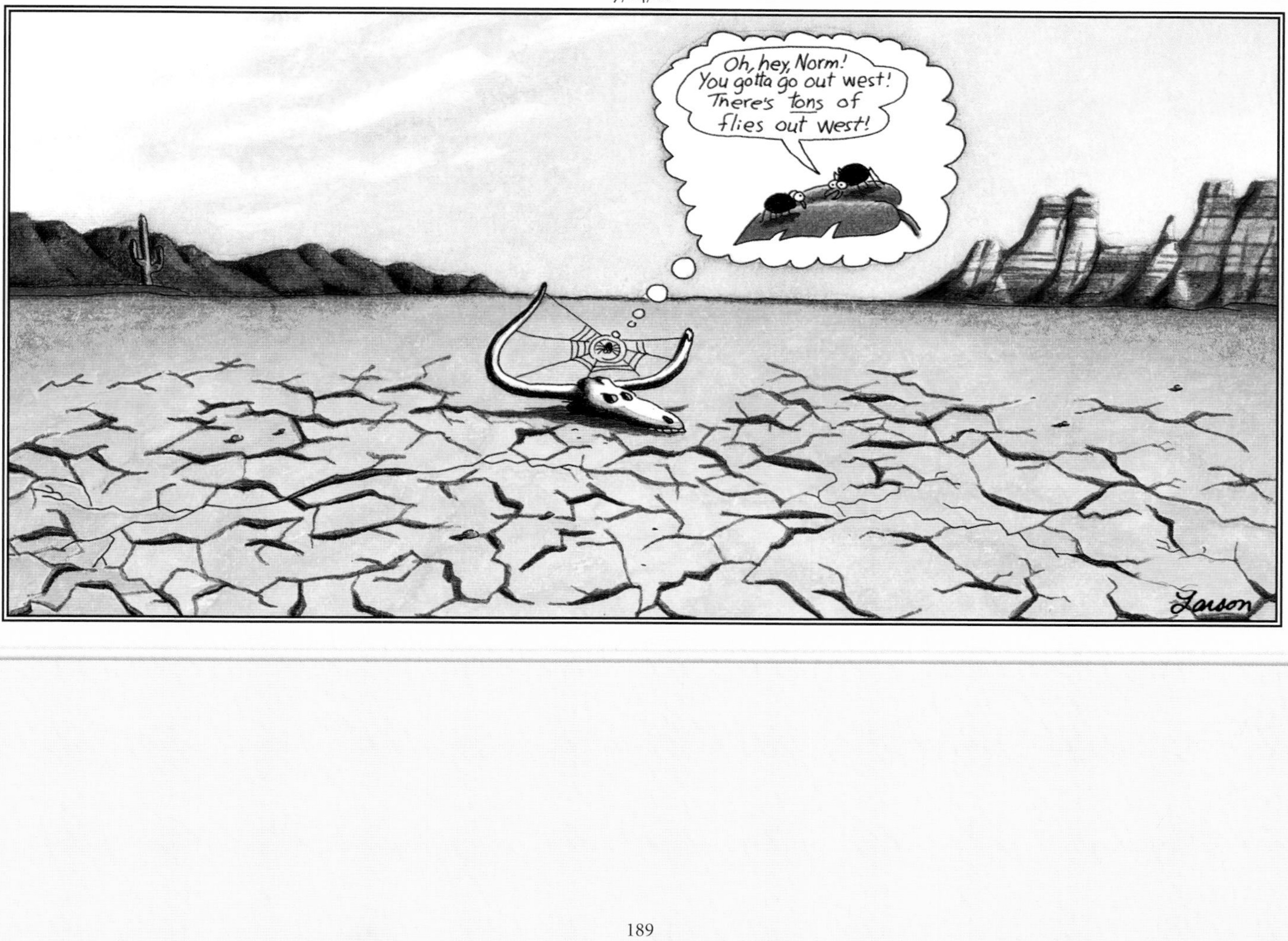
Oh, hey, Norm! You gotta go out west! There's tons of flies out west!

7/23/88

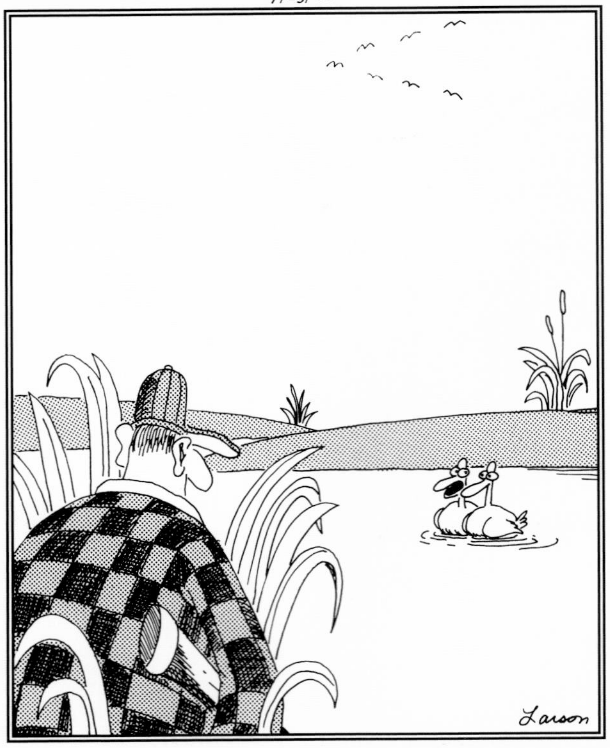
Larson

"I didn't say we were setting ducks! I said *sitting* ducks! ... I know the difference between sitting and setting, you idiot!"

7/25/88

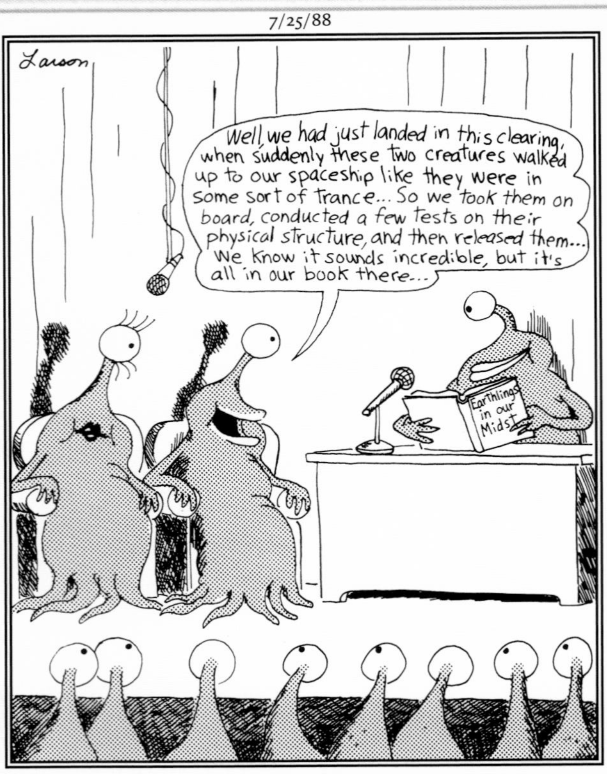
Larson
Well, we had just landed in this clearing, when suddenly these two creatures walked up to our spaceship like they were in some sort of trance... So we took them on board, conducted a few tests on their physical structure, and then released them... We know it sounds incredible, but it's all in our book there...
Earthlings in our Midst

Alien talk shows

7/26/88

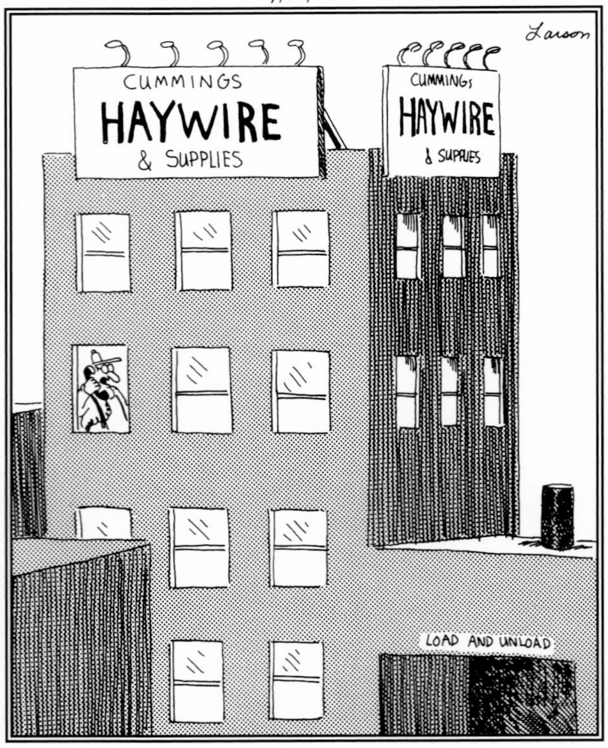
Larson
CUMMINGS HAYWIRE & SUPPLIES
CUMMINGS HAYWIRE & SUPPLIES
LOAD AND UNLOAD

"Mr. Cummings? This is Frank Dunham in Production. ... We've got some problems, Mr. Cummings. Machine No. 5 has jammed, several of the larger spools have gone off track, the generator's blown, and, well, everything seems to be you-know-what."

7/28/88

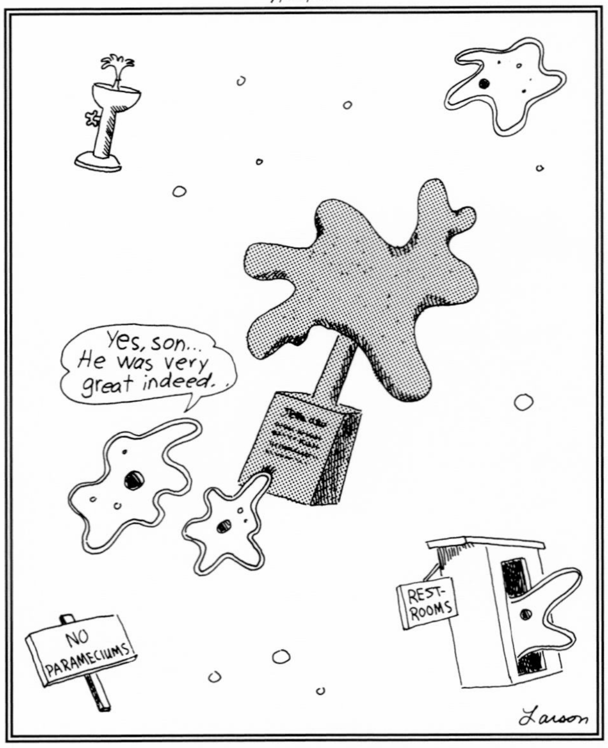
Yes, son... He was very great indeed.
REST-ROOMS
NO PARAMECIUMS
Larson

In Amoebae Park

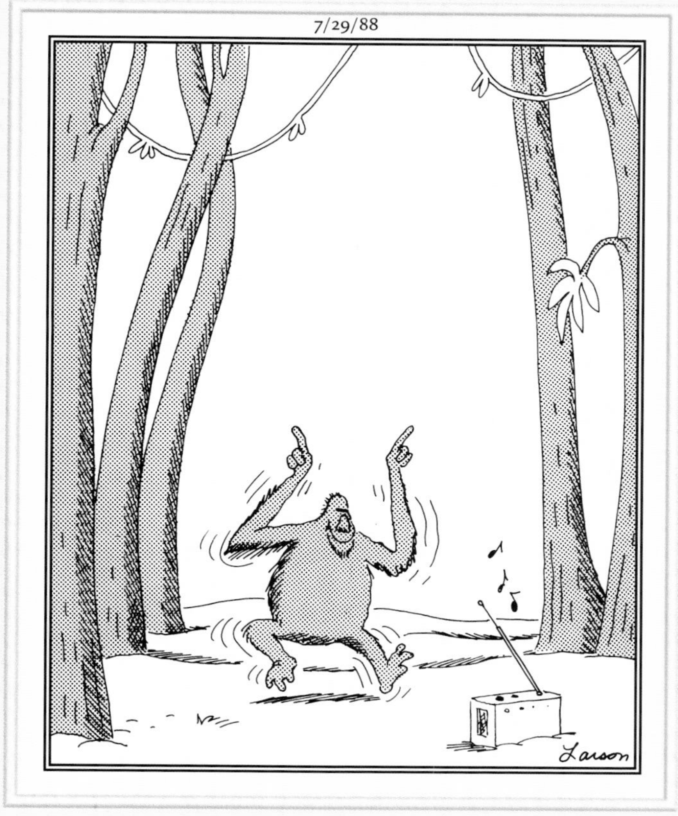
7/29/88
Larson

What sloths do when no one's around

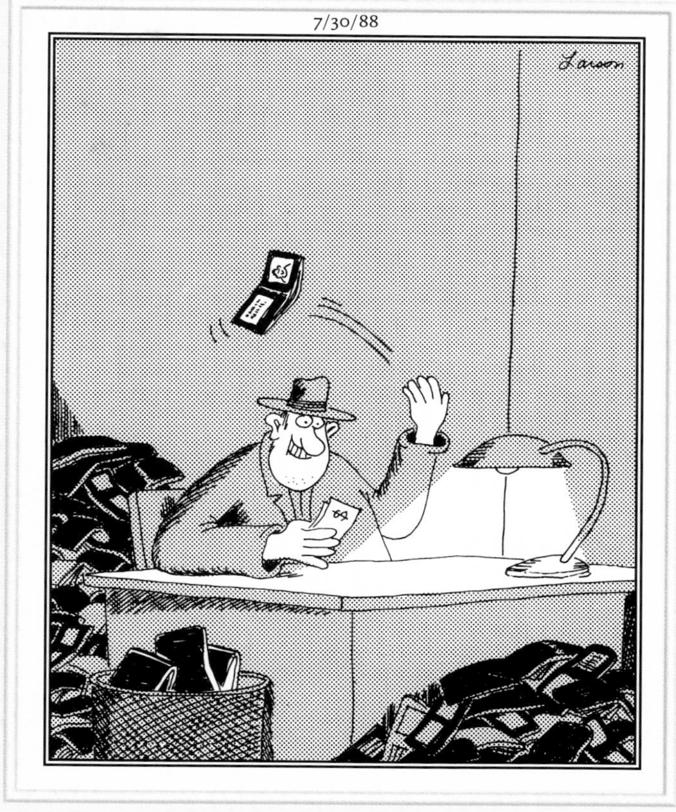
7/30/88
Larson

Karl Malden in his basement

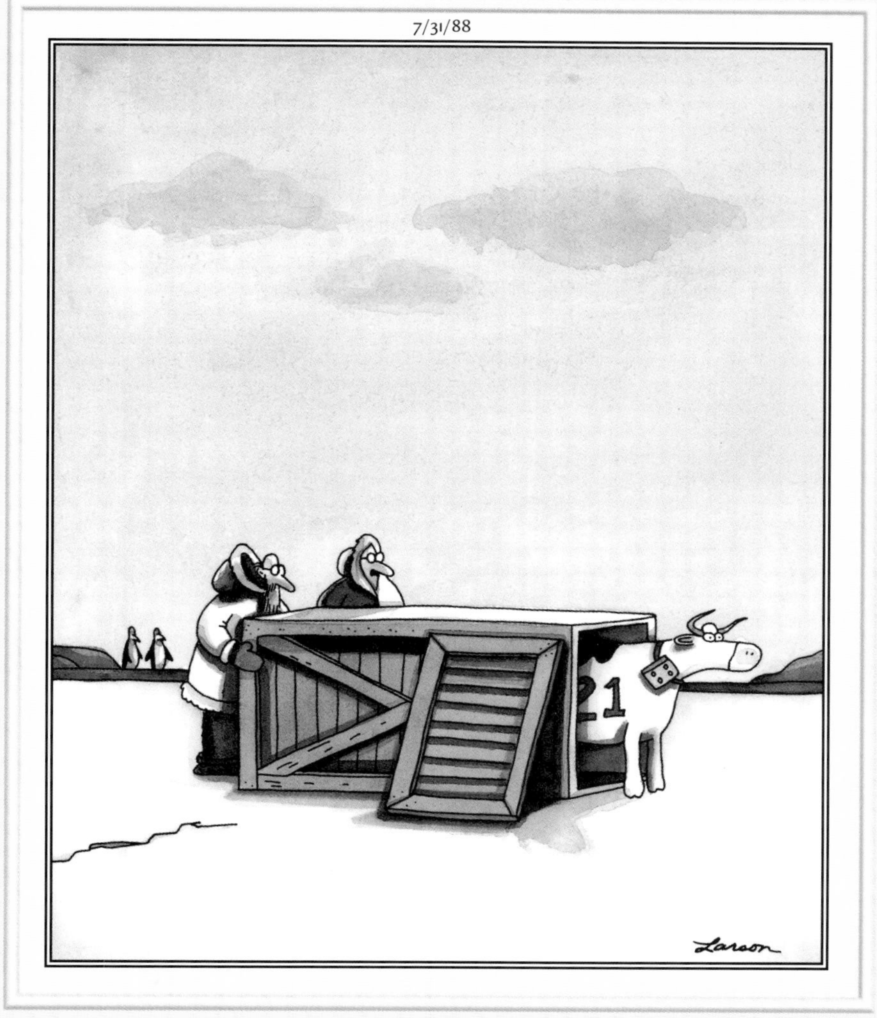
7/31/88
21
Larson

Scientists, after releasing her deep in the Antarctic, attempt to unravel the migratory secrets of the homing cow.

8/1/88

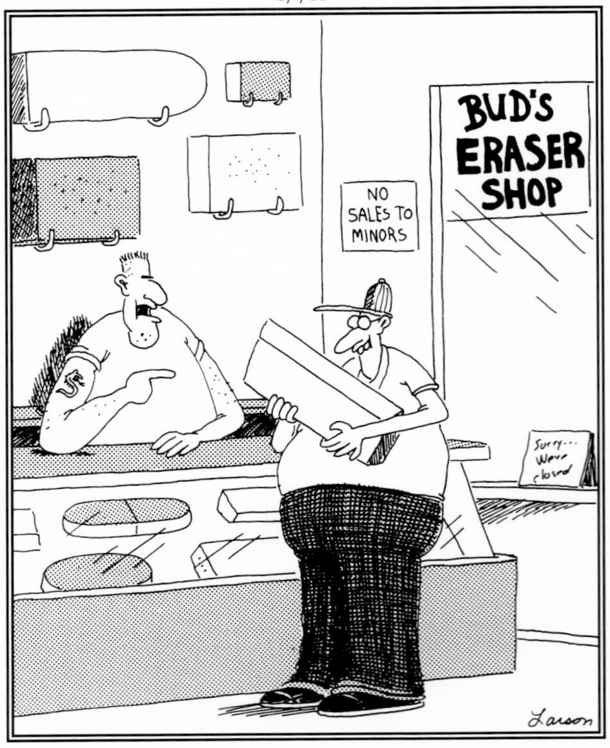
BUD'S ERASER SHOP
NO SALES TO MINORS
Larson

"Just heft that baby in your arms a little. ... I guarantee you, whether they're drawn in ink or pencil, that sucker will wipe out any characters that come around."

8/3/88

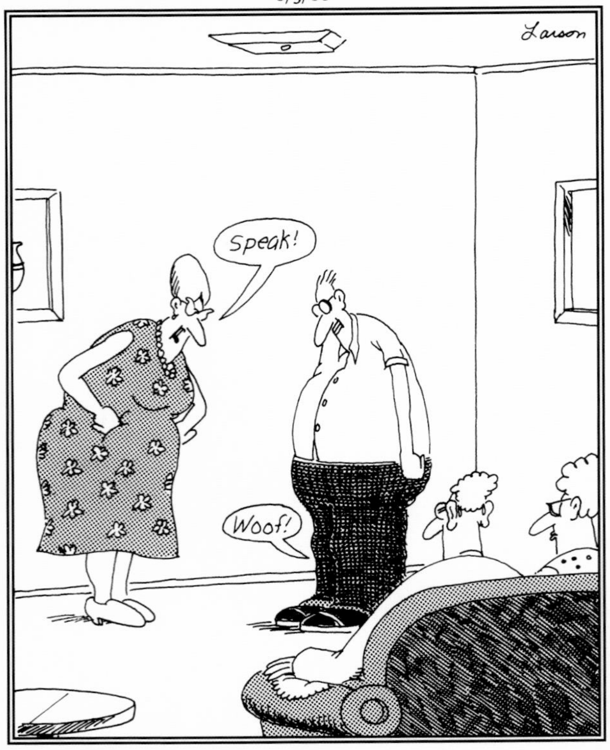
Larson
Speak!
Woof!

The Fullertons demonstrate Sidney's trick knee.

8/2/88

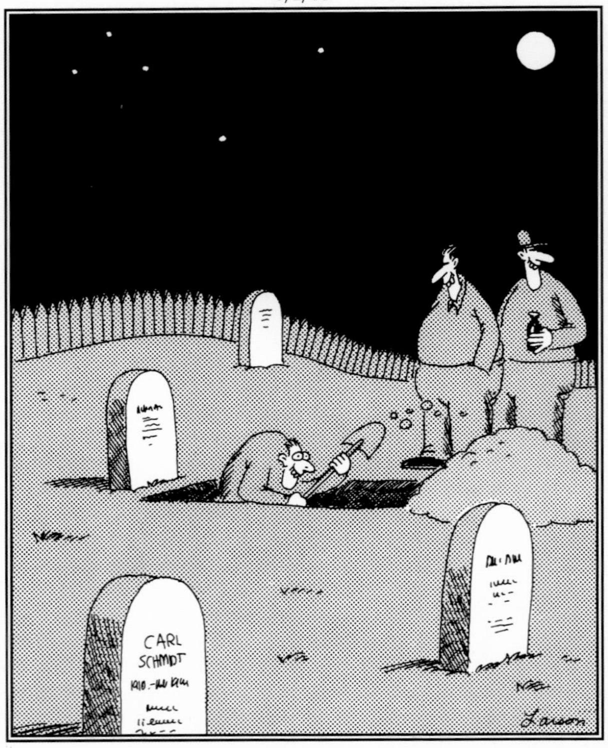
CARL SCHMIDT
Larson

Convinced by his buddies that in actual fact they were only grave "borrowing," a young Igor starts on his road to crime.

8/4/88

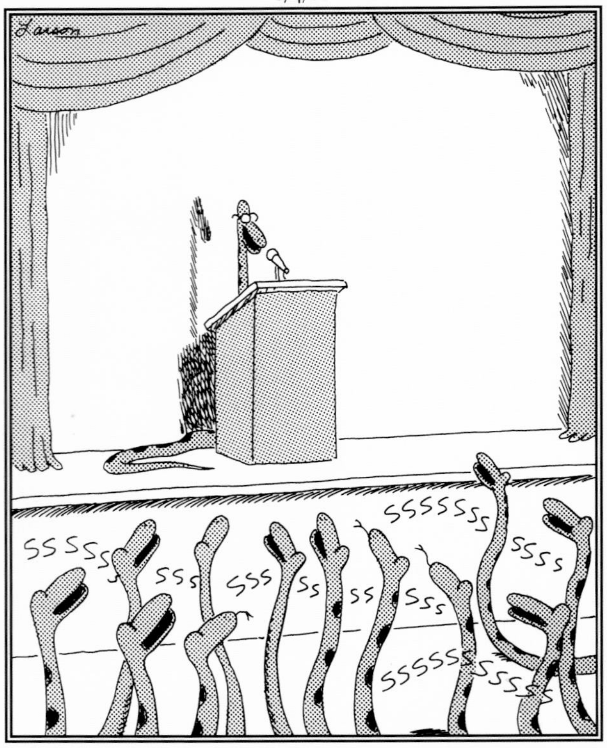
Larson
SSSSSSS
SSSSS
SSSS
SSS
SSS
SS
SS
SSS
SSSSSSSSSSS

"Why, thank you. ... Thank you very much!"

8/6/88

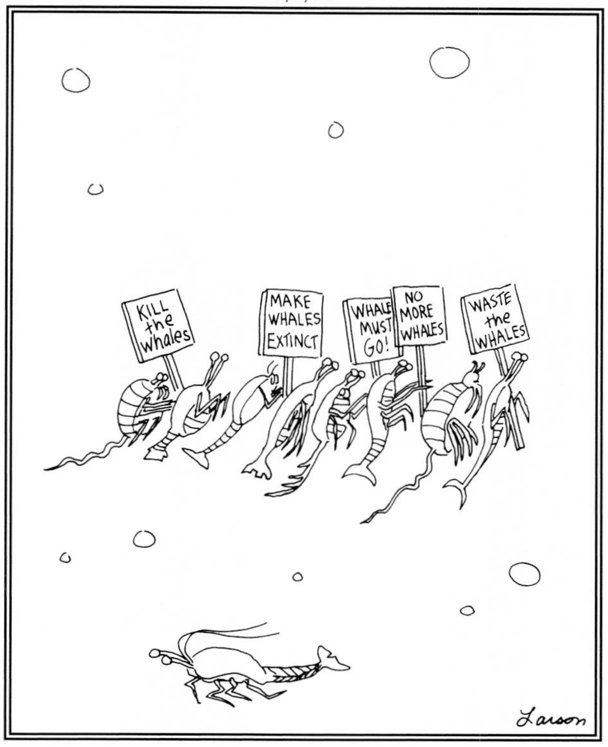
KILL the whales
MAKE WHALES EXTINCT
WHALES MUST GO!
NO MORE WHALES
WASTE the WHALES
Larson

The plankton lobby

8/11/88

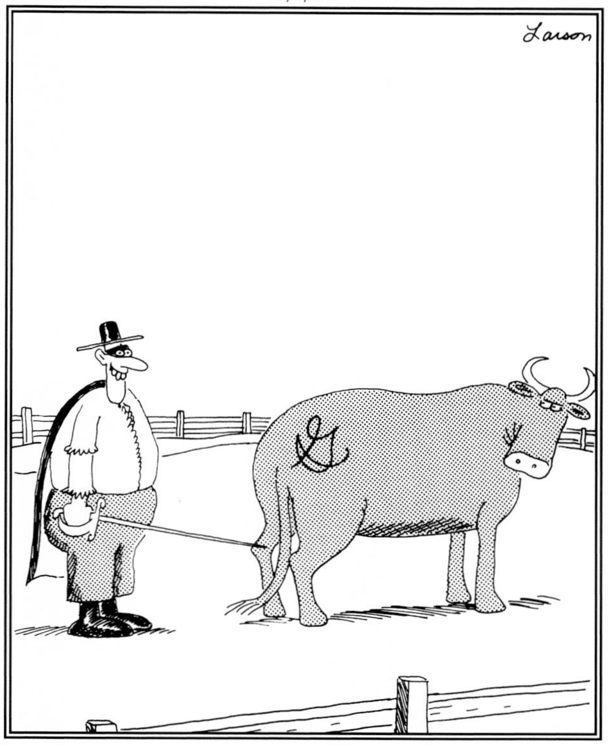
Larson

Practicing his skills wherever possible, Zorro's younger and less astute brother, Gomez, had a similar career cut short.

8/5/88

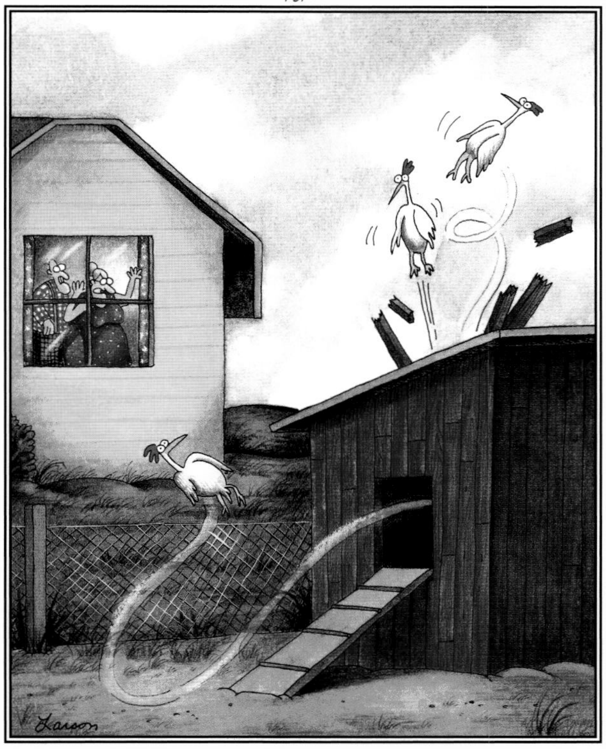
Larson

"Aaaaaaaaaaaaa! Earl! ... We've got a poultrygeist!"

8/9/88

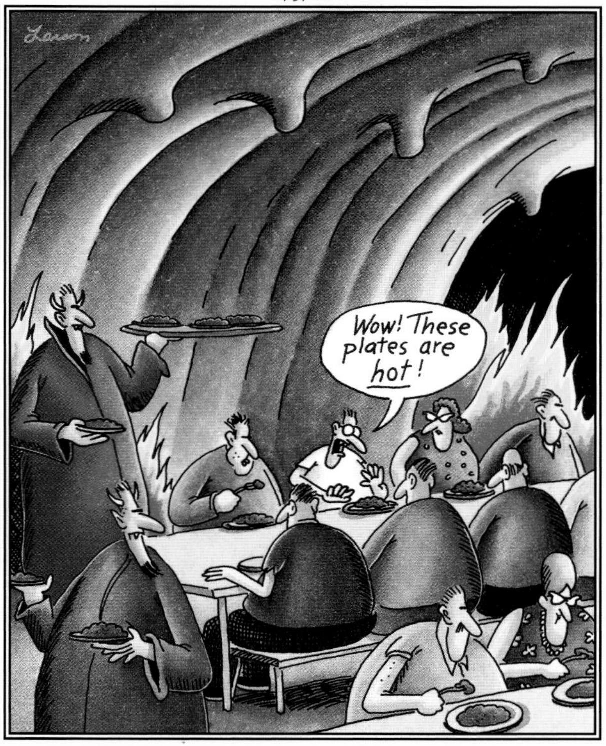
Larson
Wow! These plates are hot!

Hell's cafeteria

8/7/88

I wonder if I should report this.
ACME
GATE SMASHER
&
MOAT CROSSER

8/10/88

VERS
Hey! Buddy!..
Move that thing!
Watch it,
Buddy!

Why people named Buddy hate to drive

8/8/88

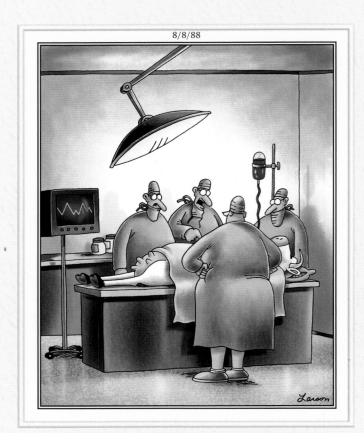

"Well, we've done everything we can; now we can only wait and see if she pulls through. ... If she doesn't, however, I got dibs on this porterhouse right here."

8/15/88

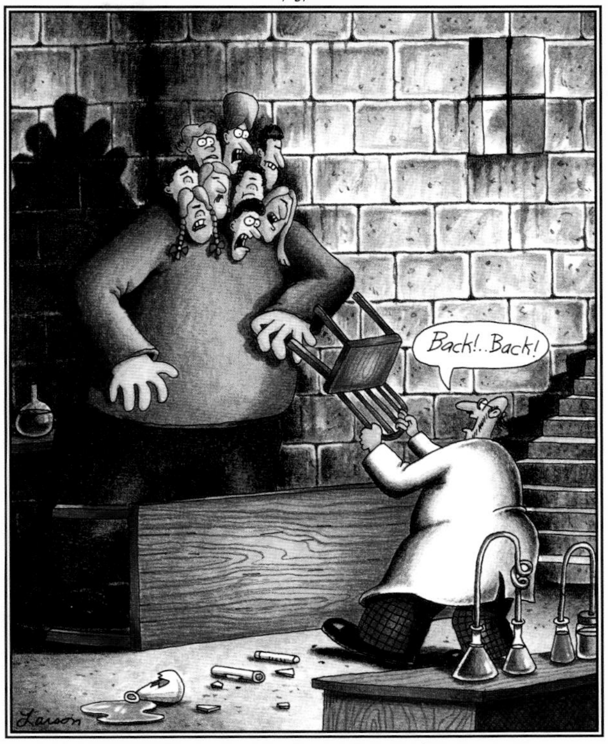
Back!..Back!

Suddenly, Dr. Morrissey's own creation, a hideous creature nine feet tall and bearing the heads of the Brady Bunch, turns against him.

8/16/88

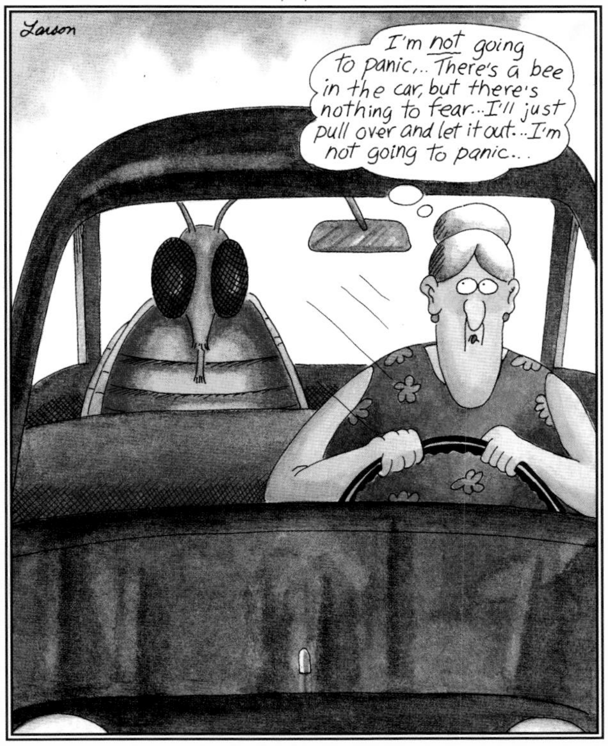
I'm not going to panic... There's a bee in the car, but there's nothing to fear...I'll just pull over and let it out...I'm not going to panic...

8/14/88

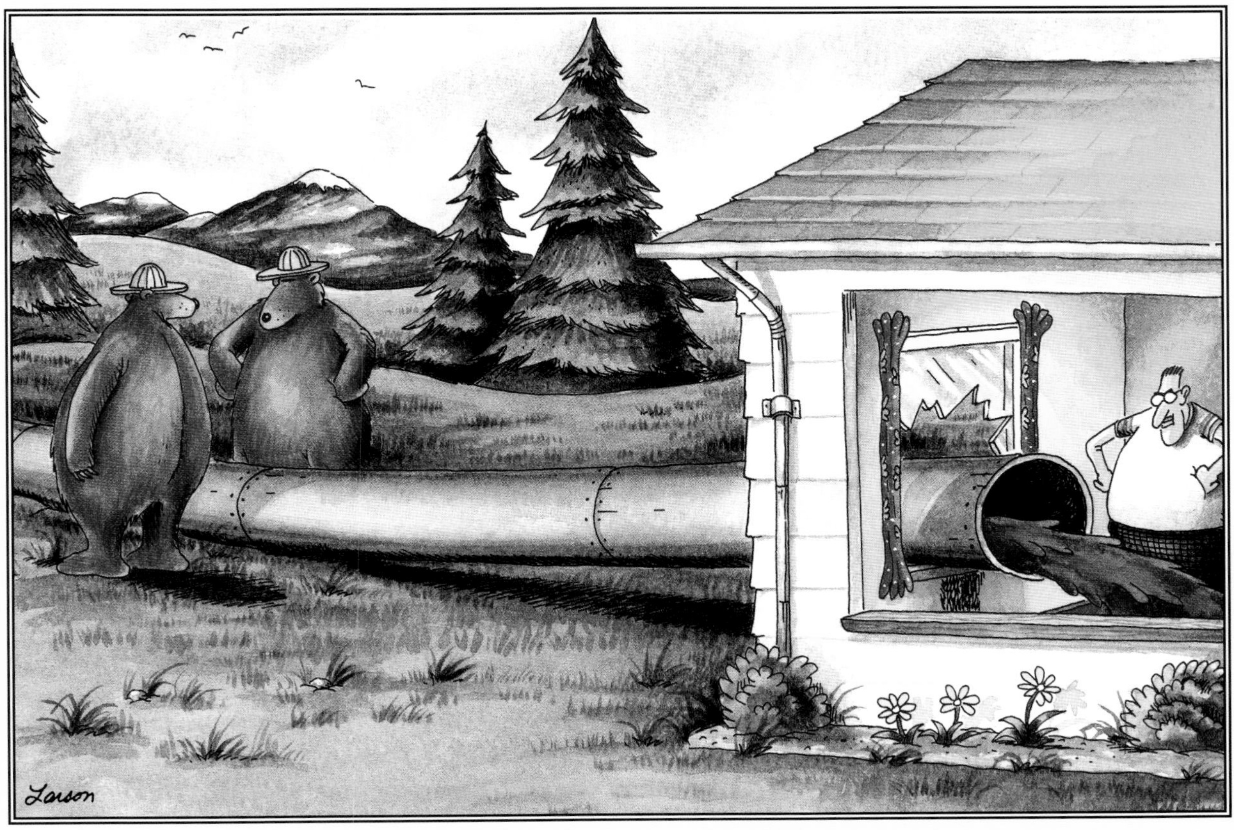

Animal waste management

8/13/88

Larson
WELCOME
POTP
ETTA
DON
BETTY
BOB
LARRY

The 25th annual "Part of the Problem" convention

8/12/88

Larson

"What? You're just going to throw the tail away? ... Why, in *my* day, we used every gol dang part of a mammoth!"

8/19/88

HOTEL
Larson

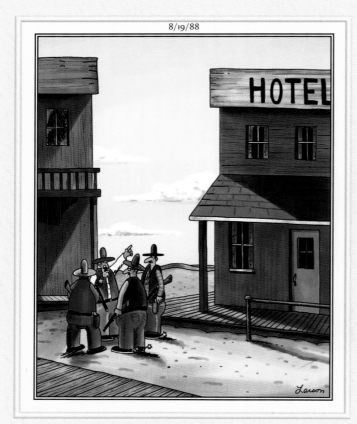

"Roy, you get up on the hotel roof there. And for godsakes, if you *are* plugged, don't just slump over and die—put some drama into it and throw yourself screaming from the edge."

8/17/88

Larson

"So! Mr. Carlisle was right! ... I put you on a short leash so you can't harass him anymore, and look what you resort to!"

8/20/88

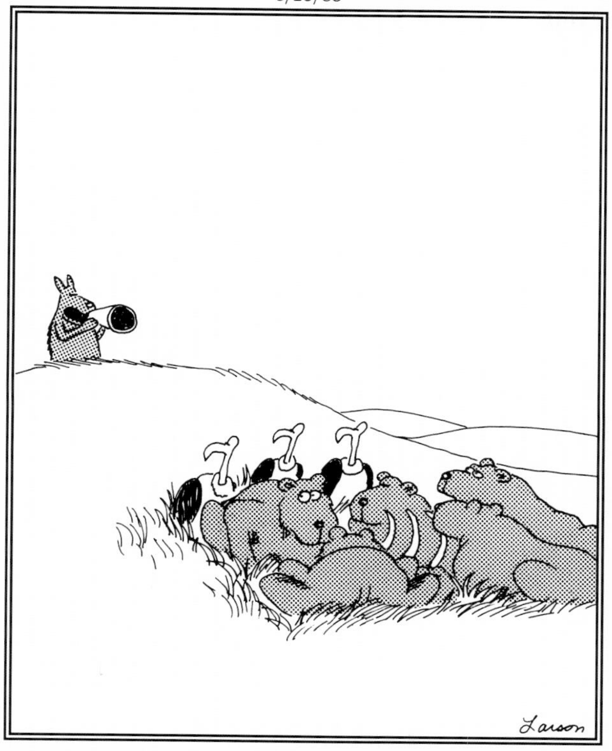

"Yo! Everyone down there! This is the jackal! I'm tired of slinking around the perimeter! ... I'm coming down to the kill! ... Is that gonna be cool with everyone? ... I don't want trouble!"

8/18/88

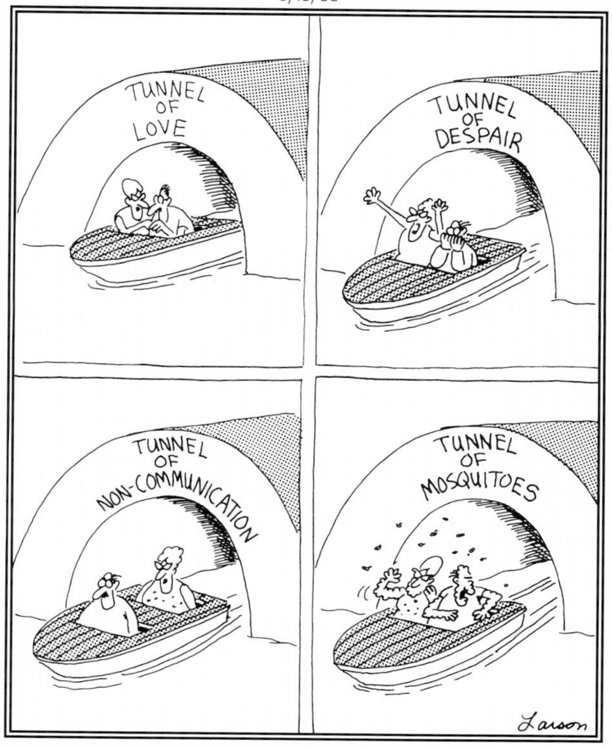
TUNNEL OF LOVE
TUNNEL OF DESPAIR
TUNNEL OF NON-COMMUNICATION
TUNNEL OF MOSQUITOES

8/22/88

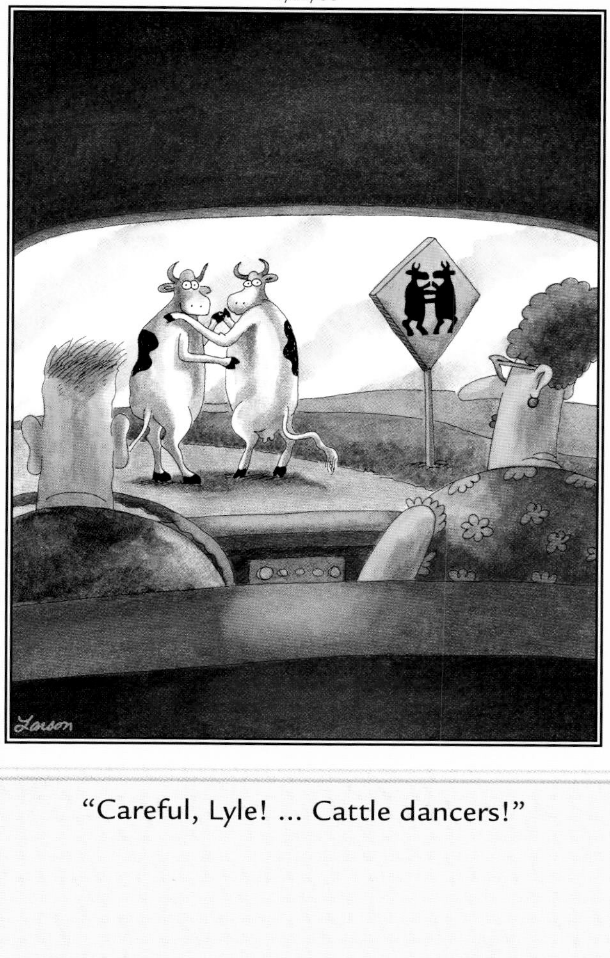

"Careful, Lyle! ... Cattle dancers!"

8/23/88

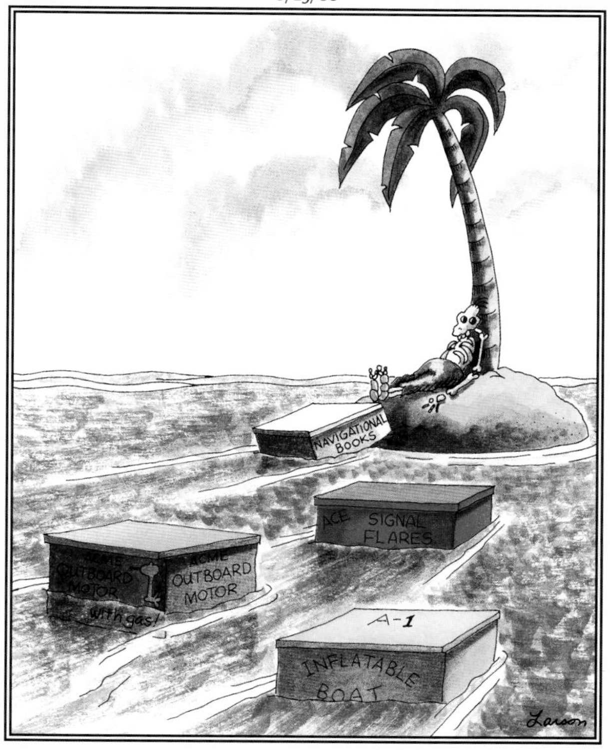
NAVIGATIONAL BOOKS
ACE SIGNAL FLARES
ACME OUTBOARD MOTOR
with gas!
A-1
INFLATABLE BOAT

8/21/88

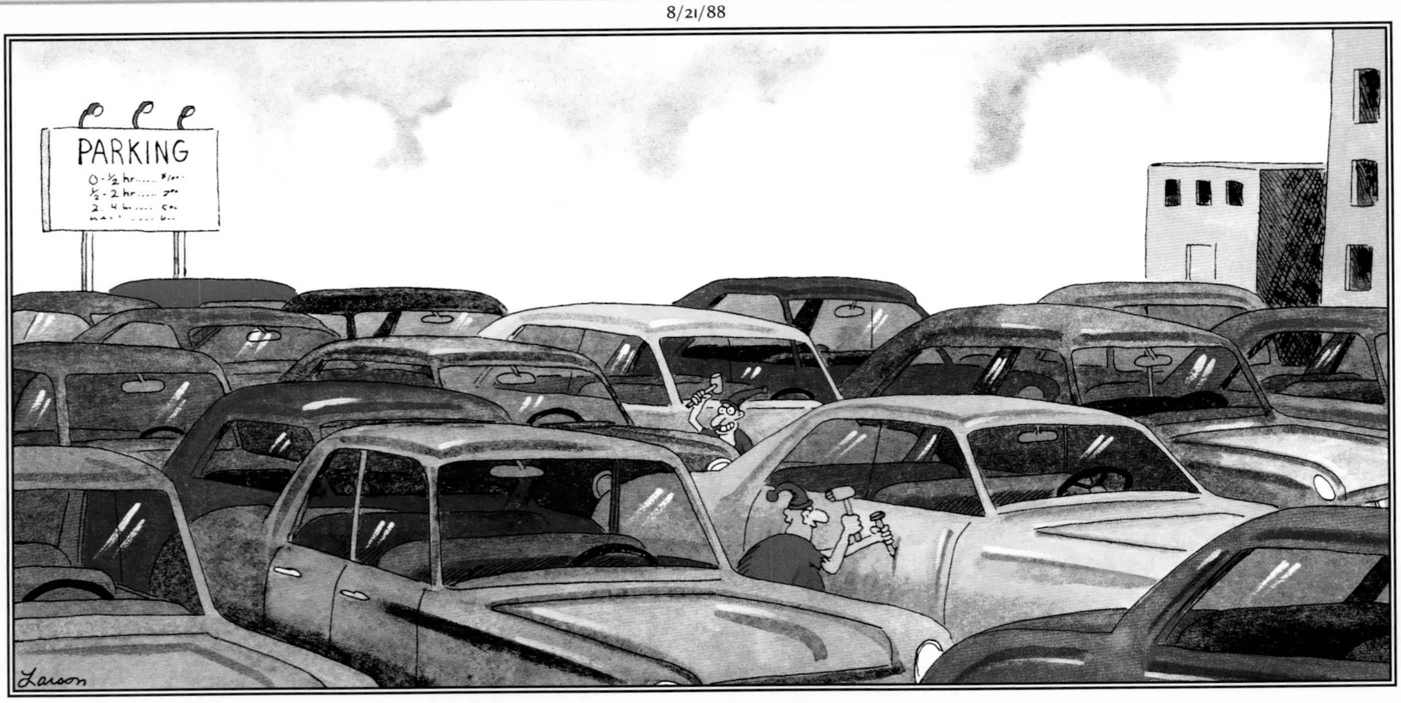
PARKING
Larson

Door ding gnomes at work

8/24/88

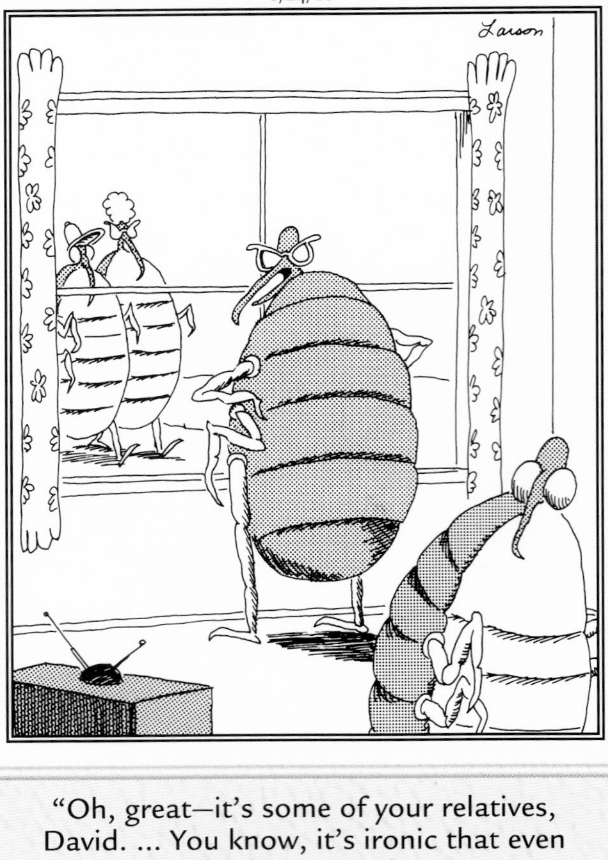
Larson

"Oh, great—it's some of your relatives, David. ... You know, it's ironic that even we lice have parasites."

8/26/88

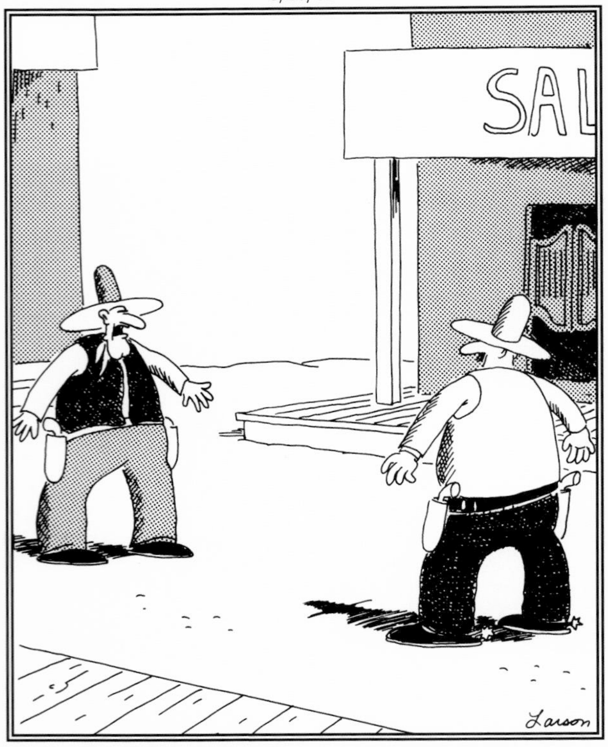
SAL
Larson

"Okay, when I say 'draw,' we draw. ... Ready? ... One, two, three—STRAW! ... Okay, just checkin' your ears. ... One, two, three—CLAW! ... Okay, DRAWbridge! ..."

8/30/88

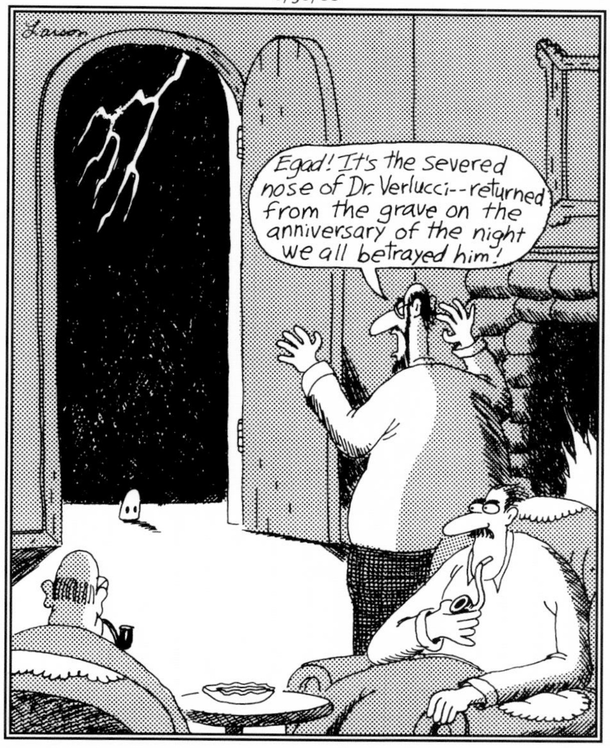
Egad! It's the severed nose of Dr. Verlucci--returned from the grave on the anniversary of the night we all betrayed him!

Scene from *Return of the Nose of Dr. Verlucci*

8/31/88

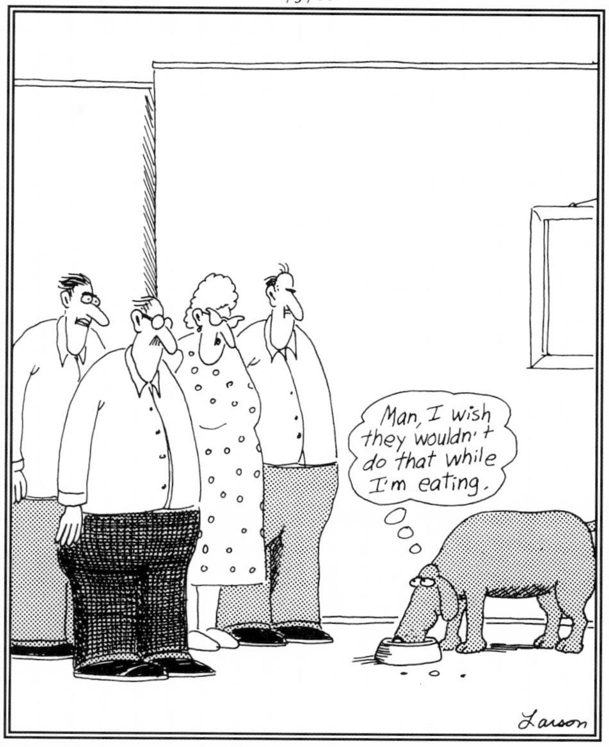
Man, I wish they wouldn't do that while I'm eating.

8/28/88

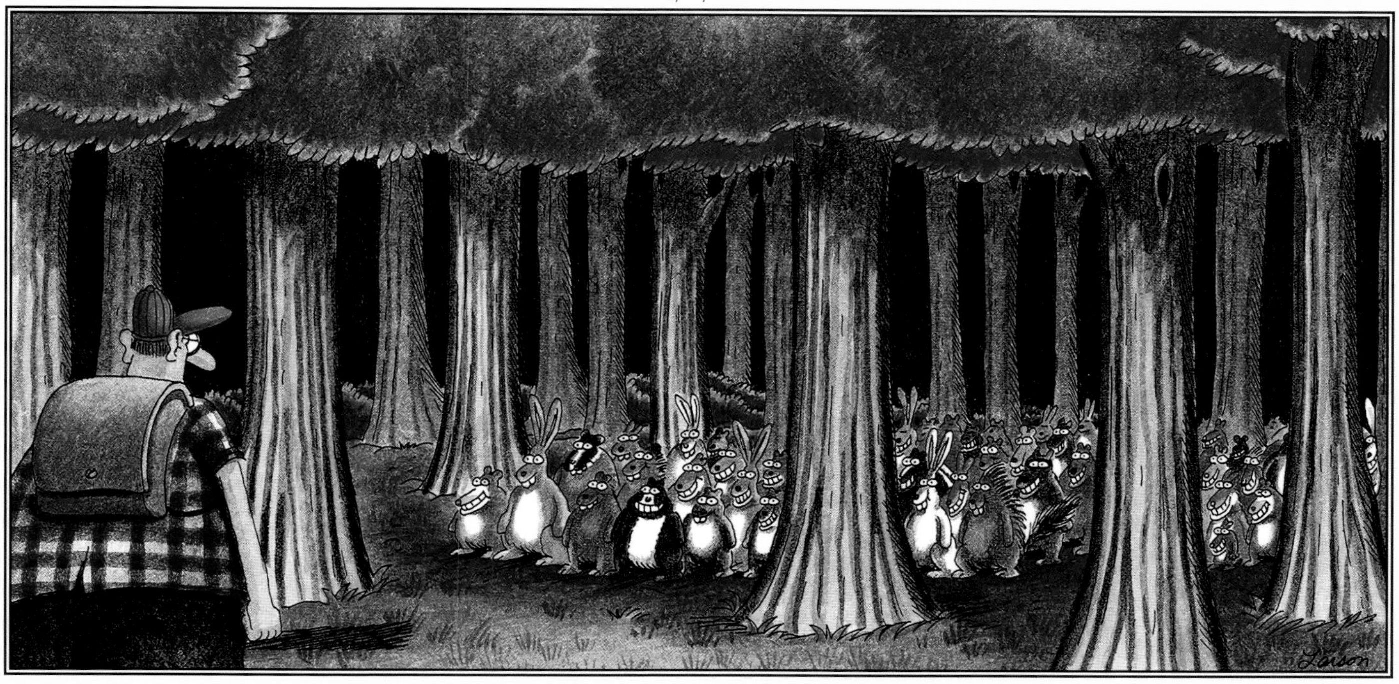

Dwayne paused. As usual, the forest was full of happy little animals—but this time, they just seemed *too* happy.

8/27/88

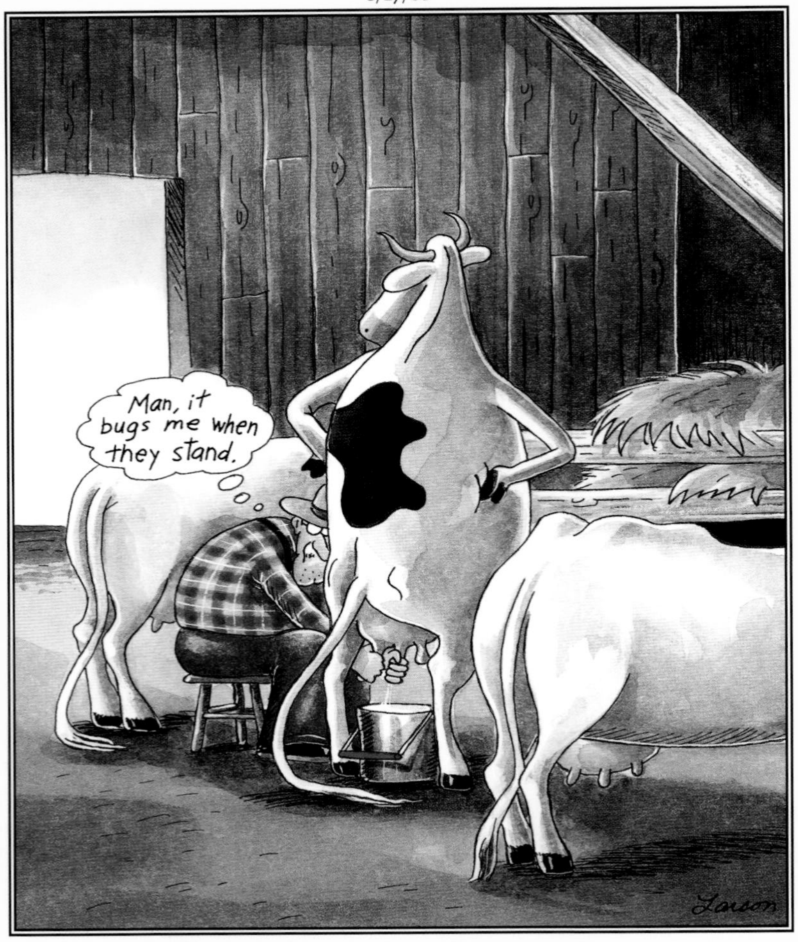
Man, it bugs me when they stand.

8/25/88

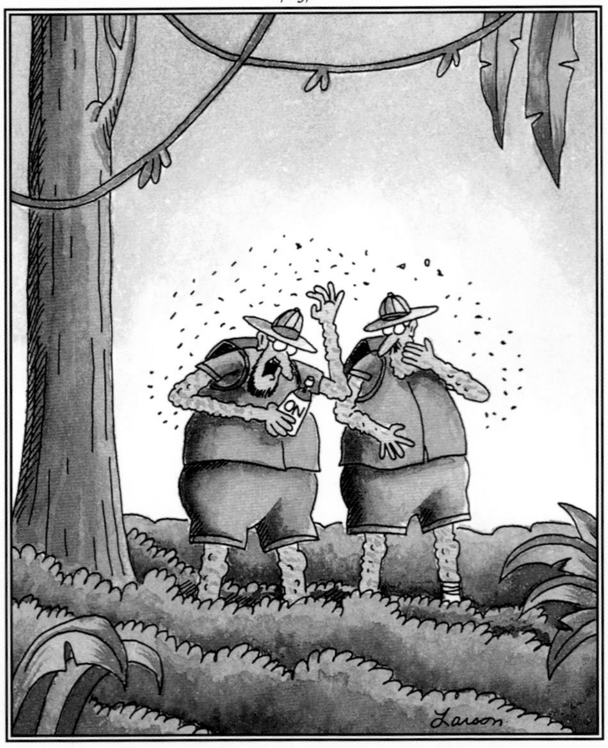

"Wait a minute! ... McCallister, you fool! *This* isn't what I said to bring!"

8/29/88

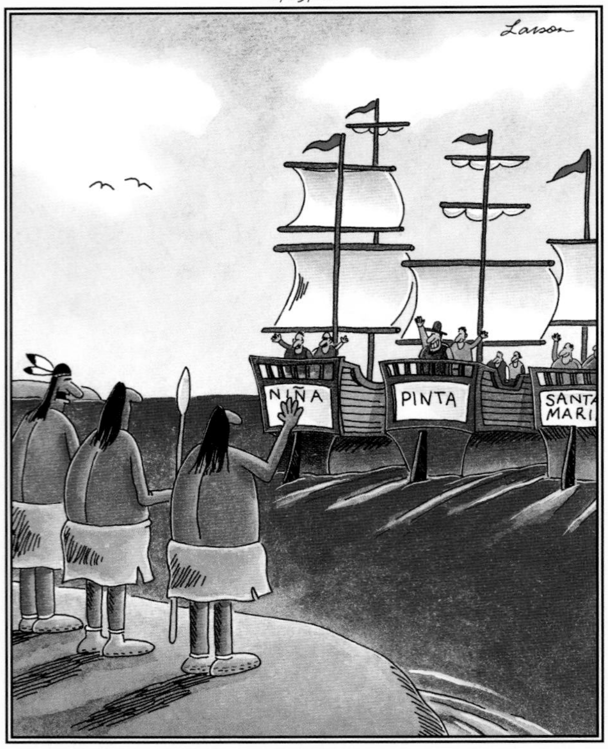
NIÑA
PINTA
SANTA MARI

"Did you detect something a little ominous in the way they said, 'See you later'?"

9/1/88

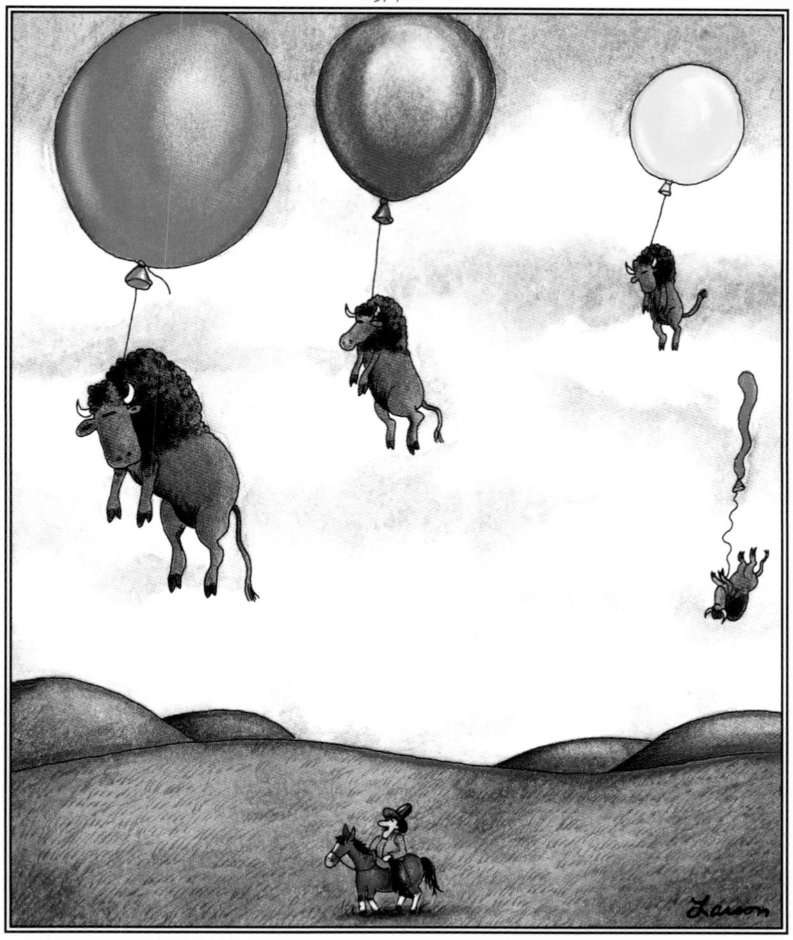
Larson

MORE FACTS OF NATURE: As part of nature's way to help spread the species throughout its ecological niche, bison often utilize a behavior naturalists have described as "ballooning."

9/4/88

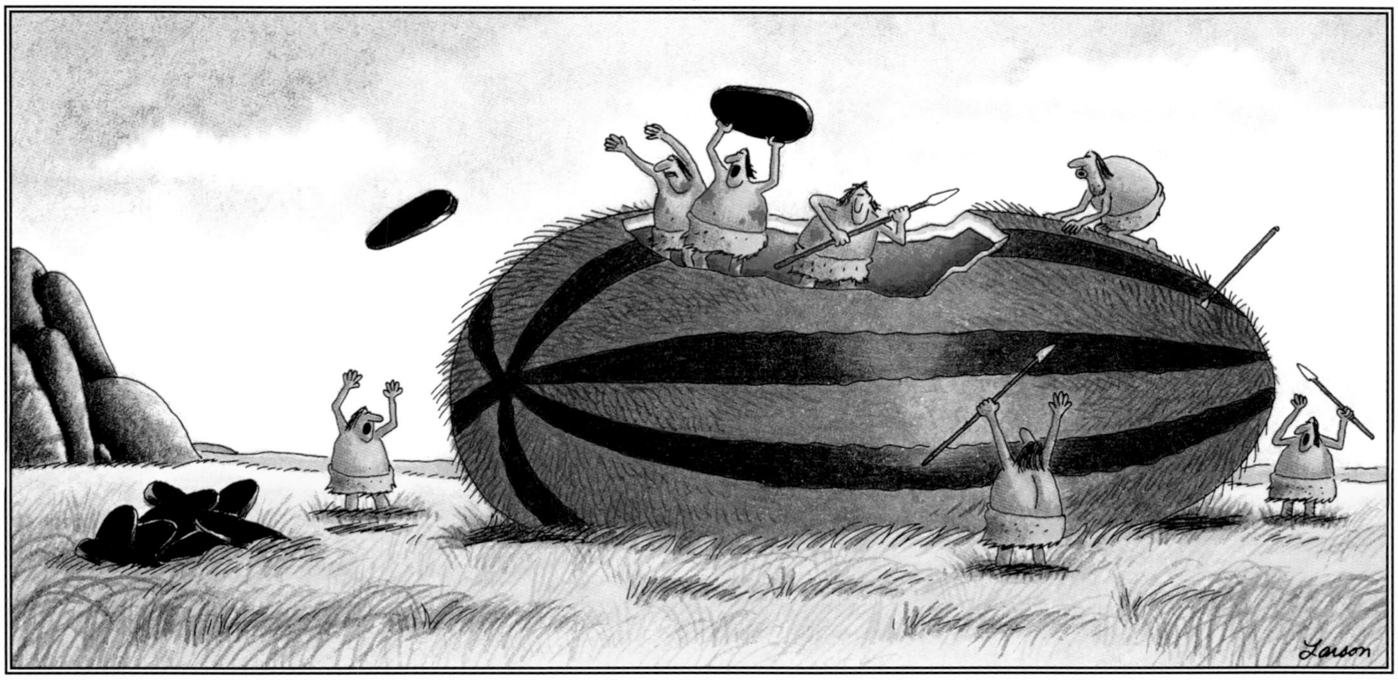
Larson

Splattered with juice and hooting excitedly, Neanderthals carve up their favorite kill, the woolly watermelon.

9/3/88

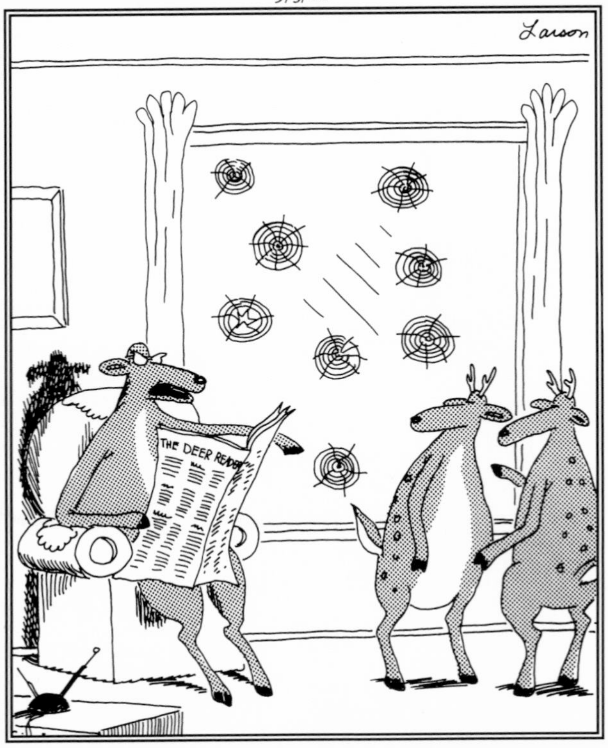

"Hey! What have I told you kids about screwing around in front of that window?"

9/2/88

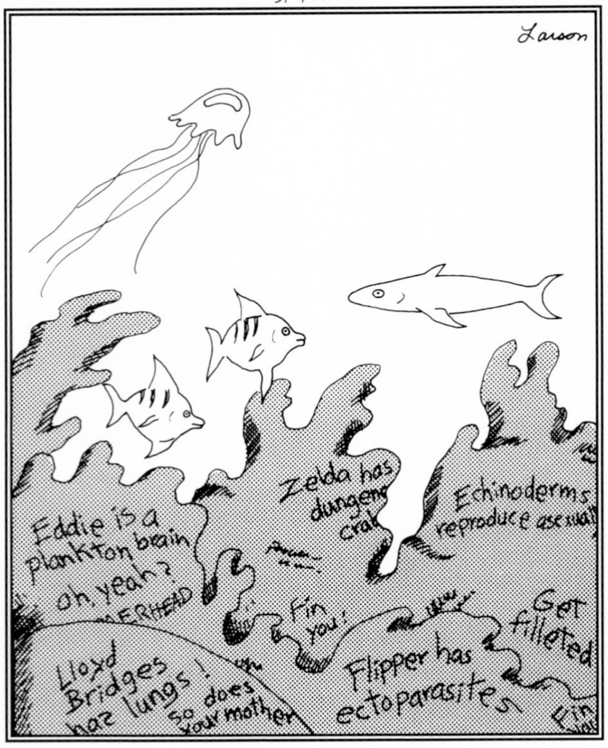
Eddie is a plankton brain
oh, yeah?
Zelda has
Echinoderms
Fin you!
Get filleted
Lloyd Bridges has lungs!
so does your mother
Flipper has ectoparasites

Coral reef graffiti

9/5/88

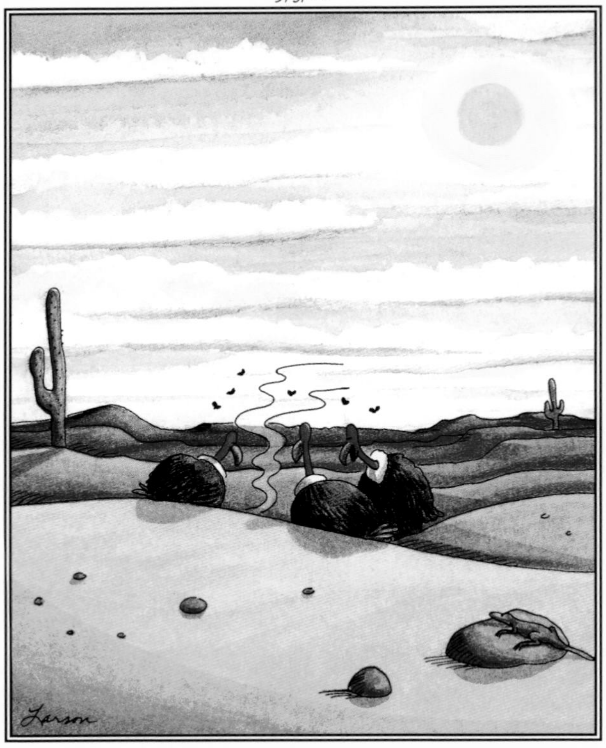

"Ooooooweeeeee! This thing's been here a looooooooong time! ... Well, thank God for ketchup."

9/6/88

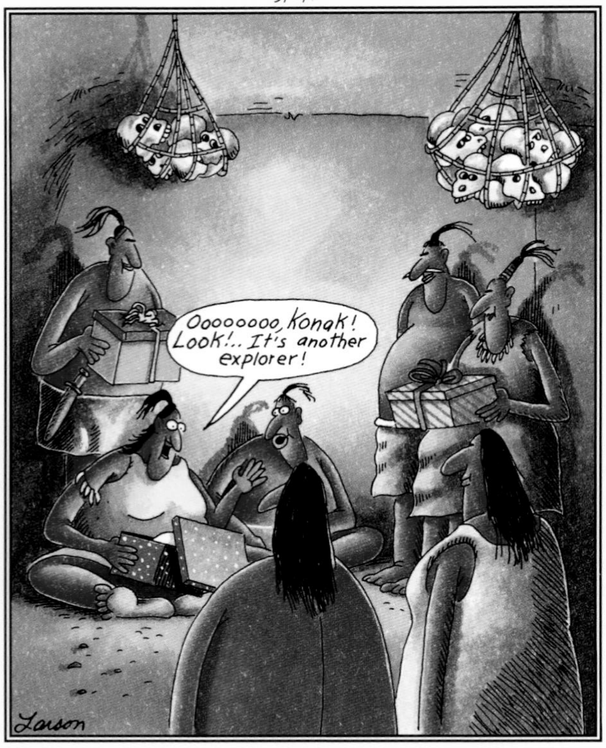
Ooooooo, Konak! Look!.. It's another explorer!

Headhunter hutwarming

9/7/88

Peelings...Nothing more than peelings...

9/10/88

The Squirrel Sentinel
LOCAL RESIDENT WINS LOTTERY
Eddie Jones says he'll
The Squirrel Sentinel
SMASHED BY CAR
CHIP AND

9/8/88

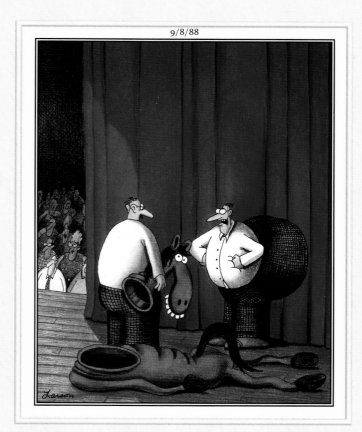

"I tell you I've *had* it! ... I'm not climbing into that getup one more time until you tell me why *I'm* always the back end!"

9/9/88

"It's Vinnie, all right. It's his nose, his mouth, his fur ... but his eyes—there's something not quite right about his eyes."

9/11/88

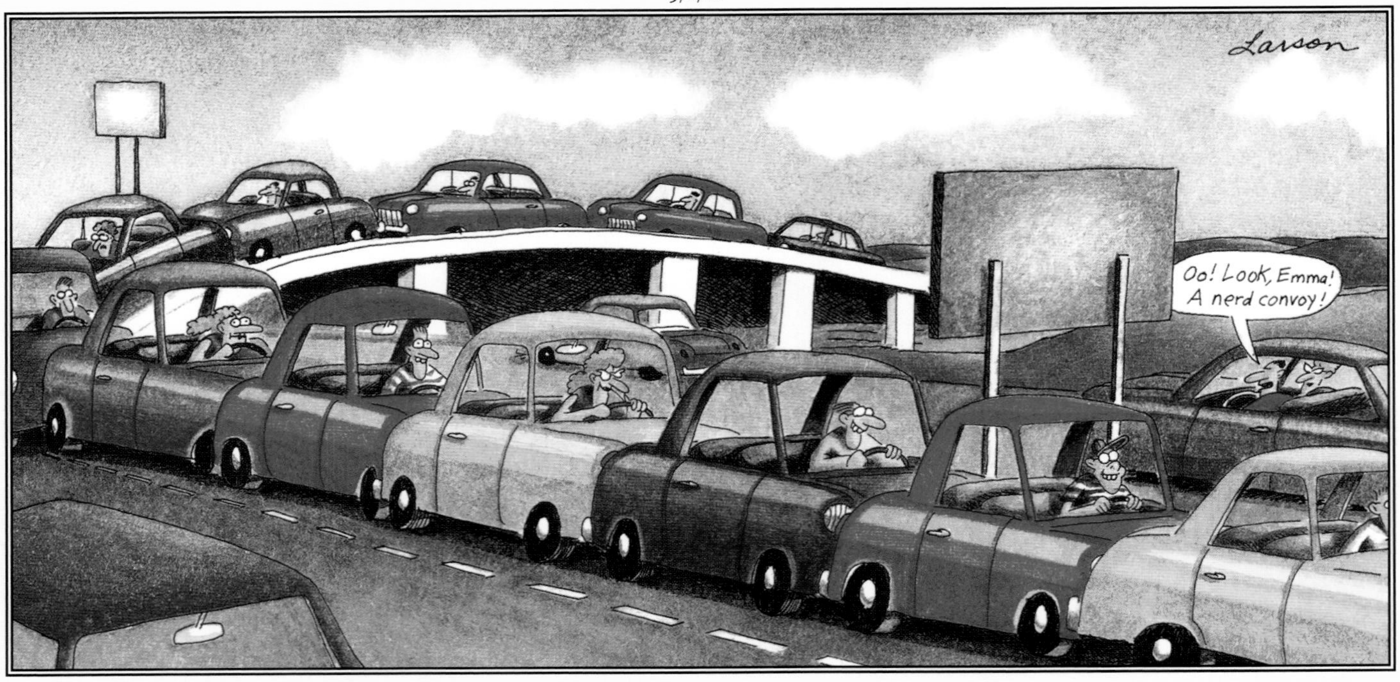
Larson
Oo! Look, Emma! A nerd convoy!

9/12/88

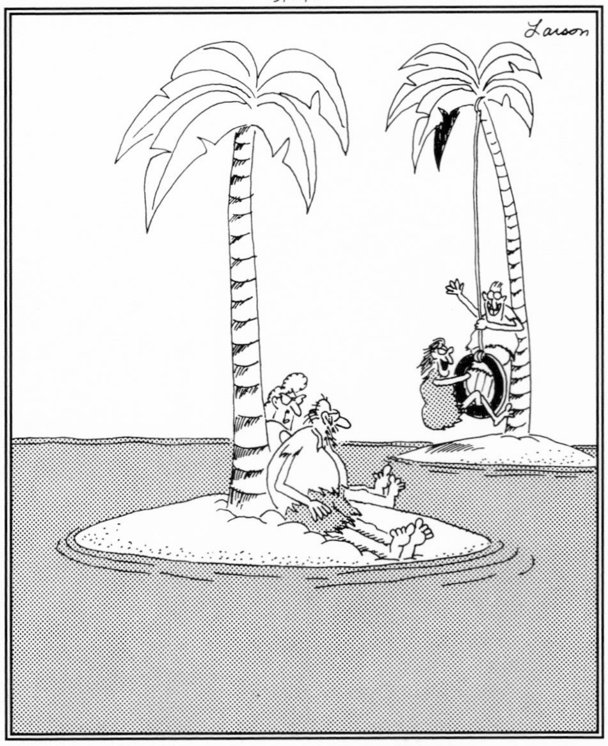
Larson

"Well, the Sullivans are out on their tire again."

9/14/88

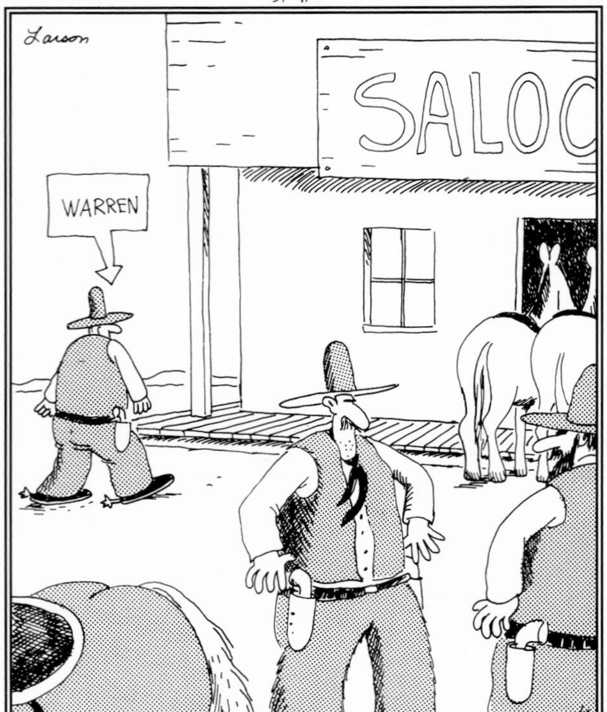
Larson
SALOO
WARREN

Warren Hagstrom: professional Western movie background street crosser

9/18/88

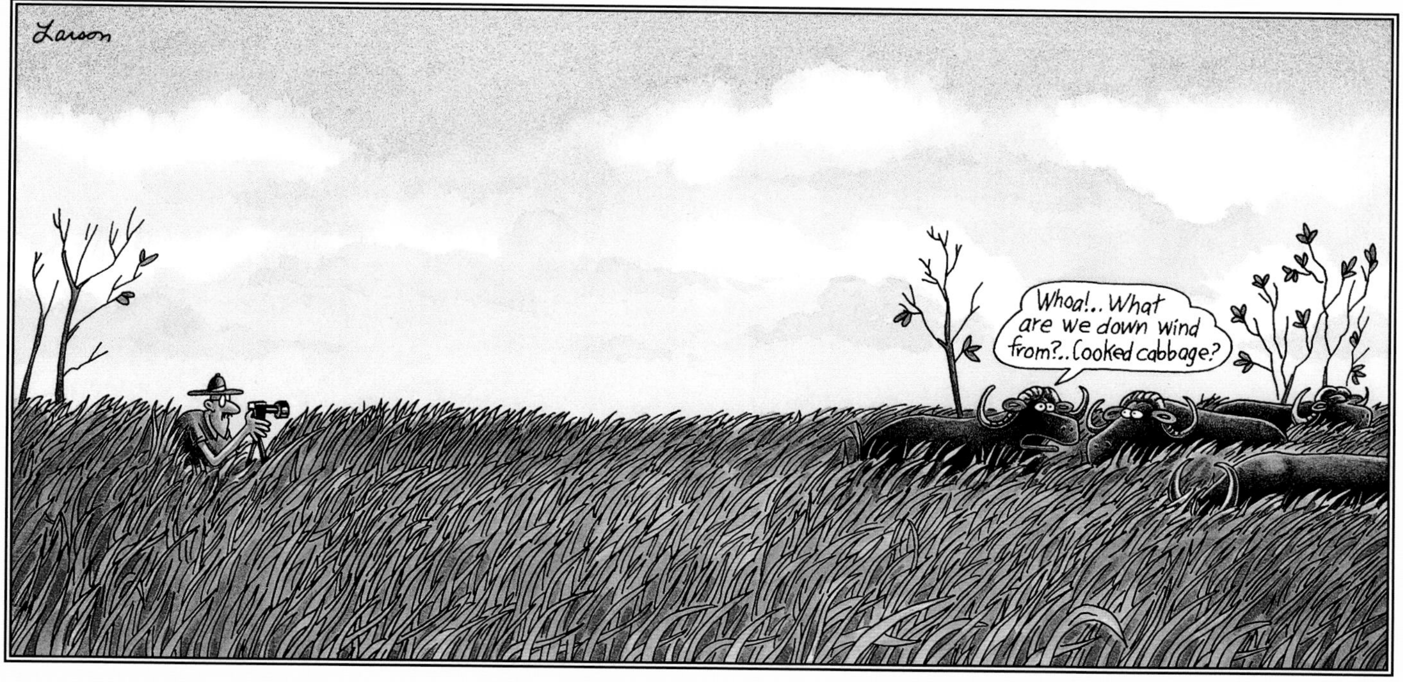
Larson
Whoa!.. What are we down wind from?.. Cooked cabbage?

9/16/88

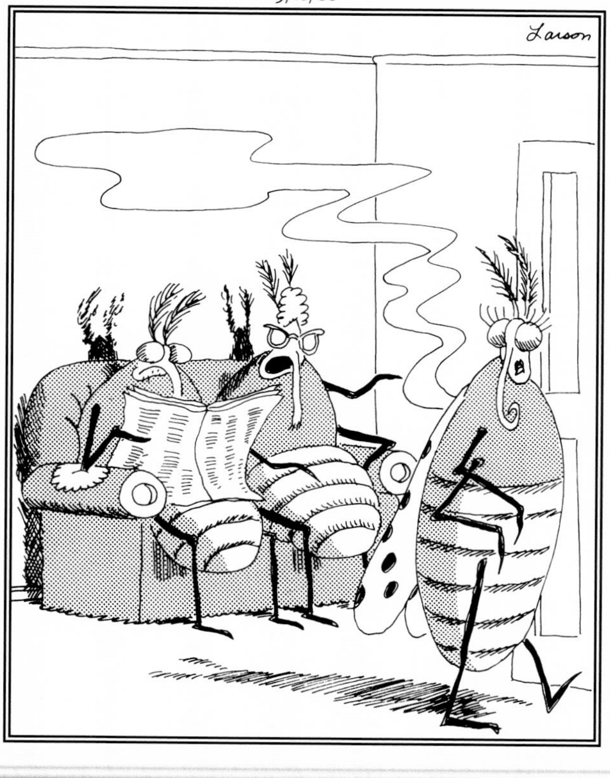
Larson

"Hold it right there, young lady! Before you go out, you take off some of that makeup and wash off that gallon of pheromones!"

9/24/88

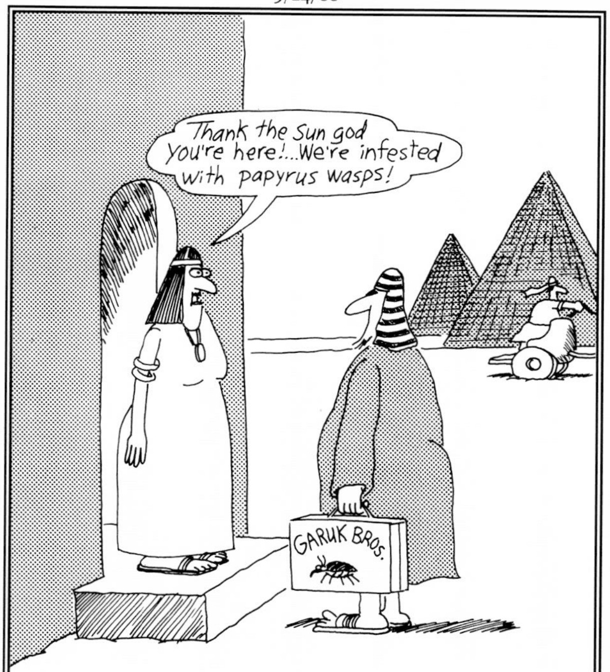
Thank the Sun god you're here!...We're infested with papyrus wasps!
GARUK BROS.
Larson

Ancient exterminators

9/13/88

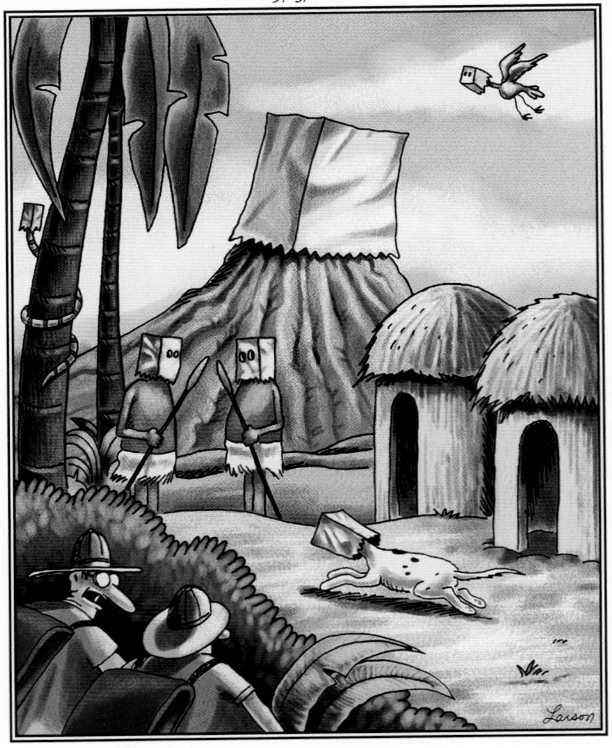
Larson

"This *must* be it, Jenkins—the legendary Ugliest Place on Earth."

9/15/88

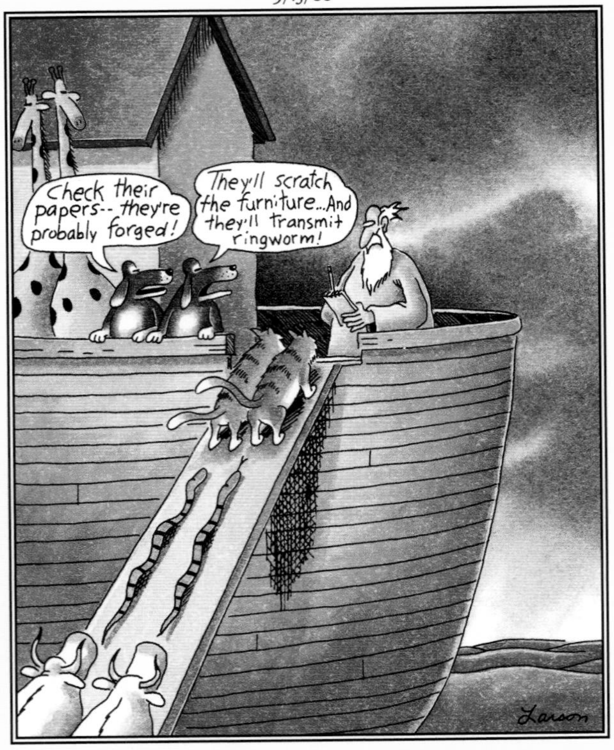
Check their papers-- they're probably forged!
They'll scratch the furniture...And they'll transmit ringworm!
Larson

9/19/88

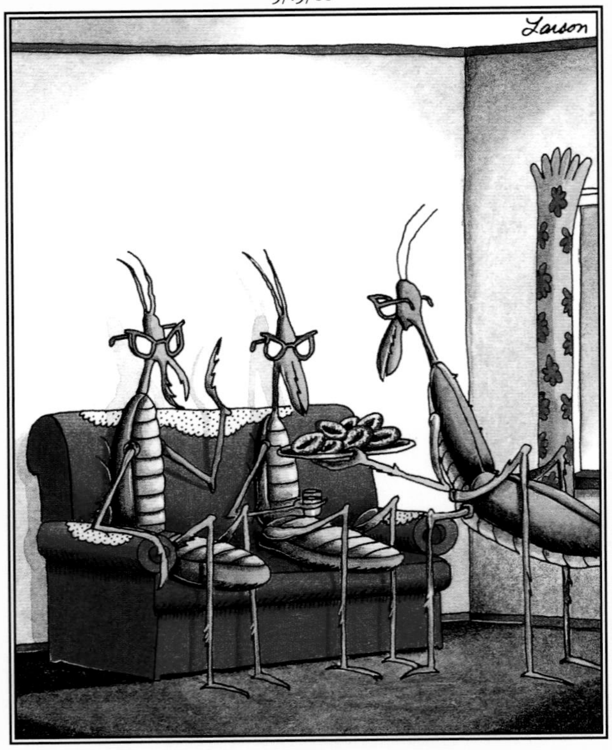
Larson

"Oh, good heavens, no, Gladys—not for me. ... I ate my young just an hour ago."

9/17/88

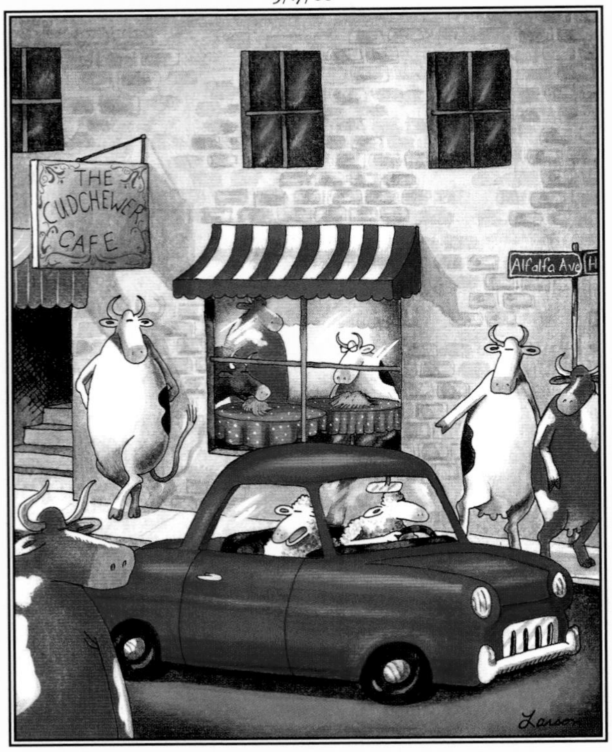
THE CUDCHEWER CAFE
Alfalfa Ave
Larson

"Drive, Ted! We've stumbled into some cowtown."

9/22/88

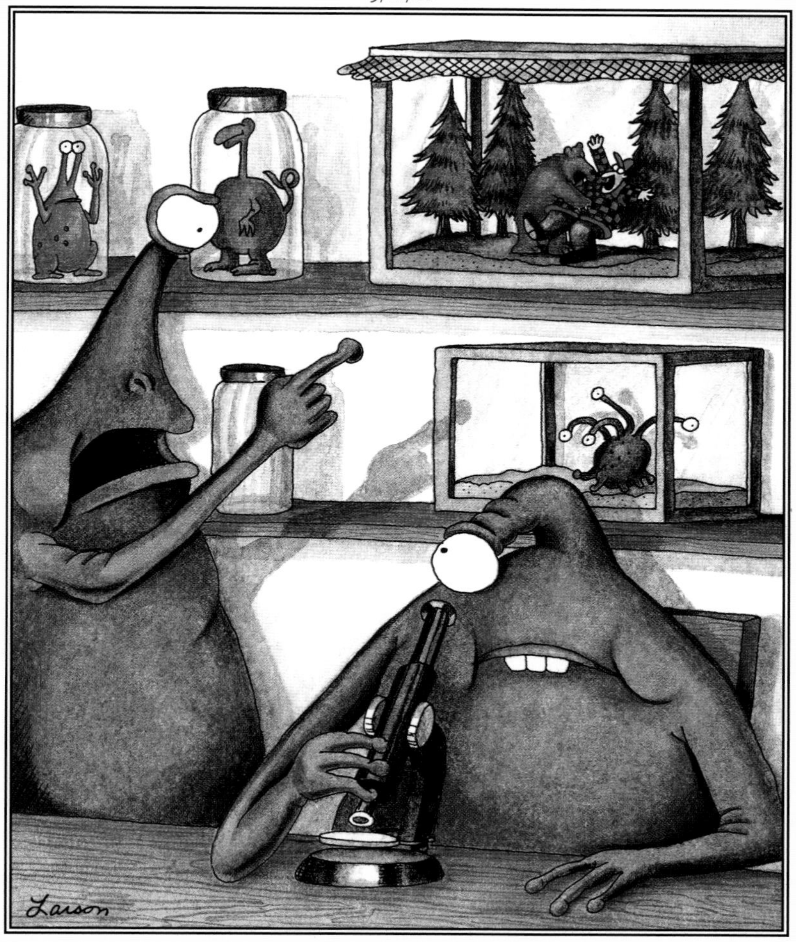

"Zorak, you idiot! You've mixed incompatible species in the earth terrarium!"

9/21/88

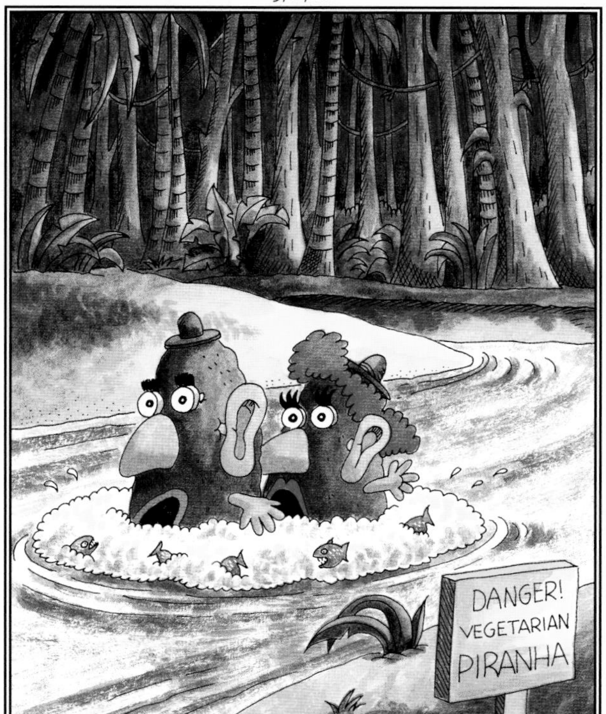
DANGER!
VEGETARIAN
PIRANHA

The Potatoheads in Brazil

9/23/88

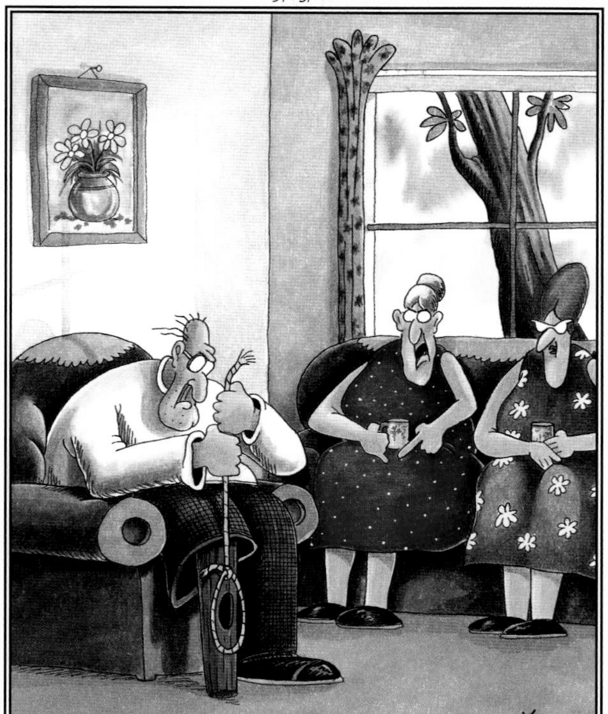

"Good heavens, Bernie! We've got company! ... And you're never going to catch that stupid squirrel anyway!"

9/20/88

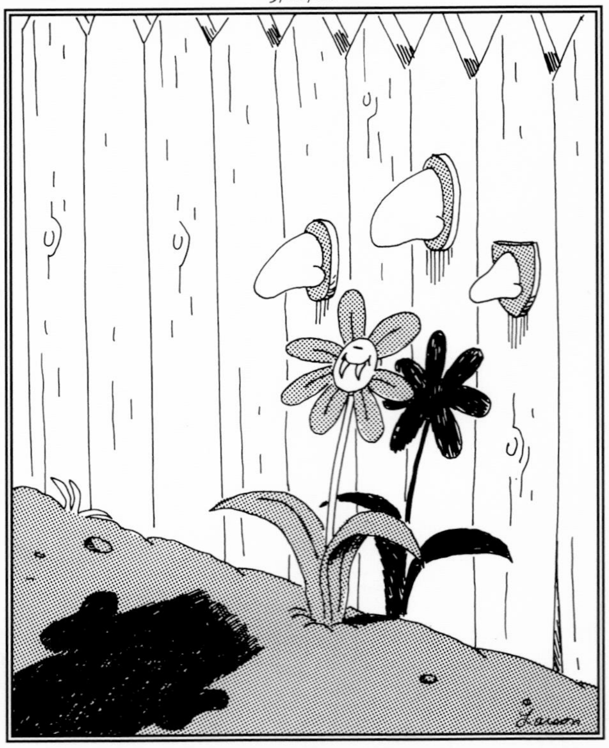

9/26/88

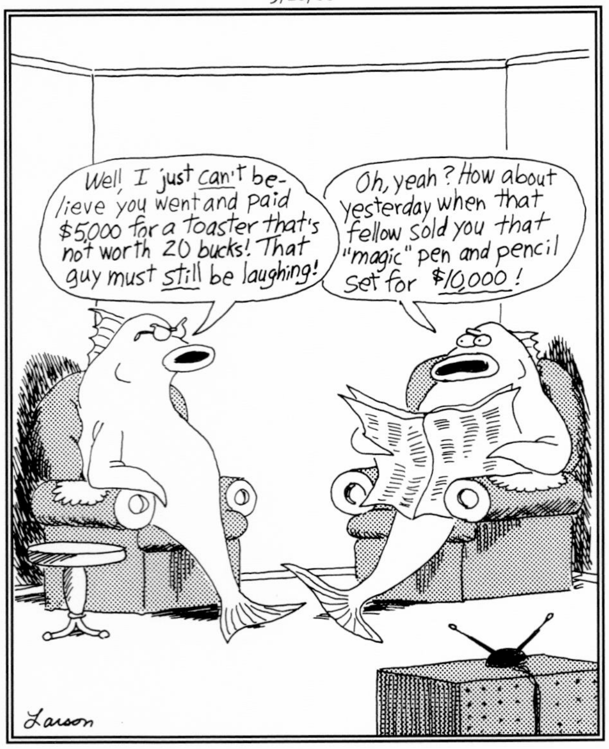
Well, I just can't believe you went and paid $5,000 for a toaster that's not worth 20 bucks! That guy must still be laughing!
Oh, yeah? How about yesterday when that fellow sold you that "magic" pen and pencil set for $10,000!

Sucker fish at home

9/25/88

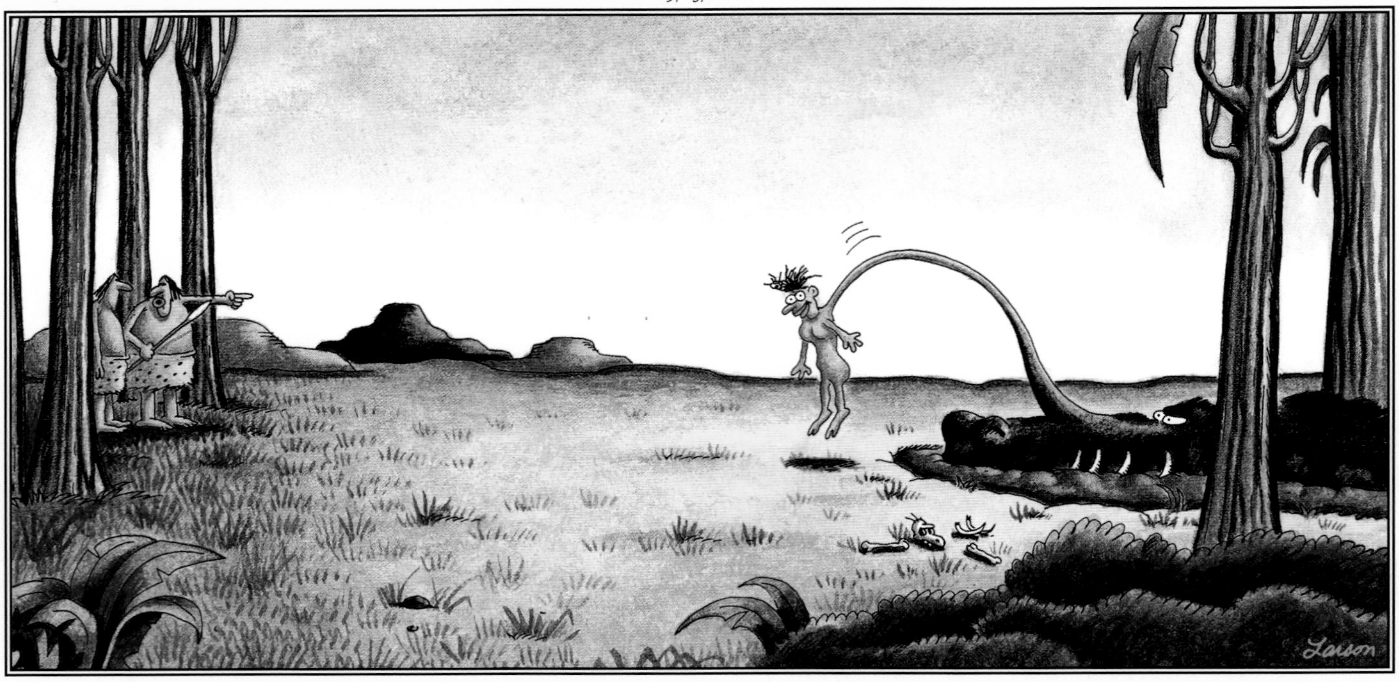

Burying itself deep in the mud, the hominideatodon, an evolutionary wonder, would slowly raise and lower its unique appendage in the hope of attracting its favorite prey.

9/27/88

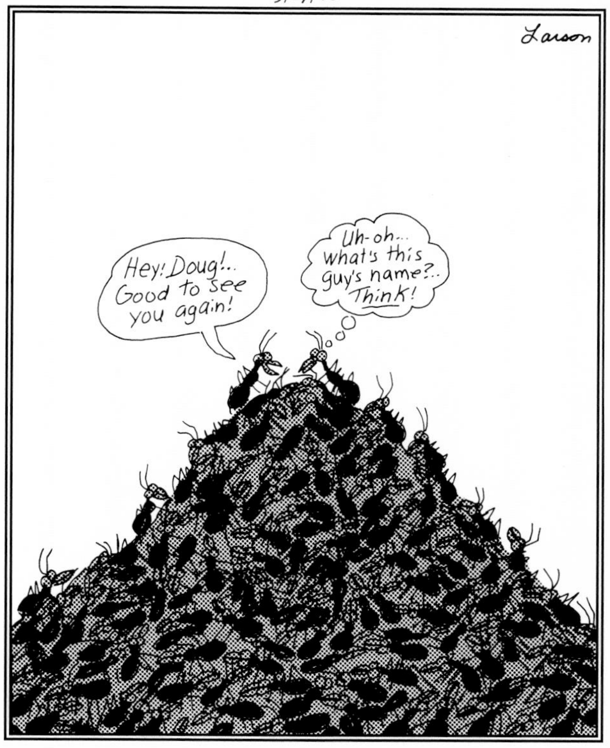
Larson
Hey! Doug!..
Good to see
you again!
Uh-oh...
what's this
guy's name?..
Think!

Awkward moments in the ant world

9/28/88

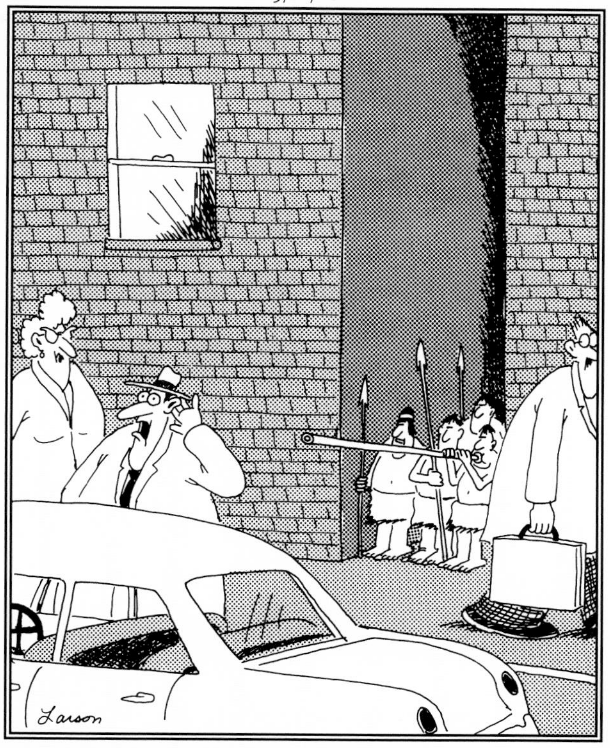
Larson

Pygmies on vacation

9/29/88

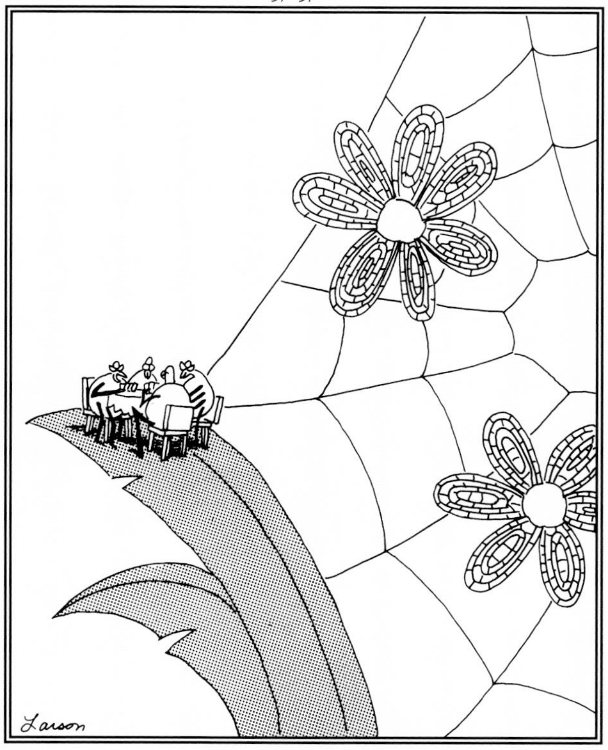
Larson

"You and Fred have such a lovely web, Edna—and I *love* what you've done with those fly wings."

9/30/88

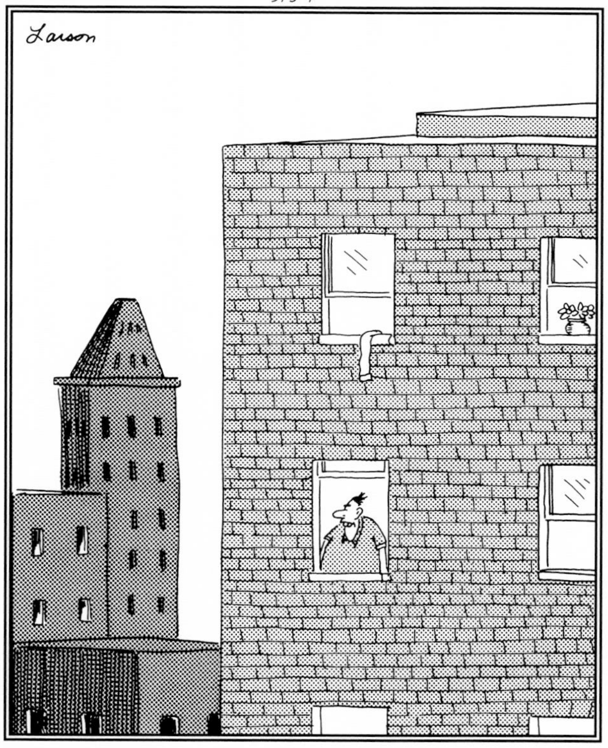
Larson

On a clear day, Eugene rose and looked around him and, regrettably, saw who he was.

10/1/88

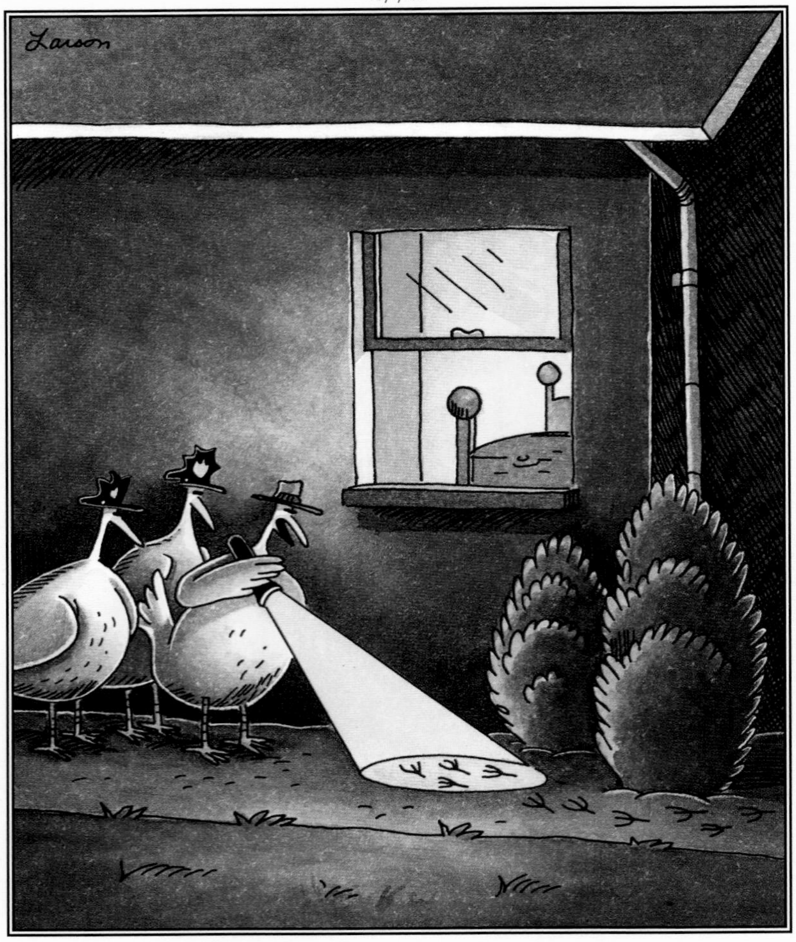
Larson

"Aha! The murderer's footprints! ... 'Course, we all leave tracks like this."

10/2/88

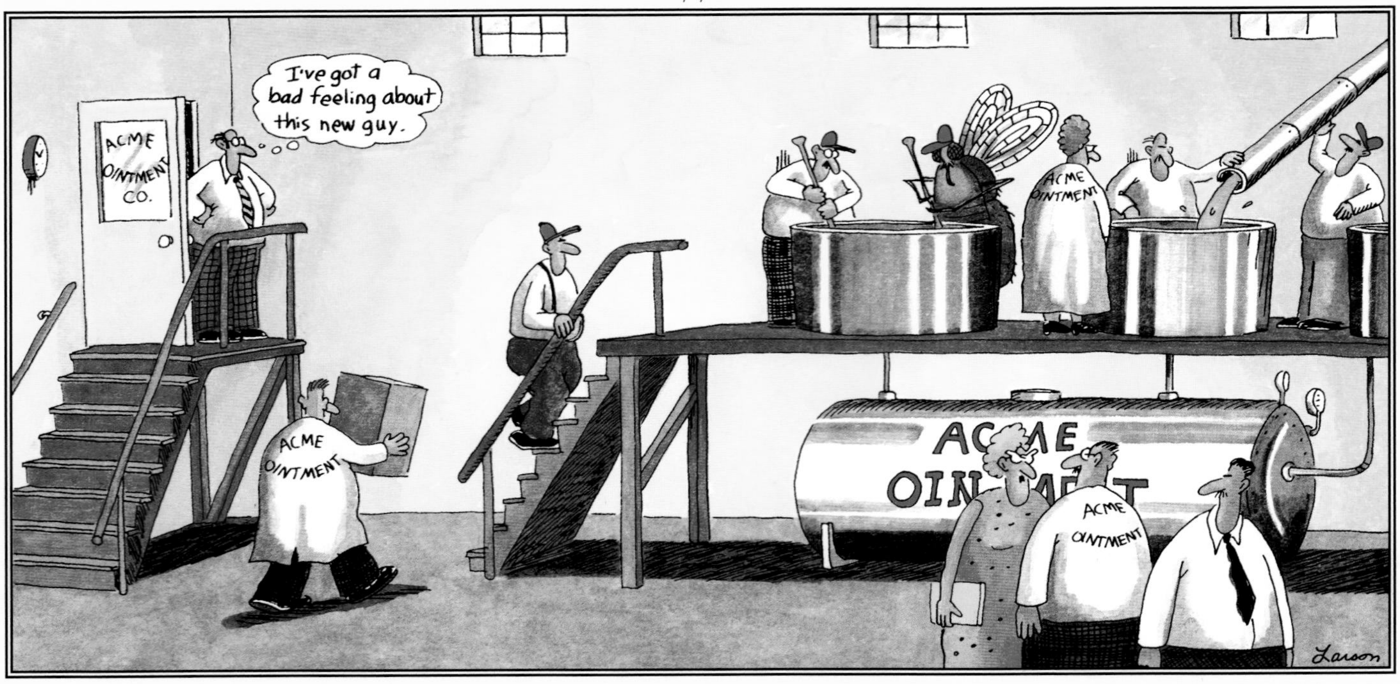
I've got a bad feeling about this new guy.
ACME OINTMENT CO.
ACME OINTMENT
ACME OINTMENT
ACME OINTMENT
Larson

10/9/88

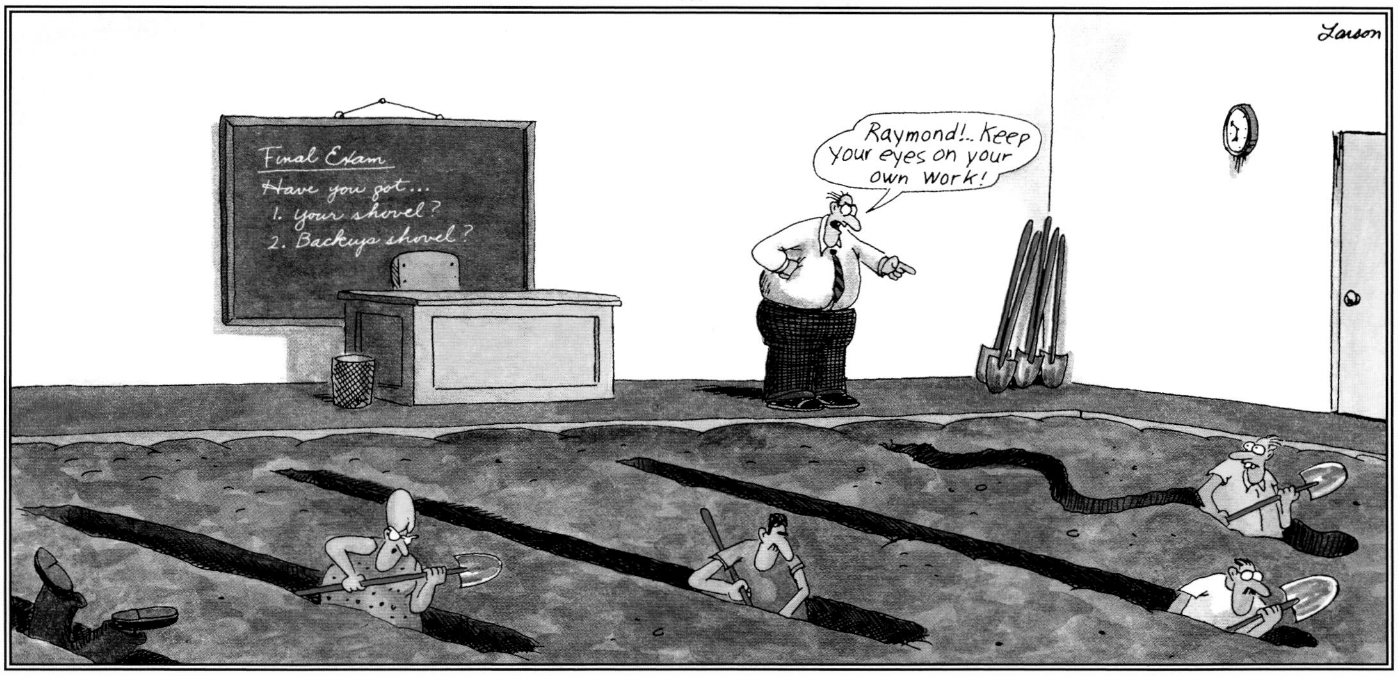
Final Exam
Have you got...
1. your shovel?
2. Backup shovel?
Raymond!.. Keep your eyes on your own work!
Larson

Ditchdiggers School

10/4/88

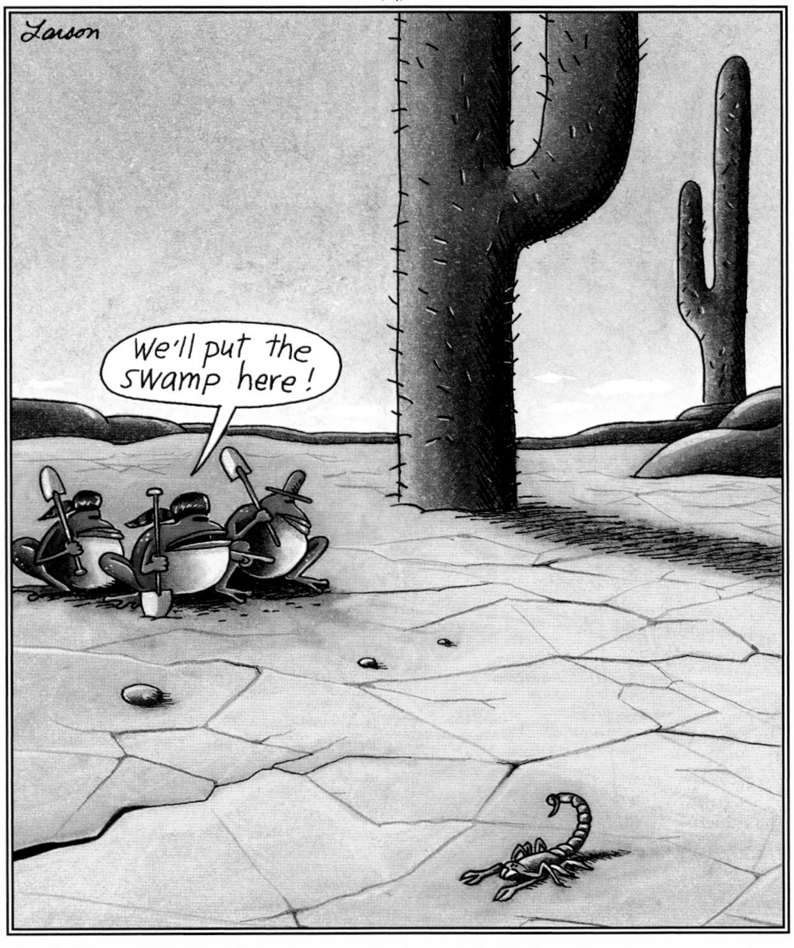
Larson
We'll put the swamp here!

Frog pioneers

10/3/88

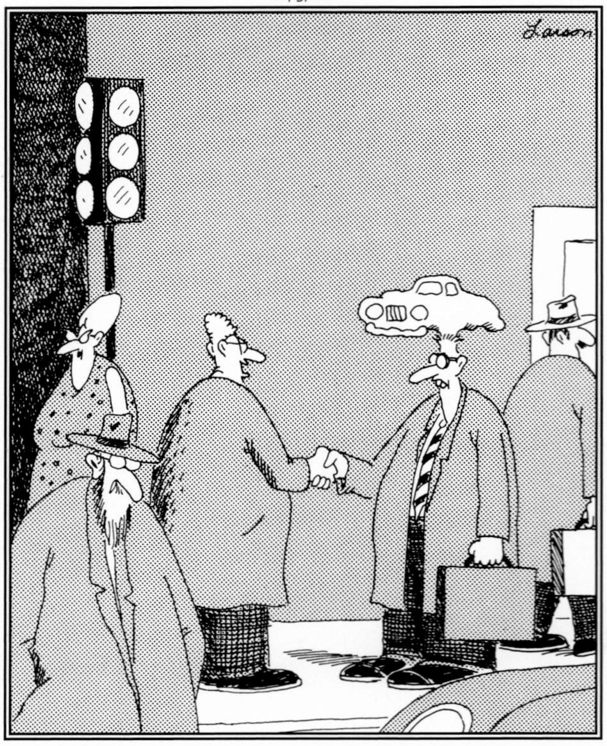
Larson

"Hey! Ernie Wagner! I haven't seen you in, what's it been—twenty years? And hey—you've still got that thing growin' outta your head that looks like a Buick!"

10/5/88

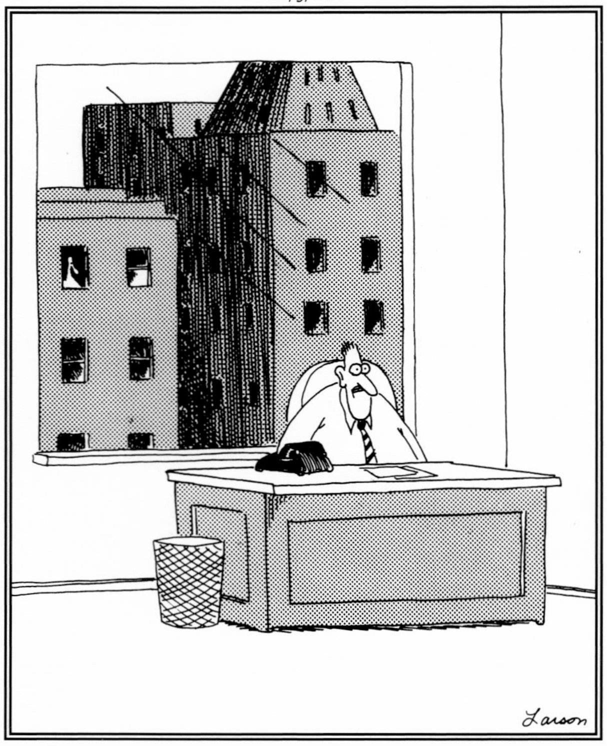
Larson

Anatidaephobia: the fear that somewhere, somehow, a duck is watching you.

10/6/88

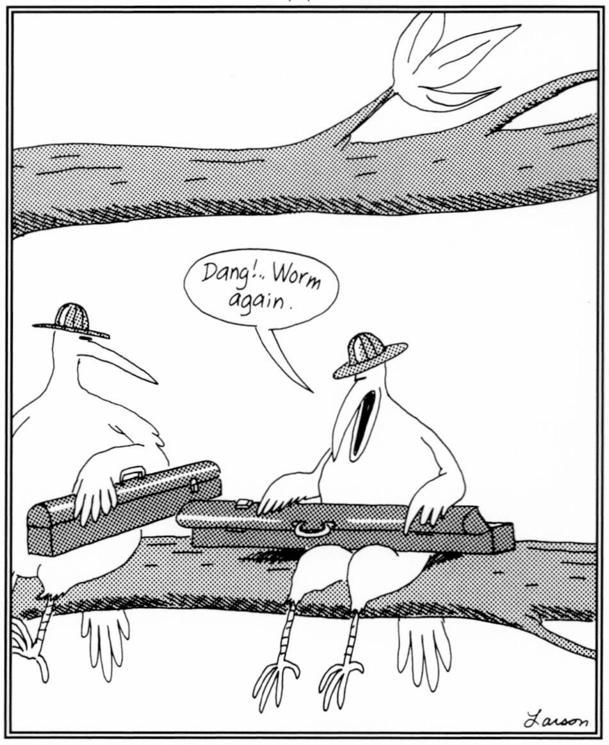
Dang!.. Worm again.
Larson

Construction birds at lunch

10/7/88

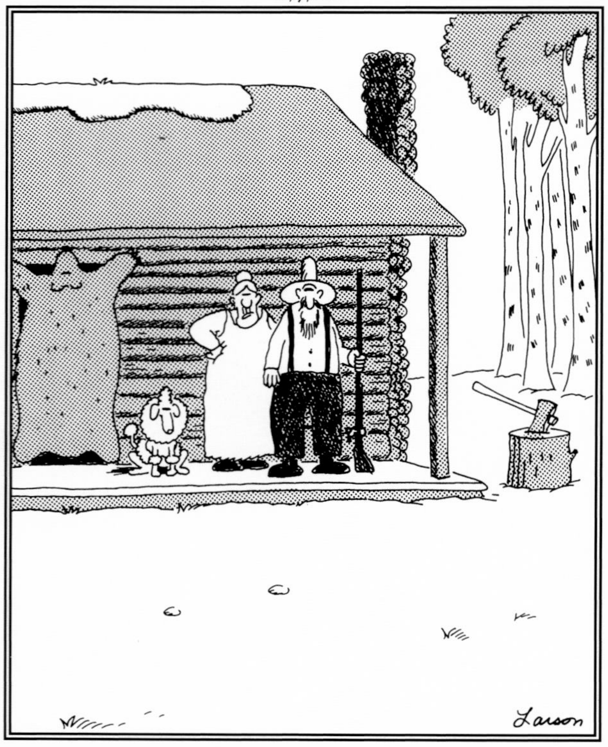
Larson

Early settlers of Beverly Hills

10/8/88

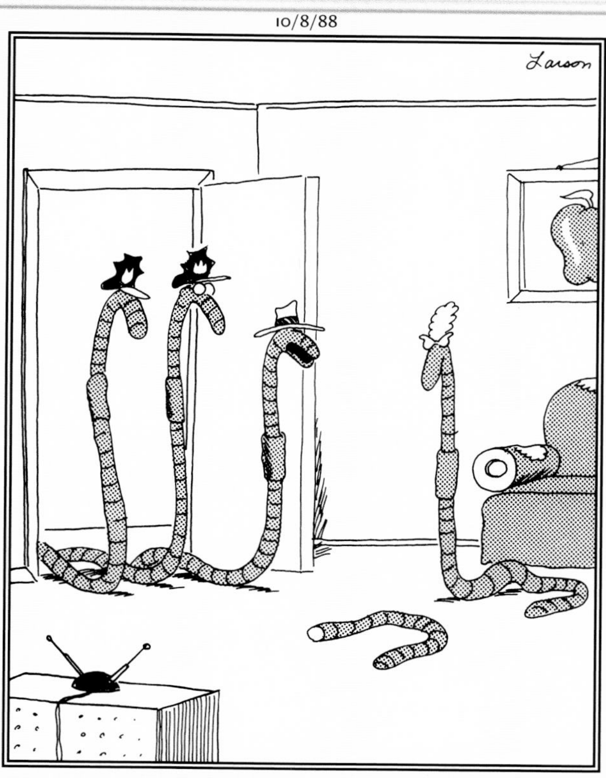
Larson

"We understand your concern, ma'am—but this just isn't enough for us to go on. Now, you find the *other* half of your husband, and then we've got a case."

10/10/88

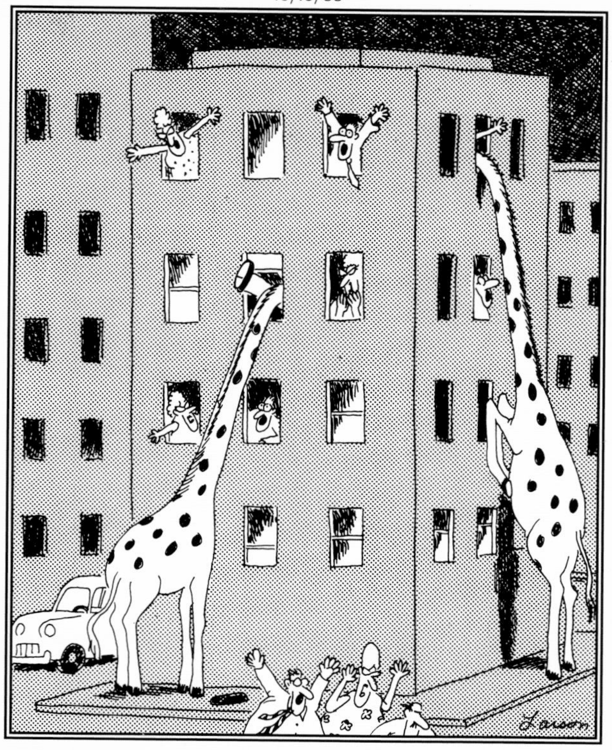
Larson

Scene from the film *Giraffes IV:* This time, they're not just looking for acacia leaves.

10/11/88

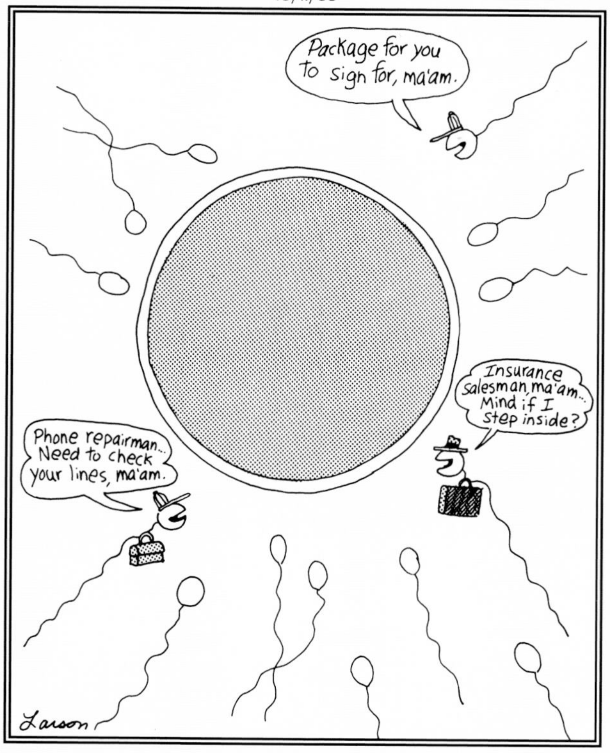
Package for you to sign for, ma'am.
Insurance salesman, ma'am... Mind if I step inside?
Phone repairman... Need to check your lines, ma'am.
Larson

How the human egg is often deceived

10/13/88

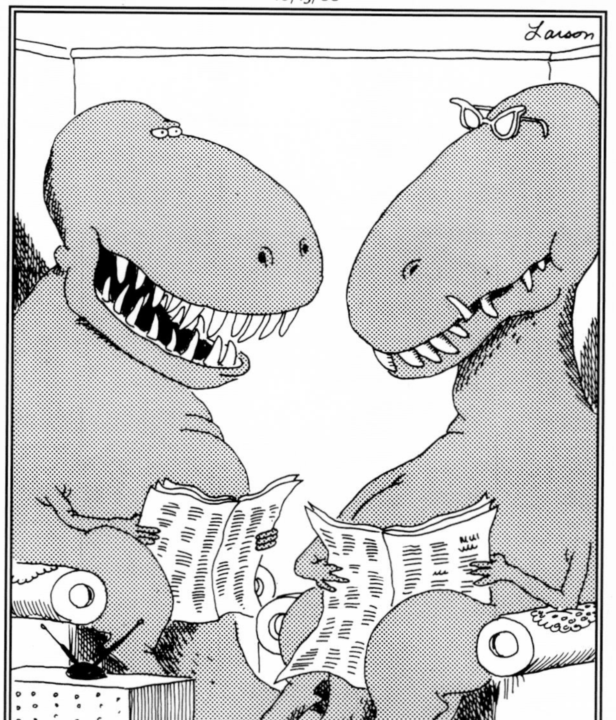
Larson

"Hey. ... Since the kids are in bed, what say we run out and kill ourselves a couple of planteaters."

10/12/88

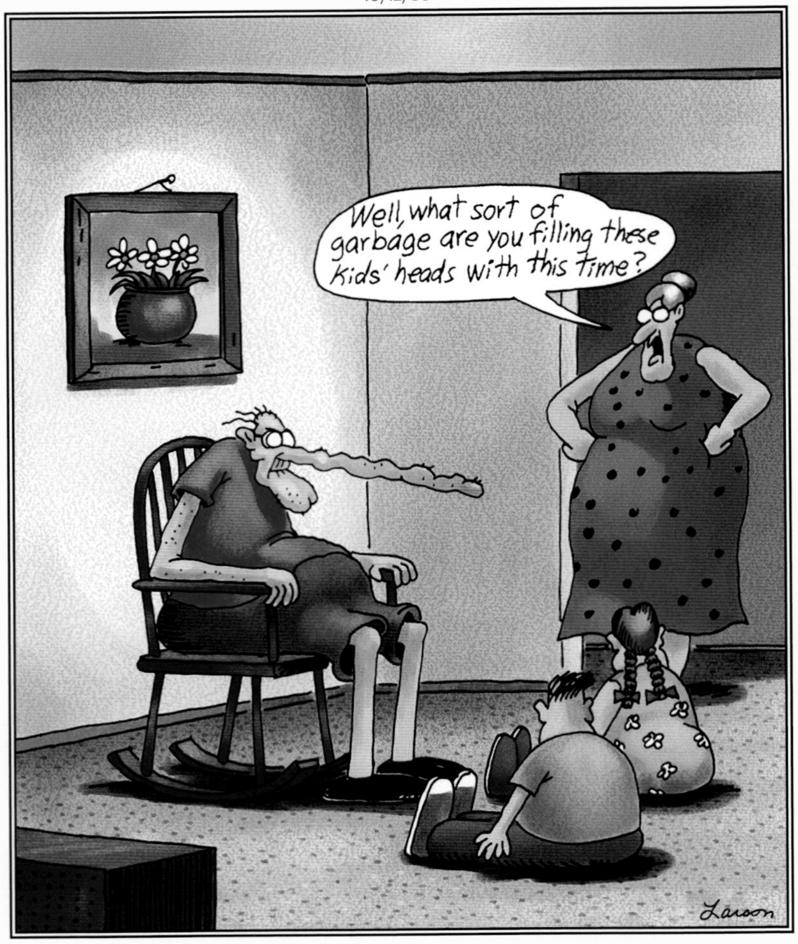
Well, what sort of garbage are you filling these kids' heads with this time?
Larson

Pinocchio in his later years

10/16/88

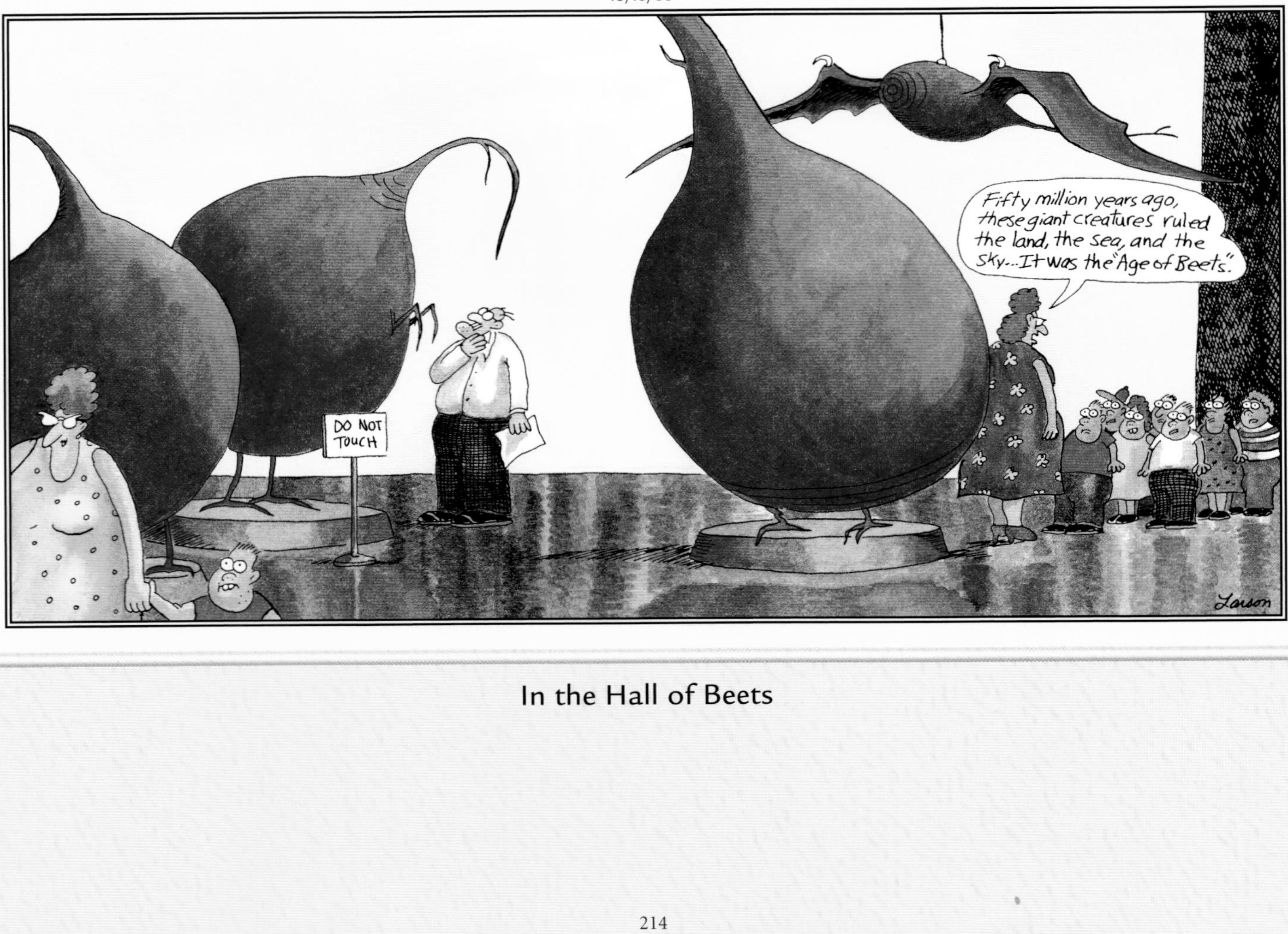
DO NOT TOUCH
Fifty million years ago, these giant creatures ruled the land, the sea, and the sky... It was the "Age of Beets."
Larson

In the Hall of Beets

10/19/88

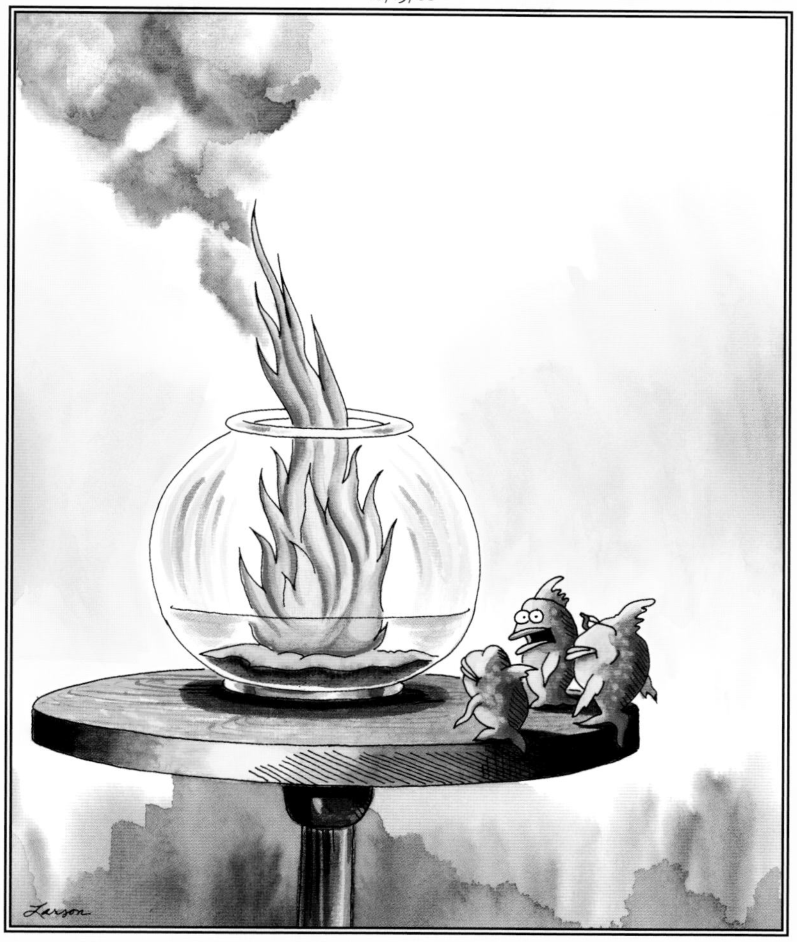
Larson

"Well, thank God we all made it out in time. ...
'Course, now we're equally screwed."

10/23/88

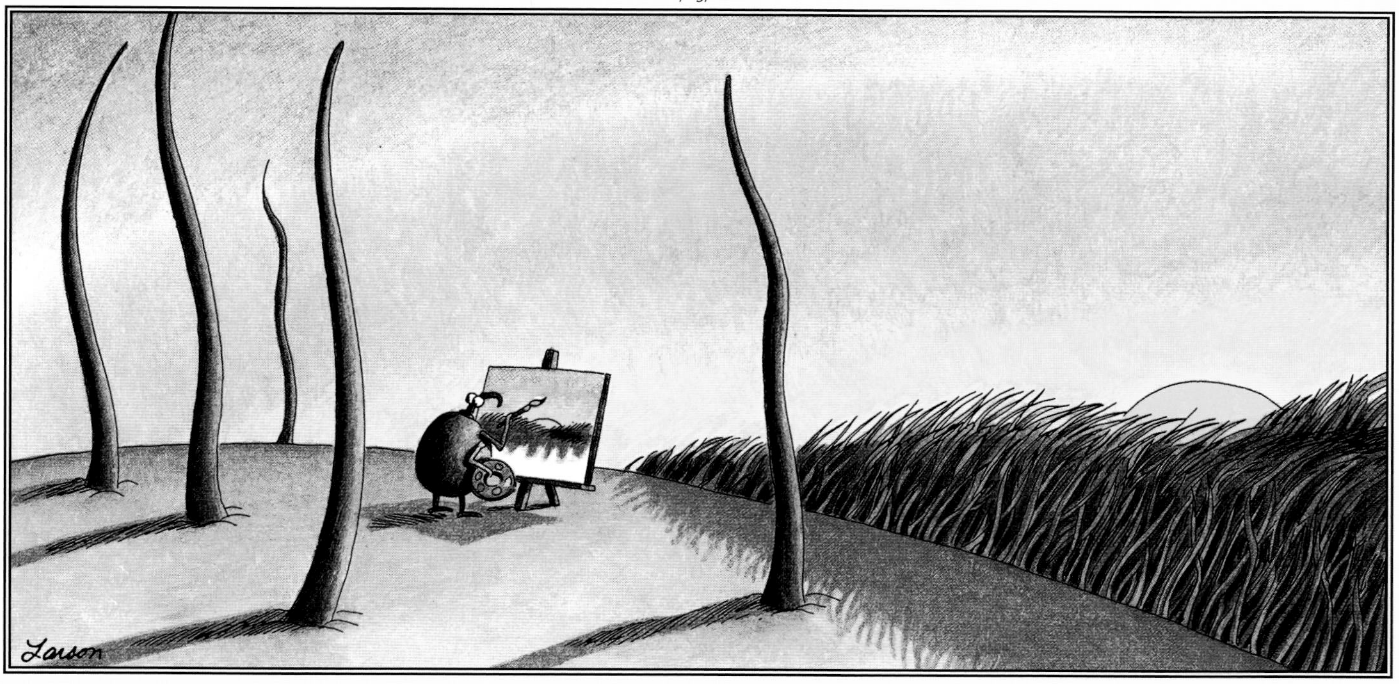
Larson

Dogscapes

10/14/88

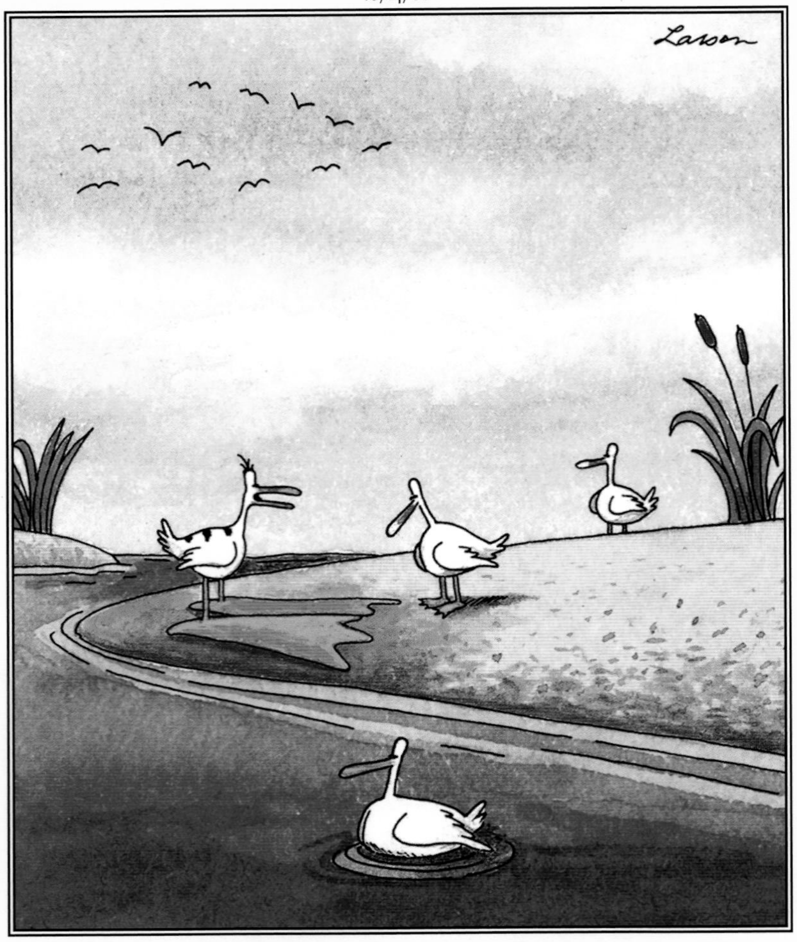

"I'm one of those species they always describe as 'awkward on land.'"

10/15/88

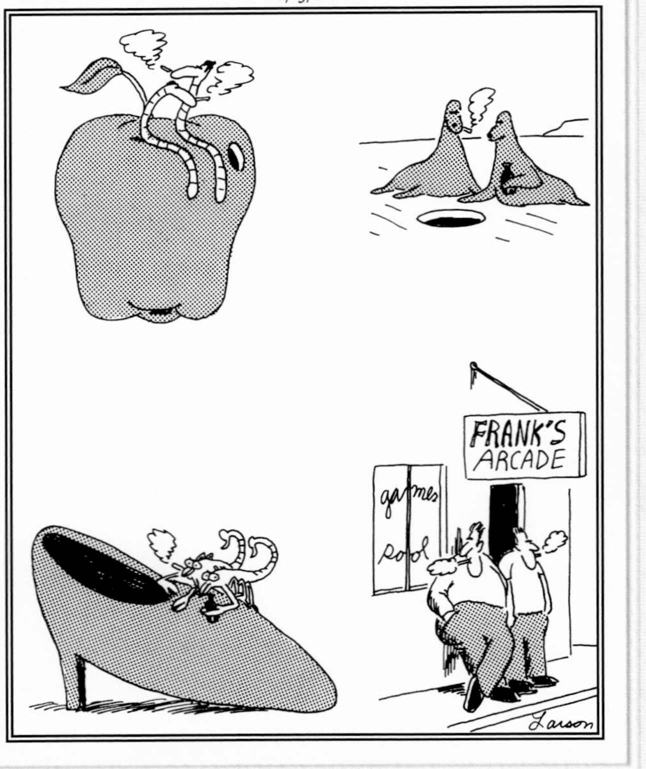
FRANK'S
ARCADE
games
pool

Animal toughs and their hangouts

10/17/88

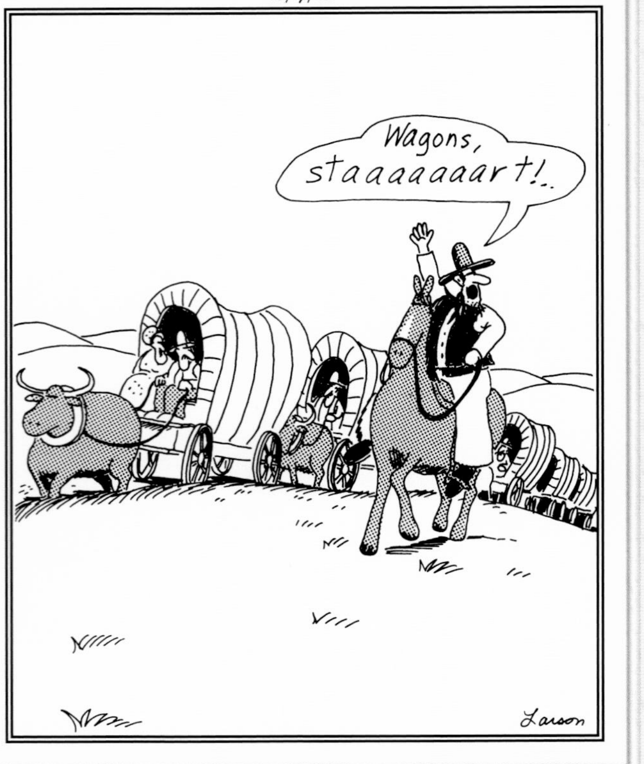
Wagons, staaaaaaart!..

Non-union wagon masters

10/22/88

The Shroud of Turin

The Shirt of Toledo

10/26/88

"Hey, Bob ... did I scare you or what?"

10/25/88

"So then I says to Borg, 'You know, as long as we're under
siege, one of us oughta moon these Saxon dogs.'"

10/18/88

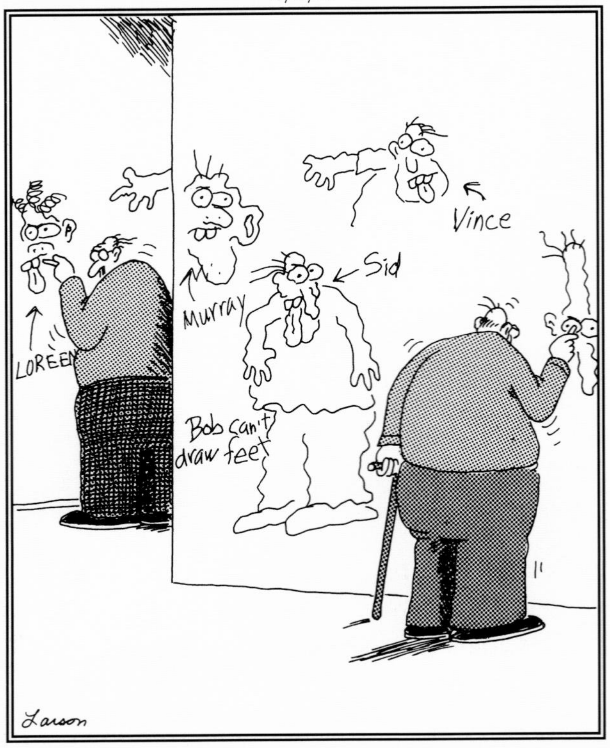
LOREEN
Murray
Sid
Vince
Bob can't draw feet

In the hallway of the Old Cartoonists' Home

10/20/88

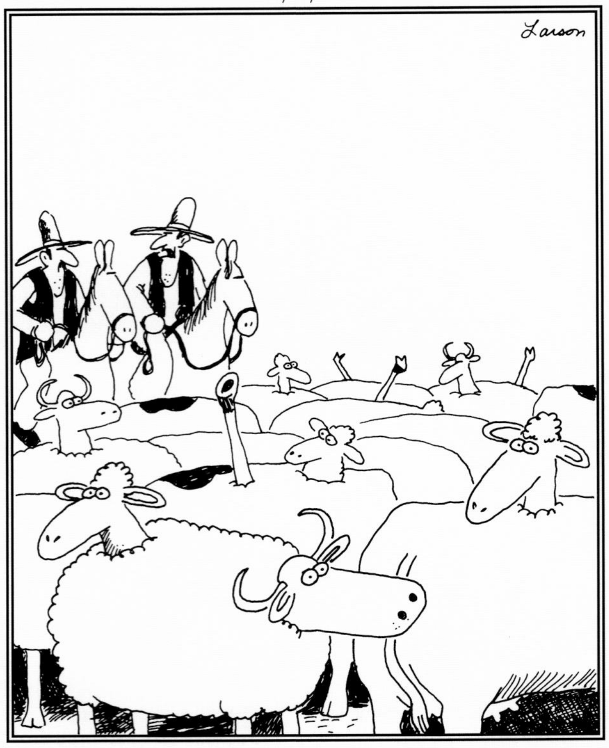

"Man, this is ugly—sheep and cattle never do mix well."

10/21/88

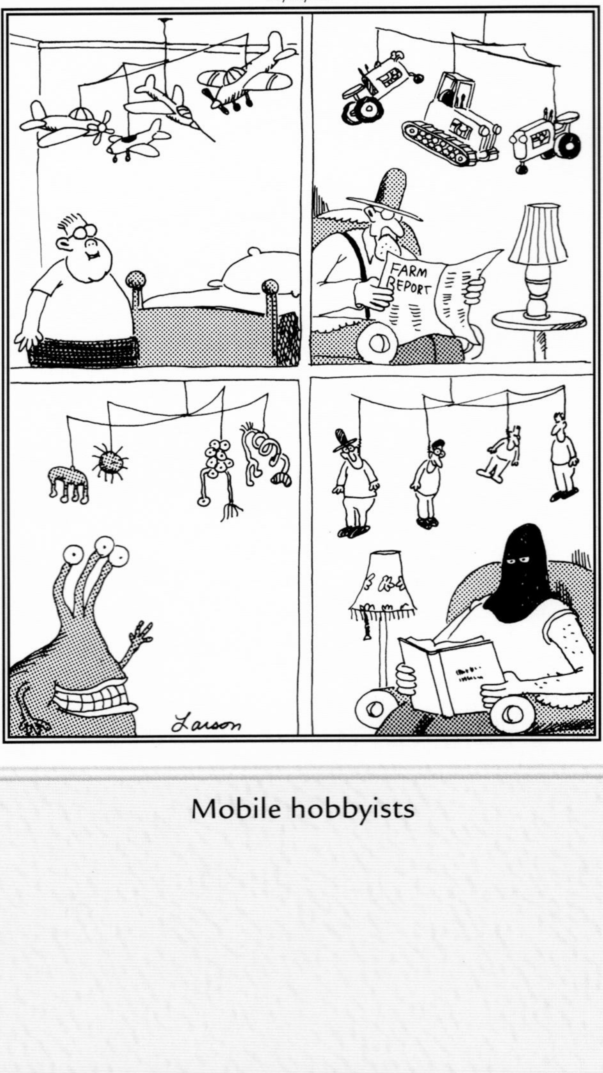
FARM REPORT

Mobile hobbyists

10/24/88

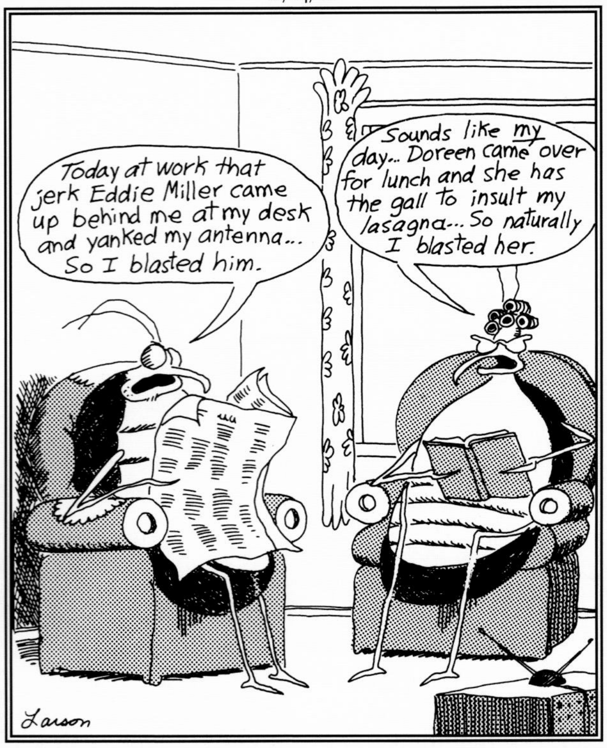
Today at work that jerk Eddie Miller came up behind me at my desk and yanked my antenna... So I blasted him.
Sounds like my day... Doreen came over for lunch and she has the gall to insult my lasagna... So naturally I blasted her.

Bombardier beetles at home

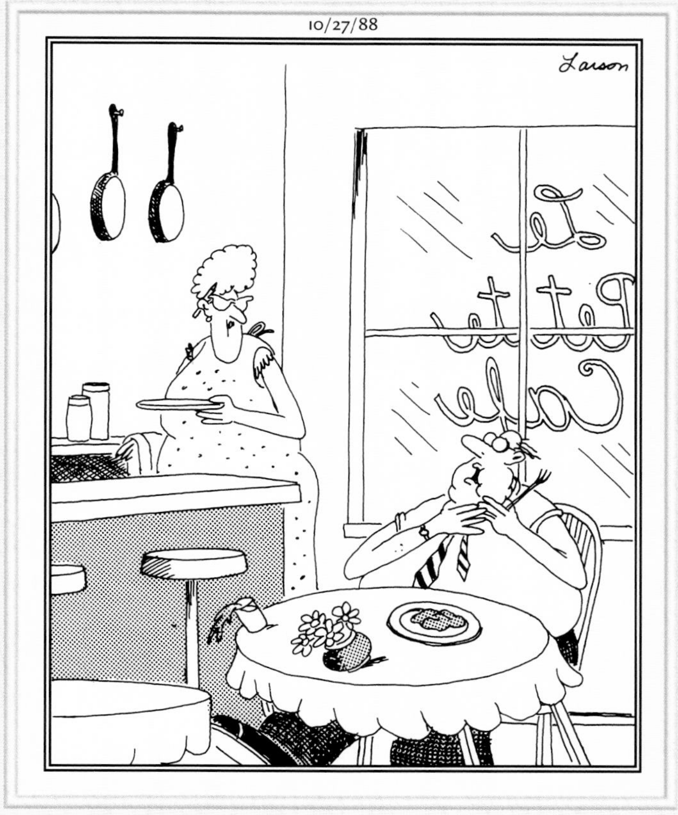
10/27/88
Larson
The crepes of wrath

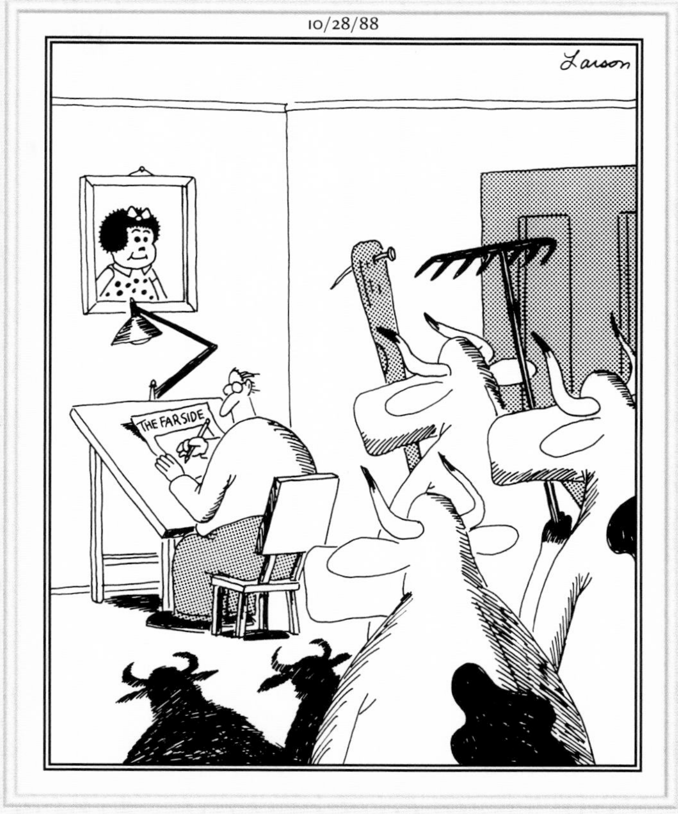
10/28/88
Larson
THE FARSIDE
The End (Act One)

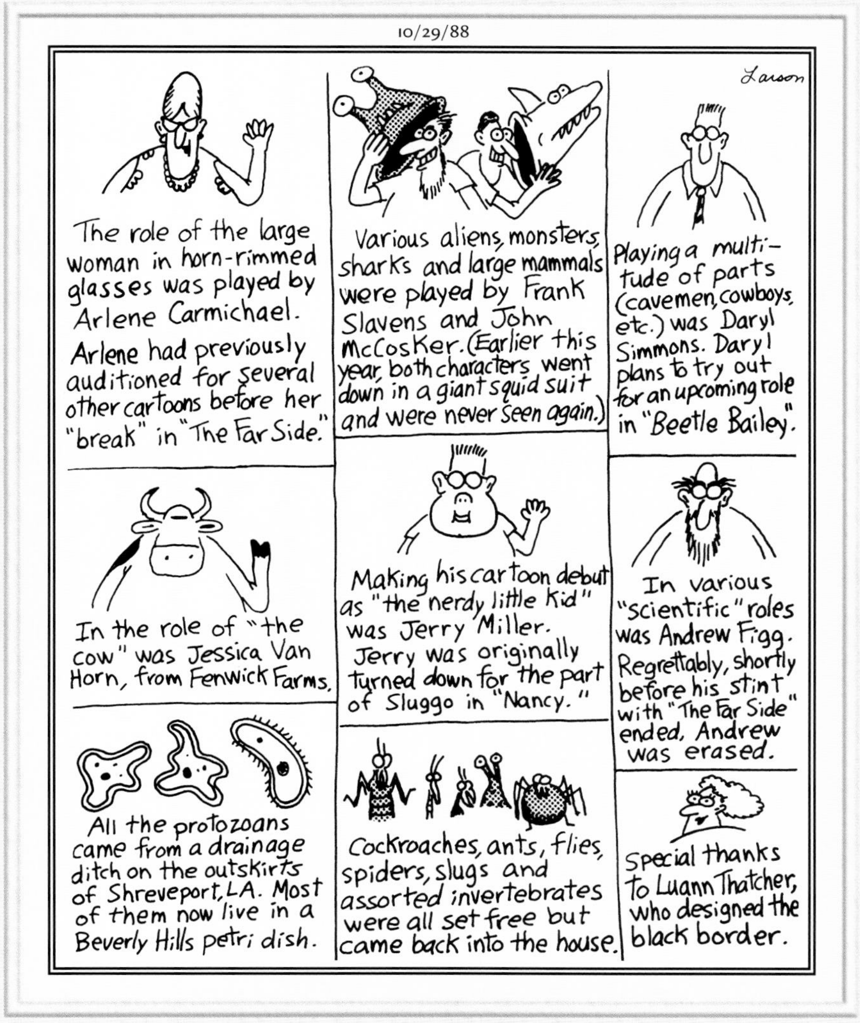
10/29/88
Larson
The role of the large woman in horn-rimmed glasses was played by Arlene Carmichael. Arlene had previously auditioned for several other cartoons before her "break" in "The Far Side."
Various aliens, monsters, sharks and large mammals were played by Frank Slavens and John McCosker. (Earlier this year, both characters went down in a giant squid suit and were never seen again.)
Playing a multitude of parts (cavemen, cowboys, etc.) was Daryl Simmons. Daryl plans to try out for an upcoming role in "Beetle Bailey".
In the role of "the cow" was Jessica Van Horn, from Fenwick Farms.
Making his cartoon debut as "the nerdy little kid" was Jerry Miller. Jerry was originally turned down for the part of Sluggo in "Nancy."
In various "scientific" roles was Andrew Figg. Regrettably, shortly before his stint with "The Far Side" ended, Andrew was erased.
All the protozoans came from a drainage ditch on the outskirts of Shreveport, LA. Most of them now live in a Beverly Hills petri dish.
Cockroaches, ants, flies, spiders, slugs and assorted invertebrates were all set free but came back into the house.
Special thanks to Luann Thatcher, who designed the black border.
The Far Side cast

Editor's note: Gary leaves for a one-year sabbatical. He returns in 1990.

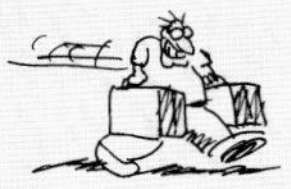

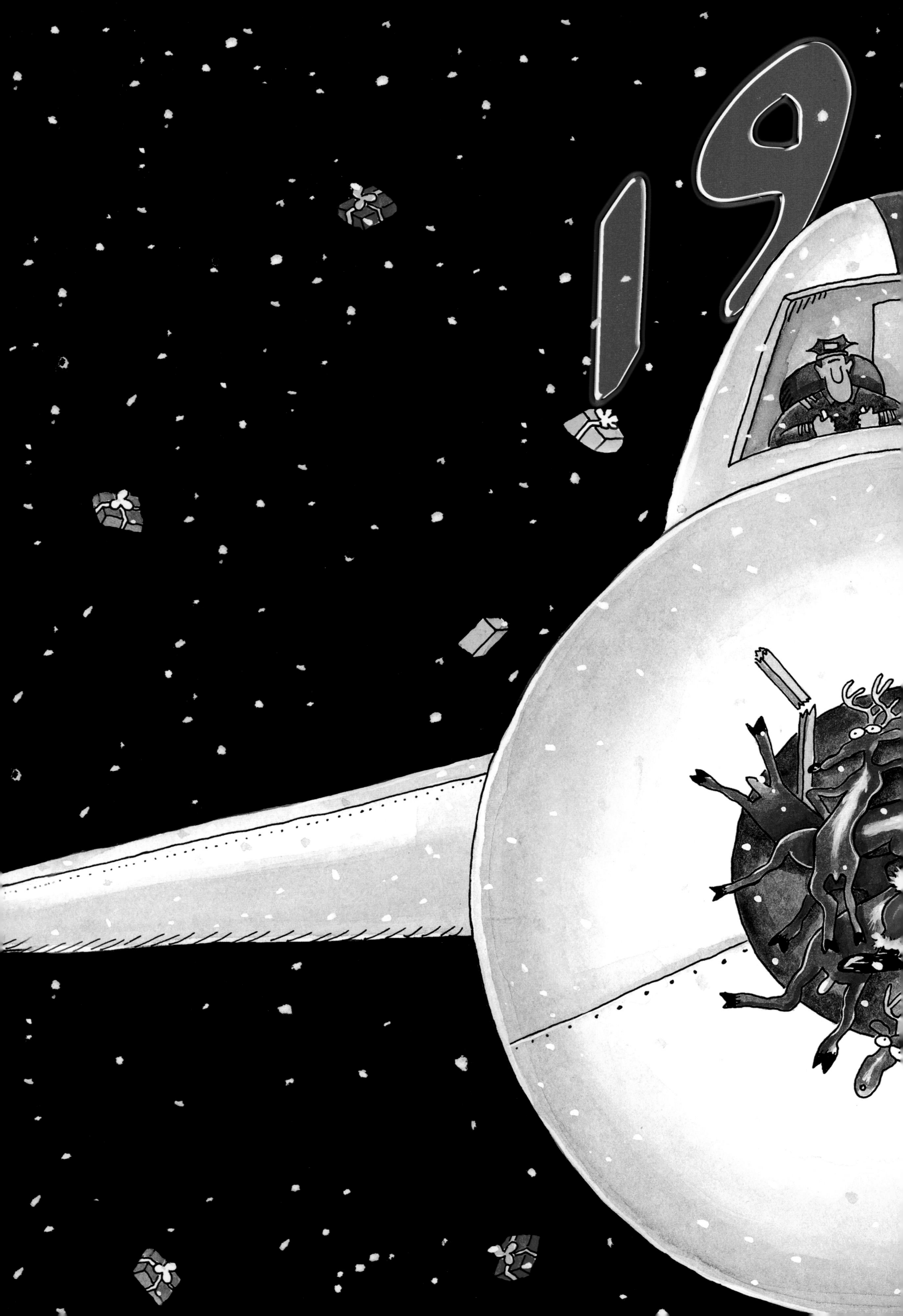
19

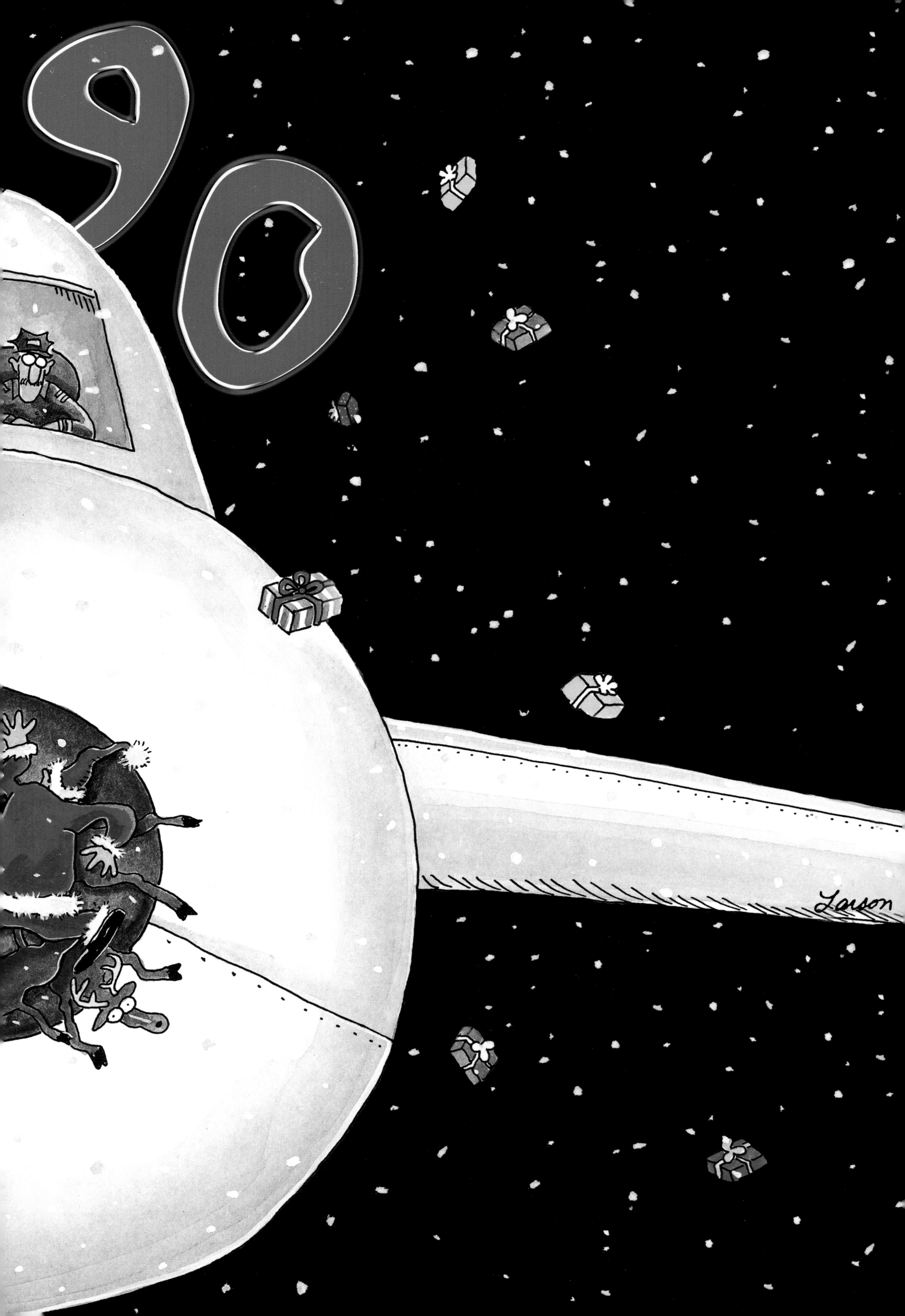
90
Larson

The Second-Most Asked Question

Before I get into this, I first must divulge what I, personally, consider to be the single-most penetrating and important question to ask any cartoonist. And no one has ever once asked me this. Get ready: *So, [name of cartoonist], tell me—what kind of pen do you use?*

Thrilling, isn't it? You can use it, if you wish, the next time you cross paths with someone who draws for a living. But I'm serious—it's the one thing I wondered about when I started out as a cartoonist. I may even ask it now. (Obviously, I never have very long conversations with other cartoonists.)

For me, everything else relates to the creative process, and I have never been able to deconstruct that invisible beast without ultimately being devoured by it.

So, please, let's move on from any exploration of that most-asked question regarding my cartoons, *Where do you get your ideas?* Not that I have ever begrudged anyone for asking it. (Hell, I guess no one's going to ask what kind of *pen* I use.) It's just that it's beyond my own understanding.

The second-place contender is an entirely *different* question, and one that has always fascinated me because I'm intrigued with why so many people have asked it: *How long does it take you to draw a cartoon?*

My initial response: Well, which cartoon are we talking about here? Does it involve amoebas or an anthill? A family of stick people or an army of Vikings? A lone vulture soaring overhead or a traffic jam in midtown? Just point the cartoon out to me and I'll scratch my head and come up with some lie.

I've suspected an ulterior motive from some people who ask me this question. I think they want to check to see if I'm *really* working. In other words, is cartooning a real job? If that's the hidden question, the answer is easy. No—it's not a real job. The guy laying asphalt in mid-July on a Louisiana highway has a real job. And I've had real jobs in my past. This was not one of them. What I did for a living was try to make that guy laying asphalt crack up once in a while so he didn't look around and notice I wasn't out there alongside him.

But I'm working on an additional theory: that this kind of question is an outgrowth of American culture. We just seem to want to quantify everything. *How much horsepower does that baby have? ... How much did they soak you for that? ... How much does that sucker weigh? ... How much time elapses before the female eats the male?* (Actually, it may not be just an American thing; I once read that some forest dwellers in Brazil distinguish between several kinds of venomous snakes based on the number of steps a bitten person can take before dropping dead. A hundred-stepper, therefore, is clearly preferred over a ten-stepper, and a one-stepper is apparently just enough time to say, "Ow! ... Hey, was that a one-stepperrrrrrrrrrrr? ...")

So (I'm back), how long *did* it take for me to draw an average cartoon? Honestly, I can't compute that with any real certainty. (See why I like that pen question so much?) First of all, I enjoyed what I did. And when you enjoy doing something, time is a disconnect. Not that you can afford to ignore the clock entirely; if you're a syndicated cartoonist under contract, you have deadlines. Mine were weekly, and the lag time between the time I submitted something and when it showed up in a newspaper was about three weeks. But I'll never complain about deadlines to that guy laying asphalt. I would lose that whining contest.

There's also a critical part of the equation that has nothing to do with the physical execution of the cartoon, and that's the time invested in just sitting, staring, and thinking. And it's difficult to know if you're not, in truth, just doing the first two. (Sometimes I think it wouldn't have been a bad thing if a Lou Grant-type person burst into my office once in a while and said, "Larson! Draw!")

Finally, on to the "Looks Are Deceiving" category, and for that I've included an example, "Houdini's final undoing." I remember all too well my long day in hell with this cartoon.

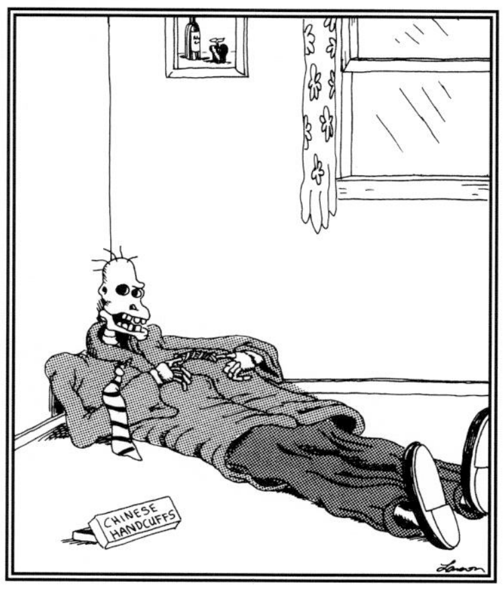
CHINESE HANDCUFFS

A simple concept, really: Houdini has apparently met his match in a pair of Chinese handcuffs, with tragic results for the famous escape artist. Now, if you will, please pretend that you are the Cartoon Coroner and take a closer look at the "deceased." What we have here is a decomposed body, with the main focus on the head. If it's too gruesome, it doesn't work. If it's too corny, it doesn't work. The expression on that face has to simultaneously capture silliness and scariness, horror and hilarity, sadness and stupidity. For me, this meant draw, erase, draw, erase, draw, erase ... for hours. I couldn't get it, although I think in the end I got sort of close. (I now see that the head should have been tilted forward just a little, dammit.) If it hadn't been for my deadline, I might be sitting there to this very day, doomed to draw Houdini's skull for the rest of my life until I, too, am discovered one day looking much like this very drawing, only perhaps funnier.

How long does it take for me to draw a cartoon? Let it go. Ask me what kind of pen I use.

1/1/90

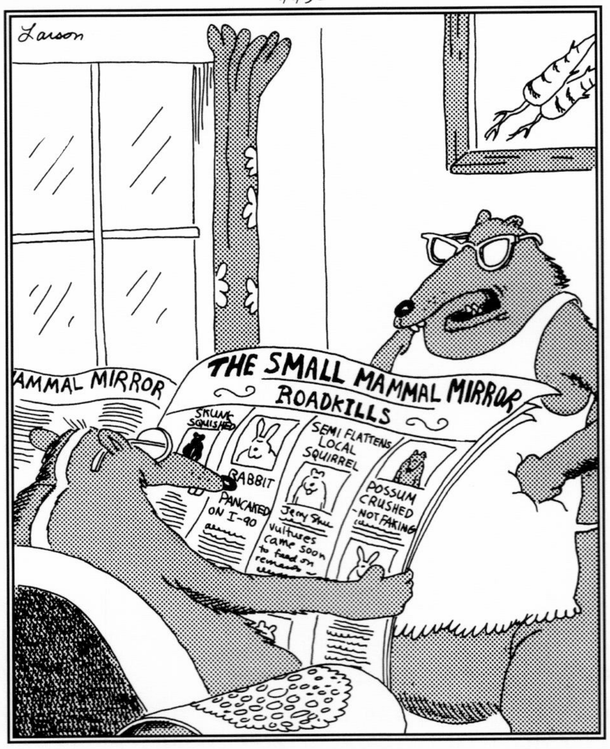
THE SMALL MAMMAL MIRROR
ROADKILLS
SKUNK SQUISHED
RABBIT PANCAKED ON I-90
SEMI FLATTENS LOCAL SQUIRREL
POSSUM CRUSHED —NOT FAKING
MAMMAL MIRROR

"You're so morbid, Jonathan—the paper comes, and that's the first section you always head for."

1/4/90

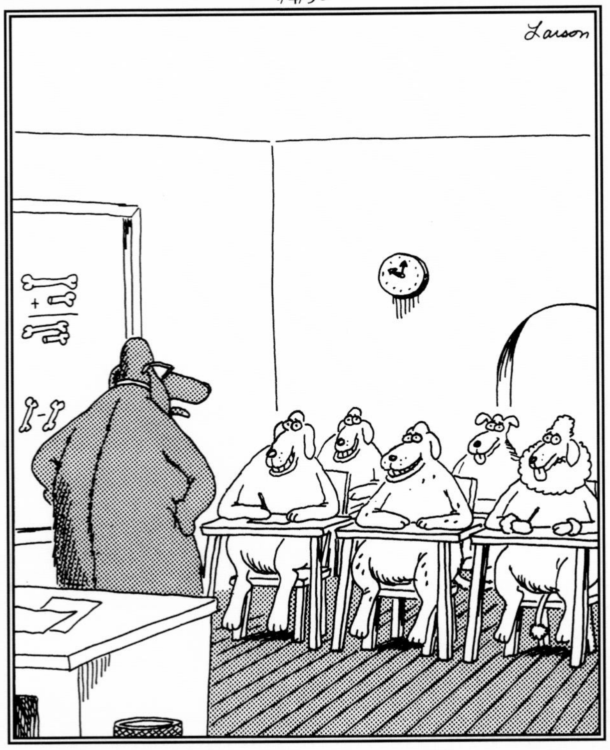

"Well, here we go again. ... Did anyone here *not* eat his or her homework on the way to school?"

1/2/90

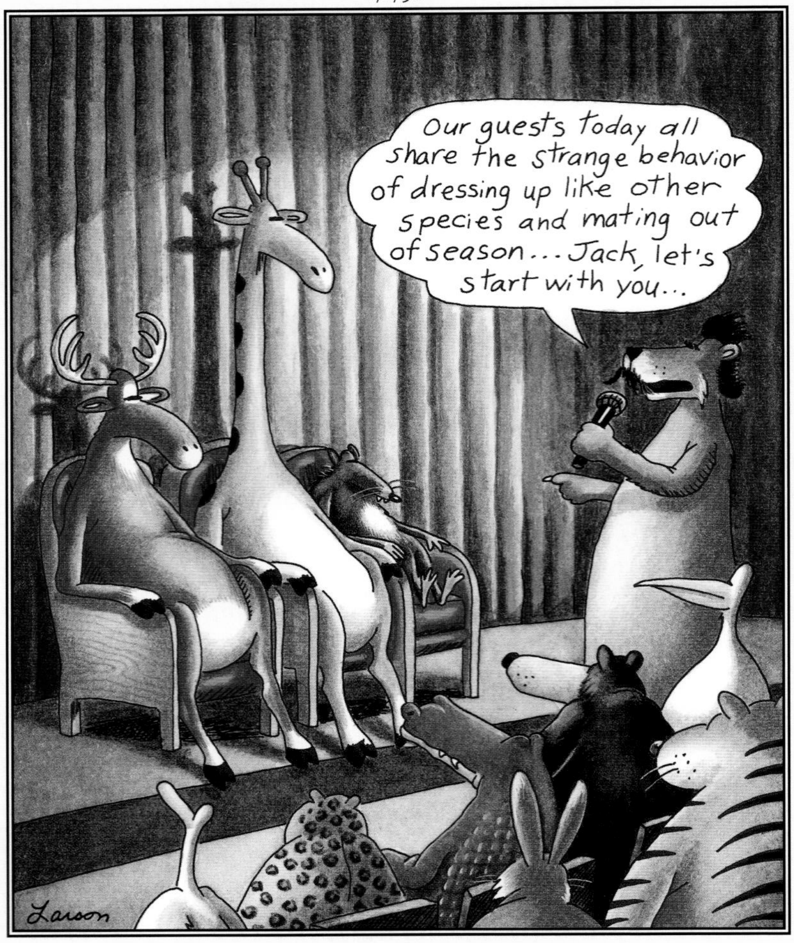
Our guests today all share the strange behavior of dressing up like other species and mating out of season... Jack, let's start with you...

Geraldo Rivera of the wild

1/3/90

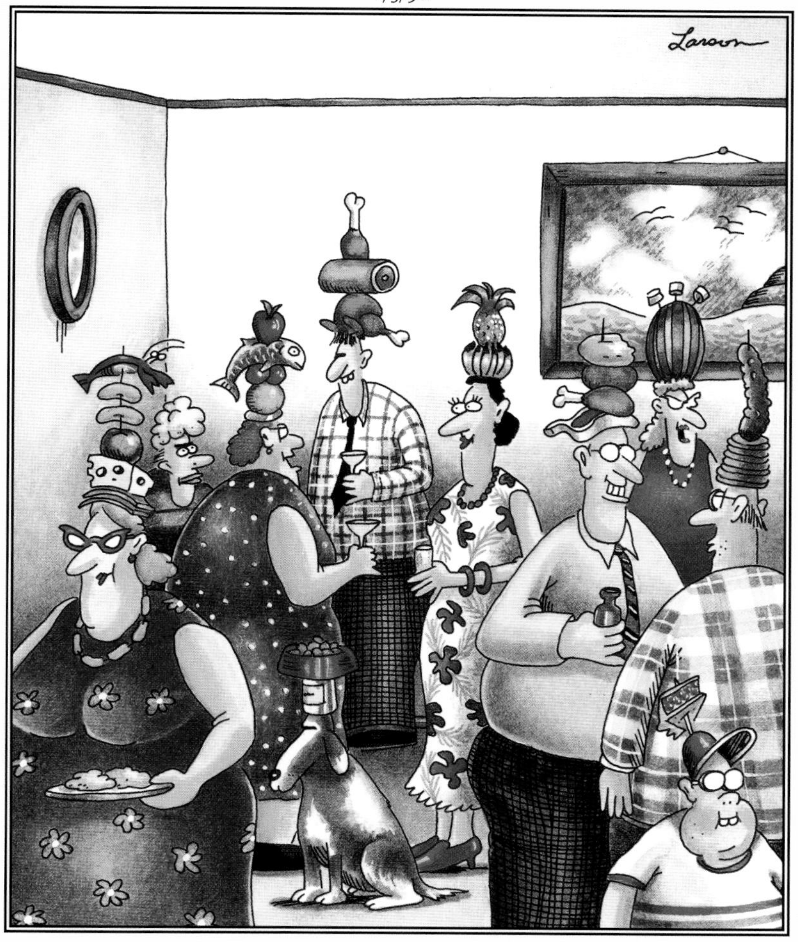
Larson

Carmen Miranda's family reunion

1/8/90

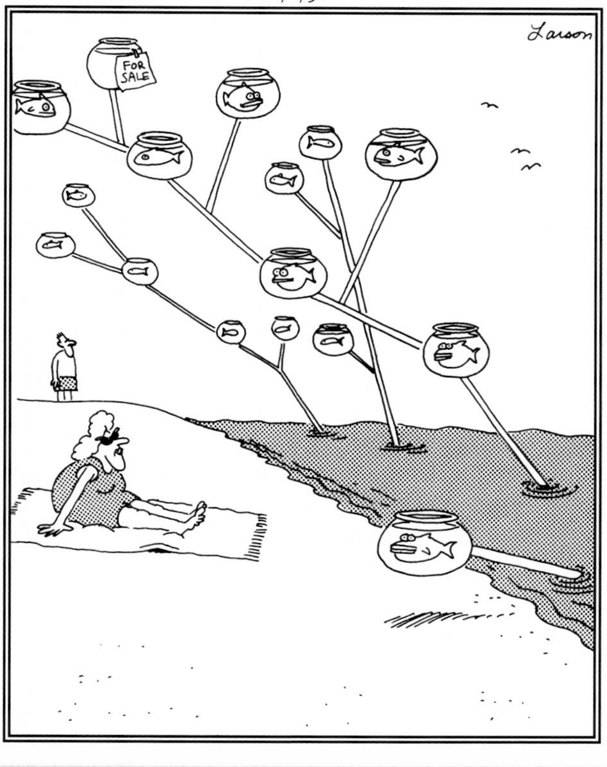
Larson
FOR SALE

Encroachment of the fish developers

1/10/90

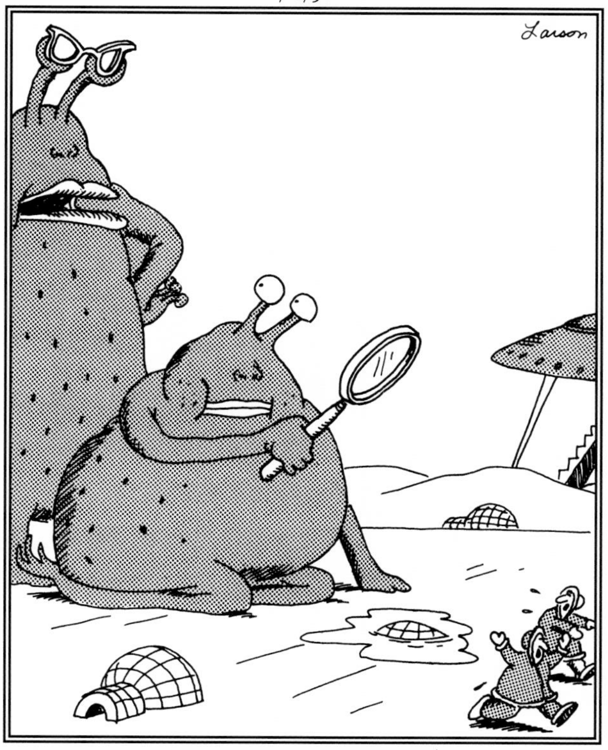
Larson

"Jimzfxxy! Do you have to mess with the organisms on every planet we visit?"

1/9/90

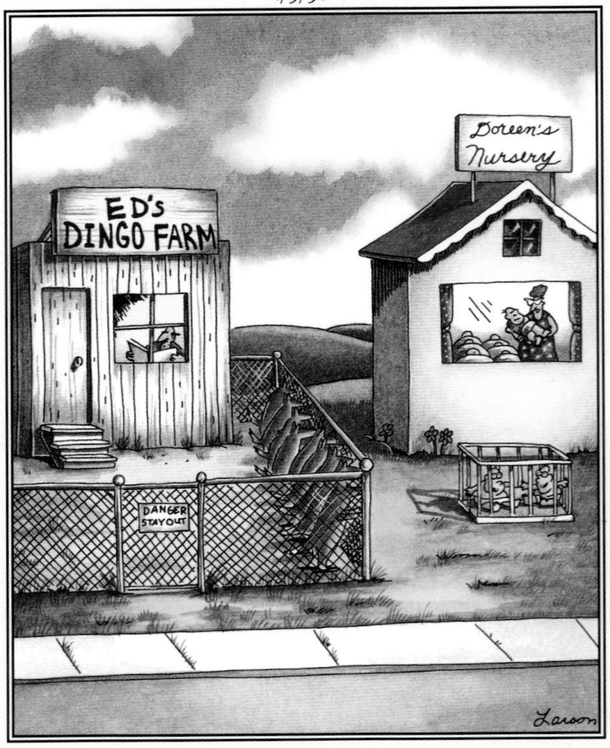
ED's
DINGO FARM
Doreen's
Nursery
DANGER
STAY OUT

Trouble brewing

1/5/90

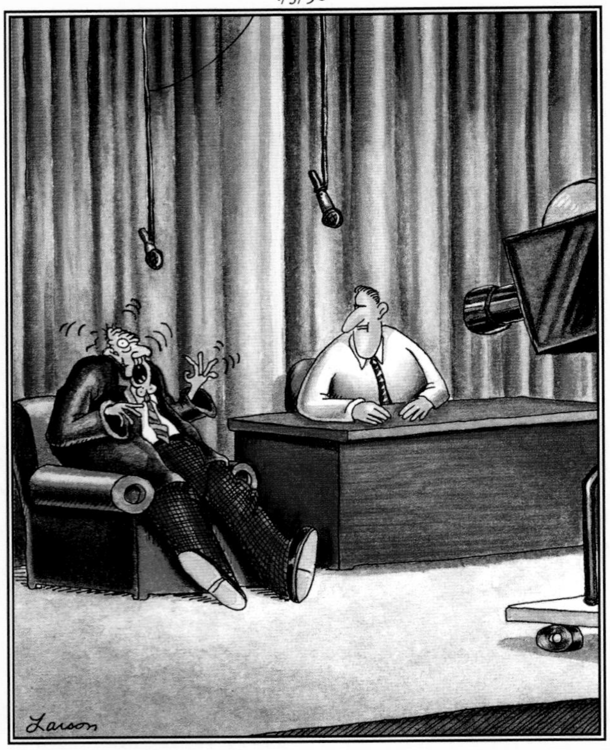

Suddenly, on a national talk show in front of millions of viewers, Dick Clark ages 200 years in 30 seconds.

1/12/90

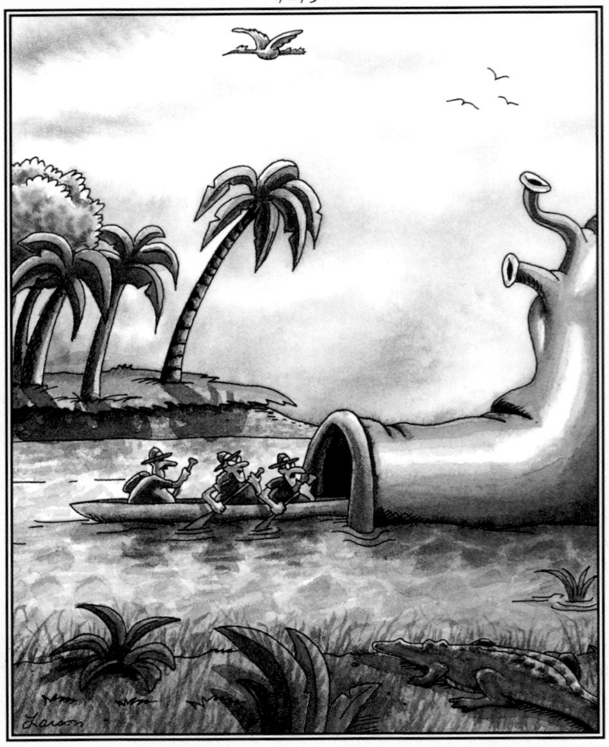

The heart of the jungle now well behind them, the three intrepid explorers entered the spleen.

1/11/90

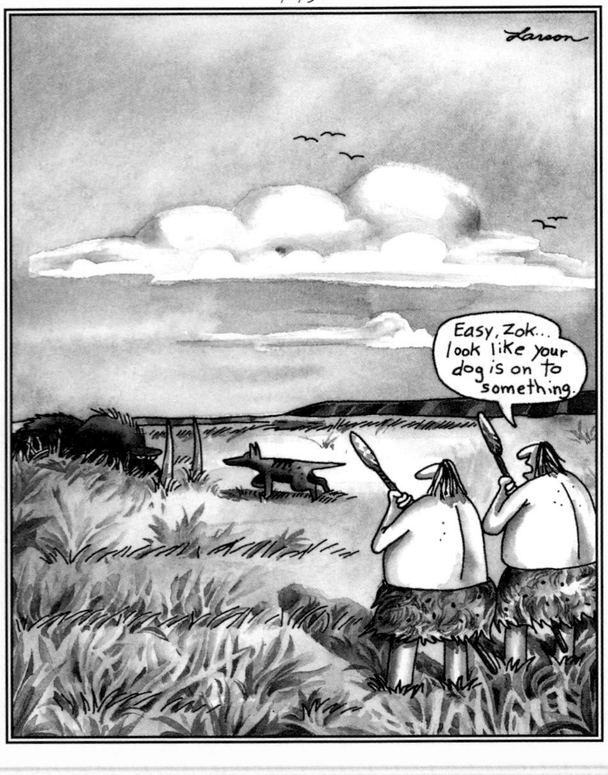
Easy, Zok... look like your dog is on to something.

Mammoth pointers

1/15/90

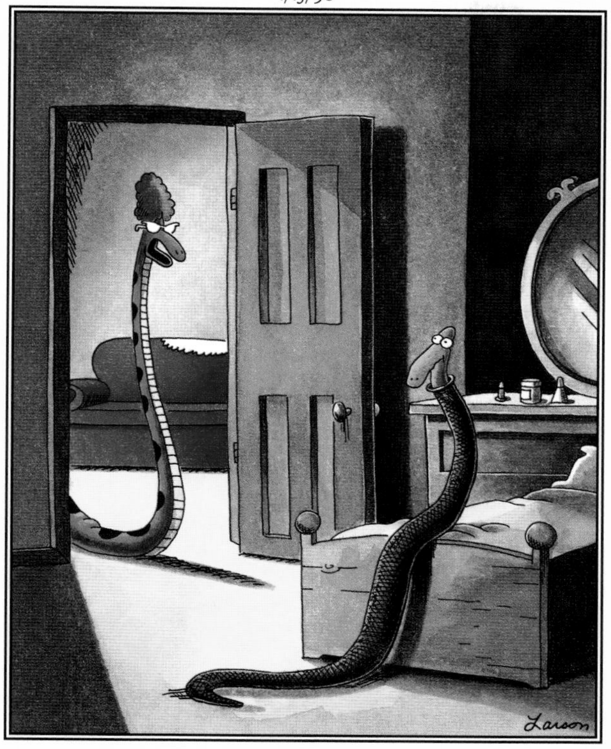

"Oh my God, Bernie! You're wearing one of my nylons?"

1/22/90

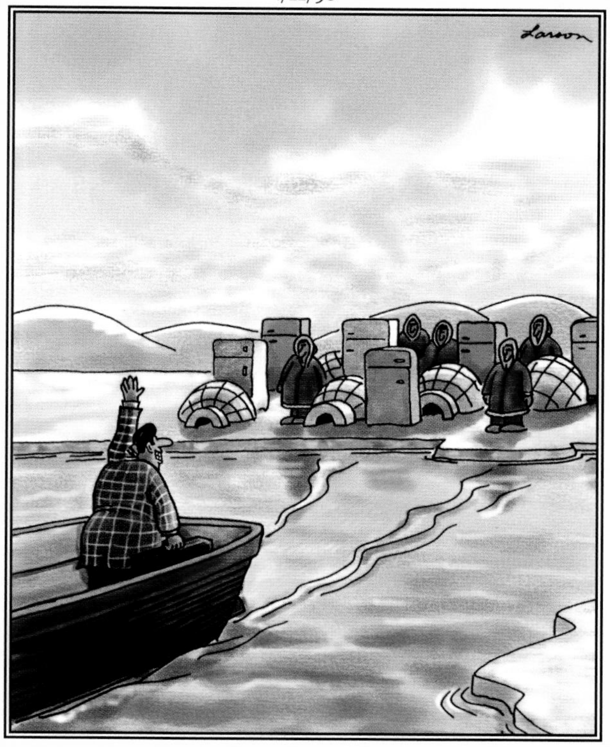

Ralph Harrison, king of salespersons

1/16/90

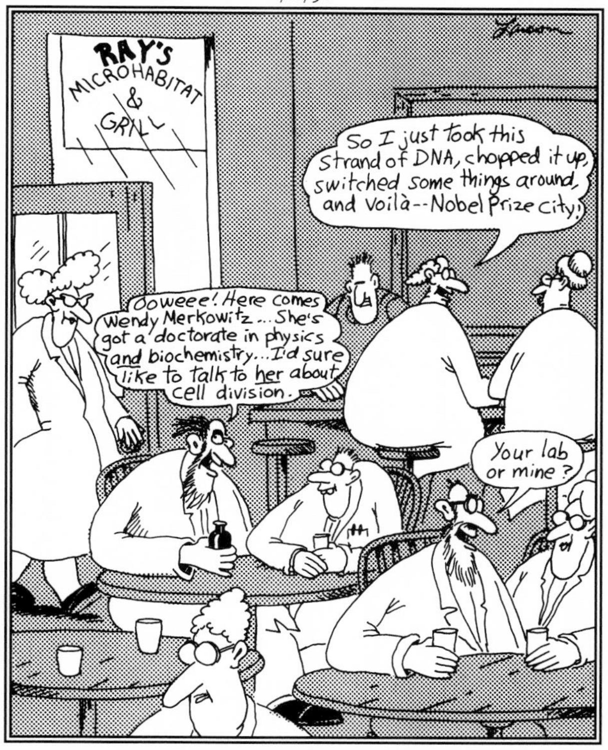
RAY'S MICROHABITAT & GRILL
So I just took this Strand of DNA, chopped it up, switched some things around, and Voilà--Nobel Prize city!
Ooweee! Here comes Wendy Merkowitz...She's got a doctorate in physics and biochemistry...I'd sure like to talk to her about cell division.
Your lab or mine?

Scientific meat markets

1/17/90

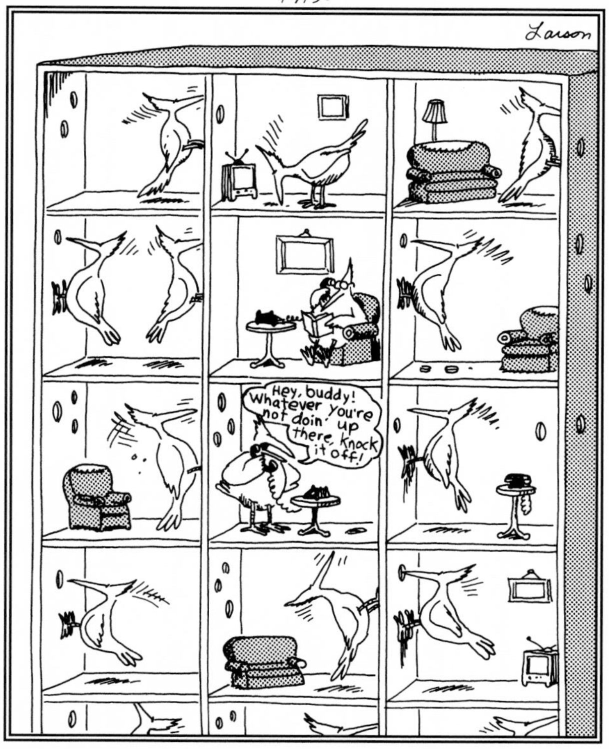
Hey, buddy! Whatever you're not doin' up there, knock it off!

1/18/90

All right! Rise from the dead, you blood-sucking morons! C'mon, c'mon!.. You lazy bunch of corpses!..
Wump! Wump! Wump!

Sunset in the vampire army

1/19/90

DERMATOLOGY

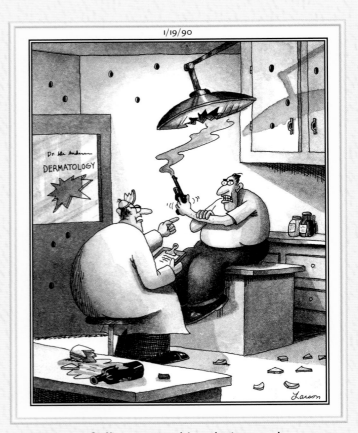

"First of all, Mr. Hawkins, let's put the gun down. ... I would guess it's an itchy trigger finger, but I want to take a closer look."

1/23/90

At the public execution of the "Ring around the collar" copywriter

January 2, 1996

Dear Gary,

I am one of your more famous unknown admirers. Fact is, you made me famous — one of the most (in)famous copywriters of all time. Yup, the execution was botched, an c'est moi, the "Ring (Wisk) around the collar" copywriter. And it's time to even the score.

My family and friends, long apprised of my dubious celebrity, have upbraided me for not demanding satisfaction. Well, no, uh, actually they just said I should get in touch with you. So here I am; unfortunately without my computer, and no spellcheck, so bear with me.

Anyhow, just to give you a little background on the man you so cavalierly prepared for hanging...
Back in the sixties, I worked at Lever Brothers in New York City as a Promotion Specialist. I created nuts-and-bolts kinds of stuff like point-of-purchase(POP) materials, contests, coupons, and the whole stinking mess of marketing crap. Meantime, a Big Name agency handled Lever's major campaigns.

I started my advertising career as an agency copywriter before going to Lever. My first real job after college was as a bona fide copywriter with what was back then the largest ad agency in the world, Interpublic. It broke-up because of the anti-trust sentiment that still had a say in those days. It became McCann-Erickson and a bunch of other topnotch agencies.

I was (at least to my own now hazy perception of those days) a hotshot at Lever, coming as I did from the "big one". Them were the days. I was in my early twenties, and just by youthful hubris and exhuberance, if nothing else, more productive, and easily as creative, as the other three Promotion Specialists combined, seasoned veterans as they may have been.

Not too surprisingly, with certain individuals at Lever my brash, call-a-spade-a-spade attitude didn't sit well—[with] two Product Managers in particular, one on Wisk and the other on the Pepsodent account. ...

As coincidence had it, about five months before I resigned from Lever, the aforementioned managers pulled off a first time coup at Lever by becoming Co-presidents of the company.

Anyway, one day, midway in my stay at Lever, my buddy Preston Doby (we had become good friends during my time there. Doby's claim to fame, other than being an heck of an artist, was his uncle, Larry, who was the first black man to play on the other major league that didn't hire Jacky Robinson), brings me over a bottle of Wisk. On its neck is a mock-up in paper of a collar and tie.

"Come up with something to say on this collar."

Doby had already drawn some blotches on the tie representing stains. Almost immediately I flashed on the idea of a dirty collar, and sing-songed, "Ring around the collar, we're out to get your dollar." I did it to the tune of that old childhood ditty from the days of the black plague:
Ring around the rosey, pocket full of posey. all fall down.

Doby responded that that wasn't exactly a product benefit, so I hit him with, "Wisk around the collar beats ring around the collar every time." And that was it.

He finished the mock-up, and I brought it to the Product Manager. Barging into his office because the door was open, I didn't notice the 'suits' on the sofa in the rear.

"What do you think of this for a POP promo?"

He gave it a thoughtful half second appraisal, and said he didn't like it. Meanwhile, as I began my last ditch appeal to sell him on it, the two guys I hadn't noticed who happened to be agency Account Execs sidled up beside me. One reached for the mock-up saying, "Hey, this isn't a bad idea!"

"We could take this little idea, and run it into a national campaign. I like it."

And that's the story. The epilogue is that this Product Manager in part for his brilliant Wisk campaign strategy and the other [guy] on Pepsodent became Co-presidents. Some of my friends in higher places at Lever told me that just about their first official act as Co-presidents was a decision to give me six months notice.

Nowadays, I'm an holistic bodywork therapist, and it's the best thing I've ever done. I'll give you a freebee if we ever cross paths. I also do a little freelance writing. I won't go so far as to say you owe me, but please write me something or call me. I'm the one that was wronged and I'm practically begging. It would make my kids real happy.

Forgivingly,

Ray

Dear Ray:

Even as I sat at my drafting table so many moons ago and drew the cartoon to which you refer, I remember thinking, "Man, I hope I don't hear from this person." And after a pause of several seconds, I thought, "No way."

And now here you are. Like the Ghost of Far Side Past.

Your letter was very enjoyable, and read like some kind of "whodunit" in the advertising world. And that Wisk commercial, when all's said and done, must have ultimately been very successful for your client -- or they wouldn't have kept driving it into our skulls for so many years.

Thanks for writing, and I'm glad to hear about your career change. (I was going to say something about how wonderful it is that you're no longer coming up with ways to irritate millions of people, and then I realized one might make that same comment about me.)

Cheers,

Gary Larson

Gary Larson

FarWorks, Inc.

1/30/90

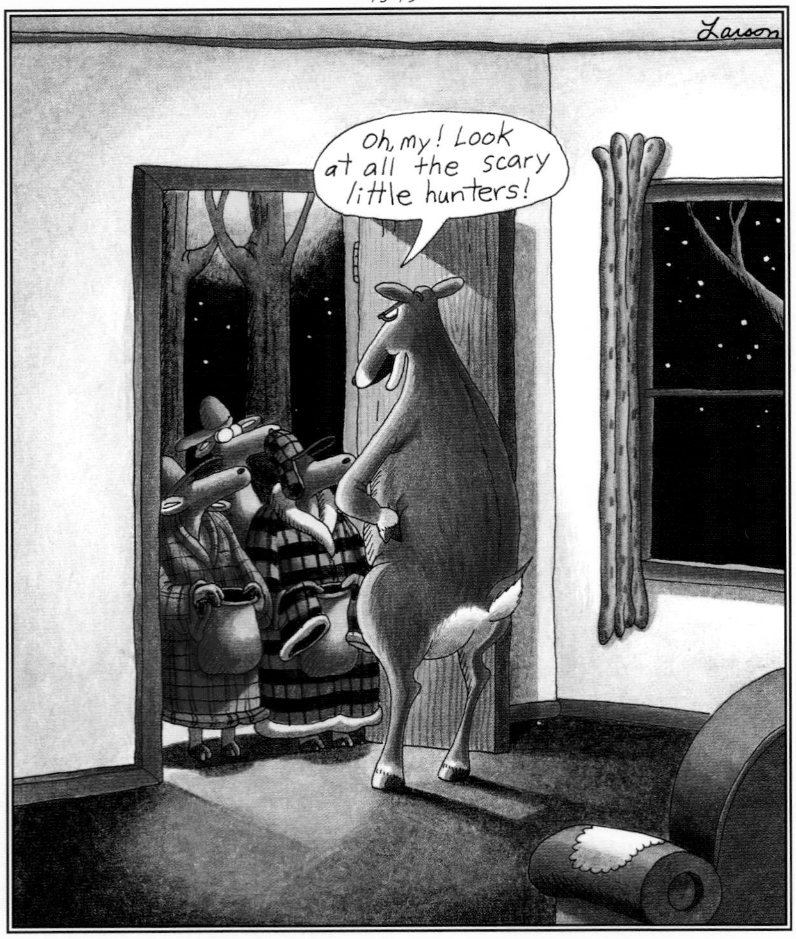
Larson
Oh, my! Look at all the scary little hunters!

Deer Halloweens

1/24/90

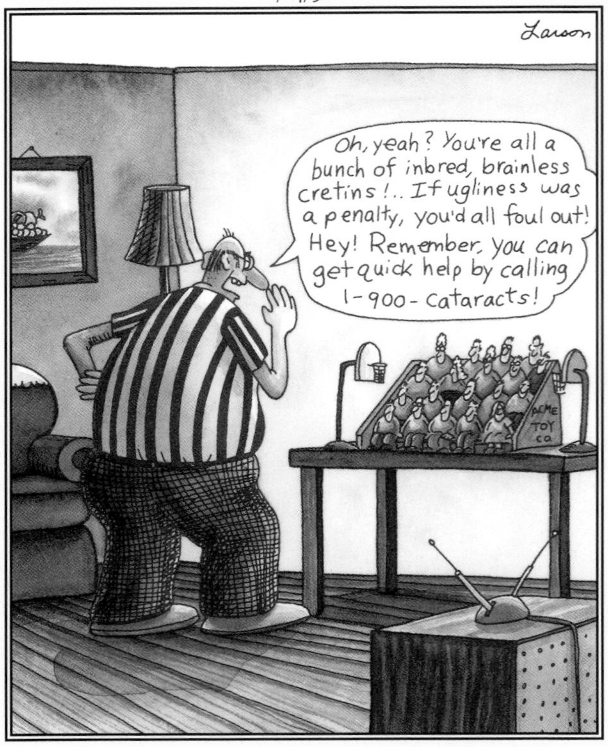
Larson
Oh, yeah? You're all a bunch of inbred, brainless cretins!.. If ugliness was a penalty, you'd all foul out! Hey! Remember, you can get quick help by calling 1-900-cataracts!

When referees go home at night

1/25/90

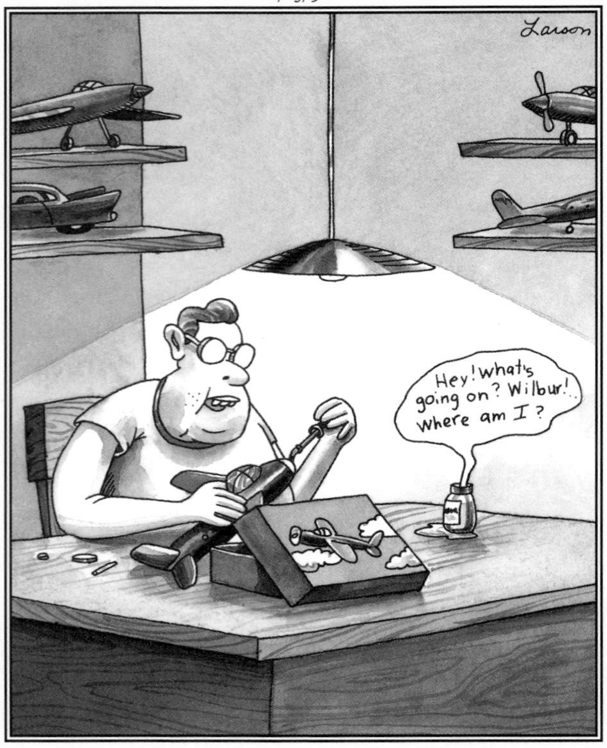
Larson
Hey! What's going on? Wilbur!.. Where am I?

Jimmy meets Mr. Ed.

1/31/90

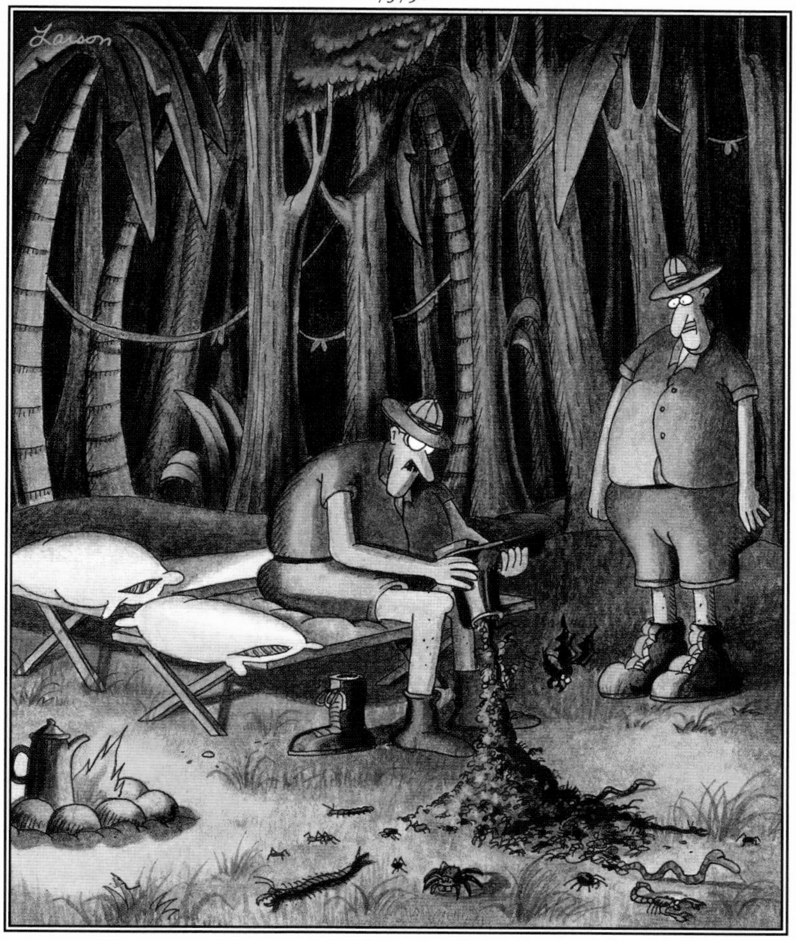

To his horror, Irving suddenly realized he had failed to check his own boots before putting them on just minutes ago.

1/29/90

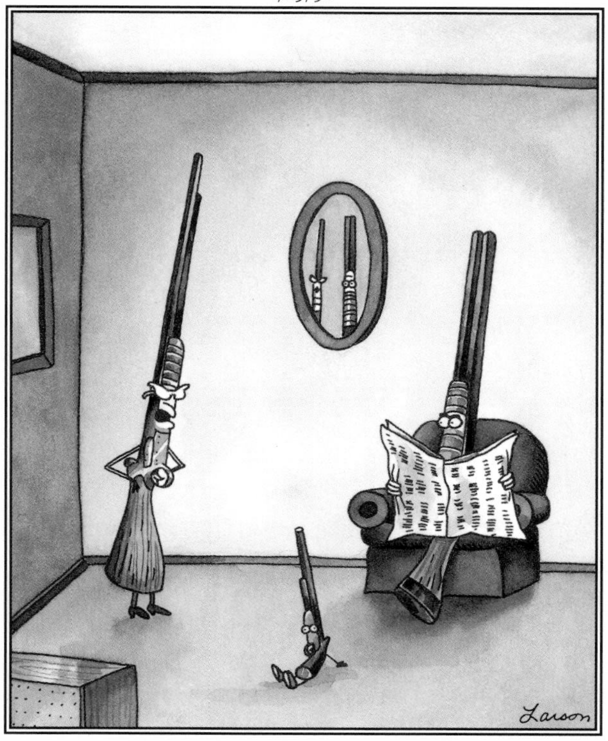

"I'm going off half-cocked? *I'm* going off half-cocked? ... Well, Mother was right—you can't argue with a shotgun."

1/26/90

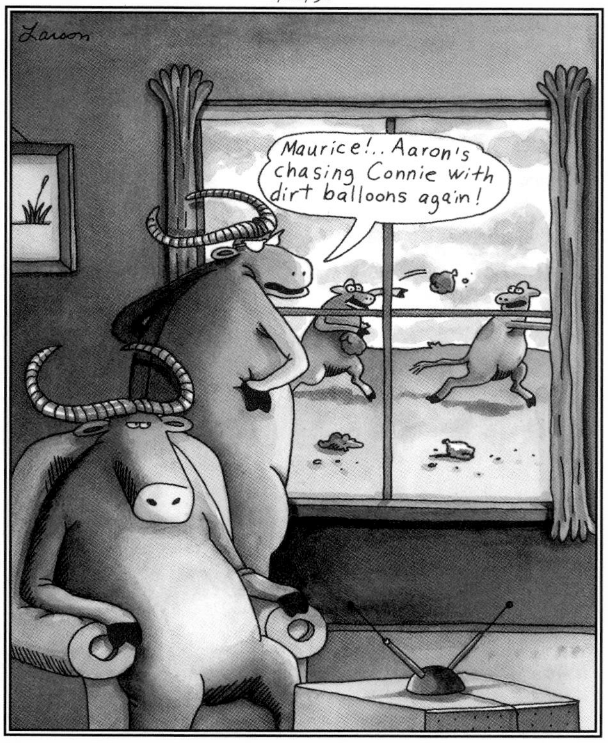
Maurice!.. Aaron's chasing Connie with dirt balloons again!

Water buffaloes at home

2/2/90

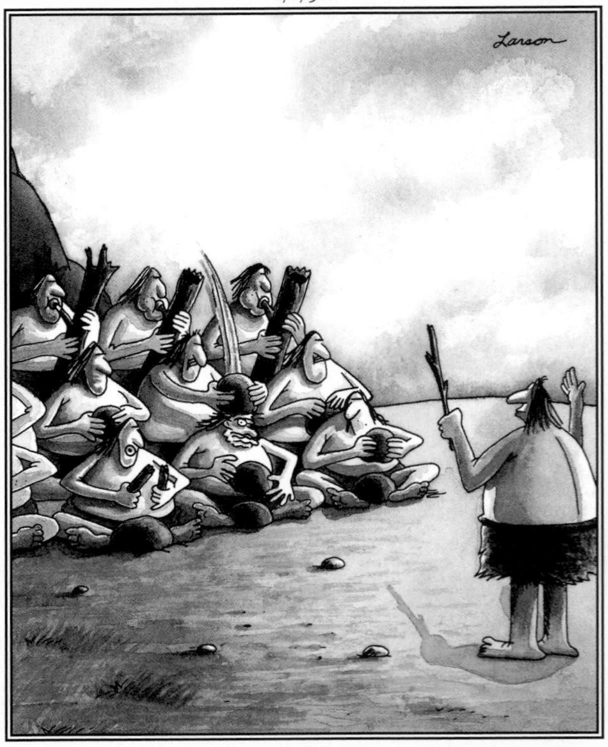
Larson

Suddenly, second-chair granite rock's jealousy of first-chair granite rock becomes uncontainable.

2/1/90

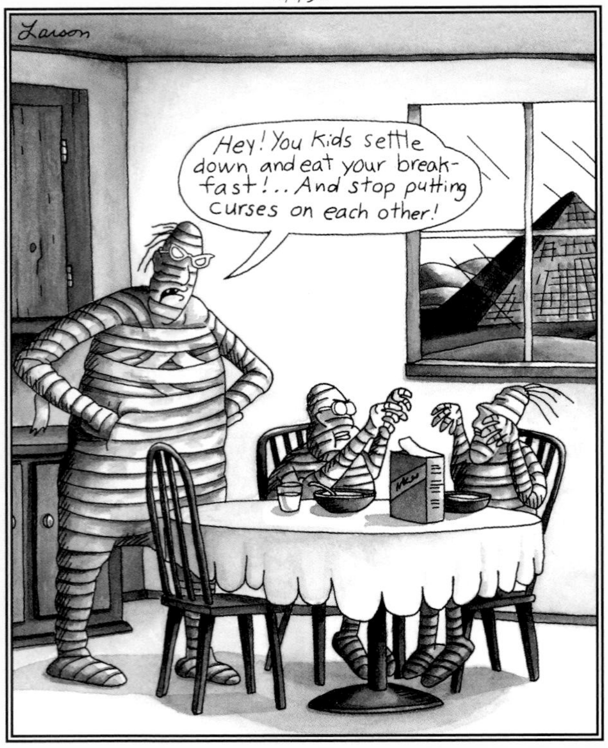
Larson
Hey! You kids settle down and eat your breakfast!.. And stop putting curses on each other!

Morning in the crypt

2/5/90

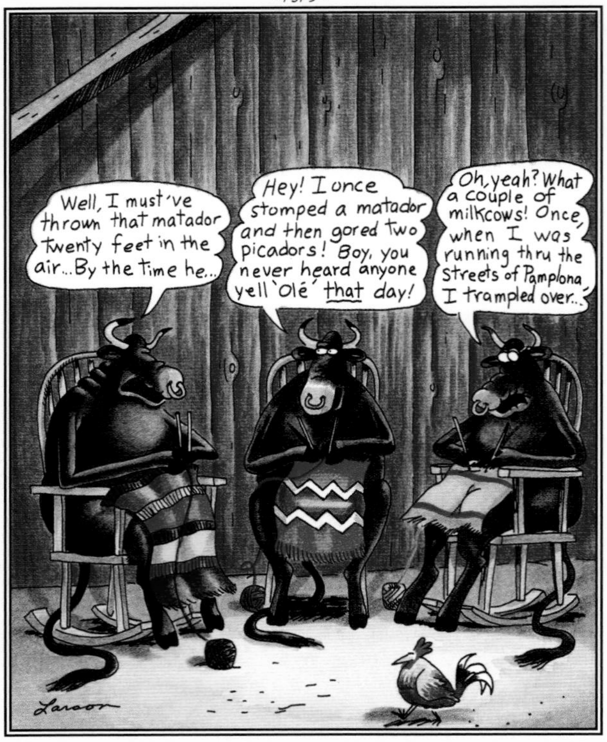
Well, I must've thrown that matador twenty feet in the air...By the time he...
Hey! I once stomped a matador and then gored two picadors! Boy, you never heard anyone yell 'Olé' that day!
Oh, yeah? What a couple of milkcows! Once, when I was running thru the streets of Pamplona I trampled over...
Larson

Bullknitters

2/7/90

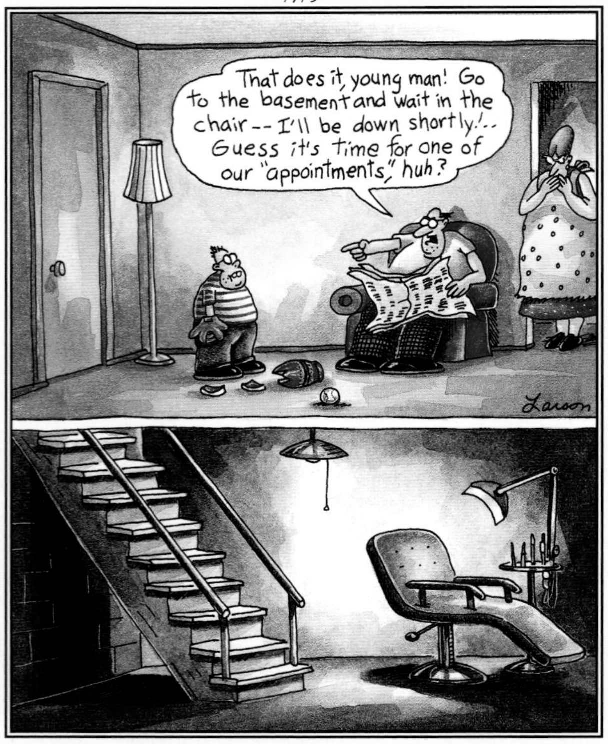
That does it, young man! Go to the basement and wait in the chair -- I'll be down shortly!.. Guess it's time for one of our "appointments," huh?
Larson

The parenting advantages of dentists

2/8/90

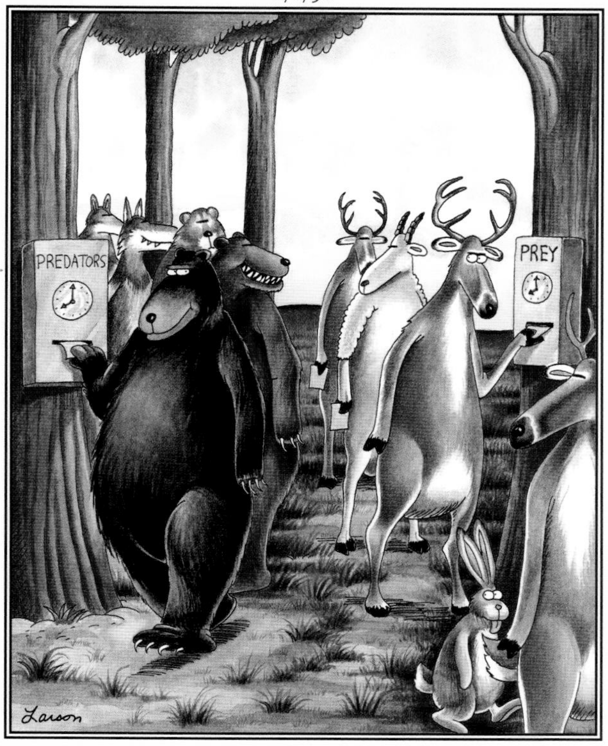
PREDATORS
PREY
Larson

Wildlife day shifts

2/6/90

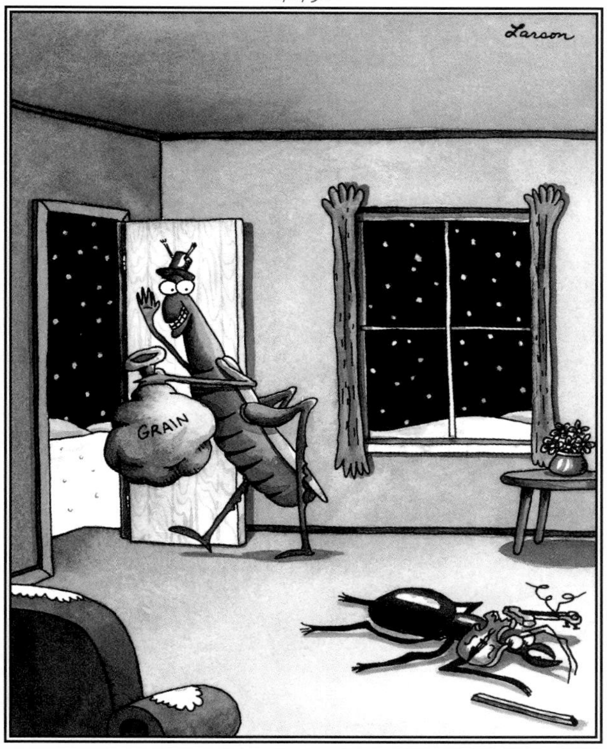
Larson
GRAIN

The untold ending to the fable,
"The Grasshopper and the Ant."

2/12/90

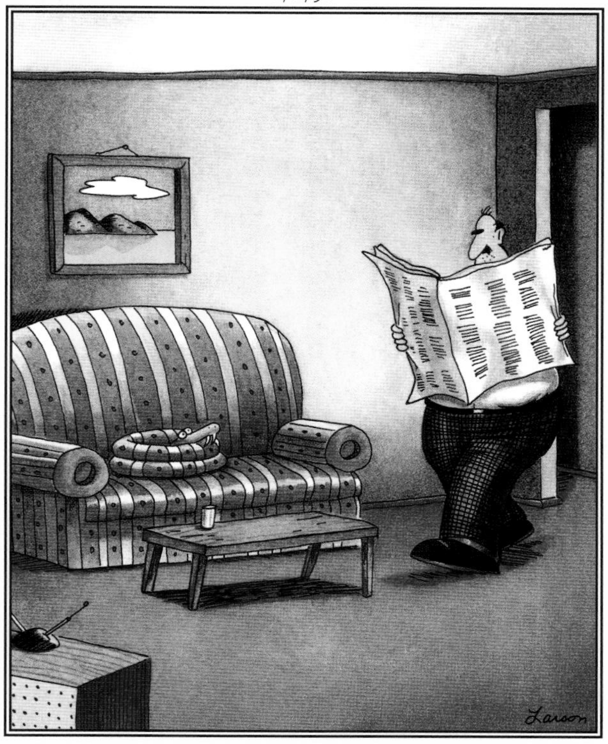
Larson

The deadly couch cobra—coiled and alert
in its natural habitat.

2/9/90

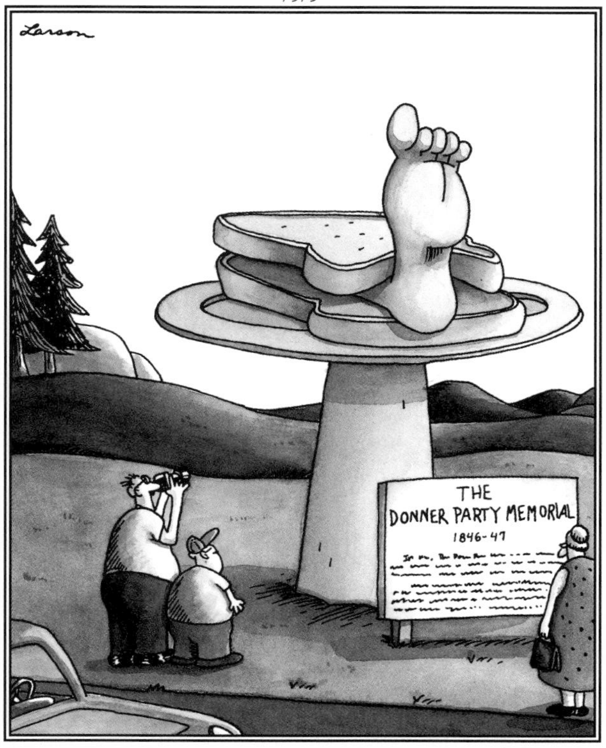
Larson
THE
DONNER PARTY MEMORIAL
1846-47

2/14/90

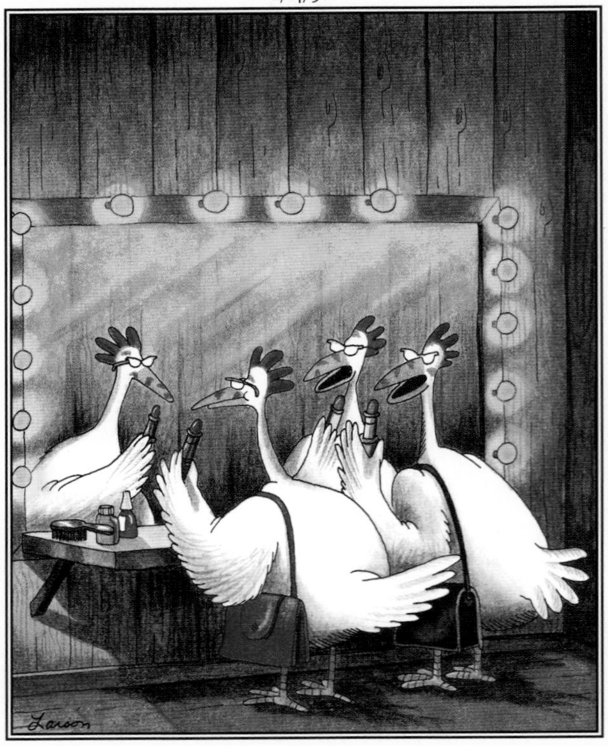

"This is no use, Wanda. It's like they say—
we just don't have lips."

2/20/90

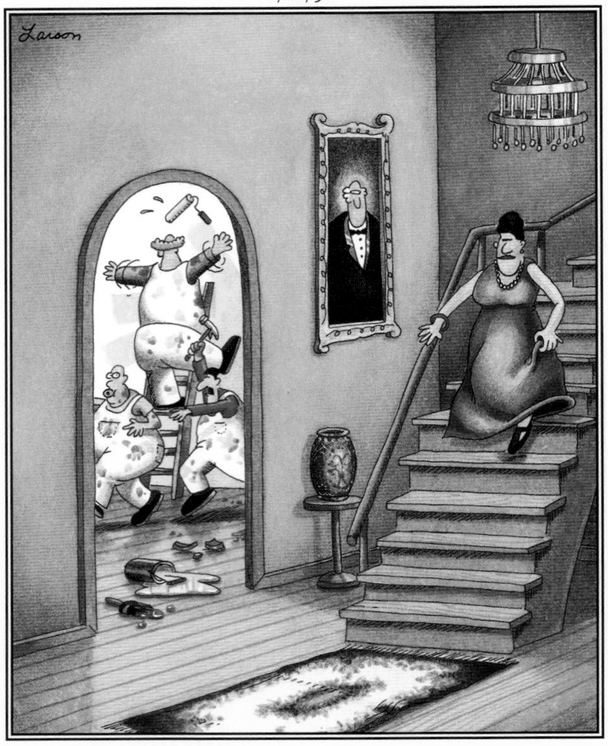

Our protagonist is about to check on the progress of her remodelers in this scene from *Leona Helmsley Meets the Three Stooges.*

2/13/90

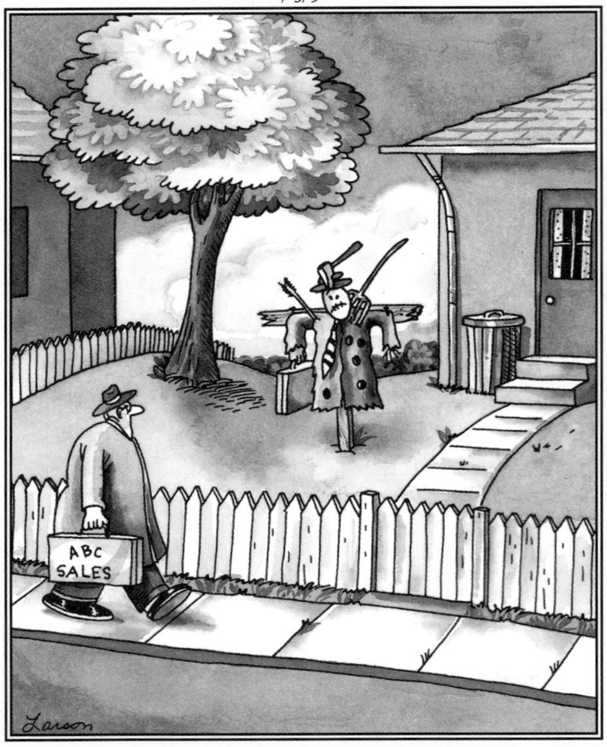
ABC
SALES

2/15/90

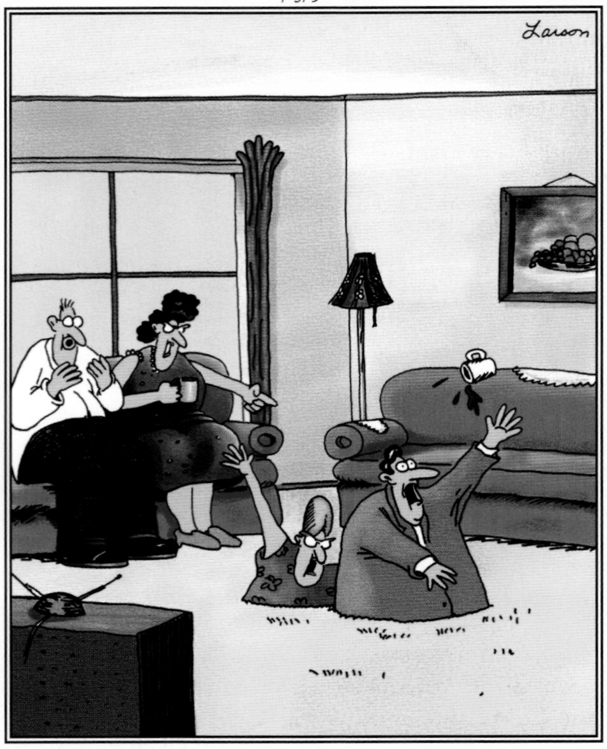

And down they went: Bob and Francine—two more victims of the La Brea Carpets.

2/21/90

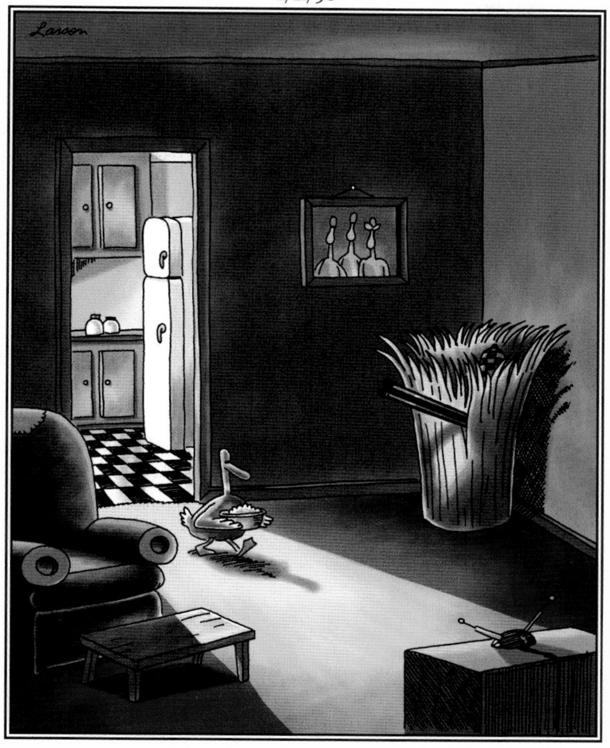
Larson

It was very late, and Raymond, fighting insomnia, went for a midnight snack. Unfortunately, he never saw the duck blind.

2/26/90

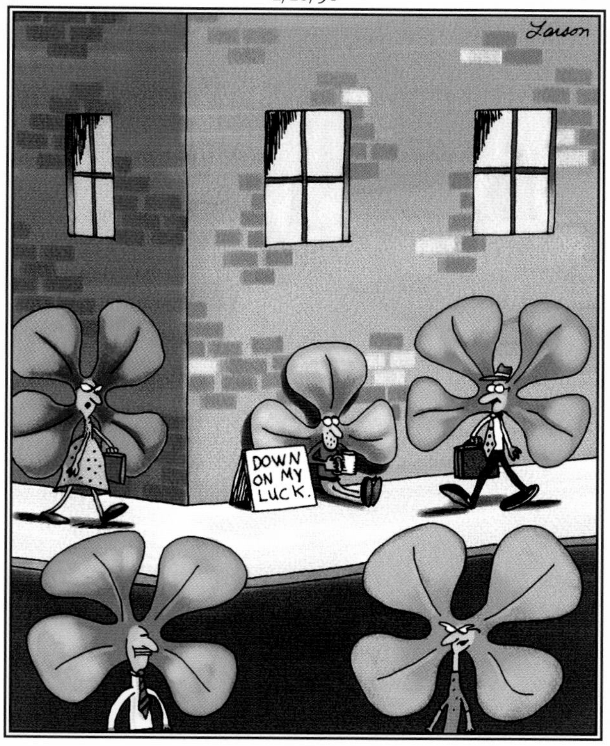
Larson
DOWN ON MY LUCK.

Life among the clover

2/16/90

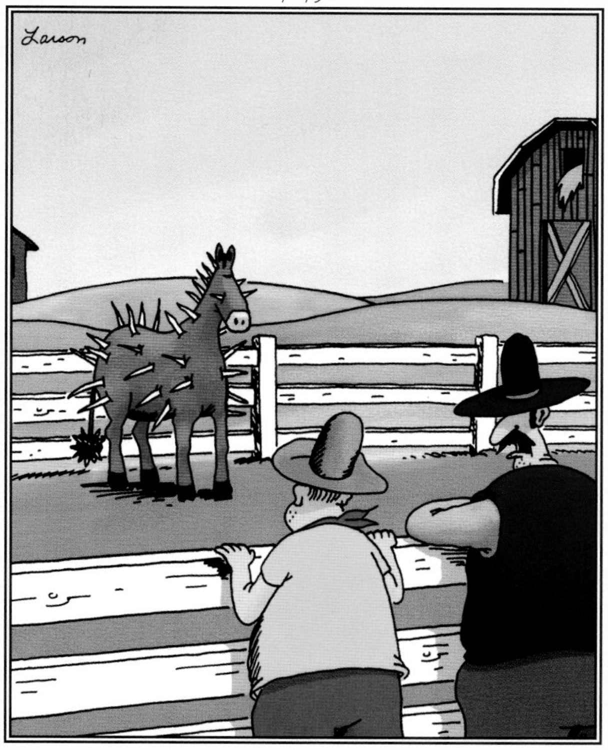
Larson

"Well, there he is, Billy—Big Red. Sure he's tough, but if you can ride him, he's yours."

2/19/90

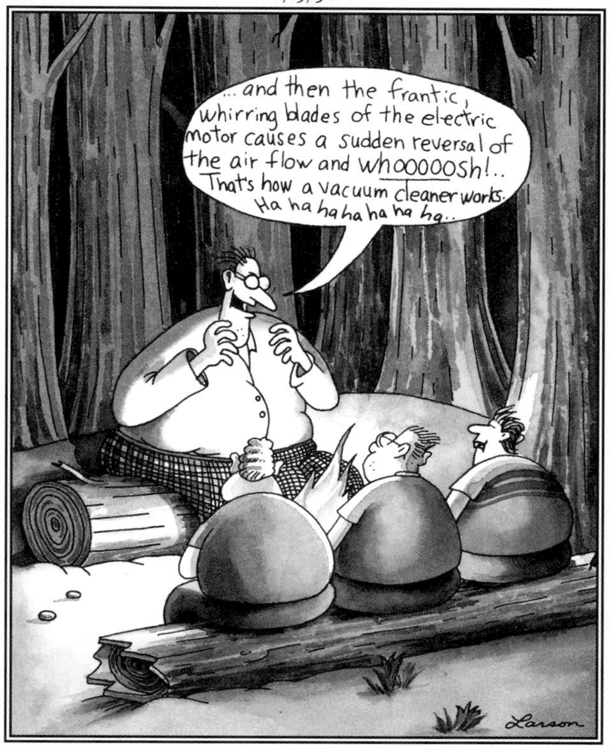
...and then the frantic, whirring blades of the electric motor causes a sudden reversal of the air flow and whoooooosh!.. That's how a vacuum cleaner works. Ha ha ha ha ha ha ha..
Larson

Tales of the Known

2/28/90

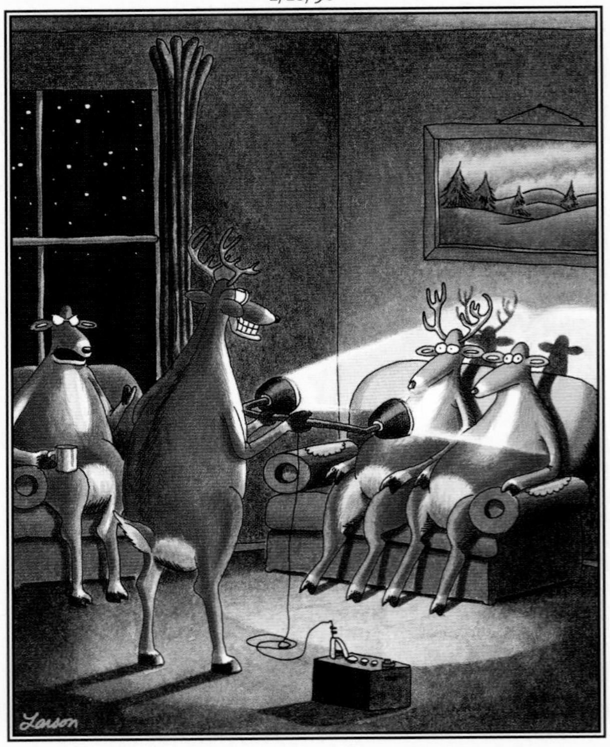

"Okay, Frank, that's enough. ...
I'm sure the Jeffersons are quite amazed
at your car headlight device."

2/23/90

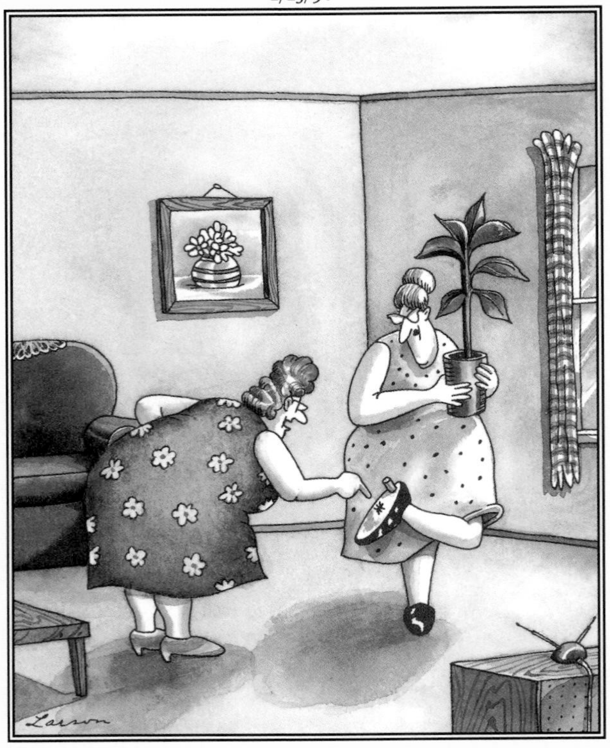

"Oooweeee! You nailed him good, Vera—to think that little ol' ant was hoping to just up and walk off with your rubber tree plant."

2/27/90

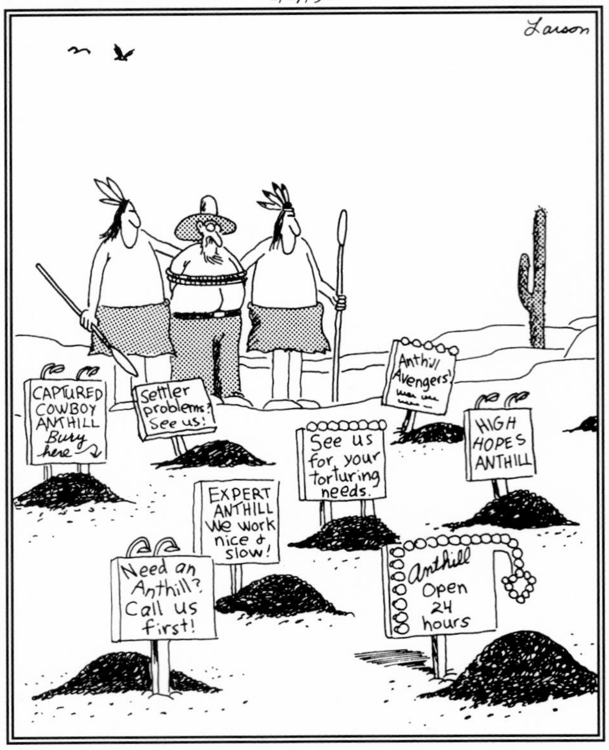
CAPTURED COWBOY ANTHILL Bury here
Settler problems? See us!
Anthill Avengers!
See us for your torturing needs.
HIGH HOPES ANTHILL
EXPERT ANTHILL We work nice & slow!
Need an Anthill? Call us first!
Anthill Open 24 hours

Competition in Nature

2/22/90

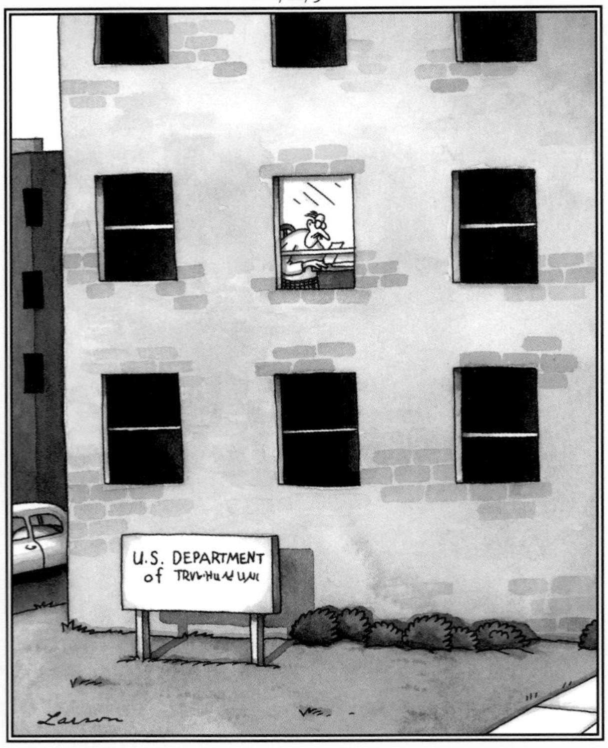
U.S. DEPARTMENT of

Civil Service History: On Oct. 12, 1979 (Columbus Day), government employee George Sullivan goes in to work for a couple of hours to, in his own words, "take care of some unfinished business."

3/12/90

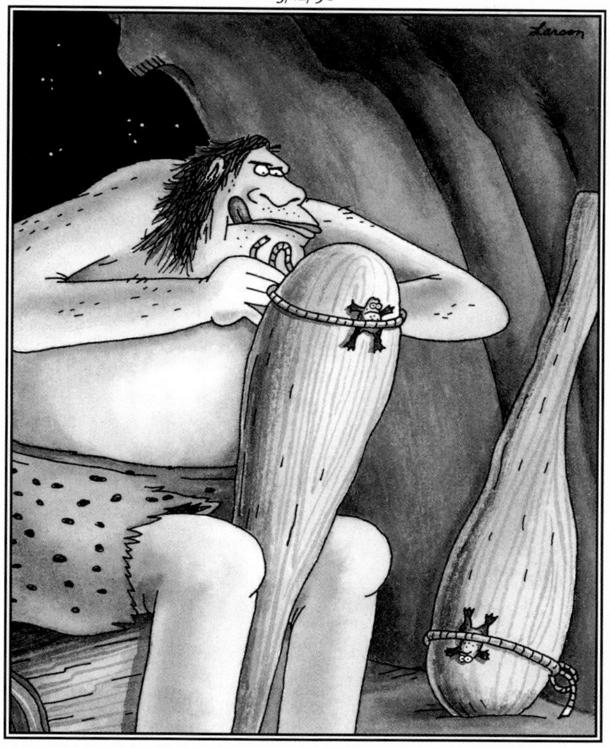

The night before the hunt, Neanderthals would carefully prepare their weaponry—often employing the help of the deadly poison-club frog.

3/5/90

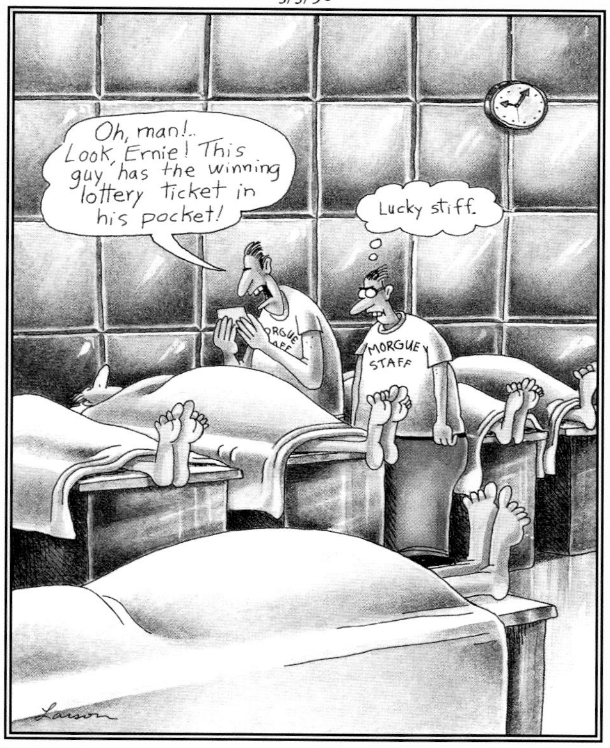
Oh, man!.. Look, Ernie! This guy has the winning lottery ticket in his pocket!
Lucky stiff.
MORGUE STAFF
MORGUE STAFF

3/16/90

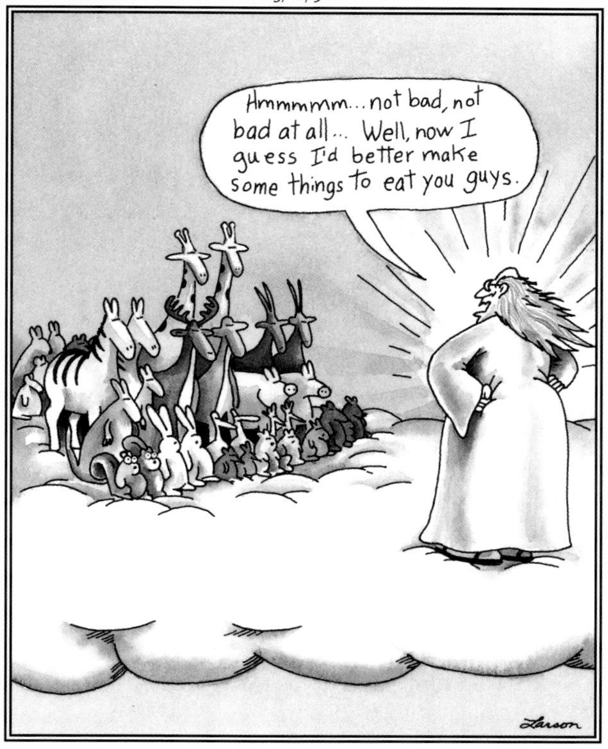
Hmmmmm...not bad, not bad at all... Well, now I guess I'd better make some things to eat you guys.

God creates the animals.

3/1/90

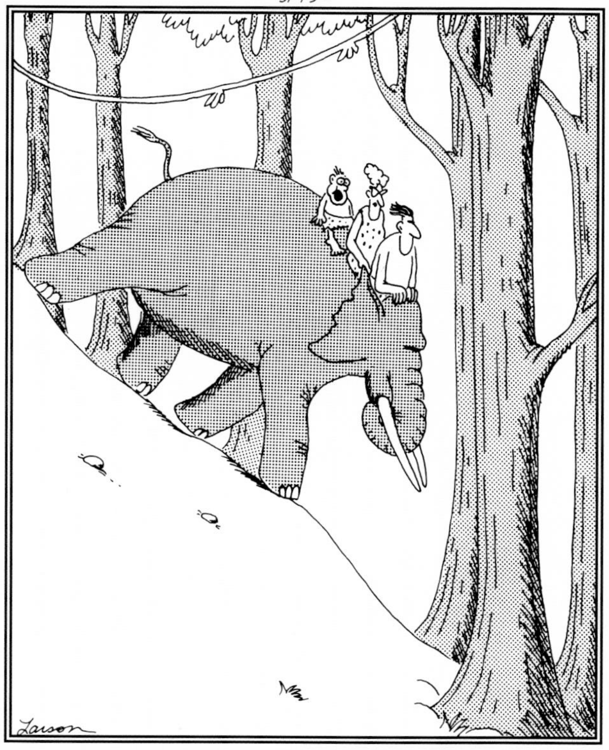

"Coast, Dad, coast!"

3/2/90

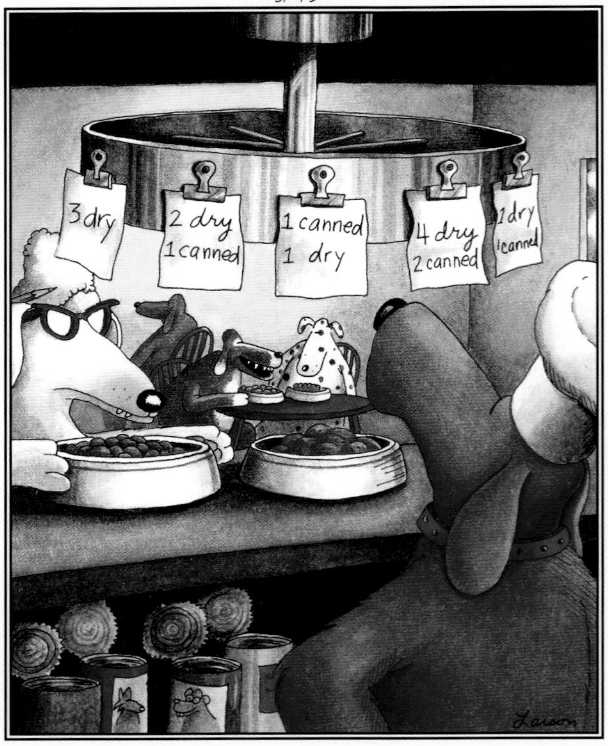
3 dry
2 dry 1 canned
1 canned 1 dry
4 dry 2 canned
1 dry 1 canned
Larson

Dog restaurants

3/6/90

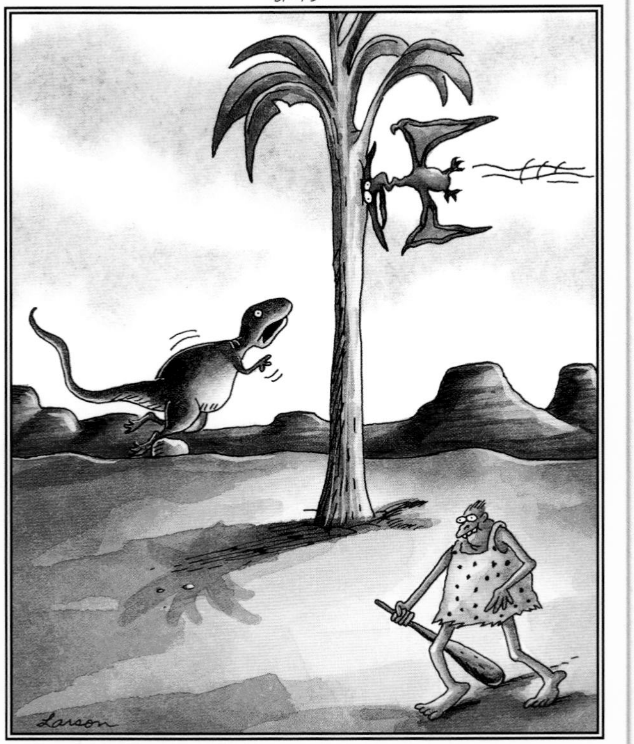
Larson

Although it lasted only 2 million years, the Awkward Age was considered a hazardous time for most species.

3/7/90

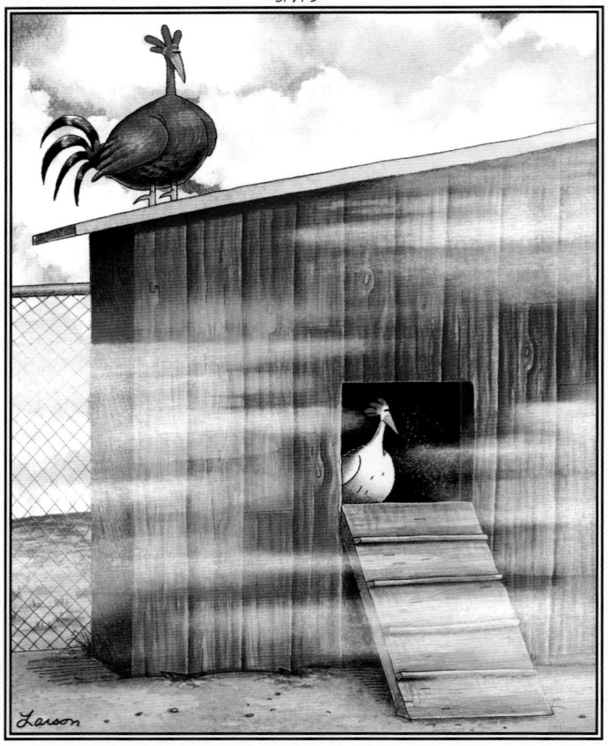
Larson

The rooster stared back at me, his power and confidence almost overwhelming. Down below, a female paused warily at the coop's entrance. I kept the camera running. They were beautiful, these *Chickens in the Mist*.

3/8/90

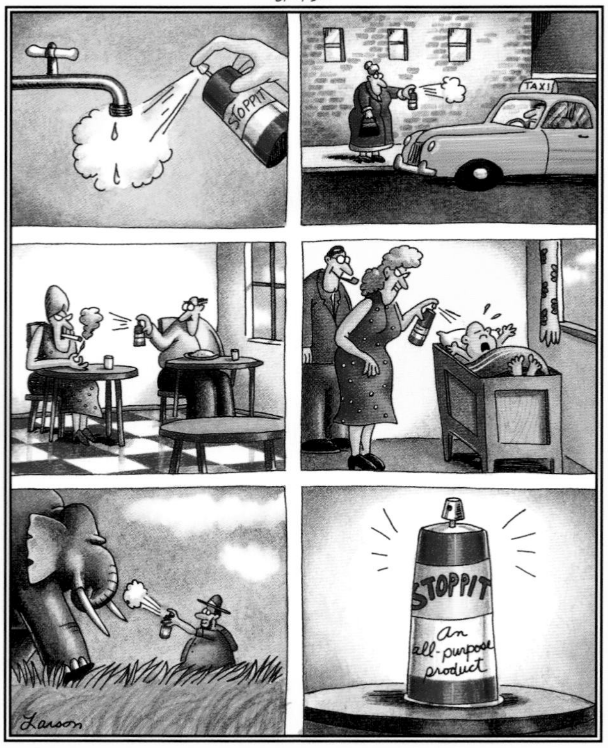
STOPPIT
TAXI
STOPPIT
an all-purpose product
Larson

3/9/90

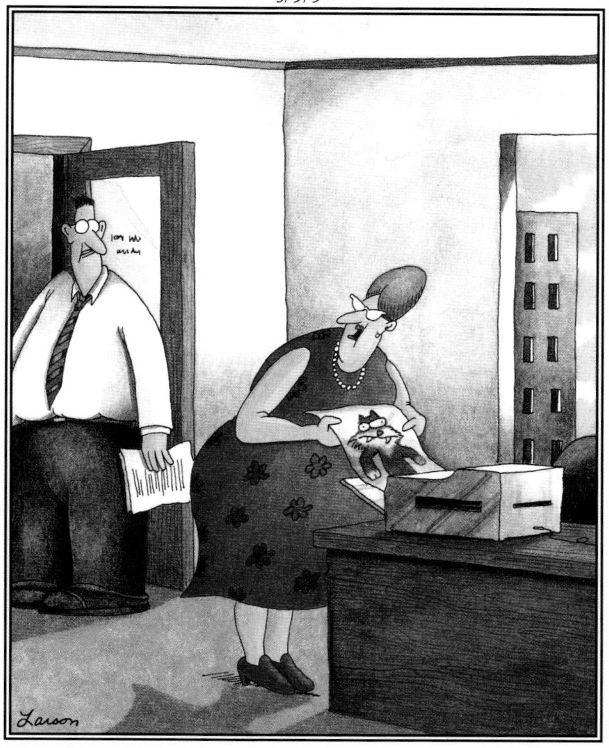

"It's a fax from your dog, Mr. Dansworth.
It looks like your cat."

3/13/90

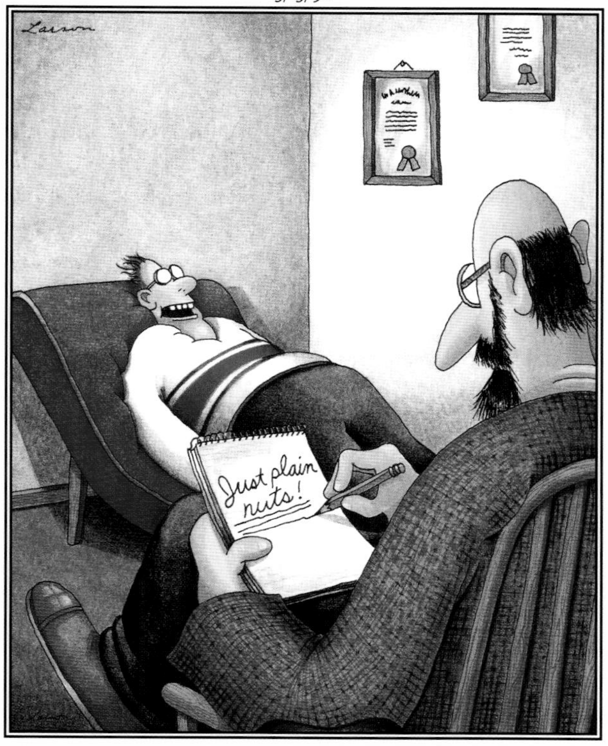
Just plain nuts!

3/14/90

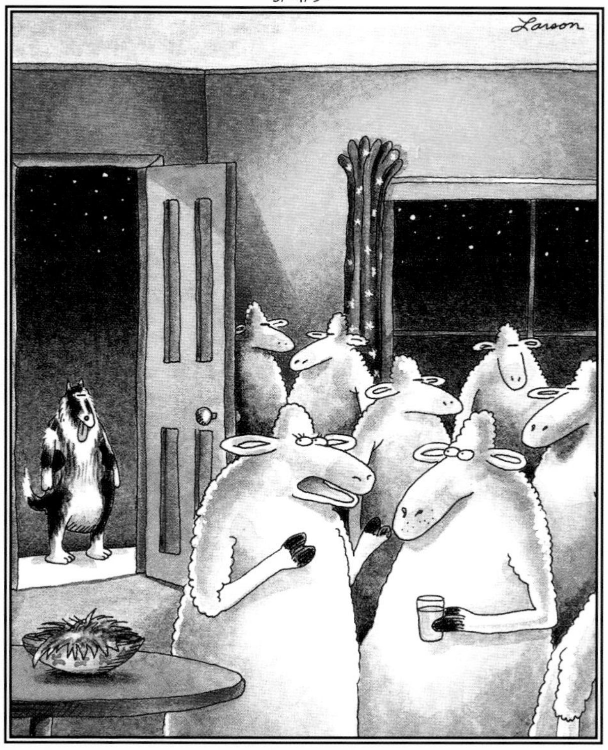

"Henry! Our party's total chaos! No one knows when to eat, where to stand, what to ... Oh, thank God! Here comes a Border collie!"

3/15/90

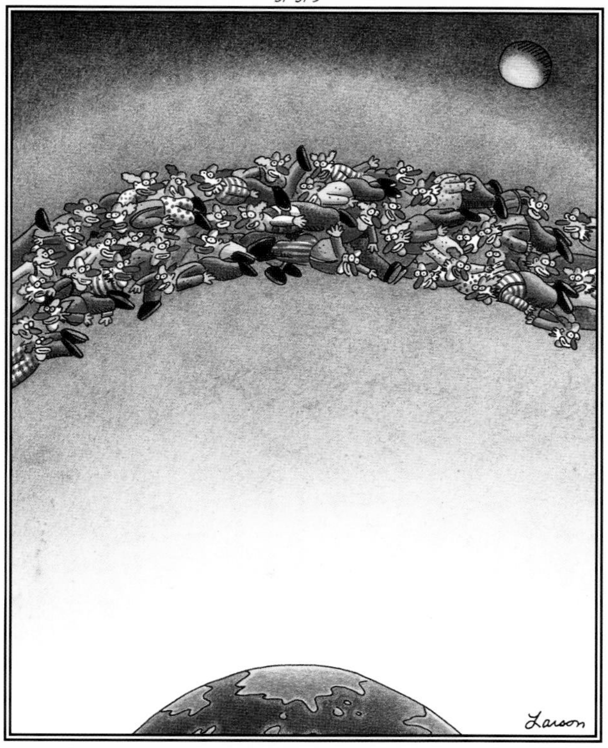

The bozone layer: shielding the rest of the solar system from the Earth's harmful effects.

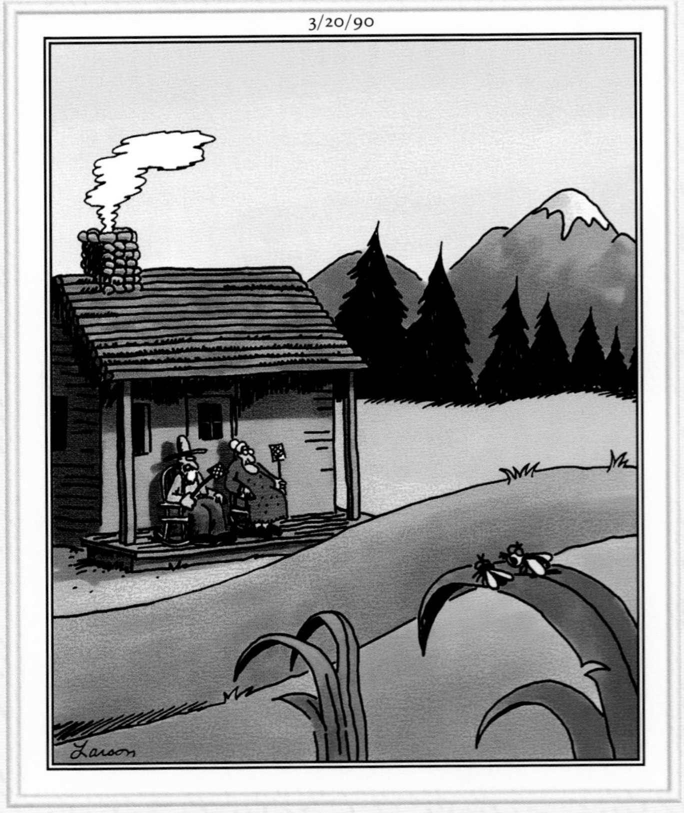
3/20/90
Larson

"Dang! Every day, more and more swatters are movin' in."

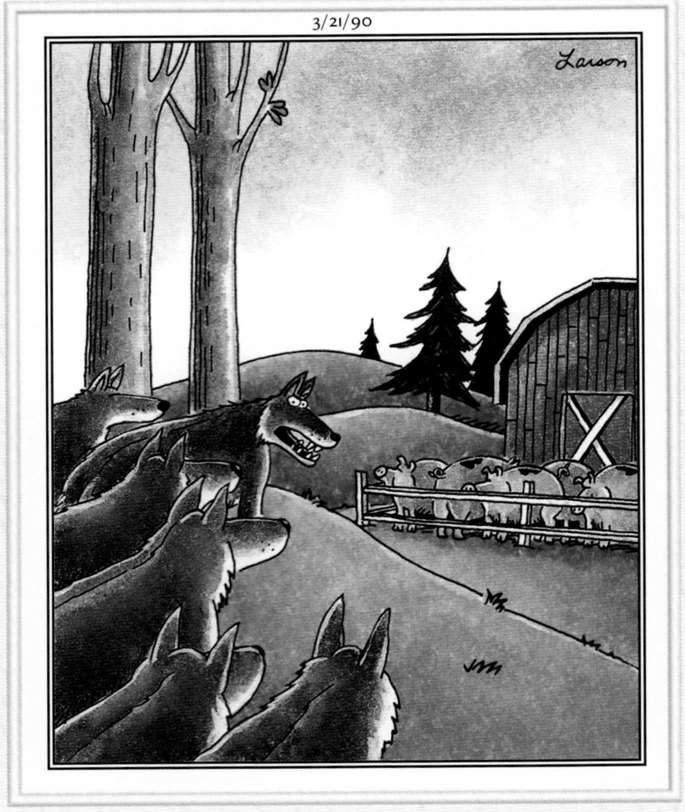
3/21/90
Larson

"I say we do it ... and trichinosis be damned!"

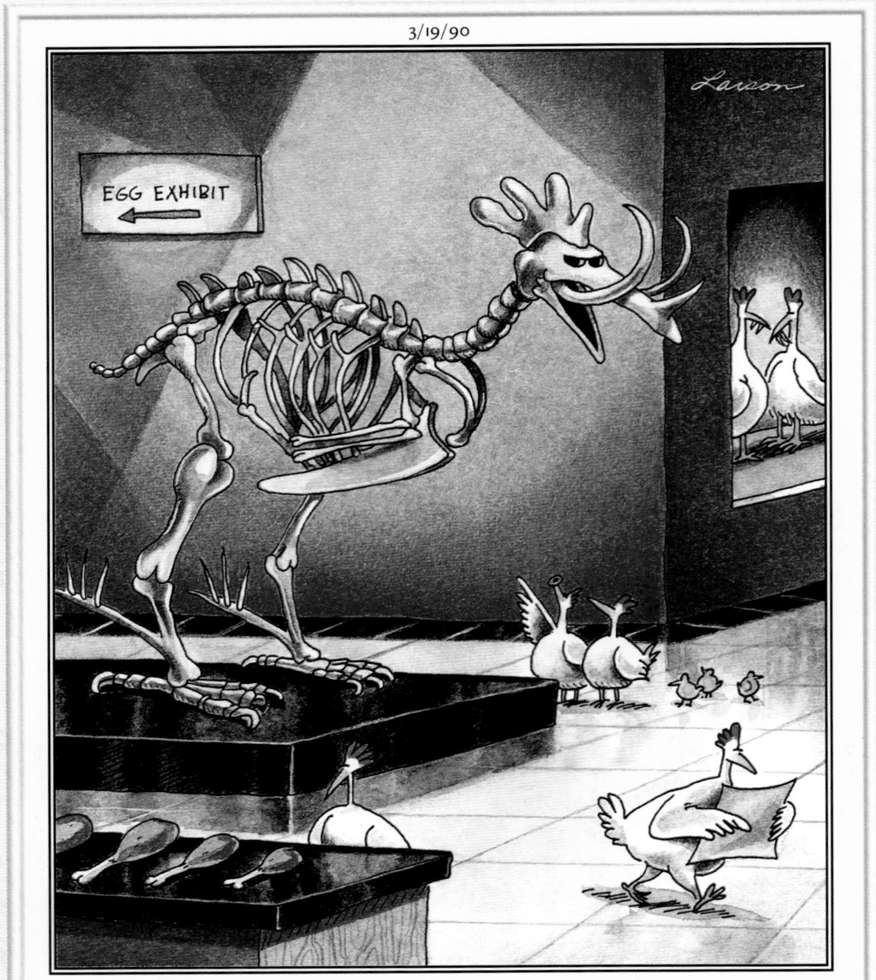
3/19/90
Larson
EGG EXHIBIT

In the Chicken Museum

3/26/90

I don't know where my life has gone, Zelda... The kids have metamorphosed, my job stinks, my dreams are unrealized, and I've only got a few more circles left around the fire.

Midlife crises in moths

3/27/90

"Oh, I don't know. Billy's been having trouble in school, and Sally's always having some sort of crisis. I tell you, Edith, it's not easy raising the dead."

3/28/90

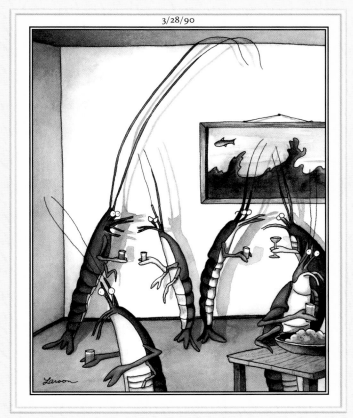

"Listen, you want to come over to my place? I get great FM."

3/29/90

Ursula, as we like to call her, was formed many years ago as a result of psychological duress. On May 7, 1983, she had a full eruption and this entire area was buried under a sea of hot acid. And, as you can see, she's still festering and gurgling to this very day.

Tapeworms visiting a stomach park

Hours later, when they finally came to, Hal and Ruby groggily returned to their yard work—unknowingly wearing the radio collars and ear tags of alien biologists.

"Okay, Zukutu—that does it! Remember, those who live in grass houses shouldn't throw spears."

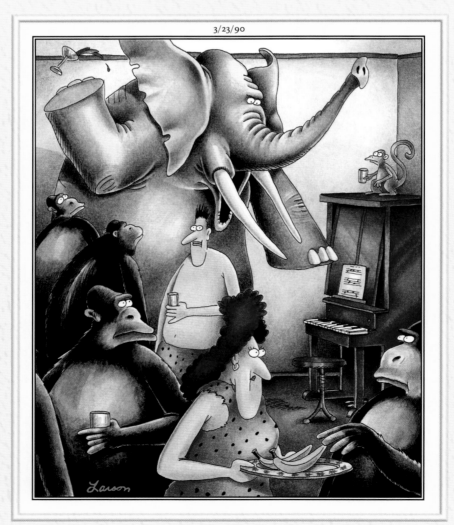

The party had been going splendidly—and then Tantor saw the ivory keyboard.

4/4/90

Larson
BOB'S STRAW DELIVERY
CITY CENTER EXIT ½ MILE
Oh, man... I've been away too long.

4/5/90

Well, shoot!.. This just isn't working!
Larson

Special Agent Gumby falls into the frustrated hands of the enemy.

4/3/90

LOOKOUT AHEAD
LOOKOUT!
Larson

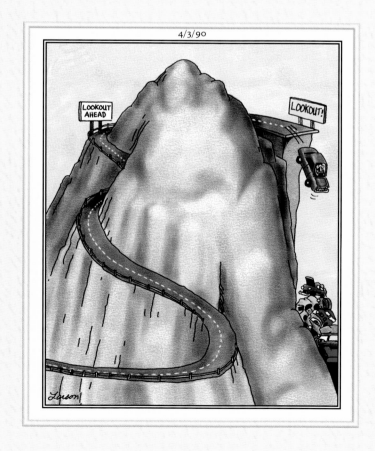

4/2/90

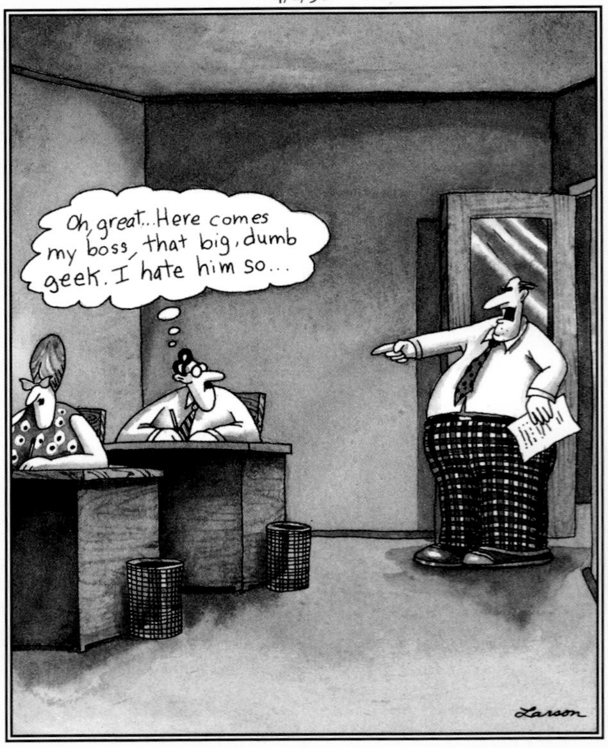
Oh, great... Here comes my boss, that big, dumb geek. I hate him so...
Larson

"Oh, yeah? Lewis, you're fired! You apparently forgot this is a cartoon, and I can read every word you think!"

4/13/90

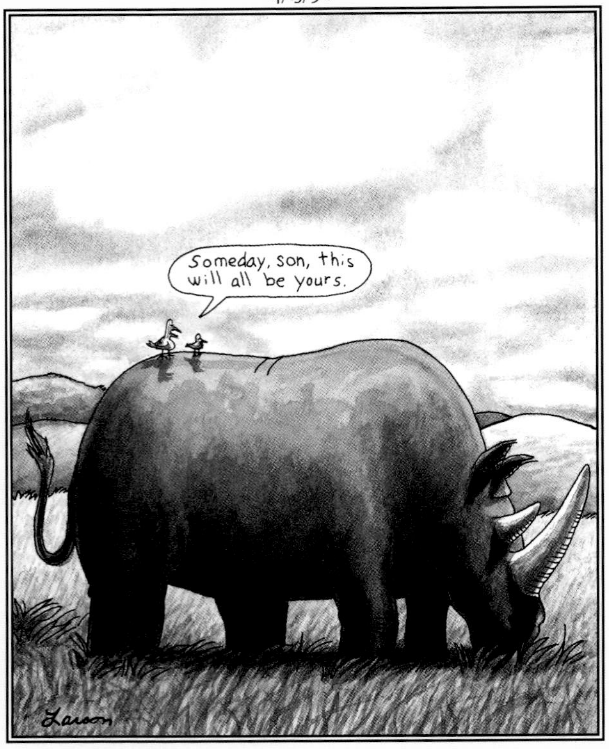
Someday, son, this will all be yours.
Larson

4/11/90

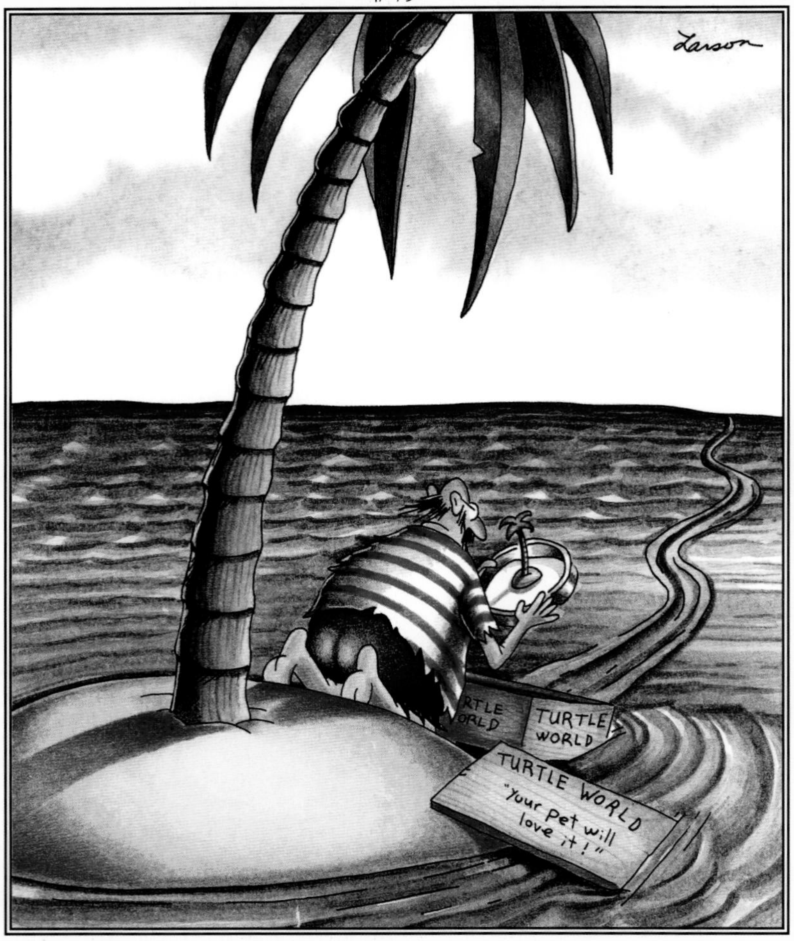
Larson
TURTLE WORLD
TURTLE WORLD
TURTLE WORLD
"Your pet will love it!"

4/12/90

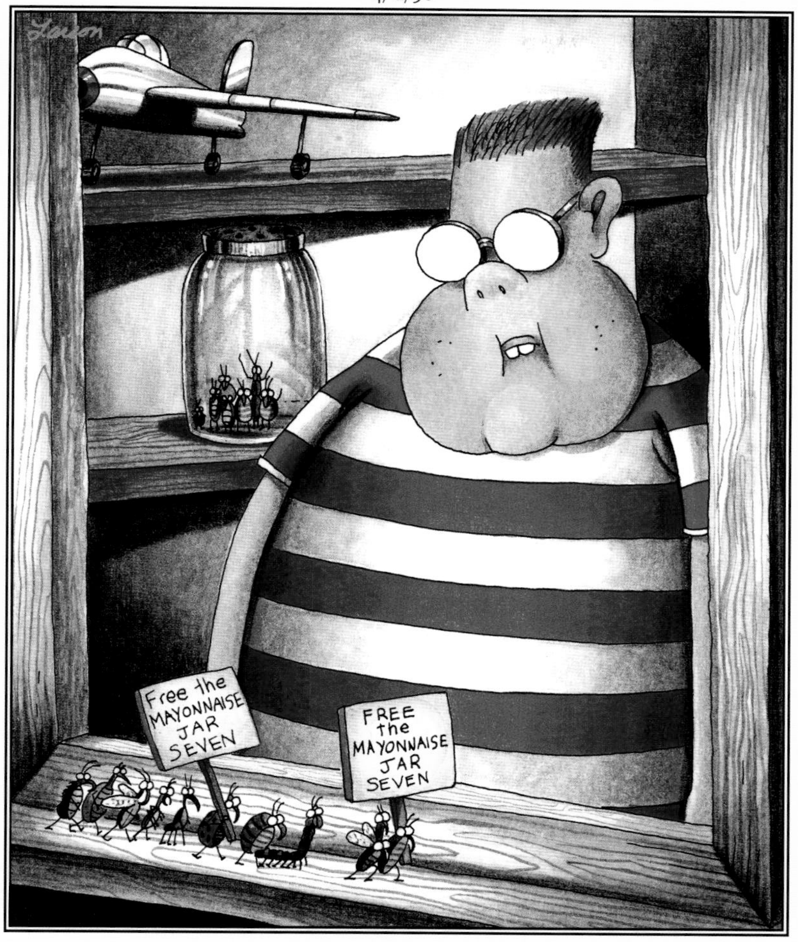
Free the MAYONNAISE JAR SEVEN
FREE the MAYONNAISE JAR SEVEN

4/9/90

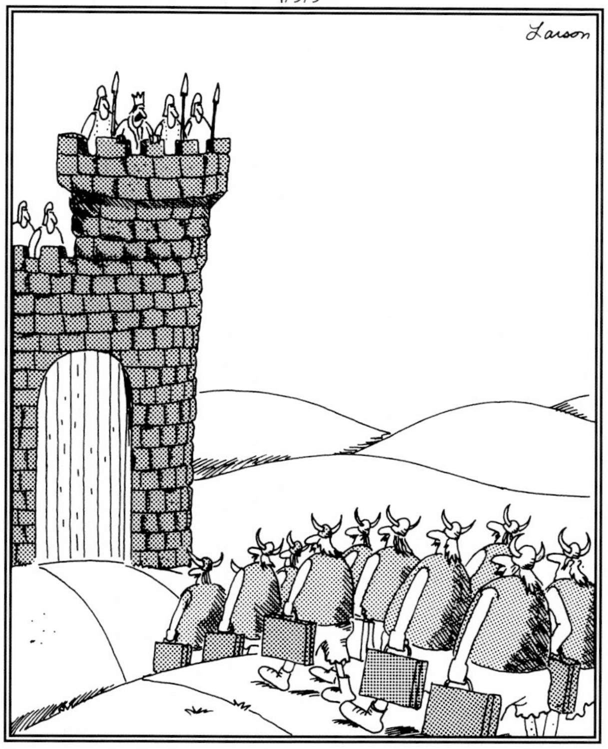

"My God! Vikings! And they mean business!"

4/10/90

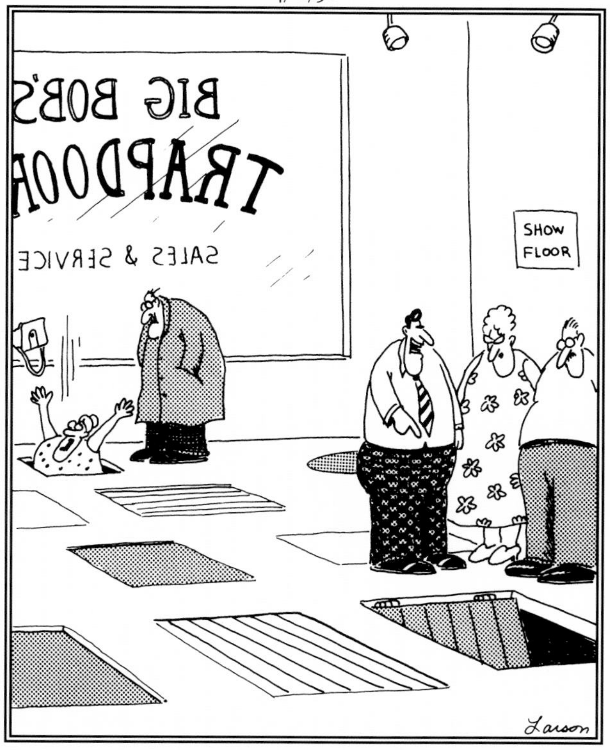
BIG BOB'S TRAPDOO
SALES & SERVICE
SHOW FLOOR

"Don't worry ... your little boy's somewhere in our service department—but let's move on and check out the TD500."

4/16/90

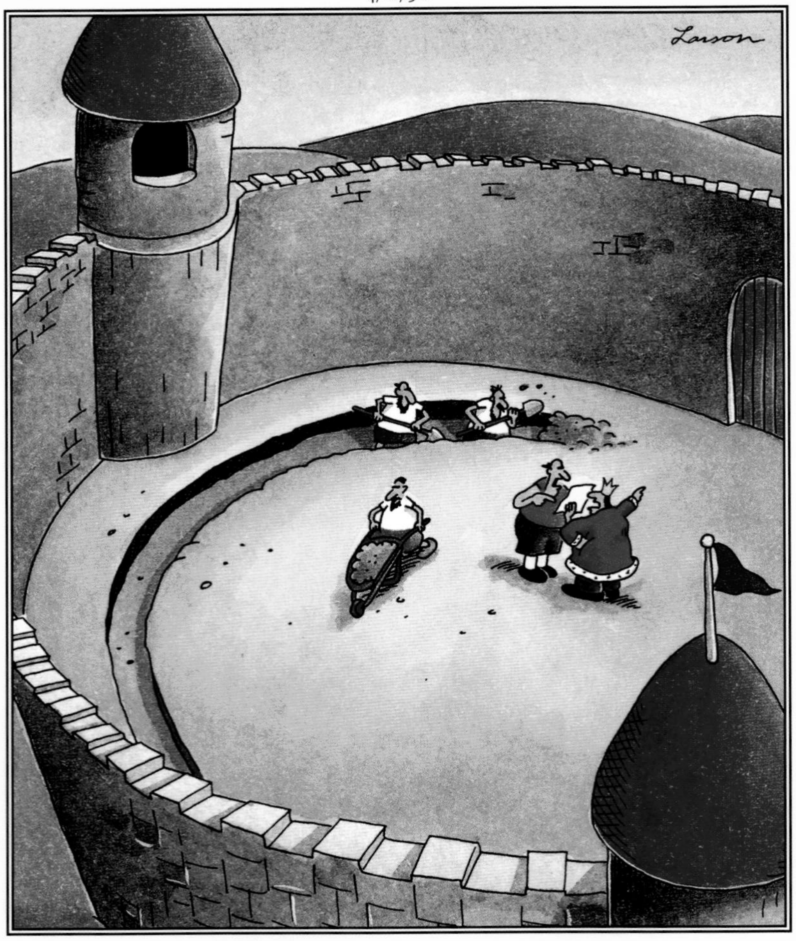
Larson

Suddenly, a heated exchange took place between the king and the moat contractor.

4/17/90

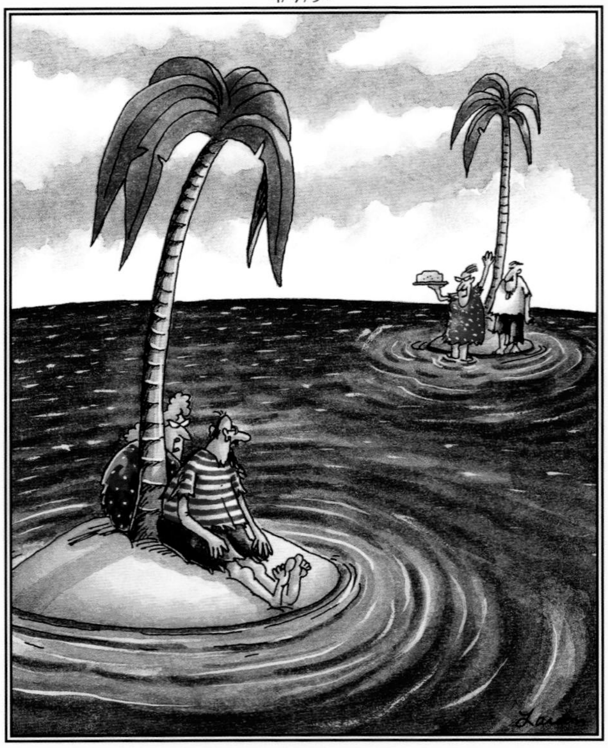

"Uh-oh. Carol's inviting us over for cake, and I'm sure it's just loaded with palm oil."

4/6/90

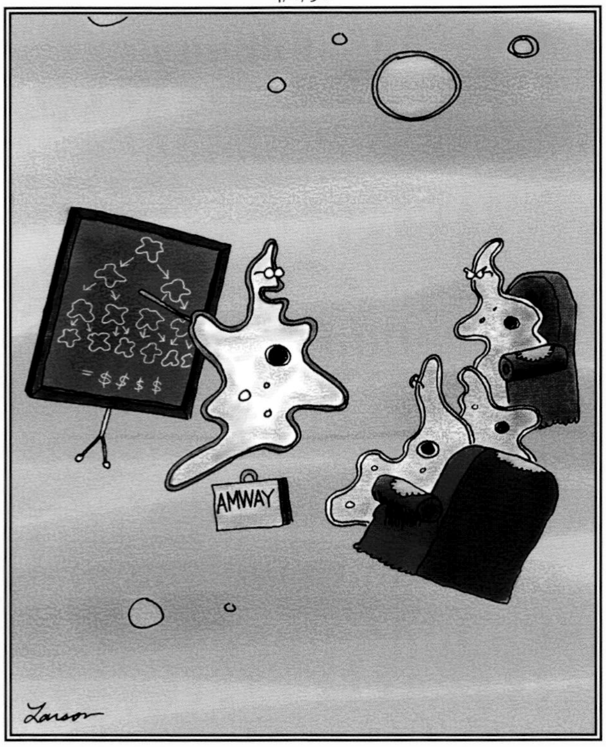
AMWAY
Larson

"And as amoebas, you'll have no problems recruiting other sales reps ... just keep dividing and selling, dividing and selling."

Inconvenience stores

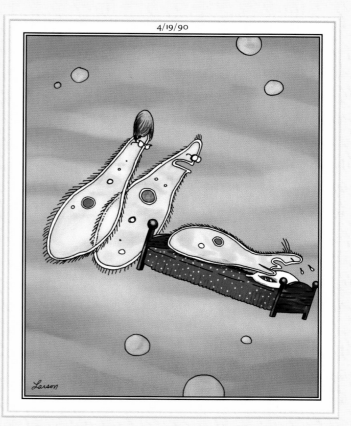

"Now Betty Sue, we know you're upset ...
breaking up with a boyfriend is always hard.
But, as they say, there are more protozoa
in the lower intestine."

"Throw him in the swamp? You idiot!
That's the *first* place they'll look."

4/22/90

Nature, Mother

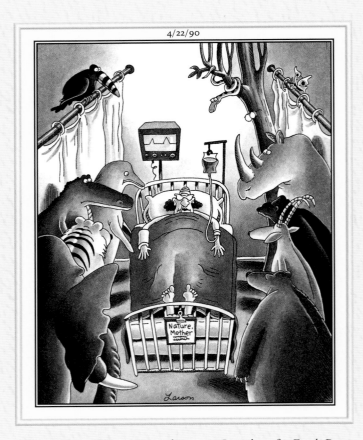

Editor's note: This is a special cartoon Gary drew for Earth Day 1990, as part of a project in which many cartoonists participated to bring more awareness to the state of the environment.

4/24/90

"Well, there he goes again ... 'Course, I guess I did the same thing at his age—checking every day to see if I was becoming a silverback."

4/25/90

And now a tragic story: Our camera was there when a swatter came down on an unidentified victim on the kitchen window. We'd like to warn our more sensitive viewers that they may prefer not to watch the following segment.
FLYWITNESS NEWS

4/30/90

C'mon, everyone... smile!
That's better.

4/23/90

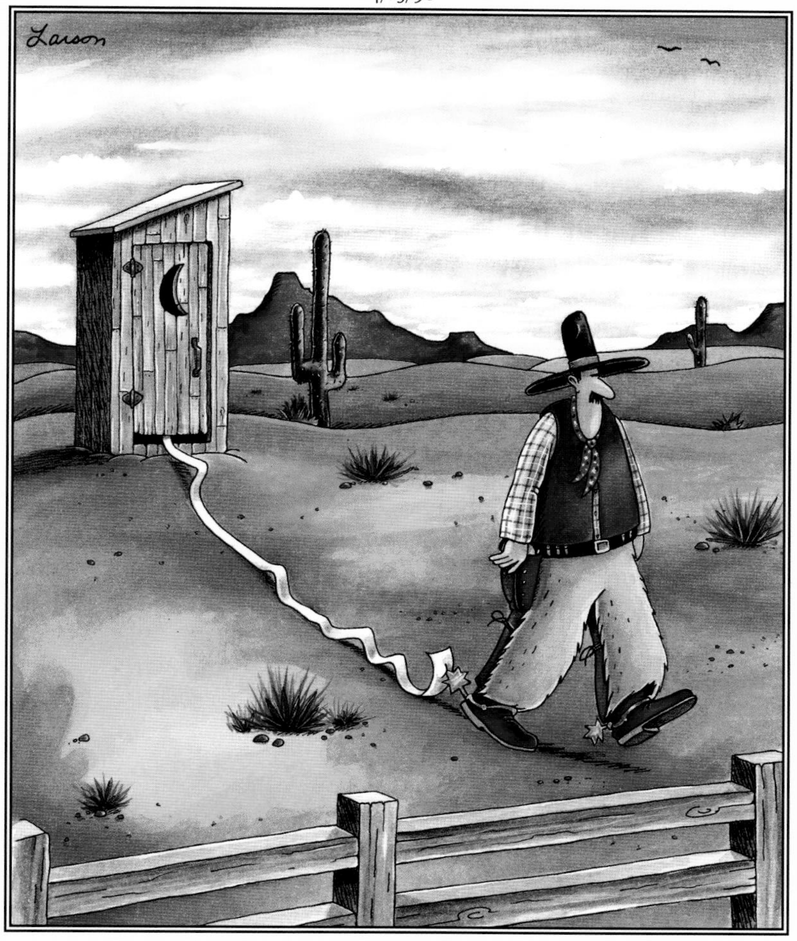

Nerds of the Old West

4/20/90

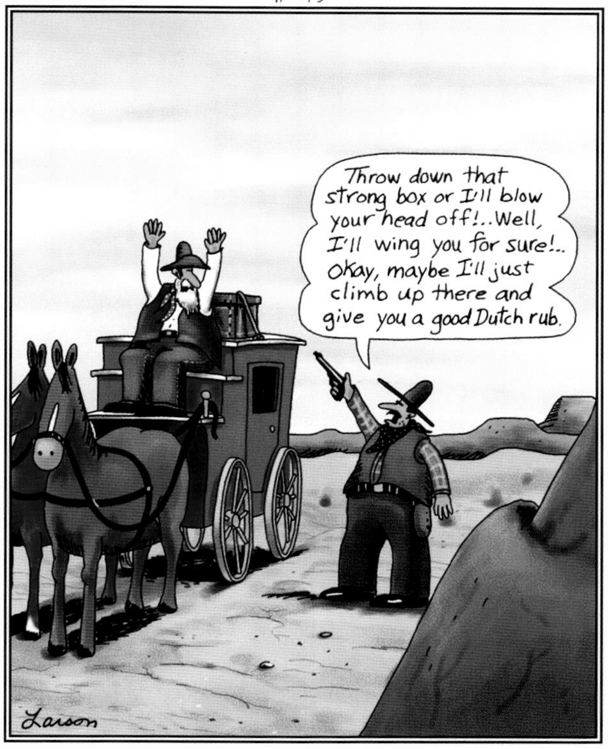
Throw down that strong box or I'll blow your head off!..Well, I'll wing you for sure!.. Okay, maybe I'll just climb up there and give you a good Dutch rub.

Semi-desperadoes

4/27/90

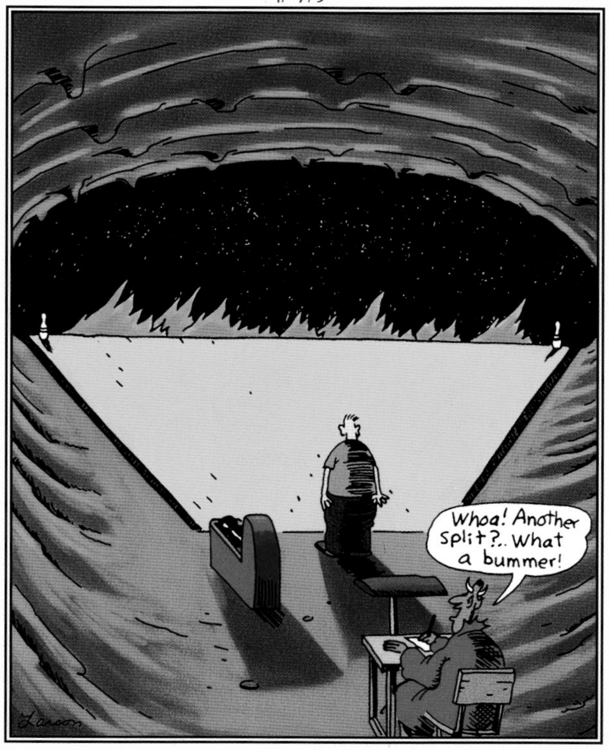
Whoa! Another split?.. What a bummer!

Bowler's hell

5/1/90

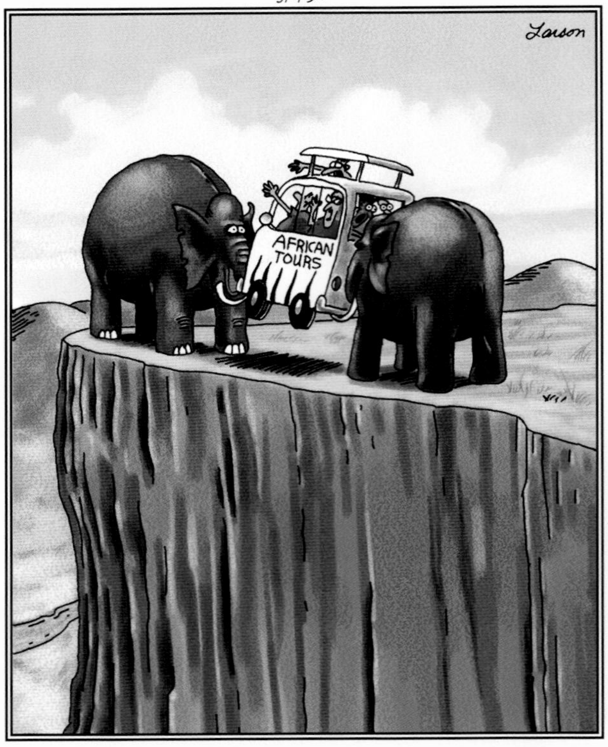
Larson
AFRICAN TOURS

"On three, Vince. Ready?"

5/2/90

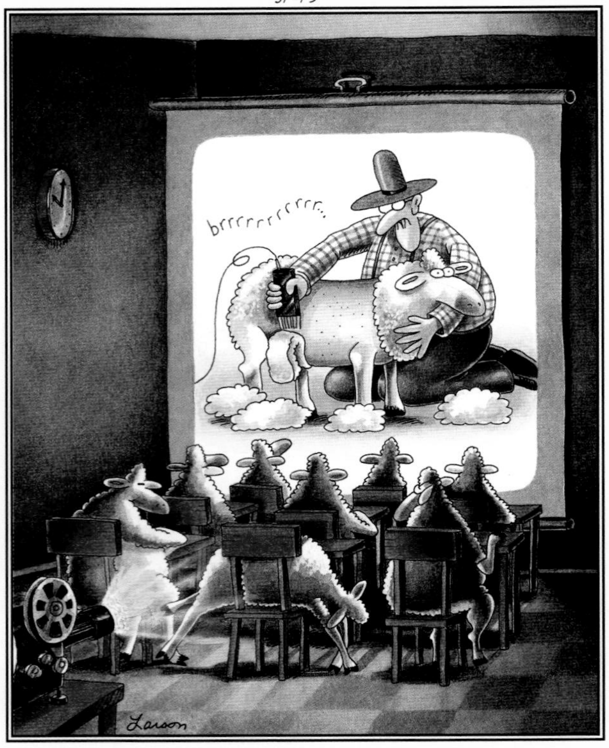
brrrrrrrrrrrr...
Larson

Sheep health classes

5/8/90

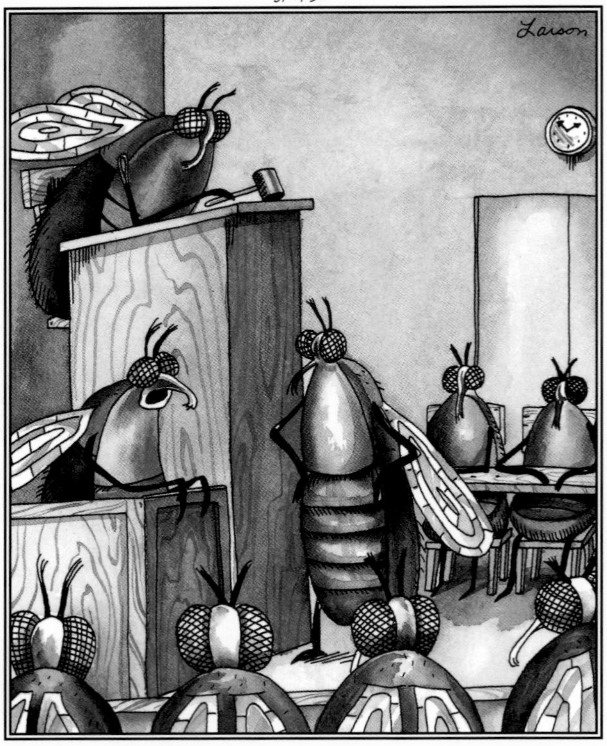
Larson

"So once they started talking, I just remained motionless, taking in every word. ... Of course, it was pure luck I just happened to be a fly on the wall."

5/3/90

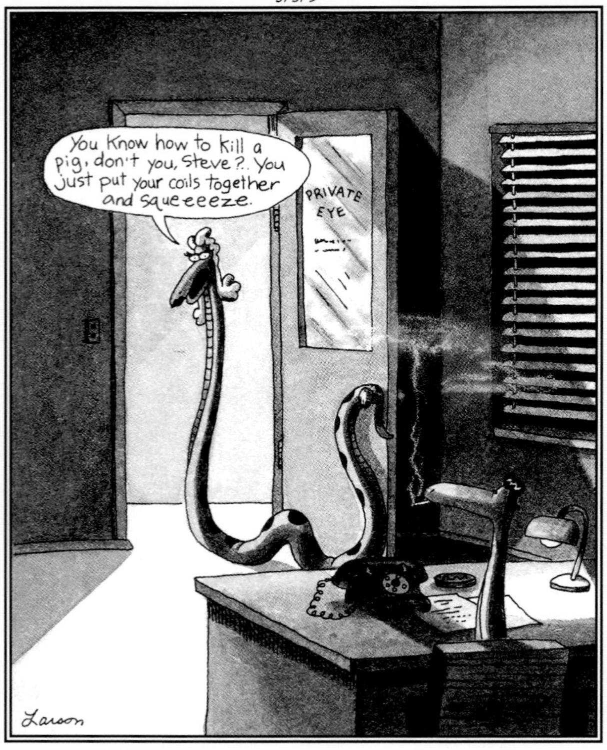
You know how to kill a pig, don't you, Steve?.. You just put your coils together and squeeeeeze.
PRIVATE EYE
Larson

Scenes from classic nature films

5/4/90

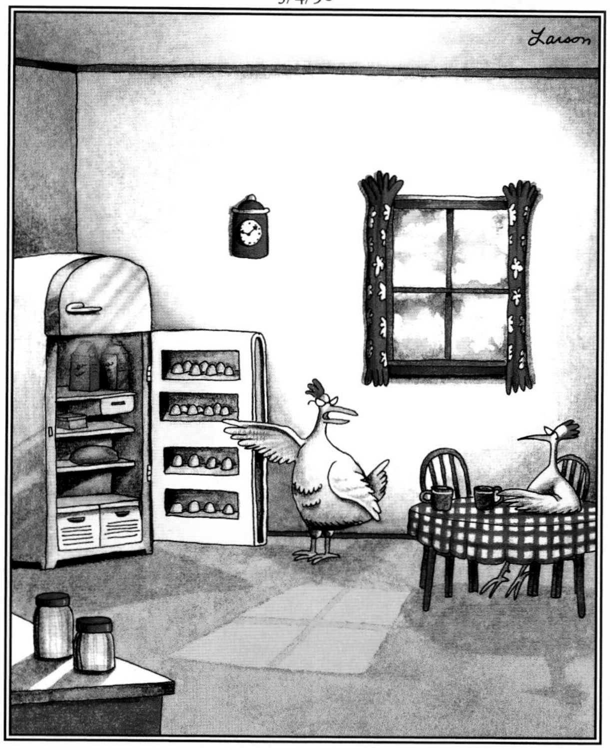
Larson

"Well, here's your problem, Marge—if you and Bob really want kids, next time try sittin' on these little guys."

5/7/90

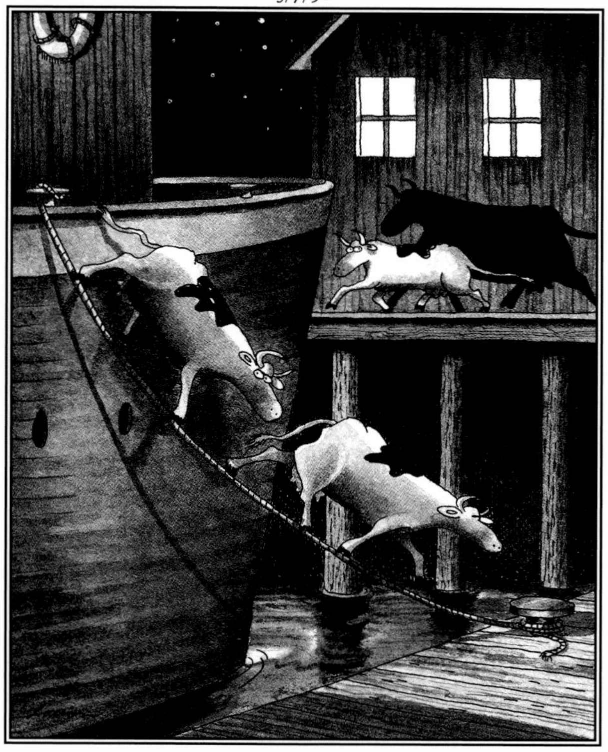

Wharf cows

5/9/90

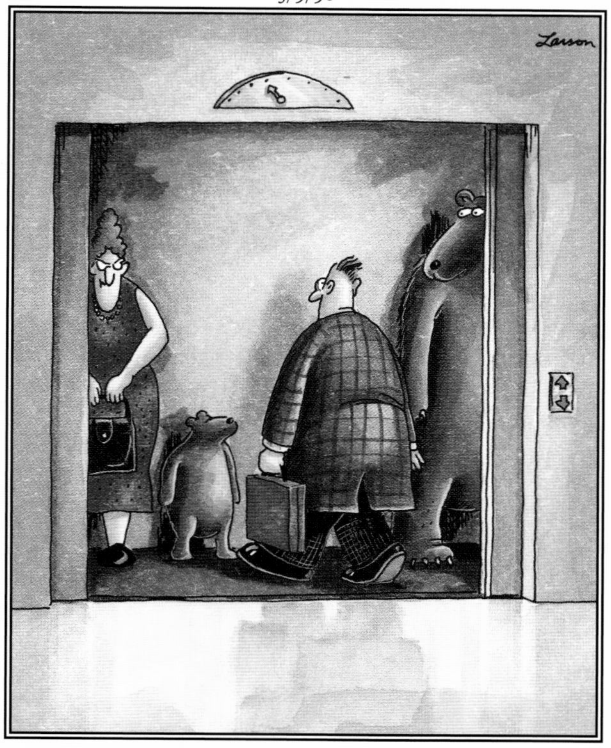
Larson

Tragedy struck when Conroy, his mind preoccupied with work, stepped into the elevator—directly between a female grizzly and her cub.

5/14/90

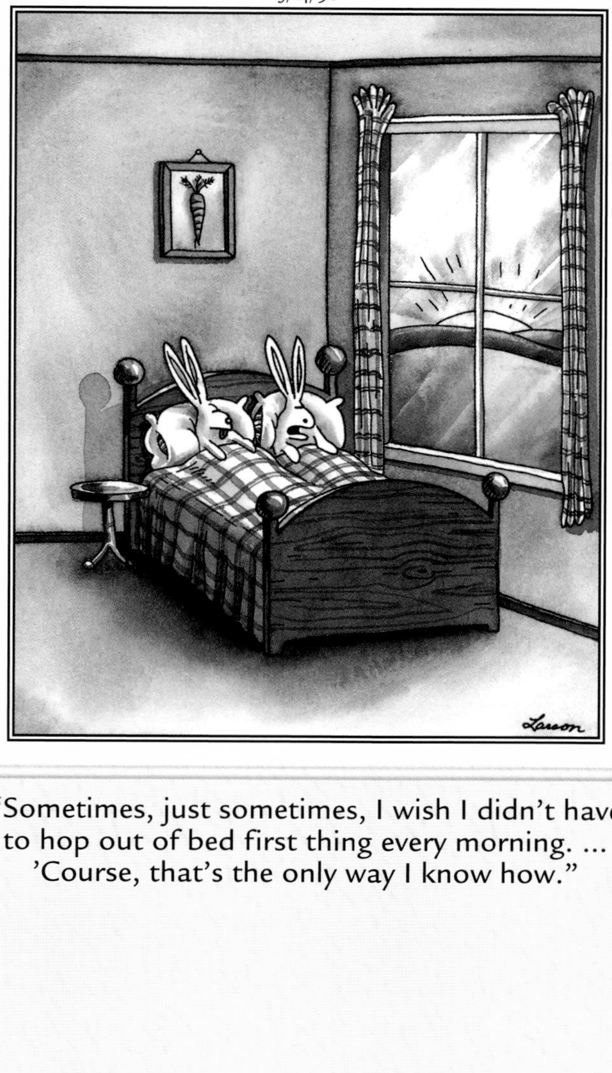
Larson

"Sometimes, just sometimes, I wish I didn't have to hop out of bed first thing every morning. ... 'Course, that's the only way I know how."

5/10/90

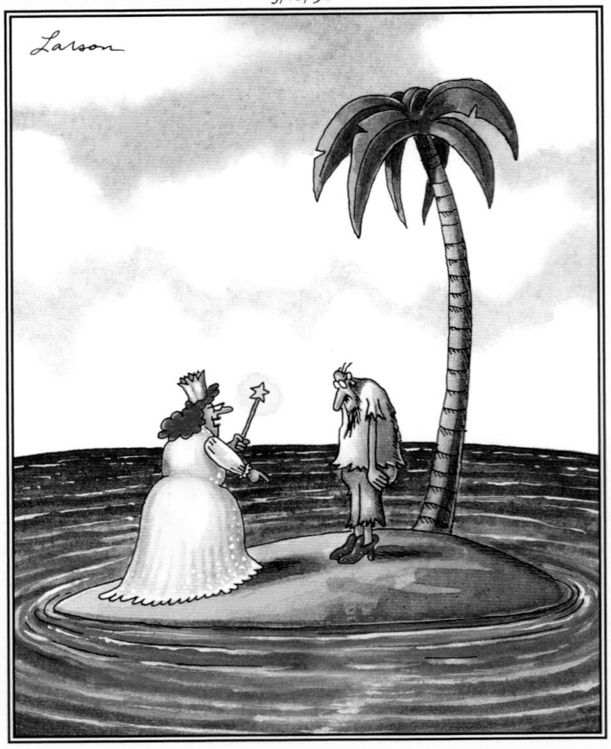

"All this time you've been able to go home whenever you desired—just click your heels together and repeat after me ..."

5/11/90

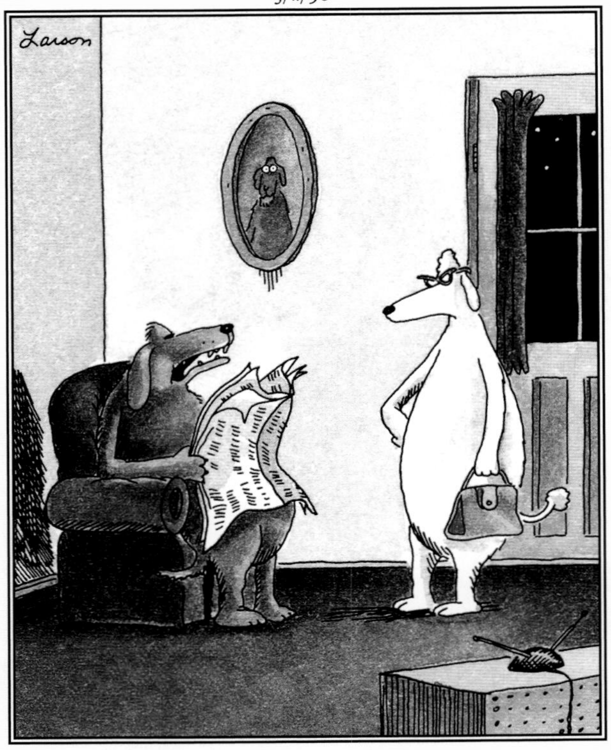

"No way am I going to that party tonight! I won't know anyone there, which means I'll be constantly introduced—and you *know* I never learned how to shake!"

5/16/90

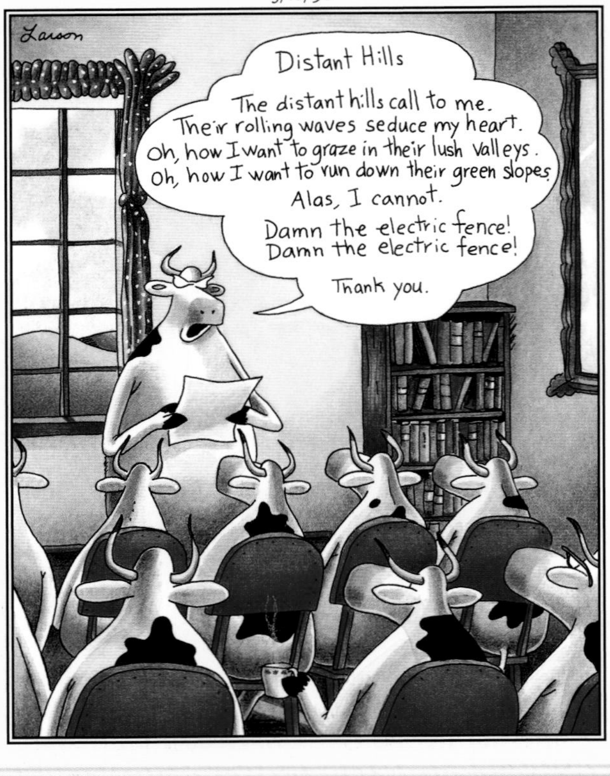
Distant Hills
The distant hills call to me.
Their rolling waves seduce my heart.
Oh, how I want to graze in their lush valleys.
Oh, how I want to run down their green slopes.
Alas, I cannot.
Damn the electric fence!
Damn the electric fence!
Thank you.

Cow poetry

5/17/90

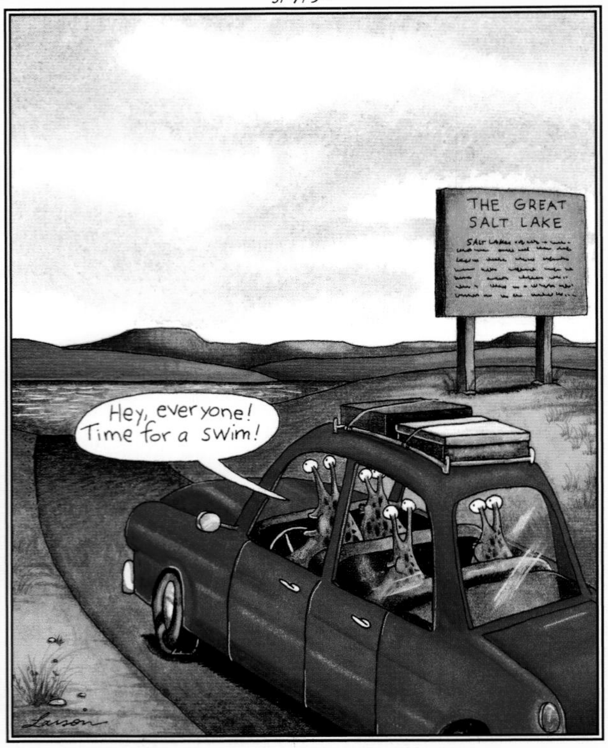
THE GREAT SALT LAKE
Hey, everyone! Time for a swim!

Slug vacation disasters

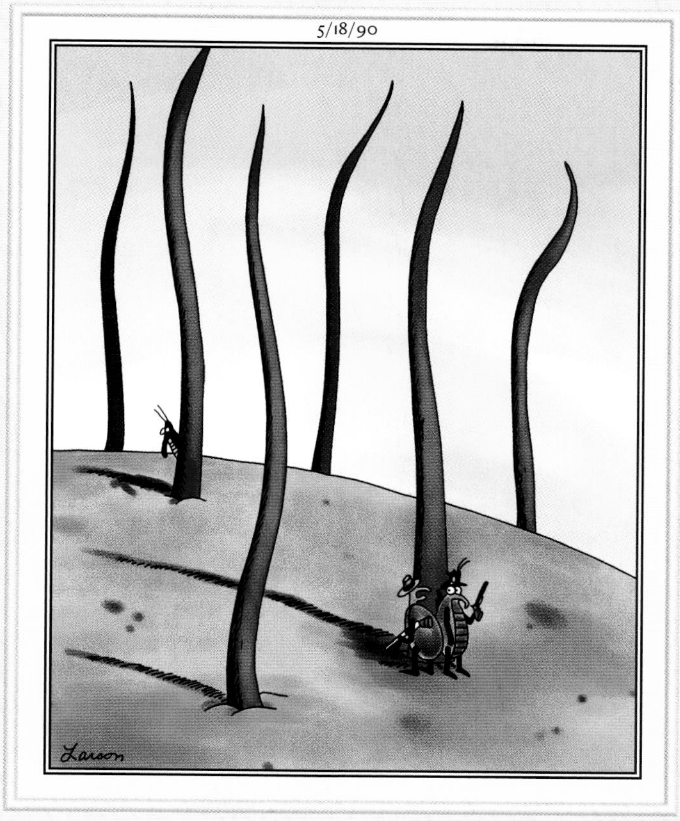
5/18/90
Larson

"Listen, before we try and take this guy, let me ask you this: You ever kill a flea before, Dawkins? ... It ain't easy."

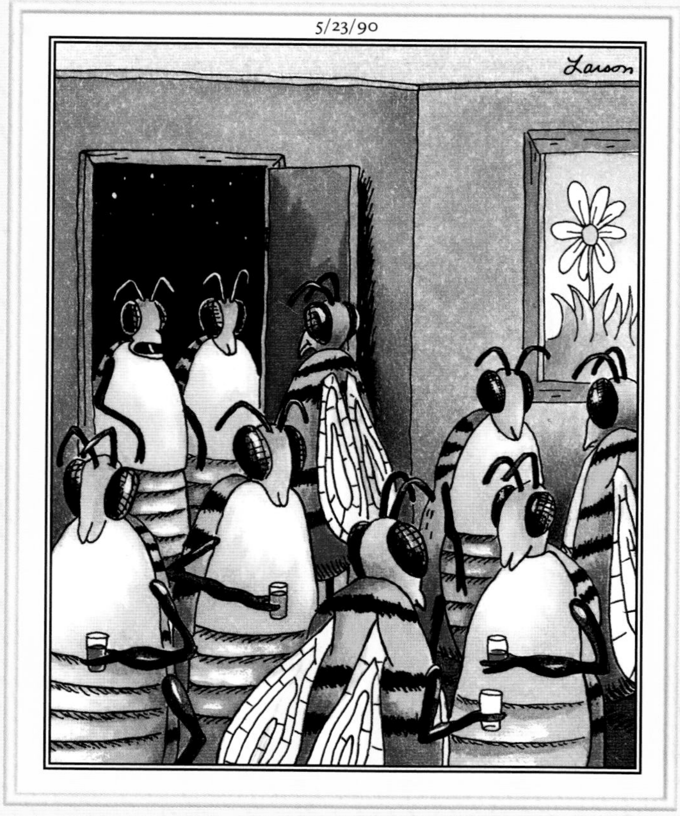
5/23/90
Larson

"Wow, this place is really packed—or maybe it's just my compound eyes."

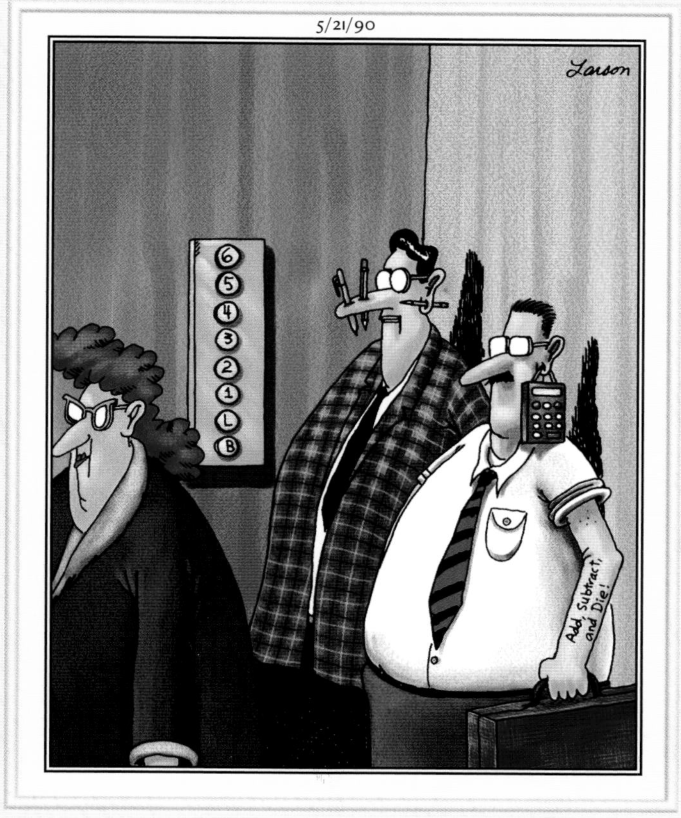
5/21/90
Larson
6
5
4
3
2
1
L
B
Add, Subtract, and Die!

Punk accountants

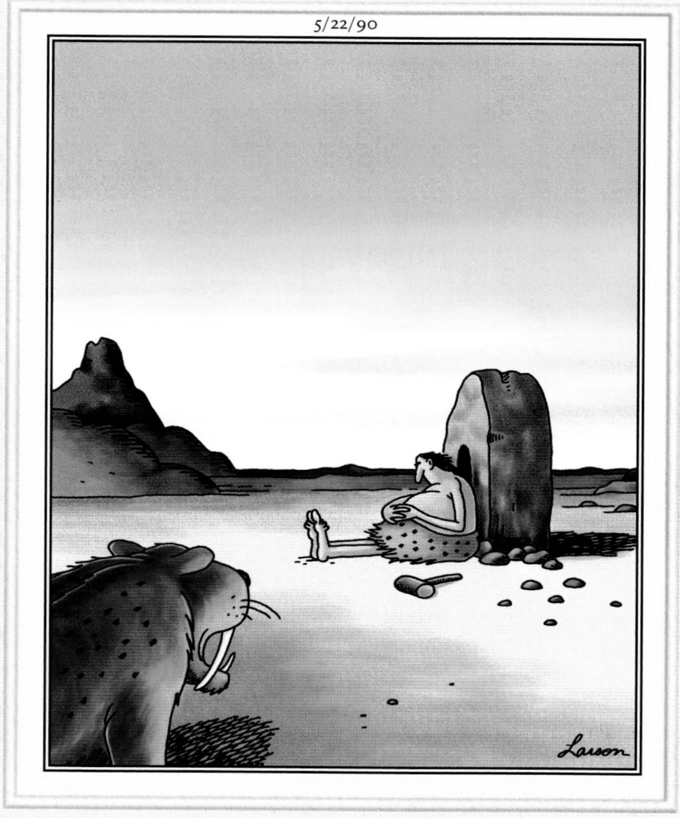
5/22/90
Larson

Thag Anderson becomes the first fatality as a result of falling asleep at the wheel.

5/15/90

All right!

As the flock of monarchs, in a silent burst of black and gold, rose from the puddle's edge, a sudden "crack" knifed through the still morning air. A spider's shotgun had found its mark.

5/24/90

Ptooey!

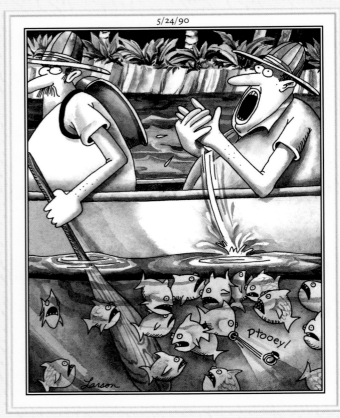

Helpful hints for the jungle traveler: Never drag your hand in piranha-infested waters.

5/25/90

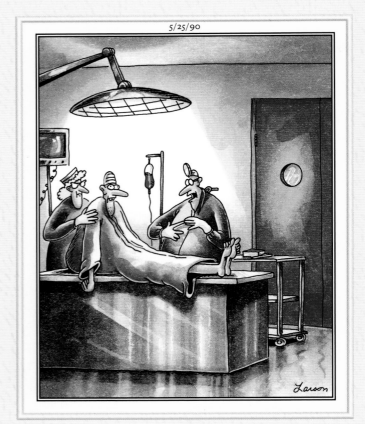

"Okay, Mr. Dittman, remember: That brain is only a temporary, so don't think too hard with it."

5/28/90

Use nice, even strokes, and always remember to make your trees look like happy trees.

5/30/90

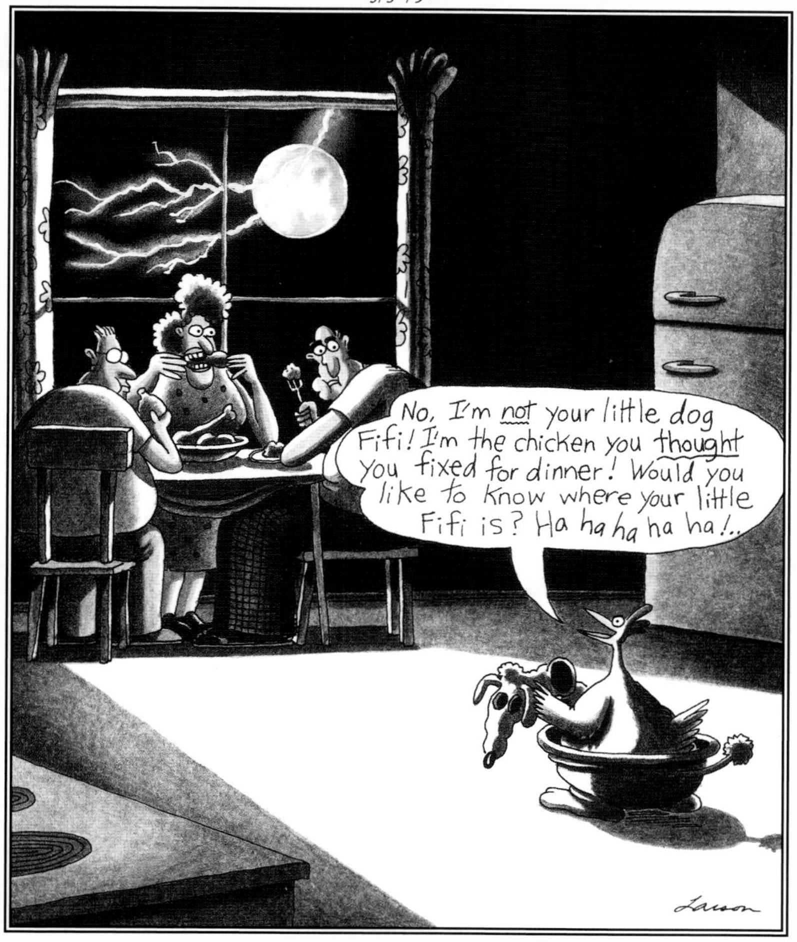
No, I'm not your little dog Fifi! I'm the chicken you thought you fixed for dinner! Would you like to know where your little Fifi is? Ha ha ha ha ha!..
Larson

Scene from *Dinner on Elm Street*

5/29/90

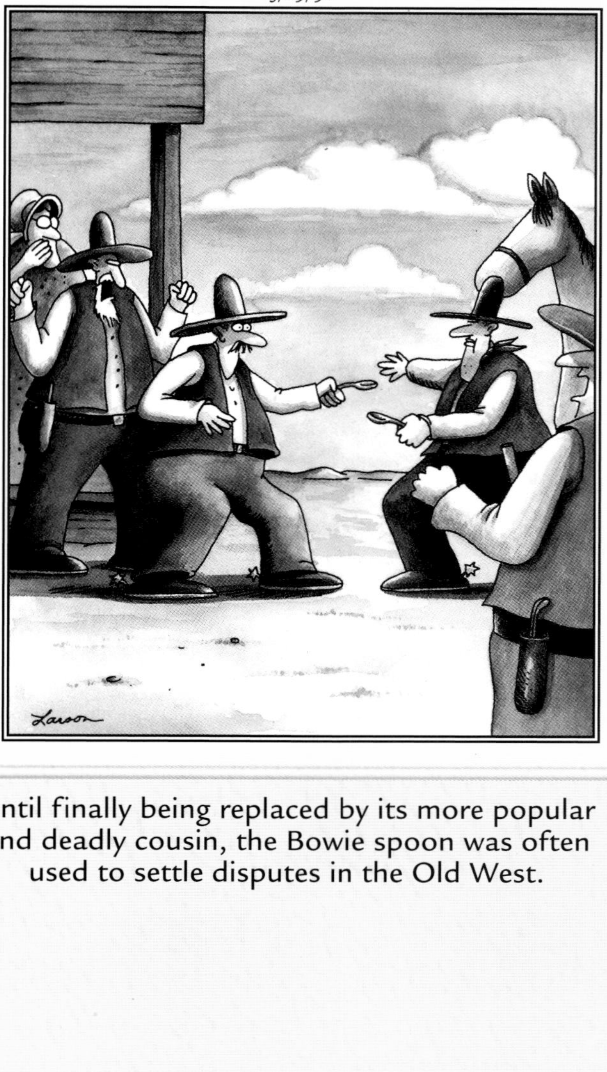
Larson

Until finally being replaced by its more popular and deadly cousin, the Bowie spoon was often used to settle disputes in the Old West.

5/31/90

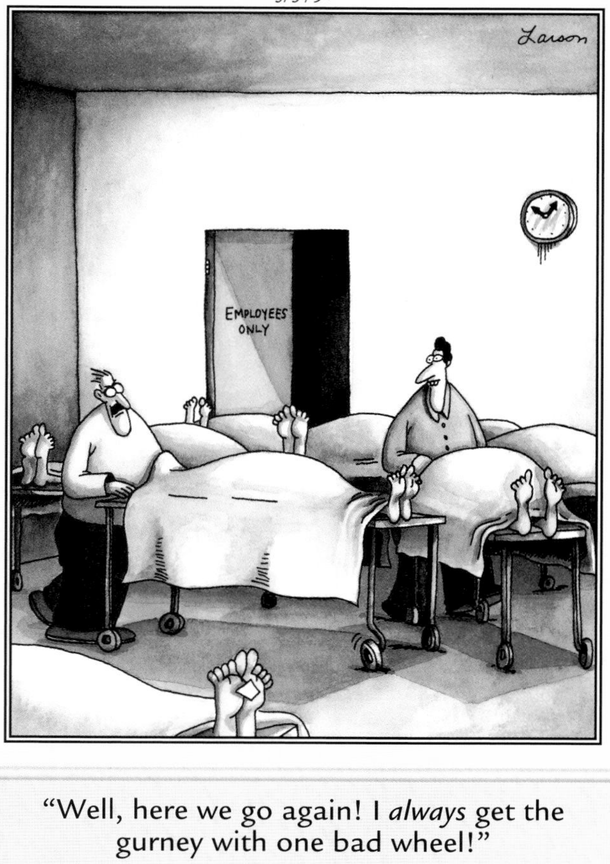
Larson
EMPLOYEES ONLY

"Well, here we go again! I *always* get the gurney with one bad wheel!"

6/1/90

Larson
Sidewinder
kangaroo rat
gila monster
sand clown

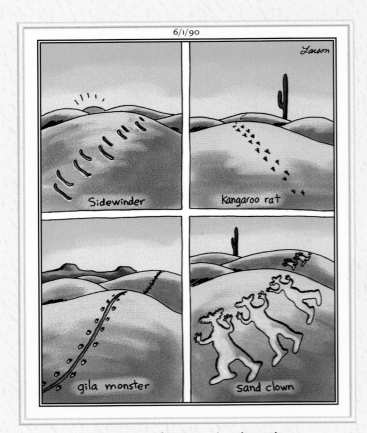

Common desert animal tracks

6/4/90

Larson
AISLE 5
TABLE SCRAPS
MISC. BONES chicken bones removed
Who Knows?
GRISTLE & FAT

6/5/90

Larson

"You need to see medicine man—me just handyman."

6/11/90

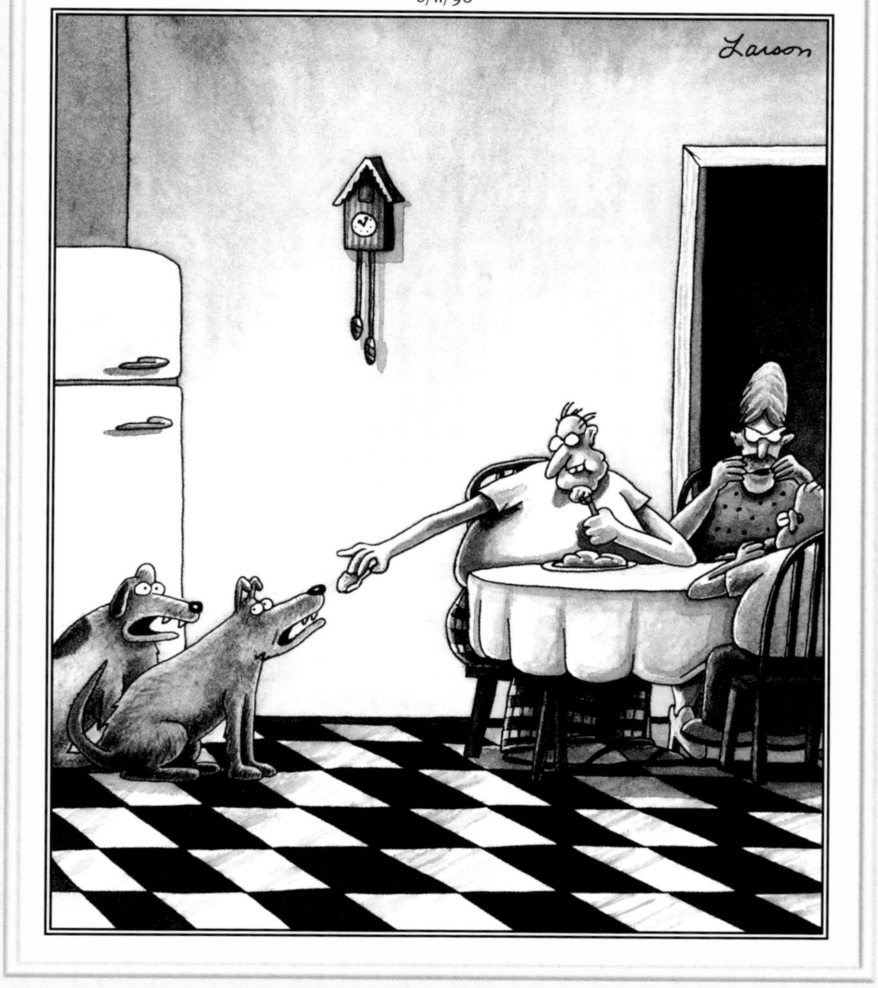
Larson

"Rex! Don't take it! Everyone knows their mouths are dirtier than our own!"

6/14/90

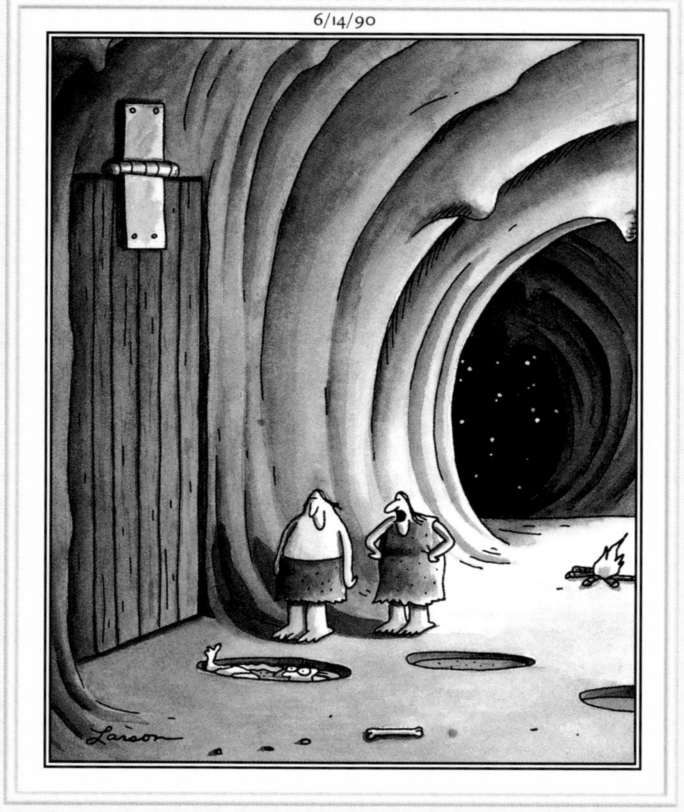
Larson

"Well, like I said, a mammoth shouldn't be allowed in the cave to begin with—but installing a swinging door was just plain crazy!"

6/15/90

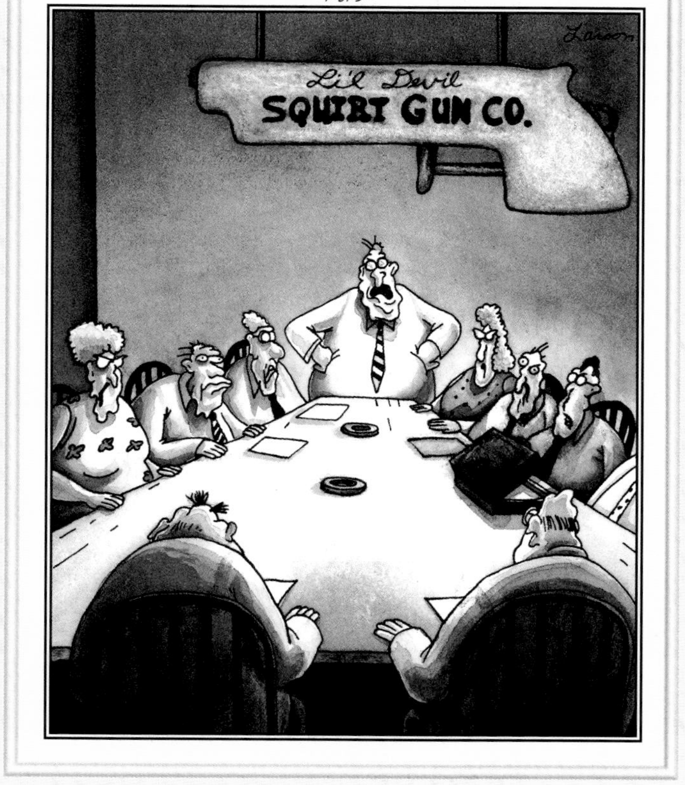
Li'l Devil
SQUIRT GUN CO.
Larson

"And one more thing about tomorrow's company picnic: Do I have to mention what happened last year when some moron sabotaged the games with a case of acid-filled LD-50s?"

6/13/90

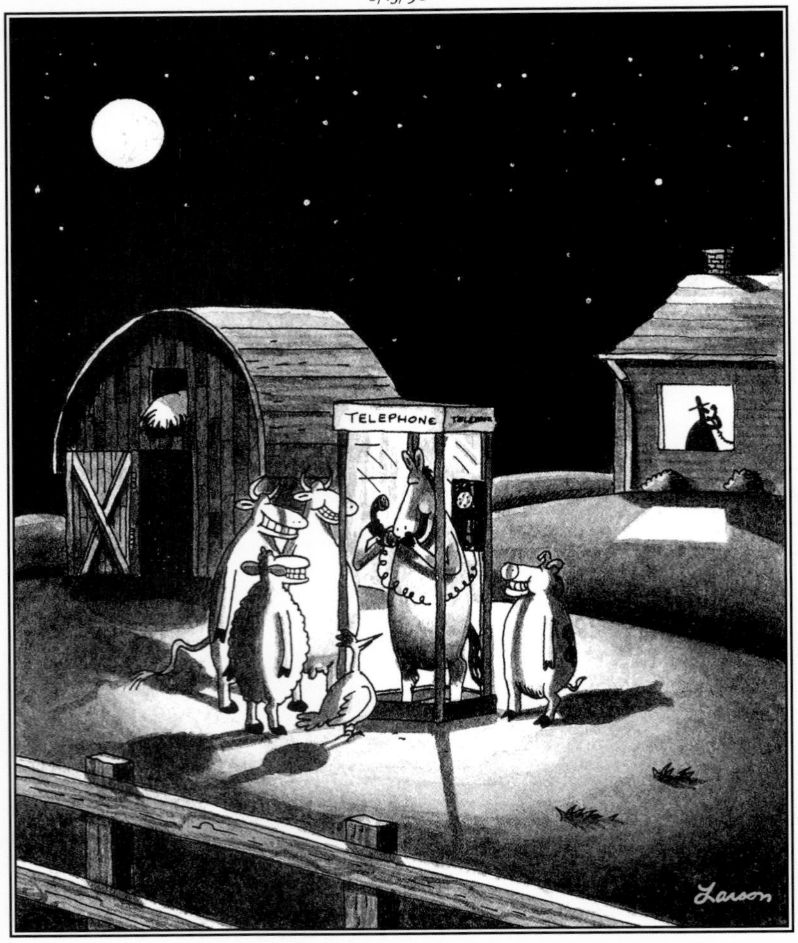
TELEPHONE
Larson

"Farmer Bob ... your barn door's open."

6/7/90

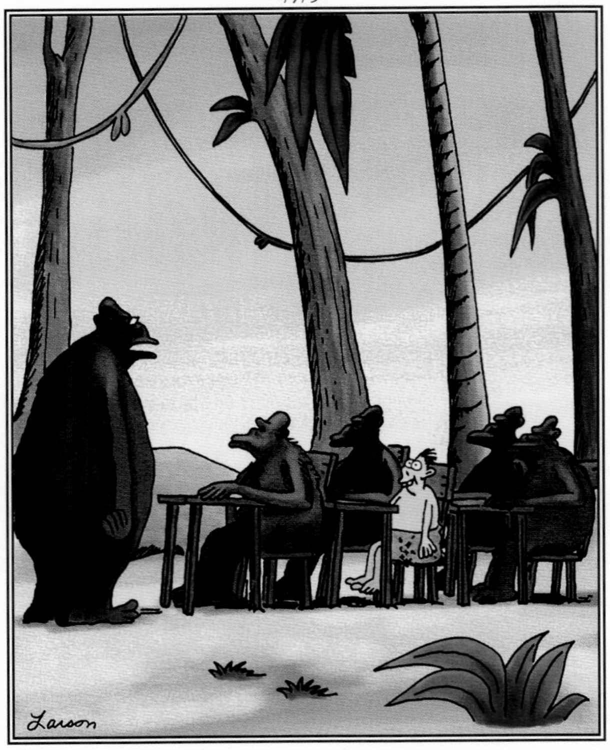
Larson

"And the really great thing about this jungle of ours is that any one of you could grow up to be King of the Apes."

6/6/90

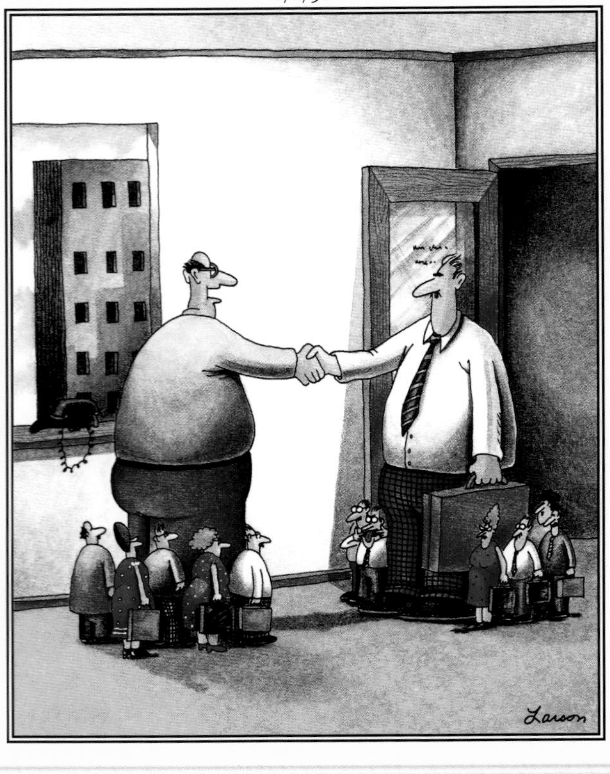
Larson

"Okay, Johnson—we've got a deal. We'll let your people and my people work out the details."

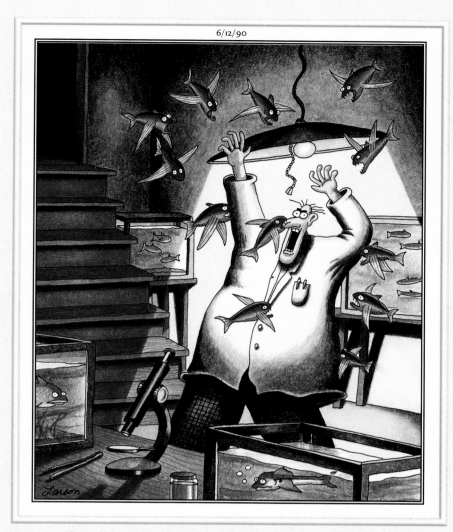

6/12/90

Larson

After flicking on the light, Professor Zurkowitz is caught off guard by the overnight success of his efforts to crossbreed flying fish and piranhas.

6/8/90

Larson
Well, here I go.
I'm outta here.
I'll be back in a jiffy.
I shall be sure to write.

March 16, 1942: The night before he leaves the Philippines, General MacArthur works on his farewell address.

6/18/90

JEOPARDY
EINSTEIN
57800
EDISON
54900
JONES
-100
Larson

"Excuse me ... I know the game's almost over, but just for the record, I don't think my buzzer was working properly."

6/19/90

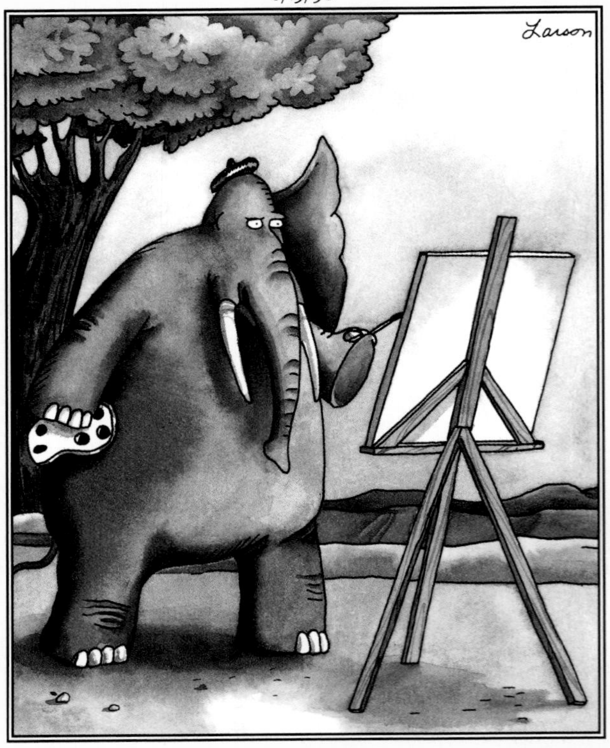
Larson

Elephan Gogh

6/22/90

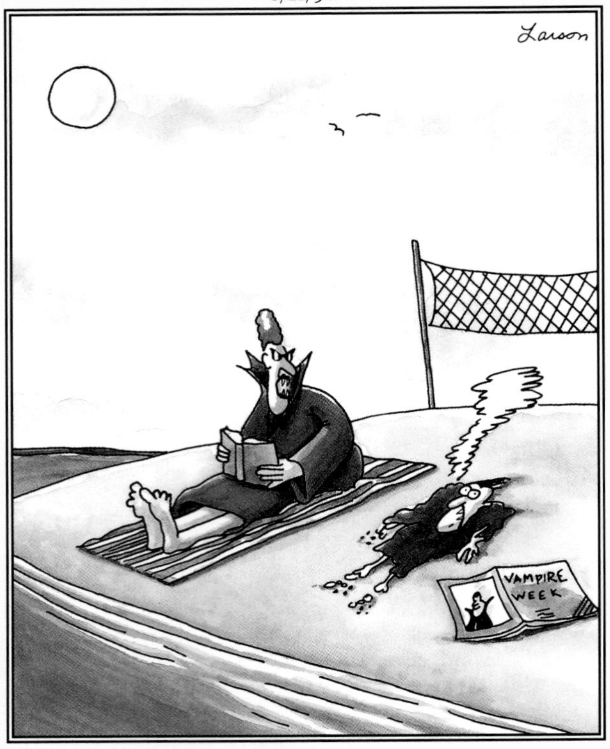
Larson
VAMPIRE WEEK

"Well, Donald—forgot your sunblock, I see."

6/20/90

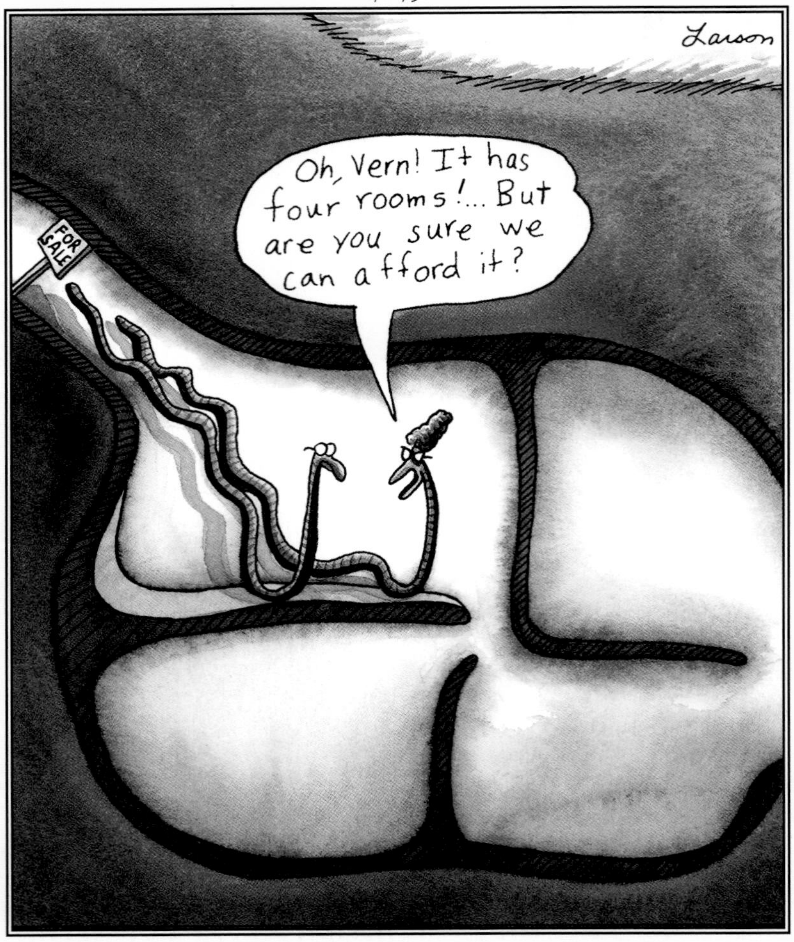
Larson
FOR SALE
Oh, Vern! It has four rooms!... But are you sure we can afford it?

Tapeworms in a cow's stomach

6/26/90

Larson

"Again? Crimony! ... How many times did I have a tentacle over the lens?"

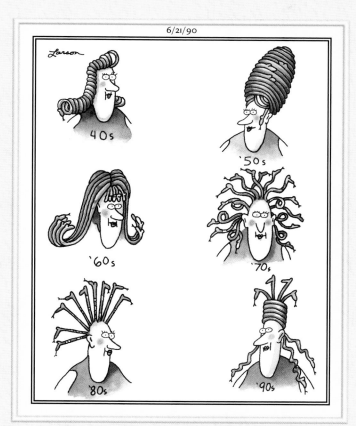

6/21/90

Larson
40s
'50s
'60s
'70s
'80s
'90s

The evolution of Medusa's hair

6/28/90

Larson
Dang! This guy's on to me... I've gotta get rid of him.

Early shell games

6/29/90

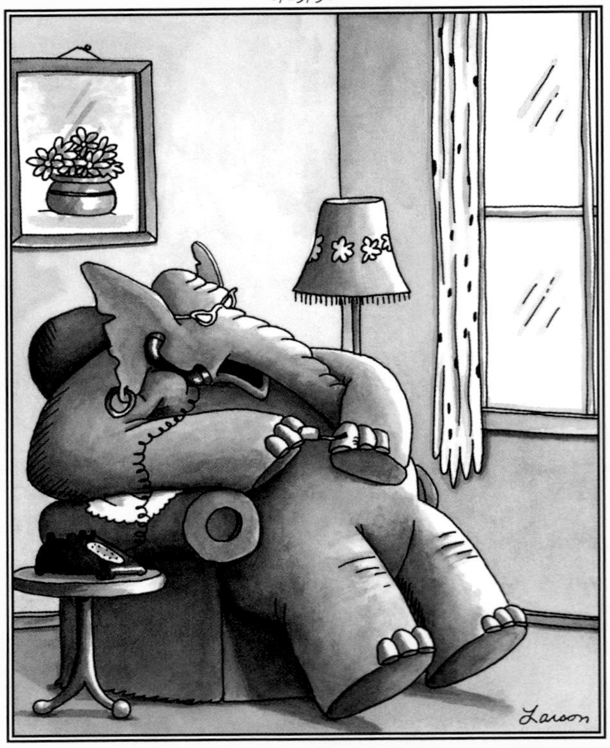
Larson

"Okay, Jane, this guy you want me to go out with—you say he lives alone, he doesn't have any friends, and he has a slight frothing problem. ... He's not a rogue, is he?"

6/25/90

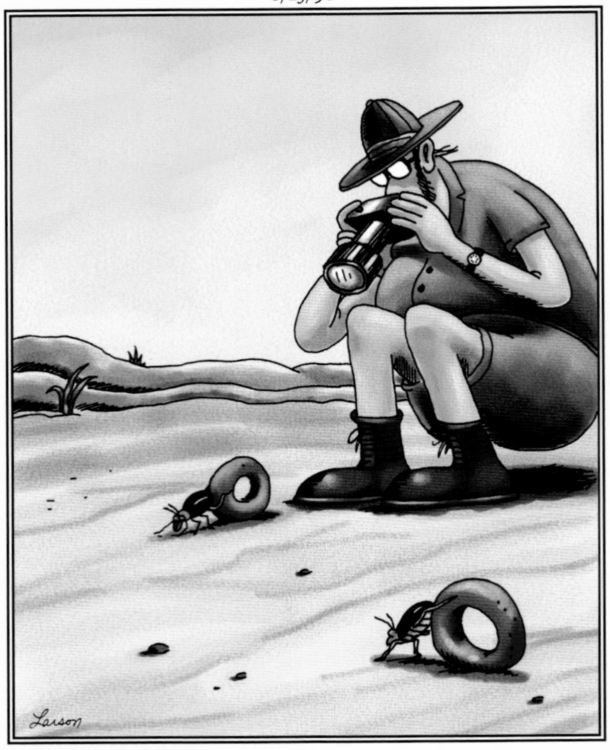
Larson

Studying the African bagel beetle

6/27/90

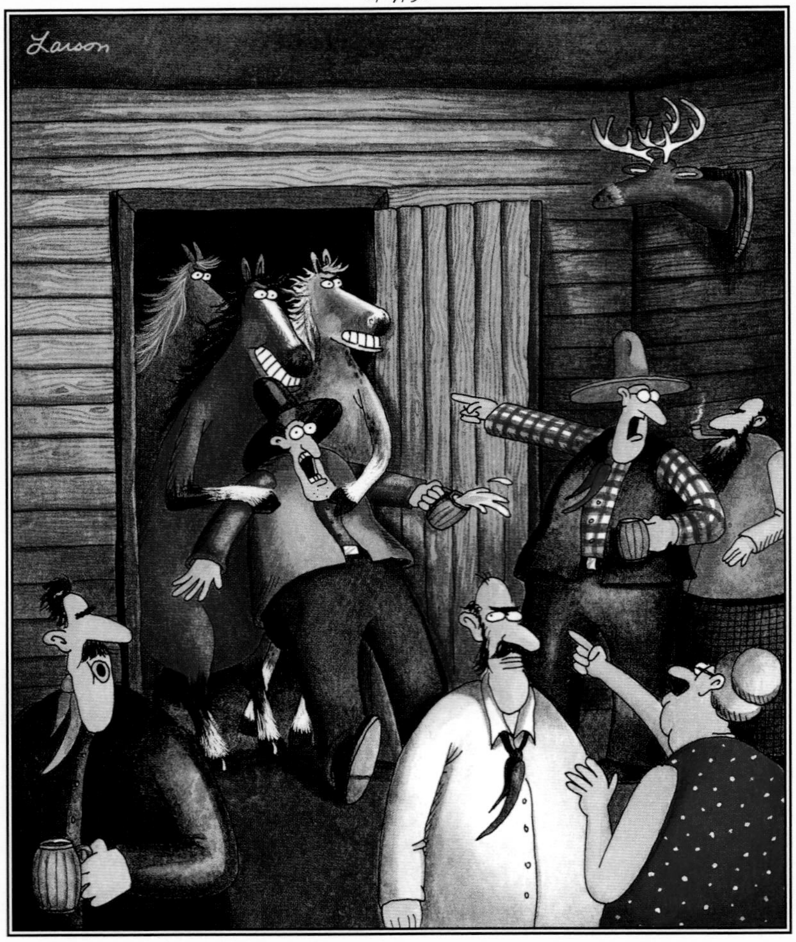
Larson

Suddenly, the door was kicked open, and with nostrils flaring and manes flying, wild horses dragged Sam away.

7/4/90

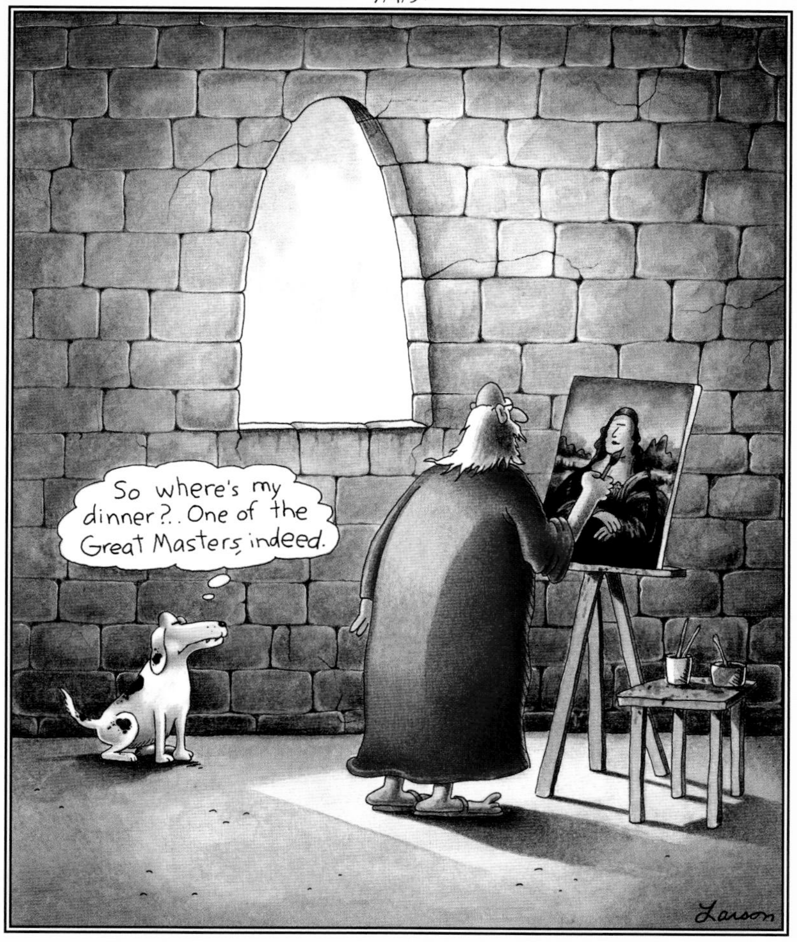
So where's my dinner?.. One of the Great Masters, indeed.
Larson

7/2/90

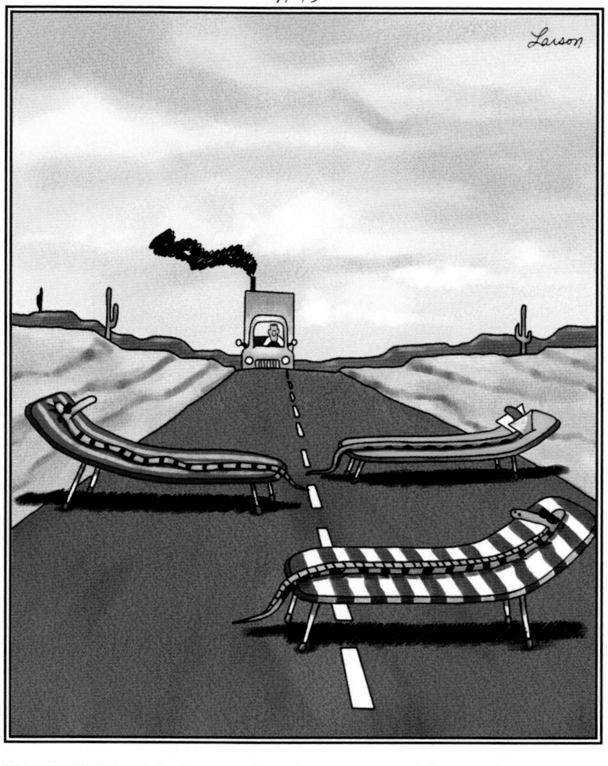
Larson

Gus saw them when he crested the hill. Snakes. Three of them, basking on the road. Probably diamondbacks.

7/6/90

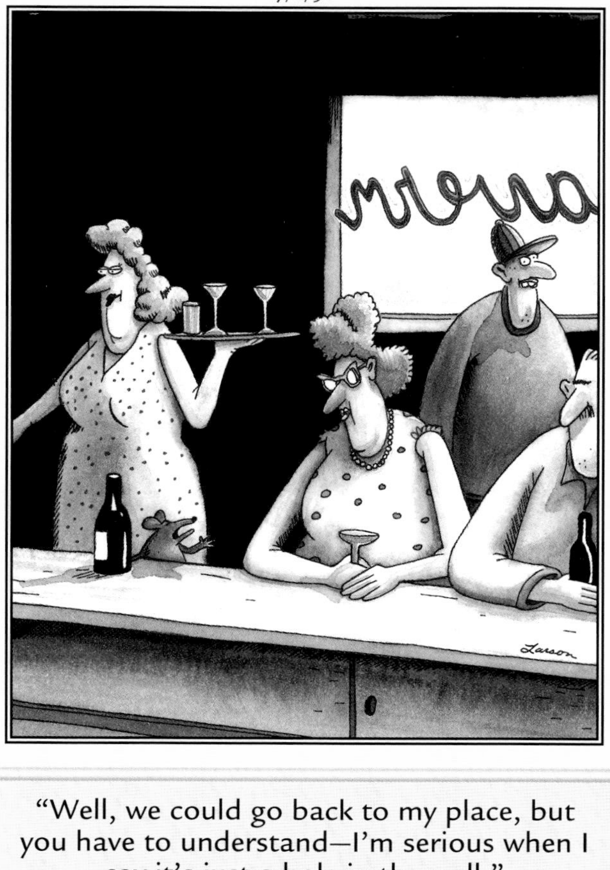
Larson

"Well, we could go back to my place, but you have to understand—I'm serious when I say it's just a hole in the wall."

7/3/90

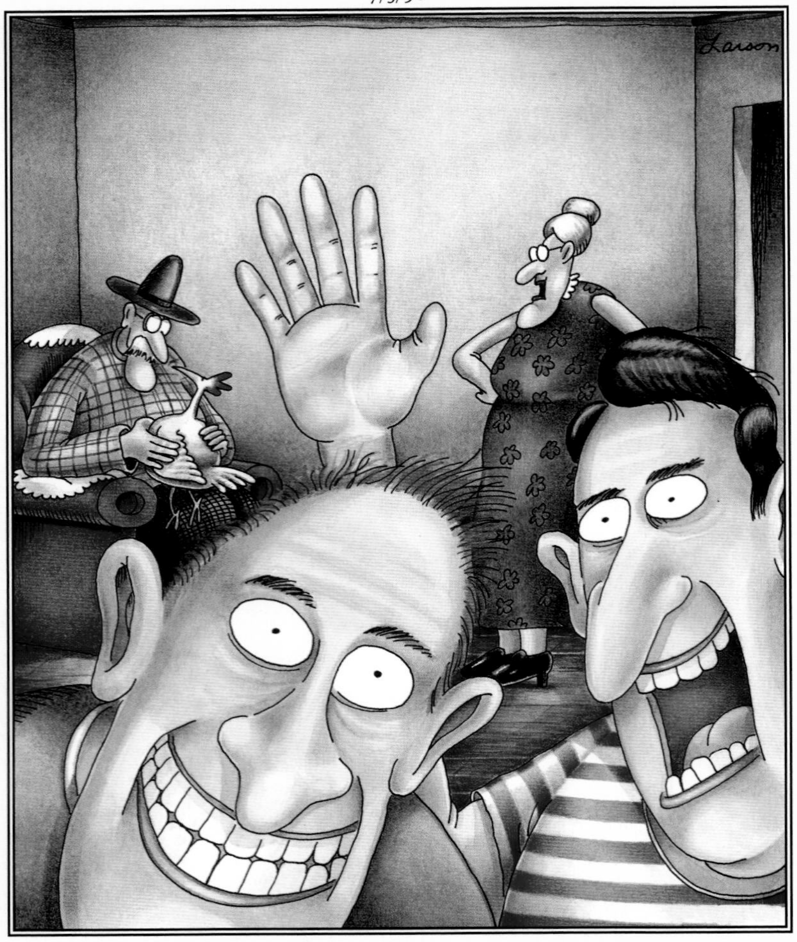
Larson

Suddenly, two bystanders stuck their heads inside the frame and ruined one of the funniest cartoons ever.

7/10/90

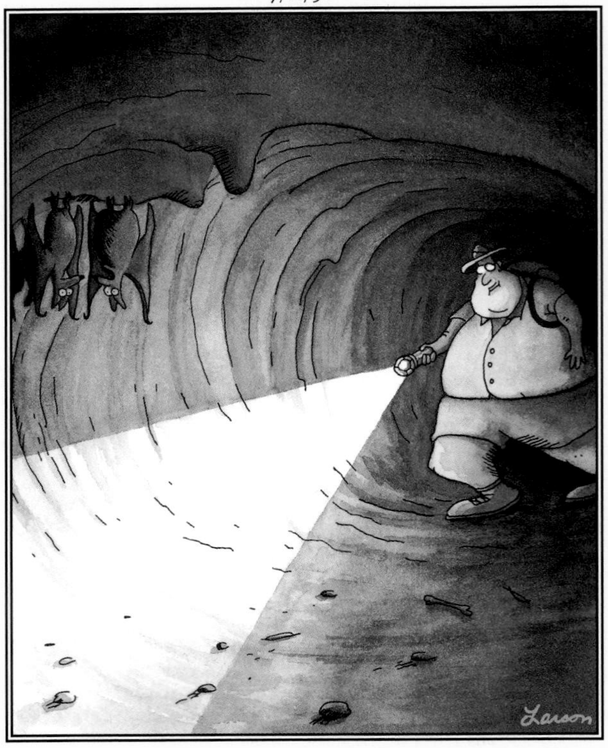
Larson

"My sonar's got it at 12 feet away and closing ... 11 feet ... 10 feet ... God, it's enormous!... Nine feet ..."

7/11/90

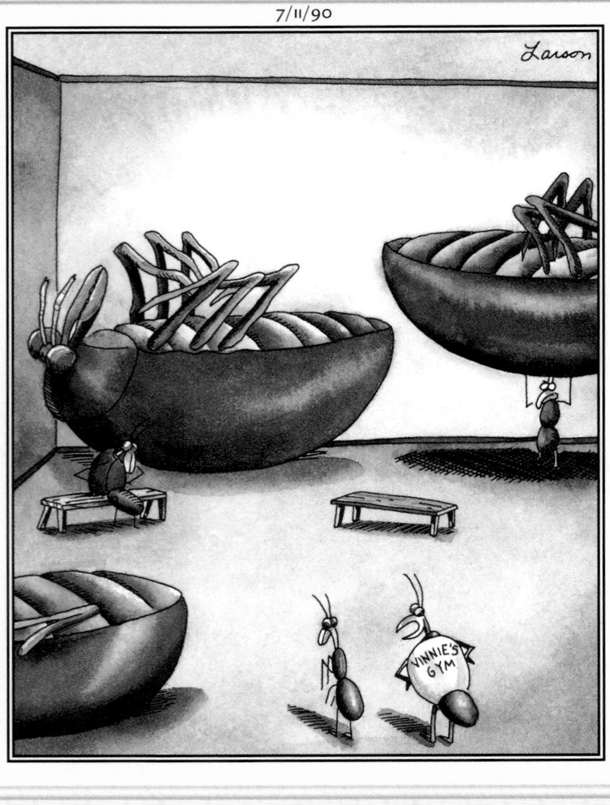
Larson
VINNIE'S GYM

"Now this is our dead beetle room, and some of these babies are 50 times an ant's body weight. ... 'Course, we'll want to start *you* out on dried ladybugs."

7/5/90

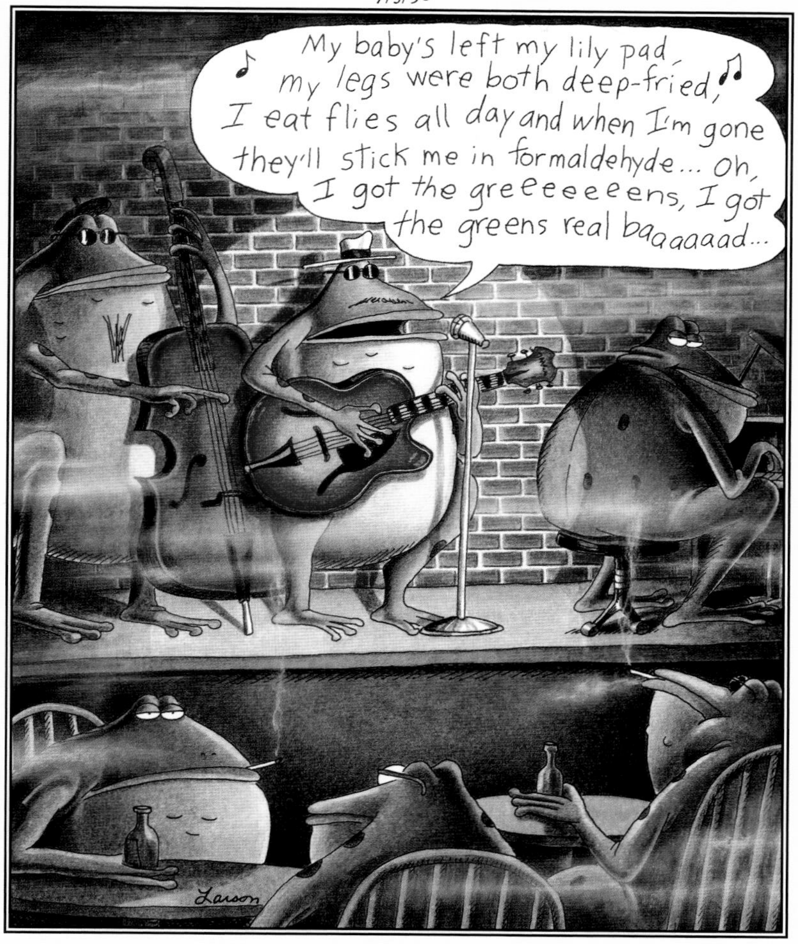
My baby's left my lily pad,
my legs were both deep-fried,
I eat flies all day and when I'm gone
they'll stick me in formaldehyde... Oh,
I got the greeeeeeens, I got
the greens real baaaaaad...
Larson

7/12/90

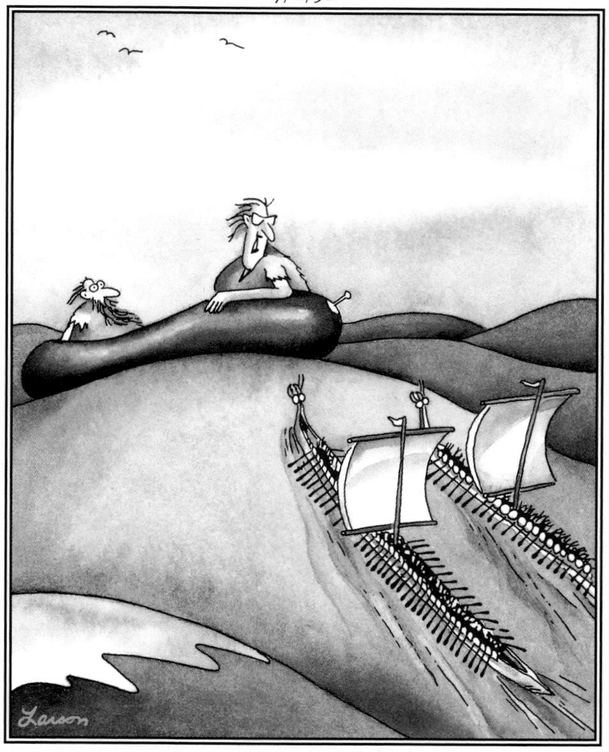
Larson

"Now what? ... Oh God, Ernie! Navy ants!"

7/19/90

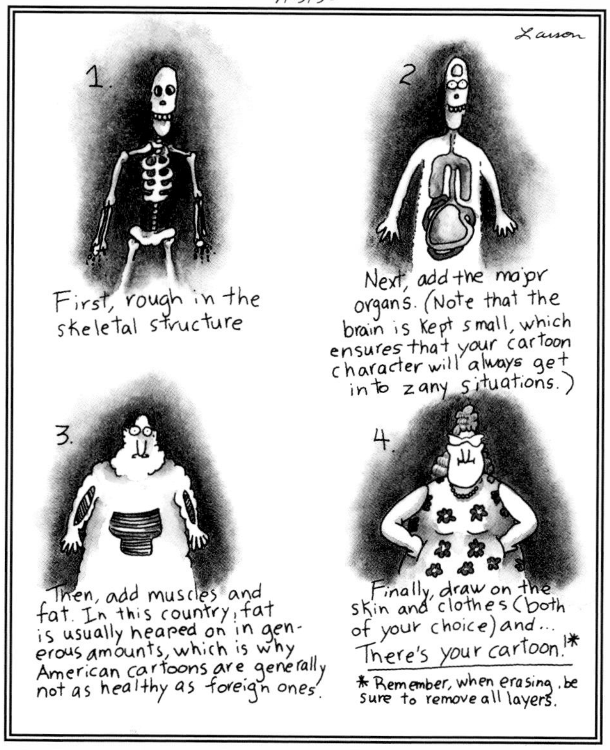
Larson
1.
First, rough in the skeletal structure
2.
Next, add the major organs. (Note that the brain is kept small, which ensures that your cartoon character will always get into zany situations.)
3.
Then, add muscles and fat. In this country, fat is usually heaped on in generous amounts, which is why American cartoons are generally not as healthy as foreign ones.
4.
Finally, draw on the skin and clothes (both of your choice) and...
There's your cartoon!*
* Remember, when erasing, be sure to remove all layers.

How to draw cartoons

7/13/90

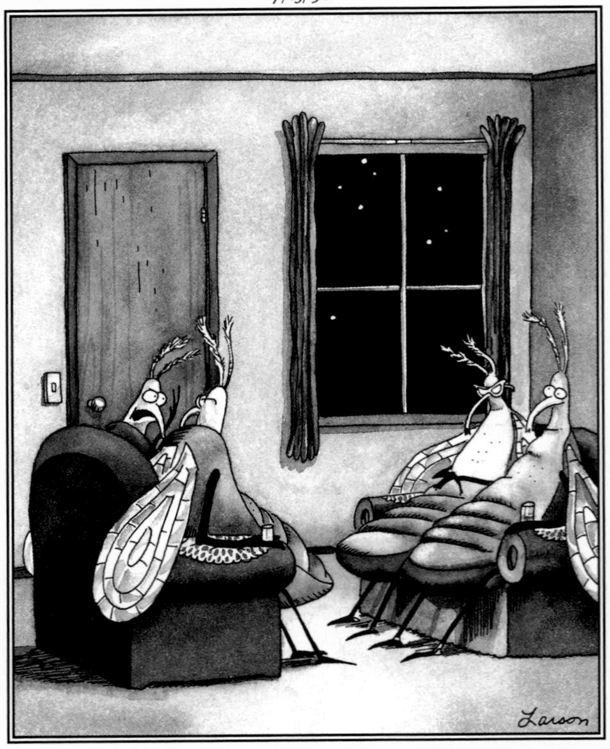
Larson

"Crimony! Talk about overstaying your welcome! ... John, open the door and turn the porch light on—see if that gets rid of them."

7/9/90

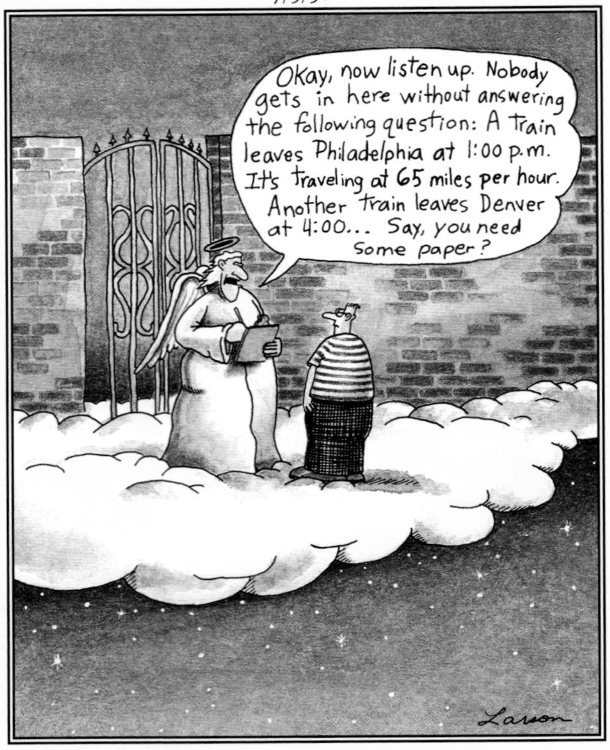
Okay, now listen up. Nobody gets in here without answering the following question: A train leaves Philadelphia at 1:00 p.m. It's traveling at 65 miles per hour. Another train leaves Denver at 4:00... Say, you need some paper?
Larson

Math phobic's nightmare

7/16/90

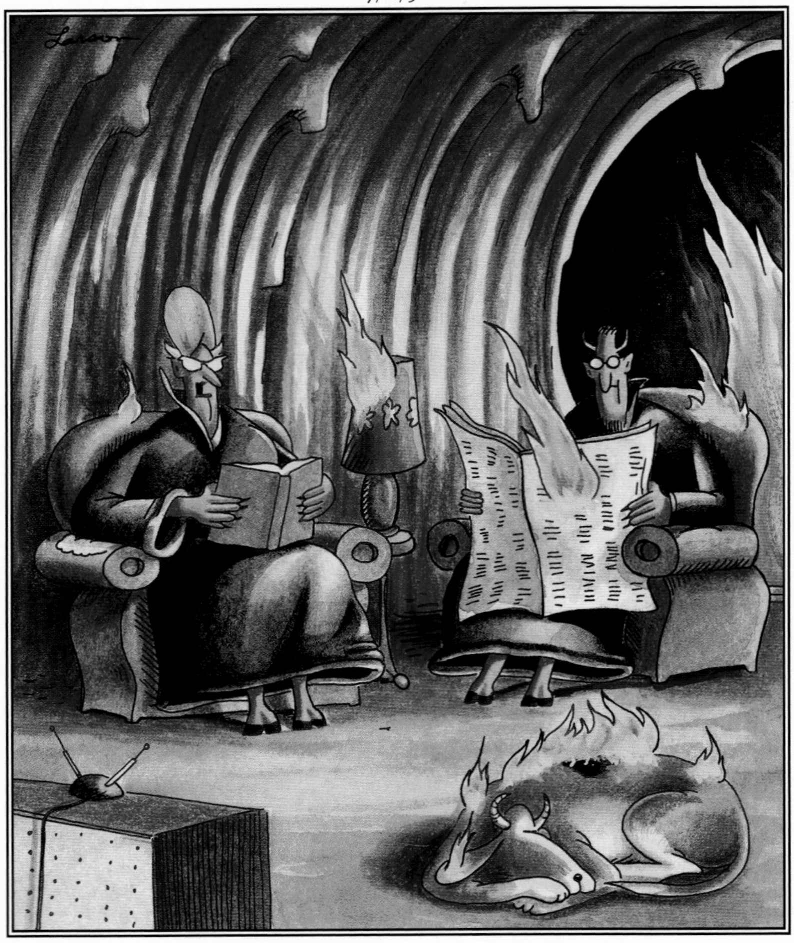
Larson

"Uh-oh, Bob, the dog's on fire. ... I think it's your turn to put him out."

7/18/90

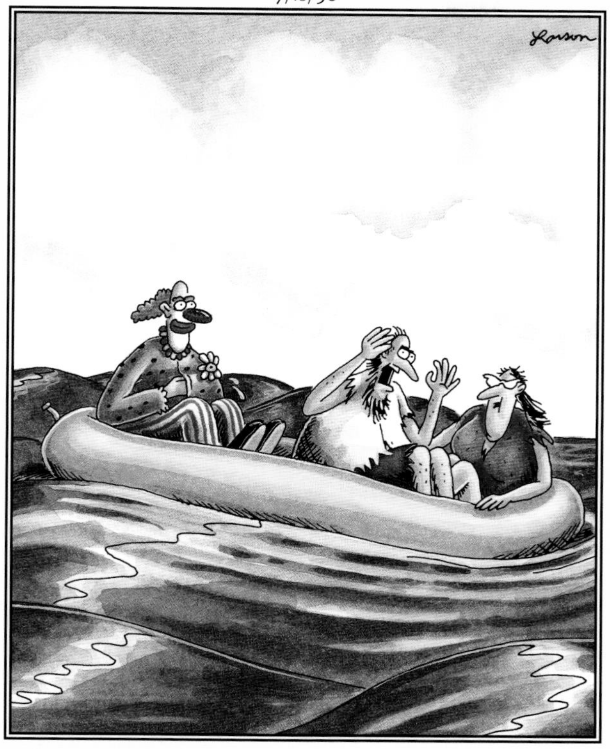
Larson

"There! I felt it again, Donna! ...
Raindrops! Raindrops!"

7/25/90

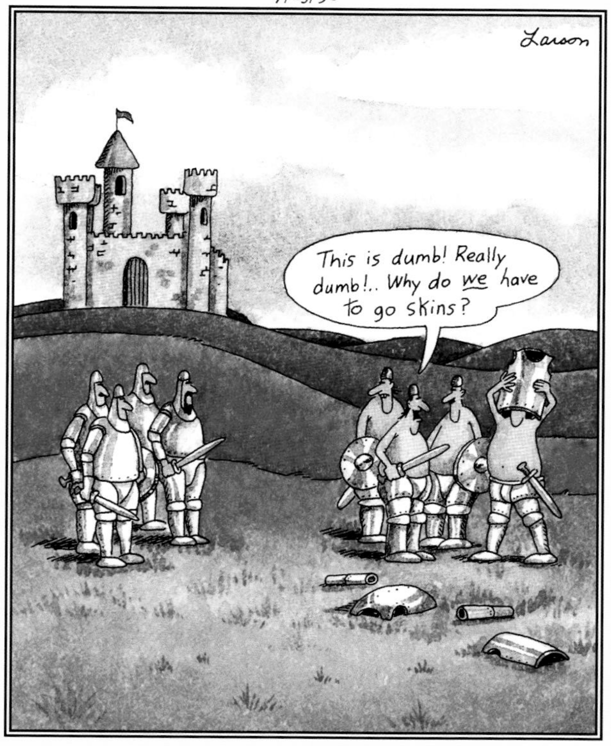
Larson
This is dumb! Really dumb!.. Why do we have to go skins?

Medieval pickup battles

7/26/90

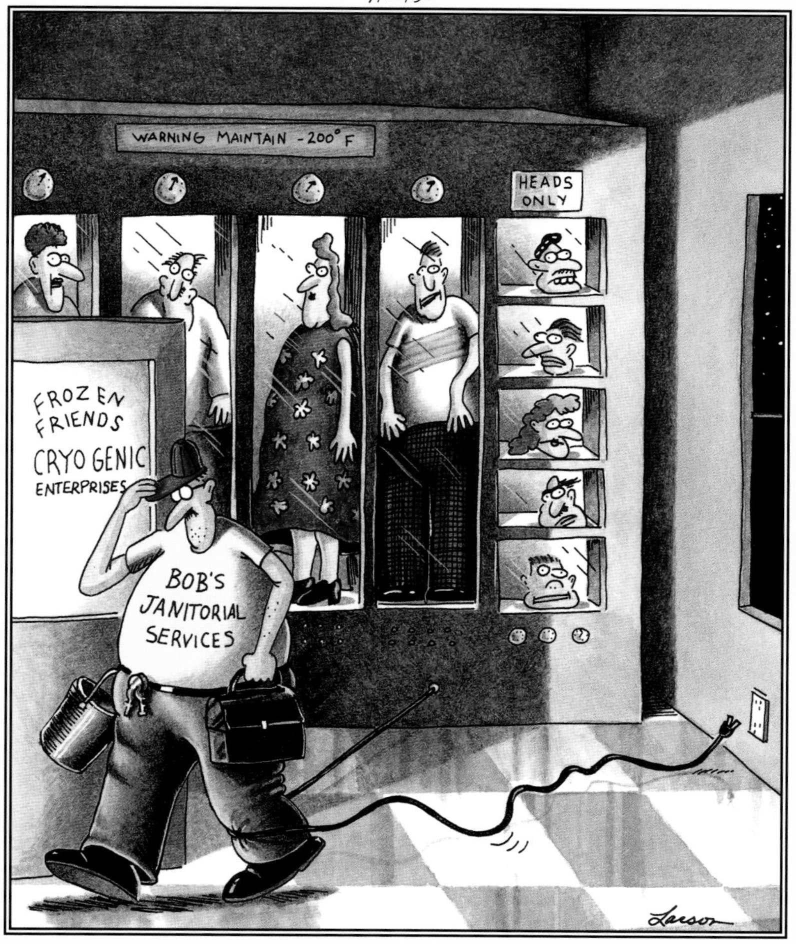
WARNING MAINTAIN -200° F
HEADS ONLY
FROZEN FRIENDS
CRYO GENIC
ENTERPRISES
BOB'S JANITORIAL SERVICES
Larson

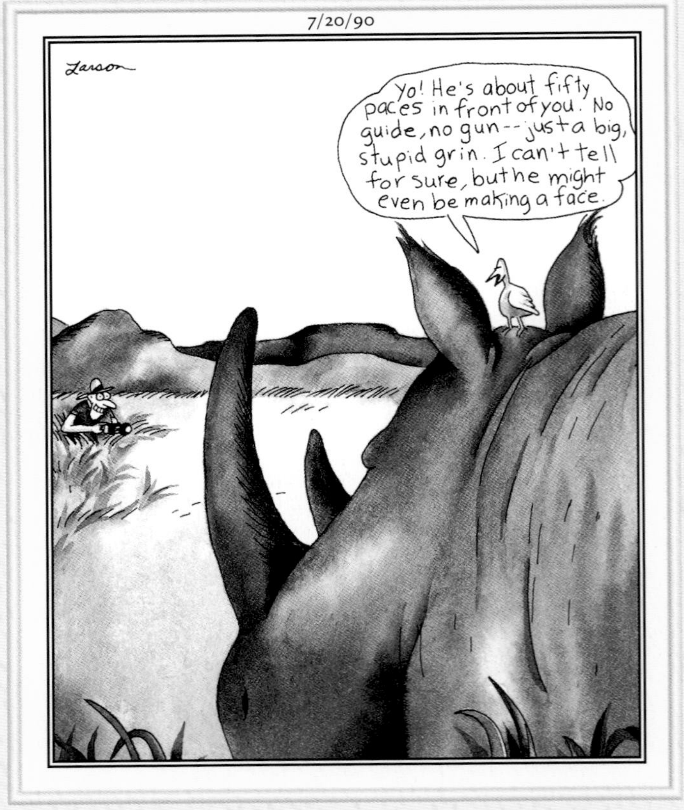
7/20/90
Yo! He's about fifty paces in front of you. No guide, no gun--just a big, stupid grin. I can't tell for sure, but he might even be making a face.

How rhinos are incited to charge

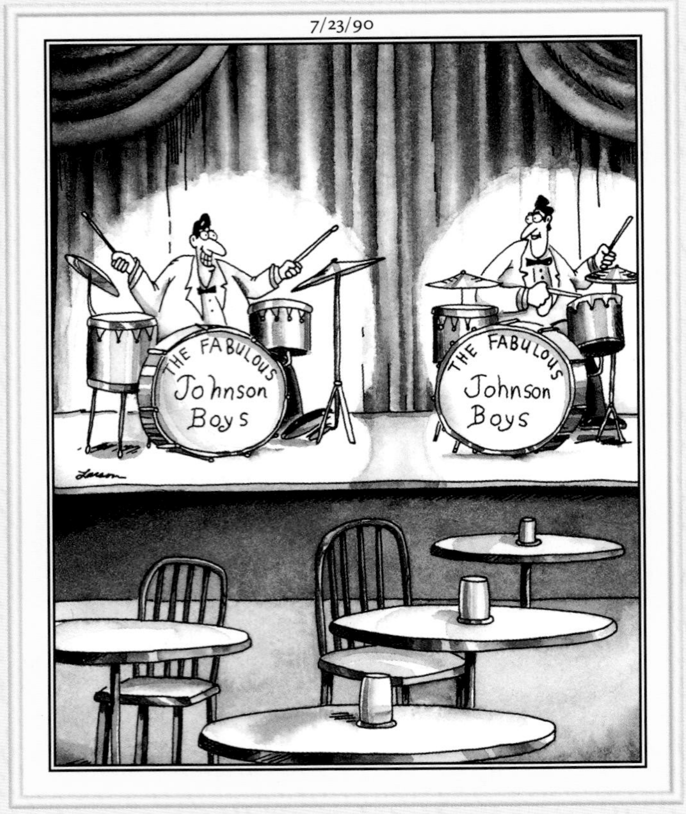
7/23/90
THE FABULOUS Johnson Boys
THE FABULOUS Johnson Boys

Failed lounge acts

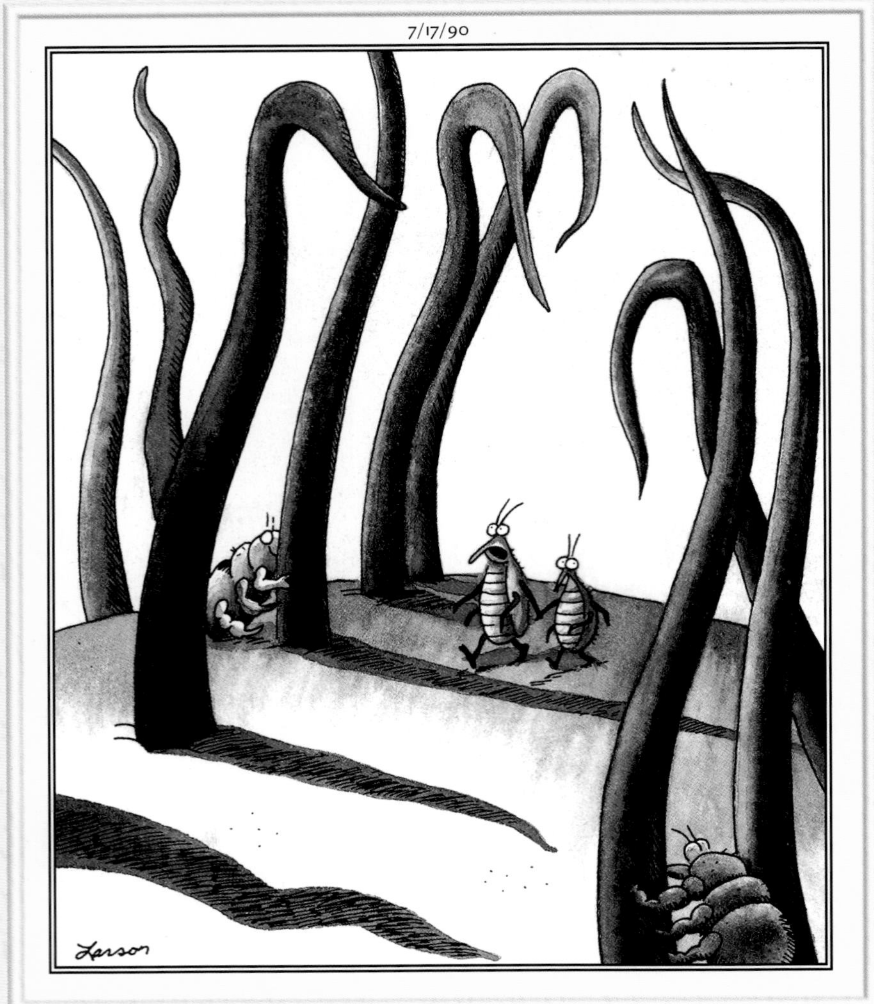
7/17/90

"Frances, I've got a feeling we're not on Toto anymore."

7/24/90

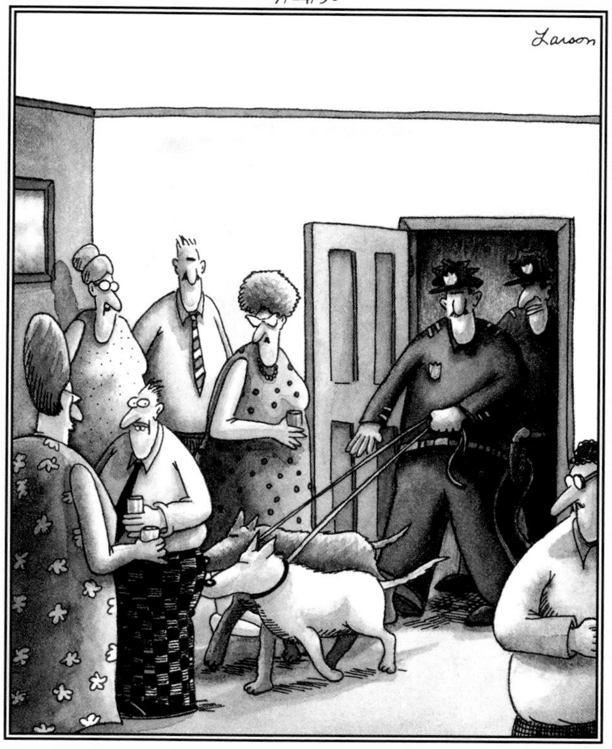

Suddenly, and to Rodney's horror, the police arrived with nerd-sniffing dogs.

7/27/90

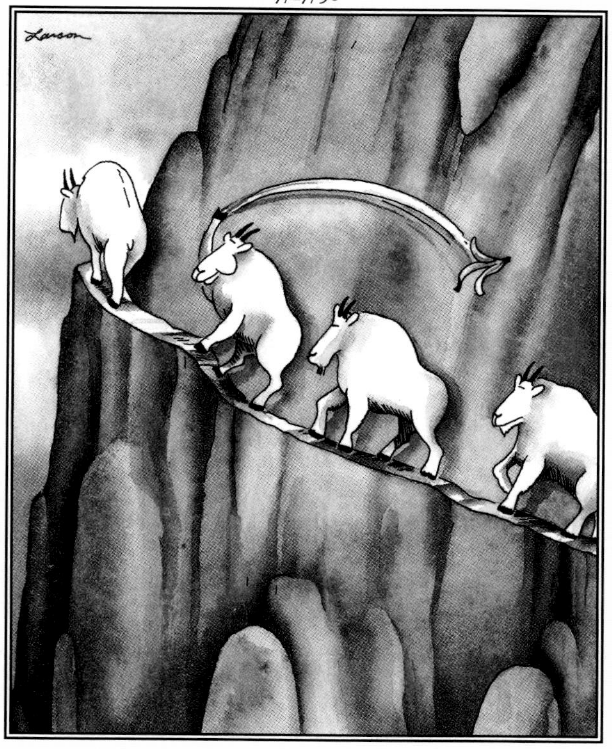

Irresponsible mountain goats

7/30/90

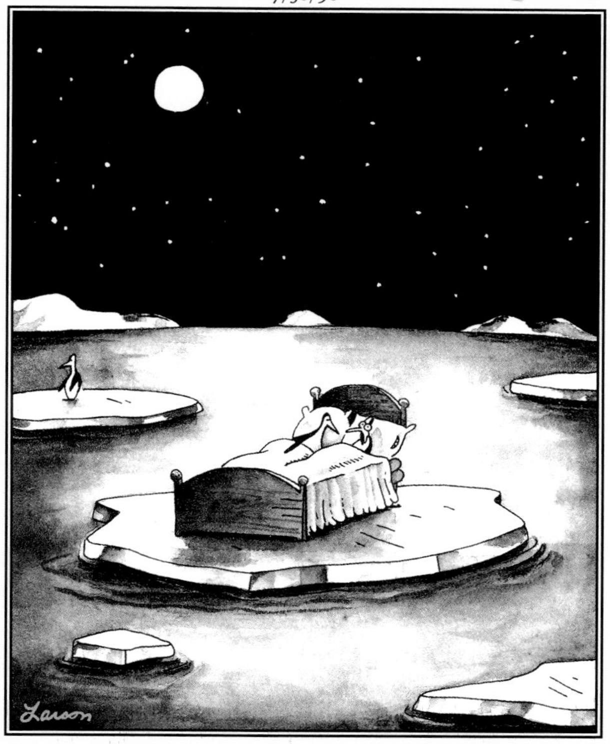

"Wowowo! ... Man, Lola, your feet are always so dang warm!"

7/31/90

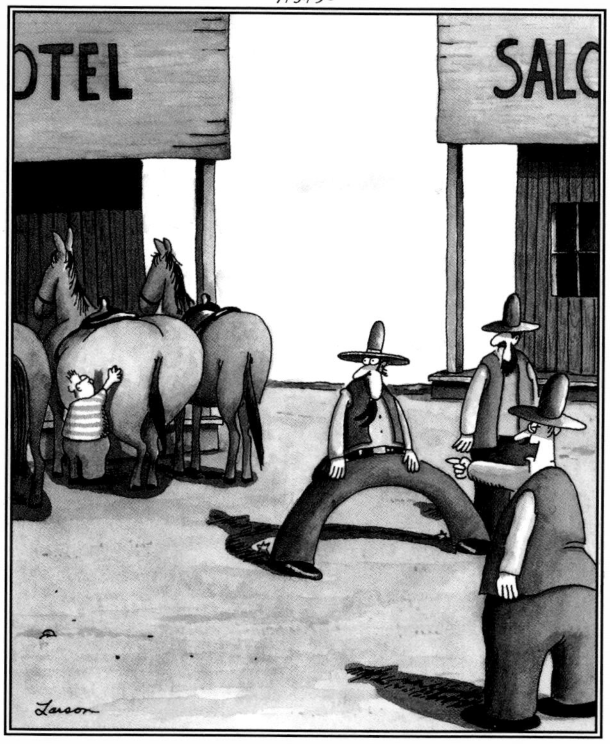
OTEL

"Dave! Ain't that your horse that kid is messin' with?"

8/1/90

"Oh, Helen! You're pregnant? That's wonderful! ... At first, I was taking you quite literally when you said you had one in the oven!"

8/2/90

"Hey! I'm *trying* to pass the potatoes! ... Remember, my forearms are just as useless as yours!"

8/6/90

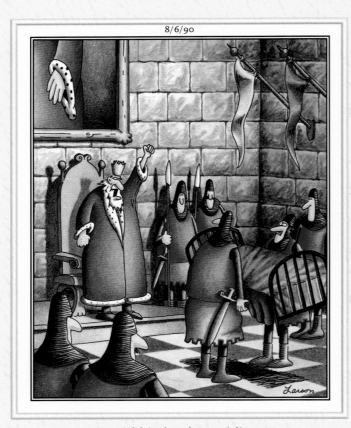

"I said his *head,* you idiots! Bring me the cur's *head!*"

8/8/90

ANDERSON'S
SCHOOL FOR
SEEING-EYE DOGS
24

"Well, scratch number 24. He did pretty good, though—right up to the jet engine test."

8/9/90

Larson
You fools! This is only his tail!.. You've fallen for the oldest trick in the books!
27

Lizard thugs

8/10/90

Larson
STUPID
I'M WITH STUPID

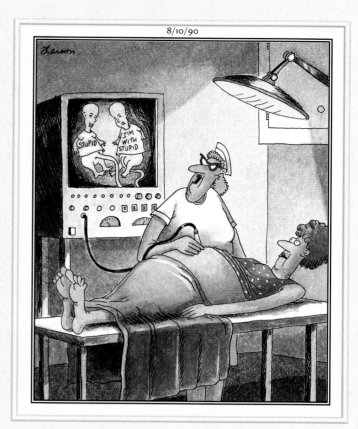

"There you go, Mrs. Eagen—you can clearly see both twins on the monitor."

8/13/90

Larson
Well, everyone passed their final exam... everyone except you, Terrance --I'm afraid you're still not complete.

Fool school

8/16/90

Larson

"Well, just look at her and *then* tell me she didn't have her jowls lifted."

8/3/90

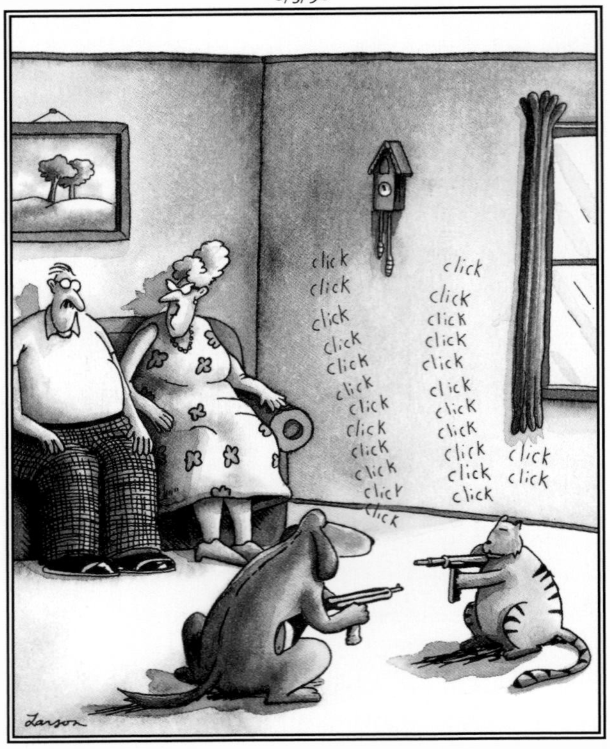
click click
click click
click click
click click
click click
click click
click click click
click click click
click click
click
Larson

"Introducing automatic weapons to a couple of dumb animals was irresponsible to begin with, Frank—but, my God! To think you almost left the bullets in!"

8/14/90

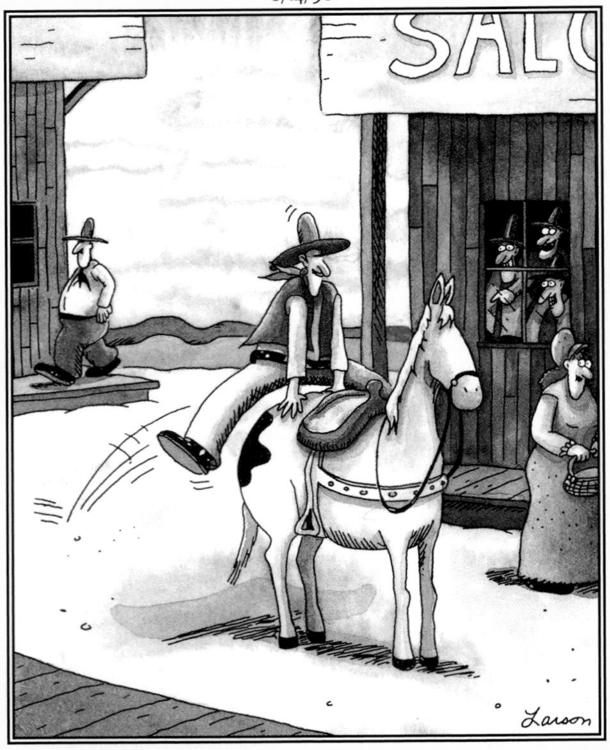
SAL
Larson

In the Old West, cowboy show-offs often fell victim to the old whoopee saddle gag.

8/7/90

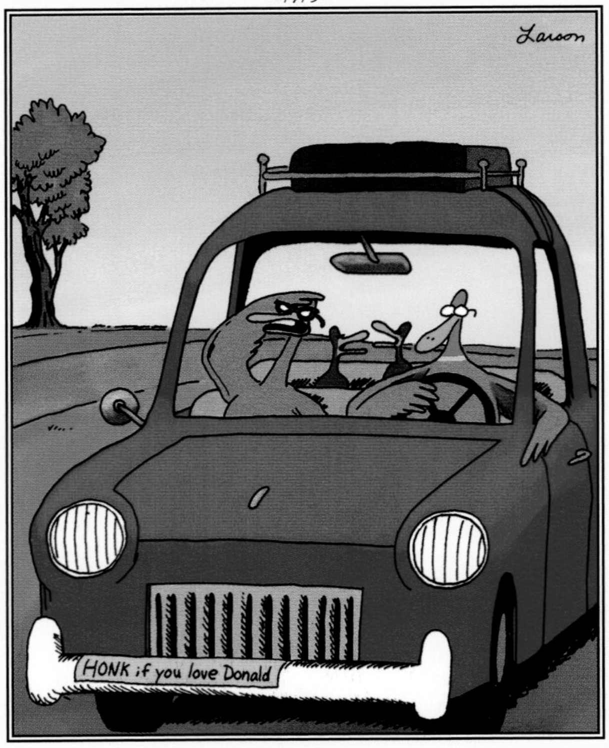
Larson
HONK if you love Donald

"Oh God, George! Stop! Stop the car! ... I've got another migration headache!"

8/15/90

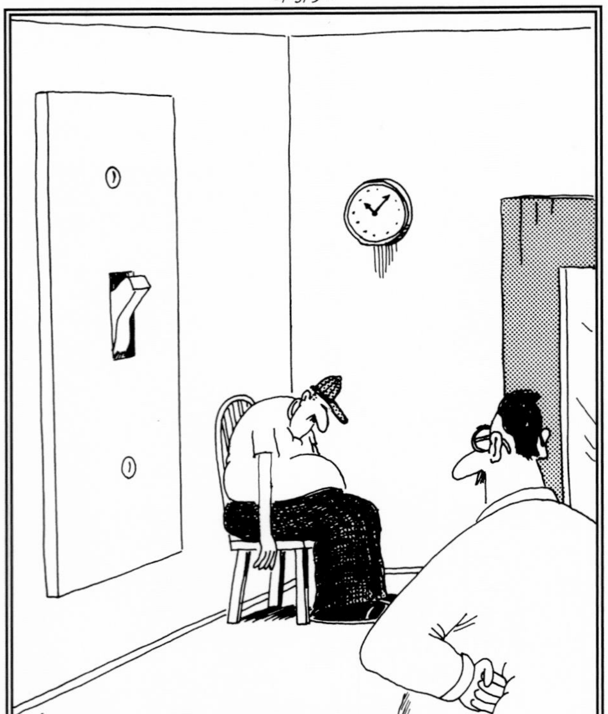
Larson

On what was to be his last day on the job, Gus is caught asleep at the switch.

8/21/90

Okay, now keep that right leg crossed for about a minute... That's it... Hold it... Hooooooold iiiiiiiit...

Leon Redbone's workout video

8/22/90

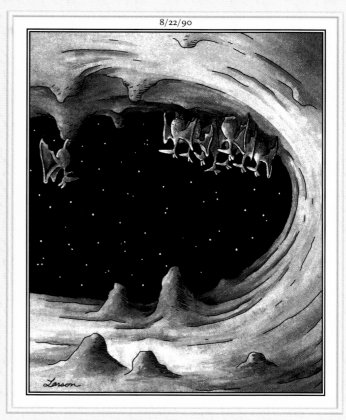

"And, during my term, I'm looking forward to a kinder, gentler cave, with a thousand points of darkness showing us the way."

8/27/90

Memo: Tonight I strike! Death to the left hand! Death! Death! Death!

Innocent and carefree, Stuart's left hand didn't know what the right was doing.

8/23/90

Rick

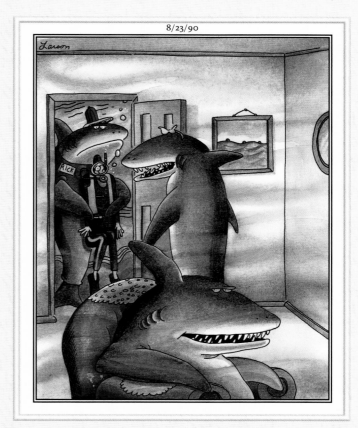

"That *was* fast! ... Gunther! The Diver Delivery guy is here."

8/17/90

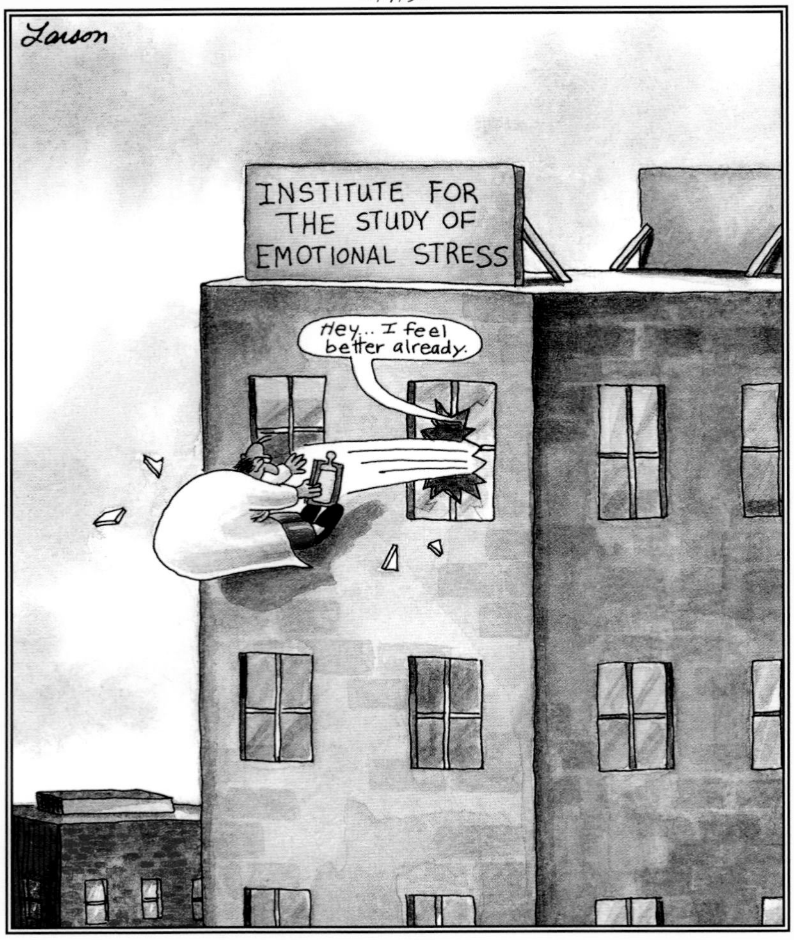
Larson
INSTITUTE FOR THE STUDY OF EMOTIONAL STRESS
Hey... I feel better already.

8/24/90

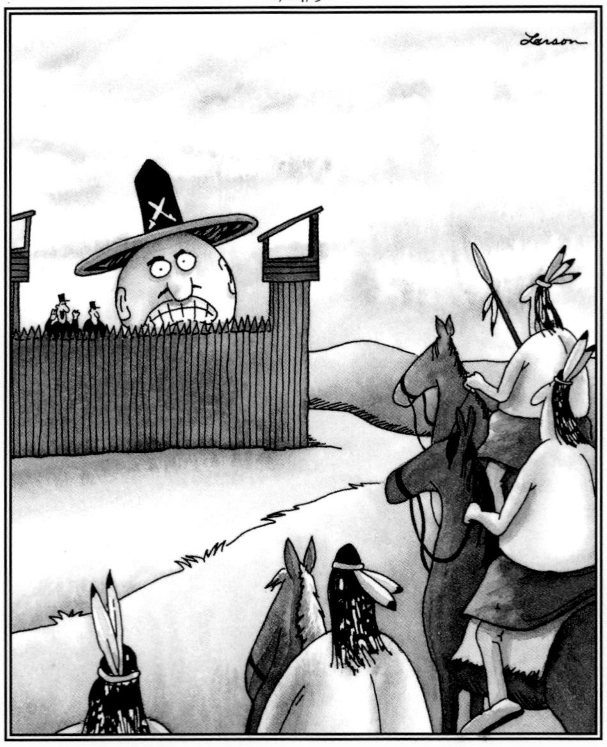
Larson

"Hey! What's the matter? ... There's only *three* of us here! C'mon! ... It's gonna be darrrrrrk soon!"

8/28/90

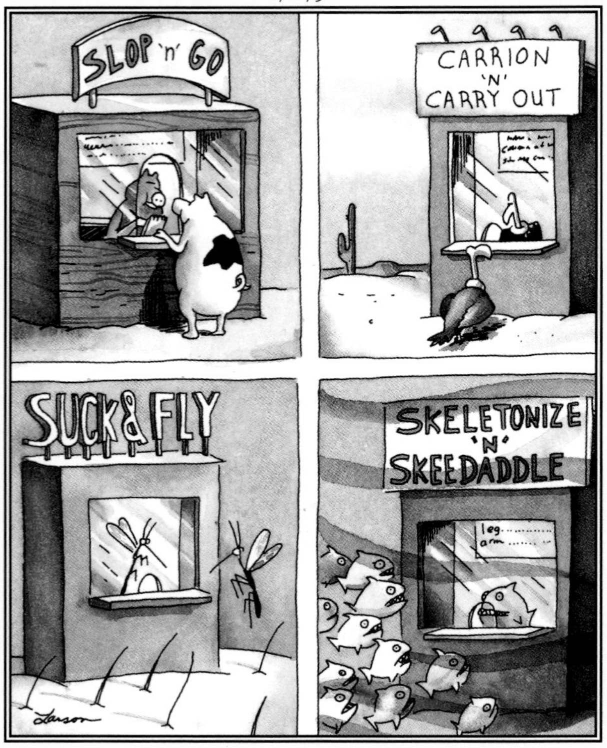
SLOP 'n' GO
CARRION 'N' CARRY OUT
SUCK & FLY
SKELETONIZE 'N' SKEEDADDLE
Larson

Animal fast-food joints

8/20/90

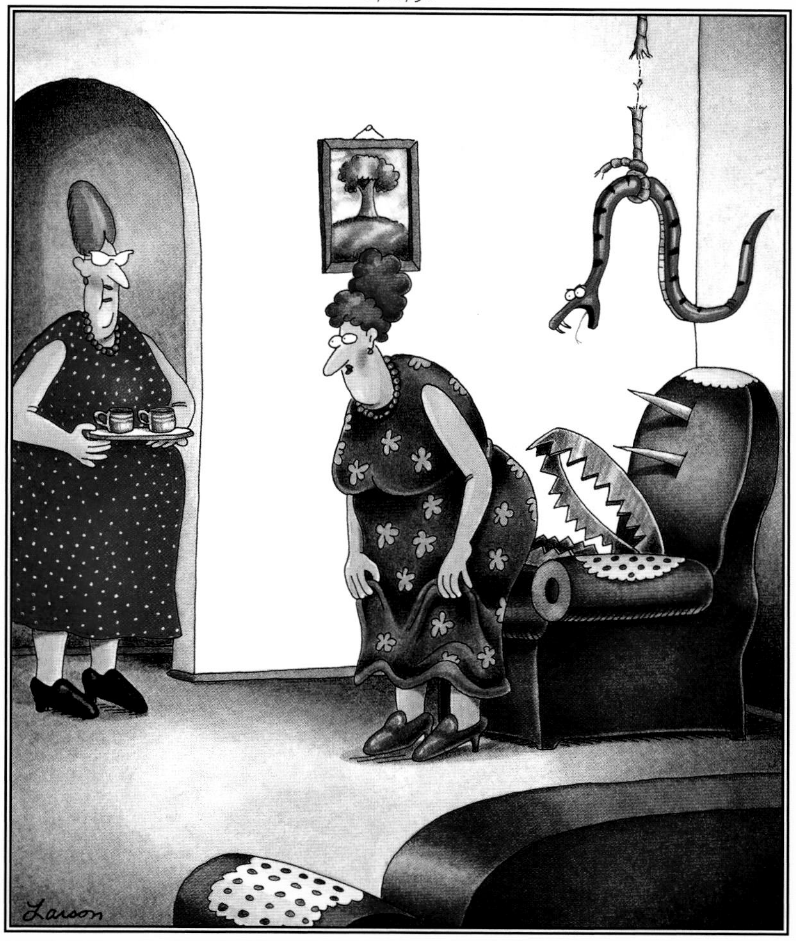

"Oh, wait, Doreen—don't sit there. ...
That chair's just not safe."

8/30/90

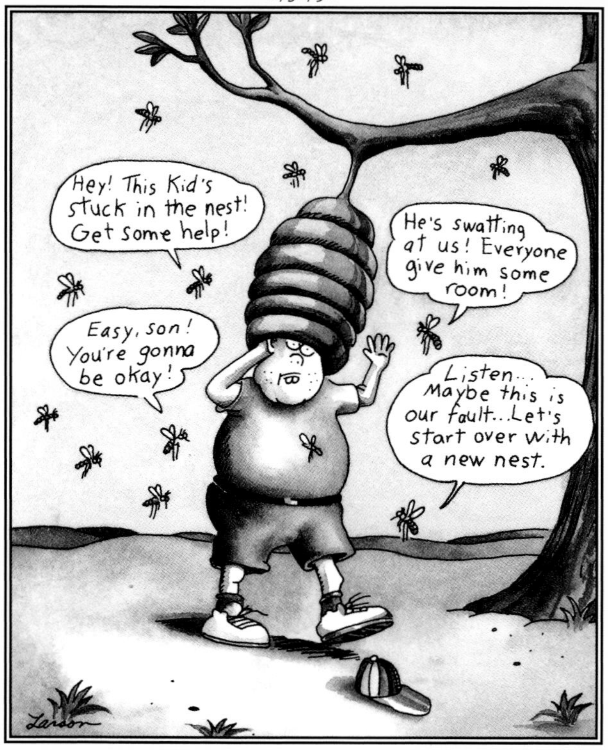
Hey! This Kid's stuck in the nest! Get some help!
He's swatting at us! Everyone give him some room!
Easy, son! You're gonna be okay!
Listen... Maybe this is our fault...Let's start over with a new nest.

Hornet goody two-shoes

8/31/90

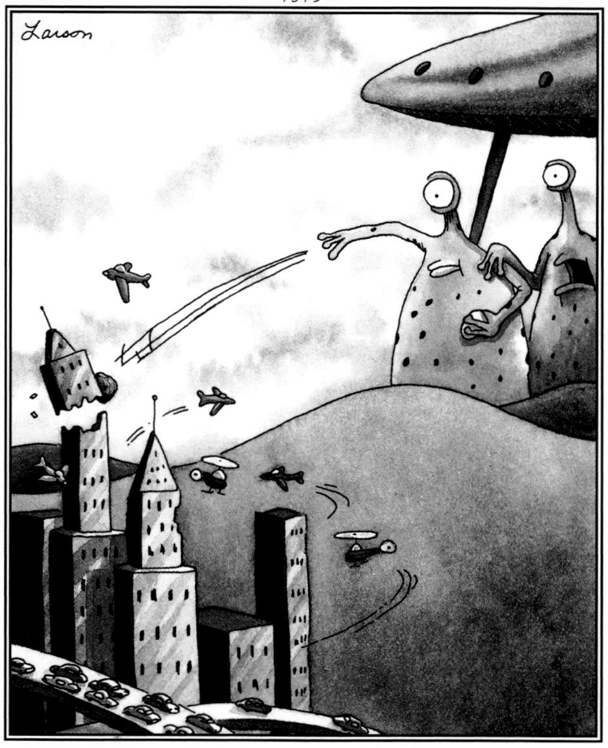

"Ooo! *That* one got 'em stirred up,
Zangorn! Let's blow!"

8/29/90

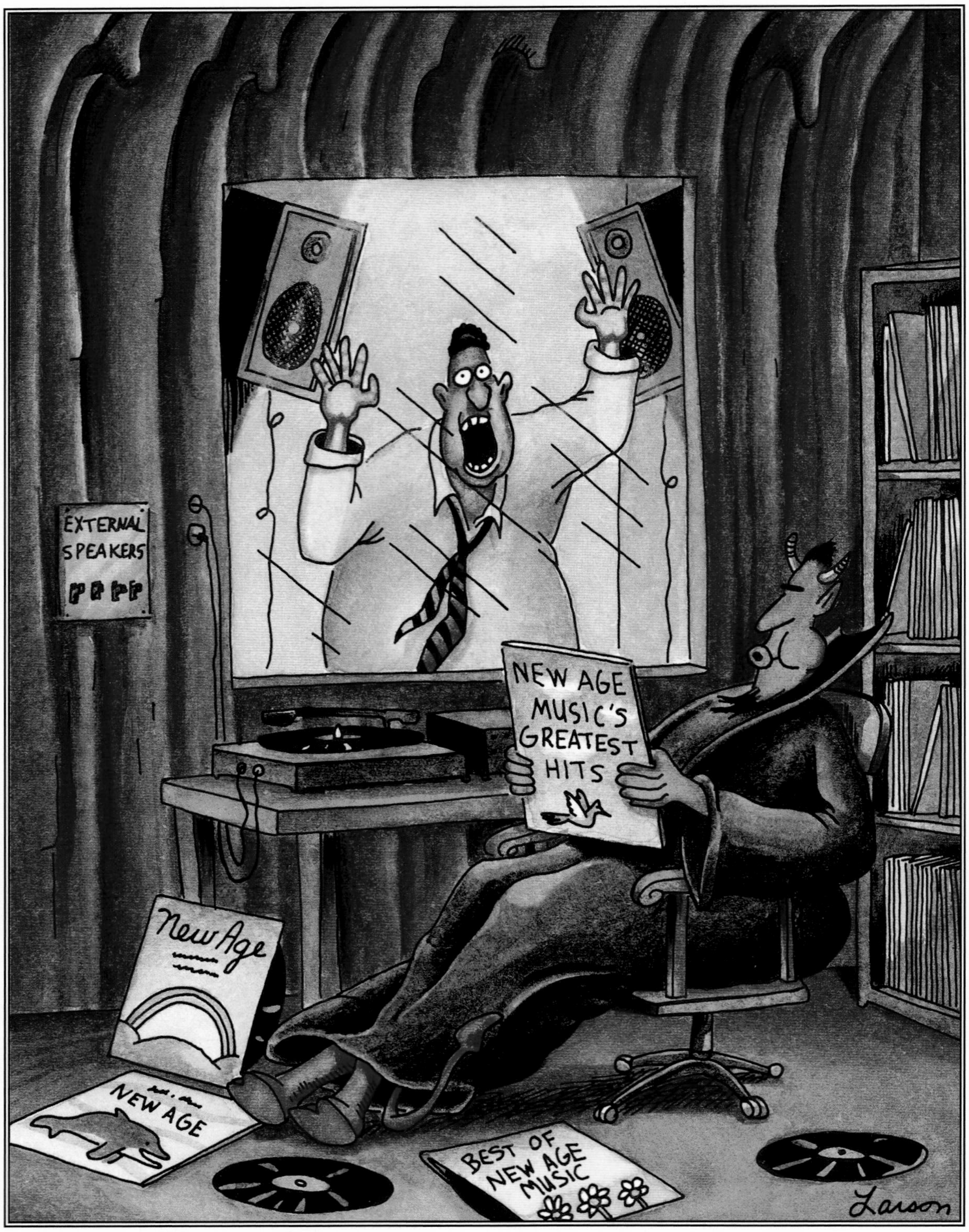
EXTERNAL
SPEAKERS
NEW AGE
MUSIC'S
GREATEST
HITS
New Age
NEW AGE
BEST OF
NEW AGE
MUSIC
Larson

Charlie Parker's private hell

Editor's note: Gary leaves for a one-month vacation.

10/1/90

Larson
BETTER COOP REALTY

"You're in luck! This place just came on the market a few days ago. ... The previous owners had their heads chopped off."

10/2/90

Dang it, Henry! I'm tired of yelling at these brats!.. They're your kids too, y'know!
DAILY BUGLE
Larson

A day in the Invisible Man's household

10/3/90

ONLY
Larson

Centipede parking lots

10/12/90

Larson
Thank God. I'm saved!

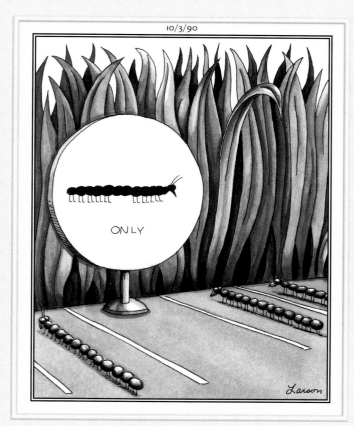

10/4/90

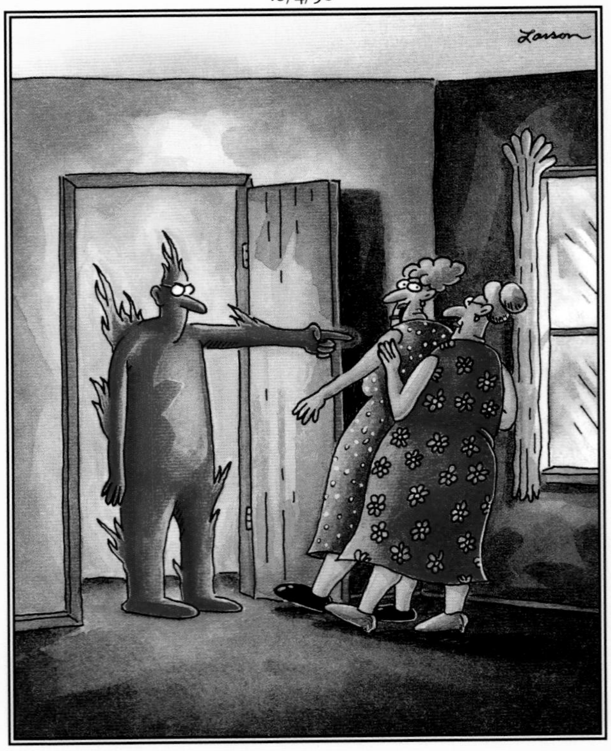
Larson

"Step back, Loretta! ... It's a red-hot poker!"

10/5/90

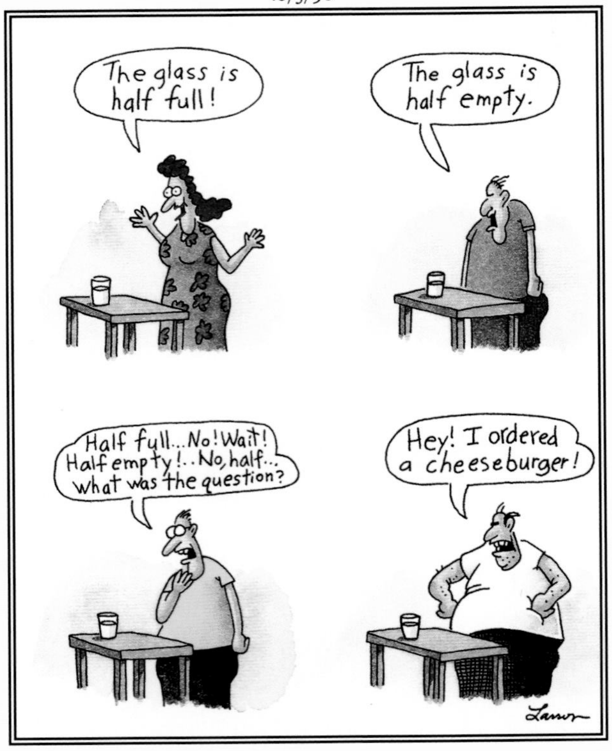
The glass is half full!
The glass is half empty.
Half full...No! Wait! Half empty!..No, half... what was the question?
Hey! I ordered a cheeseburger!
Larson

The four basic personality types

10/8/90

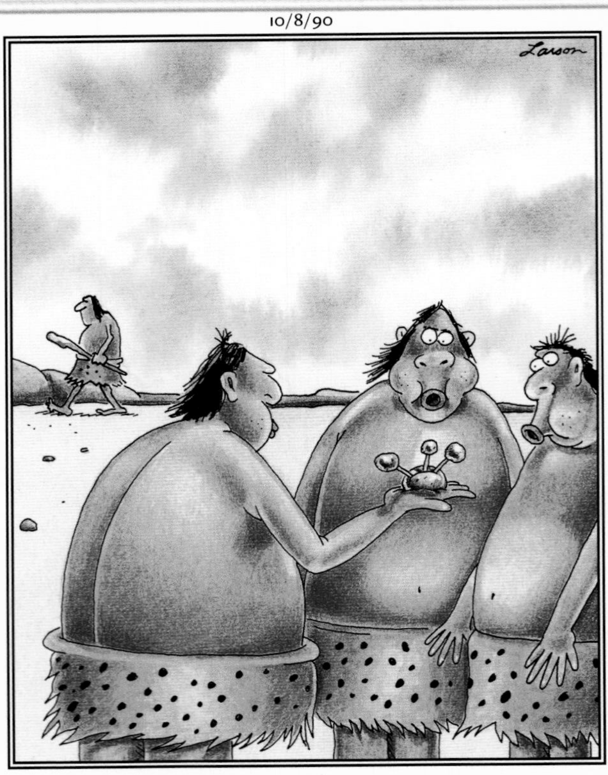
Larson

Danook shows off his Swiss Army Rock.

10/9/90

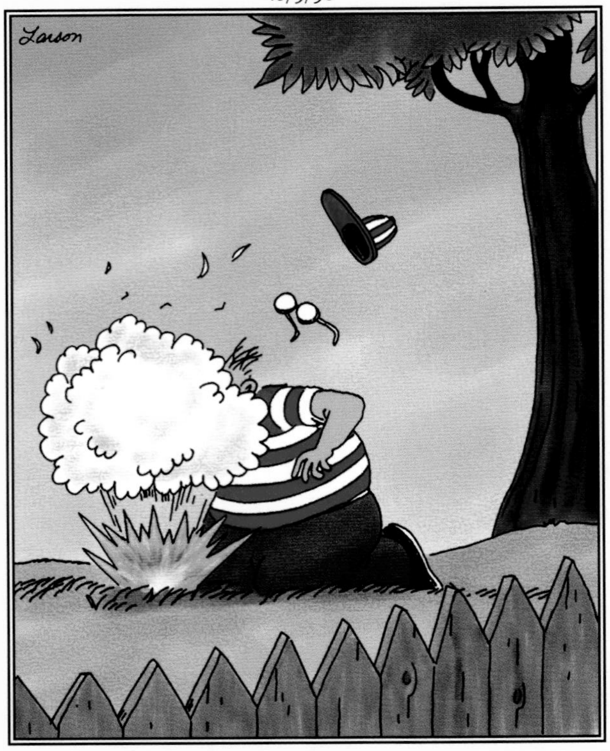
Larson

Each time the click beetle righted itself, Kyle would flip it over again—until something went dreadfully wrong.

10/17/90

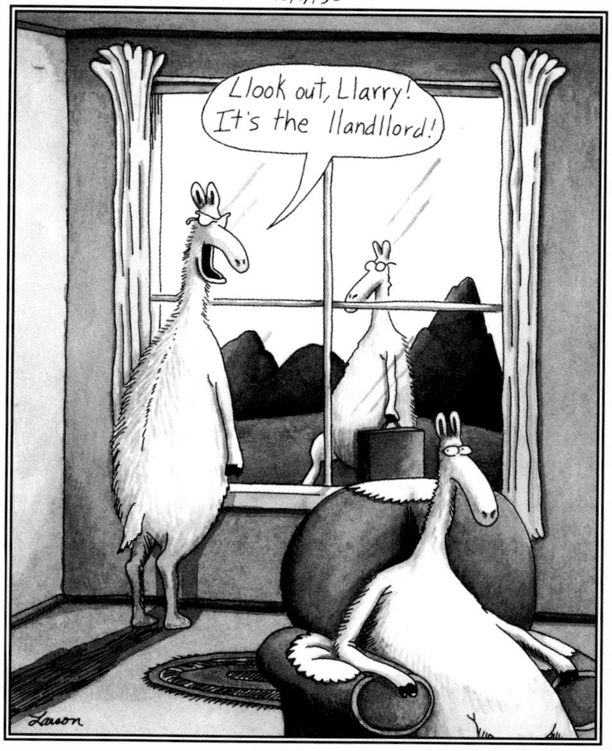
Llook out, Llarry! It's the llandllord!
Larson

Llamas at home

10/19/90

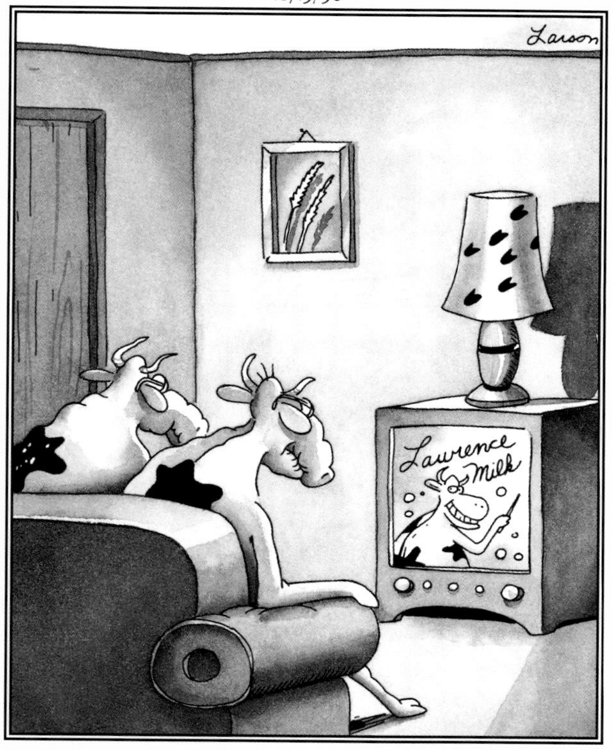
Larson
Lawrence Milk

10/16/90

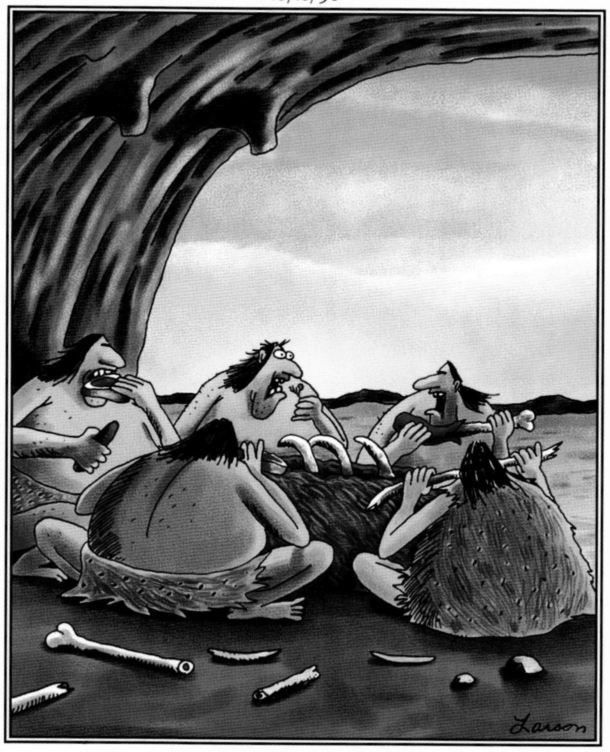
Larson

"Zak! Don't eat parsley! ... Just for looks!"

10/11/90

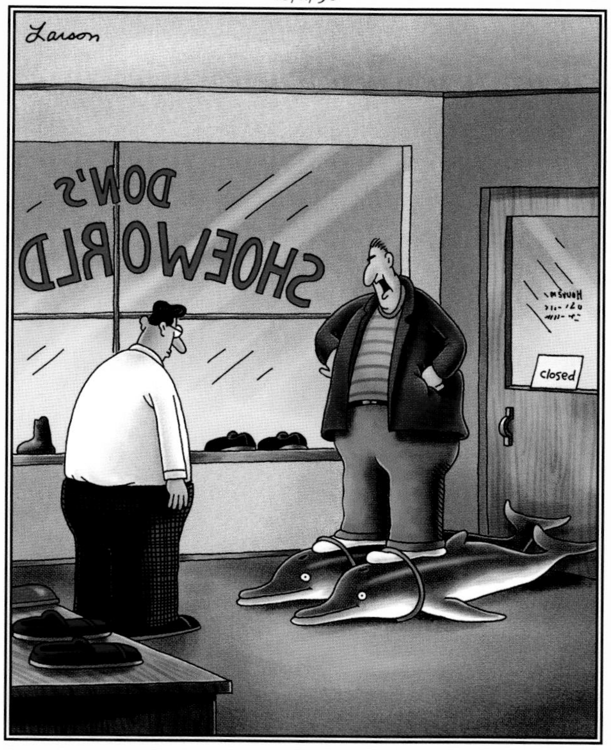
Larson
closed

"Listen—I bought these here yesterday, and the dang things won't stop squeaking!"

10/10/90

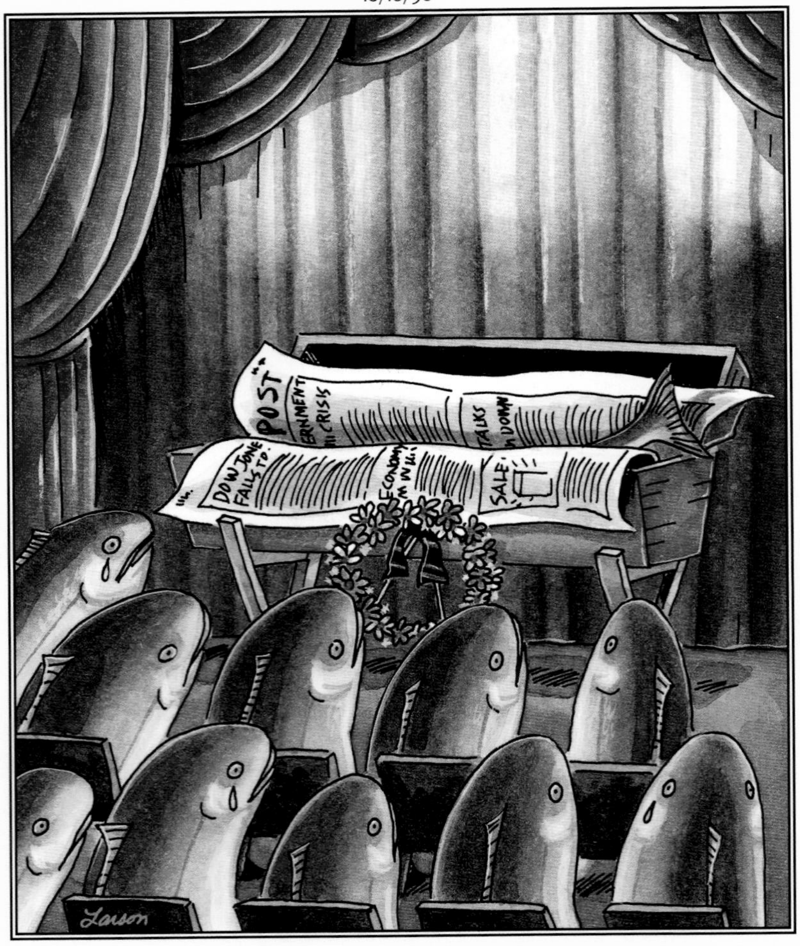
POST
SALE
Larson

Fish funerals

10/15/90

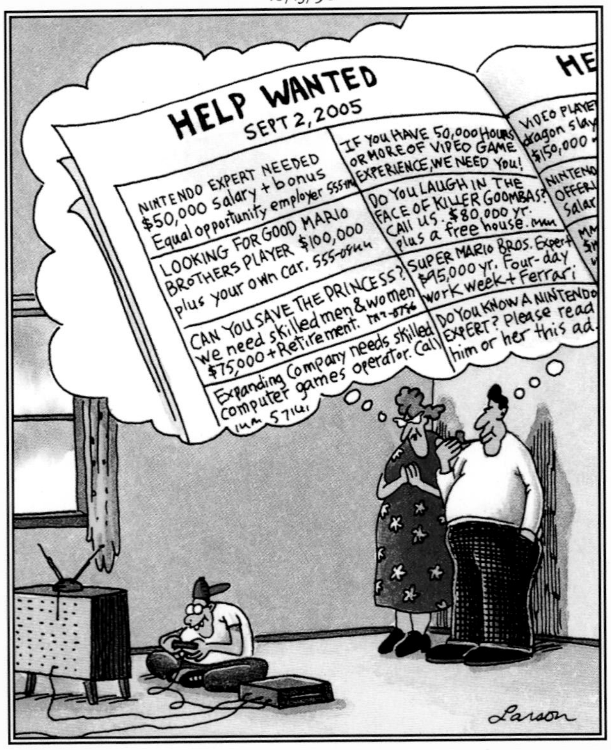
HELP WANTED
SEPT 2, 2005
NINTENDO EXPERT NEEDED $50,000 salary + bonus Equal opportunity employer
LOOKING FOR GOOD MARIO BROTHERS PLAYER $100,000 plus your own car.
CAN YOU SAVE THE PRINCESS? We need skilled men & women $75,000 + Retirement.
Expanding Company needs skilled computer games operator. Call
IF YOU HAVE 50,000 HOURS OR MORE OF VIDEO GAME EXPERIENCE, WE NEED YOU!
DO YOU LAUGH IN THE FACE OF KILLER GOOMBAS? CALL US. $80,000 yr. plus a free house.
SUPER MARIO BROS. Expert $95,000 yr. Four-day work week + Ferrari
DO YOU KNOW A NINTENDO EXPERT? Please read him or her this ad.
Larson

Hopeful parents

10/18/90

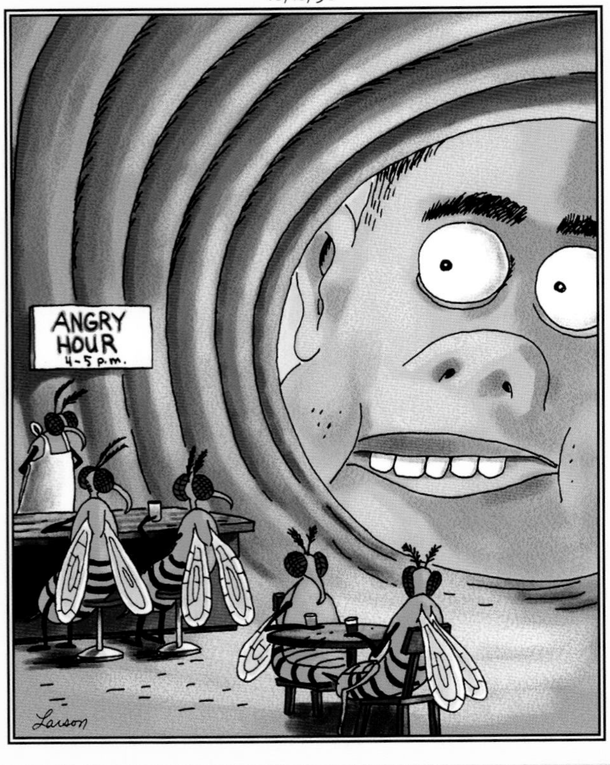
ANGRY HOUR
4-5 p.m.
Larson

It was foolish for Russell to approach the hornets' nest in the first place, but his timing was particularly bad.

10/25/90

Larson

"Barbara, you just have to come over and see all my eggs! The address is: Doris Griswold, 5 feet 4 inches, 160 pounds, brown eyes— I'm in her hair."

10/31/90

Larson

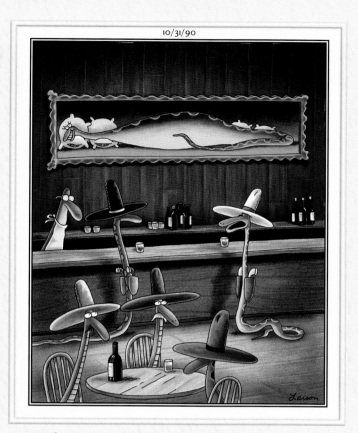

"Who are we kidding, Luke? We know this is going to be just another standoff."

10/22/90

Larson
ED'S
JACKHAMMER
SCHOOL

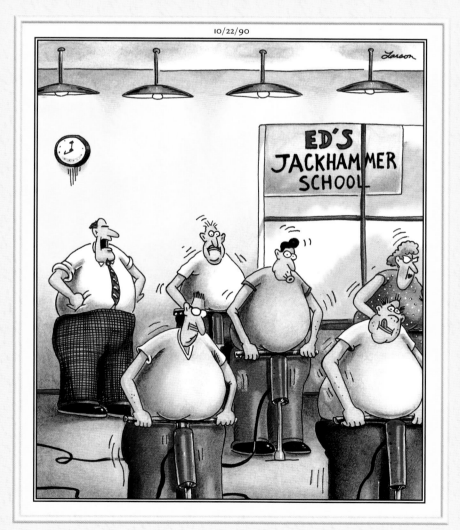

"C'mon! Keep those stomachs over the handles! Let the fat do the work! Let the fat do the work! ... That's it!"

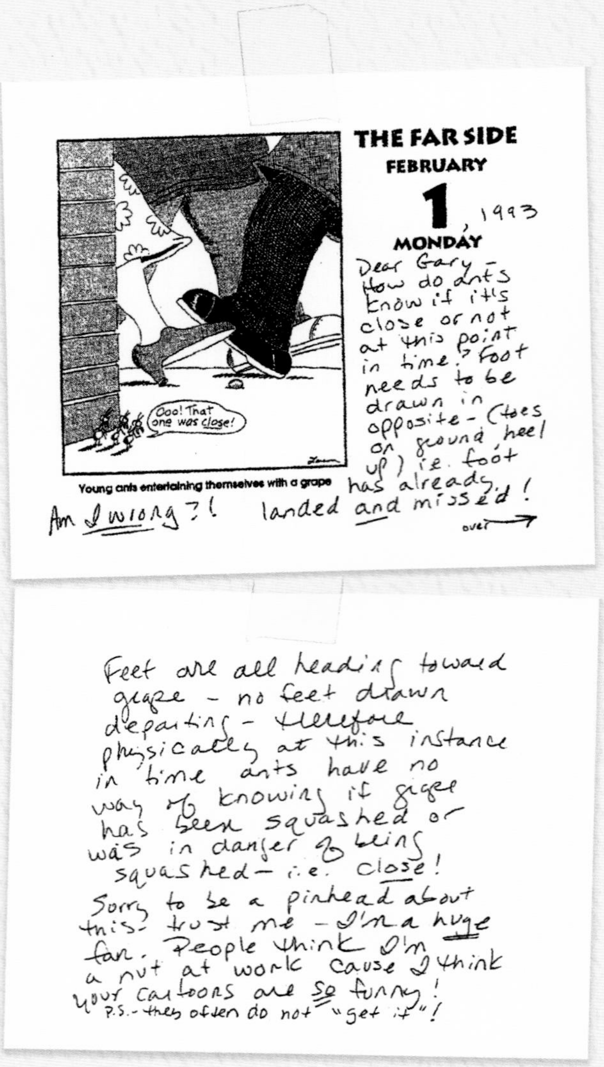
THE FAR SIDE
FEBRUARY
1, 1993
MONDAY

Ooo! That one was close!

Young ants entertaining themselves with a grape

Dear Gary – How do ants know if it's close or not at this point in time? Foot needs to be drawn in opposite – (toes on ground heel up) i.e. foot has already landed and missed! Am I wrong?!

over →

Feet are all heading toward grape – no feet drawn departing – therefore physically at this instance in time ants have no way of knowing if grape has been squashed or was in danger of being squashed – i.e. close! Sorry to be a pinhead about this – trust me – I'm a huge fan. People think I'm a nut at work cause I think your cartoons are so funny!

P.S. – they often do not "get it"!

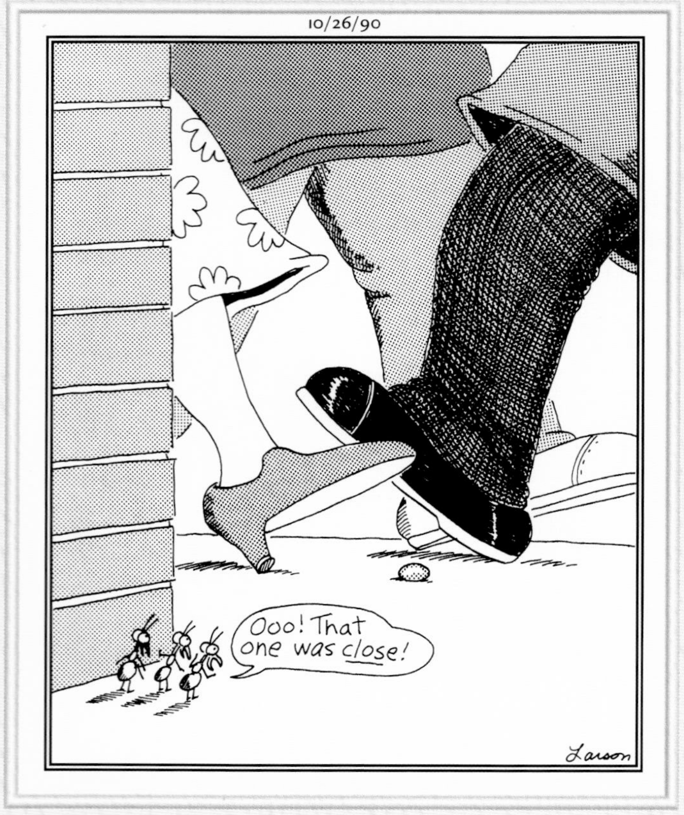
10/26/90
Ooo! That one was close!
Larson

Young ants entertaining themselves with a grape

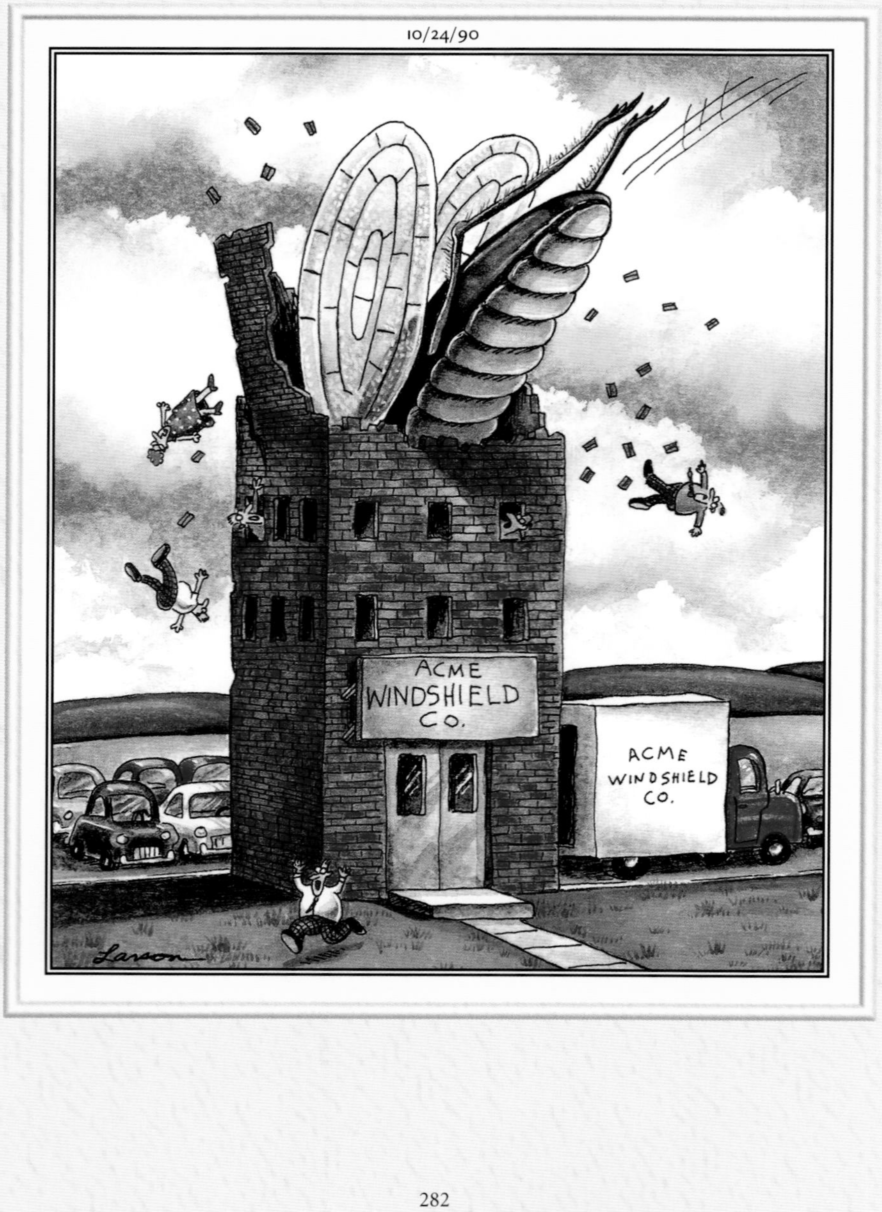
10/24/90
ACME WINDSHIELD CO.
ACME WINDSHIELD CO.
Larson

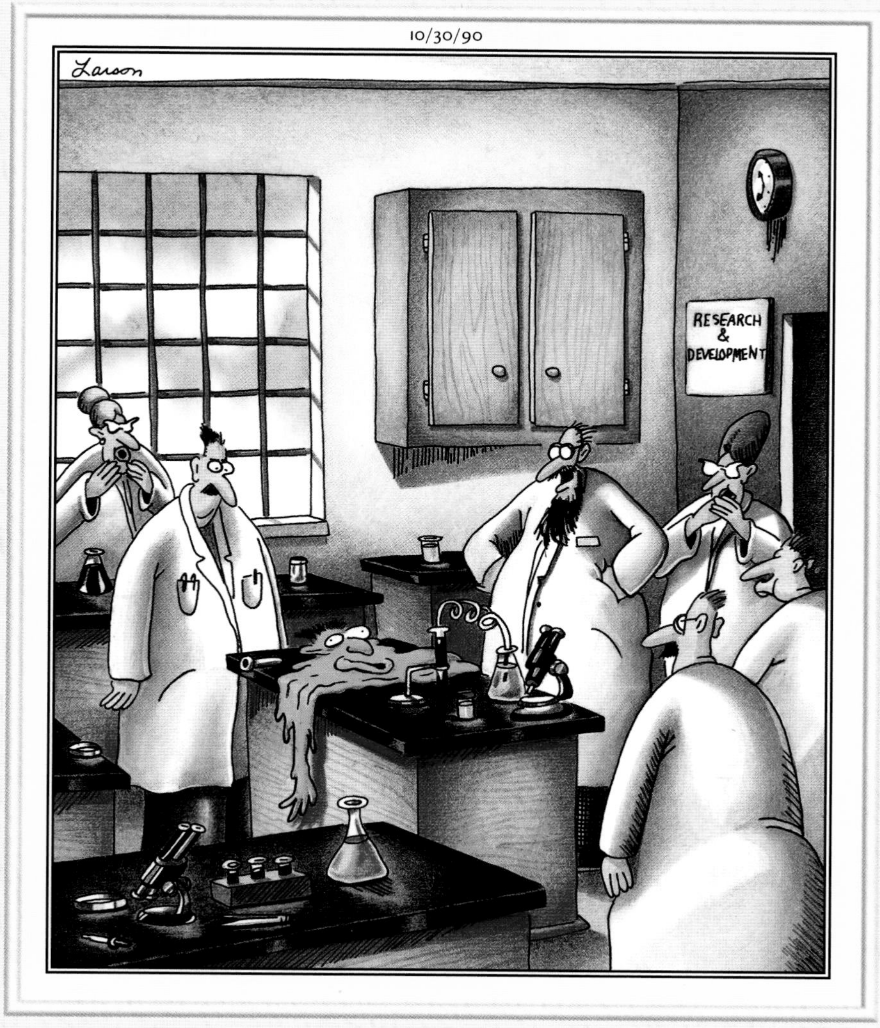
10/30/90
Larson
RESEARCH & DEVELOPMENT

"My God! It *is* Professor Dickle! ... Weinberg, see if you can make out what the devil he was working on, and the rest of you get back to your stations."

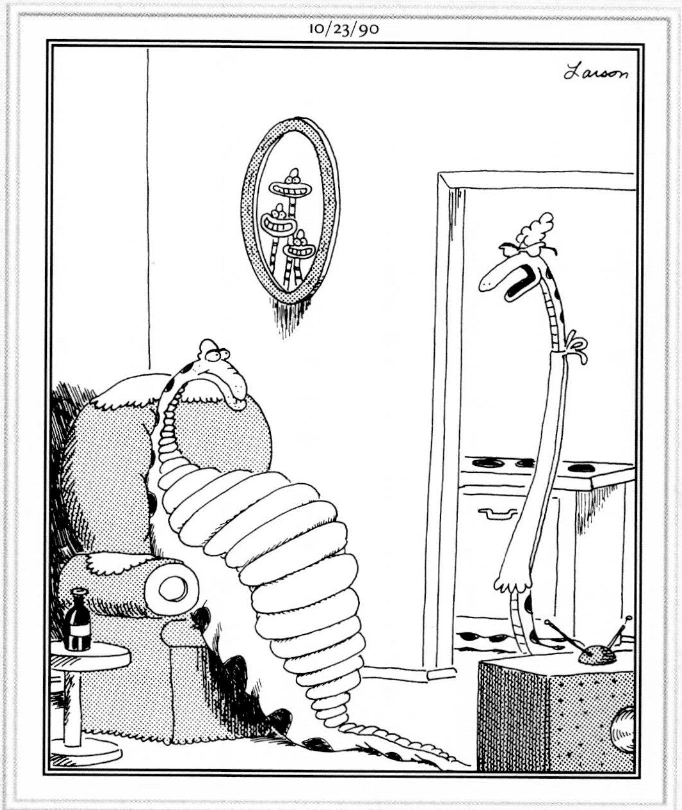
10/23/90
Larson

"Joe! You went and ate the pig I was going to serve this evening to the MacIntyres? ... Well, you just disgorge it—it should still be okay."

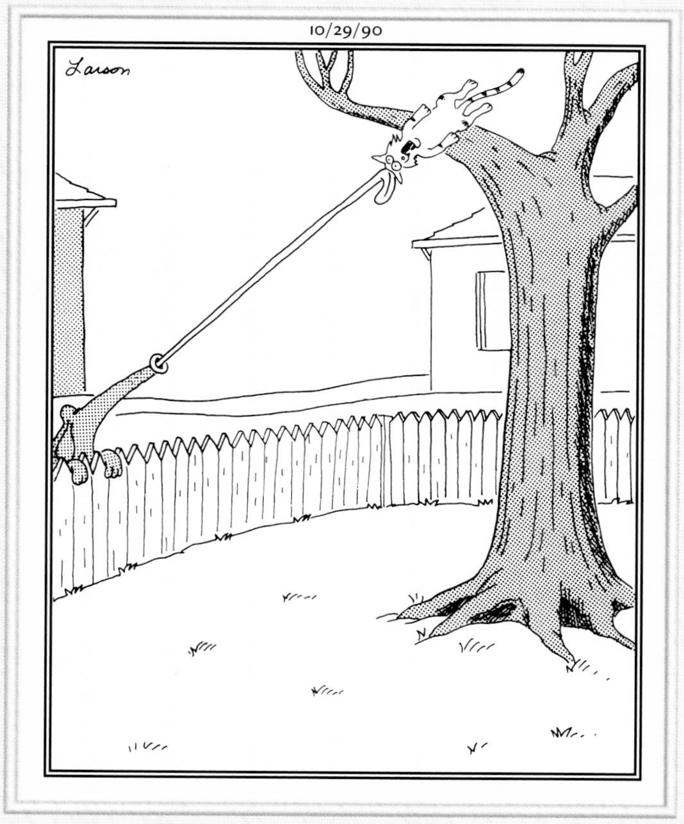
10/29/90
Larson

Aarddogs

11/1/90

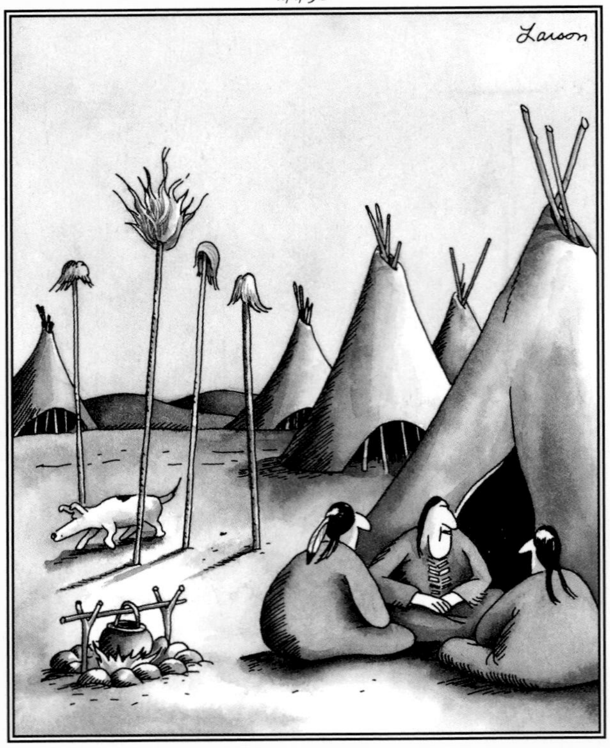

The fate of Don King's great-great-grandfather

11/5/90

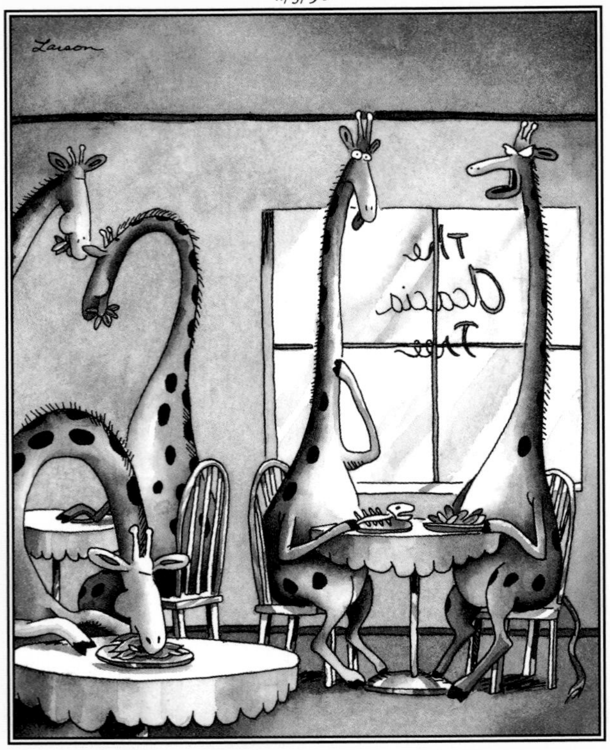

"Well, if there's a bone stuck in your throat, you deserve it! ... Do you see anyone else around here stupid enough to order fish?"

11/2/90

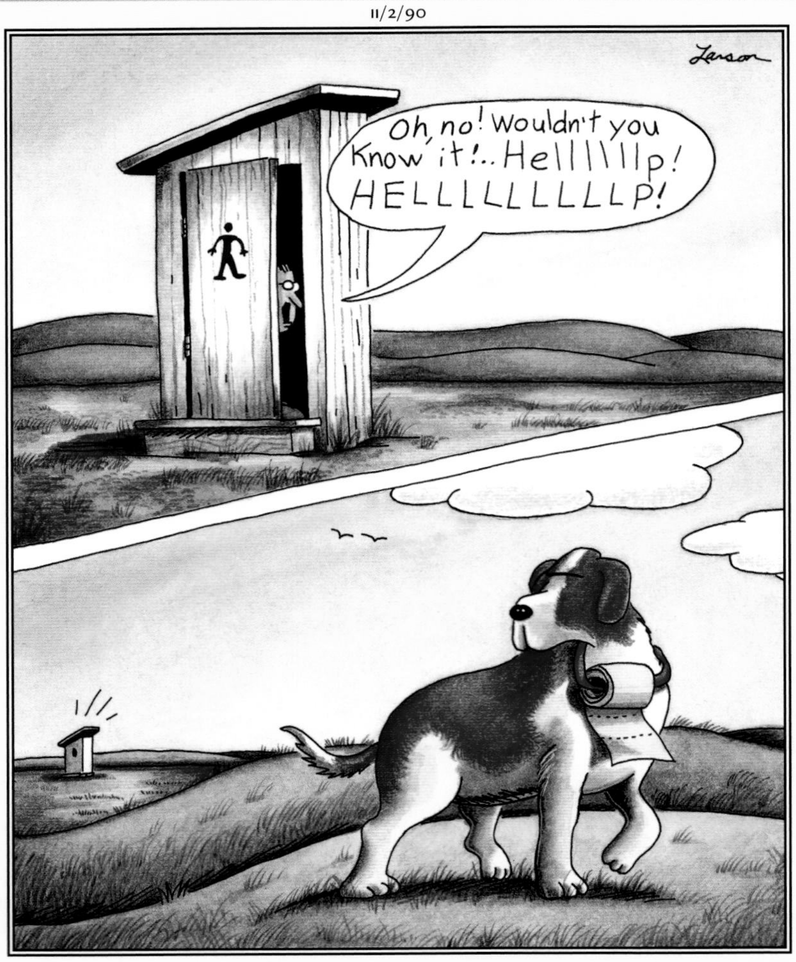
Oh, no! Wouldn't you Know it!.. Helllllllp! HELLLLLLLLLP!

Far away, on a hillside, a very specialized breed of dog heard the cry of distress.

11/7/90

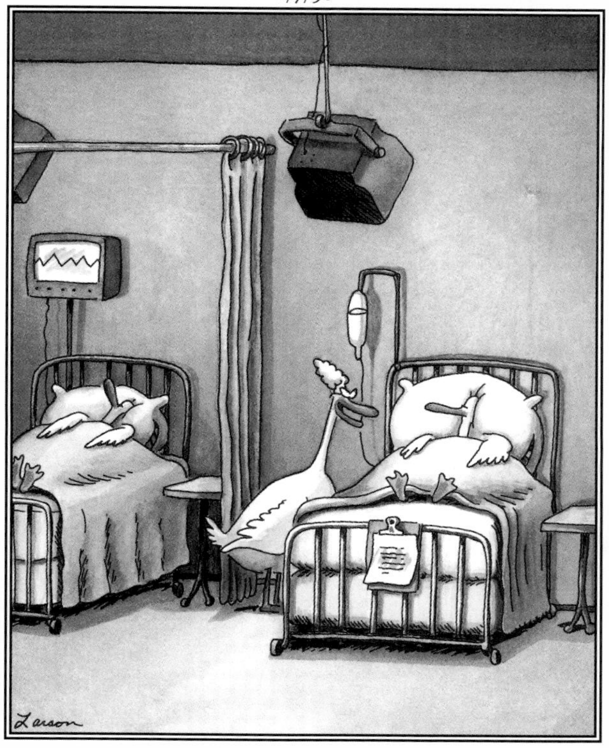

"It's just a miracle you pulled through, George. ... Why, it was only a few hours ago the whole family was deliberating on whether or not to wring your neck."

11/8/90

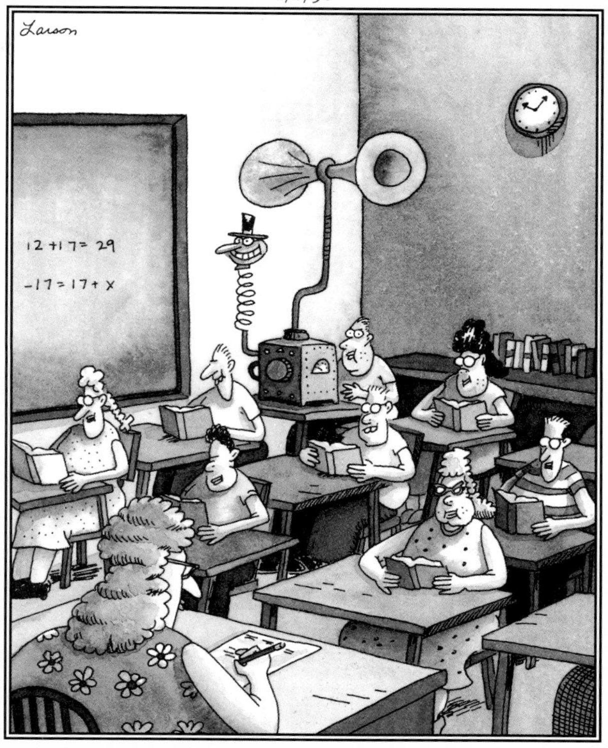
12 + 17 = 29
-17 = 17 + x

The class was quietly doing its lesson when Russell, suffering from problems at home, prepared to employ an attention-getting device.

11/12/90

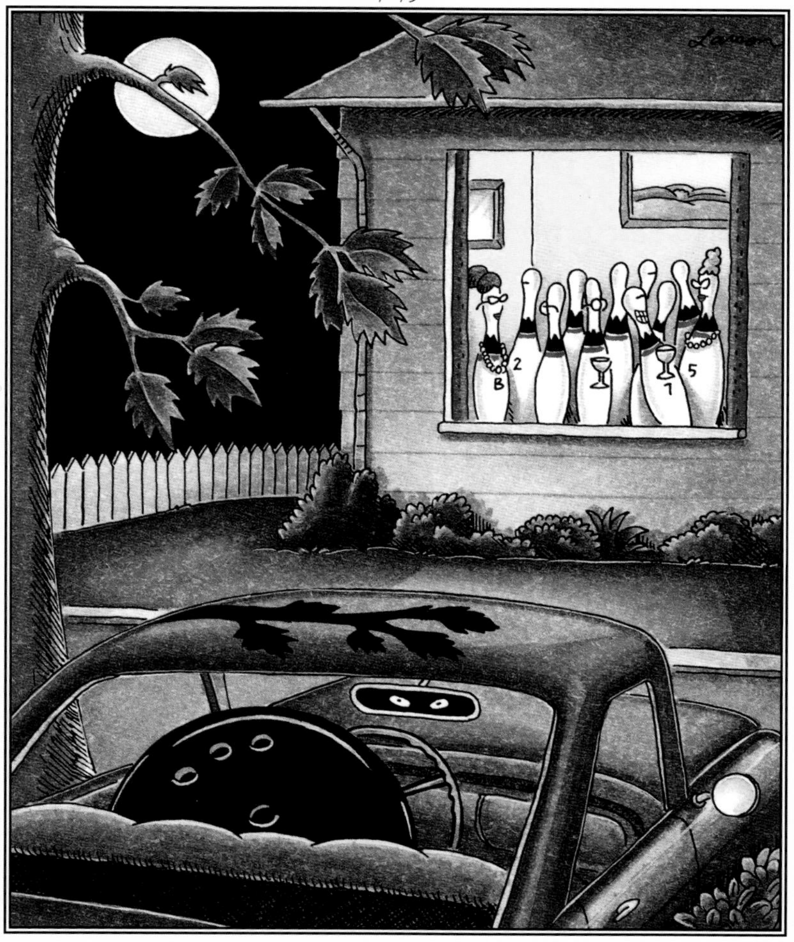

11/6/90

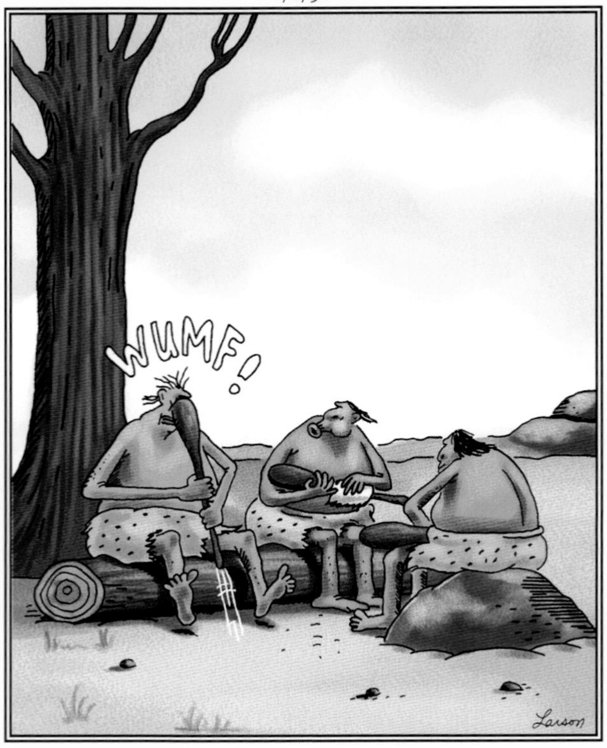
WUMF!
Larson

As the small band of hunter-gatherers sat around cleaning their weapons, one made the mistake of looking at his club straight on.

11/9/90

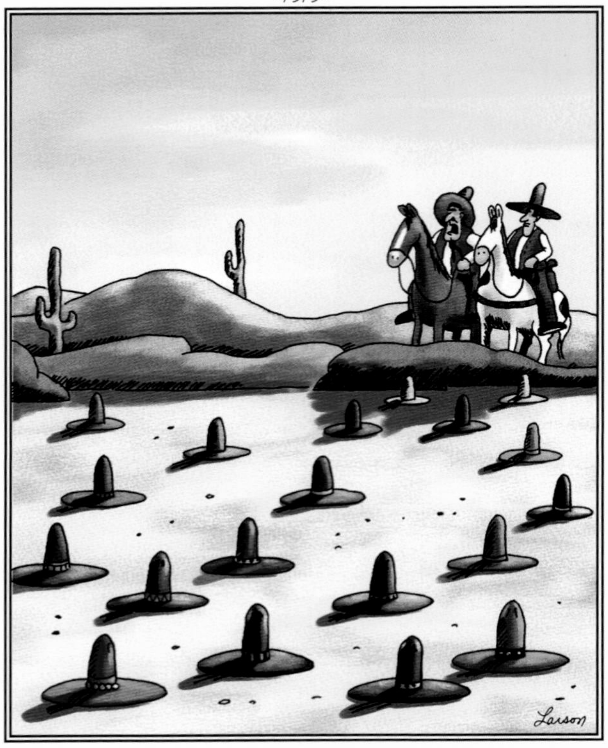
Larson

"We must be careful, Cisco! ... Thees could be the eenfamous Queeksand Beds of Chihuahua."

11/13/90

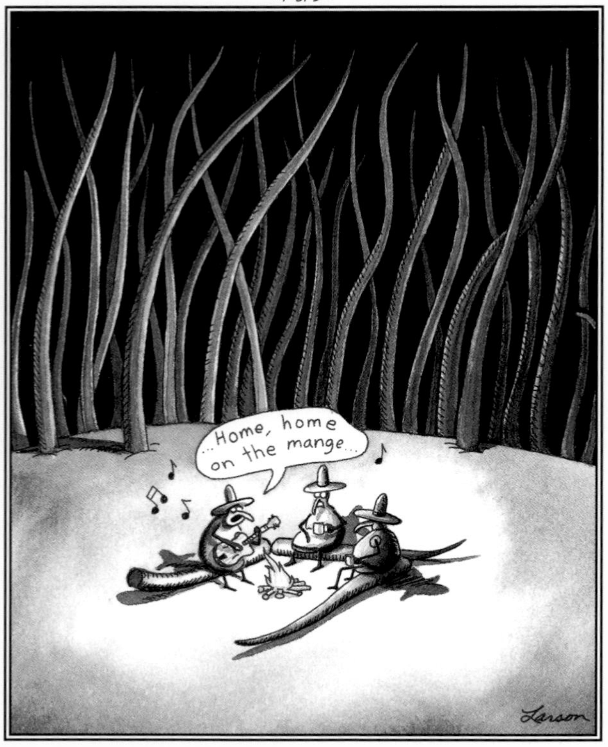
...Home, home on the mange...
Larson

Fleaboys

11/16/90

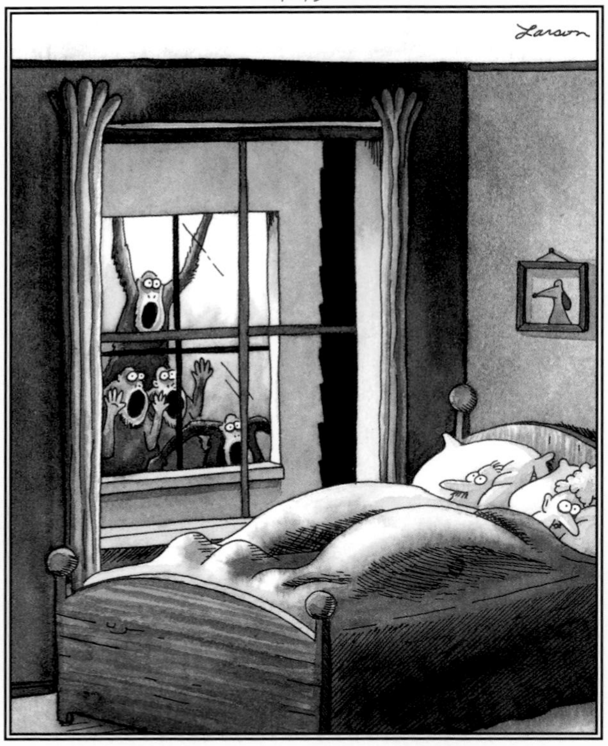
Larson

And so it went, night after night, year after year. In fact, the Hansens had been in a living hell ever since that fateful day the neighbor's "For Sale" sign had come down and a family of howler monkeys had moved in.

11/19/90

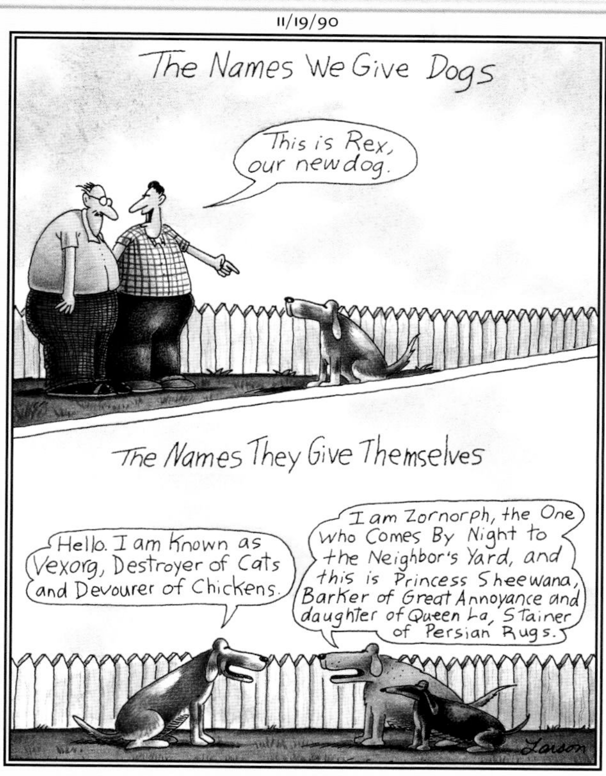
The Names We Give Dogs
This is Rex, our new dog.
The Names They Give Themselves
Hello. I am Known as Vexorg, Destroyer of Cats and Devourer of Chickens.
I am Zornorph, the One who Comes By Night to the Neighbor's Yard, and this is Princess Sheewana, Barker of Great Annoyance and daughter of Queen La, Stainer of Persian Rugs.
Larson

11/20/90

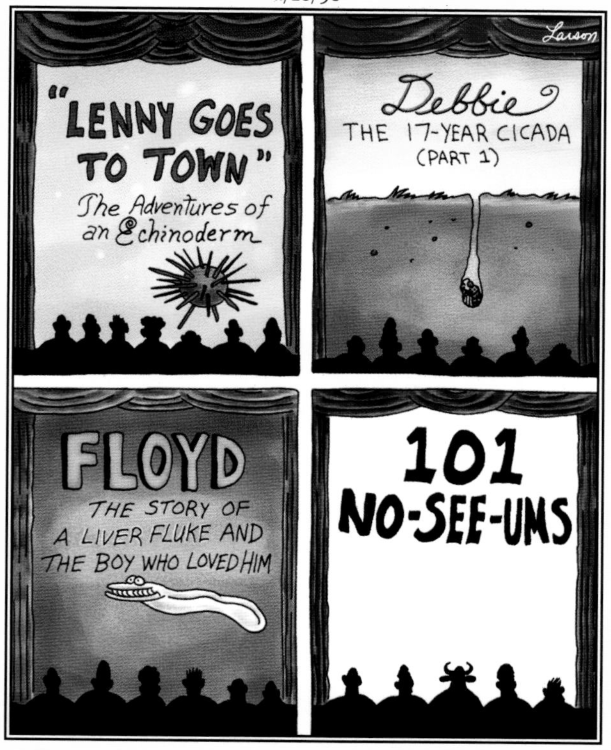
Larson
"LENNY GOES TO TOWN"
The Adventures of an Echinoderm
Debbie
THE 17-YEAR CICADA
(PART 1)
FLOYD
THE STORY OF A LIVER FLUKE AND THE BOY WHO LOVED HIM
101 NO-SEE-UMS

Nature films that Disney test-marketed but never released.

11/14/90

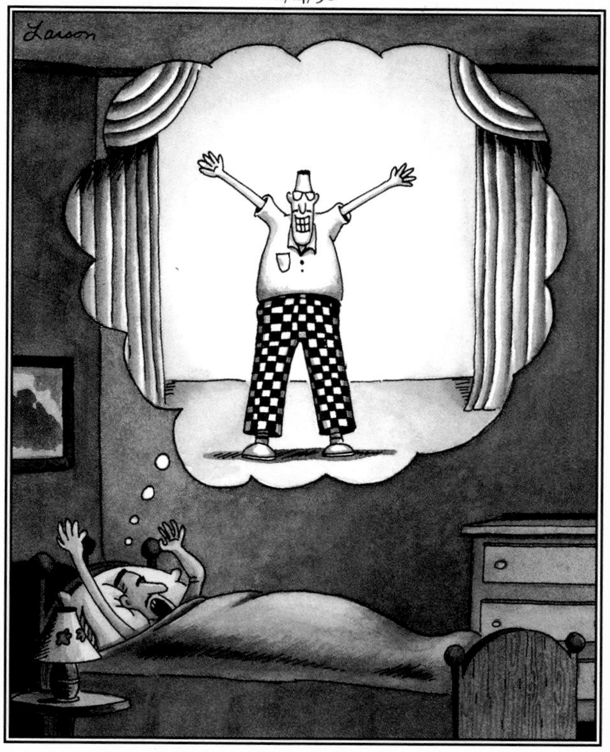
Larson

In a recurring nightmare, Arsenio Hall sees himself walk onstage wearing golf clothes.

11/15/90

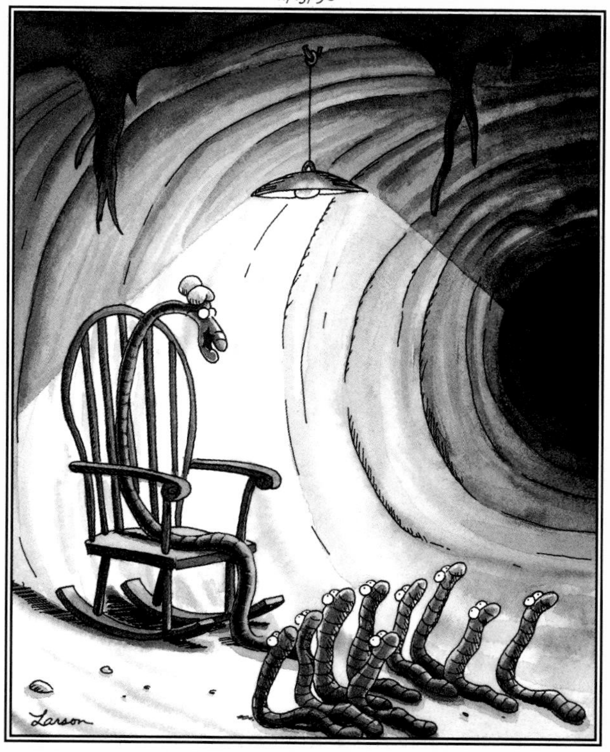
Larson

"That story again? ... Well, one stormy night, when the whole family was asleep, your grandfather quietly rose from his bed, took an ax, and made all you little grandkids."

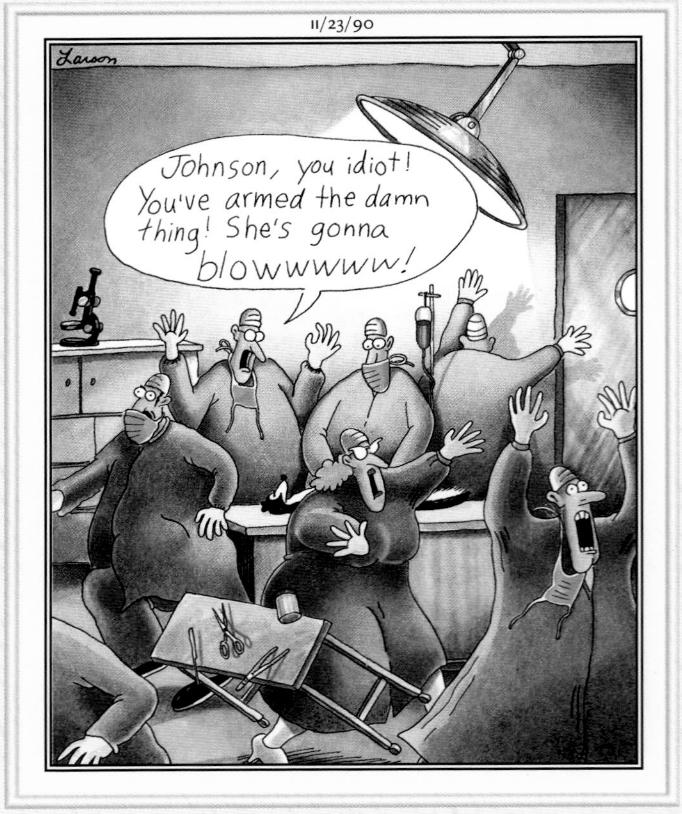
11/23/90
Johnson, you idiot! You've armed the damn thing! She's gonna blowwwwww!

Feb. 22, 1952: Veterinarians attempt the first skunk de-scenting operation.

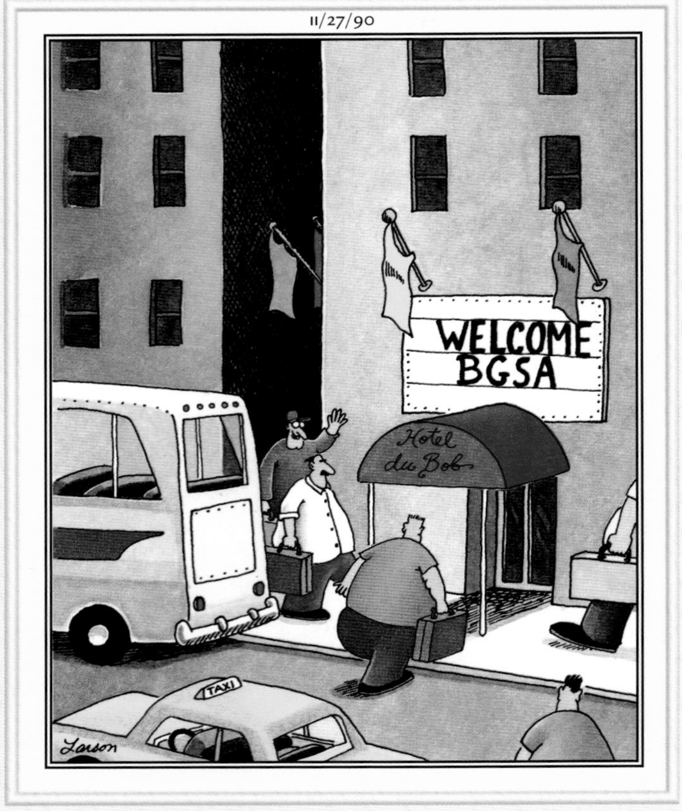
11/27/90
WELCOME BGSA
Hotel du Bob
TAXI

Buffalo, N.Y., Nov. 2-5: The annual convention of the Big Galoot Society of America

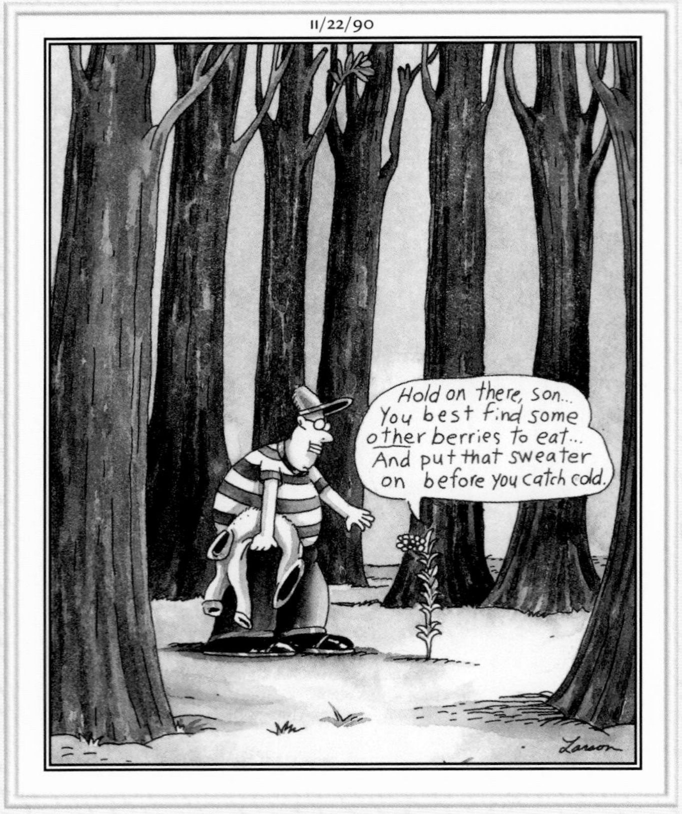
11/22/90
Hold on there, son... You best find some other berries to eat... And put that sweater on before you catch cold.

Luckily, Eddie had stumbled upon a rare variety of deadly nightshade, the amicable *Atropa belladonna congenialocus*. (Later that same day, however, he blundered into some poison oak—a flat-out intolerant species.)

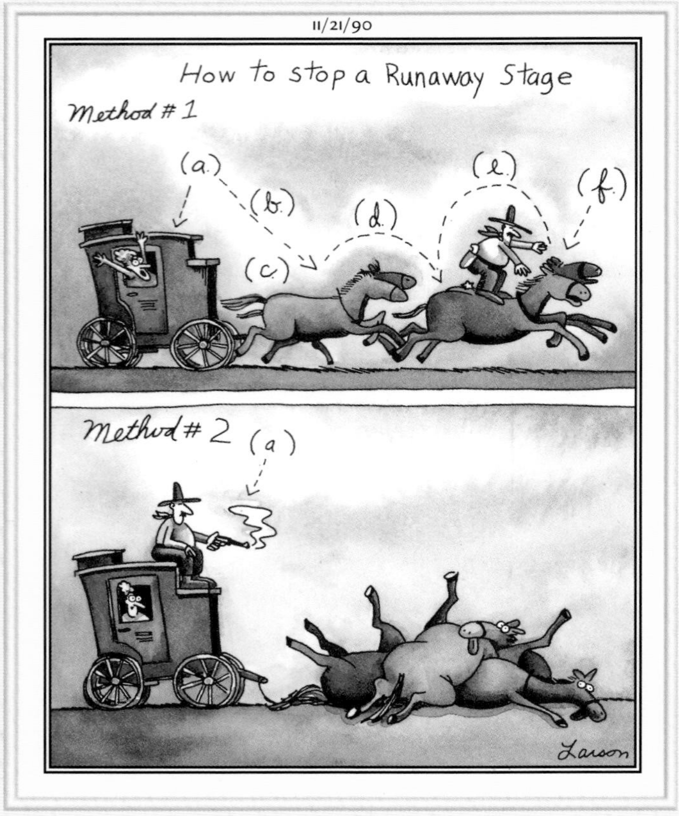
11/21/90
How to stop a Runaway Stage
Method #1
(a.)
(b.)
(c.)
(d.)
(e.)
(f.)
Method #2
(a)

From the book *Guide to Western Stuff*

11/29/90

~9~
Equine Medicine
DIAGNOSIS
TREATMENT
Broken leg
Infected eye
Splayed hoof
Runny nose
Fever
Open sores
closed sores
Swollen belly
Ornery
Swayback
Erratic heart
Hearing loss
Bad breath
Mane mange
Toothache
Nervousness
shoot
shoot
shoot
shoot
shoot
shoot
shoot
shoot
shoot
Larson

Like most veterinary students, Doreen breezes through chapter 9.

11/26/90

Man, I hate elevator music.
Larson

11/28/90

Larson

In the corner, Vance was putting the move on two females—unaware that his fake hood had begun to slip.

11/30/90

ACE
MARBLES
INC.
ACE MARBLES INC.
Larson

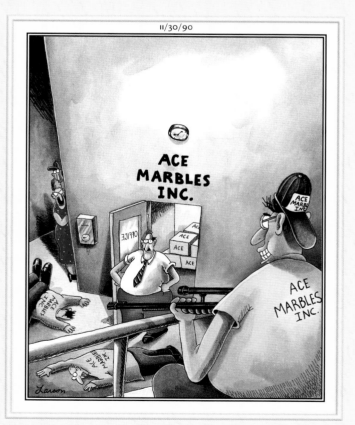

Misunderstanding his employees' screams of "Simmons has lost his marbles!" Mr. Wagner bursts from his office for the last time.

12/5/90

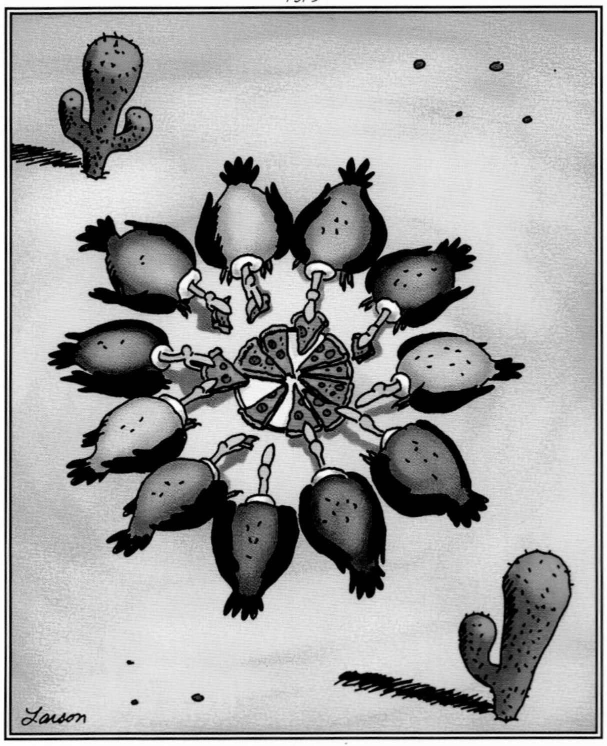
Larson

Perspectives in nature we rarely enjoy

12/10/90

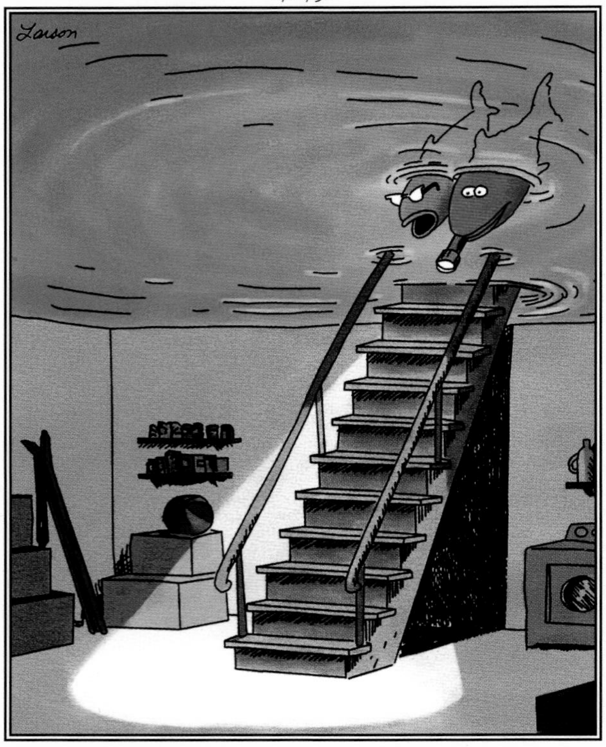
Larson

"Good heavens, John! Call someone! ...
The entire basement looks dry!"

12/4/90

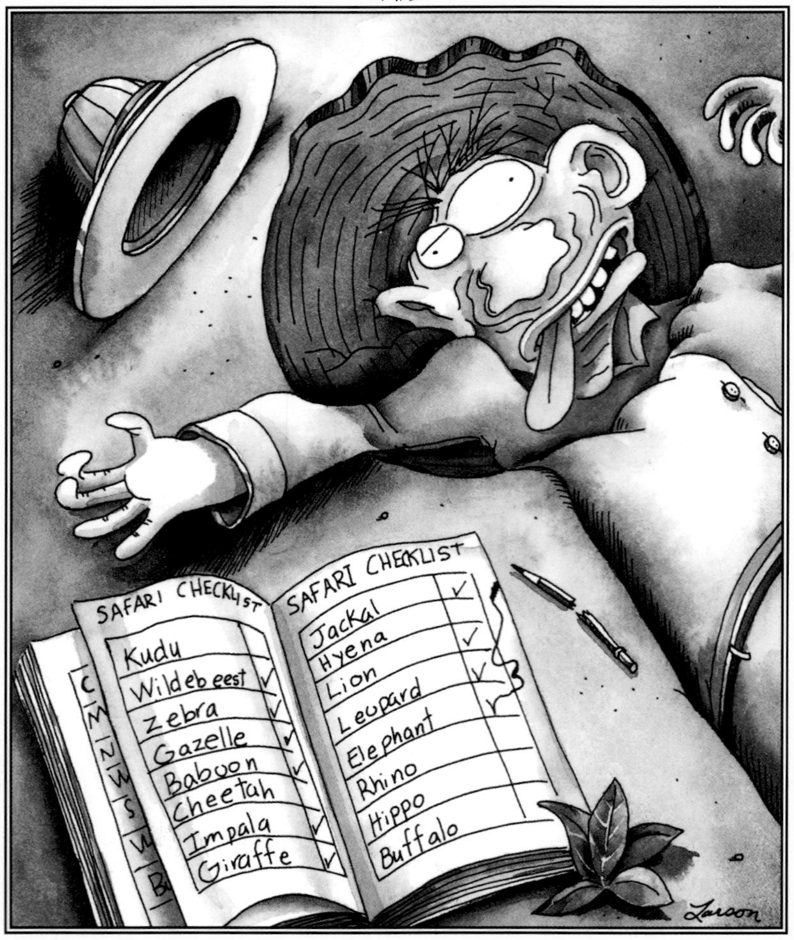
SAFARI CHECKLIST
Kudu
Wildebeest
Zebra
Gazelle
Baboon
Cheetah
Impala
Giraffe
SAFARI CHECKLIST
Jackal
Hyena
Lion
Leopard
Elephant
Rhino
Hippo
Buffalo
Larson

12/12/90

BIG BOB'S
BALLBEARINGS
BANANAS
ROLLER SKATES
&
FLOOR WAX,
INC.
OFFICE
Larson

12/11/90

hammer
anvil
stirrup
cuisinart
Larson

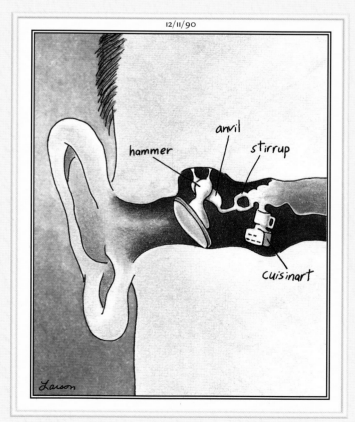

Professor Harold Rosenbloom's diagram of the middle ear, proposing his newly discovered fourth bone.

12/7/90

Larson
WOO WOO WOO WOO
WOO WOO WOO WOO...

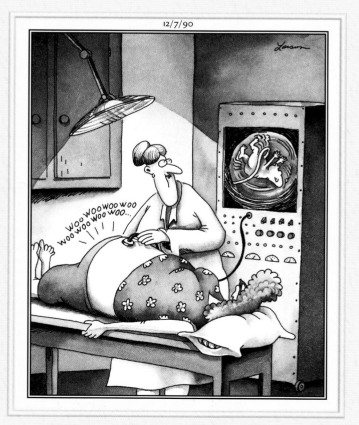

The prenatal development of Curly

"They're Neanderthals, Loona. ...
Every one of them."

"Idiot! ... You're standing on my foot!"

"Would you look at that? ... By thunder, you
couldn't do that in *our* day—yessiree, the
rocks were just a lot heavier back then."

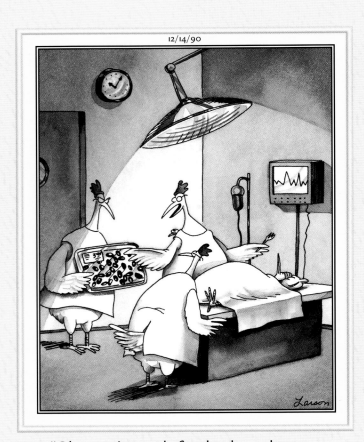

"Okay, we're ready for the donor heart. ...
Oh, very good. I see we once again have
a big selection."

12/17/90

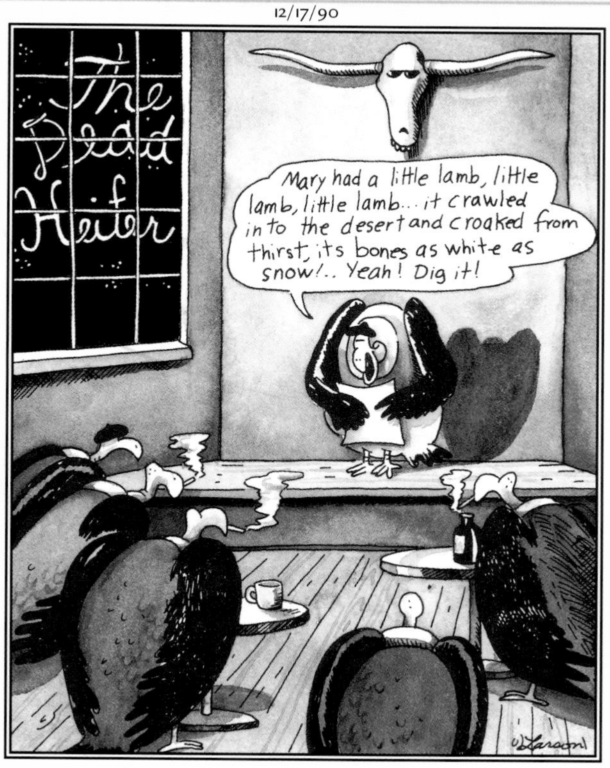
The Dead Heifer
Mary had a little lamb, little lamb, little lamb... it crawled into the desert and croaked from thirst, its bones as white as snow!.. Yeah! Dig it!

Buzzard beakniks

12/18/90

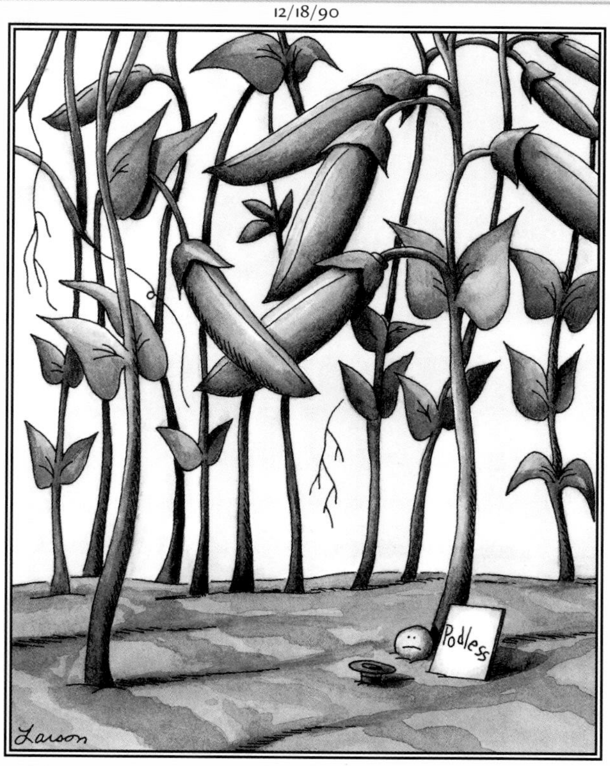
Podless

12/19/90

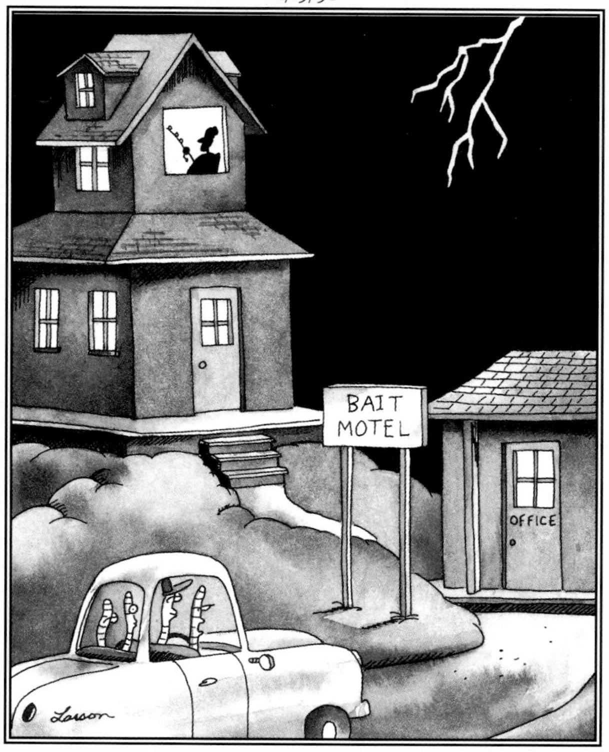
BAIT MOTEL
OFFICE

"Say, Anthony, this looks like a pleasant little place."

12/20/90

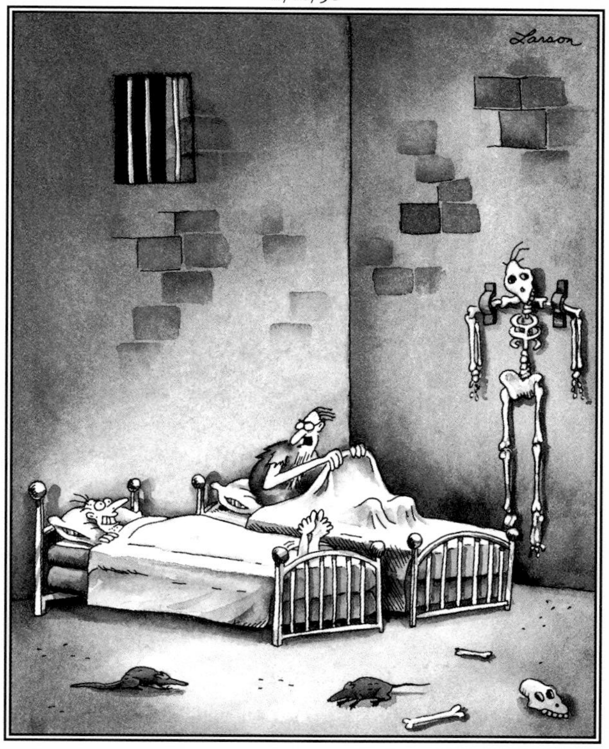

"Short-sheeted my bed, didn't you, Jenkins? ... You know, I could make your life miserable, too!"

12/21/90

"Falls down with the touch of a feather!"
COLLAPSIBLE PIANO
MR. ROSY CHEEKS CENTRIFUGE
Hi, MOM HIGH CHAIR
Brahma Buddy
Larson

Baby toys and gifts to avoid this Christmas

12/25/90

Larson

Far Side Lite: Not funny, but better for you.

12/24/90

Larson
FLY FLOSS

12/28/90

Larson

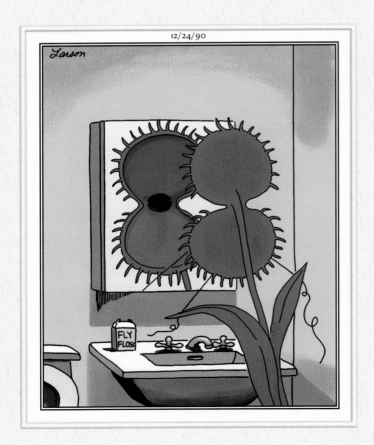

"Ben—what d'ya say we turn the power off for a while and let the little guy roam around?"

12/27/90

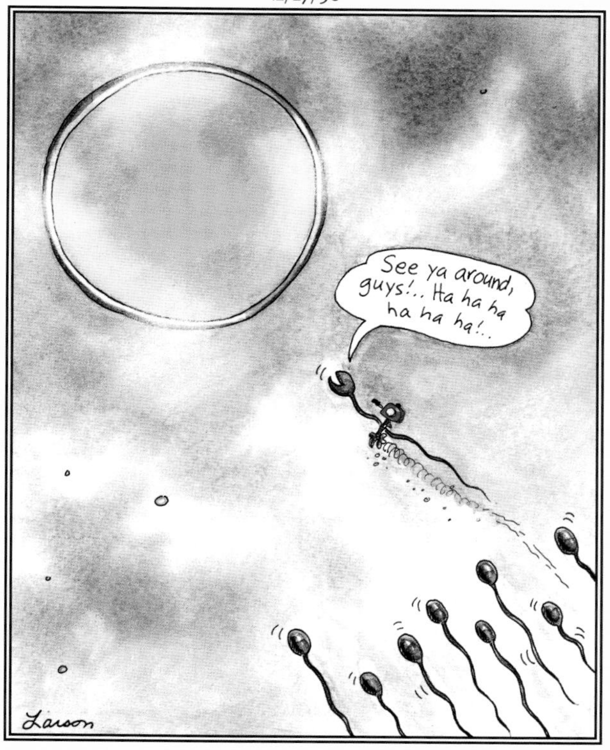
See ya around, guys!.. Ha ha ha ha ha ha!..
Larson

12/26/90

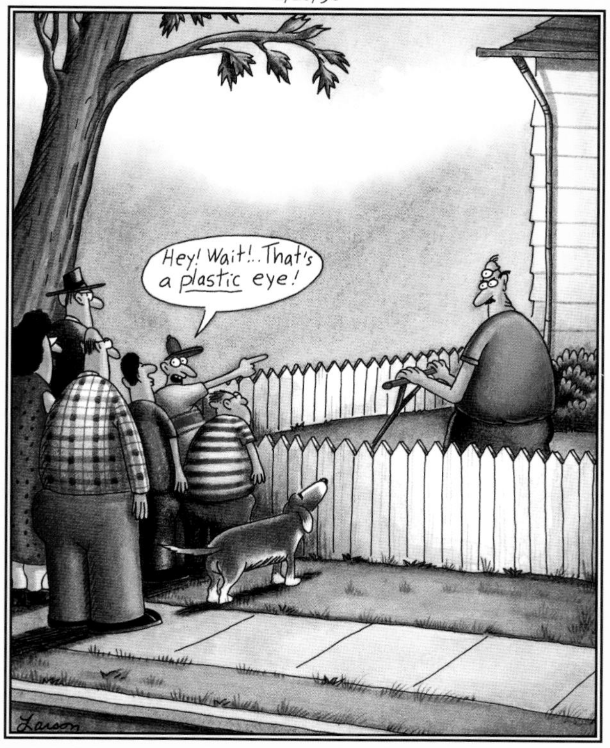
Hey! Wait!.. That's a plastic eye!
Larson

And with Johnny's revelation, Mr. Goodman's popularity in the neighborhood suddenly plummeted.

12/31/90

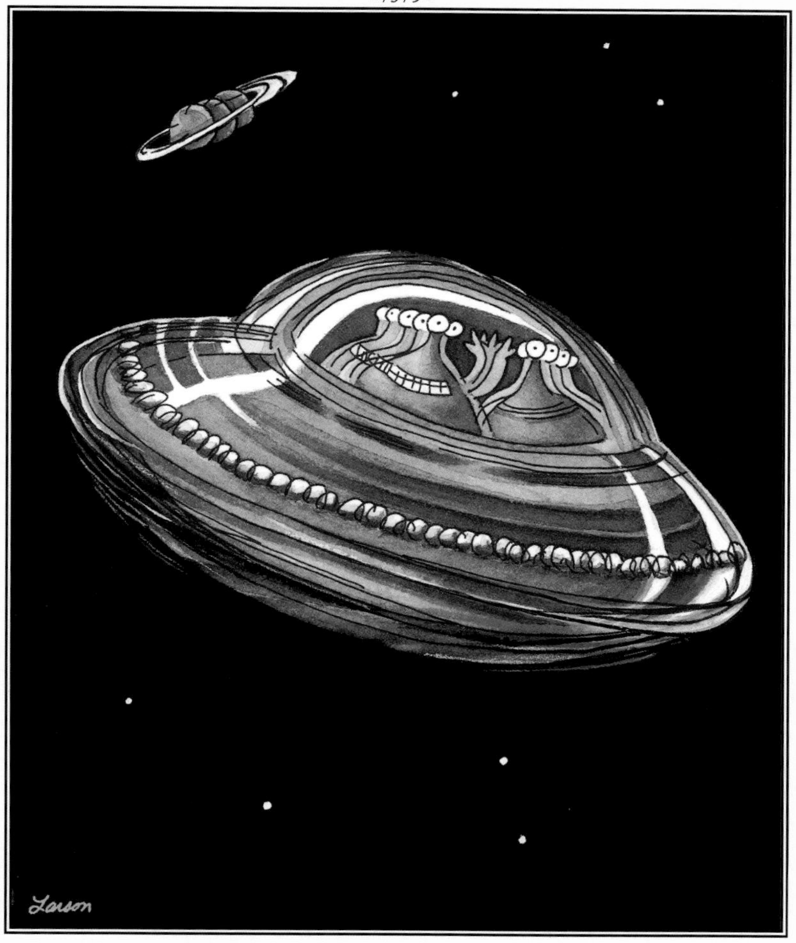
Larson

Another photograph from the Hubble Space Telescope

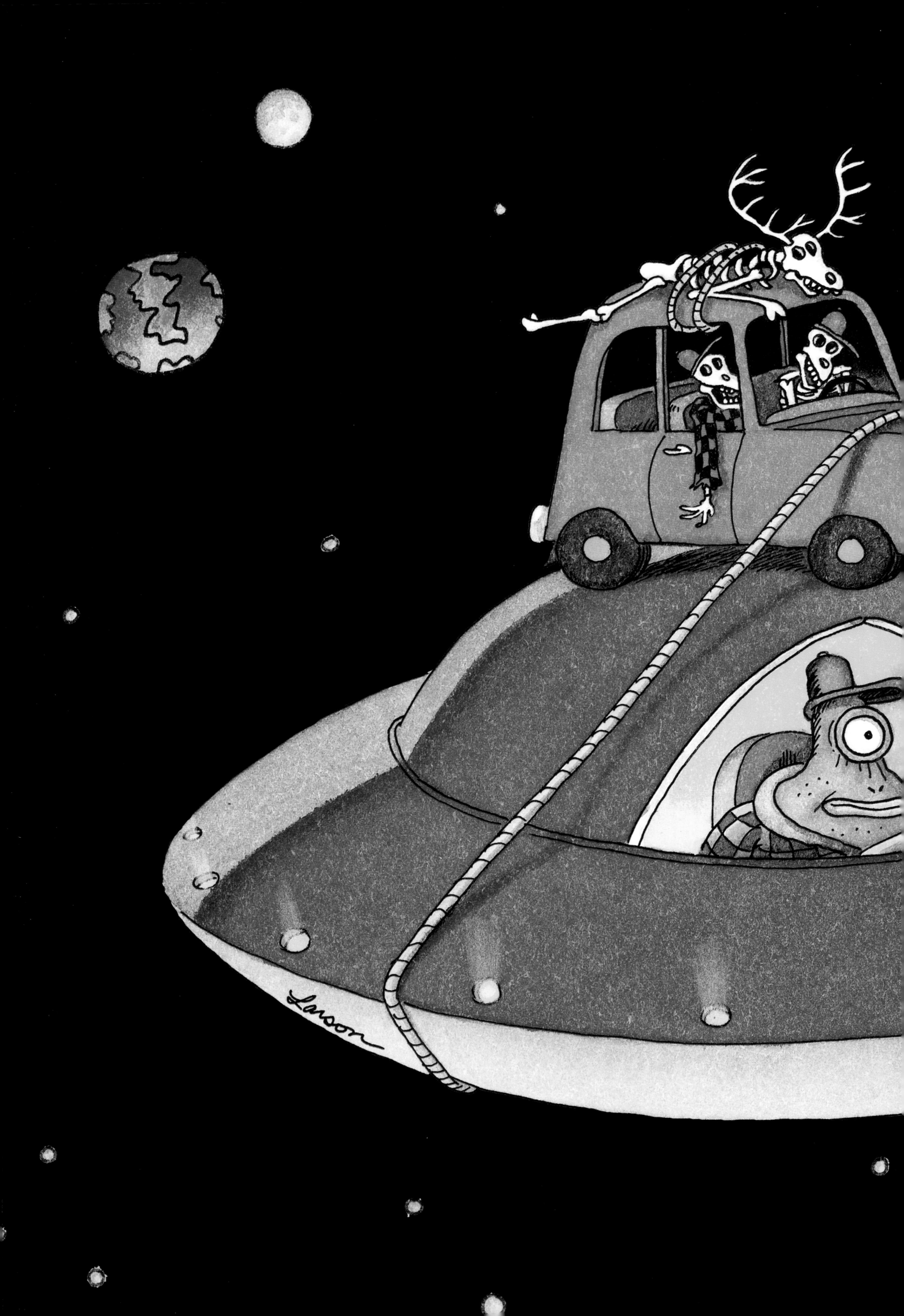
Larson

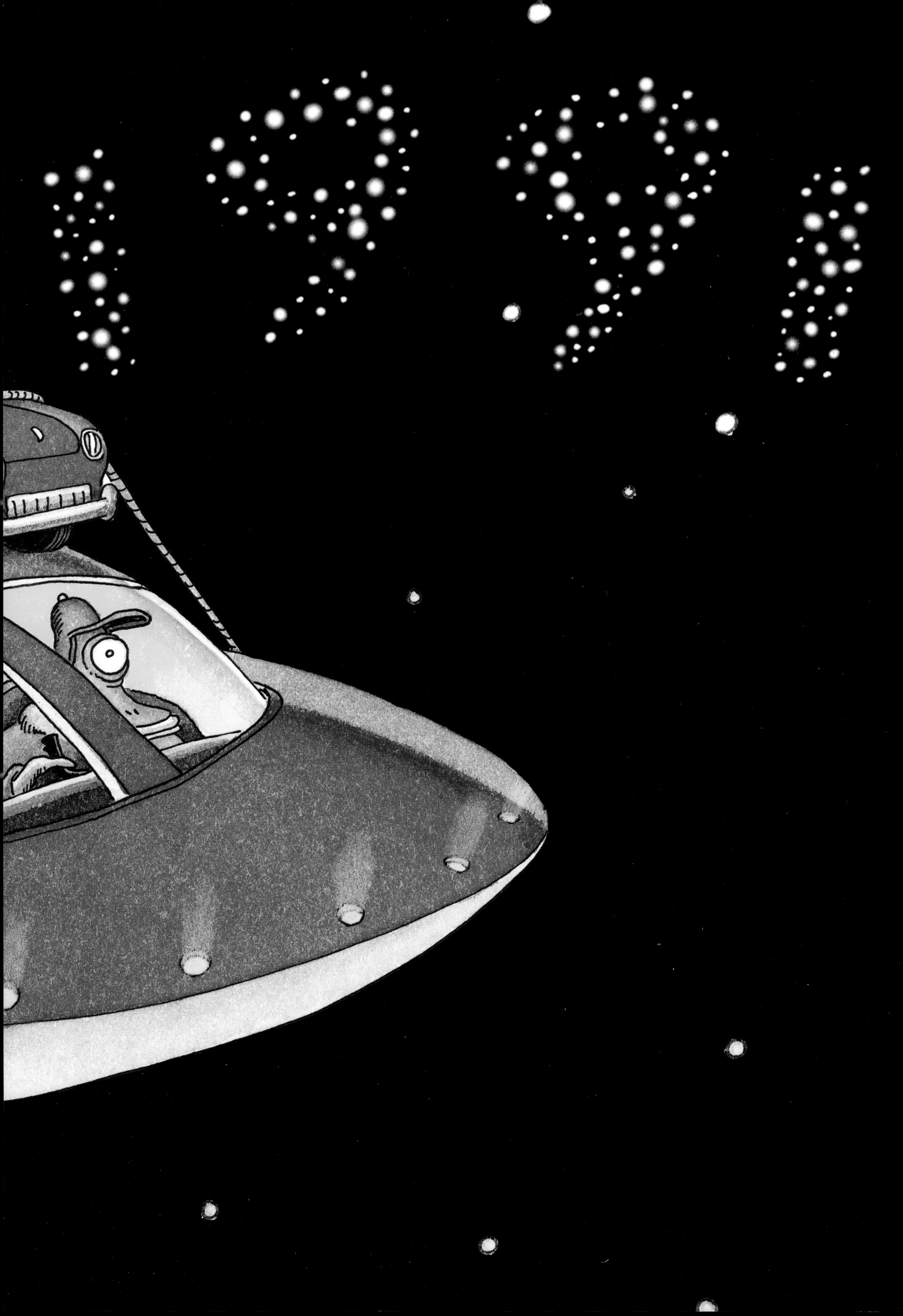

Sorry for the Confusion

For many years I had a desire to begin one of my small collections with this short preface:

*If one of my cartoons has brought joy and laughter to just
one person, if I have been able to make just <u>one</u> person
simply smile and forget their troubles for only a moment,
then that one cartoon, clearly, was not worth drawing.*

It was a joke, of course. Just a little bit of silliness. There was only one problem: I couldn't embrace this sentiment, even as a joke. It was at odds with the plain truth. I certainly never *knew* ahead of time that virtually no one would "get" a particular cartoon of mine, but if I had known, would it have killed my desire to draw it? Hard to say. One person getting it? That's tough. Two persons? I'm in.

On the other hand, I never got bogged down thinking too much about what was going on "out there." Really, a cartoonist is largely blind to reader reaction. This is the big wall that separates us from our distant and hairier cousin, the stand-up comedian. (I actually don't know if the "hairier" part is true; I'm guessing.)

Compare and contrast these two branches of the humoroid tree. For starters, we cartoonists are in ignorant bliss when we "bomb." We don't see the frozen faces or hear the collective groans or the universal "HUH?" that our little opus generated. For a comedian, however, bombing is a very public, very humiliating experience. I prefer ignorant bliss.

But the enviable side of this same coin is that comedians, perhaps at the price of such humiliating moments, are always learning from experience, throwing out jokes that didn't work, fine-tuning the ones that do. Small audiences become testing grounds for bigger audiences, and the comedians in turn are undoubtedly being shaped by the experience.

Cartoonists learn nothing from experience. There *is* no experience, really. At least none gained from "audience interaction." There *is* no audience. There's just an editor. And you, of course. There you are, probably sitting by yourself much like you are at this moment, reading your local newspaper or some other cartoon-accessorized publication. Maybe you're at home, sitting at the kitchen table, or on a bus, or in a diner, or on a park bench, or in a waiting room, or a prison cell. (I'm not joking; over my career, I've gotten more than a few fan letters from inmates, which won't surprise my detractors.)

In essence, I like to imagine you're as alone reading one of my cartoons as I was when I drew it. It's the only way I could bear it, I think. No "audience"—just you. Alone. Like me. (Now we're all depressed.)

If cartoonists do improve as the months and years go by, it's only because we're evolving from within, exploring ourselves, our characters. (There's editorial feedback, of course, but mostly at the beginning; after you've moved from your learner's permit to your license, editors make friendly, calm suggestions as you head down the road. It's only once in a while that they will actually scream and lunge for the wheel.) And there's one other evolution: We simply *draw* better with time. My first cow would have made a bad cave painting; my last cow was up there with the best Neanderthal artist you could throw at me.

Actually, I think cartoonists have more in common with writers than we do with comedians. The following writer-cartoonist parallels come to mind: loners, quiet room, favorite chair, hand puppet (just me?), and our trusty writing/drawing tools. But there is also one huge difference: If *we* blow it, we lose a day. If a writer blows it, he or she loses, what—a year? Two years? Personally, I prefer a job where I might screw up my day, not my year. (I envision most writers finally finishing a body of work, shipping it off to their publisher, and then going out that evening to a five-star restaurant and having a great meal and a bottle of vintage wine; cartoonists finish a body of work, ship it off to their publisher, and fix themselves a really big bowl of their favorite cereal. It all equates.)

So how does a confusing cartoon even come into being? It's easy. Since I'm "audience free," I just go where my mind takes me. Then my editor sees it, says to himself, "Oh, well—I've seen him do stranger things," and off it goes to your local newspaper, where you finally see it and go, "Huh?" Meanwhile, I'm back home having cereal.

For show 'n' tell, I've found a cartoon (oh, the choices) of what, in hindsight, I concede was just a little too cumbersome and obtuse. (Of course, the King of My Cartoons That Confused Everybody was one entitled "Cow tools" [Vol. 1, p. 251], but I've discussed that in a previous book and prefer not to once again relive my day in hell when that little gem was published.)

"Well, we'll never want for food, Doris. ... This rock is absolutely encrusted with oysters and mussels—all the way to the top!"

Let me be the first to acknowledge that even if you were to understand this thing, it's not exactly going to send you into gales of laughter. (Let's just call it "quiet humor," okay?) Here's the cartoon decoded: If you've managed to escape some disastrous event at sea, and then found safety on a small rock island, you would be well-advised to note where the various crustaceans and mollusks are making their little homes. Because "home" to those creatures is anywhere that is comfortably *below* high tide. (I knew I was in trouble when a marine biologist friend called me and asked me to explain this one.)

Even now, years after my retirement, I'm reminded of my reputation as The Great Confuser. One afternoon not long ago, a repair guy was at our house, trying to fix a problem with our electrical system. He tracked me down in the kitchen and started to explain to me in technical jargon what was wrong. I didn't have a clue what he was talking about, and at the end of his discourse I just looked at him and said, "Sorry, I'm confused." I didn't think he knew anything about me, but he suddenly narrowed his eyes and replied in an even tone, "Just consider it payback."

Fair enough.

1/1/91

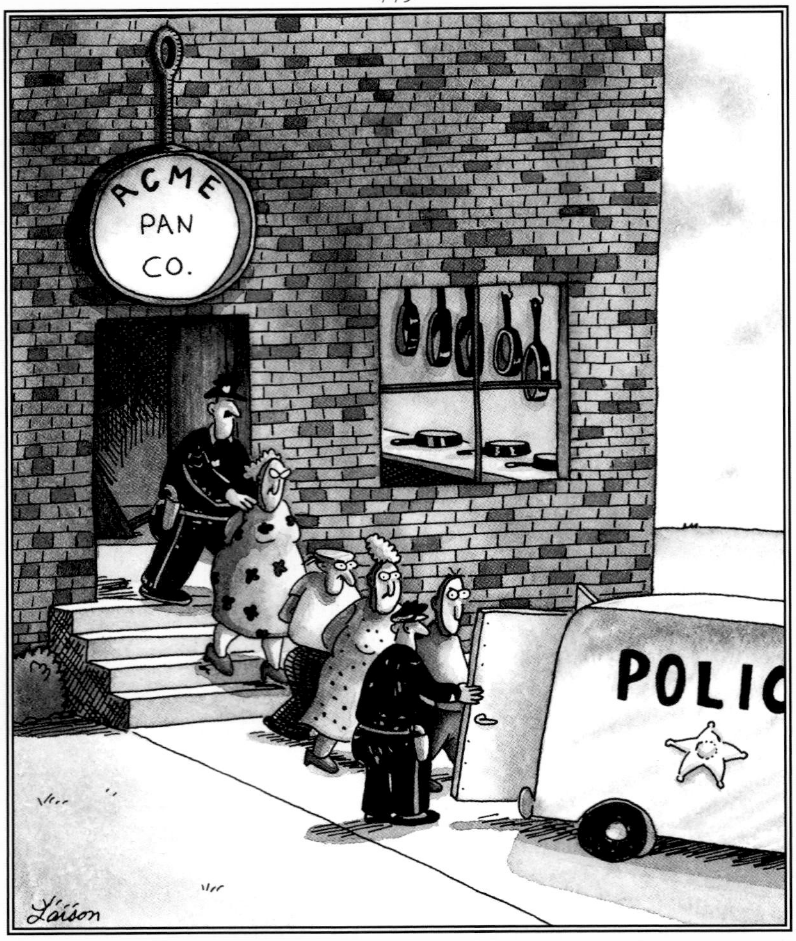
ACME
PAN
CO.
POLIC

It was over. But before the police could arrive, the rioting employees had already turned on one another, using the closest weapons at hand.

1/2/91

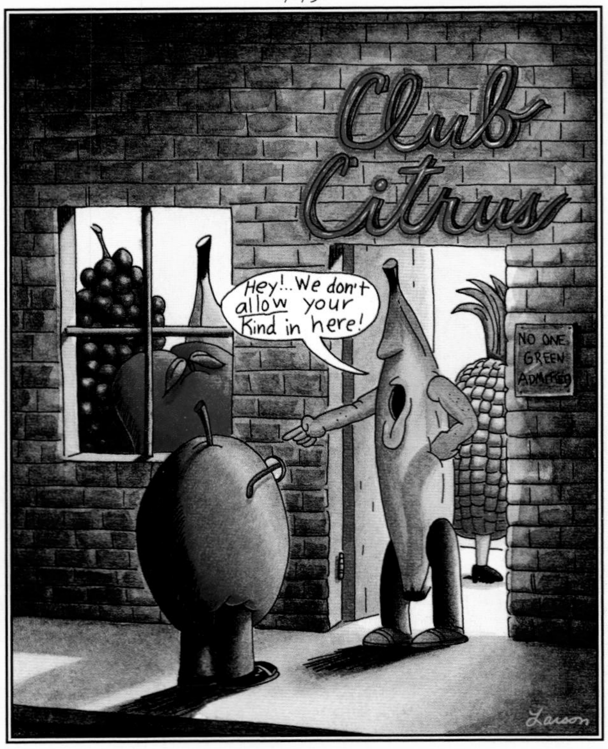
Club Citrus
Hey!.. We don't allow your kind in here!
NO ONE GREEN ADMITTED

Forbidden fruit

1/7/91

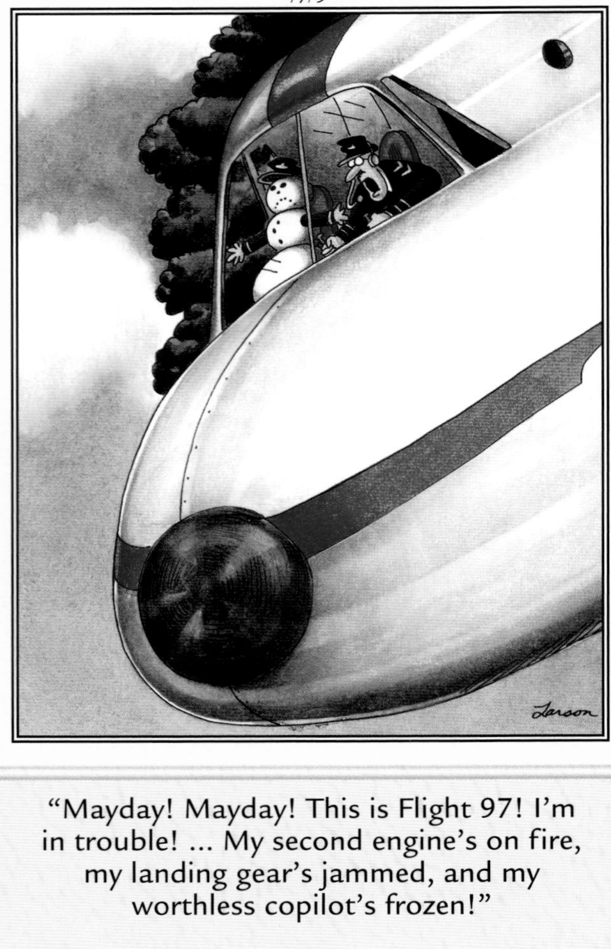

"Mayday! Mayday! This is Flight 97! I'm in trouble! ... My second engine's on fire, my landing gear's jammed, and my worthless copilot's frozen!"

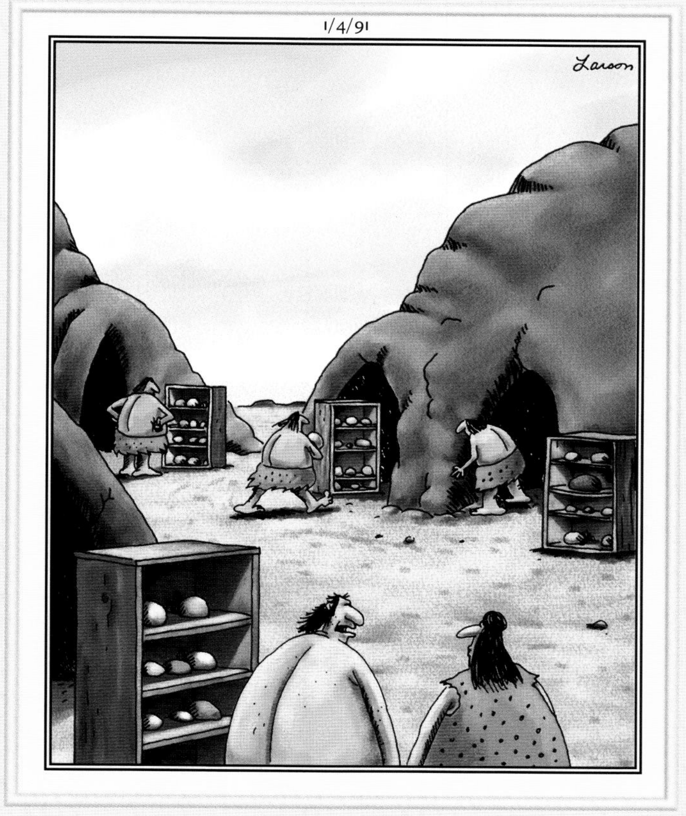
1/4/91
Larson

"You know, I used to like this hobby. ... But shoot! Seems like *everybody's* got a rock collection."

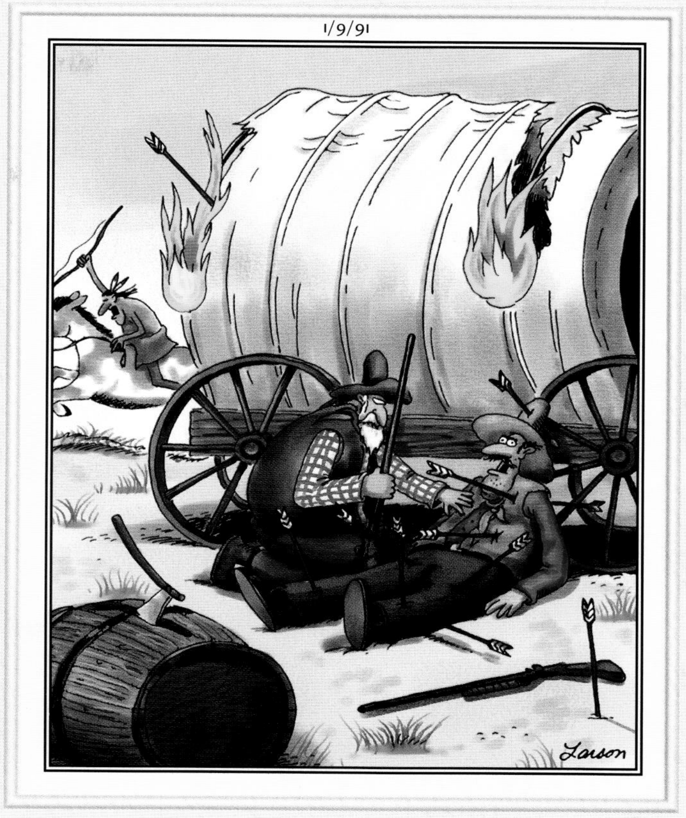
1/9/91
Larson

"Yeah, Clem, I hurt. But y'know, it's a *good* kind of hurt."

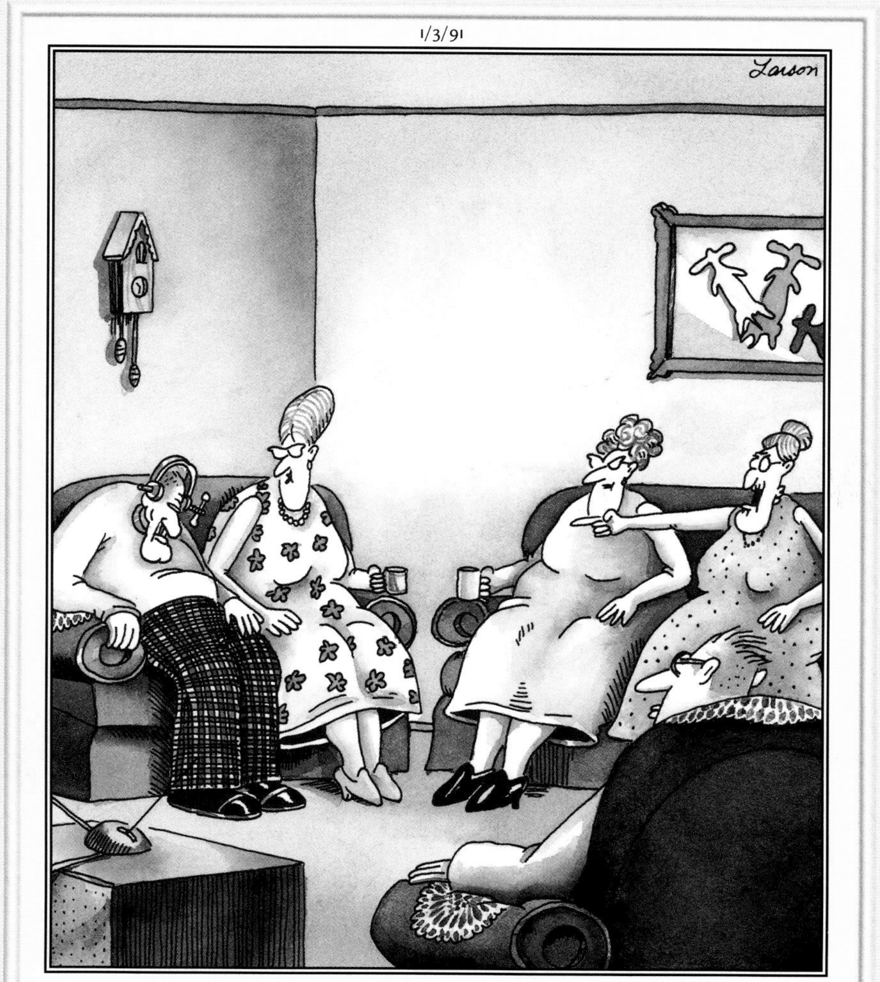
1/3/91
Larson

"Oh, for the love of—there goes Henry! ... Rita, you're closest to him—give that c-clamp 'bout a quarter turn, will ya?"

1/8/91

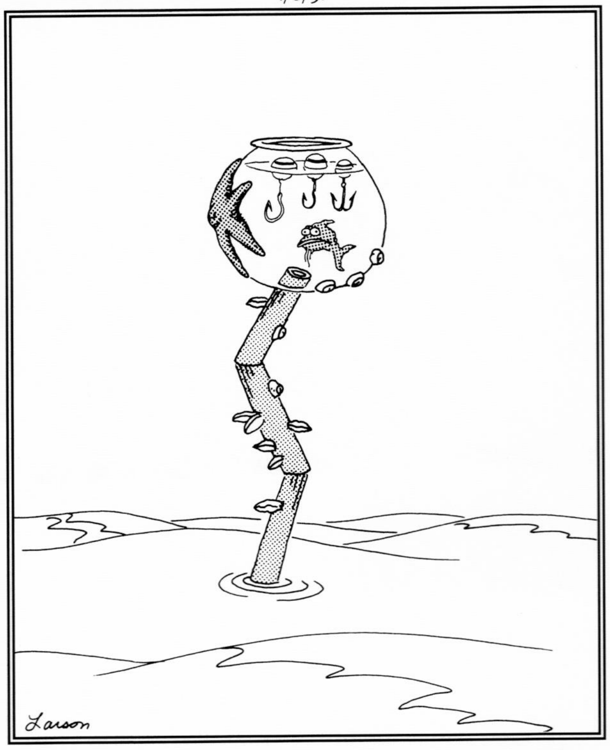
Larson

Fish dungeons

1/15/91

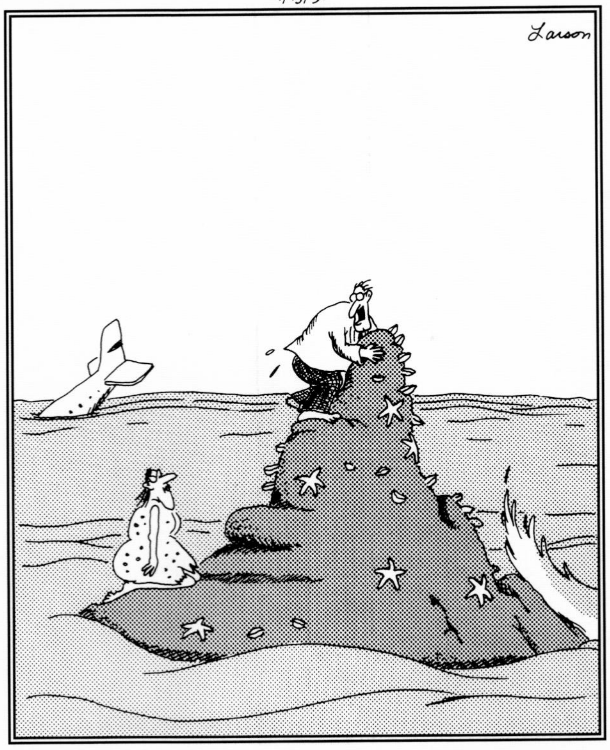
Larson

"Well, we'll never want for food, Doris. ... This rock is absolutely encrusted with oysters and mussels—all the way to the top!"

1/10/91

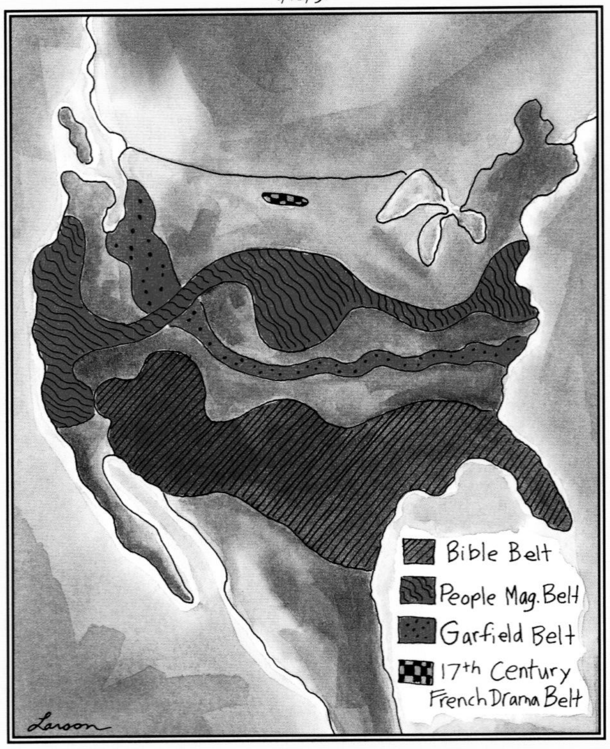
Bible Belt
People Mag. Belt
Garfield Belt
17th Century French Drama Belt
Larson

1/11/91

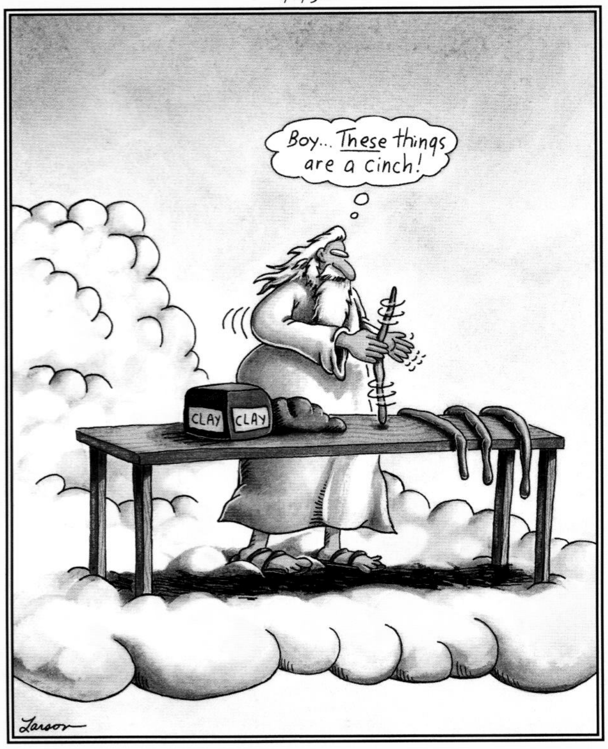
Boy... These things are a cinch!
CLAY
CLAY
Larson

God makes the snake.

1/23/91

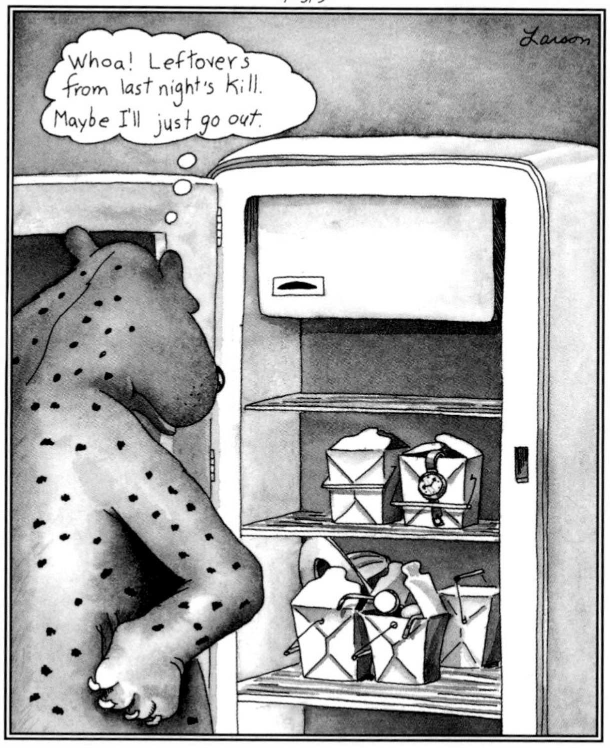
Whoa! Leftovers from last night's kill. Maybe I'll just go out.
Larson

1/28/91

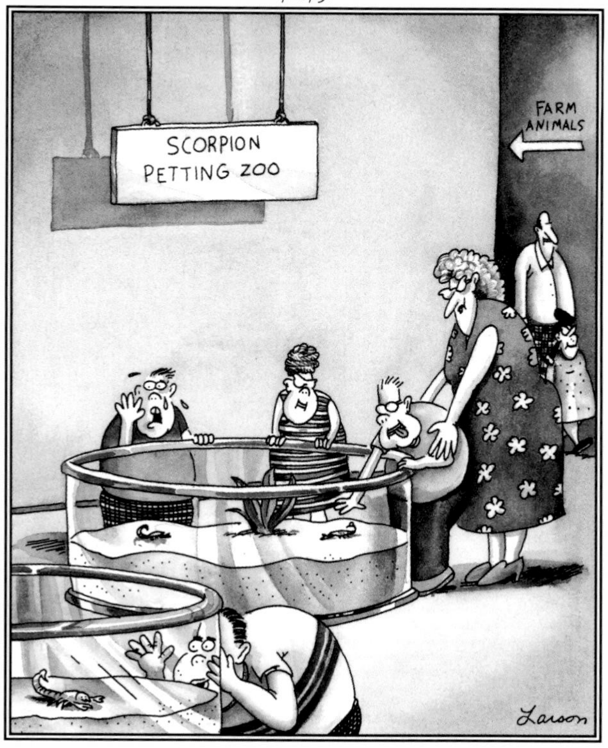
SCORPION PETTING ZOO
FARM ANIMALS
Larson

Innovative concepts in exposing city kids to nature

1/16/91

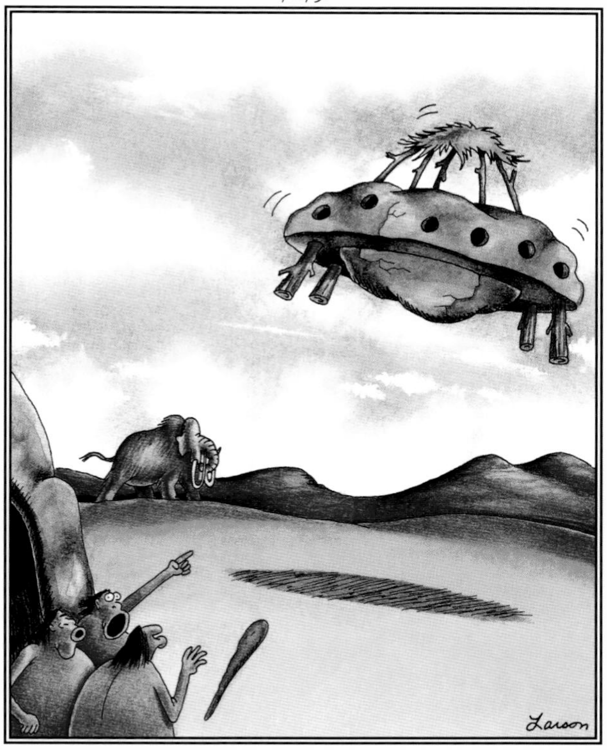
Larson

Primitive UFOs

1/14/91

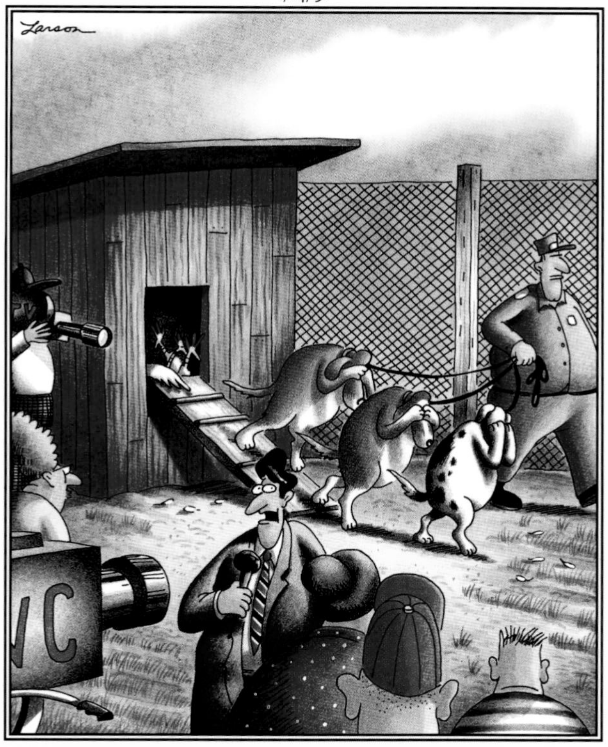
Larson

"The carnage out here is terrible, Sandy—feathers everywhere you ... Oh, here we go! The Animal Control Officer is leading the so-called Chicken Coop Three away at this very moment."

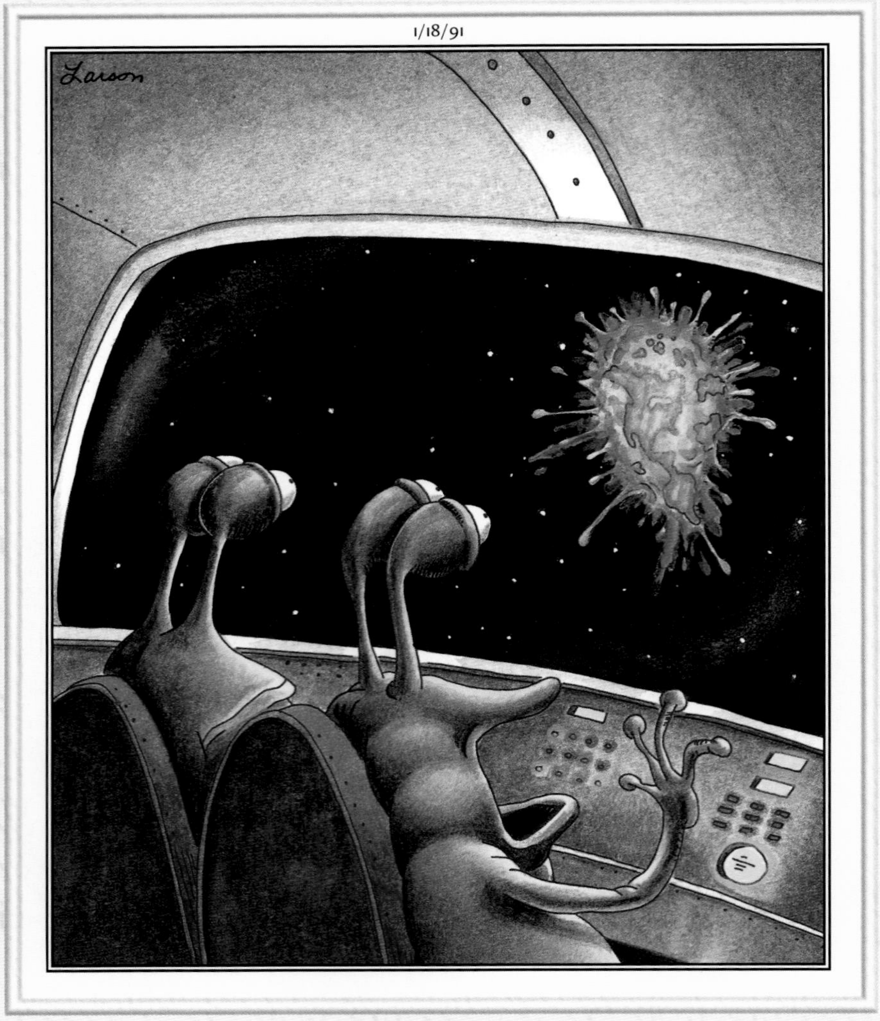
1/18/91
Larson

"Oh, gross!"

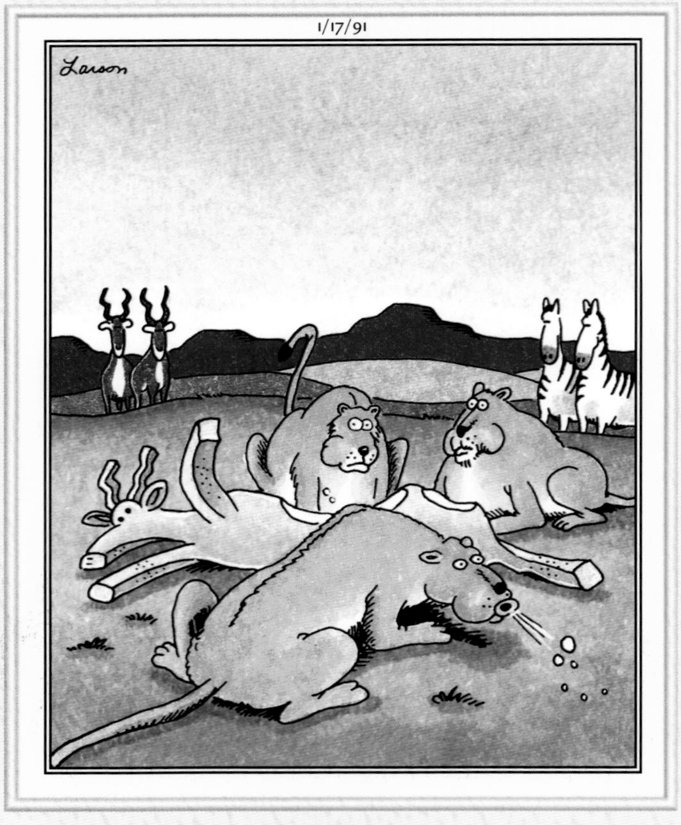
1/17/91
Larson

In sudden disgust, the three lionesses realized they had killed a tofudebeest—one of the Serengeti's obnoxious health antelopes.

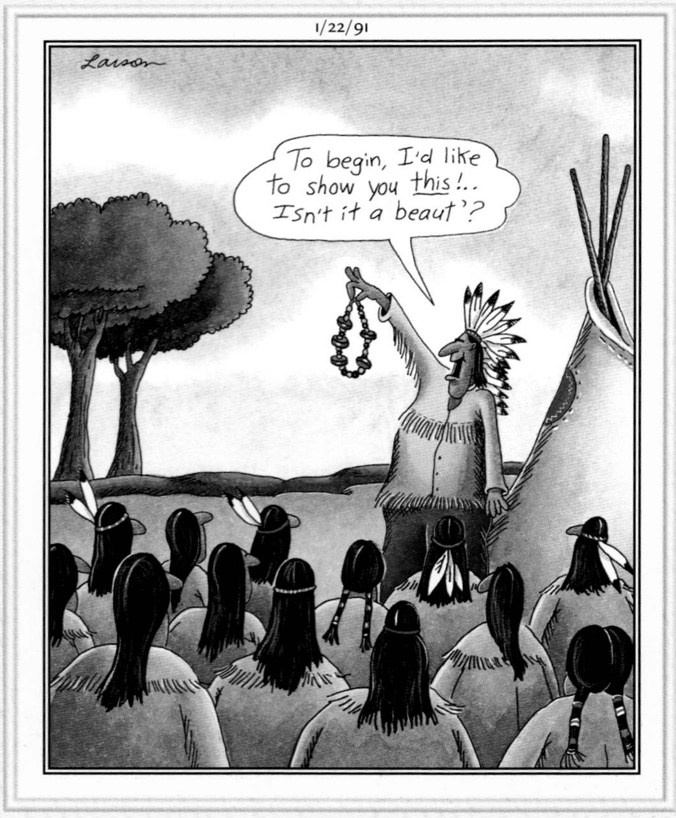
1/22/91
Larson
To begin, I'd like to show you this!.. Isn't it a beaut'?

New York, 1626: Chief of the Manhattan Indians addresses his tribe for the last time.

1/21/91
Larson

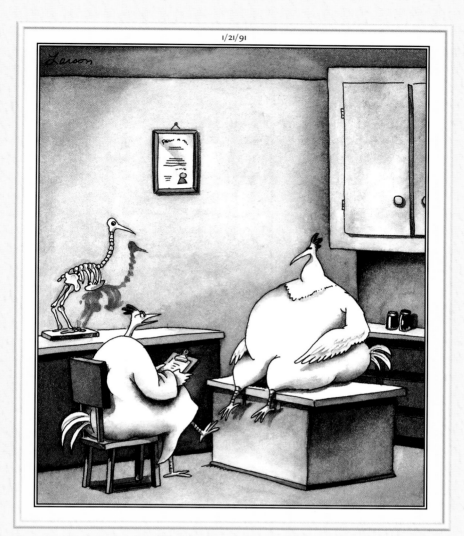

"I'm afraid it's bad news, Mr. Griswold. ... The lab results indicate your body cavity is stuffed with a tasty, breadlike substance."

1/24/91
Larson
Dang! Get inside, Ma!...Blizzard's a-comin'!

1/25/91
Larson
Hey! I told you kids to knock it off back there!... Or so help me I'll just take this car and drive it off the first cliff I come to!

Lemmings on vacation

1/31/91

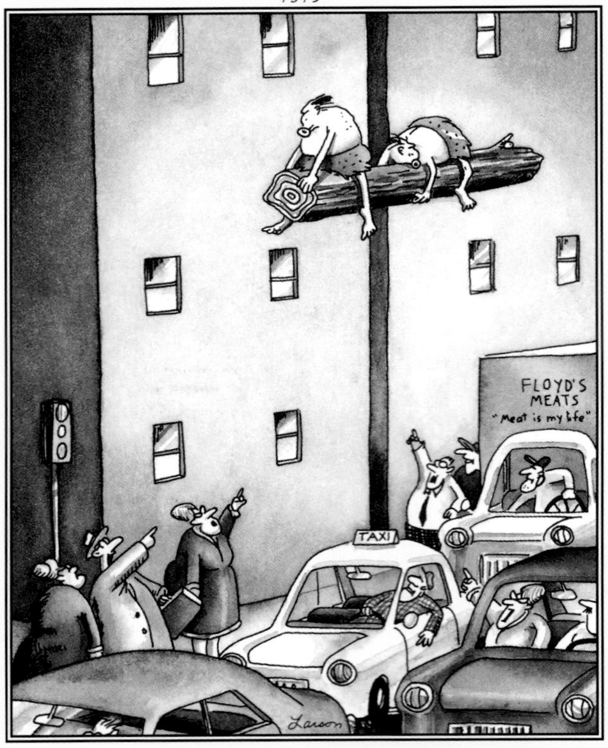
FLOYD'S
MEATS
"Meat is my life"
TAXI
Larson

Hooting excitedly, primitive scientists Thak and Gork try out their new "Time Log."

1/29/91

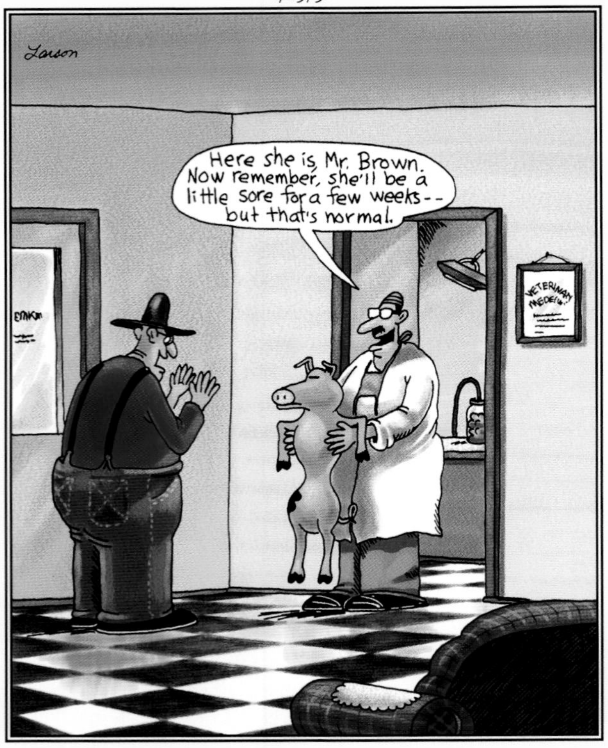
Larson
Here she is Mr. Brown. Now remember, she'll be a little sore for a few weeks-- but that's normal.

The growing field of animal liposuction

1/30/91

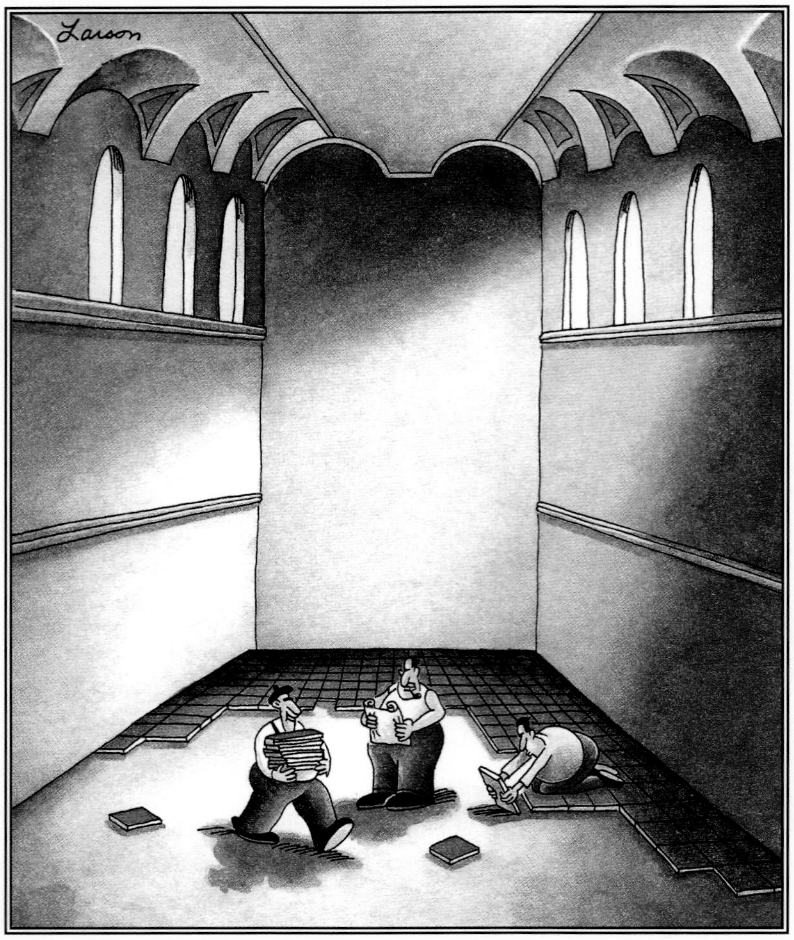
Larson

Although history has long forgotten them, Lambini & Sons are generally credited with the Sistine Chapel floor.

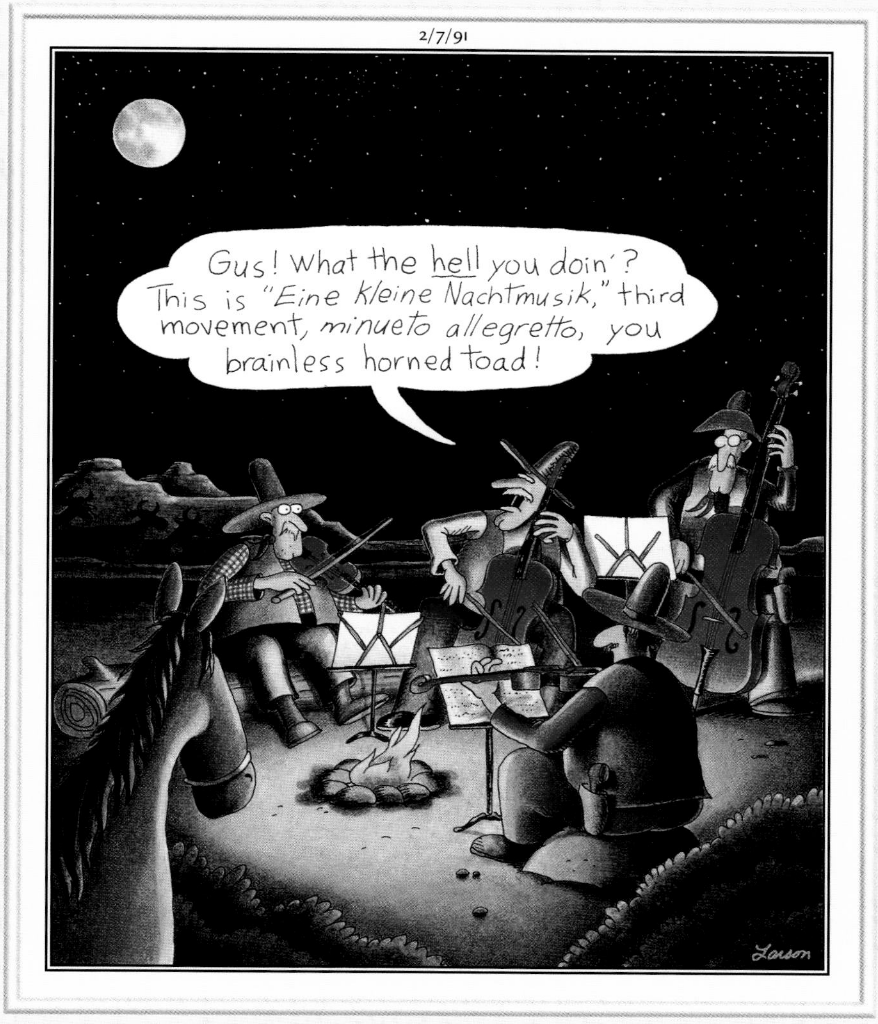
2/7/91
Gus! What the hell you doin'? This is "Eine kleine Nachtmusik," third movement, minueto allegretto, you brainless horned toad!
Larson

Cattle drive quartets

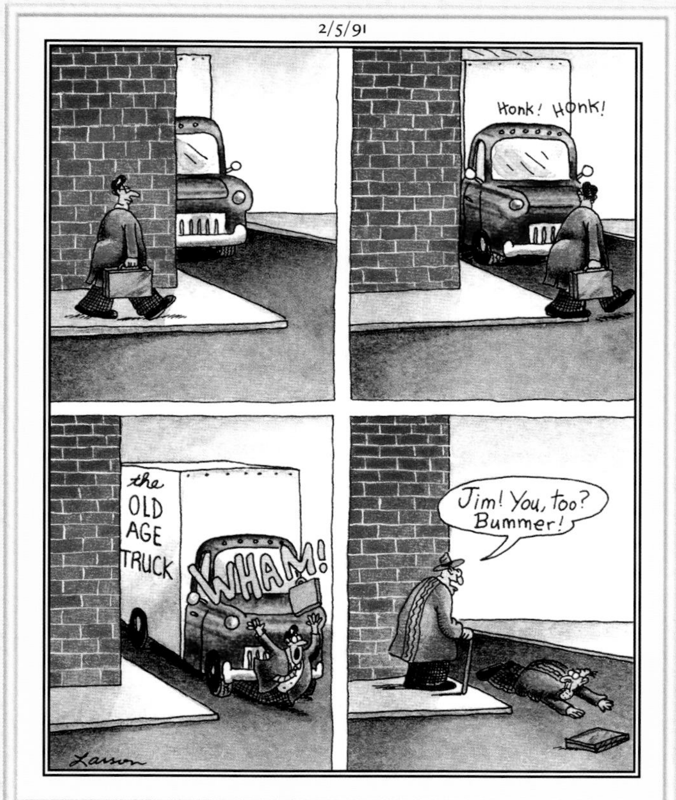
2/5/91
Honk! Honk!
the OLD AGE TRUCK
WHAM!
Jim! You, too? Bummer!
Larson

You never see it coming.

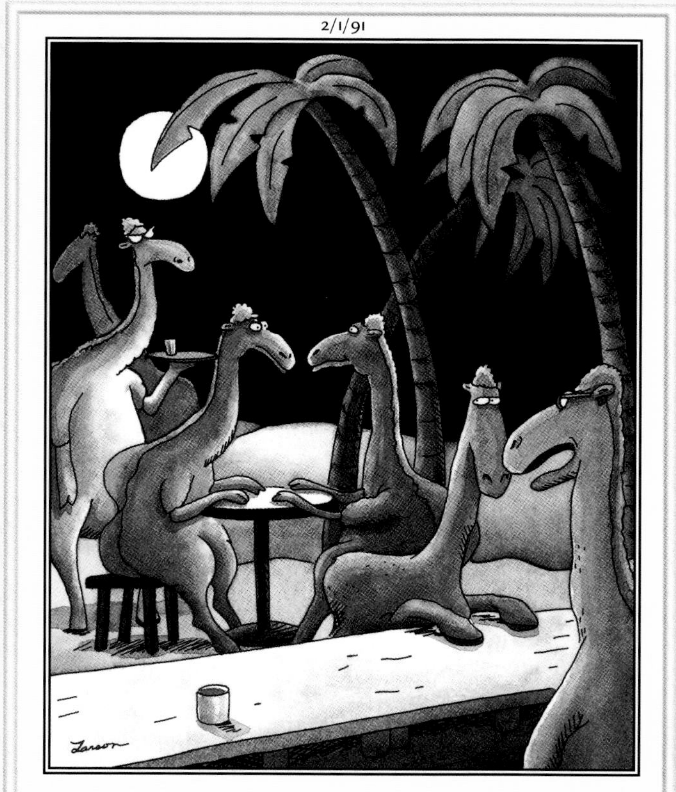
2/1/91
Larson

"Look at those two macho idiots. ... They haven't taken a drink in days—just to see which one ends up under the table."

2/4/91

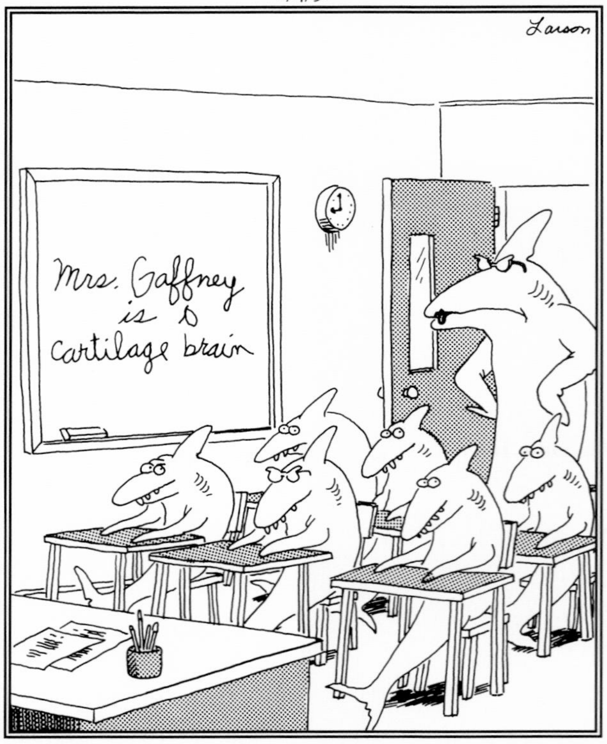
Mrs. Gaffney is a cartilage brain
Larson

2/6/91

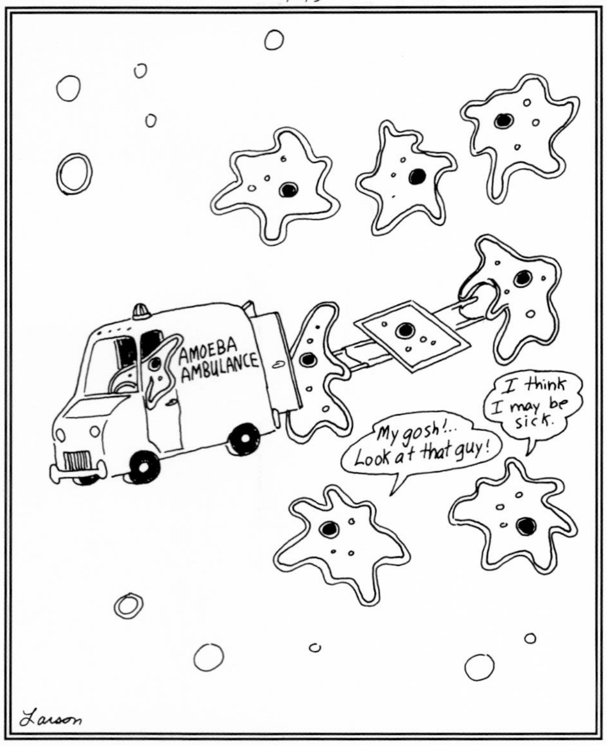
AMOEBA AMBULANCE
My gosh!.. Look at that guy!
I think I may be sick.
Larson

2/8/91

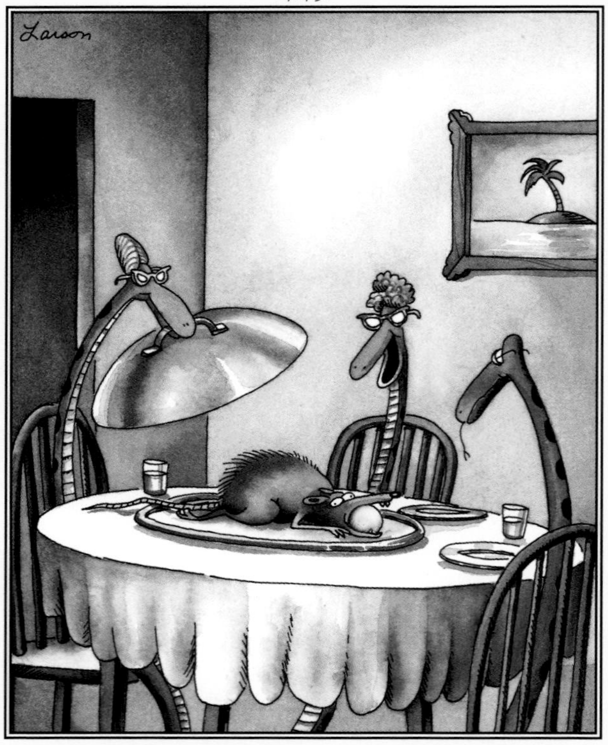
Larson

"Oh, my! Cindy! This looks exquisite! ... And look, Frank—it even has a cheeseball stuffed in its mouth!"

2/11/91

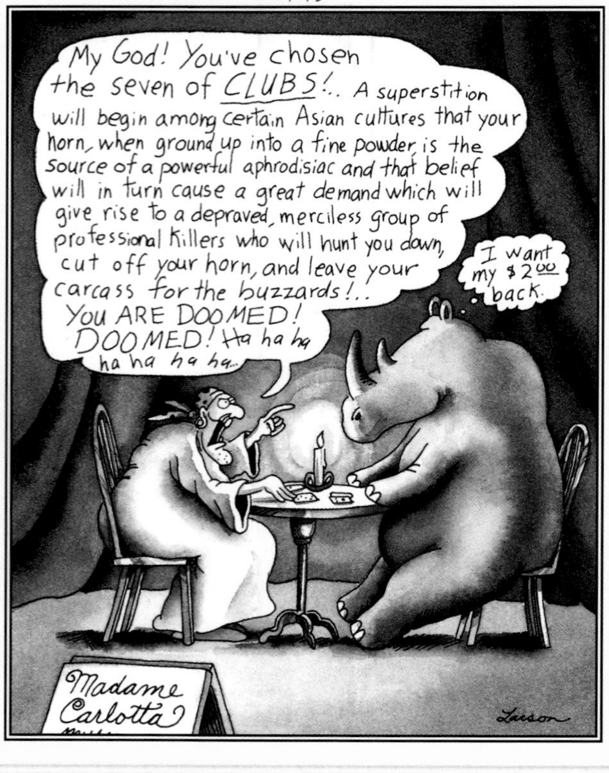
My God! You've chosen the seven of CLUBS!.. A superstition will begin among certain Asian cultures that your horn, when ground up into a fine powder, is the source of a powerful aphrodisiac and that belief will in turn cause a great demand which will give rise to a depraved, merciless group of professional killers who will hunt you down, cut off your horn, and leave your carcass for the buzzards!.. You ARE DOOMED! DOOMED! Ha ha ha ha ha ha ha..
I want my $2.00 back.
Madame Carlotta
Larson

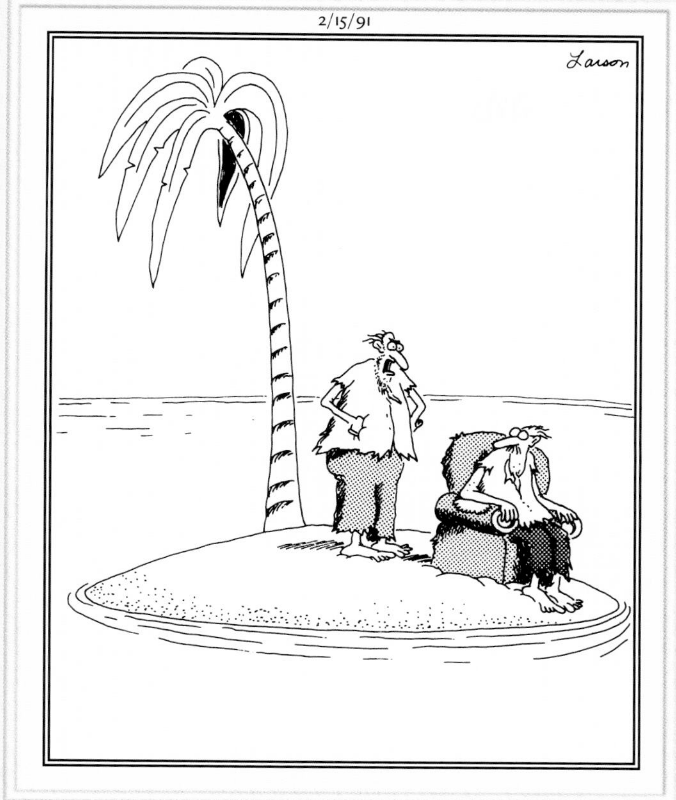

"Whoa! Whoa! Whoa! ... You're in my favorite chair again, Carl."

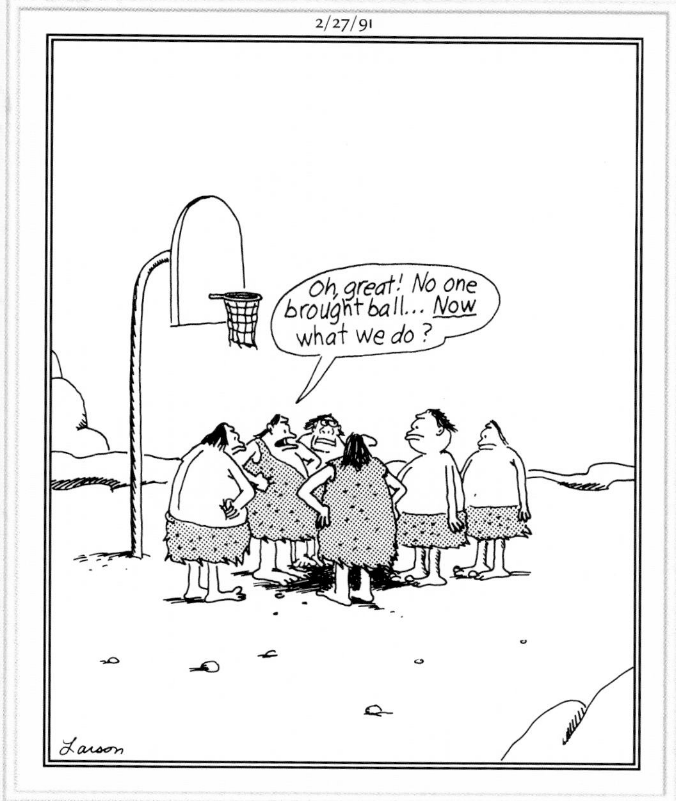
Oh, great! No one brought ball... Now what we do?

The birth of head-hunting

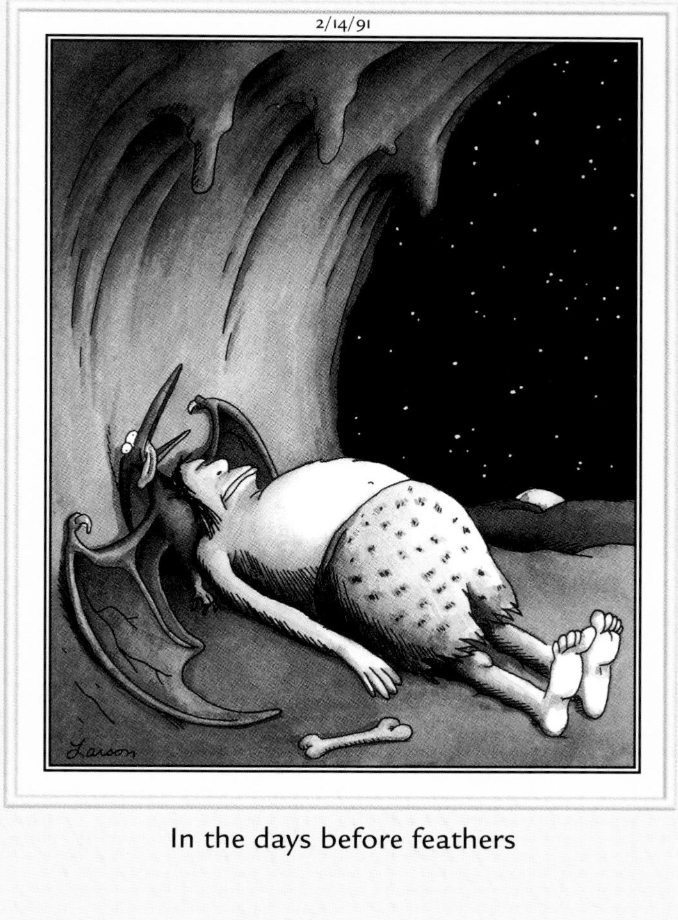

In the days before feathers

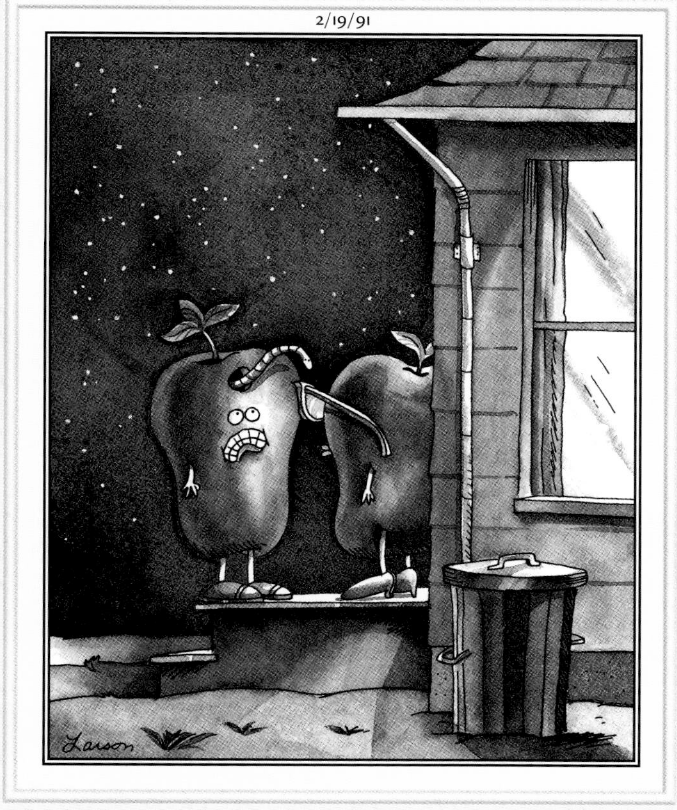

Andy looked up in horror. Right in front of Sally, a worm was emerging from his forehead—and he felt himself turning even redder.

2/12/91

Larson

"Aaaaaaa! There goes another batch of eggs, Frank! ... No wonder this nest was such a deal."

2/13/91

Larson

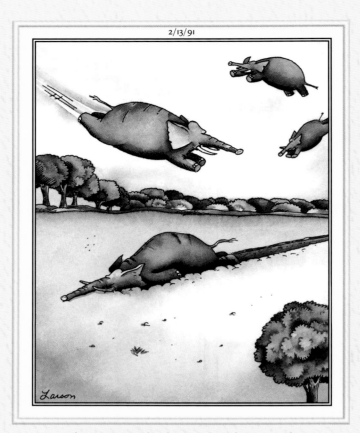

The Secret Elephant Aerial Grounds

2/18/91

Larson
Quick, Mr. Sulu!.. Get those defense shields up!

The crew of the *Starship Enterprise* encounters the floating head of Zsa Zsa Gabor.

2/25/91

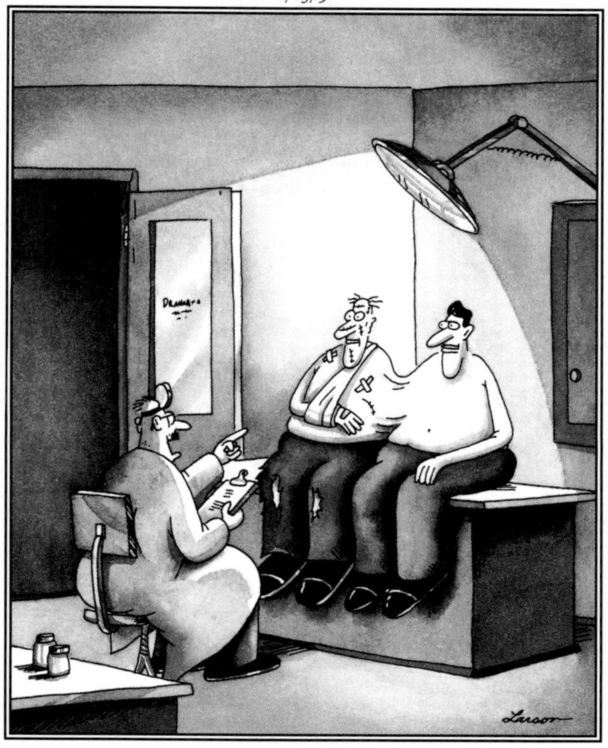

"Wait, wait, wait—I'm confused. ... Bob, *you're* the one who's claiming your Siamese twin, Frank, changes into a werewolf every full moon?"

2/21/91

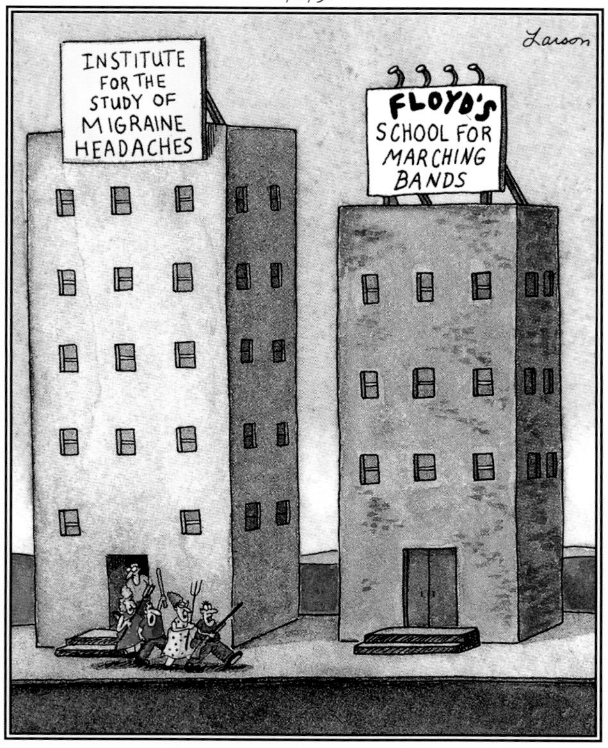
INSTITUTE FOR THE STUDY OF MIGRAINE HEADACHES
FLOYD'S SCHOOL FOR MARCHING BANDS

The dam bursts.

2/26/91

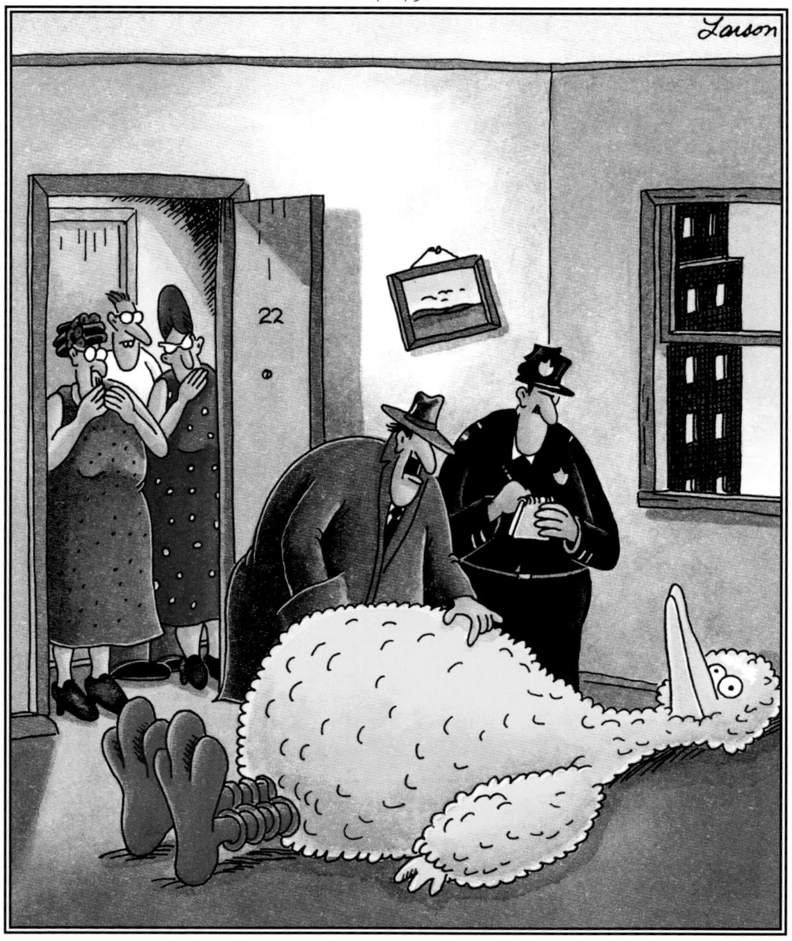
22

"Make a note of this, Muldoon. ... The wounds seem to be caused by bird shot ... big bird shot."

2/22/91
Larson
VERN'S
PEST CONT

"Okay, ma'am—it's dead. In the future, however, it's always a good idea to check your shoe each time you and the kids return home."

2/20/91
Larson
I loved the food!
Delicious
My favorite carrion
The best!
I eat here all the time

Famous patrons of Chez Rotting Carcass

2/28/91
Larson

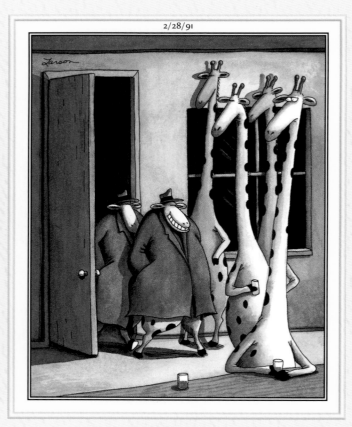

Giraffe thugs

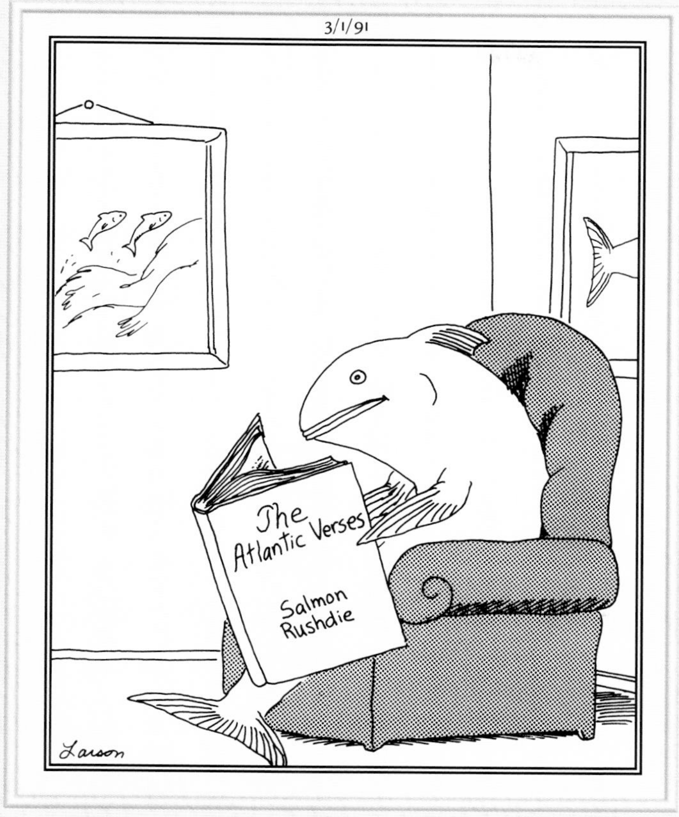
3/1/91
The Atlantic Verses
Salmon Rushdie
Larson

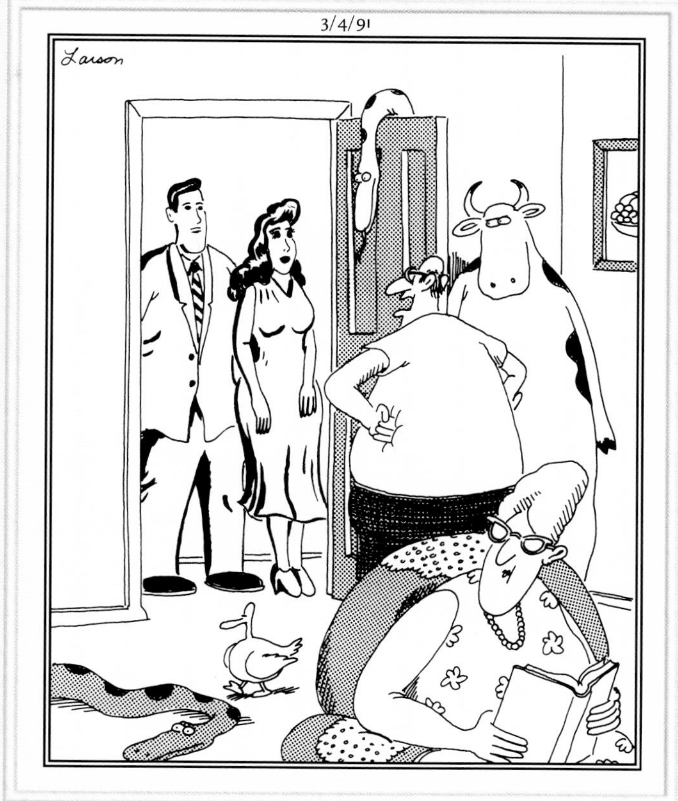
3/4/91
Larson

"Oh, man! You must be looking for *Apartment 3-G, Mary Worth,* or one of those serious-type cartoons."

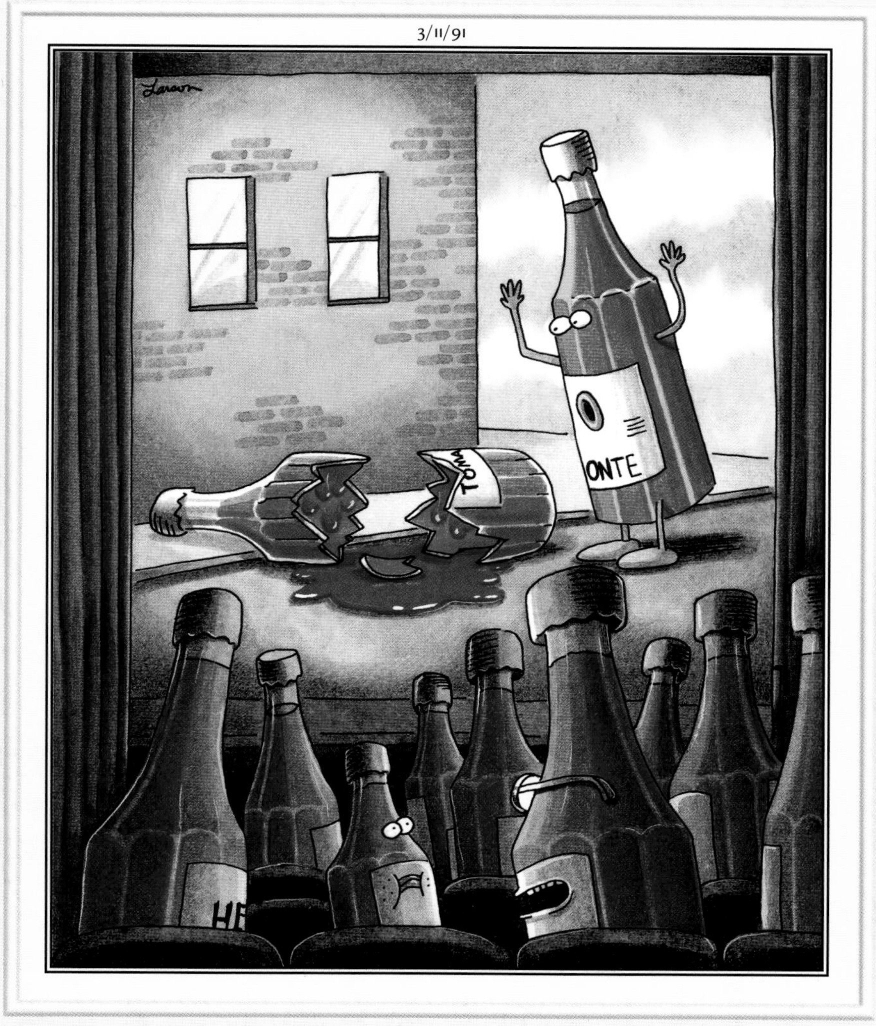
3/11/91
Larson
ONTE

"Don't worry, Jimmy—they're just actors ... and that's not real ketchup."

3/8/91
Larson
CHINESE HANDCUFFS

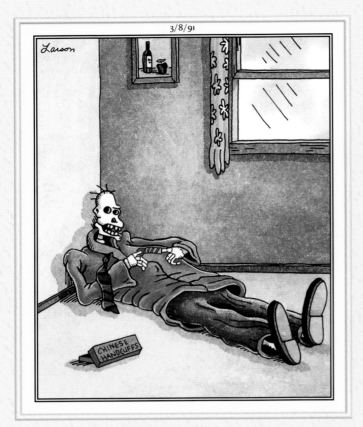

Houdini's final undoing

3/12/91
Larson

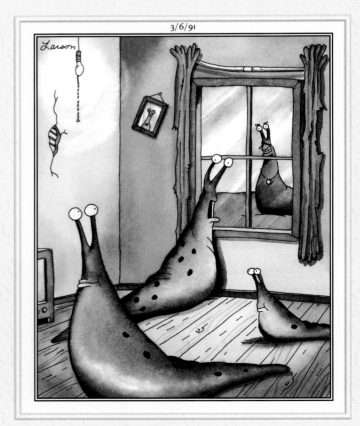

"Ticks, fleas ... ticks, fleas ... "

3/5/91
Larson

"You just take your prey, slip 'em into the flex-o-tube, flip the switch, and the Mr. Coils o' Death takes over."

3/6/91
Larson

"Uh-oh, Lenny ... it's the slimelord."

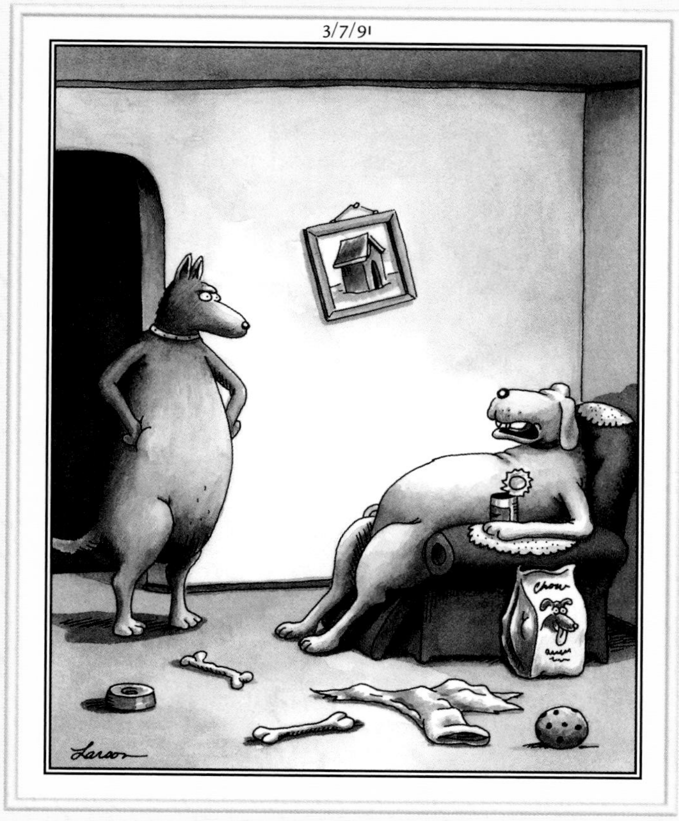
3/7/91
Larson

"Hey, look ... you knew when you married me that I was a nonworking breed."

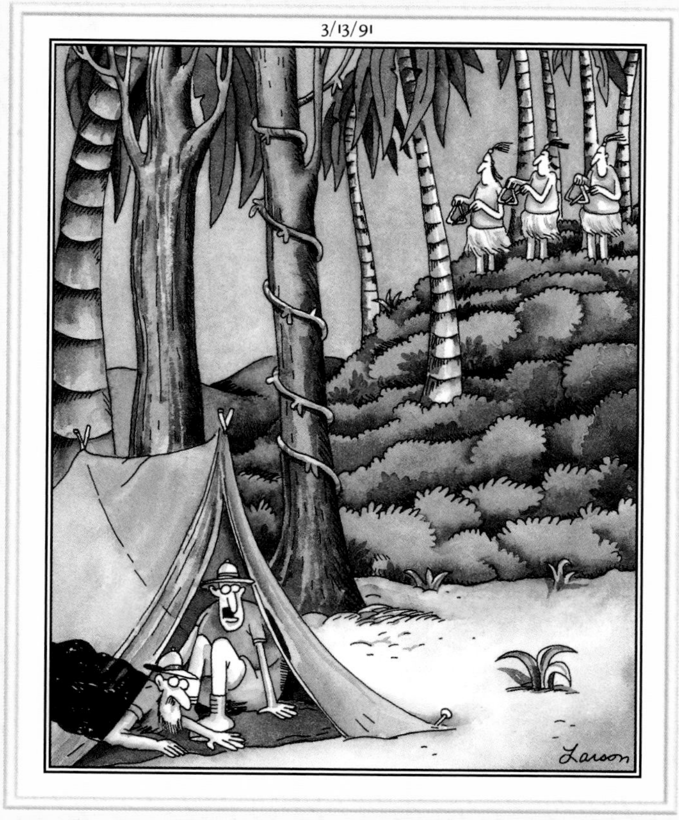
3/13/91
Larson

"Listen, Morrison! ... Oh, wait. It's okay—those are jungle *triangles!*"

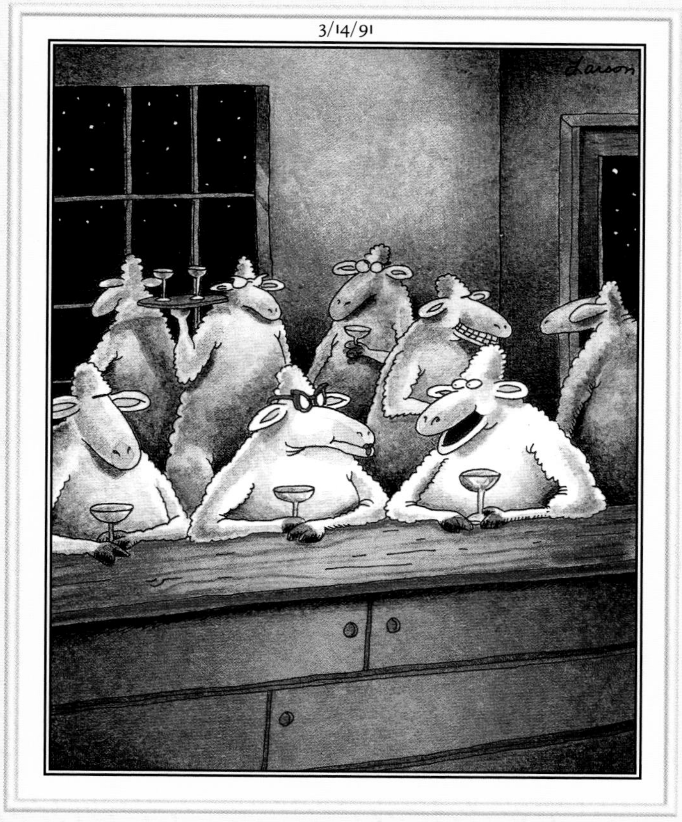
3/14/91
Larson

"Well, what d'ya know! ... *I'm* a follower, too!"

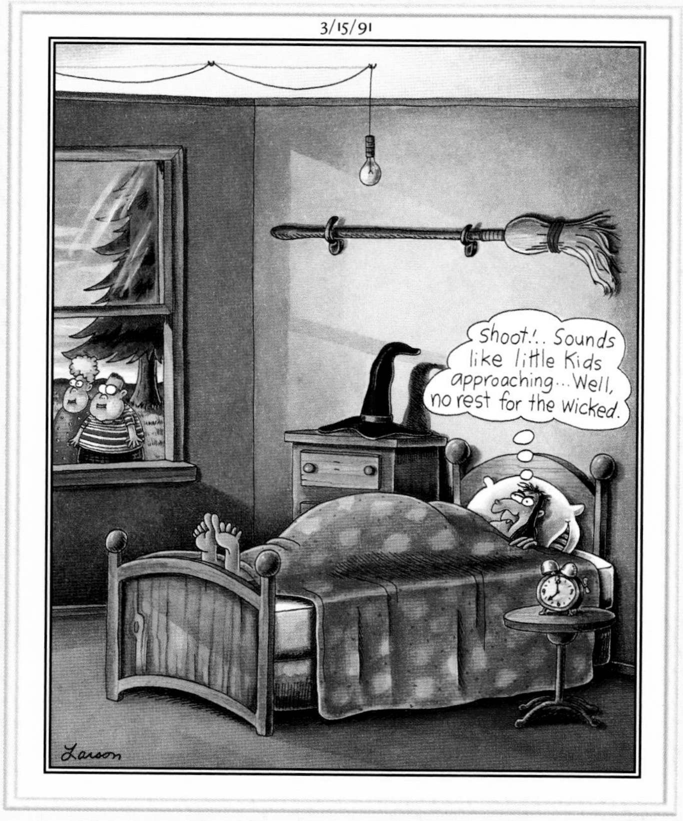
3/15/91
Shoot!.. Sounds like little Kids approaching...Well, no rest for the wicked.
Larson

3/19/91

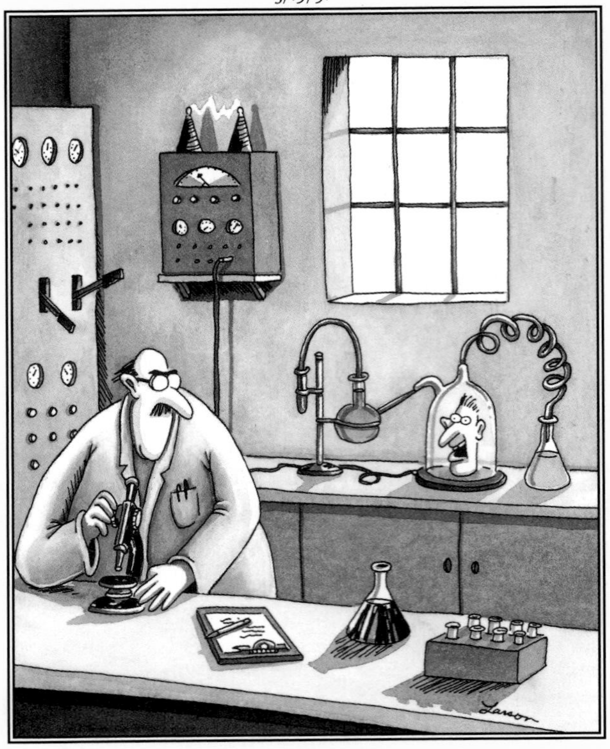

"Oh, professor ... did I tell you I had another out-of-head experience last night?"

3/27/91

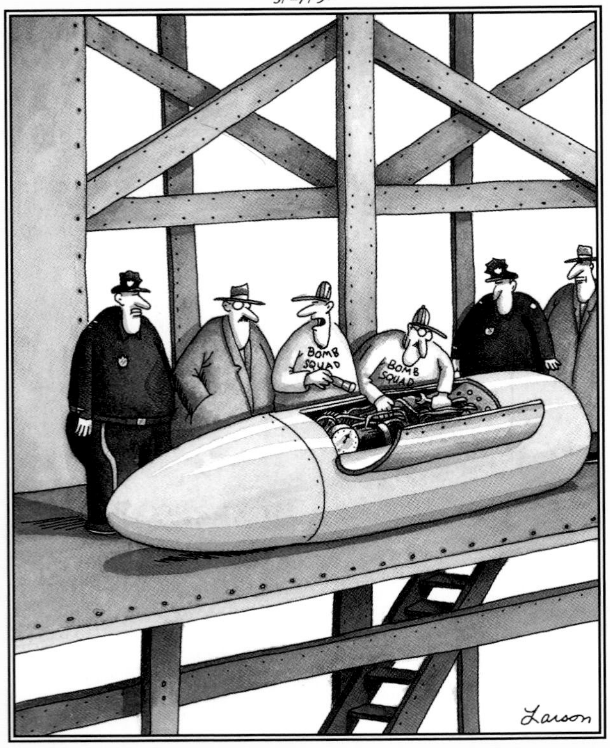
BOMB SQUAD
BOMB SQUAD

"Well, it's a delicate situation, sir. ... Sophisticated firing system, hair-trigger mechanisms, and Bob's wife just left him last night, so you *know* his head's not into this."

3/18/91

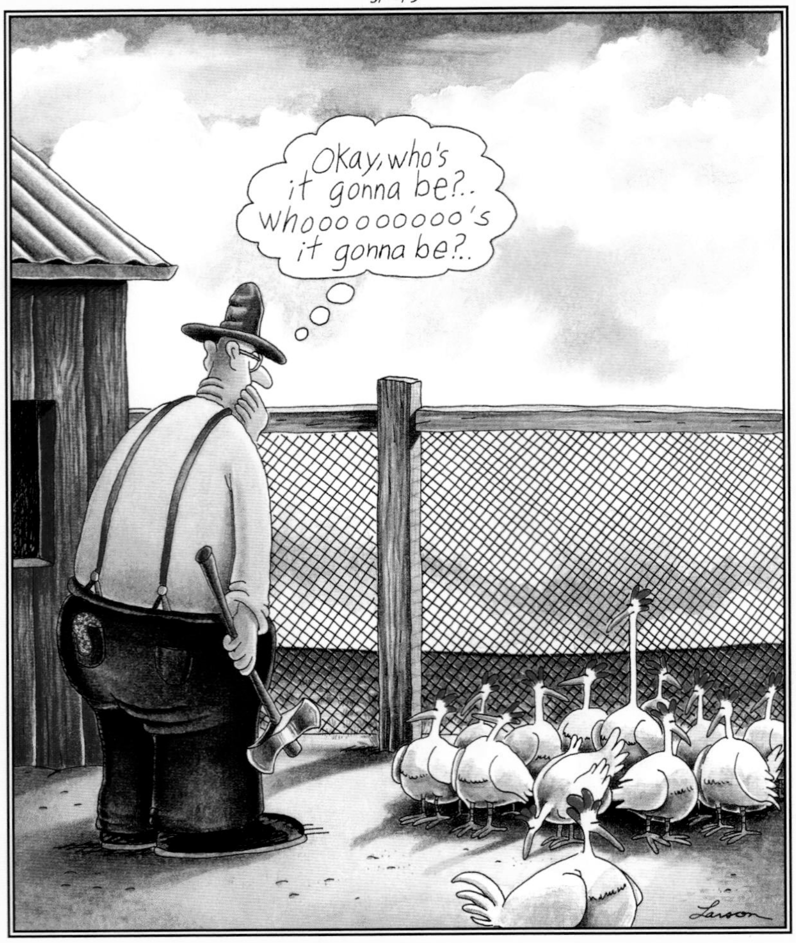
Okay, who's it gonna be?.. Whoooooooooo's it gonna be?..

3/28/91

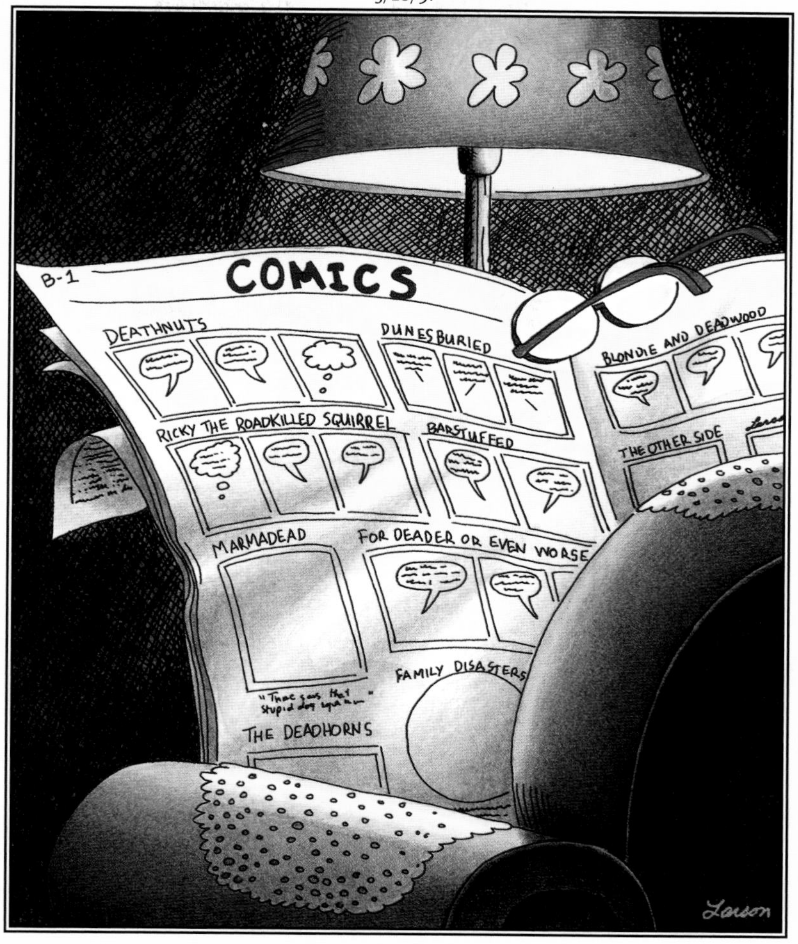
B-1
COMICS
DEATHNUTS
DUNESBURIED
BLONDIE AND DEADWOOD
RICKY THE ROADKILLED SQUIRREL
BARSTUFFED
THE OTHER SIDE
MARMADEAD
FOR DEADER OR EVEN WORSE
FAMILY DISASTERS
THE DEADHORNS
Larson

Ghost newspapers

3/22/91

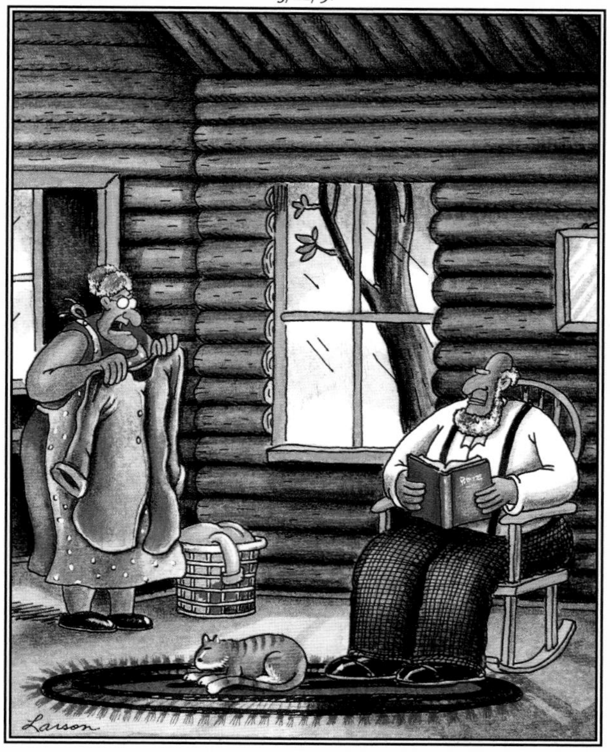
Larson

"Look at this shirt, Remus! You can zip-a-dee-doo-dah all day long for all I care, but you keep that dang Mr. Bluebird off your shoulder!"

3/26/91

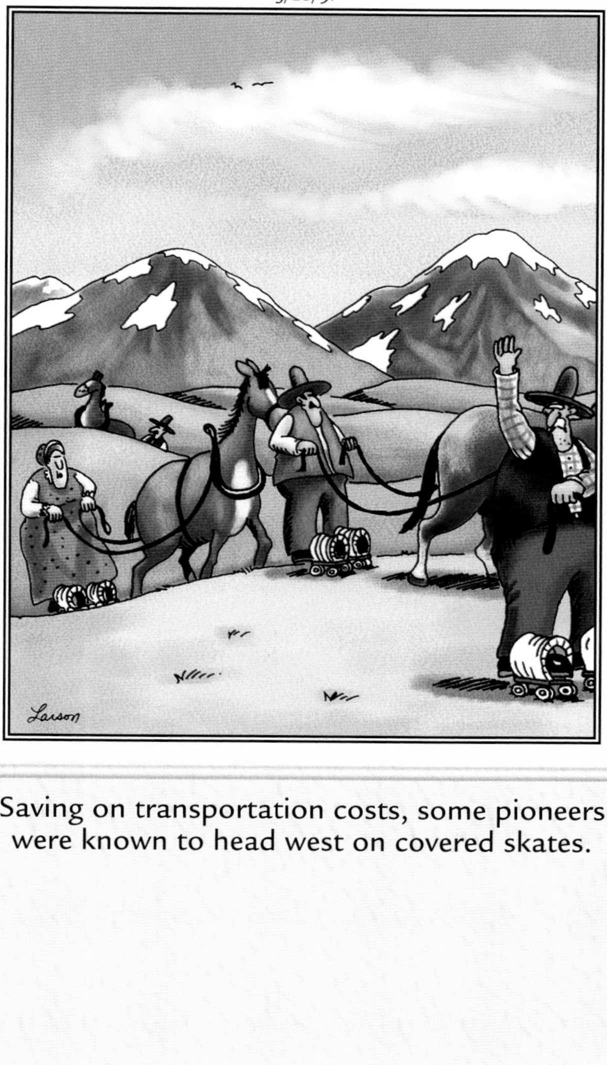
Larson

Saving on transportation costs, some pioneers were known to head west on covered skates.

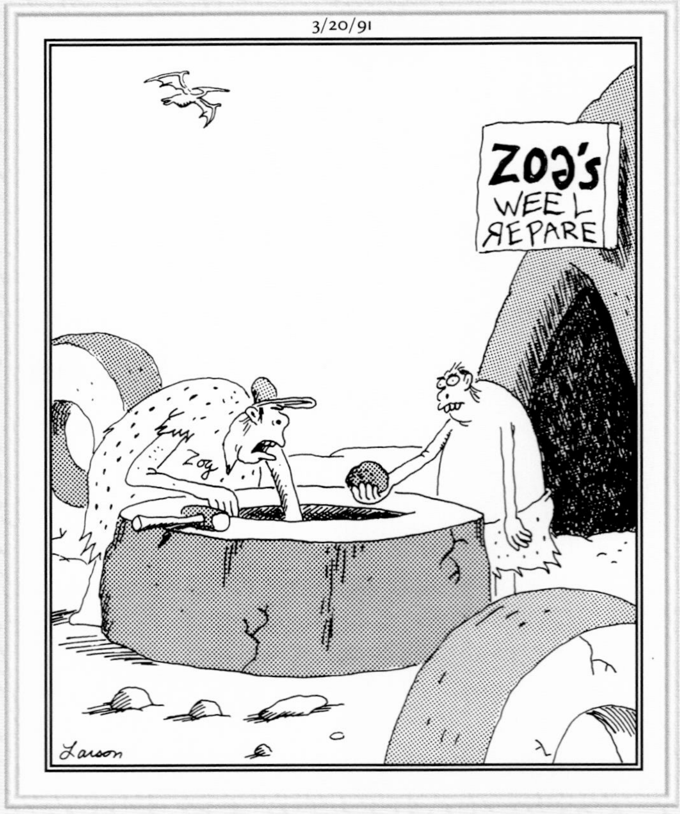
3/20/91
ZOG'S
WEEL
REPARE
Zog
Larson

"No, no, no! ... That regular rock! Me need Phillips!"

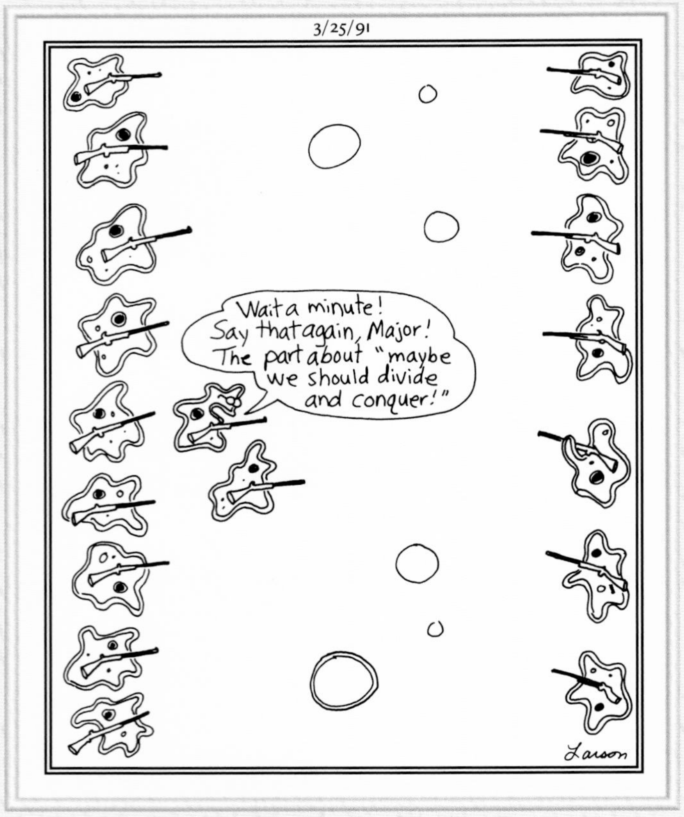
3/25/91
Wait a minute! Say that again, Major! The part about "maybe we should divide and conquer!"
Larson

Amoebas at war

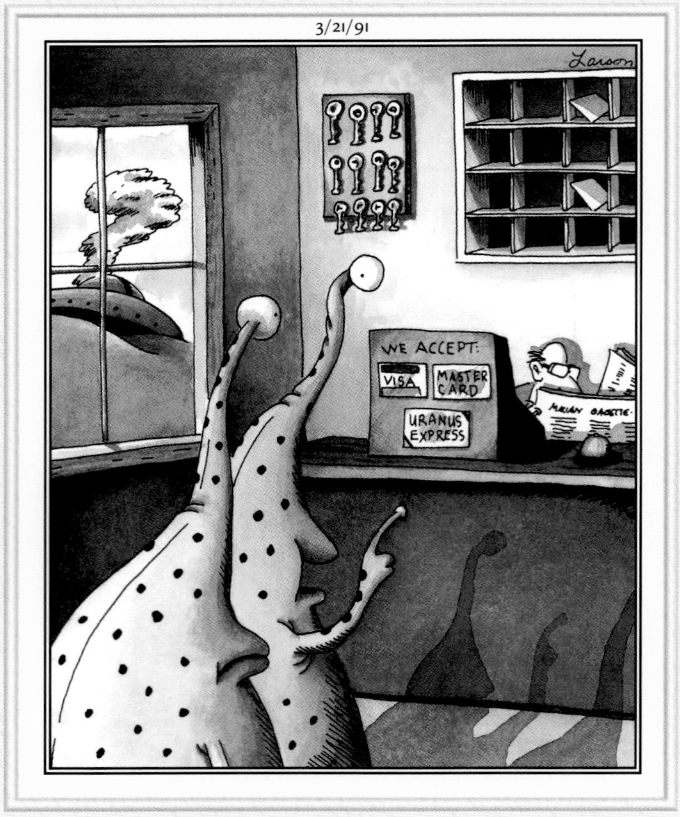
3/21/91
Larson
WE ACCEPT:
VISA
MASTER CARD
URANUS EXPRESS

"We're in luck, Zorko!"

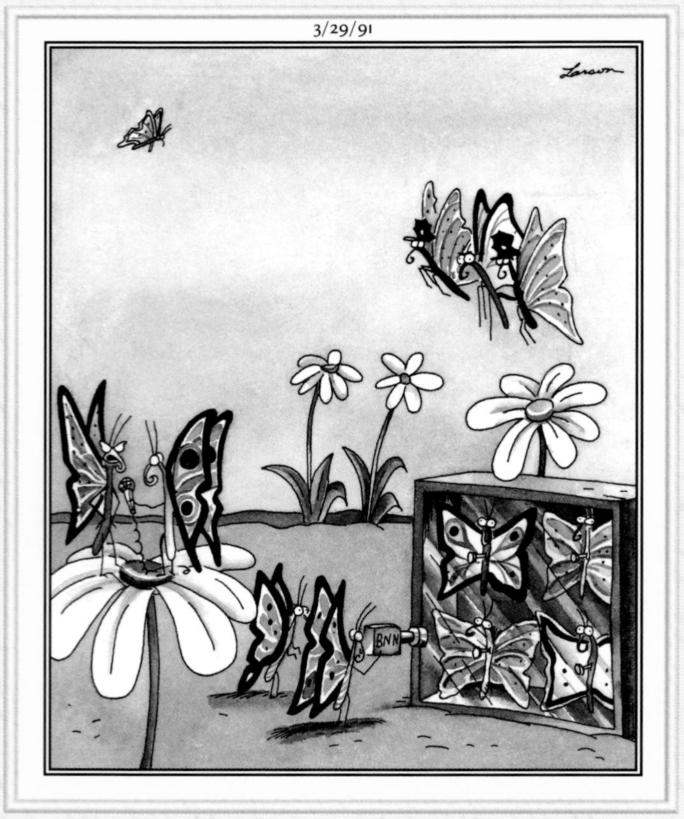
3/29/91
Larson
BNN

"Oh, the whole flower bed is still in shock. He was such a quiet butterfly—kept to himself mostly."

4/2/91

Larson

Every hour on the hour, a huge truck, made entirely of pressed ham, lumbers its way across dog heaven—and all the car chasers can decide for themselves whether or not to participate.

4/4/91

Larson

"There he is, Stan! ... On that birch tree, second branch from the top, and chattering away like crazy! ... I tell you—first come the squirrels and then come the squirrel guns."

4/1/91

Larson

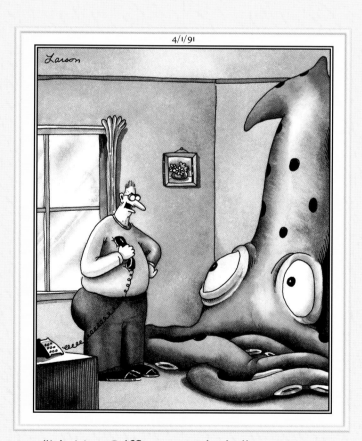

"It's Mrs. Griffin across the hall. ... Seems a giant tentacle smashed her door in today, grabbed her little shih tzu, and dragged it away. ... She called the Harrisons, but *their* squid was over at the park!"

4/5/91

Larson

"Remember this guy, Zelda? Stumbled into the den one day and just freaked out! ... Count those fang marks, everyone!"

4/8/91

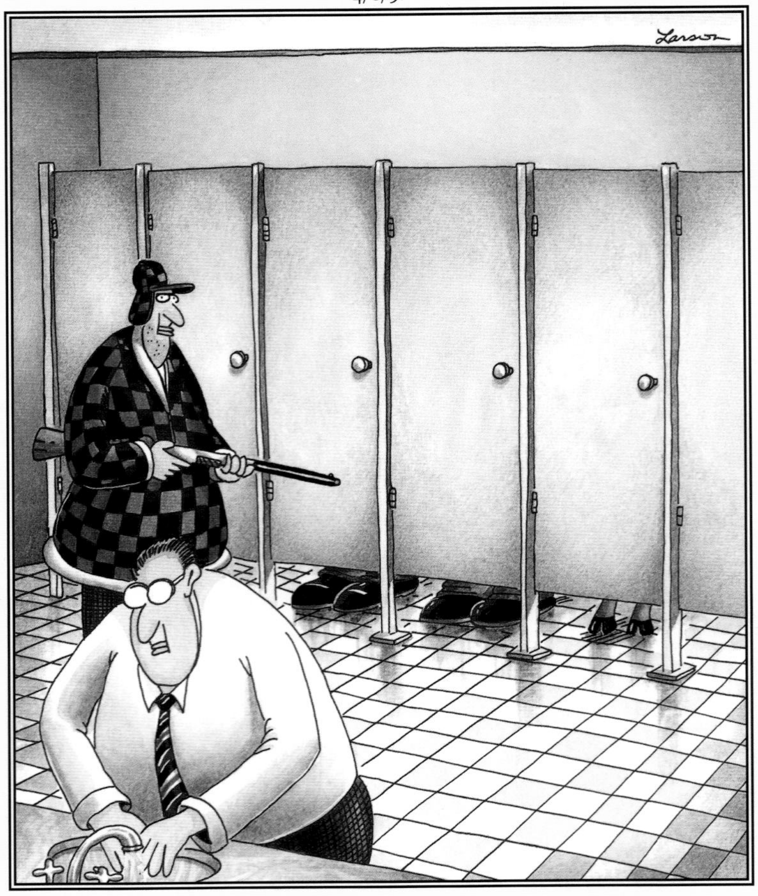
Larson

His rifle poised, Gus burst through the door, stopped, and listened. Nothing but the gentle sound of running water and the rustling of magazines could be heard. The trail, apparently, had been false.

4/11/91

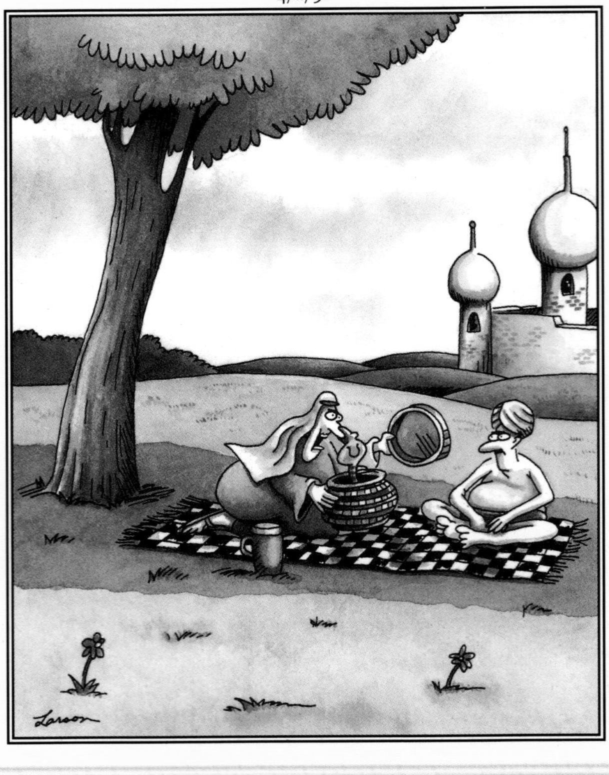
Larson

"Curse you, Ahmad! I specifically said, 'The picnic basket! Make sure you grab the *picnic* basket!'"

4/17/91

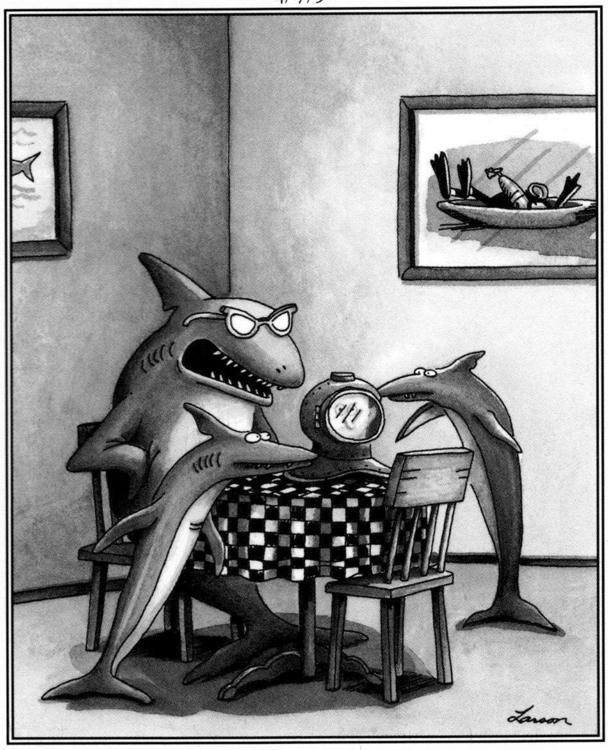
Larson

"C'mon, c'mon! You two quit circling the table and just sit down!"

4/9/91

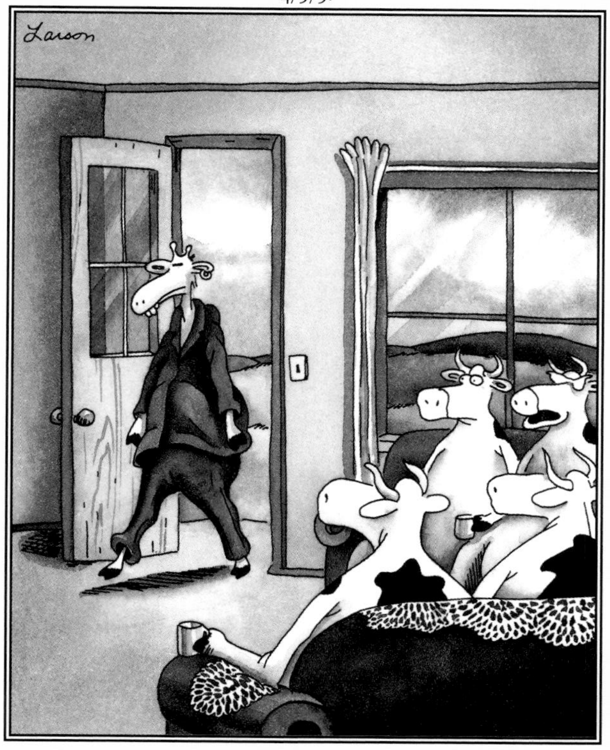
Larson

"Just ignore him. That's our rebellious young calf Matthew—he's into wearing leather clothes just for the shock value."

4/16/91

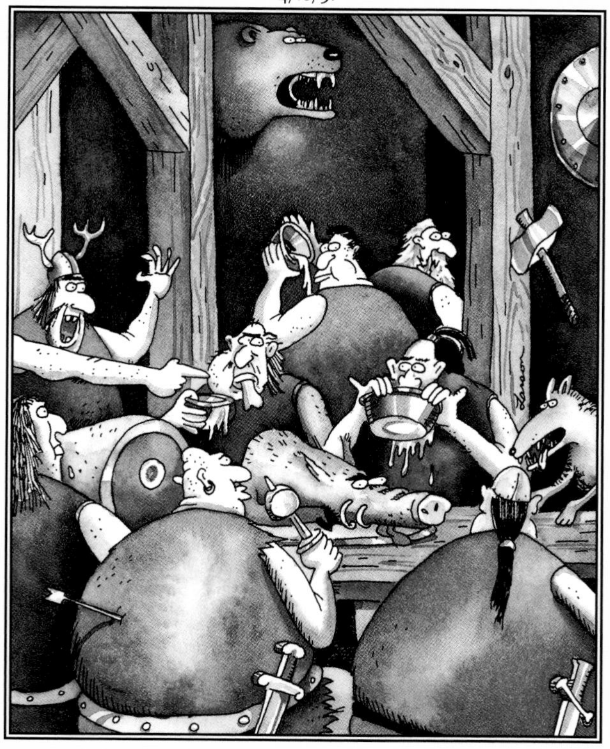
Larson

In a barbarian faux pas that quickly cost him his life, Garth is caught drinking his gruel with pinky fingers extended.

4/10/91

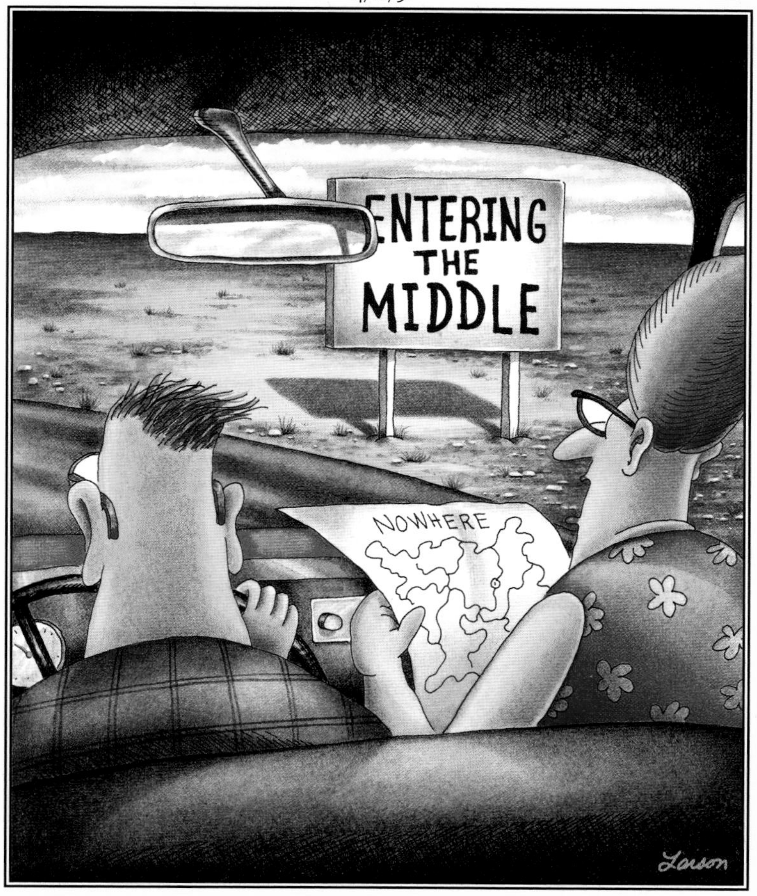
ENTERING
THE
MIDDLE
NOWHERE
Larson

"Well, this is just going from bad to worse."

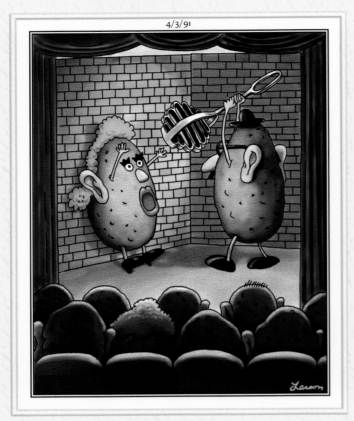

4/3/91

Masher films

4/12/91

OK, Norg... SHAKE! No, wait! Dang! OK... get ready... SHAKE! No! OK, ok... get ready...

Early but unsuccessful practical jokes

4/15/91

"Got him, Byron! It's something in the *Vespula* genus, all right—and oooowweeeee does he look mad!"

4/26/91

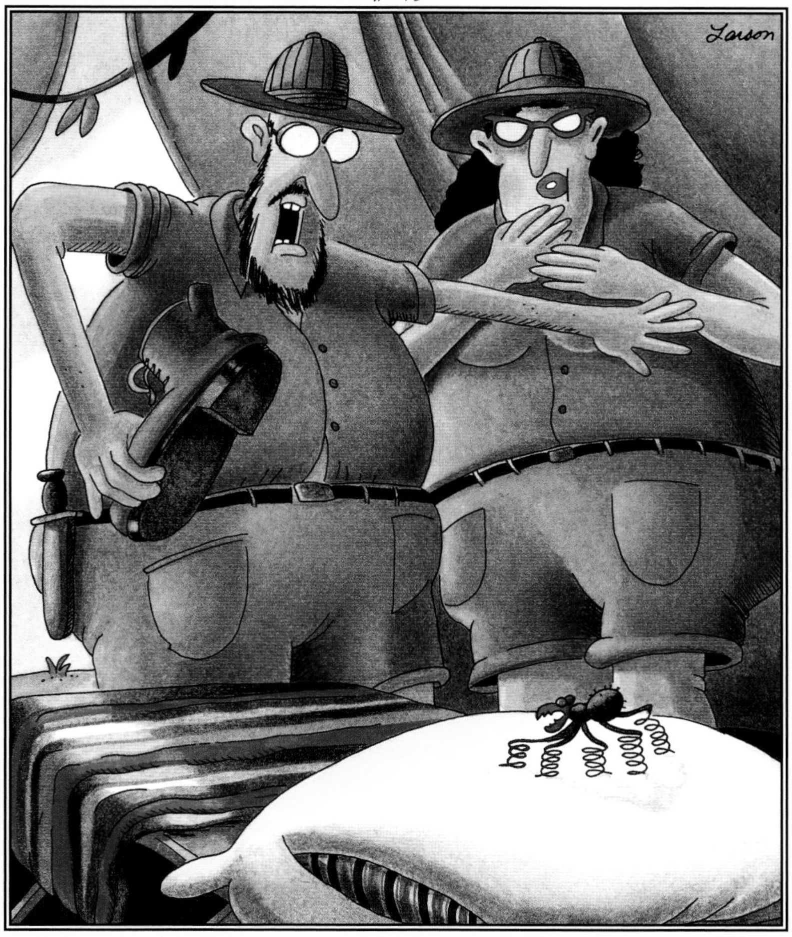
Larson

"Don't make any erratic movements, Miss Halloway. ... Not only is the truculent nature of this species amply documented, but, as you can discern for yourself, the little suckers can really jump."

4/19/91

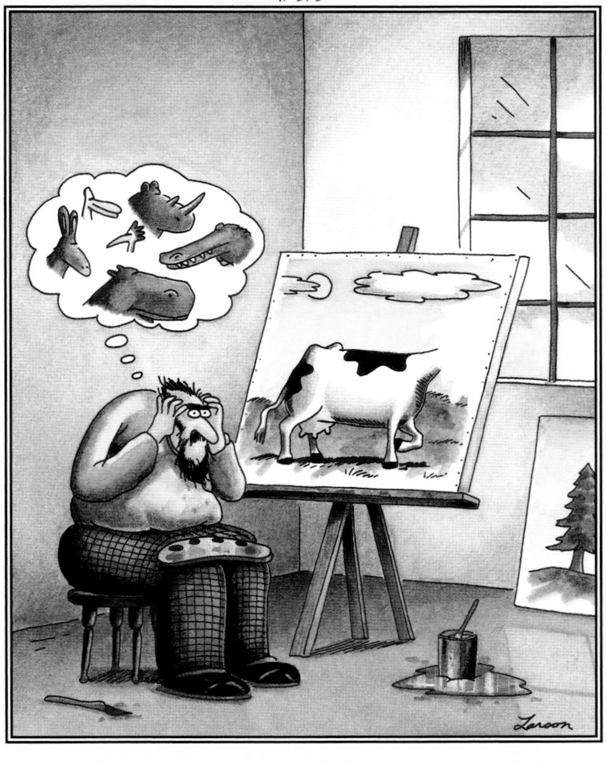
Larson

The curse of "artist's block"

4/24/91

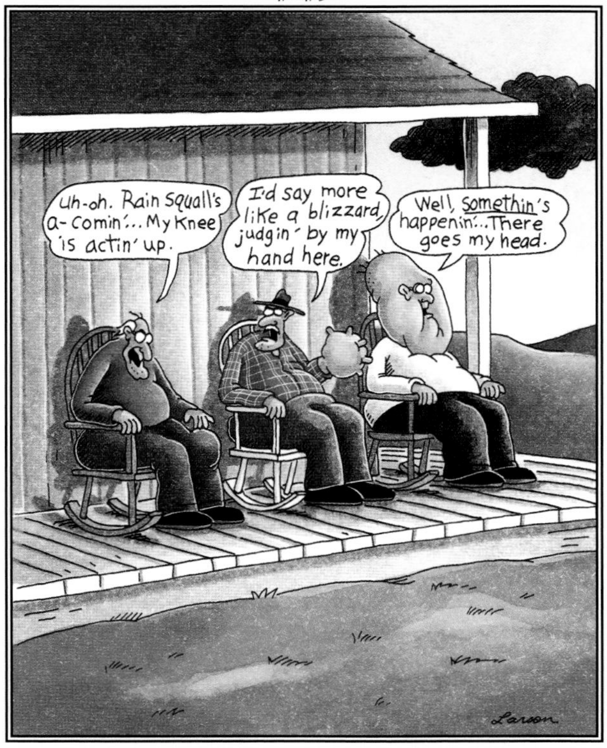
Uh-oh. Rain squall's a-comin'... My knee is actin' up.
I'd say more like a blizzard, judgin' by my hand here.
Well, somethin's happenin'... There goes my head.
Larson

Front porch forecasters

4/18/91

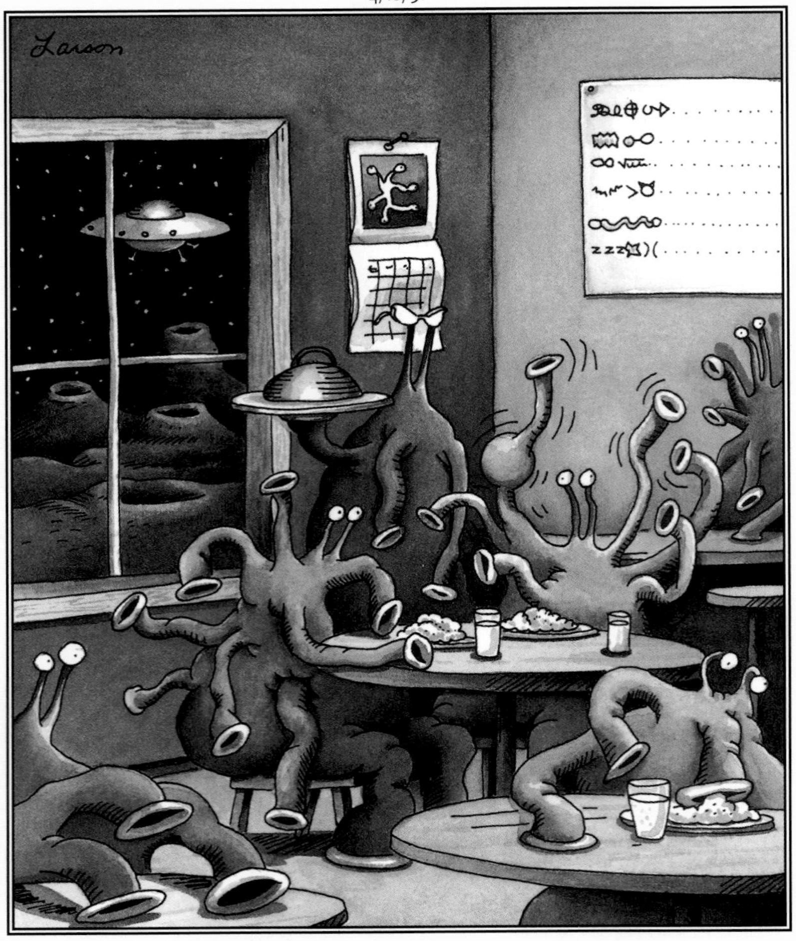
Larson

Suddenly, one of the Dorkonians began to flagellate hysterically. Something, apparently, had gone down the wrong pipe.

4/22/91

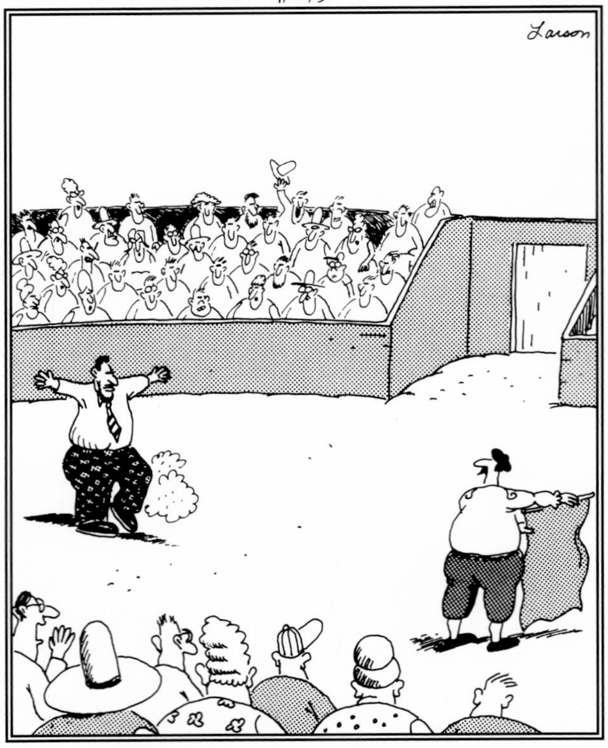
Larson

In some remote areas of the world, the popular sport is to watch a courageous young man avoid being hugged by a Leo Buscaglia impersonator.

4/23/91

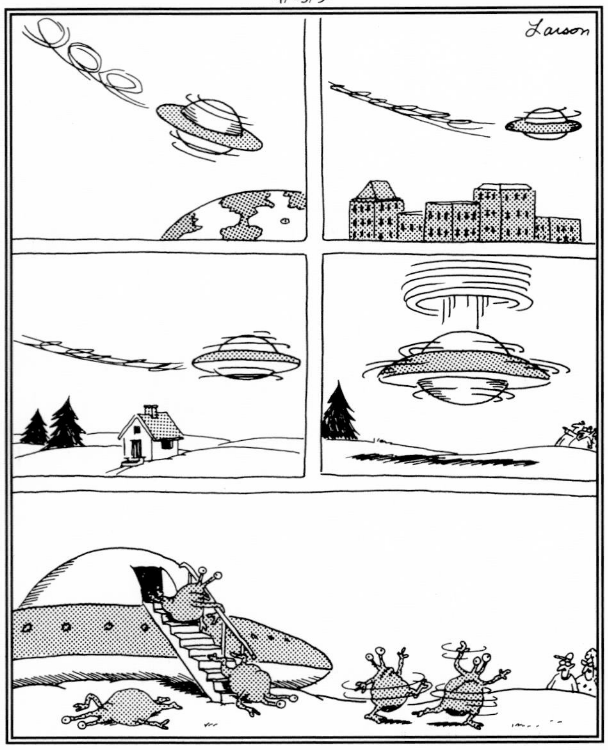
Larson

4/25/91

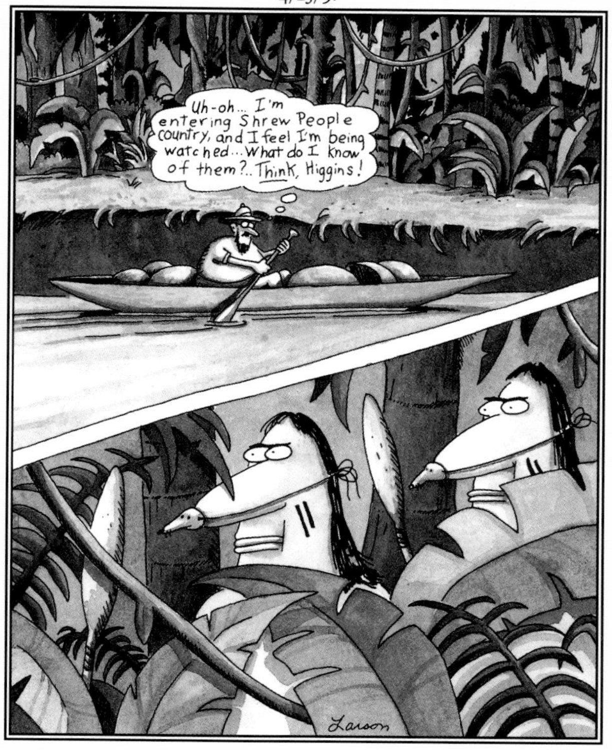
Uh-oh... I'm entering Shrew People country, and I feel I'm being watched... What do I know of them?.. Think, Higgins!

Shrew People: quick, carnivorous, usually nocturnal; smaller but more vicious than the better-known Mole People; eat five times their own body weight every day; cannibals.

4/29/91

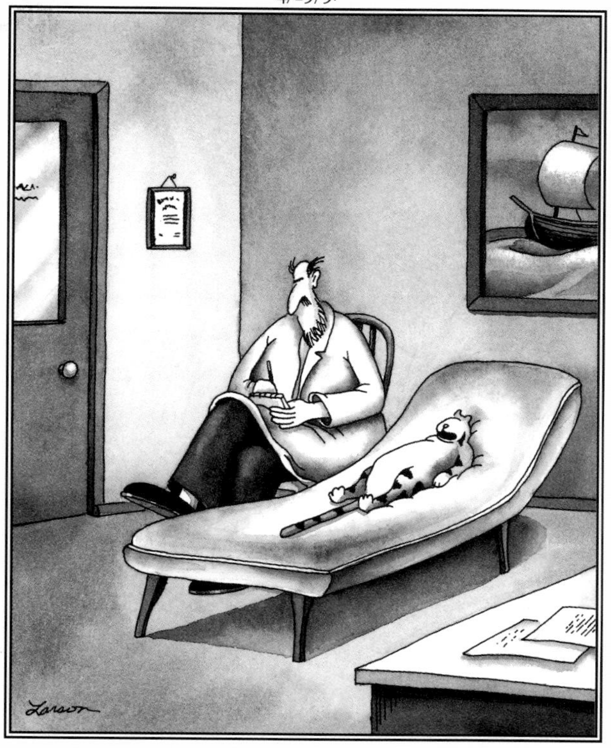

"I'm starting to feel dependent."

4/30/91

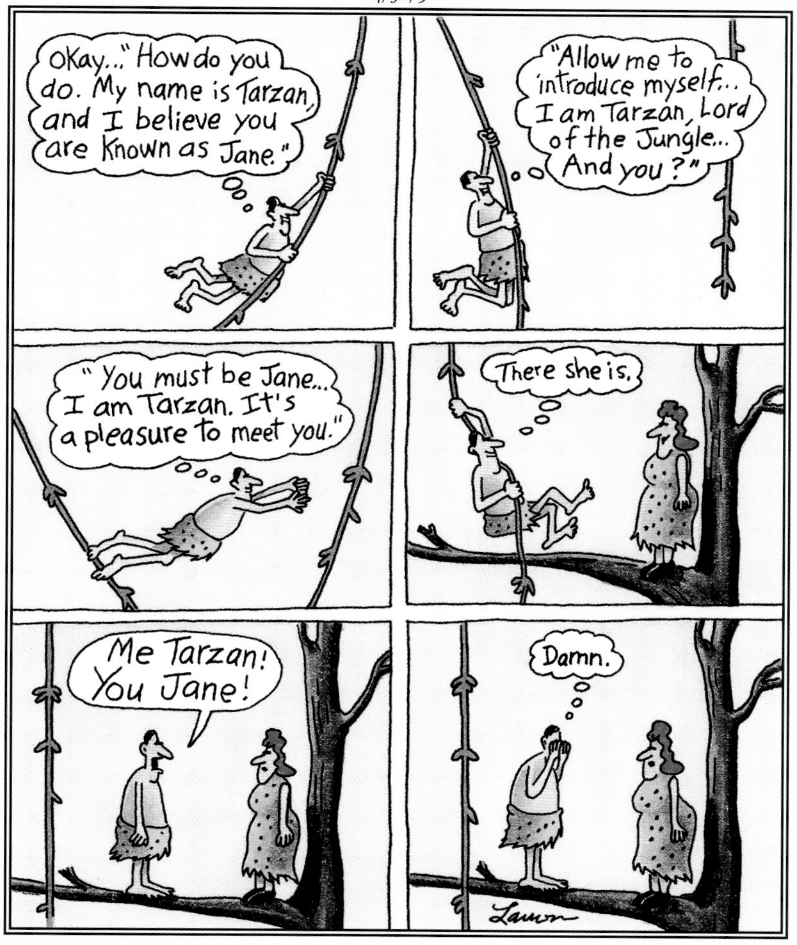
Okay..." How do you do. My name is Tarzan, and I believe you are known as Jane."
"Allow me to introduce myself... I am Tarzan, Lord of the Jungle... And you?"
"You must be Jane... I am Tarzan. It's a pleasure to meet you."
There she is.
Me Tarzan! You Jane!
Damn.

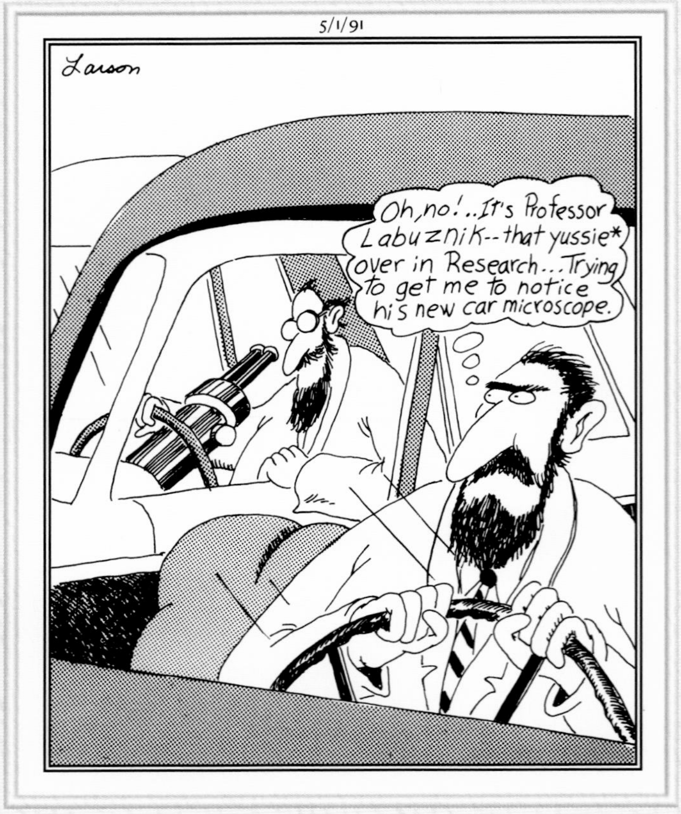
5/1/91
Larson
Oh, no!.. It's Professor Labuznik--that yussie* over in Research... Trying to get me to notice his new car microscope.

*Young urban scientist

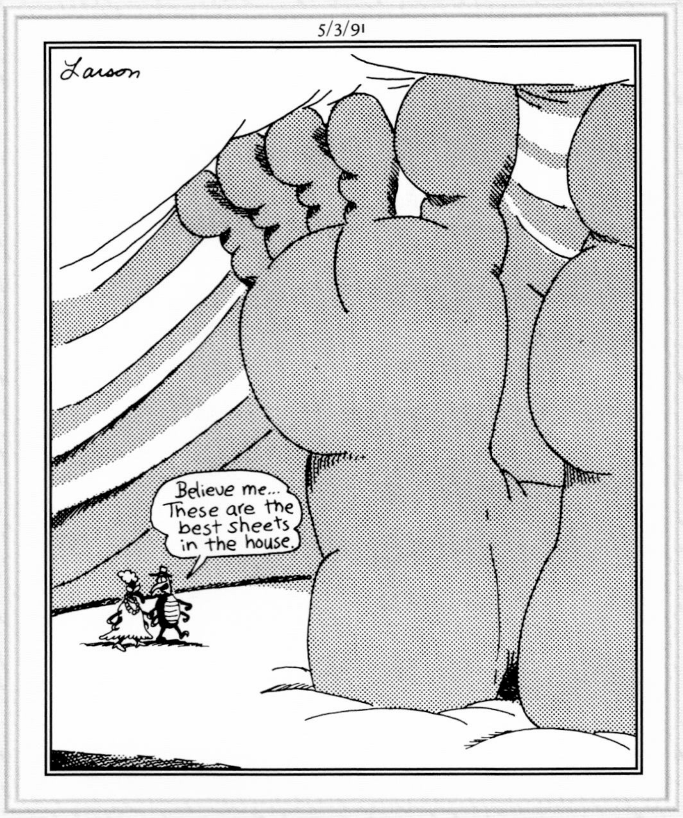
5/3/91
Larson
Believe me... These are the best sheets in the house.

Bedbug dinner theater

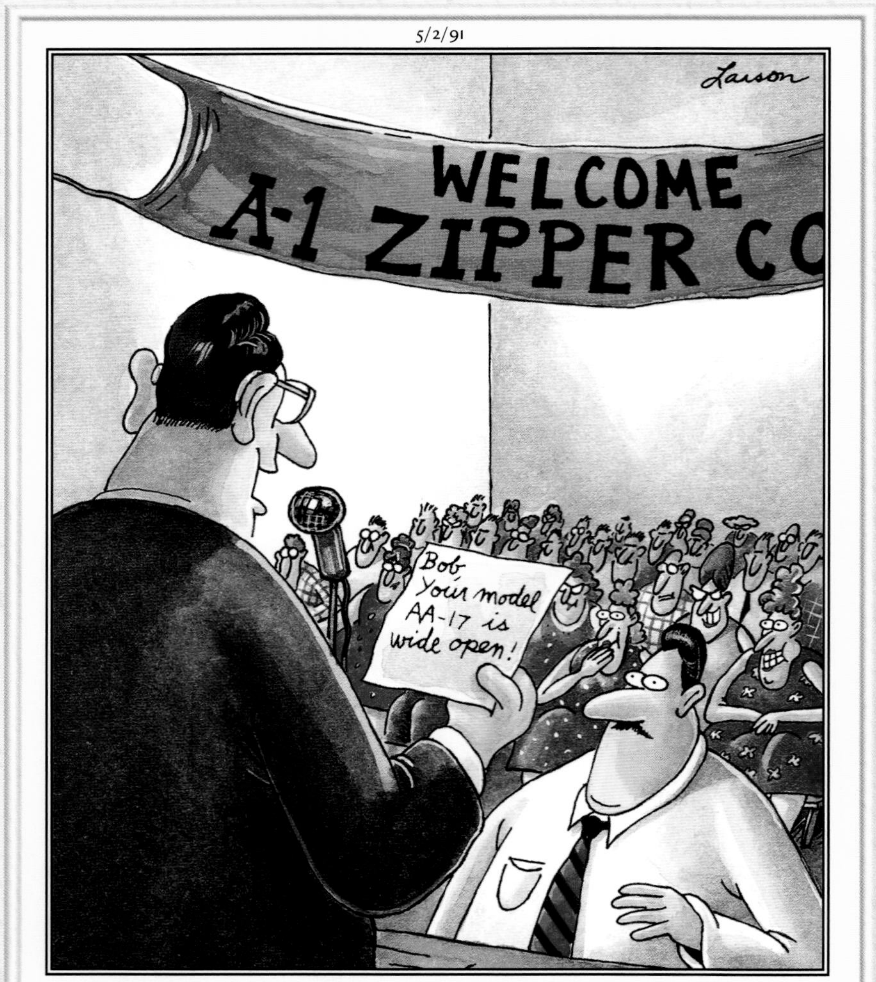
5/2/91
Larson
WELCOME
A-1 ZIPPER CO
Bob
Your model AA-17 is wide open!

"Wait a minute, friends ... Frank Stevens in marketing—you all know Frank—has just handed me a note ..."

5/6/91

DLDWWS
Furthermore, the way they portrayed the cavalry as being insensitive just made me sick!
And the buffaloes... Those buffaloes weren't really killed... That was all faked!
Larson

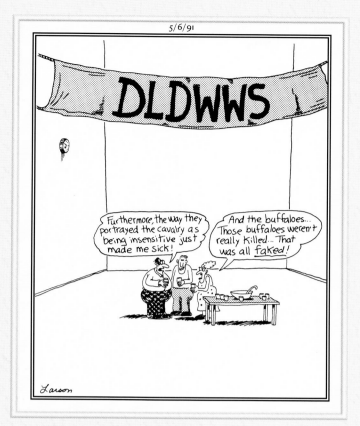

At the international meeting of the Didn't Like *Dances with Wolves* Society

5/7/91

Larson
♫ Bah bah baaah... bah bah bah-ran.. ♪

5/8/91

HONEY I ATE THE KIDS
HONEY I ATE THE KIDS
ADMISSION
Larson

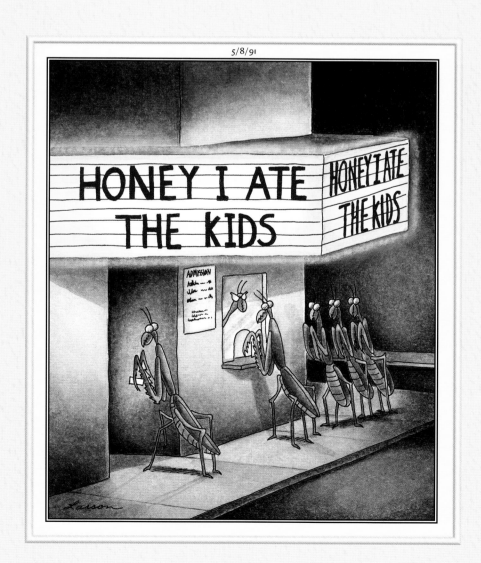

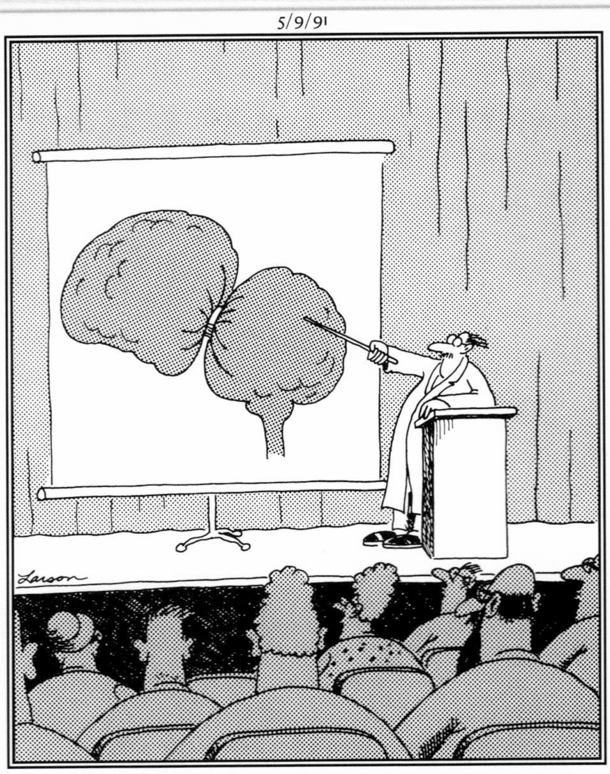
5/9/91

Professor Lundquist, in a seminar on compulsive thinkers, illustrates his brain-stapling technique.

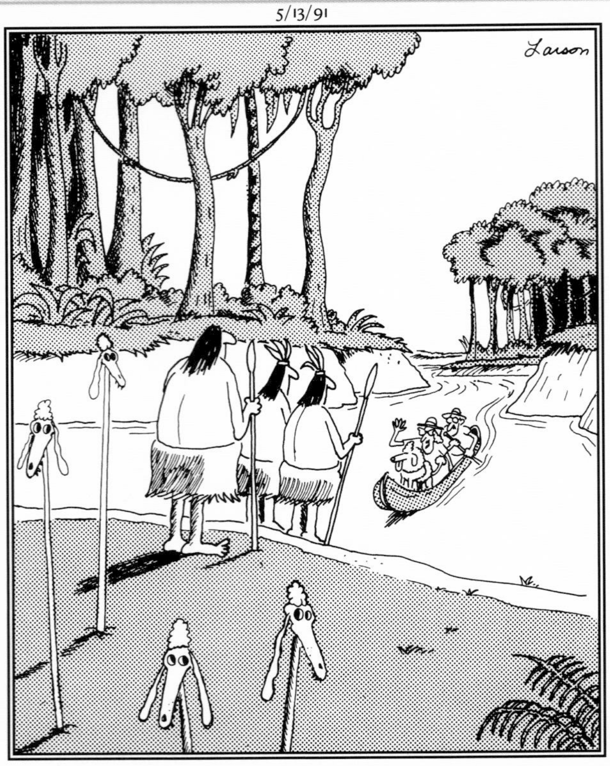
5/13/91

Although nervous, the Dickersons were well-received by this tribe of unique headhunters. It was Pooki, regrettably, that was to bear the brunt of their aggression.

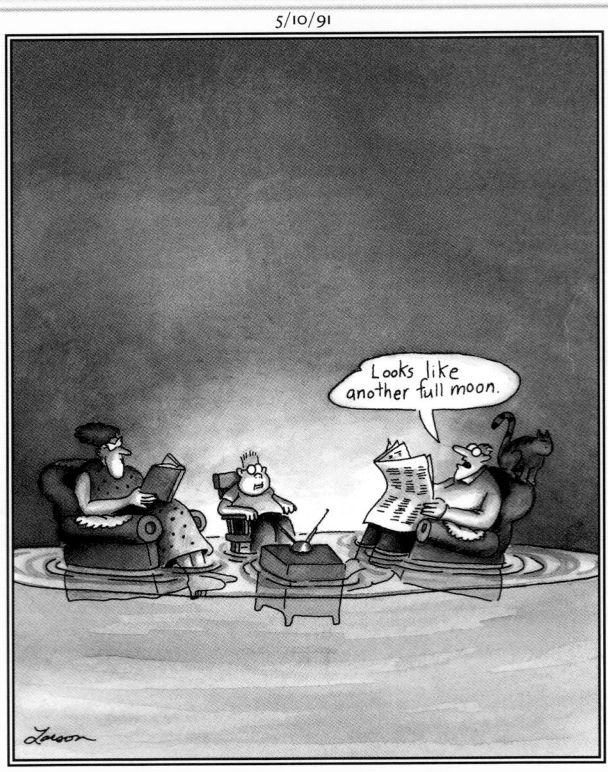
5/10/91
Looks like another full moon.

The Ty-D-Bol family at home

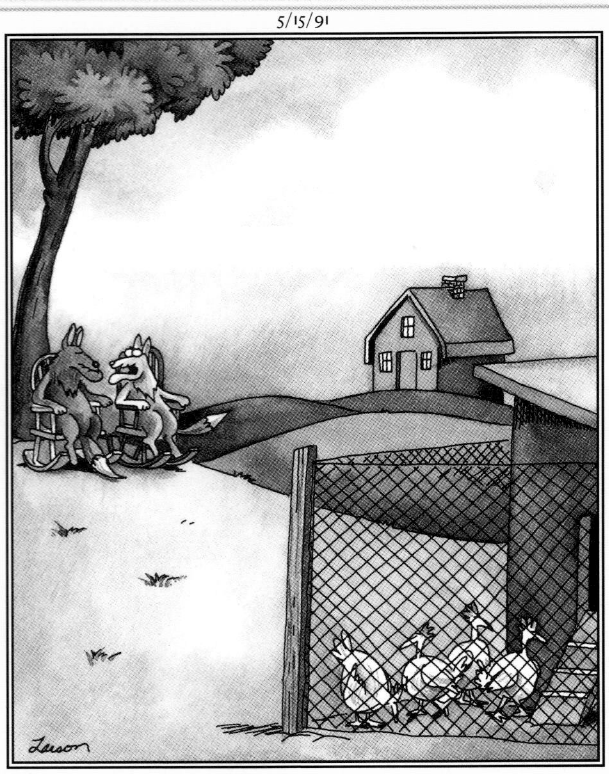
5/15/91

"Look at us, Hank. ... I tell you, there was a time when we did more than just *watch* the henhouse."

5/17/91

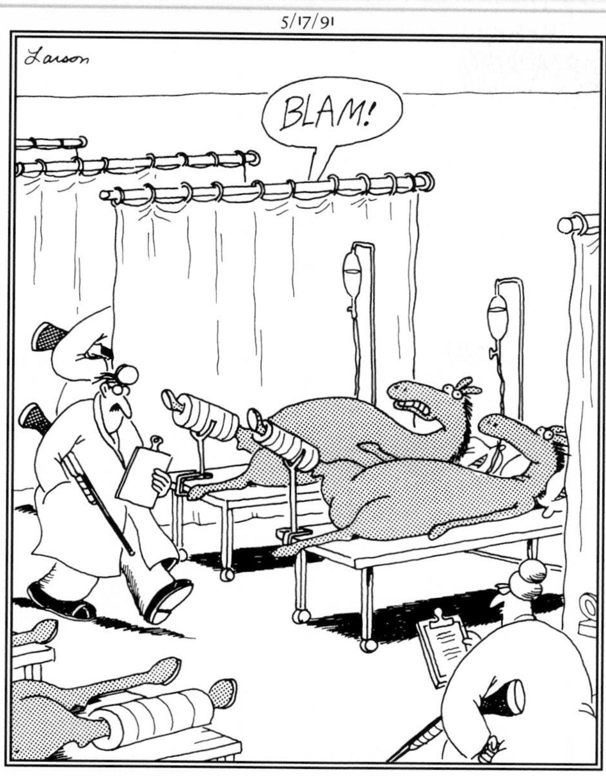
BLAM!

Horse hospitals

5/22/91

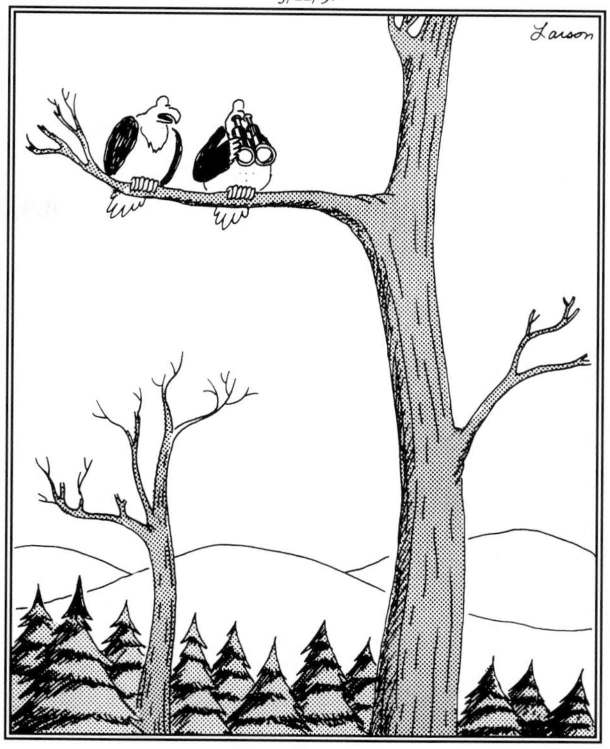

"You're cheating, Ned."

5/23/91

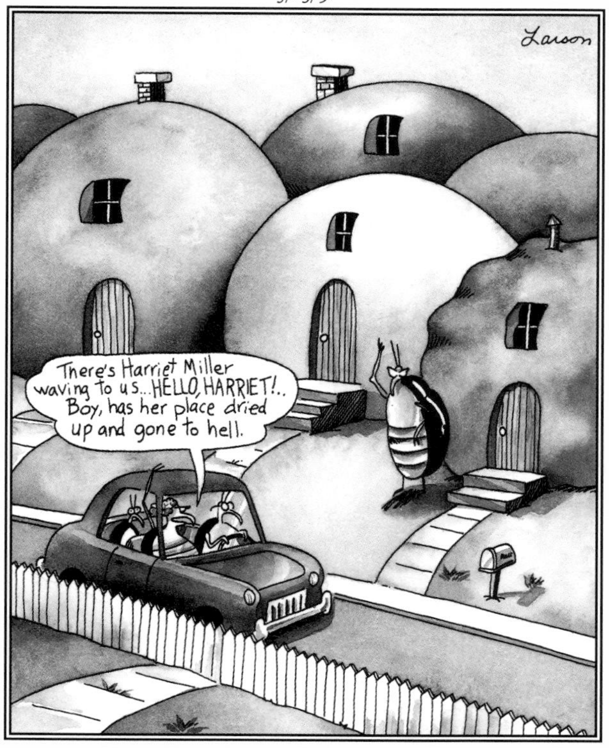
There's Harriet Miller waving to us...HELLO, HARRIET!.. Boy, has her place dried up and gone to hell.

Dung beetle neighborhoods

5/16/91

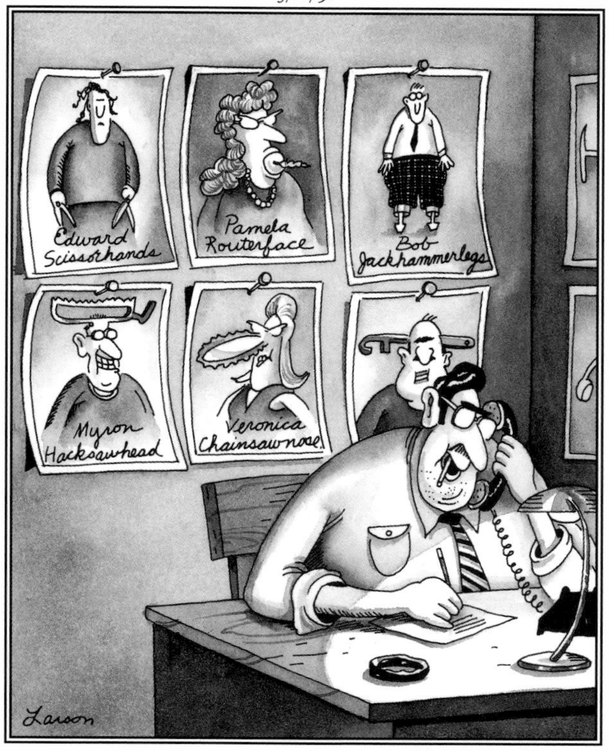
Edward Scissorhands
Pamela Routerface
Bob Jackhammerlegs
Myron Hacksawhead
Veronica Chainsawnose

"Al's All-in-One Talent Agency and Construction Company, may I help you?"

5/14/91

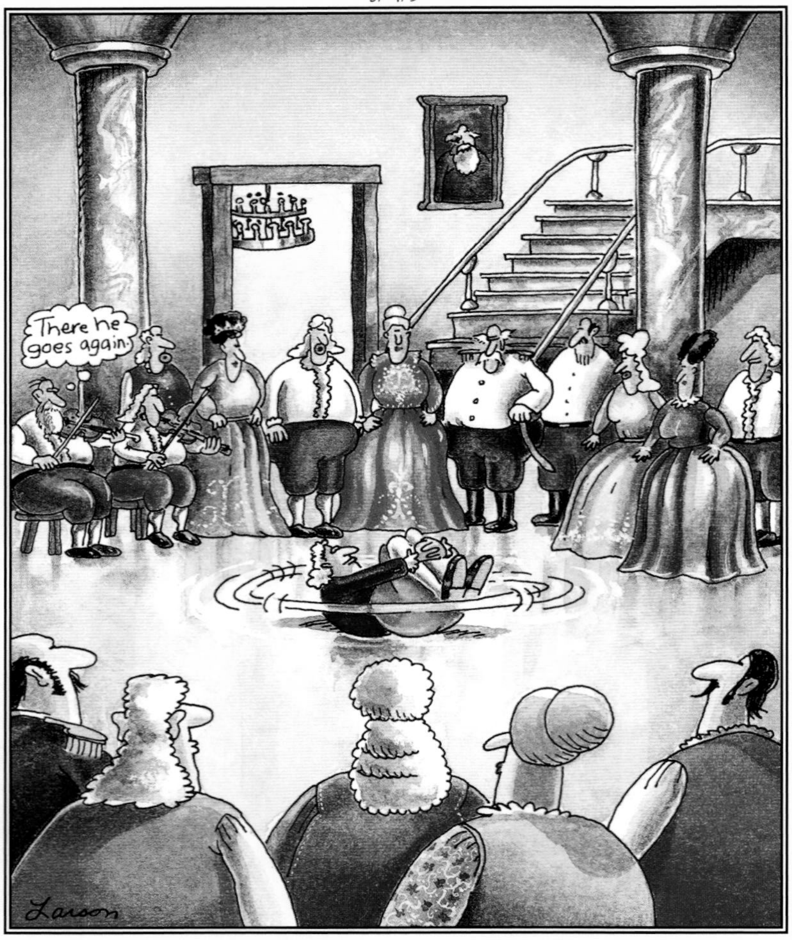
There he goes again.
Larson

George Washington: general, president, visionary,
ballroom break dancer.

5/20/91

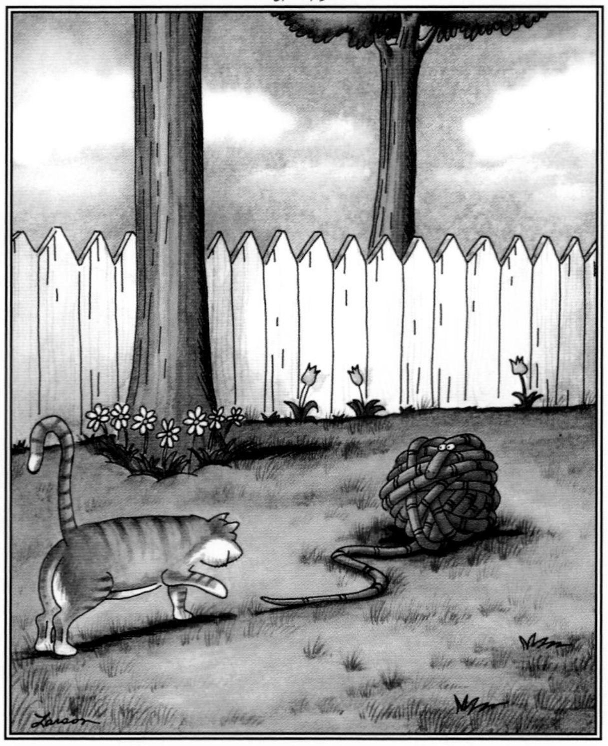
Larson

The urban catsnake and its prey

5/21/91

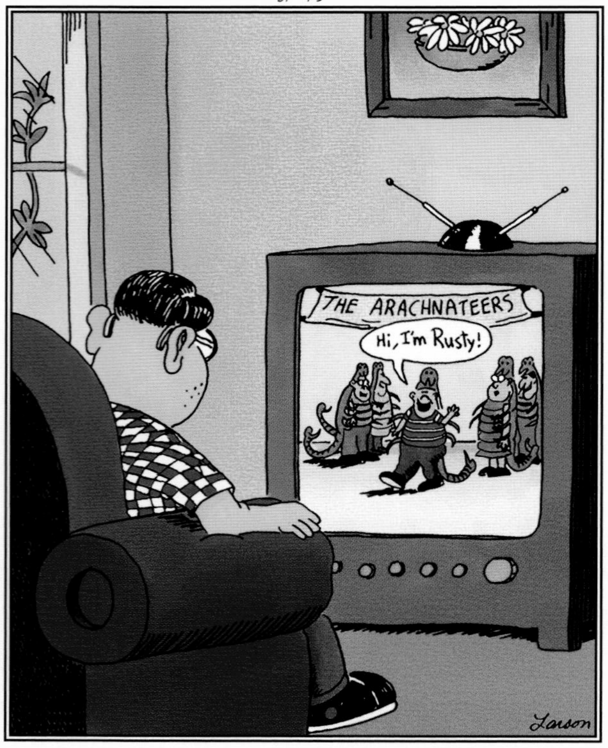
THE ARACHNATEERS
Hi, I'm Rusty!
Larson

Kids' shows that bombed

5/27/91

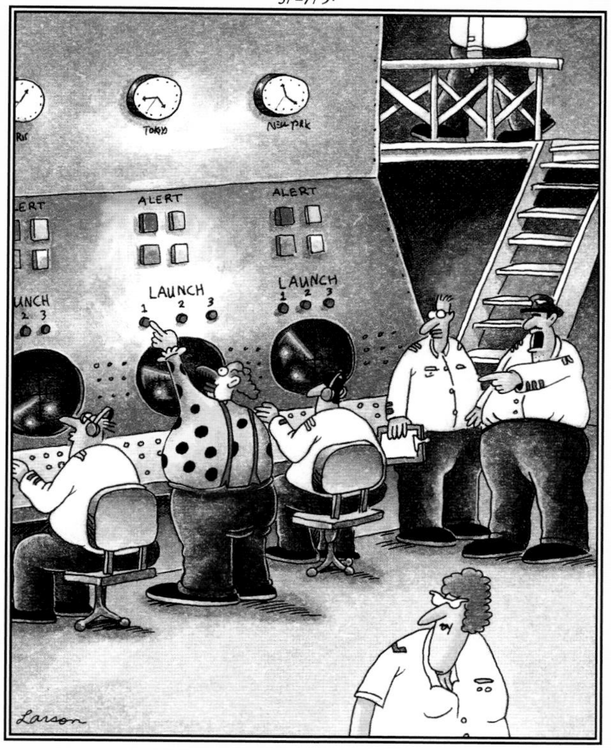
ALERT
ALERT
LAUNCH
1 2 3
LAUNCH
1 2 3
Larson

"Hey! What's that clown think he's doing?"

5/29/91

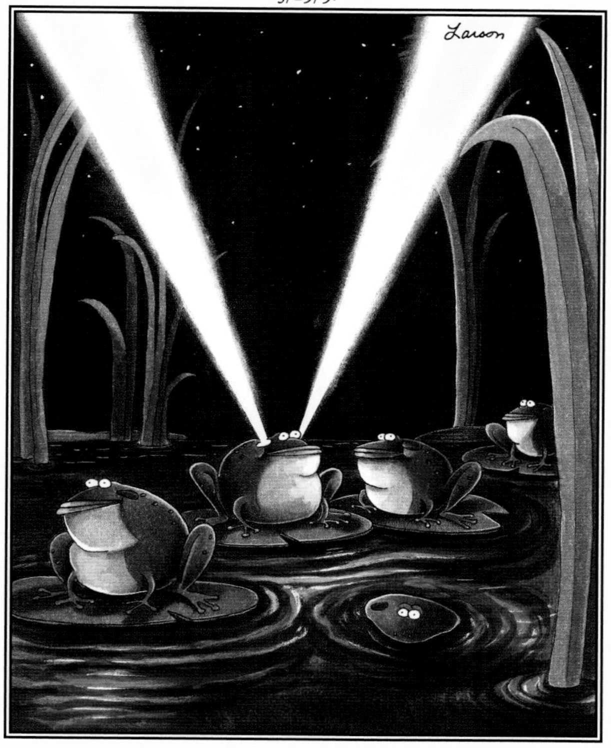
Larson

What really happened to Tinkerbell

5/31/91

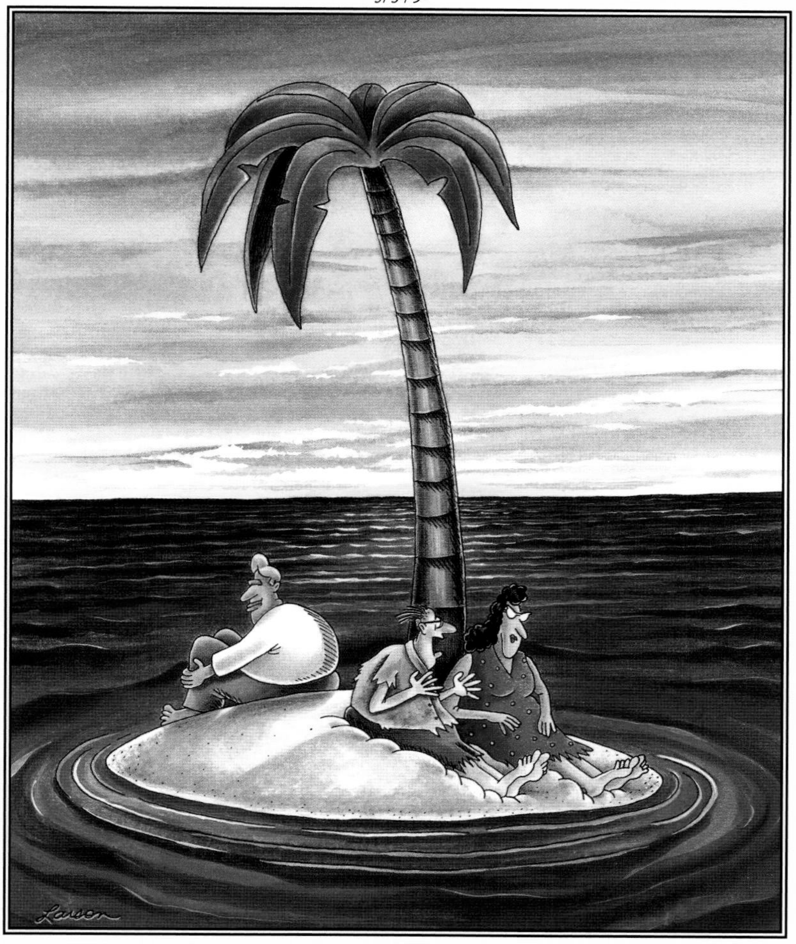
Larson

"What? You've met someone else? What are you saying? ...
Oh, my God! It's not what's-his-name, is it?"

5/24/91

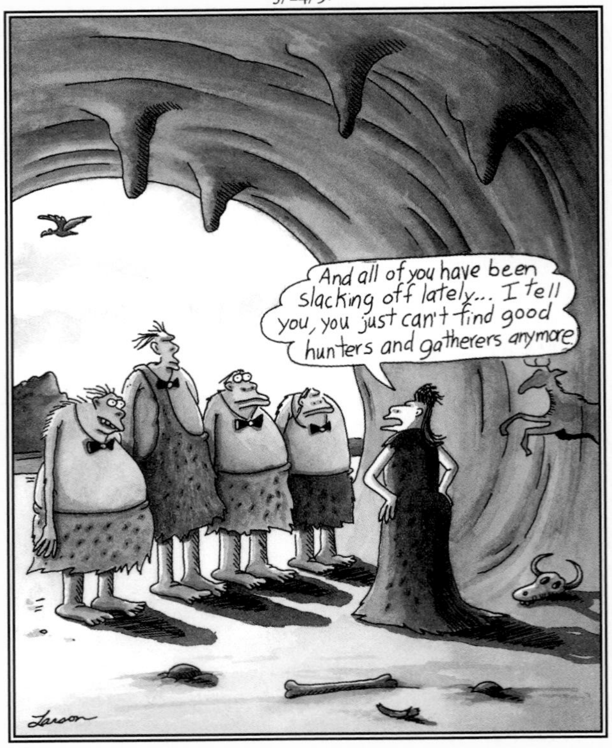
And all of you have been slacking off lately... I tell you, you just can't find good hunters and gatherers anymore.

Leona Helmsley of the Paleozoic

5/30/91

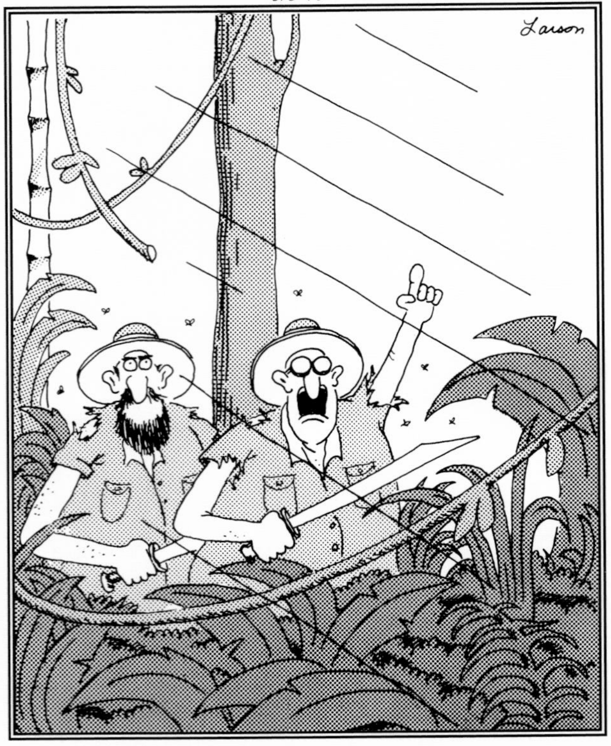

"We can't go this way either, Simmons. ... See those lines? That's the international cartoon symbol for *glass!* ... He's got us good, the dirty bugger."

5/28/91

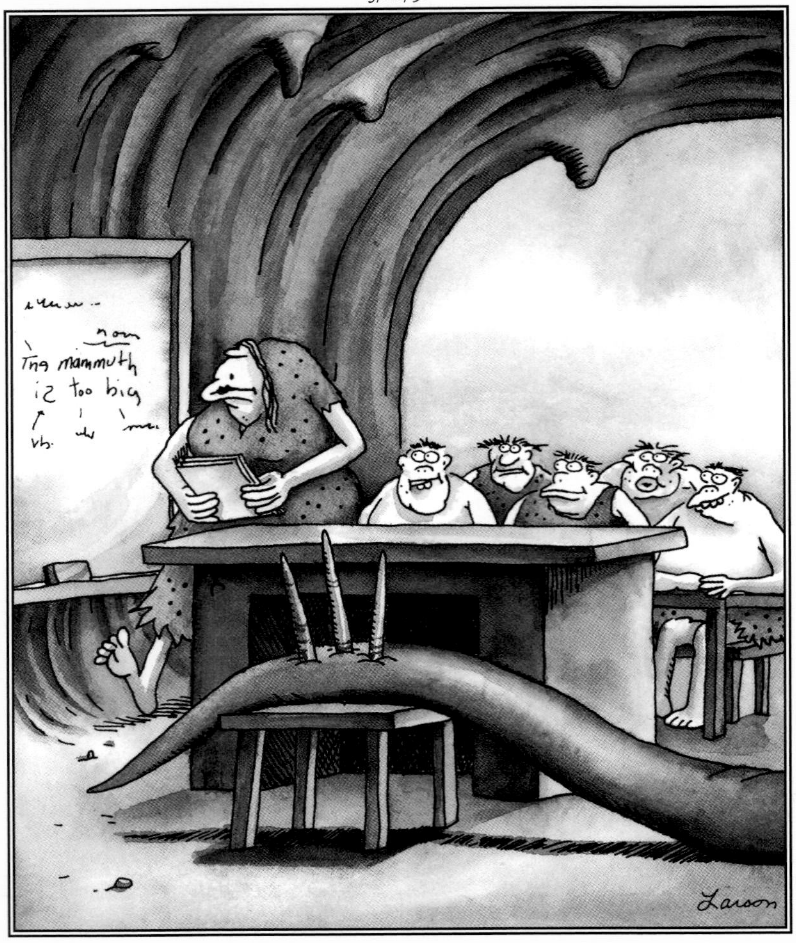
The mammuth
is too big

The hazards of teaching young Neanderthals

6/5/91

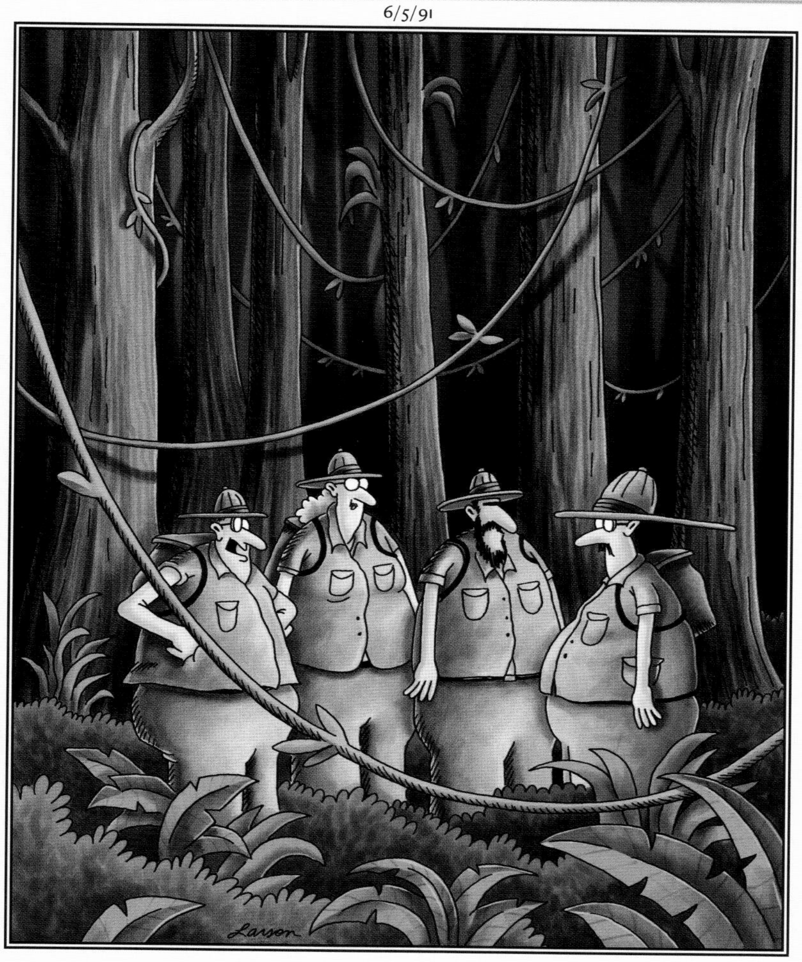

"Well, we're lost. I knew from the start that it was just plain idiotic to choose a leader based simply on the size of his or her respective pith helmet. Sorry, Cromwell."

6/3/91

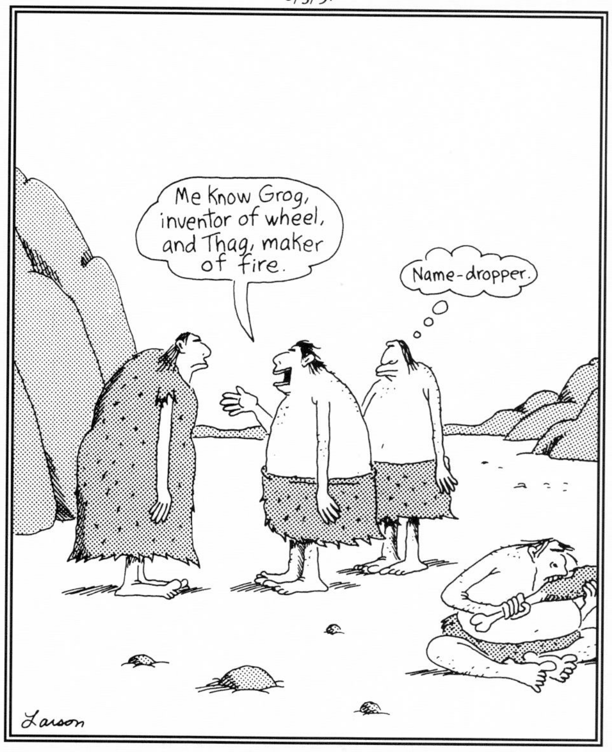
Me Know Grog, inventor of wheel, and Thag, maker of fire.
Name-dropper.

6/11/91

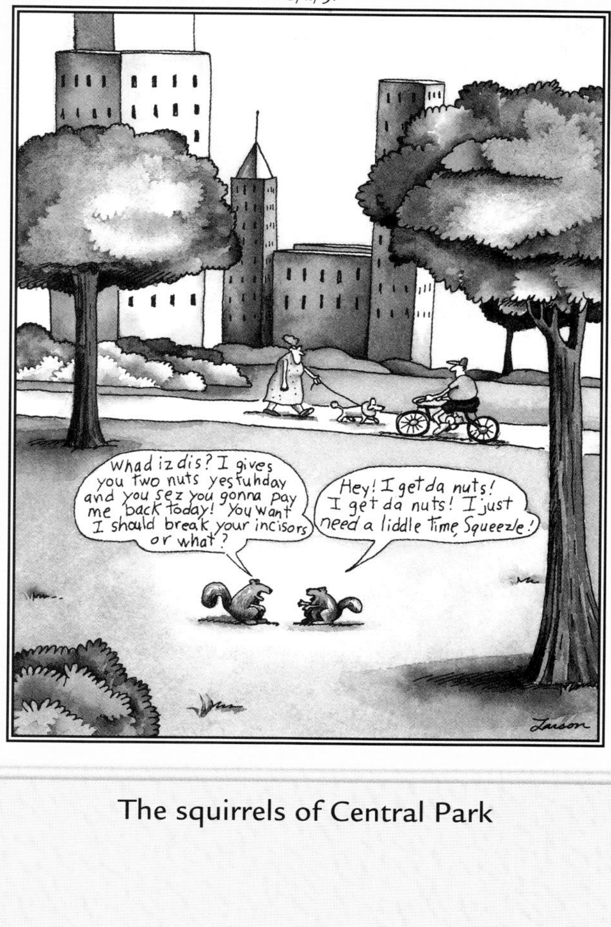
Whad iz dis? I gives you two nuts yesfuhday and you sez you gonna pay me back today! You want I should break your incisors or what?
Hey! I get da nuts! I get da nuts! I just need a liddle time, Squeezle!

The squirrels of Central Park

6/4/91

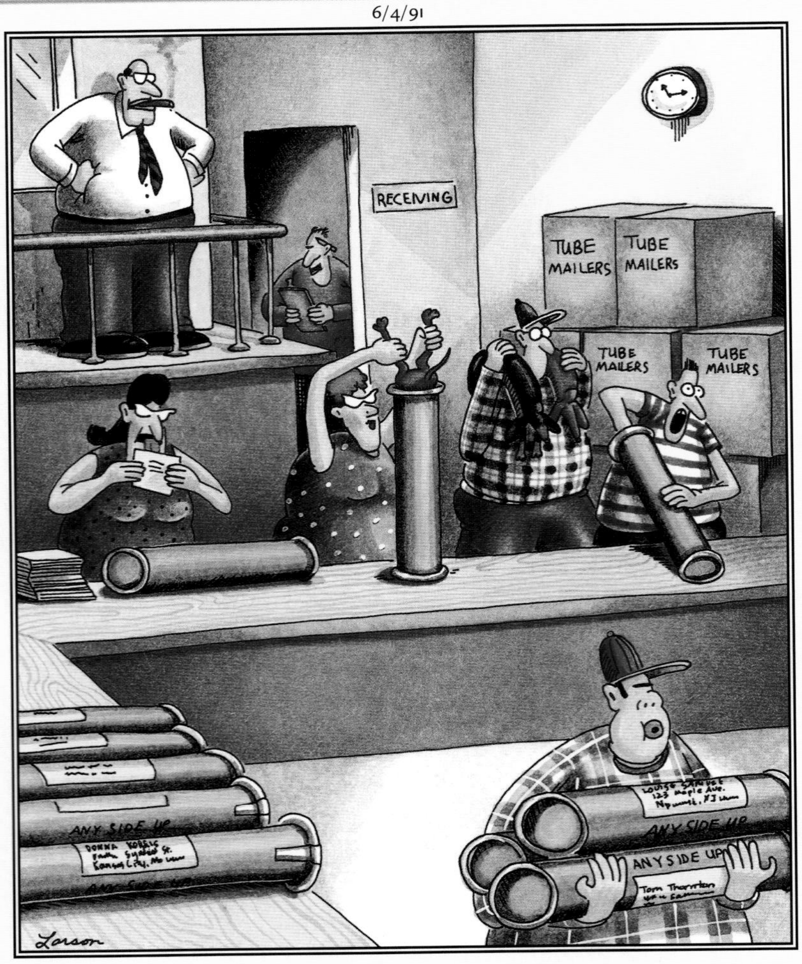
RECEIVING
TUBE MAILERS
TUBE MAILERS
TUBE MAILERS
TUBE MAILERS
ANY SIDE UP
ANY SIDE UP
ANYSIDE UP
Larson

Wiener dog distribution centers

6/6/91

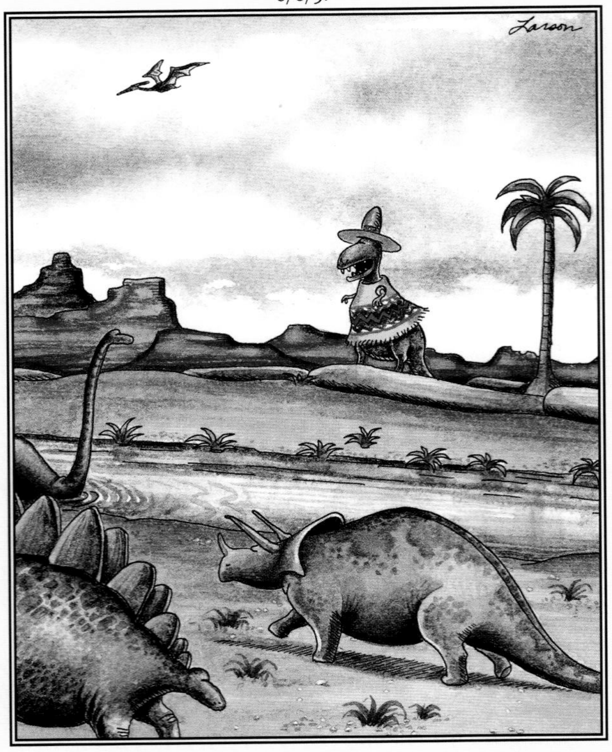
Larson

However, there was no question that, on the south side of the river, the land was ruled by the awesome *Tyrannosaurus Mex*.

6/7/91

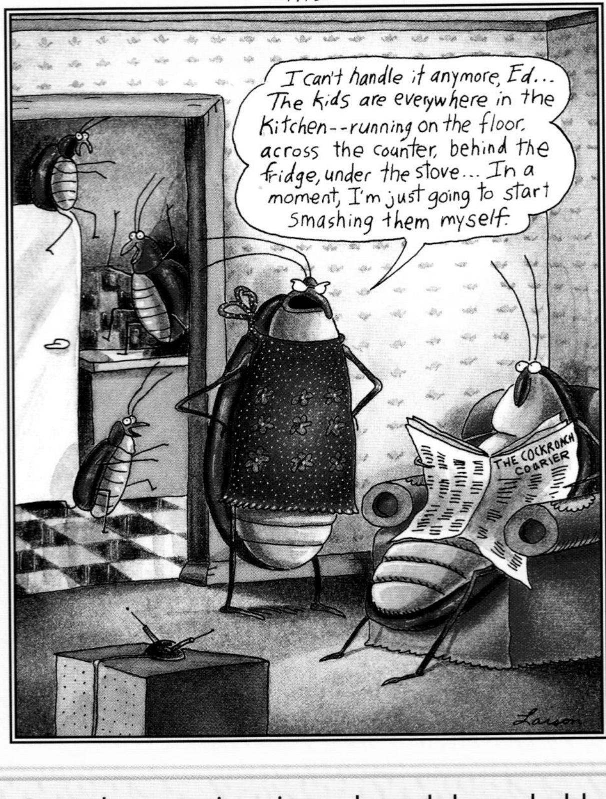
I can't handle it anymore, Ed... The kids are everywhere in the Kitchen--running on the floor, across the counter, behind the fridge, under the stove... In a moment, I'm just going to start smashing them myself.
THE COCKROACH COURIER
Larson

Saturday mornings in cockroach households

6/12/91

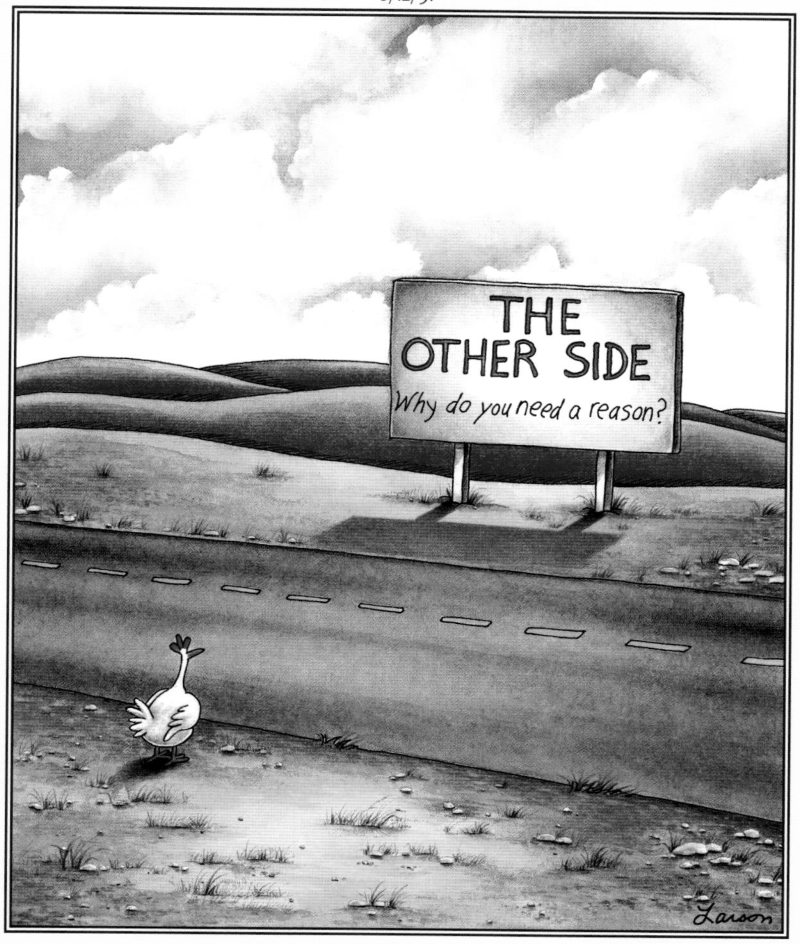
THE
OTHER SIDE
Why do you need a reason?
Larson

6/10/91

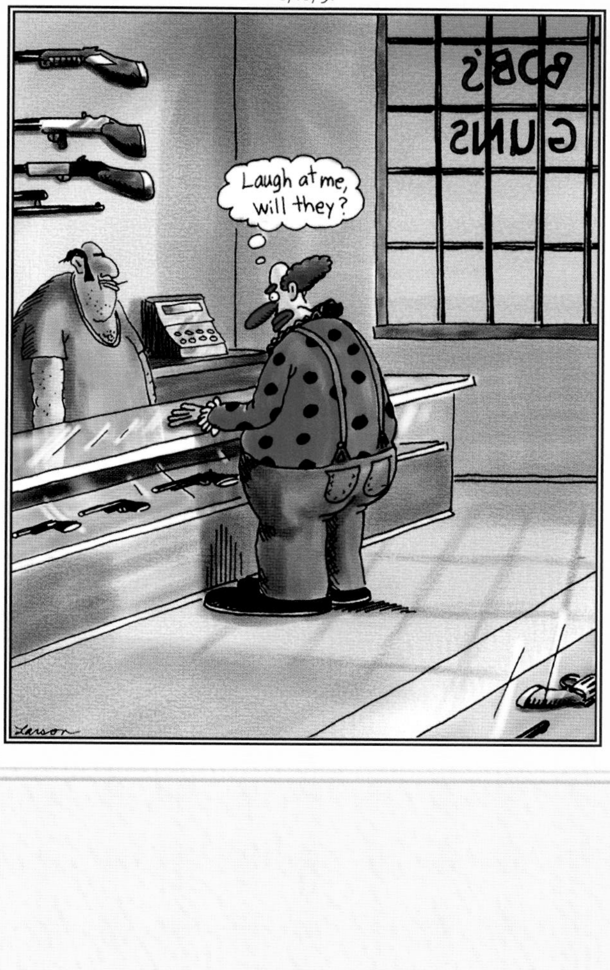
BOB'S
GUNS
Laugh at me, will they?
Larson

6/14/91

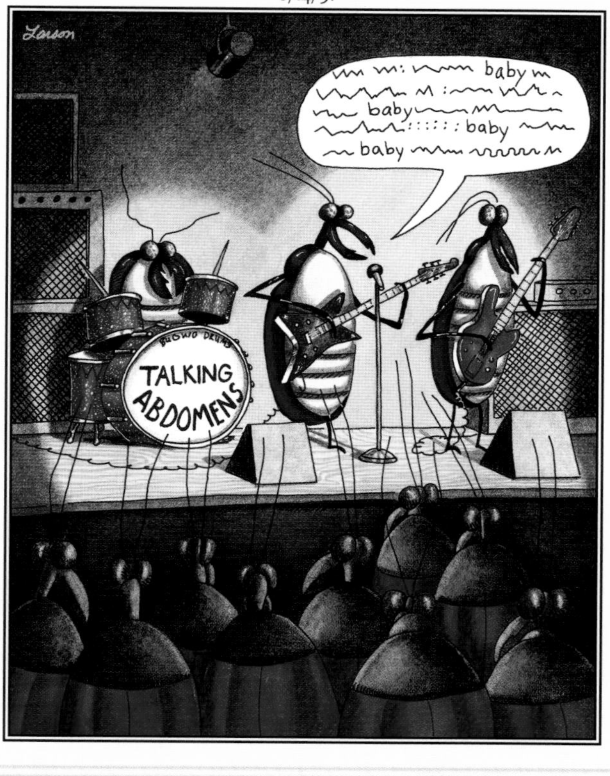
Larson
baby
baby
baby
baby
TALKING ABDOMENS

6/13/91

"The guy creeps me out, Zeena. Sure, he looks like he's just minding his own business—but he always keeps that one eye on my house."

6/17/91

"Take a good, long look at this. ... We don't know what it is, but it's the only part of the buffalo we don't use."

6/18/91

And here's my story: I, Ed Belsky, was once swallowed by a tokay gecko. I spent over an hour in the lizard's stomach, floating among half-digested flies and spiders. Fighting the stench and the powerful gastric juices, I finally clawed my way up the esophagus and out to freedom. Signed, Ed Belsky.

Insect game shows

6/20/91

Please do not feed the cartoon bears.

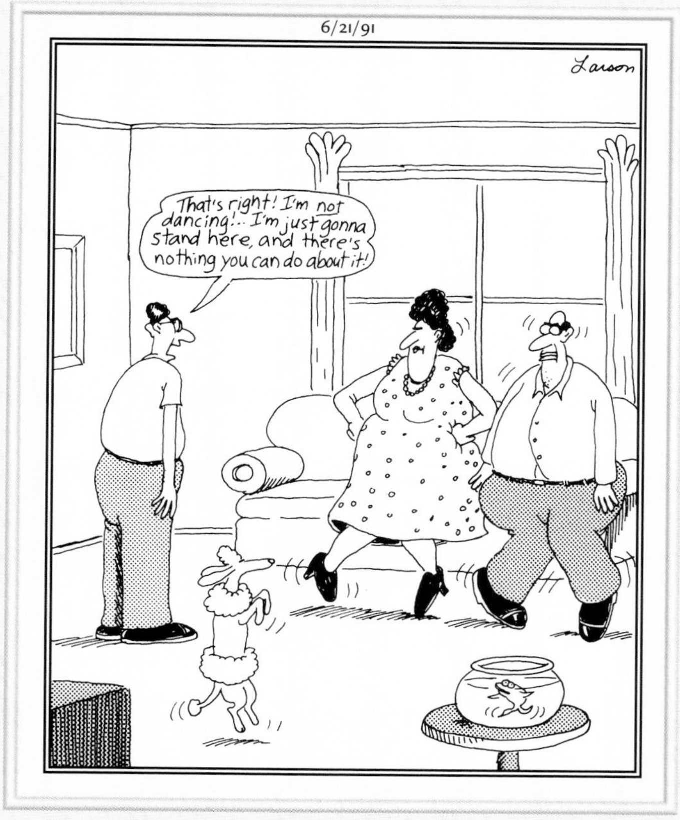
6/21/91
Larson
That's right! I'm not dancing!... I'm just gonna stand here, and there's nothing you can do about it!

Mr. and Mrs. Bojangles' rebellious son

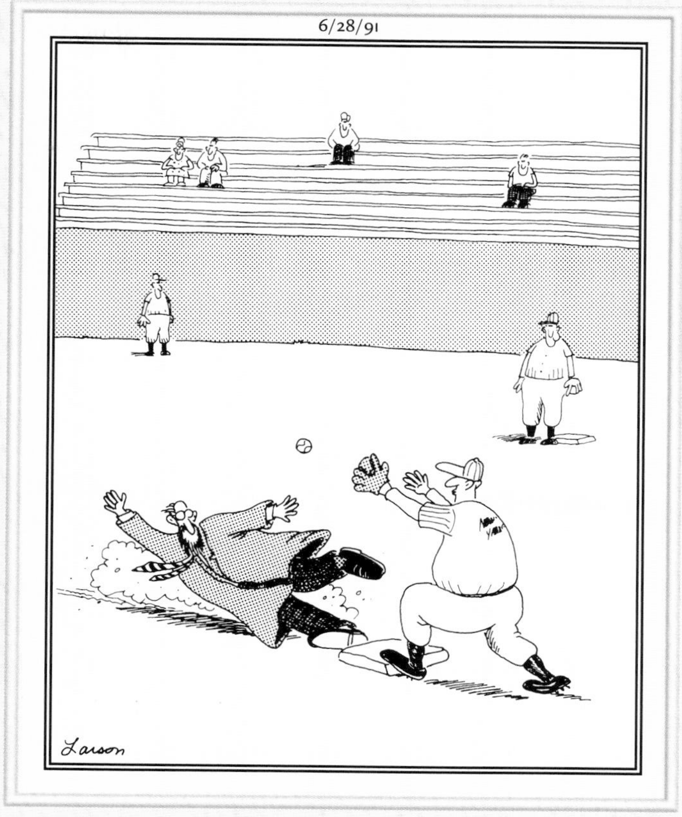
6/28/91
Larson

Freudian slide

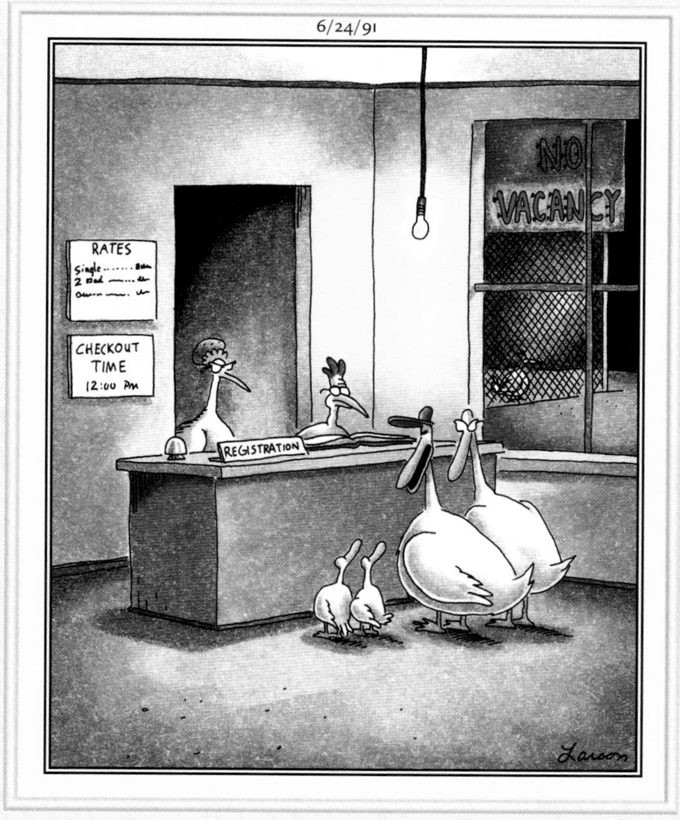
6/24/91
NO
VACANCY
RATES
CHECKOUT
TIME
12:00 PM
REGISTRATION
Larson

"Sorry, kids—they've got cable, but no pond."

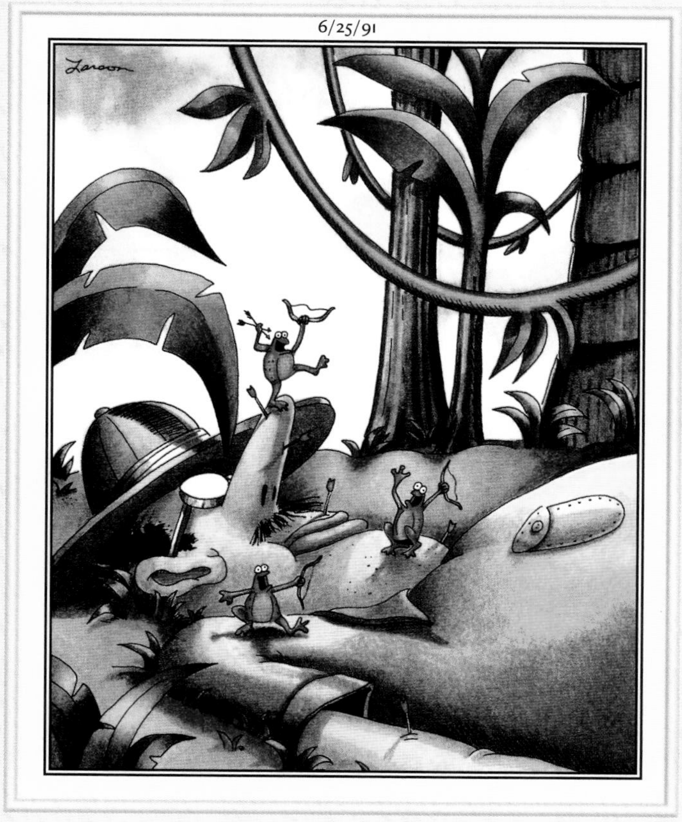
6/25/91
Larson

The rarely seen victory dance of the poison-arrow frog

6/19/91

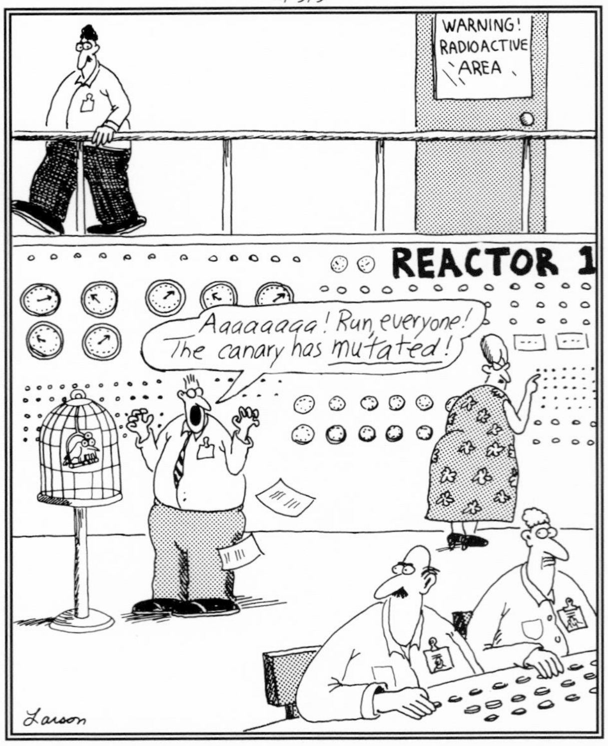
WARNING! RADIOACTIVE AREA
REACTOR 1
Aaaaaaaa! Run, everyone! The canary has mutated!

Inside a nuclear power plant

6/26/91

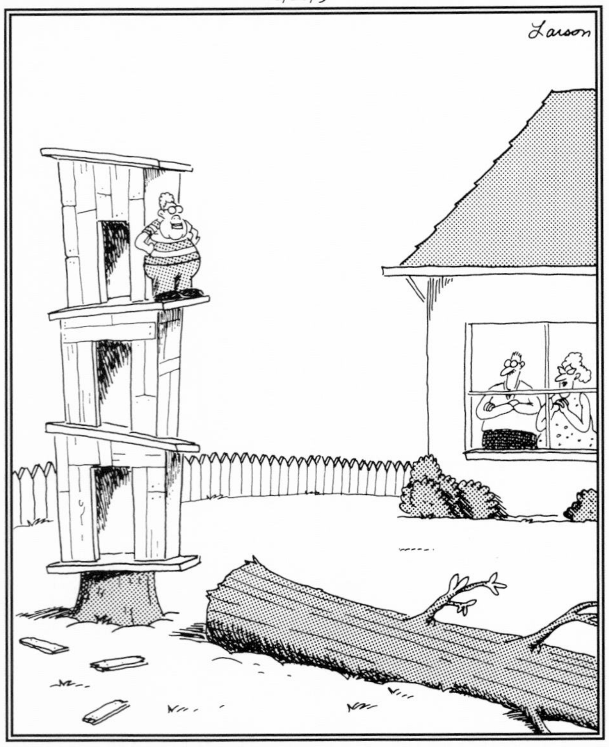

While his parents beamed, little Tommy Lundquist, future developer, surveyed the view from his newly constructed treehouse.

6/27/91

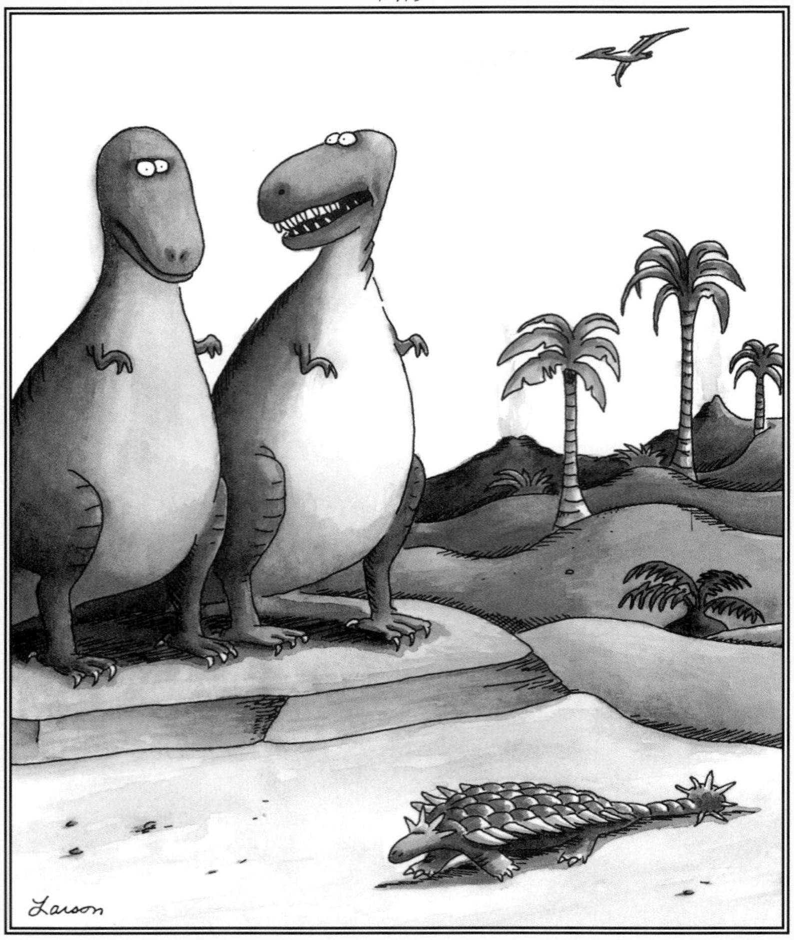

"It's roughage, and that's about it."

7/2/91

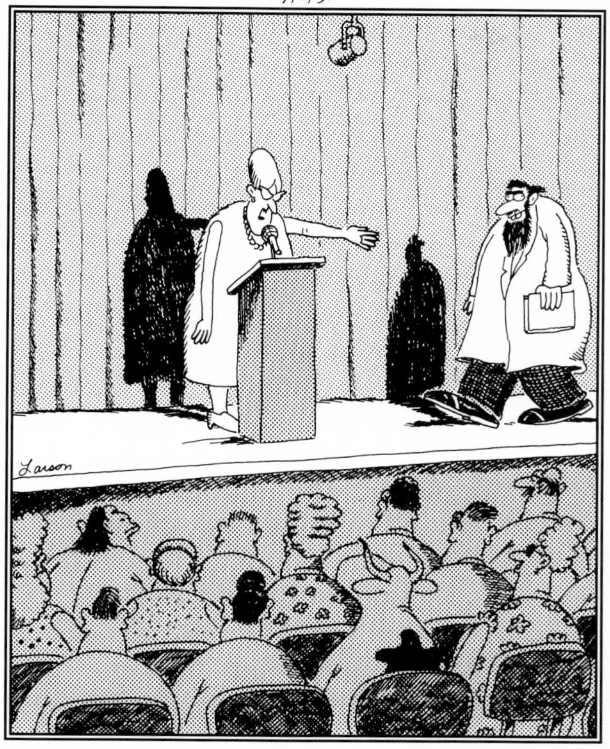
Larson

"And so please welcome one of this cartoon's most esteemed scientist-like characters, Professor Boris Needleman, here to present his paper, 'Beyond the Border: Analysis, Statistical Probability and Speculation of the Existence of Other Cartoons on The Known Comics Page.'"

7/1/91

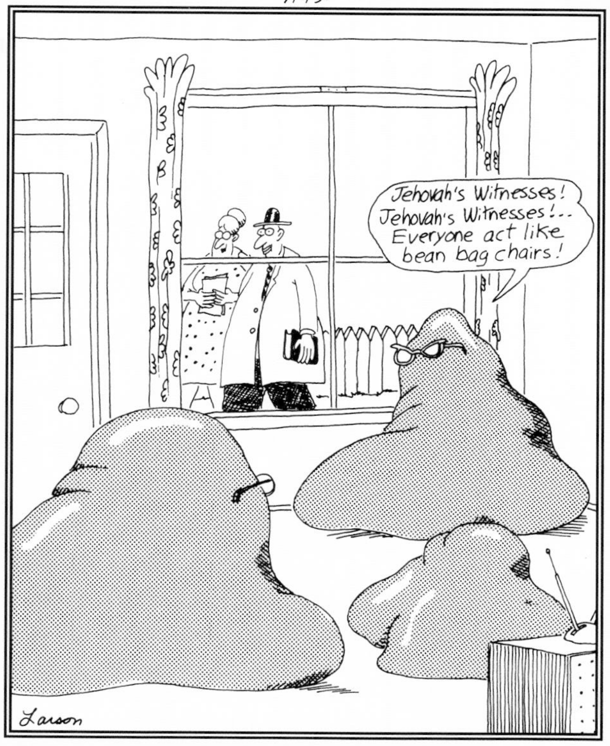
Jehovah's Witnesses! Jehovah's Witnesses!.. Everyone act like bean bag chairs!
Larson

The Blob family at home

7/4/91

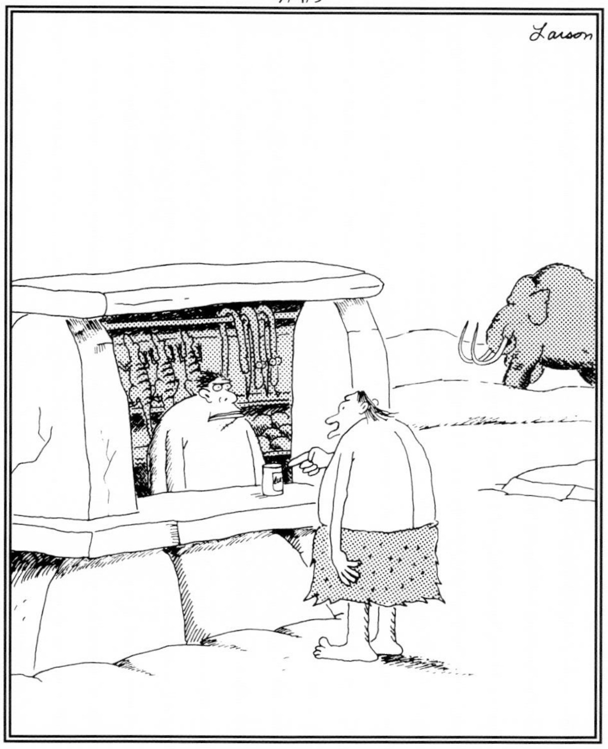
Larson

"Hey! Not this new stuff. ... Me want Jurassic Coke."

7/5/91

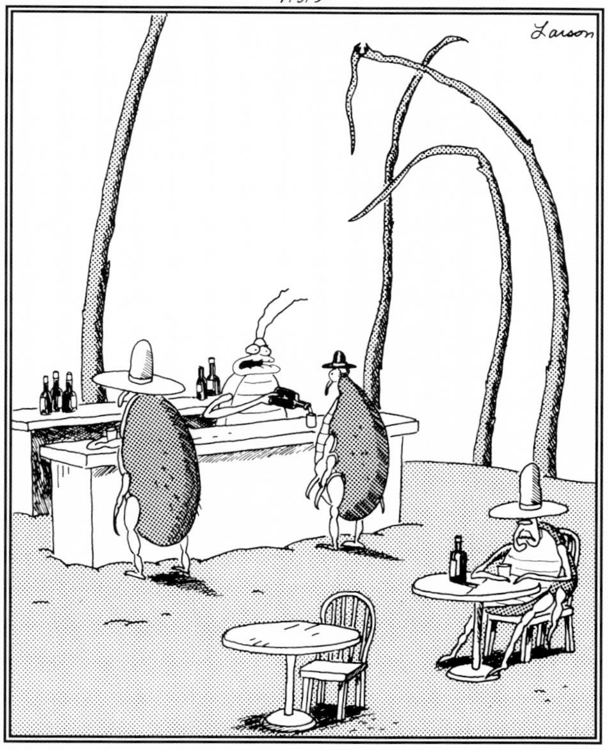
Larson

"You're a long way from Big Poodle, stranger. ... This here is Dead Skunk, and if I were you I'd just keep on movin'."

7/3/91

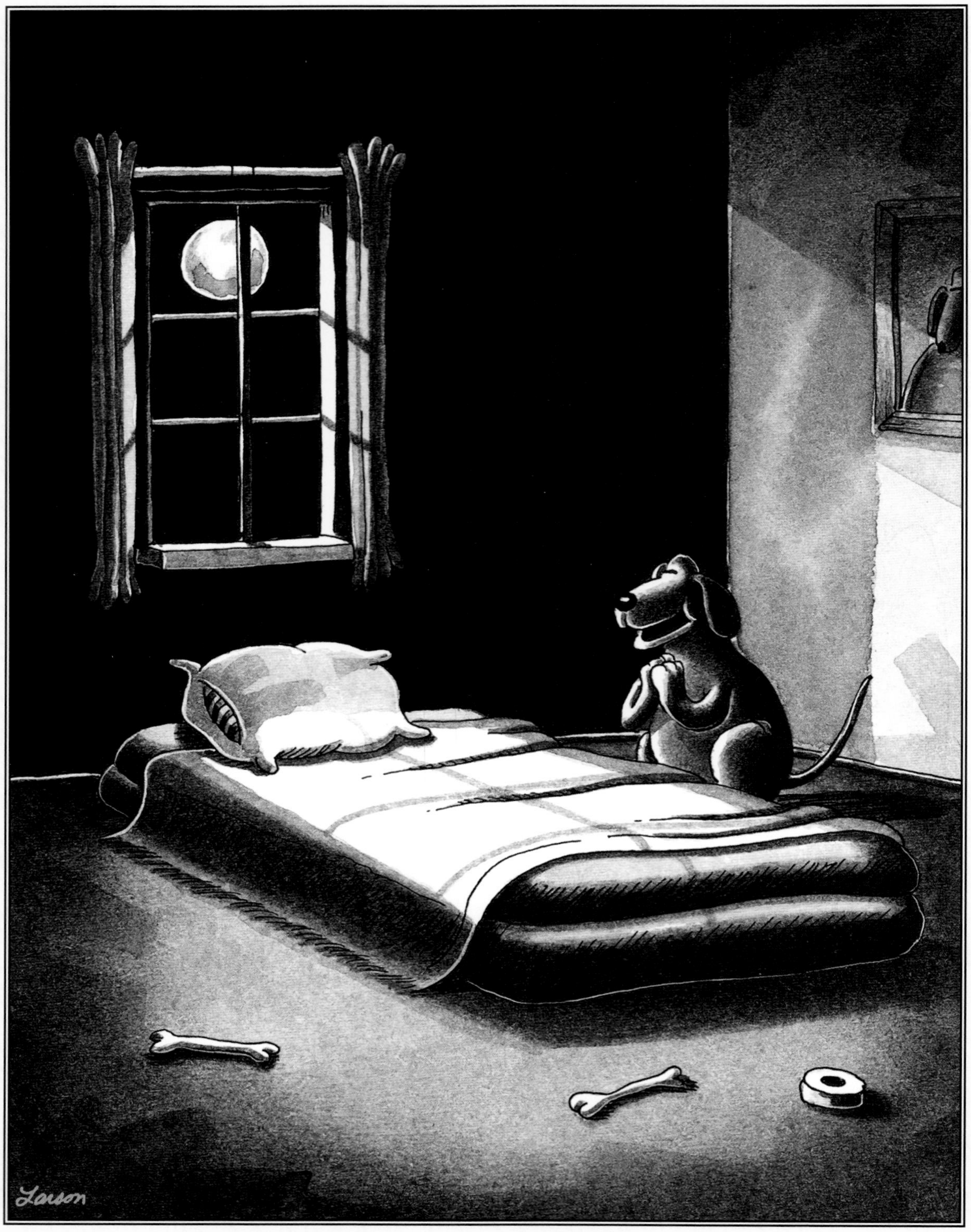
Larson

"... And please let Mom, Dad, Rex, Ginger, Tucker, me, and all the rest of the family see color."

Editor's note: Gary leaves for a one-month vacation.

8/5/91

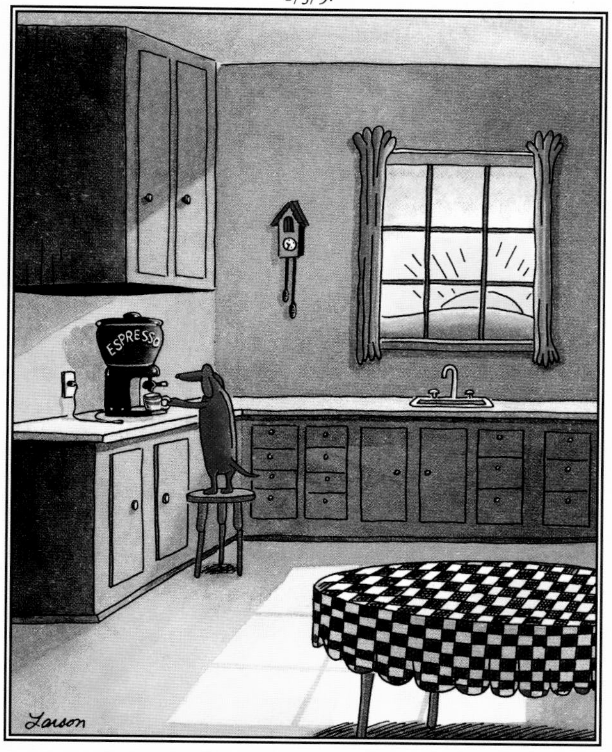
ESPRESSO

While their owners sleep, nervous little dogs prepare for their day.

8/7/91

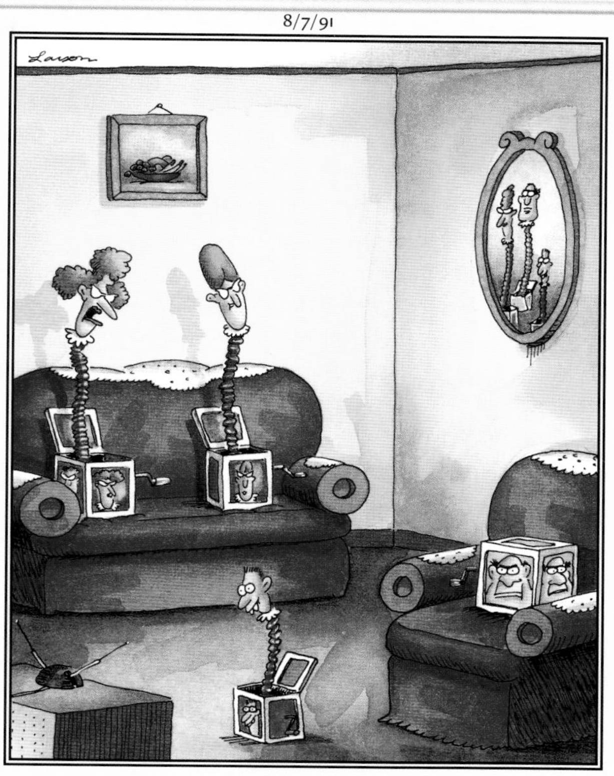

"I'm worried about Frank these days. ... It seems he just can't unwind."

8/6/91

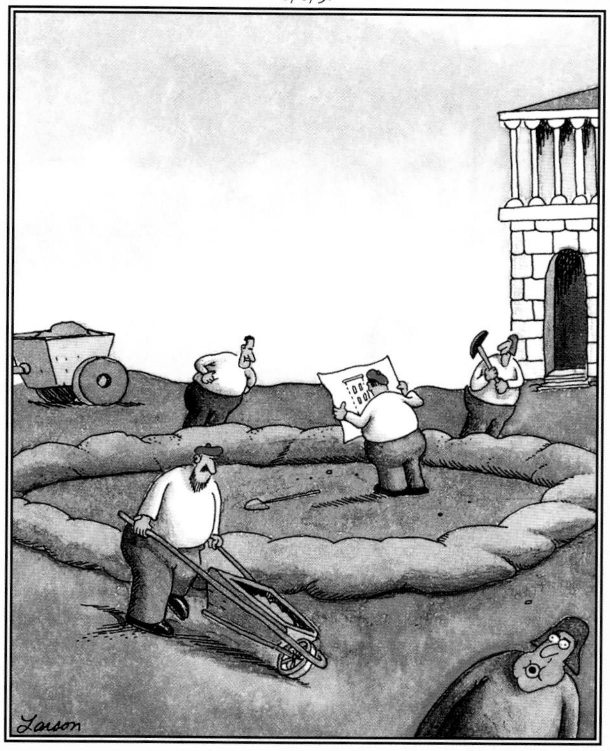

In 12th-century Pisa, Italy, the construction firm of Morrelli and Sons, whose members were all afflicted with a genetic disorder in which the left leg was considerably shorter than the right, begin work on a new tower.

8/12/91

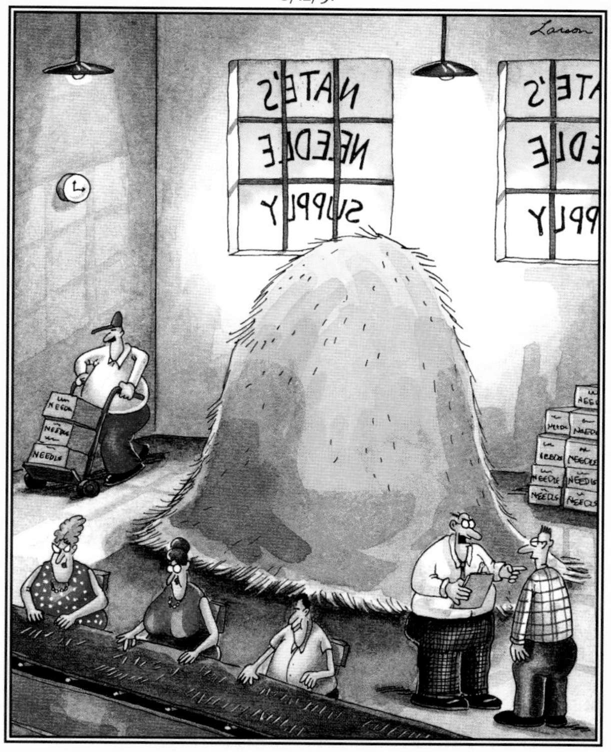
NATE'S NEEDLE SUPPLY

"According to these figures, Simmons, your department has lost another No. 2 Double N— and I want you to find it!"

8/8/91
Larson

"Bob! There's a fly on your lip! ... There he goes. ... He's back! He's back!"

8/9/91
Larson
Human: 11-13 yrs.
Dog: 6-8 mos.
Frog: 12-16 wks.
Shark: 1½-2 yrs.
Elephant: 4-6 yrs.

Awkward ages

8/13/91
Larson

"Looks like another hot one, Pa."

8/15/91
Larson

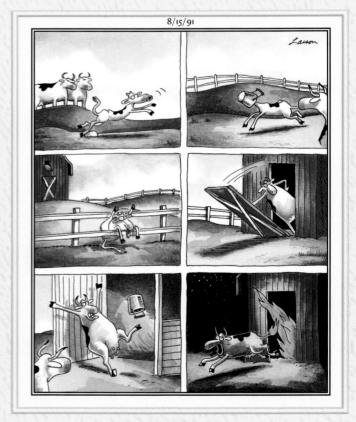

The life and times of Lulu, Mrs. O'Leary's ill-fated cow

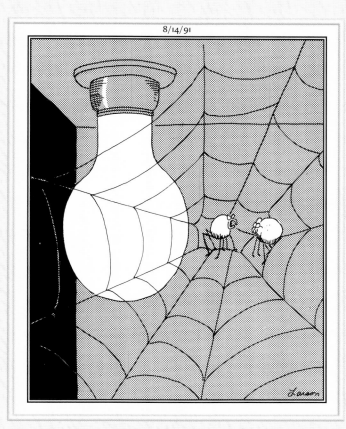

8/14/91

"Crimony! Every night you ask me what's for dinner and every night I say the same thing: 'Moths, moths, *moths!*'"

8/20/91

"And here he is, the author of the exciting autobiography, *Shoe!*"

8/19/91

The herd moved in around him, but Zach had known better than to approach these animals without his trusty buffalo gum.

8/21/91

Unwittingly, Raymond wanders into the hive's company picnic.

8/16/91

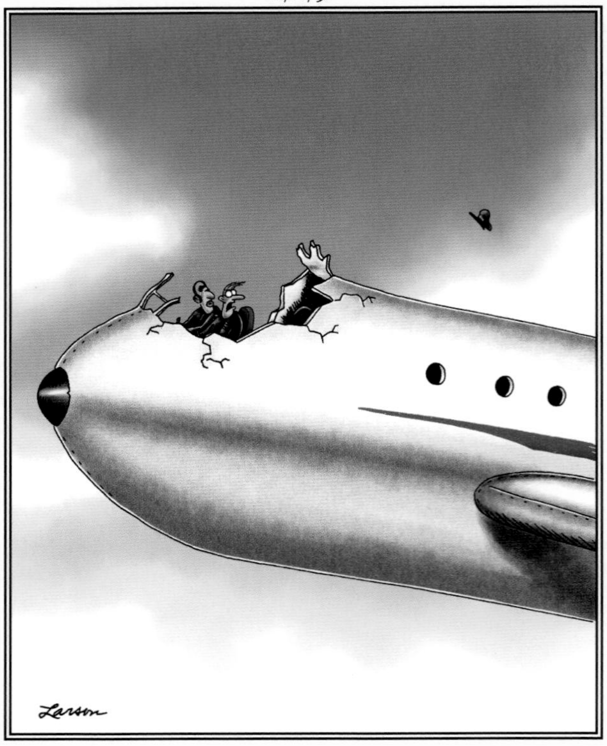

"Oh, great! Now there goes my hat!"

8/26/91

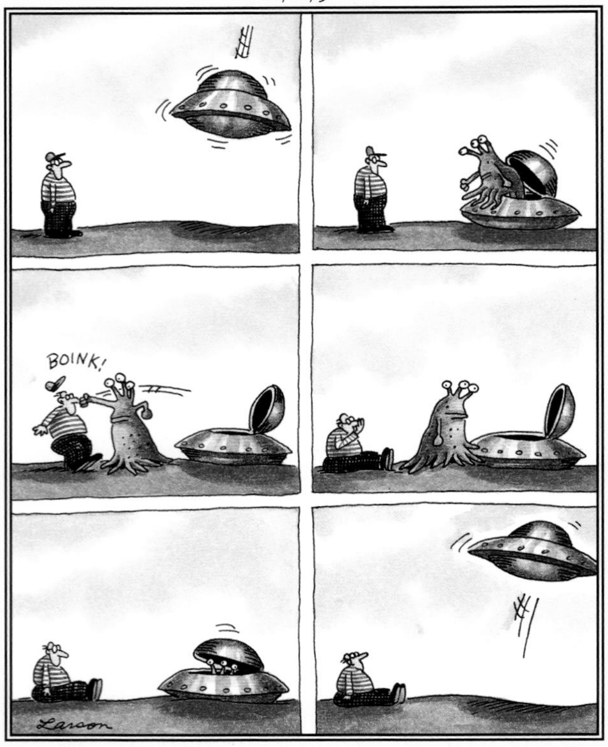
BOINK!

Henry never knew what hit him.

8/22/91

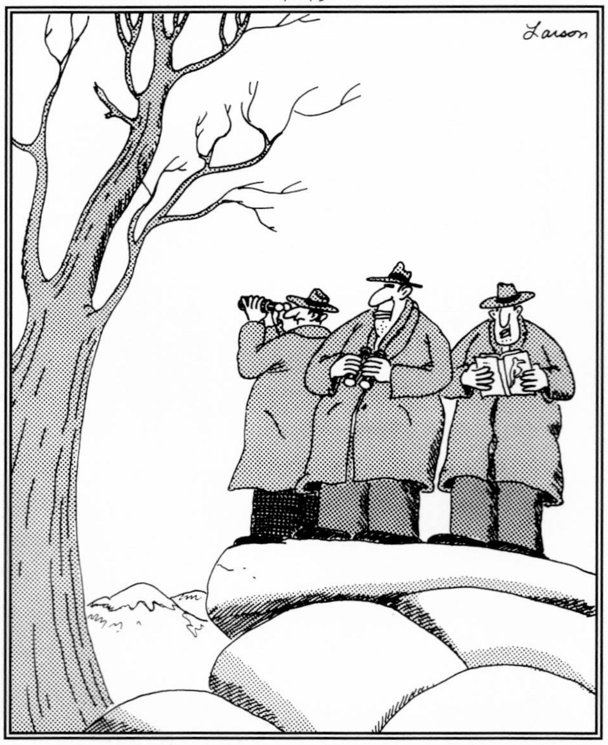

Boid watching

8/27/91

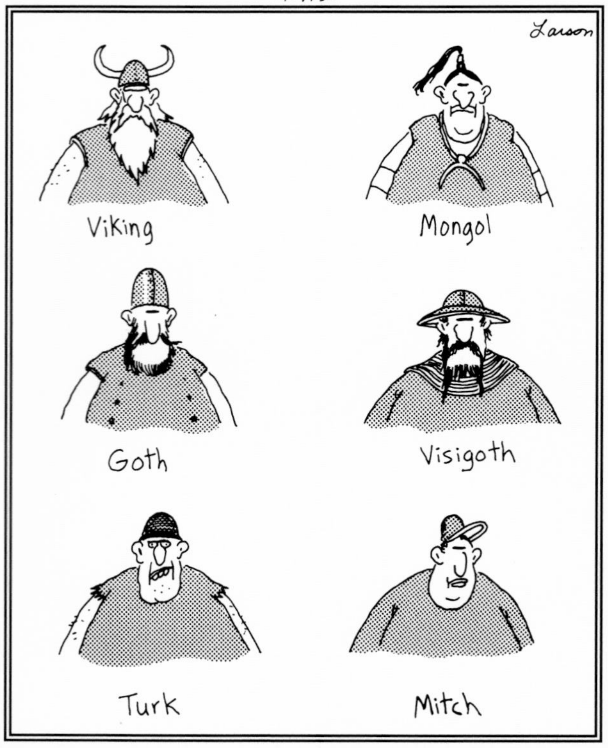
Viking
Mongol
Goth
Visigoth
Turk
Mitch

Know your barbarians.

8/28/91

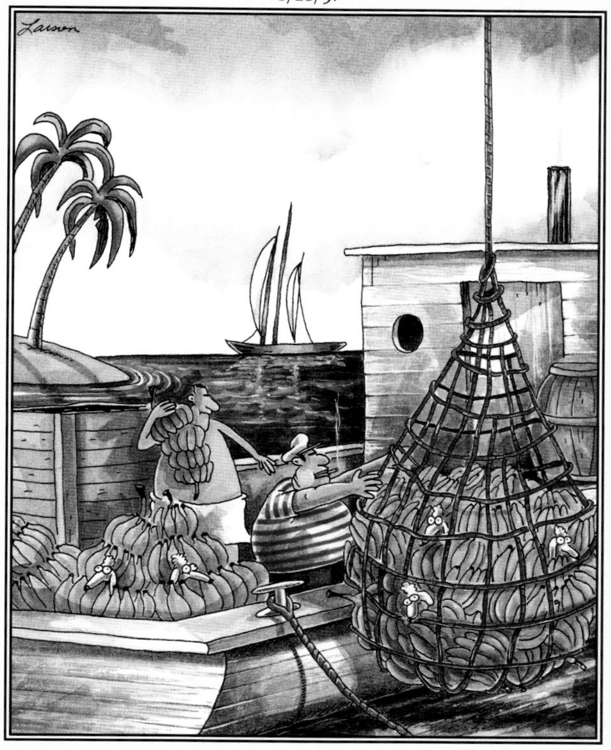

How poodles first came to North America

8/29/91

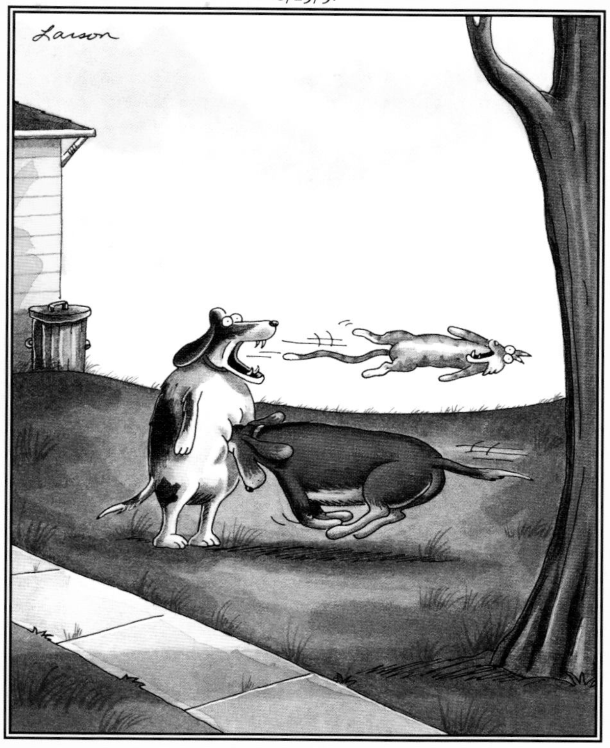

Fortunately for Sparky, Zeke knew the famous "Rex maneuver."

8/30/91

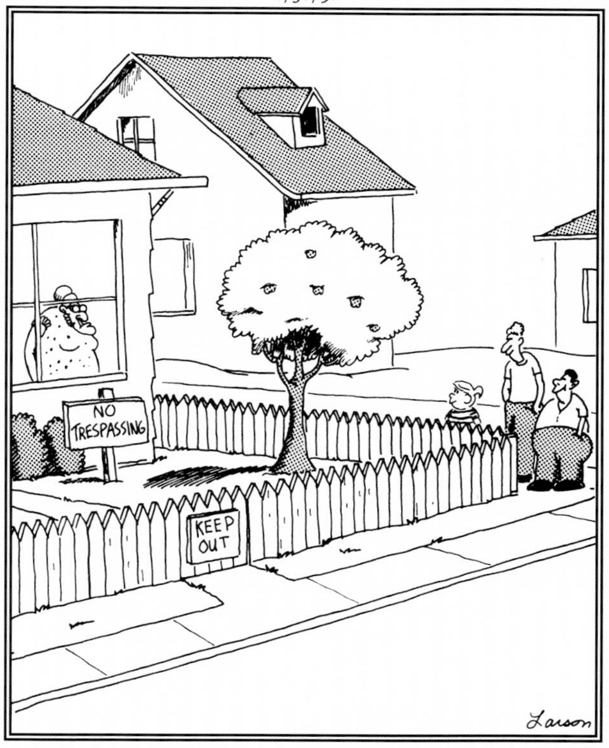
NO TRESPASSING
KEEP OUT

Mrs. MacIntyer smelled trouble. On one side of the fence was her fruit-laden apple tree; on the other was the neighborhood brat pack of Dennis the Menace, Eddie Haskell, and Damien II.

8/23/91

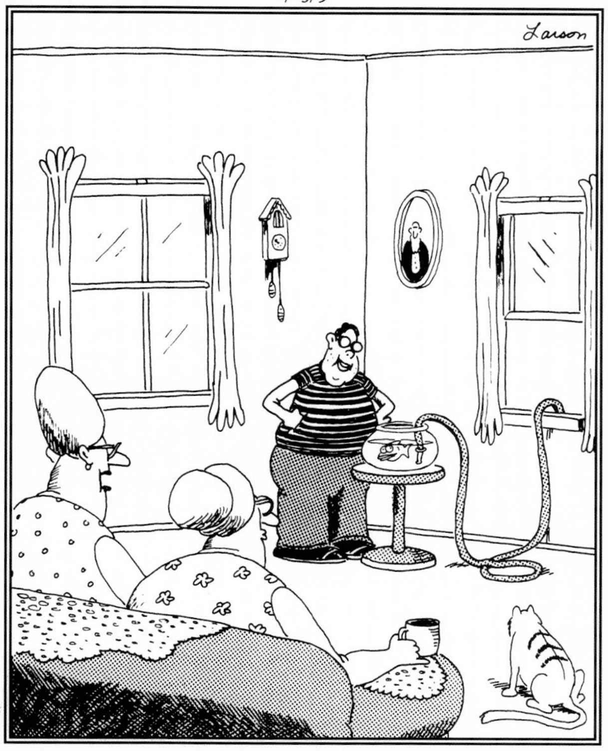

"Oh, there goes Lenny again—draining off the goldfish bowl. ... He wants to one day work for the Army Corps of Engineers, you know."

9/3/91

"Oh my God, Rogers! ... Is that? ... Is that? ... It is!
It's the MUMMY'S PURSE!"

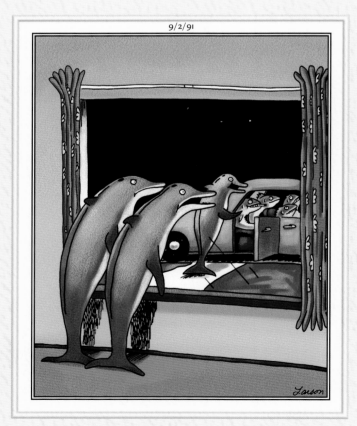

9/2/91

"Well, there he goes again. ... I suppose I
shouldn't worry, but I just get a bad
feeling about Jimmy hanging out with
those tuna punks."

9/5/91

"Well, we're ready for the males' 100-meter
freestyle, and I think we can rest assured that
most of these athletes will select
the dog paddle."

9/9/91

Larson
ONLY
MEATS

Special commuter lanes

9/11/91

Larson

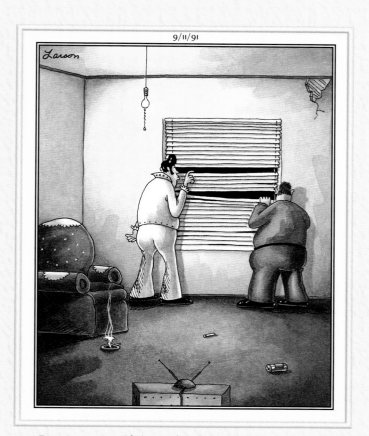

Roommates Elvis and Salman Rushdie sneak a quick look at the outside world.

9/17/91

Larson
esc
F1
Tab
A
SMITE
Z

God at His computer

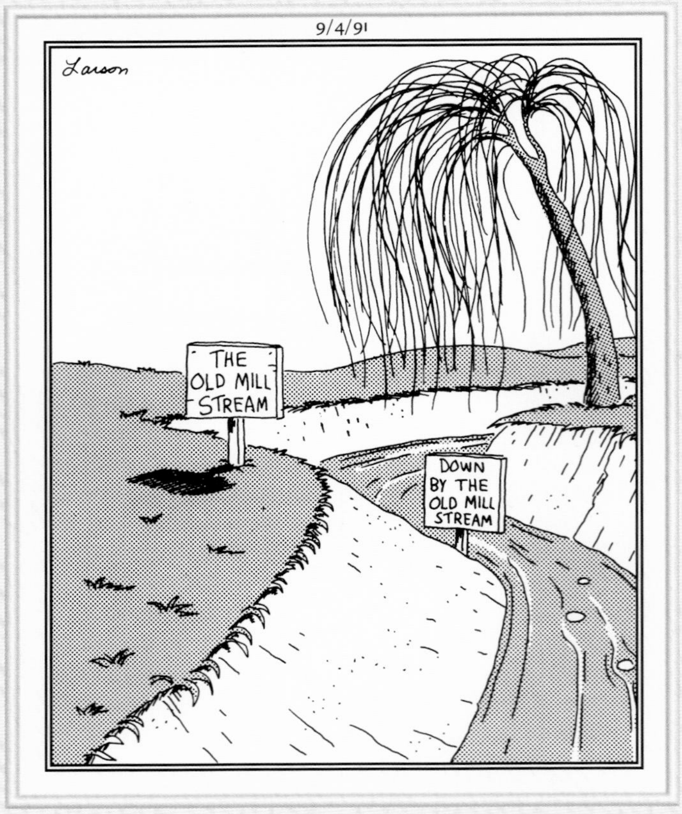
9/4/91
Larson
THE OLD MILL STREAM
DOWN BY THE OLD MILL STREAM

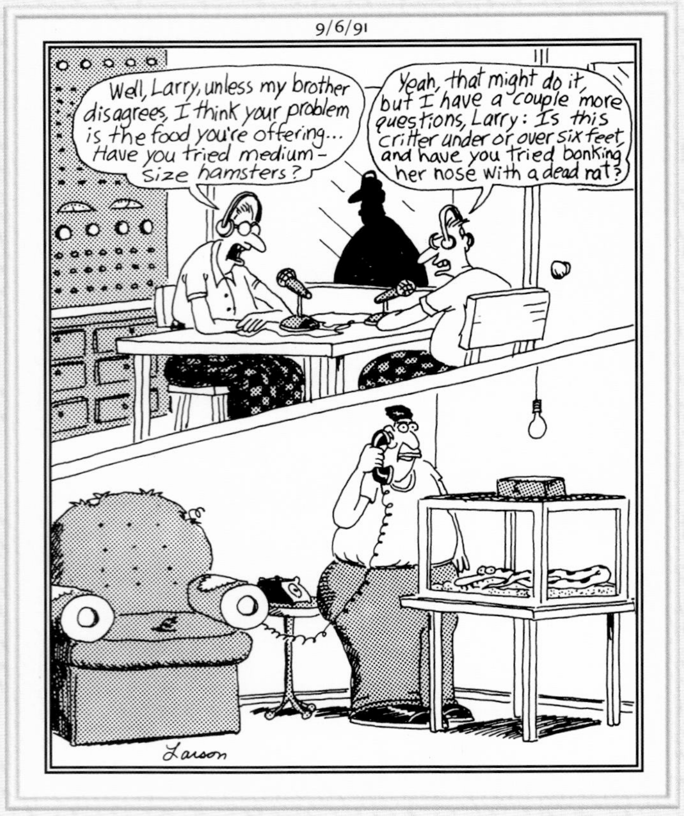
9/6/91
Well, Larry, unless my brother disagrees, I think your problem is the food you're offering... Have you tried medium-size hamsters?
Yeah, that might do it, but I have a couple more questions, Larry: Is this critter under or over six feet, and have you tried bonking her nose with a dead rat?
Larson

On the air with *Snake Talk*

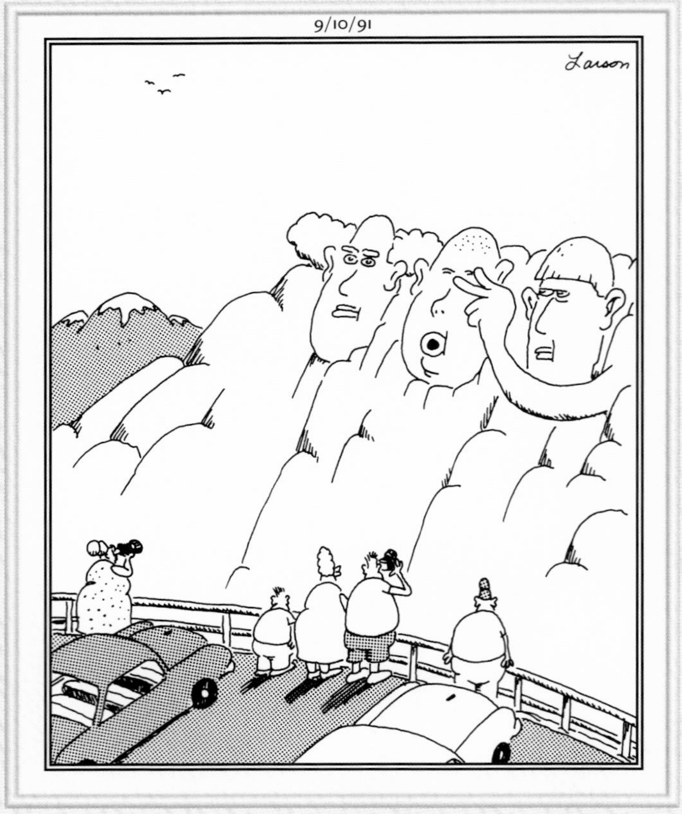
9/10/91
Larson

At Mount Stoogemore

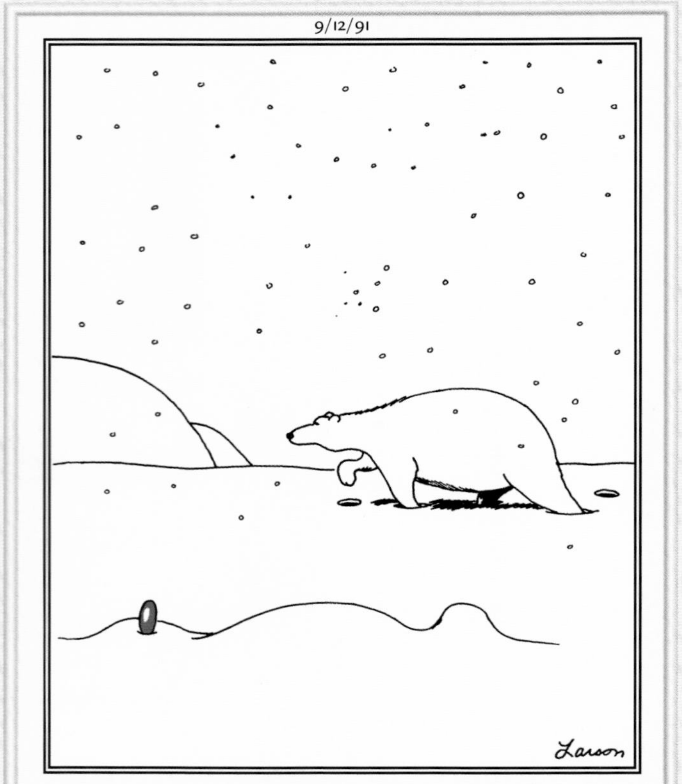
9/12/91
Larson

In its typical defensive behavior, the arctic clown remained motionless and concealed, betrayed only by its nose.

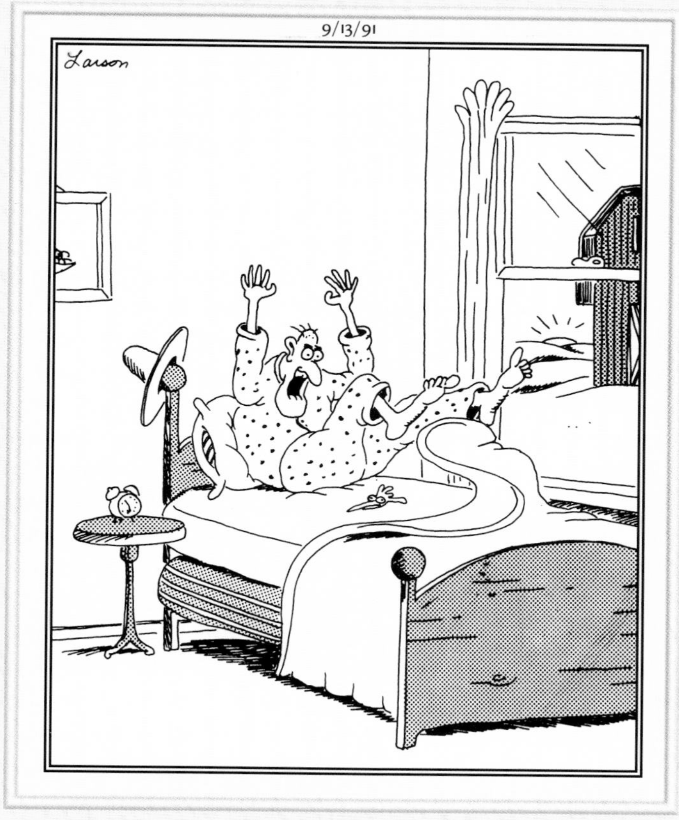
9/13/91
Larson

The farmers' Mafia sends Henry a message.

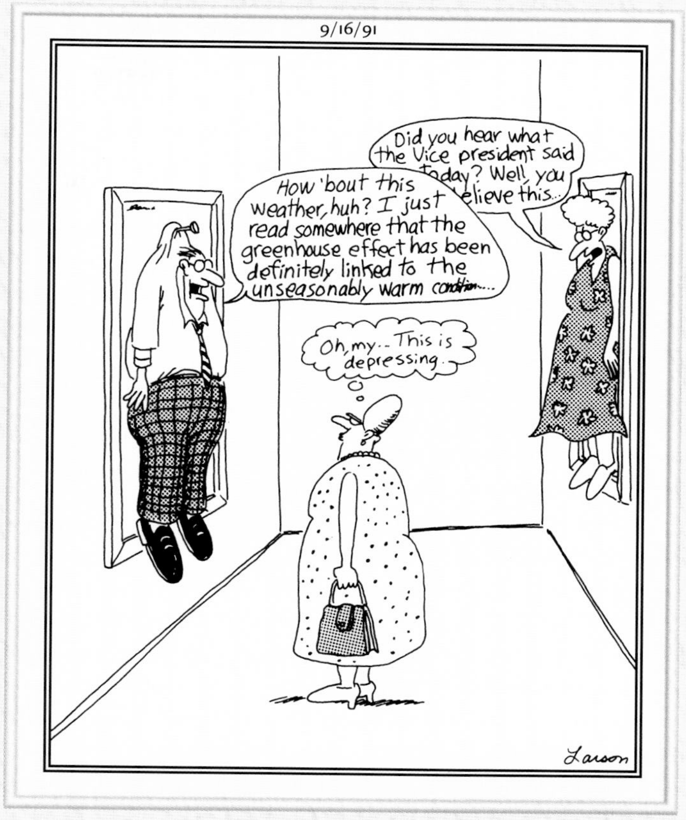
9/16/91
How 'bout this weather, huh? I just read somewhere that the greenhouse effect has been definitely linked to the unseasonably warm condition....
Did you hear what the Vice president said ...day? Well, you ...elieve this...
Oh, my... This is depressing...
Larson

The art of conversation

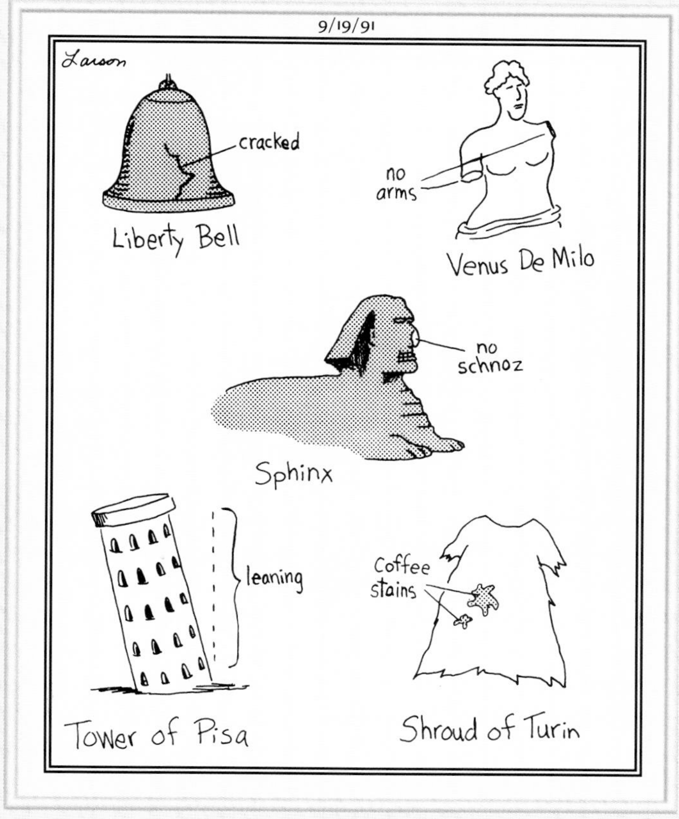
9/19/91
Larson
cracked
Liberty Bell
no arms
Venus De Milo
no schnoz
Sphinx
leaning
Tower of Pisa
Coffee stains
Shroud of Turin

Flawed cultural treasures

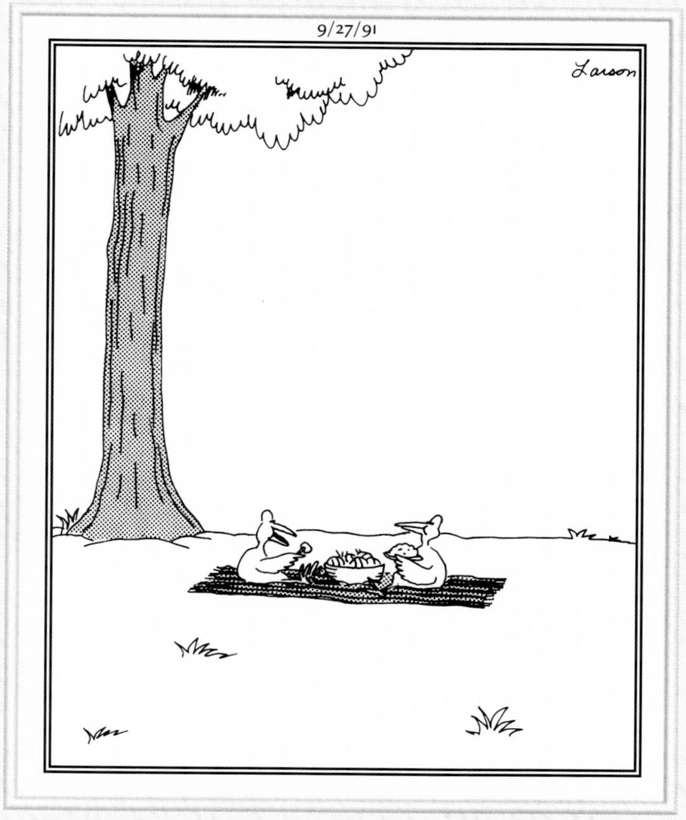
9/27/91
Larson

"Boy, that's good. But it's interesting, Bob. ... Do you think everybody's mother makes a different kind of potato bug salad?"

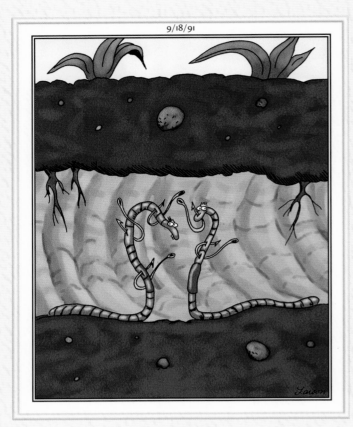

9/18/91

Punk worms

9/20/91

Oh, thank you so much for helping! We were on our way to terrorize the villagers when my monster just up and died on me... We'd still be stuck here if it wasn't for you!
Yeah, yeah... Another wet-behind-the-ears mad scientist.

9/23/91

August 11, 1959: In the heart of the Bolivian jungle, archaeologists stumble upon an ancient and heretofore unknown sacrificial altar.

9/24/91

"Whoa! Mr. Lewis! We don't know what that thing is or where it came from, but after what happened to the dog last week, we advise people not to touch it."

9/26/91

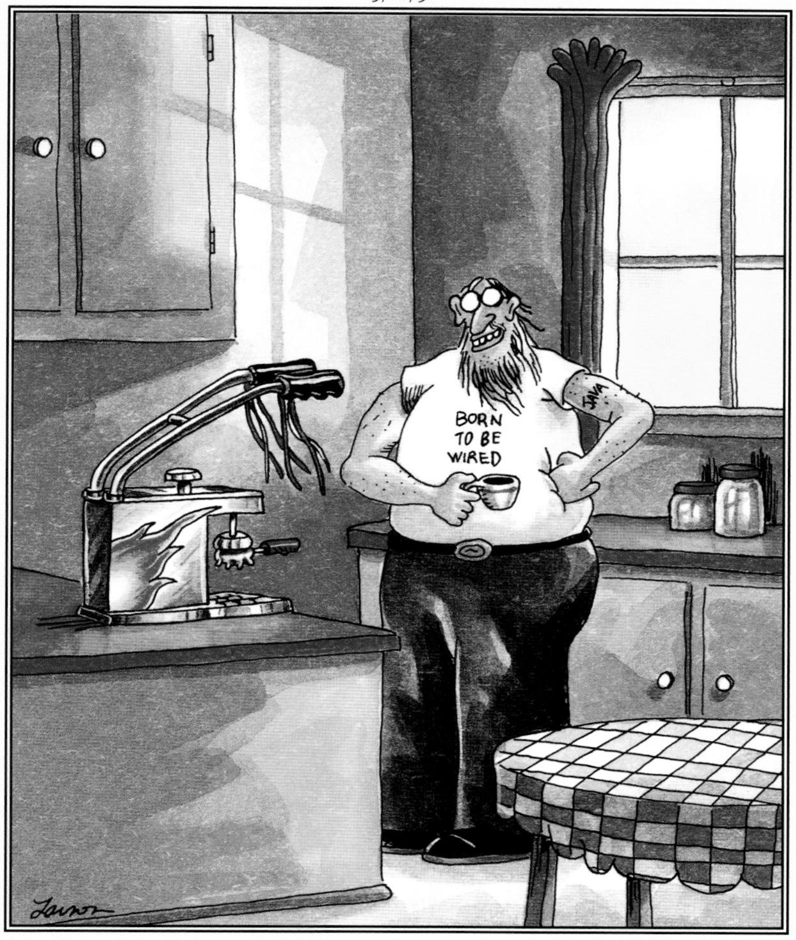
BORN TO BE WIRED
JAVA
Larson

Carl "Javahead" Jones and his chopped espresso maker

9/25/91

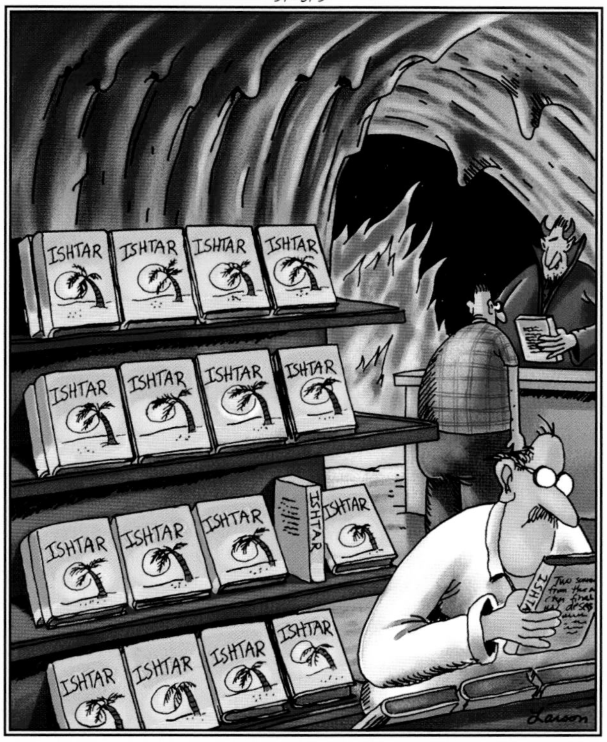
ISHTAR
Larson

Hell's video store

To whom it may concern:
When I drew the above cartoon, I had not actually seen Ishtar. *I only knew, or sensed, that it had entered the film industry lexicon as a major turkey. Years later, I saw it on an airplane, and was stunned at what was happening to me: I was being entertained. Sure, maybe it's not the greatest film ever made, but my cartoon was way off the mark. There are so many cartoons for which I should probably write an apology, but this is the only one that compels me to do so.*

—Gary Larson

9/30/91

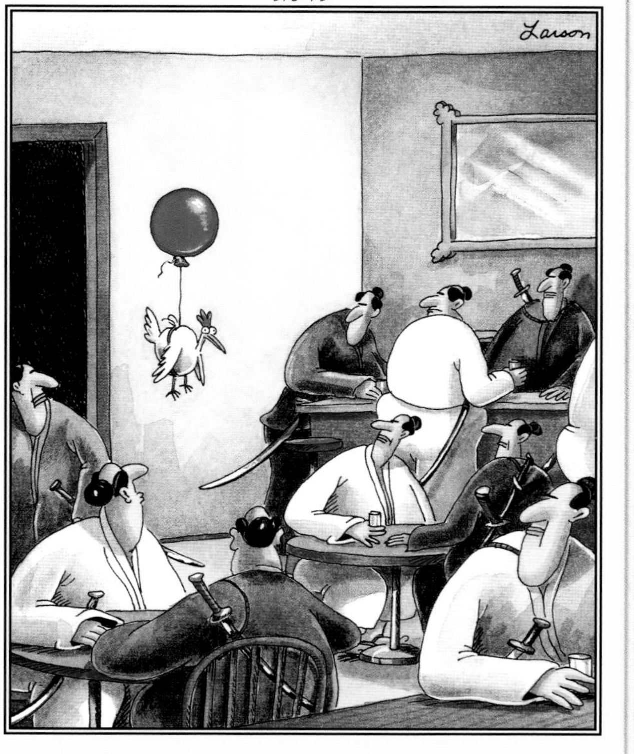
Larson

In what was destined to be a short-lived spectacle, a chicken, suspended by a balloon, floated through the samurai bar's doorway.

10/2/91

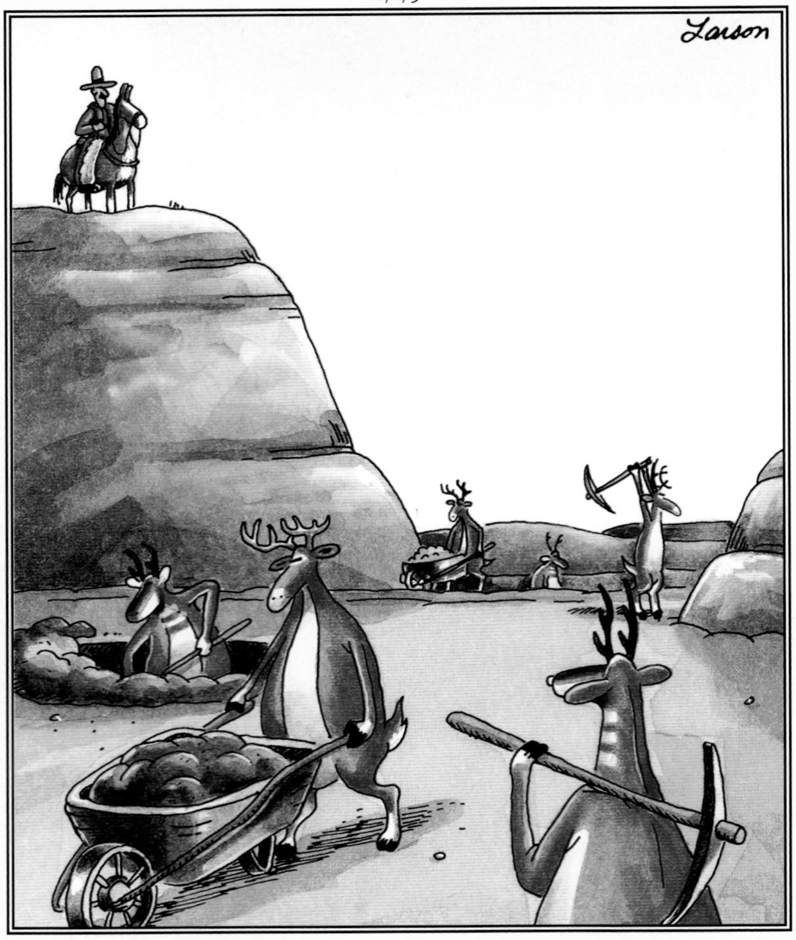
Larson

Where the deer and the antelope work

10/1/91

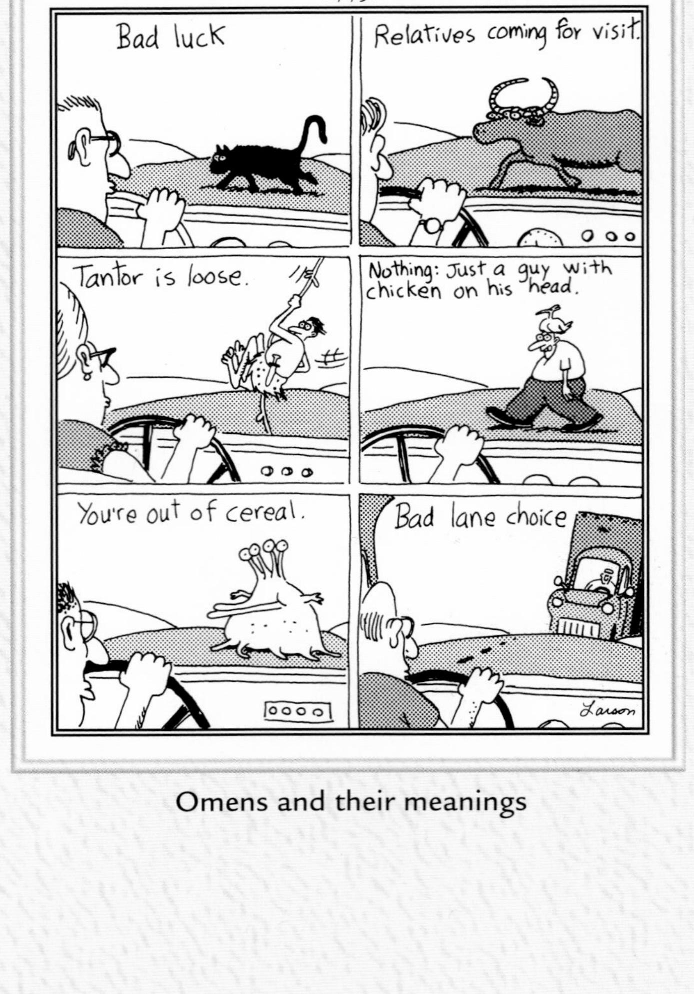
Bad luck
Relatives coming for visit.
Tantor is loose.
Nothing: Just a guy with chicken on his head.
You're out of cereal.
Bad lane choice
Larson

Omens and their meanings

10/3/91

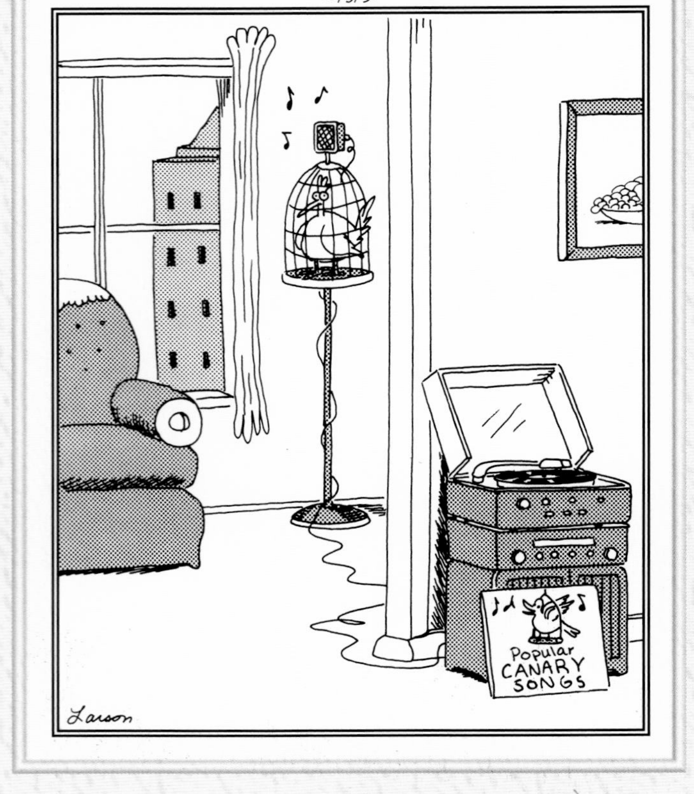
Popular CANARY SONGS
Larson

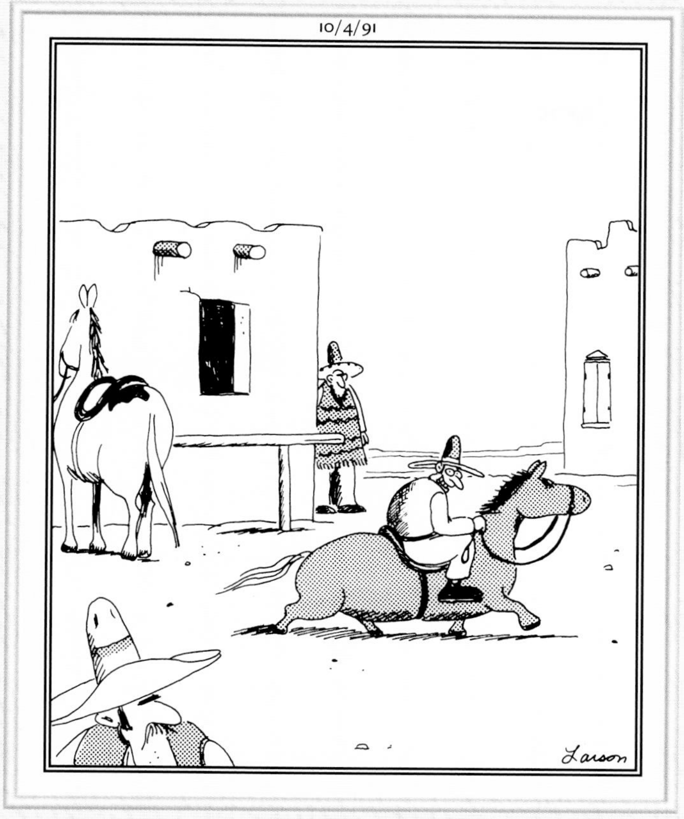
10/4/91
Larson

Durango, Mexico, circa 1880: Juan Sanchez cruises through town on the first low-rider.

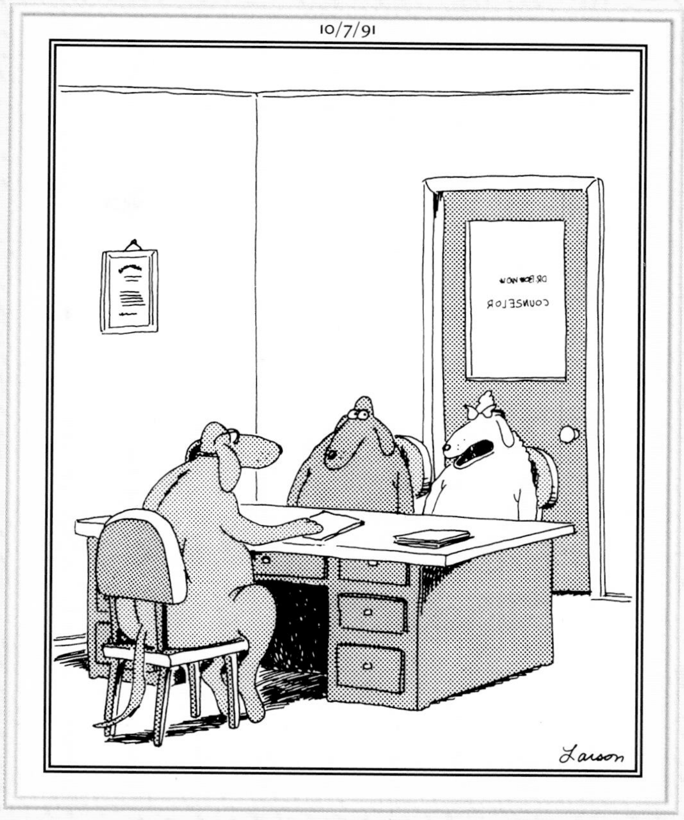
10/7/91
Larson

"You should hear him! ... First he growls and snarls at me and *then* he thinks he can make everything okay by scratching me behind the ears."

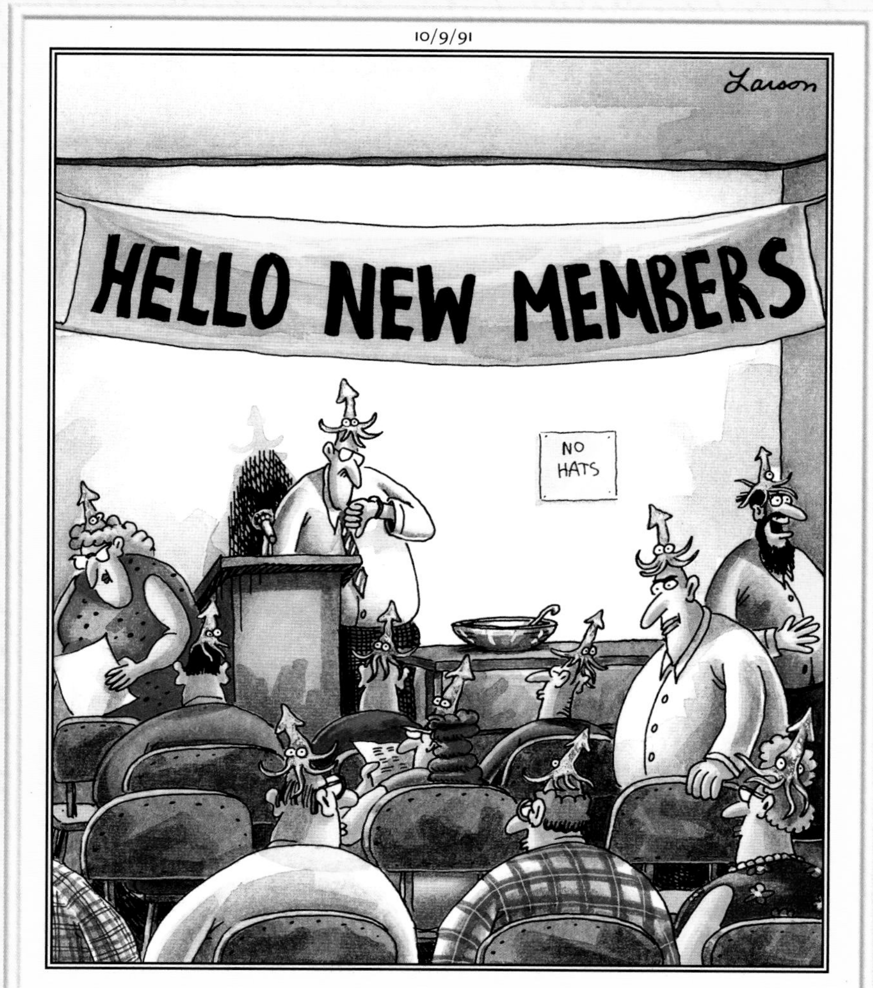
10/9/91
Larson
HELLO NEW MEMBERS
NO HATS

At the monthly meeting of Squidheads Anonymous

10/16/91

"You gotta help me, Mom. ... This assignment is due tomorrow, and Gramps doesn't understand the new tricks."

10/8/91

IS THAT A CAMERA LENS?
WILL PUT YOU TO SLEEP!

At *The Far Side*'s spy center

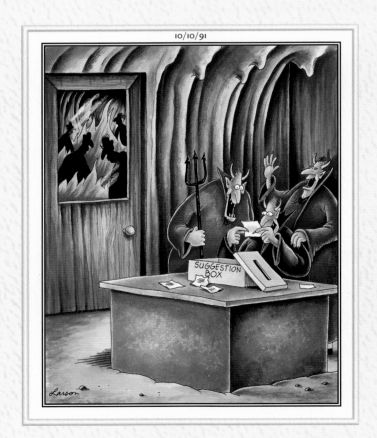

10/10/91

SUGGESTION BOX

10/14/91

"Okay, crybaby! You want the last soda? Well, let me GET IT READY FOR YOU!"

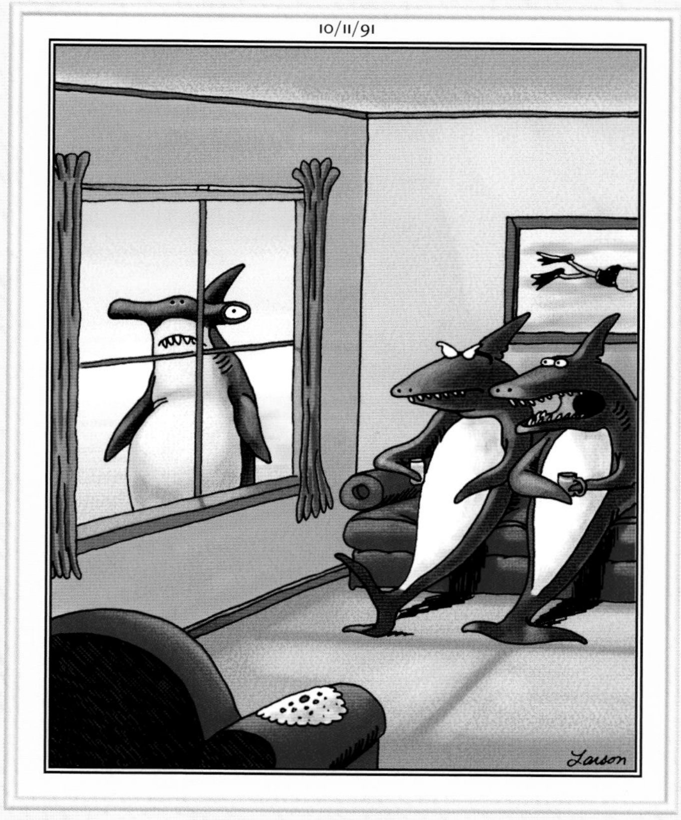
10/11/91
Larson

"My marriage is in trouble, Barbara. You ever tried communicating with a hammerhead?"

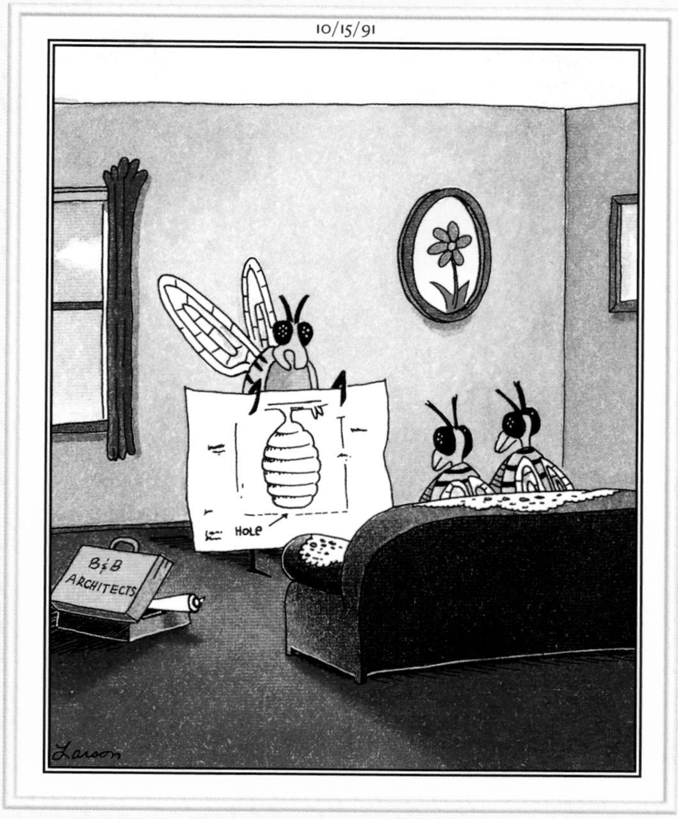
10/15/91
B&B ARCHITECTS
HOLE
Larson

"Voilà! ... Your new dream home! If you like it, I can get a crew mixing wood fibers and saliva as early as tomorrow."

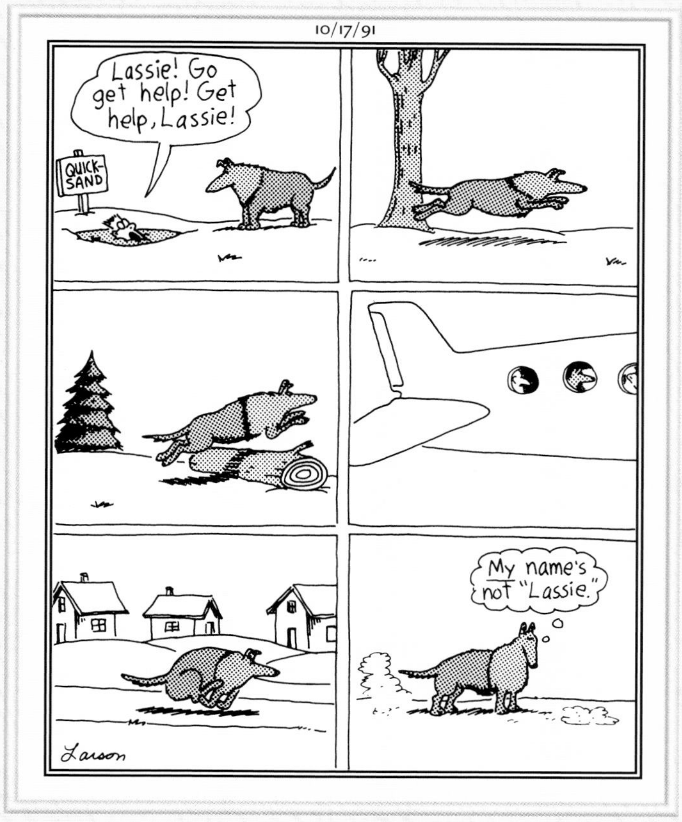
10/17/91
Lassie! Go get help! Get help, Lassie!
QUICK-SAND
My name's not "Lassie."
Larson

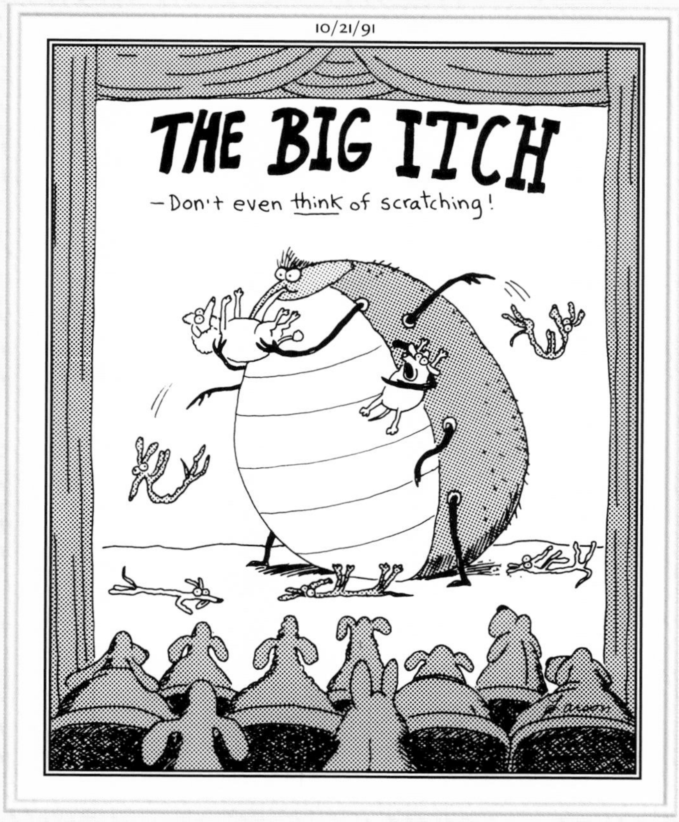
10/21/91
THE BIG ITCH
–Don't even think of scratching!

Dog previews

10/18/91

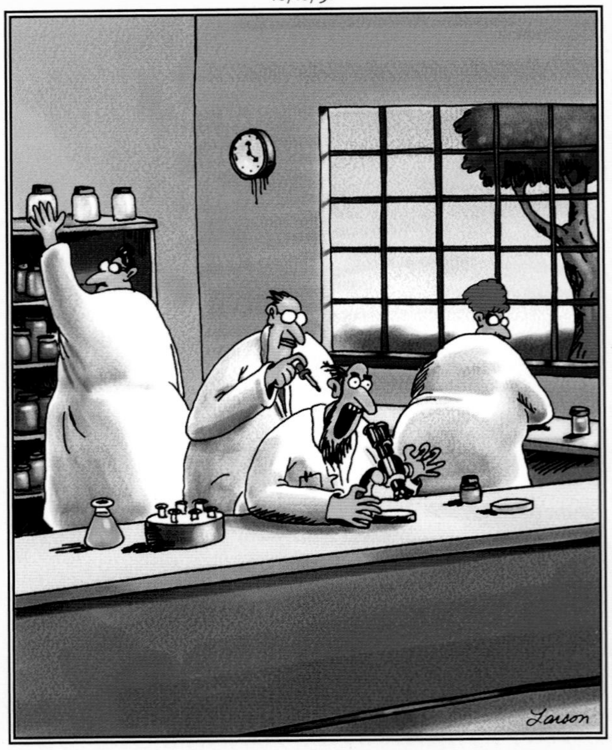
Larson

Professor Glickman, the lab practical joker, deftly places a single drop of hydrochloric acid on the back of Professor Bingham's neck.

10/24/91

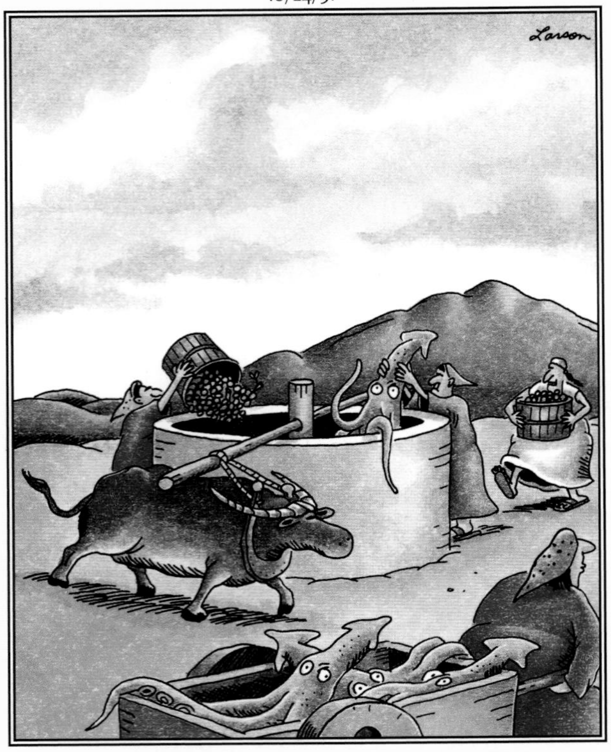
Larson

Where we get calamari blanc

10/22/91

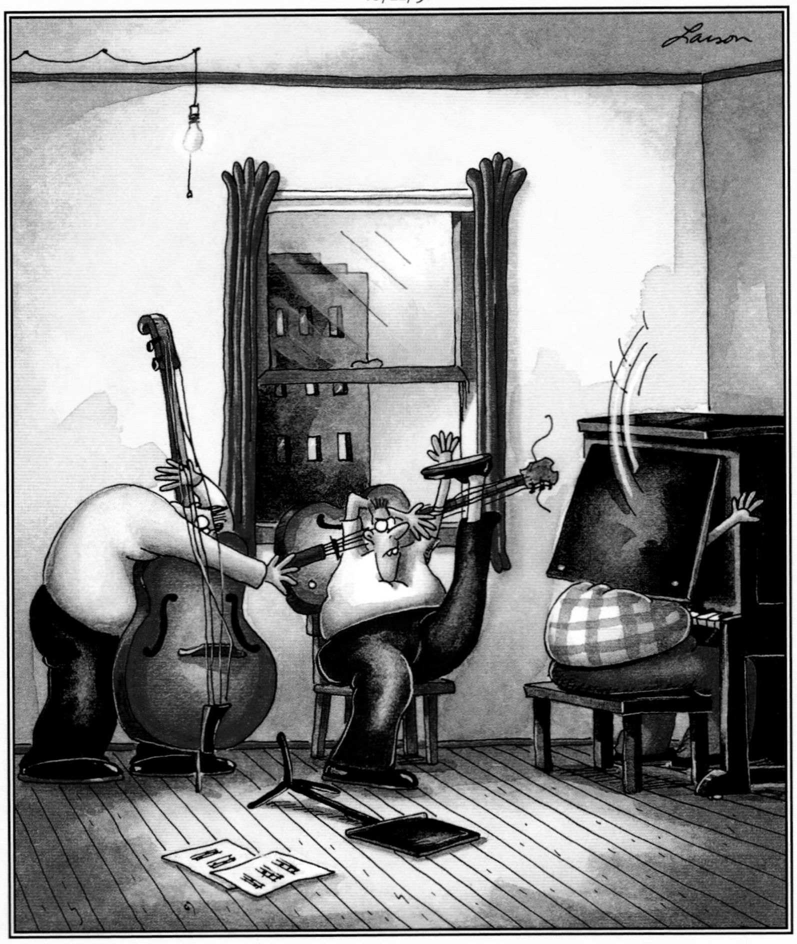
Larson

Three more careers are claimed by the Bermuda Triangle of jazz.

10/25/91

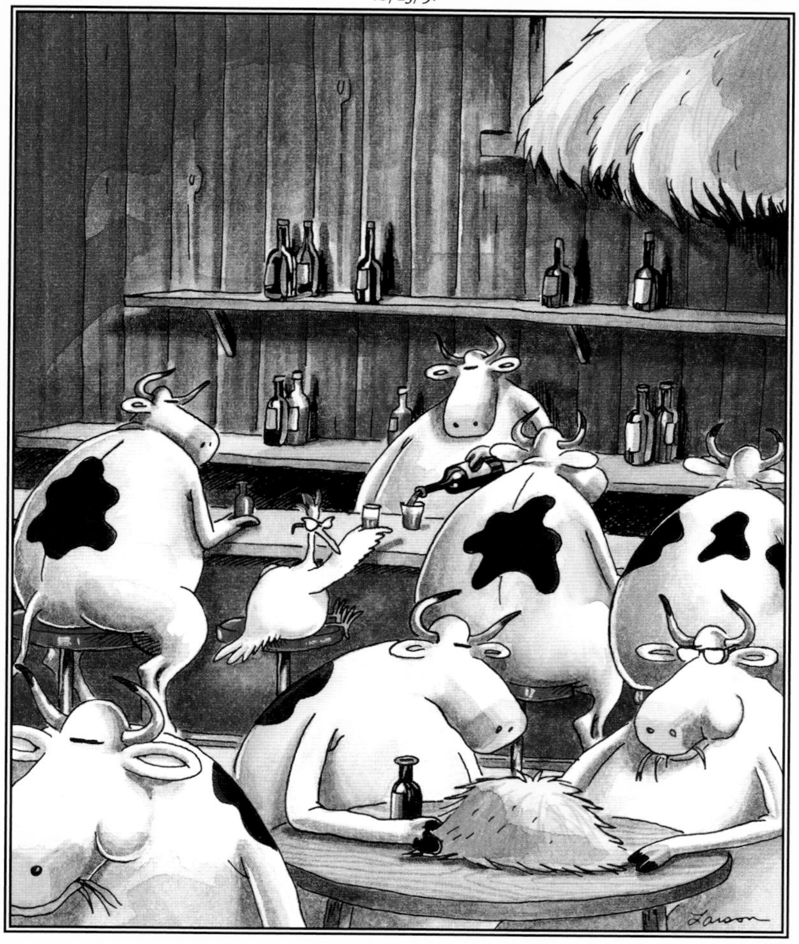

Vera looked around the room. Not another chicken anywhere. And then it struck her—this was a hay bar.

10/28/91

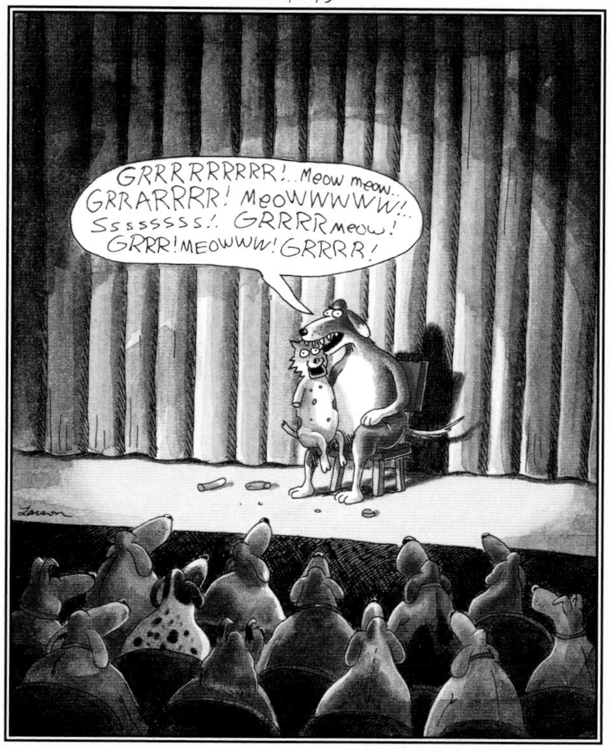
GRRRRRRRRR!..Meow meow..
GRRARRRR! MeoWWWWW!..
Sssssss!. GRRRRmeow!
GRRR!MEOWWW!GRRRR!

Dog ventriloquists

10/30/91

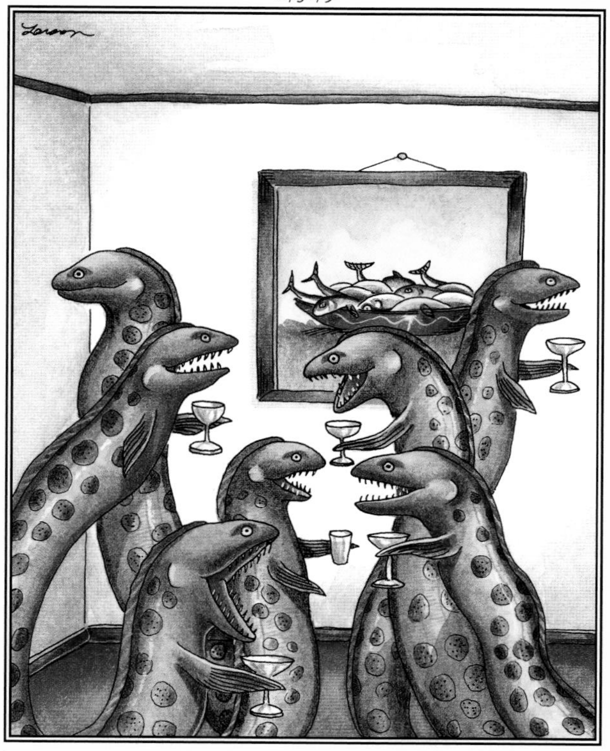

Social morays

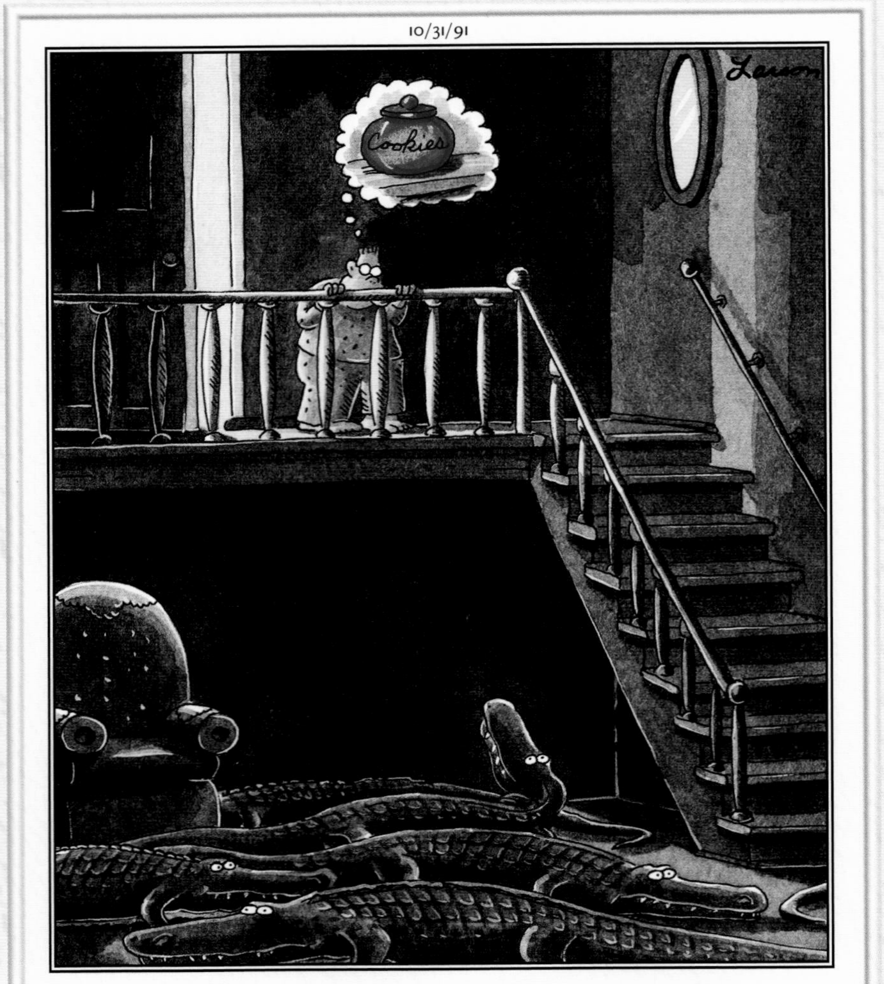
10/31/91
Larson
Cookies

The nightly crisis of Todd's stomach vs. Todd's imagination

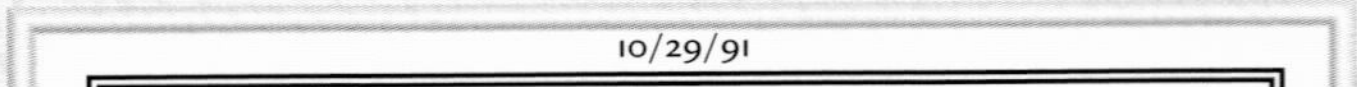
10/29/91
Larson

Stumpy didn't know how he got in this situation, but with the whole town watching, he knew he'd have to play it out.

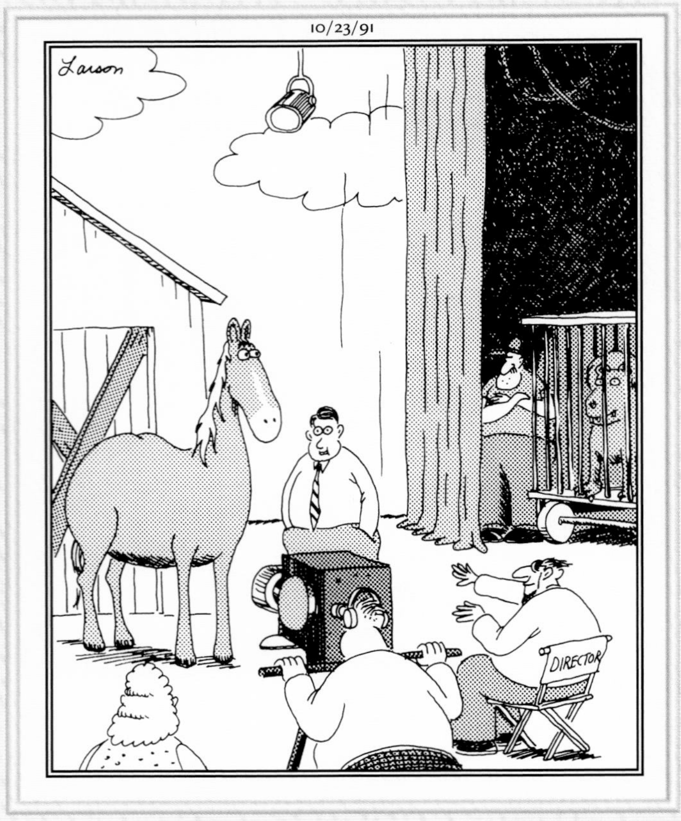
10/23/91
Larson
DIRECTOR

How Mr. Ed was made to talk

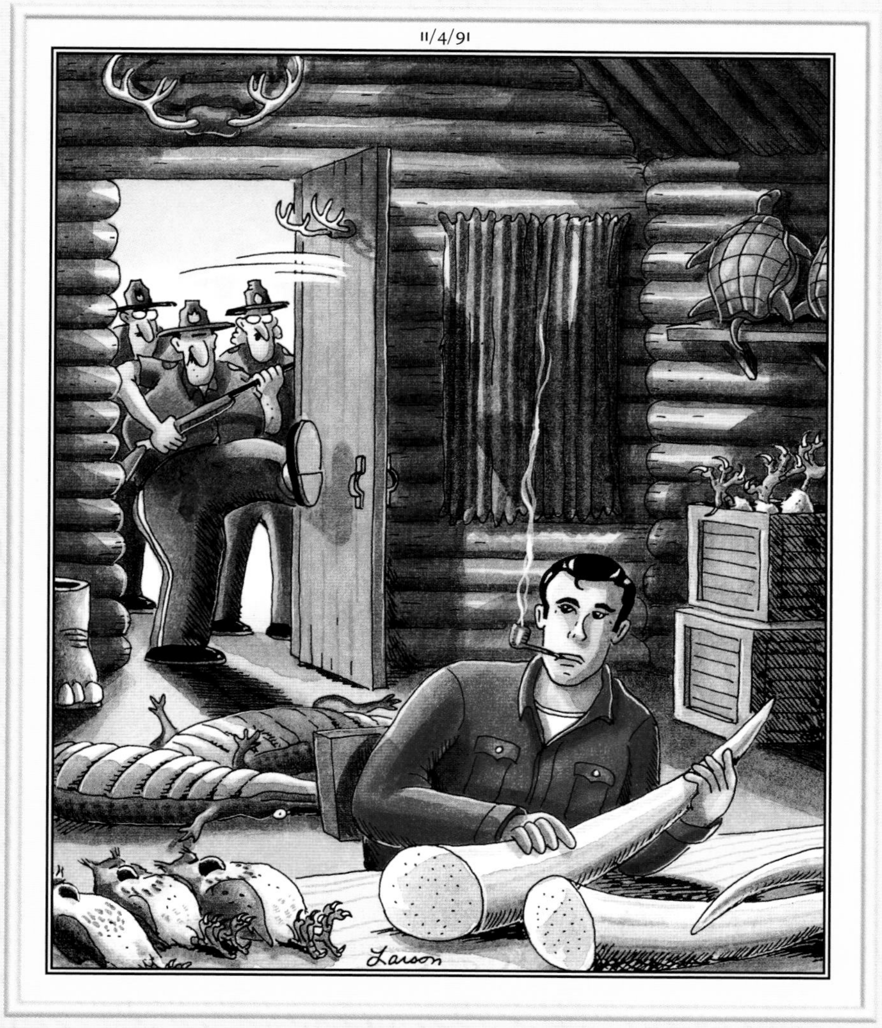
11/4/91
Larson

Suddenly, Fish and Wildlife agents burst in on Mark Trail's poaching operation.

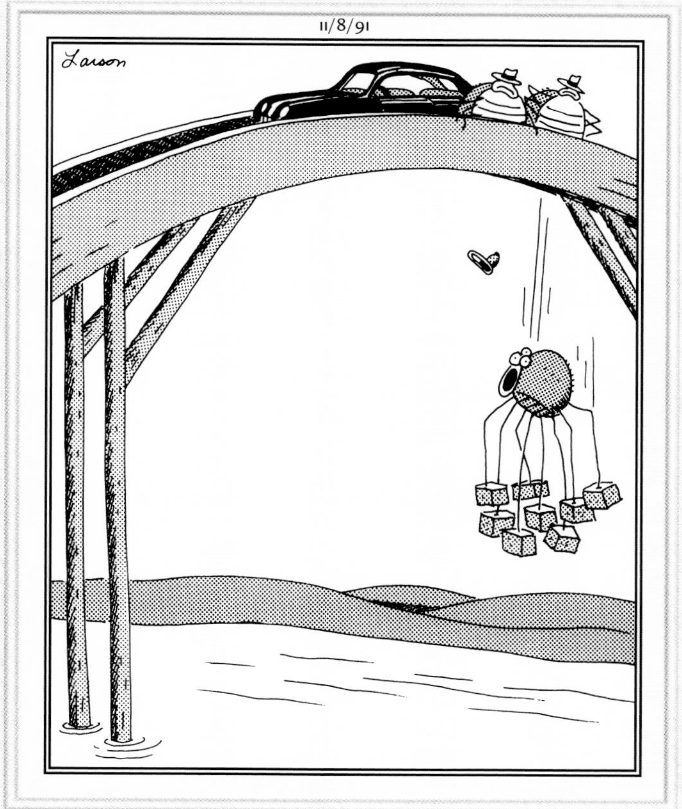
11/8/91
Larson

The spider Mafia at work

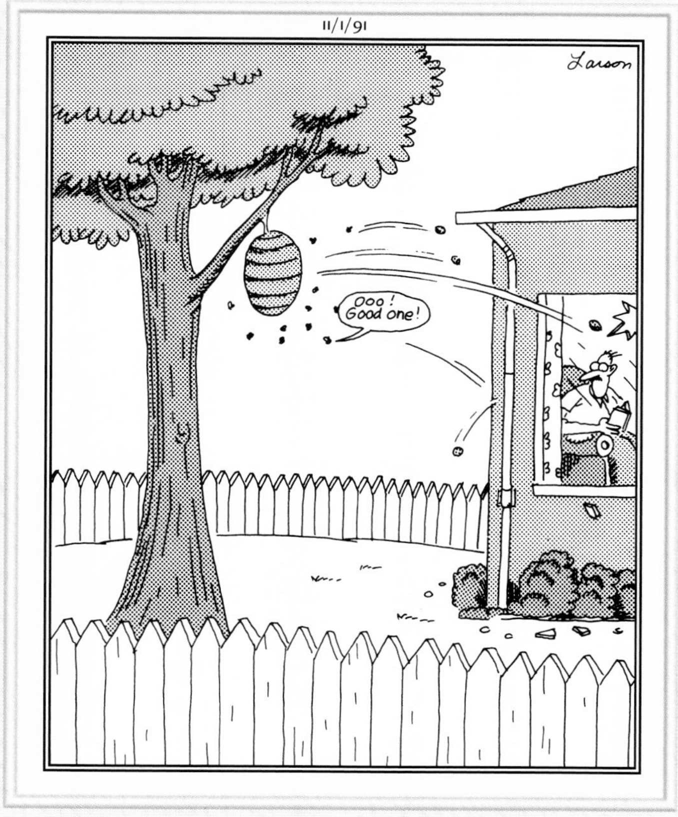
11/1/91
Larson
Ooo! Good one!

For many weeks, the two species had lived in mutual tolerance of one another. And then, without provocation, the hornets began throwing rocks at Ned's house.

"Hey! I got news for you, sweetheart! ...
I *am* the lowest form of life on earth!"

By blending in with the ostrich's eggs,
Hare Krishnas are subsequently raised
by the adult birds.

"Why don't you play some blues, Andrew?"

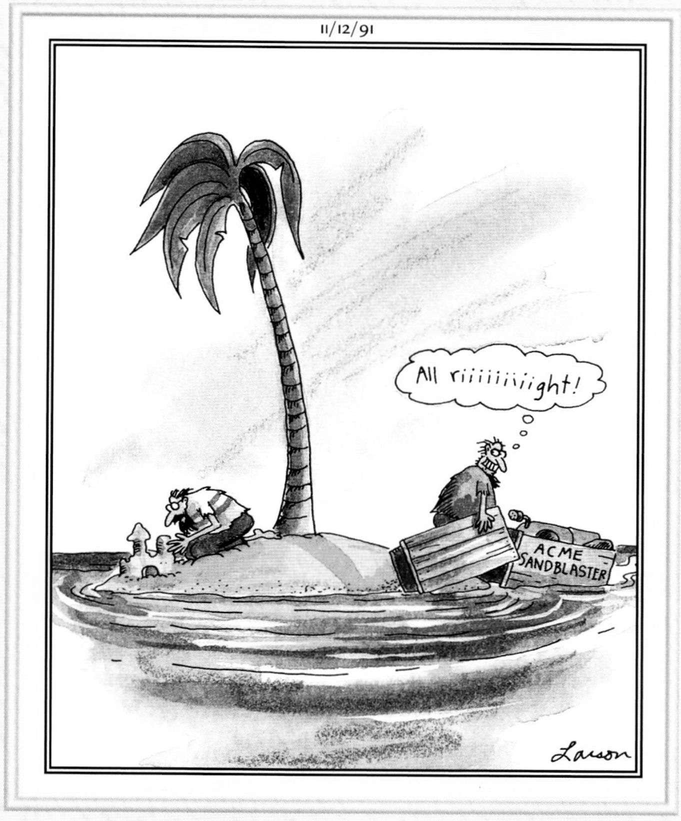
11/12/91
All riiiiiiiight!
ACME SANDBLASTER
Larson

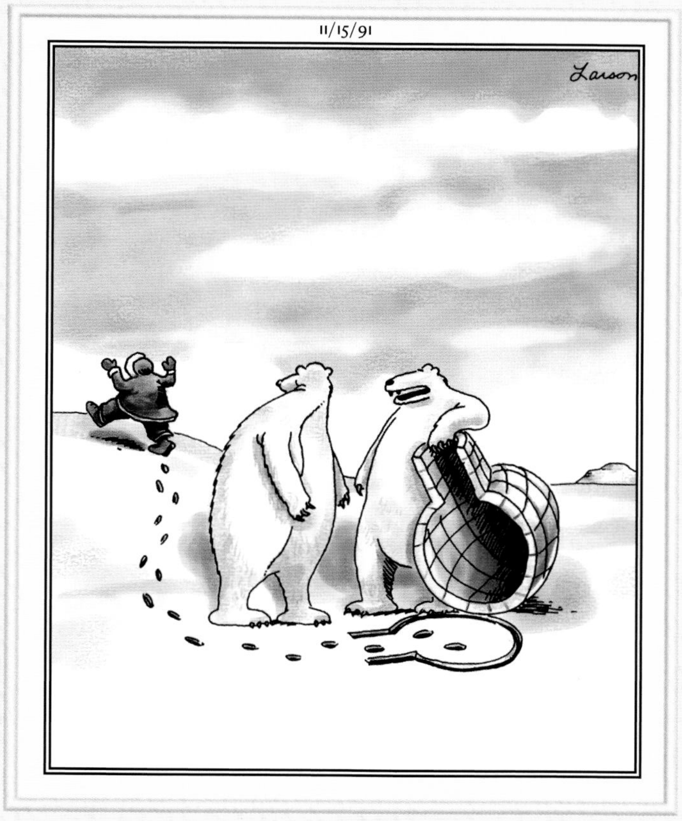
11/15/91
Larson

"I lift, you grab. ... Was that concept just a little too complex, Carl?"

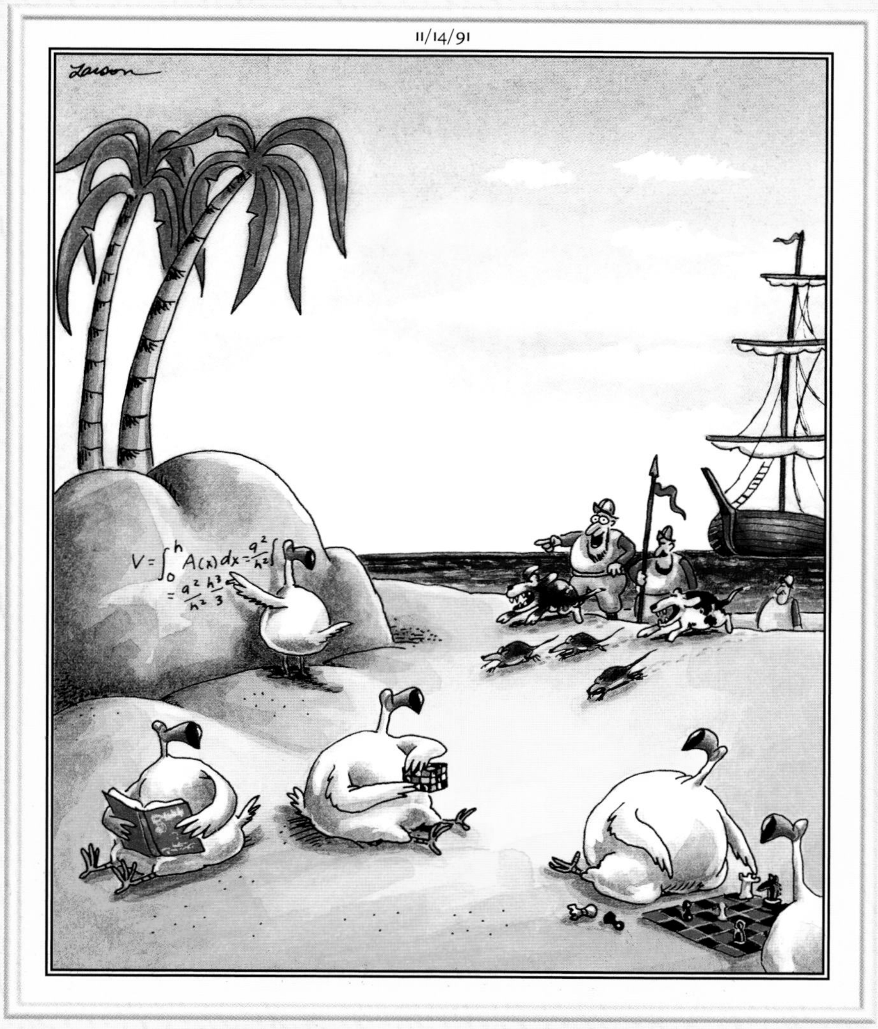
11/14/91
Larson

Unbeknownst to most ornithologists, the dodo was actually a very advanced species, living alone quite peacefully until, in the 17th century, it was annihilated by men, rats, and dogs. As usual.

11/11/91

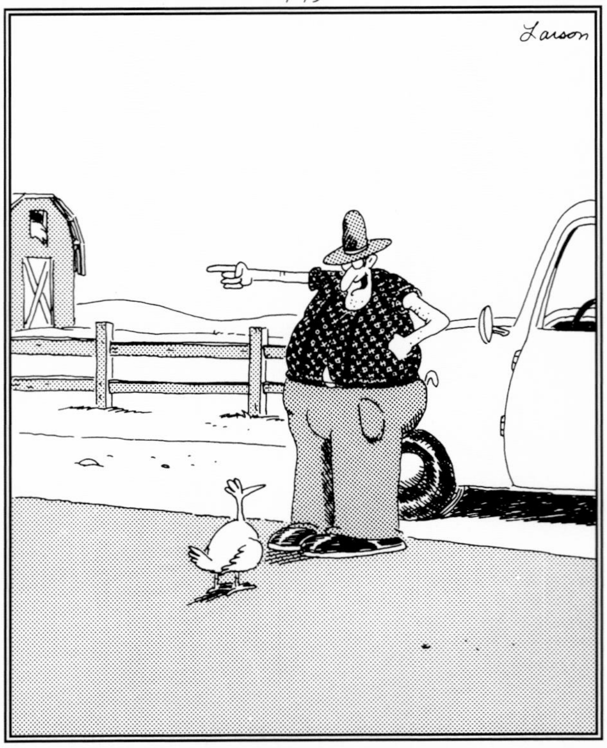
Larson

"Sure. The place you're lookin' for is straight over them hills. 'Course, that's as the crow flies, not as the chicken walks. Ha ha ha ha!"

11/13/91

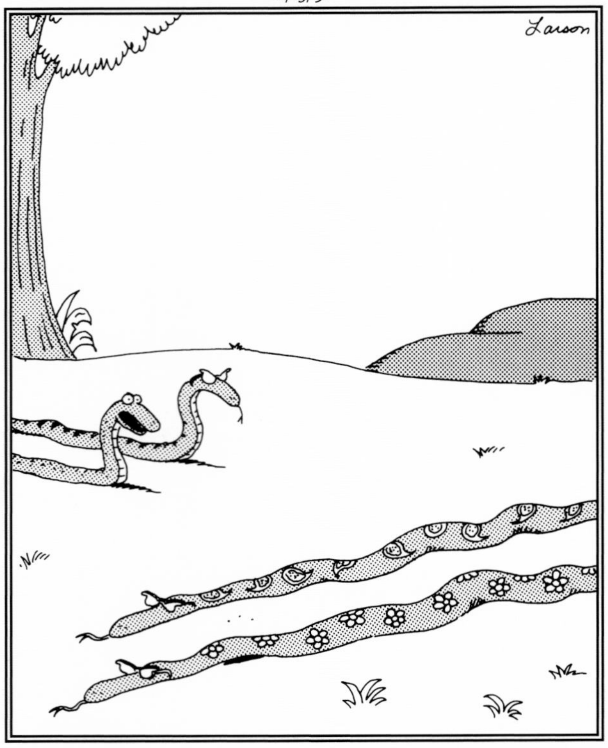
Larson

"Oh my God! ... '60s skins are back!"

11/18/91

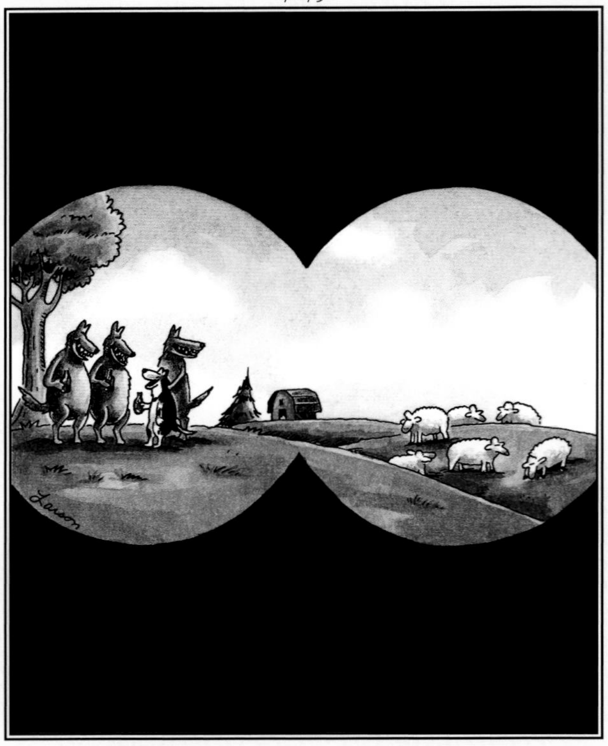
Larson

Everything was starting to come into focus for Farmer MacDougal—his missing sheep, his missing beer, and his collie, Shep, who was getting just a little too sociable for his own good.

11/20/91

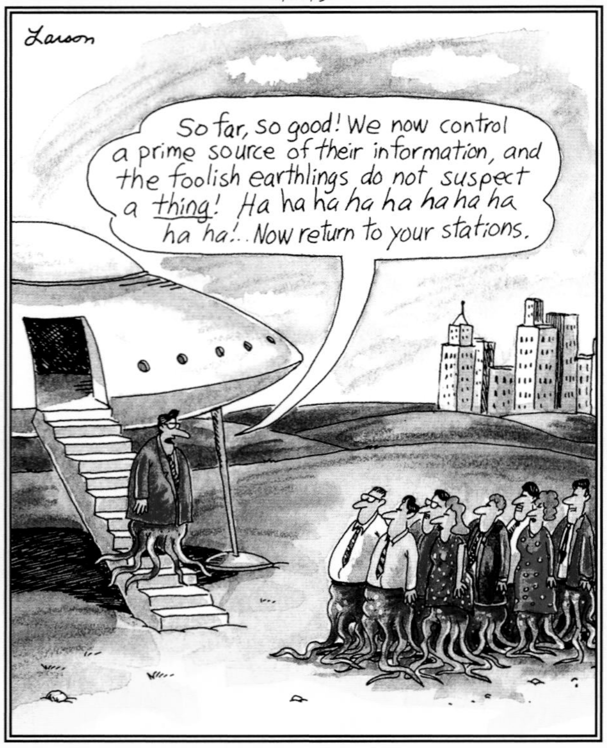
Larson
So far, so good! We now control a prime source of their information, and the foolish earthlings do not suspect a thing! Ha ha ha ha ha ha ha ha ha ha!.. Now return to your stations.

Why we see news anchorpersons only from the waist up.

11/19/91

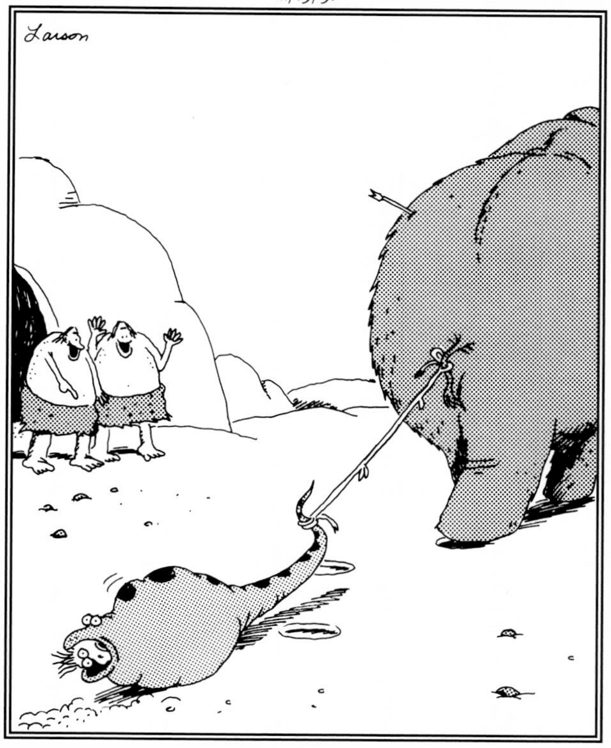
Larson

Practical jokes of the Paleolithic

To Whom it may Concern,

Help!
Normally I have no problems with understanding the Far Side. Yet the following has Stumped Not only me But the Entire office. Please Translate or at Least give me a Clue.
My work phone [redacted]

or return address Letter

Sincerly Confused,
[redacted]

UNIVERSAL PRESS SYNDICATE
4900 Main Street • Kansas City, Missouri 64112 • 816/932-6600

April 26, 1994

Dear Mr. [redacted]

Gary Larson passed along to me your letter asking about a FAR SIDE cartoon in his Off-the-Wall calendar.

The panel you didn't understand is a twist on the putting-a-man-in-his-place joke. The two cavemen in the background have pulled a practical joke on the third caveman. Somehow the two men put the third into the snake, and then tied the snake to the mammoth's tail. They then must have angered the mammoth by sticking a spear in its hide, which caused the mammoth to take the caveman on a very bumpy ride.

The situation is not unlike someone putting a smart aleck into a car trunk and taking him on a joyride. But this cartoon takes place thousands of years ago.

I hope this explanation helps. Thanks for taking the time to write.

Sincerely,

Jake Morrissey
Associate Editor

11/29/91

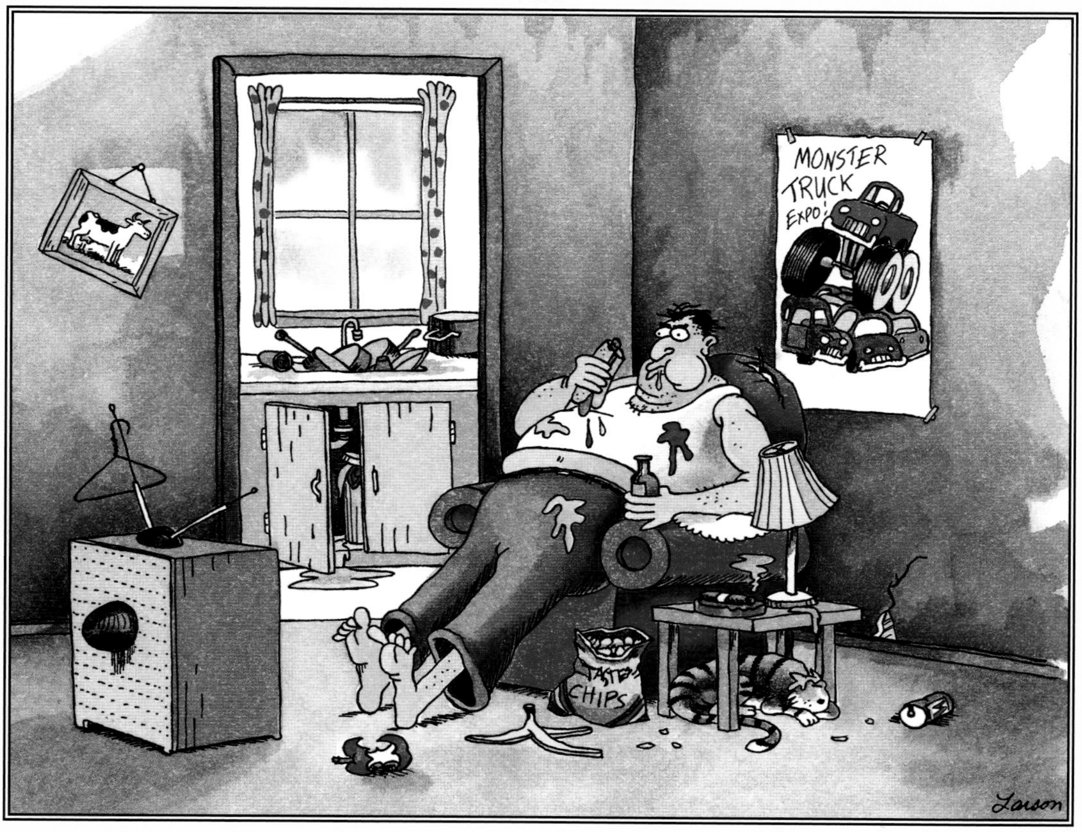
MONSTER TRUCK EXPO!
TASTEE CHIPS
Larson

Giorgio Armani at home

11/25/91

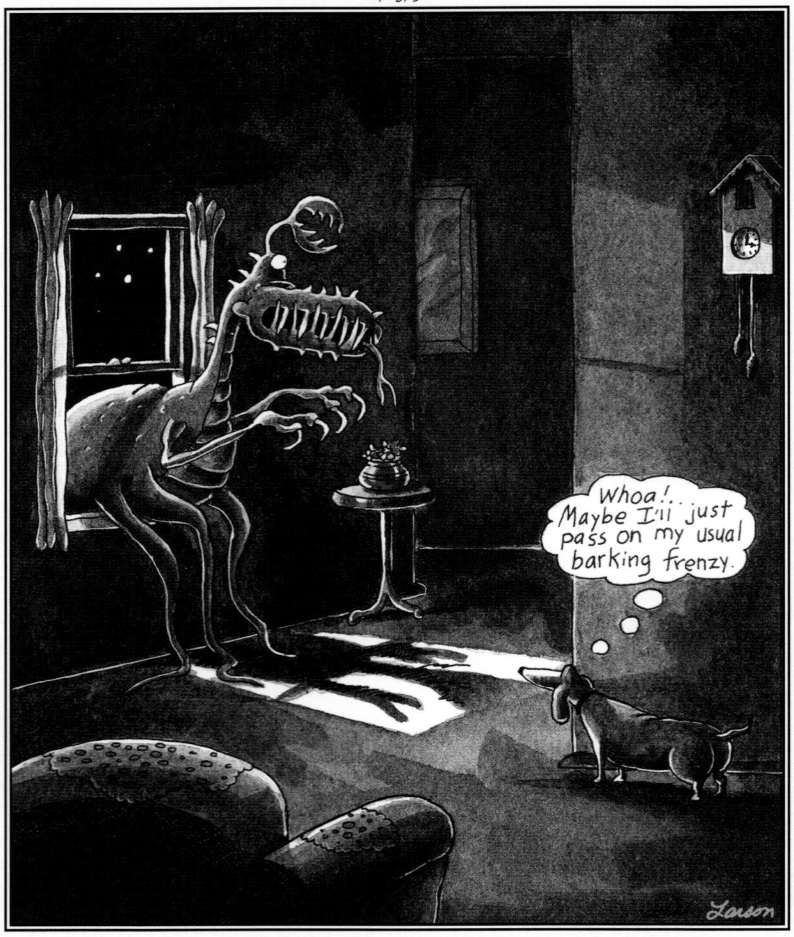
Whoa!.. Maybe I'll just pass on my usual barking frenzy.
Larson

11/21/91

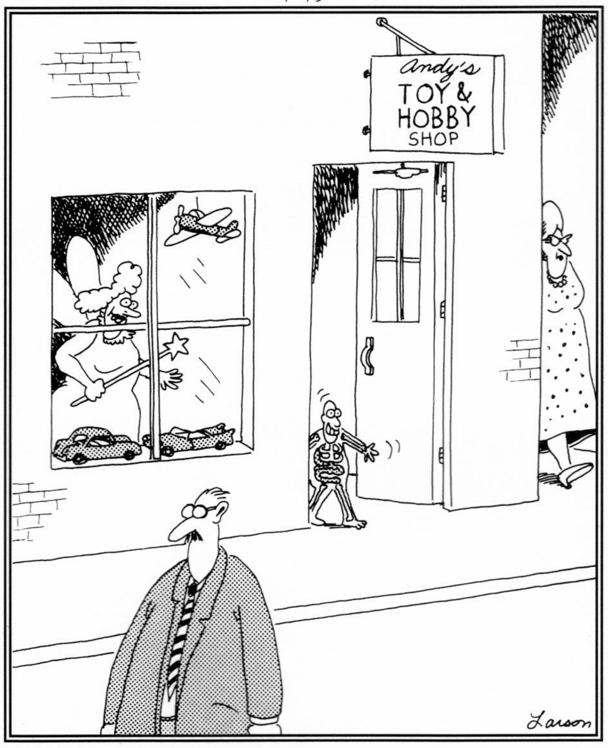
Andy's
TOY & HOBBY SHOP
Larson

His wish to be a real person granted, the Visible Man takes his first steps into the real world—not suspecting that most people, upon seeing him, would either faint or throw up.

11/22/91

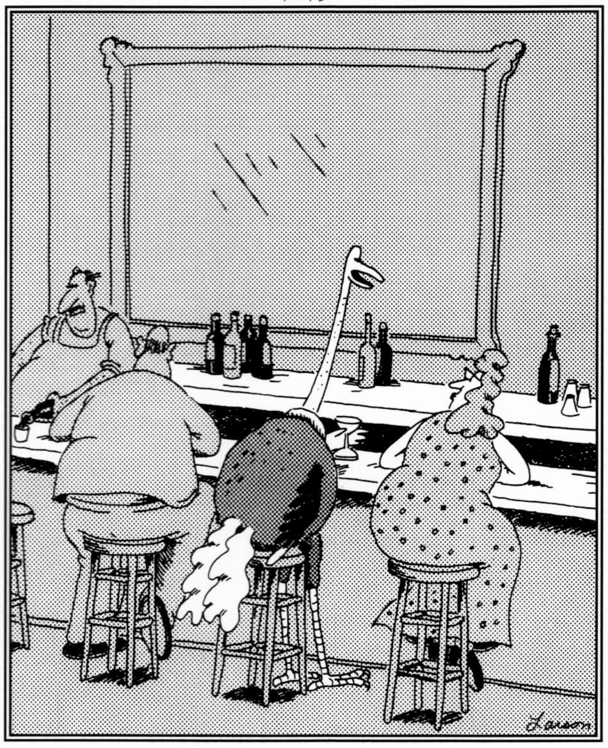
Larson

"Well, according to the dictionary, I'm just a large, flightless bird from East Africa. ... But believe me, Doris—once you get to know me, you'll see I'm much, much more than that."

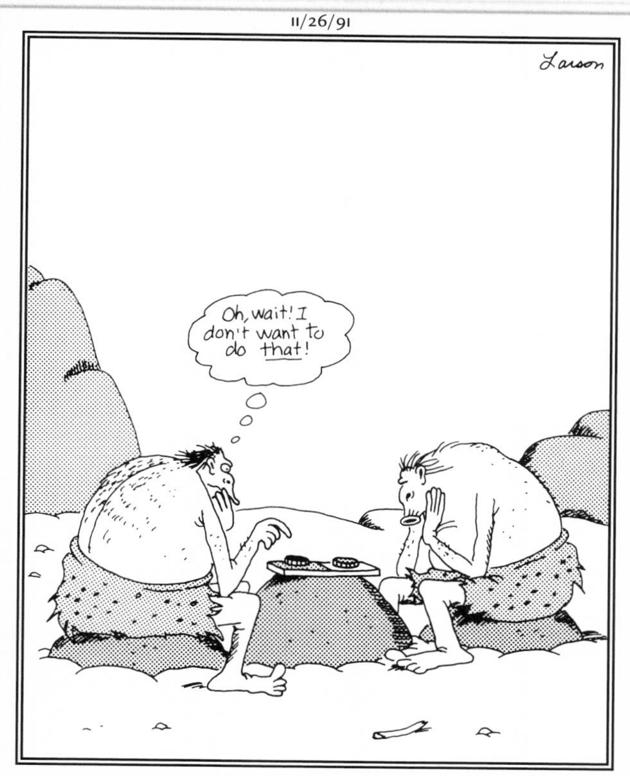
11/26/91
Larson
Oh, wait! I don't want to do that!

Early checkers

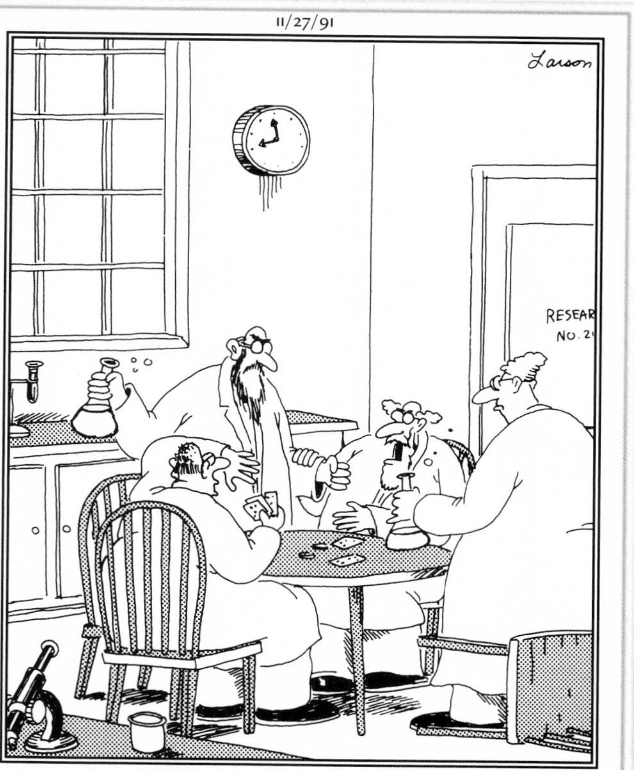
11/27/91
Larson
RESEAR
NO. 2

"Whoa! Whoa! C'mon, you guys! This is just a friendly game of cards—ease up on those acid-filled beakers."

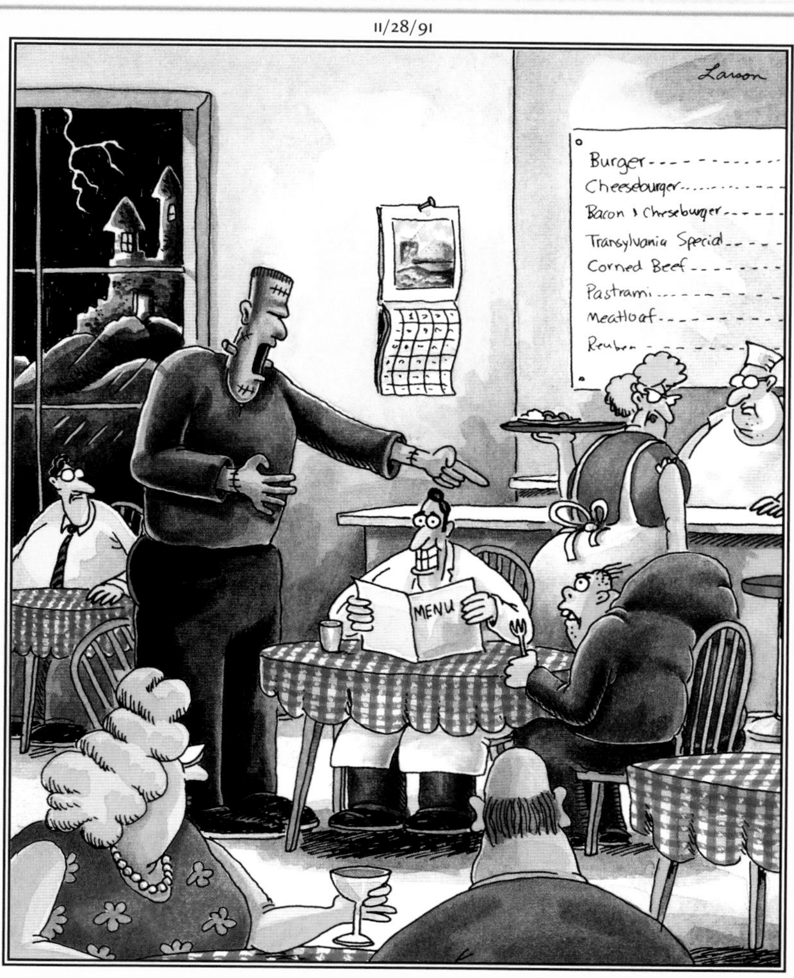
11/28/91
Larson
Burger
Cheeseburger
Bacon & Cheeseburger
Transylvania Special
Corned Beef
Pastrami
Meatloaf
MENU

"Oh, yeah? Well, I'd rather be a living corpse made from dismembered body parts than a hunchbacked little grave robber like you!"

12/2/91
Larson

"You're a cold fish, Raymond."

12/3/91
♪ Country roads, ♪ take me home, to the place, I ♫ ran over my dog!
Larson

John Denver on the comeback trail

12/4/91
KARATE SCHOOL
Larson

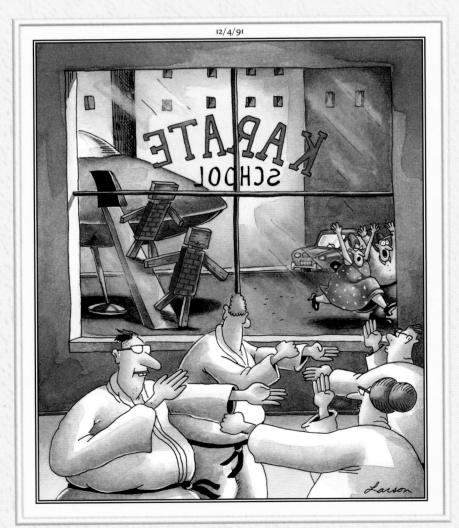

The class abruptly stopped practicing. Here was a chance to not only employ their skills, but also to save the entire town.

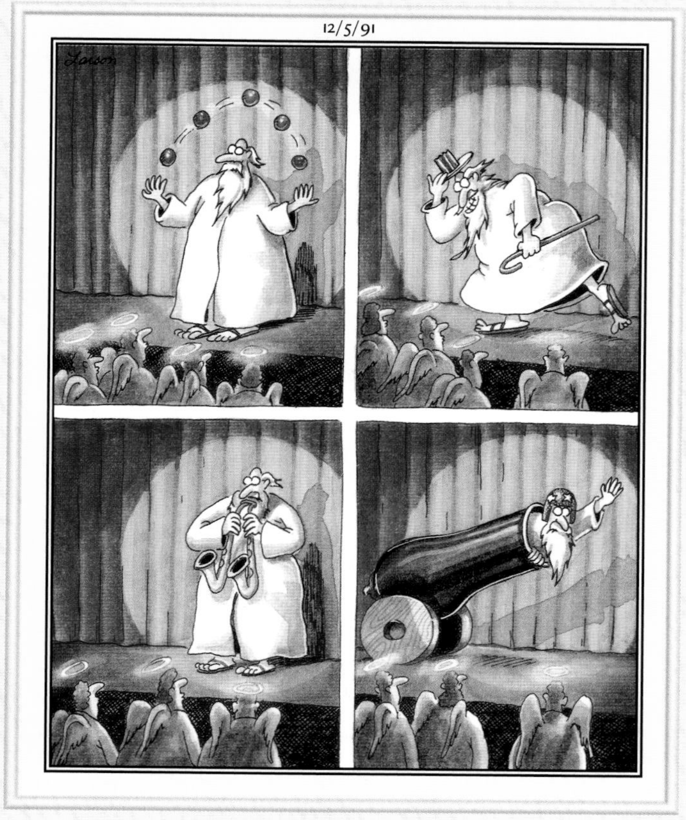
12/5/91
Larson

Acts of God

August 23, 1994

Mr. Victor H. Hanson II
Birmingham, Alabama

Dear Sir:

The reason this letter is being sent directly to you instead of to "Reader's Opinions" is that I am not interested in seeing my letter or my name in the paper, but I am very greatly concerned with a deplorable situation which you can, if you will, very easily set right.

I do not believe that you are the sort of man who would mock God, or who would enjoy seeing others hold the Almighty up to ridicule—but the "Far Side" cartoon which appears daily in the BIRMINGHAM NEWS does just this on a recurring basis. Some time ago—perhpas two years ago—God was pictured in a series of cartoons entitled THE ACTS OF GOD, which appeared in a Sunday edition of the NEWS, as performing such acts as juggling and being shot out of a cannon, for the entertainment of the angels.

Less than a week ago—in last Friday's paper, I believe—He was ridiculed as an apparently clumsy creator who was delighted to find that snakes were quite easy to make using modeling clay.

It is not surprising that a warped mind would enjoy ridiculing Almighty God—what is surprising is to find a respectable family newspaper such as the BIRMINGHAM NEWS providing a platform for that warped mind.

Surely, Mr. Hanson, you do not wish to make it appear that mocking God is an ordinary, respectable, acceptable thing to do, do you? Then will you not please cease to publish the "Far Side" cartoons in the NEWS?

Yours truly,

[redacted]

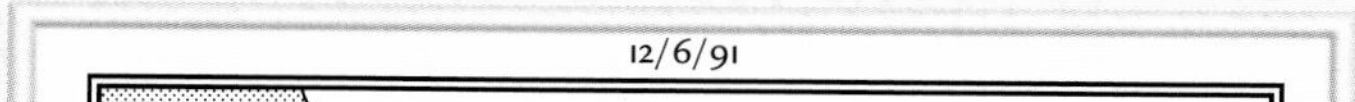
12/6/91
Larson

Of course, prehistoric neighborhoods always had that one family whose front yard was strewn with old mammoth remains.

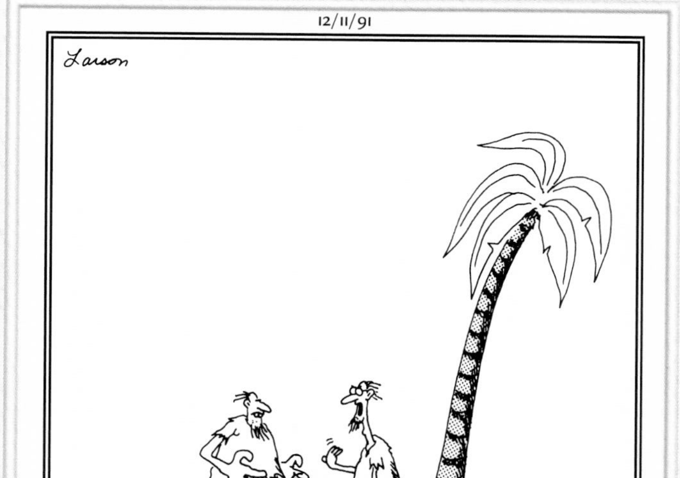
12/11/91
Larson

"Yeah, Vern! You heard what I said! And what are you gonna do about it? Huh? C'mon! What are ya gonna do? Huh? C'MON!"

12/9/91

...gently down the stream... Port Side!.. Row row row your boat...
Larson

Slave-ship entertainers

12/10/91

Larson

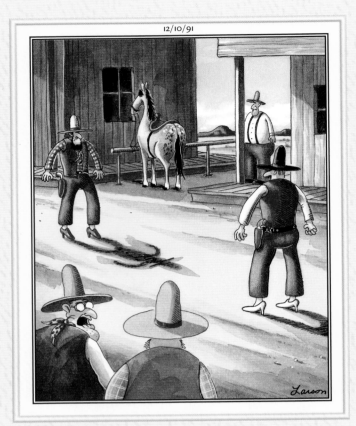

"I tell ya, Ben—no matter who wins this thing, Boot Hill ain't ever gonna seem the same."

12/17/91

Larson

Until his medical license was suspended, cosmetic surgeon Dr. Irwin Blumenfeld left many of his patients with the tragic side effect known as "buffalo nose."

12/12/91

Larson

If pets wore hats: a study in animal personalities and styles

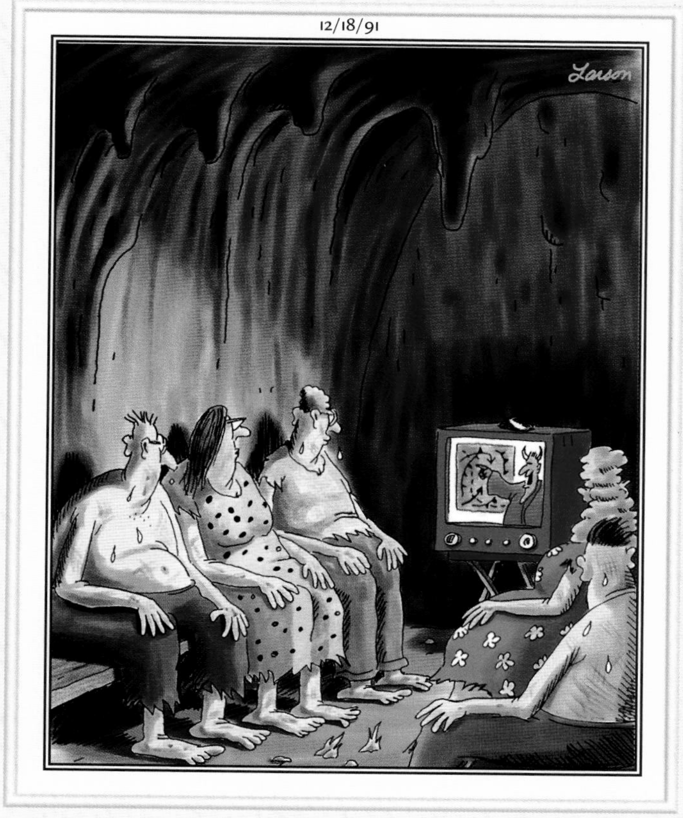
12/18/91
Larson

"And now the weather—well, doggone it, but I'm afraid that cold front I told you about yesterday is just baaarrrely going to miss us."

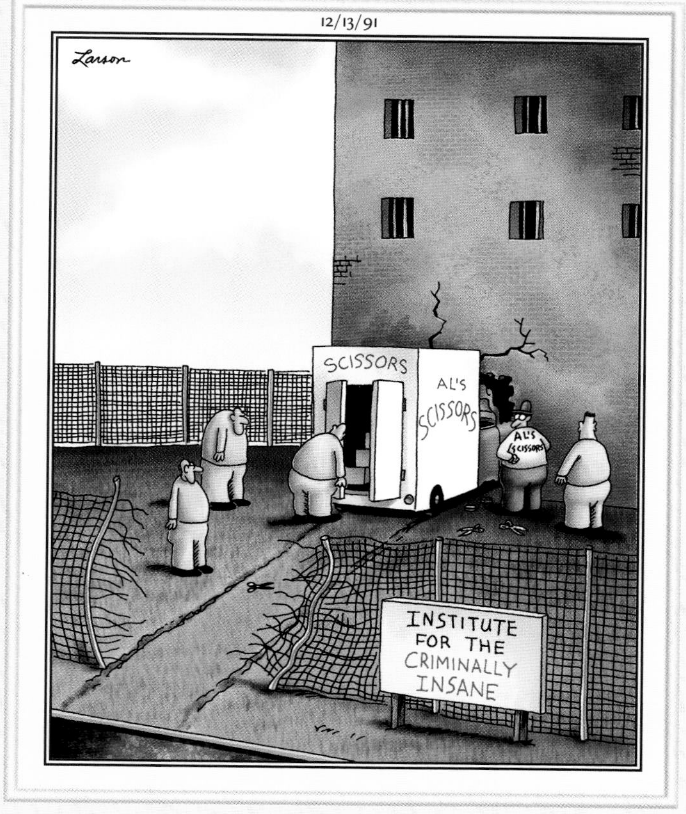
12/13/91
Larson
SCISSORS
AL'S SCISSORS
INSTITUTE FOR THE CRIMINALLY INSANE

And then Al realized his problems were much bigger than just a smashed truck.

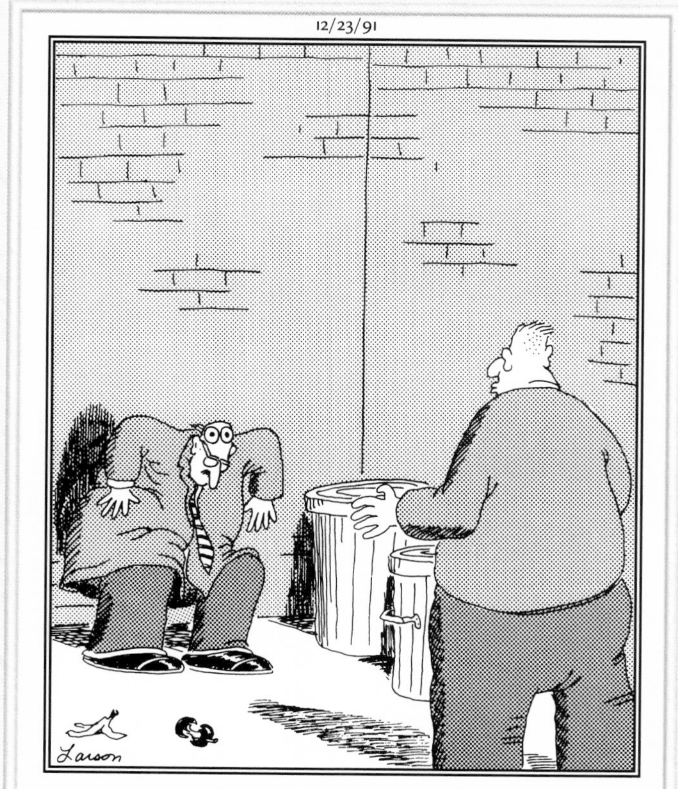
12/23/91
Larson

Cornered and sensing danger, Sidney flares his "eye spots."

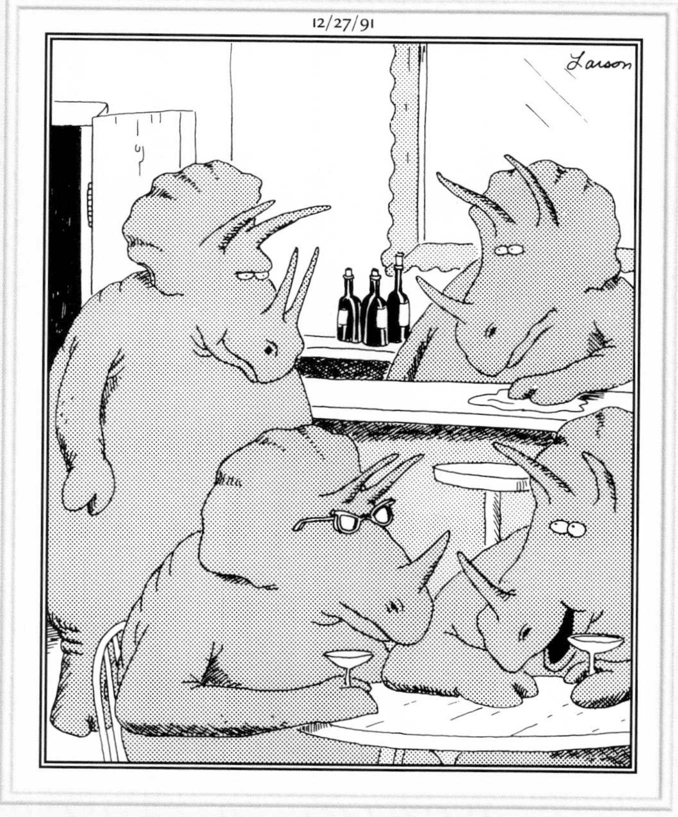
12/27/91
Larson

"Oooooo! Check it out, Edith! It's a *quadra*ceratops!"

12/16/91

Larson

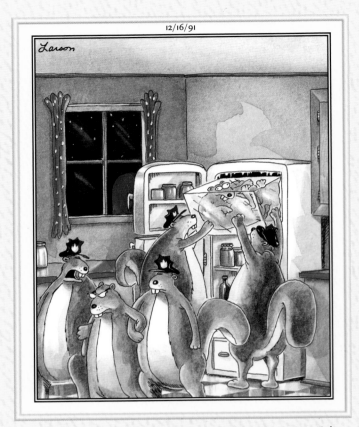

"Come with us, ma'am—and if I were you, I'd get a good lawyer. No one's gonna buy that my-husband-was-only-hibernating story."

12/19/91

Larson

"Latte, Jed?"

12/20/91

Larson

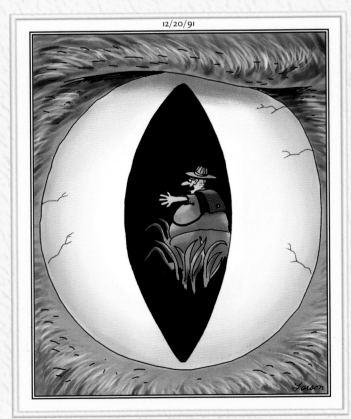

"My gun, Desmond! I sense this striped man-eater is somewhere dead ahead, waiting to ambush us! ... Ohhhhhh, he thinks he's so clever."

12/24/91

Larson
Chef Floyd

"Waiter! What's that soup doin' on my fly?"

12/25/91

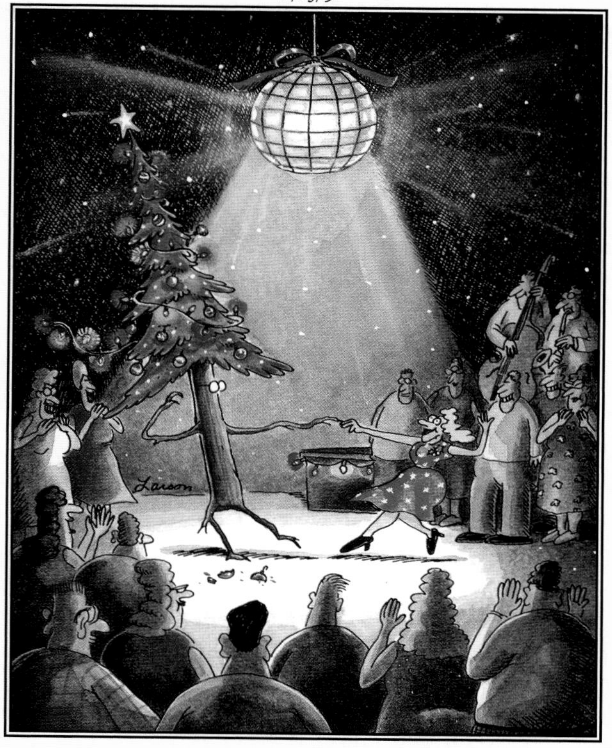

Carl had never had so much fun in his whole life, and he knew, from this moment on, that he would never again be a lone pine tree.

12/26/91

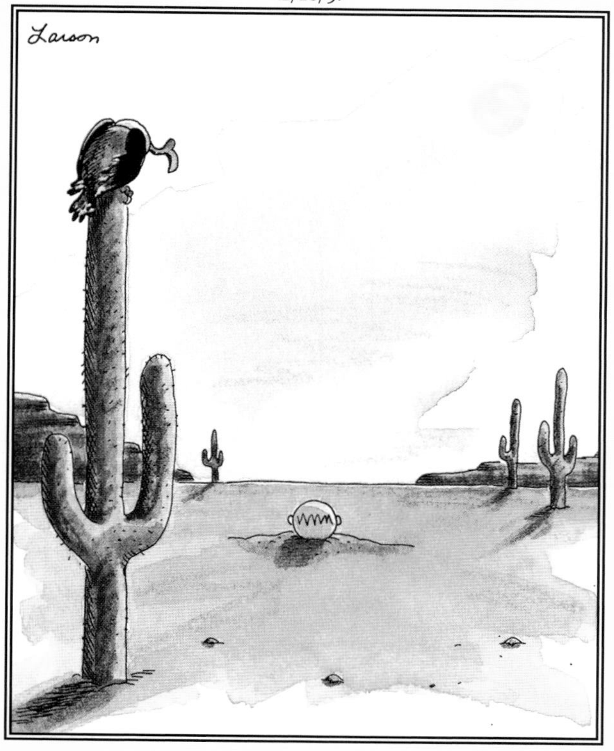

Charlie Brown in Indian country

12/30/91

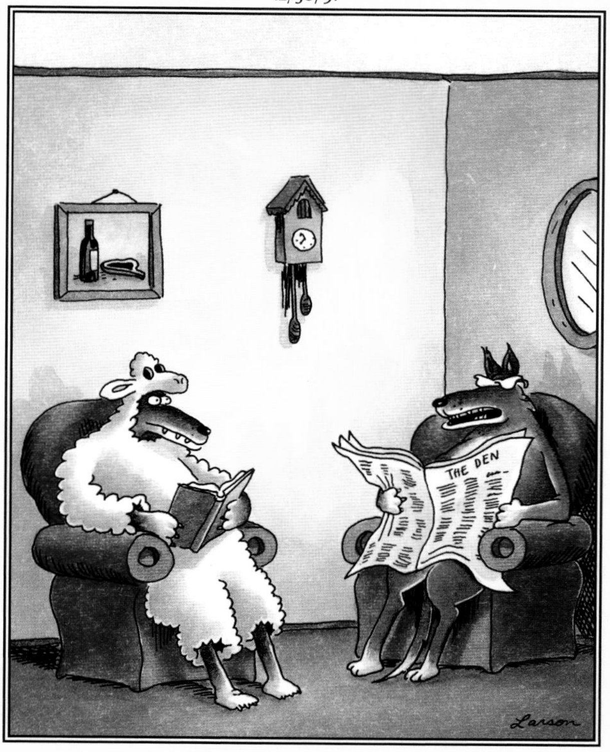
THE DEN

"I'm starting to worry about you, Earl. ... Stalking sheep in that outfit is one thing, but wearing it around the house is just a little bit kinky."

12/31/91

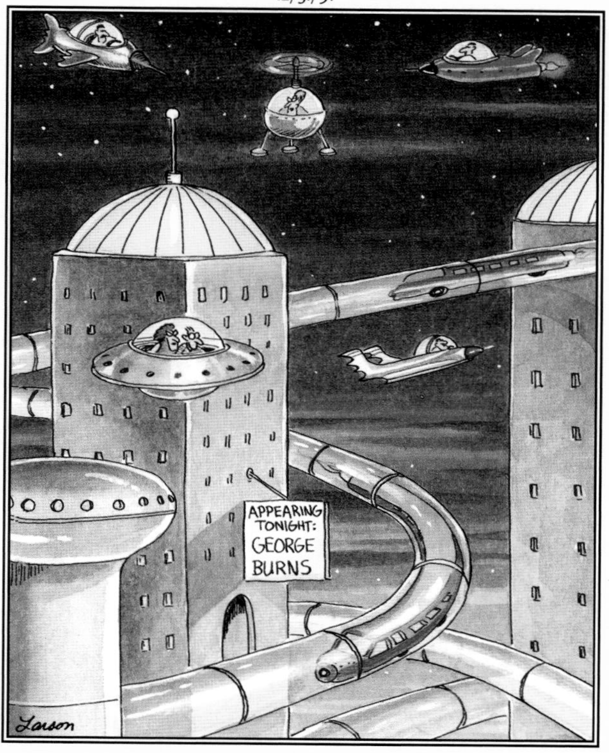
APPEARING TONIGHT: GEORGE BURNS

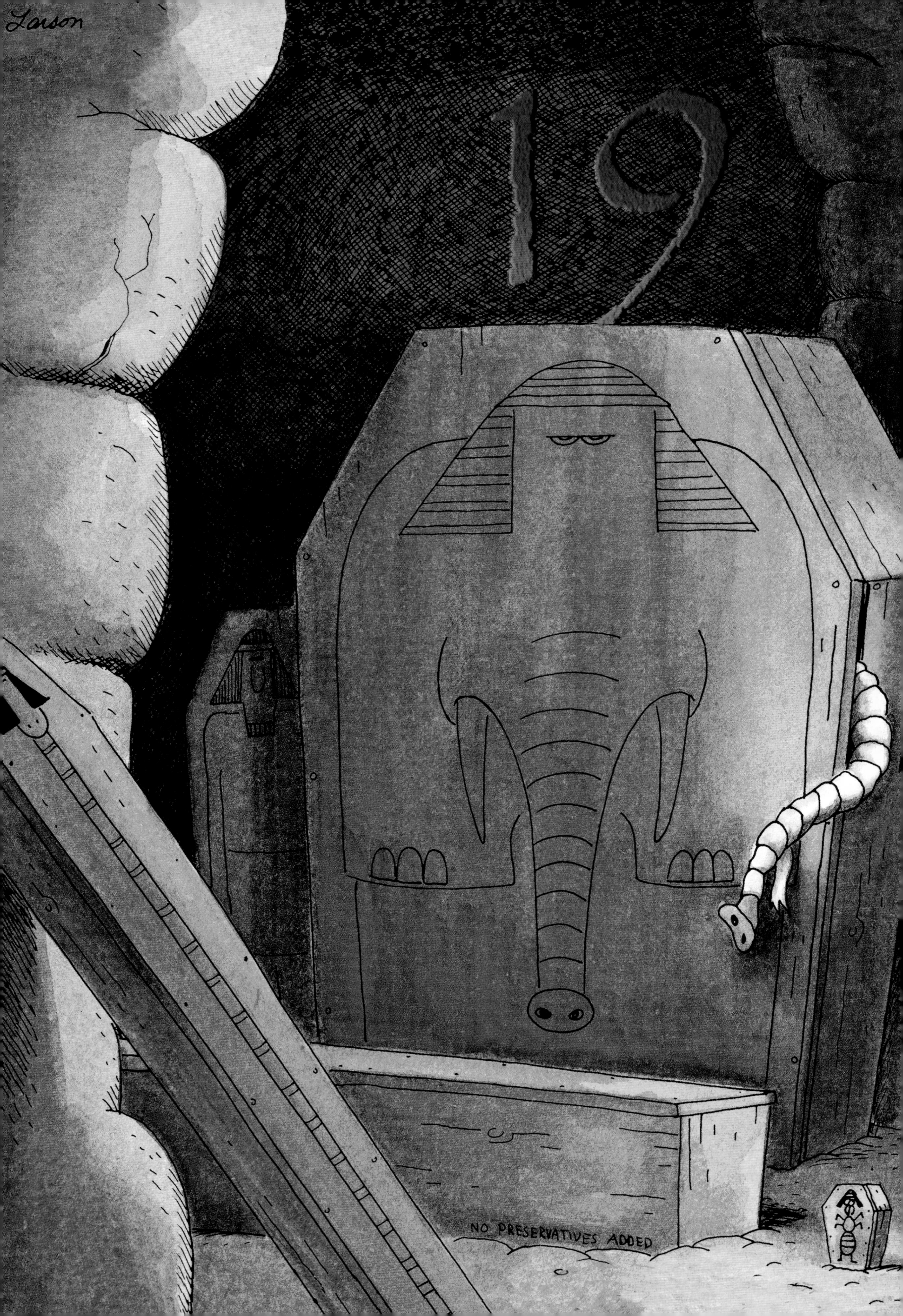
Larson
19
NO PRESERVATIVES ADDED

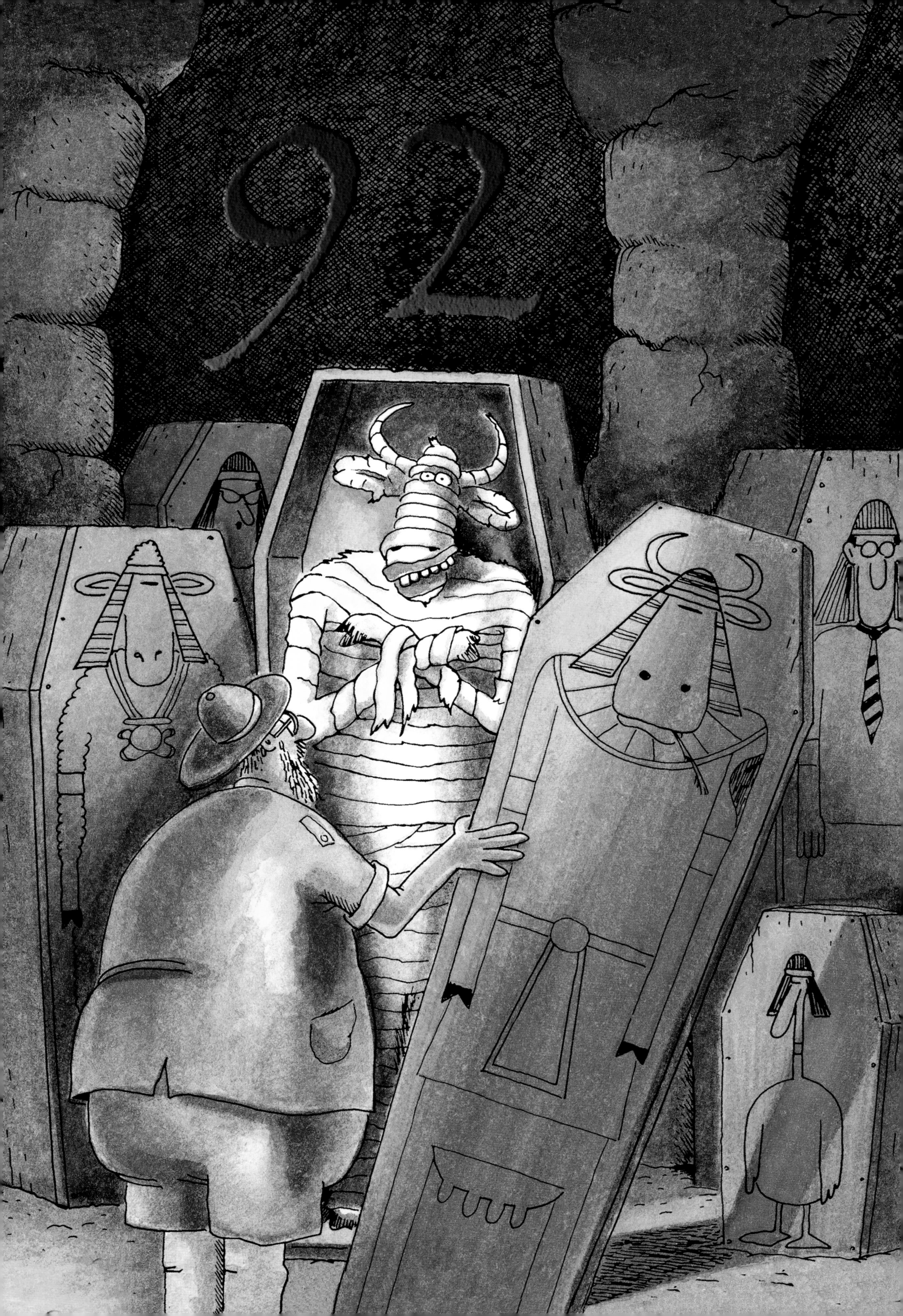
92

The Minefields of Mirth

Having started this essay several times, I realize this subject could easily have required a third volume for this collection, which is already approaching critical mass. But maybe I can touch on just a few examples of how, in my experience, the simple formula:

$$\text{drawing (d)} + \text{words (w)} = \text{cartoon (c)}$$
can turn into:
$$d + w = \pi \text{ in my face.}$$

First, there is the offensive variable: Inadvertently offending people (speaking for myself, I swear it was always inadvertent, although I admit to sometimes holding my breath when certain cartoons went "out the door") and reading their angry letters is a tough experience when you're first starting out young and enthusiastic, with visions of sugar cows in your head. Sometime after you receive your second or third "How DARE you!" letter, it begins to dawn on you that your own mother may not be the best gauge of how the rest of the world will always respond to you.

But eventually you learn the Big Truth: There's no avoiding this variable. You learn pretty fast in the humor business that offending some people is simply inevitable. (Unless I'm mistaken, even Dean Martin sang, "Everybody offends somebody sometime.") I suppose you could step around this particular land mine by drawing a strip like *Nancy,* although I'd be willing to bet that in his lifetime even Ernie Bushmiller got a letter or two suggesting that Sluggo was fostering some "social cancer."

How easy is it to offend someone? Try this: I once knew someone who expressed indignation over the cartoonist's universal symbol for cursing. You know, the "&*#@*$#!" you sometimes see when, say, a character hits his thumb with a hammer? Maybe just a simple "#@!" would have been okay with this person, but a full, in-your-face "&*#@*$#!" was apparently too much to handle. For the record, I don't believe I ever said "&*#@*$#!" in any of my cartoons, except once when I made fun of the device.

Some land mines you unwittingly plant yourself, without a clue in the world of what you're doing. For example, the word "boink."

Warning to other cartoonists: Do not use "boink" as a sound effect for something smacking into something else. I didn't know this. I used it more than once. "Boink," as it turns out, can be considered a verb. (Especially by the Brits, who first brought the boink issue to my attention.) And as a verb, "boink" is a bad thing to say. Unless, of course, you *meant* to say "boink." Then I suppose "boink" is a beautiful thing, if perhaps not the most romantic way of expressing the thing that "boink" means, as a verb, you see. Whatever. Let's drop it.

Then there are the small, factual details that I sometimes overlooked. I suppose these are more equivalent to stumbling in a cartoon rather than actually falling, but frankly it used to bug the hell out of me when I did it. Case in point: Cassius Marcellus Coolidge.

It was a dark and stormy night. I was working on a cartoon based on that famous-for-being-kitschy painting, *Dogs Playing Poker* (Vol. 2, p. 423). I had to come up with a name for the artist. No use in checking the painting's history, I decided—*Dogs Playing Poker* is just one of those artifacts of American pop culture that's always been around, right? It's just *Dogs Playing Poker* by the standard "artist unknown."

So I came up with the name "Gus Nickerson" for the long-forgotten artist. The cartoon gets published, years go by, and one morning I'm having breakfast and reading the *New York Times,* and wham!—there it is, front page: a human interest story about the life and times of Cassius Marcellus Coolidge, creator of *A Friend in Need,* the painting's real title, based on the fact that one dog is helping another cheat. Artist known.

Why did (and does) this bug me so much? Because these are the sort of small, arcane insights I enjoy capturing, like getting the right genus name on some insect. It wouldn't matter if only a handful of people would have discovered the cartoon's small "bonus." For me, that's what makes it fun. And in truth, it bugged me for another reason. If you think about it, *A Friend in Need* is arguably as famous (in this country, at least) as the *Mona Lisa* by what's-his-name, and I just didn't give Mr. Coolidge his proper due.

Then there's "Jimmy" Frankenstein (Vol. 1, p. 228). It jumped into my head that the mad scientist's name was "James Frankenstein." I have no explanation for this error. ("Jim Frankenstein" sounds more plausible as Victor's brother, who perhaps became a mad insurance salesman.)

Now allow me a brief excursion into the world of foreign translations. Here, the wheels can come off a cartoon completely and the whole shebang will plummet off a cliff in an entertaining ball of fire.

The translators usually are fairly successful at taking my sometimes very American clichés and expressions and finding their own native language equivalent. Of course, sometimes there's an impasse. And when a *cultural* gap opens up, well, that's when the fireball-over-the-cliff thing can happen. From Boot Hill to Eddie Haskell, some subjects just won't cut it in the *Le Journal Officiel de la Republique Français.*

Consider a cartoon I did on the subject of Babe the Blue Ox. (Vol. 1, p. 175). My German editors, naturally, had never heard of Paul Bunyan and his colorful sidekick. They took "blue" to mean "depressed." So in the German interpretation, hunters have mistaken the fabled animal for a big, "depressed" mule deer.

I'll simply show two other suggested translations below. These also are German, but I hasten to add that this problem wasn't unique to the Germans; I just liked these examples.

Original Caption

"Nik! The fireflies across the street—I think they're mooning us!"

Proposed Translation

"Nik! The fireflies across the street—I think they're trying to take the piss out of us!"

Original Caption

"Okay, folks! ... It's a wrap!"

Proposed Translation

"Okay, folks! ... The gift is ready!"

I need to call this a "wrap" myself. And I haven't even touched on the cartoons I drew that were simply misinterpreted. (Now we're moving into a theoretical volume four.) But, in the end, looking back at all the glitches, the near-misses, the gaffes, the should've/could'ves, I'm content. You know, ink happens.

1/1/92

Larson

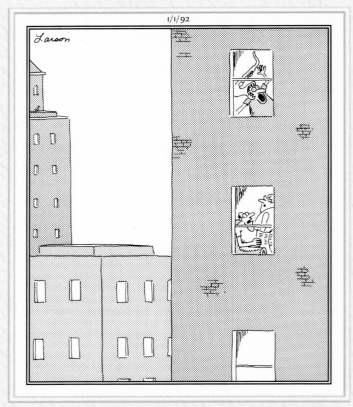

"Whoa! Listen to that, Marge! ... I said that kid was playing a mean sax!"

1/2/92

HAMSTER
HAVEN
Larson

"Those snakes? Oh, they're just signing, honey."

1/6/92

Larson

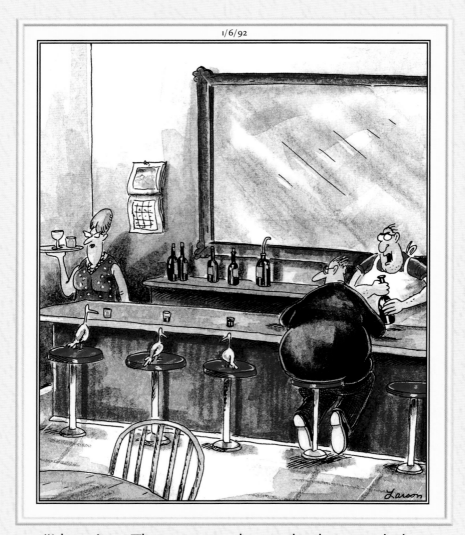

"I hate 'em. They mess on the stools, they attack the mirror and—of course—they drink like birds."

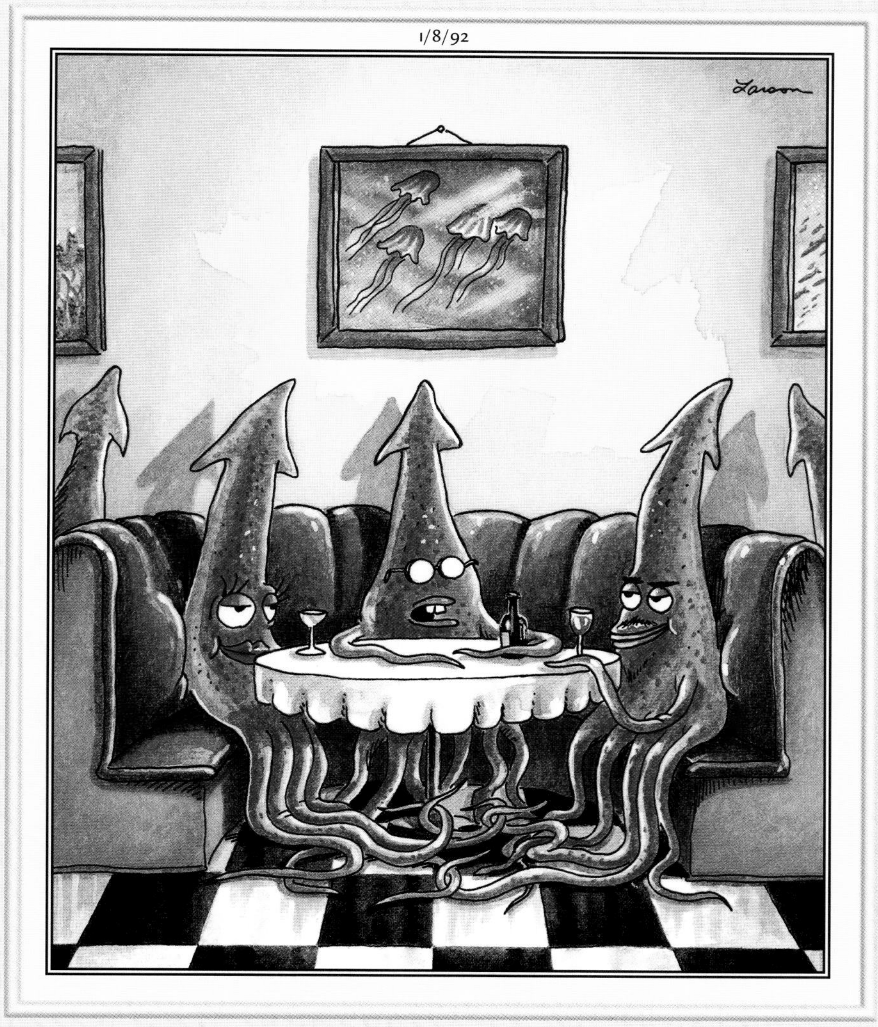
1/8/92
Larson

Darren was unaware that, under the table, his wife and Raymond were playing "tentaclies."

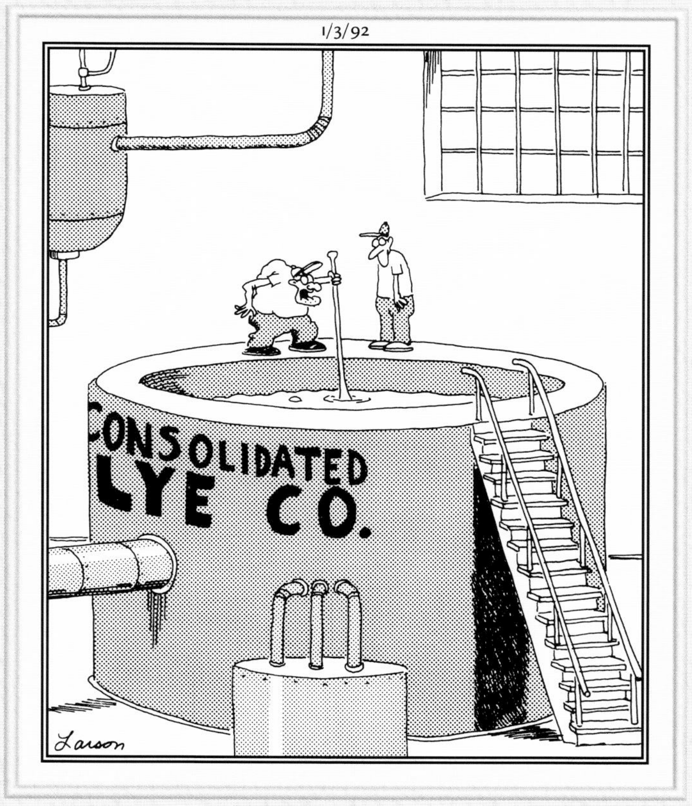
1/3/92
CONSOLIDATED
LYE CO.
Larson

"New guy, huh? Well, up here, you walk the edge! And the edge is a fickle hellcat. ... Love her, but never trust her, for her heart is full of *lye!*"

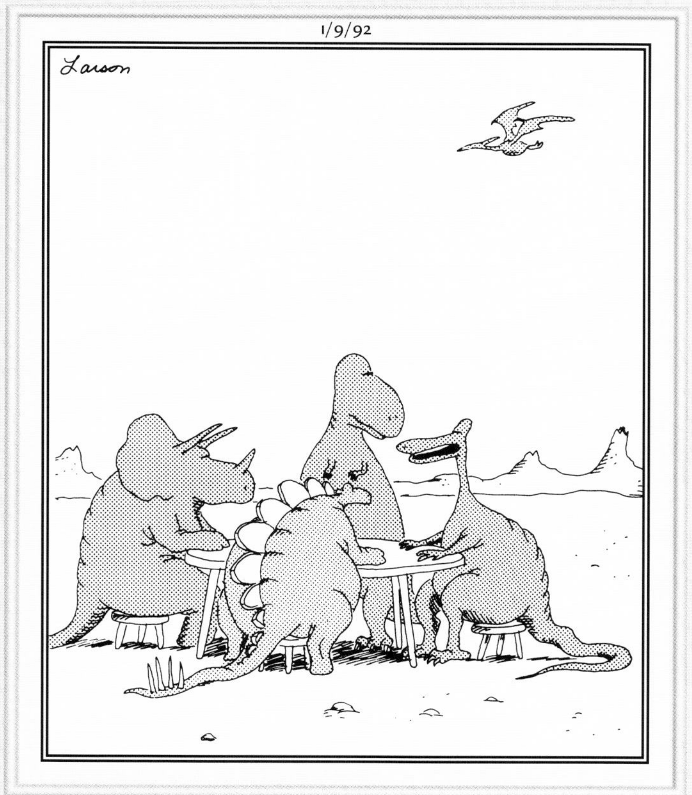
1/9/92
Larson

"Well, time for our weekly brainstem-storming session."

1/13/92

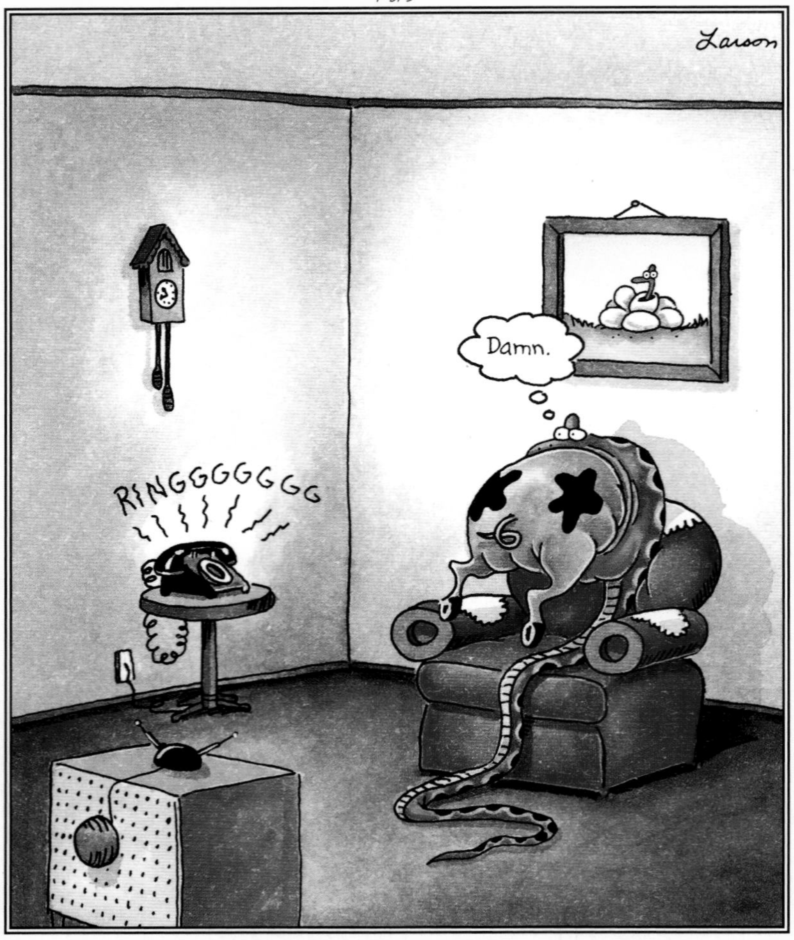
Damn.
RINGGGGGGG

1/15/92

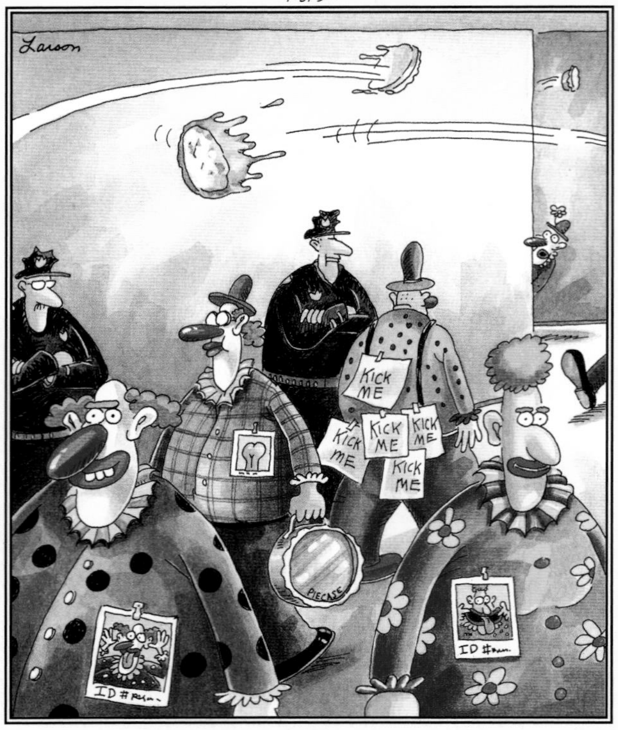
KICK ME
KICK ME
KICK ME
KICK ME
KICK ME
KICK ME
PLEASE

In the corridors of Clowngress

1/7/92

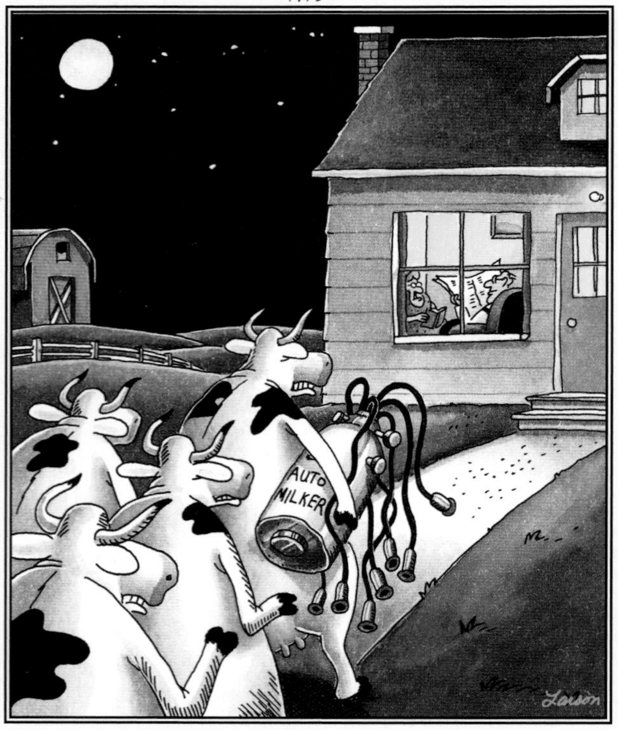
AUTO MILKER

That night, their revenge was meted out on both Farmer MacDougal and his wife. The next day, police investigators found a scene that they could describe only as "grisly, yet strangely hilarious."

1/16/92

Uh-oh.

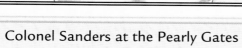

Colonel Sanders at the Pearly Gates

1/17/92

CARRION KING
NOTHING FRESH!

1/20/92

Floral Anatomy

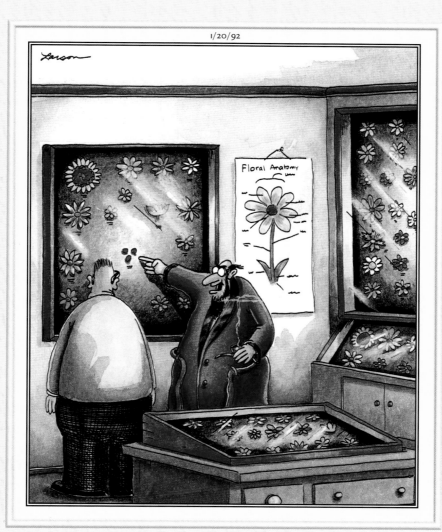

"And here's the jewel of my collection, purchased for a king's ransom from a one-eyed man in Istanbul. ... I give you—Zuzu's petals."

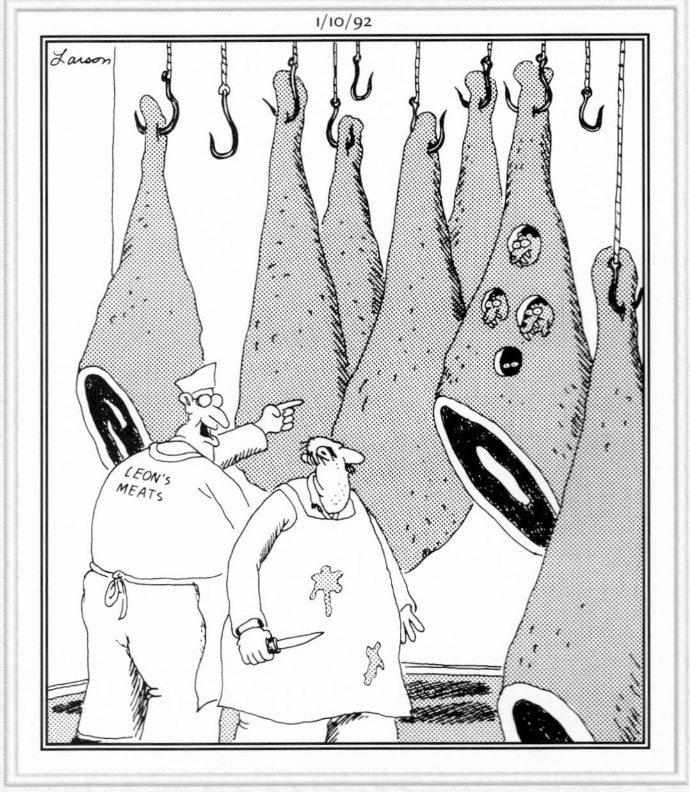
1/10/92
Larson
LEON'S
MEATS

"Ooo! Look, Leon! An entire family of meatchucks!"

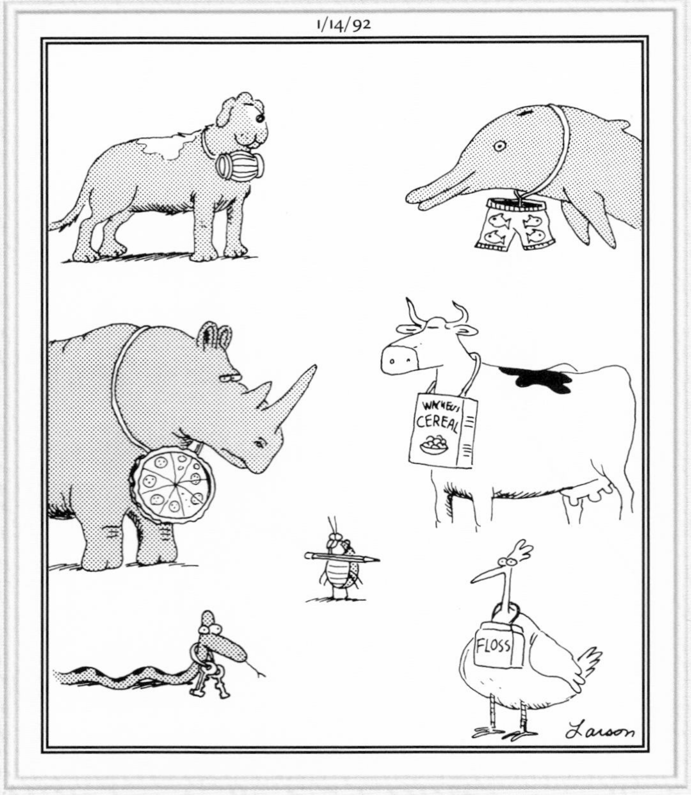
1/14/92
CEREAL
FLOSS
Larson

Some of our more common rescue animals

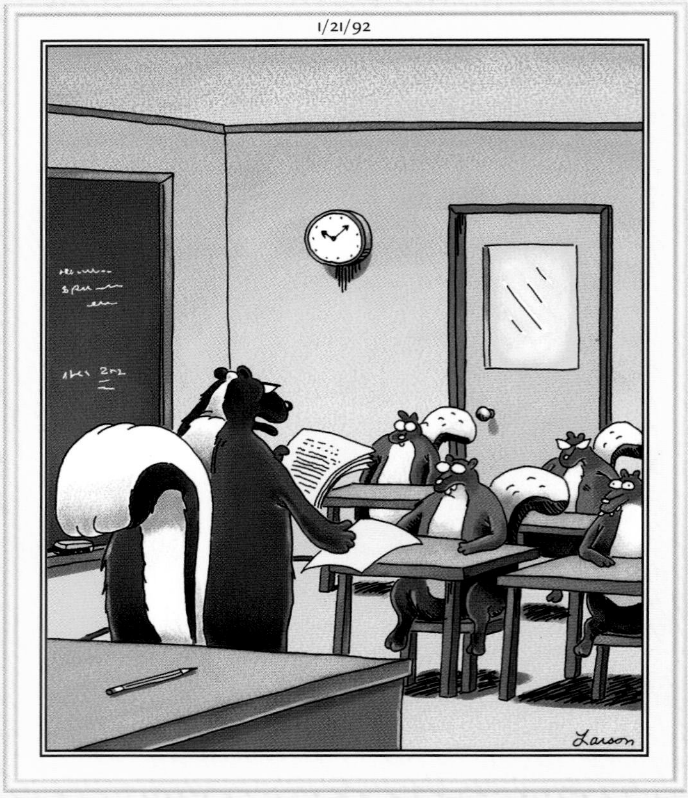
1/21/92
Larson

"Okay, let's start the exam. Stinking caps on, everyone—stinking caps on."

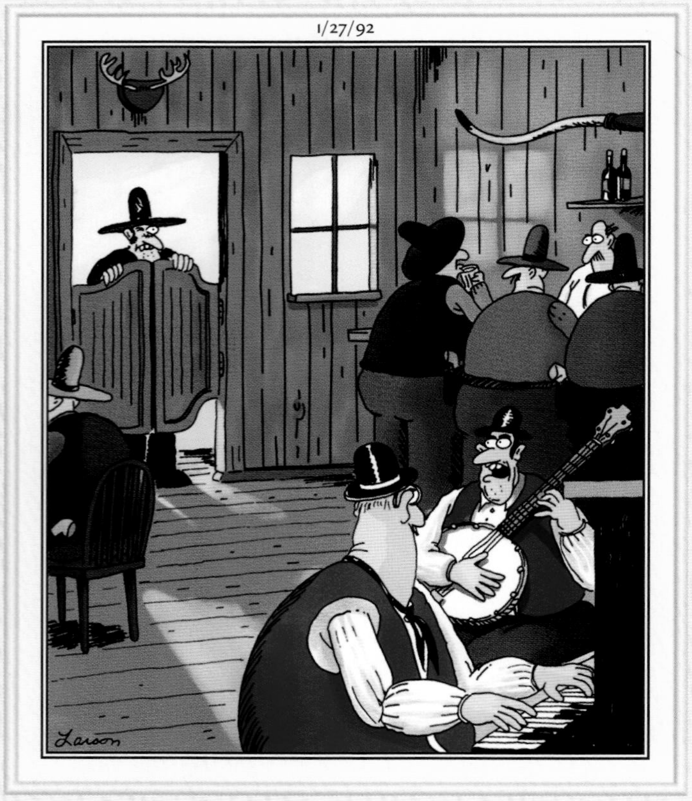
1/27/92
Larson

"Bad guy comin' in, Arnie! ... Minor key!"

1/22/92

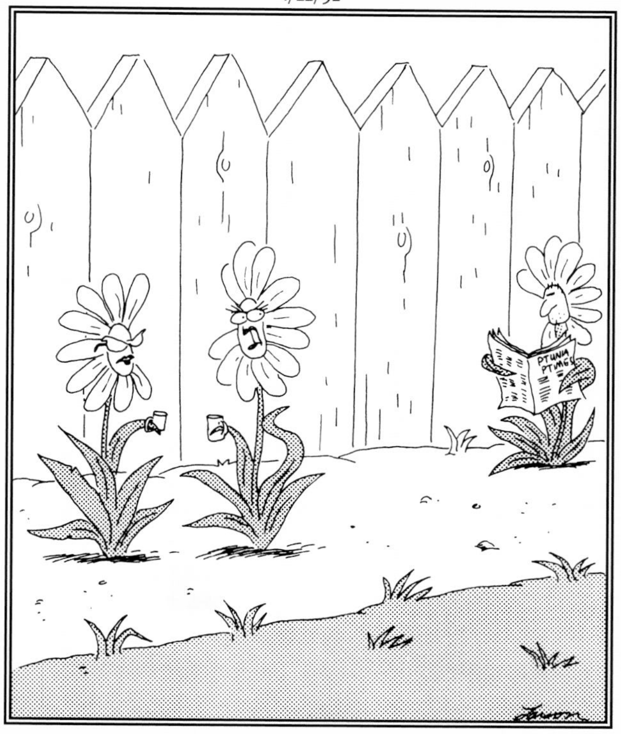

"I don't have any hard evidence, Connie, but my intuition tells me that Ed's been cross-pollinating."

1/23/92

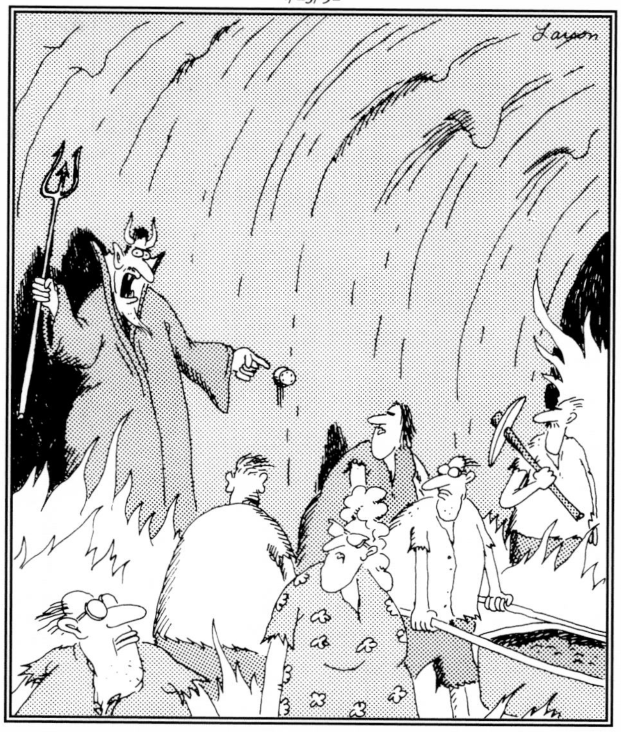

"Hey! Hey! Hey! ... Who's the wise guy that just turned down the thermostat?"

1/29/92

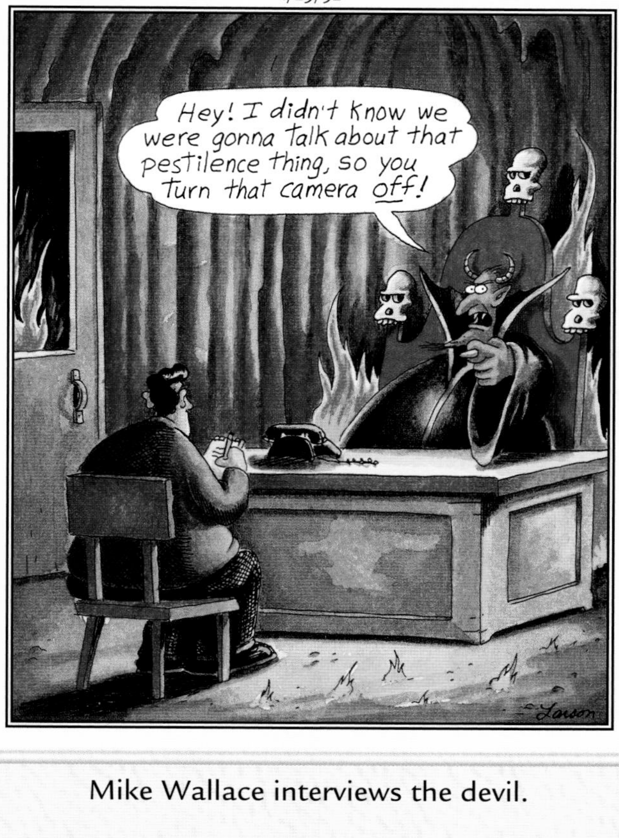
Hey! I didn't know we were gonna talk about that pestilence thing, so you turn that camera off!

Mike Wallace interviews the devil.

1/31/92

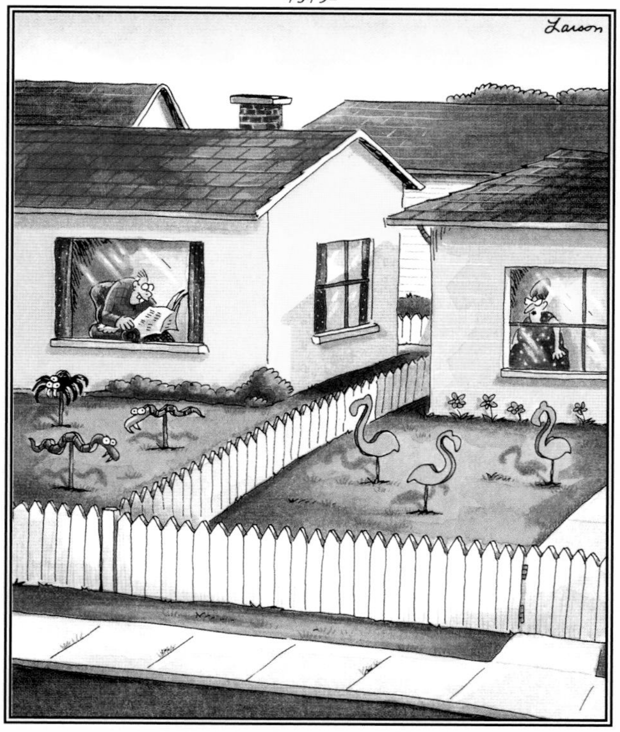

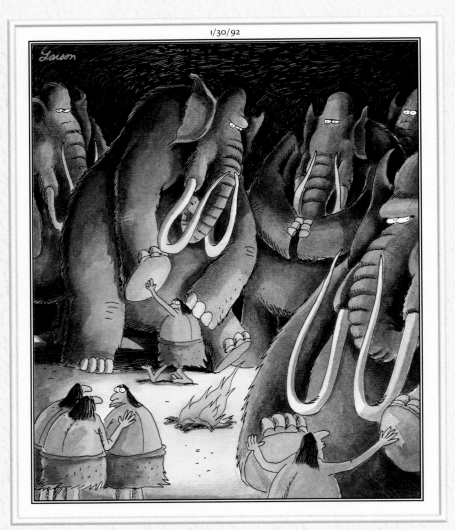

1/30/92

Larson

Tomorrow, they would be mortal enemies. But on the eve of the great hunt, feelings were put aside for the traditional Mammoth Dance.

1/24/92

DEADER 'N A DOORNAIL
ALMOST AS DEAD AS A DOORNAIL
ABOUT HALF AS DEAD AS A DOORNAIL
MUCH, MUCH DEADER 'N A DOORNAIL
Larson

Hospitals to avoid

1/28/92

Now here we come to our simulated kitchen floor test... If Miss Cranshaw doesn't like what she sees, back it goes.
Larson

Inside tours of Acme Fake Vomit, Inc.

2/4/92

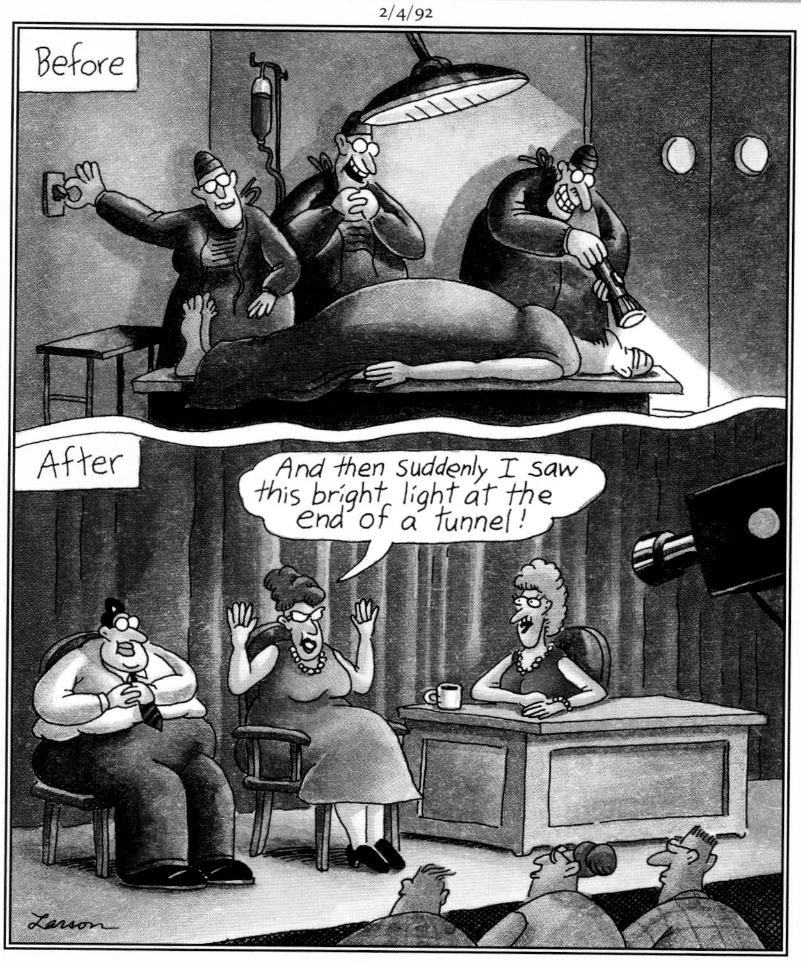
Before
After
And then suddenly I saw this bright light at the end of a tunnel!
Larson

2/3/92

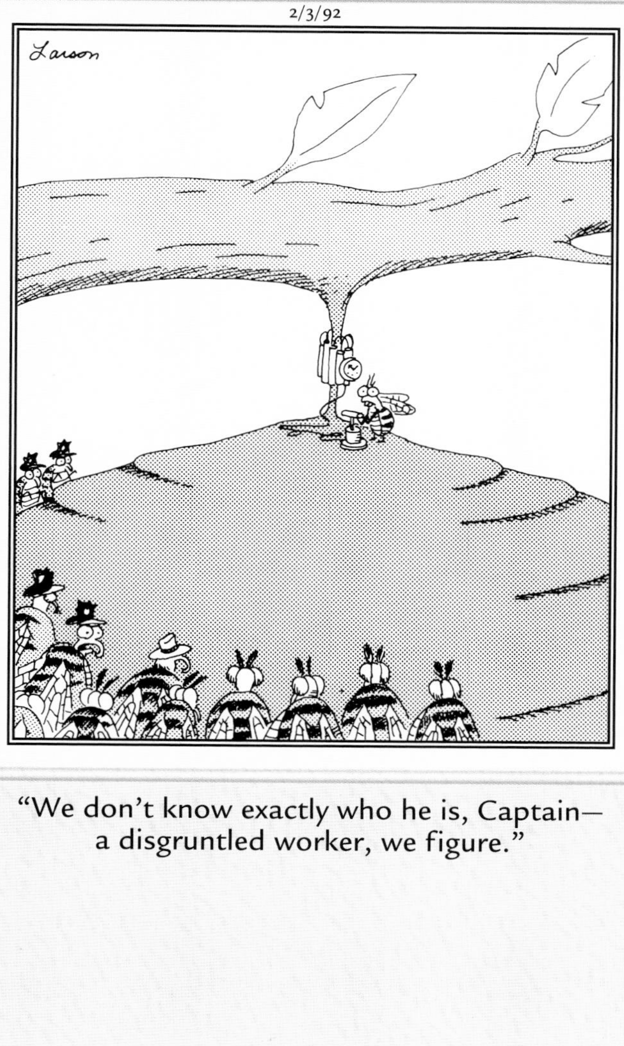
Larson

"We don't know exactly who he is, Captain—
a disgruntled worker, we figure."

2/7/92

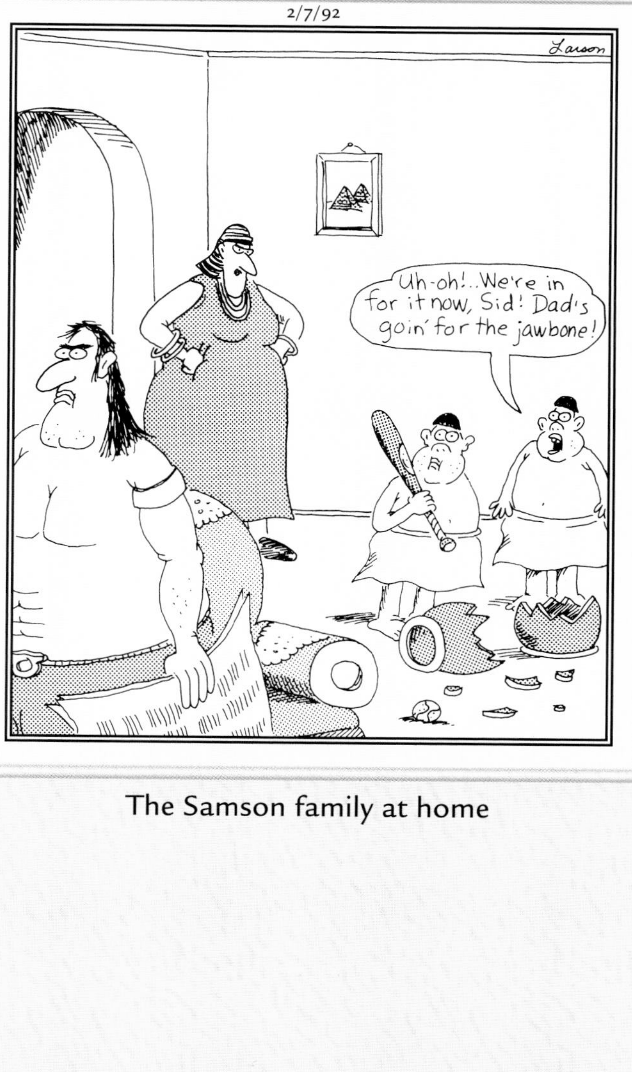
Larson
Uh-oh!..We're in for it now, Sid! Dad's goin' for the jawbone!

The Samson family at home

2/5/92

Larson

“Hey ... this could be the chief.”

2/6/92

Larson

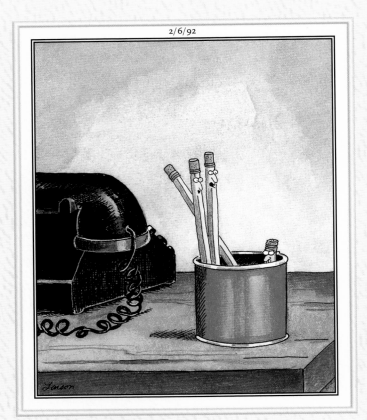

“Man, *there’s* an old-timer with one foot in the wastebasket.”

2/10/92

Larson
224

“Same as the others, O’Neill. The flippers, the fishbowl, the frog, the lights, the armor. ... Just one question remains: Is this the work of our guy, or a copycat?”

2/14/92

Larson

“Those, sire, are the uncommon folk.”

2/11/92

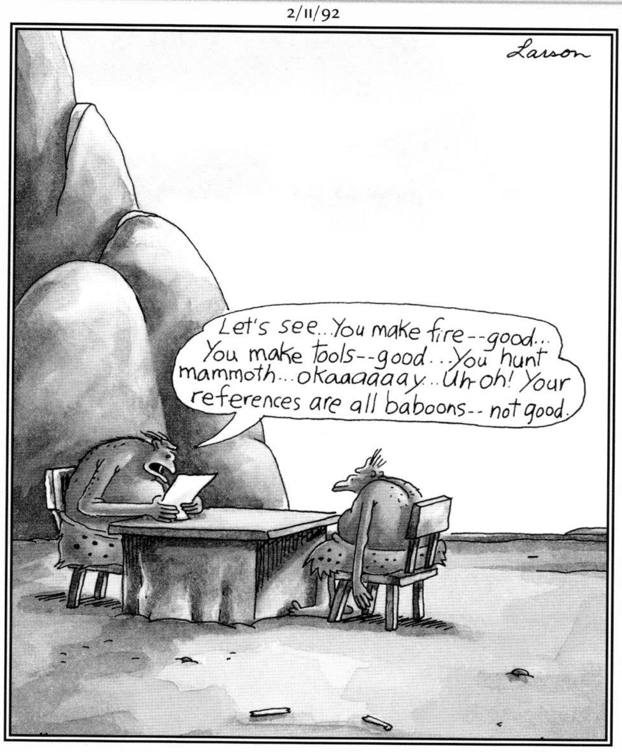
Let's see.. You make fire--good.. You make tools--good.. You hunt mammoth...okaaaaaay..Uh-oh! Your references are all baboons-- not good.

Primitive résumés

2/20/92

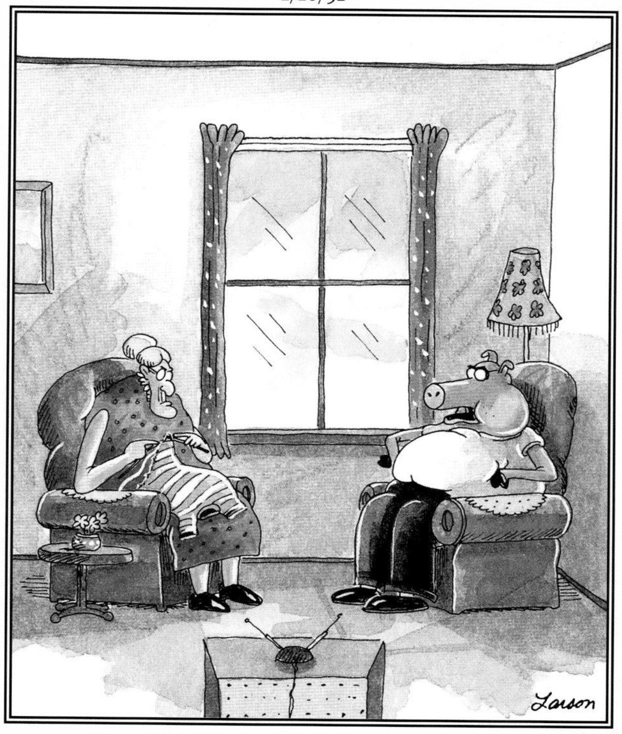

"Hey! So I made the wrong decision! ... But you know, I really wasn't sure I *wanted* to swing on a star, carry moonbeams home in a jar!"

2/18/92

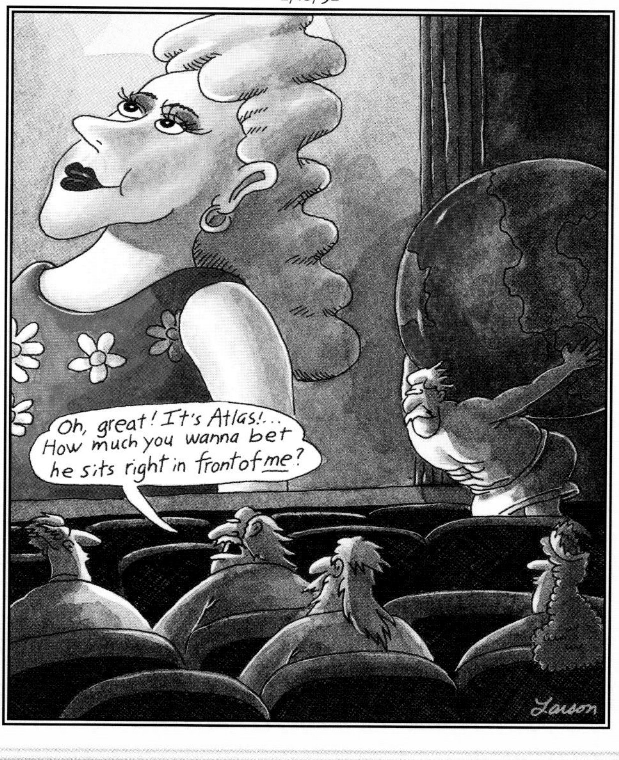
Oh, great! It's Atlas!.. How much you wanna bet he sits right in front of me?

Theater of the gods

2/19/92

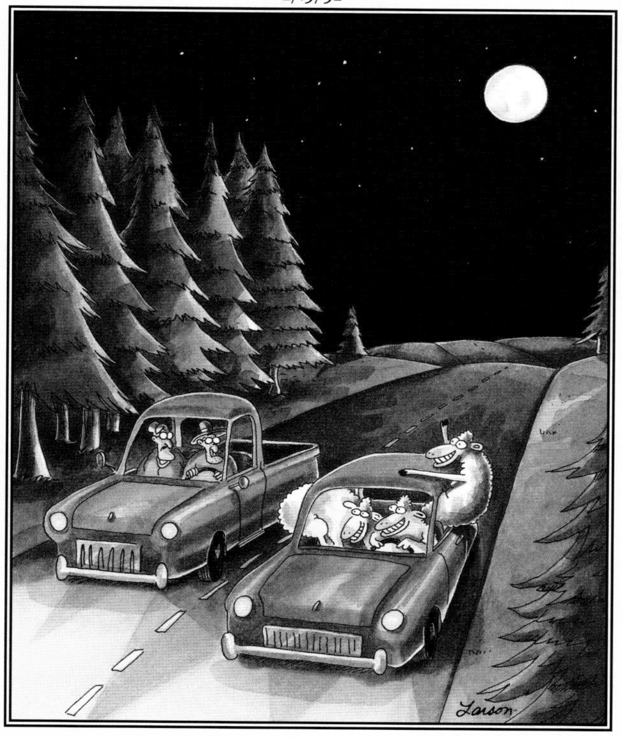

Sheep that pass in the night

2/12/92

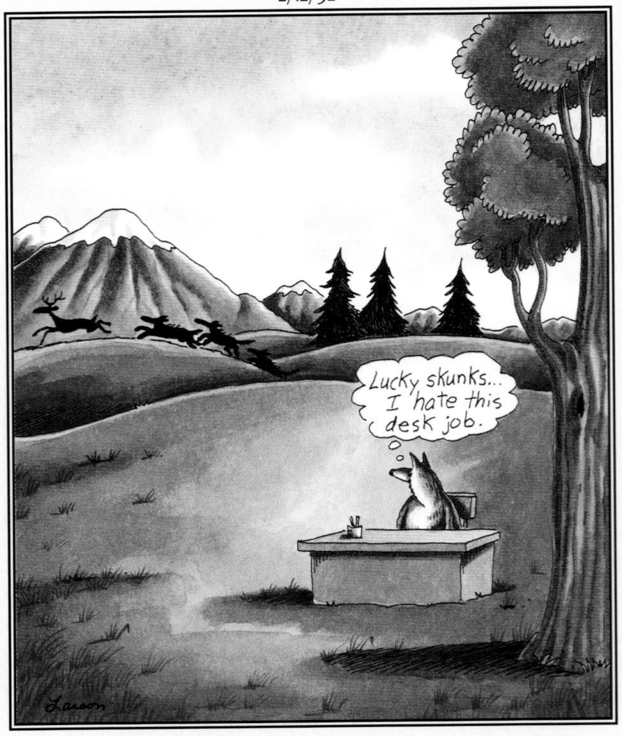
Lucky skunks... I hate this desk job.
Larson

2/13/92

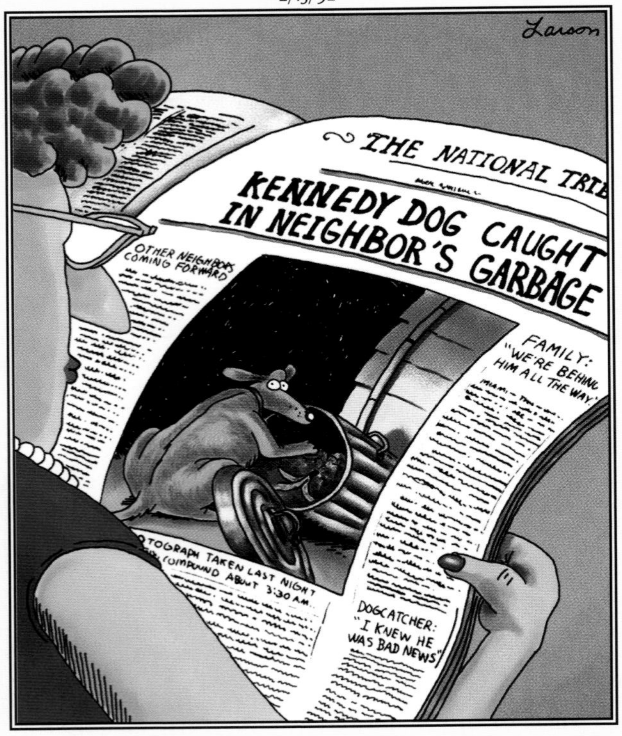
Larson
THE NATIONAL TRIB
KENNEDY DOG CAUGHT IN NEIGHBOR'S GARBAGE
OTHER NEIGHBORS COMING FORWARD
FAMILY: "WE'RE BEHIND HIM ALL THE WAY"
OTOGRAPH TAKEN LAST NIGHT
COMPOUND ABOUT 3:30 A.M.
DOGCATCHER: "I KNEW HE WAS BAD NEWS"

2/17/92

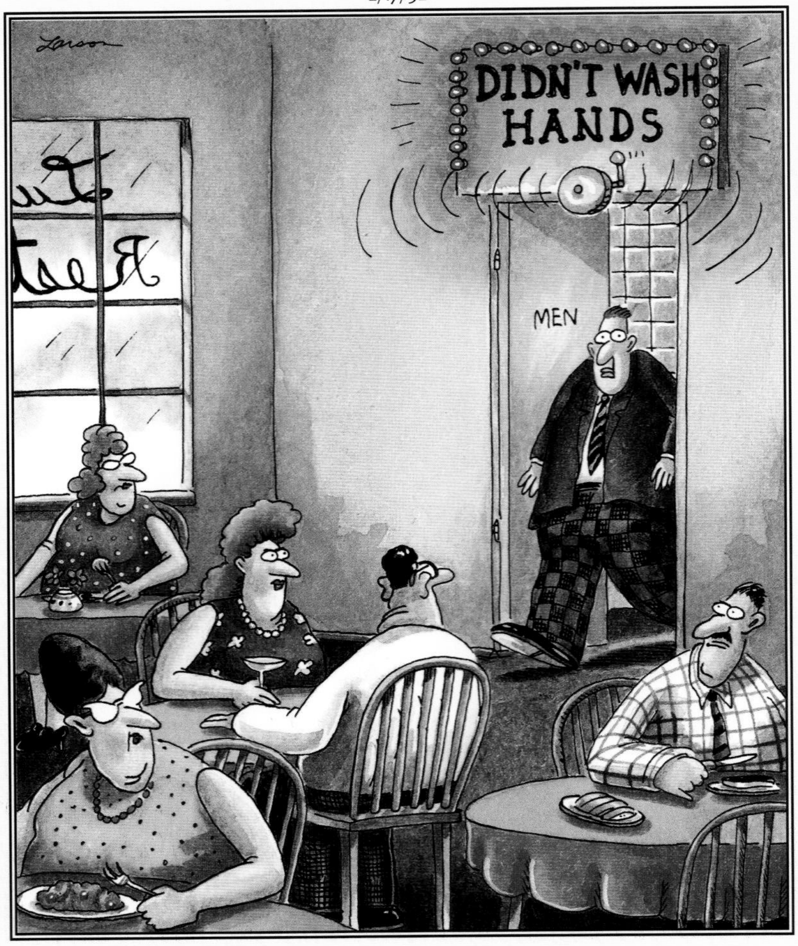
Larson
DIDN'T WASH HANDS
MEN

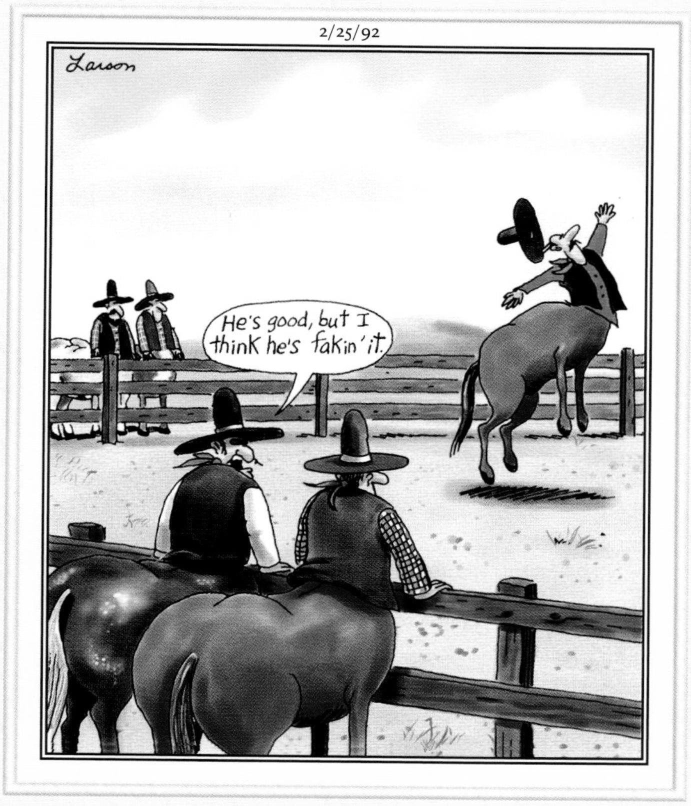
2/25/92
Larson
He's good, but I think he's fakin' it.

Centaur rodeos

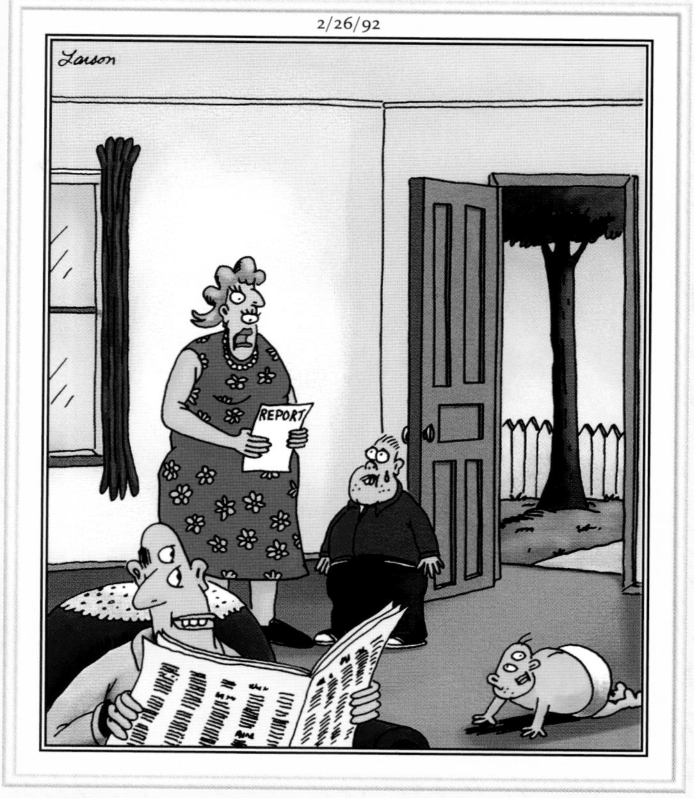
2/26/92
Larson
REPORT

“Good heavens! Pablo got an ‘F’ in art! ... Well, I'm just going to go down to that school myself and meet this teacher face to face!”

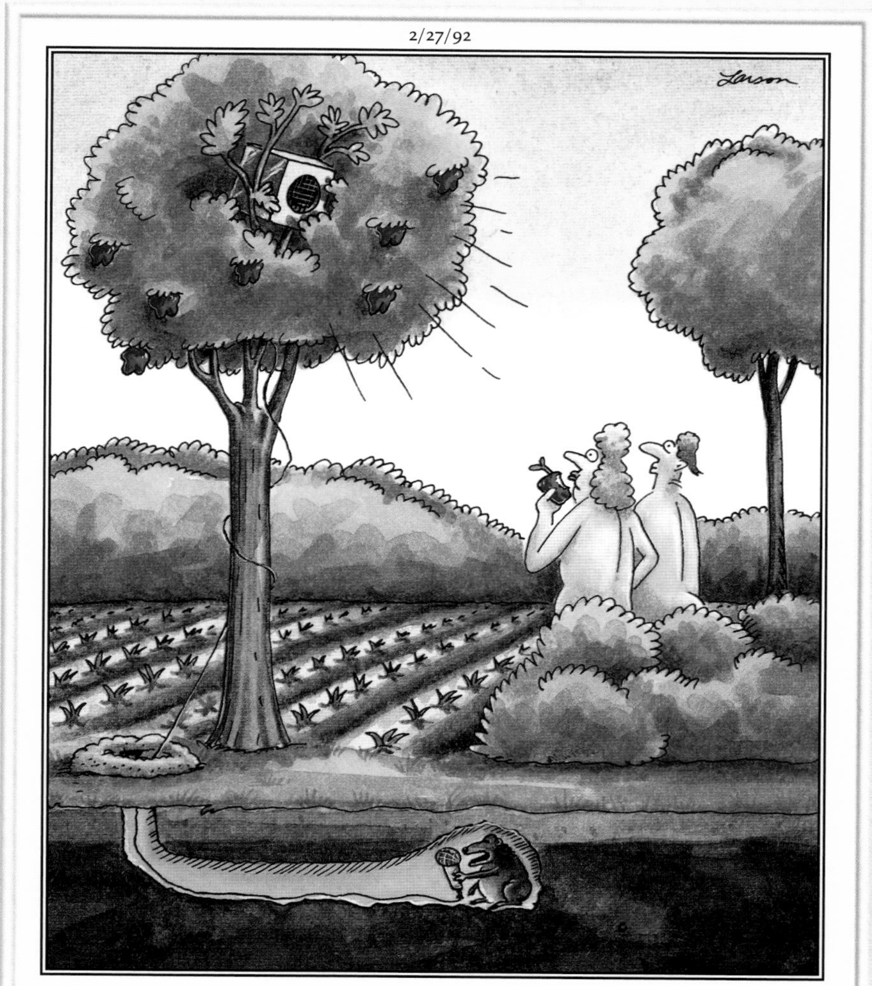
2/27/92
Larson

“Eat my apple, will you? LEAVE MY GARDEN! BEGONE! ... And take all the mole traps with you!”

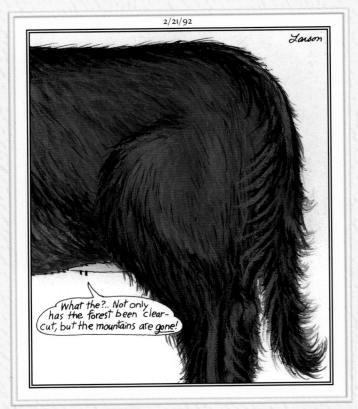

2/21/92

What the?.. Not only has the forest been clear-cut, but the mountains are gone!

Environmental disasters in a flea's world

2/24/92

OPEN
MILK
ACACIA-O
HAVE YOU SEEN ME?

2/28/92

Okay, Johnny--your turn! Ready? Now keep that tail up! Okay, here I come, Johnny!

Scorpion school

3/9/92

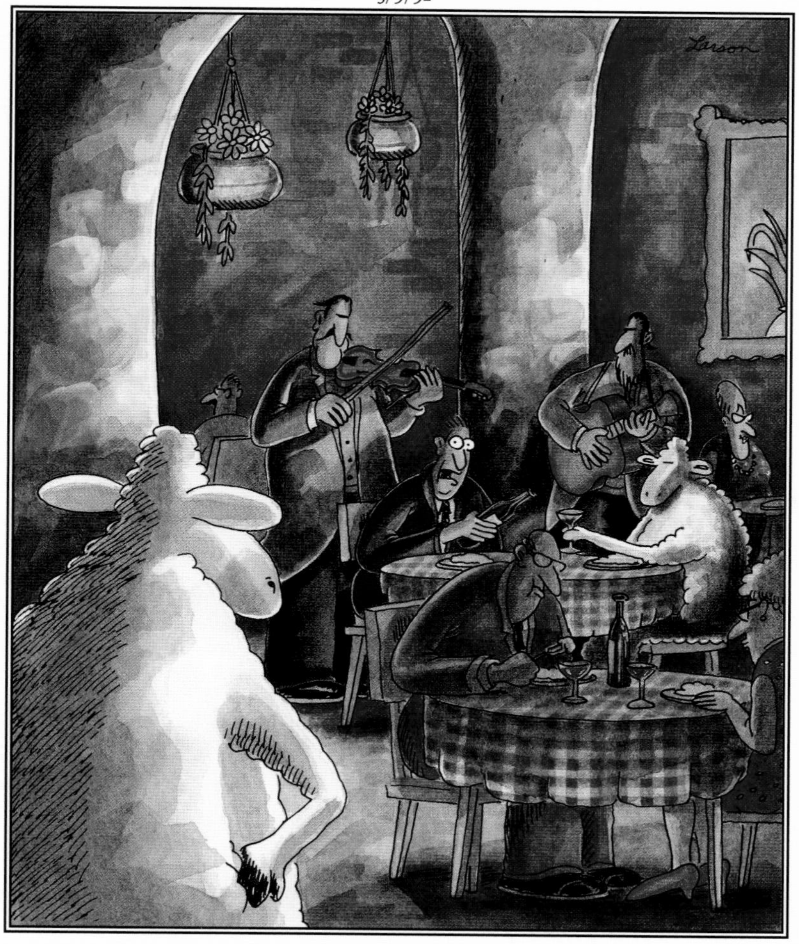
Larson

"Oh my God! It's Yvonne!"

3/2/92

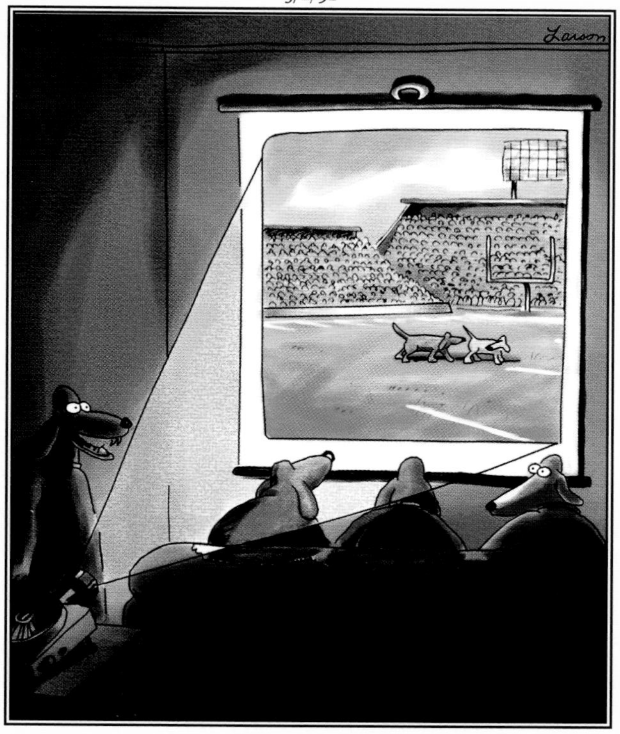
Larson

"Oh, Misty always hates me showing this slide. ...
It's halftime at the '88 Detroit-Chicago
game when we first met."

3/6/92

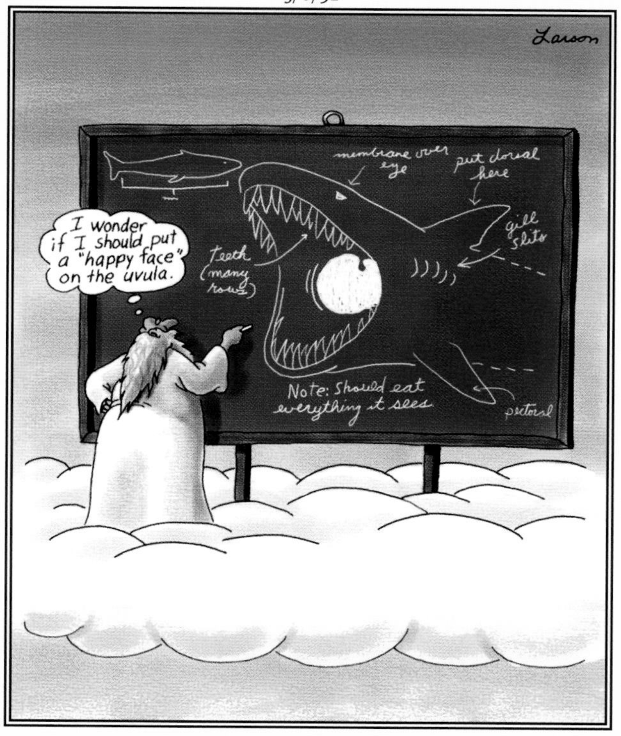
Larson
I wonder if I should put a "happy face" on the uvula.
membrane over eye
put dorsal here
gill slits
Teeth (many rows)
Note: Should eat everything it sees.
pectoral

God designs the great white shark.

3/3/92

"Waiter, is that a *hair* in my salad?"

3/4/92

Yo! Is this the place that ordered the Mother of all Pizzas?
Larry

In Saddam Hussein's war room

3/5/92

YELLOWSTONE PARK

In an ancient custom of retribution, the ranger Mafia sends Ted to "sleep with the bears."

3/11/92

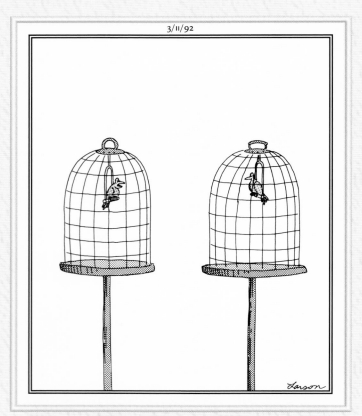

"Oh, yeah? Well, maybe I'll just come over there and rattle *your* cage!"

3/13/92

Larson
O. ceratophthalma
M. kaempferi
U. uca
F. MacDougal
M. longicarpus

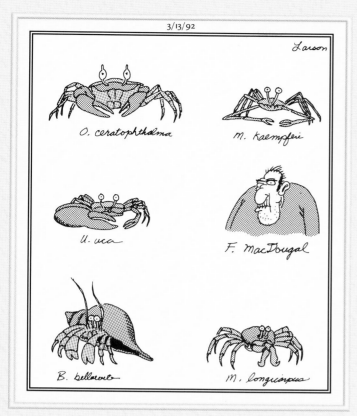

Some of our common crabs

3/23/92

Larson
GRANDPA JONES and 500 Strings
SINATRA & PRINCE ☆ The Duets ☆
METALLICA AND THE ANDEAN PAN PIPE PLAYERS
THE CHIPMUNKS NEW AGE ALBUM
PUBLIC ENEMY NO. 1 Does Cole Porter
NEW KIDS ON THE BLOCK (By themselves)

Albums to avoid

3/24/92

Larson

Crossing the village, Mowaka is overpowered by army ants. (Later, bystanders were all quoted as saying they were horrified, but "didn't want to get involved.")

3/27/92

Larson

When Seeing Eye dogs dream

3/10/92

J.W. STEVENS
Mr. Stevens...There's another salesperson out here... Should I push him out the door?

Sumo temporaries

3/12/92

I should make Dodge by sunup...unless I hit a cactus.

Lacking a horse, Jed was compelled to just drift along with the tumbling tumbleweed.

3/16/92

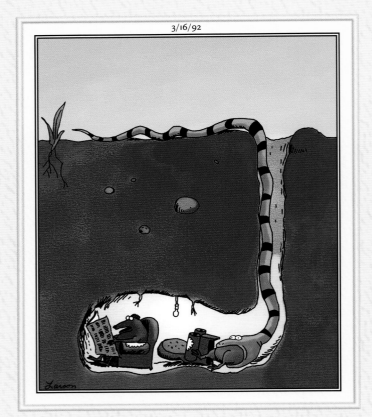

"Well, I'll be darned. ... Says here 70 percent of all accidents happen in the hole."

3/17/92

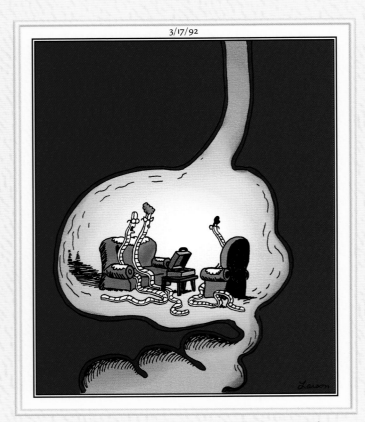

"Well, I'm not sure we can afford stomach insurance—right now we're trying to put the kids through the small intestine."

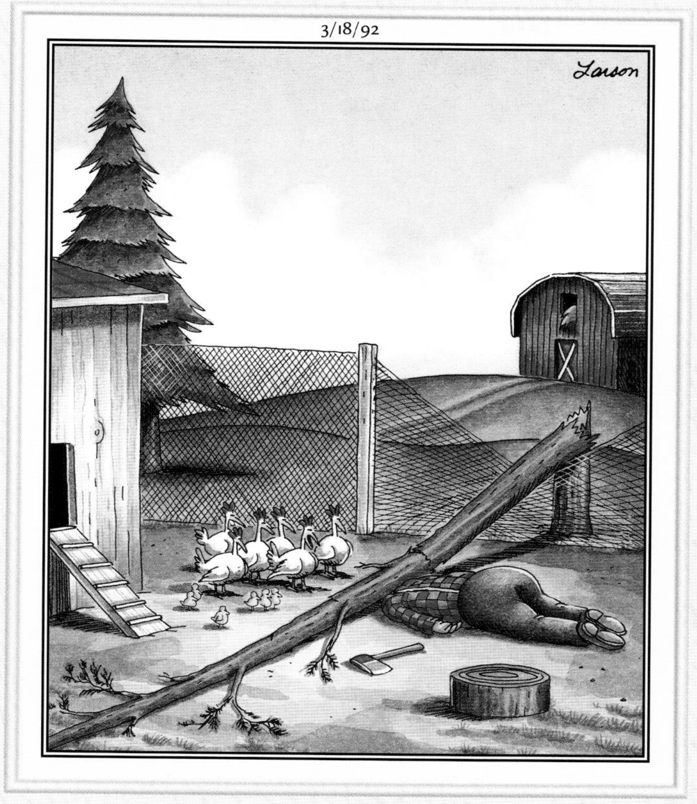
3/18/92
Larson

"Lord, we thank thee."

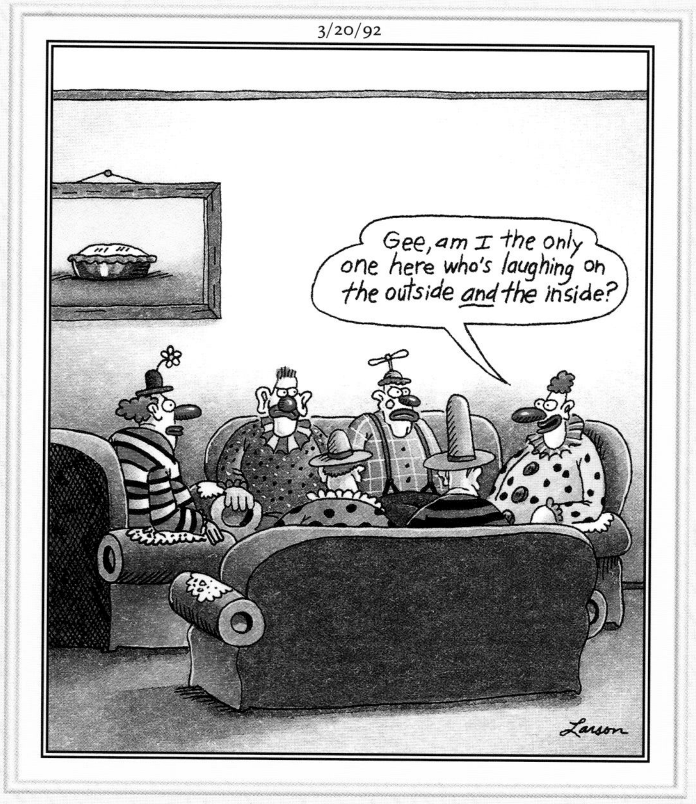
3/20/92
Gee, am I the only one here who's laughing on the outside and the inside?
Larson

Clown therapy sessions

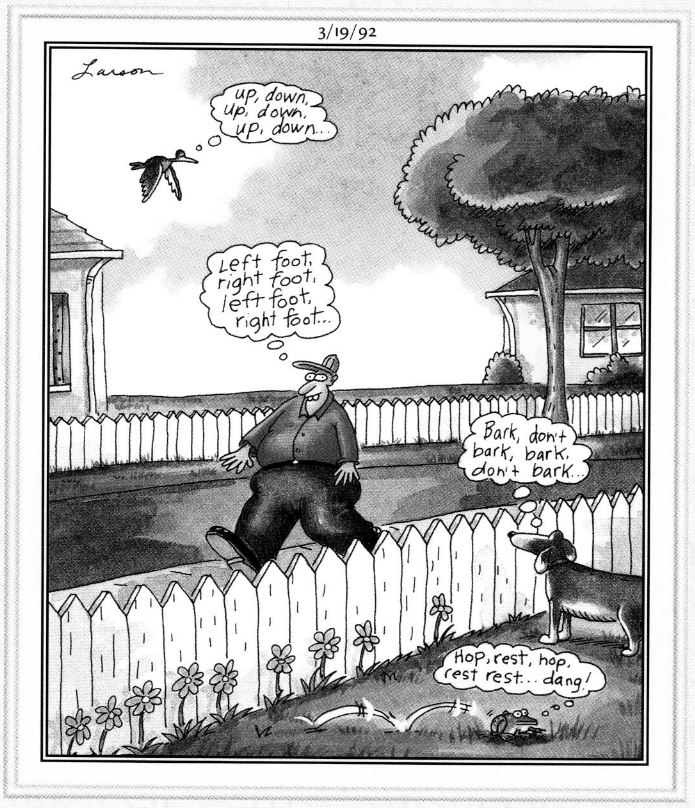
3/19/92
Larson
up, down, up, down, up, down...
Left foot, right foot, left foot, right foot...
Bark, don't bark, bark, don't bark...
Hop, rest, hop, rest rest... dang!

Basic lives

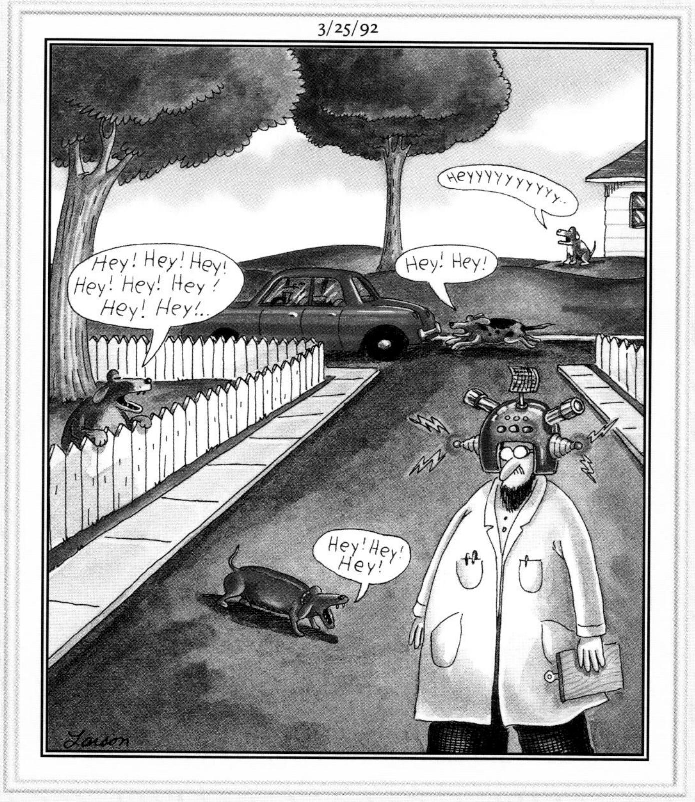
3/25/92
Heyyyyyyyyyy.
Hey! Hey! Hey! Hey! Hey! Hey! Hey! Hey!..
Hey! Hey!
Hey! Hey! Hey!
Larson

Donning his new canine decoder, Professor Schwartzman becomes the first human being on Earth to hear what barking dogs are actually saying.

3/31/92

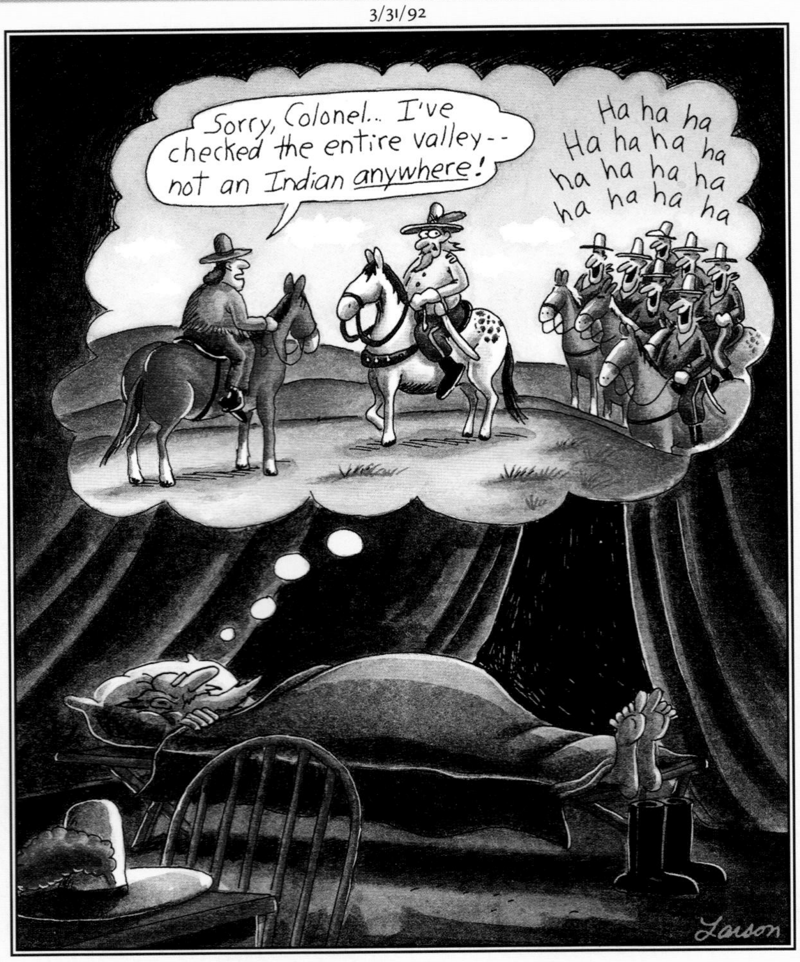
Sorry, Colonel.. I've checked the entire valley-- not an Indian anywhere!
Ha ha ha Ha ha ha ha ha ha ha ha ha ha ha ha ha ha
Larson

Custer's recurrent nightmare

3/26/92

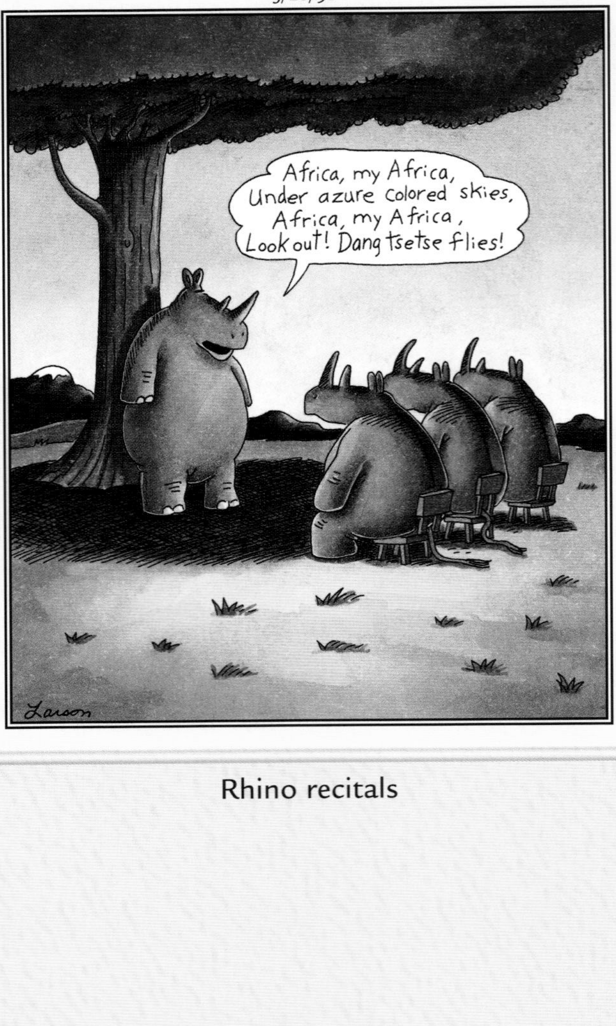
Africa, my Africa, Under azure colored skies, Africa, my Africa, Look out! Dang tsetse flies!
Larson

Rhino recitals

3/30/92

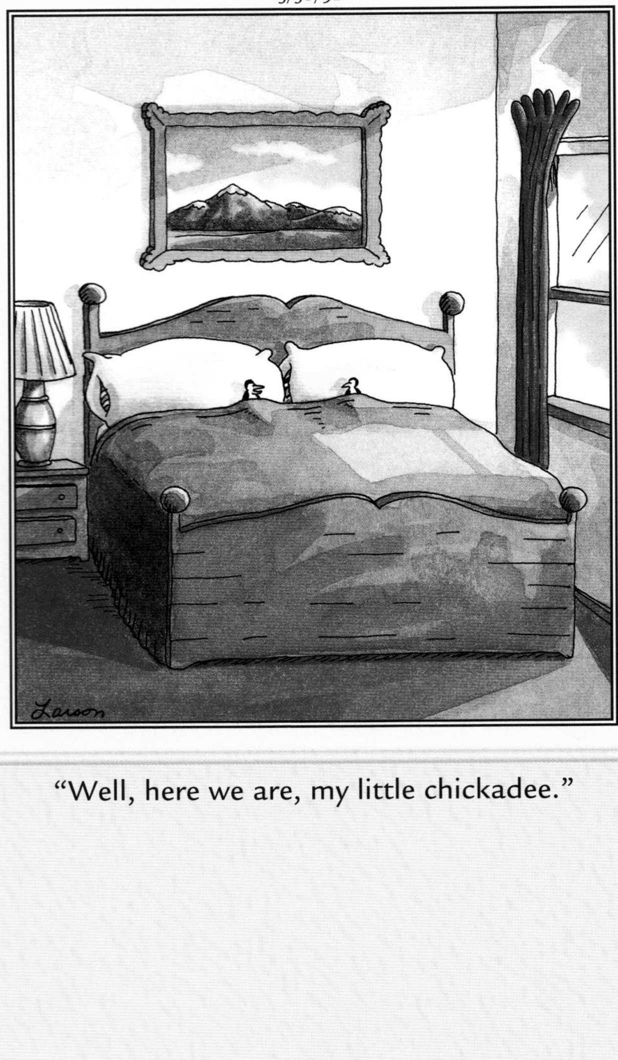
Larson

"Well, here we are, my little chickadee."

4/1/92

Larson
POOF!

While vacationing in Africa, Pinocchio had his longtime wish to be a real boy suddenly and unexpectedly granted.

4/9/92

Well, here we go again.
Larson

Medieval chicken coops

4/2/92

Larson
E
DAGZI
MTOFC
RUBKQW
OPHTHALMOLOGY

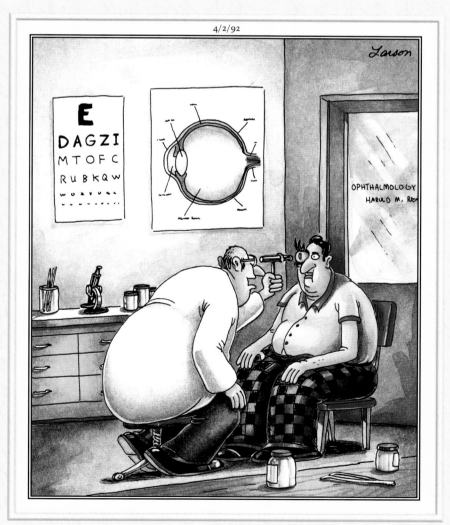

"Oh, this is wonderful, Mr. Gruenfeld—I've only seen it a couple of times. You have corneal corruption. ... Evil eye, Mr. Gruenfeld, evil eye."

4/3/92

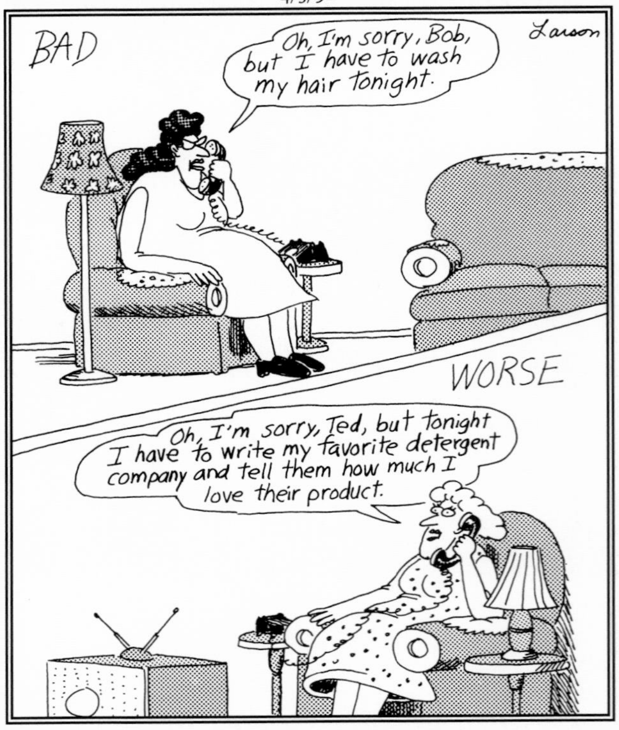
BAD
Oh, I'm sorry, Bob, but I have to wash my hair tonight.
WORSE
Oh, I'm sorry, Ted, but tonight I have to write my favorite detergent company and tell them how much I love their product.
Larson

Date rejection lines

4/6/92

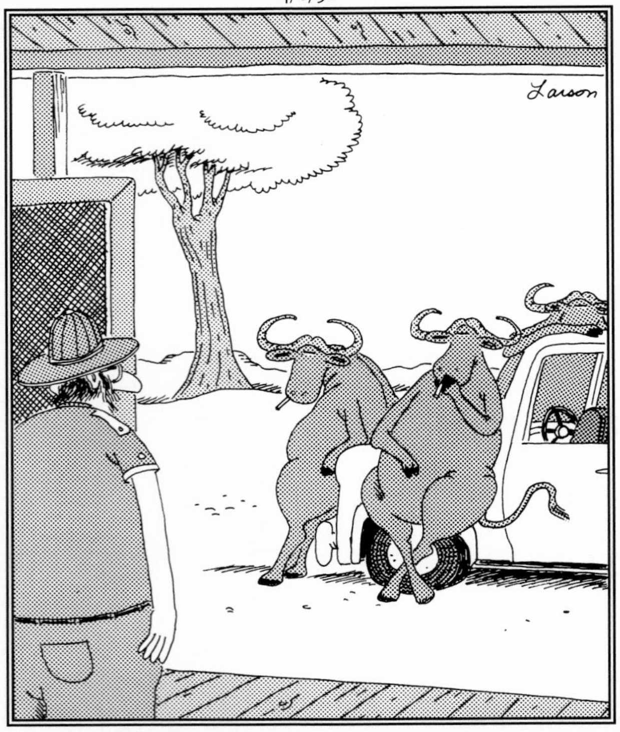
Larson

As Nyles left the safari club, his stomach suddenly knotted up. Foolishly, he had ignored the warnings not to park his Land Rover in this part of Tanzania.

4/7/92

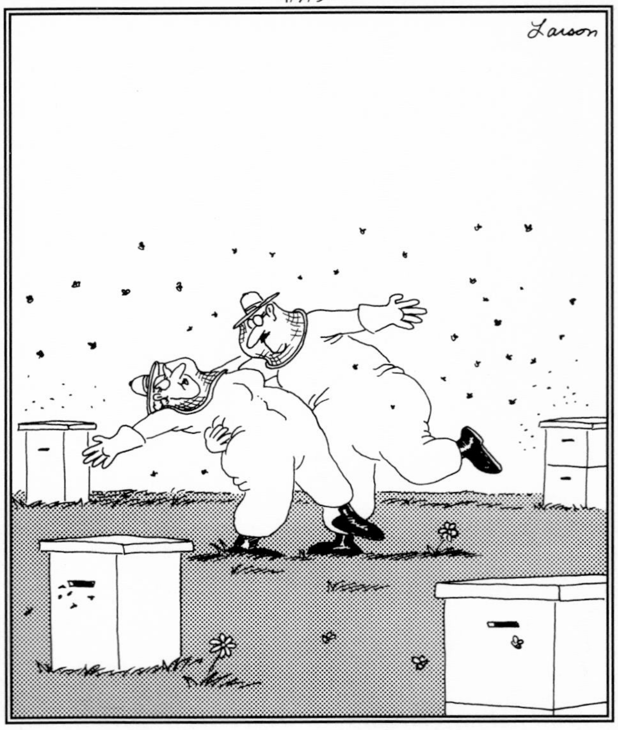
Larson

Dance of the beekeepers

4/8/92

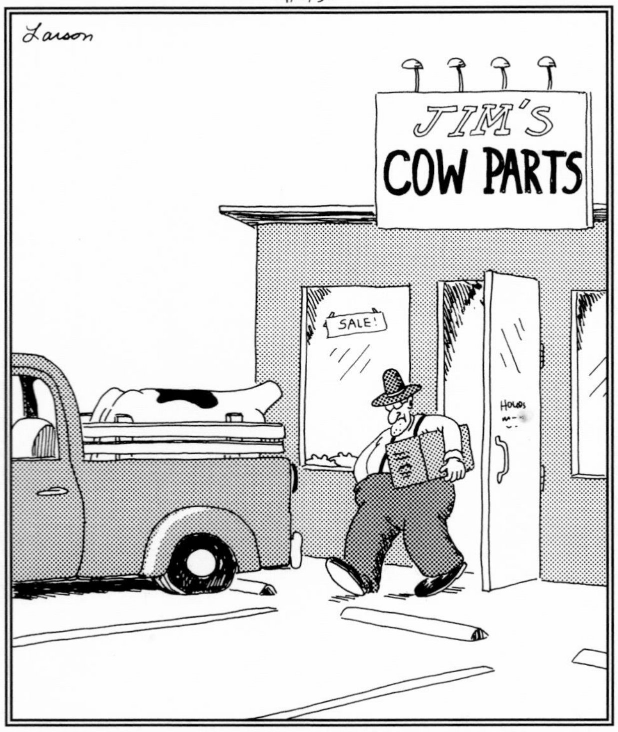
Larson
JIM'S
COW PARTS
SALE!

4/14/92

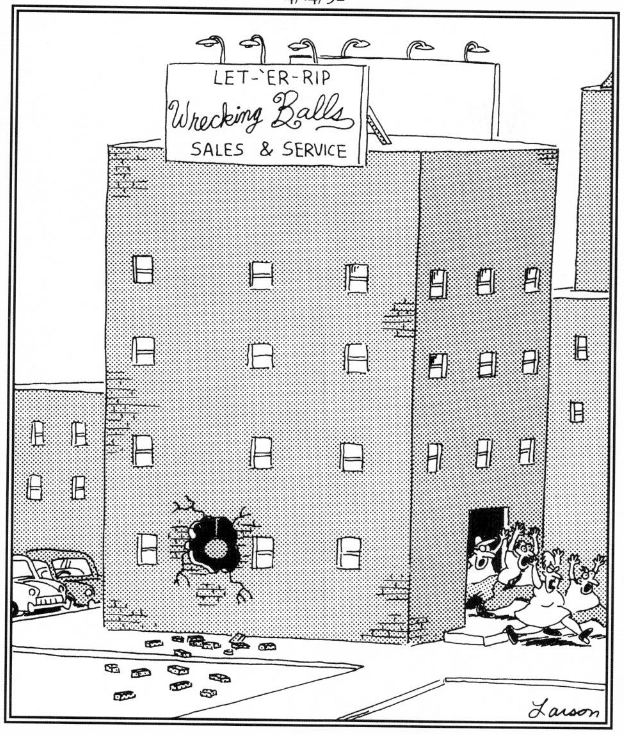
LET-'ER-RIP
Wrecking Balls
SALES & SERVICE

Up until that moment, Raymond had been a rather shy employee with a nervous twitch. Up until that moment.

4/10/92

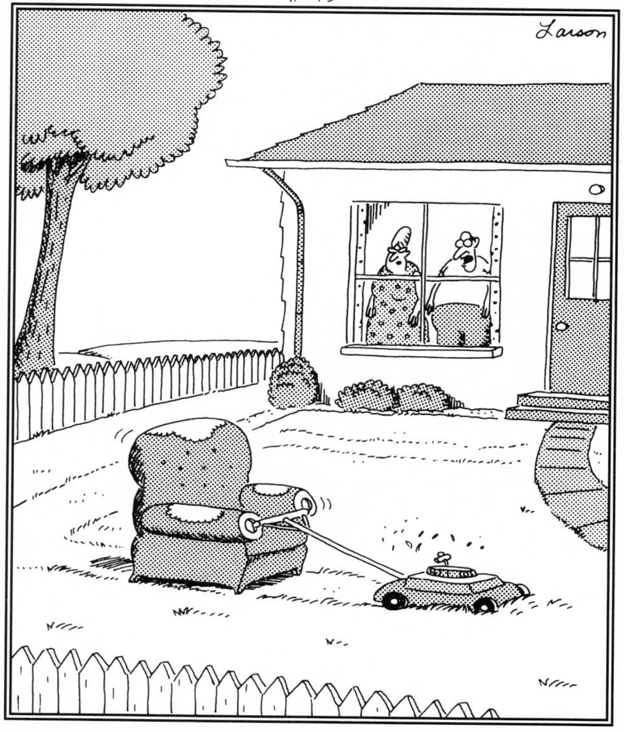

"Holy cow! What's gotten into our La-Z-Boy?"

4/28/92

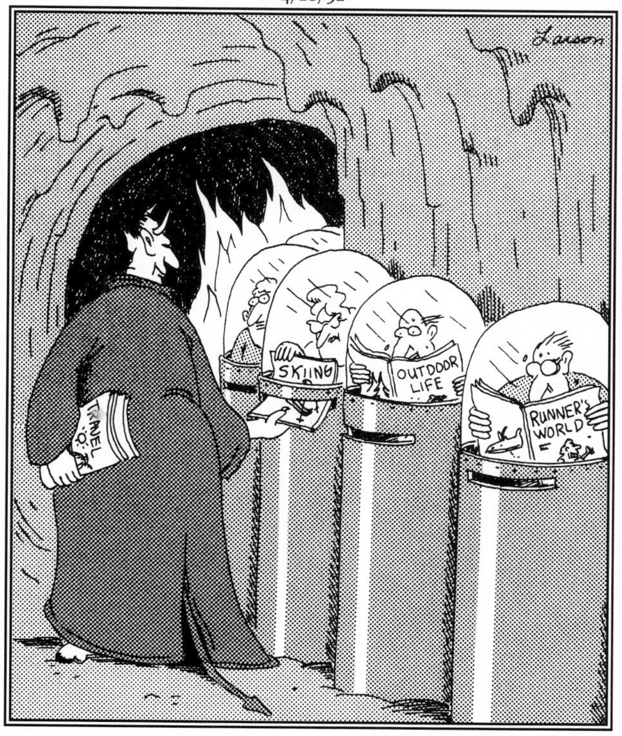
SKIING
OUTDOOR LIFE
RUNNER'S WORLD

Concepts of hell

4/30/92

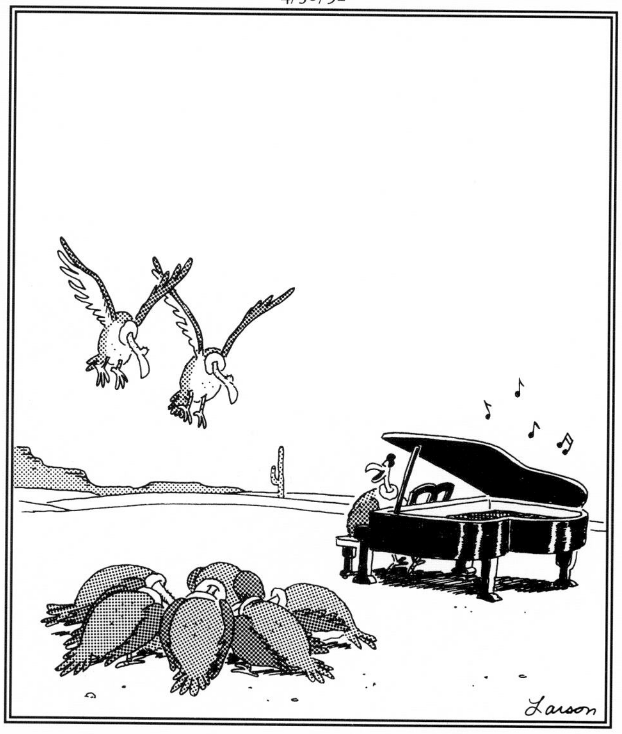

"Hey! It's Frank and Cindy! ... Haven't seen you folks for a while!"

4/13/92

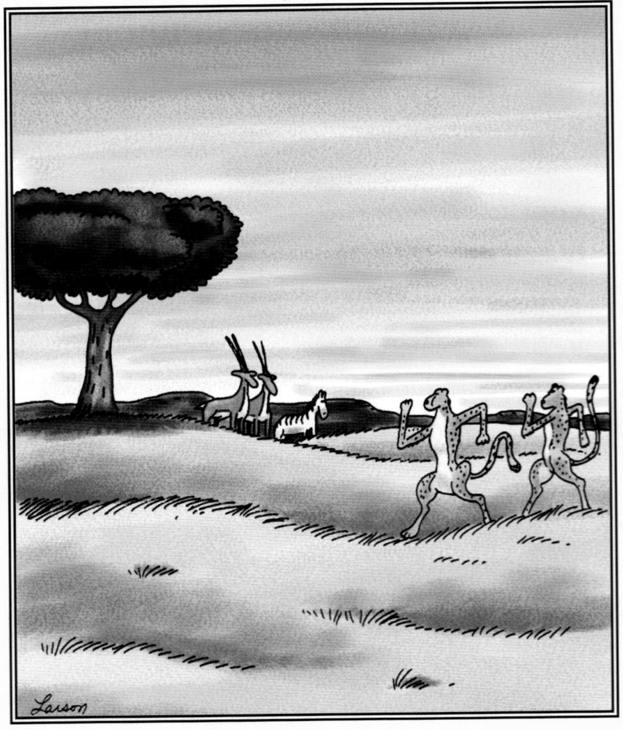

Alert, but far from panicked, the herbivores studied the sudden arrival of two cheetah speedwalkers.

4/15/92

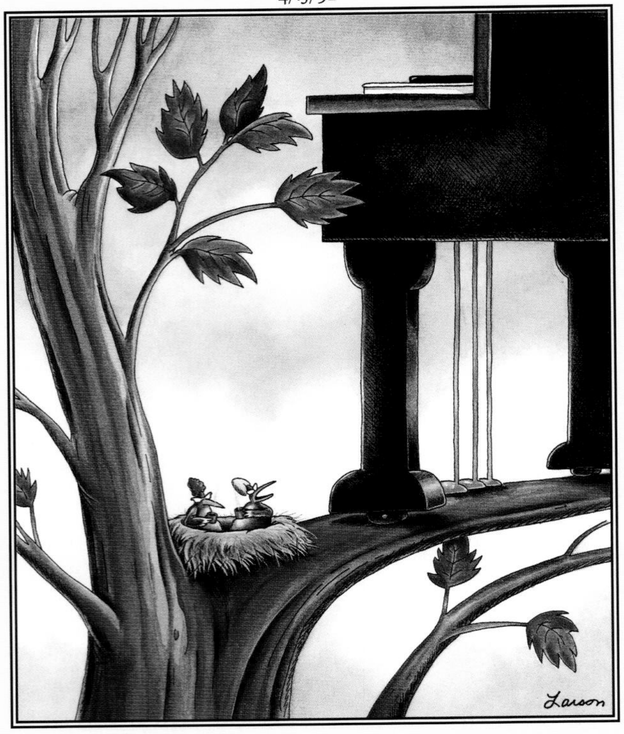

"Oh, my word, Helen! You play, *too?* ... And here I always thought you were just a songbird."

4/16/92

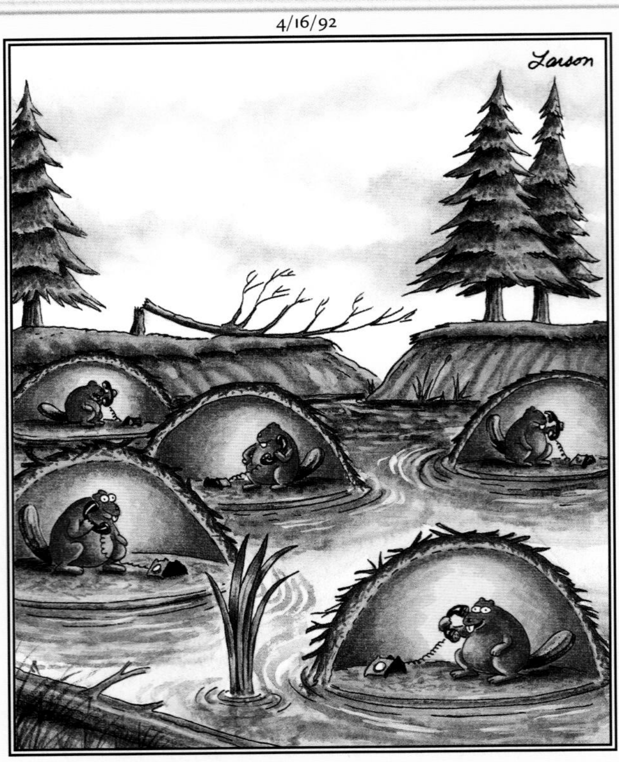

In the rodent family, the beaver is the king of the busy signal.

4/17/92

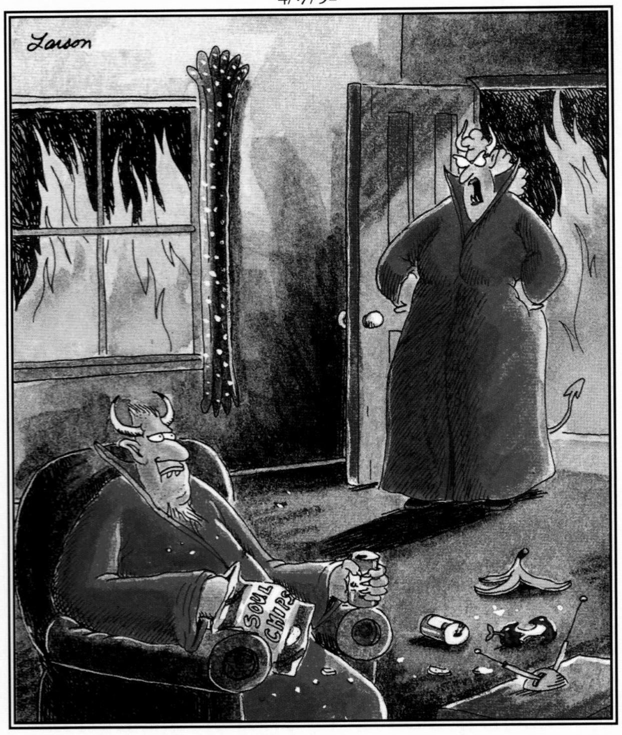
SOUL CHIPS

"For crying out loud! Look at this place! ... Well, this is one little satanic ritual that's coming to an end!"

4/20/92

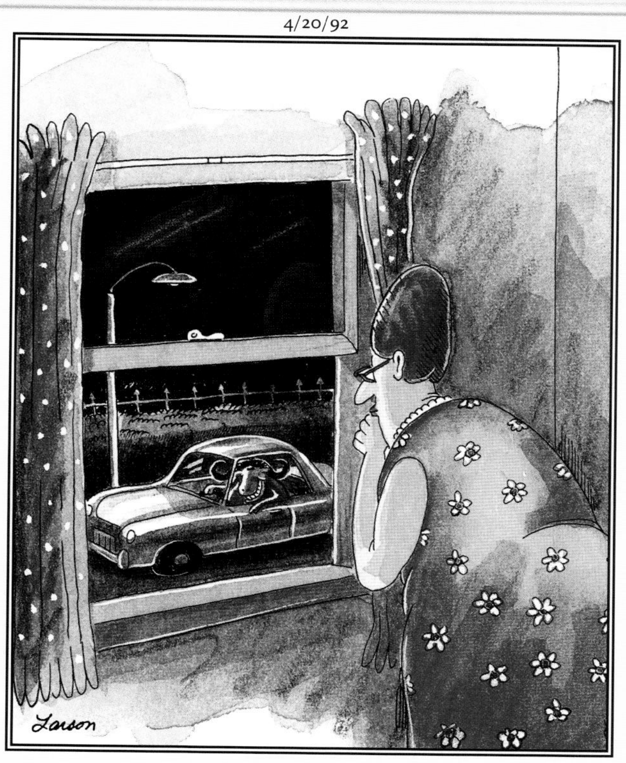
Larson

Scene from *Cape Buffalo Fear*

4/21/92

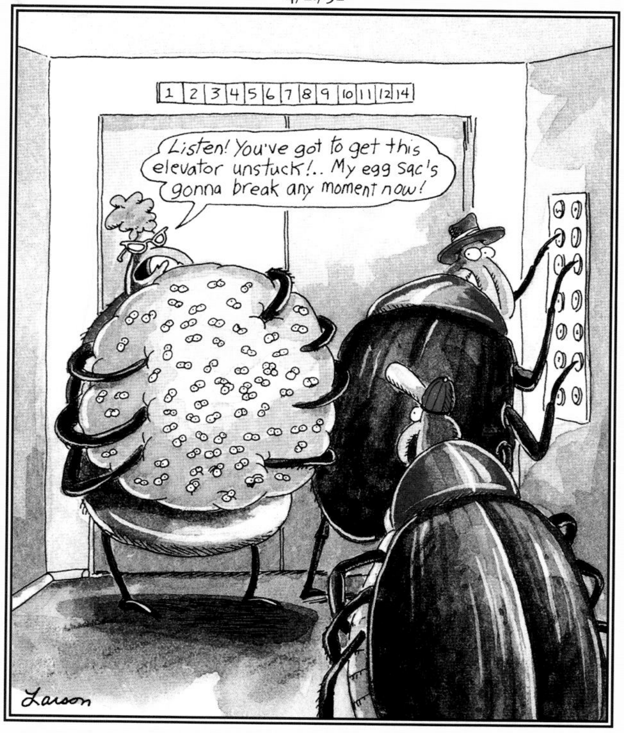
1 2 3 4 5 6 7 8 9 10 11 12 14
Listen! You've got to get this elevator unstuck!.. My egg sac's gonna break any moment now!
Larson

High drama at the Arthropod Trade Center

4/22/92

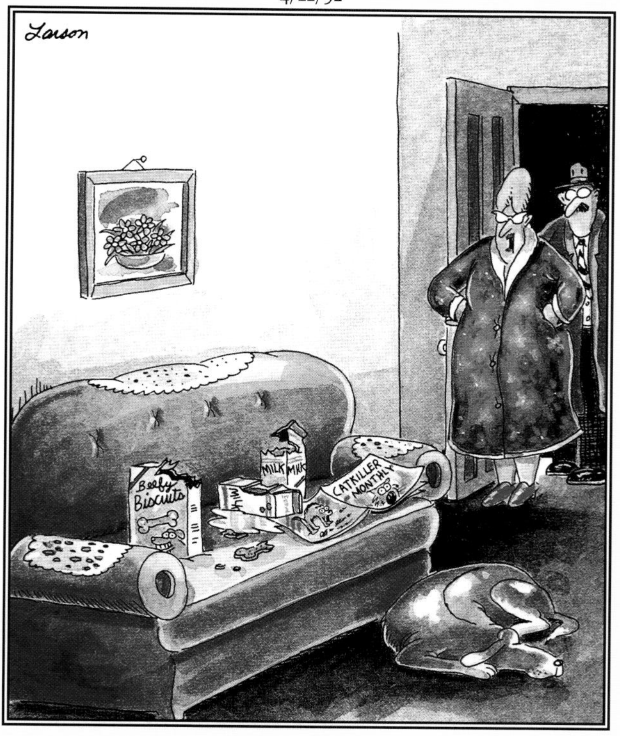
Larson
Beefy Biscuits
MILK
CATKILLER MONTHLY

"Dang! That dog's been up on the sofa again, Hank—I just know it!"

4/23/92

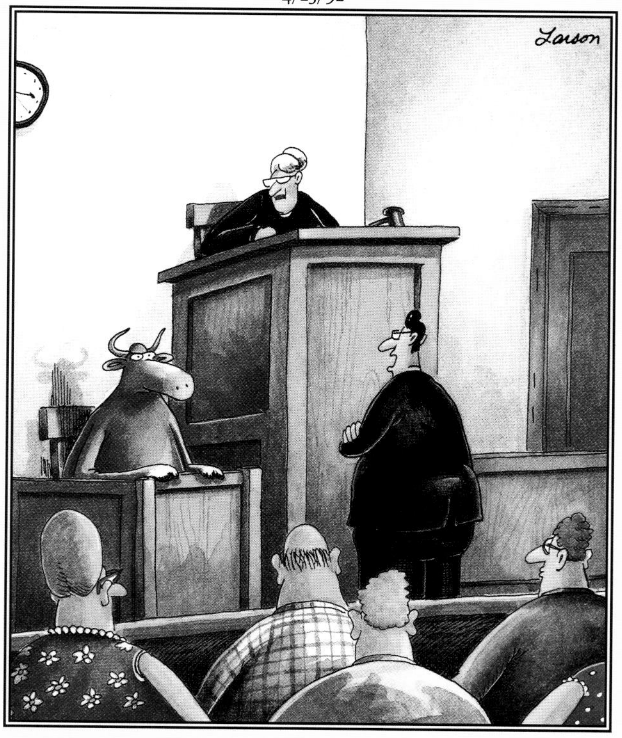
Larson

"Look. We know *how* you did it—*how* is no longer the question. What we now want to know is *why*. ... Why now, brown cow?"

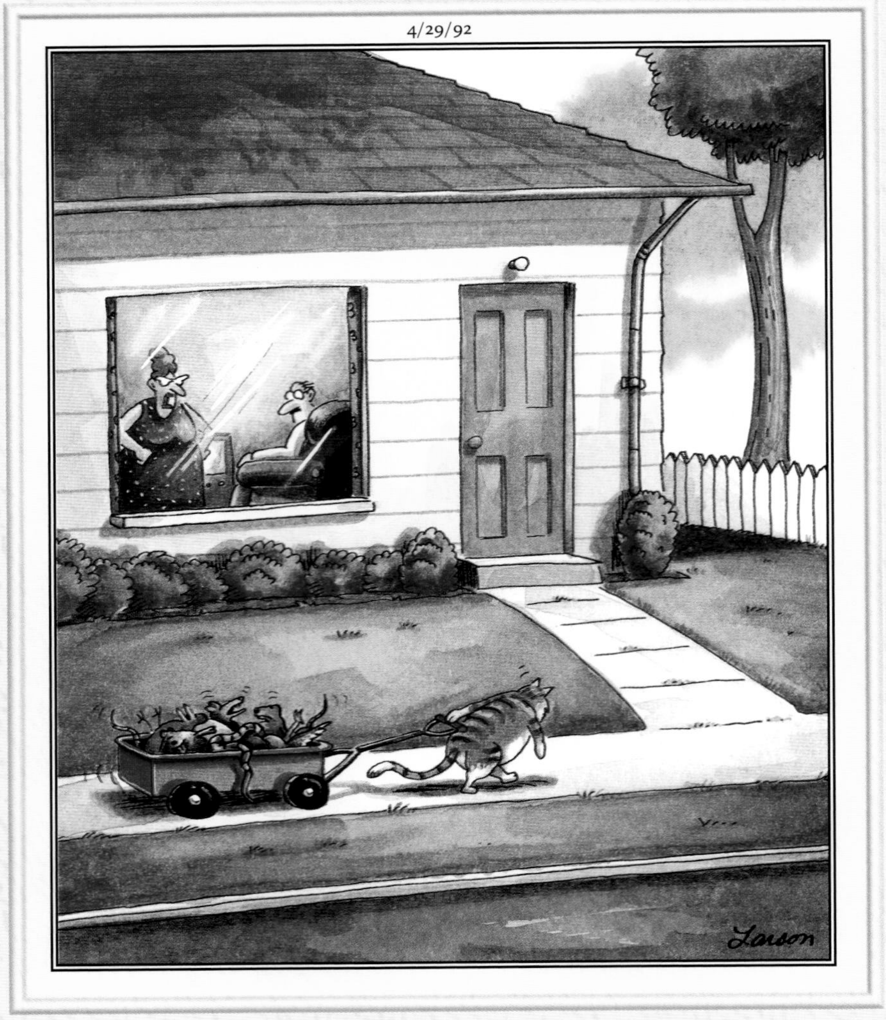
4/29/92
Larson

"Keep the door shut, Ernie! I just *know* that dang cat is going to try dragging that thing into the house."

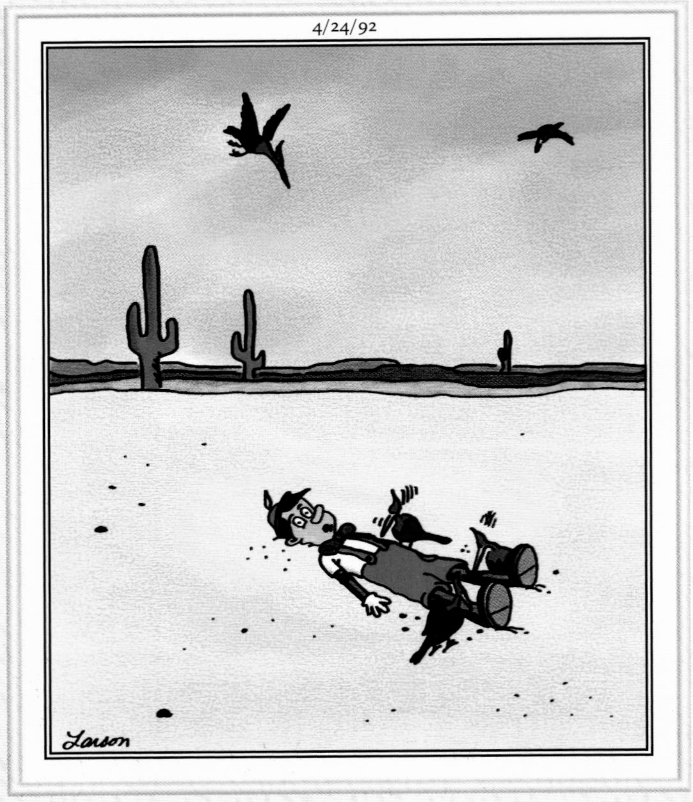
4/24/92
Larson

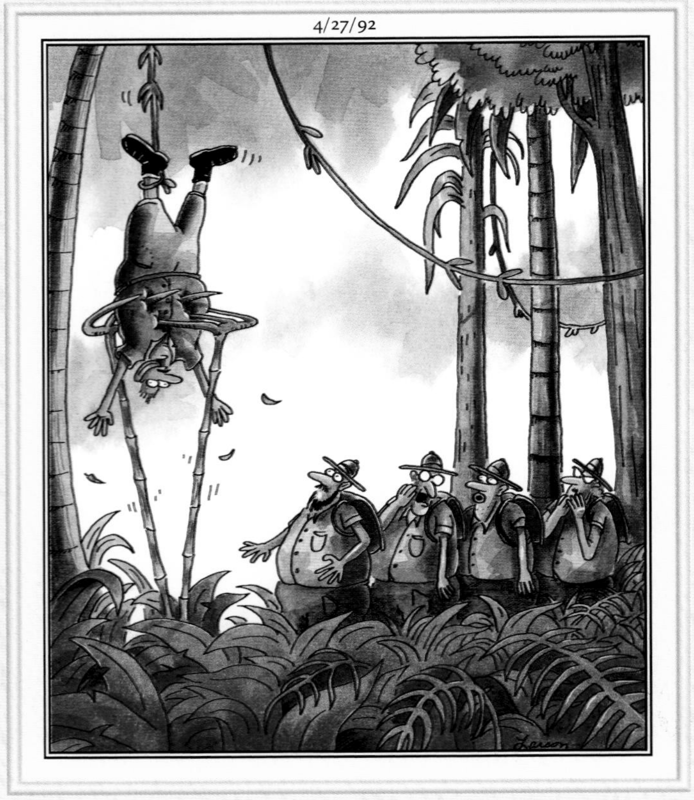
4/27/92

"That's why I never walk in front."

5/4/92

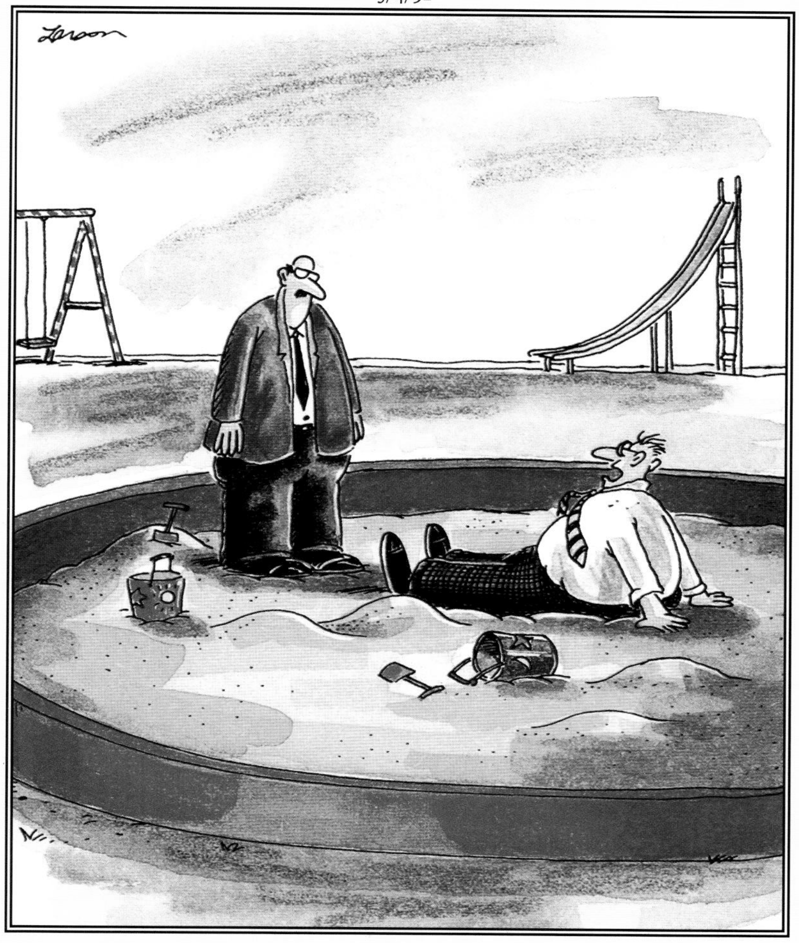

"Okay, McFadden. ... So *that's* the way you wanna play."

5/6/92

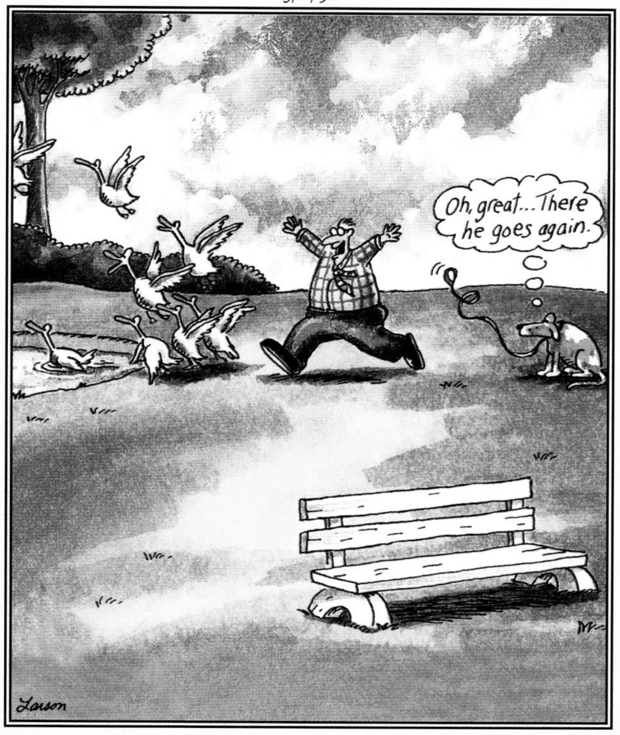
Oh, great... There he goes again.

5/7/92

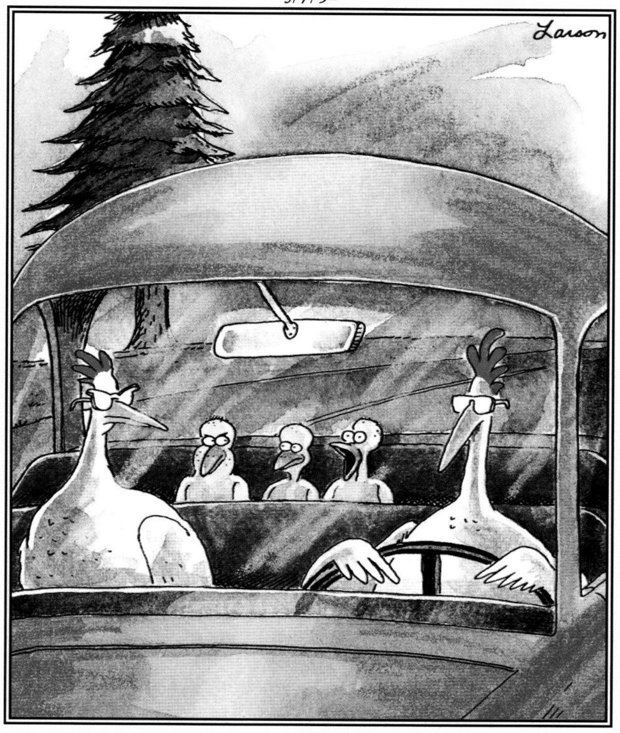

"Mom! We were all singing 'She'll Be Comin' 'Round the Mountain,' but Randy won't stop with the 'whack, whack' part!"

5/1/92

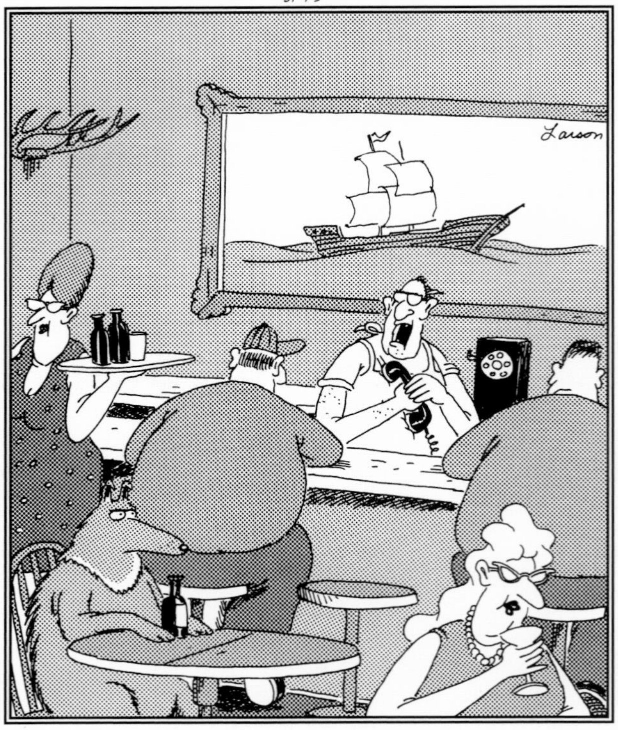

"LASSIE! ... COME HOME! ...
LASSIE COME HOME!"

5/5/92

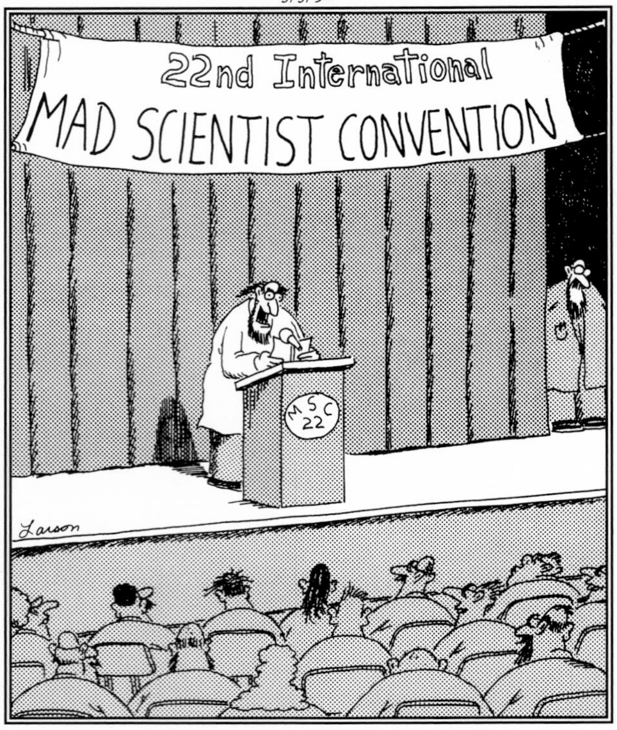
22nd International
MAD SCIENTIST CONVENTION
M.S.C.
22

"So please welcome our keynote speaker, Professor Melvin Fenwick—the man who, back in 1952, first coined the now common phrase: 'Fools! I'll destroy them all!'"

5/8/92

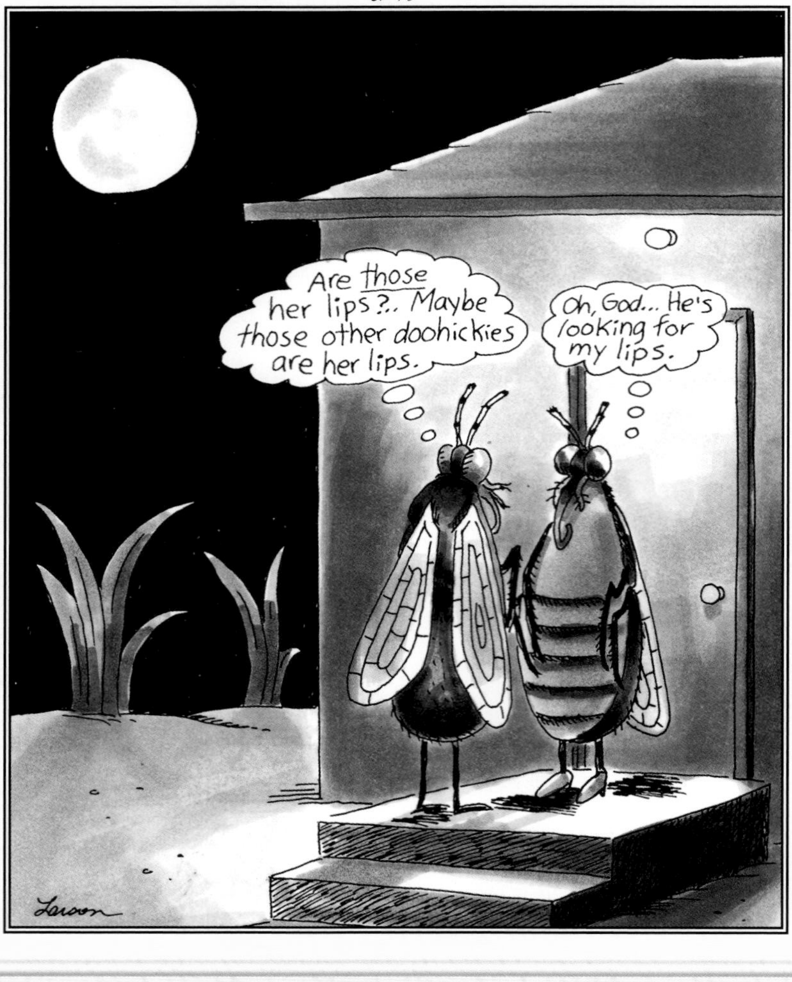
Are those her lips?.. Maybe those other doohickies are her lips.
Oh, God... He's looking for my lips.

Fly dates

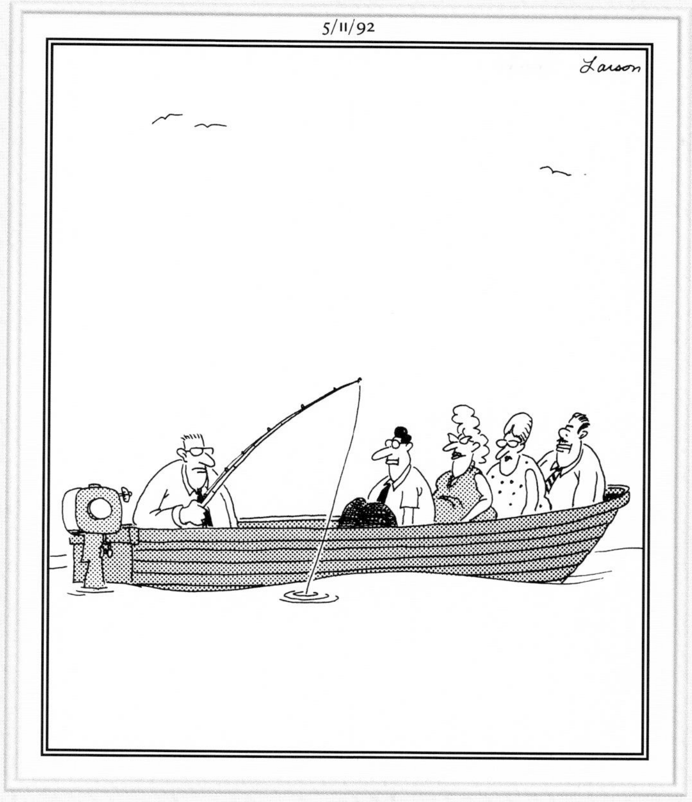
5/11/92
Larson

J. W. Miller with his staff and rod

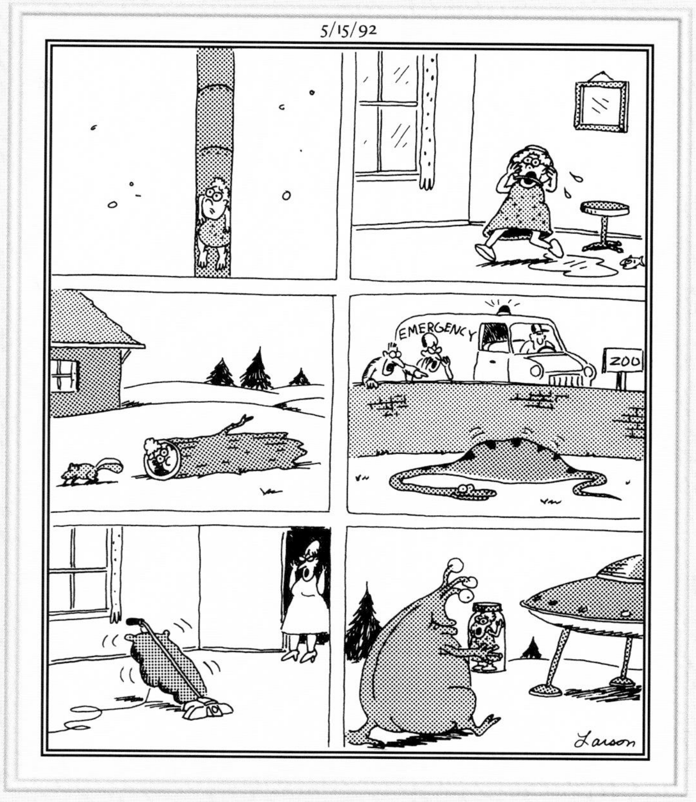
5/15/92
EMERGENCY
ZOO
Larson

The life and times of baby Jessica

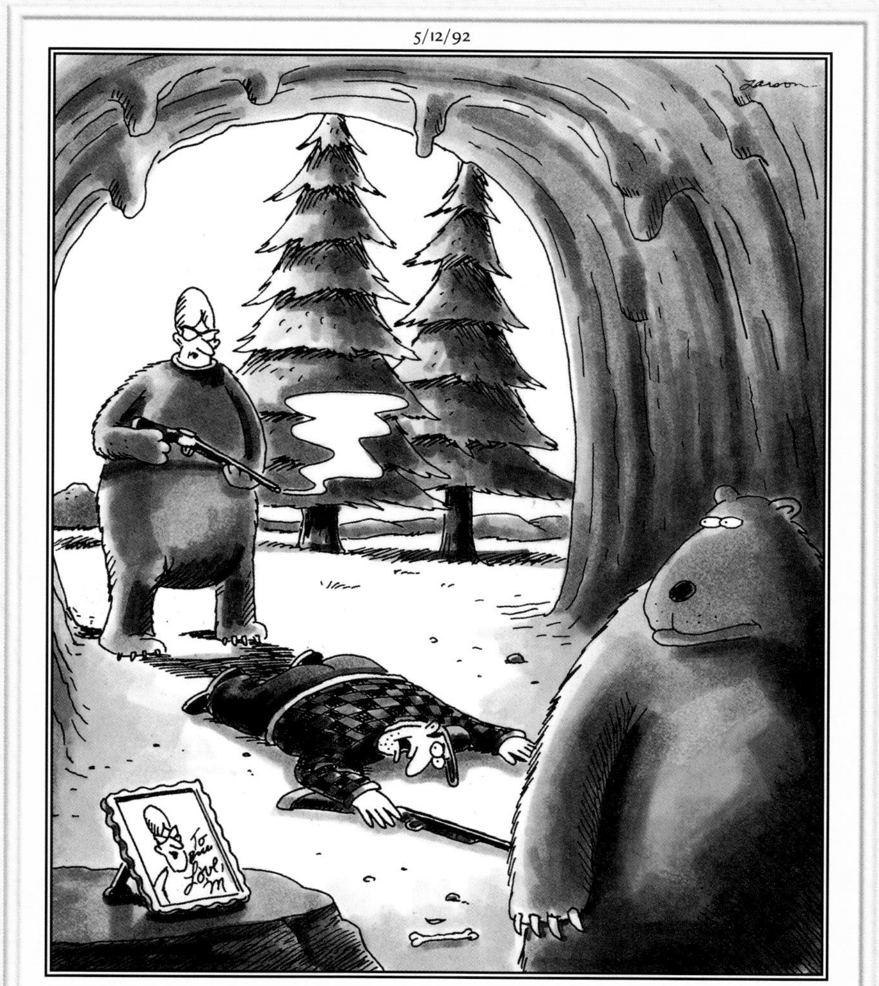
5/12/92
Larson

"Margaret! You? ... I ... should ... have ... knowwwwwnnnnnn ... "

5/14/92

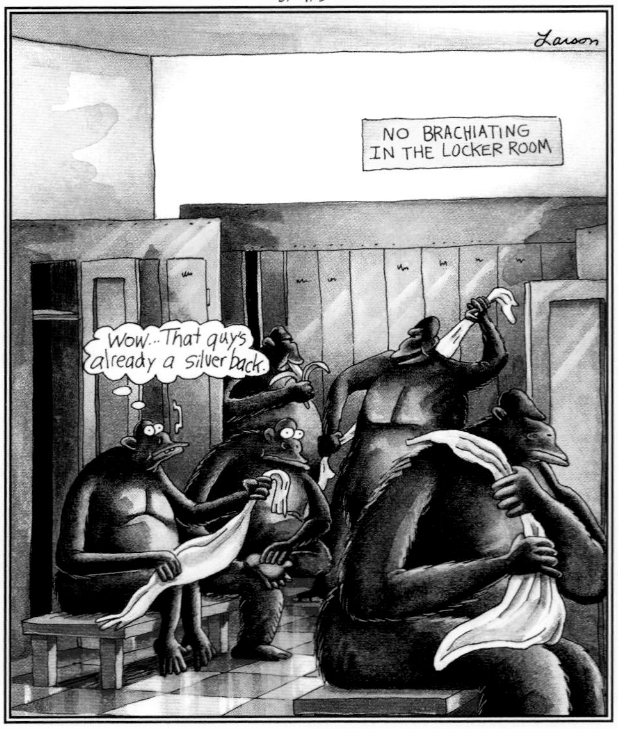
Larson
NO BRACHIATING IN THE LOCKER ROOM
Wow... That guy's already a silver back.

Junior high gorillas

5/13/92

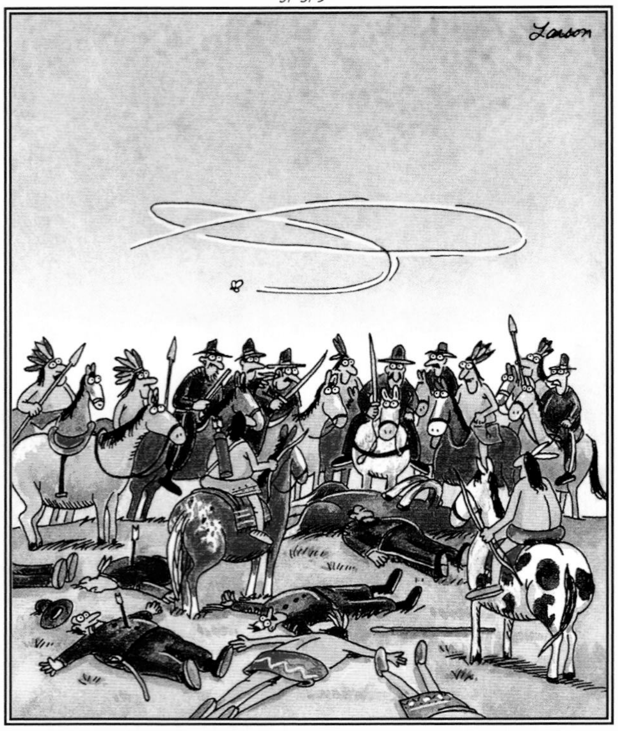
Larson

The action suddenly stopped while both sides waited patiently for the hornet to calm down.

5/18/92

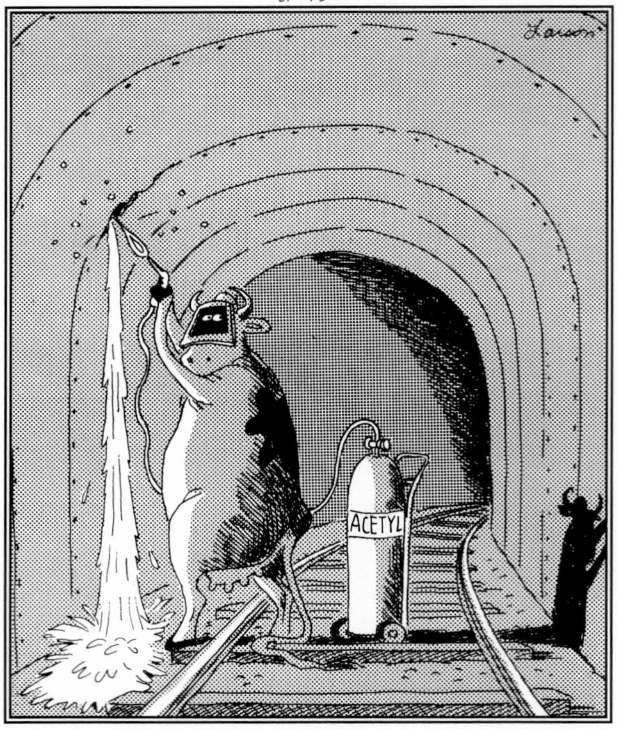
Larson
ACETYL

In a tunnel under the Chicago River, a descendant of Mrs. O'Leary's cow follows her calling.

5/20/92

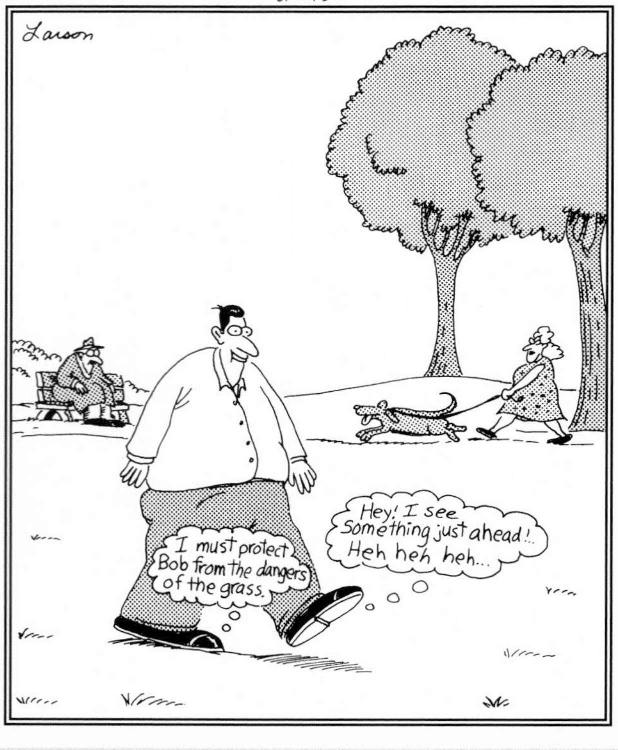
Larson
I must protect Bob from the dangers of the grass.
Hey! I see something just ahead!.. Heh heh heh...

Good and evil shoes

5/21/92

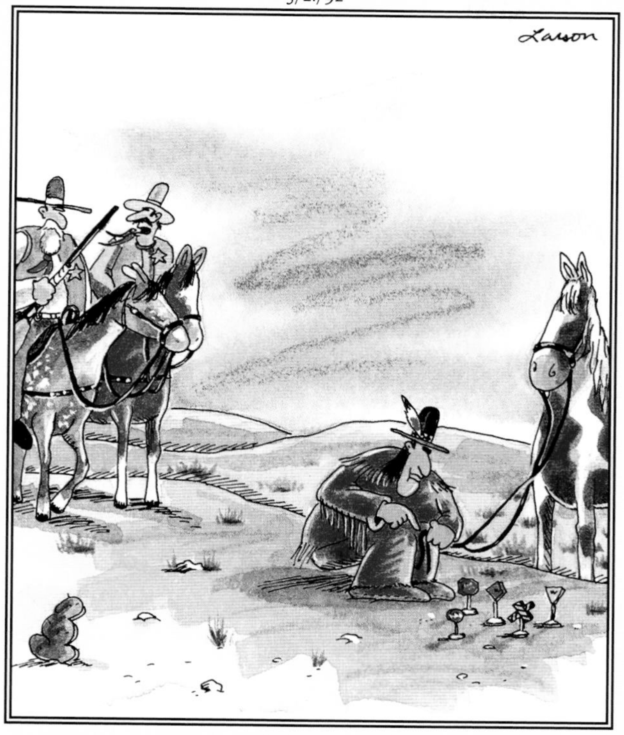
Larson

"Now we'll find the varmint for sure. ...
Red Cloud can read even the smallest trail signs."

5/19/92

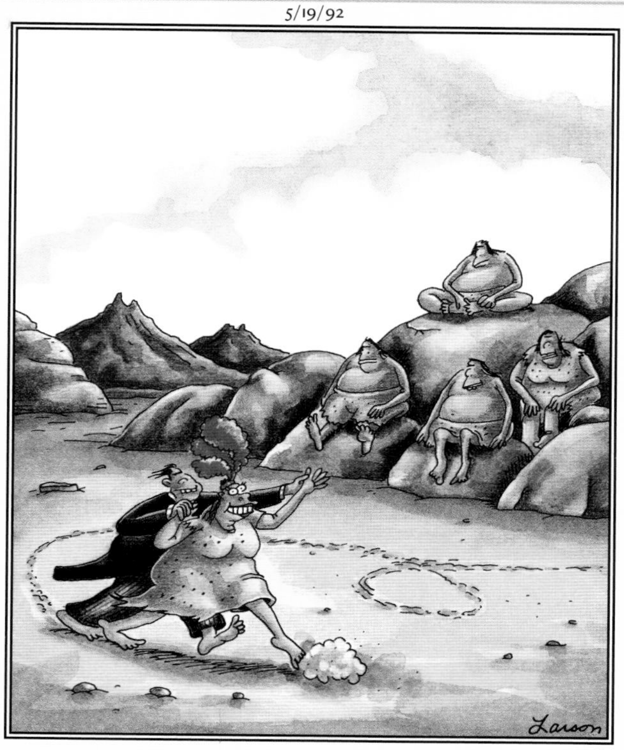
Larson

The first Dirt Capades

5/22/92

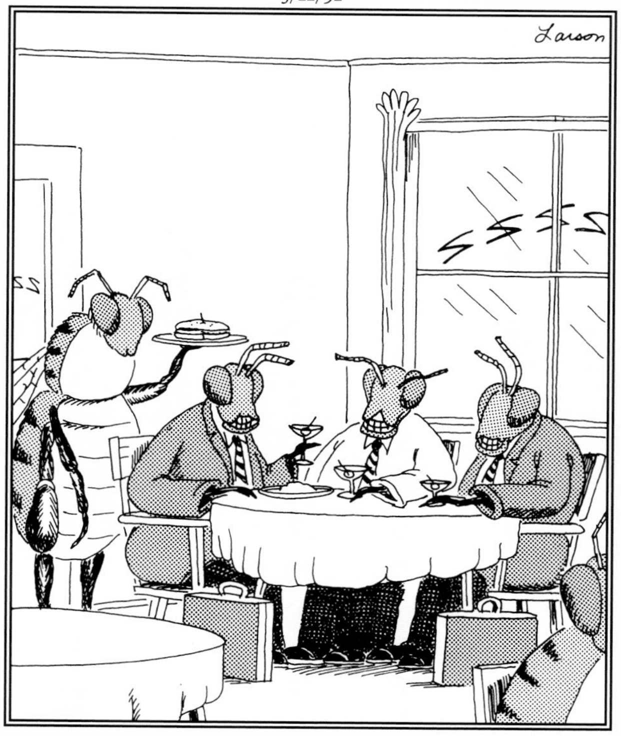
Larson

Beeswax lunches

5/29/92

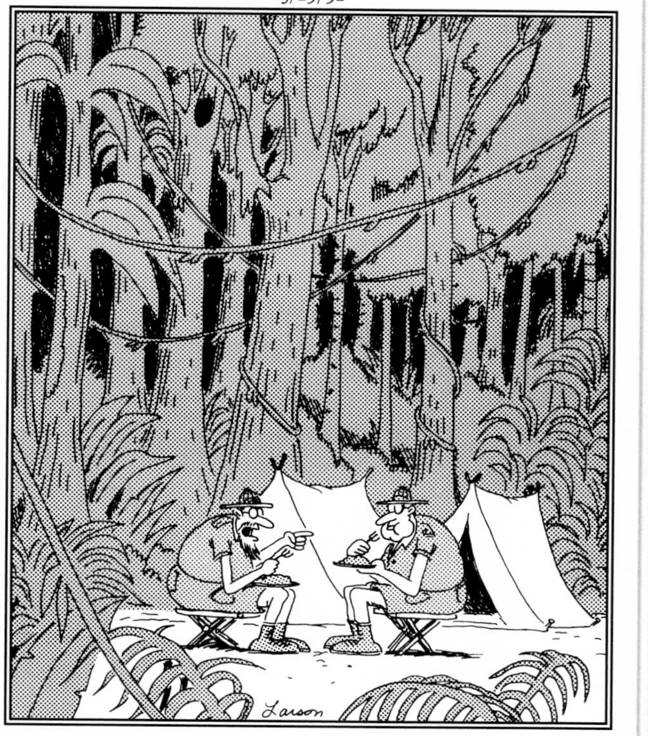
Larson

"Curse you, Flannegan! Curse you to *hell!* ...
There, I've said it."

5/25/92

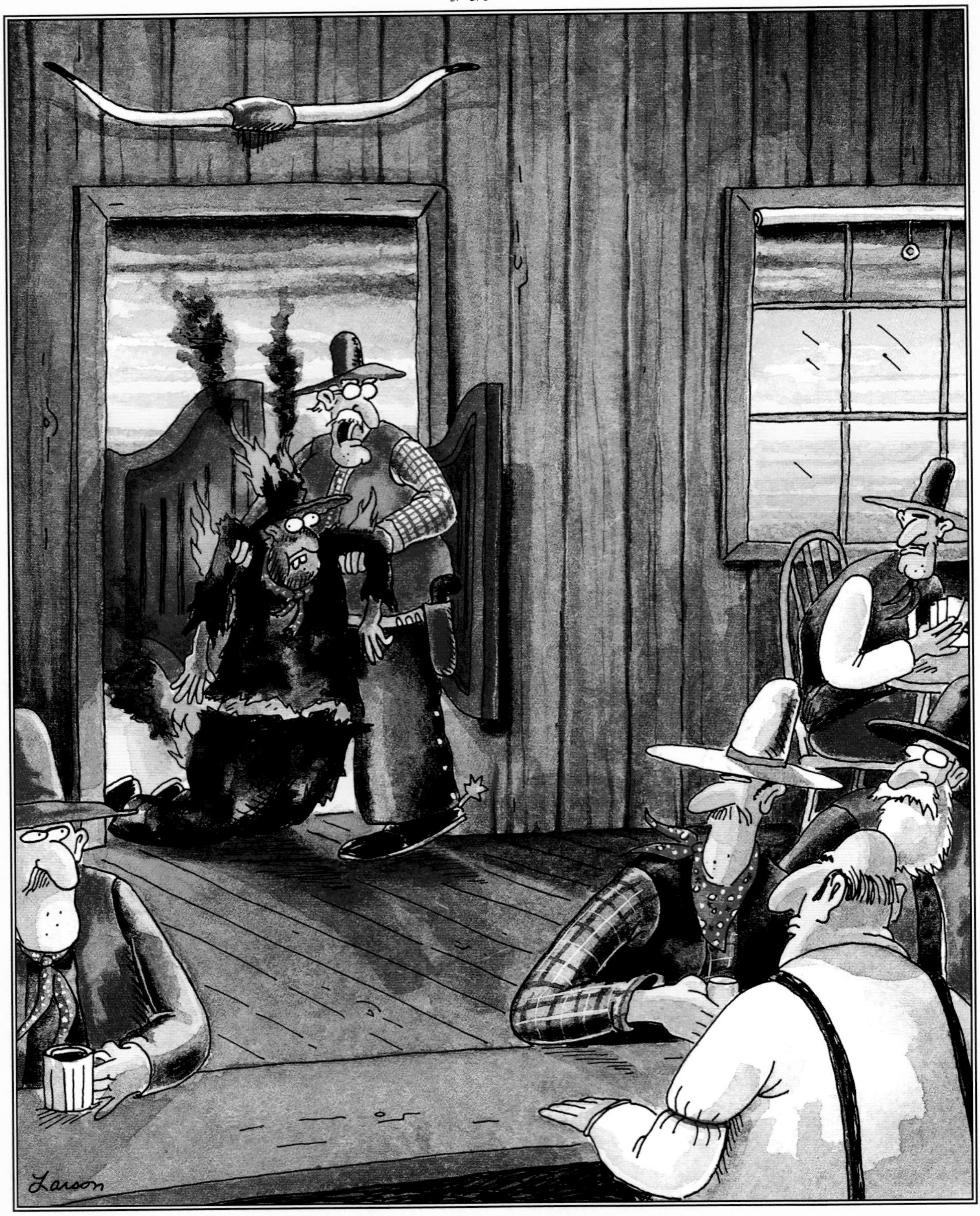
Larson

"Give me a hand here, boys! It's young Will Hawkins! ...
Dang fool tried to ride into the sunset!"

5/27/92

Larson

"I wouldn't do that, bartender. ... Unless, of course, you think you're fast enough."

5/26/92

AS IS
Larson

It wasn't until he got home that Sahib realized the thing had no front end.

5/28/92

Larson

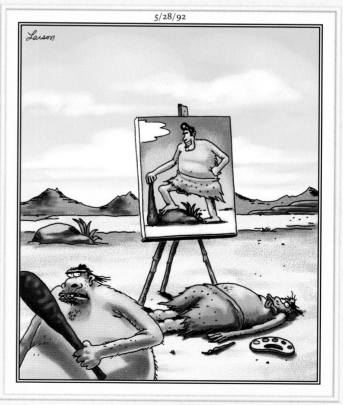

Modern art critic

6/1/92

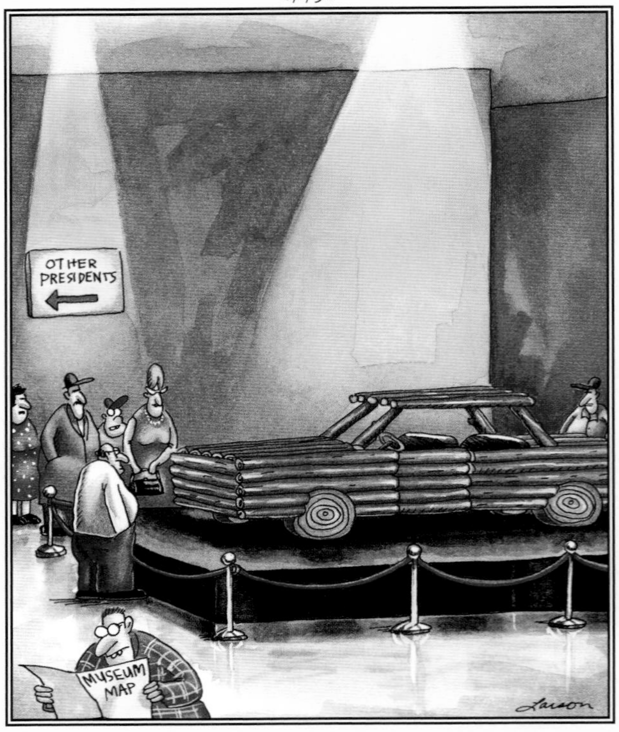
OTHER PRESIDENTS
MUSEUM MAP
Larson

Abraham Lincoln's first car

6/4/92

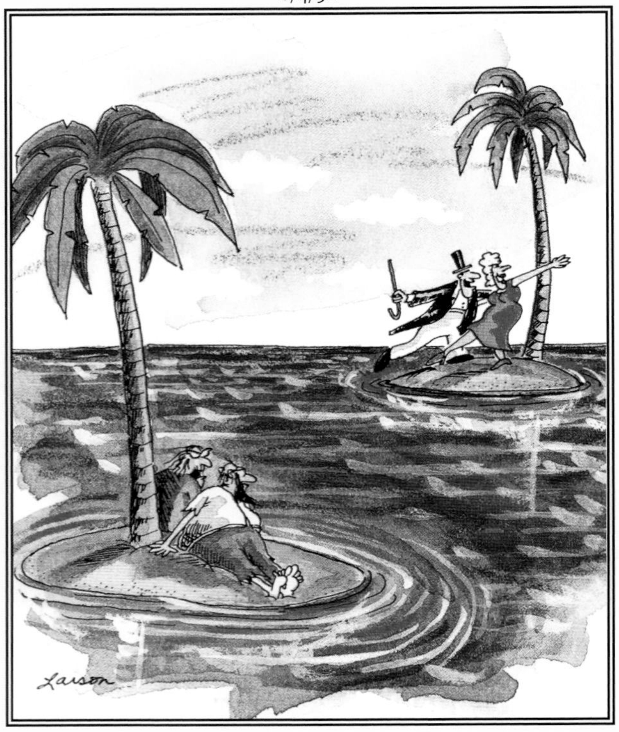
Larson

"Well, there they go again. The Stenbergs are always acting like life is one big musical."

6/2/92

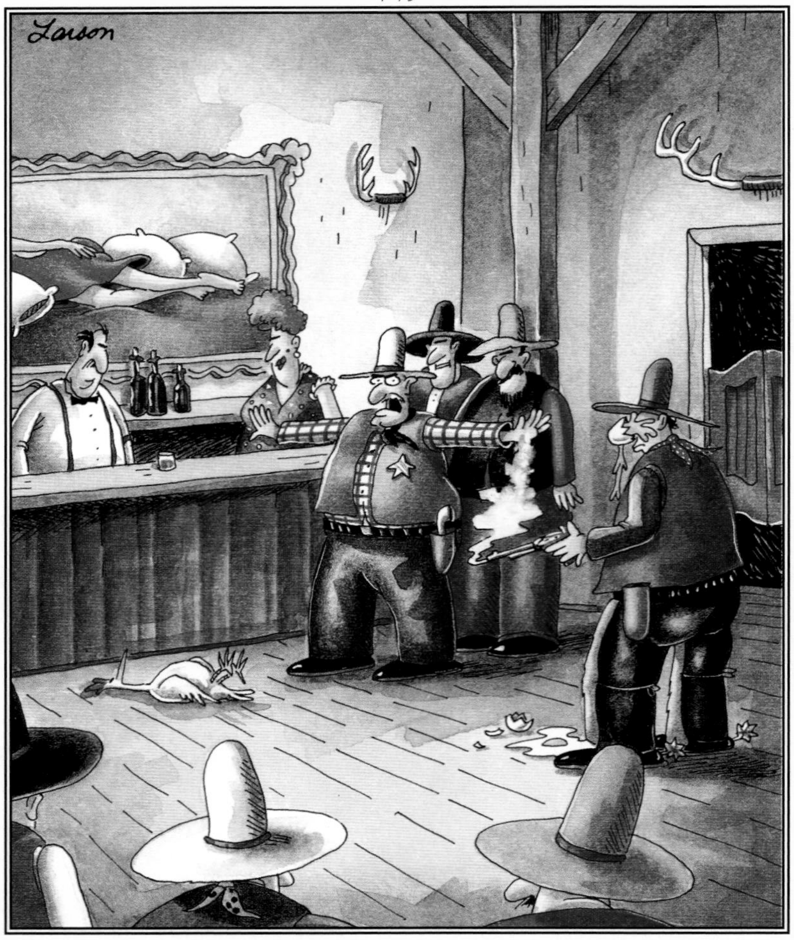
Larson

"Okay, everyone just stand back! ... Anyone see what happened here?"

6/3/92

Larson

High above the hushed crowd, Rex tried to remain focused. Still, he couldn't shake one nagging thought: He was an old dog and this was a new trick.

6/8/92

Larson

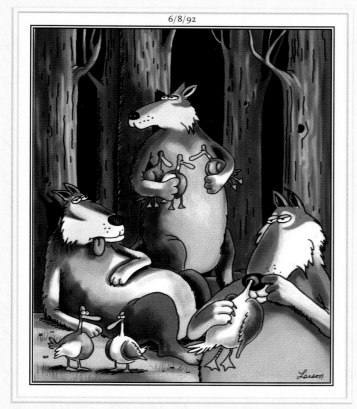

Some wolves, their habitat destroyed and overwhelmed by human pressures, turn to snorting quack.

6/9/92

Larson
bonk! bonk!
bonk!
bonk!

6/10/92

"Look here, McGinnis—hundreds of bright copper kettles, warm woolen mittens, brown paper packages tied up with string. ... Someone was after a few of this guy's favorite things."

6/5/92

"Look at the hordes down there, Phil. ... Have I ever told you what they look like? Huh? ... Have I?"

6/12/92

fly leech tick

echinoderm Madonna musk ox

Reagan mosquito cockroach

giant squid Jagger yak

Lips of the animal kingdom

6/15/92

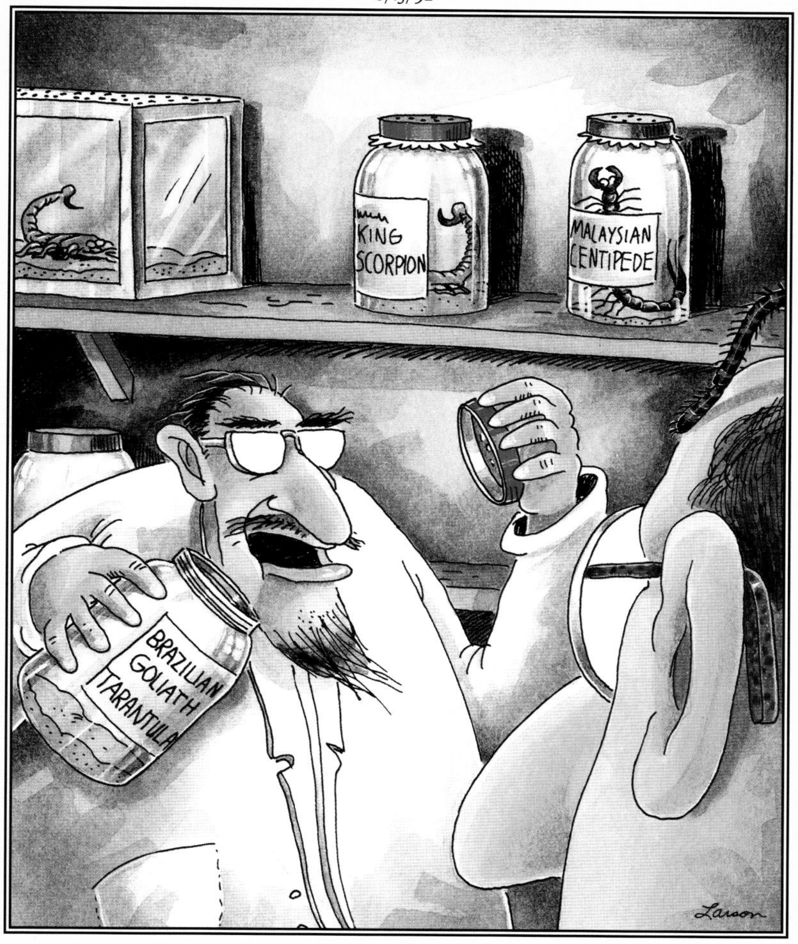
KING
SCORPION
MALAYSIAN
CENTIPEDE
BRAZILIAN
GOLIATH
TARANTULA
Larson

"*There* you are, my darling ... Rawlings! Don't move!"

6/16/92

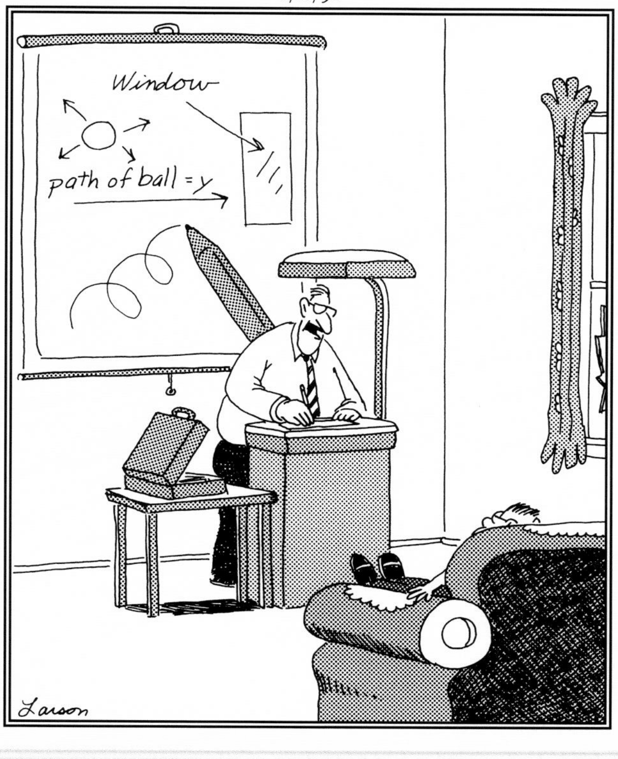
Window
path of ball = y
Larson

Eventually, Billy came to dread his father's lectures over all other forms of punishment.

6/18/92

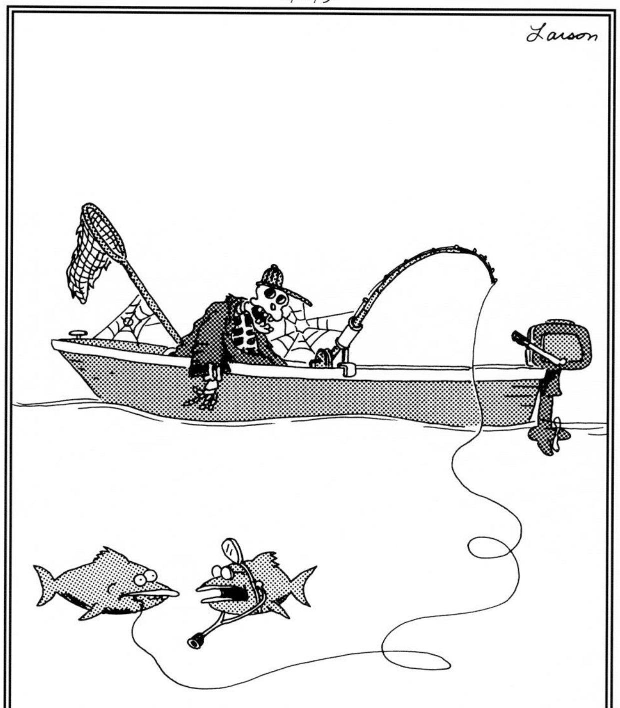
Larson

"Well, first the bad news—you're definitely hooked."

6/19/92

Larson
happy
depressed
angry
pensive
excited
suicidal

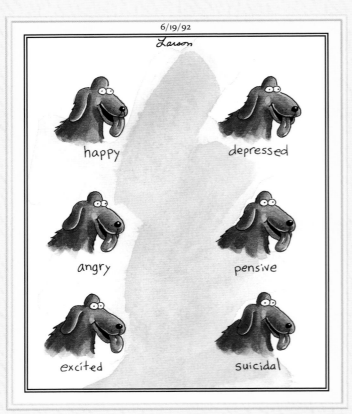

How to recognize the moods of an Irish setter

6/22/92

Larson

"Man, the Kellermans have a lot of nerve! ... If it wasn't for our screens, they'd probably walk right in!"

6/11/92

Larson
Shoot!.. I'm gonna go back and try this **again**.

6/17/92

Larson
page 1
NAME REX
1. A Siamese, traveling at three feet per second, tries to climb a 20 ft. tree while being chased by a rottweiler who is running at the same rate.

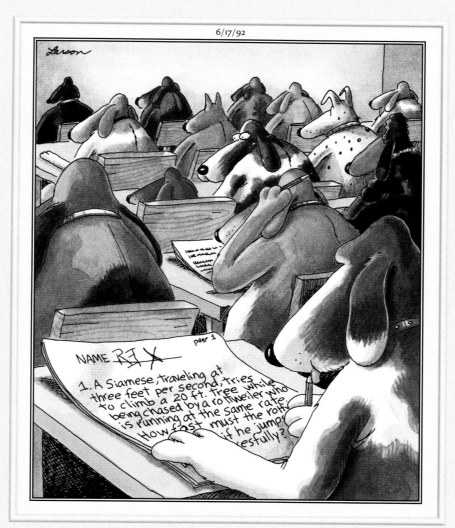

Before their admission to any canine university, dogs must first do well on the CATs.

6/23/92

Larson

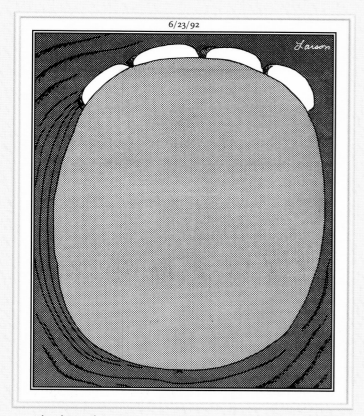

The last thing you see of an annoyed elephant

6/24/92

RUBY'S CAFE
Today's Special
Turtle Soup!
w/roll + coffee
Larson

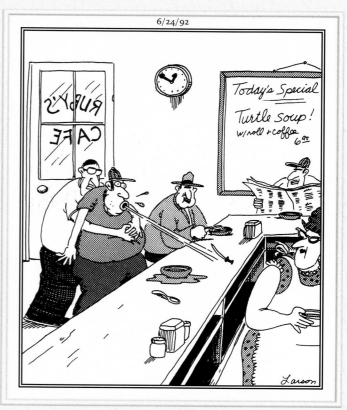

As suddenly as it started, Joe's gagging is alleviated when a small ninja sword is dislodged from his throat.

6/25/92

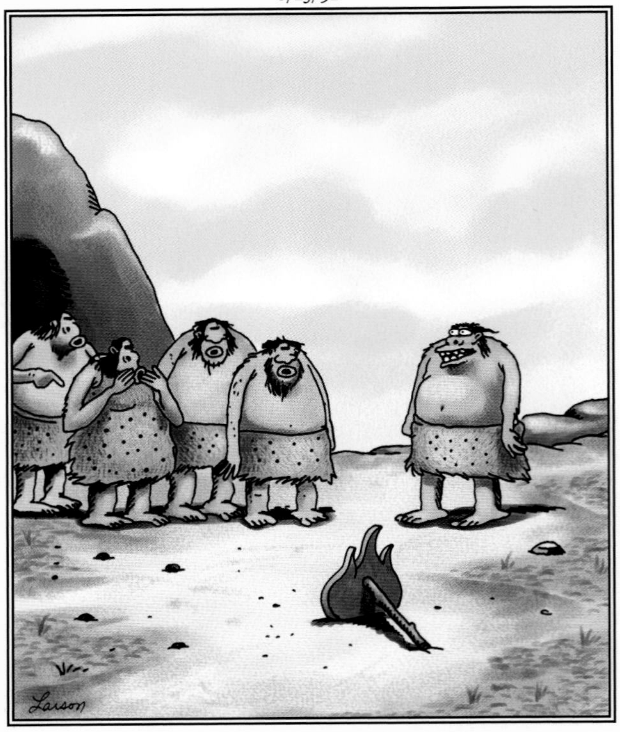
Larson

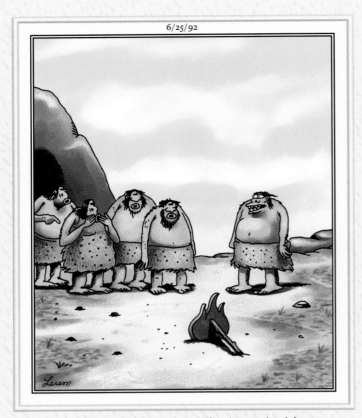

Zorg dupes the entire tribe in an incident later known as "firegate."

6/26/92

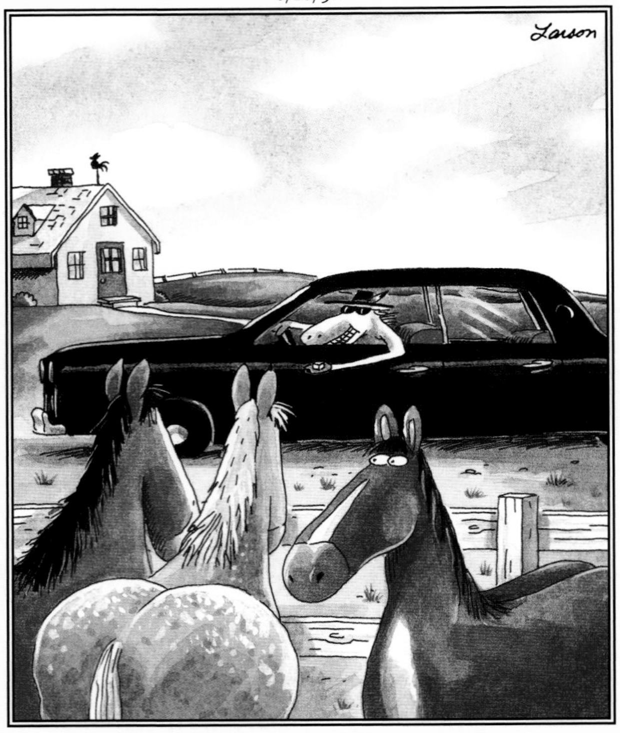
Larson

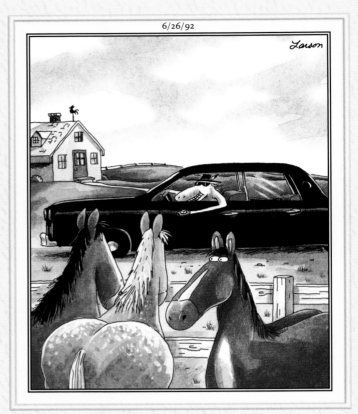

Every afternoon a sugar cube dealer would slowly cruise the corral looking for "customers."

6/29/92

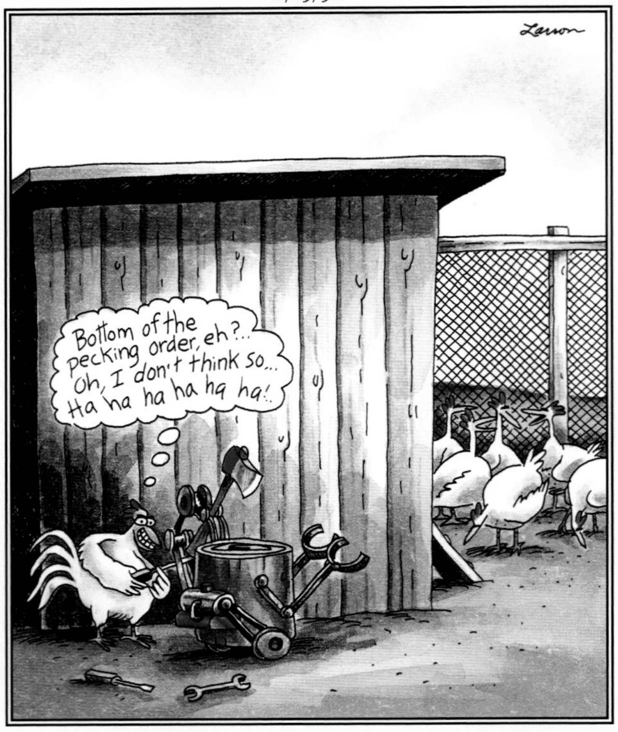
Larson
Bottom of the pecking order, eh?... Oh, I don't think so... Ha ha ha ha ha ha!

6/30/92

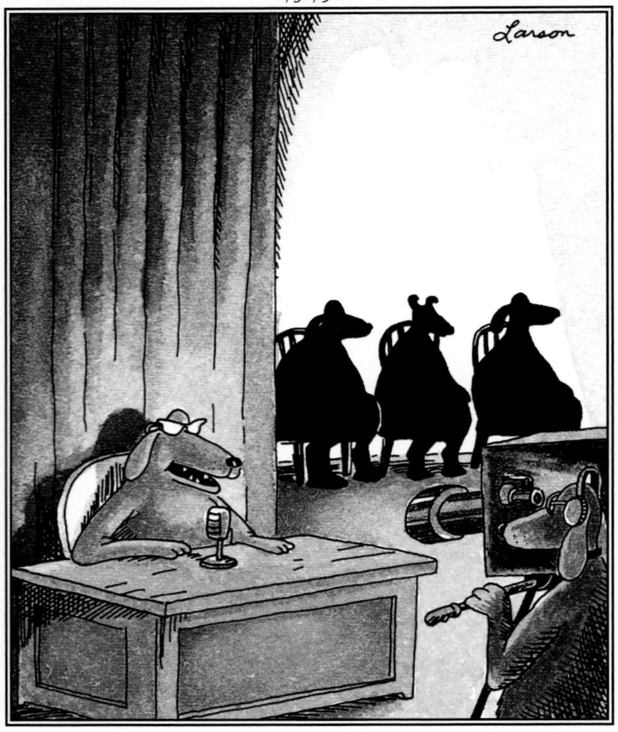
Larson

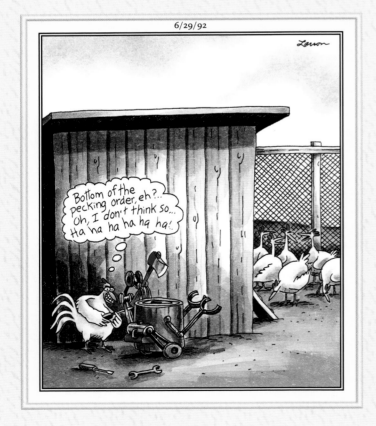

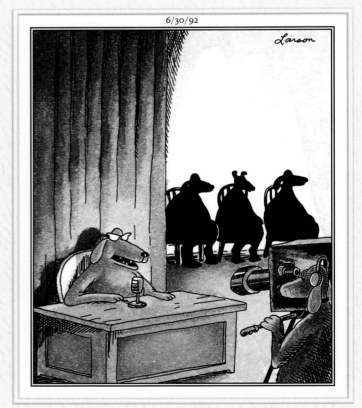

"Dogs that drink from the toilet bowl—right after this message."

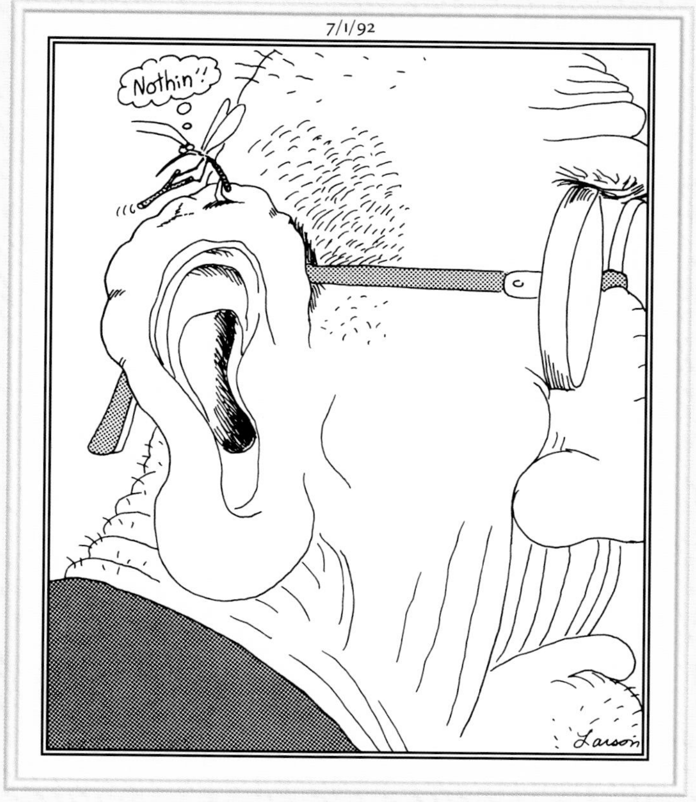
7/1/92
Nothin'!
Larson

Insect witching rods

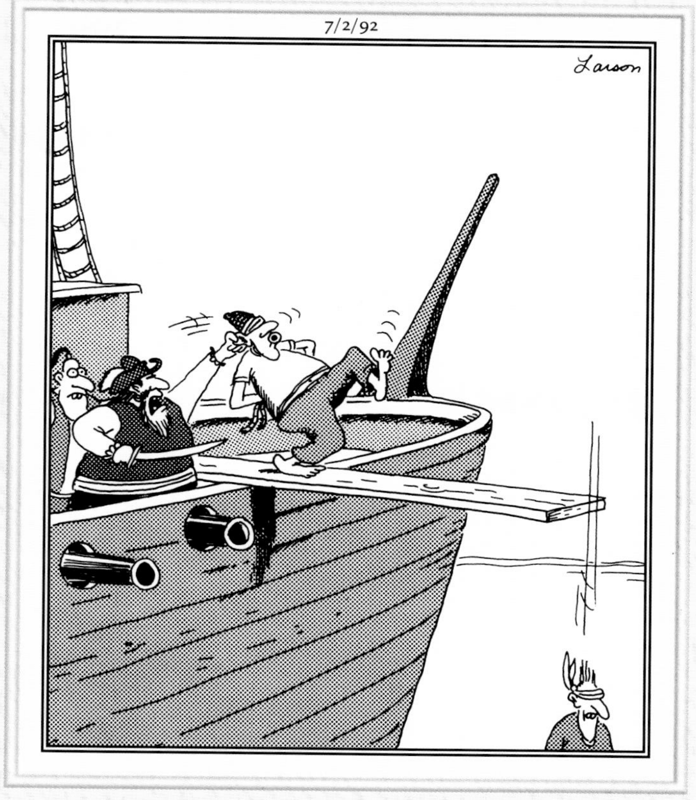
7/2/92
Larson

"Whoa whoa whoa, young man! You *walk* the plank like everyone else!"

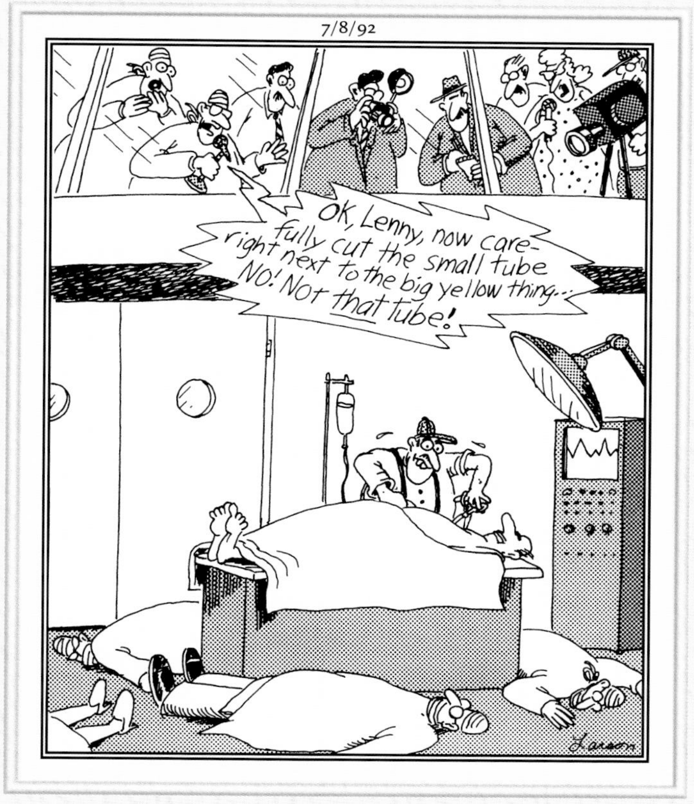
7/8/92
OK, Lenny, now carefully cut the small tube right next to the big yellow thing... NO! Not that tube!
Larson

With the surgical team passed out, and with help from the observation deck, hospital custodian Leonard Knudson suddenly became responsible for bringing Mr. Gruenfeld "home."

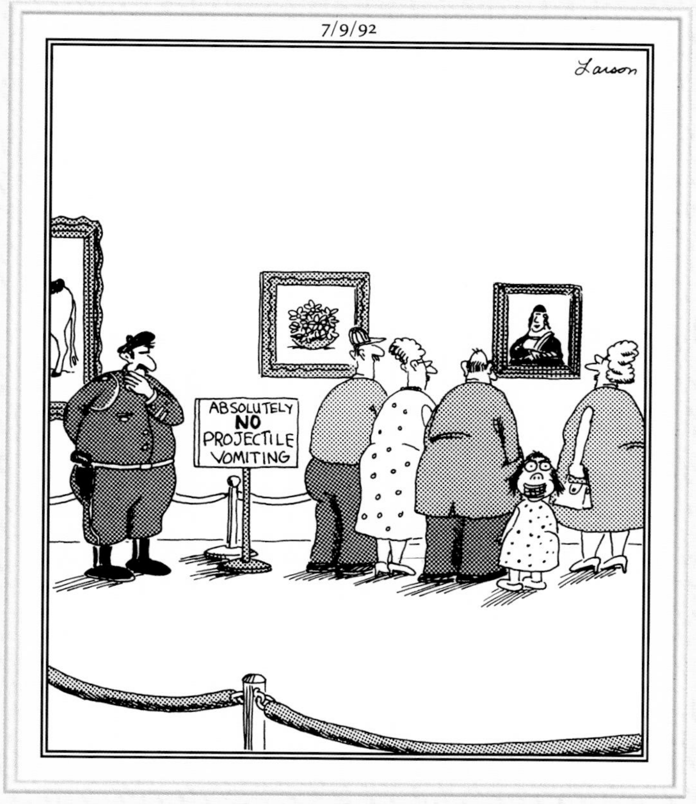
7/9/92
Larson
ABSOLUTELY NO PROJECTILE VOMITING

A Louvre guard is suddenly unsettled by the arrival of Linda Blair.

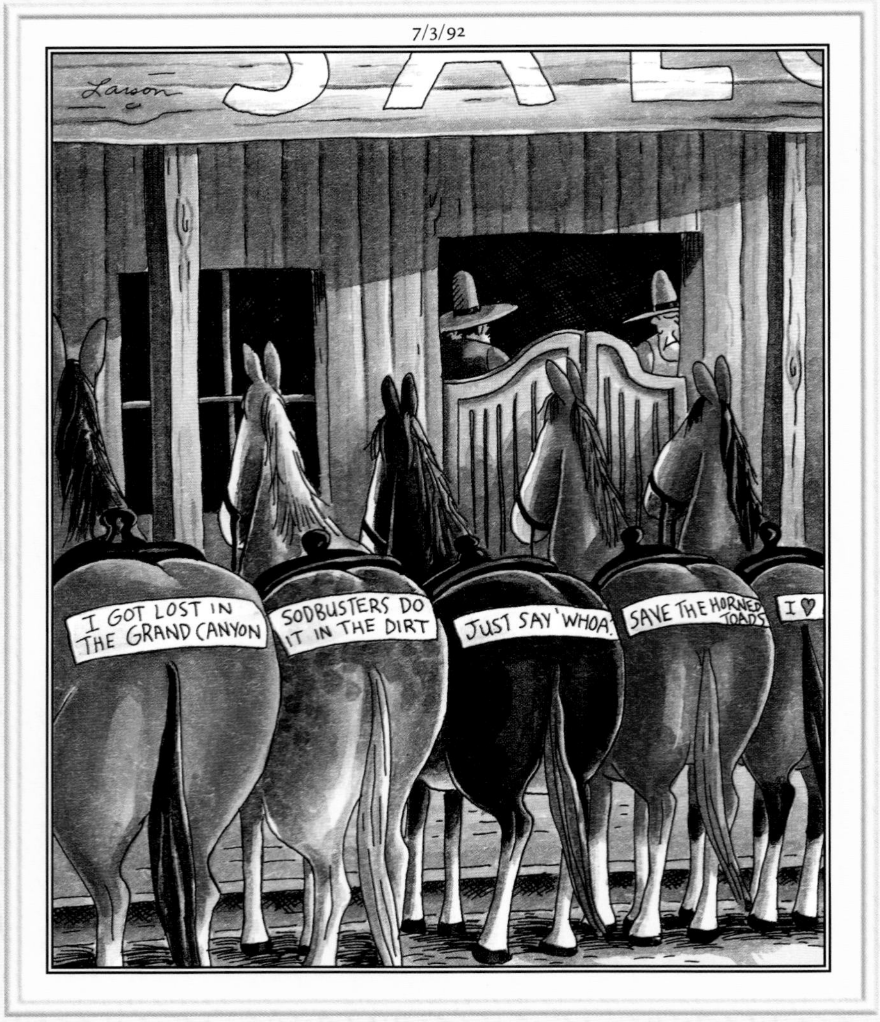
7/3/92
I GOT LOST IN THE GRAND CANYON
SODBUSTERS DO IT IN THE DIRT
JUST SAY 'WHOA'
SAVE THE HORNED TOADS
I ♥

Common rumper stickers of the Old West

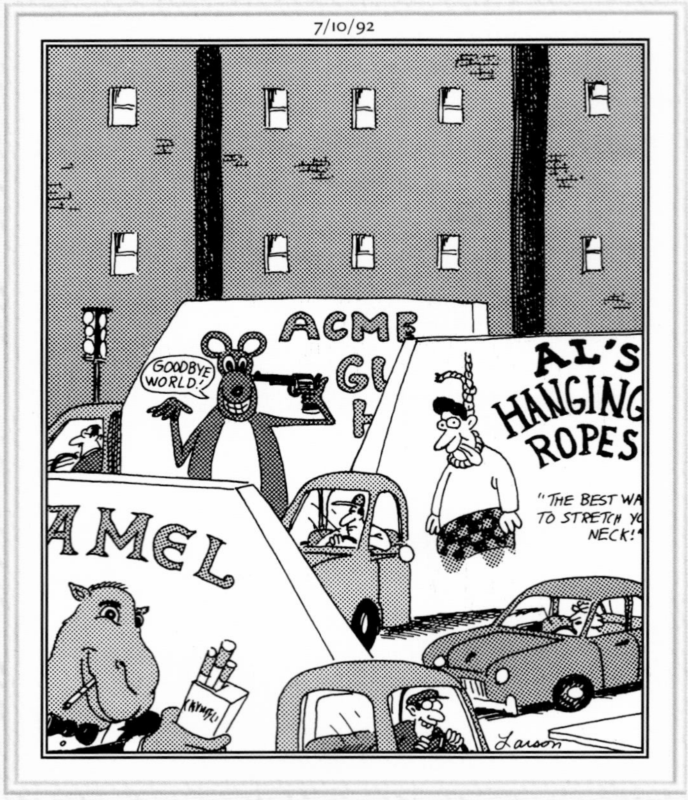
7/10/92
ACME
GOODBYE WORLD!
AL'S HANGING ROPES
"THE BEST WA TO STRETCH YO NECK!"
AMEL

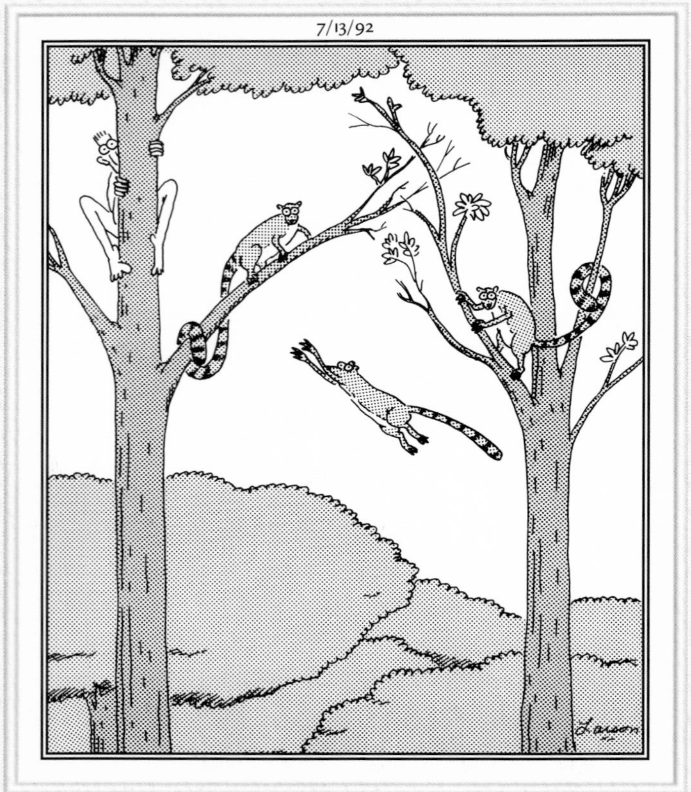
7/13/92

Although never achieving the fame of Tarzan, his African counterpart, Larry of the Lemurs was a common sight to natives of Madagascar.

7/16/92

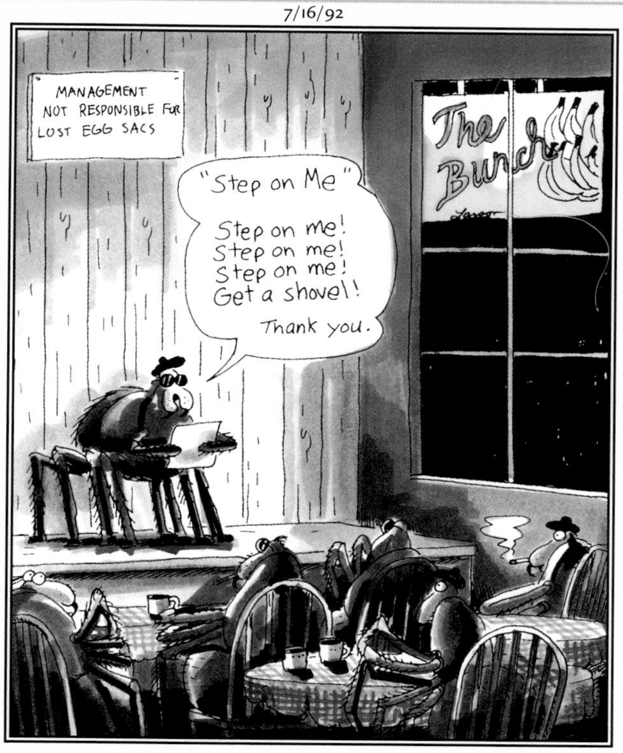
MANAGEMENT NOT RESPONSIBLE FOR LOST EGG SACS
"Step on Me"
Step on me!
Step on me!
Step on me!
Get a shovel!
Thank you.
The Bunch

Tarantula coffeehouses

7/14/92

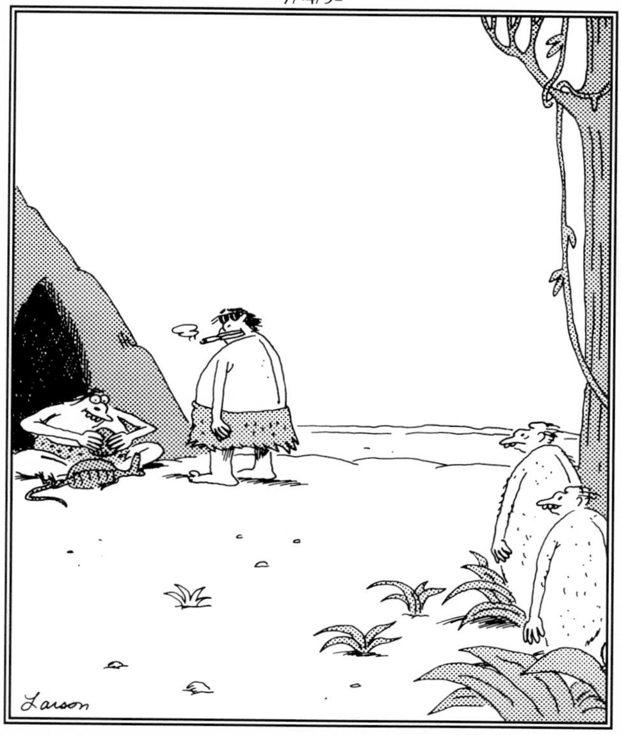

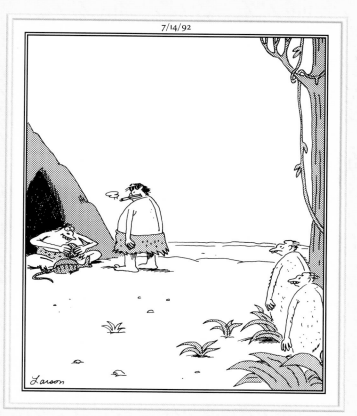

Drawn by the pulsating sound of a rock thumping on a dead armadillo, two australopithecines stood at the forest edge. Instantly, Thag's agent knew they had a crossover hit.

7/6/92

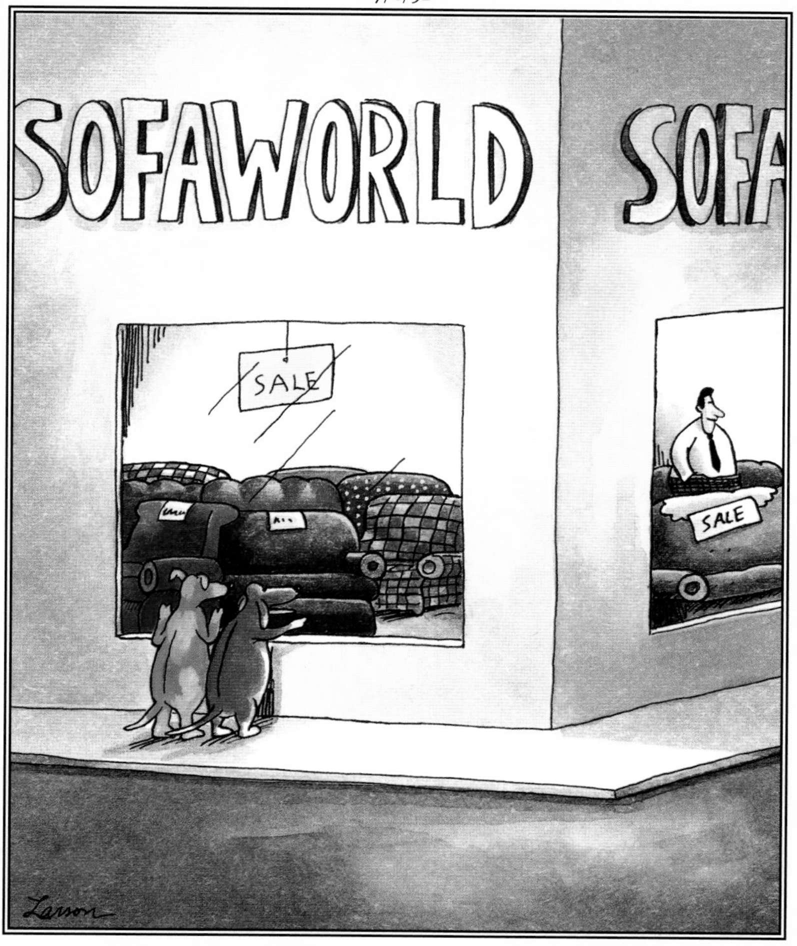
SOFAWORLD
SOFA
SALE
SALE

"Oo! *I'd* get up on that big fuzzy one!"

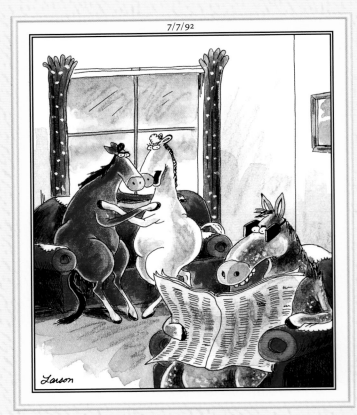

7/7/92

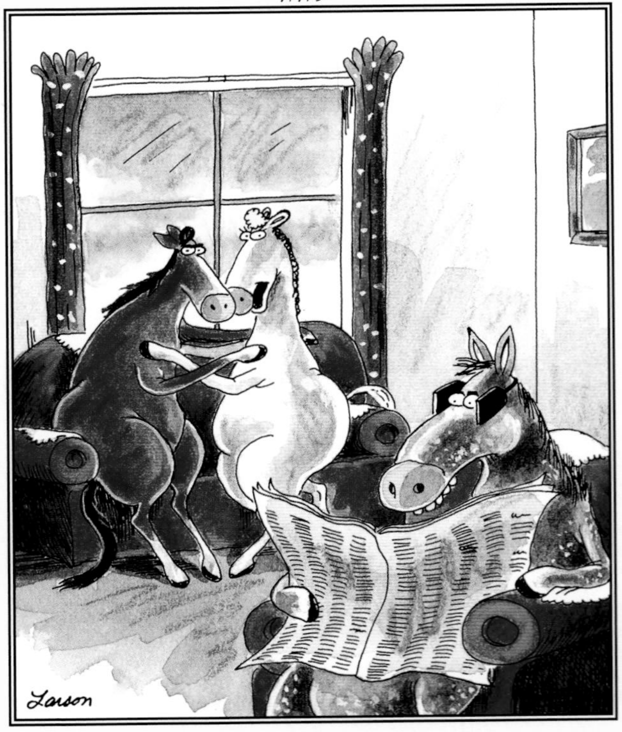
Larson

"We can't go on like this, Ramone. ... One day, George is bound to take his blinders off."

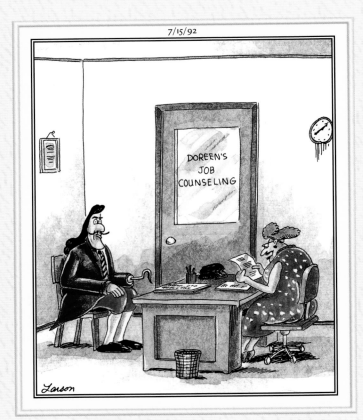

7/15/92

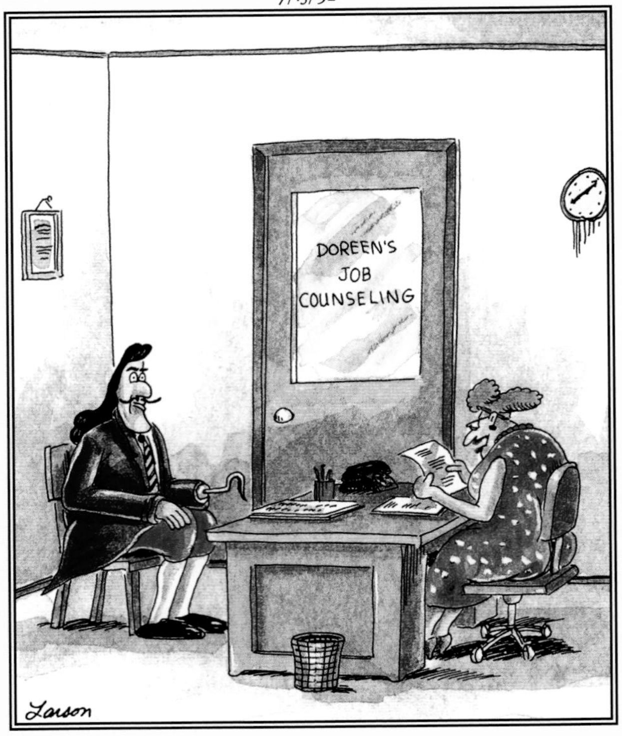
DOREEN'S
JOB
COUNSELING
Larson

"Okay, Mr. Hook. Seems you're trying to decide between a career in pirating or massage therapy. Well, maybe we can help you narrow it down."

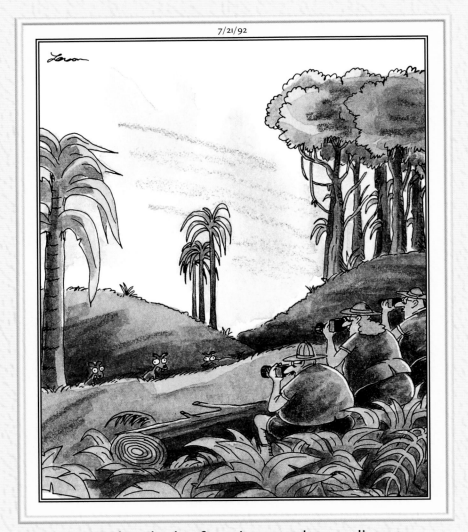

7/21/92

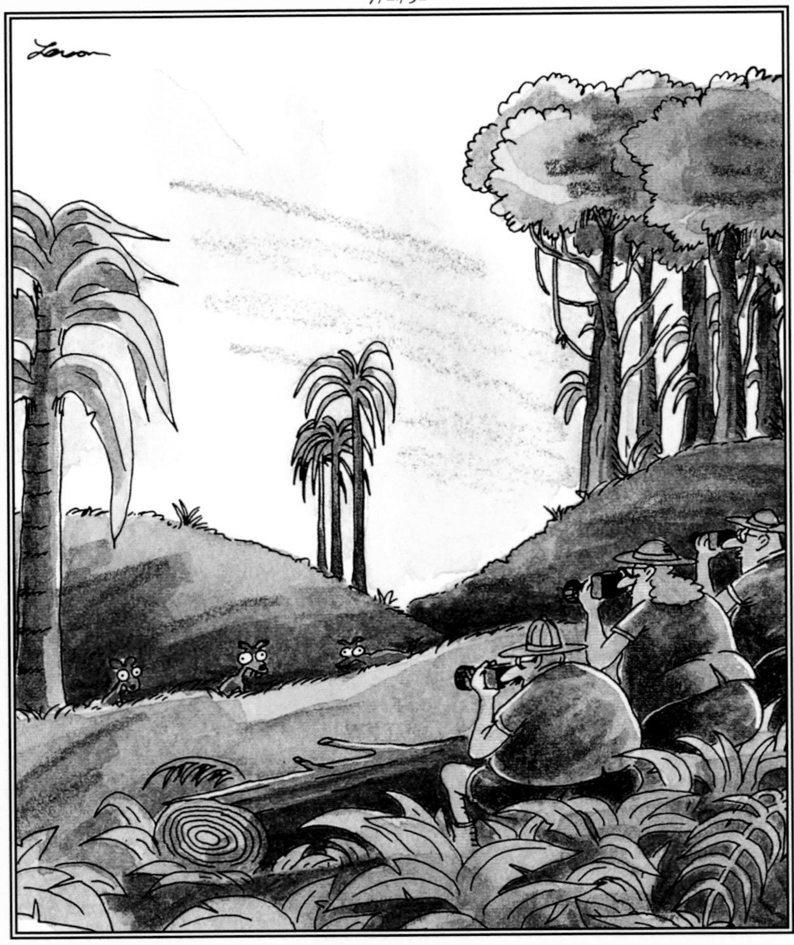
Larson

Every year, hundreds of tourists travel great distances to get a glimpse of the few remaining mountain Chihuahuas.

7/23/92

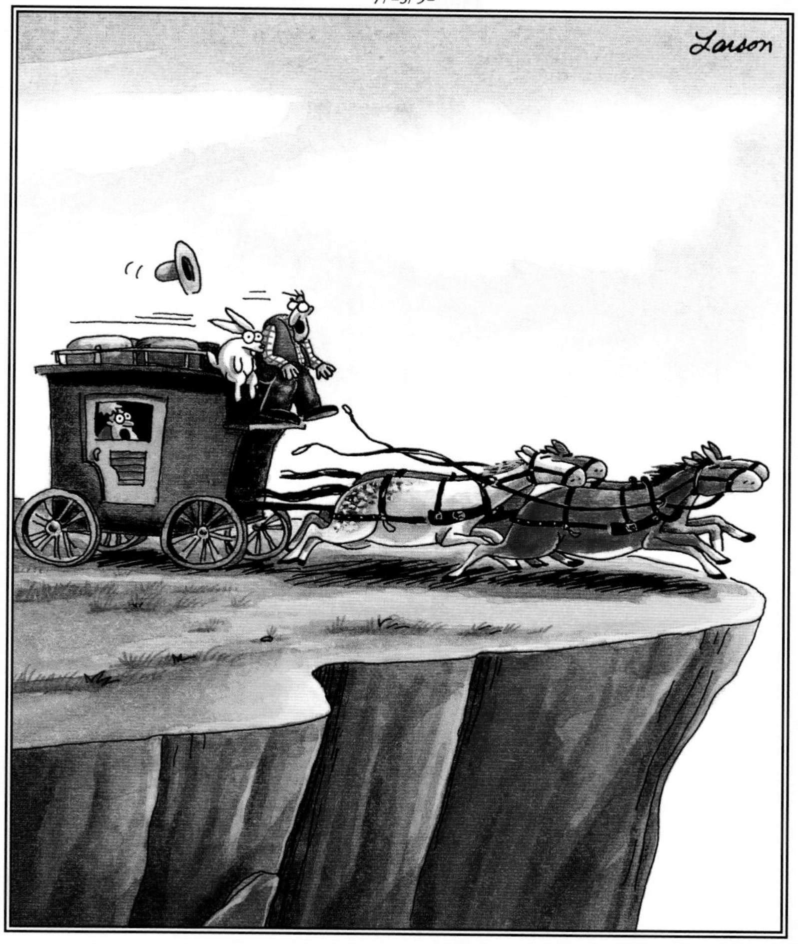

"Go ahead and jump, Sid! Hell, I *know* you're thinkin' it!"

7/20/92

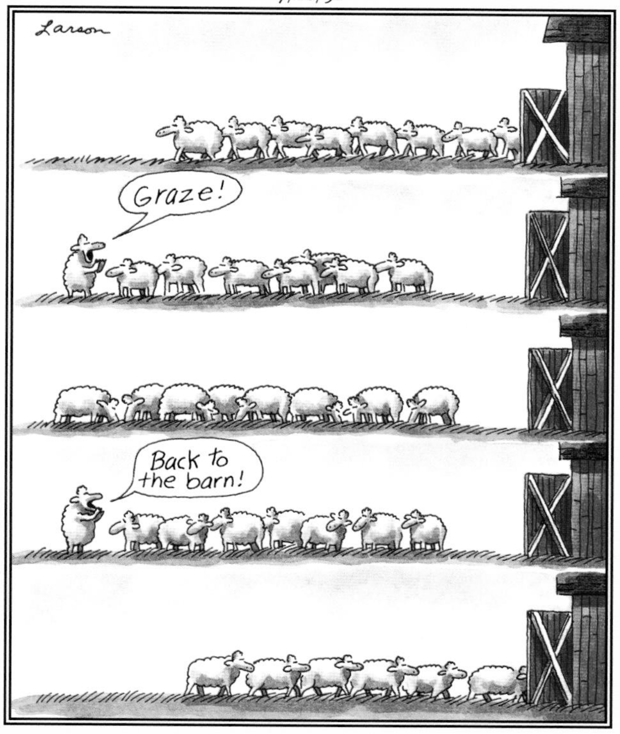
Graze!
Back to the barn!

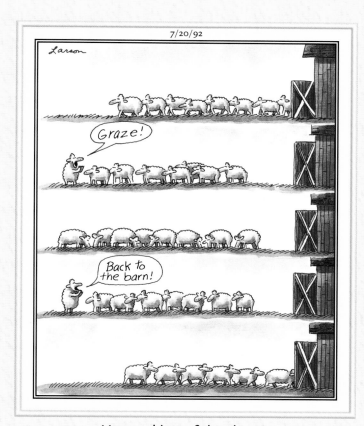

He was king of the sheep.

7/29/92

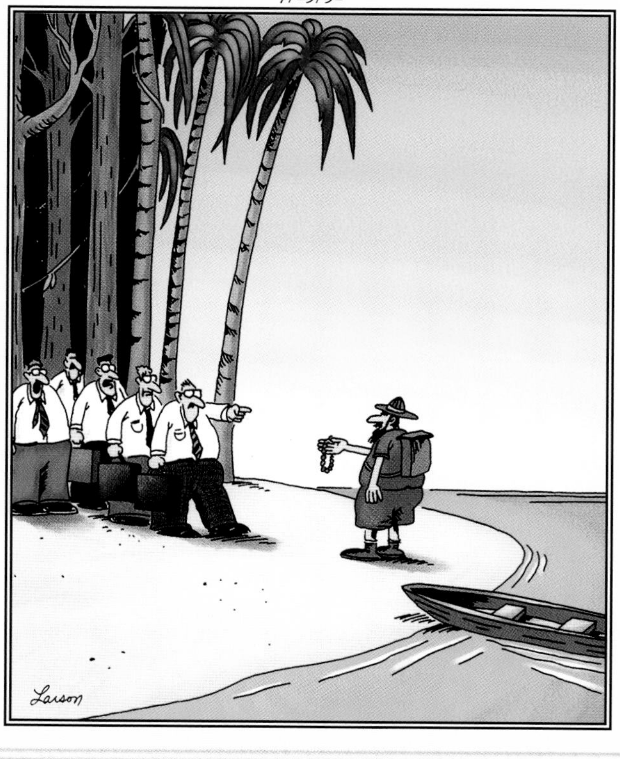

Wellington held out some beads and other trinkets, but the islanders had sent their fiercest lawyers—some of whom were chanting, "Sue him! Sue him!"

7/17/92

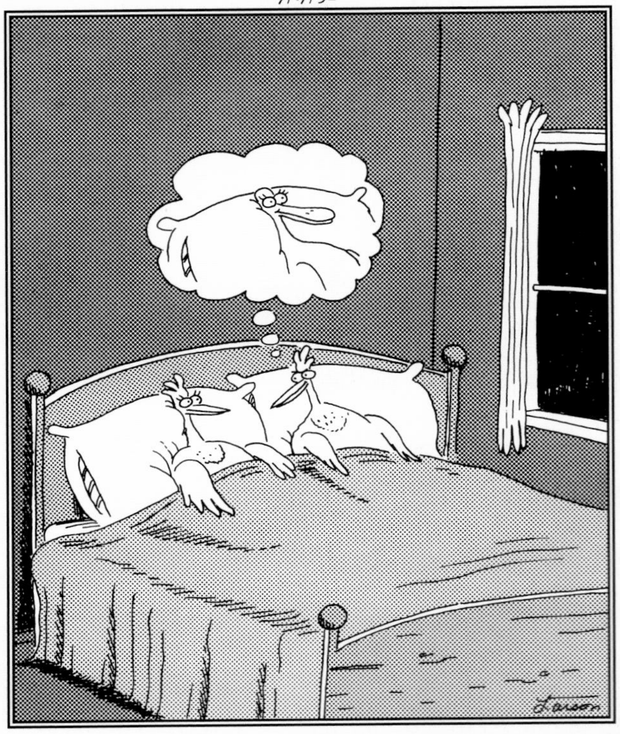

Chicken sexual fantasies

7/22/92

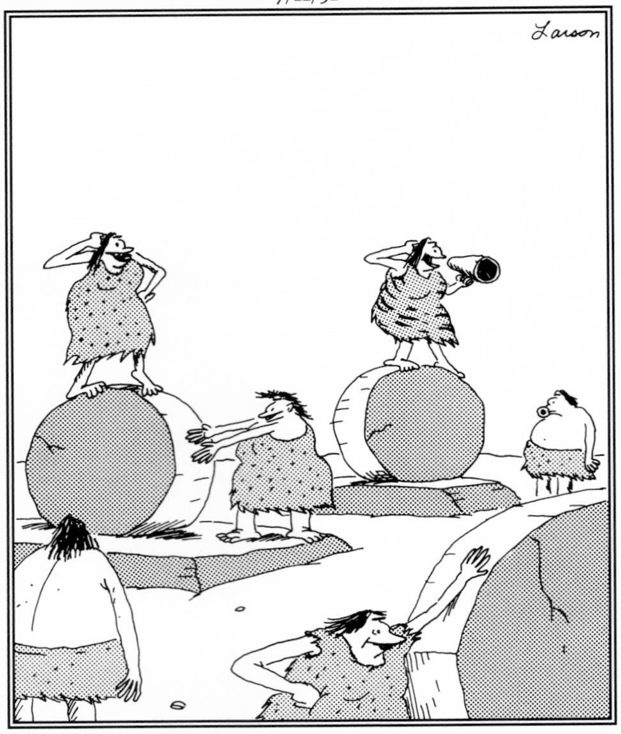

Early spokesmodels

7/24/92

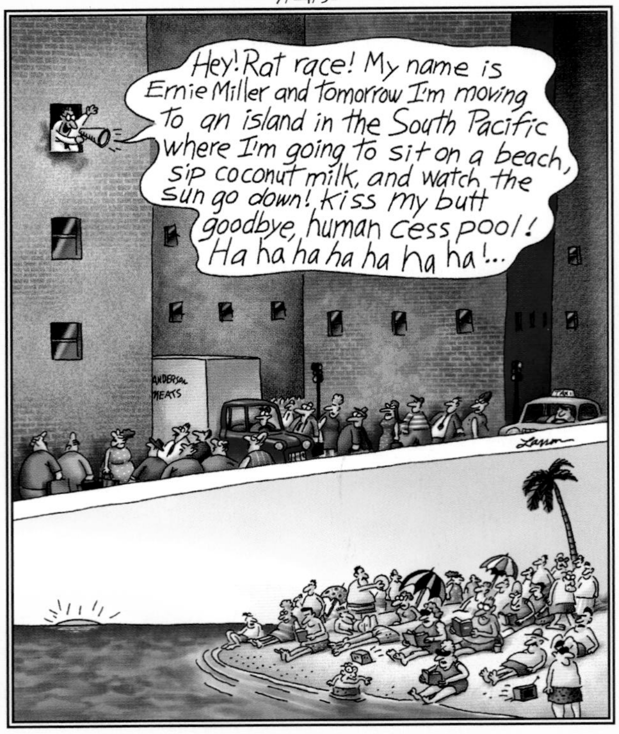
Hey! Rat race! My name is Ernie Miller and tomorrow I'm moving to an island in the South Pacific where I'm going to sit on a beach, sip coconut milk, and watch the sun go down! Kiss my butt goodbye, human cess pool! Ha ha ha ha ha ha ha!..

7/27/92

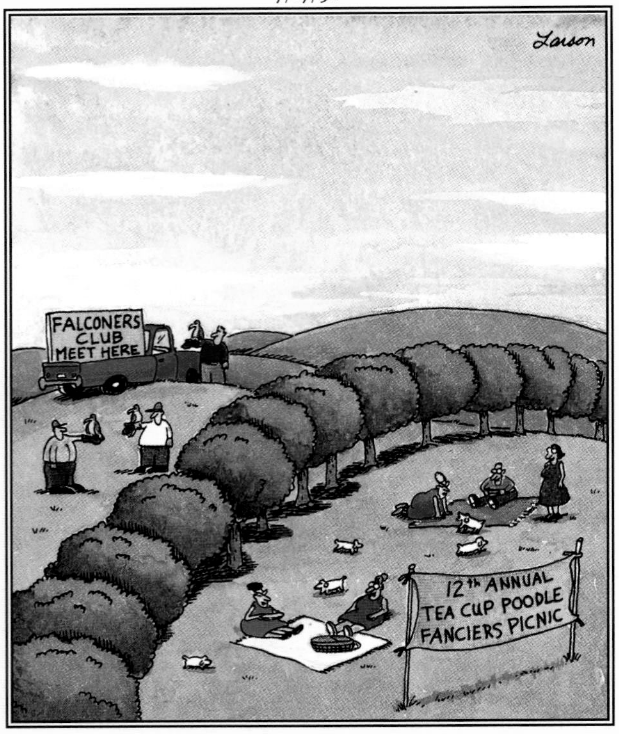
FALCONERS CLUB MEET HERE
12th ANNUAL TEA CUP POODLE FANCIERS PICNIC

Trouble brewing

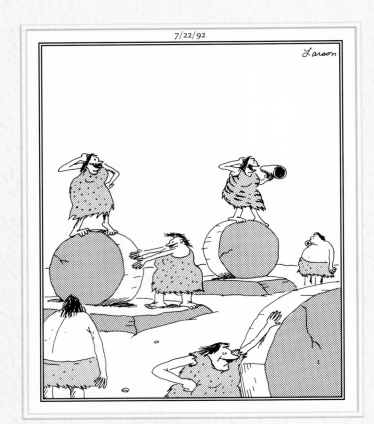

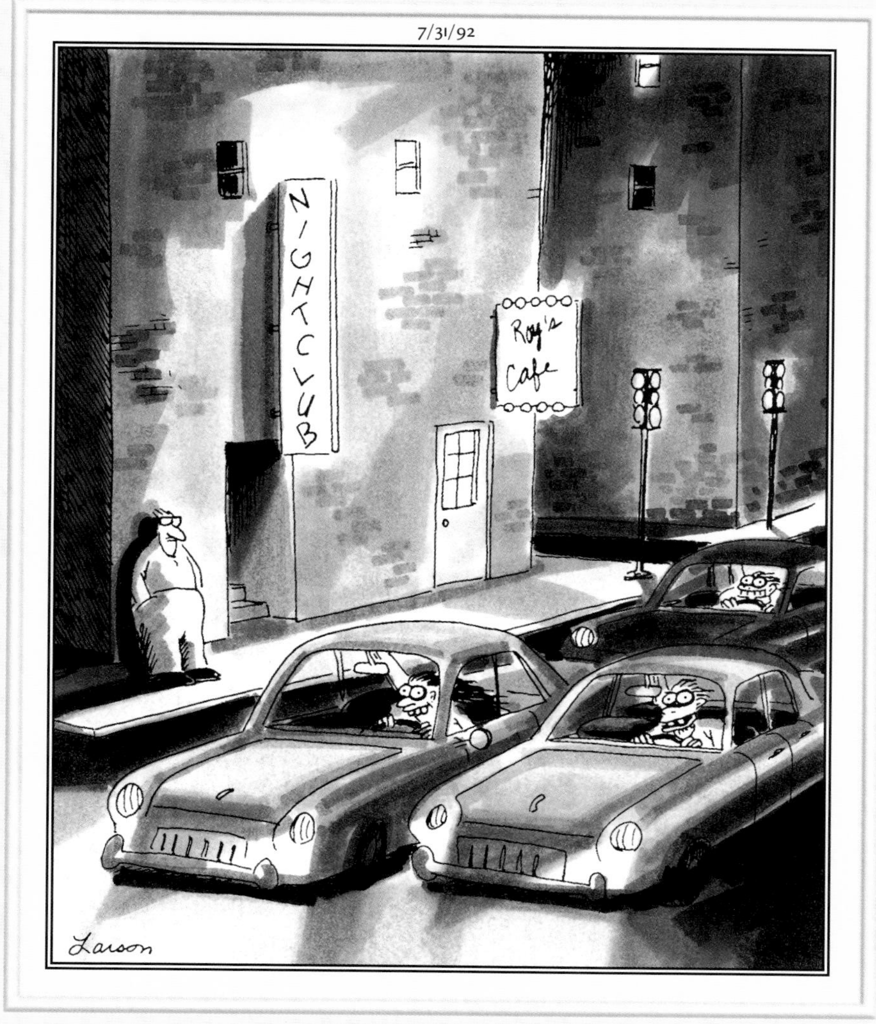
7/31/92
NIGHTCLUB
Roy's Cafe
Larson

Zoombies: the driving dead

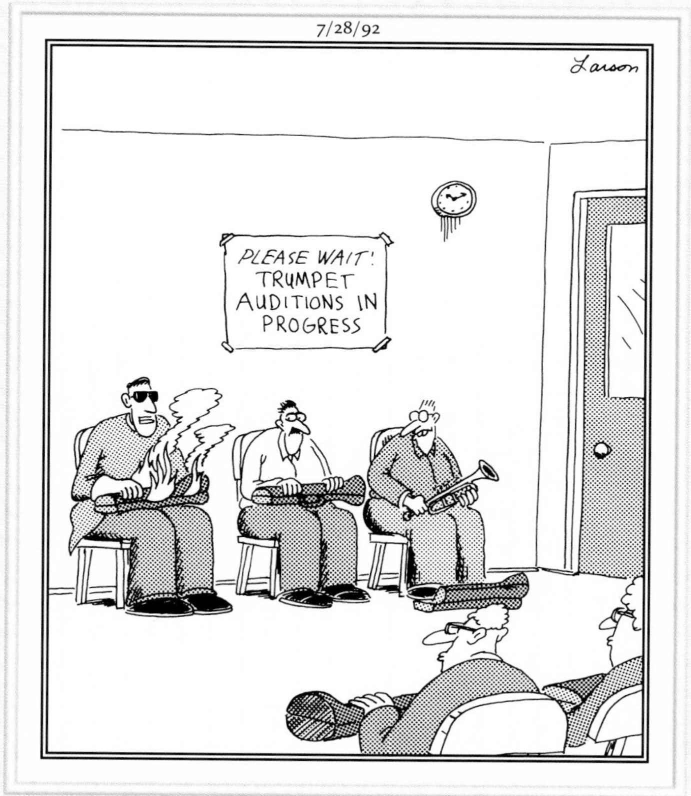
7/28/92
Larson
PLEASE WAIT: TRUMPET AUDITIONS IN PROGRESS

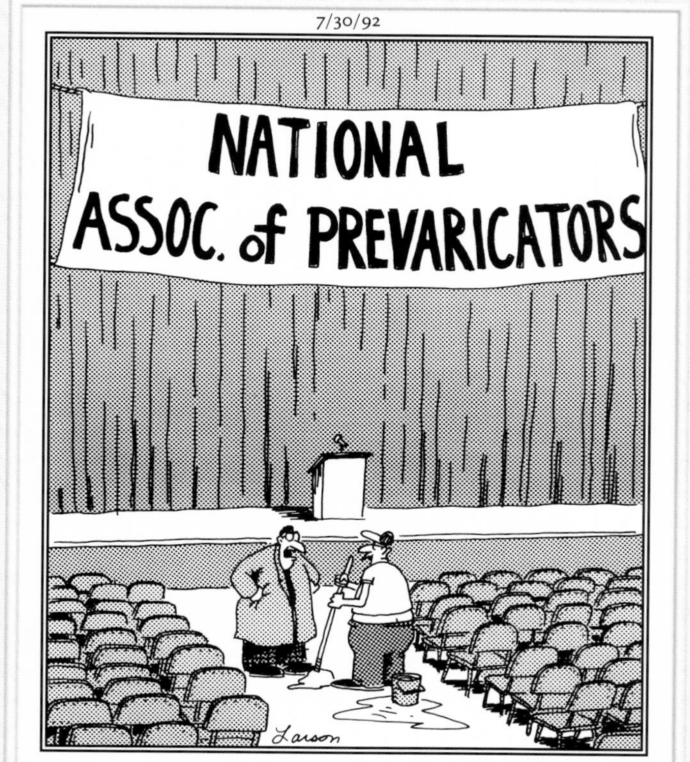
7/30/92
NATIONAL ASSOC. of PREVARICATORS
Larson

"Yesterday? I was told the meeting was *today!*"

8/4/92

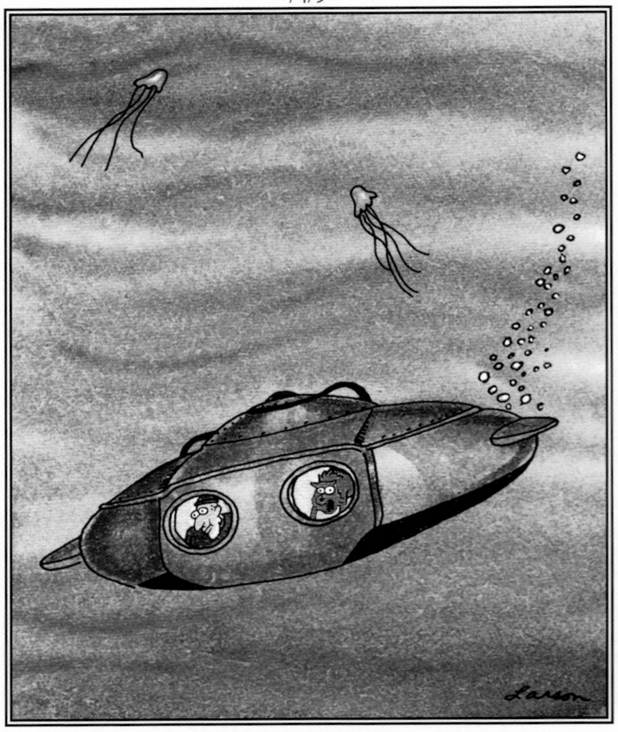

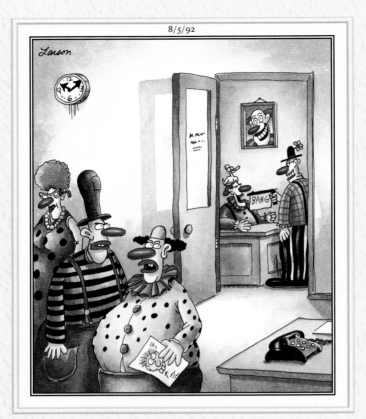

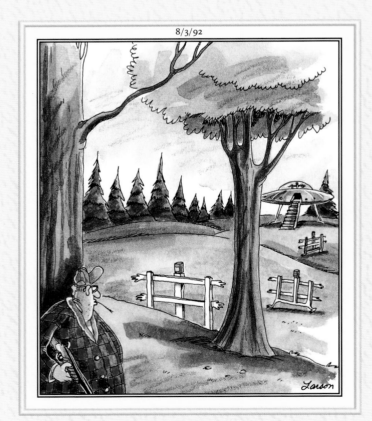

The living hell of Maurice, Jacques Cousteau's cat

8/5/92

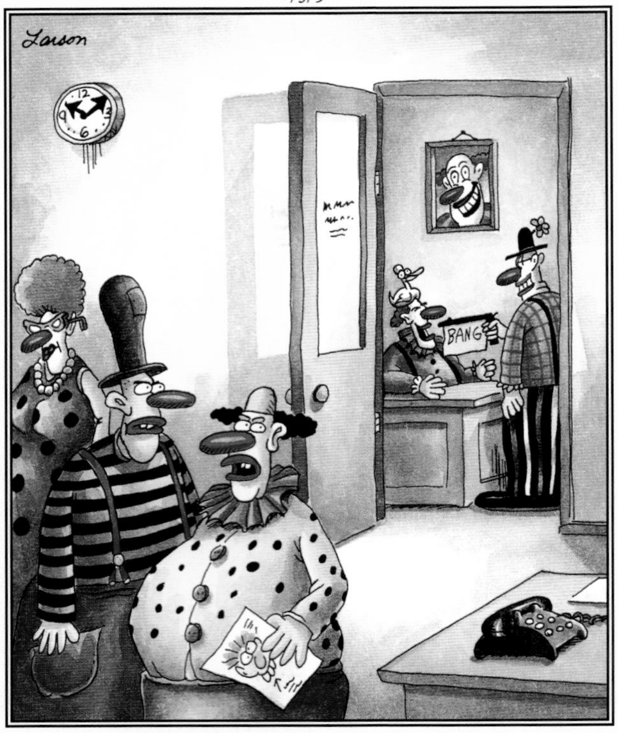
BANG

"Well, there goes Binky with the boss again. ... What a red-noser!"

8/3/92

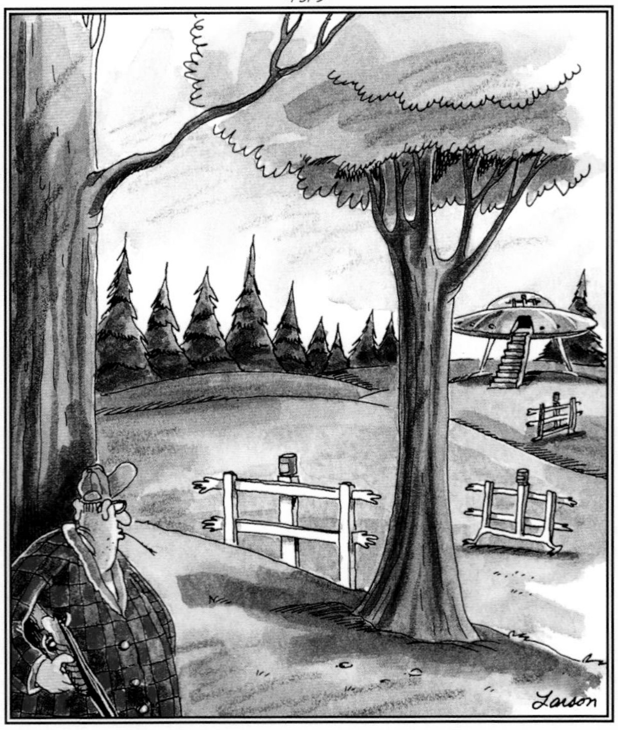

The Zeonions came with the answers to many secrets of the universe. Vern, regrettably, came with thick glasses and his deer rifle.

8/6/92

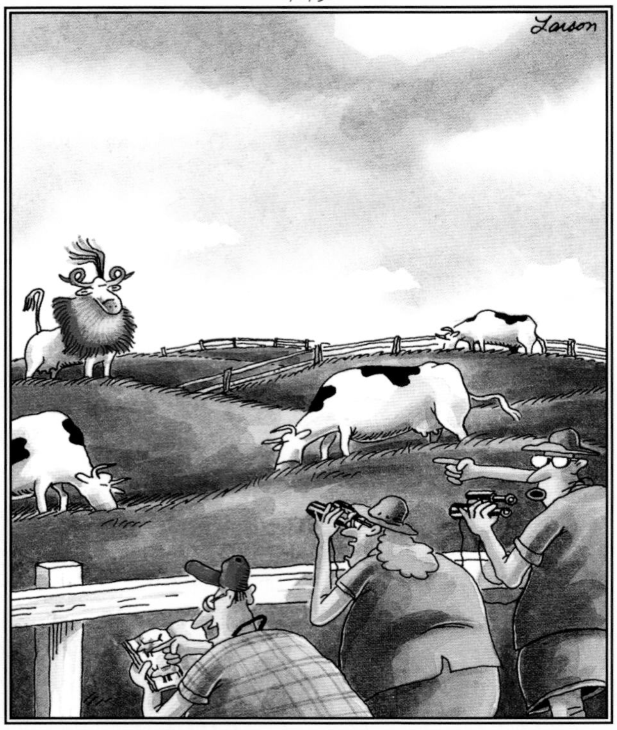

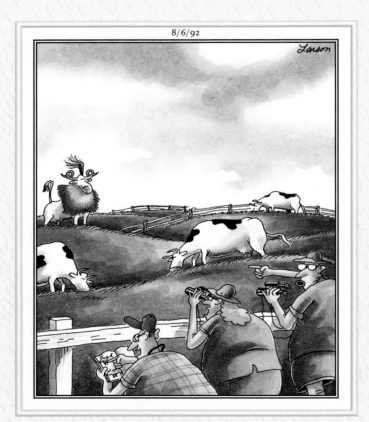

And then the bovine watchers were given a real treat. On a small knoll, in full splendor, there suddenly appeared a Guatemalan cow of paradise.

8/10/92

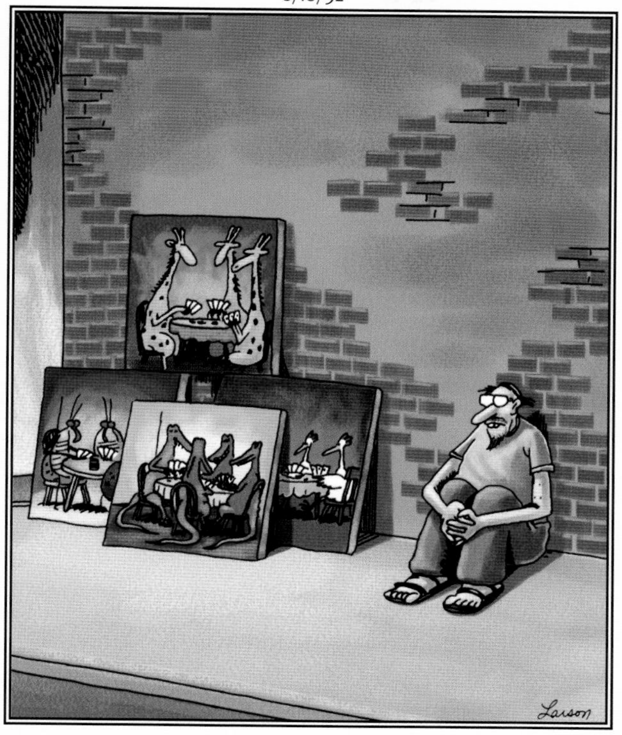

Long before his rise to fame, artist Gus Nickerson experimented with many variations on a single theme—until that fateful day when a friend said, "Gus ... have you tried *dogs* playing poker?"

8/11/92

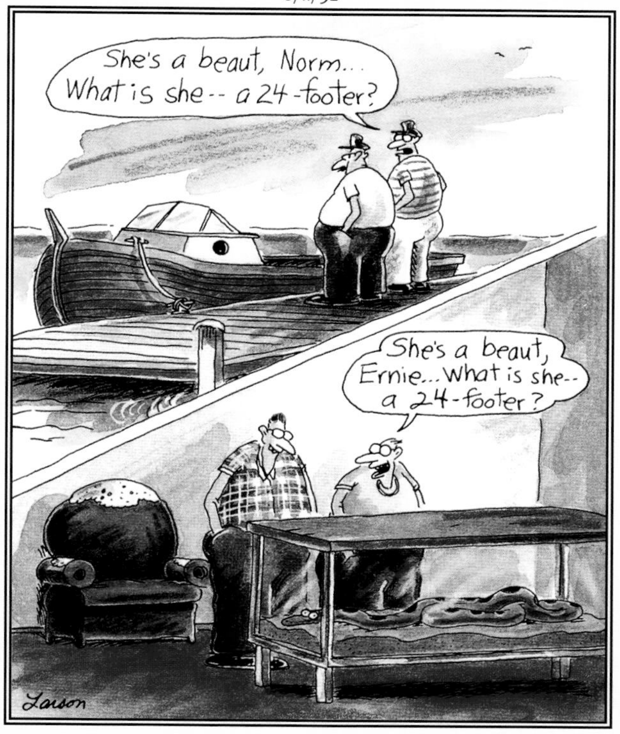
She's a beaut, Norm... What is she-- a 24-footer?
She's a beaut, Ernie... What is she-- a 24-footer?

Where the respective worlds of boating and herpetology converge.

8/12/92

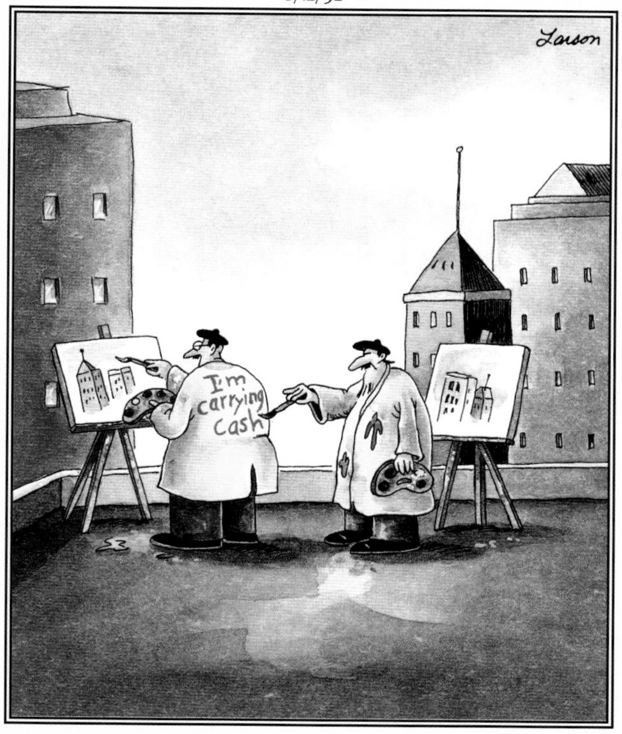
I'm carrying cash

8/13/92

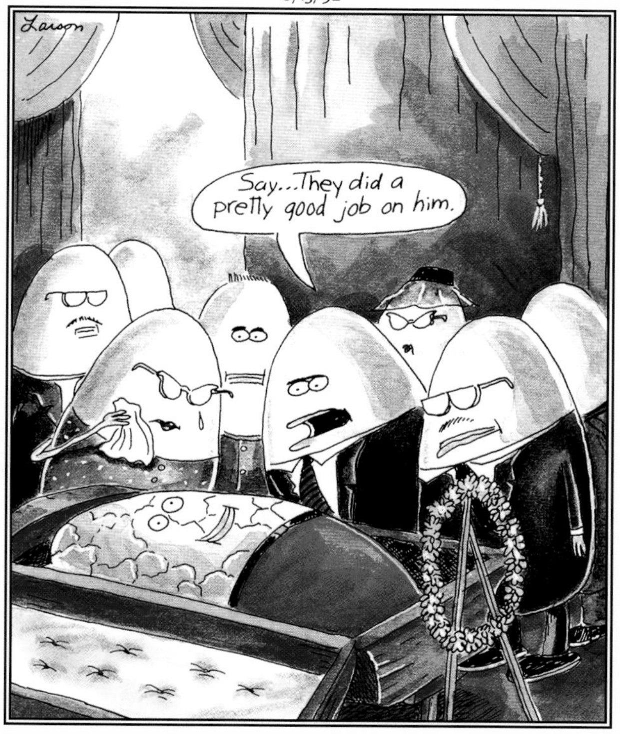
Say...They did a pretty good job on him.

At Humpty's funeral

8/7/92

Offensive quotient = 3x-yn in midwest states
42 hate letters predicted
OK This should be hilarious.
Snake radius must not exceed
move woman 4 mm. right
12 flowers on dress
9 cross-hatches
7 snake coils
Larson

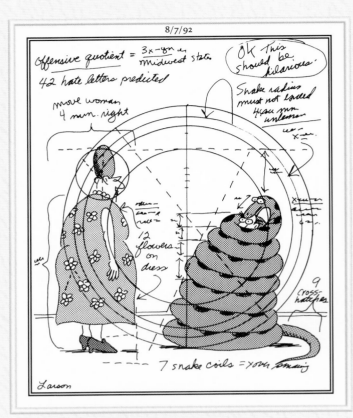

Revealing some of the mathematical computations every cartoonist must know.

8/14/92

My God!.. He's got something green stuck between his teeth.
Larson

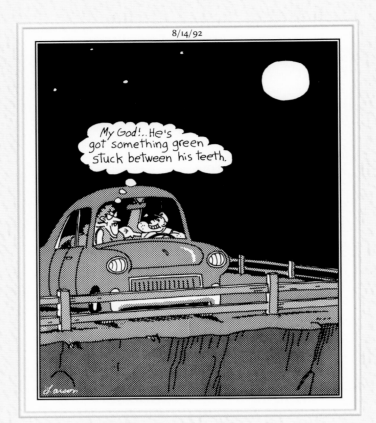

Popeye on the dating scene

8/18/92

THE SHARK'S HEAD INN
Larson

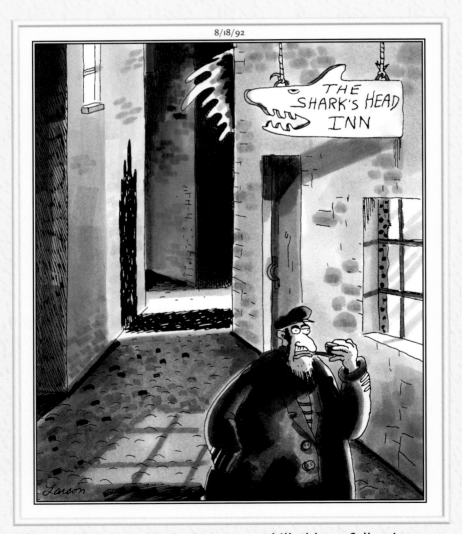

That night, Captain MacIntyre was killed by a following sea.

8/17/92

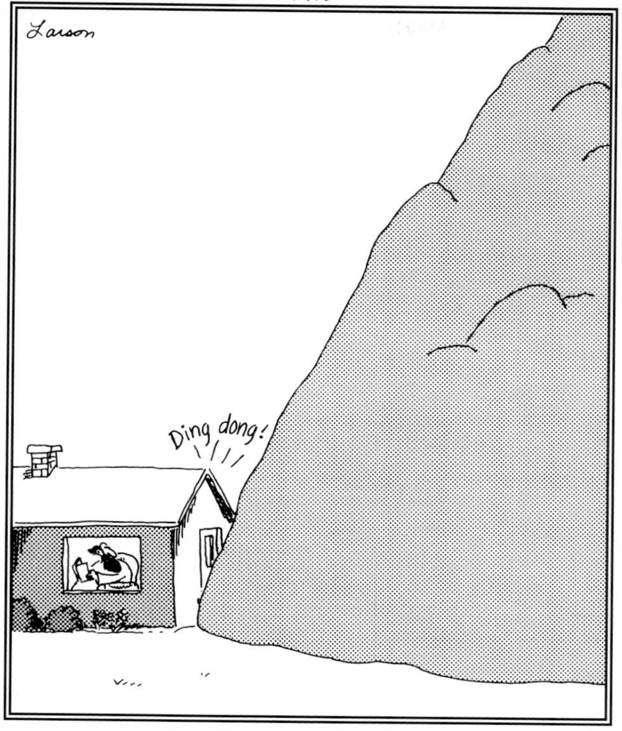
Larson
Ding dong!

Again the doorbell chimed. With his wife out of town, and not expecting any visitors, Mohammed began to grow uneasy.

8/19/92

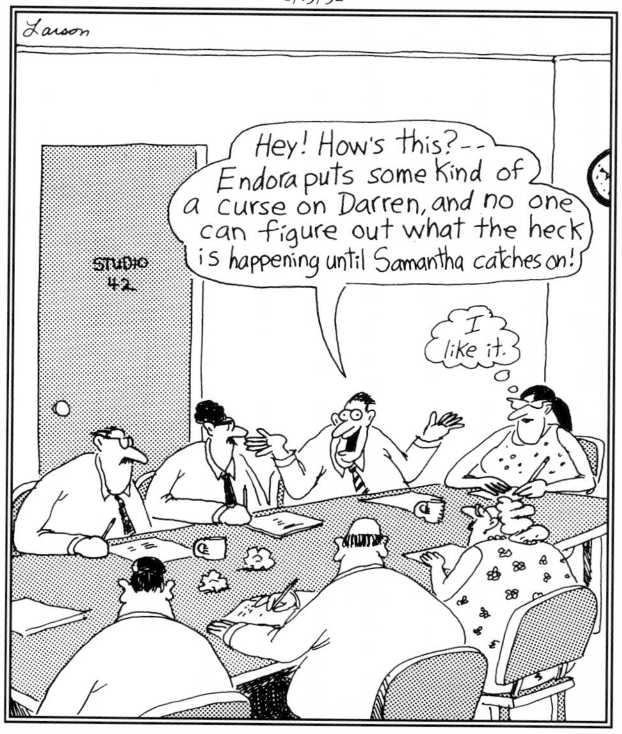
Larson
STUDIO 42
Hey! How's this?-- Endora puts some kind of a curse on Darren, and no one can figure out what the heck is happening until Samantha catches on!
I like it.

The writers for *Bewitched* sit down for their weekly brainstorming session.

8/21/92

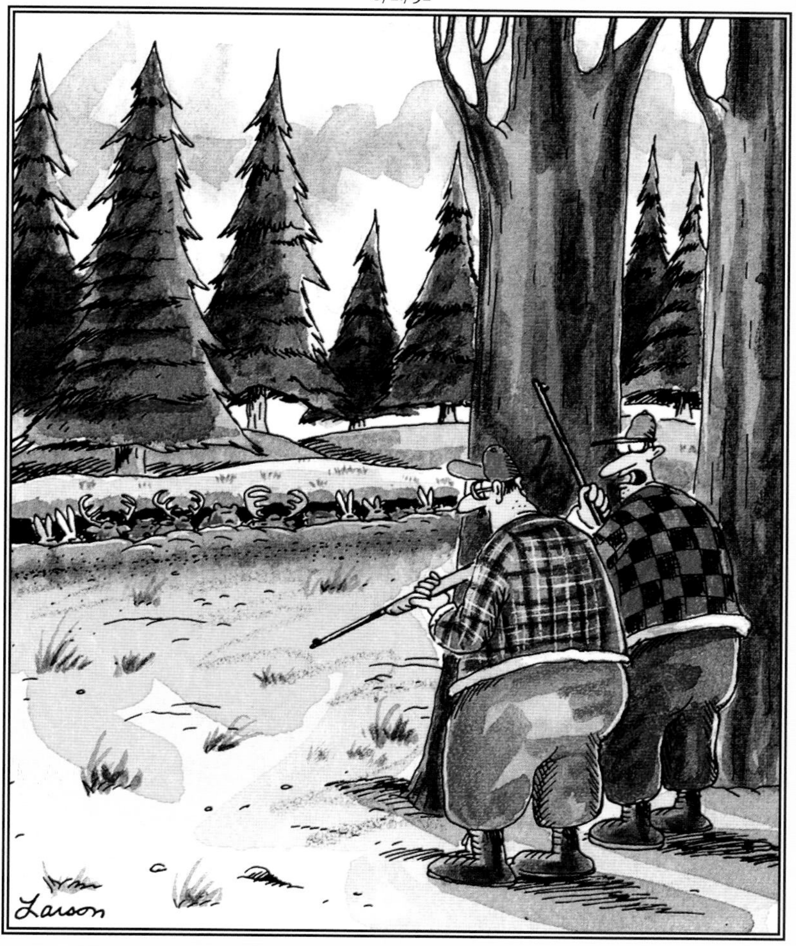
Larson

"I've never seen this before, Roy! ... They've all stopped running!"

8/24/92

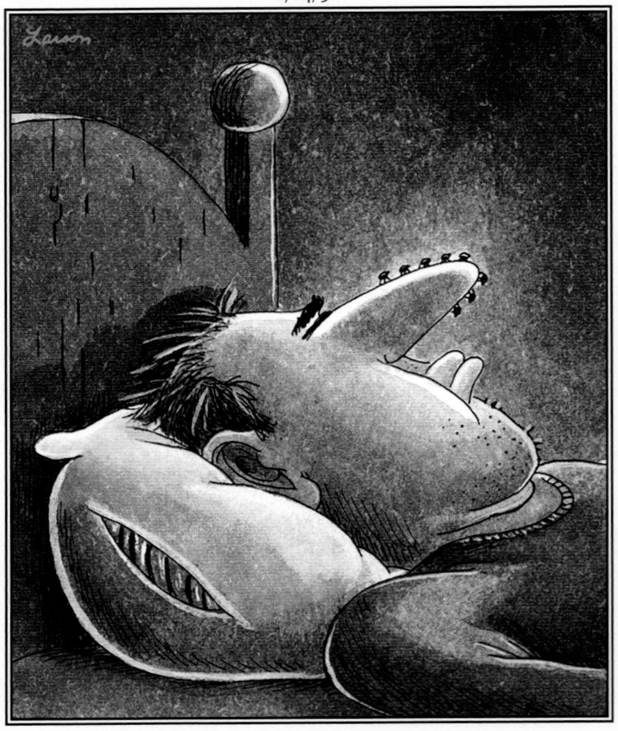

Every August, the fleas would test their endurance in the grueling Tour de Frank.

8/26/92

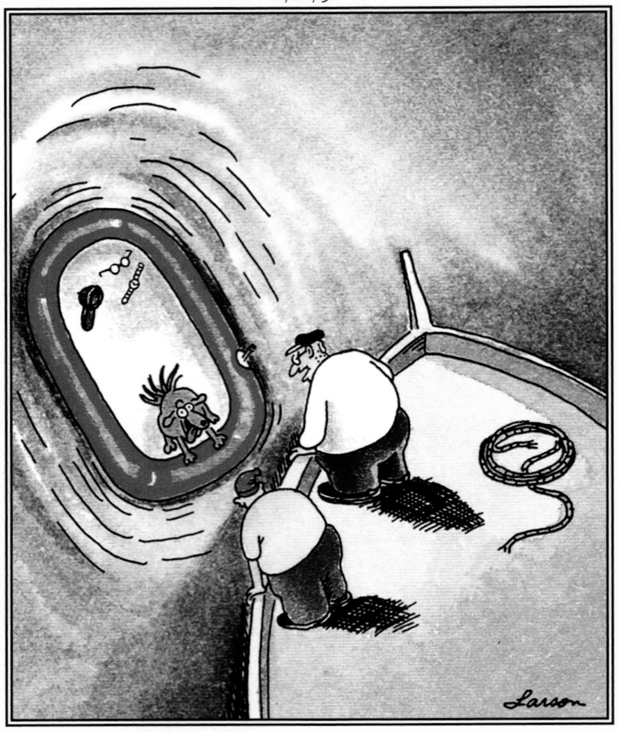

"Hey, boy! How ya doin'? ... Look at him, Dan. Poor guy's been floating out here for days, but he's still just as fat and happy as ever."

8/20/92

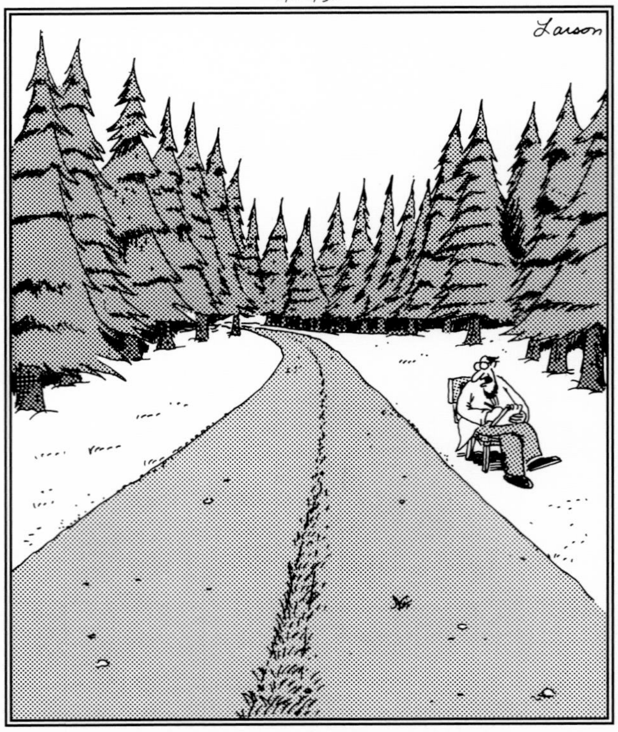

"Now now now. ... You won't be a lonely road forever, you know."

8/25/92

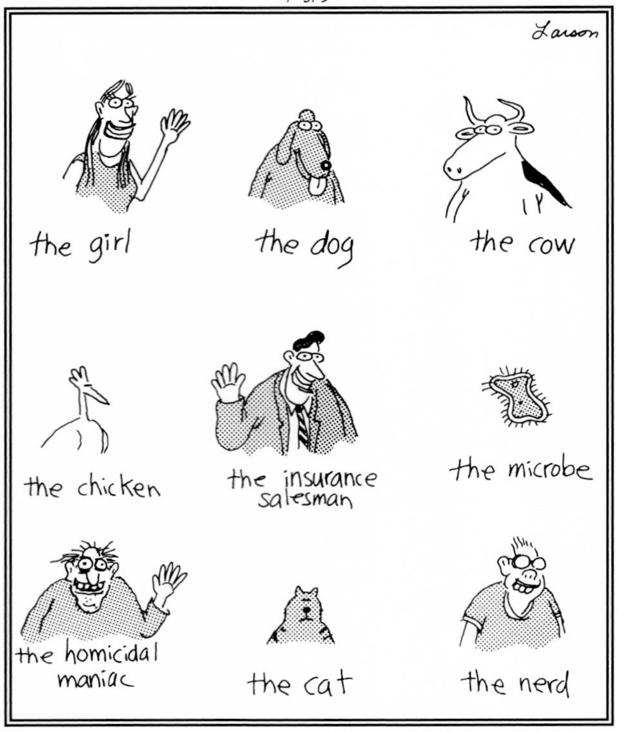
the girl
the dog
the cow
the chicken
the insurance salesman
the microbe
the homicidal maniac
the cat
the nerd

Things from Ipanema

8/27/92

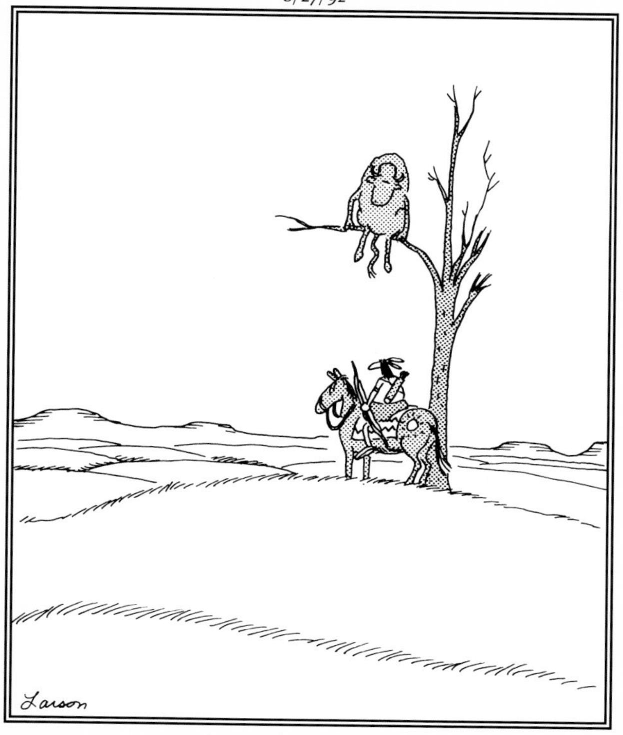
Larson

8/31/92

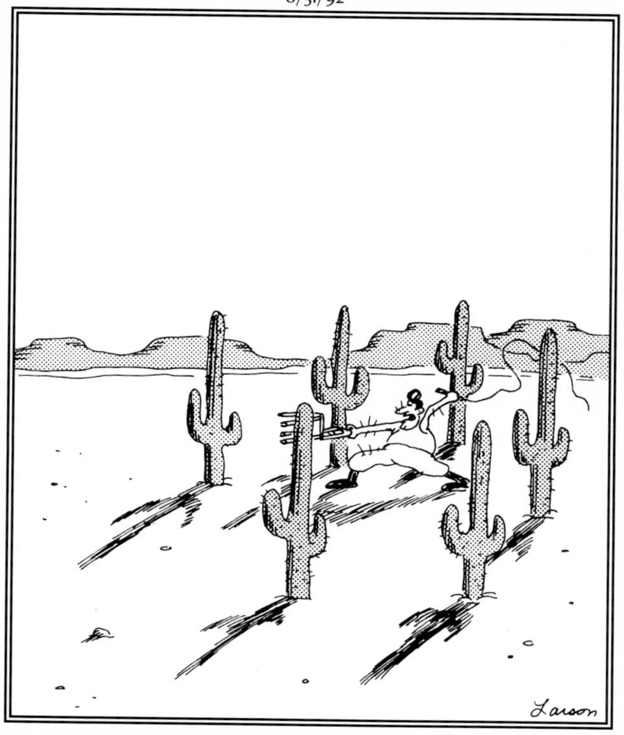
Larson

Andre Lafleur: cactus tamer
(later killed in central Arizona)

8/28/92

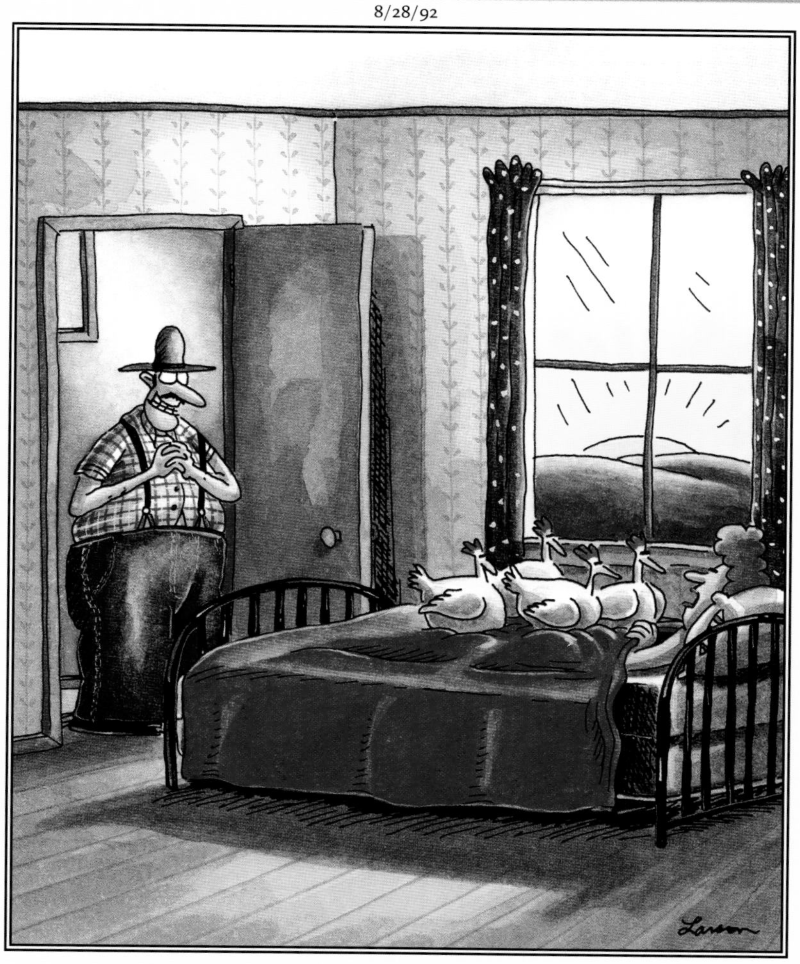
Larson

"This is it, Maurice! I've warned you to keep your hens off me!"

9/1/92

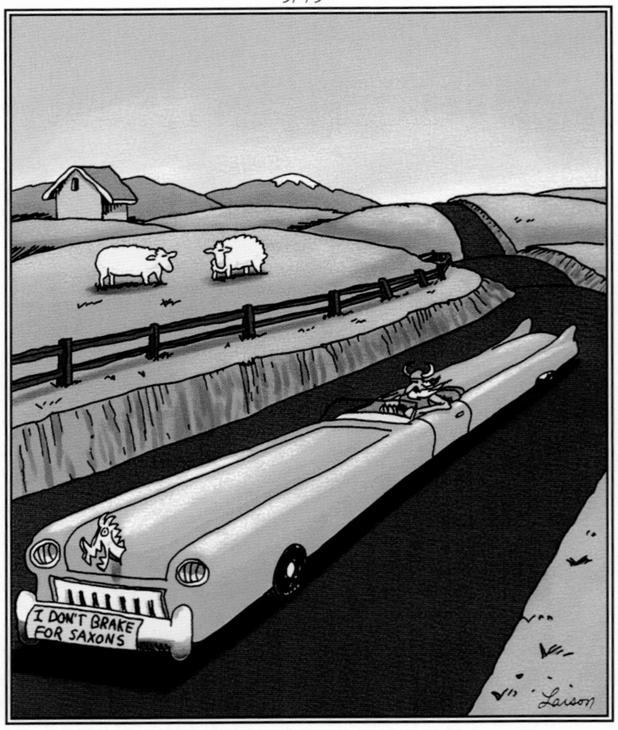
I DON'T BRAKE FOR SAXONS
Larson

The Viking longcar was once the scourge of European roadways.

9/4/92

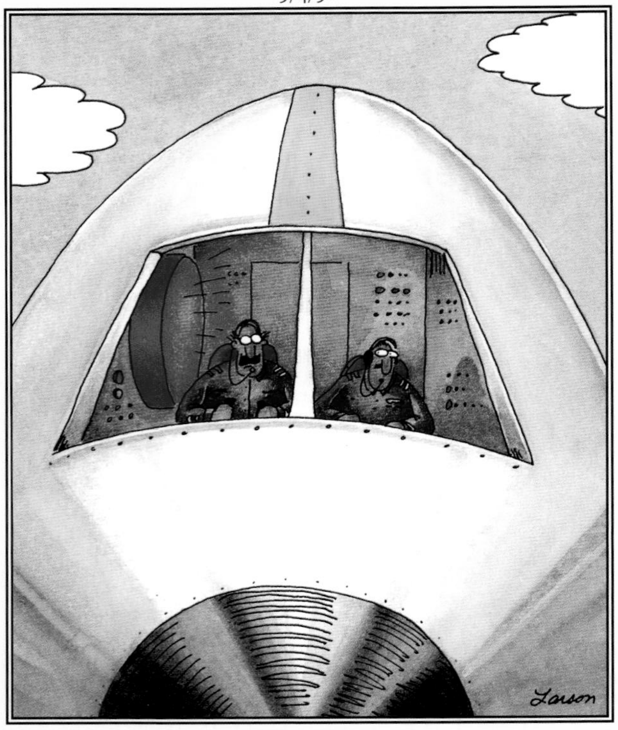
Larson

"I'm afraid we're going to have to head back, folks. ... We've got a warning light on up here, and darn if it isn't the big one."

9/3/92

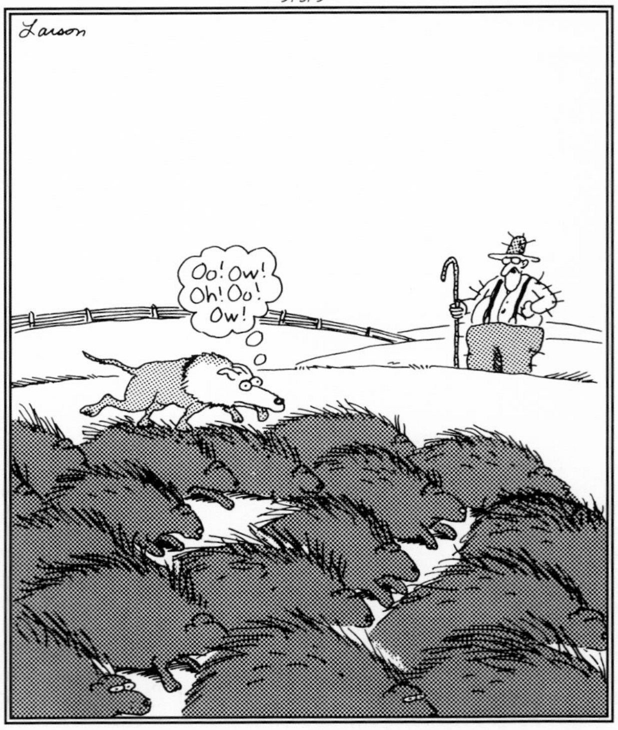
Larson
Oo! Ow! Oh! Oo! Ow!

Indispensable workers on any porcupine ranch, these amazing dogs will sometimes run across the backs of their charges.

9/8/92

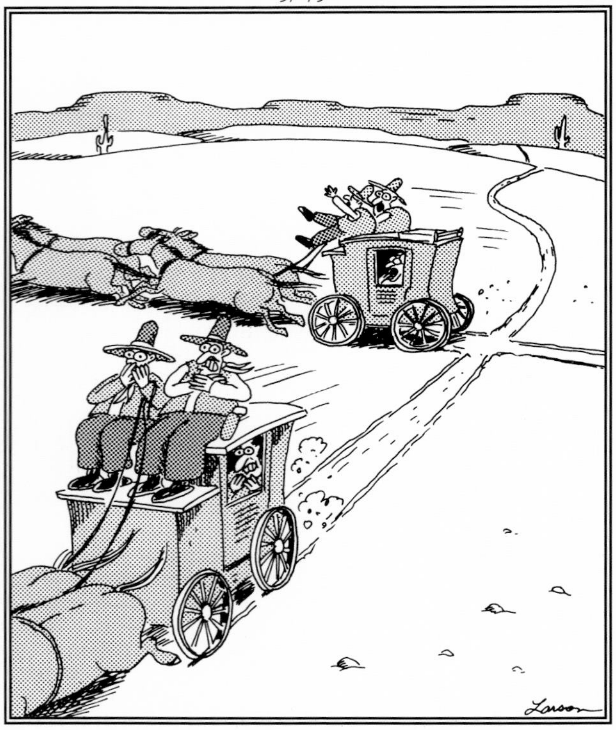
Larson

Near misses of the Old West

9/2/92

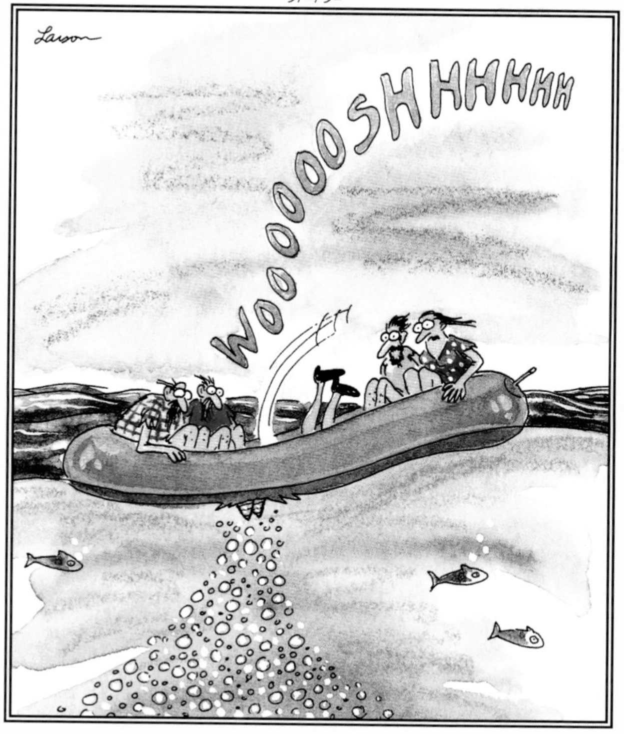
Larson
WOOOOOOOSHHHHHH

To the horror of the lifeboat's other members, Madonna loses her balance and falls on her face.

9/7/92

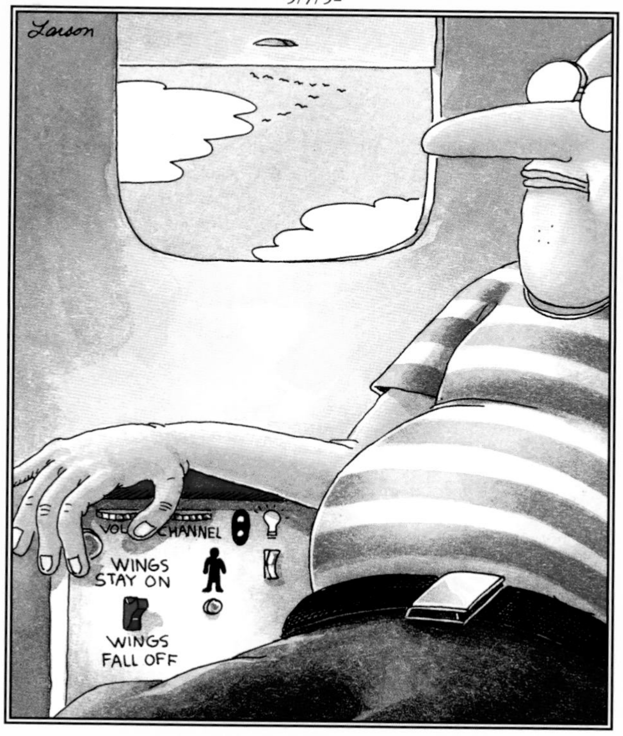
Larson
VOL CHANNEL
WINGS STAY ON
WINGS FALL OFF

Fumbling for his recline button, Ted unwittingly instigates a disaster.

9/16/92

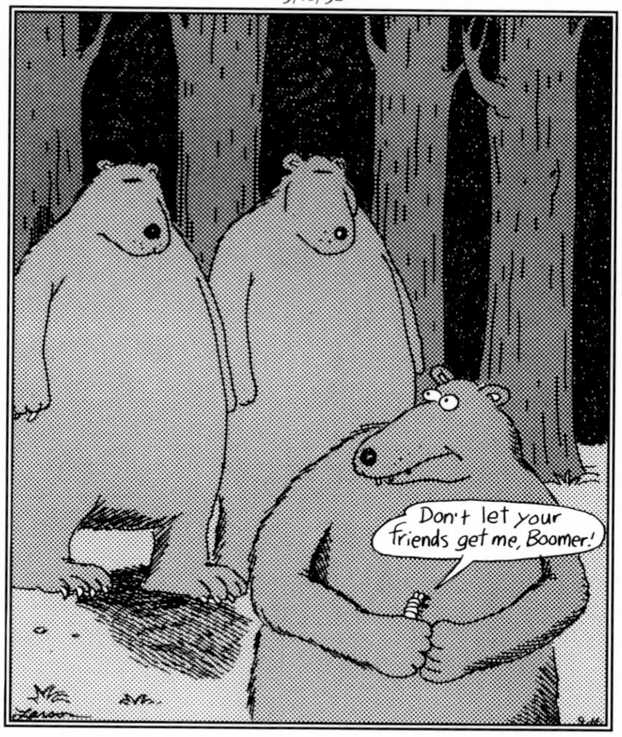
Don't let your friends get me, Boomer!
Larson

Boomer and Doug's relationship was never fully accepted by the other bears, who regarded all grubs in a much more traditional way.

9/17/92

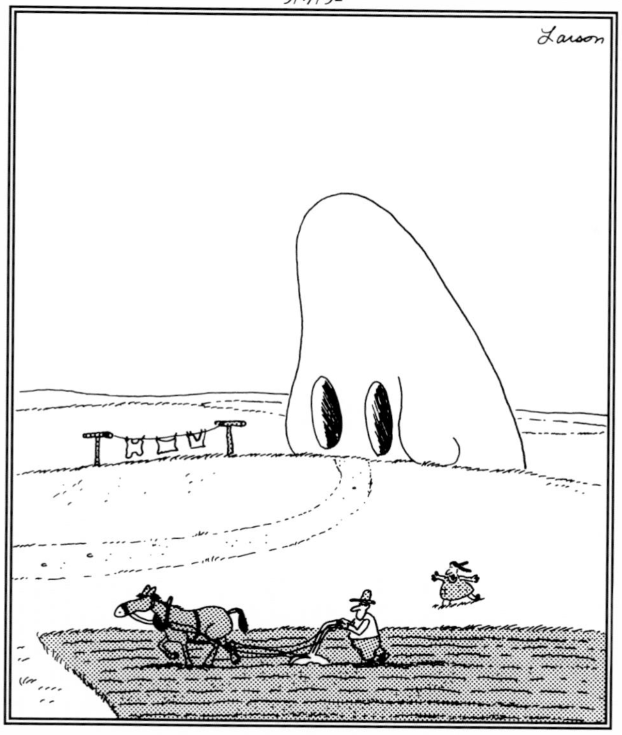
Larson

Laura runs to greet her pa in this scene from *Big Nose on the Prairie*.

9/9/92

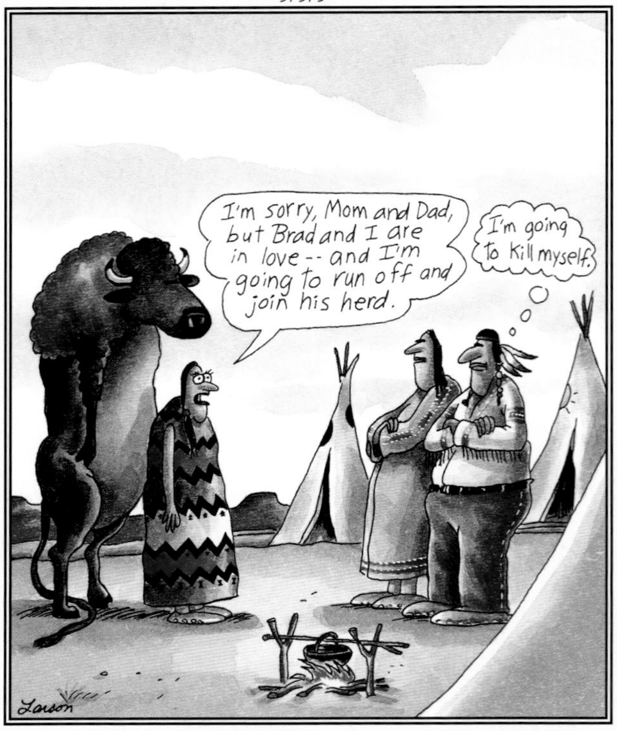
I'm sorry, Mom and Dad, but Brad and I are in love -- and I'm going to run off and join his herd.
I'm going to kill myself.
Larson

Red Cloud's ultimate nightmare

9/14/92

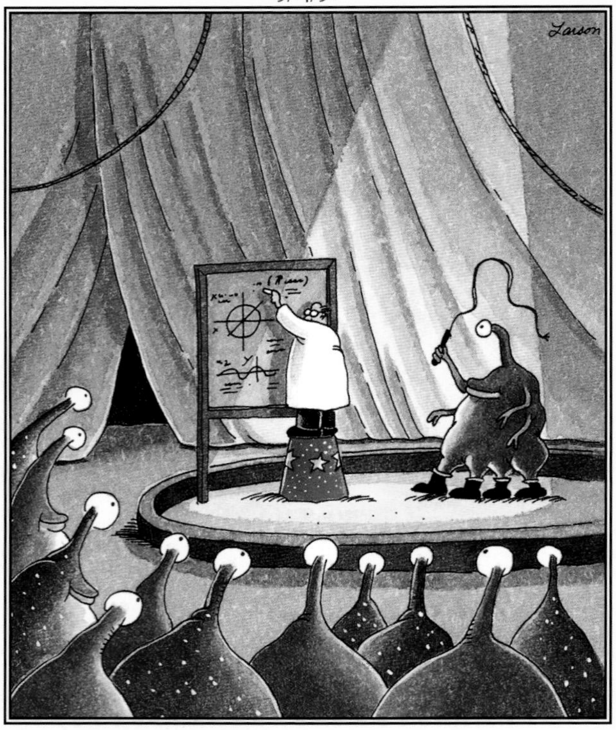
Larson

Abducted by an alien circus company, Professor Doyle is forced to write calculus equations in center ring.

9/10/92

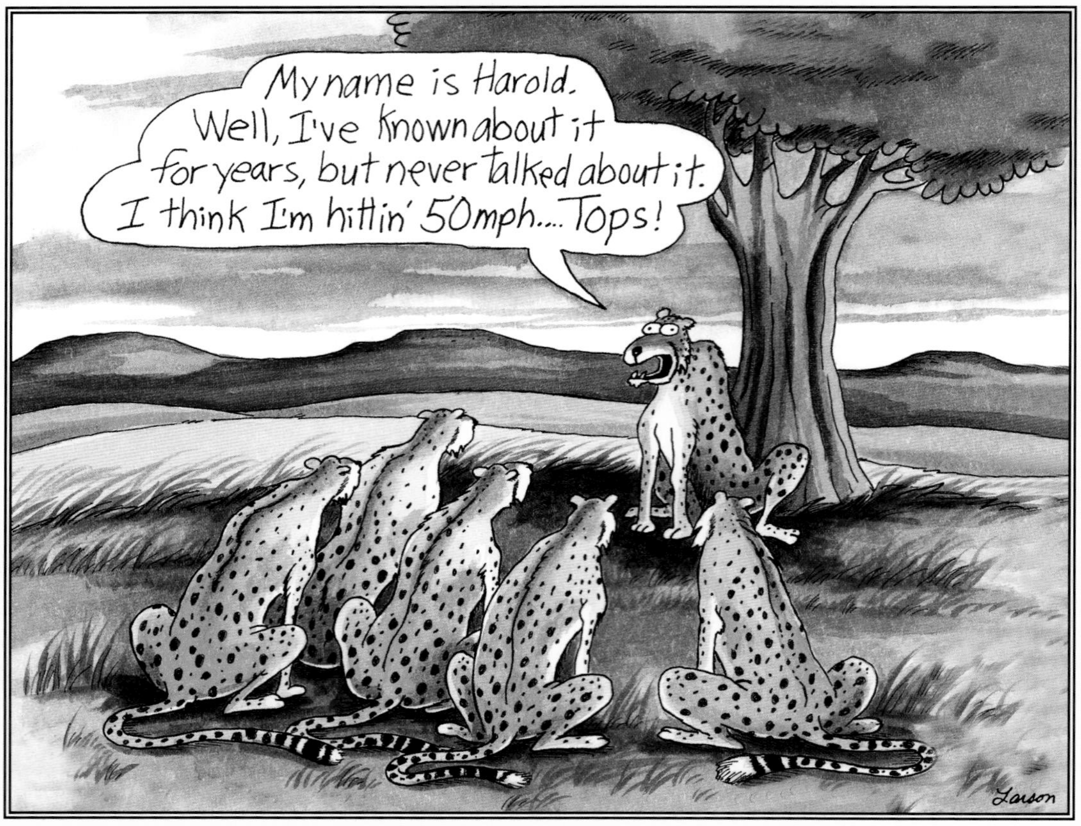
My name is Harold. Well, I've known about it for years, but never talked about it. I think I'm hittin' 50mph.... Tops!
Larson

At Slow Cheetahs Anonymous

9/11/92

Calf delinquents

9/15/92

"Remember, Calloway, this is their biggest and best warrior—so stay alert! When you knock him down, he's gonna come right back at ya!"

9/18/92

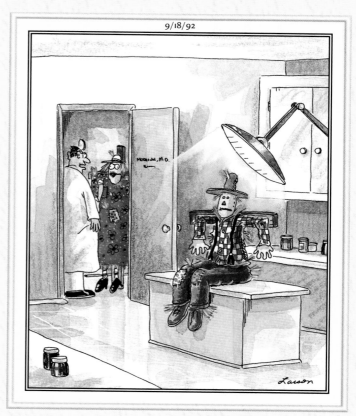

"It's not good, ma'am. ... He's got field mice."

9/23/92

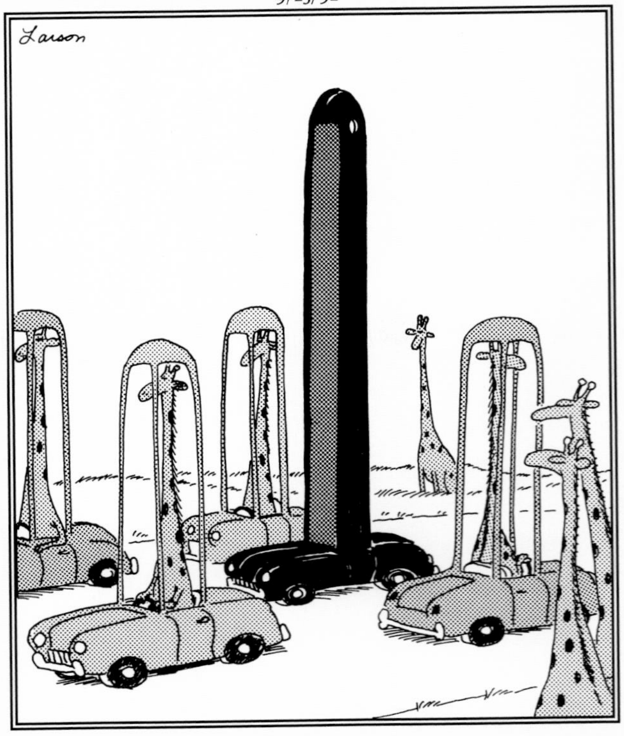

Giraffe limos

9/22/92

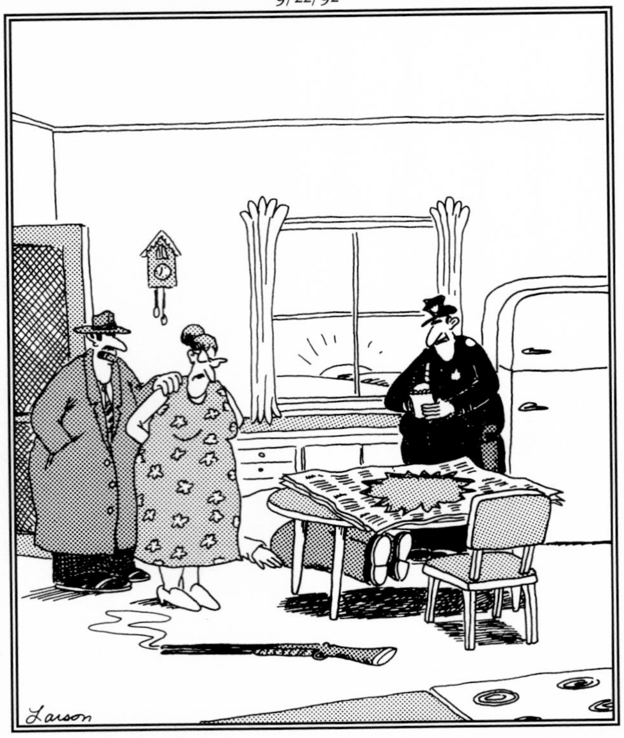

"Okay, ma'am, you said you warned your husband to put the newspaper down or you'd blow him away. ... Did he respond?"

9/21/92

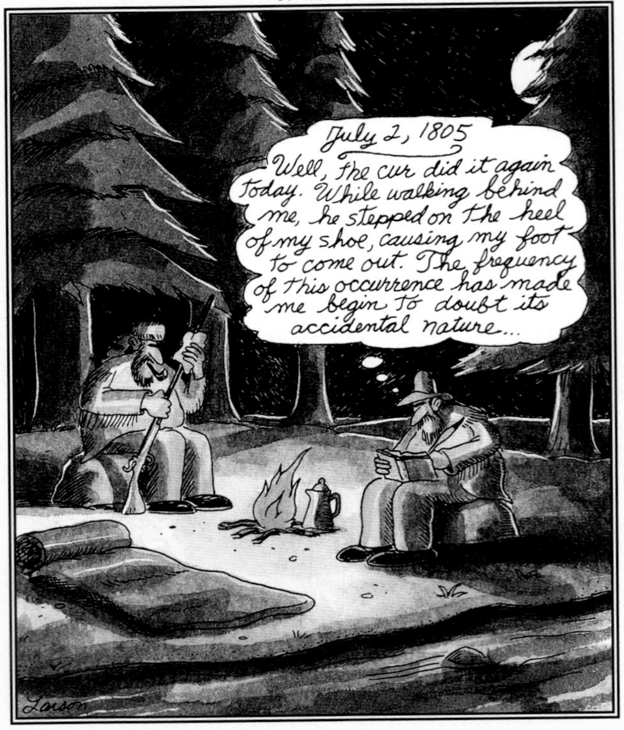
July 2, 1805
Well, the cur did it again today. While walking behind me, he stepped on the heel of my shoe, causing my foot to come out. The frequency of this occurrence has made me begin to doubt its accidental nature...

Tensions mount on the Lewis and Clark expedition.

9/24/92

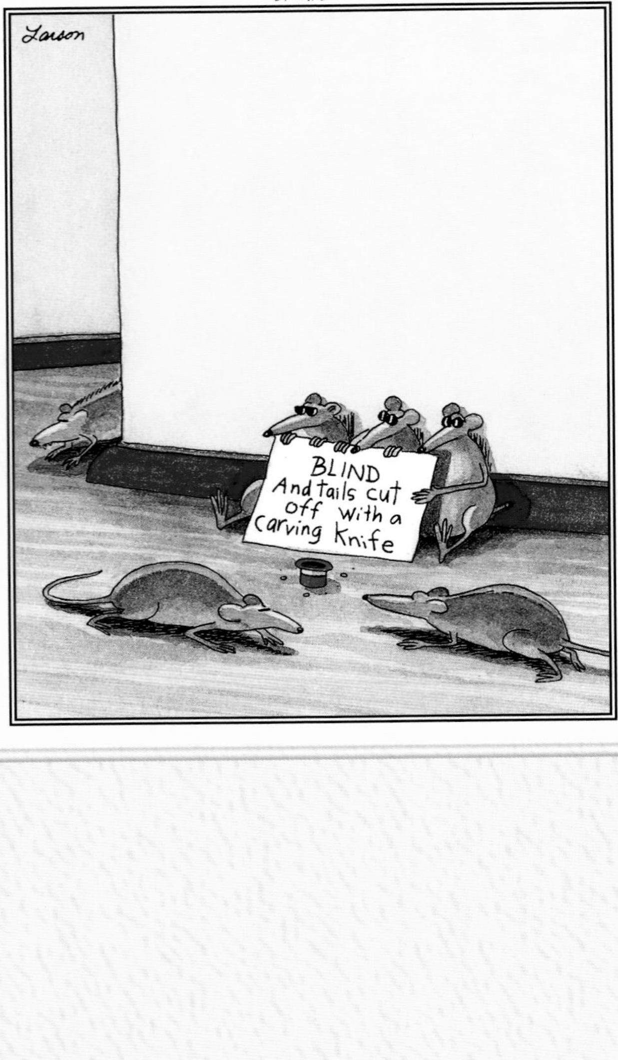
BLIND
And tails cut off with a Carving Knife

"So, Mr. Pig—you built that fire *after* you heard
my client coming down your chimney? ... Did
you know my client is an endangered species,
Mr. Pig, while you yourself are nothing more
than a walking side of ham?"

At the professional stick chaser's training camp

Suddenly, the cops stepped into the clearing,
and the spamshiners knew they were busted.

"Aaaaaaaaaa! It's Sid! ... Someone snuffed him!"

10/2/92

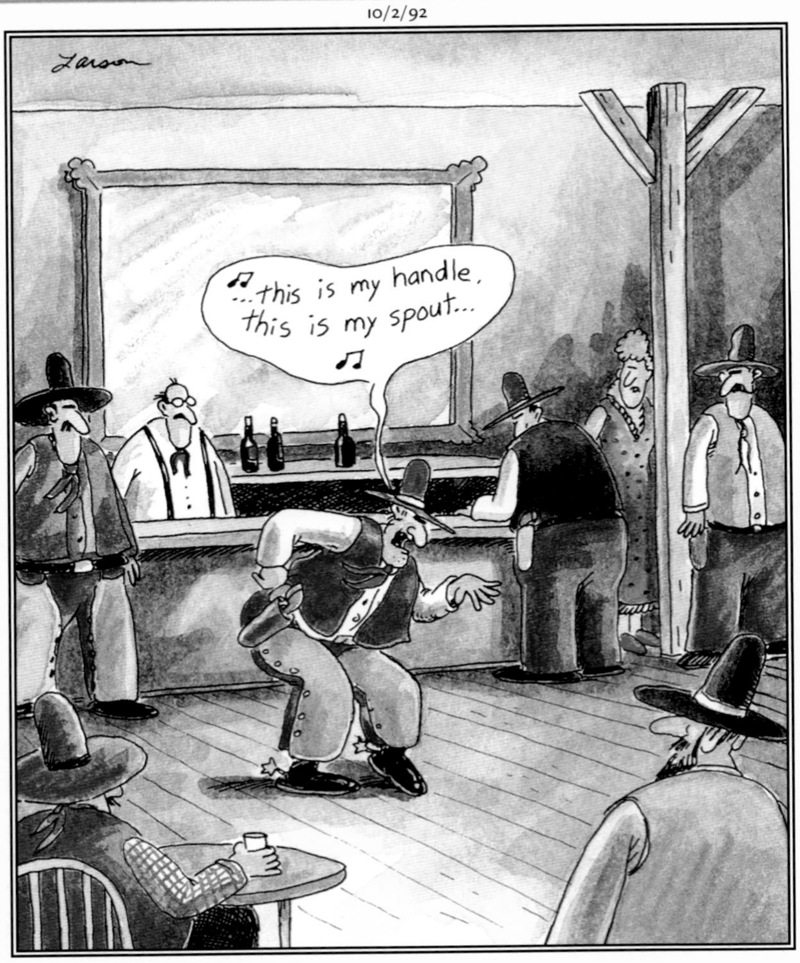
Larson
♫ ...this is my handle,
this is my spout... ♫

It was always a bizarre spectacle, but no one ever, *ever,* ridiculed the Teapot Kid.

10/5/92

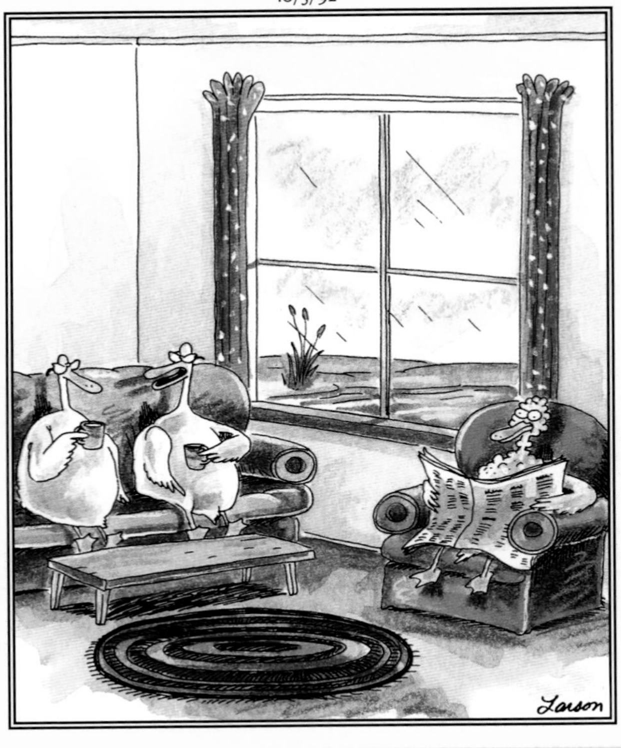
Larson

"Oh, it's just Hank's little cross to bear—
he's allergic to down and that's that."

10/6/92

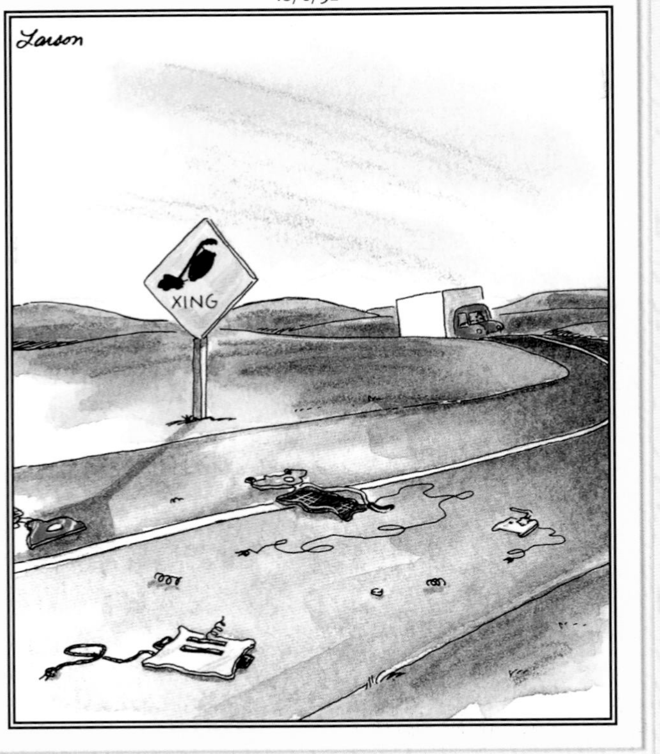
Larson
XING

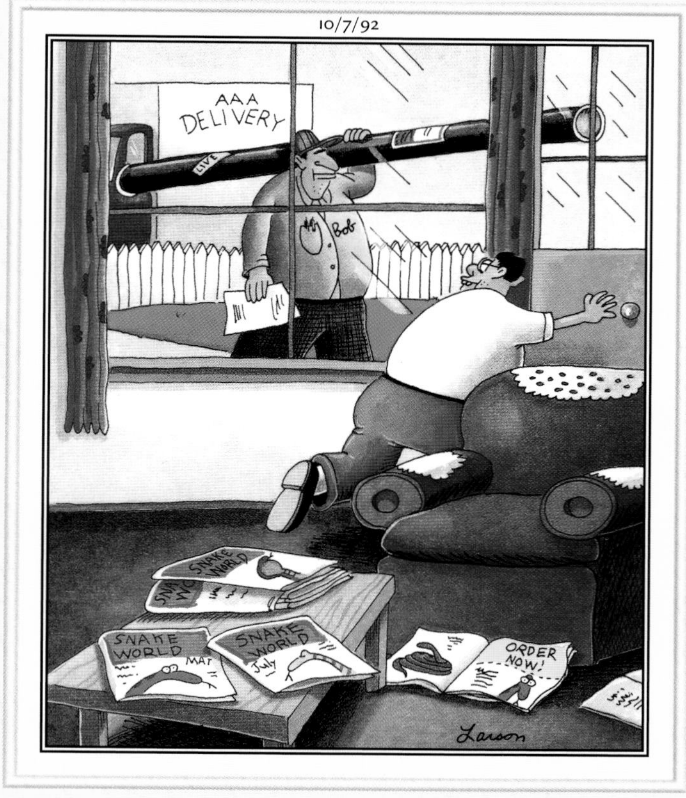
10/7/92
AAA
DELIVERY
SNAKE WORLD
SNAKE WORLD
ORDER NOW!
Larson

A big day for Jimmy

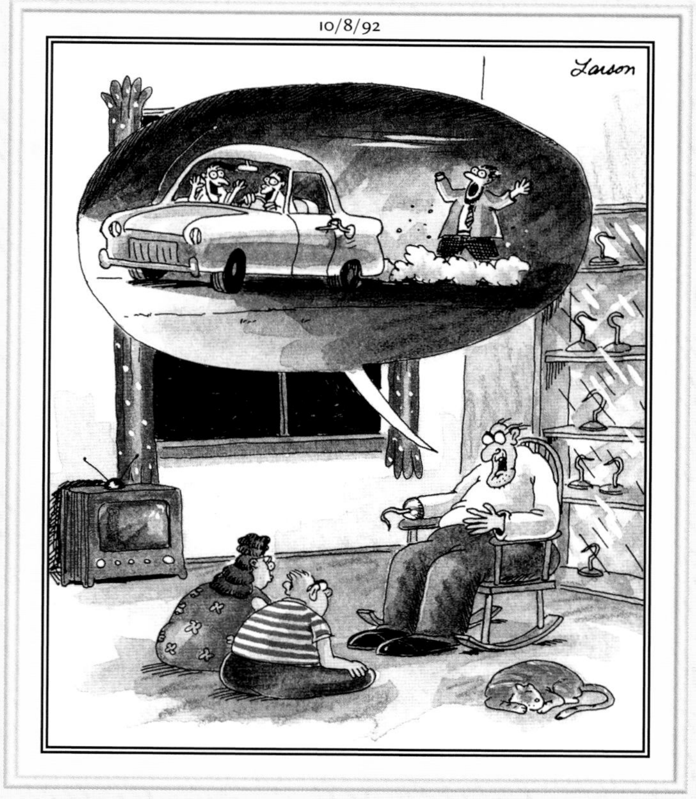
10/8/92
Larson

Years later, Harold Zimmerman, the original "Hookhand" of campfire ghost stories, tells his grandchildren the "Tale of the Two Evil Teenagers."

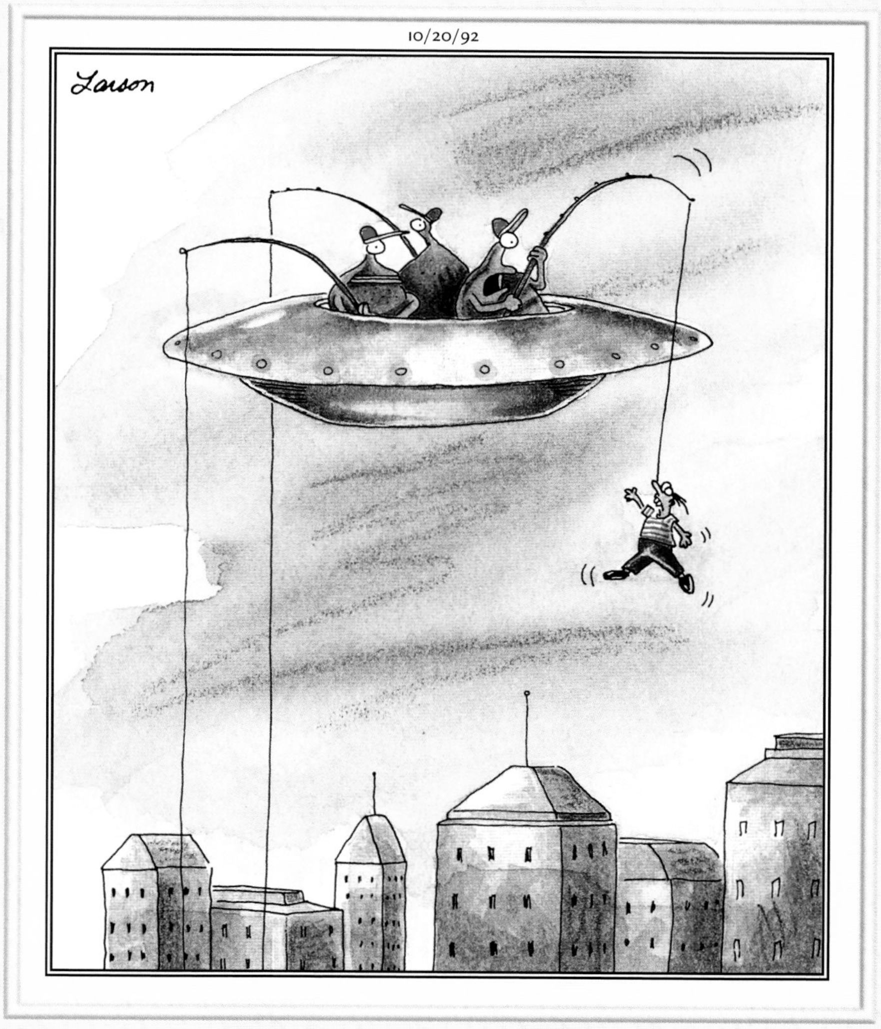
10/20/92
Larson

"Nerd! ... Dang!"

10/1/92

NATIONAL CONFERENCE OF PEOPLE WHO FOLLOW PARANOIACS

EDDIE'S BINOCULARS

HENDERSON'S MASKS & THINGS

ACME BIG NOSE & GLASSES

RALLN'S EXTRA-QUIET SHOES

CARL'S CAMOUFLAGE

10/13/92

"Fools! They made me into a free-range chicken ... and man, I never looked back."

10/12/92

Historical note: For many years, until they became truly nasty, Vikings would plunder, loot, and then egg the houses of coastal villagers.

10/14/92

Explorers from another cartoon are captured and tortured by the savage Farsidians.

10/15/92

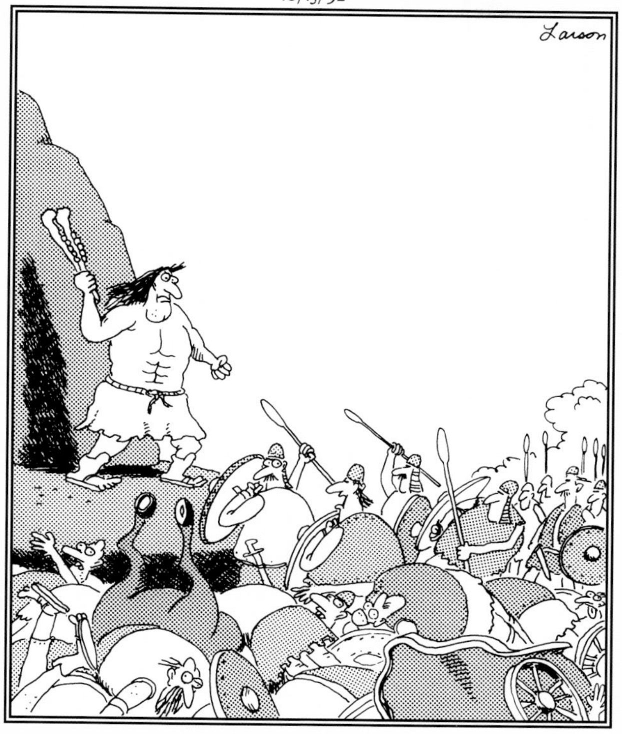

"Cornelius! I've been watching him! ... Beware of the jawbone!"

10/16/92

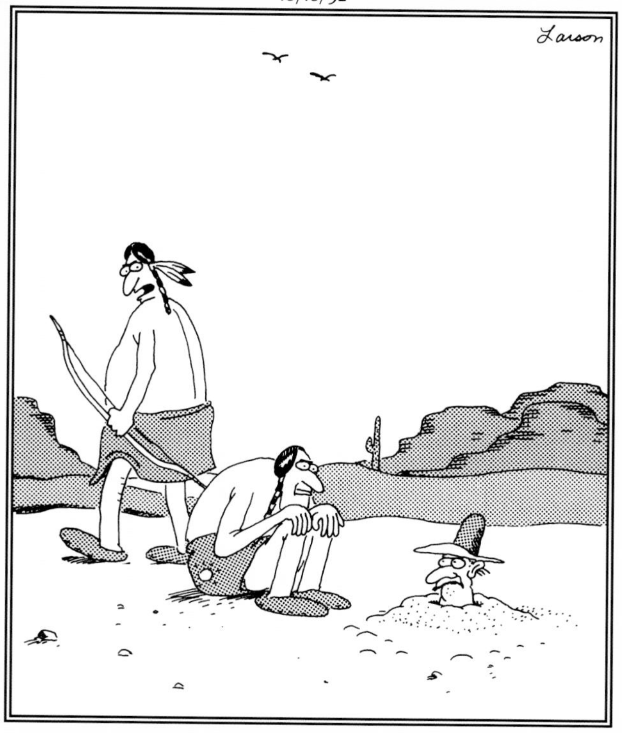

"Little Bear! A watched head never gets eaten by ants."

10/19/92

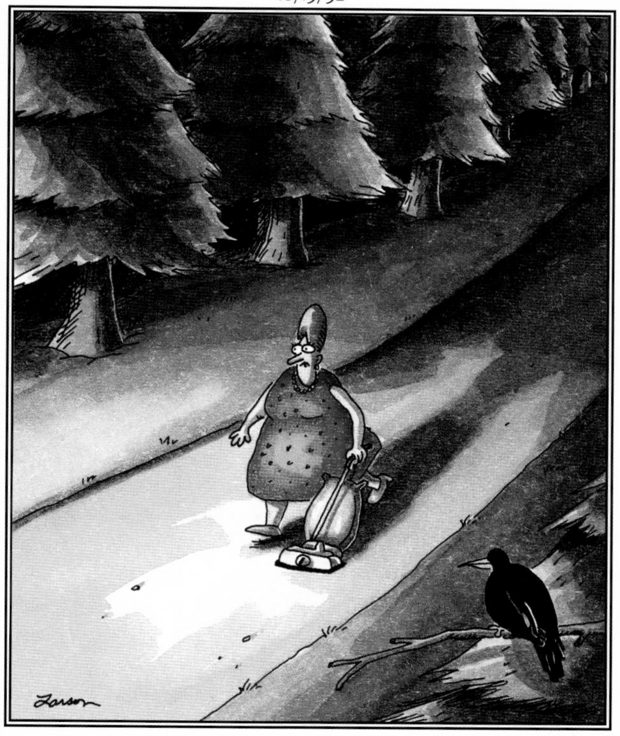

The woods were dark and foreboding, and Alice sensed that sinister eyes were watching her every step. Worst of all, she knew that Nature abhorred a vacuum.

10/22/92

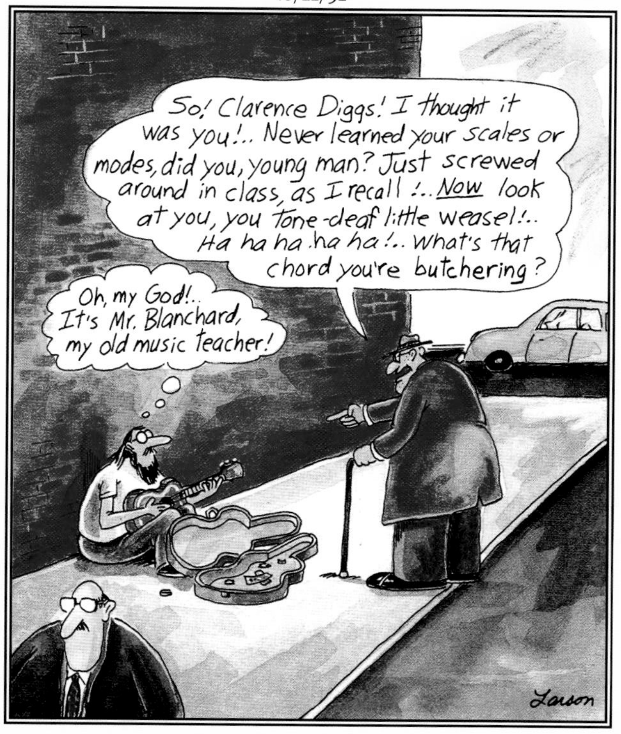
So! Clarence Diggs! I thought it was you!.. Never learned your scales or modes, did you, young man? Just screwed around in class, as I recall!.. Now look at you, you tone-deaf little weasel!.. Ha ha ha ha ha!.. What's that chord you're butchering?
Oh, my God!.. It's Mr. Blanchard, my old music teacher!

10/9/92

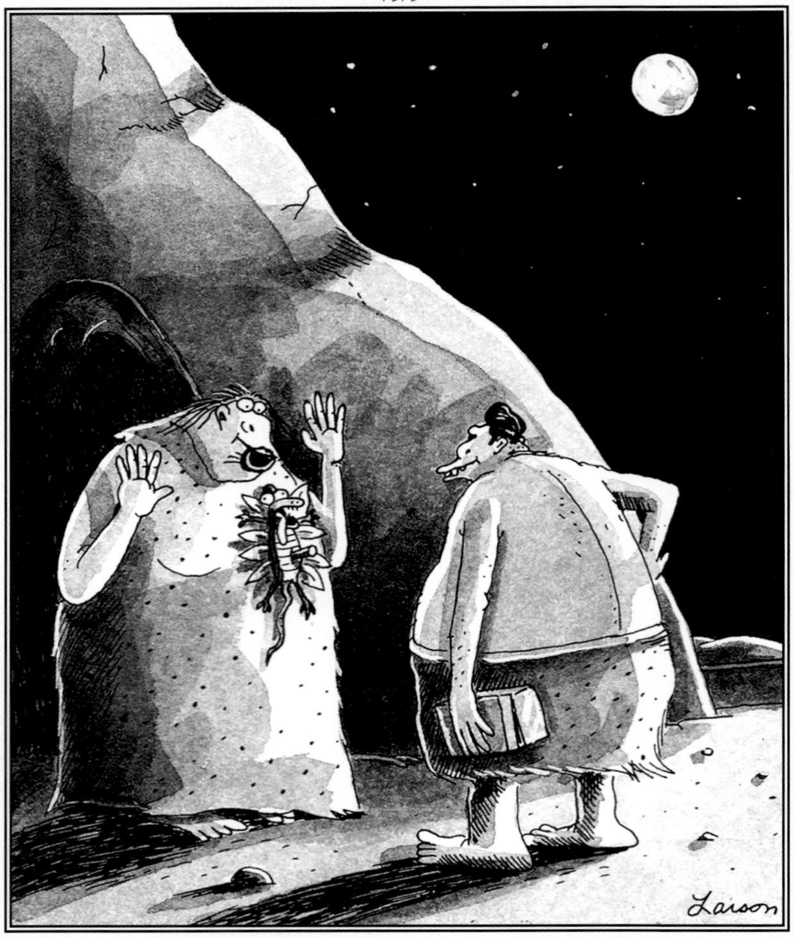
Larson

Early corsages

10/23/92

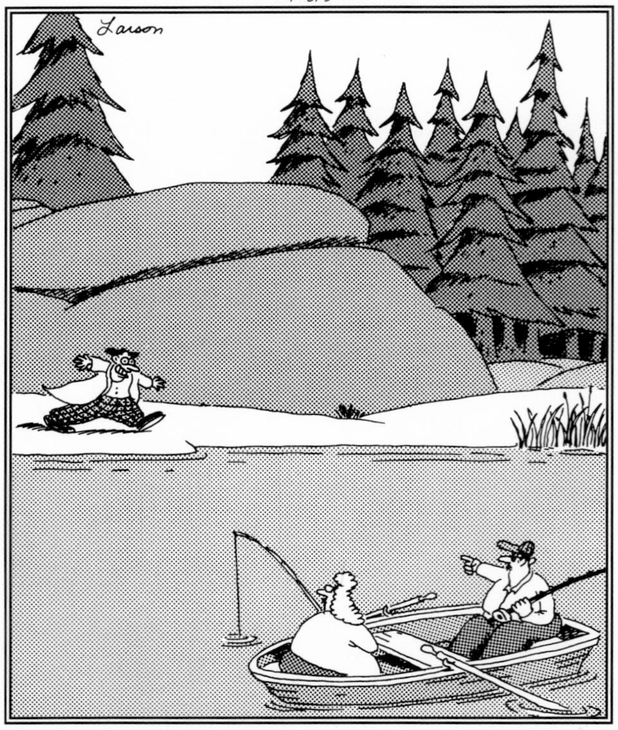
Larson

Suddenly, there he was, running along the far shore right in front of Bob and Vera, who would always remember they once saw the legendary "Character of the Lake."

10/21/92

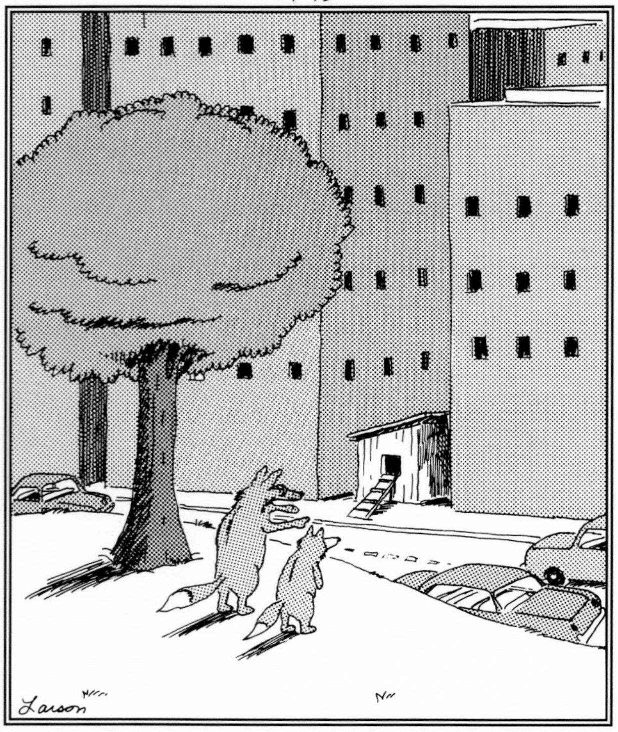
Larson

"Well, I'll be! It's still there! The henhouse I used to watch as a kid!"

Editor's note:
Gary leaves for a one-month vacation.

11/25/92

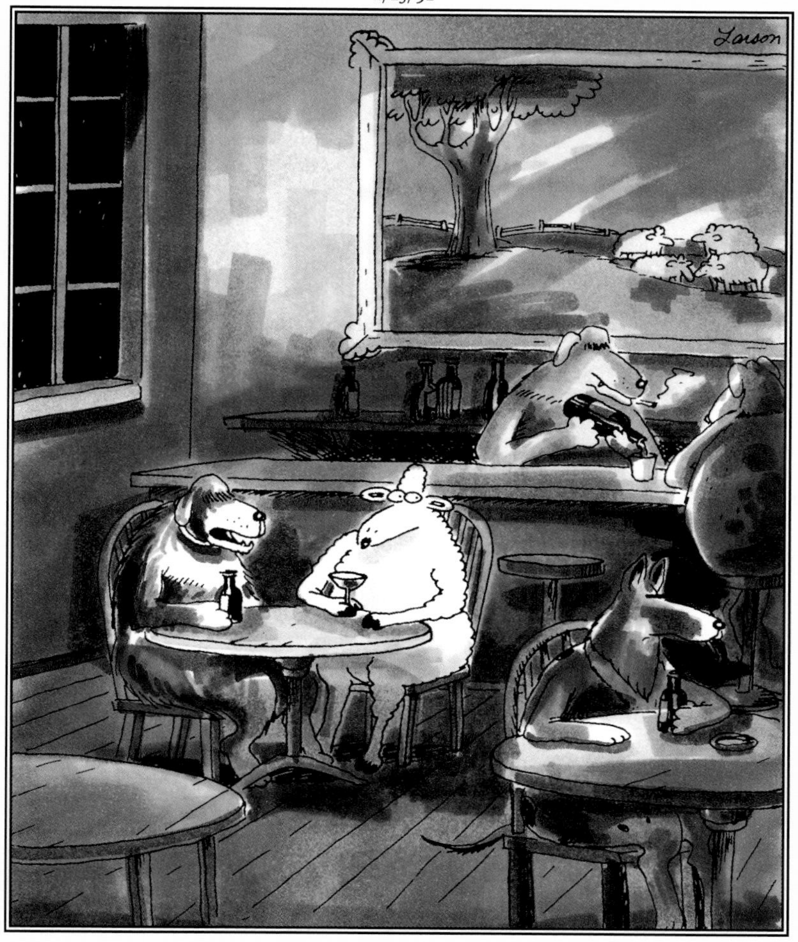
Larson

"Confession time, Mona—I've lead you astray."

11/23/92

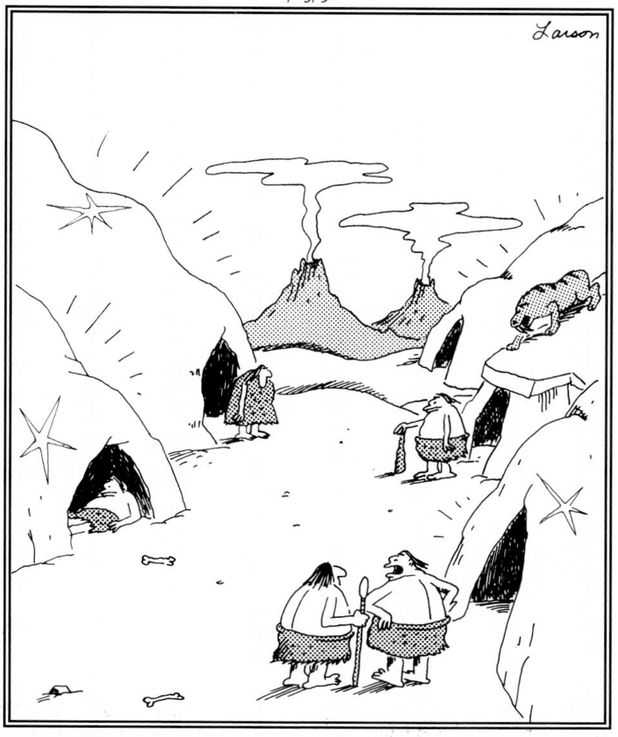
Larson

"One good thing about living in this age—
all the caves are brand-new."

11/24/92

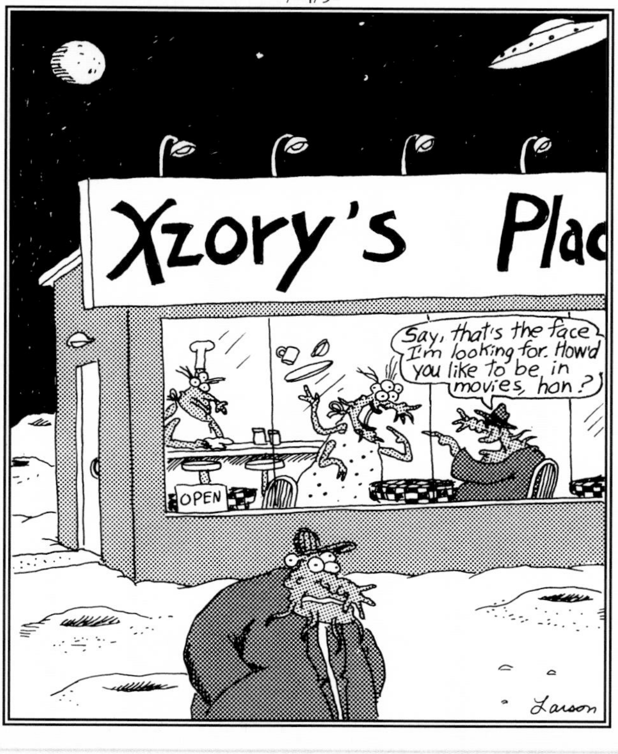
Xzory's Plac
Say, that's the face I'm looking for. How'd you like to be in movies, hon?
OPEN
Larson

Alien corner cafes, where sometimes
dreams do come true.

11/26/92

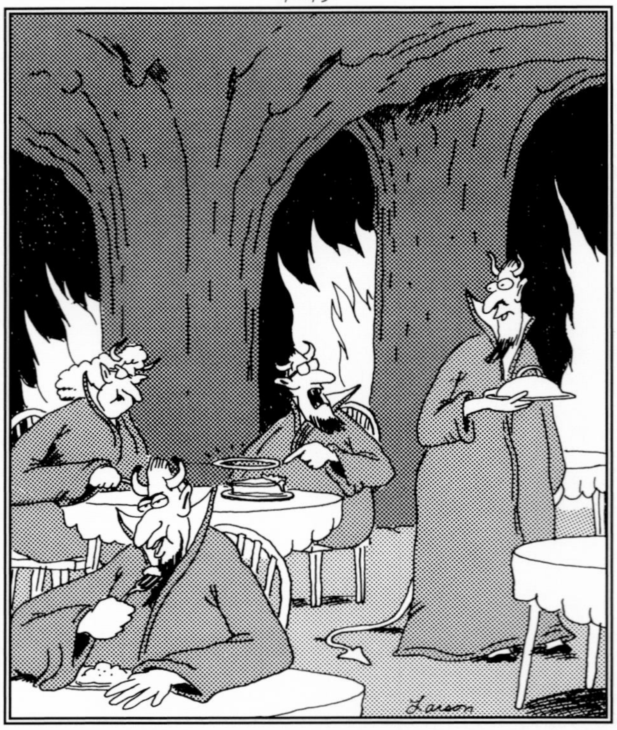
Larson

"What the? ... Waiter! This looks like a little slice of heaven!"

11/27/92

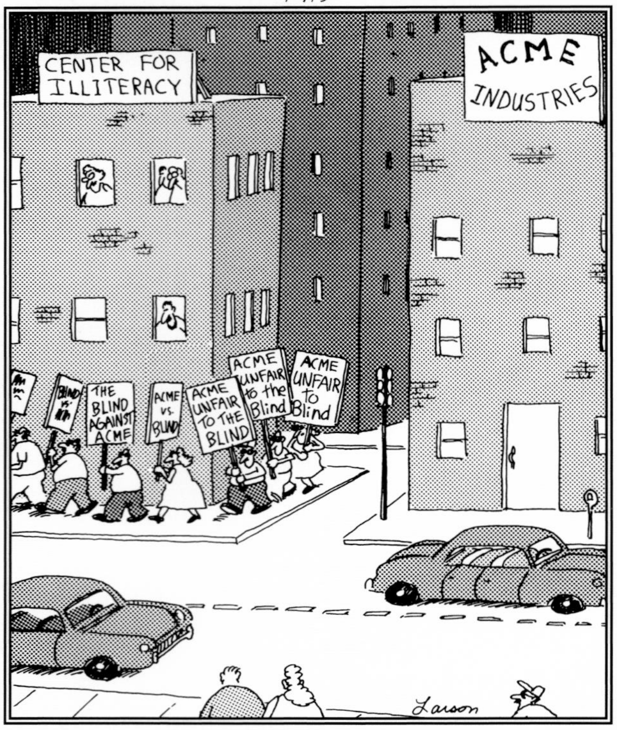
CENTER FOR ILLITERACY
ACME INDUSTRIES
THE BLIND AGAINST ACME
ACME vs. BLIND
ACME UNFAIR TO THE BLIND
ACME UNFAIR to the Blind
ACME UNFAIR to Blind
Larson

For several hours, confusion reigned.

11/30/92

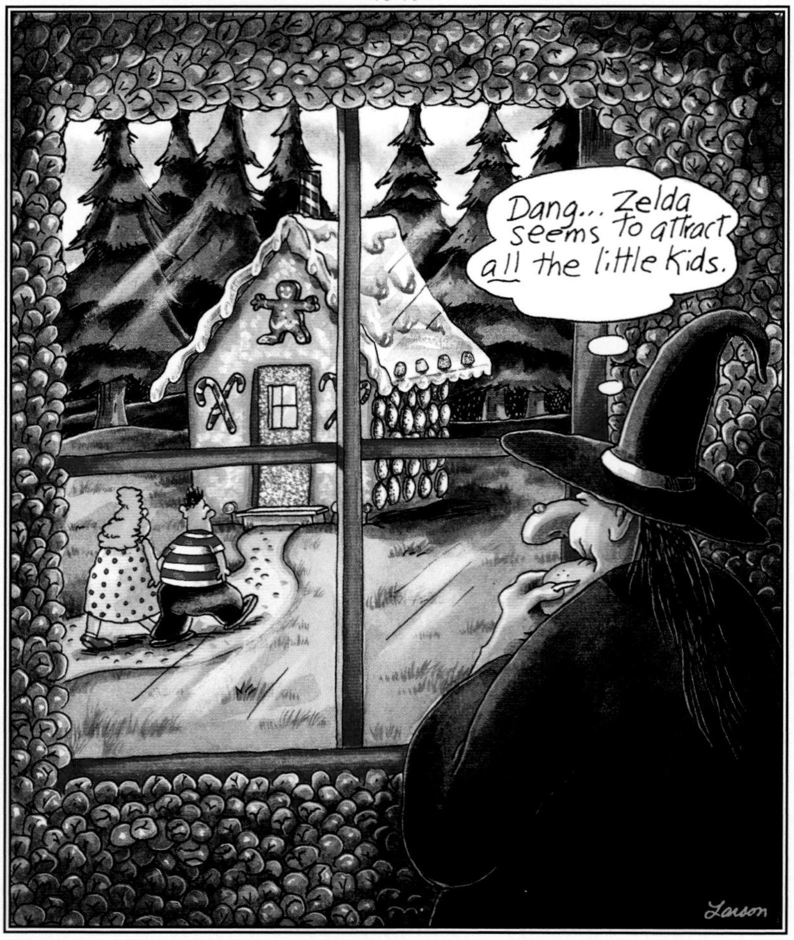
Dang... Zelda seems to attract all the little kids.
Larson

Later, Edna was forced to sell her Brussels sprout house.

12/7/92

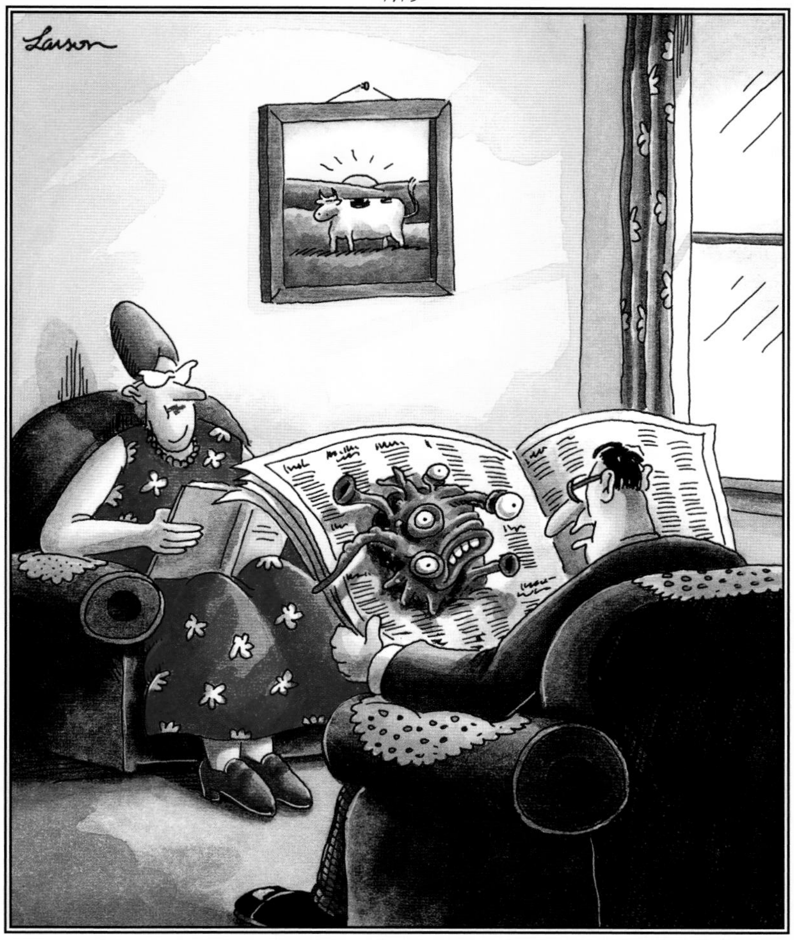

"Hey, Lola. ... Did you see this thing in the paper?"

12/3/92

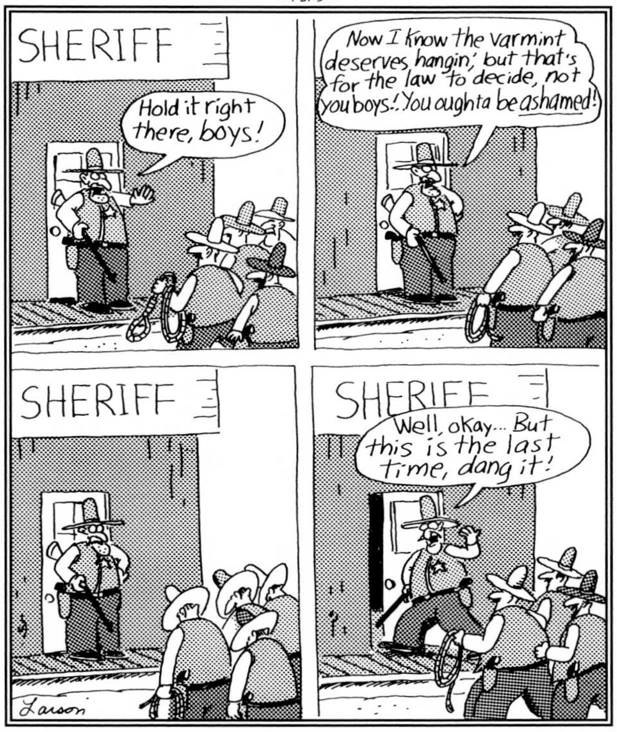
SHERIFF
Hold it right there, boys!
Now I know the varmint deserves hangin', but that's for the law to decide, not you boys! You oughta be ashamed!
SHERIFF
SHERIFF
Well, okay... But this is the last time, dang it!

12/18/92

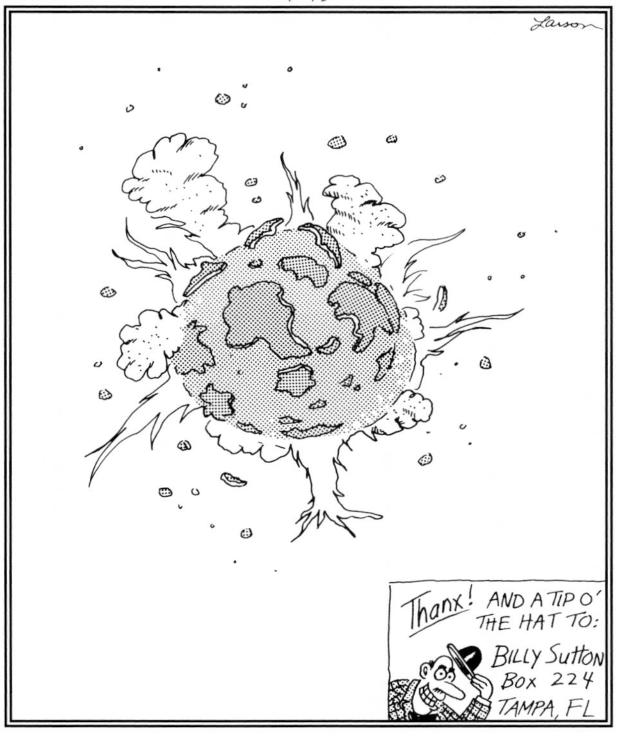
Thanx! AND A TIP O' THE HAT TO:
BILLY SUTTON
Box 224
TAMPA, FL

Suddenly, the whole world blows up.

12/8/92

"Sheriff! Ben Wiggins is ridin' into town, and he's wearin' that same little chiffon number that he wore when he shot Jake Sutton!"

12/1/92

Ooooo... This not be cheap.

Early plumbers

12/2/92

"Be patient, Leona, be patient. ... Zebras won't take a drink until they know it's absolutely safe."

12/4/92

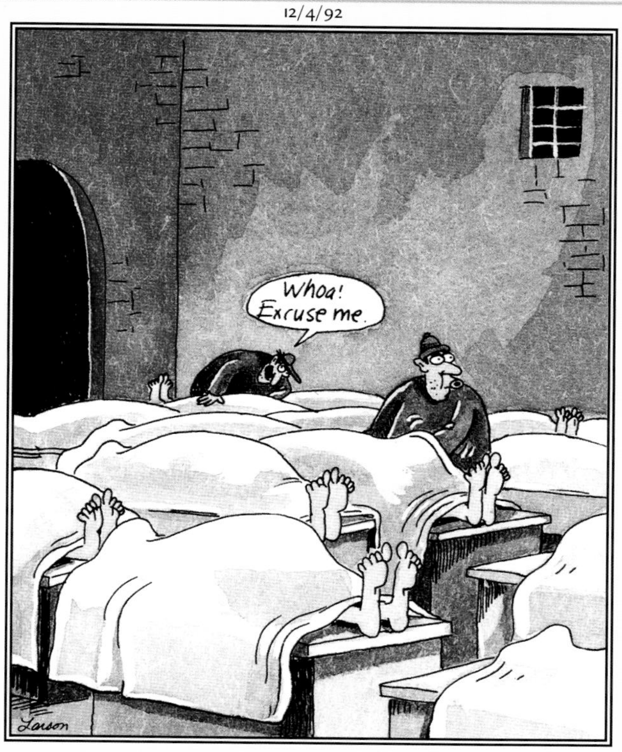
Whoa! Excuse me.

Pickpockets of the Rue Morgue

12/9/92

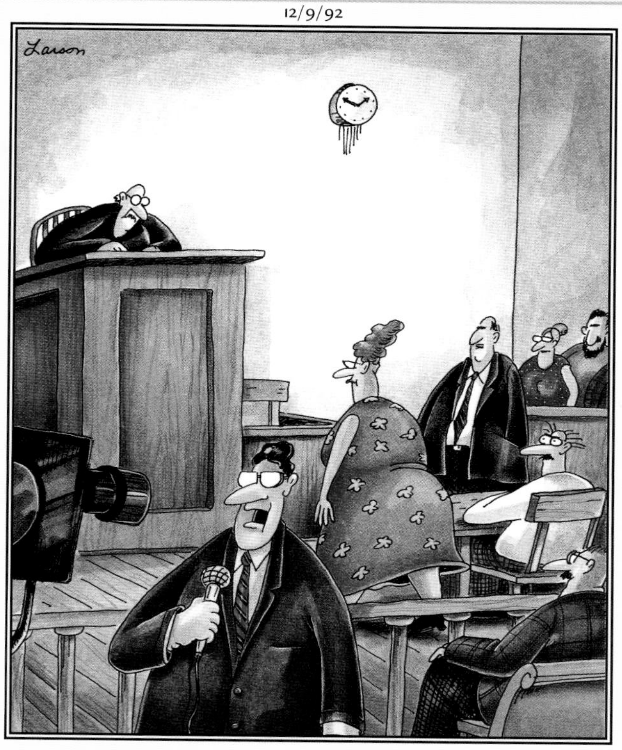

"In this dramatic turn of events, testimony against Mr. Pumpkineater is about to be given by his sister, Jeannie Jeannie Eatszucchini."

12/11/92

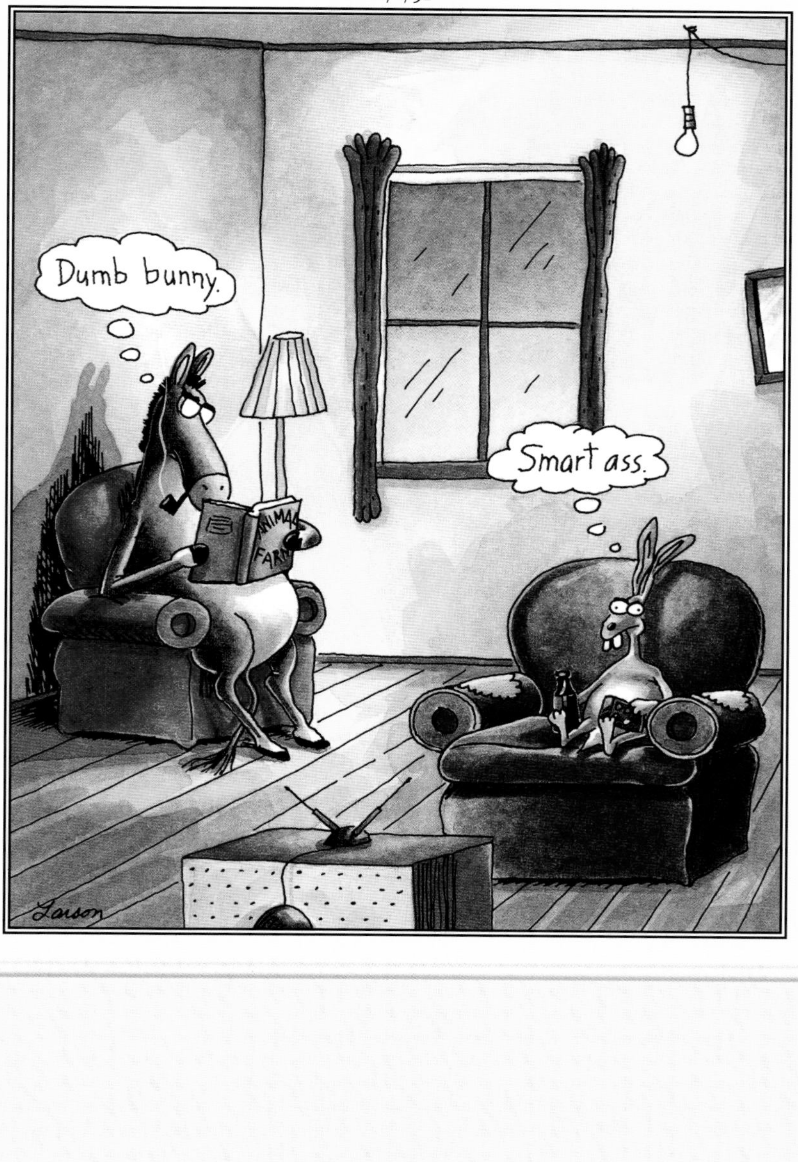
Dumb bunny.
Smart ass.

12/14/92

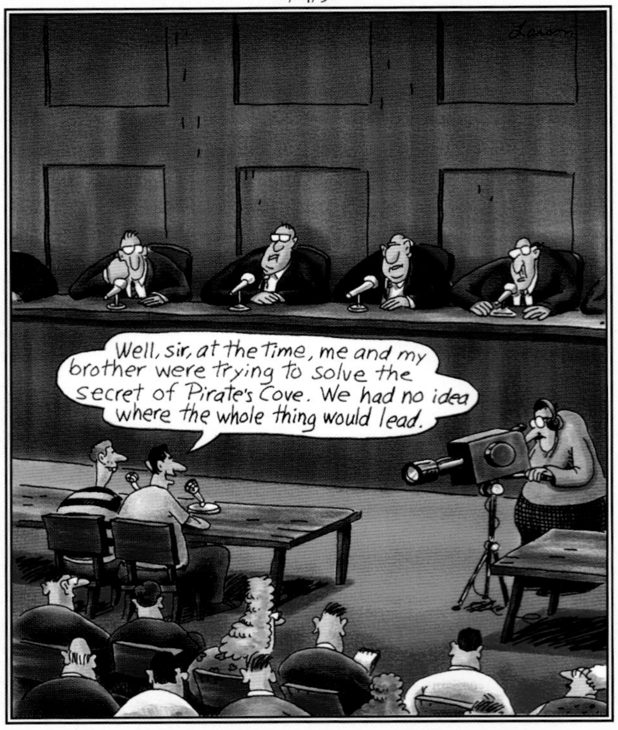
Well, sir, at the time, me and my brother were trying to solve the secret of Pirate's Cove. We had no idea where the whole thing would lead.

Testifying before a Senate subcommittee, the Hardy boys crack the Iran-contra scandal.

12/10/92

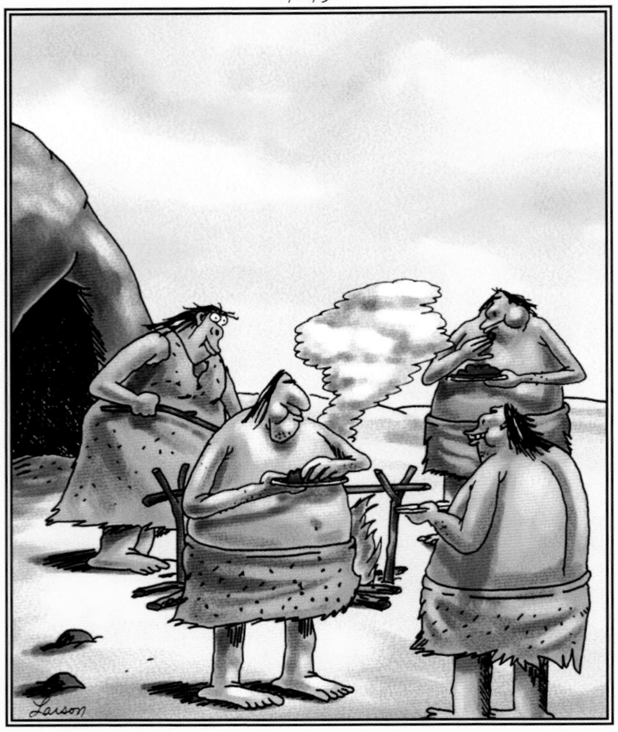

Origin of the expression "Puttin' on the dog"

12/15/92

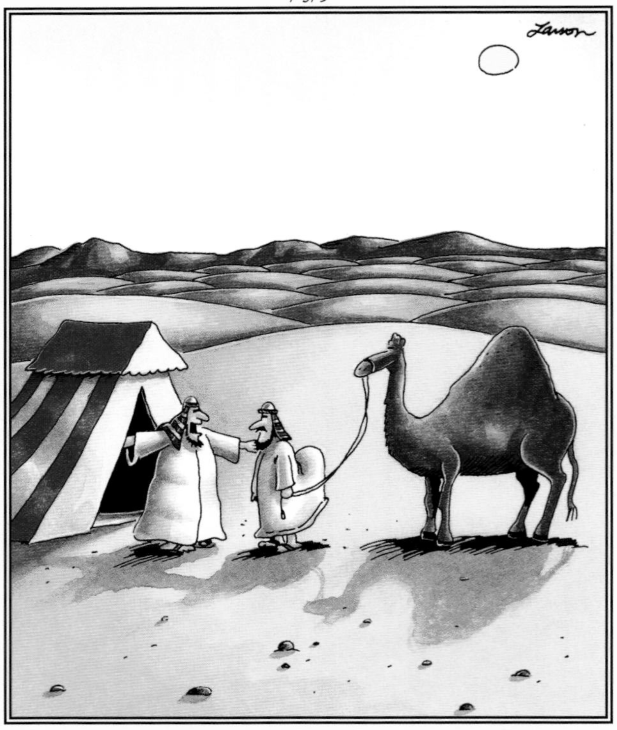

"Abdul, my old friend! Come in, come in! ... Have you traveled far?"

12/16/92

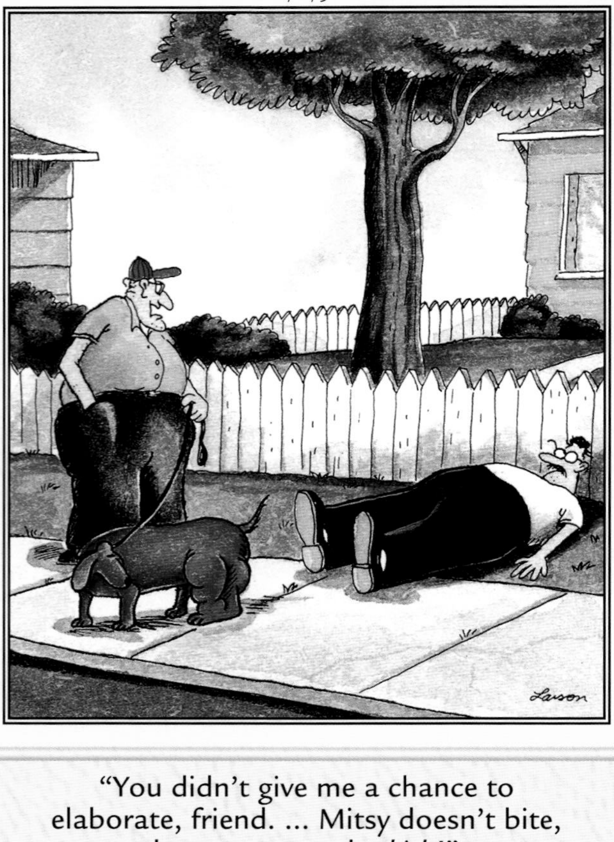

"You didn't give me a chance to elaborate, friend. ... Mitsy doesn't bite, but man, can she *kick!*"

12/17/92

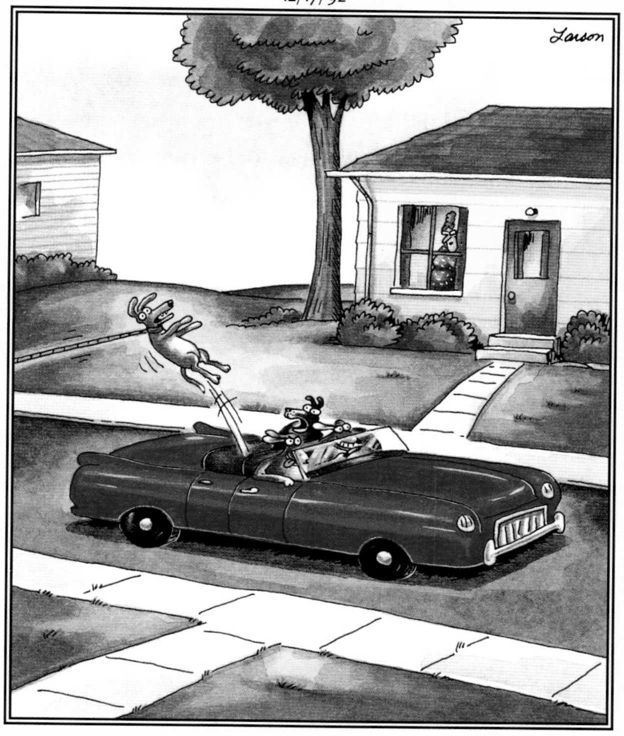
Larson

Careening through the neighborhood with reckless abandon, none of them suspected that Tuffy was still tied up.

12/25/92

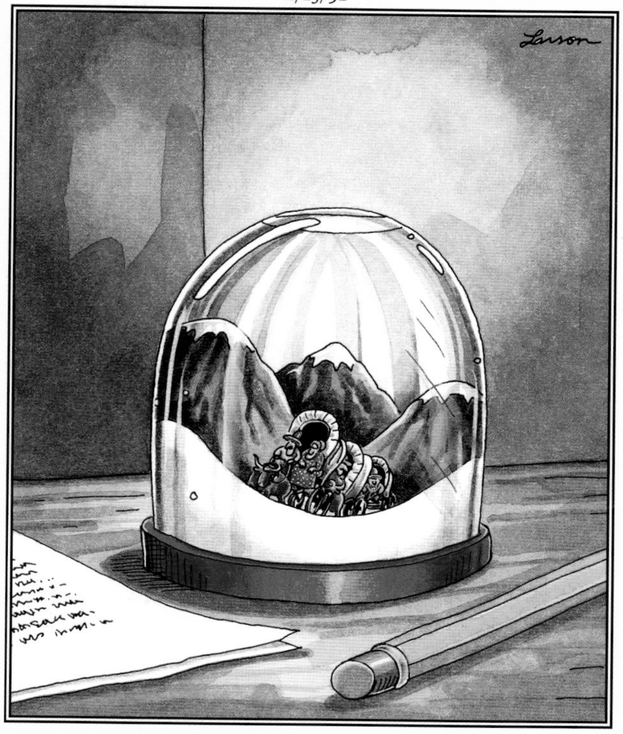
Larson

The ever-popular Donner Party snow dome

12/28/92

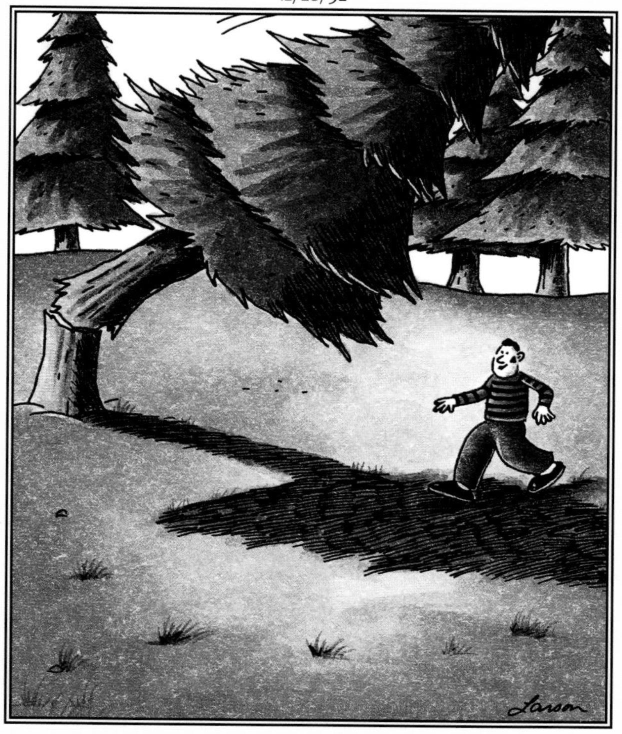
Larson

Question: If a tree falls in the forest and no one's around, and it hits a mime, does anyone care?

12/29/92

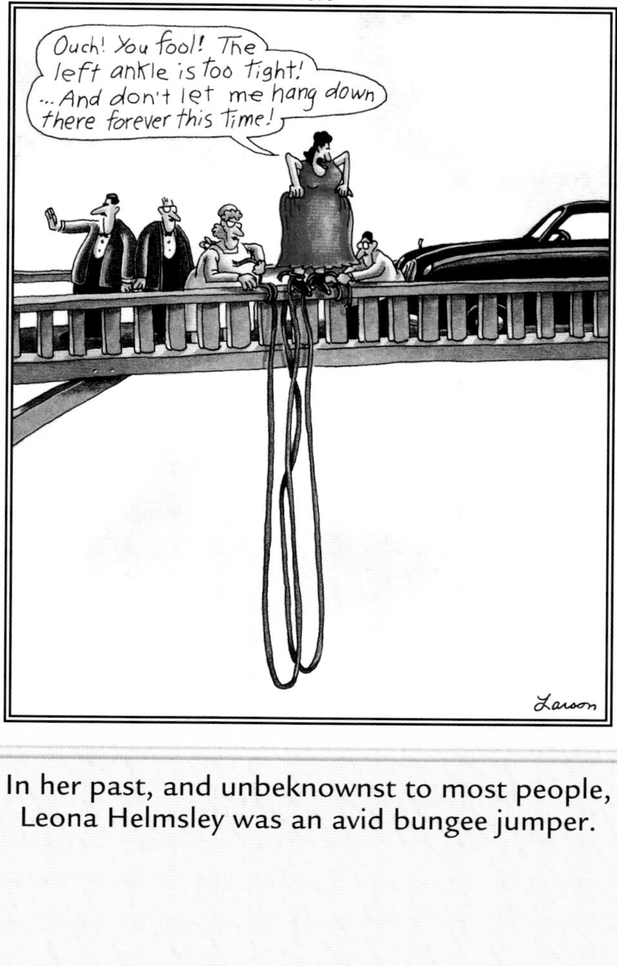
Ouch! You fool! The left ankle is too tight! ...And don't let me hang down there forever this time!
Larson

In her past, and unbeknownst to most people, Leona Helmsley was an avid bungee jumper.

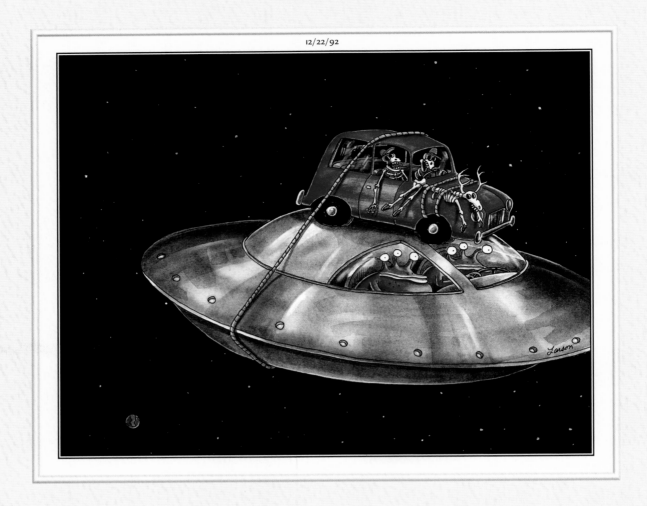

12/22/92

12/21/92

Cossack accountants

12/23/92

The Philadelphia Air Quartet

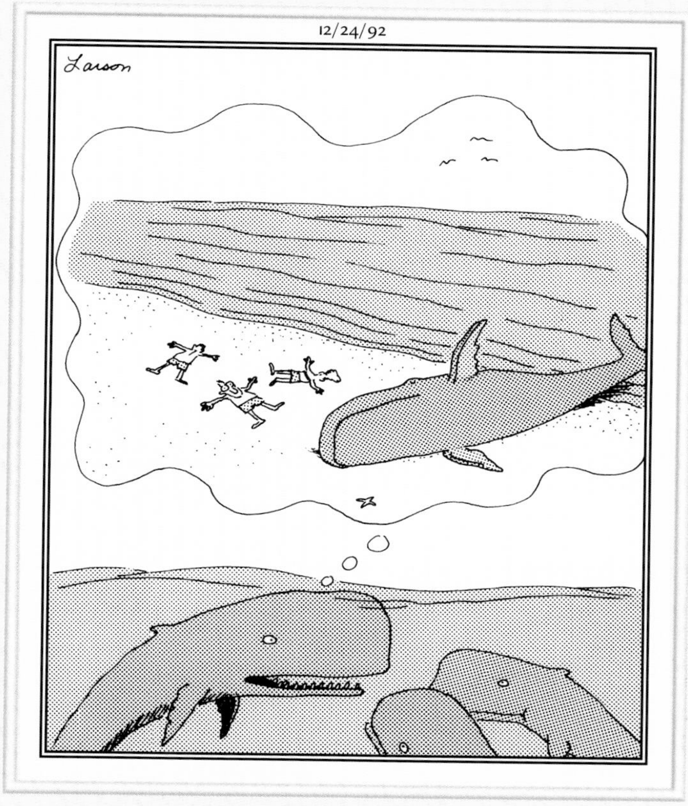
12/24/92
Larson

"And so there I was—beached! I could hear voices around me, but I couldn't go forward or back. And then it hit me: I could *roll!*"

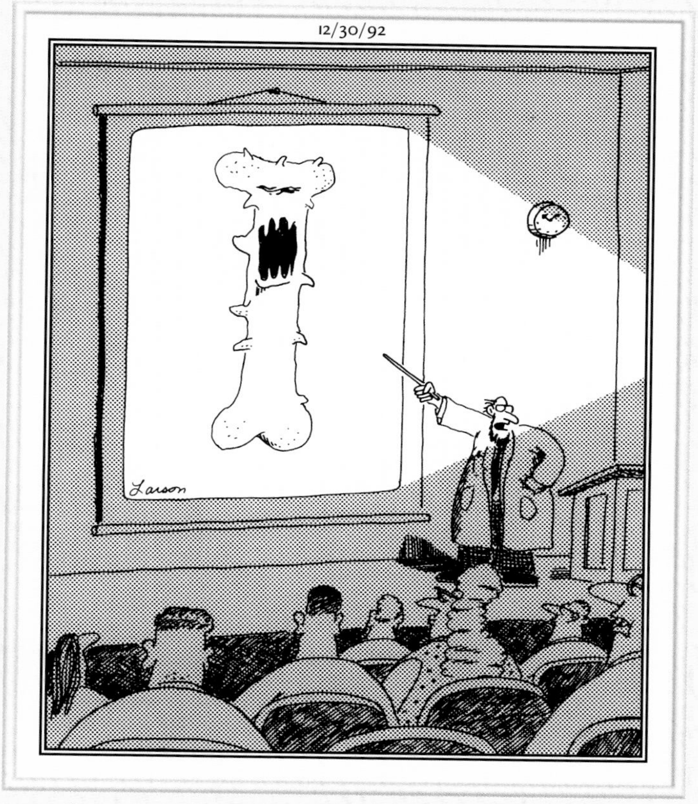
12/30/92
Larson

"Now, moving on from the so-called funny bone, we come to this little guy—and you tickle *him* at your own peril."

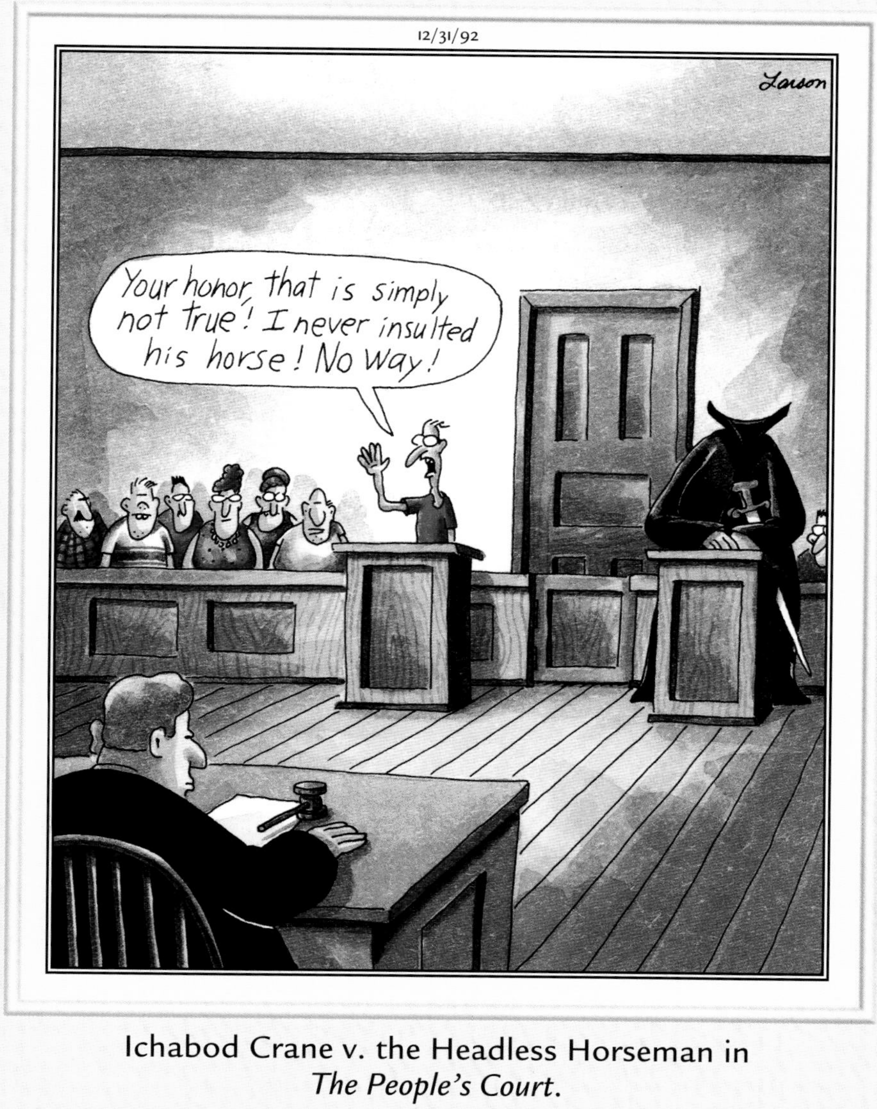
12/31/92
Larson
Your honor, that is simply not true! I never insulted his horse! No way!

Ichabod Crane v. the Headless Horseman in *The People's Court*.

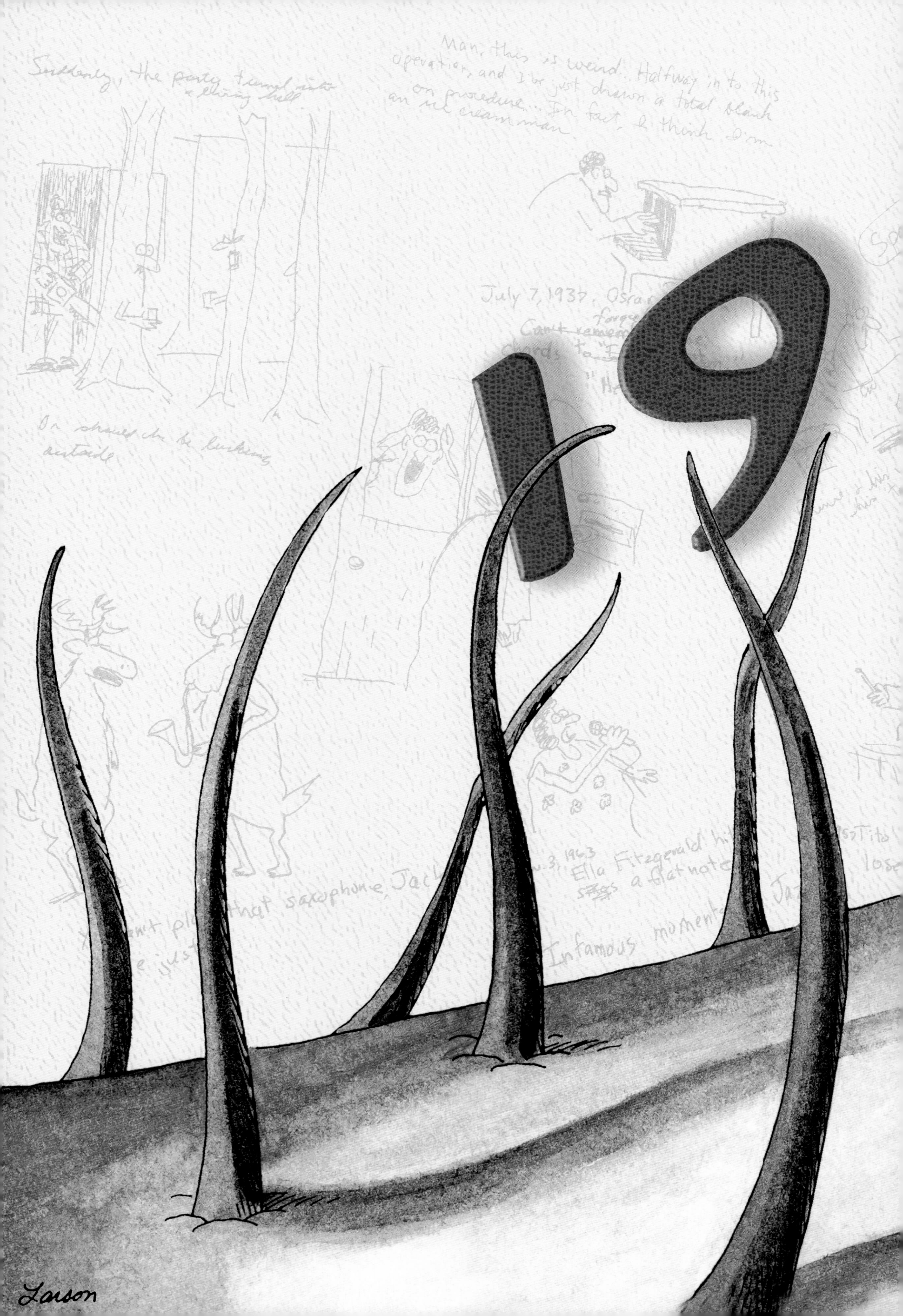

19
Infamous moments
Larson

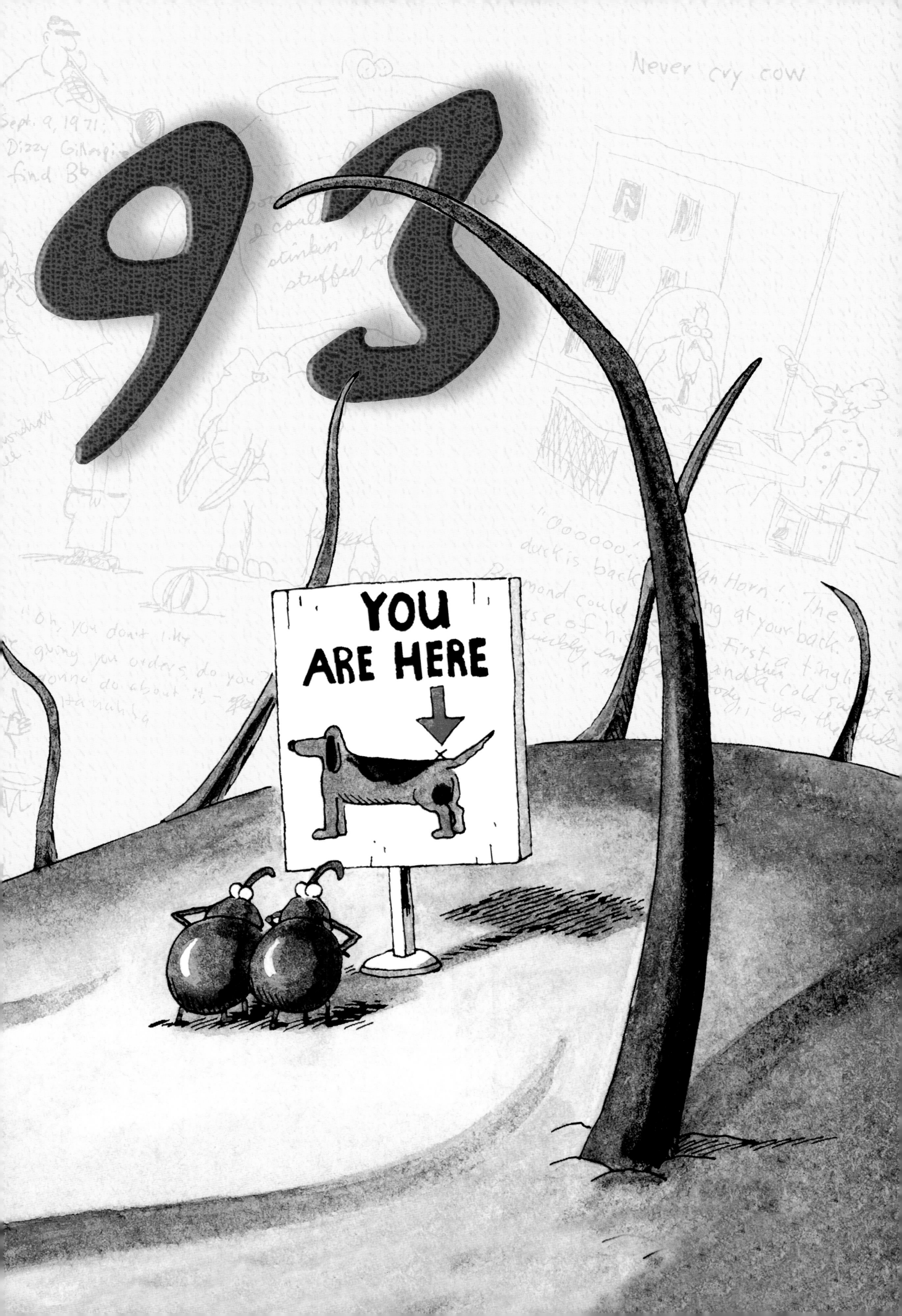
93
Never cry cow
YOU
ARE HERE

I Remember...

- ... the magic cow that granted me three wishes.

- ... the phone call from Alice Smith, a magazine editor who bought my first cartoons and kick-started my interest in cartooning.

- ... the first check I ever received for drawing the above-mentioned cartoons. When a friend saw it, he advised me to frame it, not cash it. (I held off on the latter for about an hour.)

- ... my first "office," a phone booth at Fisherman's Wharf in San Francisco, where I hung out and made calls to Chronicle Features, my future syndicate and where my portfolio had been temporarily impounded.

- ... realizing I had truly "arrived" when I got my electric pencil sharpener. (Listen, it was a big moment for me. It had suction cup feet, a see-through shavings container, and a light that told you when your lead was sharp! Yes, I had gone pro.)

- ... the time a woman, dressed in a rabbit suit, showed up at a book signing and hit me with a cream pie. (I think it was actually intended to be a "friendly" pie-in-the-face, but the episode was a little, well, awkward.) And since I had to leave directly for the airport and the pie had actually missed my face but not my shirt, on the flight home I'm sure everyone around me thought I was wearing banana cologne.

- ... some of the things that fans brought with them for me to sign, perhaps the most memorable being a large, stuffed shark. I suppose the runner-up might be the guy who brought in his bowling ball, along with an electric engraver.

- ... my first complaint letter, from a mother who demanded I tell her how she was supposed to explain to her five-year-old the meaning of my cartoon showing Santa Claus writing a cookbook called *Nine Ways to Serve Venison*.

- ... the time a foreign publisher took my first book cover, which looked like this:

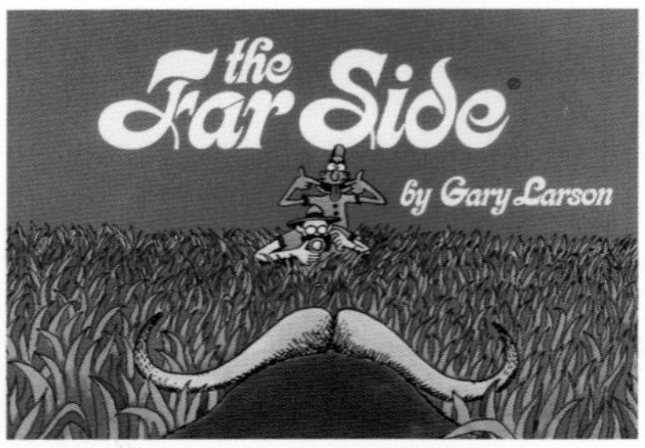
the Far Side
by Gary Larson

and made it look like this:

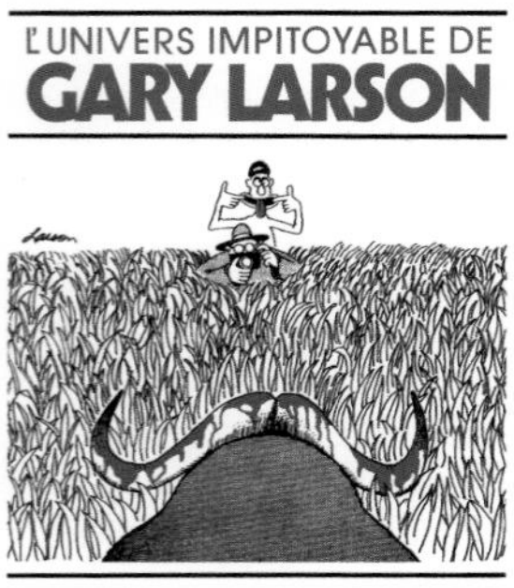
L'UNIVERS IMPITOYABLE DE
GARY LARSON

- … the time I drew what I believe *may* have been the first naked butt (Vol. 2, p. 217) to appear on the comic pages of mainstream newspapers. (Not that this was ever one of my goals, but you have to grab these awards on your own because no one hands them out.)

- … the absolute worst cartoon I ever drew and which still makes me cringe. (I thought about revealing it, but I fear I'd start hearing, "Oh, you're wrong— *that's* not your worst cartoon.")

- … the time a TV reporter began an interview with: "Tell me, Mr. Larson, where *is* The Far Side, and is it difficult to travel there and back?" (*Twilight Zone* theme music, please.)

- … the time a stranger, a woman, learned where I lived, knocked on my door, and asked for an autograph. I went to a room in the back of the house to get a pen, turned around, and there she was, standing right next to me, holding a butcher knife. (I made up the butcher knife part—this one seemed to need a little "something.")

- … my first book signing, and a young man showed up with a photo album containing every cartoon I had ever drawn, cut out and neatly glued down and arranged in chronological order. Ask any cartoonist: Anyone who cuts out one of your cartoons has just paid you the greatest compliment. (I liked this guy.)

- … the letter from another cartoonist's attorney threatening me with a lawsuit on behalf of his client, who claimed I had stolen his idea that had been published previously in a campus newspaper some 3,000 miles away from where I lived, BUT, of course, his client was willing to let the entire matter drop for $50,000. (I passed, but thought about sending the guy an electric pencil sharpener as a small consolation prize.)

- … the cartoon called "Cow tools" (Vol. 1, p. 251) that took me to hell and back because everyone tried to decipher something in the cartoon that was undecipherable, which was supposed to be the joke, which then became a joke on me, which wasn't funny anymore, which forced me to write a press release, which gave me a good lesson about drawing confusing cartoons, which lasted about a week.

- … the night in Washington, D.C., after a crazy book signing when I couldn't find my publisher's rep and, searching for her, wandered out onto the sidewalk where I encountered a bunch of people who immediately crowded around me trying to get their *Far Side* books signed, and a car pulled up to the curb, a guy yelled, "Gary! Quick! Get in!" so I did, we took off, and I found myself in a car full of more fans who were delighted I had joined them.

- … the time I sat across a dinner table from Charles Addams, and neither of us said a word to the other. (I was intimidated; he suffered from narcolepsy.)

- … the time I unwittingly wore a T-shirt that had one of my own cartoons on it into a grocery store. At the checkout stand, my shirt sparked a conversation between the clerk and the box boy, with the clerk saying to the box boy, "Did you know Gary Larson comes into the store every once in a while? … yeah … big bear of a guy … very friendly … not weird at all … blah blah blah … ." Still talking to the box boy, he handed me my change, and as I walked away he said something to the kid about pointing me out next time I'm in the store. (Officially, I would describe myself as more deer-size than bear-size.)

- … the time I incurred the wrath of some Eskimos. (I'm still not exactly sure why.)

- … the time I incurred the wrath of some cat lovers. (I know why.)

- … the time I incurred the wrath of mental health organizations. (Shouldn't they have been reaching out to me?)

- … the many times I incurred the wrath of Amnesty International. (They don't like cartoons about dungeons and people being tortured in them.)

- … the time I incurred the wrath of some Christian fundamentalists. (I know why, but I was at more risk from the cat lovers.)

- … the time I realized I needed to get an unlisted phone number. (Now you know why.)

1/4/93
WELCOME
BUTLERS of the WORLD
ANNUAL BANQUET
Larson

"God, Collings, I hate to start a Monday with a case like this."

1/5/93
Larson

The Angel of Migraines

1/7/93
Larson

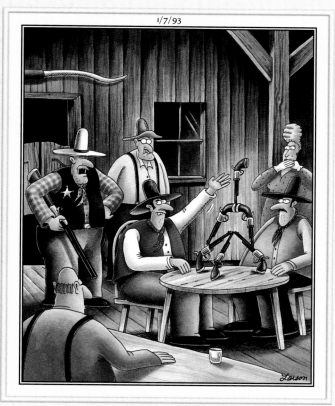

"Okay, boys—that'll be enough. ... We don't allow any gunplay in this town."

1/1/93

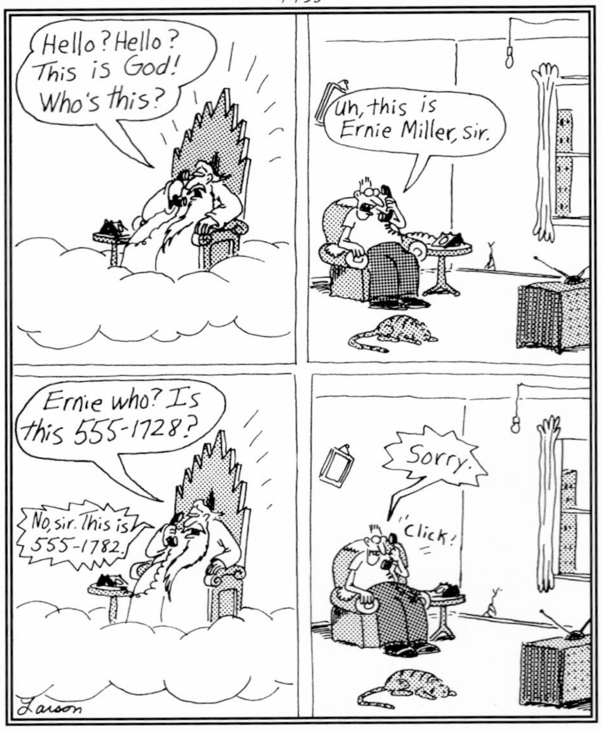
Hello? Hello? This is God! Who's this?
Uh, this is Ernie Miller, sir.
Ernie who? Is this 555-1728?
No, sir. This is 555-1782.
Sorry.
Click!
Larson

And for the rest of his life, Ernie told his friends that he had talked with God.

1/6/93

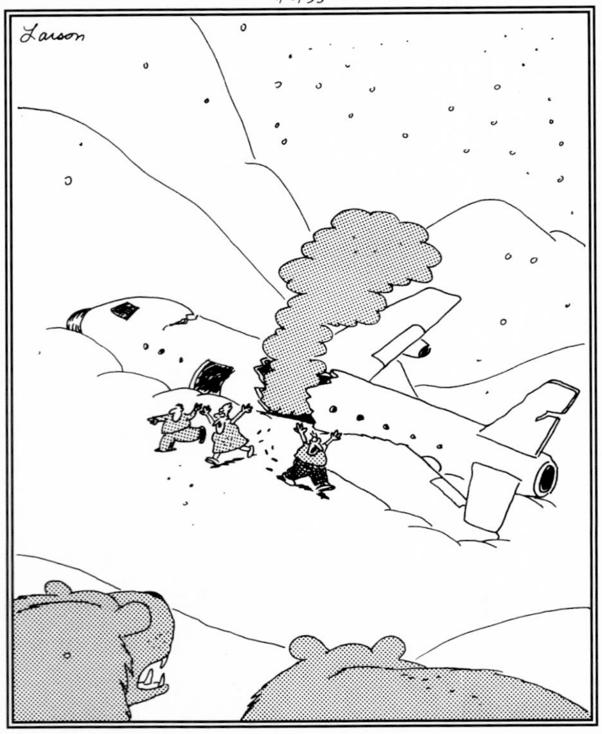
Larson

"Uh-oh. ... Looks like the usual airplane food."

1/8/93

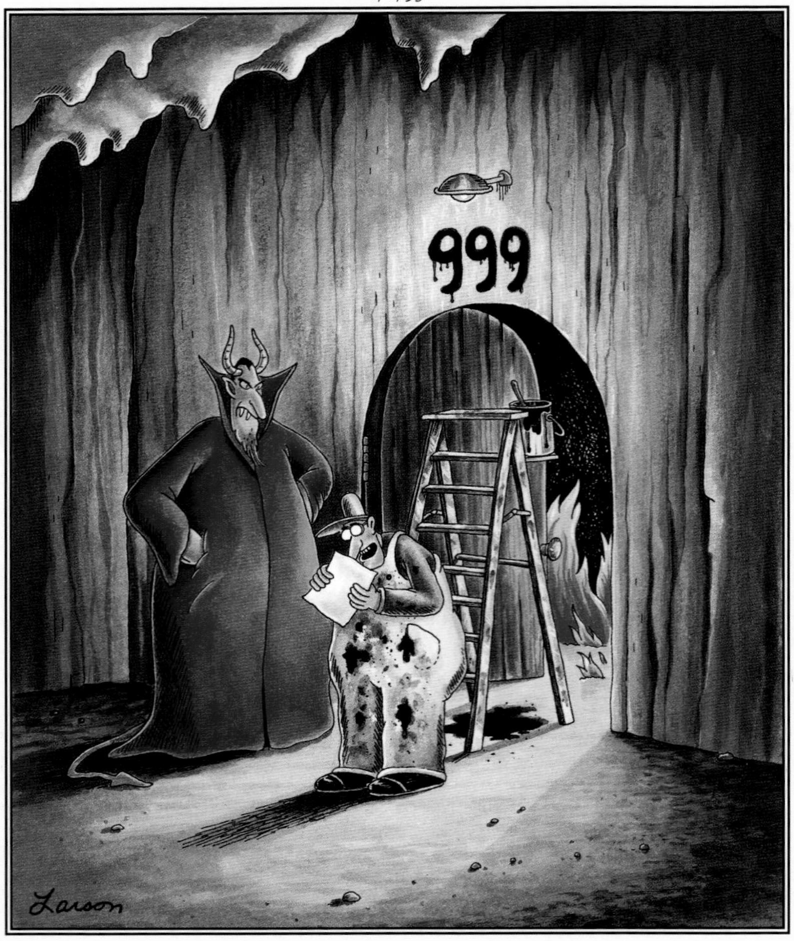
999
Larson

"Well, I'll be. ... I must've been holding the dang work order like *this!*"

1/15/93

Larson
My friends, feast your eyes on *Parides hahneli* -- the Holy Grail of butterflies! And she's mine, all mine!

Regrettably, Professor DeWitt's boasting fell on too many jealous ears, and that night, as he stumbled from the bar, he was etherized by an unknown assailant and "relieved" of his trophy.

1/20/93

Larson

Scenes that make a crow smile

1/11/93

Larson
THIS IS NOT A STEP

1/12/93

Larson
Toy with me, will they?

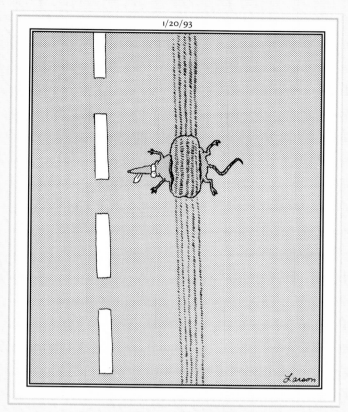

1/14/93

Moses parting his hair

1/13/93

TRANSOIL

A tragedy occurs off the coast of
a land called Honah-Lee.

1/21/93

STINK SCENT
2nd Floor
WATCH YOUR CRAWL

Snake department stores

1/22/93

RUBY'S CHOWDER HUT
That? Well, back in '62, we had a real minus tide, and that young fool went out on Deadgull Point, braggin' 'bout how he was gonna be the one to dig up Big Clyde.. Ha! Big Clyde siphoned Mr. Hotshot Clamdigger right out of his boots!

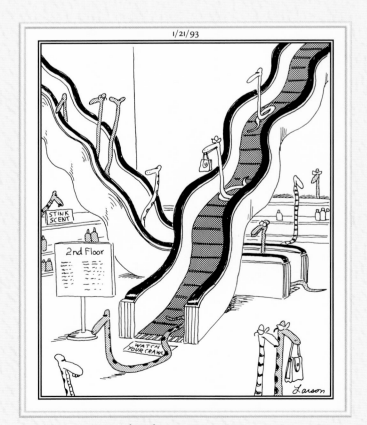

Bivalve lore

1/19/93

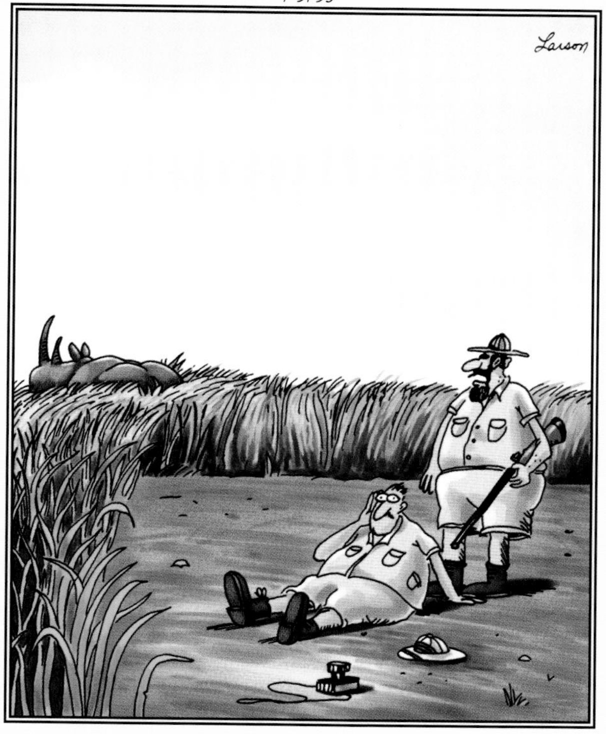

"You're damn lucky, Saunders. ... If that rhino had really respected you as an enemy, he'd have done a helluva lot more than just walk up and slap your face."

1/18/93

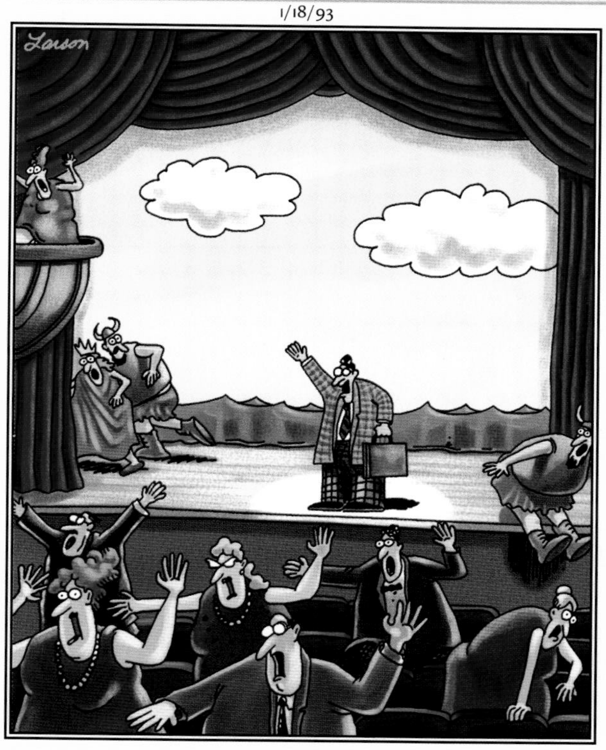

Scene from *Insurance Salesman of the Opera*

1/25/93

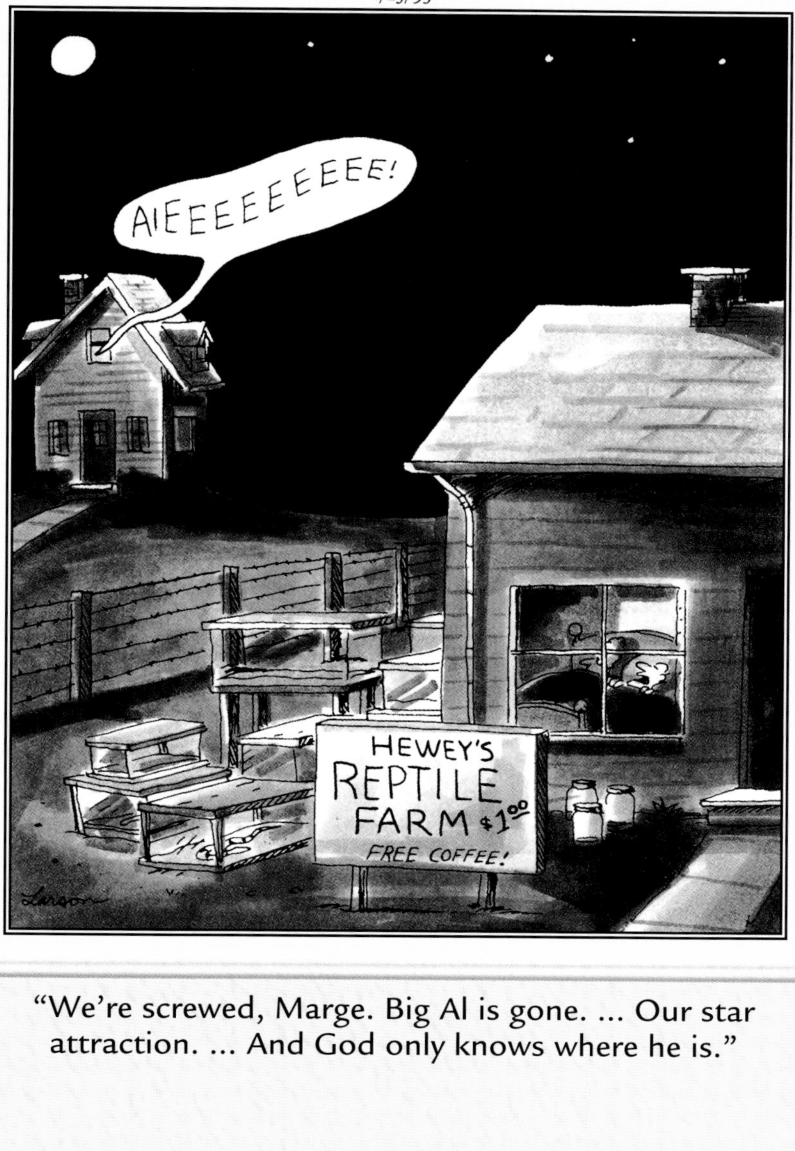
AIEEEEEEEEE!
HEWEY'S REPTILE FARM $1.00
FREE COFFEE!

"We're screwed, Marge. Big Al is gone. ... Our star attraction. ... And God only knows where he is."

1/26/93

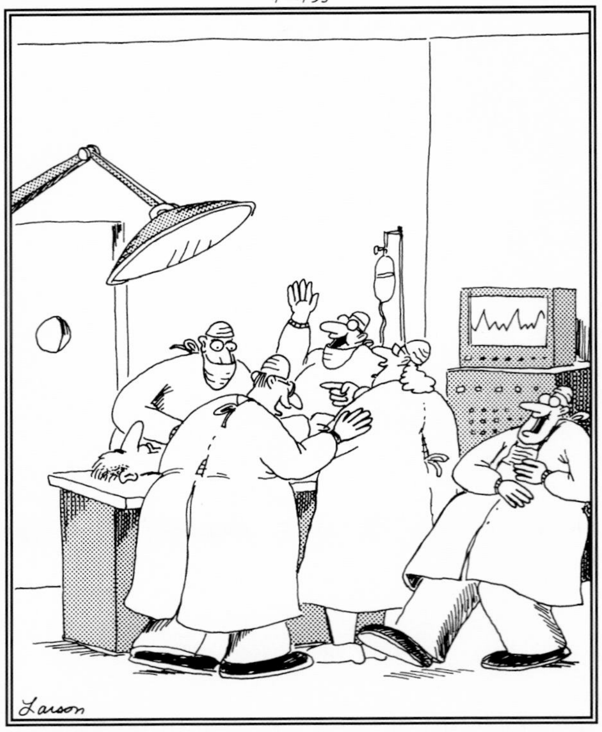
Larson

Carlton falls for the old rubber-scalpel gag.

1/27/93

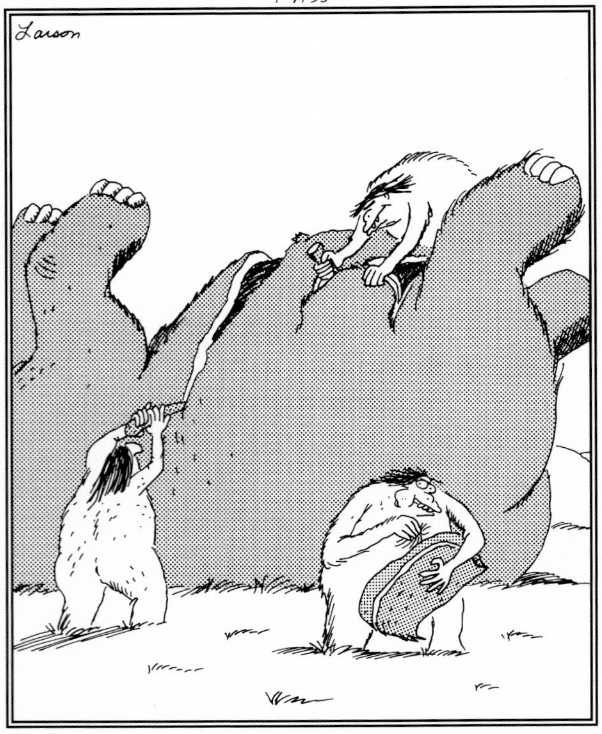
Larson

With no one looking, Koona would secretly sprinkle on a few sprouts.

1/28/93

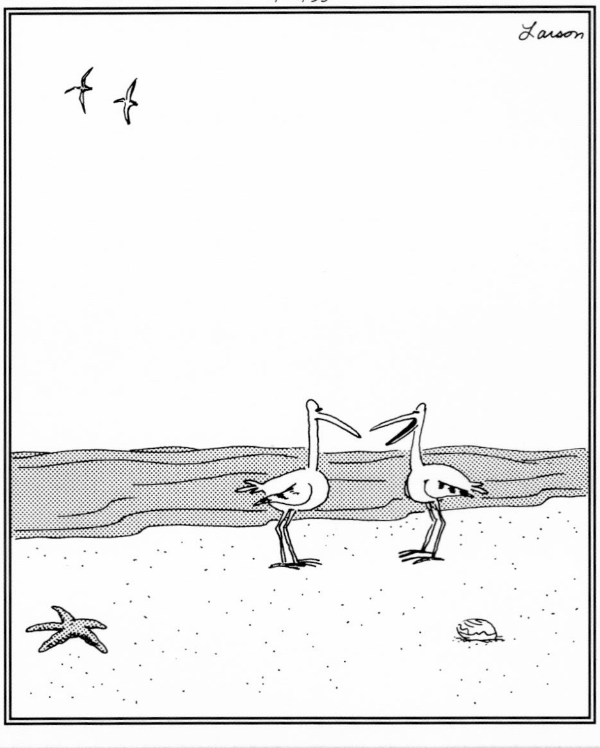
Larson

"You're not fooling me, Ned. ... Taking a long walk on the beach sounds romantic, but I know you're just looking for crustaceans."

1/29/93

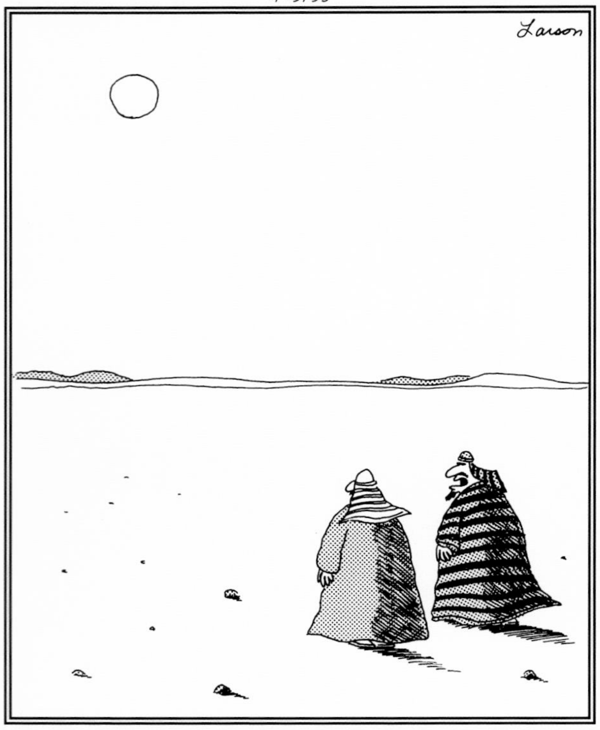
Larson

"Our camels are dead, we have no water, and yet we must cross this desert if we are to survive. ... For the love of Allah, Omar, do you ever trim your nose hairs?"

2/1/93

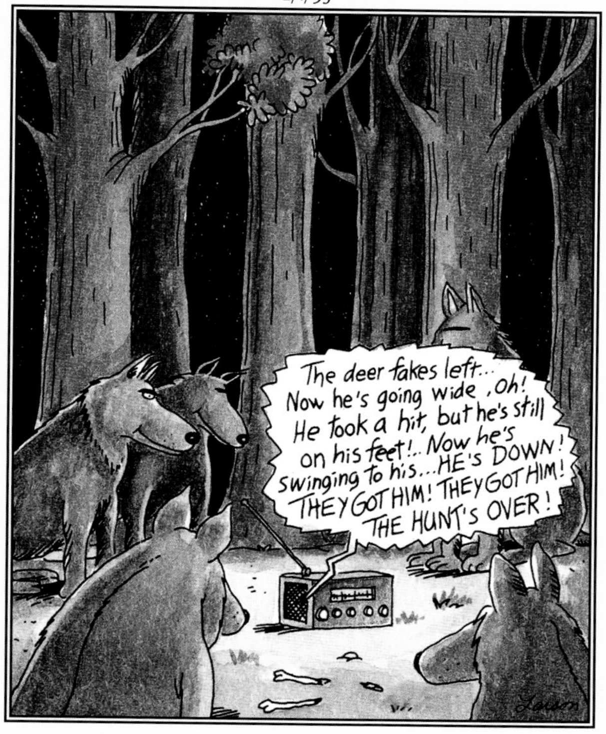
The deer fakes left... Now he's going wide, oh! He took a hit, but he's still on his feet!.. Now he's swinging to his... HE'S DOWN! THEY GOT HIM! THEY GOT HIM! THE HUNT'S OVER!

Monday night in the woods

2/2/93

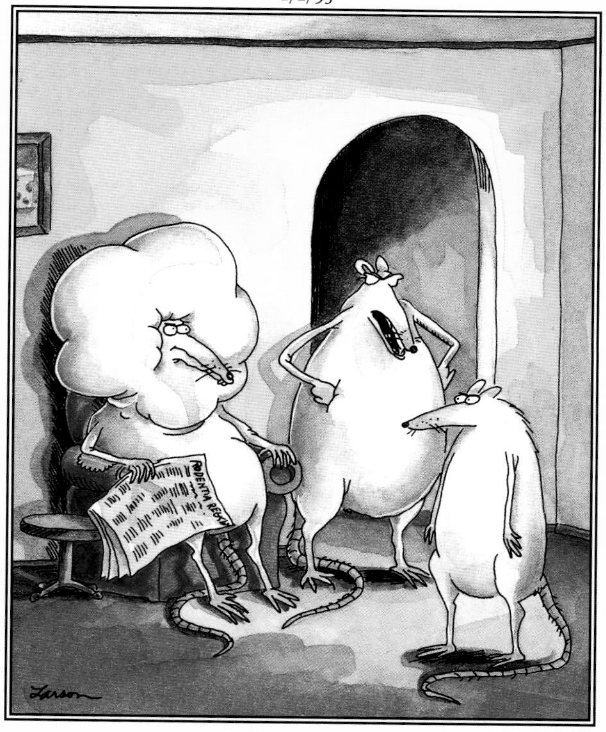

"Quit school? *Quit school?* You wanna end up like your father—a career lab rat?"

2/3/93

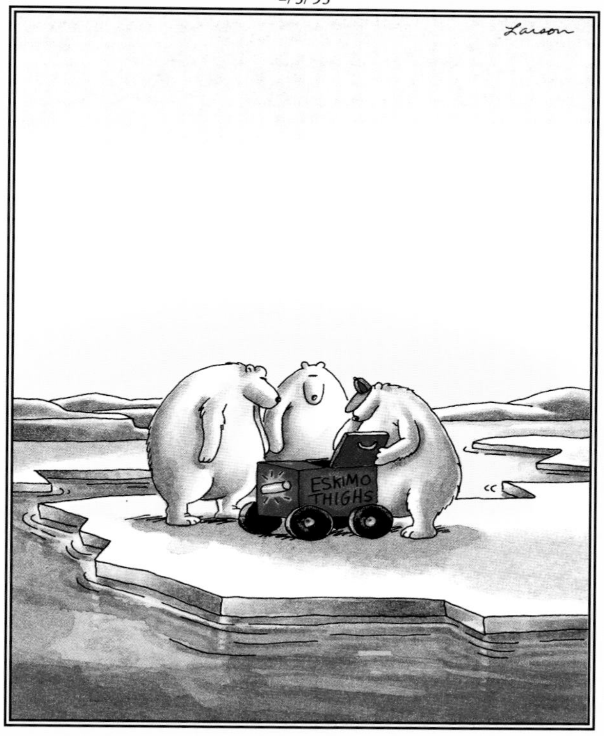
ESKIMO THIGHS

2/4/93

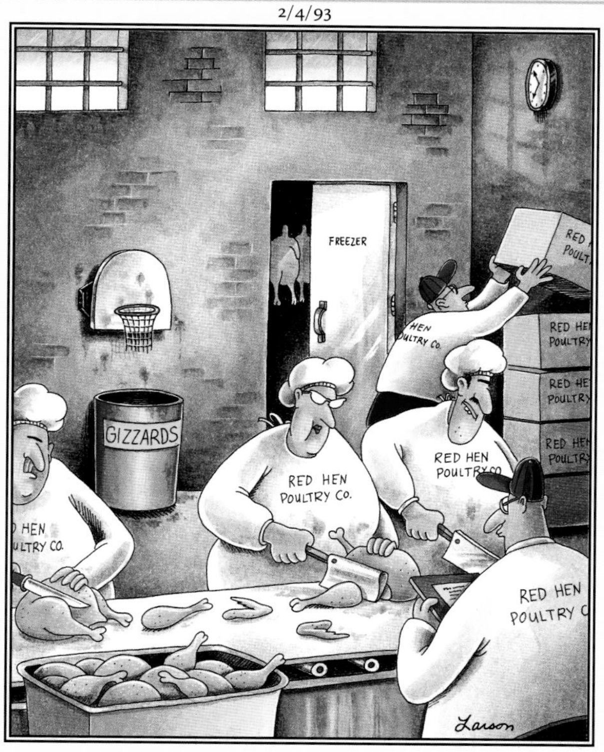
FREEZER
GIZZARDS
RED HEN POULTRY Co.
RED HEN POULTRY Co.

2/5/93

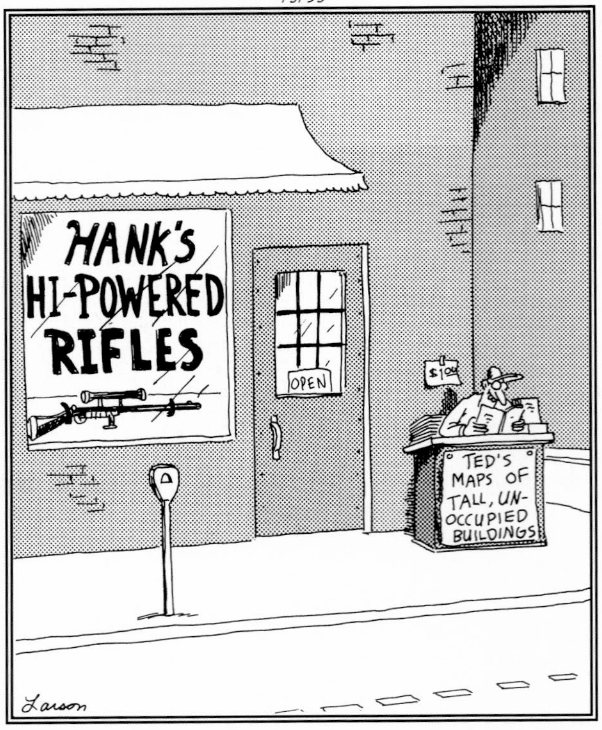
HANK'S HI-POWERED RIFLES
OPEN
TED'S MAPS OF TALL, UN-OCCUPIED BUILDINGS
Larson

2/10/93

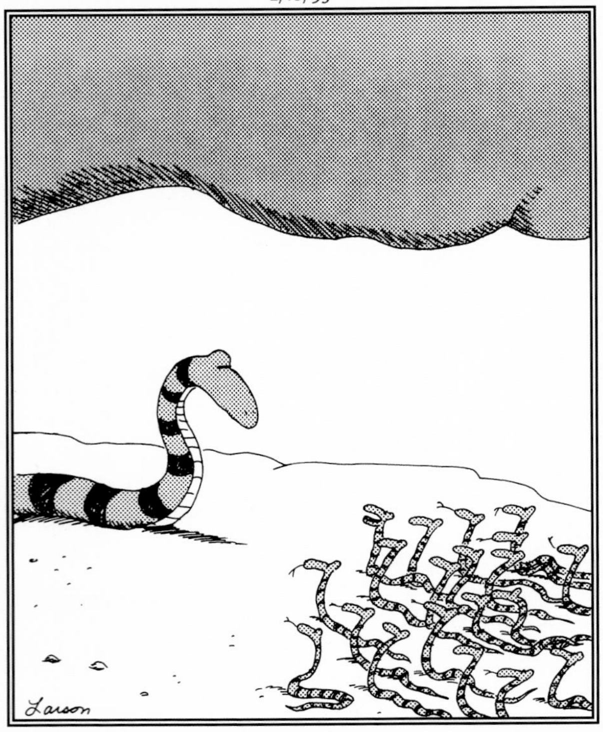
Larson

"No, really, Mom—who do you like best?"

2/8/93

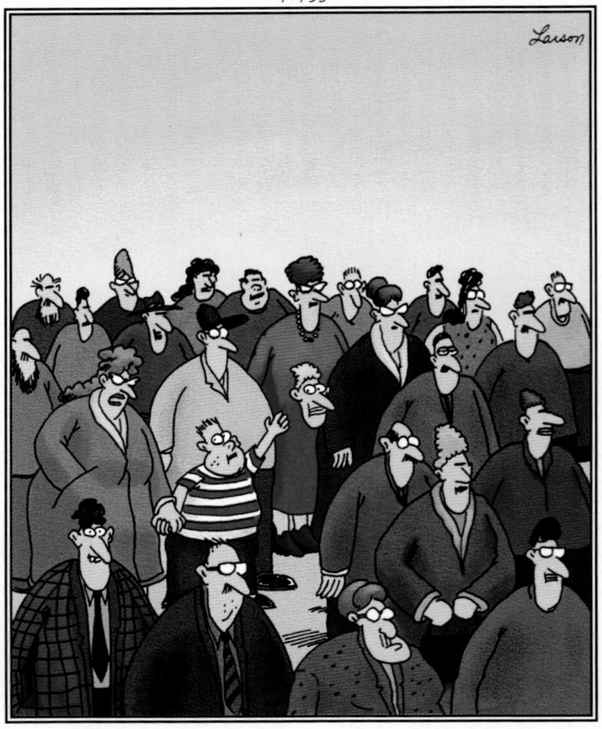
Larson

"Don't touch it, honey ... it's just a face in the crowd."

2/9/93

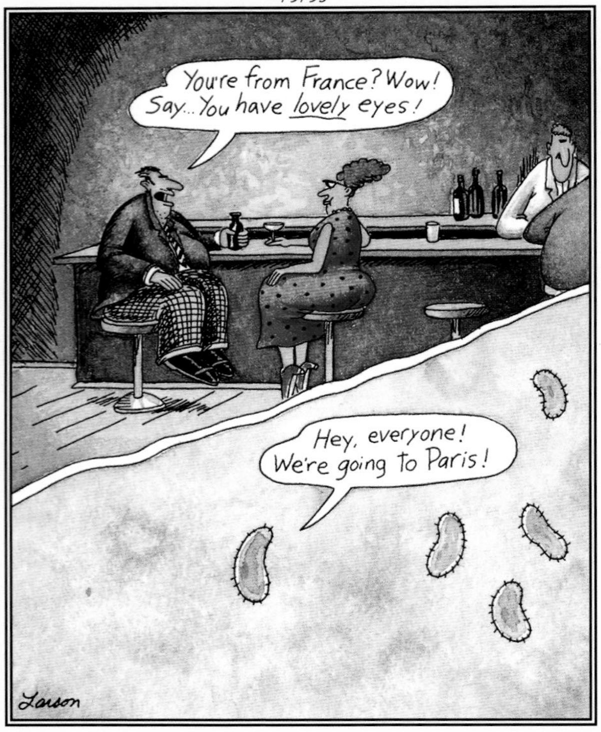
You're from France? Wow! Say... You have lovely eyes!
Hey, everyone! We're going to Paris!
Larson

Be a virus, see the world.

2/16/93

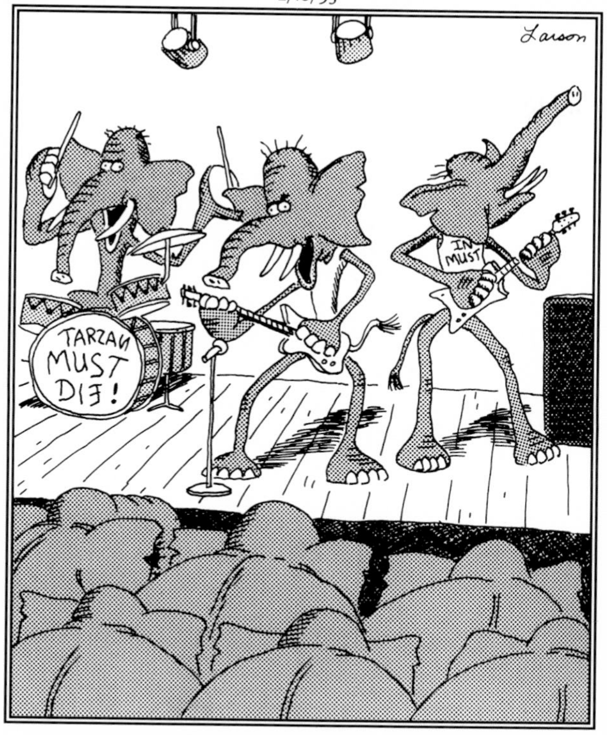
TARZAN
MUST
DIE!
IN
MUST

The Angry Young Pachyderms

2/17/93

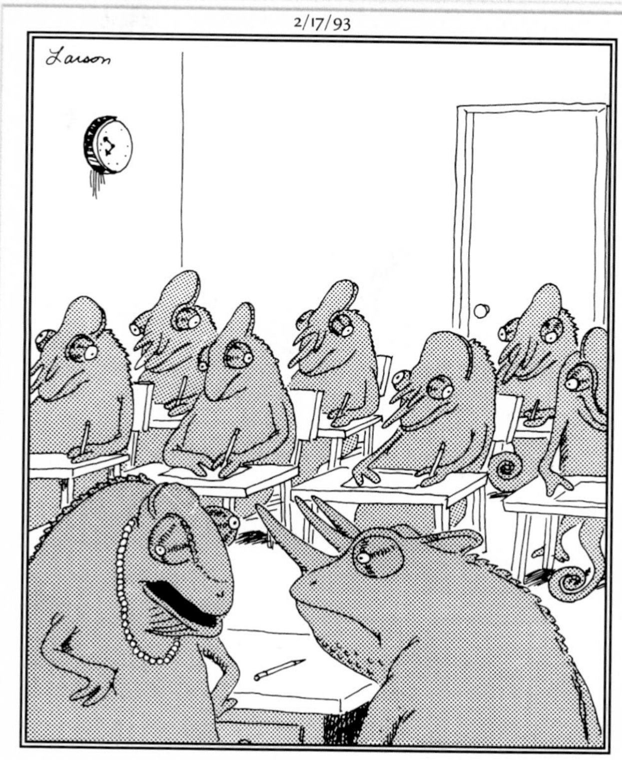

"Well, Douglas! I noticed during the exam your eyes weren't exactly rotating in their sockets."

2/12/93

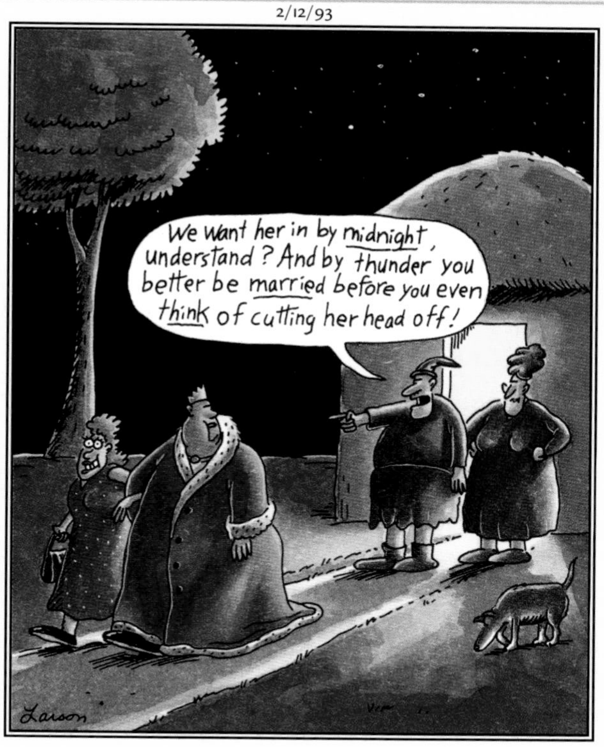
We want her in by midnight, understand? And by thunder you better be married before you even think of cutting her head off!

Henry VIII on the dating scene

2/11/93

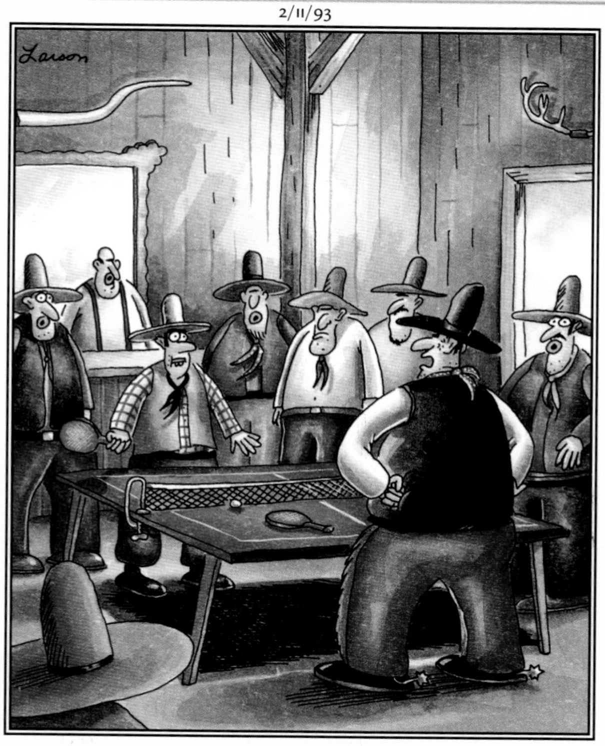

"Well, kid, ya beat me—and now every punk packin' a paddle and tryin' to make a name for himself will come lookin' for *you!* ... Welcome to hell, kid."

2/15/93

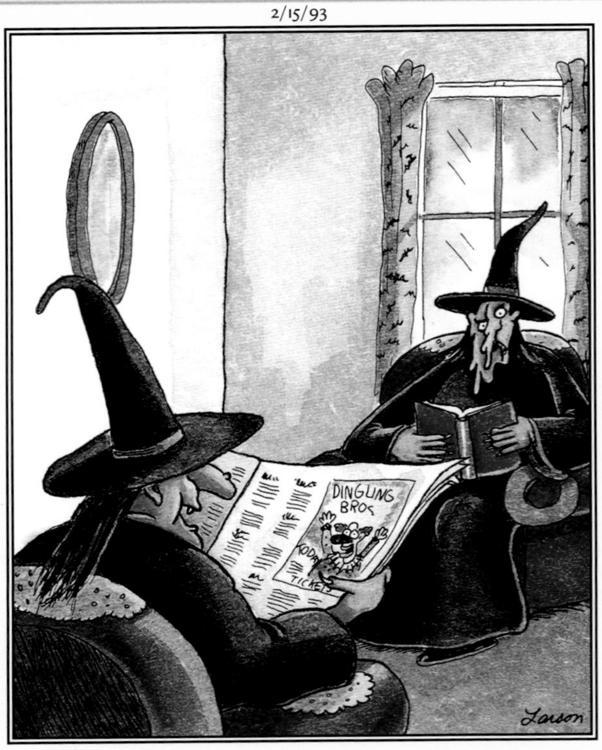
DINGLING BROS
Larson

"Hey, Ruby! The circus is back in town! Remember when we went last year and that clown asked you to smell his boutonniere?"

2/19/93

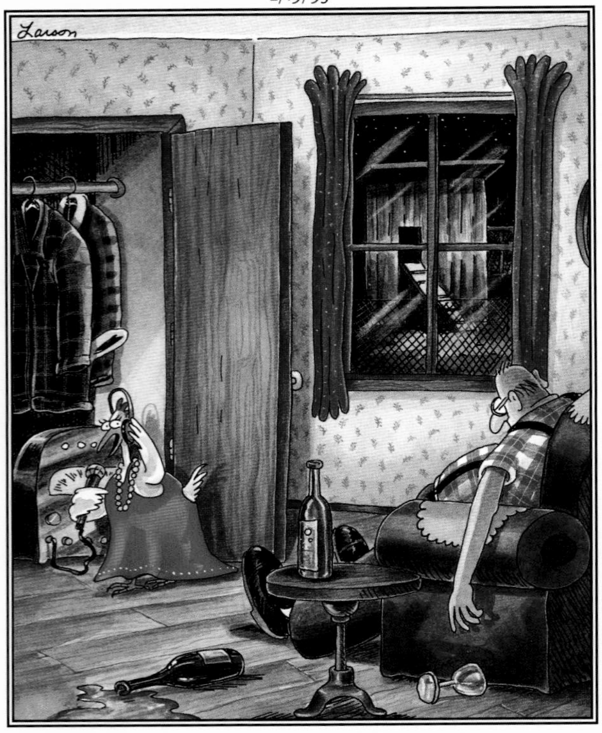
Larson

She was known as Madame D'Gizarde, and, in the early '40s, she used deceit, drugs, and her beguiling charms to become the bane of chicken farmers everywhere.

2/18/93

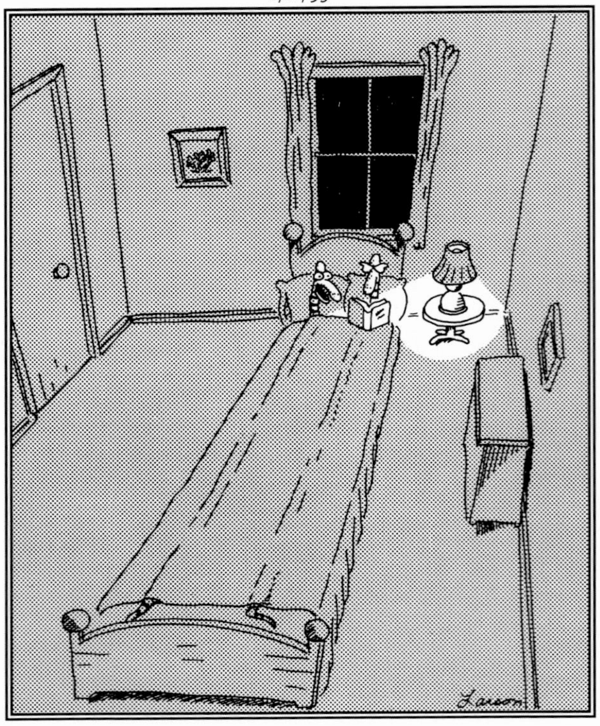
Larson

"Oh, man. ... Is that another one of those hiss-and-tell books?"

2/23/93

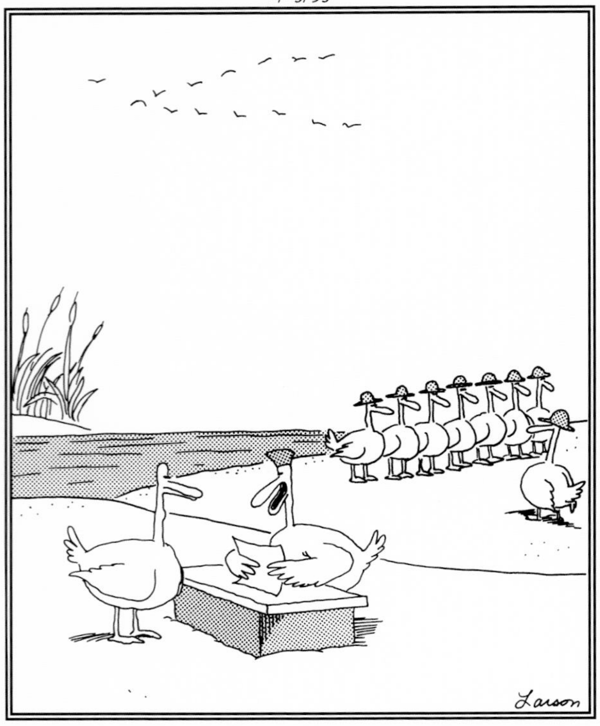
Larson

"Can't use ya, son ... says here your feet aren't flat."

2/22/93

BORDER

"Excuse me, sir, but could your entire family please step out of the car? ... Your faces are not in order."

2/24/93

"Look, if it was electric, could I do this?"

2/25/93

DANGER
WATCH
YOUR NOSE
C'mon! C'mon!
GRRRR!.. C'mon!

How attack-wiener dogs are trained

2/26/93

Hummingbirds, of course, have to watch nature films with the action greatly speeded up.

3/3/93

"Oh, the box of dead flies? Ramone gave them to me Saturday night during his courtship display. ... Of course, they were already sucked dry."

3/1/93

"Norm? This is Mitch. ... You were right—I found my drill."

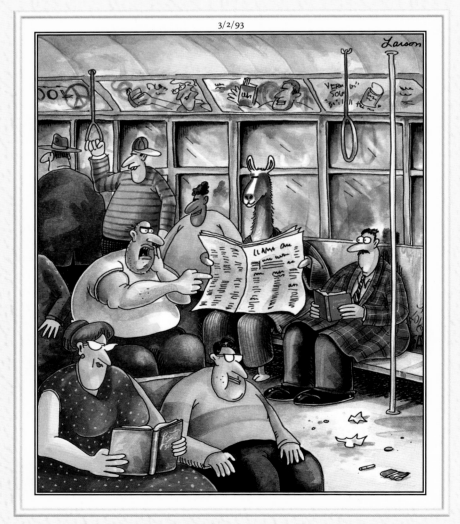

3/2/93

"Hey! You! ... Yeah, you! I ain't gonna tell you again—quit spittin' on me!"

3/9/93

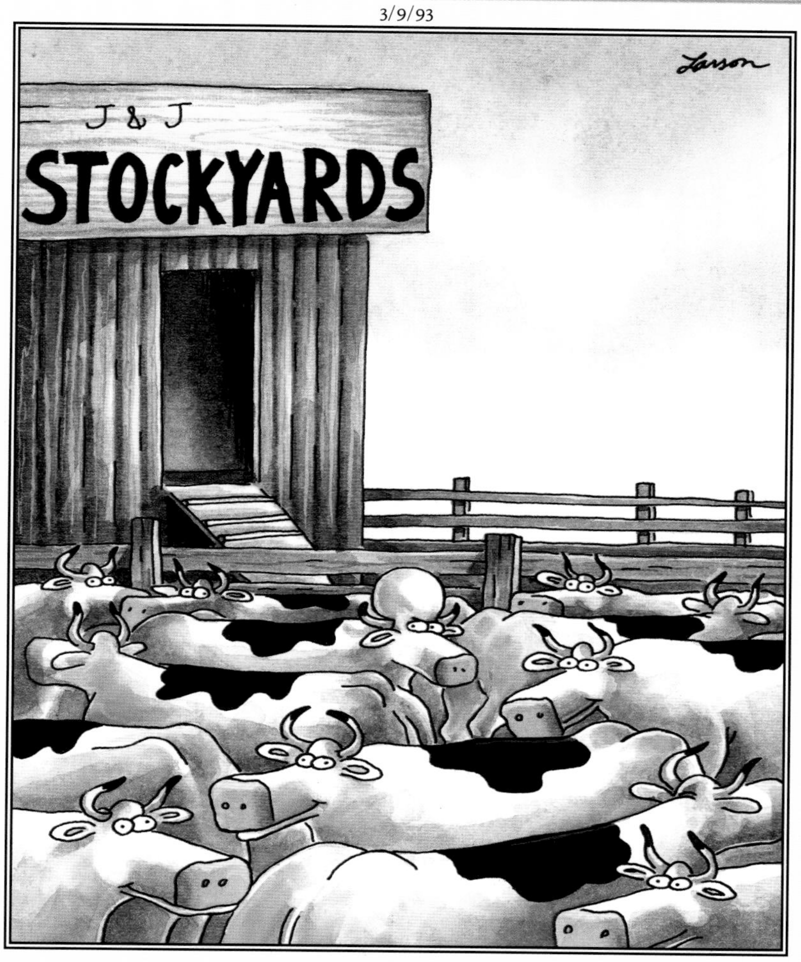
J & J
STOCKYARDS
Larson

Only Claire, with her oversized brain,
wore an expression of concern.

3/4/93

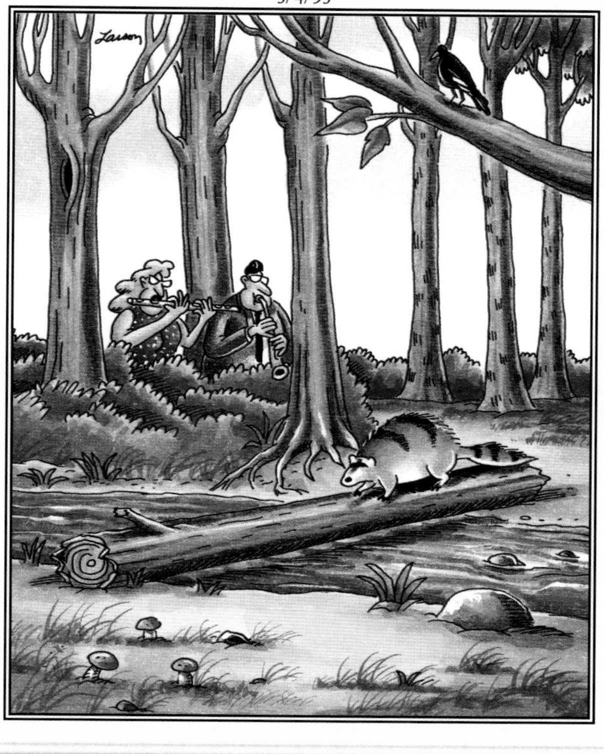

On this particular day, Rory the raccoon was hunting frogs at his favorite stream, and the pleasant background music told him that Mr. Mountain Lion was nowhere around.

3/8/93

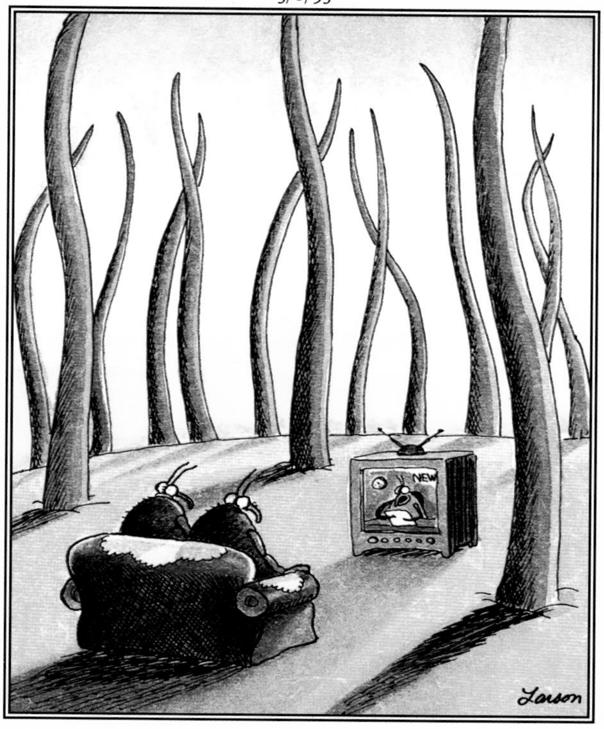
NEW
Larson

"Several more deaths have been reported in the neck area, and although the authorities won't comment, some residents are blaming the new collar."

3/5/93

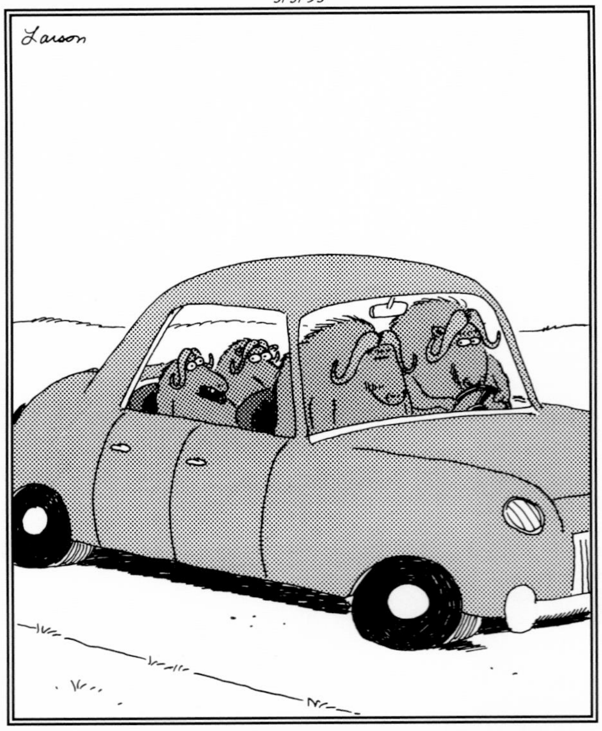

"It wasn't *me,* Dad! It was Randy's musk glands!"

3/10/93

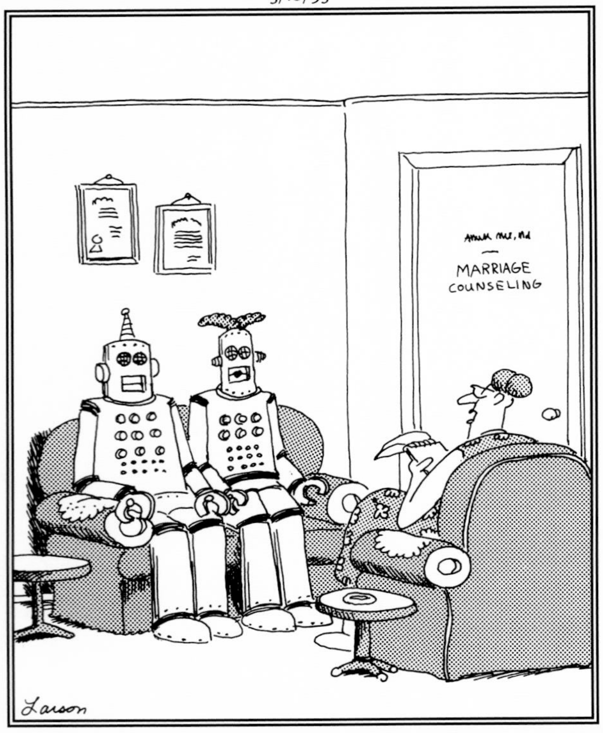
MARRIAGE
COUNSELING

"The problem, as I see it, is that you both are extremely adept at pushing each other's buttons."

3/15/93

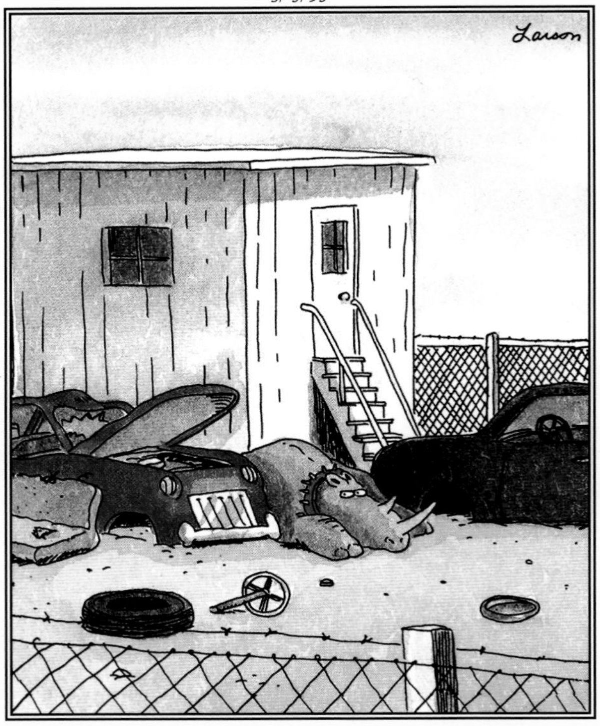

Several times more dangerous than his African cousin, the junkyard rhino offers the ultimate in property protection.

3/12/93

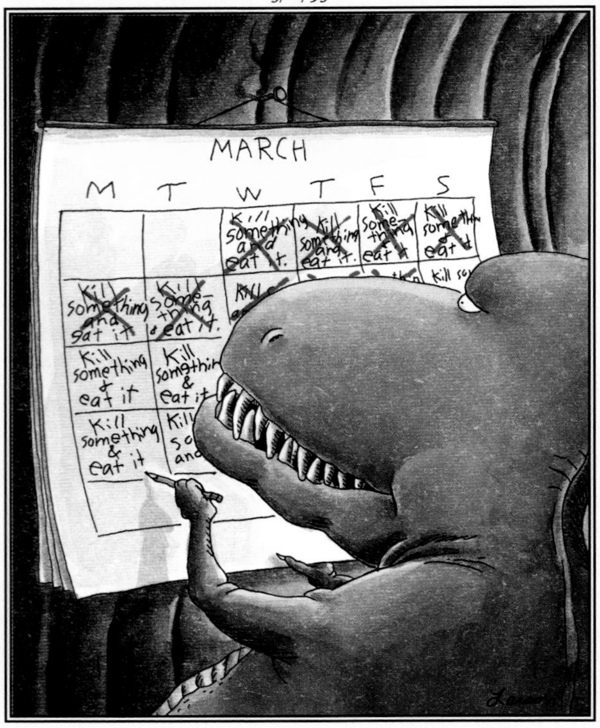
MARCH
M T W T F S
Kill something & eat it

Jurassic calendars

3/11/93

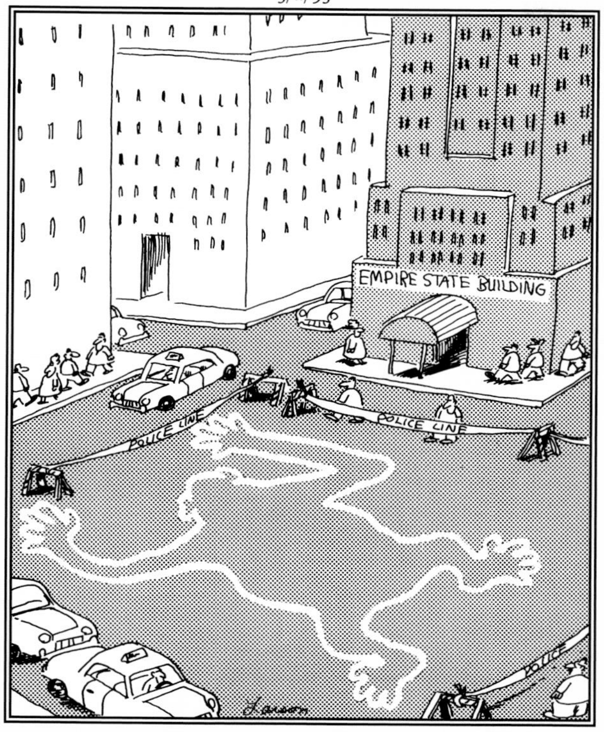
EMPIRE STATE BUILDING
POLICE LINE
POLICE LINE

3/18/93

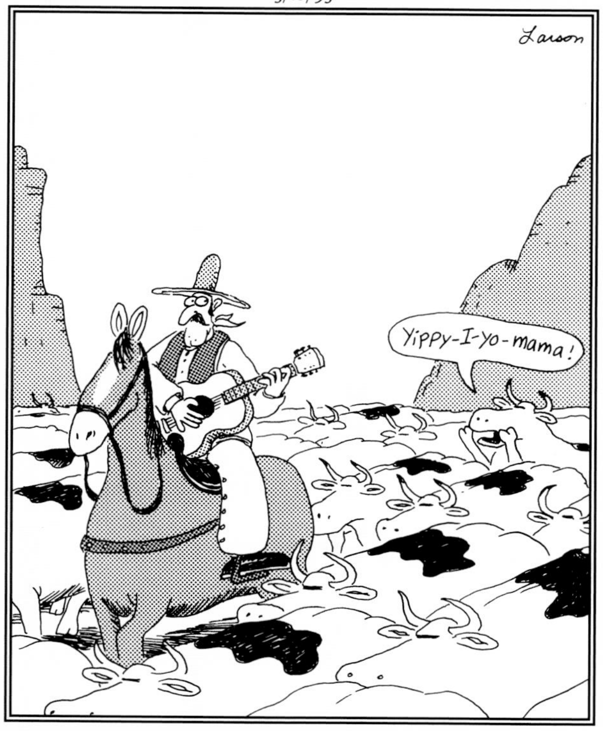
Yippy-I-yo-mama!

3/16/93

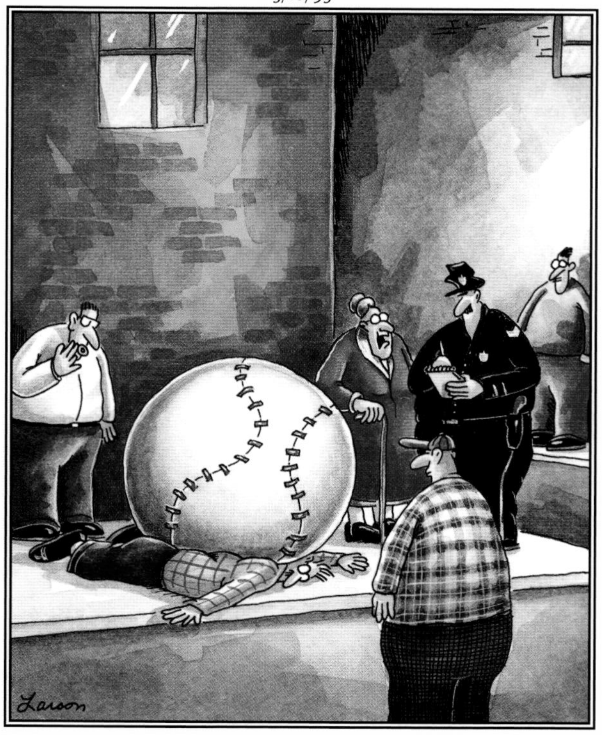

"And then, WHAM! This thing just came right out of left field."

3/17/93

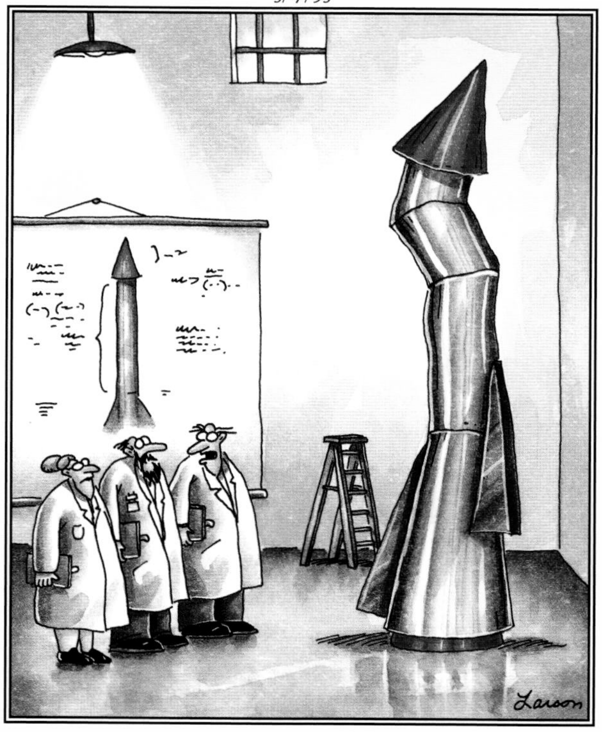

"It's time we face reality, my friends. ... We're not exactly rocket scientists."

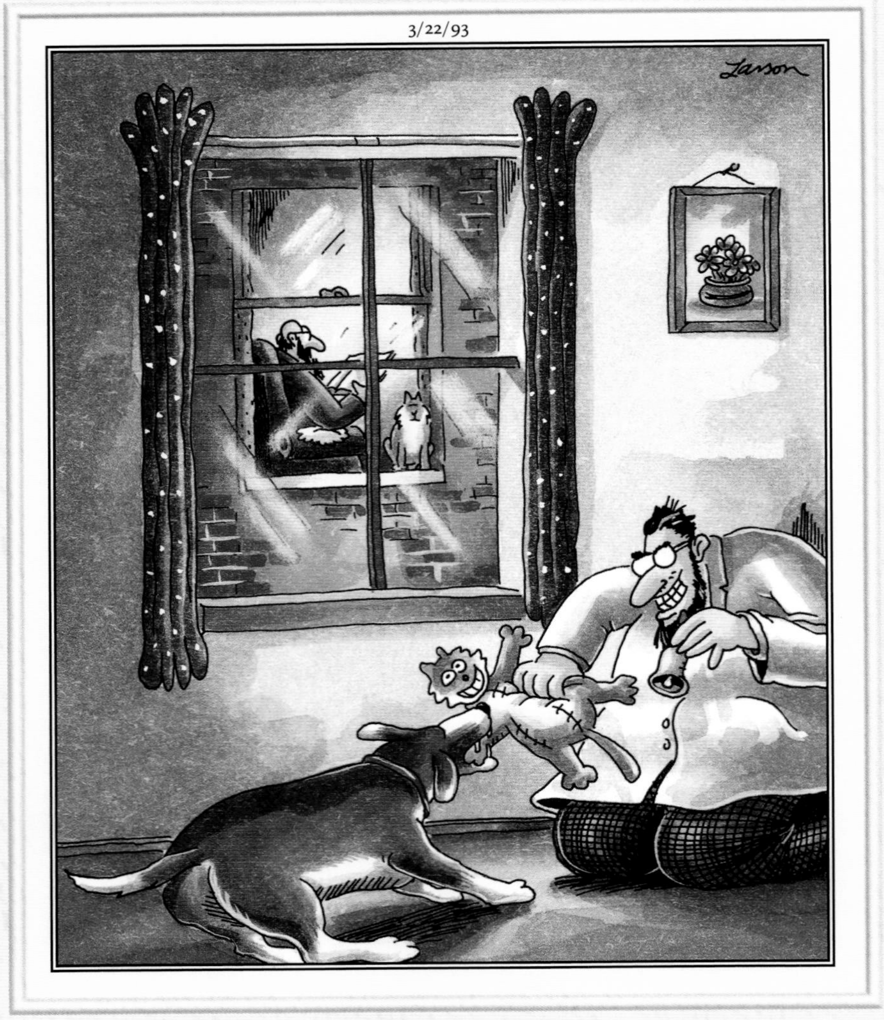
3/22/93
Larson

Unbeknownst to most students of psychology, Pavlov's first experiment was to ring a bell and cause his dog to attack Freud's cat.

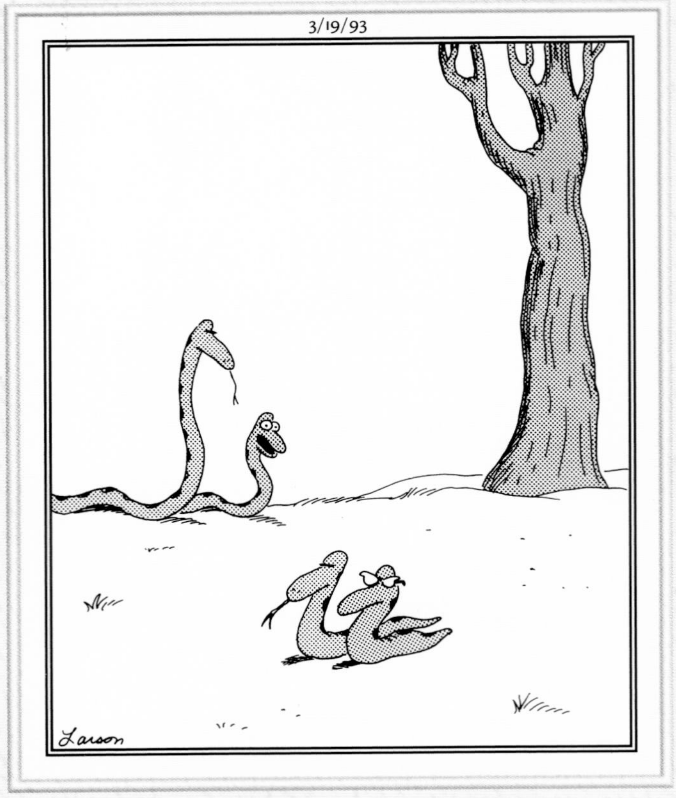
3/19/93
Larson

"Look, Dad! ... Snidgets!"

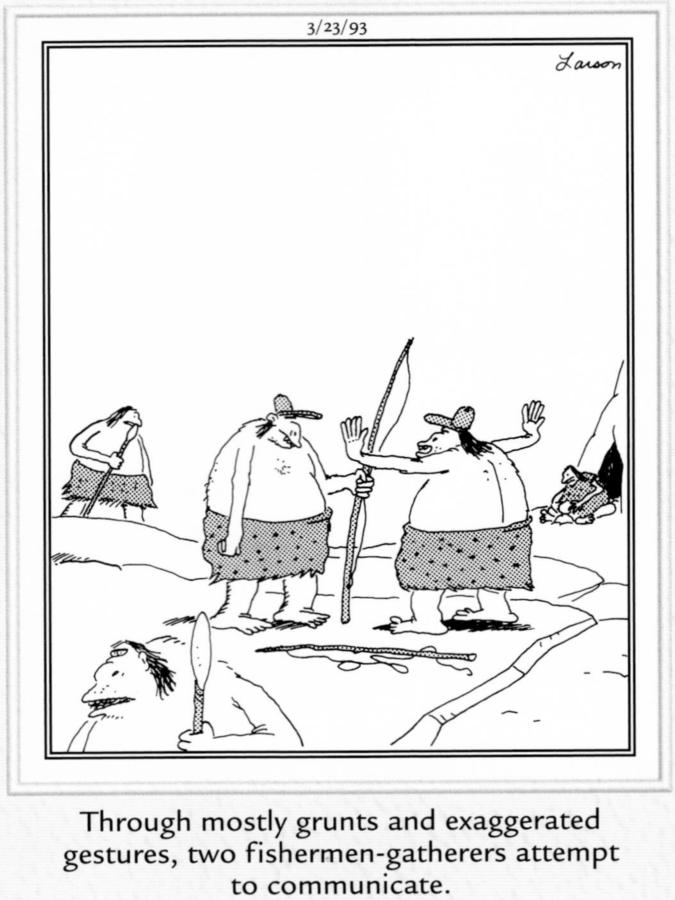
3/23/93
Larson

Through mostly grunts and exaggerated gestures, two fishermen-gatherers attempt to communicate.

3/29/93

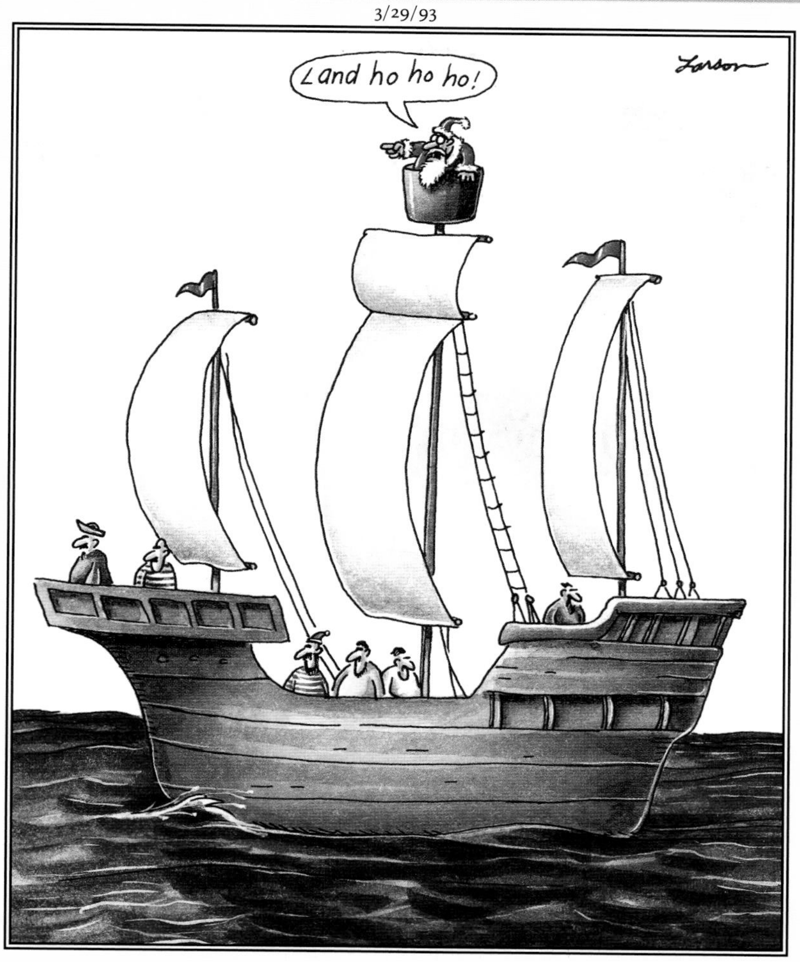
Land ho ho ho!
Larson

Santa arrives in the New World.

3/25/93

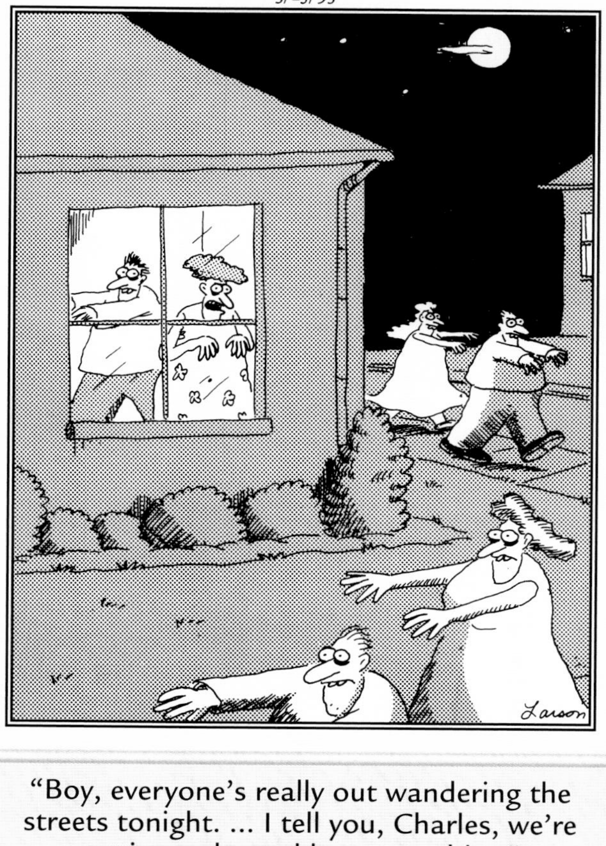
Larson

"Boy, everyone's really out wandering the streets tonight. ... I tell you, Charles, we're getting to be real home zombies."

3/26/93

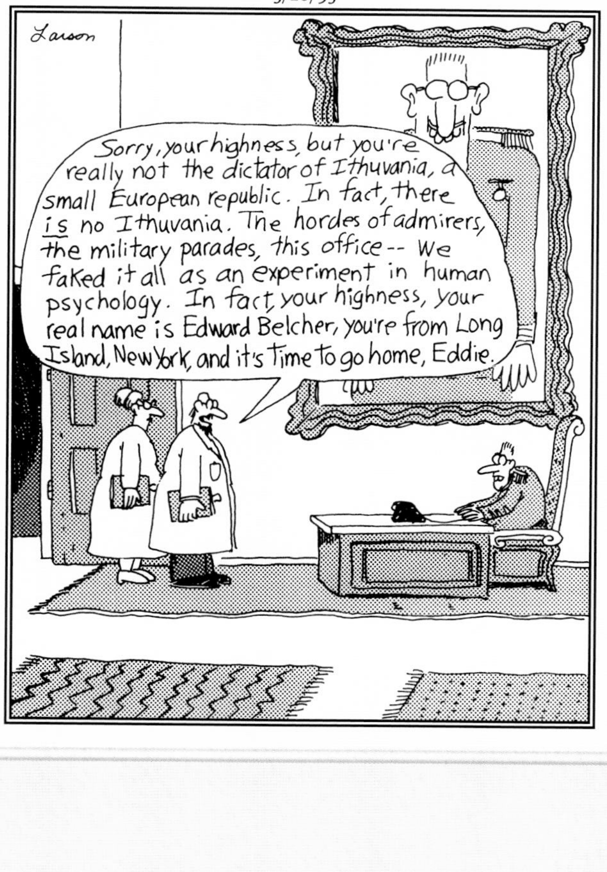
Larson
Sorry, your highness, but you're really not the dictator of Ithuvania, a small European republic. In fact, there is no Ithuvania. The hordes of admirers, the military parades, this office -- We faked it all as an experiment in human psychology. In fact, your highness, your real name is Edward Belcher, you're from Long Island, New York, and it's time to go home, Eddie.

3/24/93

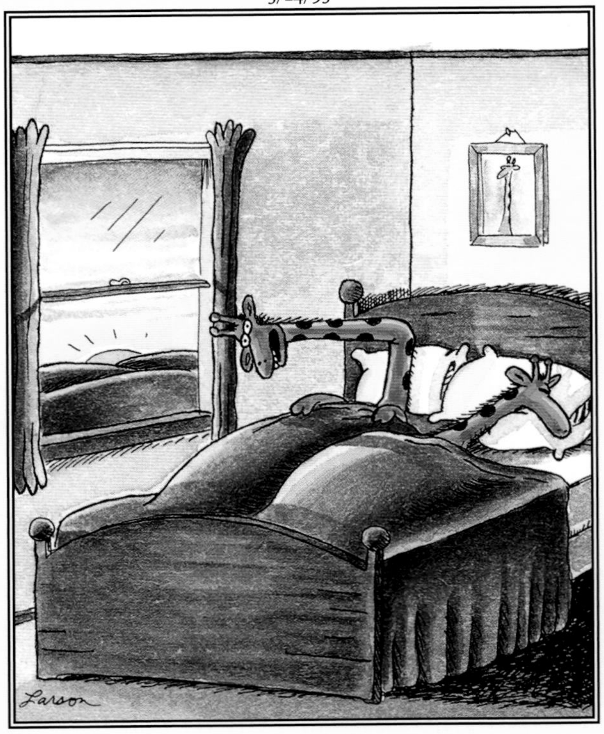

"Dang! ... Stiff neck!"

3/30/93

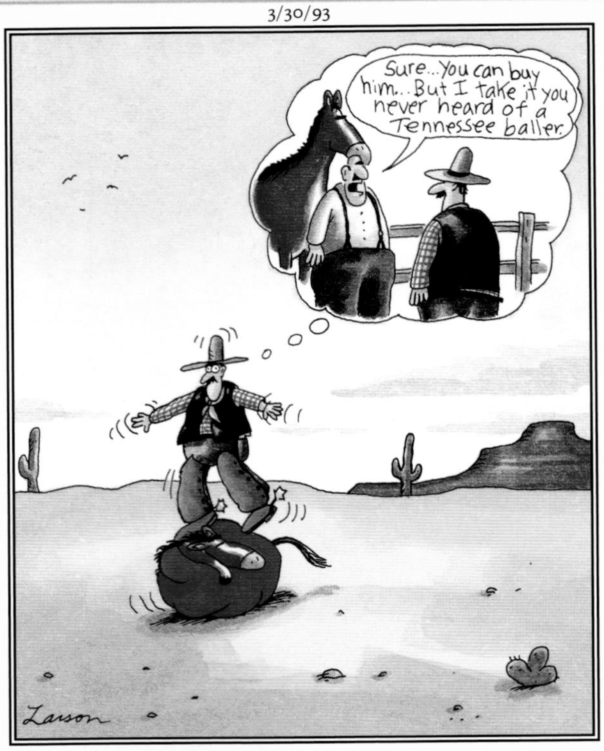
Sure... You can buy him... But I take it you never heard of a Tennessee baller.

3/31/93

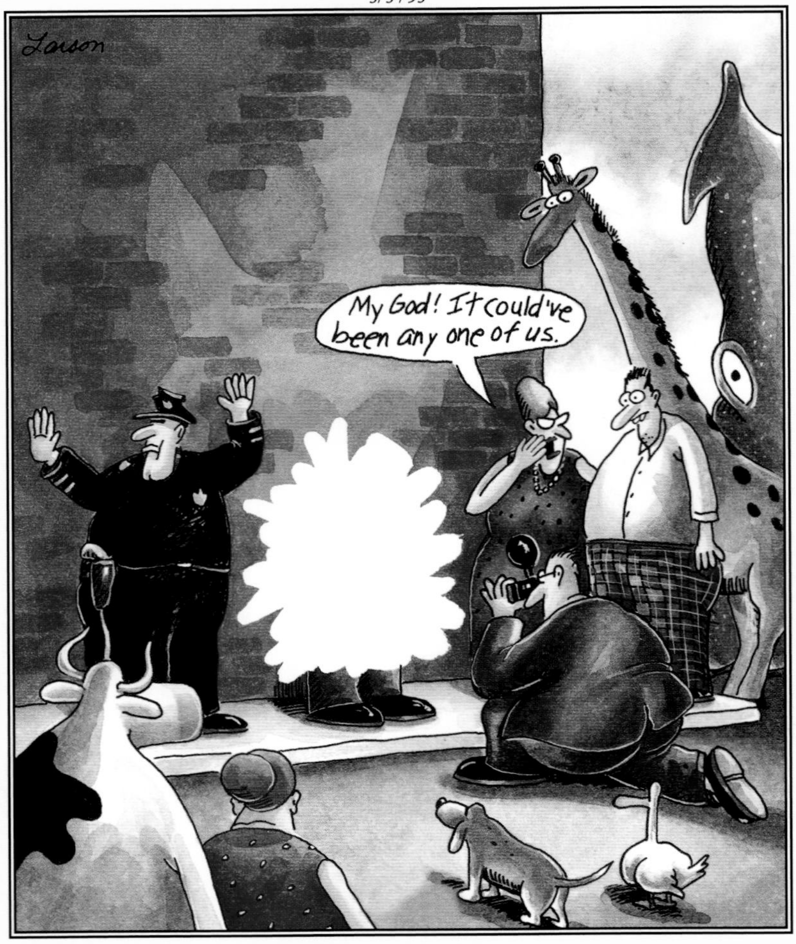
My God! It could've been any one of us.

Drive-by erasings

4/2/93

ON
OFF

"Hey, who's that? ... Oh—Mitch, the janitor. Well, our first test run has just gotten a little more interesting."

4/1/93

This is it, Kids... The mouth.

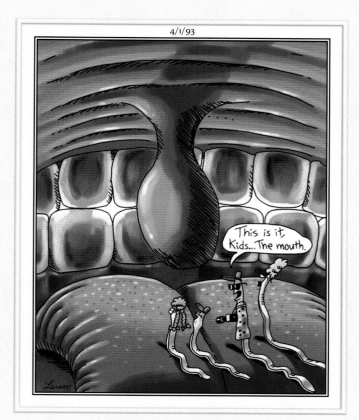

Tapeworms on vacation

4/5/93

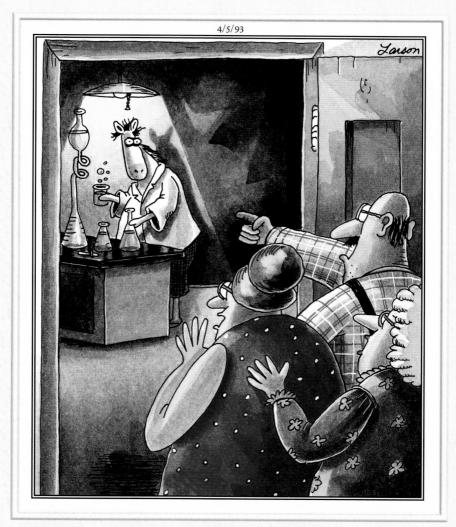

Scene from *Dr. Jekyll and Mr. Ed*

4/6/93

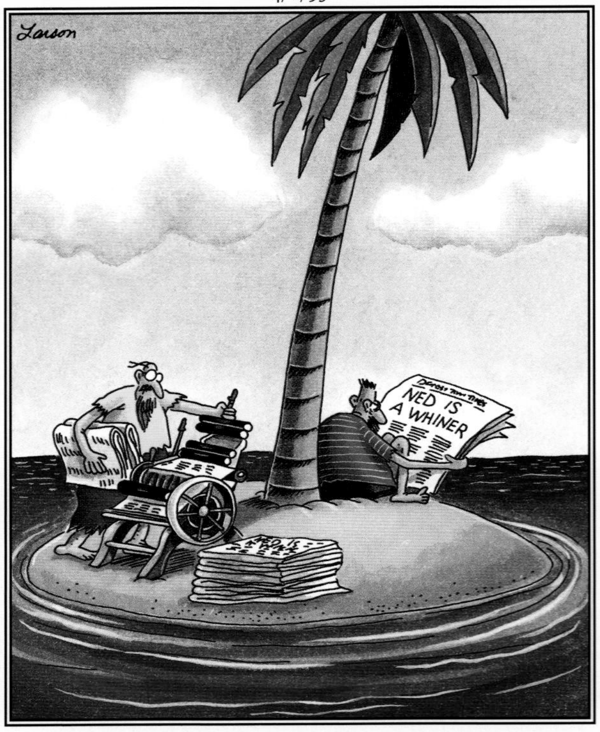
Larson
NED IS A WHINER

Hot off the press, the very first edition of the *Desert Island Times* caused the newspaper to quickly fold.

4/7/93

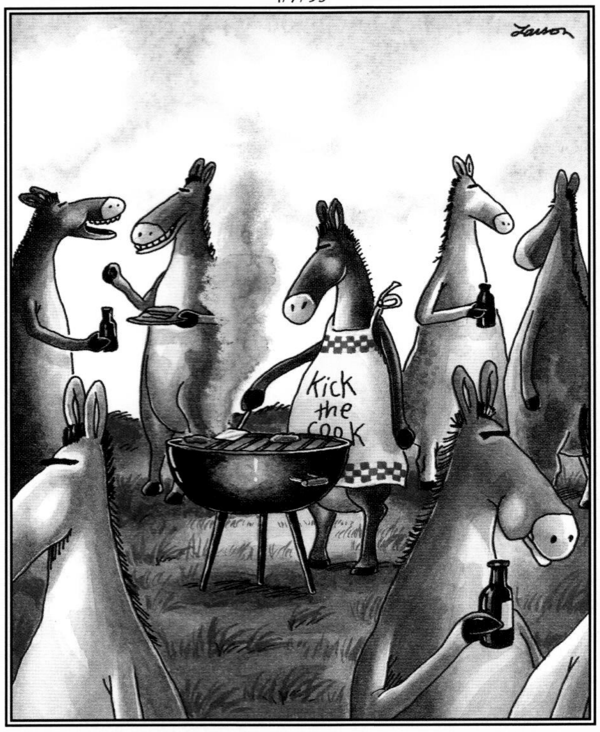
Larson
Kick the cook

4/8/93

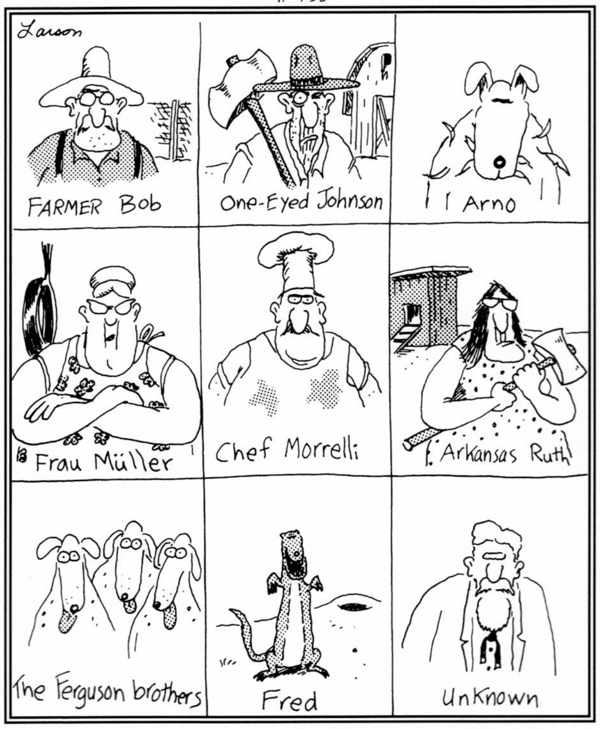
Larson
FARMER Bob
One-Eyed Johnson
Arno
Frau Müller
Chef Morrelli
Arkansas Ruth
The Ferguson brothers
Fred
Unknown

Chicken serial killers

4/12/93

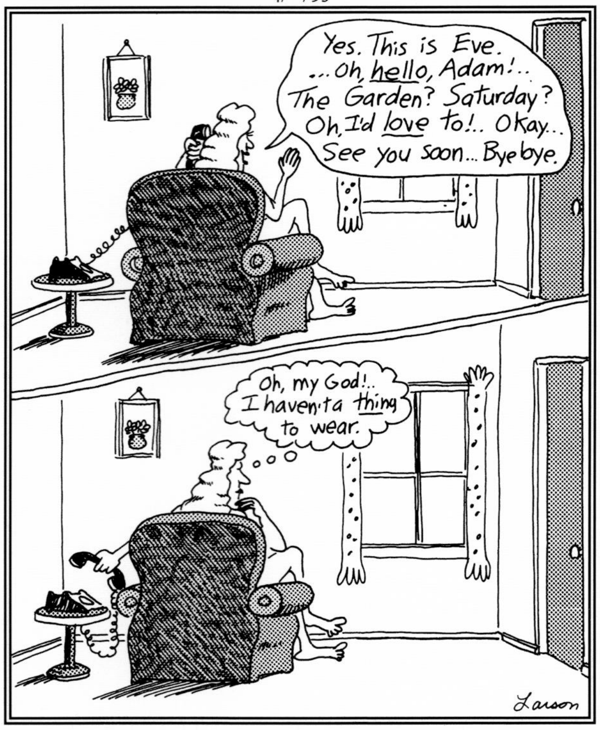
Yes. This is Eve. ...Oh, hello, Adam!.. The Garden? Saturday? Oh, I'd love to!.. Okay... See you soon... Bye bye.
Oh, my God!.. I haven't a thing to wear.
Larson

4/9/93

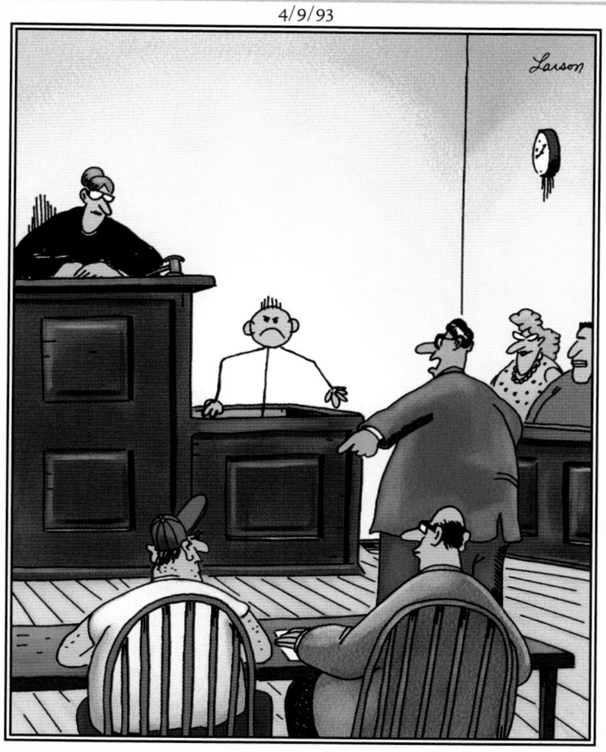

"One more time: You were at the park, enjoying the afternoon, when you distinctly heard the defendant turn to his dog and say, 'Look, boy! A stickman!'"

4/14/93

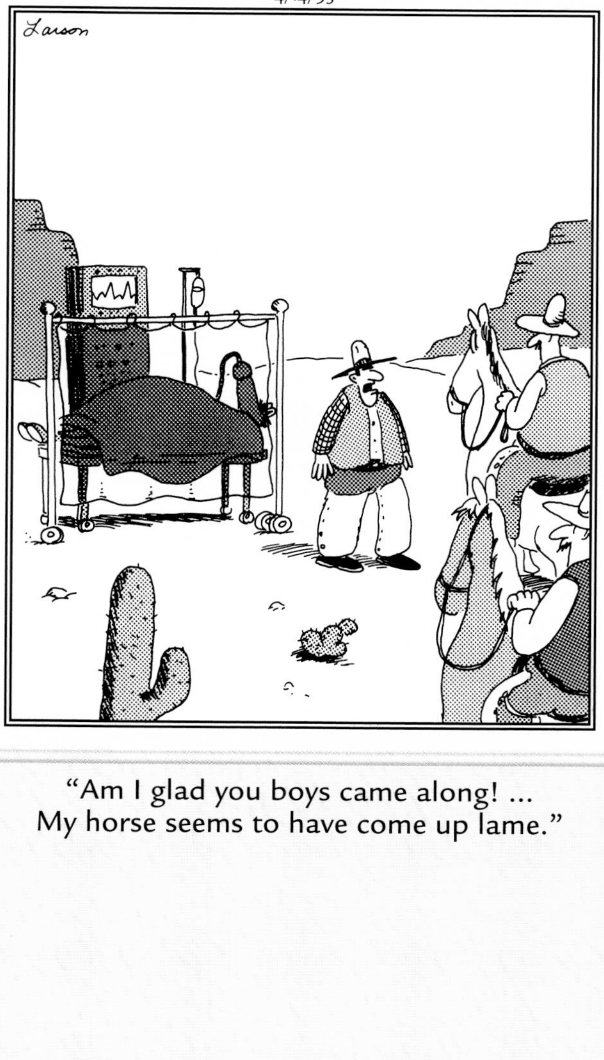

"Am I glad you boys came along! ... My horse seems to have come up lame."

4/15/93

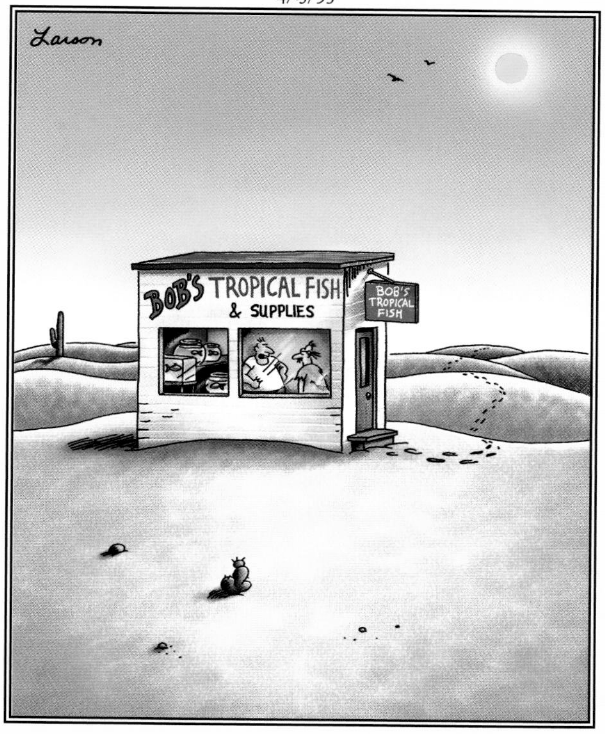
BOB'S TROPICAL FISH
& SUPPLIES
BOB'S TROPICAL FISH

"Hey! You're not lookin' to buy anything, are you? ... I think you best just keep movin', buddy."

4/16/93

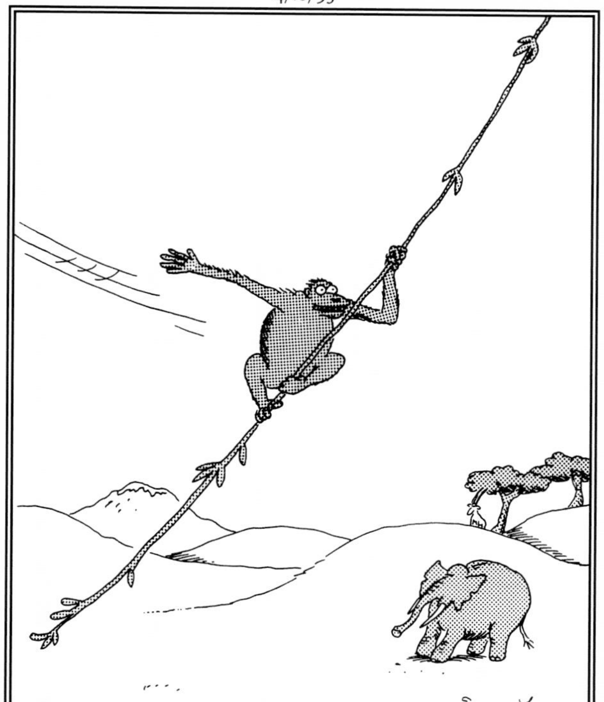

He had seen Tanzania, and most of Mozambique was already behind him. There was no mistake. Chippy had done what most chimps only dream about: He had caught the Perfect Vine.

4/13/93

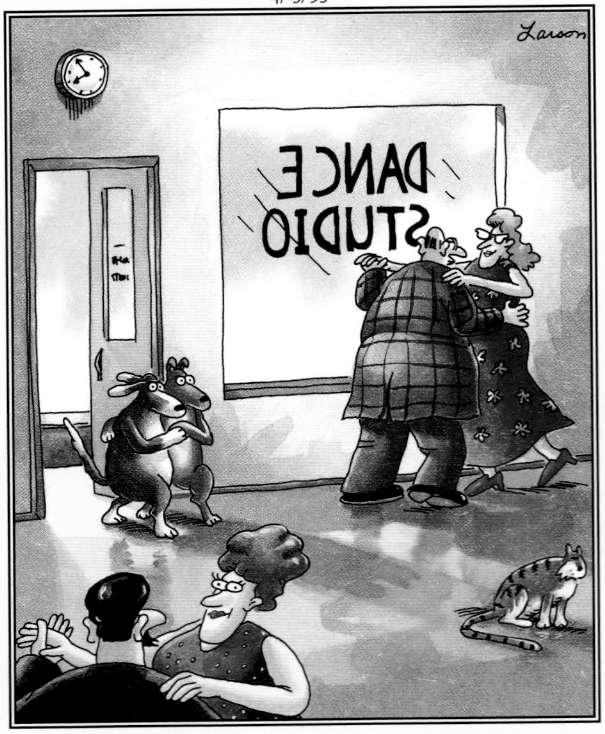
DANCE
STUDIO

As witnesses later recalled, two small dogs just waltzed into the place, grabbed the cat, and waltzed out.

4/21/93

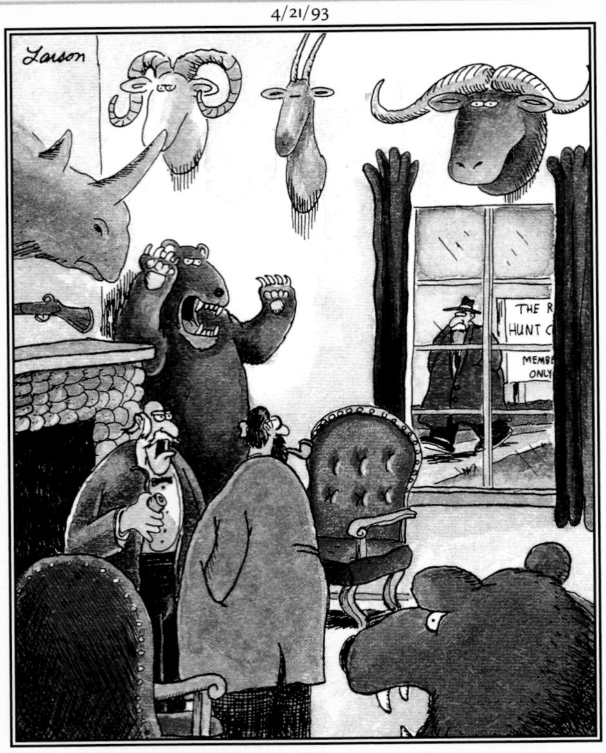

"Oh, God! Here comes Finchley! ... He's out of the closet, you know—says he kills only for food, not for sport."

4/22/93

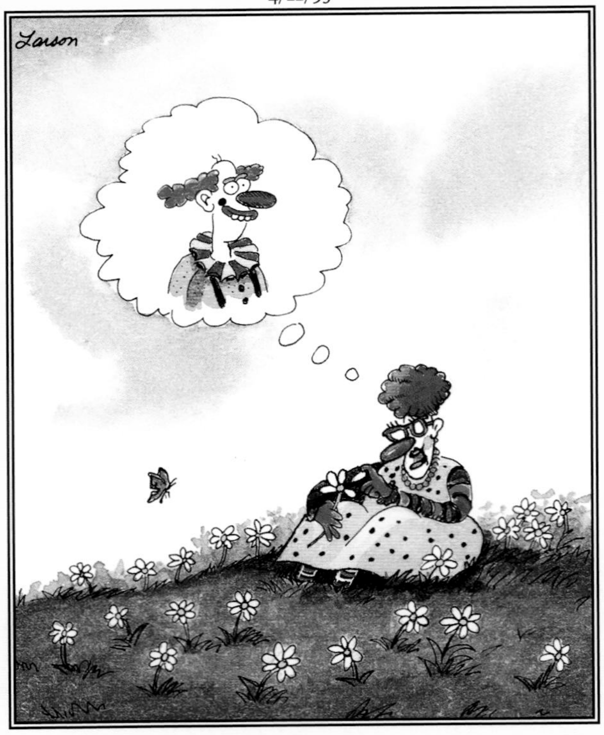

"He kids me ... he kids me not. ... He kids me ... he kids me not. ..."

4/19/93

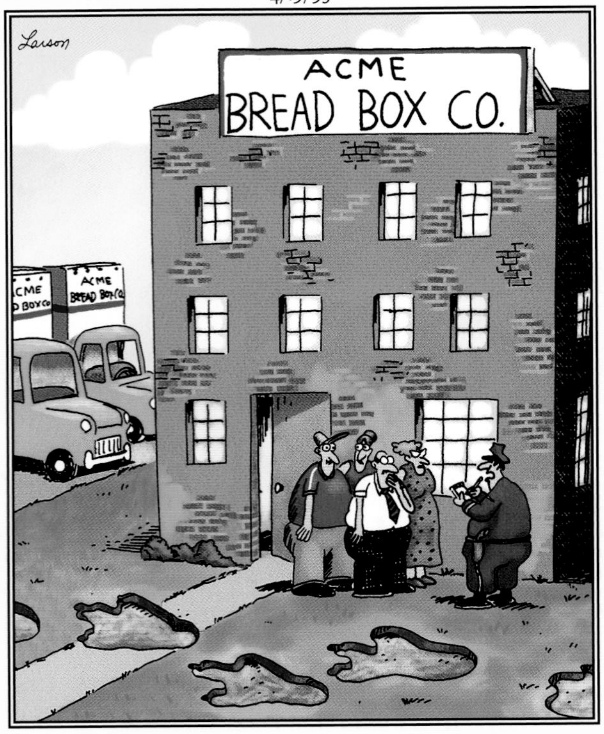
ACME
BREAD BOX CO.

"Okay, okay! Calm down, everyone! ... This monster—would you say he was bigger or smaller than your building? ... You can talk it over."

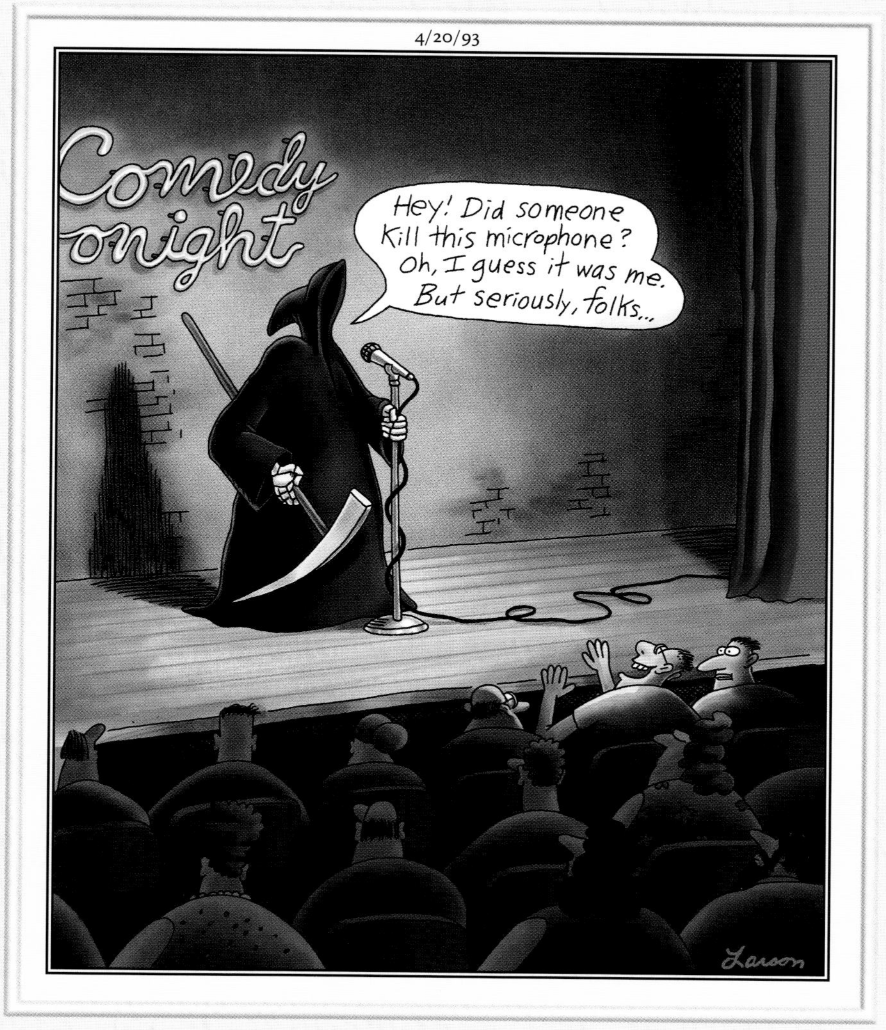
4/20/93
Comedy Tonight
Hey! Did someone Kill this microphone? Oh, I guess it was me. But seriously, folks...
Larson

Only Bernard, in the front row, had the nerve
to laugh at Death.

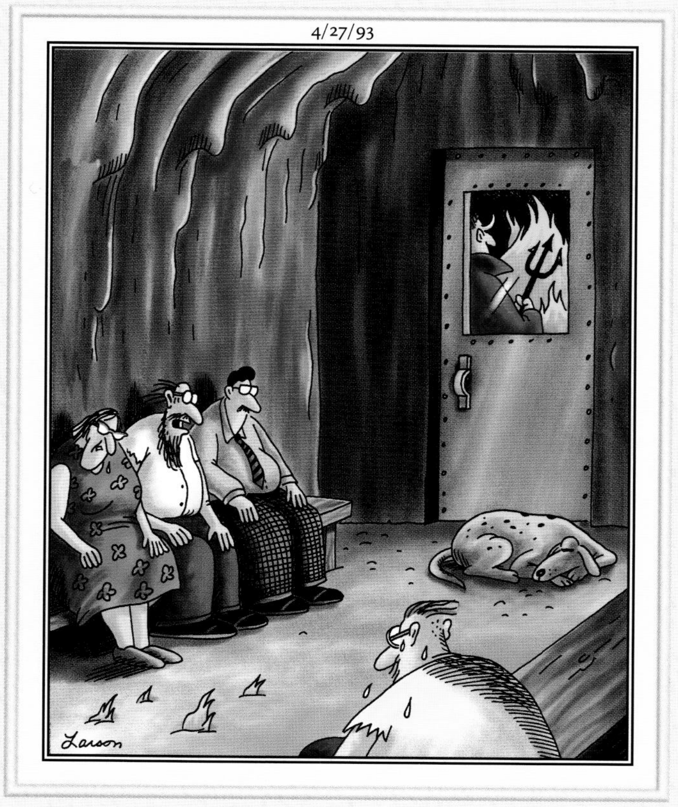
4/27/93
Larson

"*His* story? Well, I dunno. ... I always assumed
he was just a bad dog."

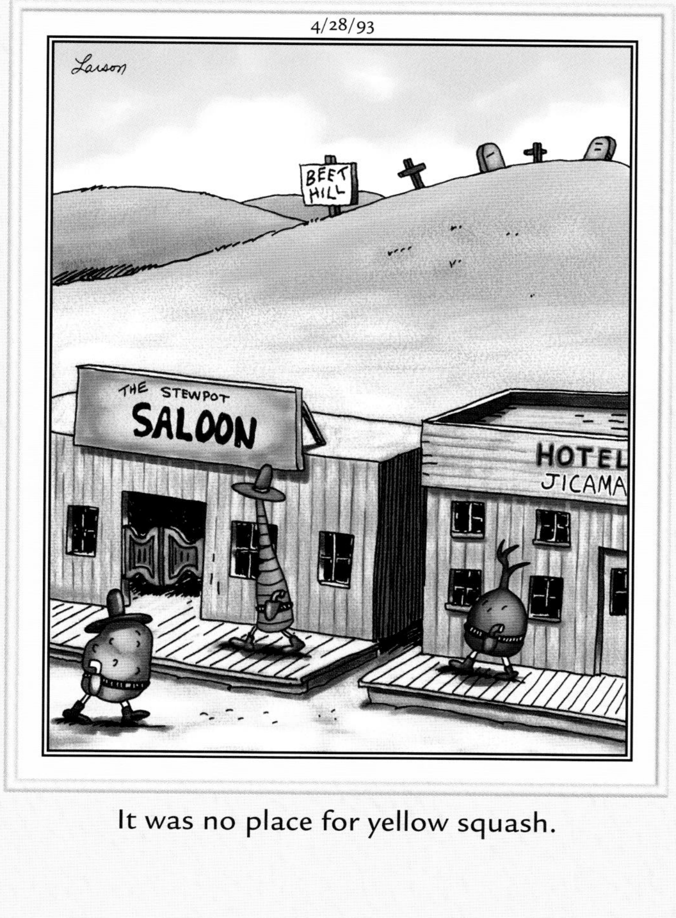
4/28/93
Larson
BEET HILL
THE STEWPOT SALOON
HOTEL JICAMA

It was no place for yellow squash.

4/23/93

Larson

"Man, these pups today with all their fancy balls and whatnot. ... Why, back in our day, we had to play with a half-rotted cat's head."

4/26/93

Larson

"We've done it! They've linked up! ... Man, Feldman must be freaking out— he even hates spiders."

4/29/93

Larson
LIBRARY

Back in his college days, Igor was known as the HBOC.

4/30/93

Larson
quack quack quack quack quack quack
Chicken!
quack quack quack

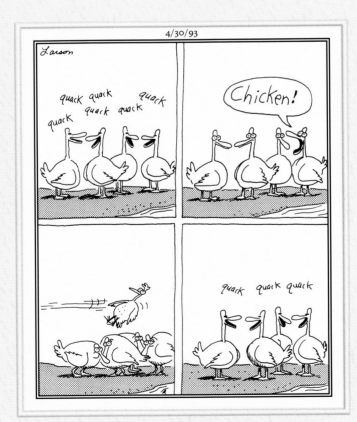

"And so," the interviewer asked, "Do you ever have trouble coming up with ideas?" "Well, sometimes," the cartoonist replied.

5/5/93

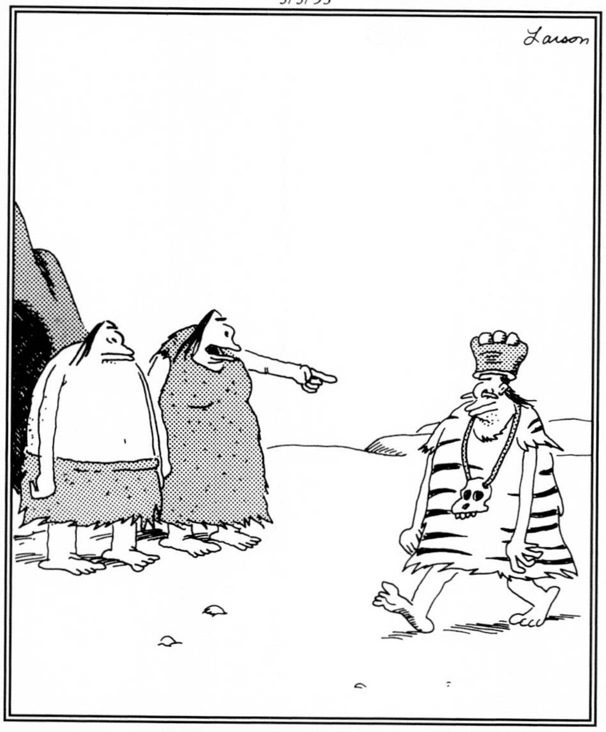
Larson

"Whoa! Look at Zagar! ...
He dressed to the twos!"

5/6/93

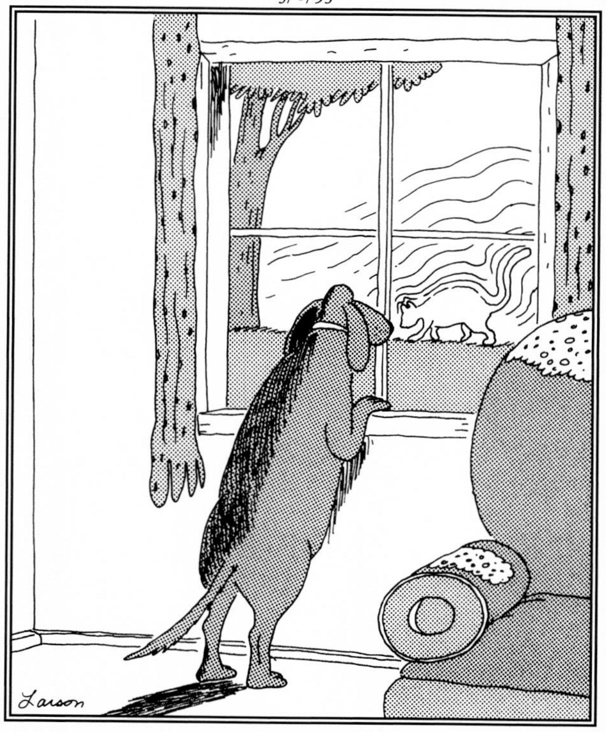
Larson

On hot days, dogs are often subject to the
phenomenon of cat mirages.

5/4/93

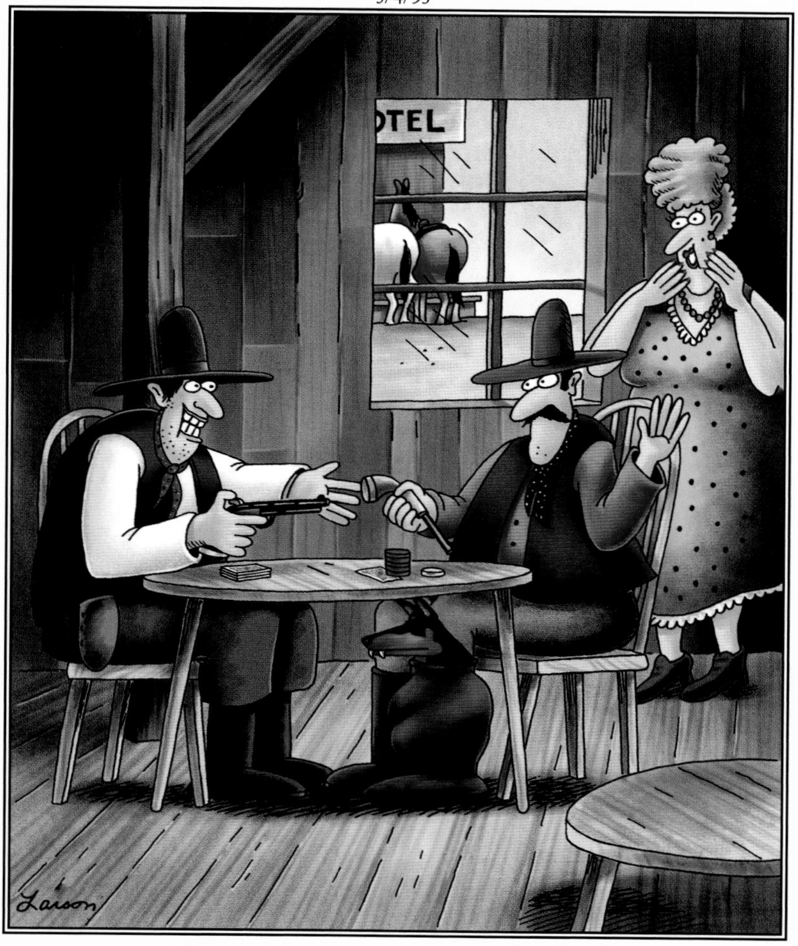
OTEL
Larson

What the stranger didn't know, of course, was that
Sam always kept a Dobie in his boot.

"Okay, time for lunch. ... And Dwayne here will be dismissing
you by row number, since he's the alpha wolf today."

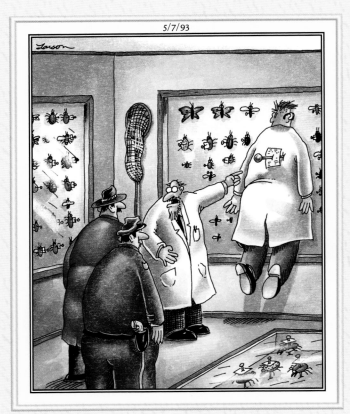

"Professor LaVonne had many enemies in the
entomological world, detective, but if you
examine that data label, you'll find exactly when
and where he was—shall we say—'collected.'"

The magnificent Lipizzaner cows

5/13/93

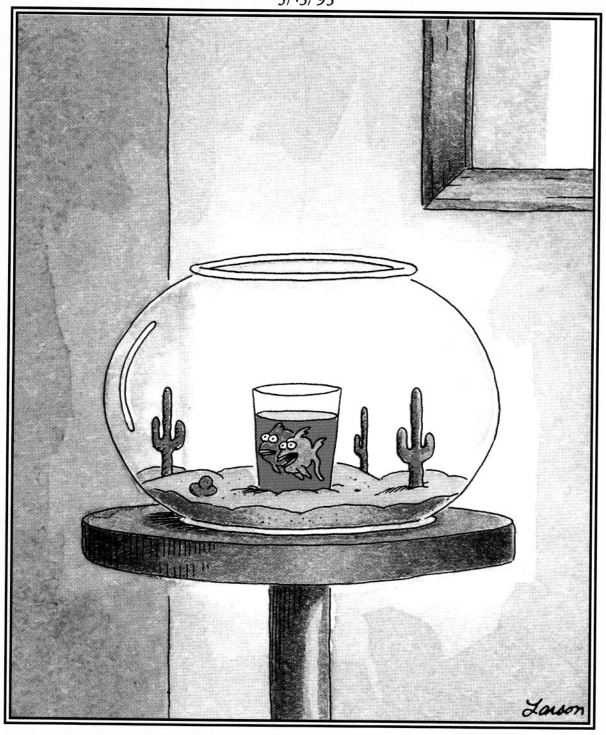
Larson

"I love the desert."

5/14/93

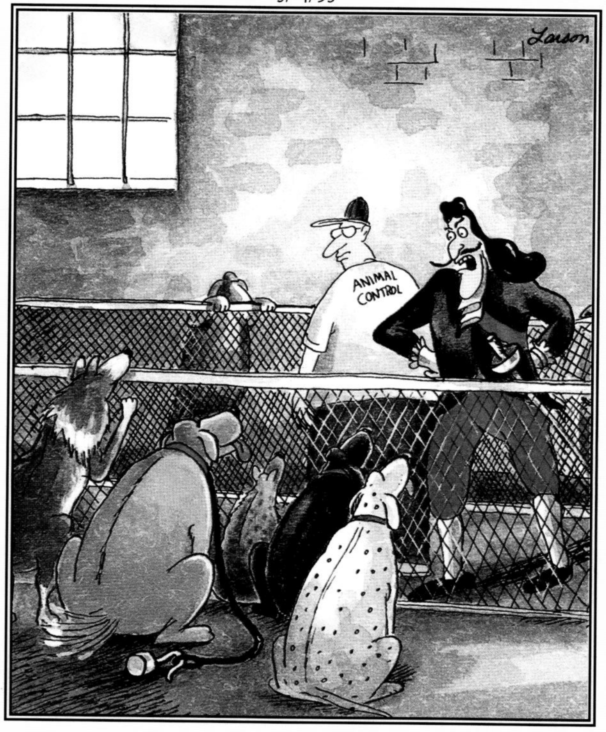
Larson
ANIMAL CONTROL

"*There* he is! ... Bruno! Bad dog!"

5/11/93

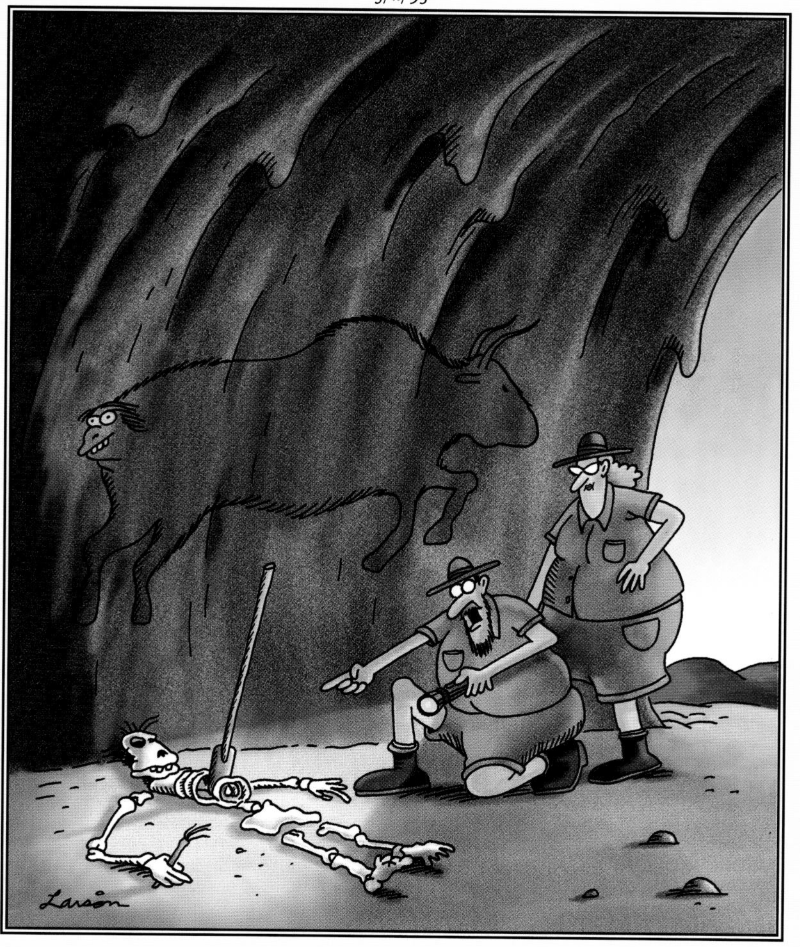
Larson

"Amazing! The mummified remains of a prehistoric cave-painter, still clutching his brush! ... Seems he made an enemy, though."

5/10/93

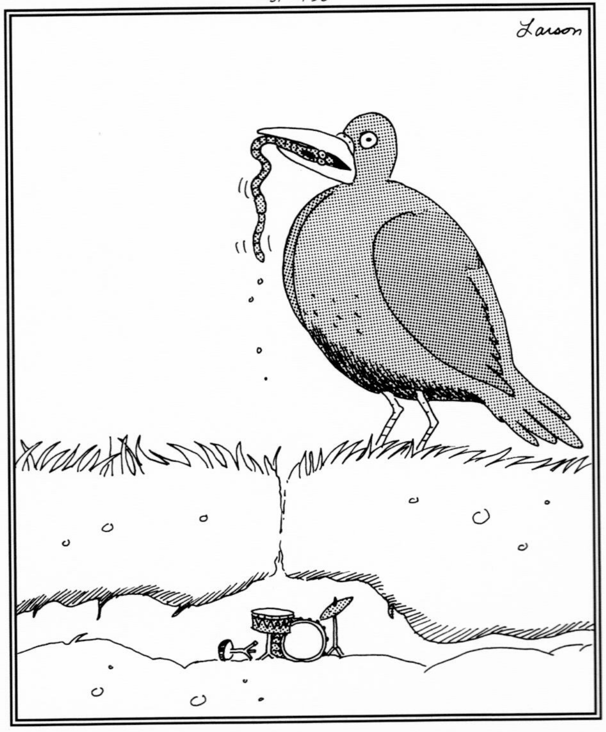
Larson

5/17/93

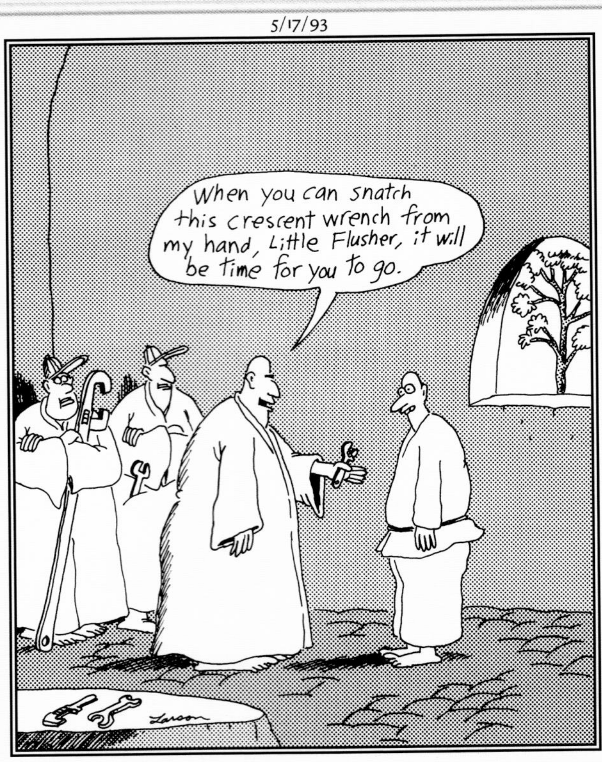
When you can snatch this crescent wrench from my hand, Little Flusher, it will be time for you to go.
Larson

The Shaolin School of Plumbing

5/19/93

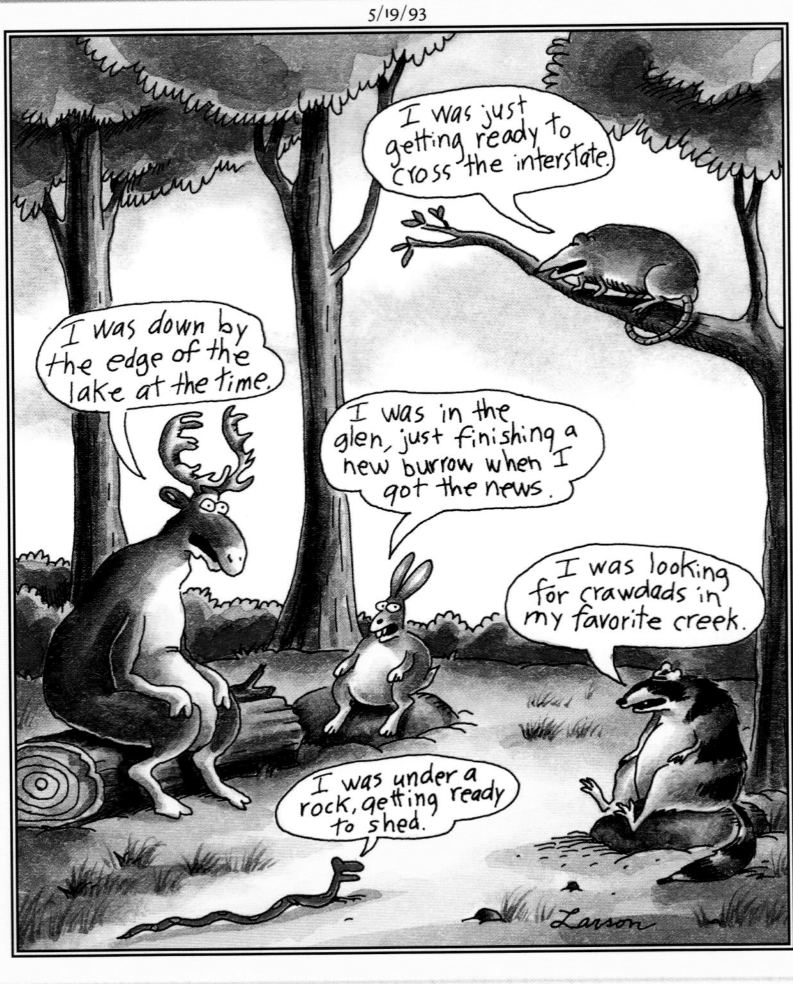
I was just getting ready to cross the interstate.
I was down by the edge of the lake at the time.
I was in the glen, just finishing a new burrow when I got the news.
I was looking for crawdads in my favorite creek.
I was under a rock, getting ready to shed.
Larson

More facts of nature: All forest animals, to this very day, remember exactly where they were and what they were doing when they heard that Bambi's mother had been shot.

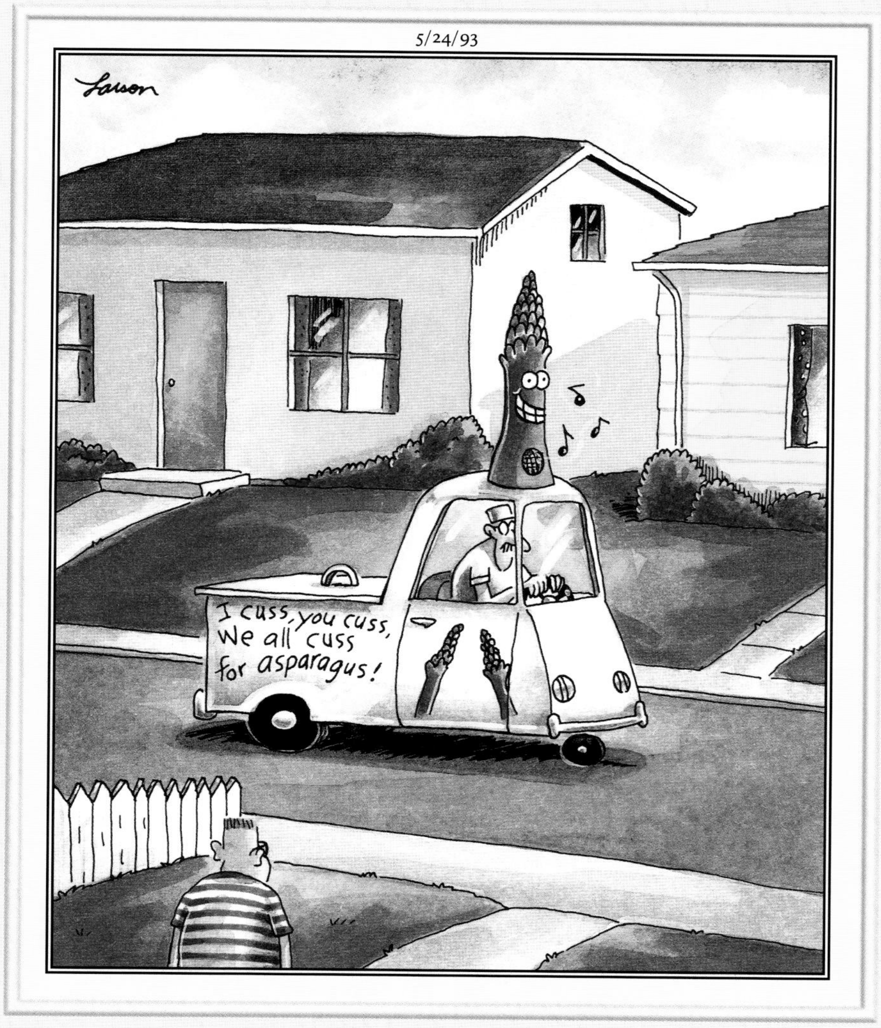
5/24/93
Larson
I cuss, you cuss,
We all cuss
for asparagus!

Failed marketing ploys

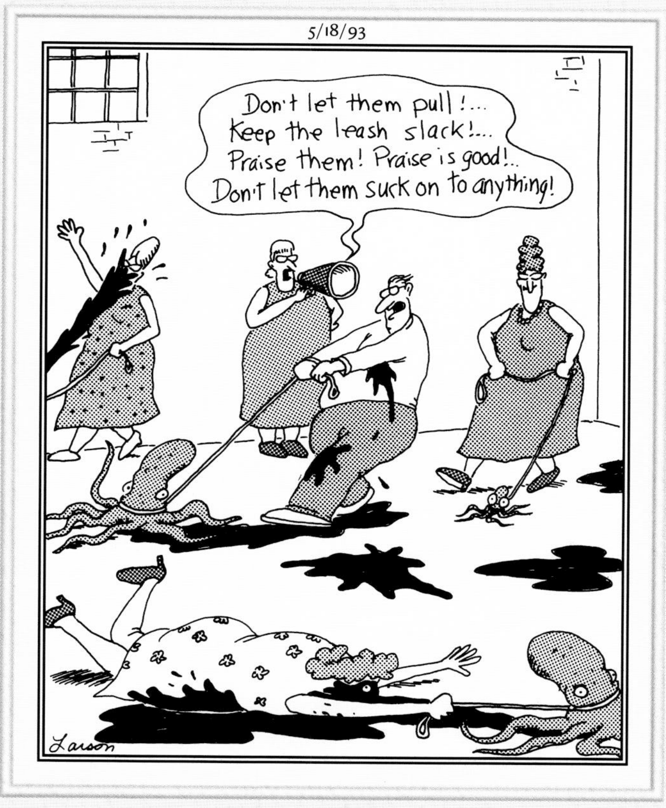
5/18/93
Don't let them pull!...
Keep the leash slack!...
Praise them! Praise is good!..
Don't let them suck on to anything!
Larson

Octopus obedience school

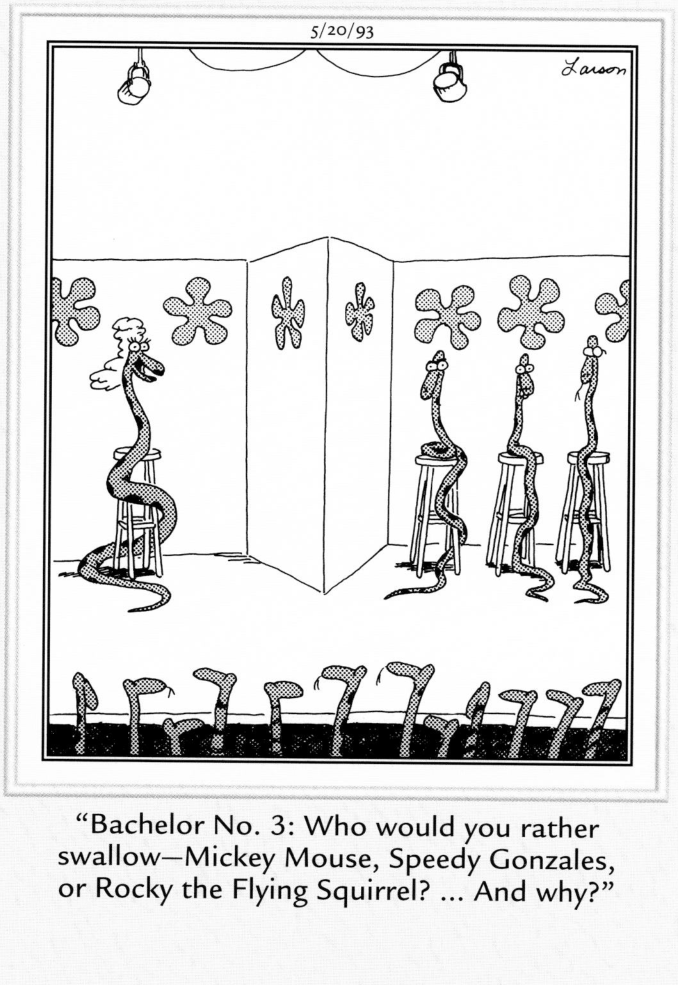
5/20/93
Larson

"Bachelor No. 3: Who would you rather swallow—Mickey Mouse, Speedy Gonzales, or Rocky the Flying Squirrel? ... And why?"

5/26/93

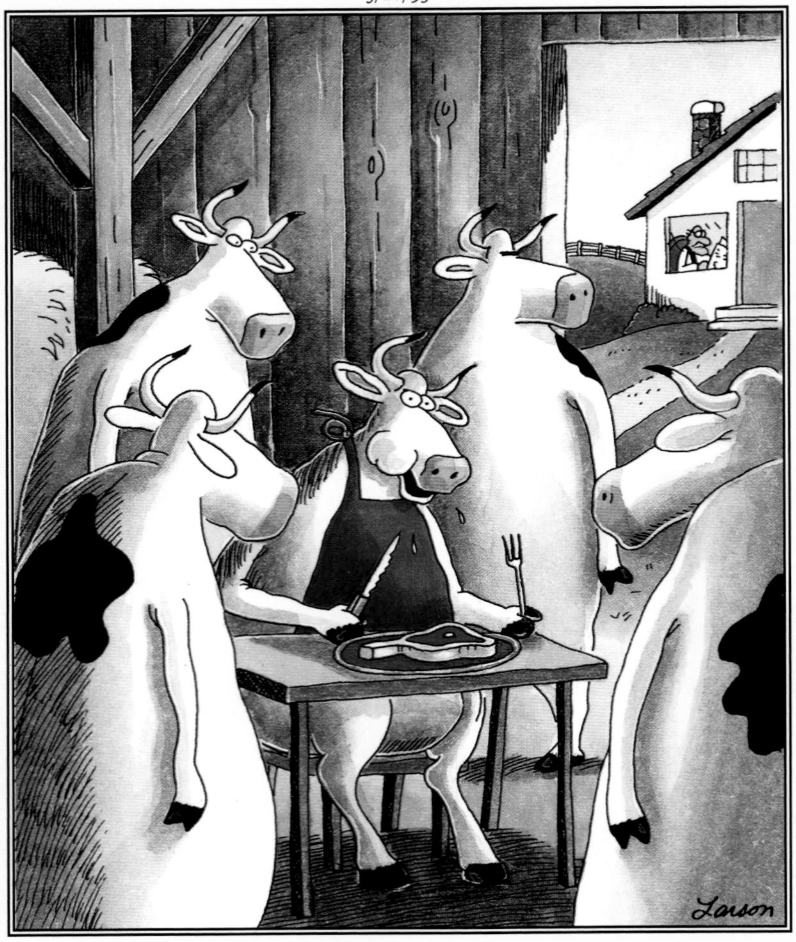

"Mmmmmm ... interesting ... interesting. ... Well, I'd say we taste a little like chicken."

5/21/93

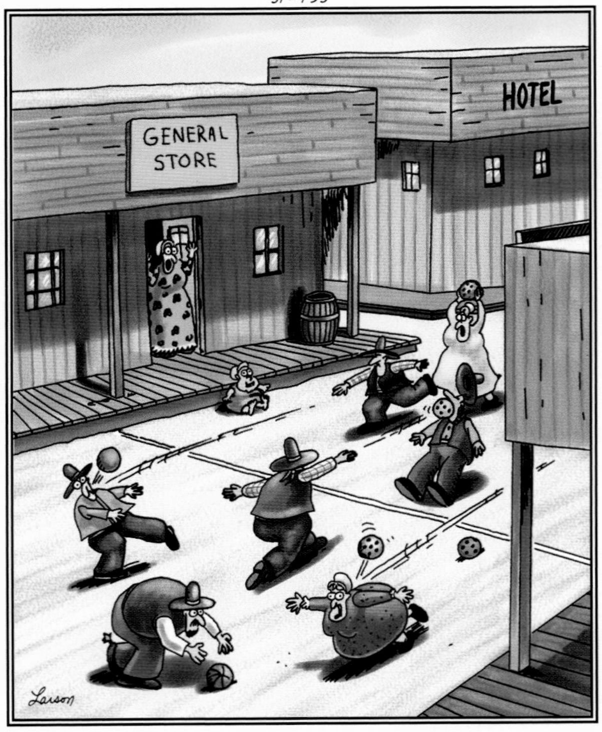
GENERAL STORE
HOTEL

It was a tough frontier town; but later, after the arrival of the Earp brothers, things calmed down, and the town's name was shortened to simply Dodge City.

5/27/93

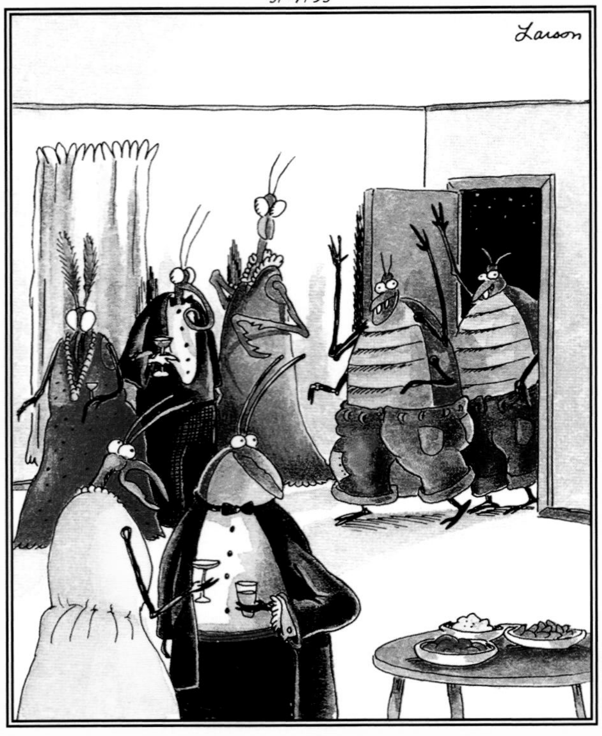

"Oh, my God! Dung beetles! ... And in their filthy dungarees, of course!"

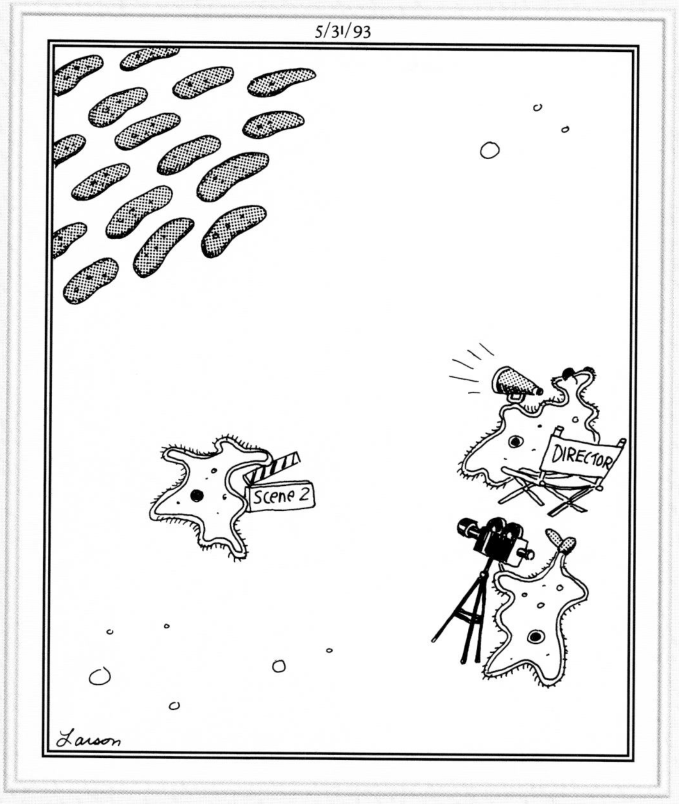
5/31/93
DIRECTOR
Scene 2
Larson

"Okay! When I say 'action,' all you bacteria charge the camera! ... Remember, this is the biggest scene in the whole movie—relatively speaking!"

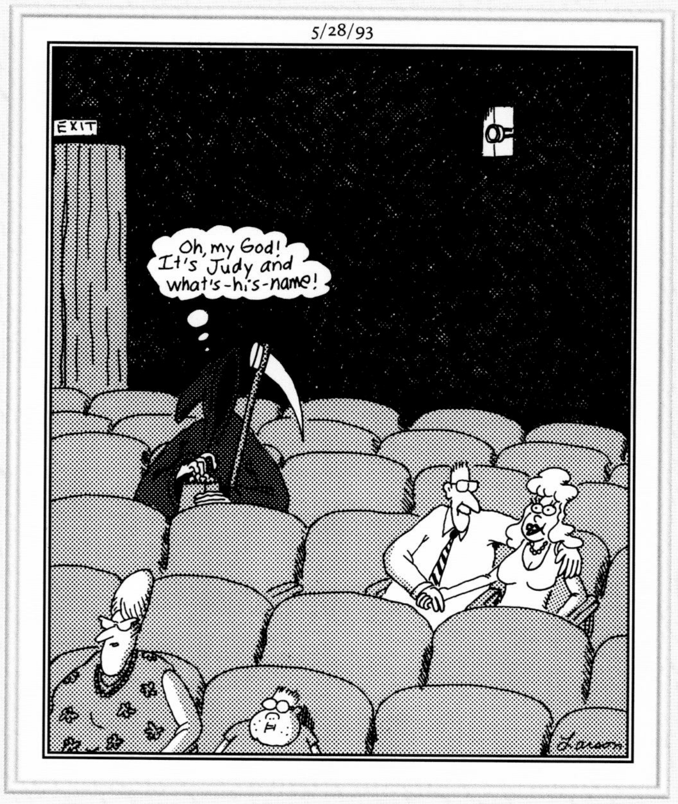
5/28/93
EXIT
Oh, my God! It's Judy and what's-his-name!
Larson

As his eyes grew accustomed to the dark, Death suddenly noticed his girlfriend sitting with Dr. Jack Kevorkian.

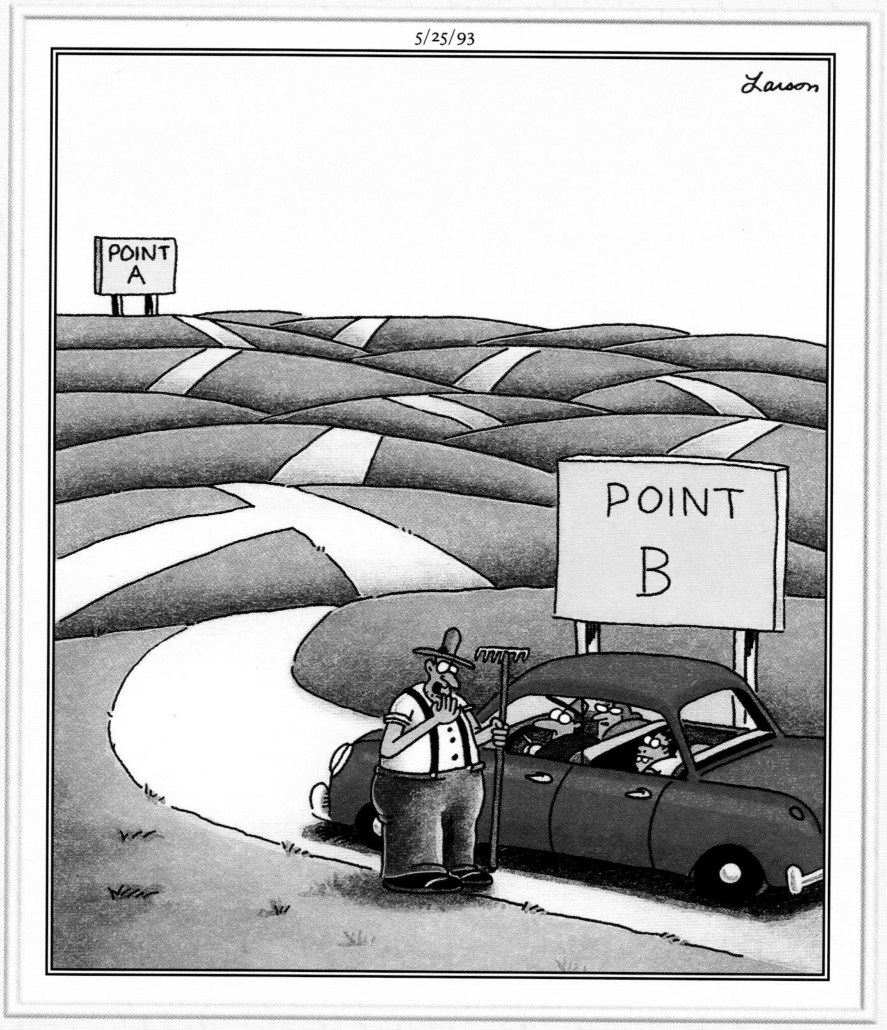
5/25/93
Larson
POINT A
POINT B

"Well, lemme think. ... You've stumped me, son. Most folks only wanna know how to go the other way."

6/1/93

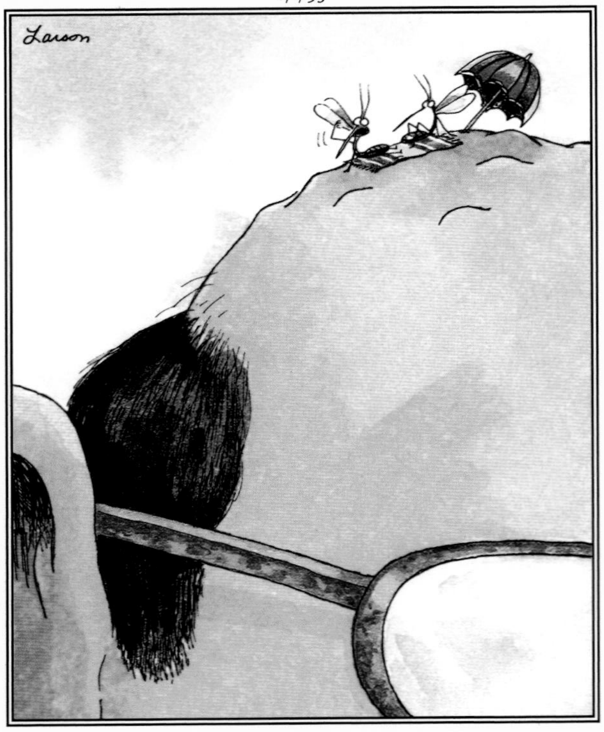
Larson

"Wow. ... That's ironic. I think something bit me."

6/3/93

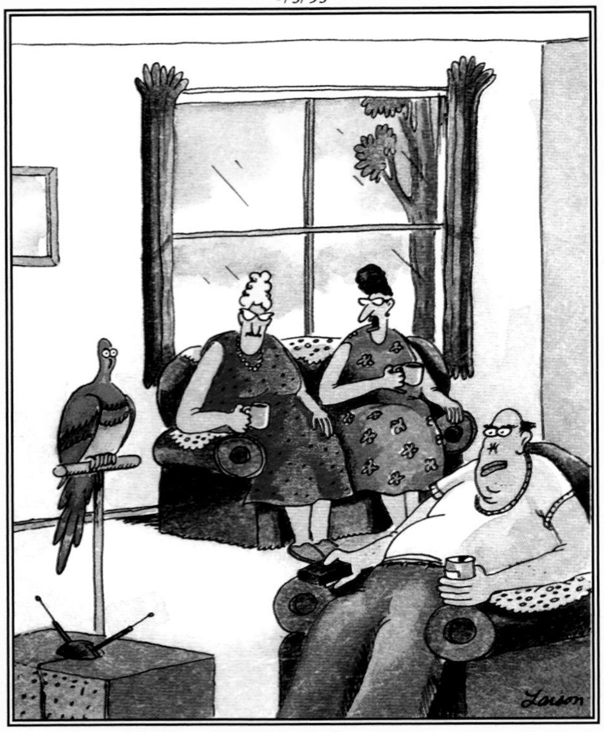
Larson

"Oh, boy, was *that* an ugly day. ... Roy instantly took the bird in to be debeaked, all the way yelling, 'Tit for tat! Tit for tat!'"

6/4/93

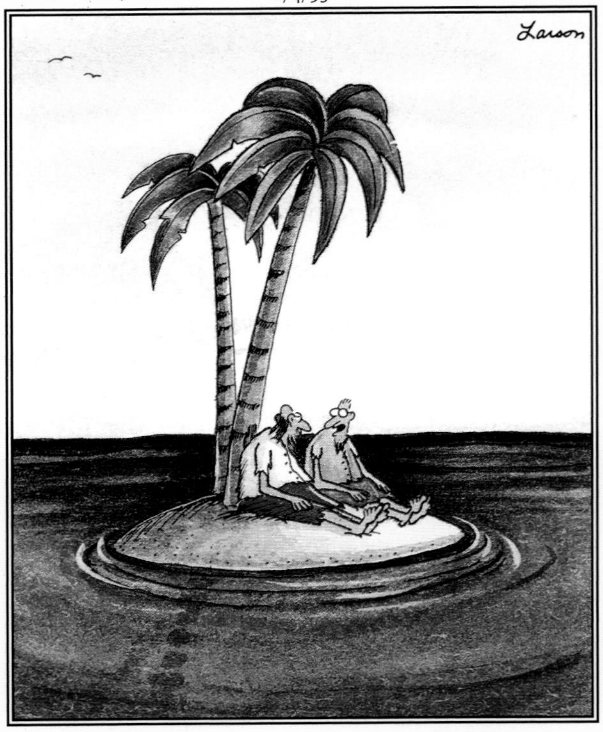
Larson

"Thanks for being my friend, Wayne."

6/7/93

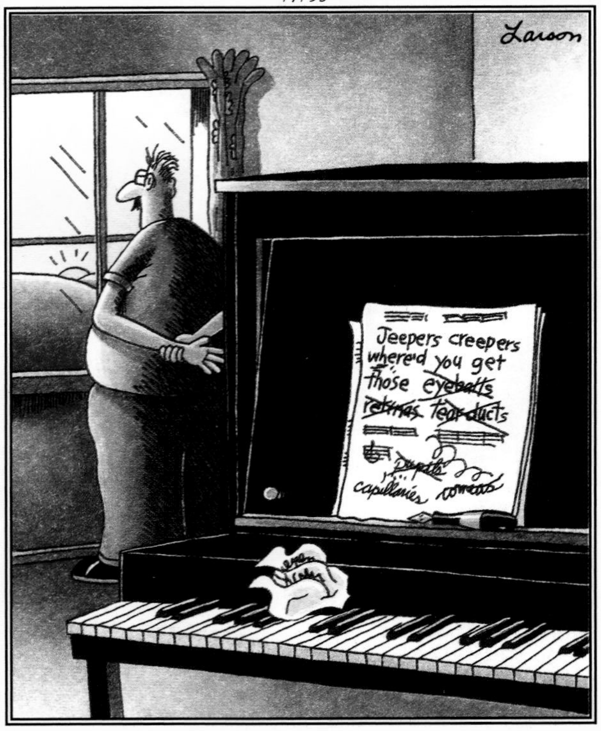
Larson
Jeepers creepers
where'd you get
those eyeballs
retinas tear ducts
pupils
capillaries corneas

The curse of songwriter's block

6/8/93

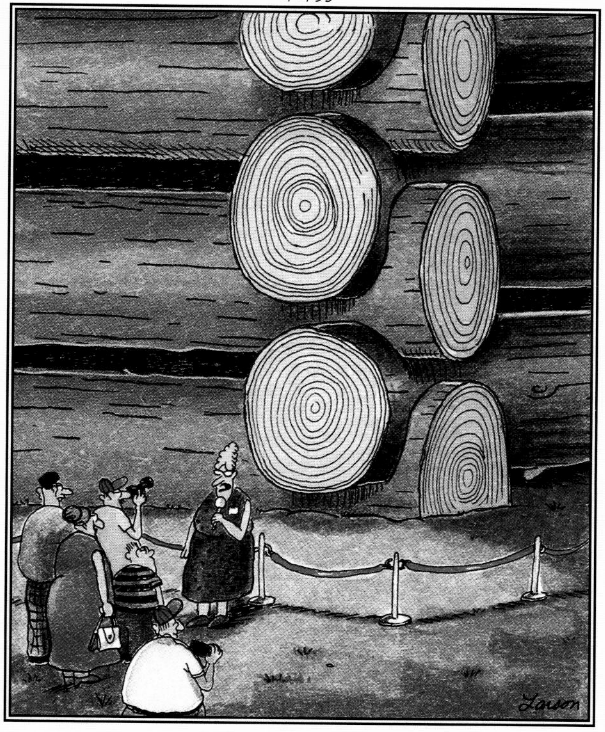

"Of course, one of the more popular myths is that our 16th president was born in a little log cabin."

6/9/93

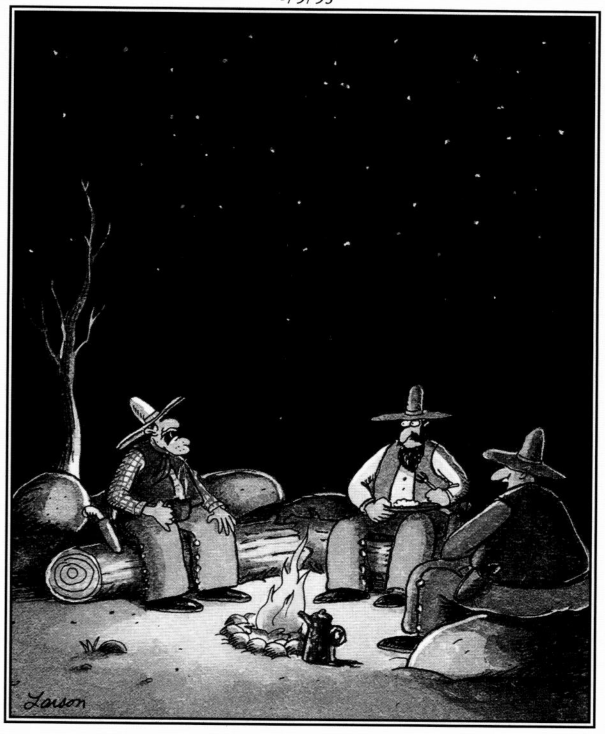

"You know, boys, sometimes I stare up at the stars like this and I wonder ... I wonder wonder who ... who wrote *The Book of Love?*"

6/10/93

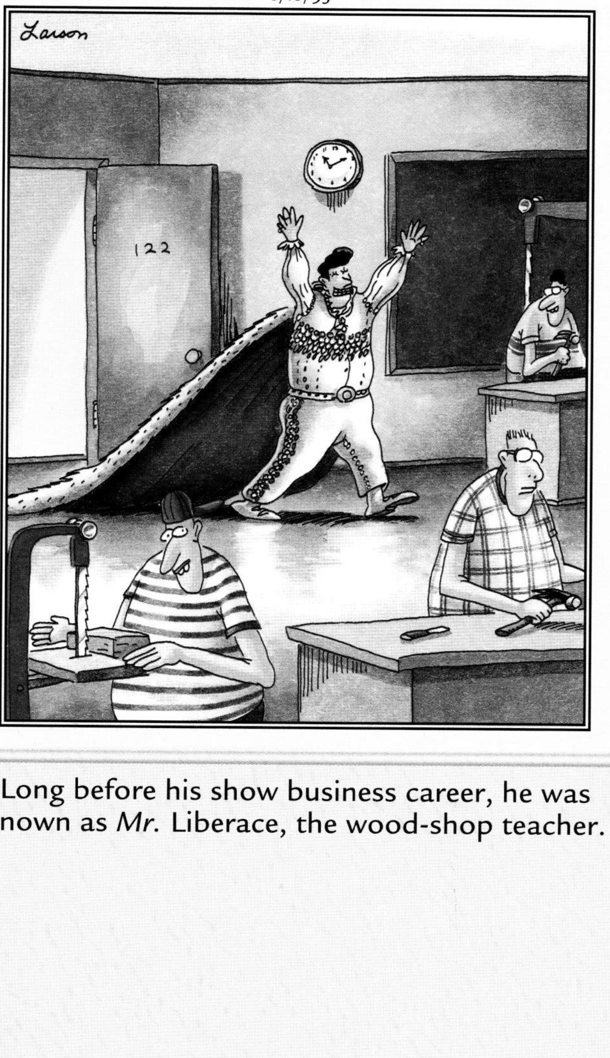
122

Long before his show business career, he was known as *Mr.* Liberace, the wood-shop teacher.

6/11/93

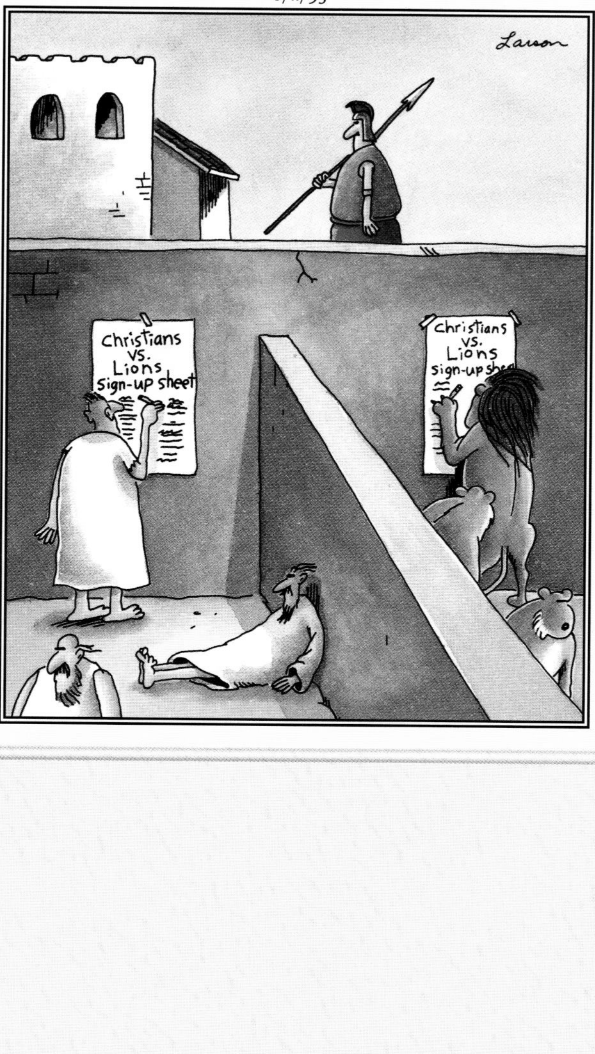
Christians vs. Lions Sign-up sheet
Christians vs. Lions

6/2/93

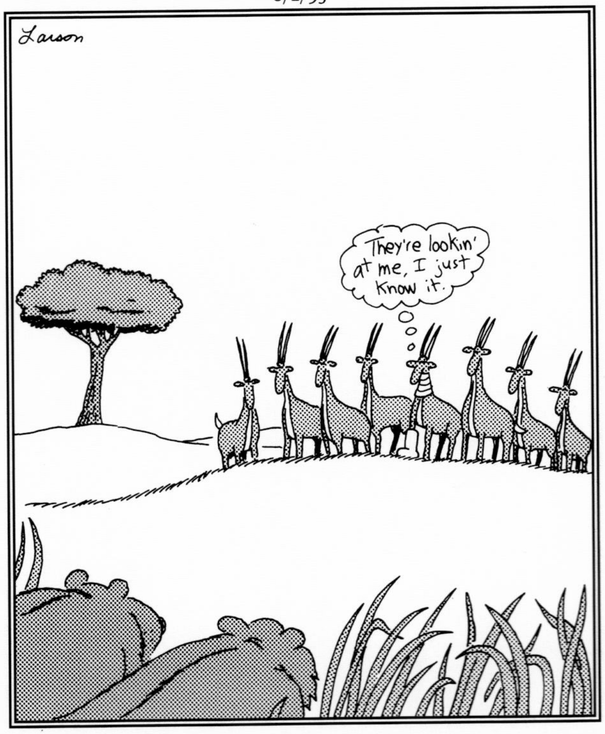
Larson
They're lookin' at me, I just know it.

6/15/93

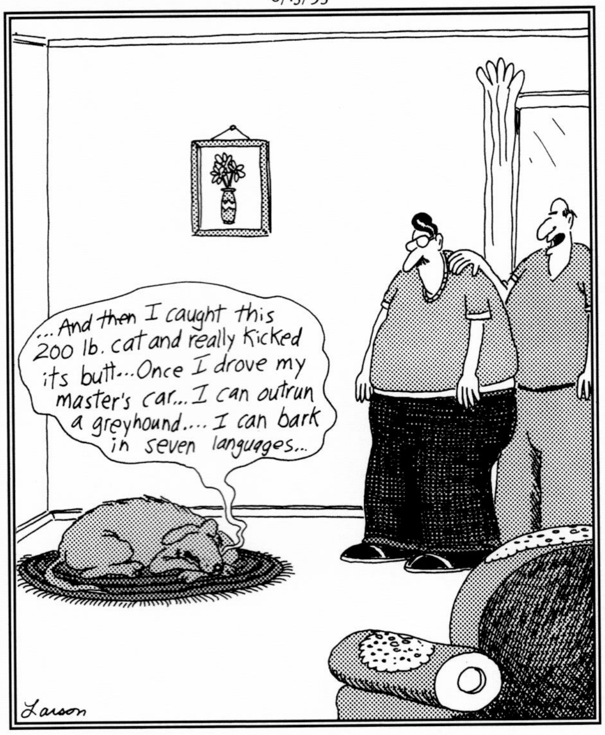
...And then I caught this 200 lb. cat and really kicked its butt...Once I drove my master's car...I can outrun a greyhound.... I can bark in seven languages...
Larson

"Edgar! Leave him be! ... Always best to let sleeping dogs lie."

6/14/93

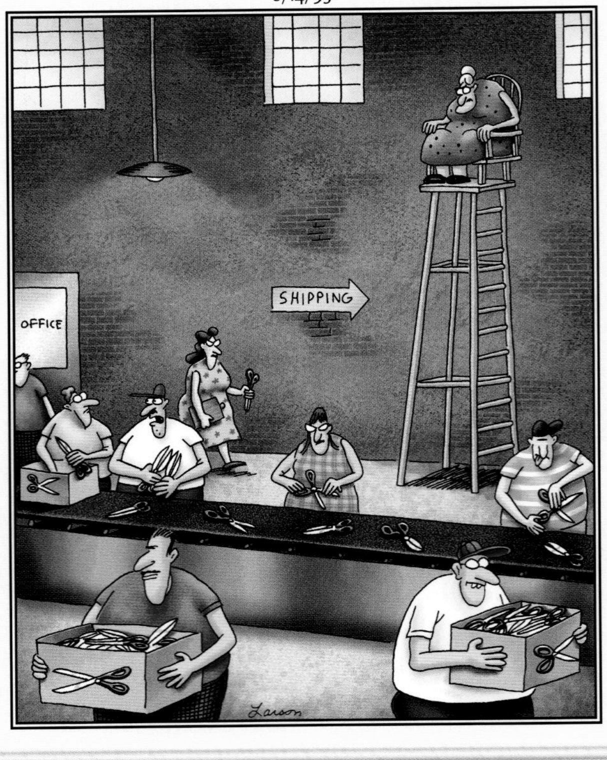
SHIPPING
OFFICE
Larson

"You must be new here! ... That's Miss Crutchfield, and she's there to make sure *nobody* runs with scissors."

6/18/93

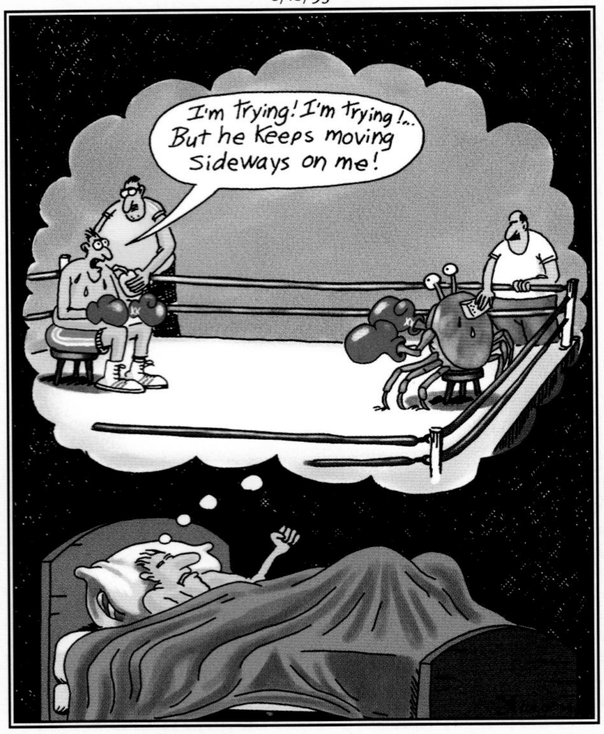
I'm trying! I'm trying!... But he keeps moving sideways on me!

Boxer nightmares

6/21/93

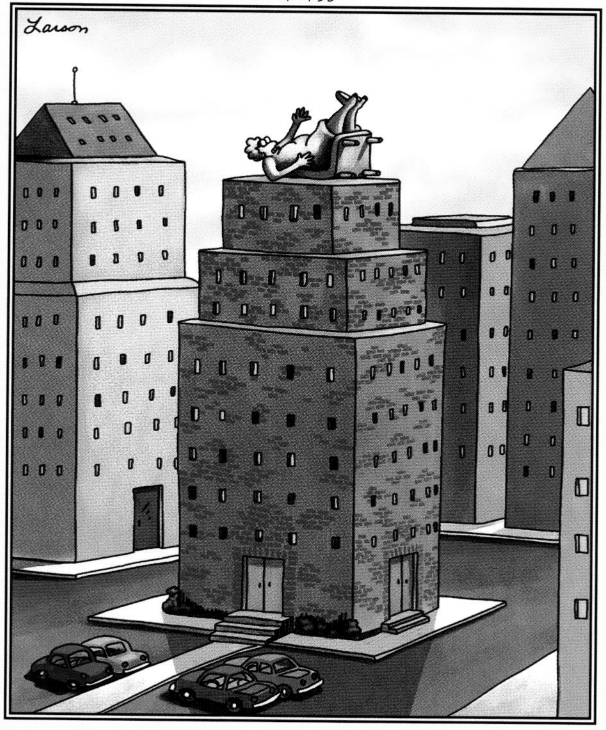
Larson

At the I've Fallen and I Can't Get Up Building

6/25/93

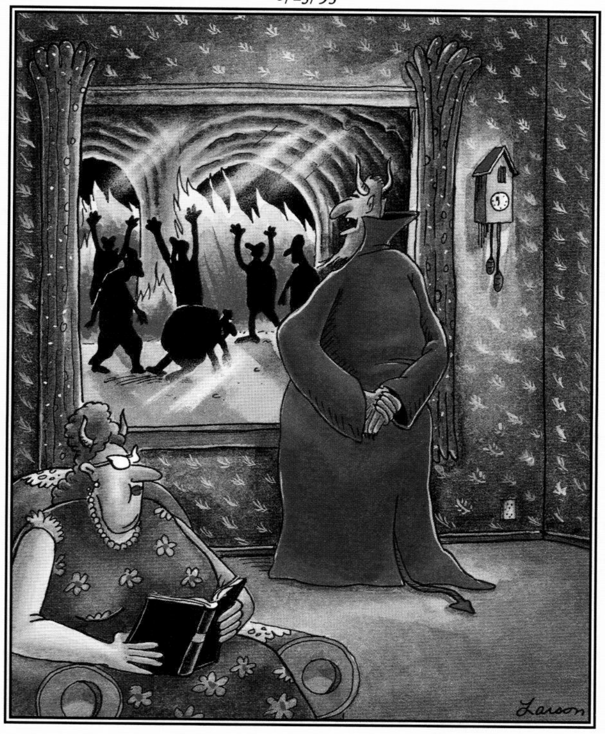
Larson

"Tell me, Margaret. ... Am I a butthead?"

6/16/93

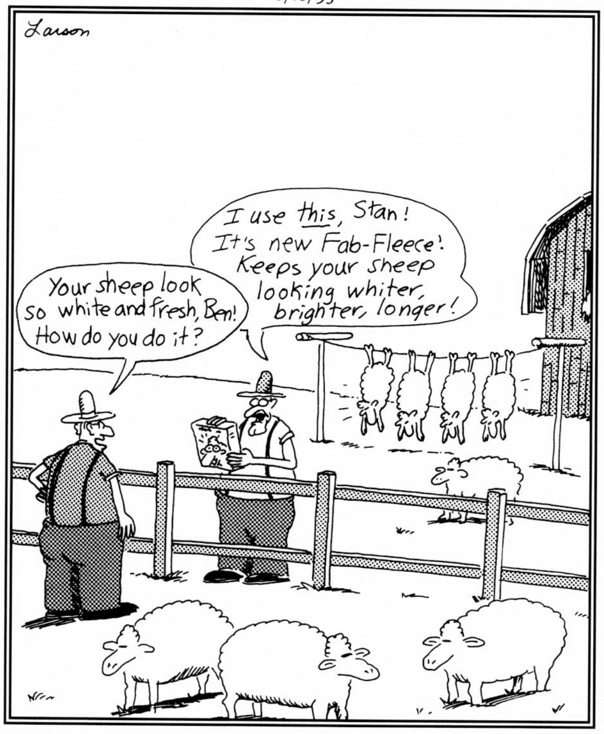
Larson
Your sheep look so white and fresh, Ben! How do you do it?
I use this, Stan! It's new Fab-Fleece! Keeps your sheep looking whiter, brighter, longer!

Now at your local feed store

6/17/93

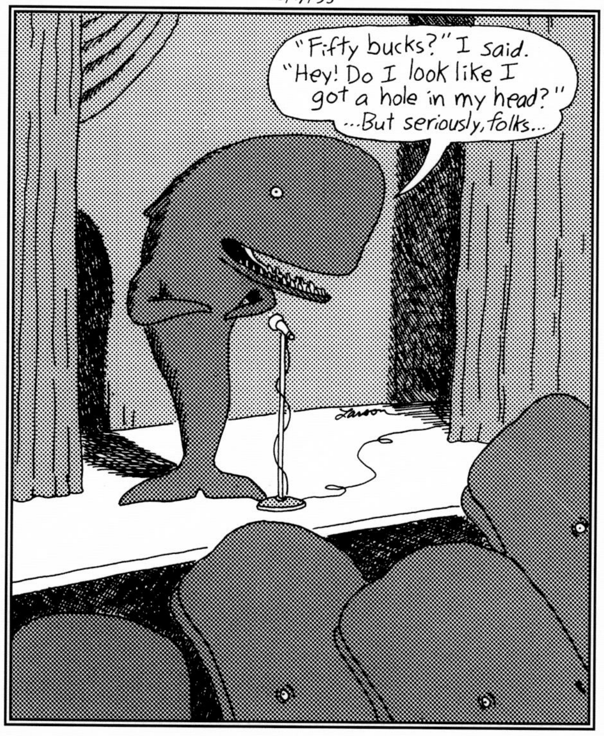
"Fifty bucks?" I said. "Hey! Do I look like I got a hole in my head?" ...But seriously, folks...
Larson

6/22/93

"Twarn't the alien's fault, sheriff. ...
Ol' Jeb Halloway kept stickin' his head in
one of the critter's orifices and yellin',
'Jimmie crack-corn! Jimmie crack-corn!'"

6/23/93

ROADKILL
TOURS

"As you can see, most of these things are
jackrabbits, but keep your eyes peeled for
armadillo as well. ... We're about five miles
now from the dead steer."

6/24/93

egg
nest
brain
heart
wishbone
keys
lunchbox

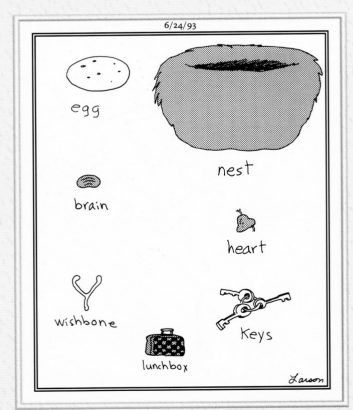

Structures, organs, and accessories (shown
actual size) pertaining to *Mellisuga helenae,*
the world's smallest hummingbird.

6/28/93

MITCHELL'S
PIANO REPAIR

"Oh, this is so exciting! ... You know,
no one's played that thing for years!"

June 1993

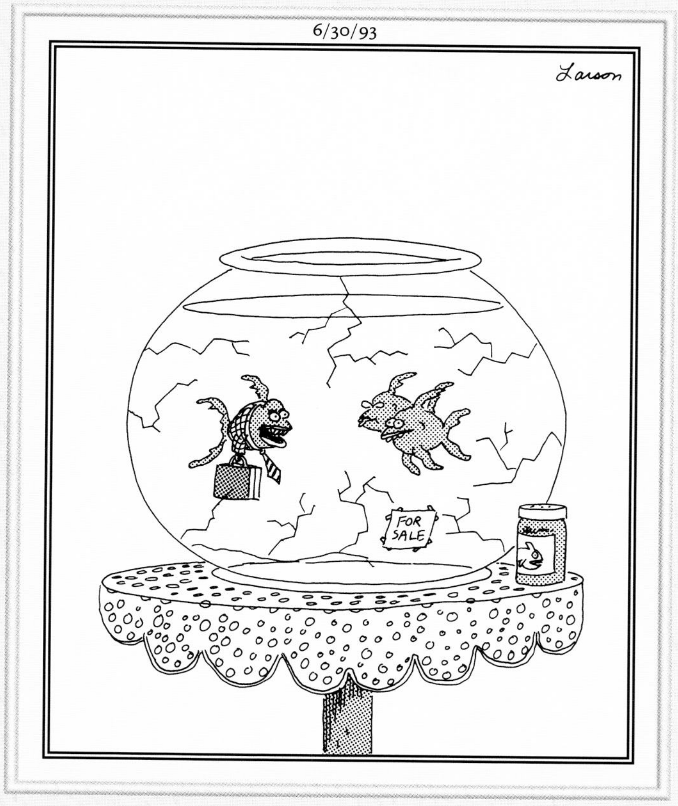
6/30/93
Larson
FOR SALE

"Hey, you'll love it! All she needs is some gravel, a few plants, and maybe one of those miniature human skeletons."

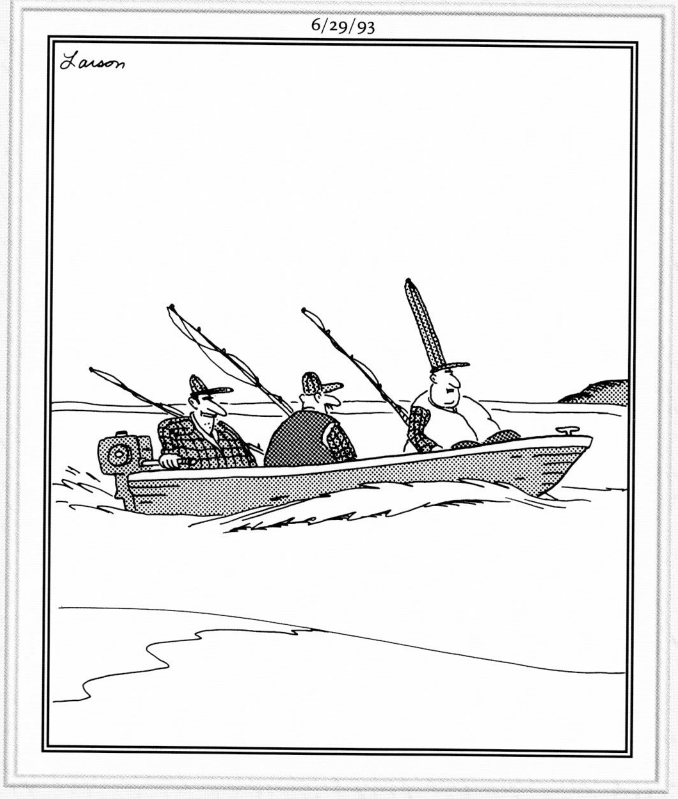
6/29/93
Larson

Vern, Chuck, and the pope go fishing.

July 1993

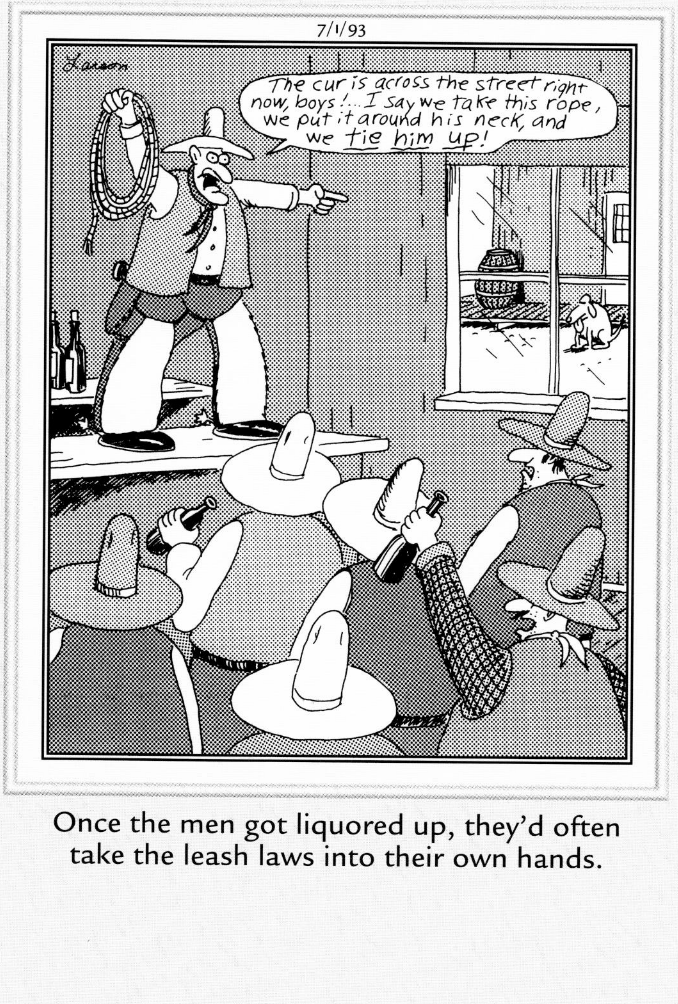
7/1/93
Larson
The cur is across the street right now, boys!... I say we take this rope, we put it around his neck, and we tie him up!

Once the men got liquored up, they'd often take the leash laws into their own hands.

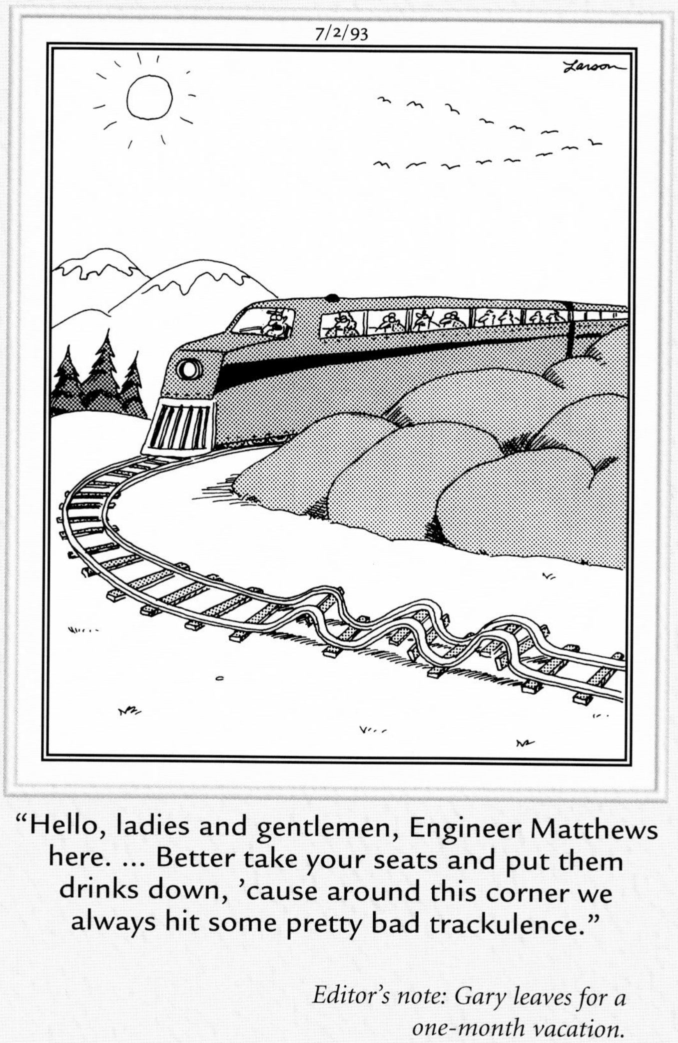
7/2/93
Larson

"Hello, ladies and gentlemen, Engineer Matthews here. ... Better take your seats and put them drinks down, 'cause around this corner we always hit some pretty bad trackulence."

Editor's note: Gary leaves for a one-month vacation.

8/2/93

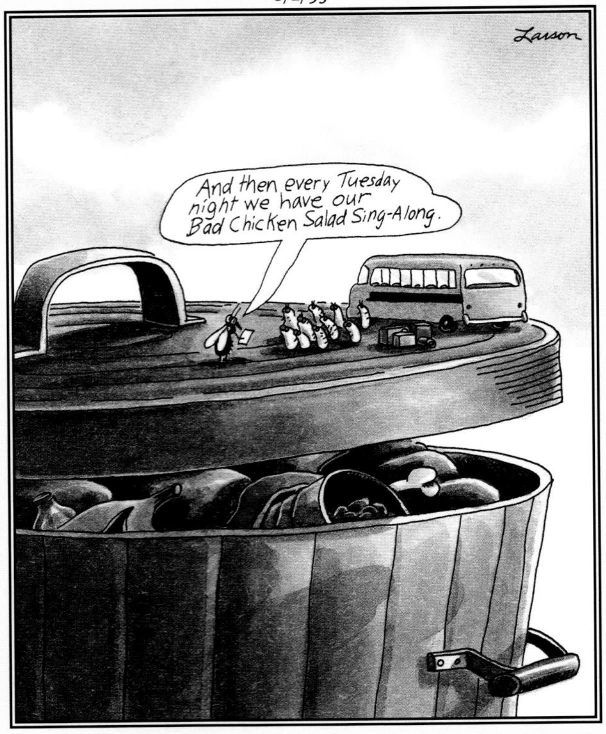
And then every Tuesday night we have our Bad Chicken Salad Sing-Along.

The first day at fly summer camp

8/3/93

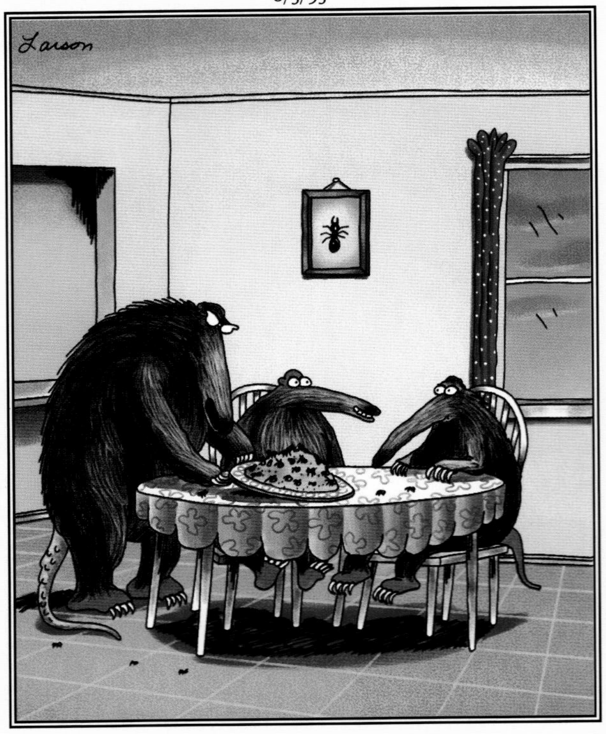

"Okay, kids, here we go. ... And I believe Danny's right, Randy—it's his turn to eat the queen."

8/4/93

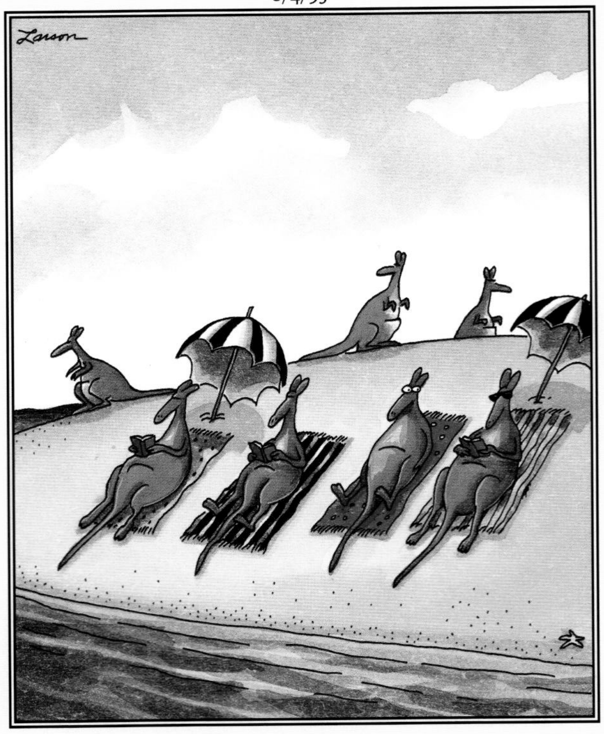

Incredibly, Morty had forgotten to bring a pocketbook.

8/5/93

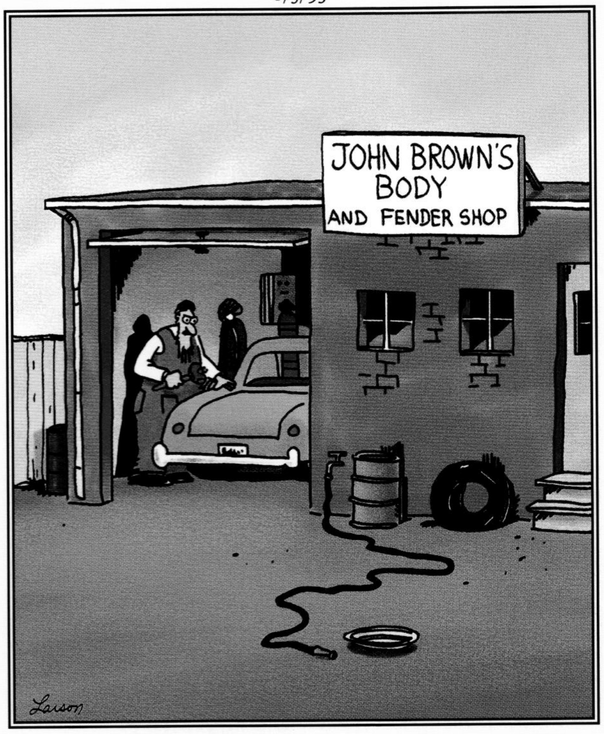
JOHN BROWN'S BODY
AND FENDER SHOP

8/6/93

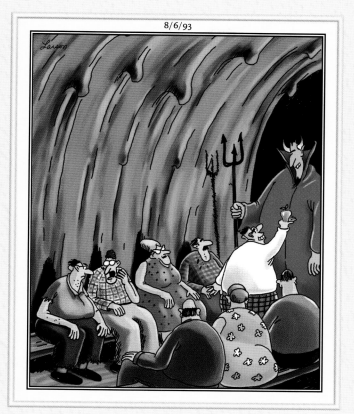

"There he goes again. ... Satan's pet."

8/12/93

He heard the sound again. Little Jimmy squinted his eyes in the dark and stared at the clock. It was 4:00 in the morning. "Who'd be coming around at this ungodly hour?" he asked himself. Again, he heard the sound. But, this time, it was closer.... closer...

Tales of the Early Bird

8/18/93

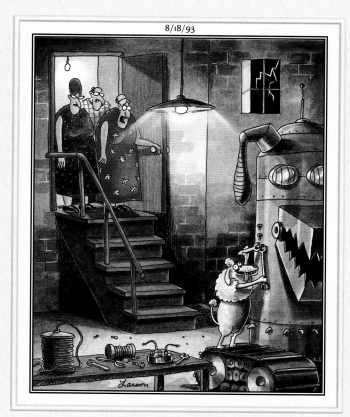

"And down here we keep Fluffy. ...
We're afraid he may have gone mad."

8/19/93

This is your egg.
This is your egg covered with bugs.

8/9/93

Larson
Oo! Igor!... Come here and look at this brain coral!

Dr. Frankenstein vacations in Hawaii.

8/10/93

Larson
NUTS! NUTS! GET 'EM!... NUTS! NUTS! GET 'EM!...

Before starting their day, squirrels must first pump themselves up.

8/11/93

Larson

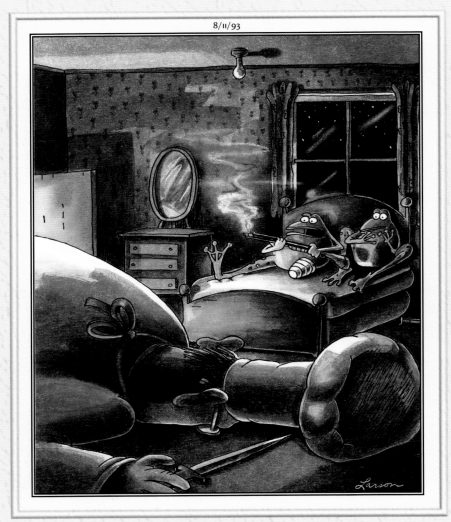

"Ha! That finishes it! ... I always knew he'd be back one day to get the other one!"

8/13/93

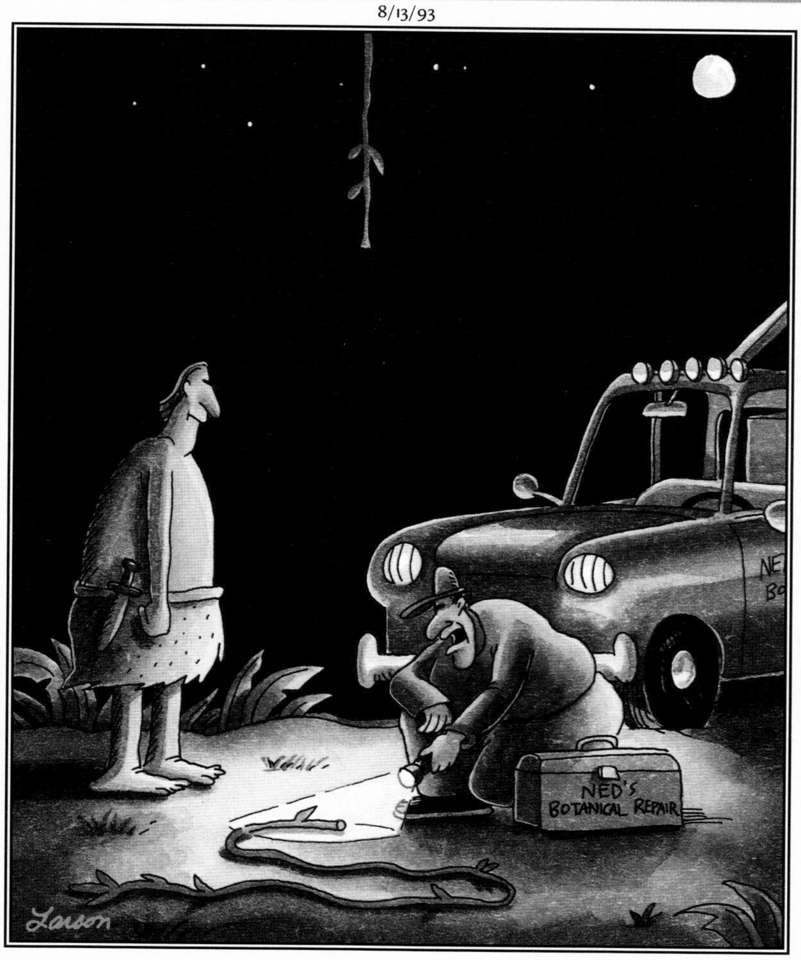
NED'S BOTANICAL REPAIR

"Whoa! ... Think I found the problem, buddy."

8/16/93

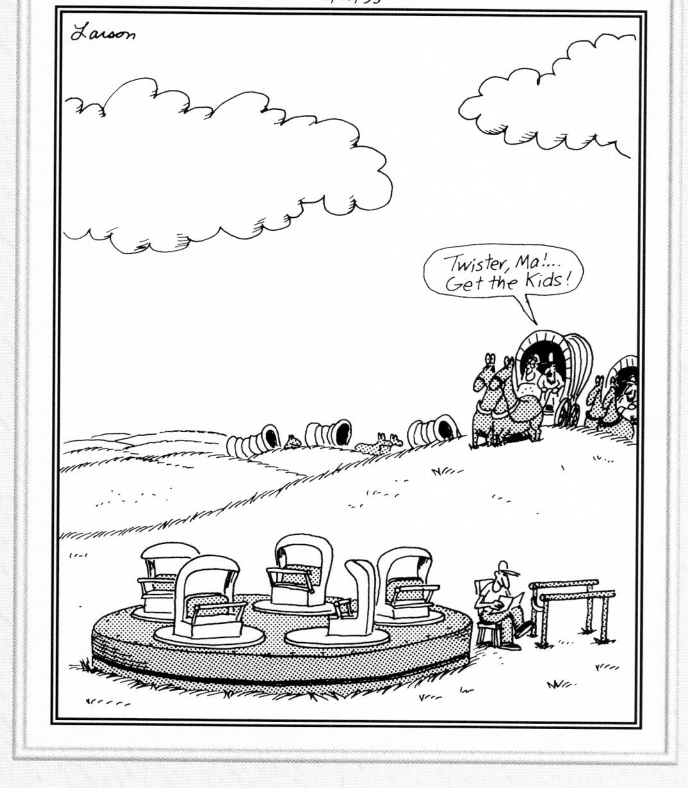
Twister, Ma!... Get the Kids!

8/20/93

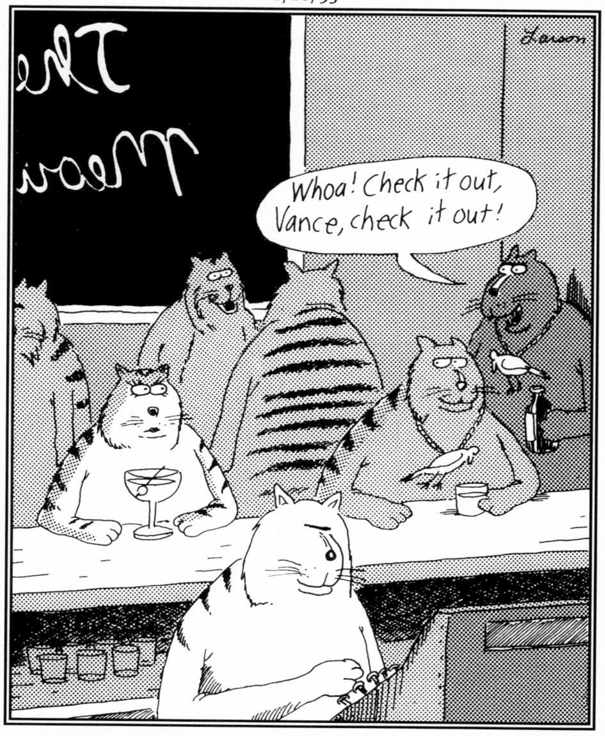
Whoa! Check it out, Vance, check it out!

With one glance, Luanne sized up the two males in their goldfinch necklaces.

8/17/93

"Talk about rubbing it in! Not only did we arrive late, but they *deliberately* left his organ-donor card."

8/27/93

"Pardon me, boys—is that the Chattanooga Iron Horse?"

8/23/93

"My dad can act deader than your dad."

8/26/93

"You're a right-brained sort of person, Mr. Sommersby—very creative, artistic, etc. ... Unfortunately, I think I also see why you're having trouble figuring out your gas mileage."

8/25/93

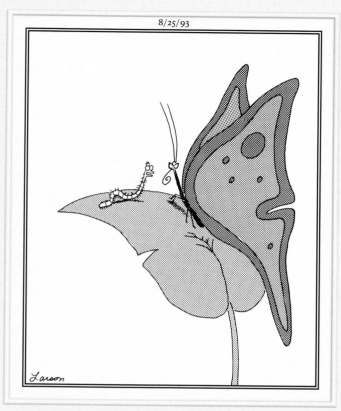

"How could you think that? ... I've *always* been attracted by your personality."

8/31/93

"Excuse me, but may I assume you're not Dr. Livingstone?"

8/24/93

Well, there he goes again... Y'know, Randy just isn't a team player.

8/30/93

Ironically, Barnum's and Bailey's respective kids—Sid and Marty—both ran away one night to join corporate America.

Back home in his native India, Toomba tells and retells
the story of his daring escape from the Cleveland Zoo.

Prairie dog developers

"Time out, please! ... Eyelash!"

9/8/93

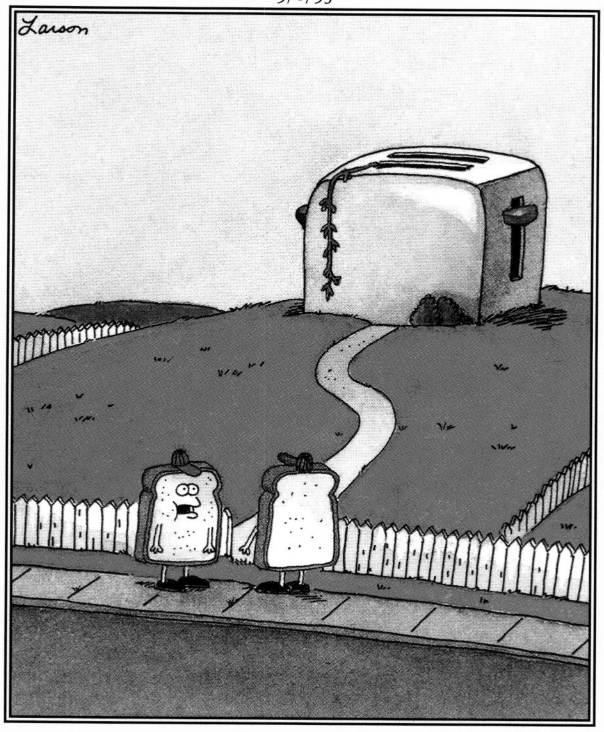

"I dunno, Andy. ... Mom said we were never to go near the old Sutter place."

9/7/93

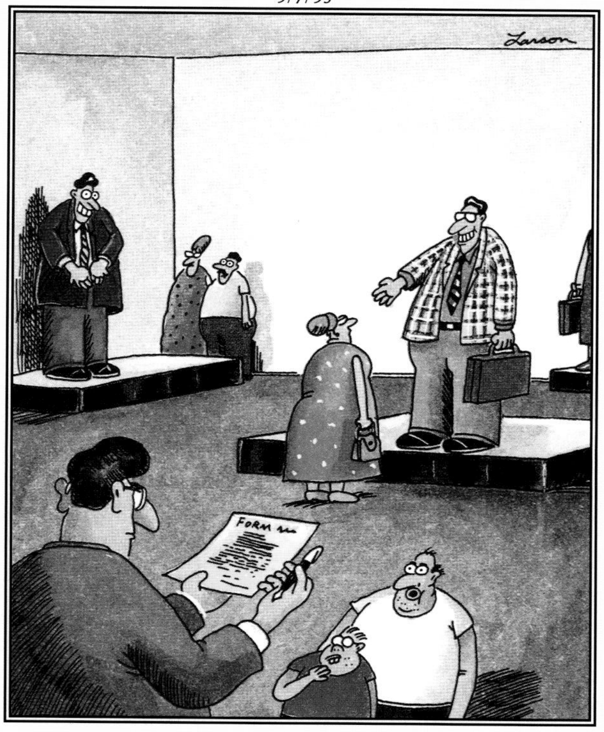
FORM

At the Insurance Agents Wax Museum

9/6/93

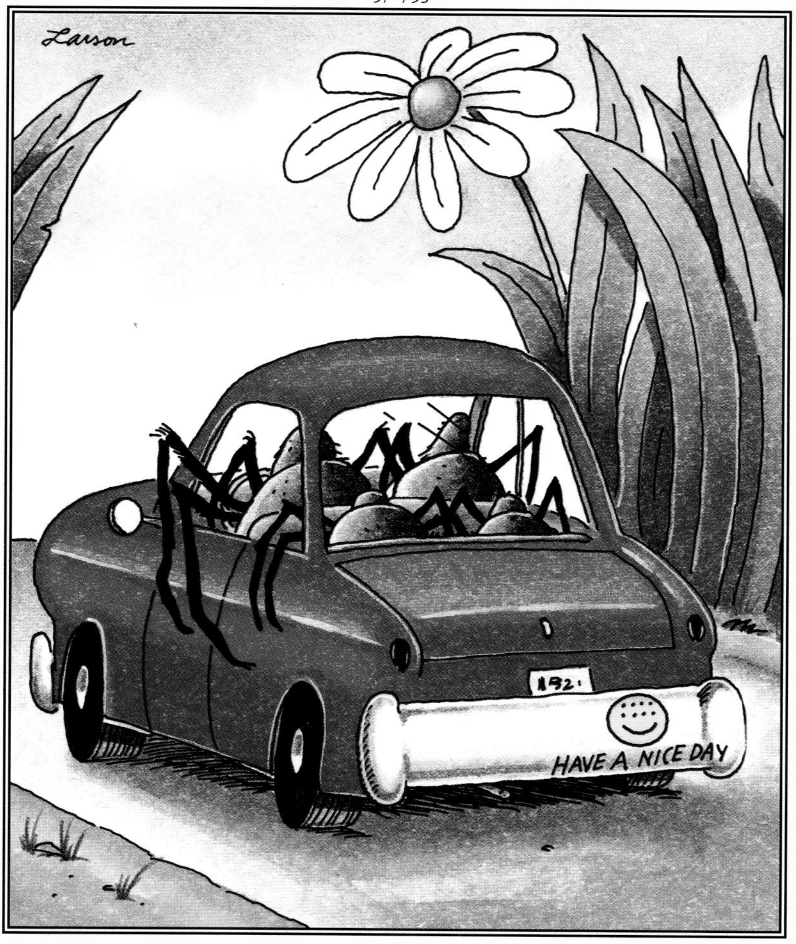
HAVE A NICE DAY

9/10/93

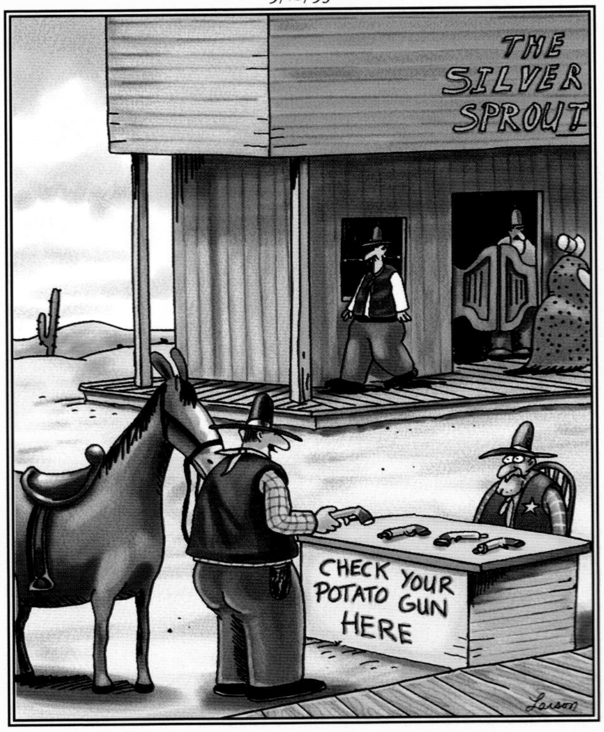
THE SILVER SPROUT
CHECK YOUR POTATO GUN HERE
Larson

Vegetarian towns of the Old West

9/16/93

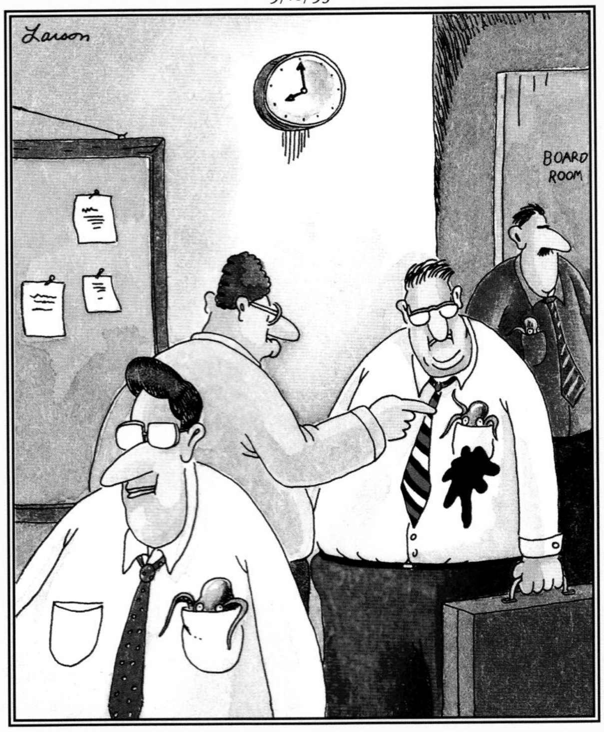
Larson
BOARD ROOM

Once again, Vernon has a good shirt ruined by a cheap pocket octopus.

9/14/93

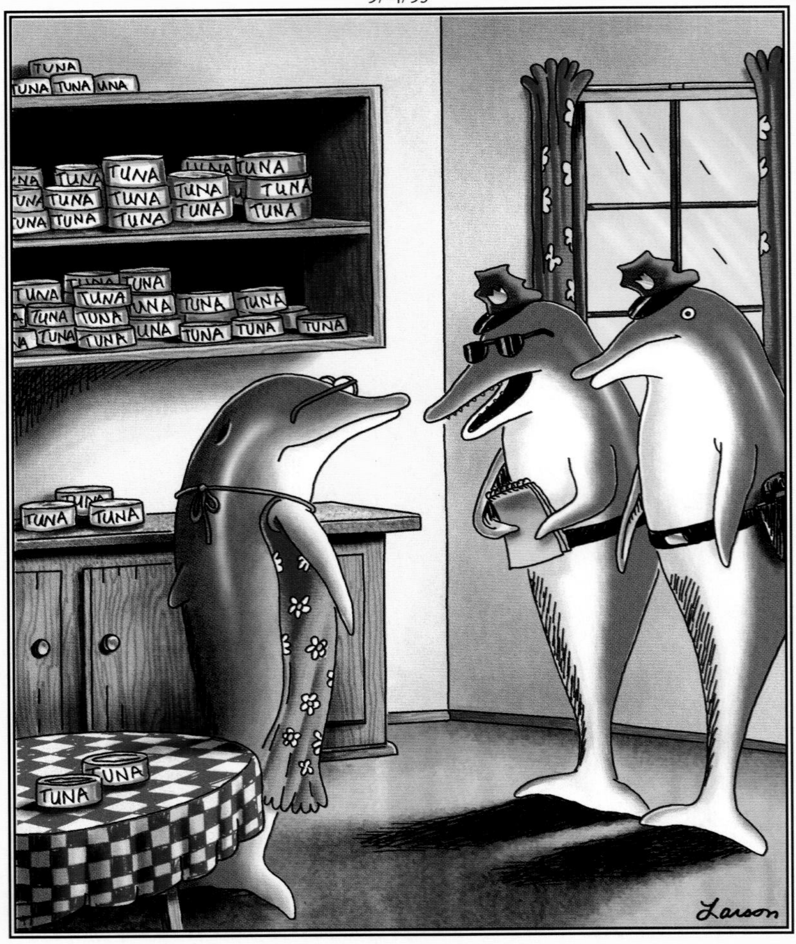
TUNA
Larson

"Sorry, ma'am, but your neighbors have reported not seeing your husband in weeks. We just have a few questions, and then you can get back to your canning."

9/15/93

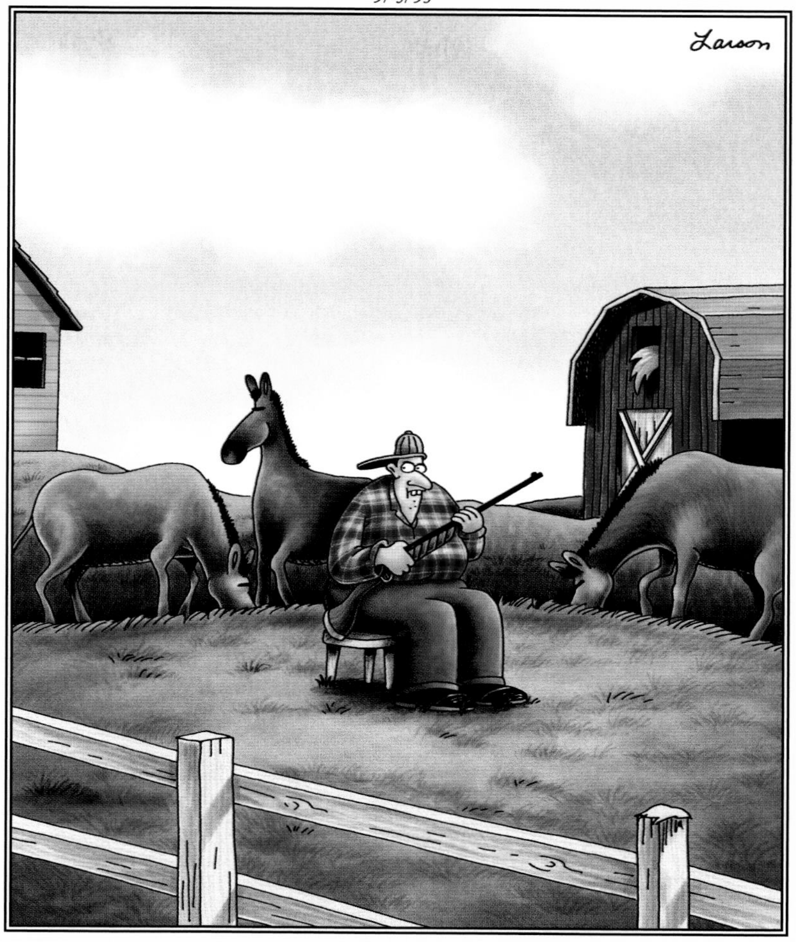
Larson

Misunderstanding his dying father's advice, Arnie spent several years protecting the family mules.

9/21/93

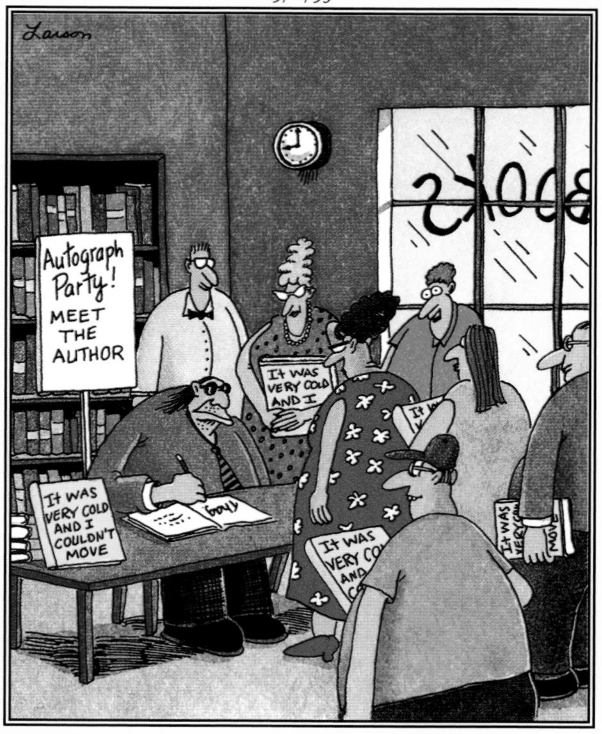
Larson
Autograph Party! MEET THE AUTHOR
It WAS VERY COLD AND I COULDN'T MOVE

After being frozen in ice for 10,000 years, Thag promotes his autobiography.

9/23/93

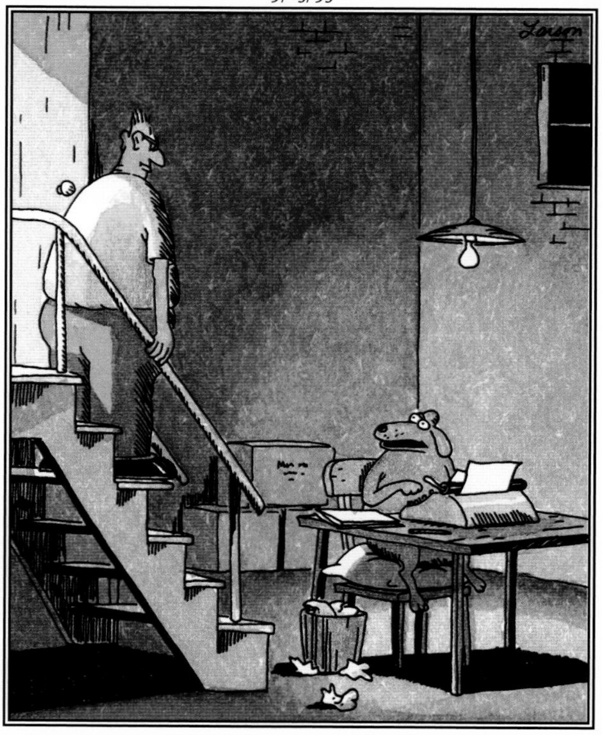
Larson

"I wouldn't laugh, Jack. ... I know things about you."

9/9/93

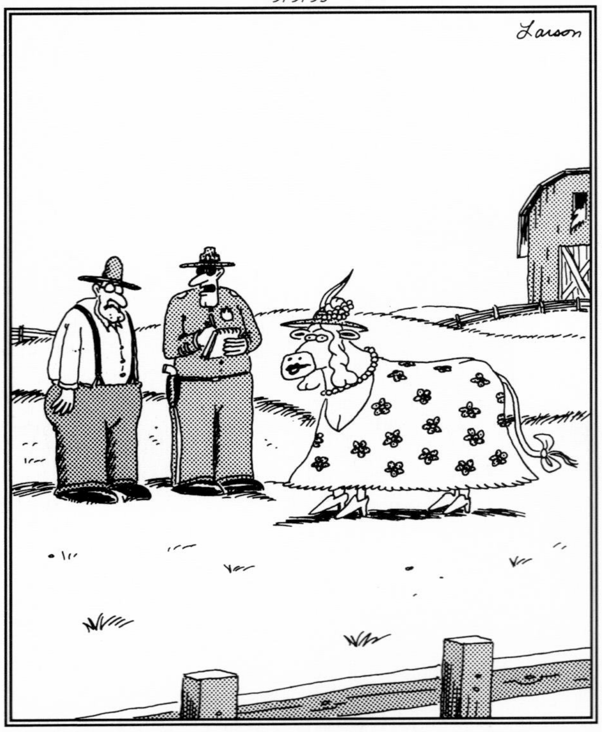

"You were hit last night by some kind of cult, Mr. Gilbert. ... Not the sickest cult I've ever seen, but a cult nonetheless."

9/13/93

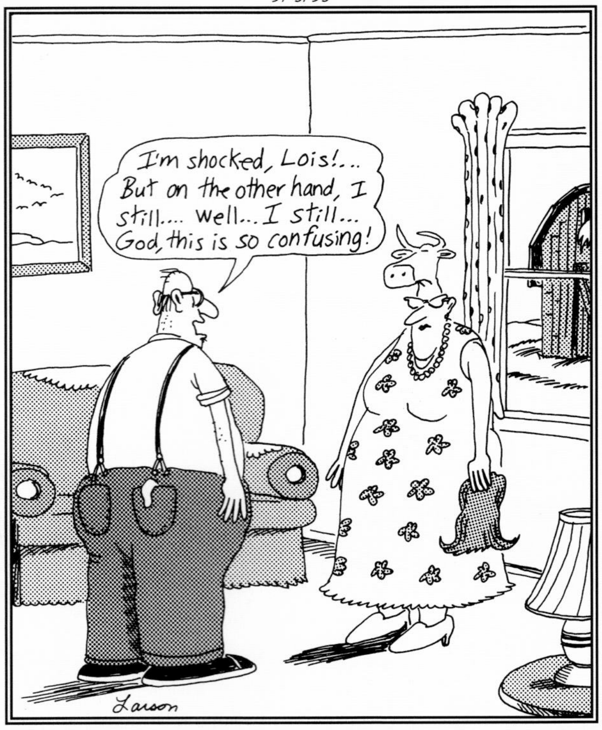
I'm shocked, Lois!... But on the other hand, I still.... well... I still... God, this is so confusing!

Scene from *The Crying Game II: The Rural Version*

9/22/93

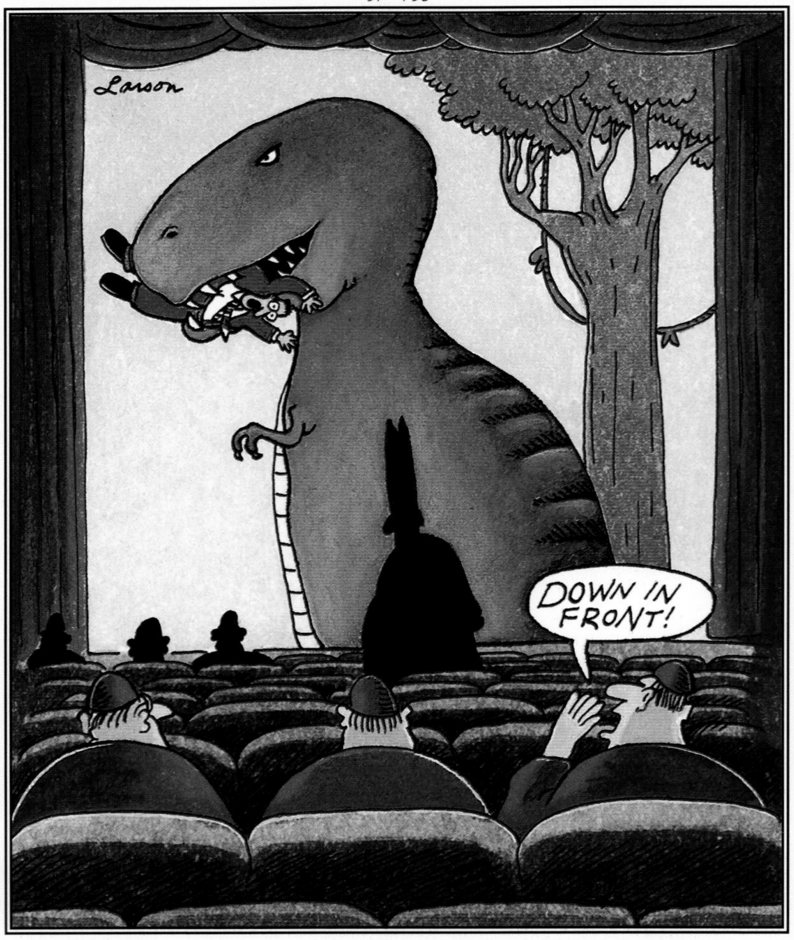
DOWN IN FRONT!

At the Vatican's movie theater

9/17/93

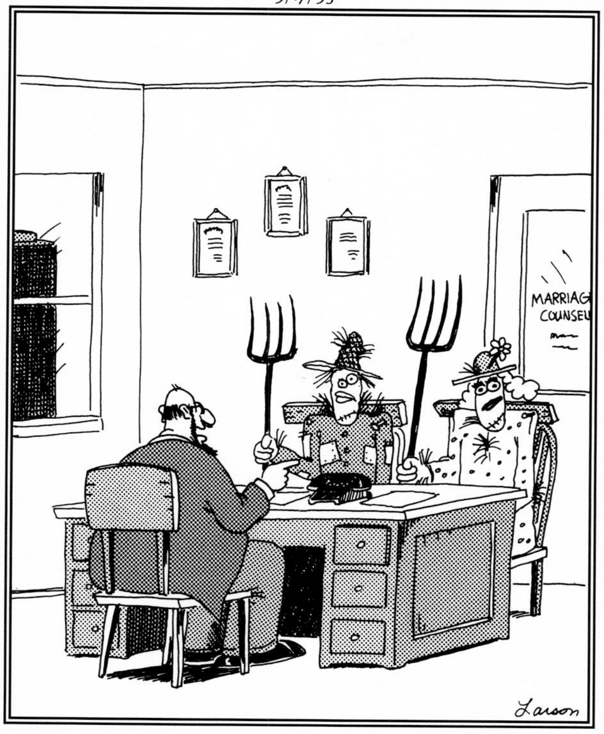
MARRIAGE COUNSEL
Larson

"Now, you can't really hurt each other with those things, so next time you bicker, just go ahead and vent your anger—you'll both feel better."

9/20/93

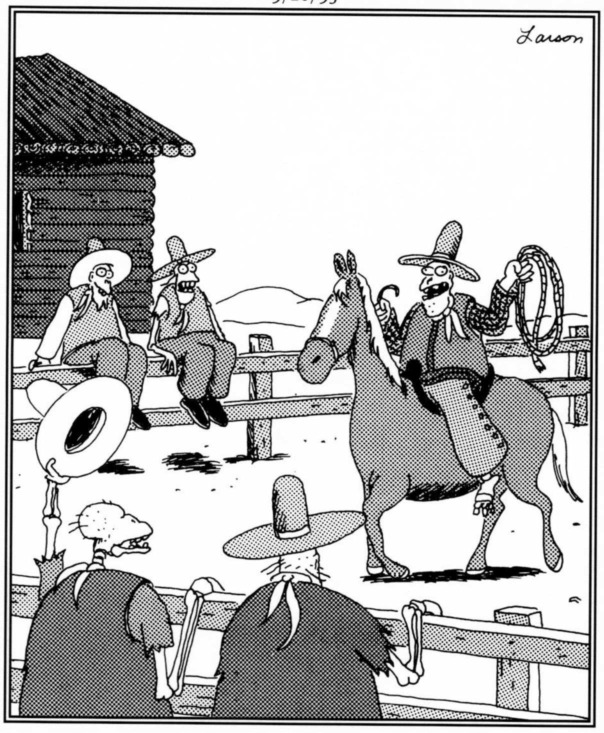
Larson

Vacationing from their jobs of terrorizing young teenagers, zombies will often relax at a Western dead ranch.

9/29/93

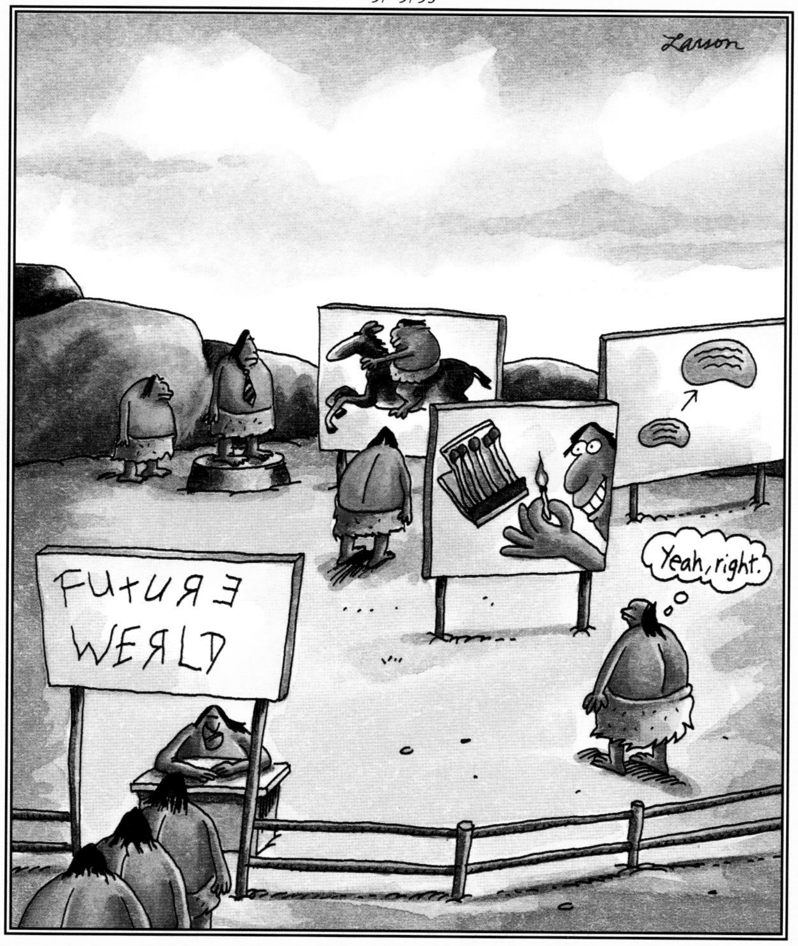
Larson
FUTURE WERLD
Yeah, right.

Primitive theme parks

9/30/93

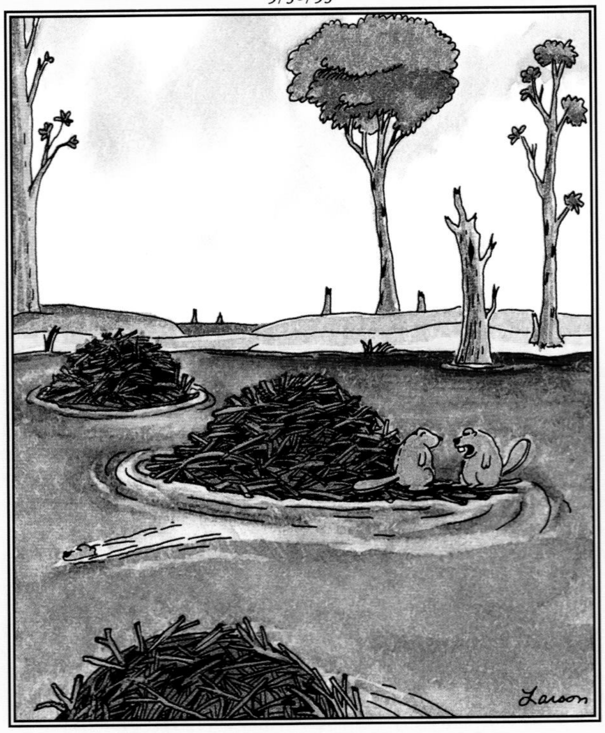
Larson

"Hey. Quit complaining. ... We *all* live out in the sticks."

9/24/93

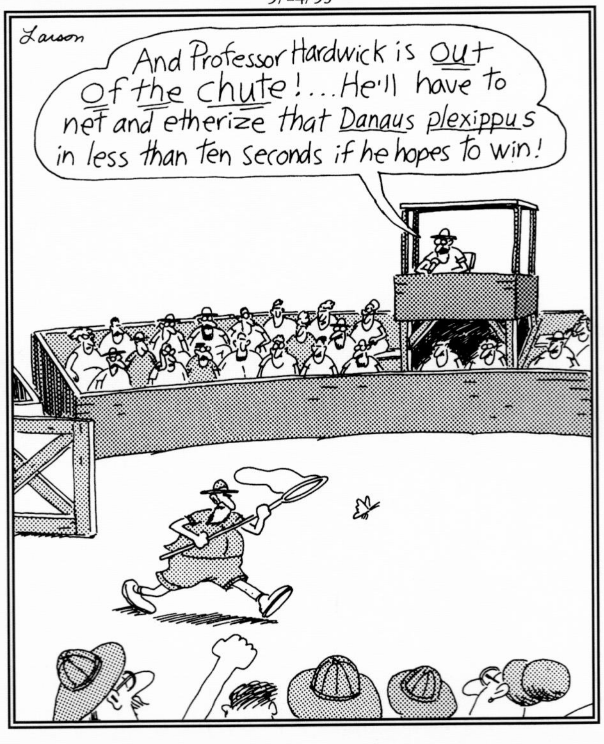
Larson
And Professor Hardwick is out of the chute!...He'll have to net and etherize that Danaus plexippus in less than ten seconds if he hopes to win!

Entomological rodeos

9/28/93

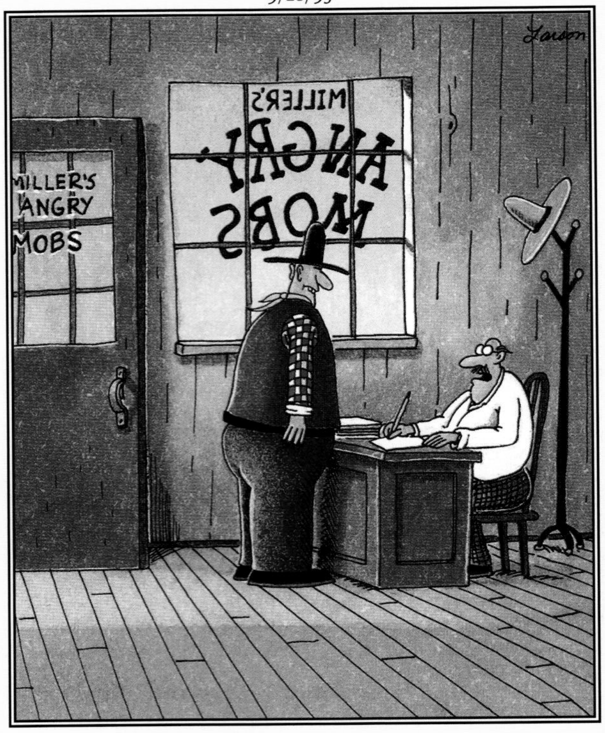
Larson
MILLER'S ANGRY MOBS

"Okay, Bill. Tuesday night, 8 o'clock, over at the sheriff's office where they're holdin' your brother's killer. ... You want that with extra hollerin'?"

9/27/93

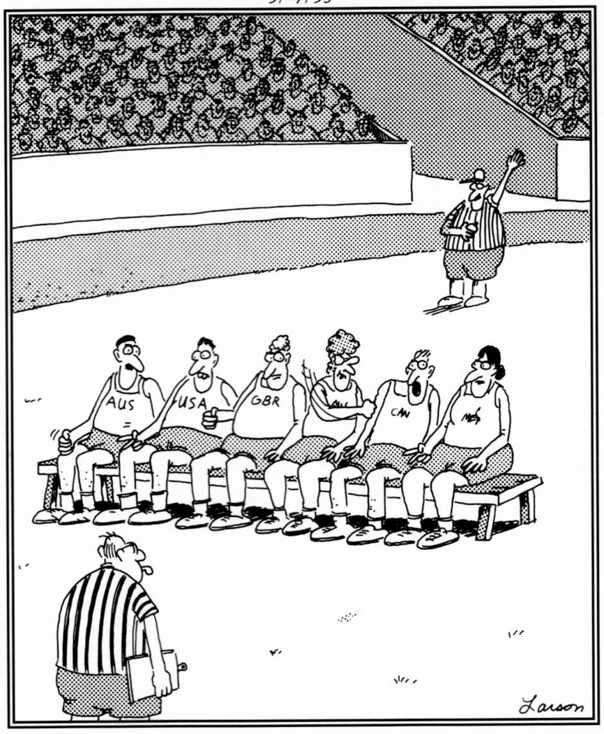
AUS
USA
GBR
CAN
Larson

Tension mounts in the final heat of the paper-rock-scissors event.

10/5/93

"Okay, Professor Big Mouth, we've all chipped in—here's the hundred bucks! ... But remember, you gotta kiss her on the *lips!*"

10/7/93

"Listen, Noreen—*you* wanna be the photographer next time, be my guest."

10/6/93

"Contagious? Contagious?" I asked the doctor. "*Really* contagious," he tells me.

So that's it! As of this morning, I quit my medication!... Homicidal tendencies be damned!

And then I realized the guy was actually a ventriloquist, and it was his dummy who was giving me the exam.

You're sitting in it now.

Classic conversation stoppers

10/1/93

"It's Jim Wilkins, Dave. Same as the others. Trussed up like a Christmas present with his hunting license stuffed in his mouth. ... I want this bear, Dave. I want him bad."

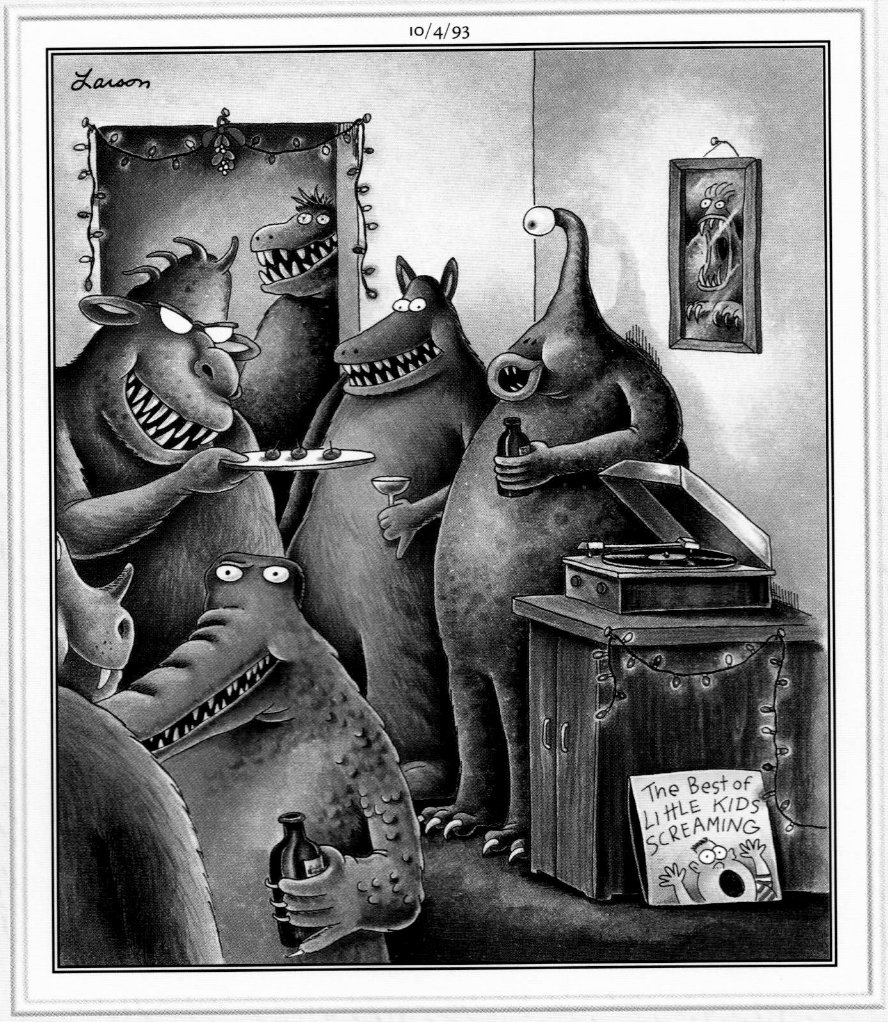
10/4/93
Larson
The Best of
Little Kids
Screaming

Later, when one of the monsters cranked up the volume, the party really got going.

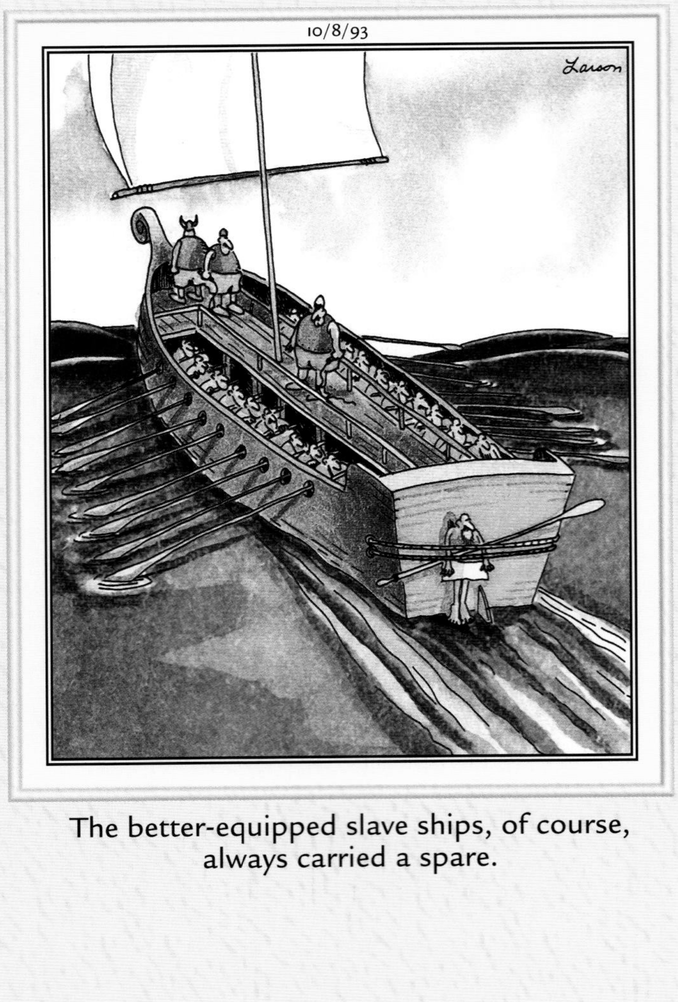
10/8/93
Larson

The better-equipped slave ships, of course, always carried a spare.

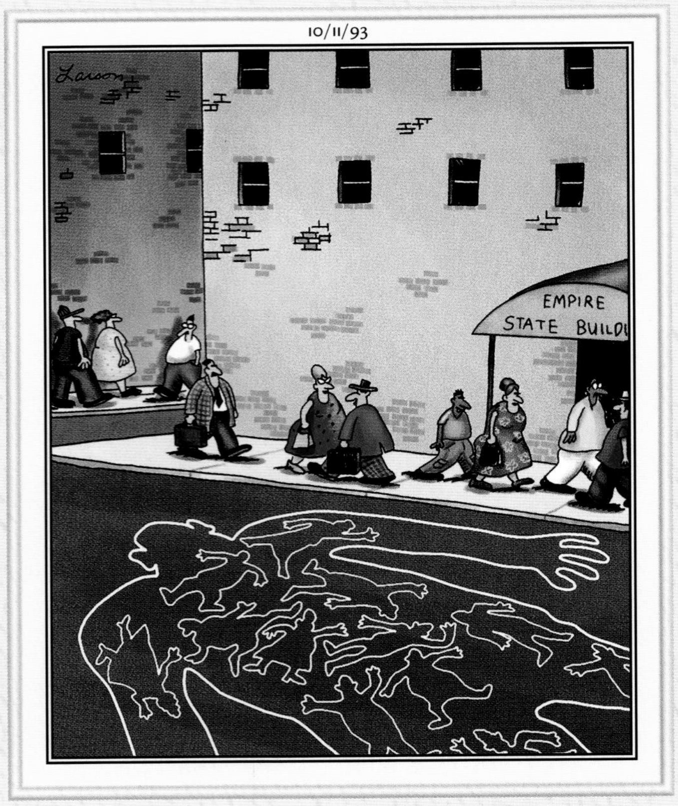
10/11/93
Larson
EMPIRE
STATE

A few days following the King Kong "incident," New Yorkers return to business as usual.

10/12/93

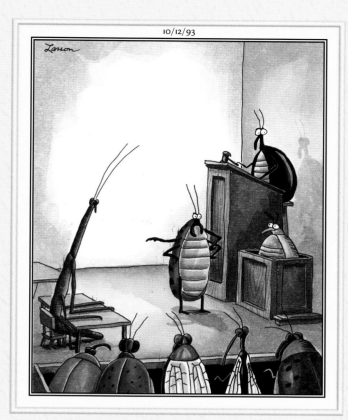

"Most interesting, ma'am—you've identified the defendant as the one you saw running from the scene. I take it, then, that you're unaware that my client is a *walking* stick?"

10/13/93

EXPERIENCE
AUG '63 - Nov '67:
Jumped around a lot and went "woohoo, woohoo, woohoo!"
JAN. '68 - Sept. '83:
Jumped around a lot and went "woohoo, woohoo, woohoo!"
Oct. '84 - present:
After short stint in politics, jumped around a lot and went, "woohoo, woohoo!"
SPECIAL SKILLS: Can be blown away by shotgun at close range without dying
Jumping around a lot

Daffy's résumé

10/14/93

Hang on, Omak! We'll get you out!...Just scream when we're getting close!

Eskimo rescue units

10/15/93

HERPETOLOGY
INVENTORY OF REPTILES & AMPHIBIANS

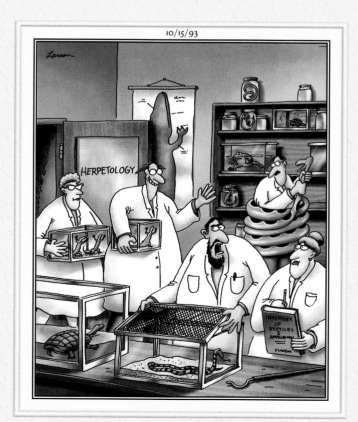

"Oh, God! It's that creepy Ted Sheldon and Louise Dickerson. ... They're skinkheads, you know."

10/19/93

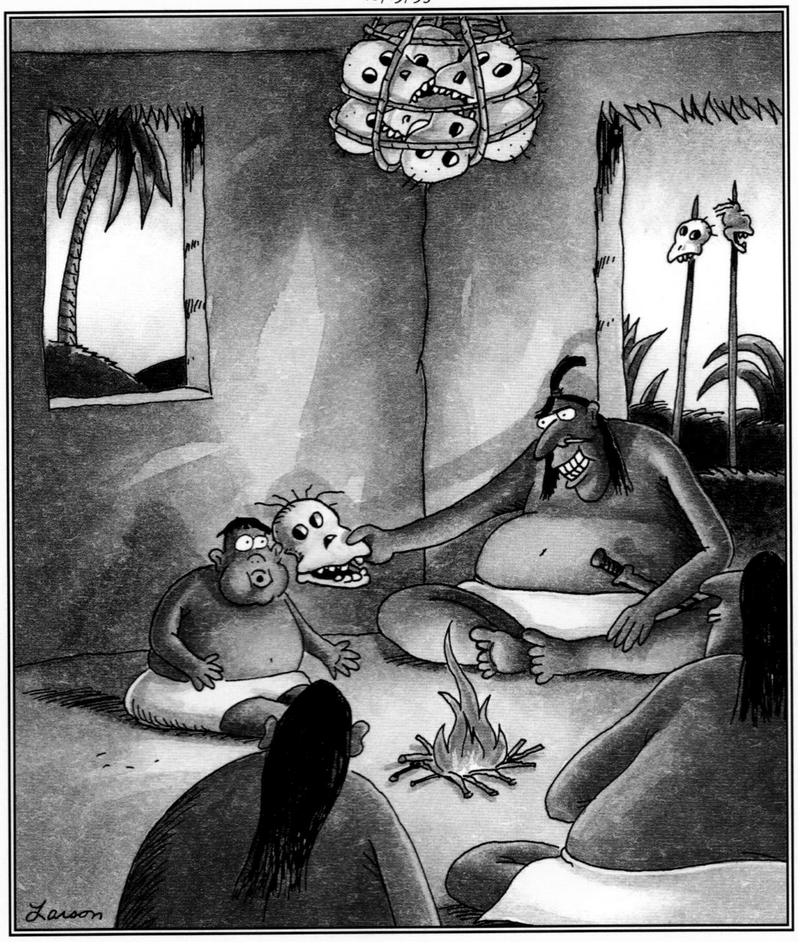

The whole family always enjoyed the way Uncle Numanga could reach over and “find” a skull in little Jerog’s ear.

10/22/93

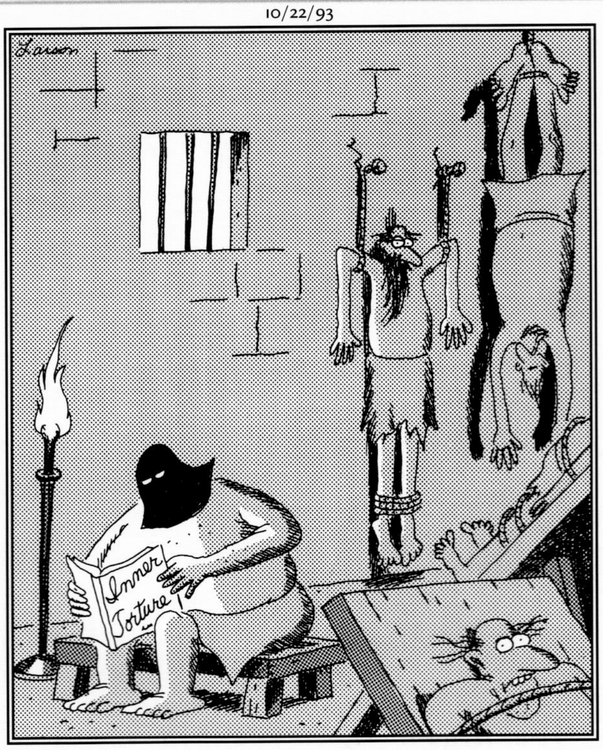
Larson
Inner Torture

10/25/93

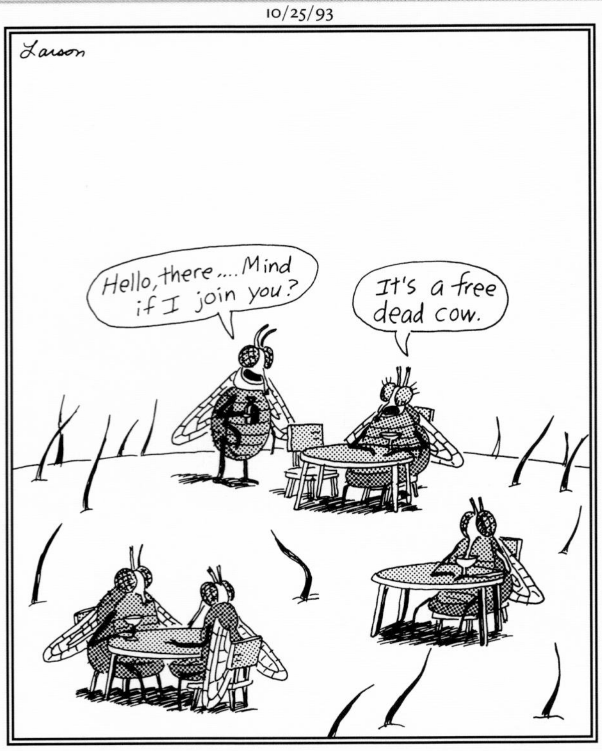
Larson
Hello, there.... Mind if I join you?
It's a free dead cow.

10/21/93

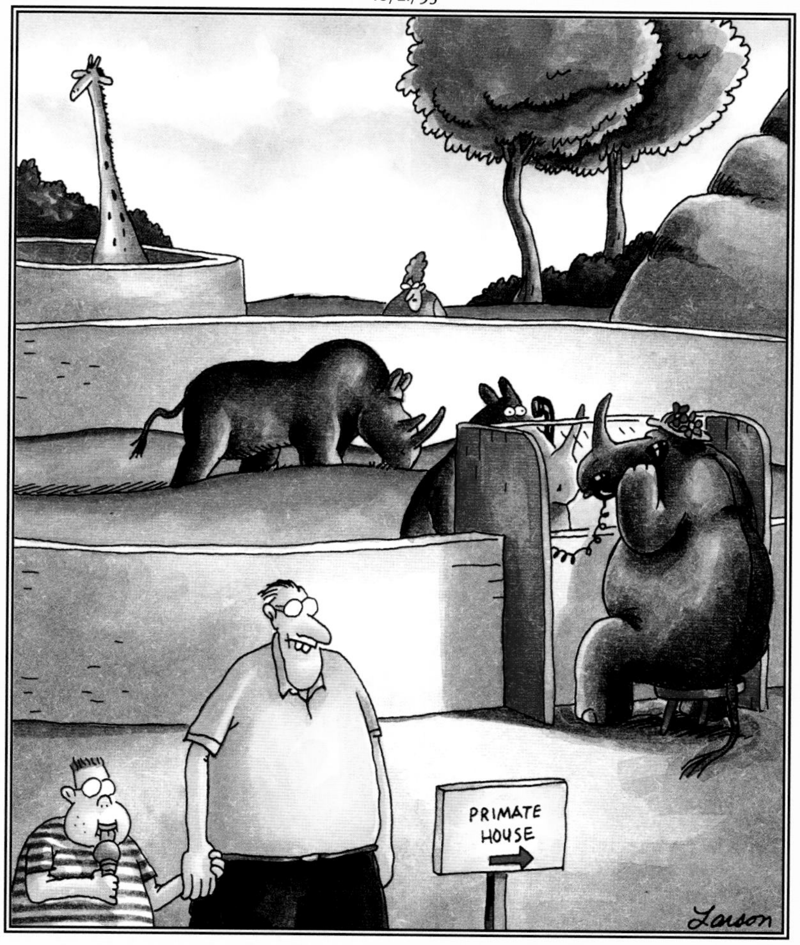
PRIMATE HOUSE
Larson

10/26/93

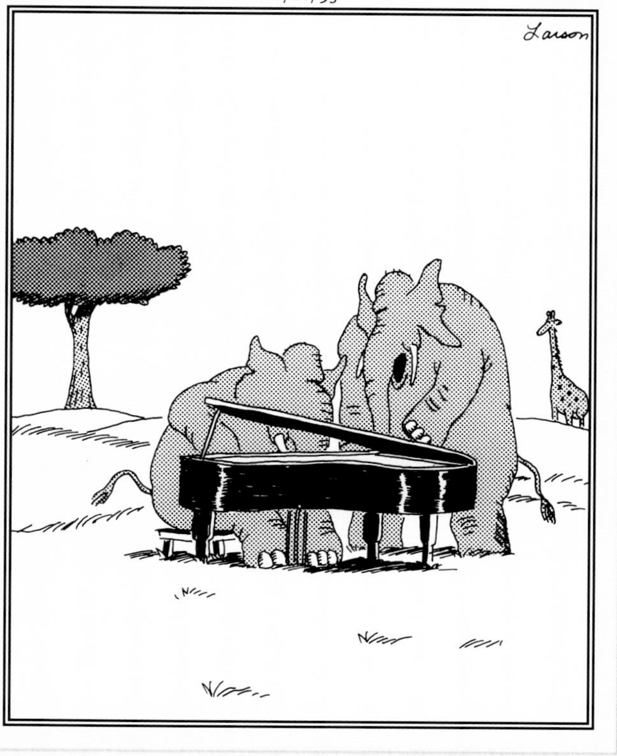
Larson

"Smash your left hand down about right here three times, then twice up in this area, then three times right about here. ... That's 'Louie Louie.'"

10/27/93

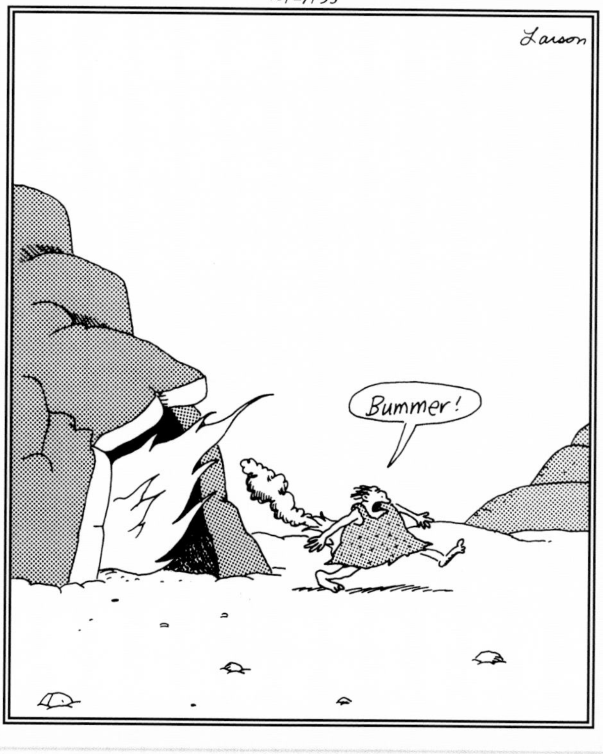
Larson
Bummer!

Some anthropologists believe that the discoveries of fire, shelter, and language were almost simultaneous.

10/18/93

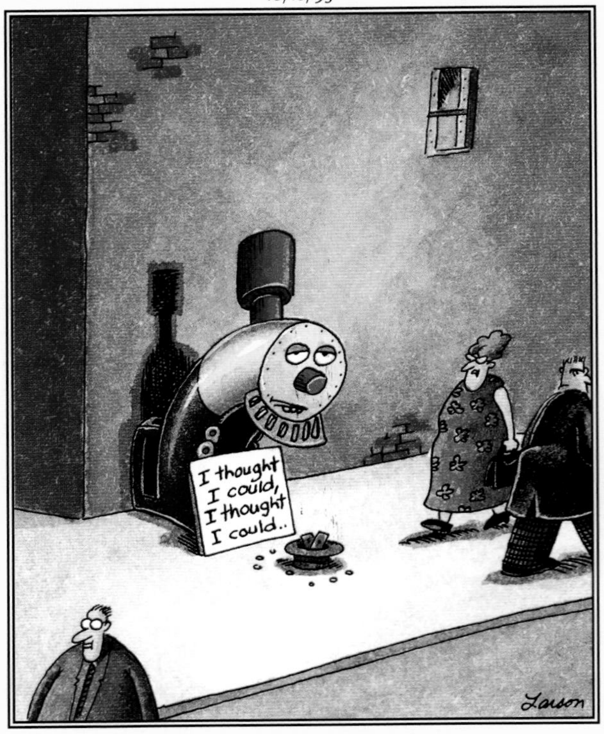
I thought
I could,
I thought
I could..

10/20/93

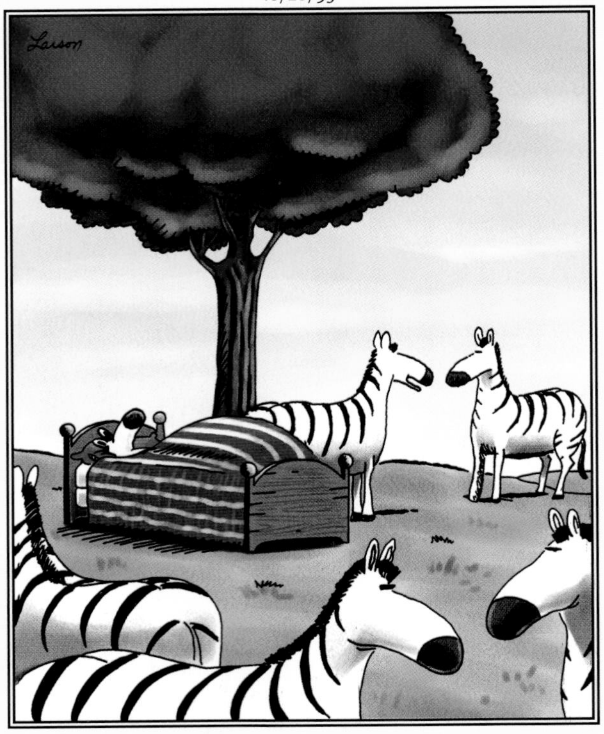

"Could you come back later? He's catching a few Y's right now."

10/28/93

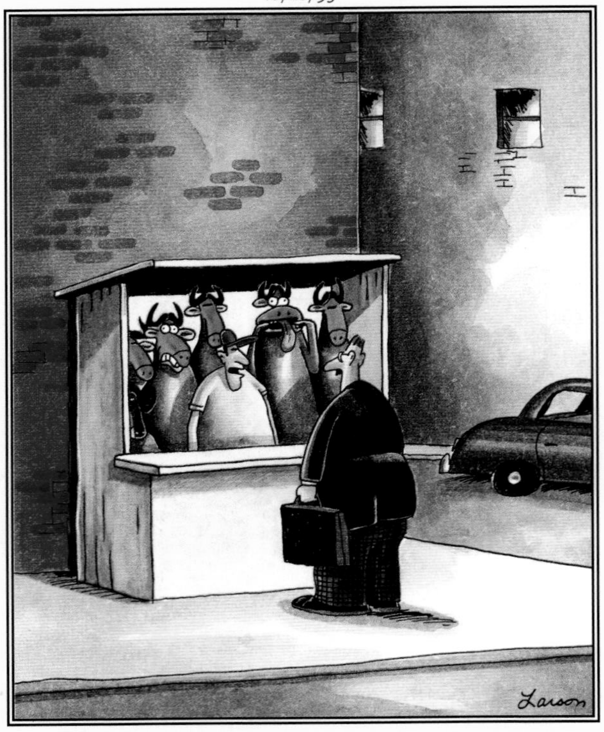

"Well, I've got good gnus and I've got bad gnus."

10/29/93

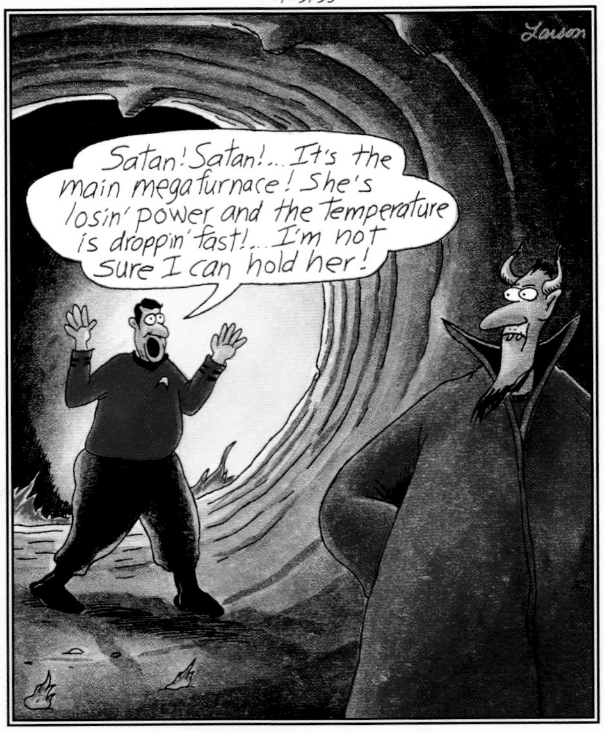
Satan! Satan!... It's the main megafurnace! She's losin' power and the temperature is droppin' fast!... I'm not sure I can hold her!

Scotty in hell

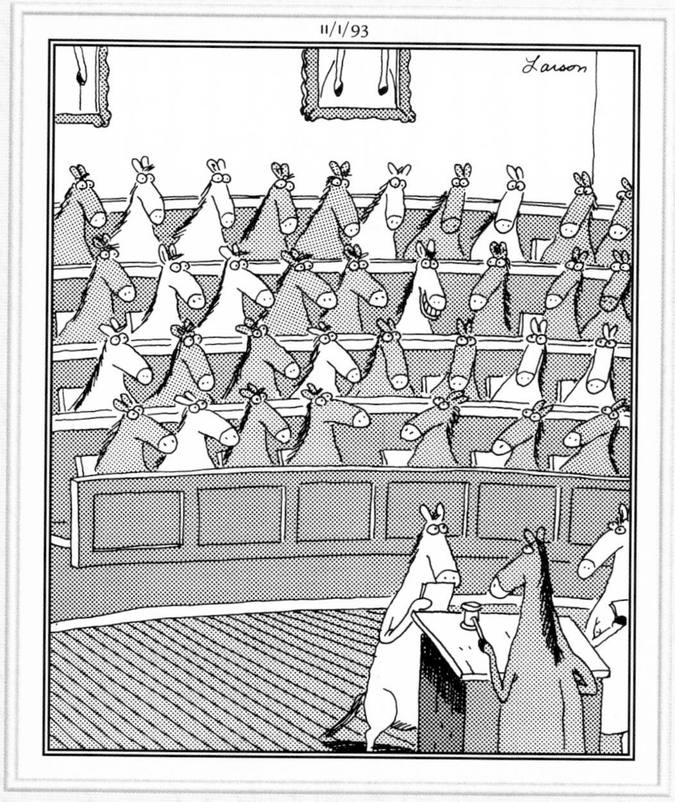
11/1/93
Larson

The entire parliament fell dead silent. For the first time since anyone could remember, one of the members voted "aye."

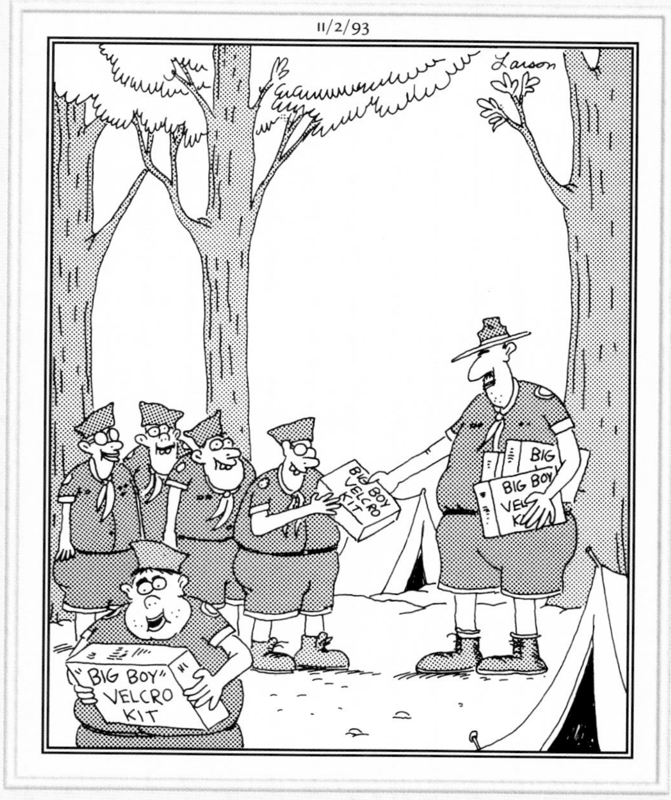
11/2/93
Larson
BIG BOY VELCRO KIT
"BIG BOY" VELCRO KIT

Fortunately, even the Boy Scouts who fail knot-tying get to go camping.

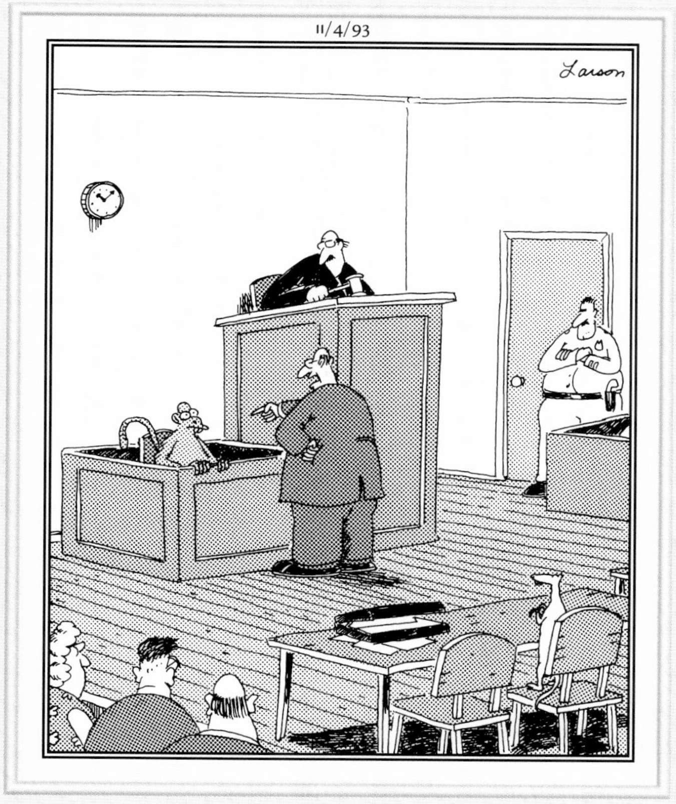
11/4/93
Larson

"Well, sir, my client says *he* wasn't having any fun, and that *you* just kept chasing him and chasing him around this mulberry bush, and that's when—out of self-defense—he decided to pop you one."

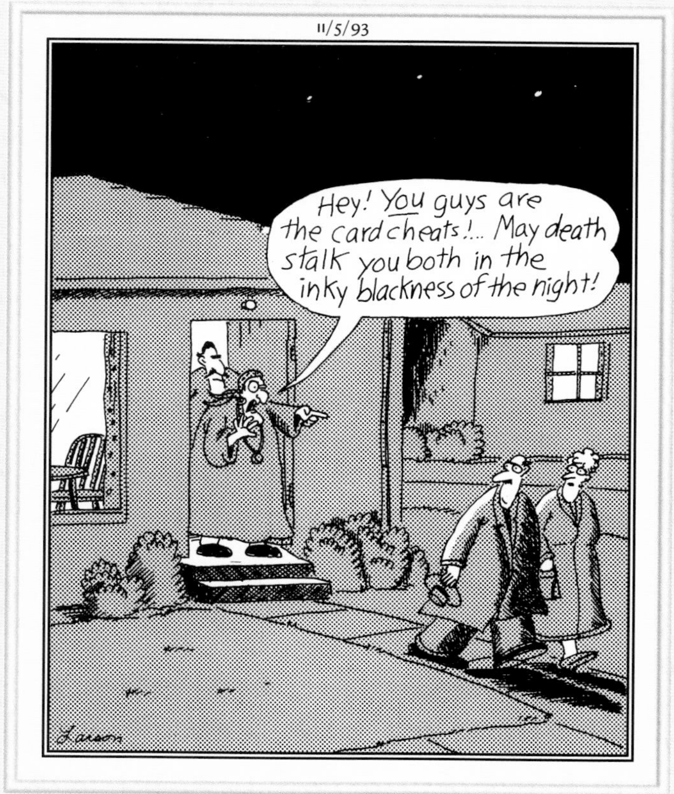
11/5/93
Hey! You guys are the card cheats!... May death stalk you both in the inky blackness of the night!
Larson

It had started off as a pleasant evening, but, as the Caldwells were soon to discover, it was a mistake to try and trump the old gypsy woman.

"This is it, son—my old chomping grounds. ...
Gosh, the memories."

"And then one of the little kids shined his
flashlight into the corner of the basement, and
there they saw these strange jars. ... Some said
'creamy,' some said 'crunchy.'..."

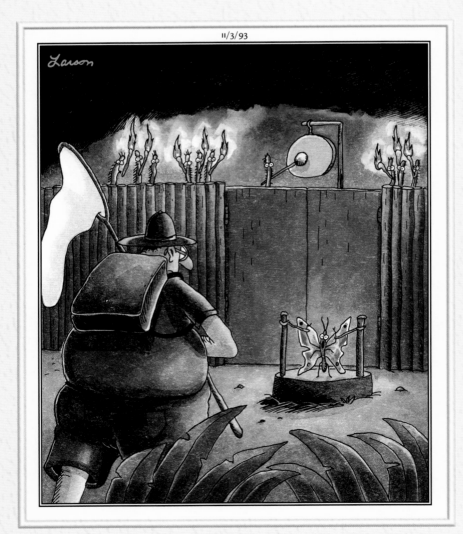

Summoned by the gonging, Professor Crutchfeld
stepped into the clearing. The little caterpillars had
done well this time in their offering.

11/16/93

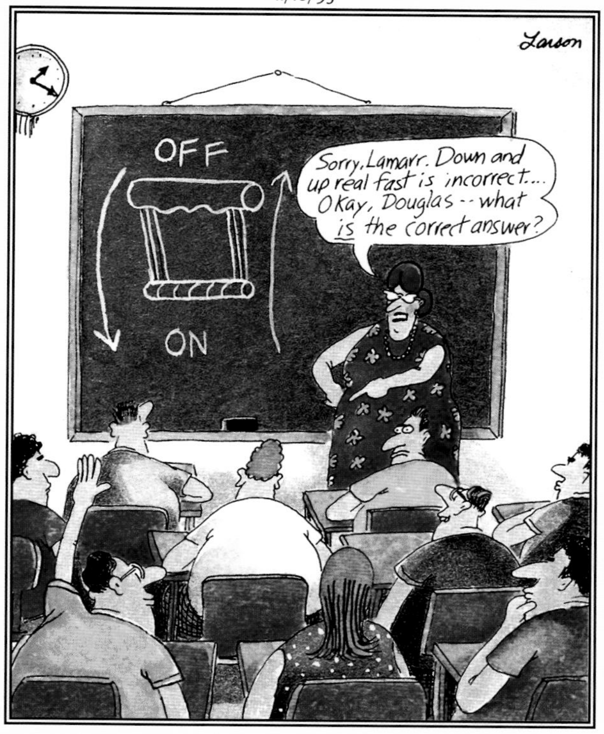
Larson
OFF
ON
Sorry, Lamarr. Down and up real fast is incorrect.... Okay, Douglas -- what is the correct answer?

At Electric Chair Operators Night School

11/30/93

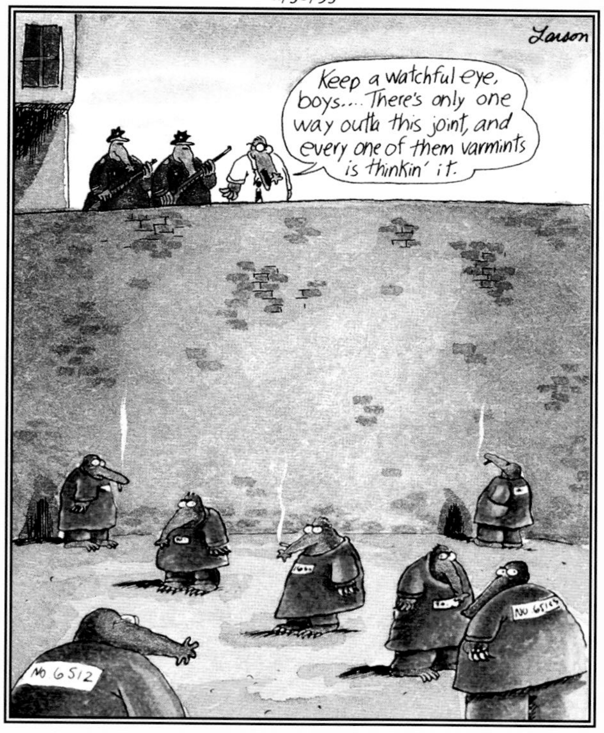
Larson
Keep a watchful eye, boys.... There's only one way outta this joint, and every one of them varmints is thinkin' it.
No 6512

At the Federal Mole Penitentiary

11/8/93

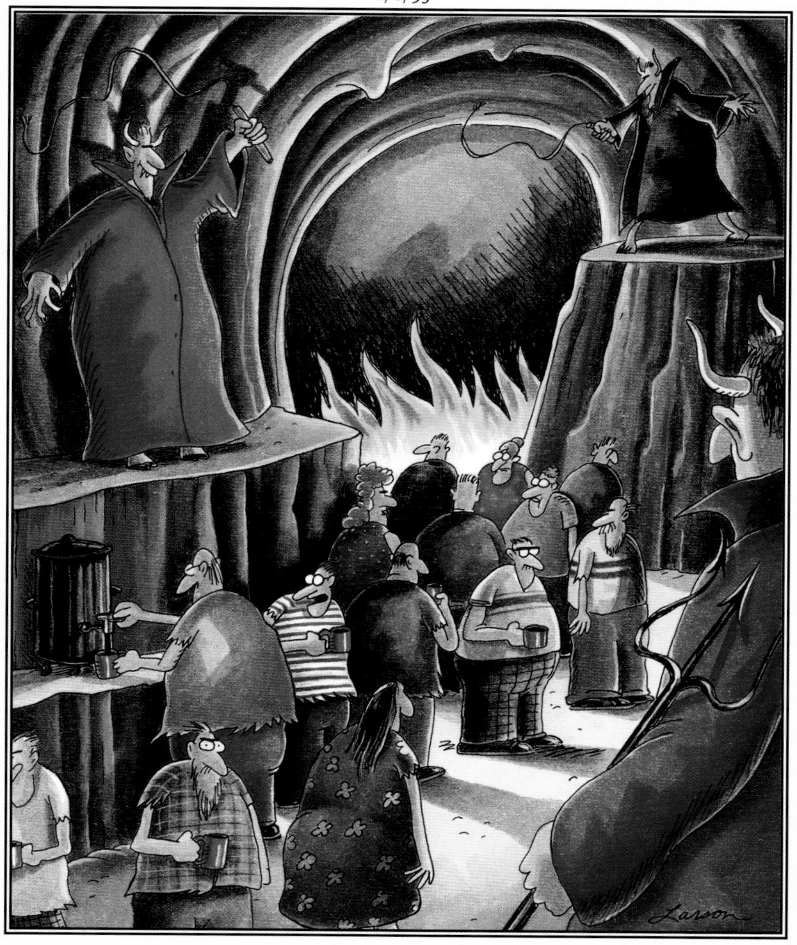
Larson

"Oh, man! The coffee's *cold!* They thought of *everything!*"

11/11/93

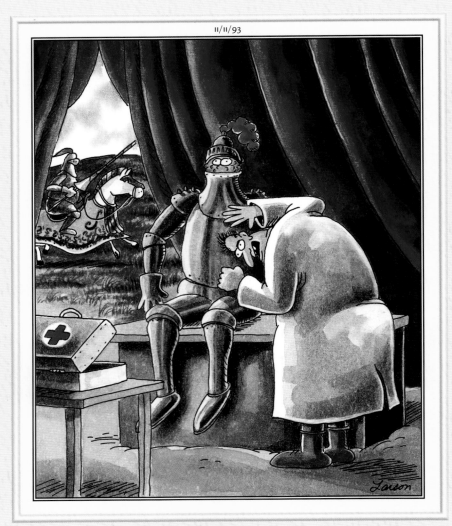

"Ooo! You're right, Sir Dwayne! If I knock right here,
I can make him start buzzing. ... Ooo, and he's *angry!*"

11/9/93

Douglas is ejected from the spoon band.

11/12/93

Backing out of the driveway, Mr. Peabody
suddenly brought his car to a stop. He had
already heard a peculiar "thump," and now
these crushed but familiar-looking glasses
further intrigued him.

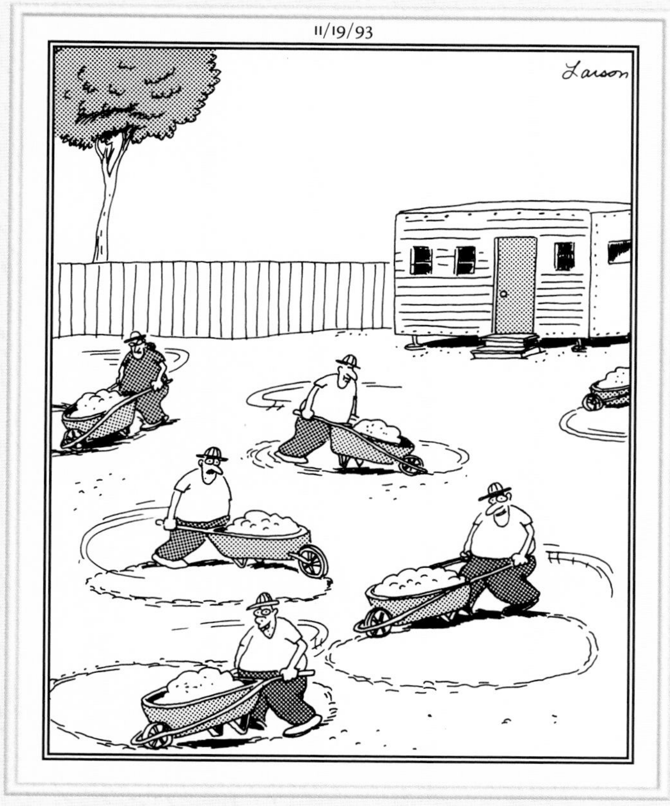
11/19/93
Larson

New Age construction workers

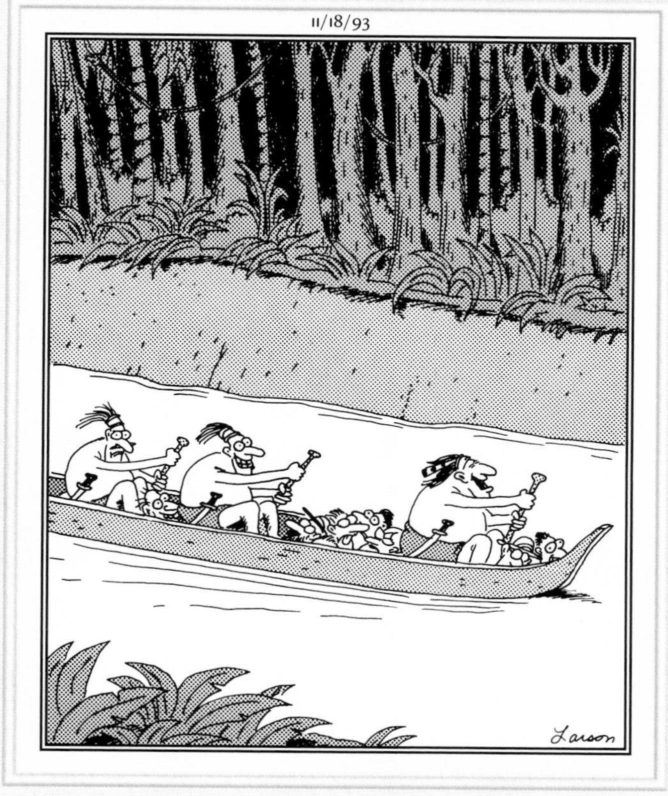
11/18/93
Larson

It had been a wonderfully successful day, and the dugout was filled with the sound of laughter and the fruits of their hunting skills. Only Kimbu wore a scowl, returning home with just a single knucklehead.

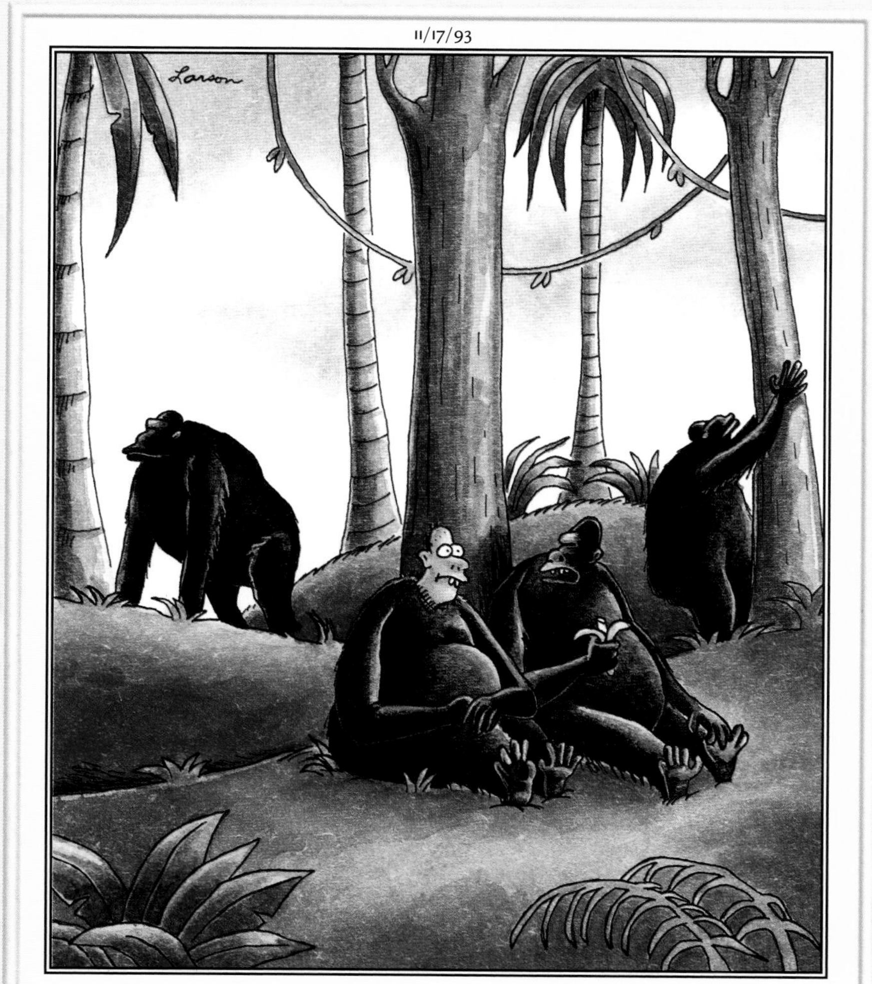
11/17/93
Larson

"Look. If you're so self-conscious about it, get yourself a gorilla mask."

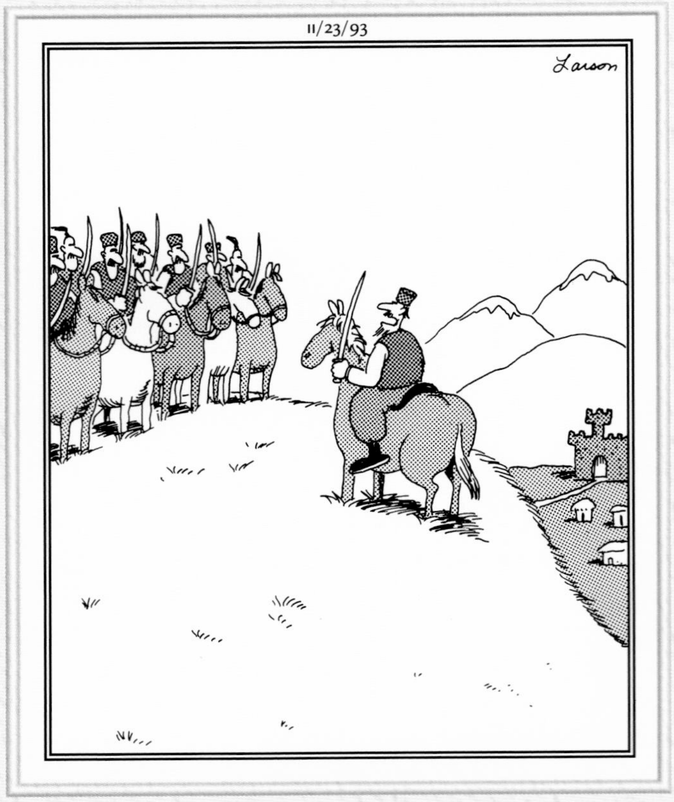
11/23/93
Larson

"Listen up, my Cossack brethren! We'll ride into the valley like the wind, the thunder of our horses and the lightning of our steel striking fear in the hearts of our enemies! ... And remember—stay out of Mrs. Caldwell's garden!"

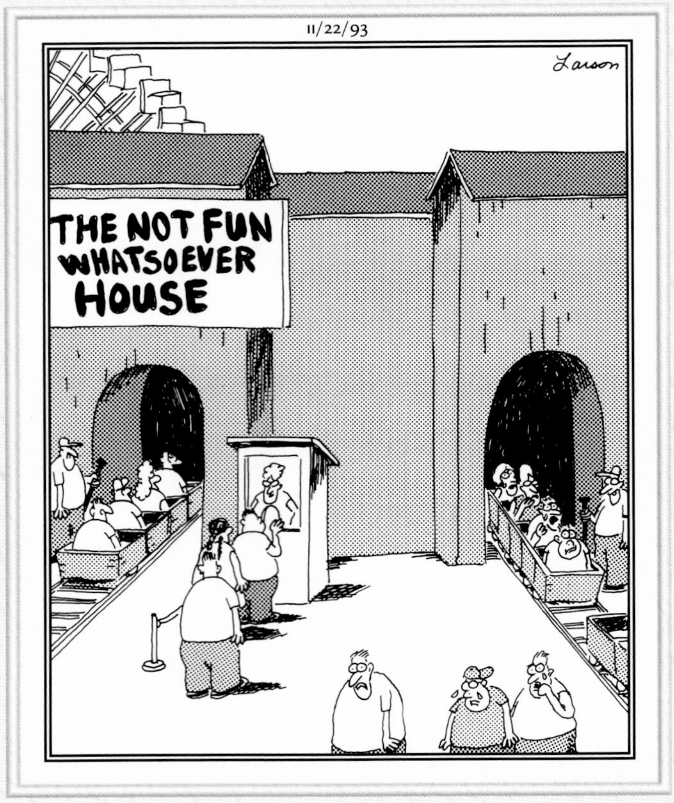
11/22/93
Larson
THE NOT FUN
WHATSOEVER
HOUSE

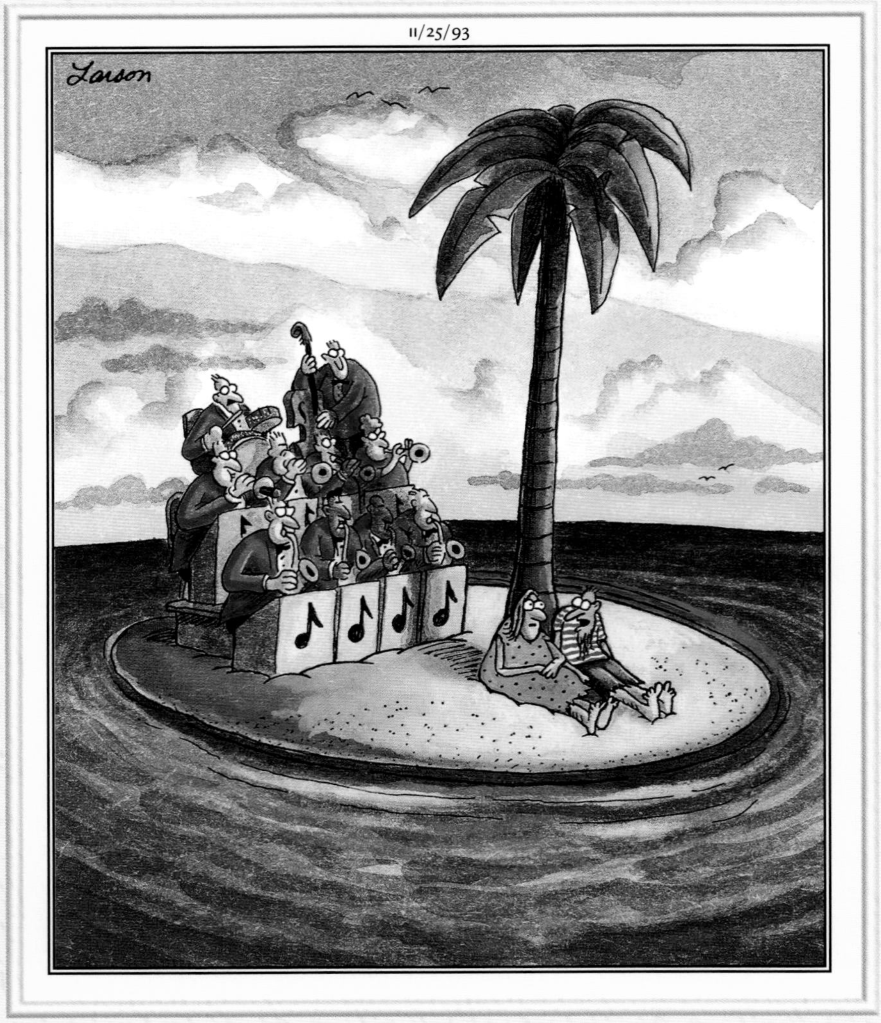
11/25/93
Larson

"Care to dance, Ms. Hollings?"

11/29/93
Larson

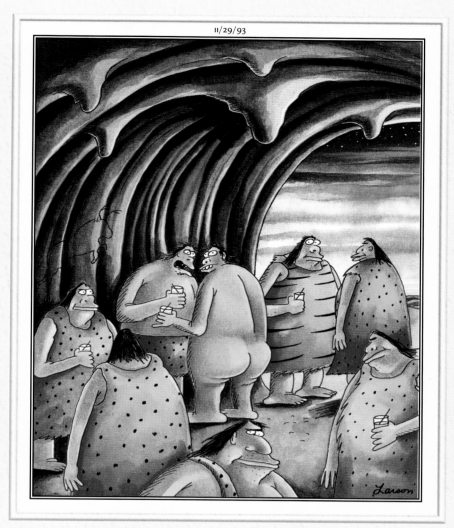

"A word of advice, Durk: It's the Mesolithic. We've domesticated the dog, we're using stone tools, and no one's *naked* anymore."

11/24/93
Duffy's
Bird Seed
Larson

"Frankie! When didja get out? ... Gee, I bet you been sittin' in da cage wonderin' where me and da loot wuz! ... Oh, Frankie, Frankie ... heh heh heh ... Want some coffee, Frankie?"

11/26/93
Larson

Fortunately, both Ali and his camel knew to take refuge during a desert Spam storm.

12/2/93

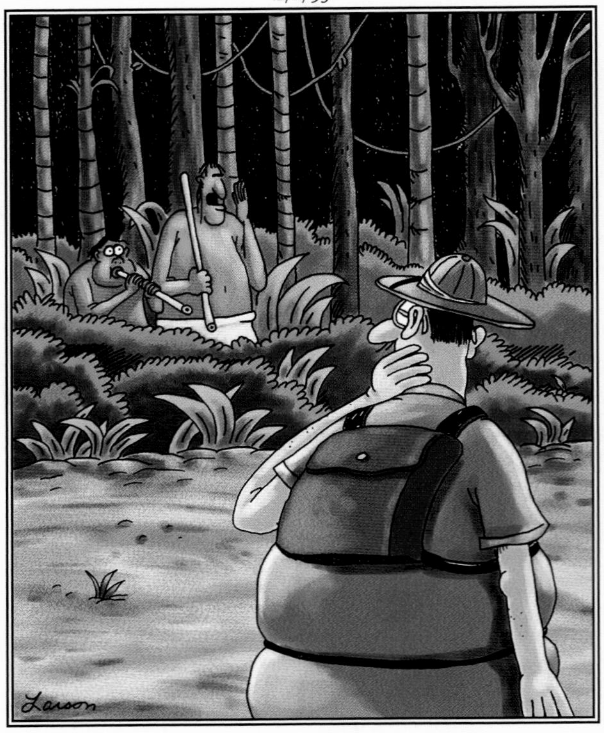

"It's okay! Dart not poisonous. ... Just showin' my kid the ropes!"

12/3/93

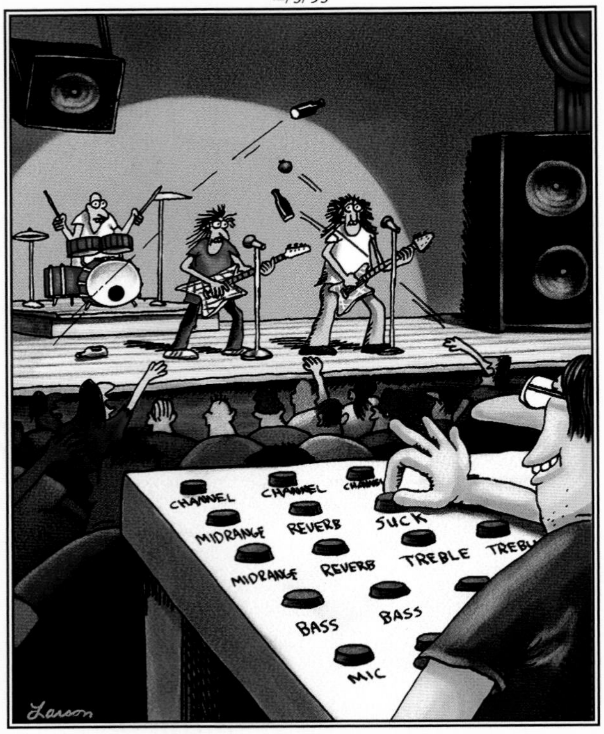
CHANNEL
CHANNEL
MIDRANGE
REVERB
SUCK
MIDRANGE
REVERB
TREBLE
BASS
BASS
MIC

Raymond's last day as the band's sound technician.

12/6/93

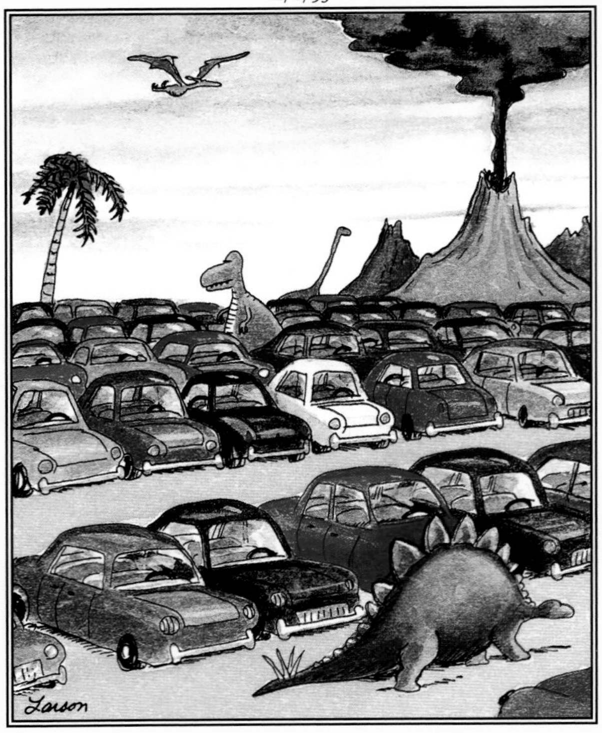

Jurassic parking

12/7/93

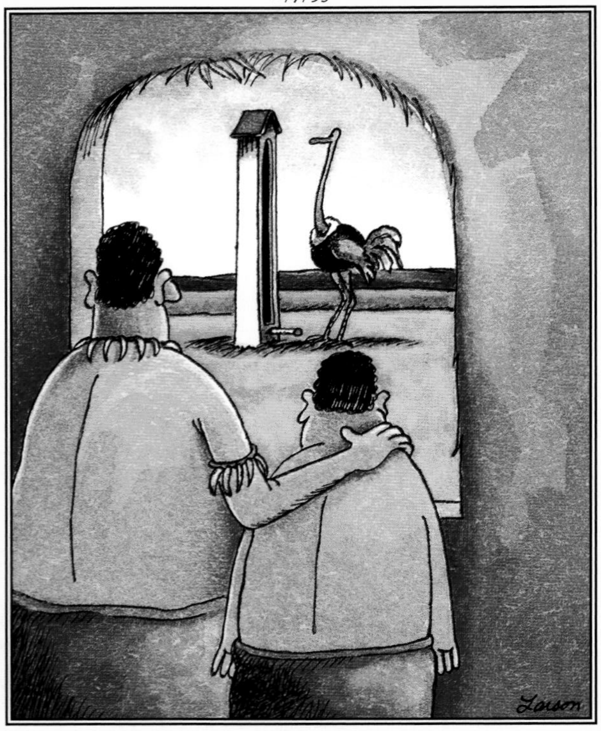

It was a special moment, as father and son watched their weekend project attract its first tenant.

12/14/93

"Dang it, Morty! ... You're always showing this picture of me you took at 7 o'clock in the morning!"

12/9/93

Iggy knew he was extremely lucky to get a room with a view.

12/8/93

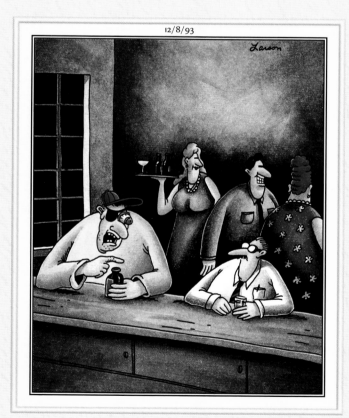

"Just keep starin', buddy, and I'll show ya my *bad* eye!"

12/15/93

Here it is again, William! Front page!.. "Lewis and Clark Expedition Declared a Success!".. See what I mean? His name is always first!... I tell you, son, if you don't do somethin' about this now, you'll be playin' second fiddle in the hist'ry books!

Clark's mother

12/13/93

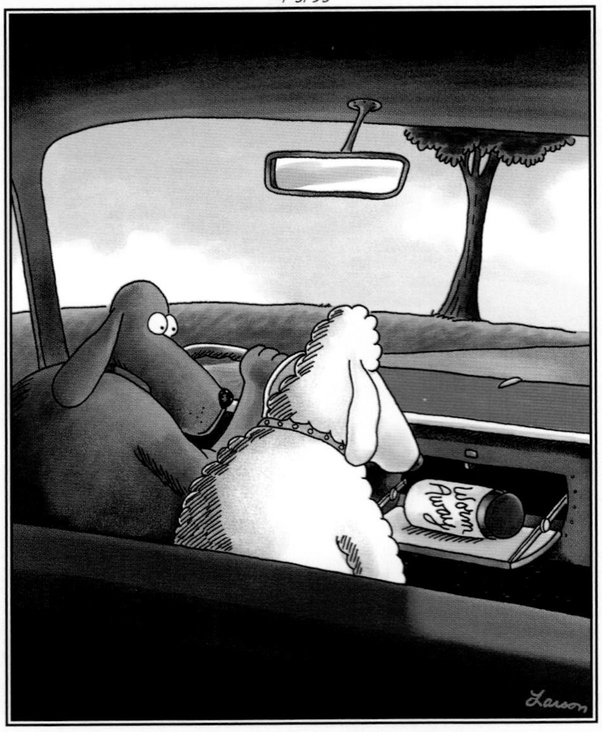
Worm Away
Larson

Suddenly, the car struck a pothole, the glove box flew open, and Sparky knew the date was basically over.

12/16/93

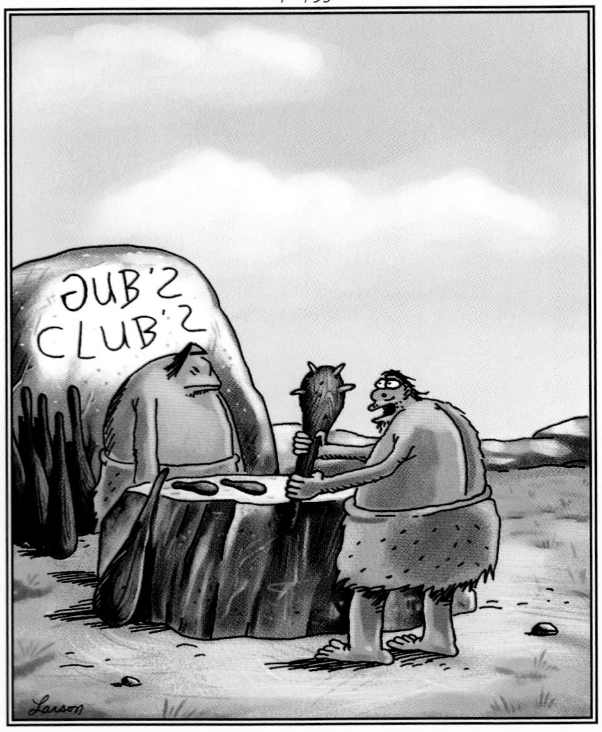
GUB'S
CLUB'S
Larson

"No, no. ... Not this one. Too many bells and whistles."

12/1/93

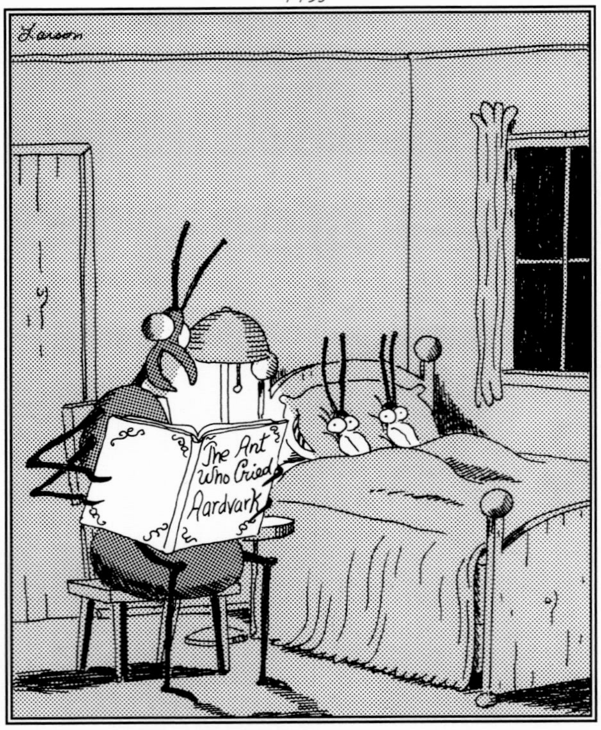
Larson
The Ant Who Cried Aardvark

12/10/93

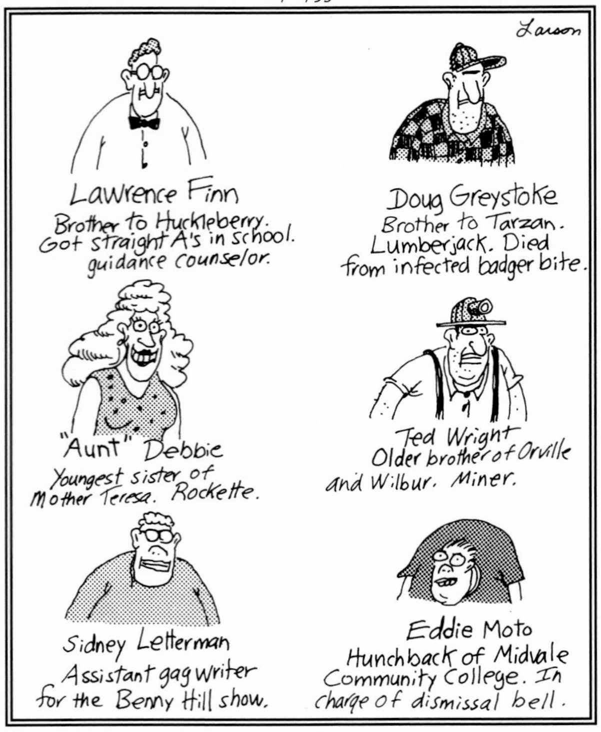
Larson
Lawrence Finn
Brother to Huckleberry. Got straight A's in school. guidance counselor.
Doug Greystoke
Brother to Tarzan. Lumberjack. Died from infected badger bite.
"Aunt" Debbie
Youngest sister of Mother Teresa. Rockette.
Ted Wright
Older brother of Orville and Wilbur. Miner.
Sidney Letterman
Assistant gag writer for the Benny Hill show.
Eddie Moto
Hunchback of Midvale Community College. In charge of dismissal bell.

In their sibling's shadow

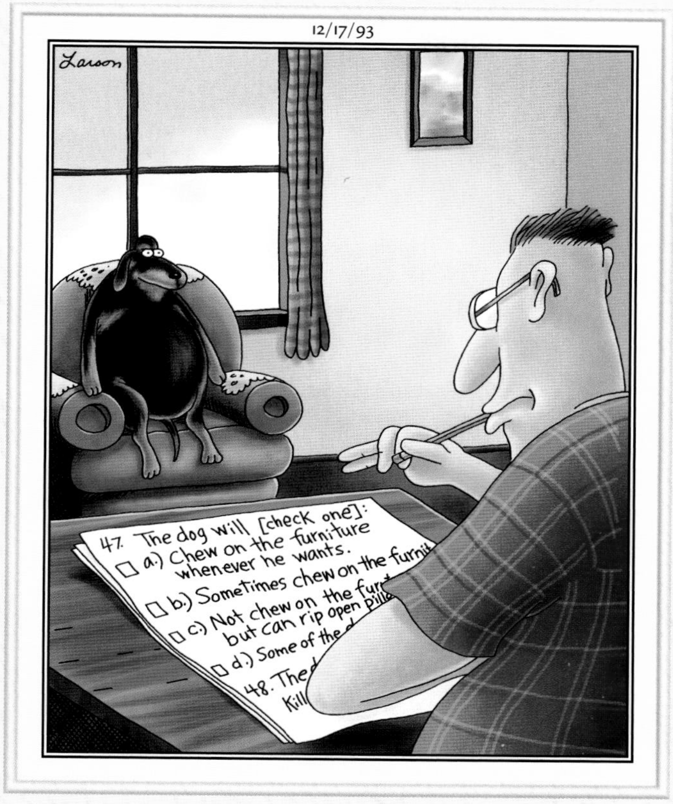
12/17/93
47. The dog will [check one]:
a.) Chew on the furniture whenever he wants.
b.) Sometimes chew on the
c.) Not chew on the
48. The

The questions were getting harder, and Ted could feel Lucky's watchful glare from across the room. He had been warned, he recalled, that this was a breed that would sometimes test him.

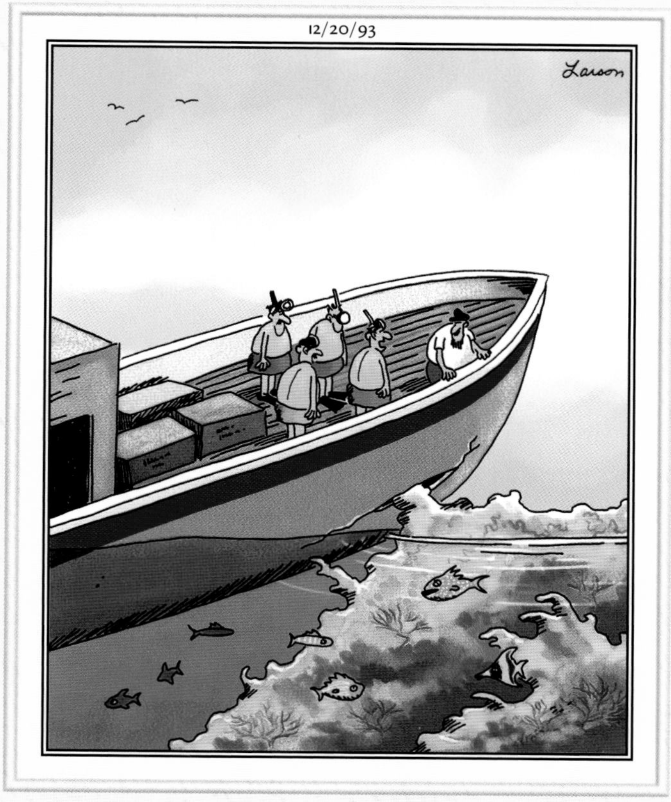
12/20/93

"Excuse me, Captain, but while we're waiting, would you like to join the crew and myself for a little snorkeling?"

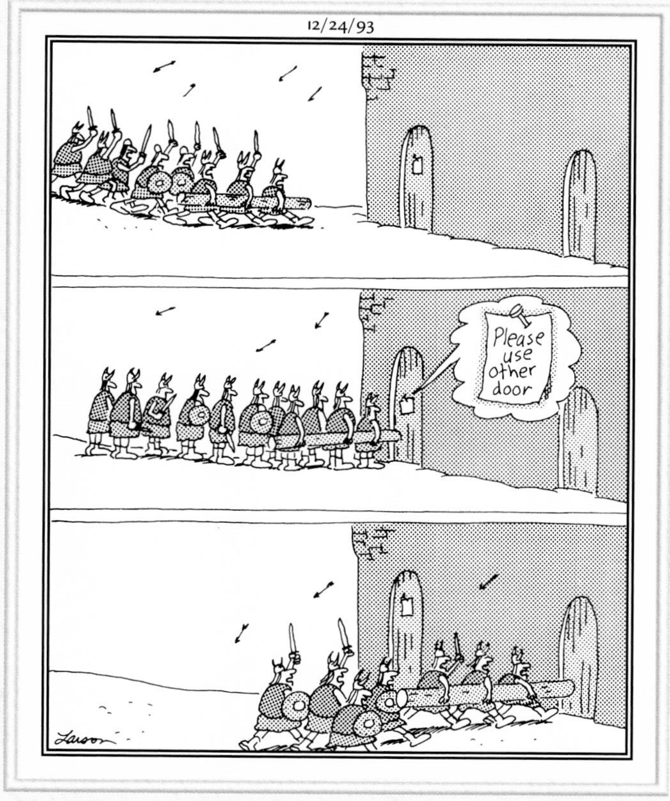
12/24/93
Please use other door

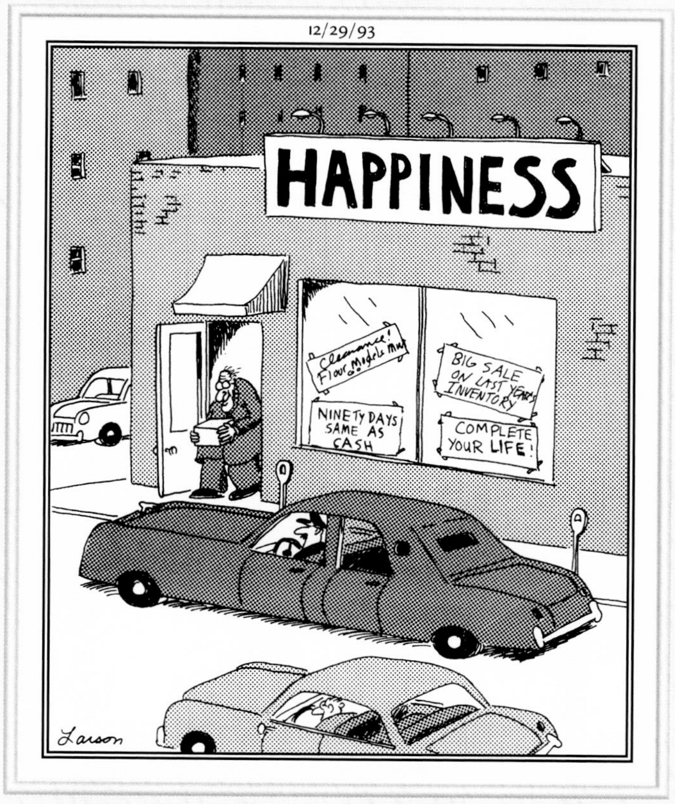
12/29/93
HAPPINESS
NINETY DAYS SAME AS CASH
BIG SALE ON LAST YEAR'S INVENTORY
COMPLETE YOUR LIFE!

His few friends had told him he could never buy it, but Mr. Crawley surmised that they just didn't know where the store was.

12/21/93

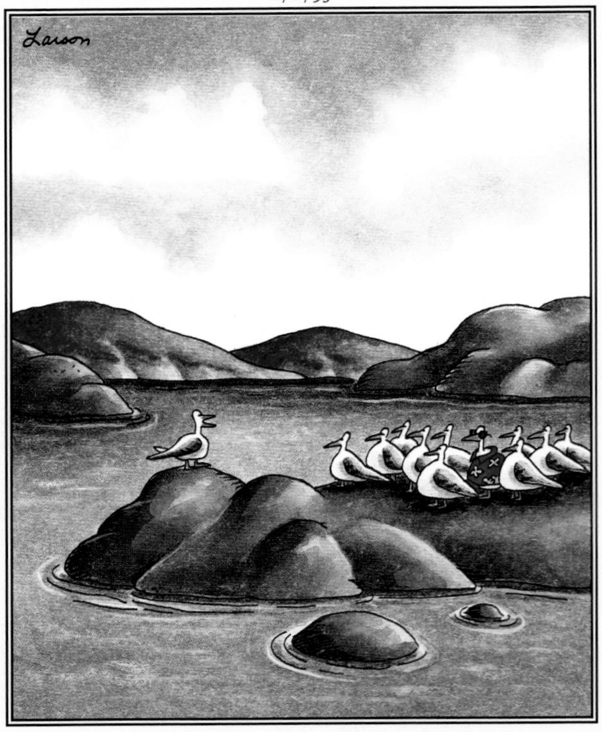
Larson

"Okay, everyone, we'll be departing for Antarctica in about 15 minutes. ... If anyone thinks he may be in the wrong migration, let us know now."

12/22/93

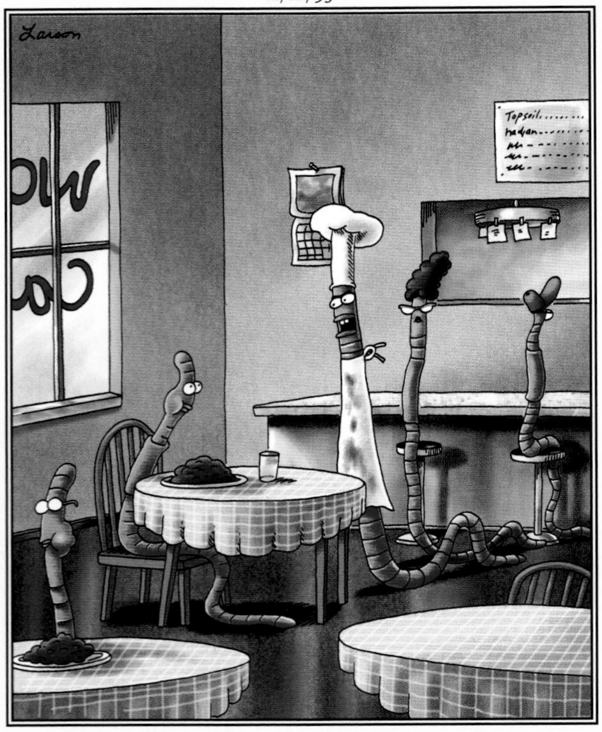
Larson

"I've been told you don't like my dirt!"

12/23/93

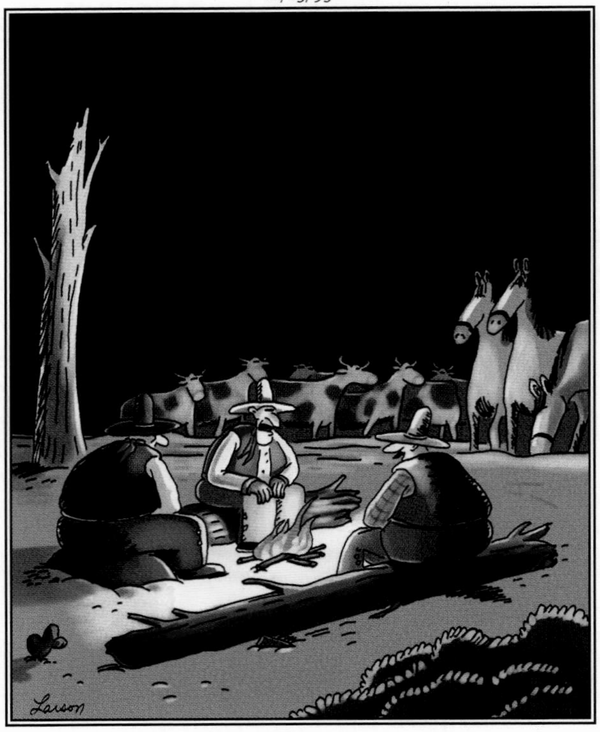
Larson

"Okay, I got one—do you say 'darn it' or 'dern it'?"

12/28/93

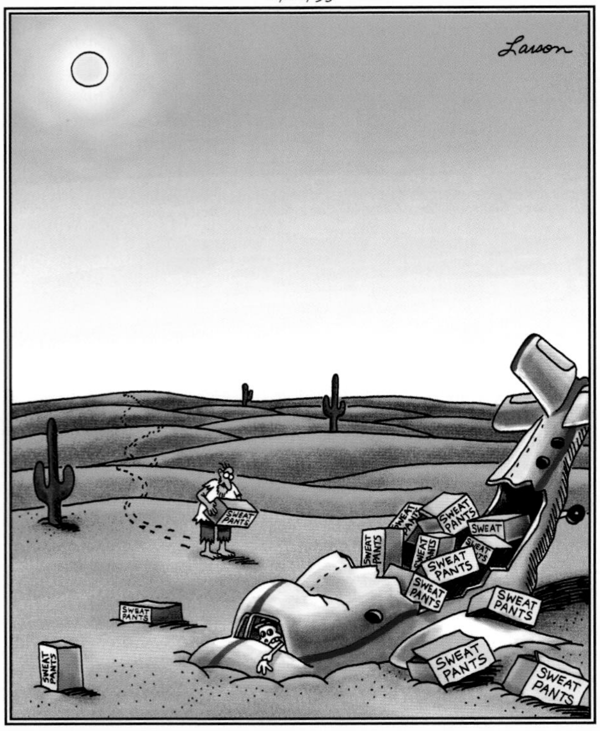
Larson
SWEAT PANTS

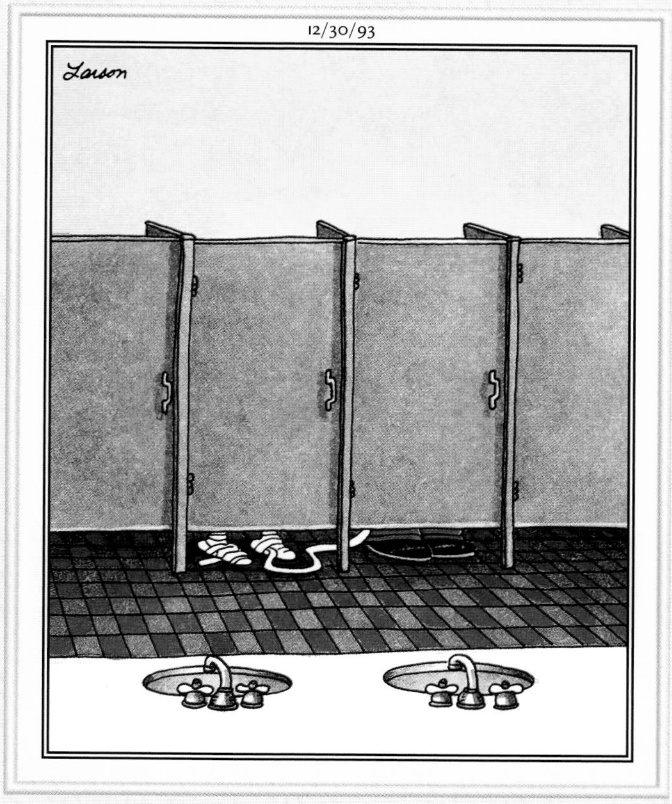
12/30/93
Larson

It was an innocent mistake, but nevertheless, a moment later Maurice found himself receiving the full brunt of the mummy's wrath.

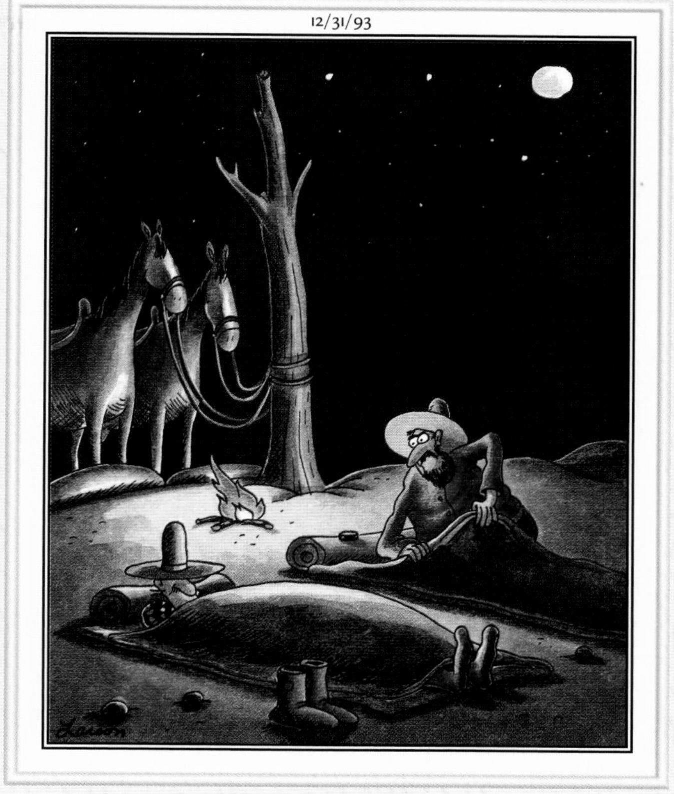
12/31/93

Zeke froze. For the longest time, all he could do was stare at the chocolate mint that "someone" had placed on his bedroll.

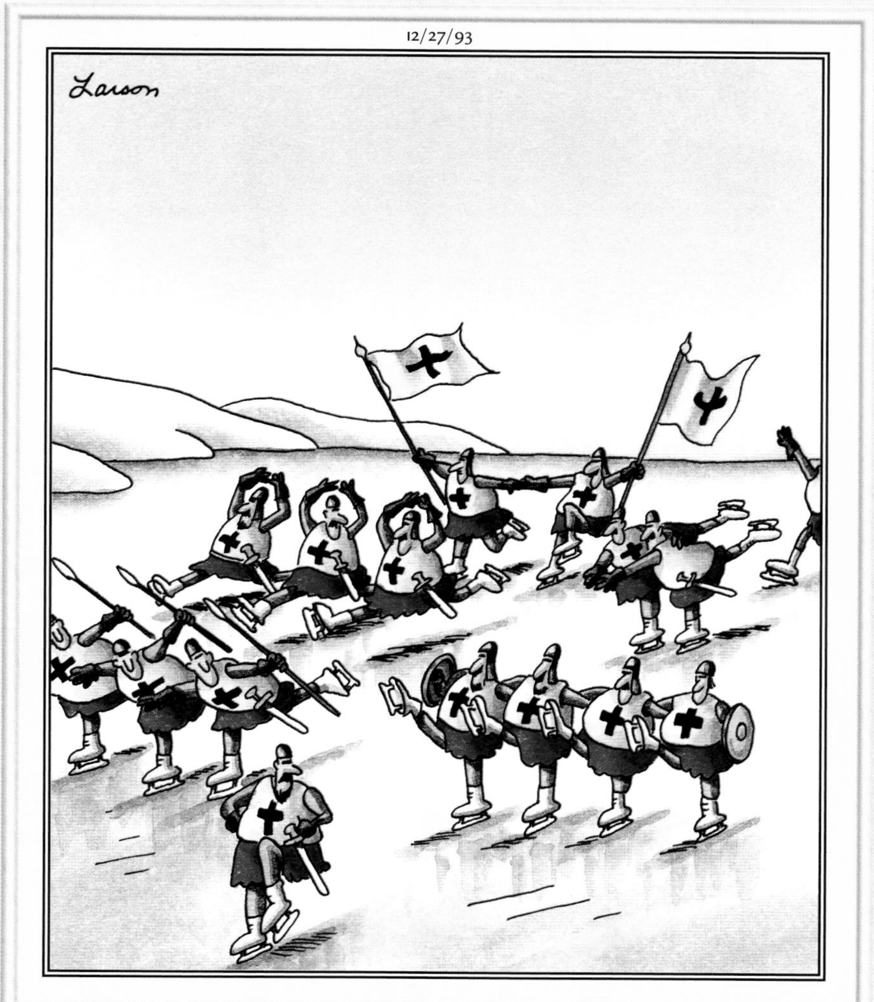
12/27/93
Larson

The Ice Crusades

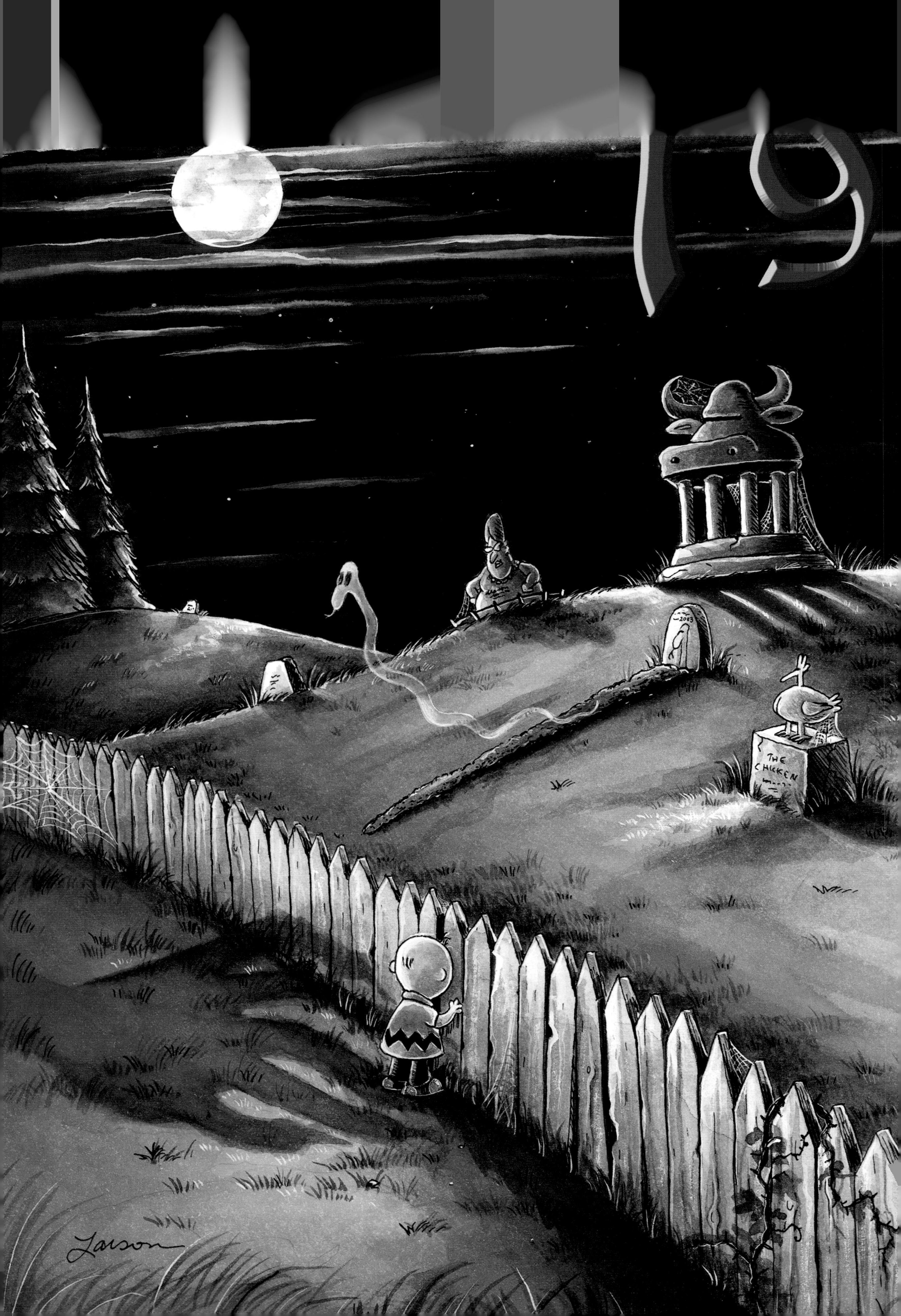
19
THE CHICKEN
Larson

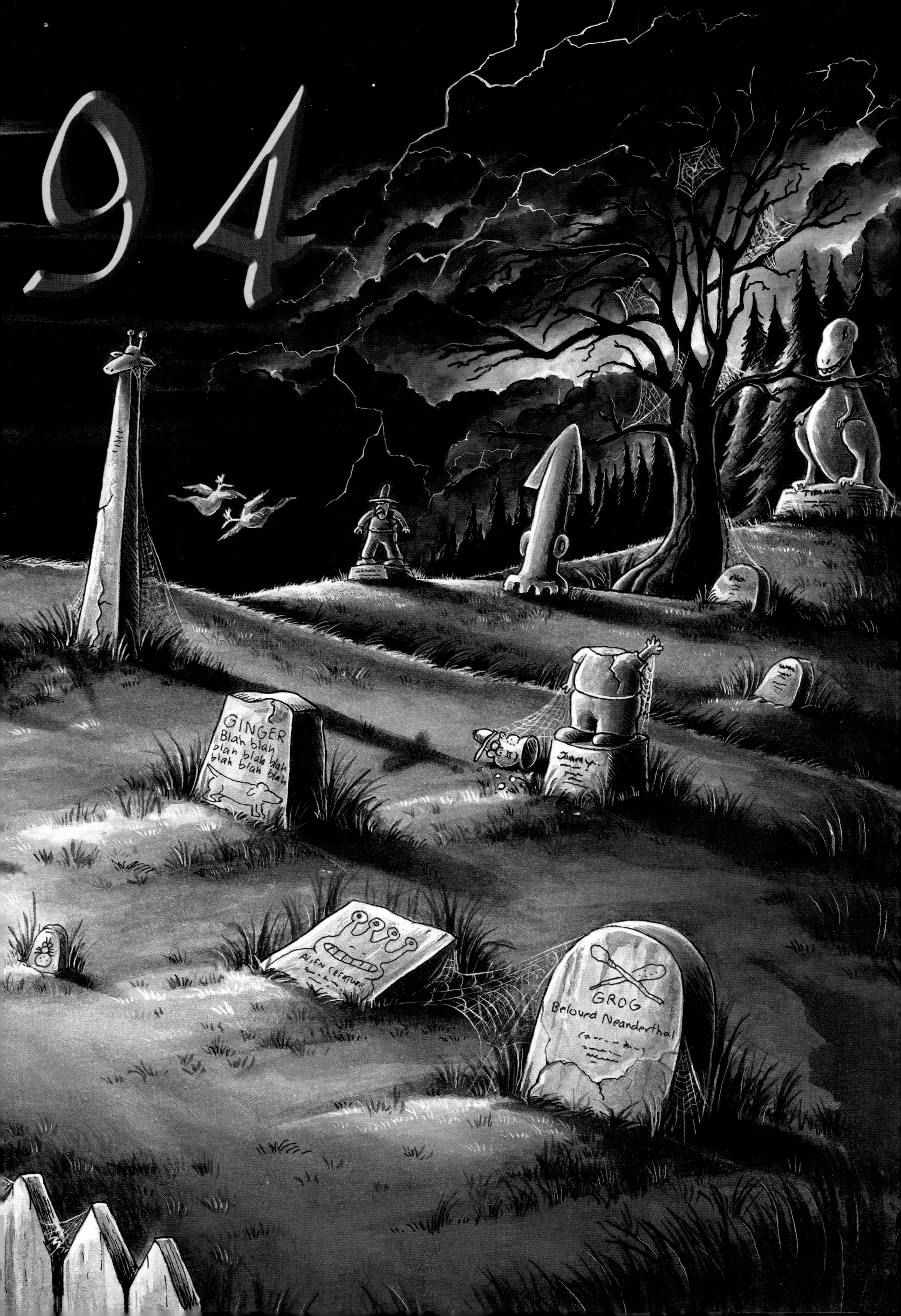
94
GINGER
Blah blah
blah blah blah
blah blah blah
Jimmy
ALIEN CREATURE
GROG
Belovd Neanderthal

Final Thoughts

There's a little cartoon—a doodle, really—that I came across in one of my old sketchbooks while working on this two-volume, 18-pound hernia giver. And despite the fact that I believe there's a rule somewhere that you're not supposed to laugh at your own work, this one caught me off guard. I confess: I laughed.

What I was looking at was a tavern scene where the customers and staff are all praying mantises. One mantis dressed in a rumpled coat and tie is sitting by himself at the bar, clutching a stiff drink. He has no head. And, with a voice that emanates from somewhere down below his empty collar, he angrily blurts out just one word to the mantis bartender: "Women!"

It's a cartoon that never got further than my sketchbook, and I'm not sure why. I admit, you would have to know something about the sex lives of mantises to recognize the thin slice of natural history buried in among all the other anthropomorphic silliness, but I doubt that would have stayed my hand. I do see a note to myself on the same page questioning whether this male mantis would most likely blurt out "Women!" or "Females!" and I bet that was my undoing. These sorts of decisions usually started off as minor details, grew in significance, and finally sent me into the Don't-Draw-This Abyss. (Actually, I could have just referred to Cartoon Rule #359, which clearly states that "… anything walking around with a missing head shall be deemed funny, with the exception of a puppy or the Pope.")

On another page, I found my half-doodled, half-described idea of a nightclub filled with assorted invertebrates. The dance floor is packed with creatures, all having a good time (I like the imagery already, complete with disco ball), but at a table in the foreground sits a slug couple, dressed to the nines, looking hip, but—as always—compelled to wait for a slow song.

And then I stumbled upon my crude little sketch of the astrophysicists' convention. The scene is an auditorium, and everyone is seated as one of the guest speakers begins his presentation. Only there's apparently been a mistake. The speaker is a farmer, in overalls and brim hat, and he is giving a talk on String Bean Theory.

I'll stop there, but this is just a way of divulging the one thing that haunts me now. Not every day, and sometimes not for weeks, but sooner or later it creeps into my brain, stays a while, and leaves a lingering sadness after it's gone. It is this: What else didn't I draw? What other ideas and characters are doomed to remain everlastingly in my inkwell, never to have *The Far Side* marquee hoisted over their heads, left to wander forever in the Land of the Undrawn?

C'est la vie, I suppose. If you were to ask me today if I miss cartooning (and I do hear it a lot), my answer is no, not really. As they say, been there done that. Plus, for me, there was always the unforeseen nature of this thing, which no doubt made it easier to eventually let it go. (When Career Day comes to your high school, you don't walk around looking for the Cartoon Guy.)

Do I think I might return to the drafting table one day? Well, they say never say never, so I'll take that advice. If that haunting problem I mentioned becomes more frequent, who knows—maybe I'll need to exorcise some ghosts. (At least I should work up that praying mantis cartoon; damn, I'm sorry I missed that one.)

Serendipity has handed me a way to wrap this up. I'm sitting here writing my final essay for this book, and every few minutes I lift my eyes from the computer monitor and stare out the window overlooking the garden. But I'm not looking at the garden. I'm watching the small spiders that have spun webs between the leaded panes and the brick frame. There are four of them, and they're catching gnats like they know it's the gnat warden's day off.

This is really a show. They're extremely small, these spiders, but the gnats—and they're as thick as, well, gnats—are considerably smaller. There are so many, the spiders aren't even bothering to throw a few holding threads around their prey. They're just grabbing and sucking down gnats, one after the other. I can't help but imagine that somewhere within the primitive, ganglionic mass that serves as a spider's brain, these little guys are experiencing a sensation that equates to what my dad, an avid fisherman, feels when a salmon strikes his line: Hot damn! Another one!

The parallels are interesting, now that I think about it: My dad's invisible fishing line/the spider's invisible web; my dad's net/the spider's holding threads; my dad sitting alone in his boat, patiently waiting for a strike/the spiders sitting alone in their webs, patiently waiting for the same signal. There's only one conclusion: My dad's really just like a big spider and all these little spiders are really just like my dad. (All we need now is for one of these little gnats to start screaming "Help me!" and this will get really weird.)

I'm telling you this because I'm guessing—or hoping—you may know me a little by now. My mind seems to wander. I started off wistfully describing a few cartoons I wish I had drawn, wondering about the ones yet to be imagined, and what happens?—I get cut off by some little spiders.

Here's where I think I must simply admit the truth: I want to stop writing about cartoons and thinking about cartoons. I just want to watch these little spiders. This is how I started as a cartoonist—drawn to the little story—and this is how I'll end.

And if you run into my dad, please don't squish him.

1/3/94

Larson
NEVER NEVER LAND
NEVER SAY NEVER LAND
SOMETIMES BUT NOT ALWAYS LAND
SAY IT DON'T SPRAY IT LAND
NEWARK

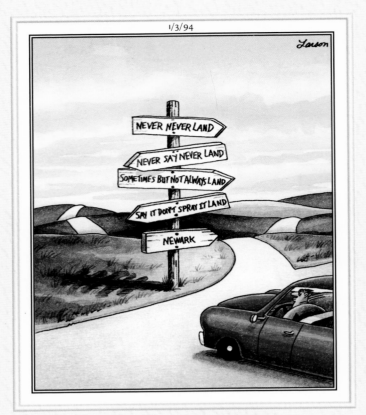

Crucial decisions along life's highway

1/5/94

Larson

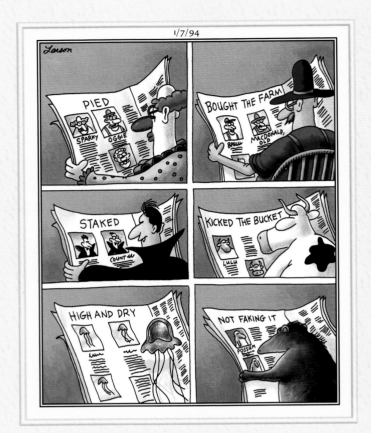

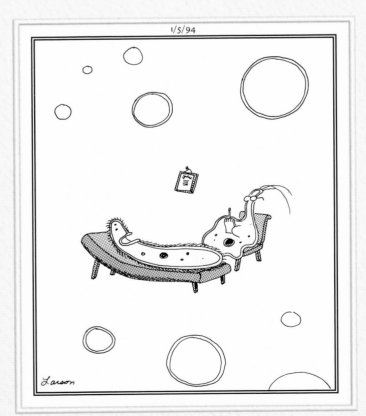

"Well, I just feel like I'm living under a microscope."

1/7/94

Larson
PIED
SPARKY
OGGIE
BOUGHT THE FARM
MACDONALD, OLD
STAKED
COUNT
KICKED THE BUCKET
LULU
HIGH AND DRY
NOT FAKING IT
POSSUM

Specialized obituaries

1/12/94

Larson

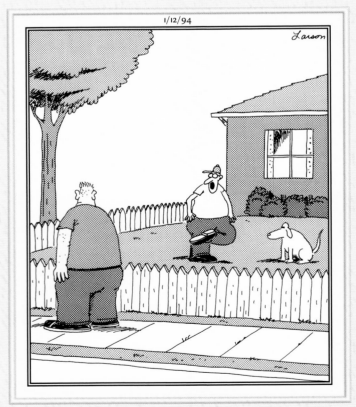

"Oh, not *you,* mister! ... I was referring to something here from my dog, Nimka."

1/4/94

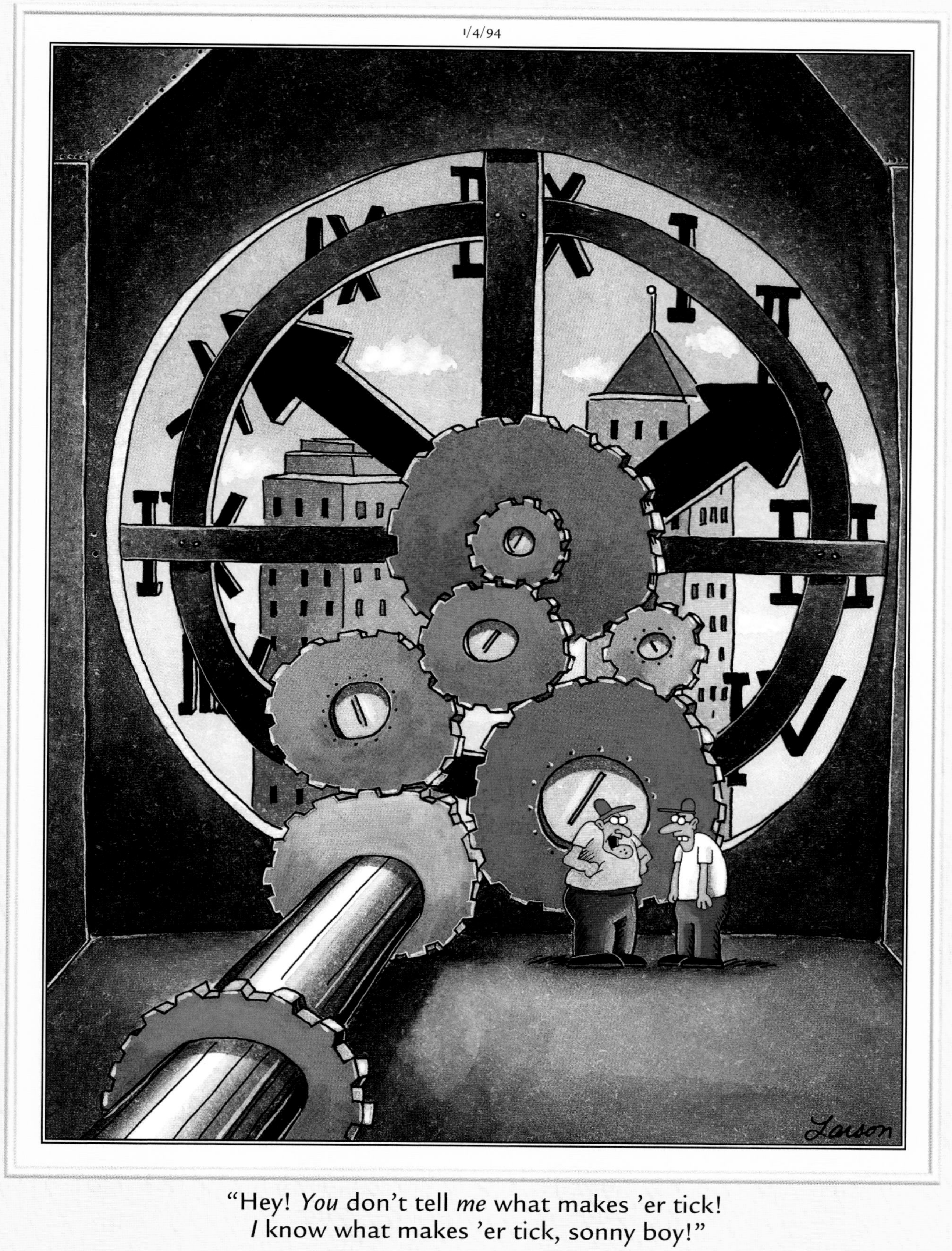
Larson

"Hey! *You* don't tell *me* what makes 'er tick! *I* know what makes 'er tick, sonny boy!"

1/6/94

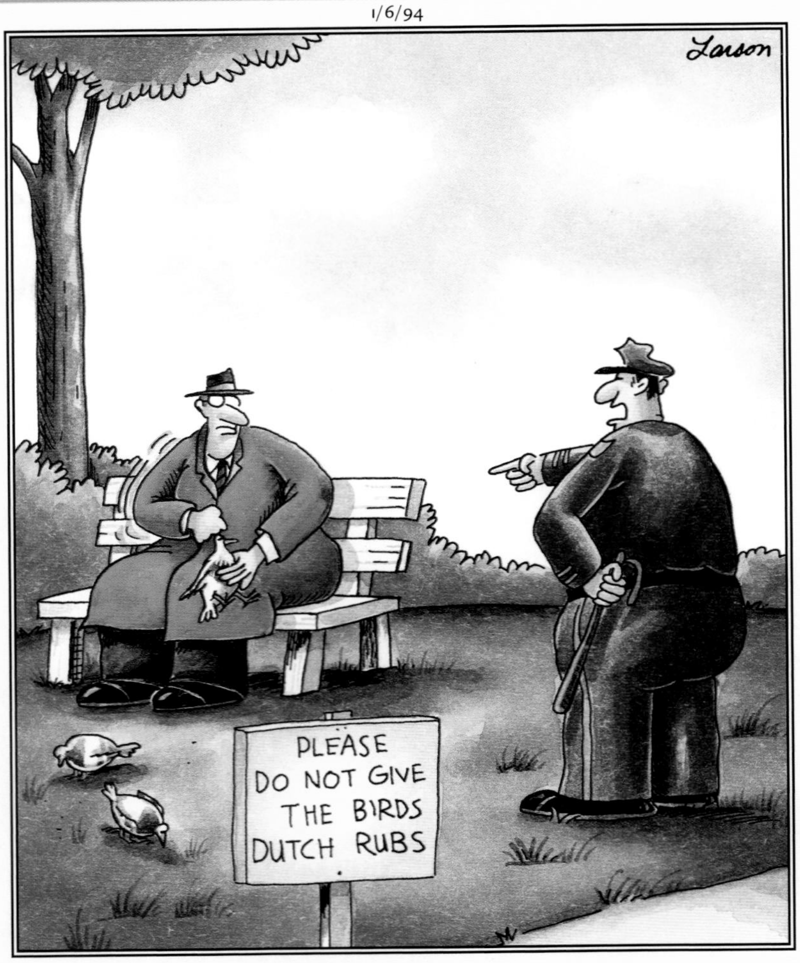
Larson
PLEASE DO NOT GIVE THE BIRDS DUTCH RUBS.

"Hey! ... You!"

1/10/94

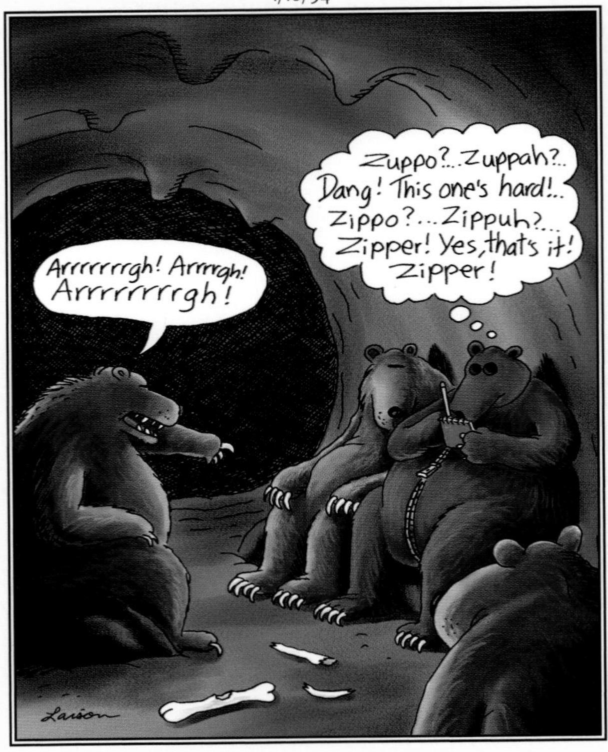
Arrrrrrrgh! Arrrgh! Arrrrrrrrgh!
Zuppo?..Zuppah?.. Dang! This one's hard!.. Zippo?...Zippuh?.. Zipper! Yes, that's it! Zipper!
Larson

Professor Wainwright's painstaking field research to decode the language of bears comes to a sudden and horrific end.

1/17/94

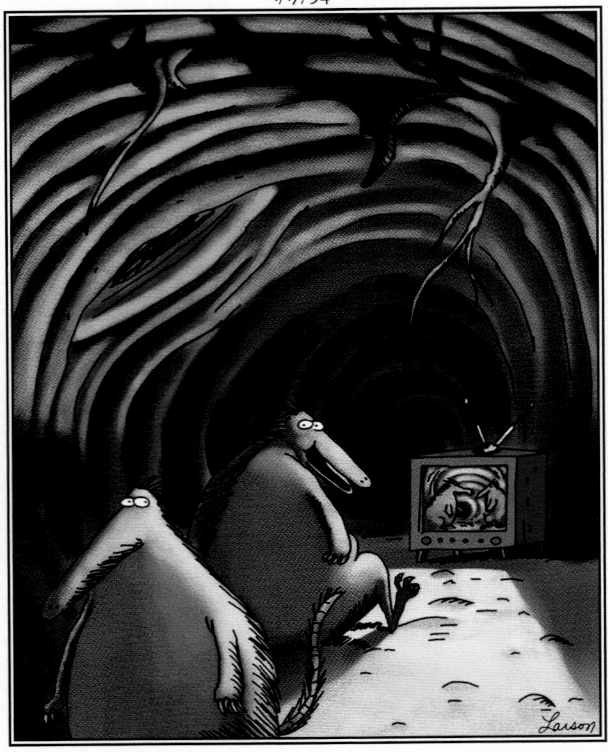
Larson

"Vera! Come quick! Some nature show has a hidden camera in the Ericksons' burrow! ... We're going to see their entire courtship behavior!"

1/19/94

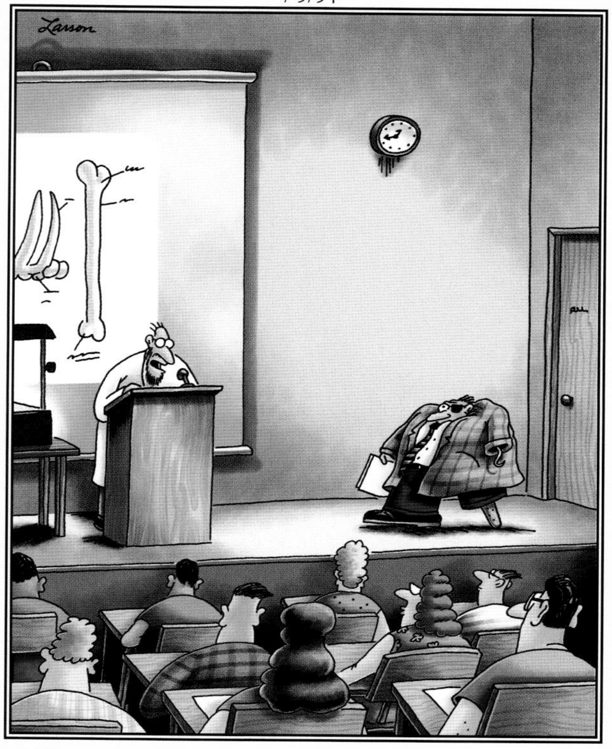
Larson

"Today, our guest lecturer is Dr. Clarence Tibbs, whose 20-year career has culminated in his recent autobiography, *Zoo Vet—I Quit!*"

1/13/94

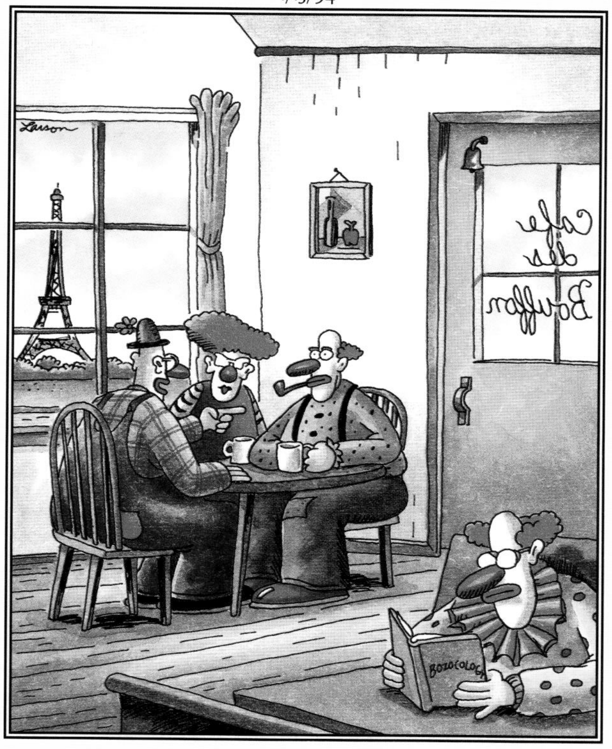
Larson

Expatriates, they migrated in the 1920s to Paris's Left Bank, gathering in their favorite haunts and discussing the meaning of cream pies and big shoes. They were, in fact, the original Boclownians.

1/11/94

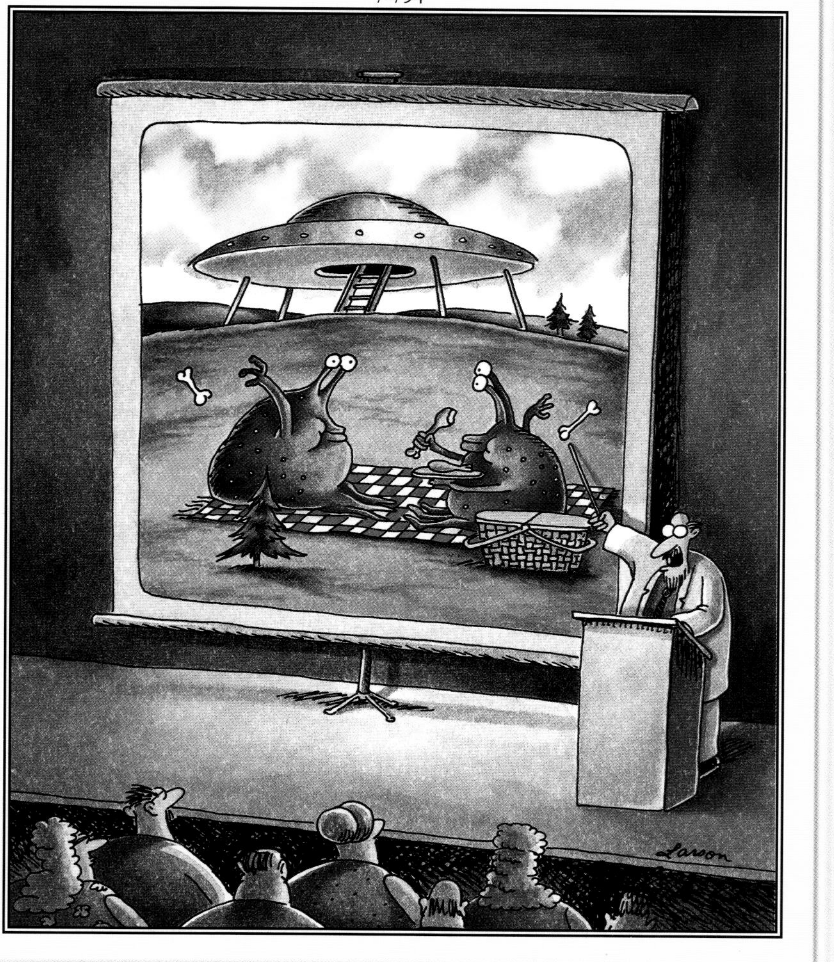
Larson

Professor Ferrington and his controversial theory that dinosaurs were actually the discarded "chicken" bones of giant, alien picnickers.

1/14/94

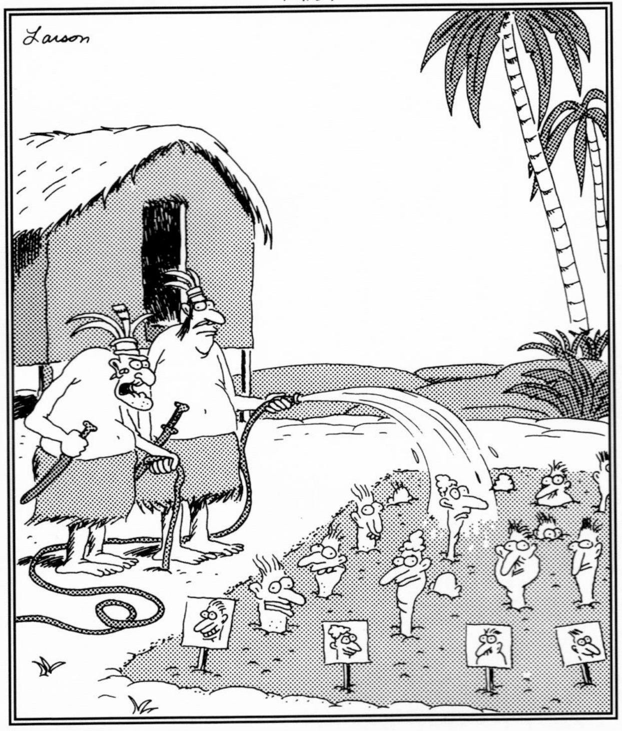
Larson

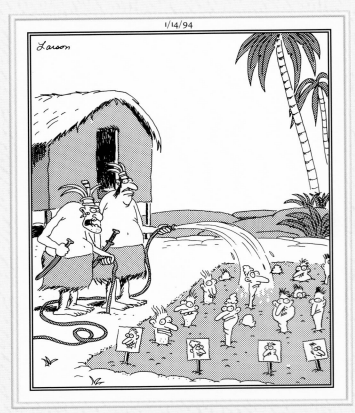

"This just makes me sick! ... *Sick!* ... Why, in my day, we collected *wild* heads from the jungle! ... These things are all *sissies!*"

1/18/94

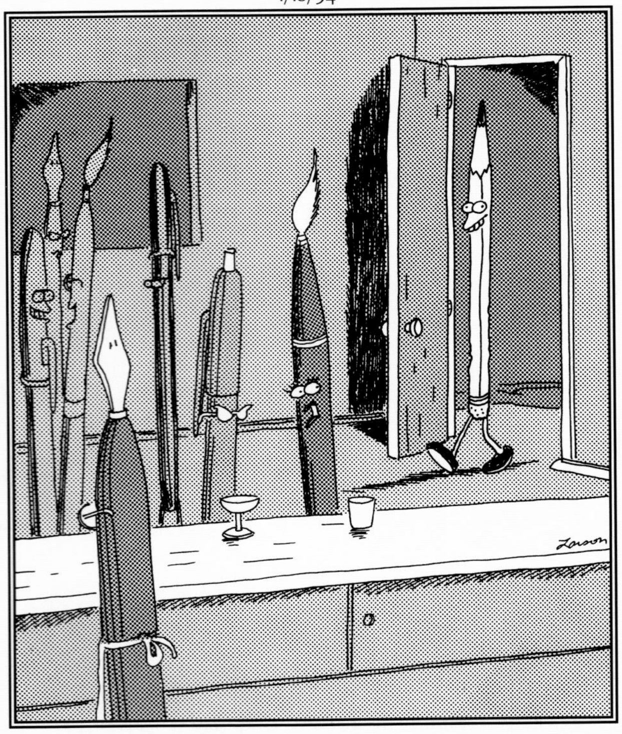
Larson

"Oh my God, Alice! ... Heading right for us! A chewed-up No. 2 pencil!"

1/27/94

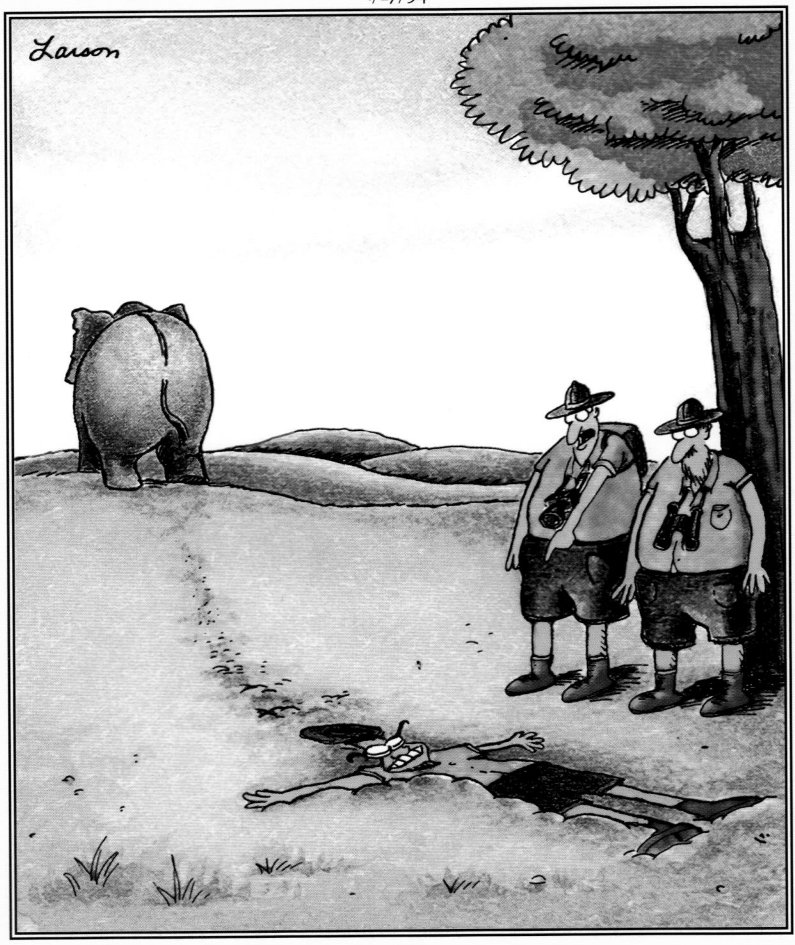
Larson

"Oh, and *that* makes me feel even worse! ... I laughed at Dinkins when he said his new lenses were indestructible."

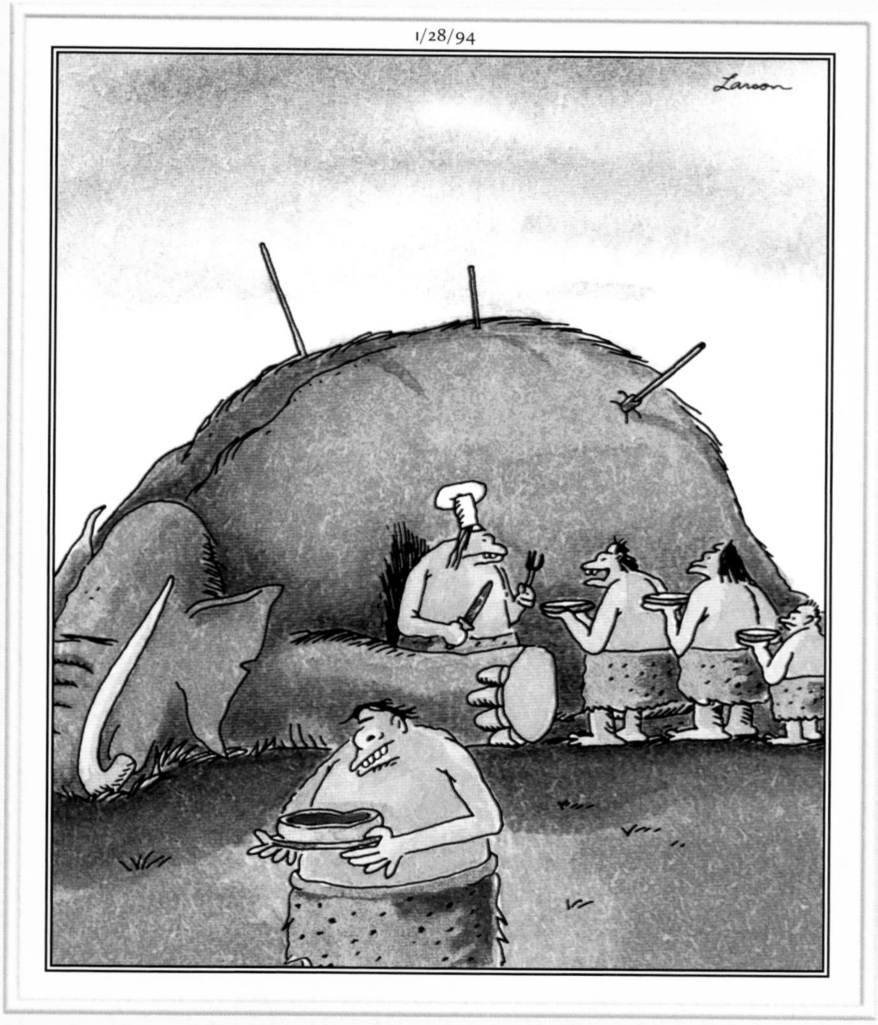
1/28/94
Larson

"Uh, let's see ... I'll try the mammoth, please."

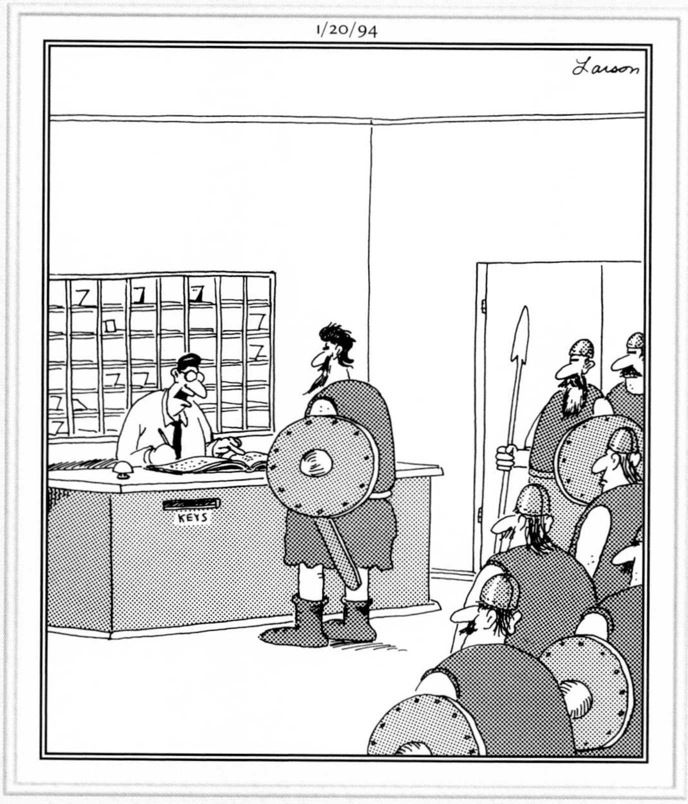
1/20/94
Larson
KEYS

"I'm sorry, sir, but the reservation book simply says 'Jason.' ... There's nothing here about Jason *and* the Argonauts."

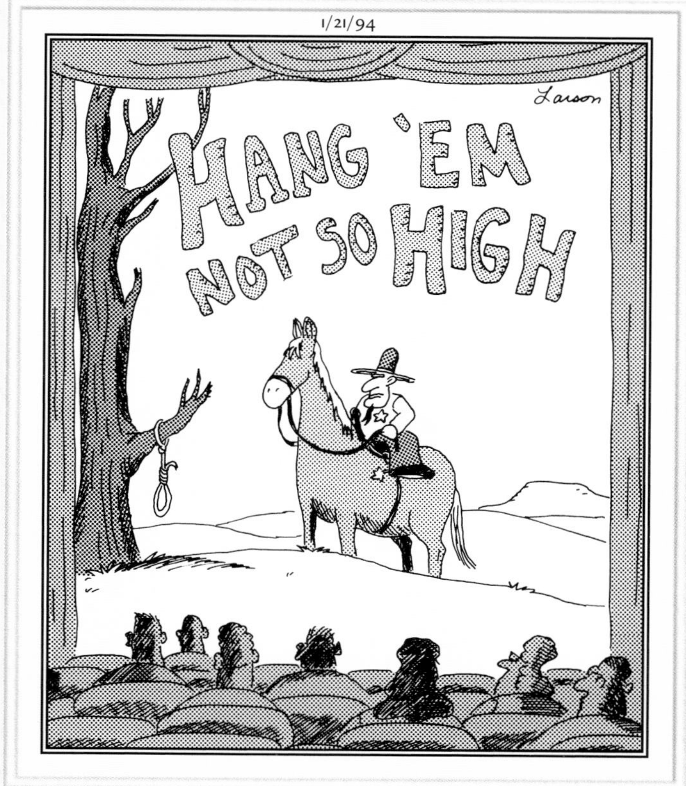
1/21/94
Larson
HANG 'EM NOT SO HIGH

Midget Westerns

1/25/94

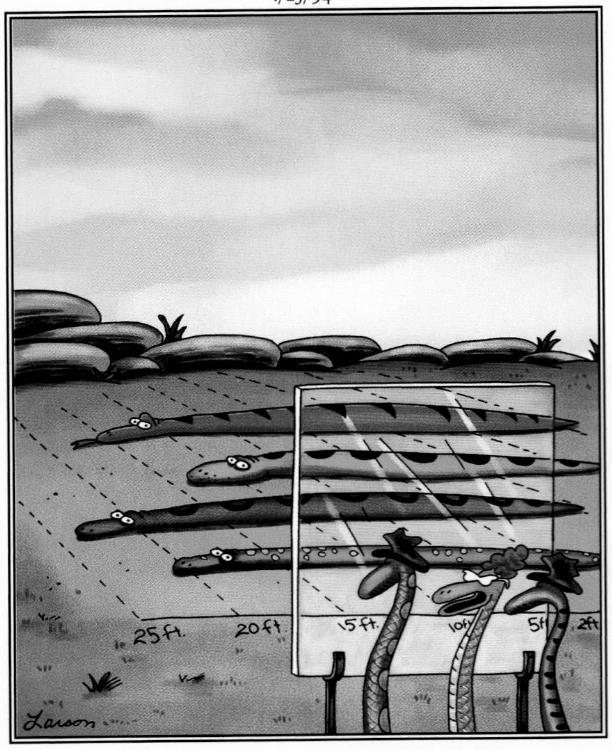
25 ft.
20 ft.
15 ft.
Larson

"That's him, officer. Second from the end—the 12-footer!"

1/31/94

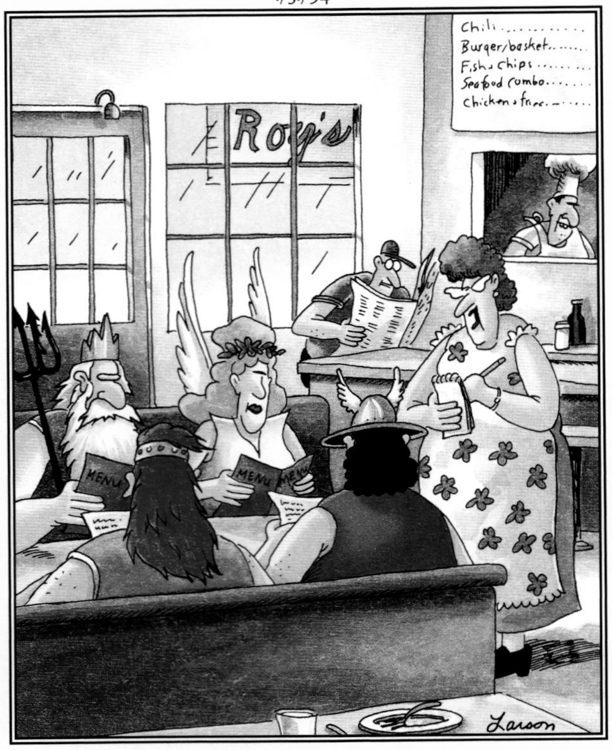
Roy's
MENU
Larson

"Well, I'd recommend either the chicken-fried steak or maybe the seafood platter. But look—I gotta be honest with ya—nothin' we serve is exactly what I'd call food for the gods."

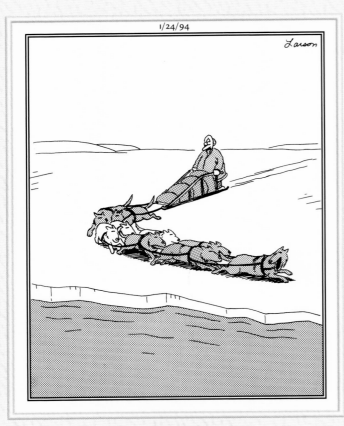

1/24/94

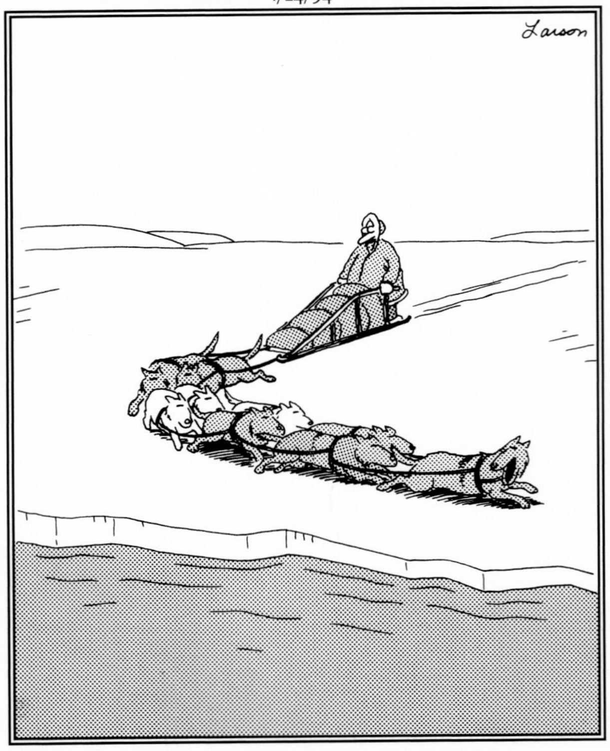
Larson

"Crack the whip!"

1/26/94

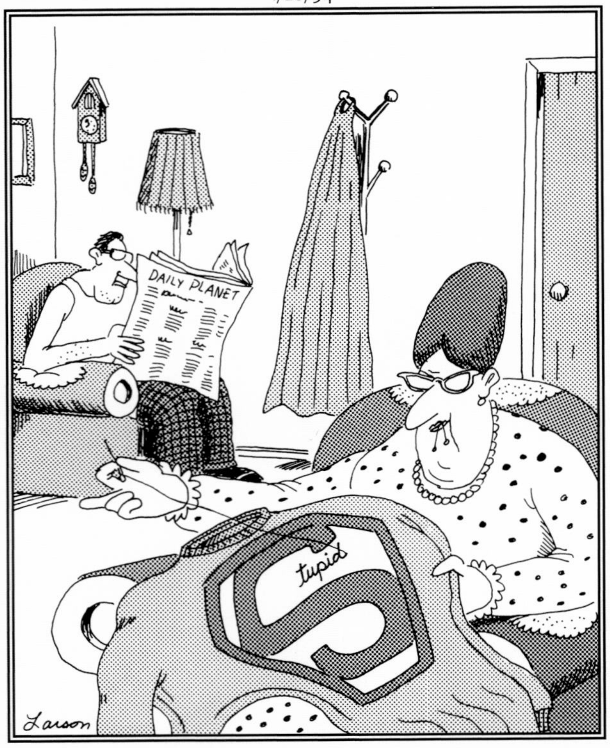
DAILY PLANET
tupid
Larson

After many years of marital bliss, tension enters the Kent household.

2/1/94

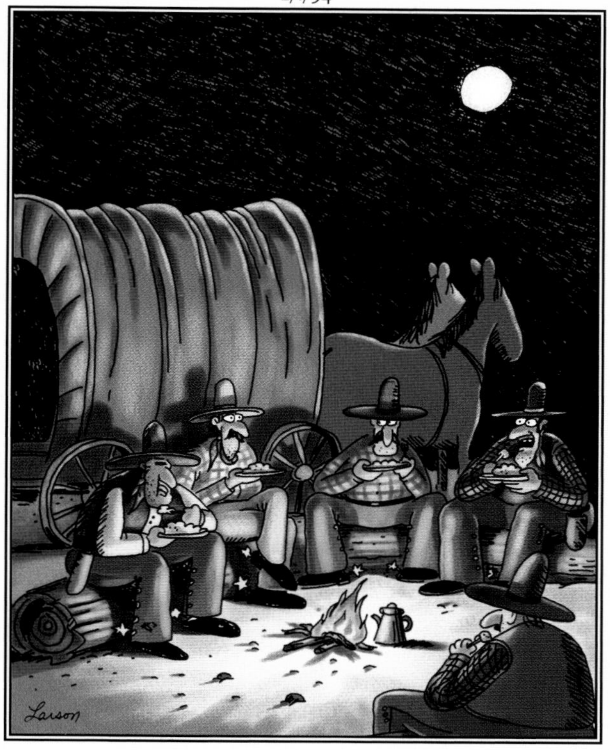

"Frank ... don't do that."

2/8/94

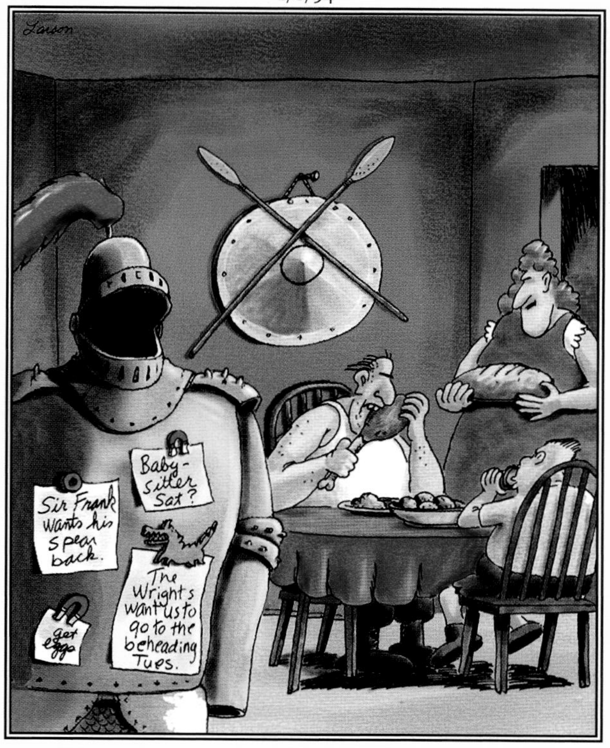
Baby-sitter Sat?
Sir Frank wants his spear back.
The Wrights want us to go to the beheading Tues.
get eggs

In medieval times, a suit of armor often served as a family's message center.

2/2/94

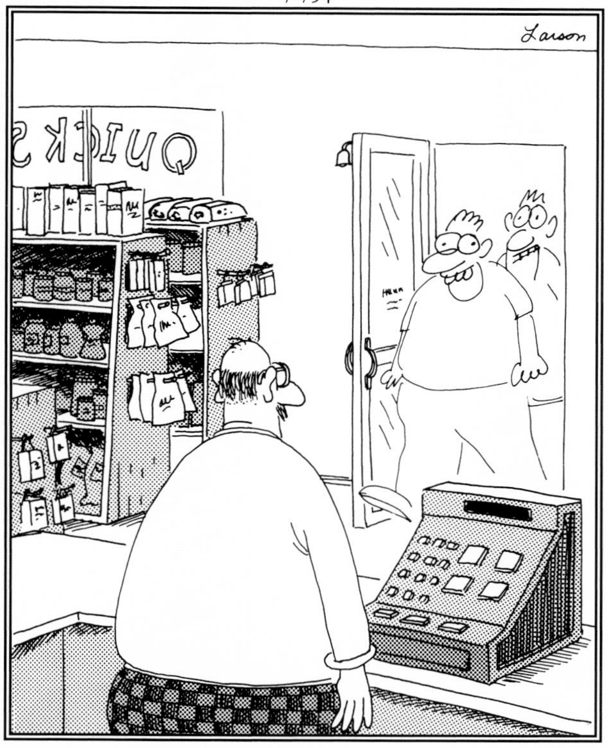

Leonard felt his skin suddenly crawl. Coming through the door were a couple of real sketchy characters.

2/3/94

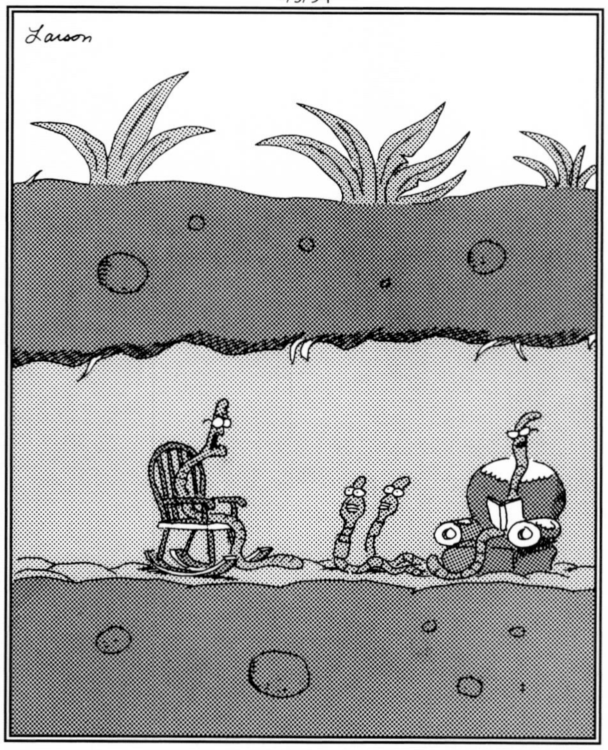

"You little softies! When *I* was your age, I had to crawl 14 inches to the surface and back! Every day! ... Through *hardpan,* by thunder!"

2/4/94

Larson

"Come on, Johnny—don't be chicken. ...
After it's over, we'll all be strawbrothers."

March 17, 1994

Attn: Mr. Gary Larson
Los Angeles Times
Times Mirror Square
Los Angeles CA 90053

Dear Mr. Larson,

I want to thank you for many years of laughter at your "Far
Side" cartoons. I have been a fan for a long time- and read your
work first when I pick up the LA Times.

I also want to express my recent sadness at your choice of the
enclosed cartoon. It is the first time I have ever felt offended
by any of your work and felt the need to write.

I'm sure you didn't mean any harm, but I found that the
depiction of a crucifixion scene and the casual reference to
"strawbrothers" struck at the core of my convictions as a follower
of Jesus Christ.

I came to a belief in Christianity as a young adult, and
discovered that the central teaching of my new faith was the death
and resurrection of Jesus to pay the penalty for my sin against God
and His will for the people and world He created.

To treat something so meaningful to me and millions of others
around the world in such a casual fashion is very painful.

I will not stop enjoying your work and look forward to many
more years of your creative genius. Please take this letter as
constructive feedback. There are some things in life that really
should not be treated so casually.

Keep up the good work.

Sincerely,

Steve Morgan

Editor's note: These are three scarecrows. No religious themes were intended.

2/10/94

Larson

"Well, as usual, there goes Princess Luwana—
always the center of attention. ... You know,
underneath that outer wrap, she's held
together with duct tape."

2/11/94

Larson

"Well, here he comes ... Mr. Never-Makes-a-Dud."

2/15/94

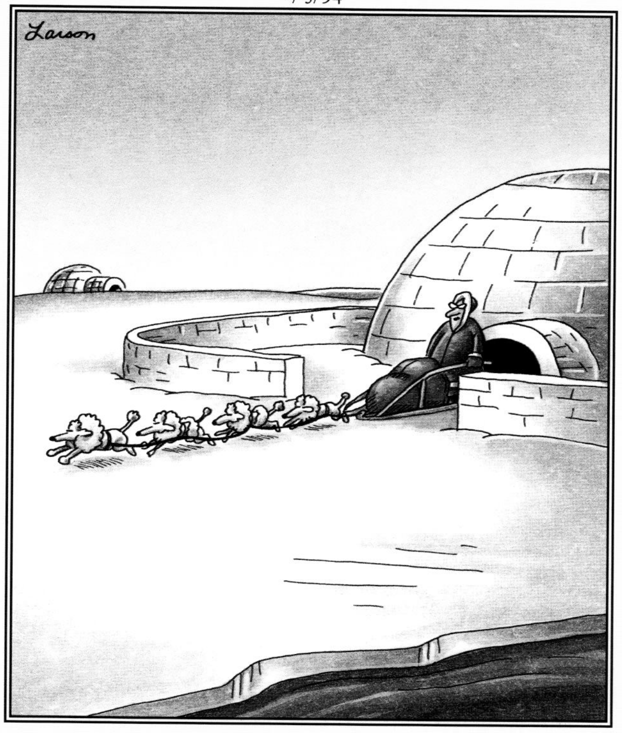
Larson

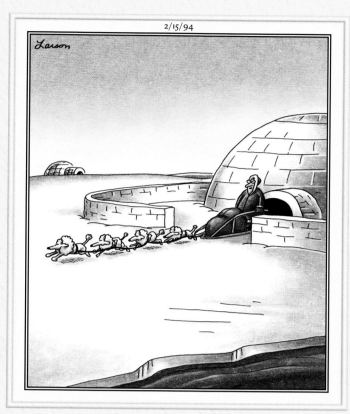

Beverly Hills of the North Pole

2/14/94

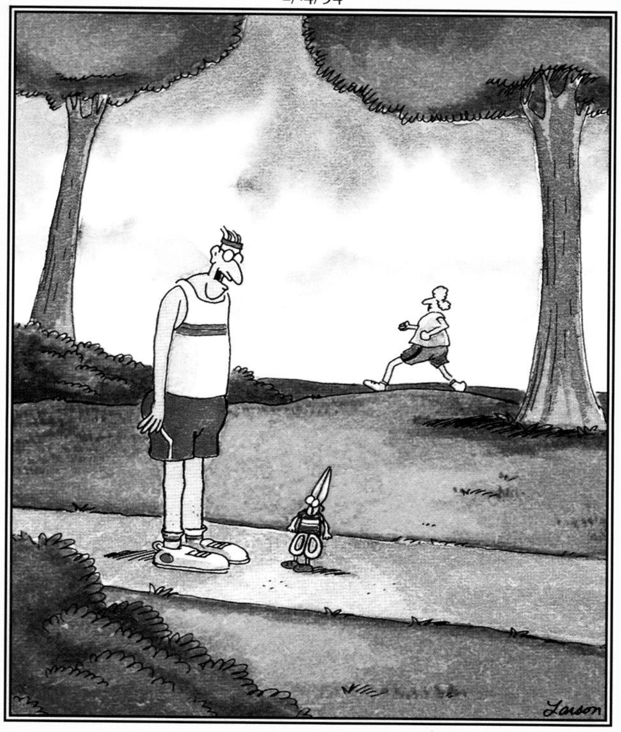
Larson

"Sorry, Kevin, but my friends have all advised me not to run with you anymore."

2/7/94

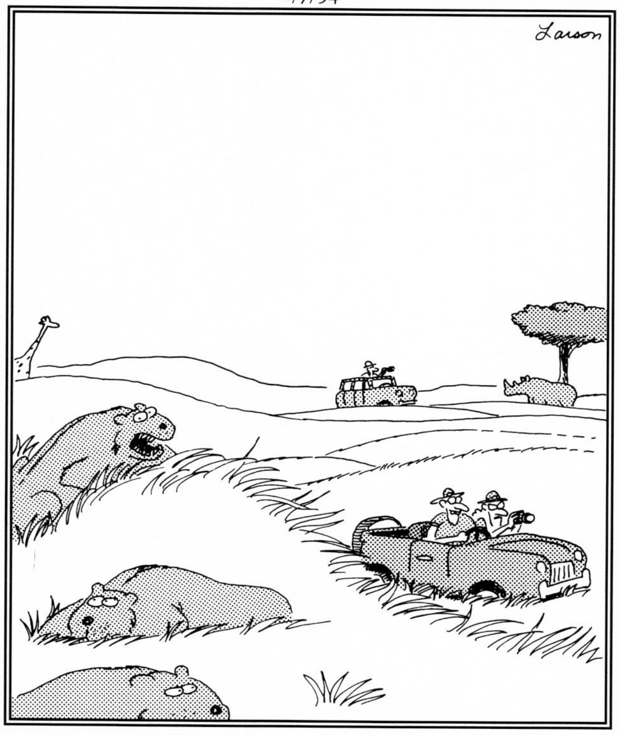
Larson

"Convertible! Convertible!"

2/9/94

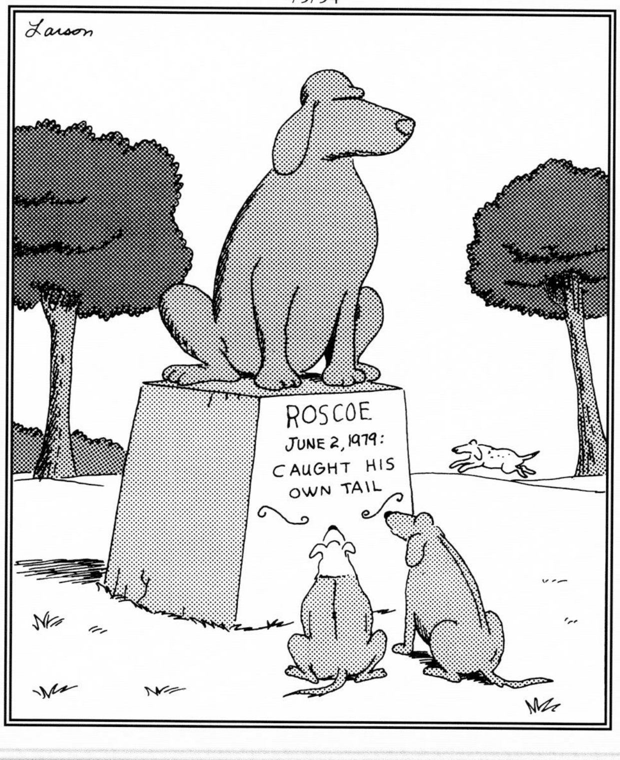
Larson
ROSCOE
JUNE 2, 1979:
CAUGHT HIS
OWN TAIL

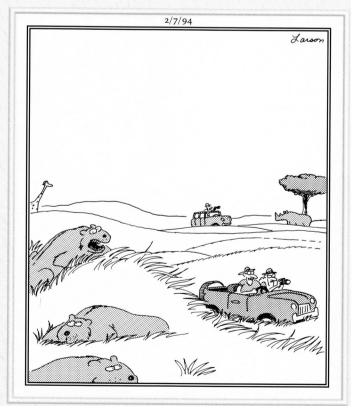

2/23/94

Larson

"Sorry, Bobby, but you know the rule—no swimming for a week after eating."

2/16/94

Larson

10th Annual **PSYCHICS** CONFERENCE

For the most part, the meeting was quite successful. Only a slight tension filled the air, stemming from the unforeseen faux pas of everyone showing up in the same dress.

2/18/94

Larson

Thirty years had passed, and although he had no real regrets about marrying Wendy, buying a home, and having two kids, Peter found his thoughts often going back to his life in Never-Never-Land.

2/22/94

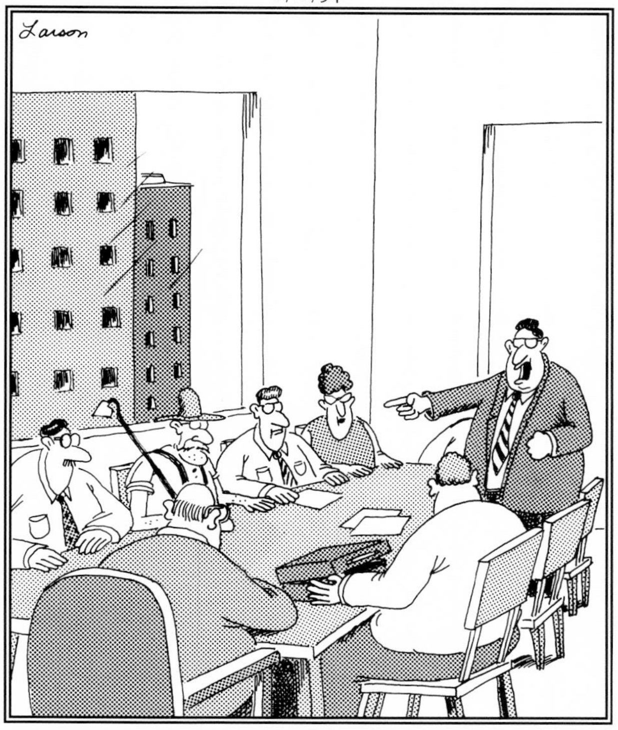
Larson

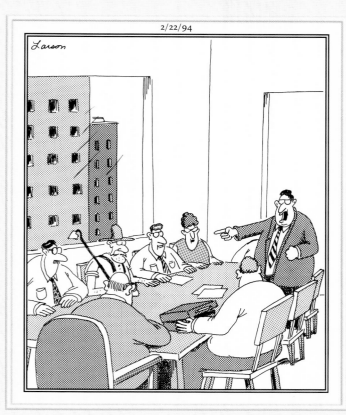

"What? MacDougal is being promoted over me? ... Well, that does it! I won't take no orders from no stinkin' sodbuster!"

2/24/94

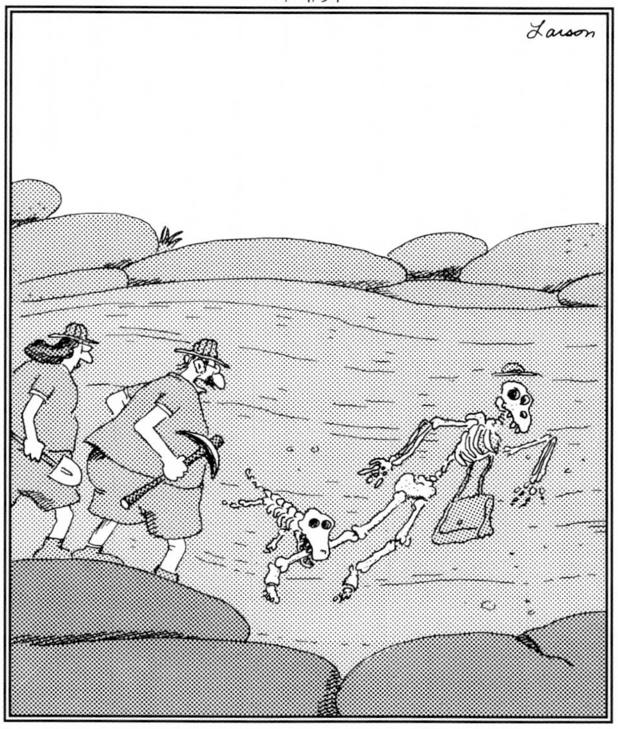
Larson

"What a find, Ms. Dinkins! ... It's Mailman, all right—but remarkably, this specimen is fully intact, with a *Canis nipponicus* still attached!"

2/25/94

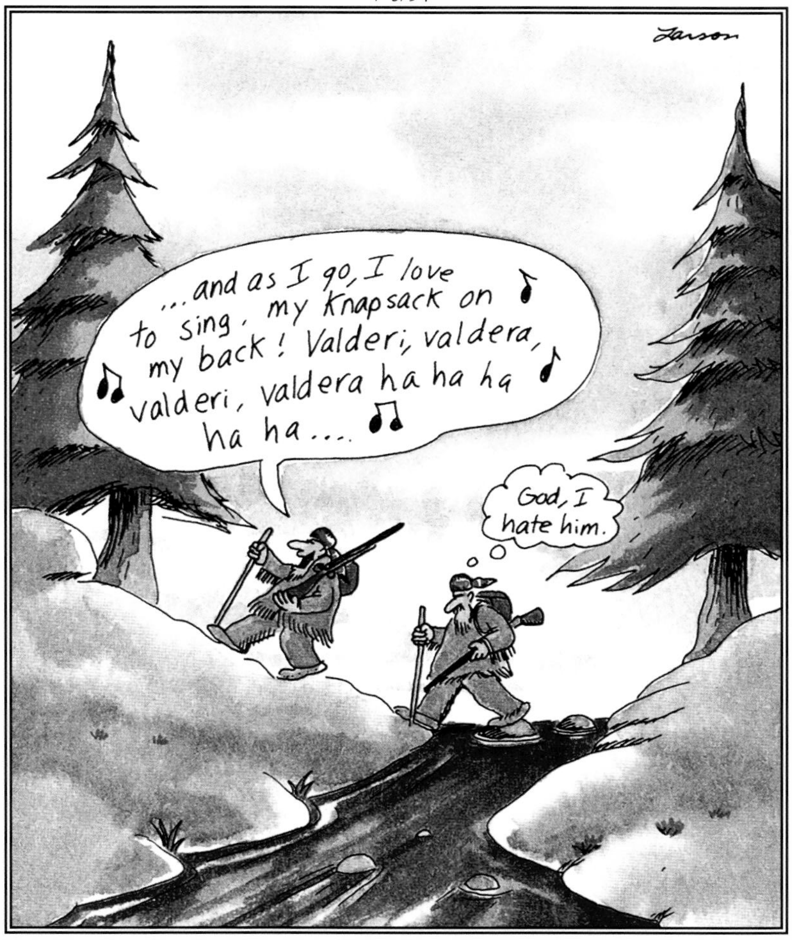
Larson
...and as I go, I love to sing, my knapsack on my back! Valderi, valdera, valderi, valdera ha ha ha ha ha....
God, I hate him.

More tension on the Lewis and Clark expedition

2/28/94

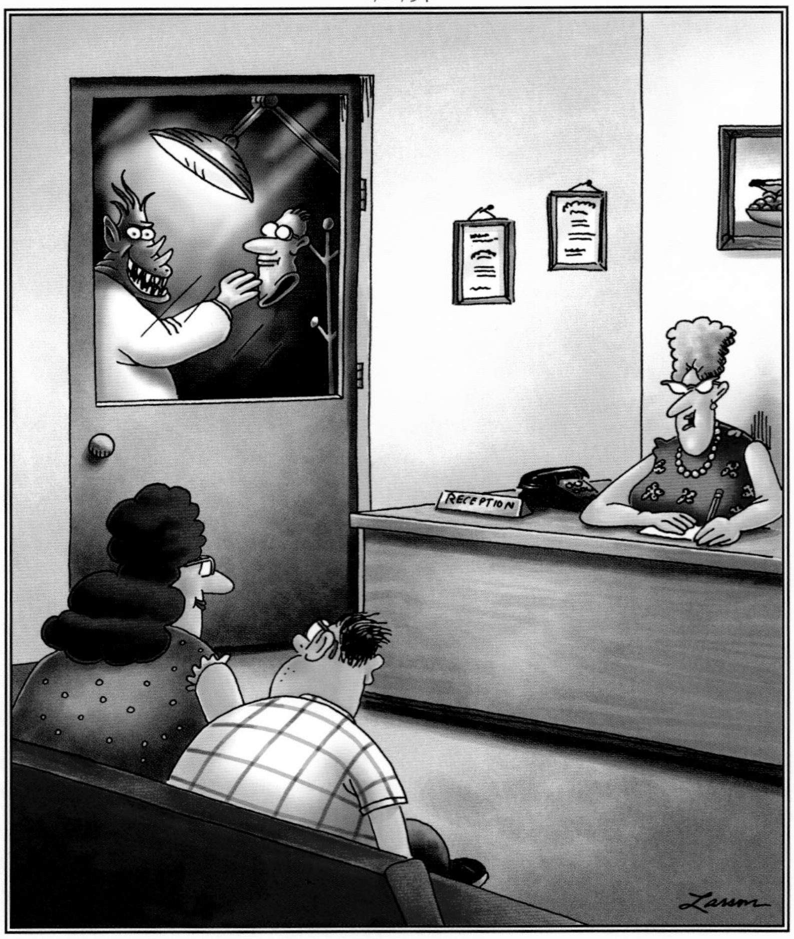
RECEPTION
Larson

"The dentist just buzzed me, Mrs. Lewellyn—he's ready to see Bobby now."

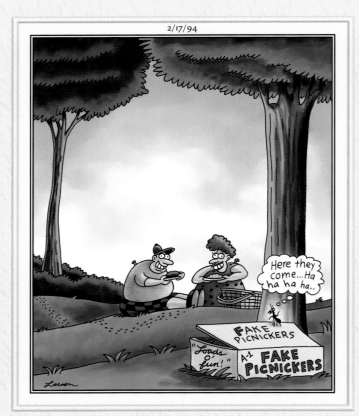

2/17/94

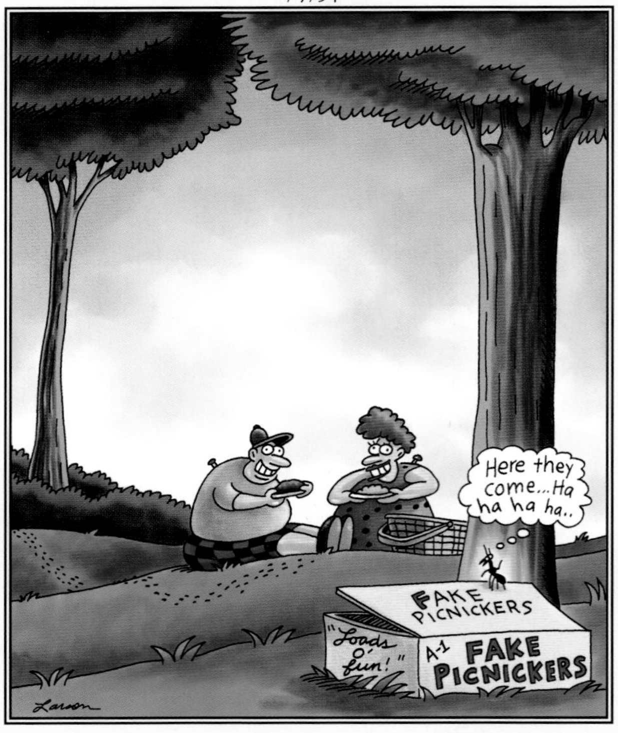
Here they come...Ha ha ha ha..
FAKE PICNICKERS
"Loads of fun!"
A-1 FAKE PICNICKERS
Larson

This time his practical jokes had gone too far, and Wally was finally booted off the hill.

2/21/94

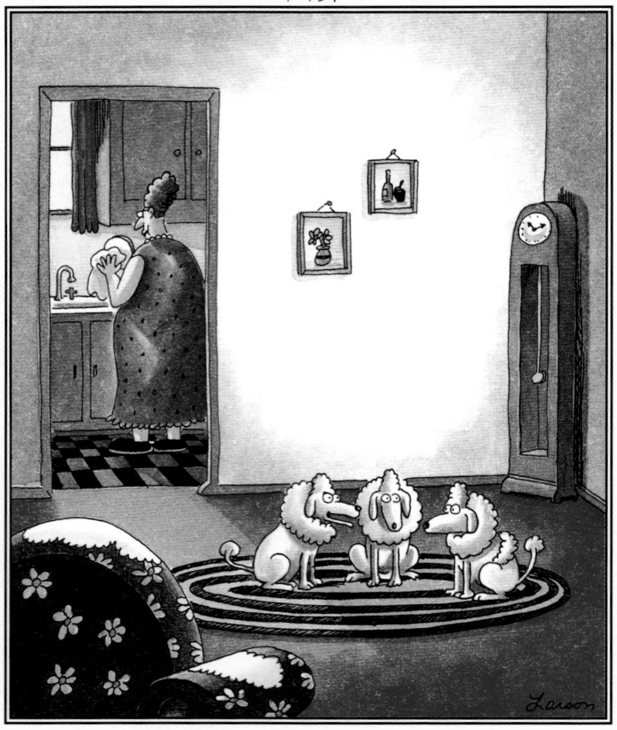
Larson

"Well, yes, that is the downside, Fluffy. ... Once we kill her, the pampering will end."

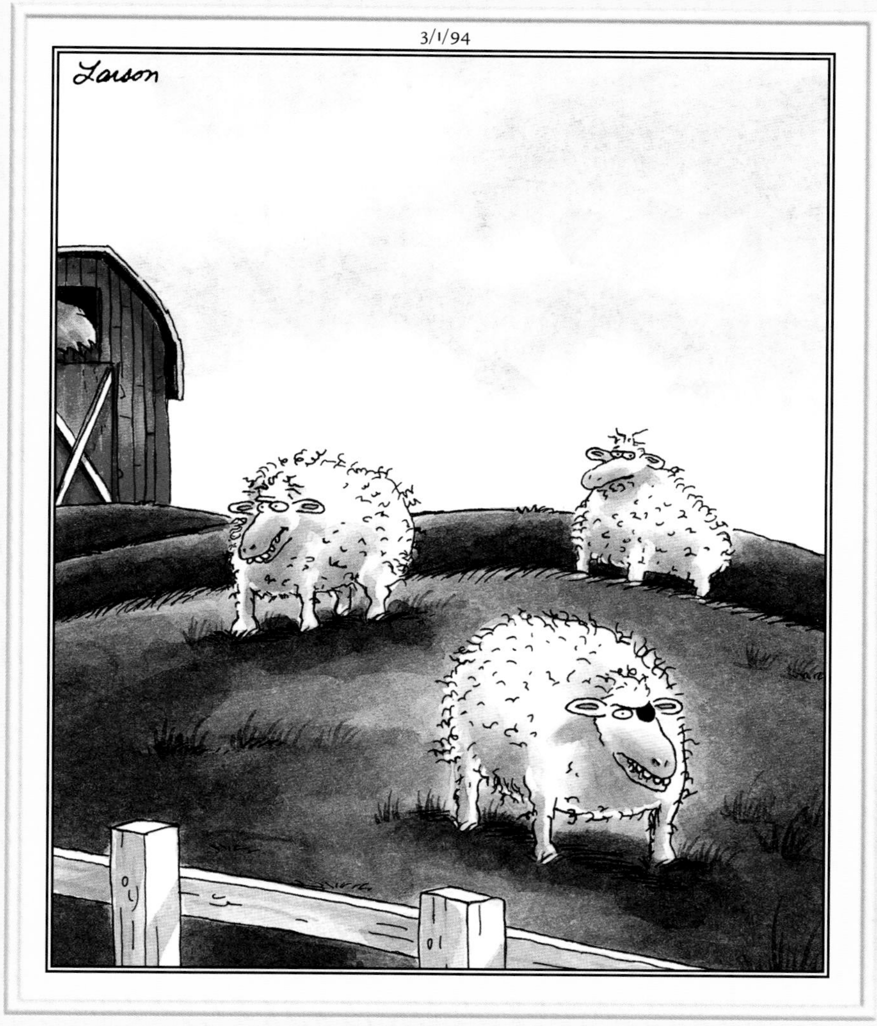
3/1/94
Larson

It's a known fact that the sheep that give us steel wool have no natural enemies.

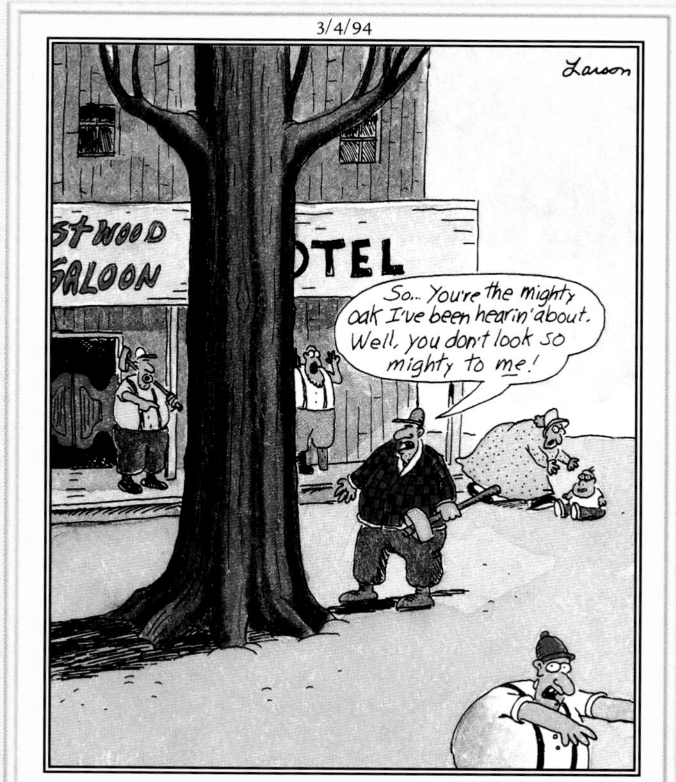
3/4/94
Larson
STWOOD
SALOON
OTEL
So... You're the mighty oak I've been hearin' about. Well, you don't look so mighty to me!

He stood there—unflinching, tall, and silent as always. But as Gus soon found out, this outward calm belied the "Widowmaker's" reputation.

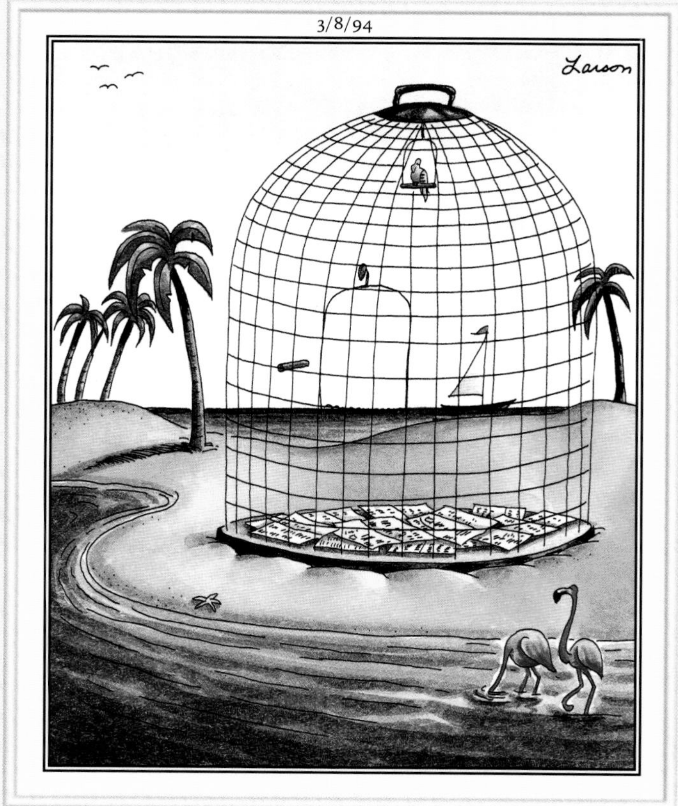
3/8/94
Larson

Winning the lottery had changed his life, but at times Chico still felt strangely unfulfilled.

3/2/94

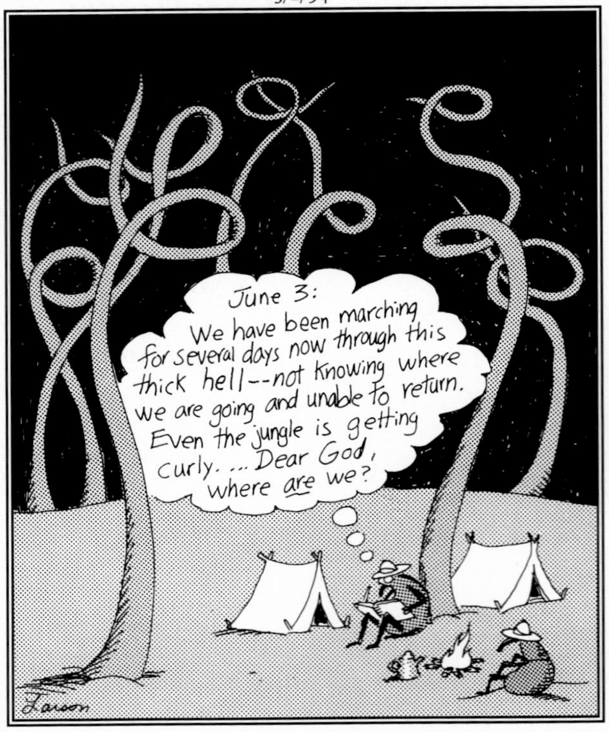
June 3:
We have been marching for several days now through this thick hell--not knowing where we are going and unable to return. Even the jungle is getting curly. ... Dear God, where are we?

3/3/94

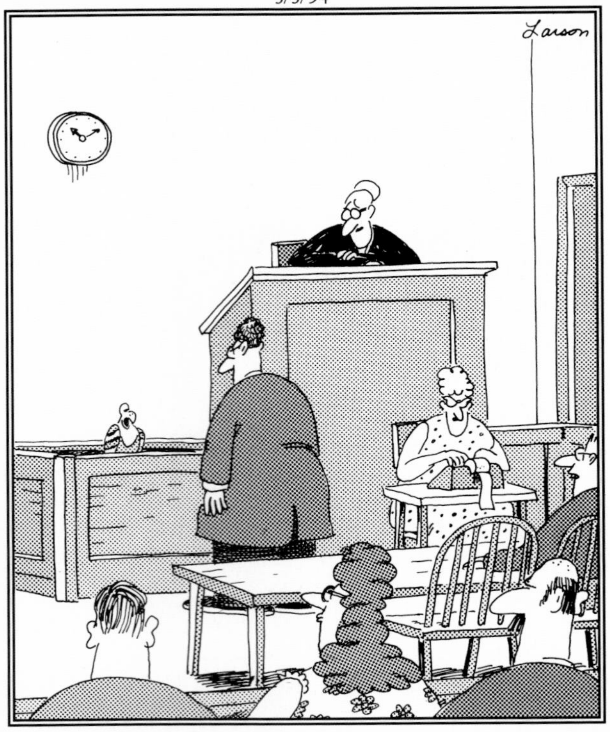

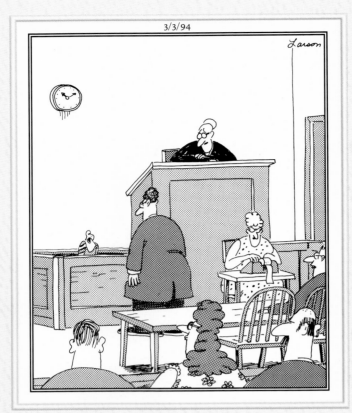

"No, I never said that. ... Well, I actually *did* say it, but *after* he said it. He said it, *then* I said it. I'm a mimic—that's what I do."

3/9/94

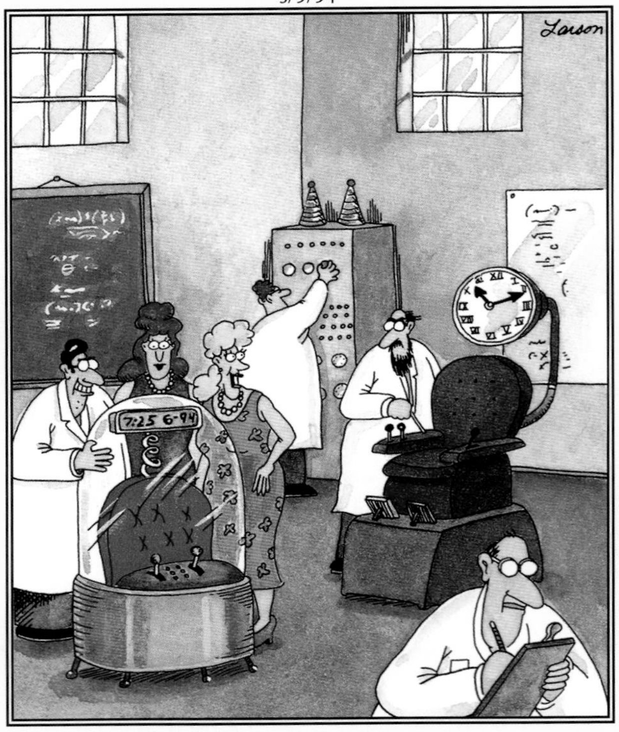
7:25 6-94

"Oh, Professor DeWitt! Have you seen Professor *Weinberg's* time machine? ... It's digital!"

3/10/94

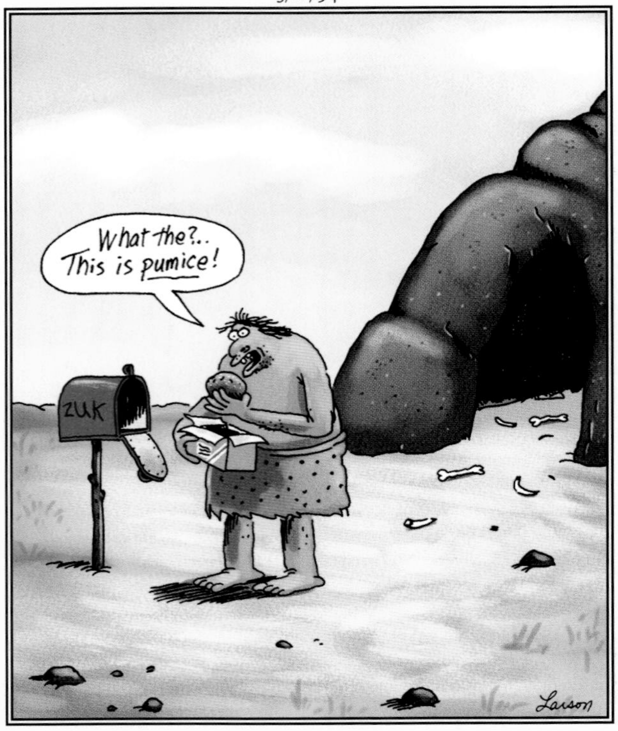
What the?..
This is pumice!
ZUK

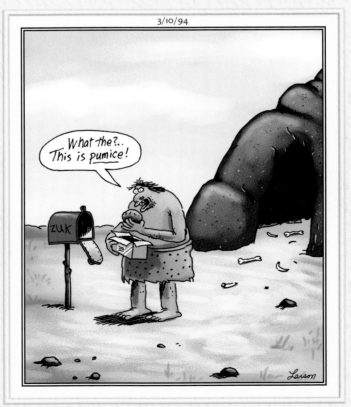

Primitive mail fraud

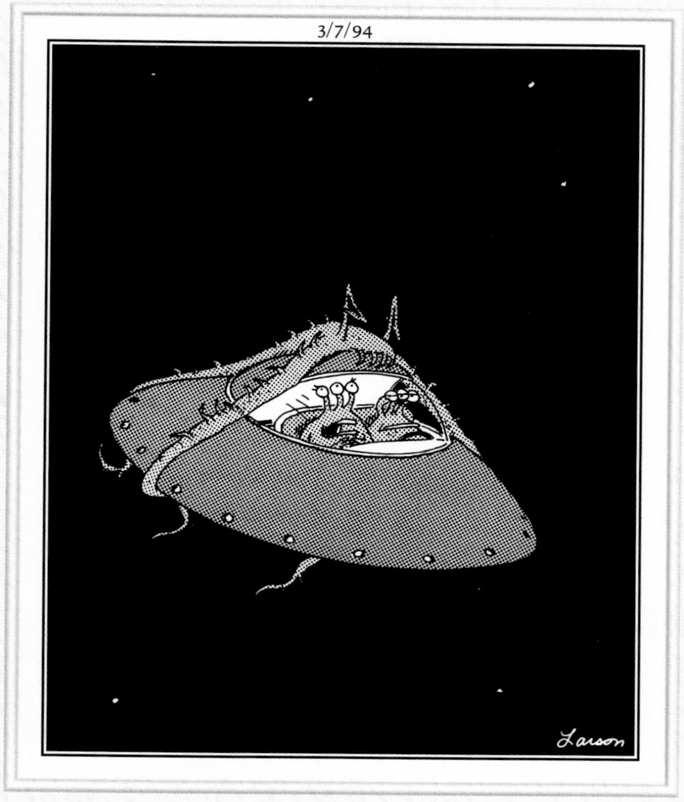
3/7/94
Larson

"Aaaaaaaaaa! ... Oh, sorry—it's just the dog."

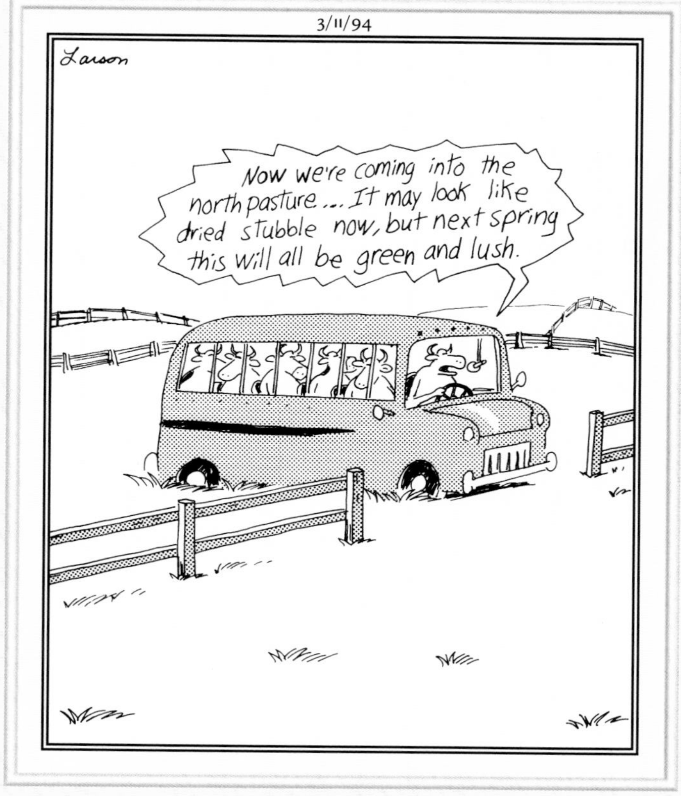
3/11/94
Larson
Now we're coming into the north pasture... It may look like dried stubble now, but next spring this will all be green and lush.

Basic field trips

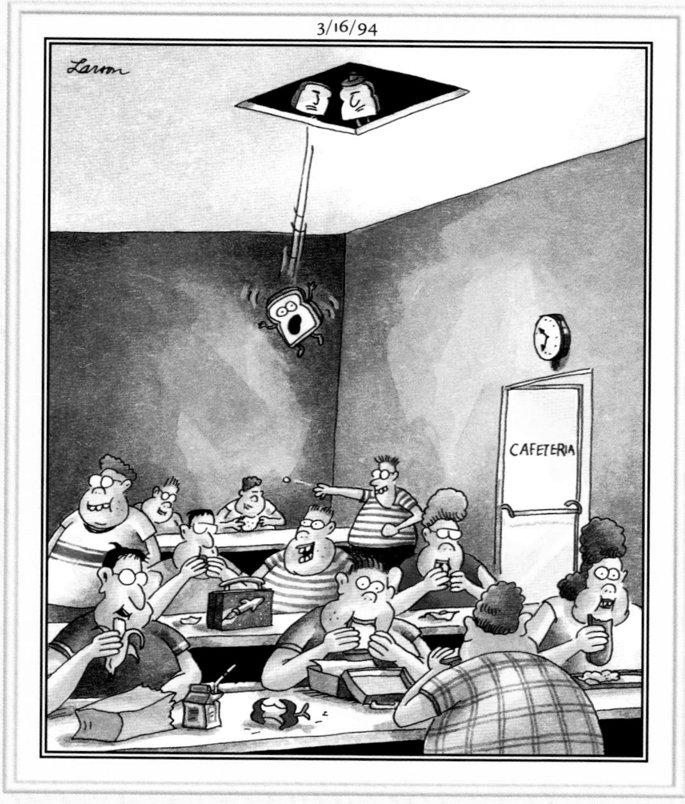
3/16/94
Larson
CAFETERIA

The sandwich Mafia sends Luigi to "sleep with the fourth-graders."

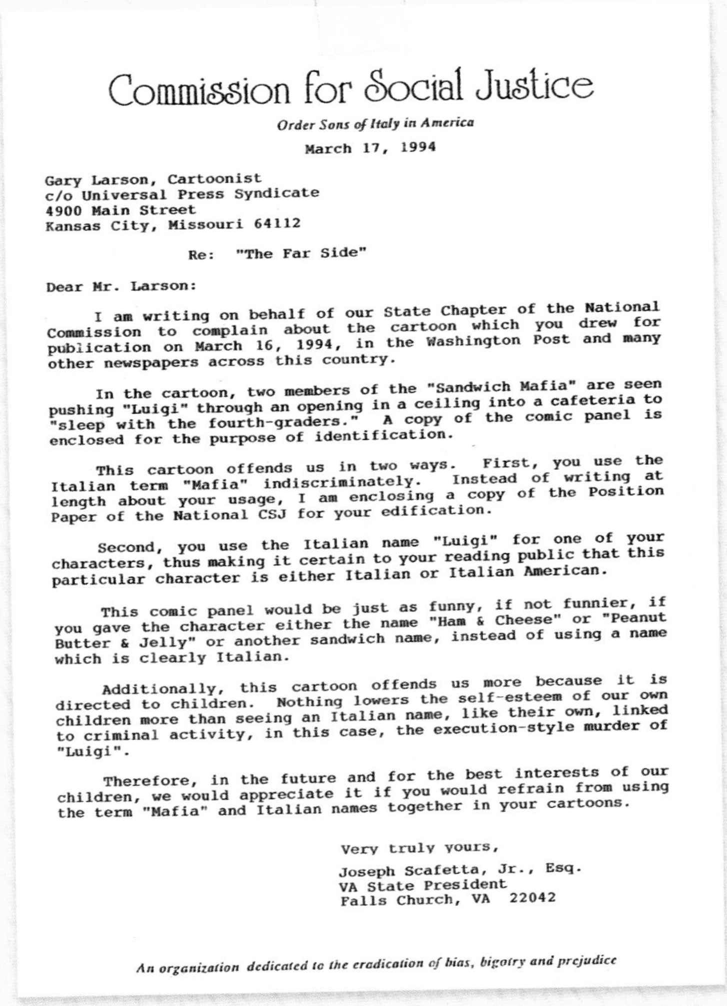

Commission for Social Justice

Order Sons of Italy in America

March 17, 1994

Gary Larson, Cartoonist
c/o Universal Press Syndicate
4900 Main Street
Kansas City, Missouri 64112

Re: "The Far Side"

Dear Mr. Larson:

I am writing on behalf of our State Chapter of the National Commission to complain about the cartoon which you drew for publication on March 16, 1994, in the Washington Post and many other newspapers across this country.

In the cartoon, two members of the "Sandwich Mafia" are seen pushing "Luigi" through an opening in a ceiling into a cafeteria to "sleep with the fourth-graders." A copy of the comic panel is enclosed for the purpose of identification.

This cartoon offends us in two ways. First, you use the Italian term "Mafia" indiscriminately. Instead of writing at length about your usage, I am enclosing a copy of the Position Paper of the National CSJ for your edification.

Second, you use the Italian name "Luigi" for one of your characters, thus making it certain to your reading public that this particular character is either Italian or Italian American.

This comic panel would be just as funny, if not funnier, if you gave the character either the name "Ham & Cheese" or "Peanut Butter & Jelly" or another sandwich name, instead of using a name which is clearly Italian.

Additionally, this cartoon offends us more because it is directed to children. Nothing lowers the self-esteem of our own children more than seeing an Italian name, like their own, linked to criminal activity, in this case, the execution-style murder of "Luigi".

Therefore, in the future and for the best interests of our children, we would appreciate it if you would refrain from using the term "Mafia" and Italian names together in your cartoons.

Very truly yours,

Joseph Scafetta, Jr., Esq.
VA State President
Falls Church, VA 22042

An organization dedicated to the eradication of bias, bigotry and prejudice

3/14/94

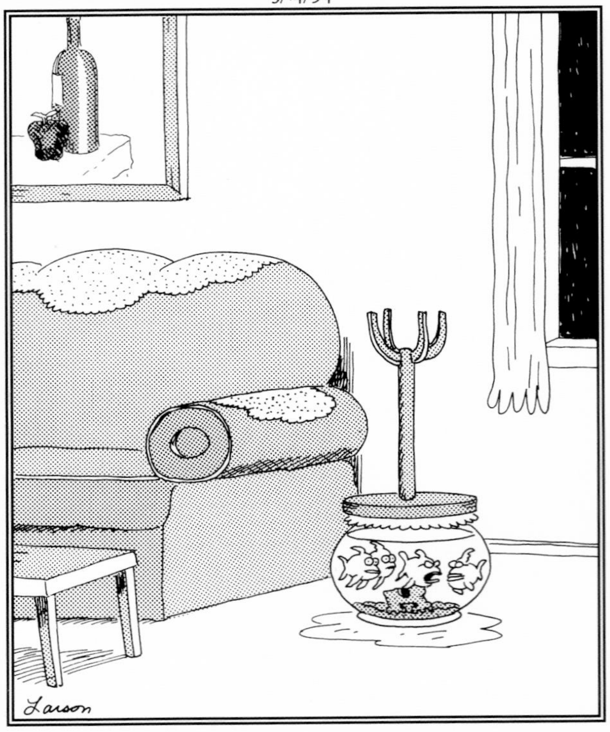
Larson

"It's a cute trick, Warren, but the Schuberts are here for dinner, so just 'abracadabra' this thing back to where it was."

3/15/94

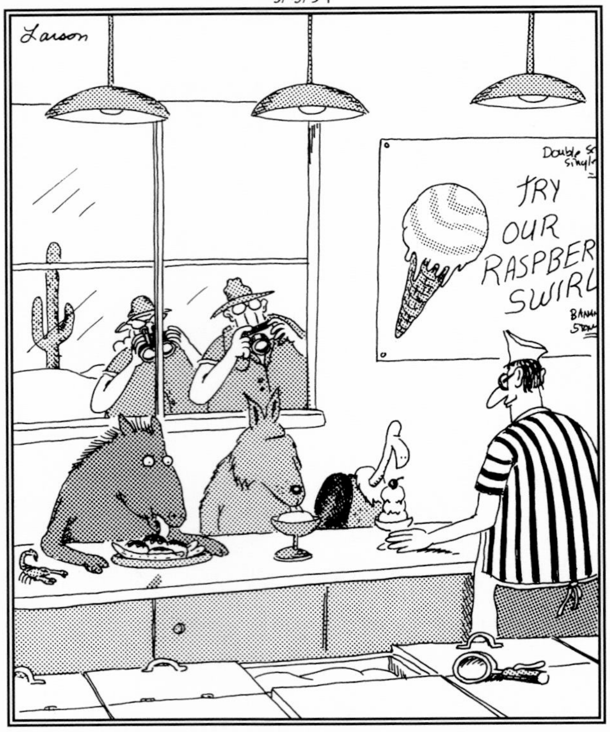
Larson
TRY
OUR
RASPBER
SWIRL

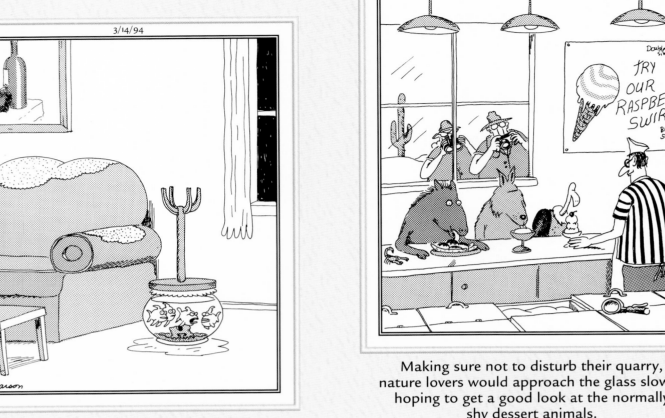

Making sure not to disturb their quarry, nature lovers would approach the glass slowly, hoping to get a good look at the normally shy dessert animals.

3/17/94

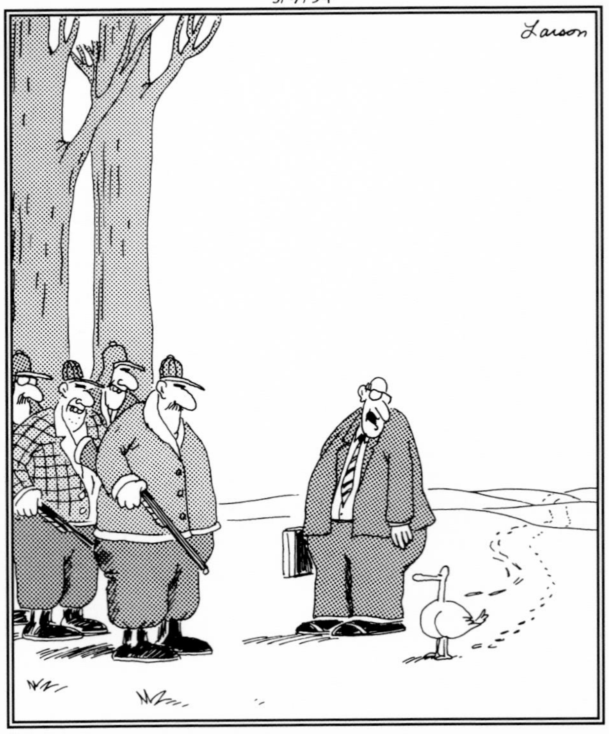
Larson

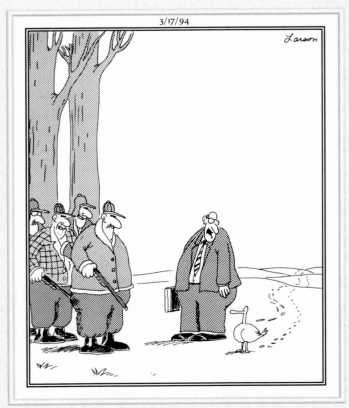

"I'm sorry, Sidney, but I can no longer help you. ... These are not my people."

3/18/94

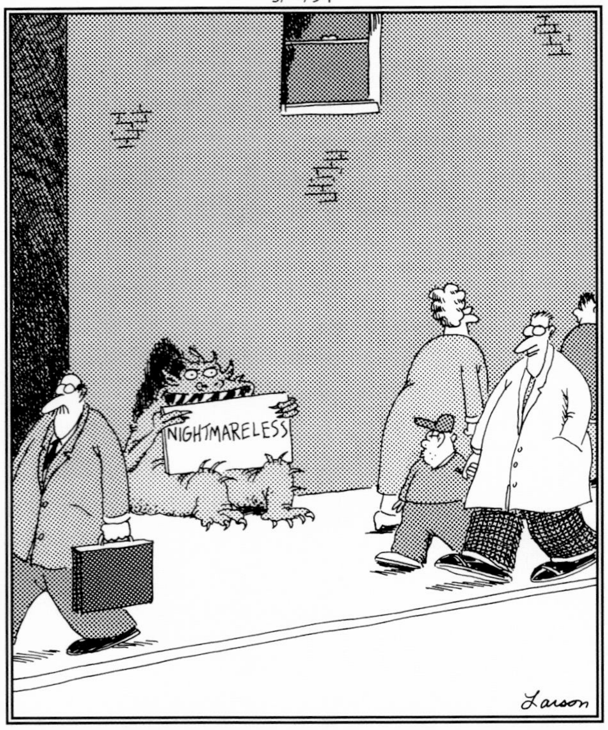
NIGHTMARELESS
Larson

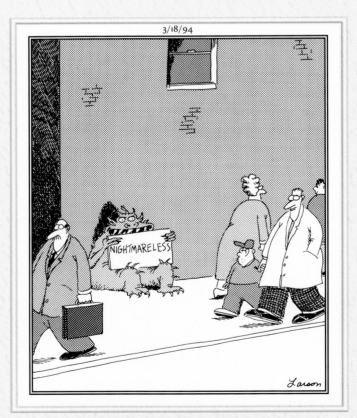

Not heeding his father's advice to avoid eye contact, Joey makes a "contribution."

Editor's note: Gary leaves for a one-month vacation.

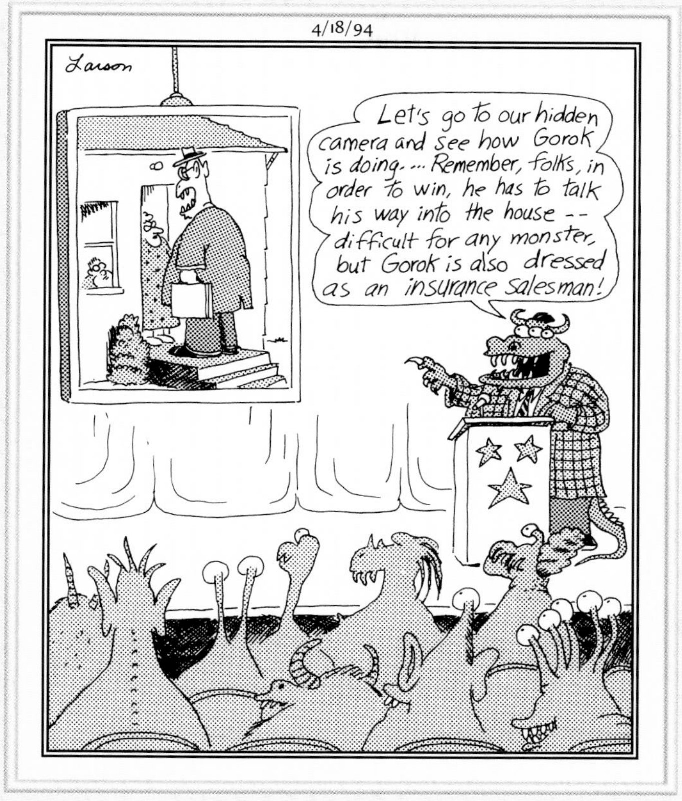
4/18/94
Larson
Let's go to our hidden camera and see how Gorok is doing.... Remember, folks, in order to win, he has to talk his way into the house -- difficult for any monster, but Gorok is also dressed as an insurance salesman!

Monster game shows

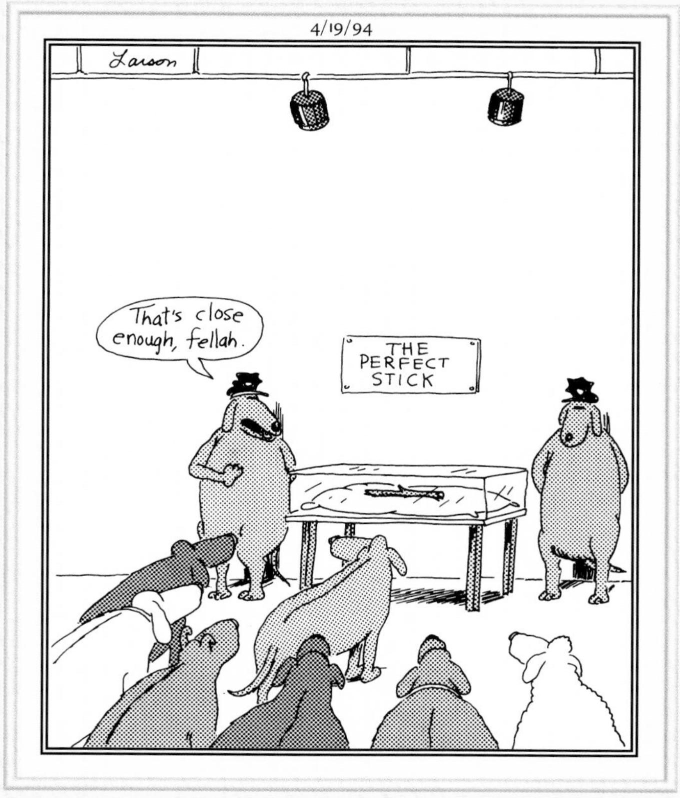
4/19/94
Larson
That's close enough, fellah.
THE PERFECT STICK

At the Dog Museum

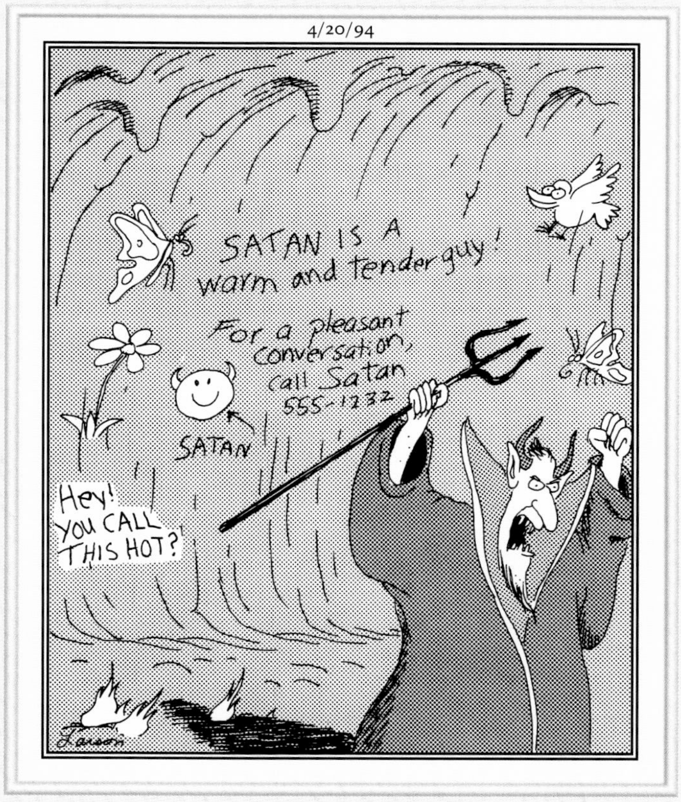
4/20/94
SATAN IS A warm and tender guy!
For a pleasant conversation, call Satan 555-1232
SATAN
Hey! YOU CALL THIS HOT?
Larson

Graffiti in hell

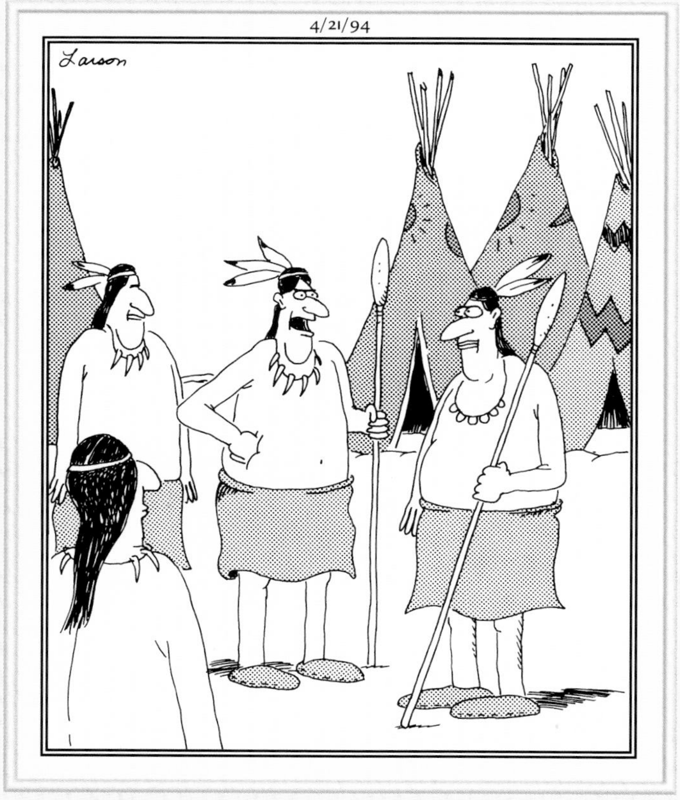
4/21/94
Larson

"Well, Red Cloud, it just so happens I *did* go ask the chief! ... A bear claw necklace is a symbol of honor, a Grizzly Adams fingernail necklace is not!"

"So let's go over it again: You're about a mile up, you see something dying below you, you circle until it's dead, and down you go. Lenny, you stick close to your brothers and do what they do."

"Oh, and a word of warning about Mueller over there. ... He's got a good head on his shoulders, but it's best not to mention it."

"So, Professor Sadowsky, you're saying that your fellow researcher, Professor Lazzell, knowing full well that baboons consider eye contact to be threatening, handed you this hat on that fateful day you emerged from your Serengeti campsite."

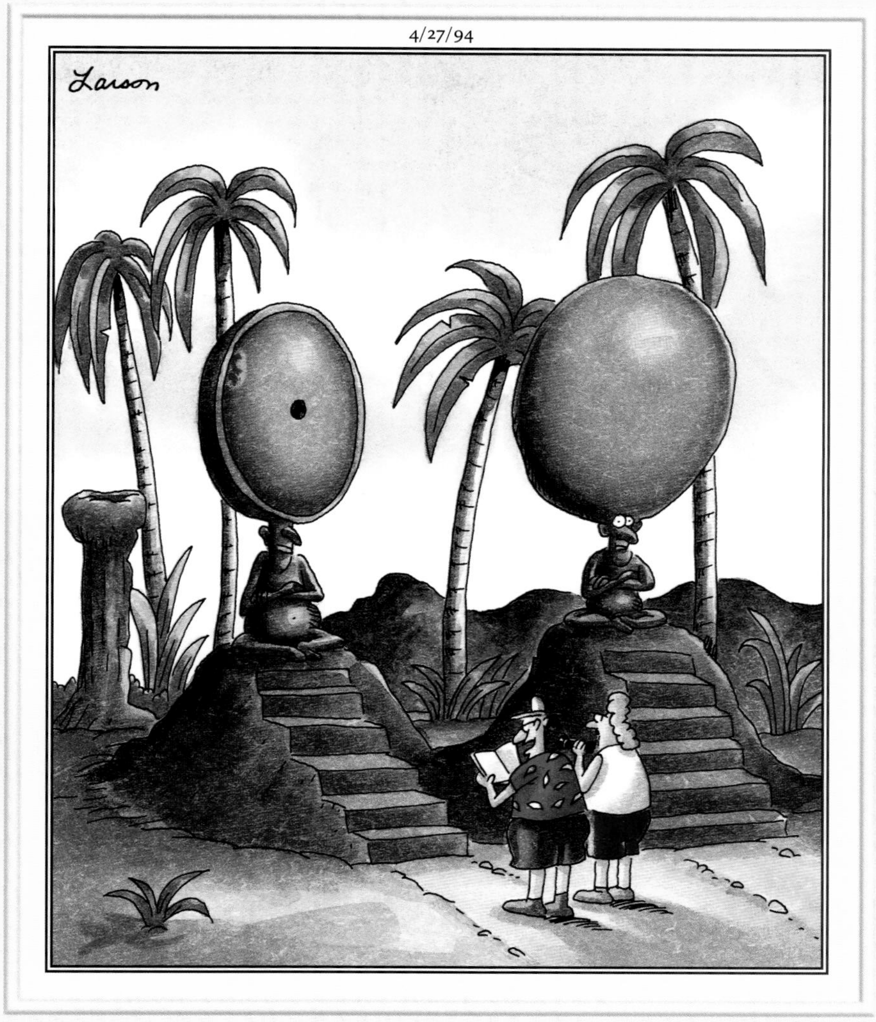
4/27/94
Larson

"Well, this guidebook is worthless! It just says these people worshipped two gods: one who was all-knowing and one who was all-seeing—but they don't tell you which is which, for crying out loud!"

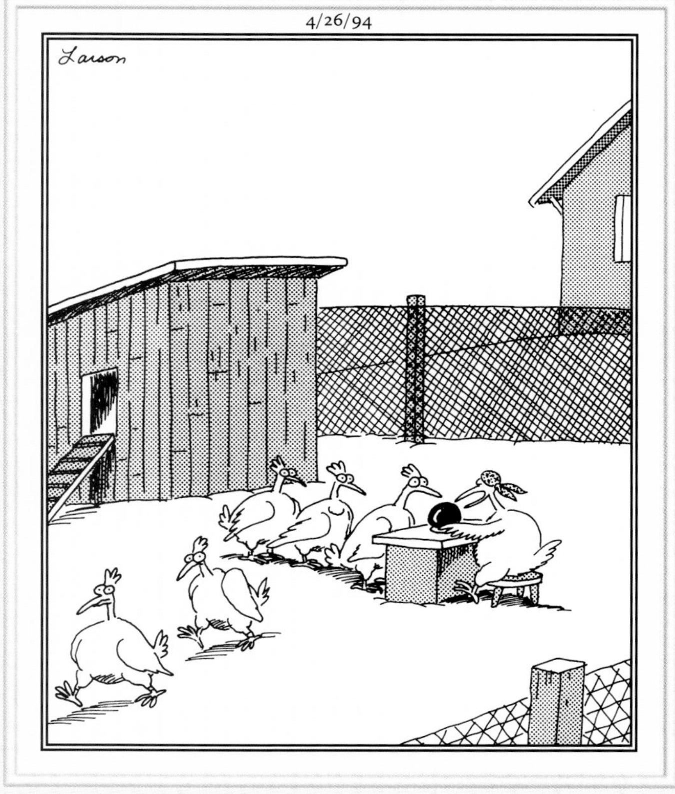
4/26/94
Larson

"Whoa! Another bad one! ... I see your severed head lying quietly in the red-stained dirt, a surprised expression still frozen in your lifeless eyes. ... Next!"

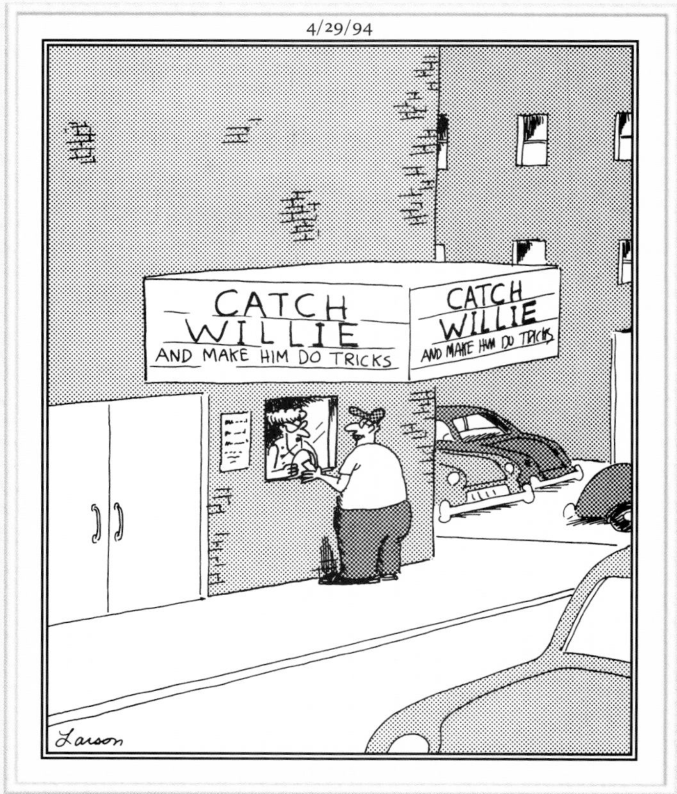
4/29/94
CATCH WILLIE
AND MAKE HIM DO TRICKS
CATCH WILLIE
AND MAKE HIM DO TRICKS
Larson

5/2/94

Larson
28. How much wood would a woodchuck chuck if a wood-chuck could chuck wood?
(a.) 250 board feet
(b.) 500 board feet
(c.) 1,000 board feet

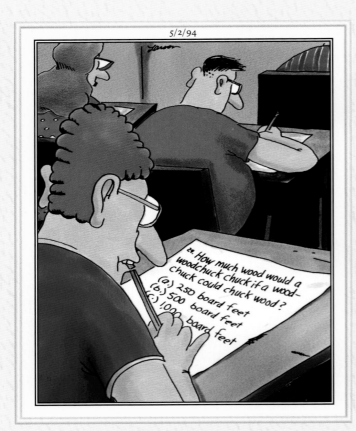

The Wildlife Management finals

5/4/94

Larson
CAT CHAZING
Gardun digging
garbidge dumping

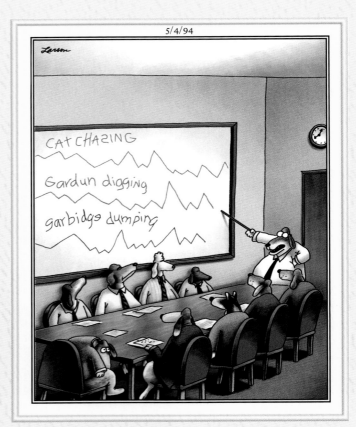

"Now, if you all would examine the chart, you will notice that—well, well ... seems Mr. Sparky has found something more engrossing than this meeting."

5/3/94

IT'S A MAD, MAD, MAD, MAD, MAD, MAD INTESTINAL TRACT
Larson

5/5/94

Larson

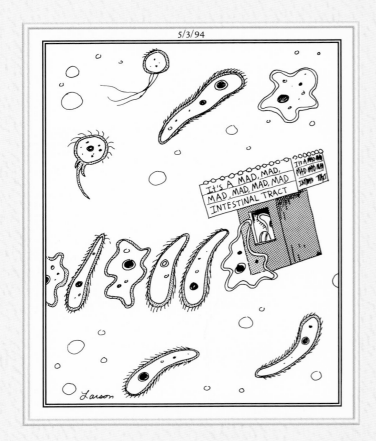

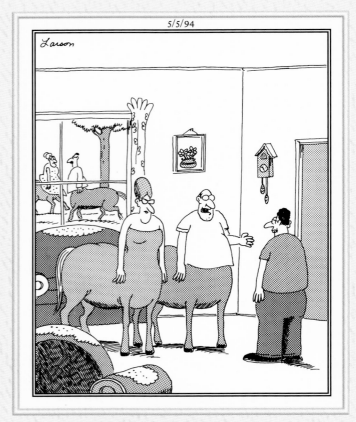

"Sorry, son, but for you to understand what happened, you have to first understand that back in the '60s we were all taking a lot of drugs."

5/6/94

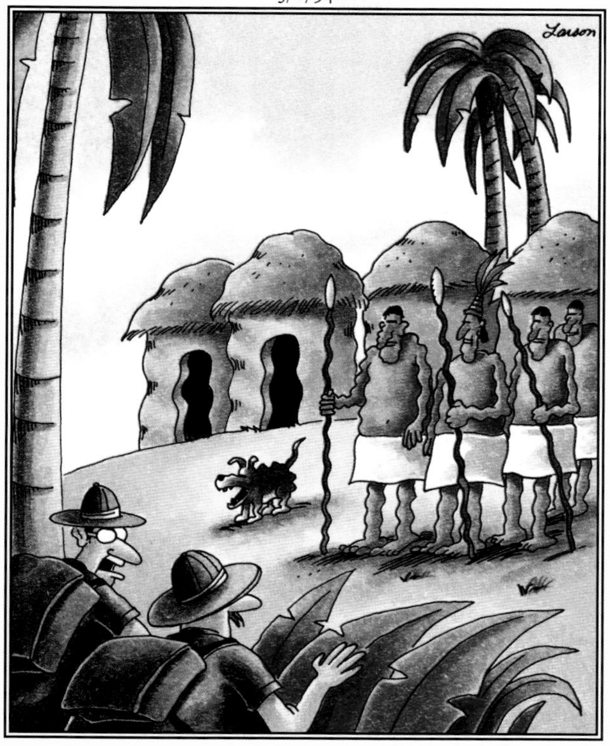

"Now watch your step, Osborne. ...
The Squiggly Line people have an inherent
distrust for all smoothliners."

5/9/94

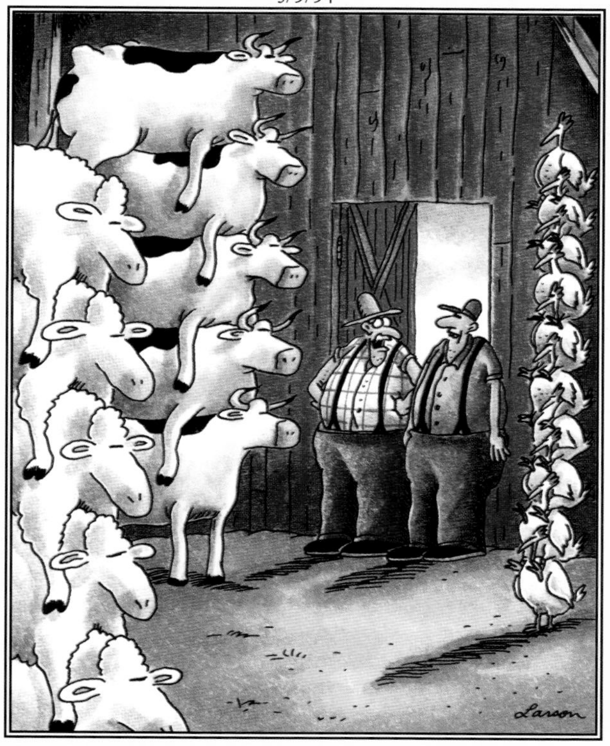

"It's the only way to go, Frank. Why, my
life's changed, ever since I discovered
Stackable Livestock®."

5/10/94

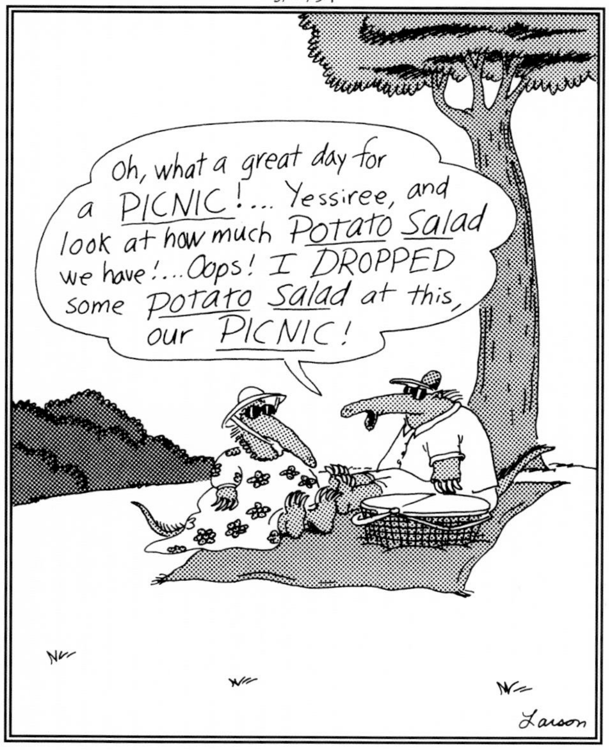
Oh, what a great day for a PICNIC!... Yessiree, and look at how much Potato Salad we have!...Oops! I DROPPED some Potato Salad at this, our PICNIC!

Hunting techniques of the modern anteater

5/11/94

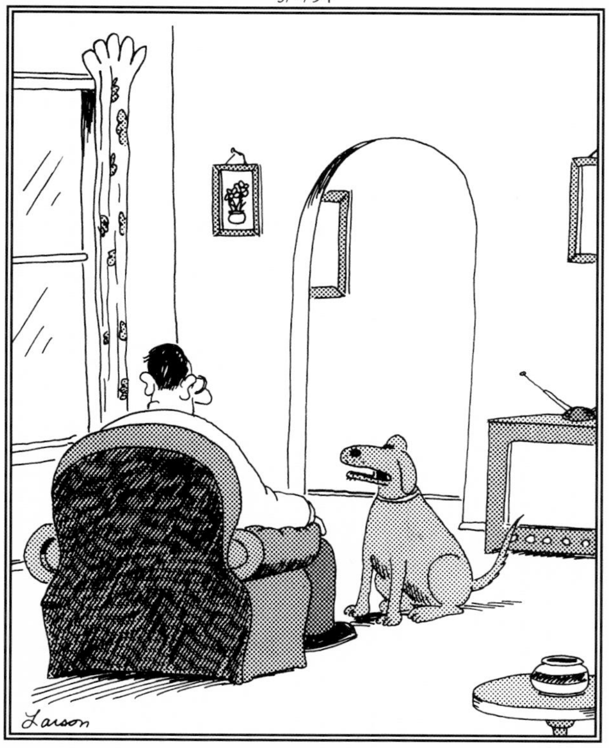

"The truth is, Stan, I'd like a place of my own."

5/12/94

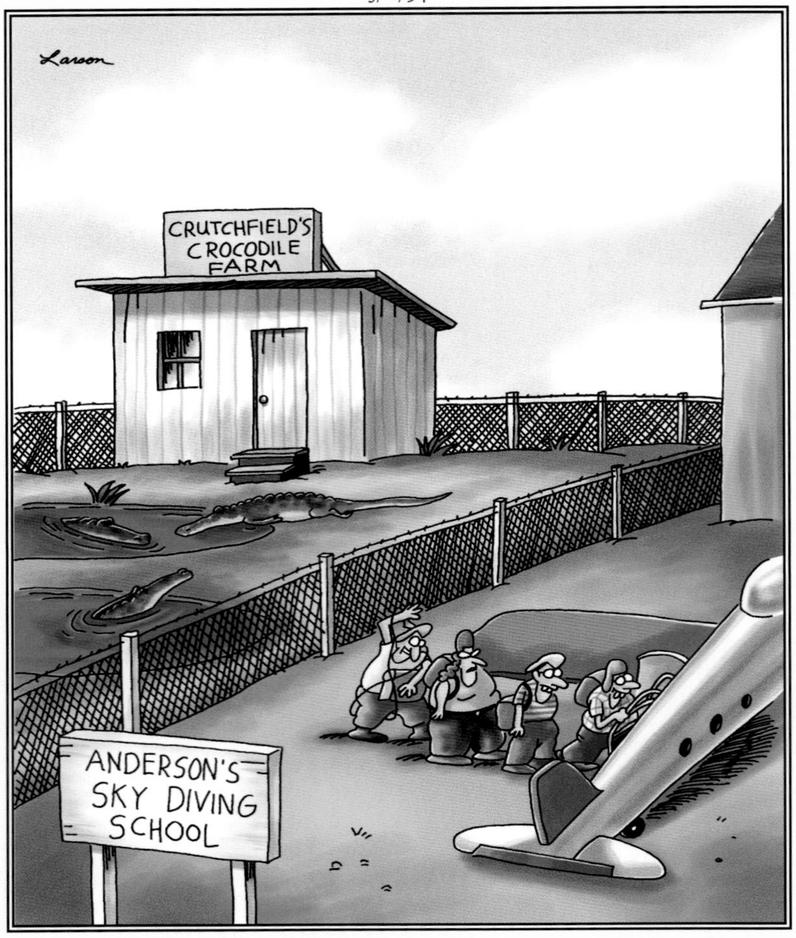
Larson
CRUTCHFIELD'S CROCODILE FARM
ANDERSON'S SKY DIVING SCHOOL

More trouble brewing

5/13/94

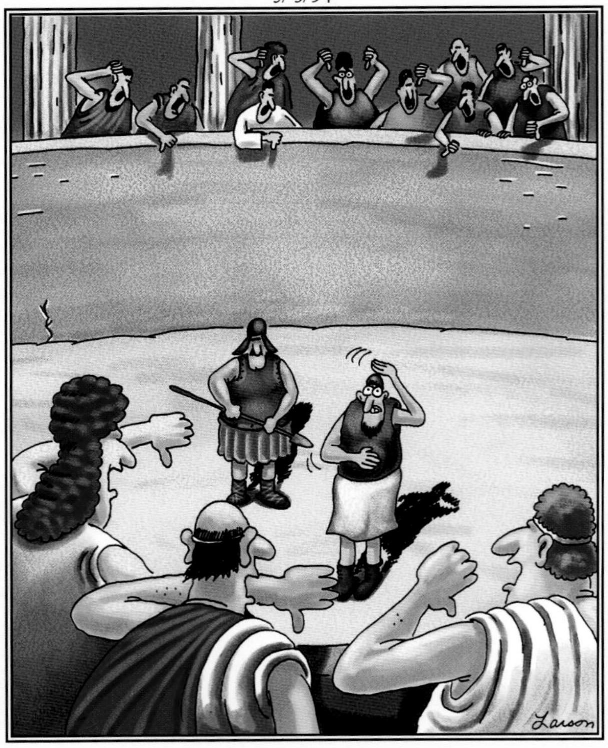
Larson

In the stadiums of ancient Rome, the most feared trial was the rub-your-stomach-and-pat-your-head-at-the-same-time event.

5/23/94

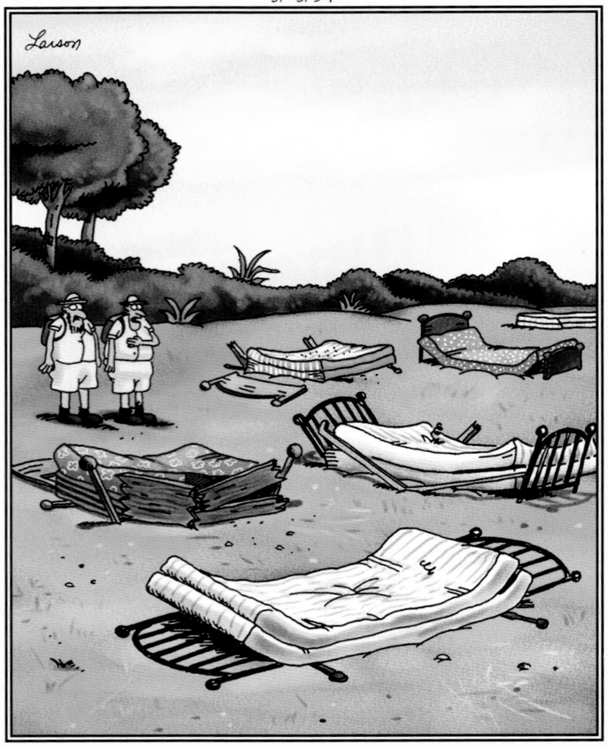
Larson

"My God, Carlson! After years of searching, this is an emotional moment for me! ... Voilà! I give you the Secret Elephant Breeding Grounds!"

5/24/94

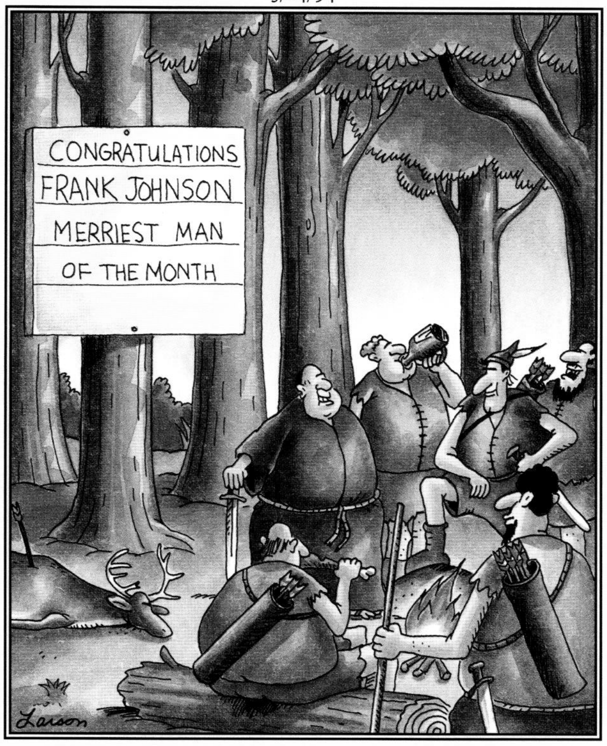
CONGRATULATIONS
FRANK JOHNSON
MERRIEST MAN
OF THE MONTH
Larson

5/26/94

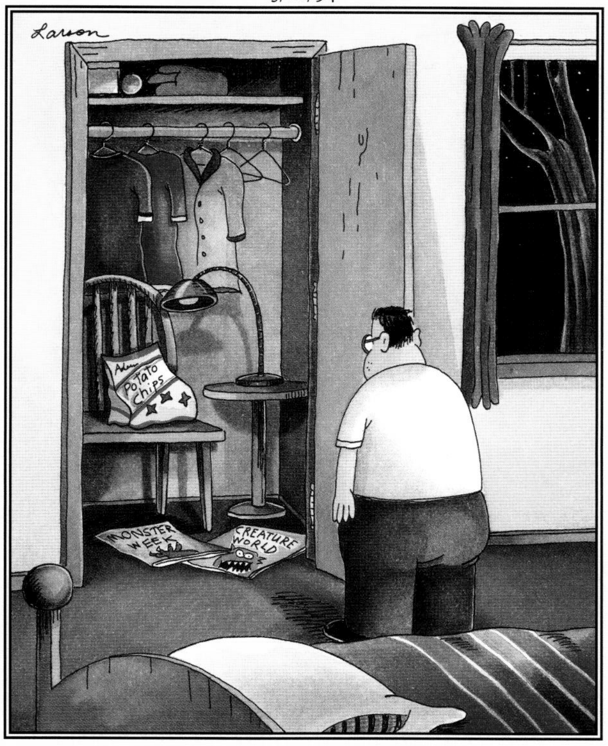
Larson
Potato Chips
MONSTER WEEK
CREATURE WORLD

For the time being, the monster wasn't in Ricky's closet. For the time being.

5/18/94

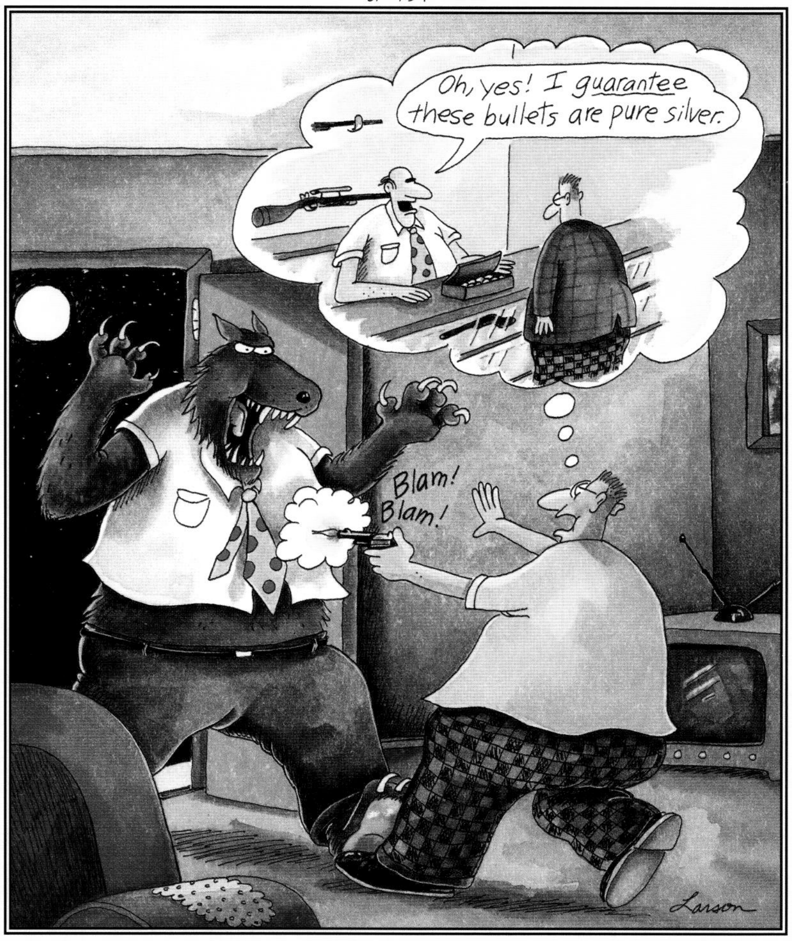
Oh, yes! I guarantee these bullets are pure silver.
Blam! Blam!
Larson

Moments before he was ripped to shreds, Edgar vaguely recalled having seen that same obnoxious tie earlier in the day.

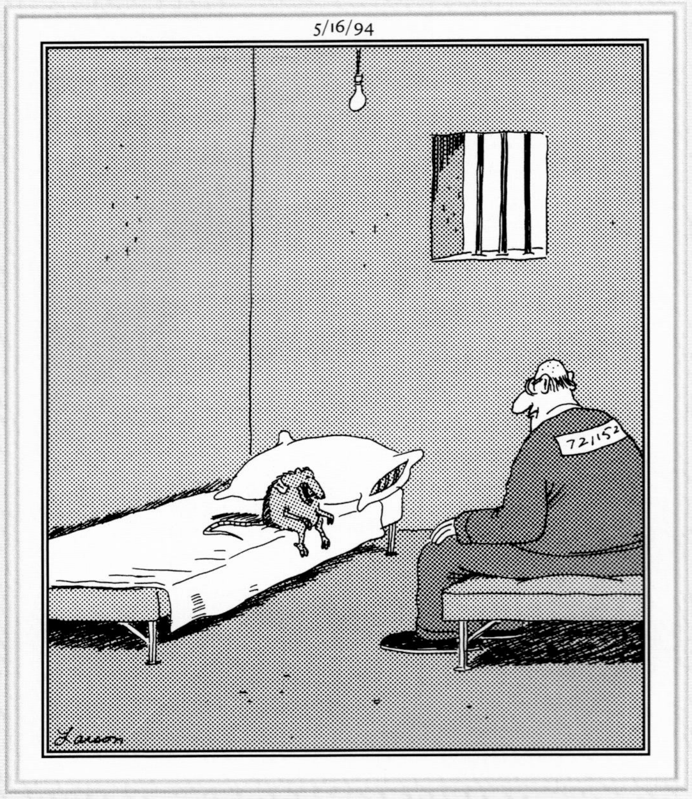
5/16/94
Larson

"I *would* have gotten away scot-free if I had just gotten rid of the evidence. ... But, shoot—I'm a pack rat."

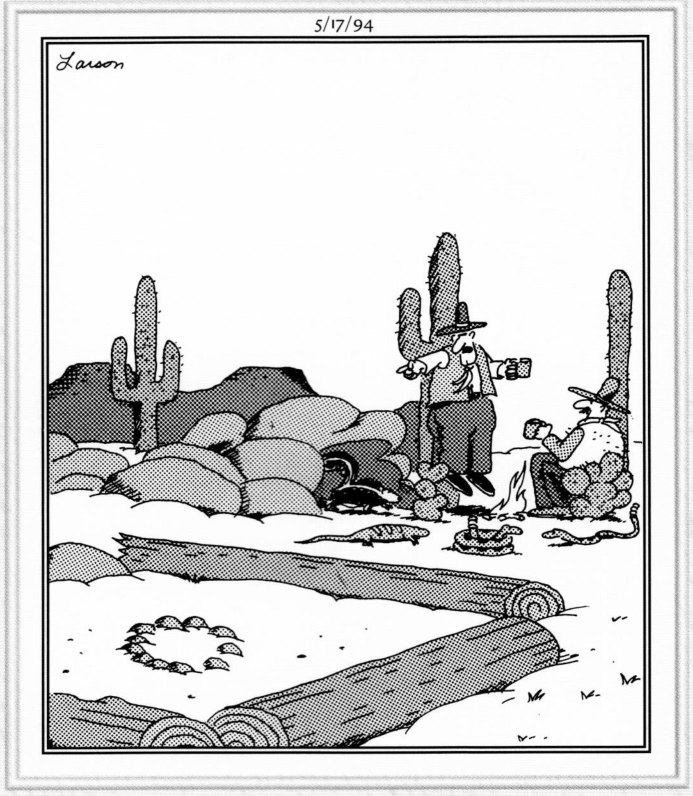
5/17/94
Larson

"Oh, man, Clem! To add insult to injury, I see a great campsite right over yonder."

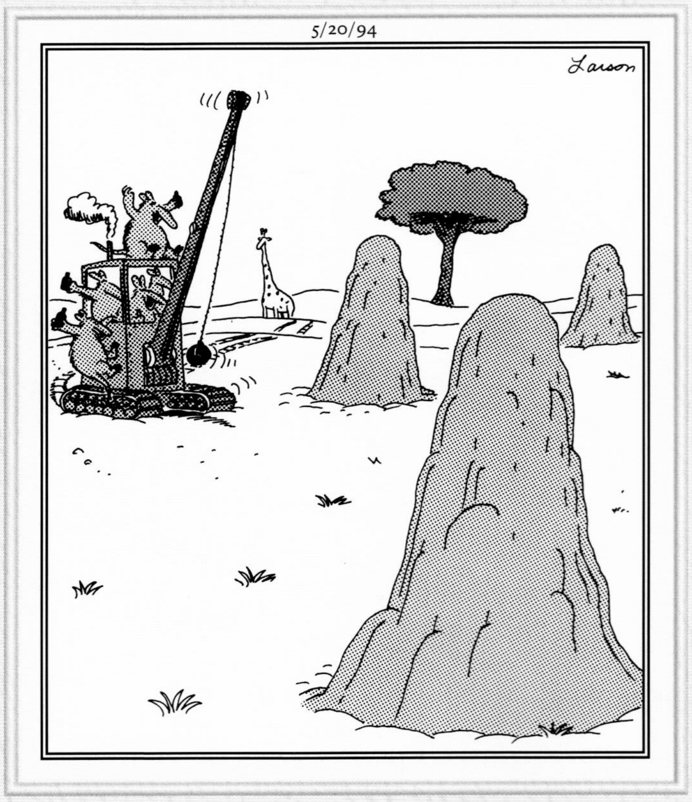
5/20/94
Larson

Like frozen sentries of the Serengeti, the century-old termite mounds had withstood all tests of time and foe—all tests, that is, except the one involving drunken aardvarks and a stolen wrecking ball.

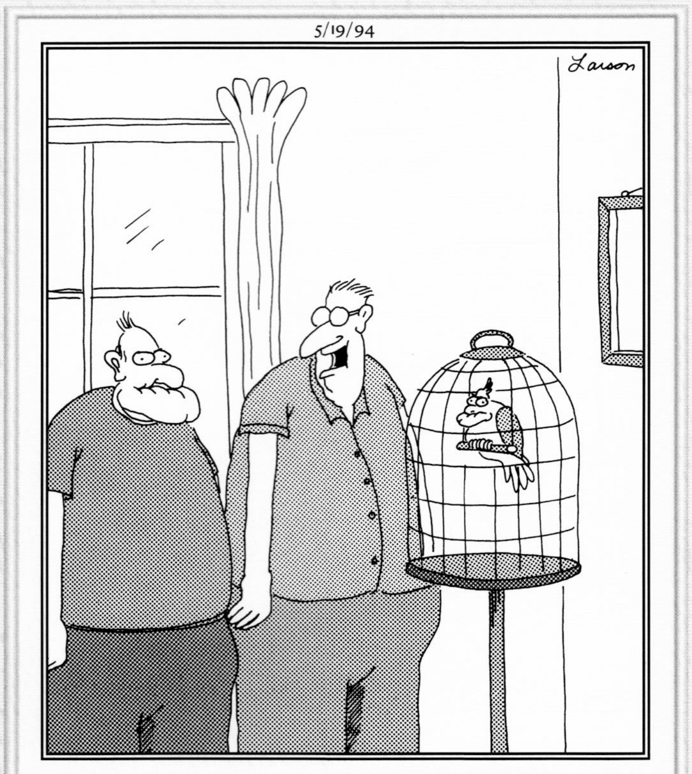
5/19/94
Larson

"Boy, Henry ... he really *can* do you!"

5/25/94

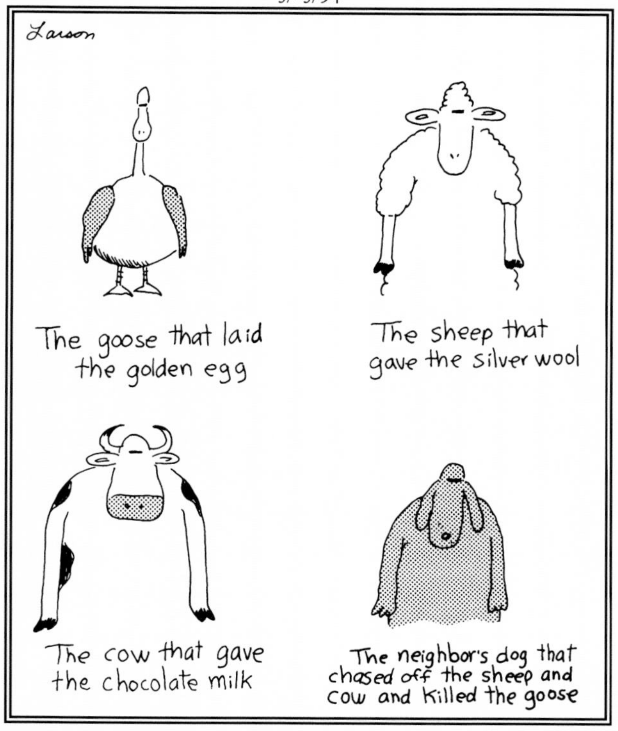
Larson
The goose that laid the golden egg
The sheep that gave the silver wool
The cow that gave the chocolate milk
The neighbor's dog that chased off the sheep and cow and killed the goose

5/27/94

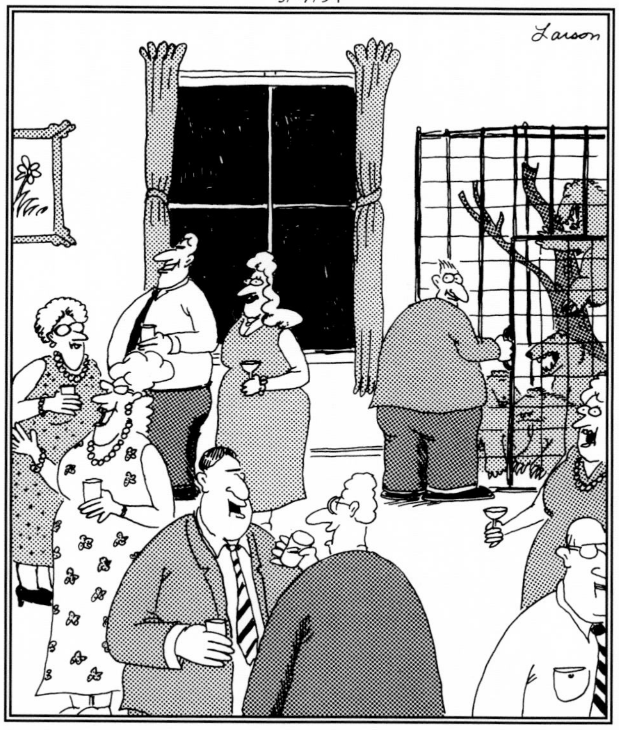
Larson

The party was going along splendidly—and then Morty opened the door to the wolverine display.

5/31/94

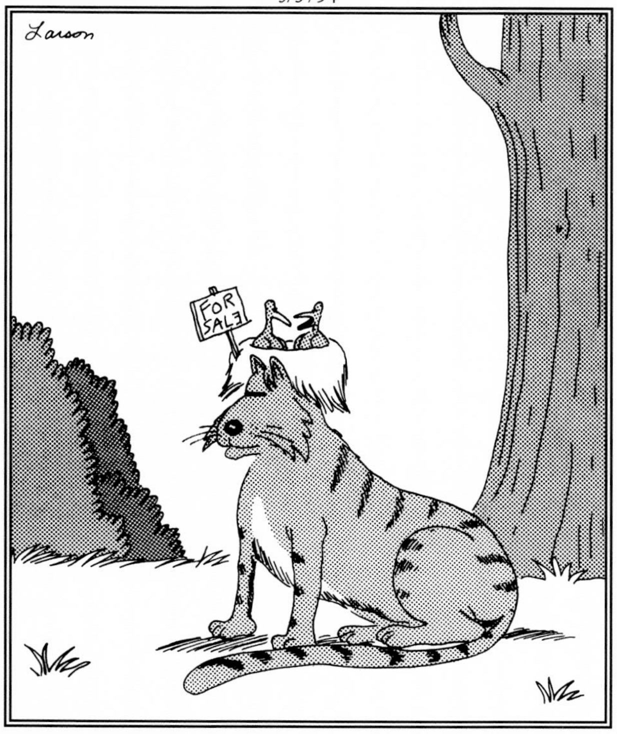
Larson
FOR SALE

"Hey, we'll be lucky if we *ever* sell this place! ... Well, it's like everyone says—location, location, location."

5/30/94

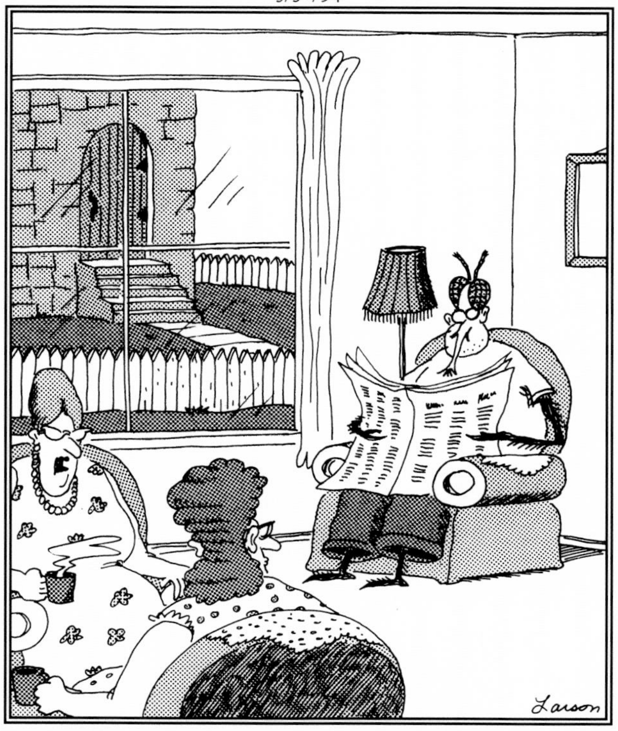
Larson

"So George says, 'I'm goin' over there and tellin' that guy to shut that equipment off!'... So *I* said: 'George, that guy's a mad scientist. Call the cops. Don't go over there alone.'... Well, you know George."

6/2/94

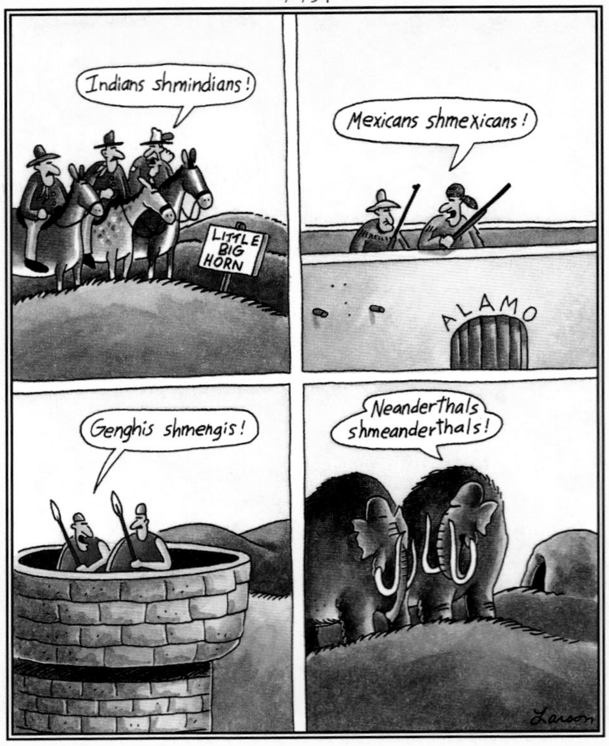
Indians shmindians!
LITTLE BIG HORN
Mexicans shmexicans!
ALAMO
Genghis shmengis!
Neanderthals shmeanderthals!

History shmistory

6/3/94

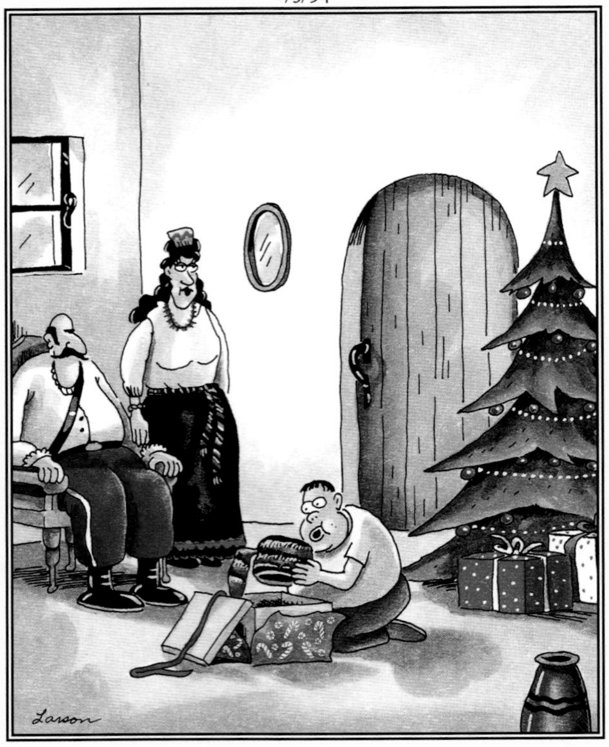

Mexico City, Christmas morning, 1837: Santa Anna's son, Juan, receives the original Davy Crockett hat.

6/6/94

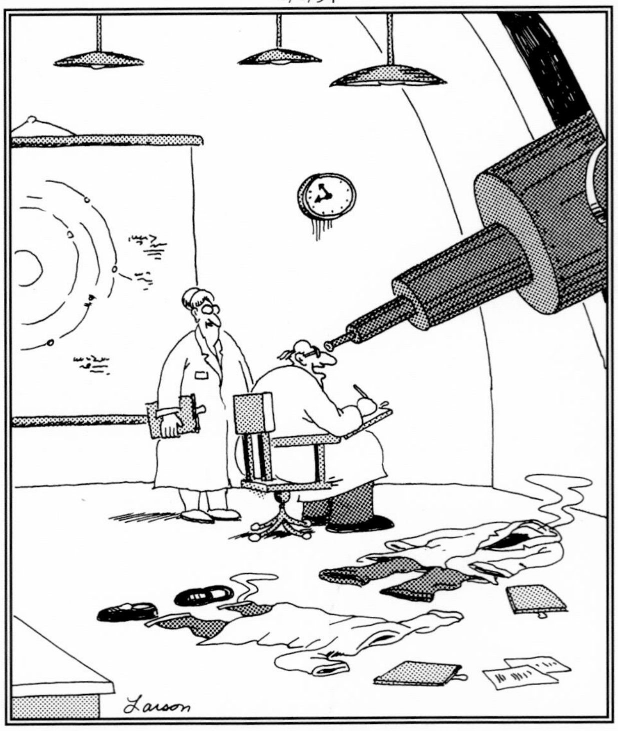

"First that cretin Foster and now that jerk Cummings has instantly evaporated! ... I tell you, Ms. Goodman, without a doubt, I'm looking at an authentic, full-fledged wishing star!"

6/1/94

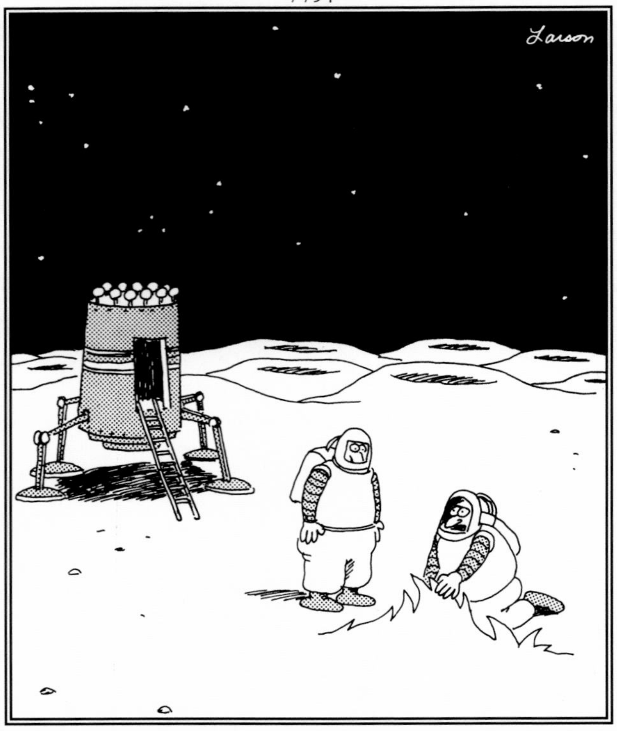

"Say. ... It's only a *paper* moon."

6/7/94

"AIM AT THE BEST!"
SHIPPING

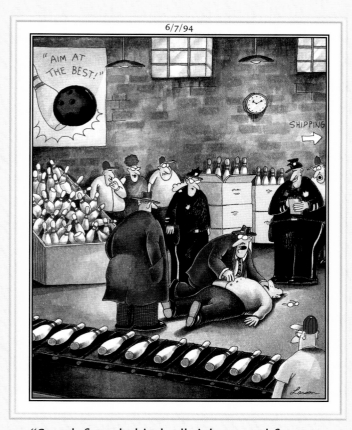

"Struck from behind, all right ... and from my first examination of the wound, I'd say this was done by some kind of heavy, blunt object."

6/10/94

"So, they tell me you fancy yourself a tuba player."

6/13/94

B

Humboys

6/14/94

"You know, you and I could make primitive music together."

6/9/94

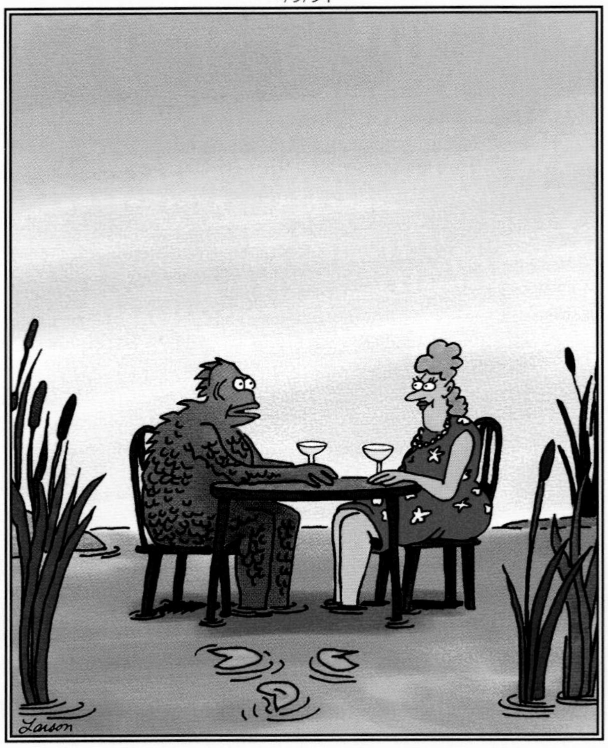
Larson

"Well, actually, Doreen, I rather resent being called a 'swamp thing.'... I prefer the term 'wetlands-challenged-mutant.'"

6/8/94

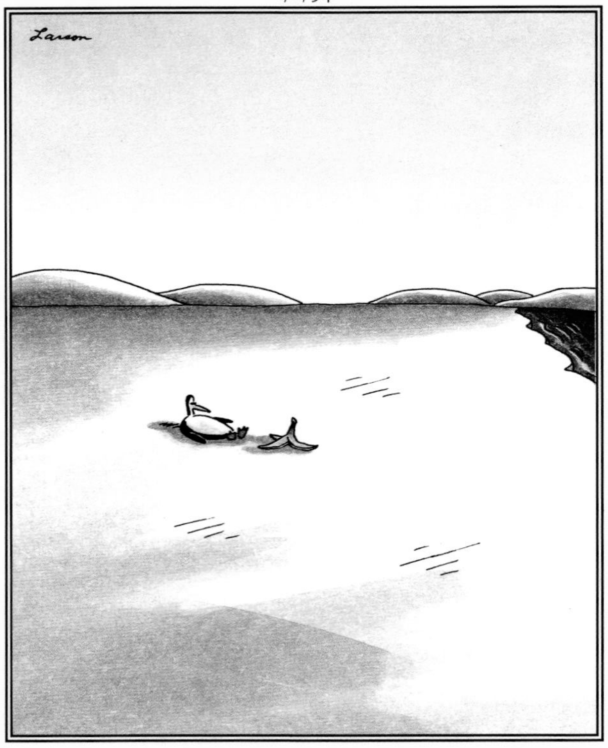
Larson

6/15/94

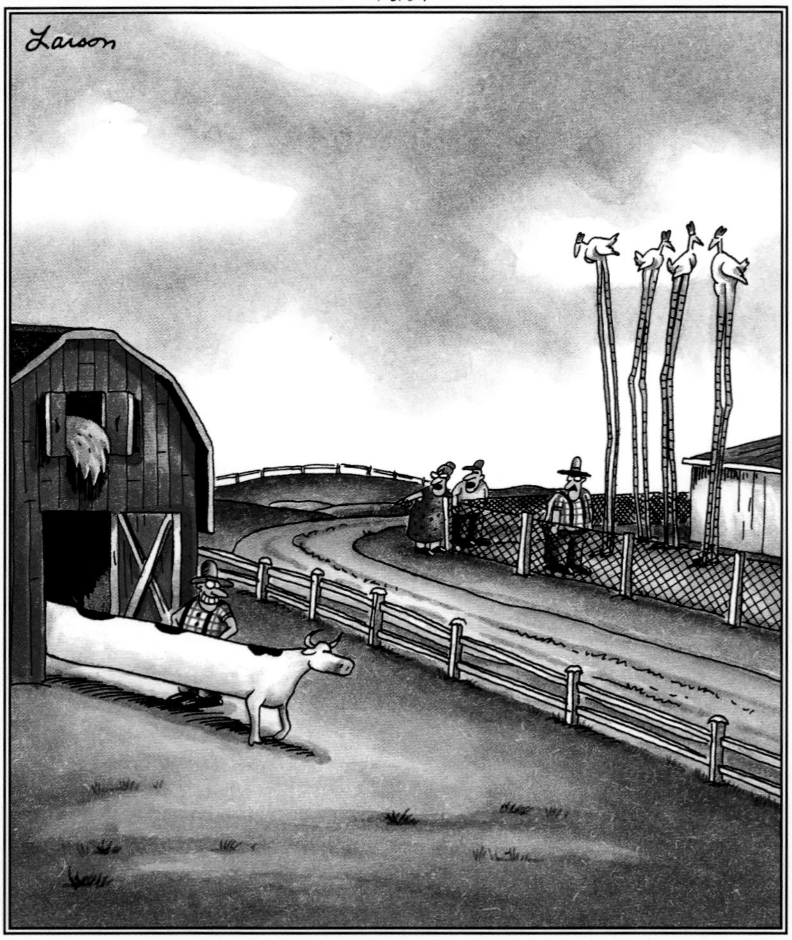
Larson

For a long time, Farmer Hansen and his tall chickens enjoyed immense popularity—until Farmer Sutton got himself a longcow.

6/16/94

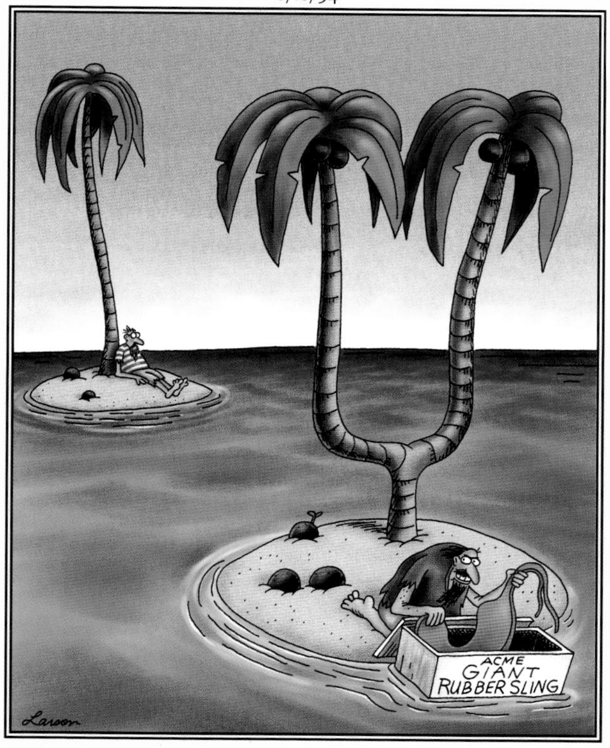
ACME
GIANT
RUBBER SLING
Larson

6/20/94

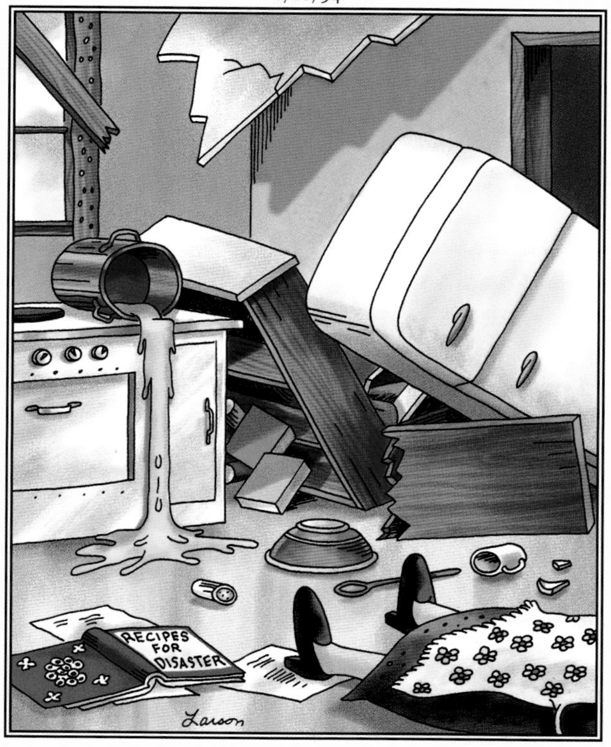
RECIPES
FOR
DISASTER
Larson

6/17/94

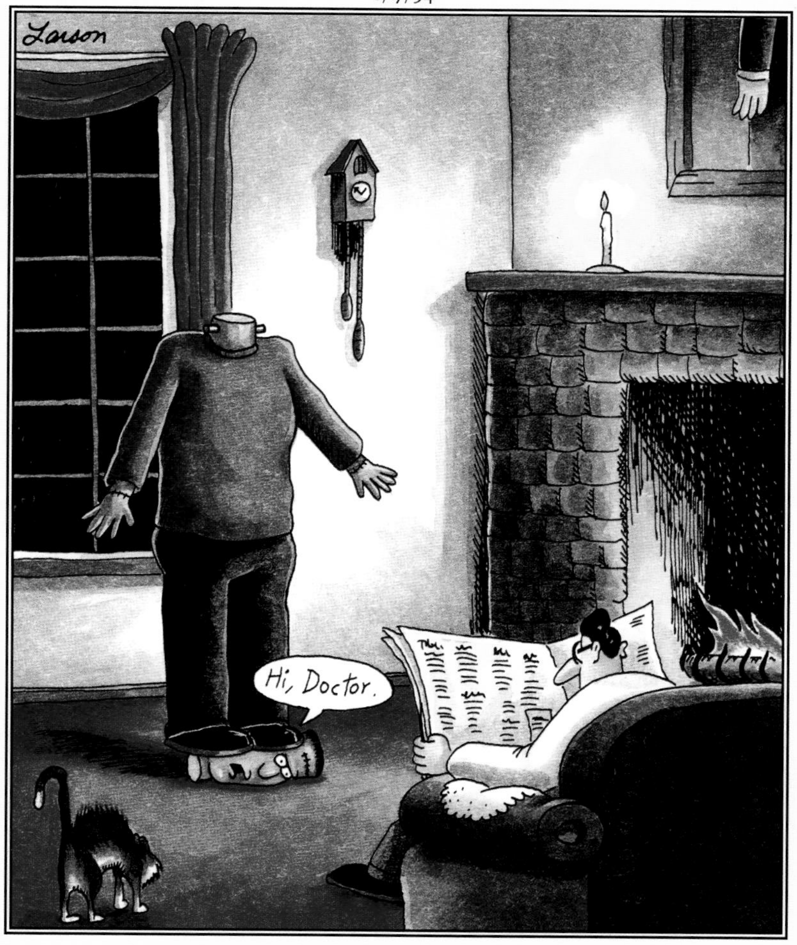
Larson
Hi, Doctor.

In an effort to show off, the monster would sometimes stand on his head.

6/22/94

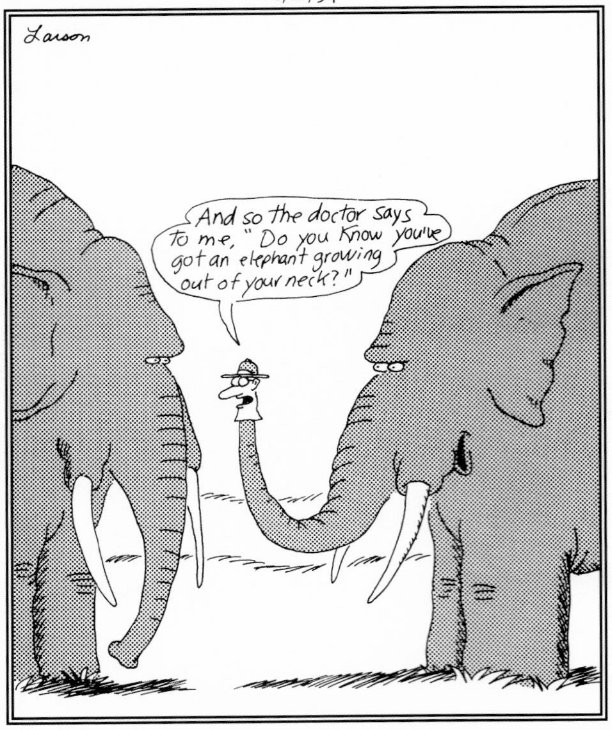
And so the doctor says to me, "Do you know you've got an elephant growing out of your neck?"

When things got slow in the midday heat, Arnie would often break out his trunk puppet.

6/23/94

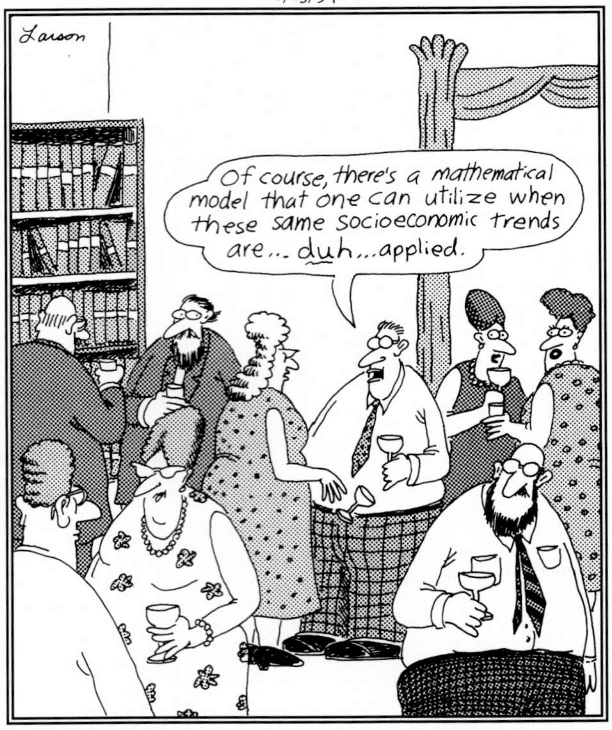
Of course, there's a mathematical model that one can utilize when these same socioeconomic trends are... duh... applied.

Suddenly the Mensa partygoers froze when Clarence shockingly uttered the "D" word.

6/21/94

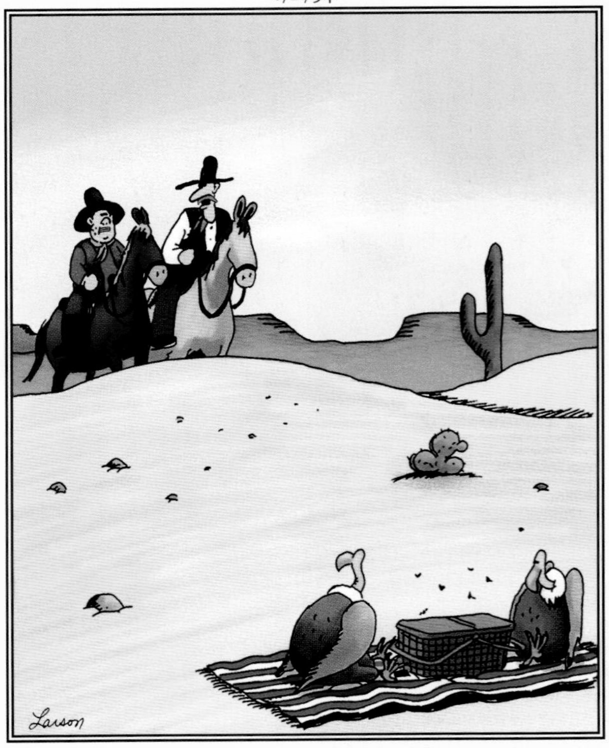

"It's a buzzard picnic, son—and you best remember to never take a look-see inside one of them baskets."

6/24/94

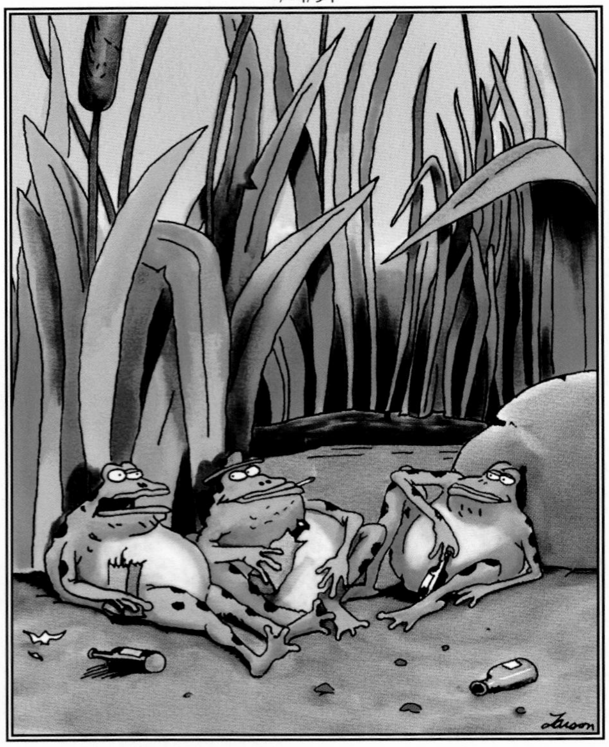

"Yeah. I remember Jerry. Good friend of mine. ... You know, I never understood a single word he said, but he always had some mighty fine wine."

6/27/94

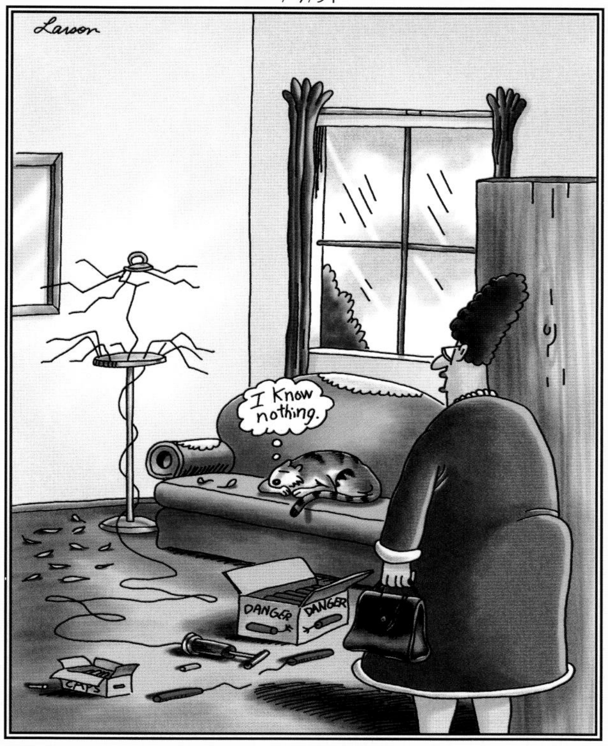
I Know nothing.
DANGER
DANGER

6/29/94

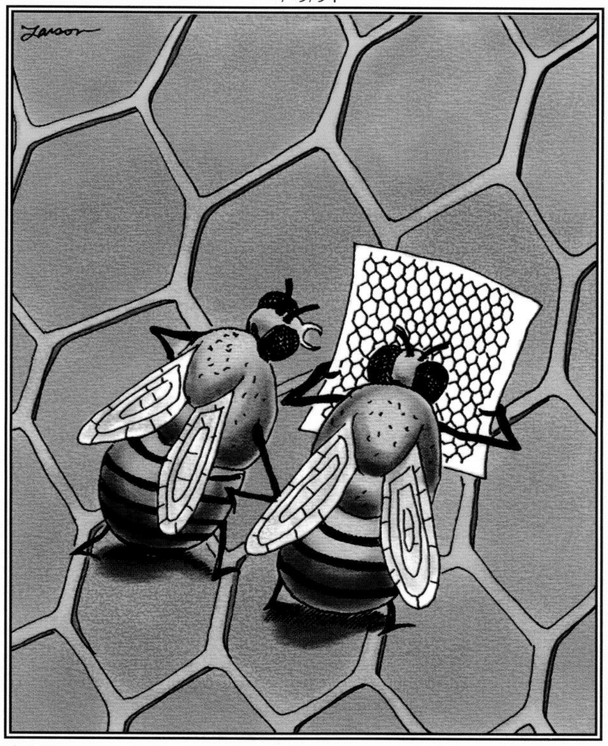

"Face it, Fred—you're lost."

6/28/94

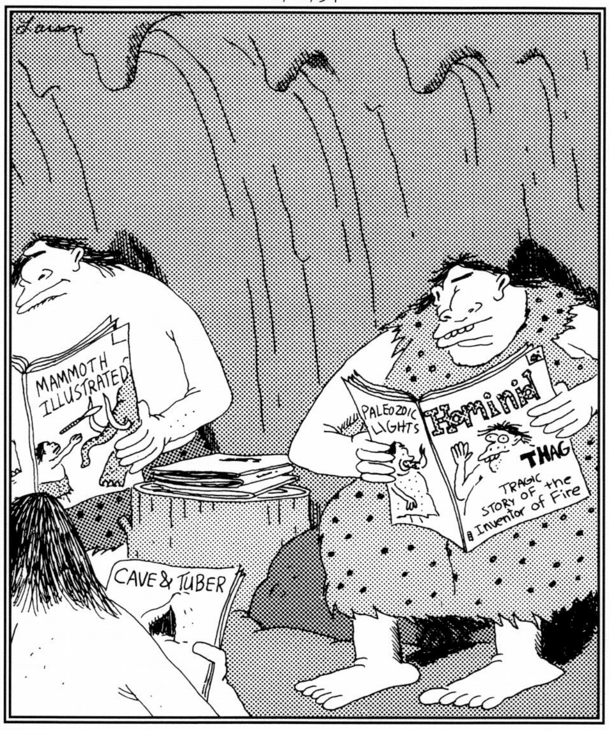
MAMMOTH ILLUSTRATED
PALEOZOIC LIGHTS
Hominid
THAG
TRAGIC STORY OF the Inventor of Fire
CAVE & TUBER

Primitive waiting rooms

6/30/94

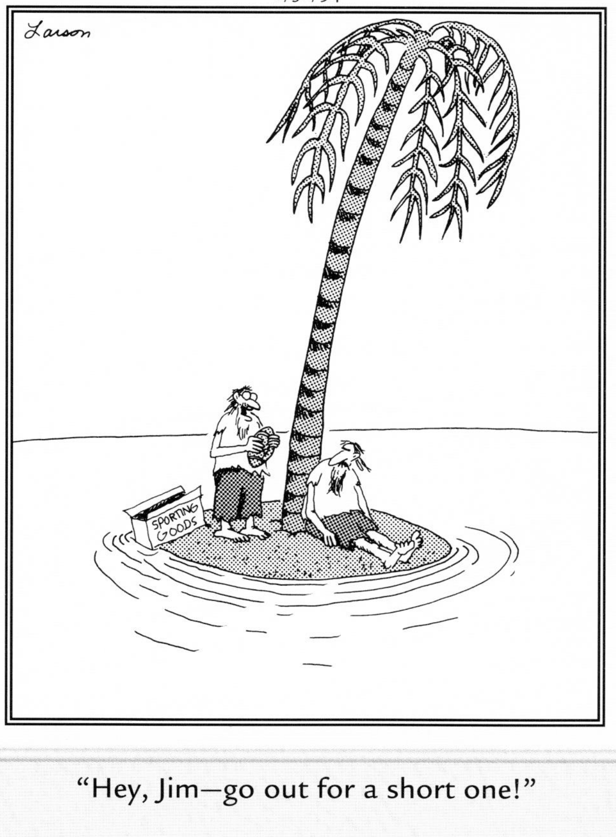
SPORTING GOODS

"Hey, Jim—go out for a short one!"

7/1/94

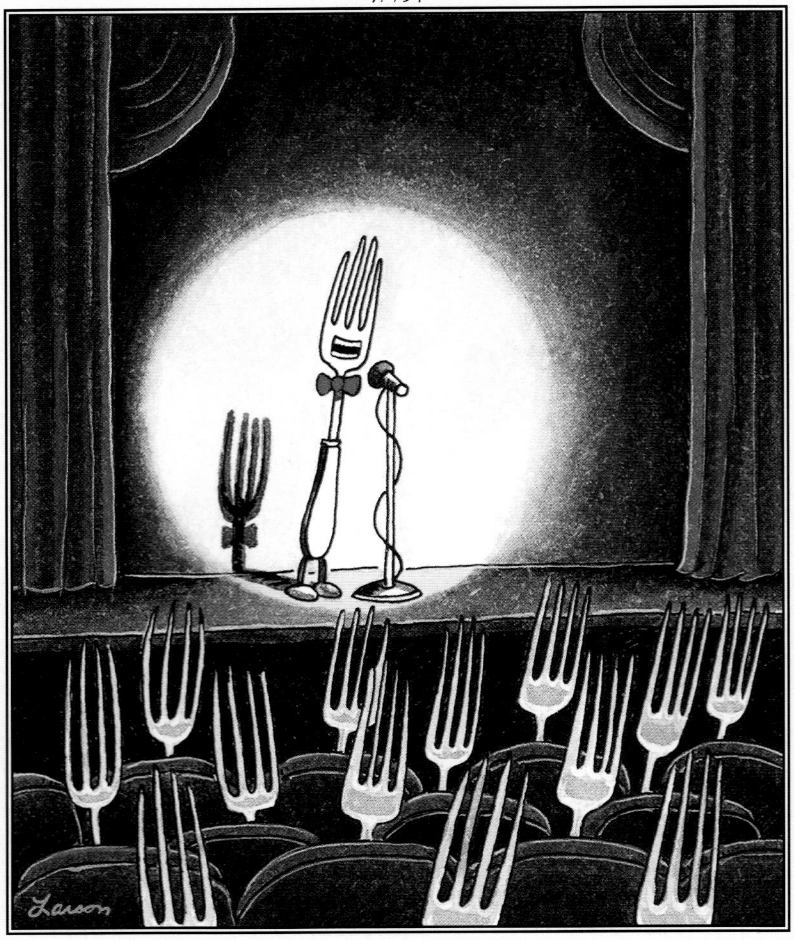
Larson

"... And so the bartender says, 'Hey! That's not a soup spoon!'... But seriously, forks ..."

7/4/94

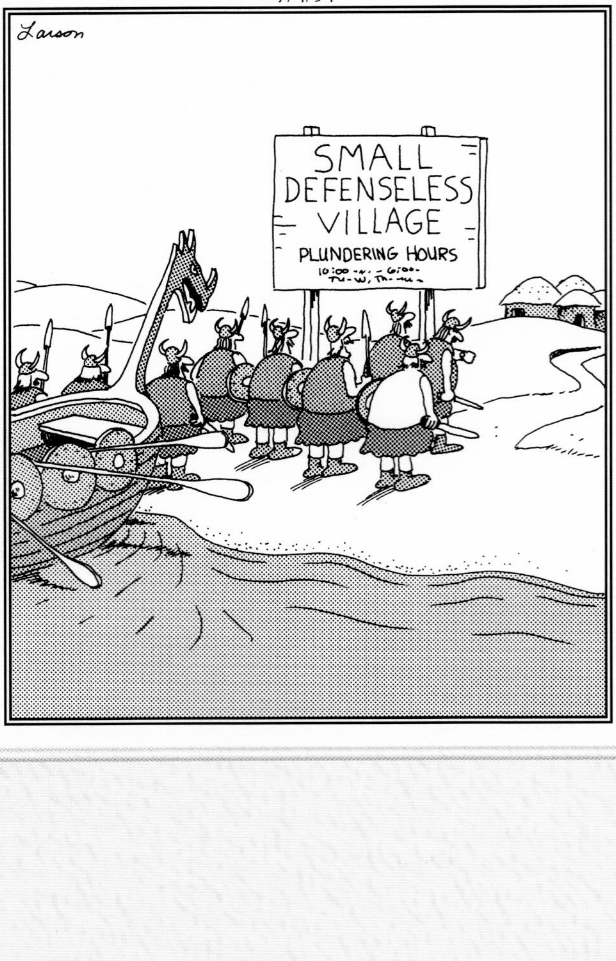
Larson
SMALL DEFENSELESS VILLAGE
PLUNDERING HOURS

7/5/94

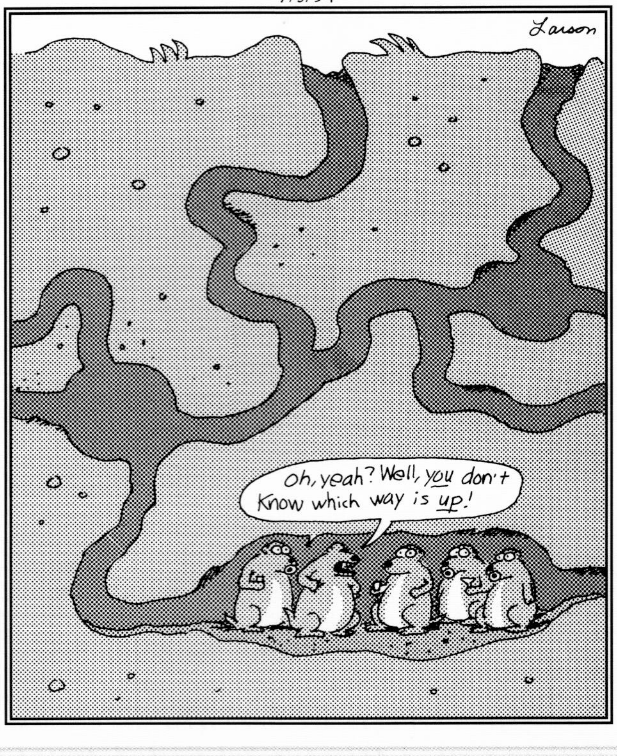
Larson
Oh, yeah? Well, you don't know which way is up!

The ultimate gopher insult

7/6/94

ZOO
DANGER
PIT VIPER
TROPICAL HOUSE employees only
ZOO STAFF
Larson

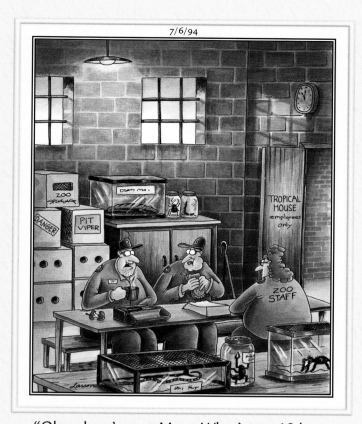

"Okay, here's one, Marv: What's got 12 legs, six eyes, a hairy thorax, was found dead in its display case this morning, and goes 'crunch' inside a submarine sandwich?"

7/12/94

Larson

"I'm sorry, Delores—I didn't think you'd truly ever leave! ... But where will you go?"

7/14/94

Larson

"Yeah, I just got back! And the wizard I mentioned? He gave me a new brain! ... It's on the coffee table as we speak!"

7/20/94

Larson

"Sorry, Virgil—that's all you get. ... I don't know how you got hold of a dribble glass in the first place, but it's just your bad luck."

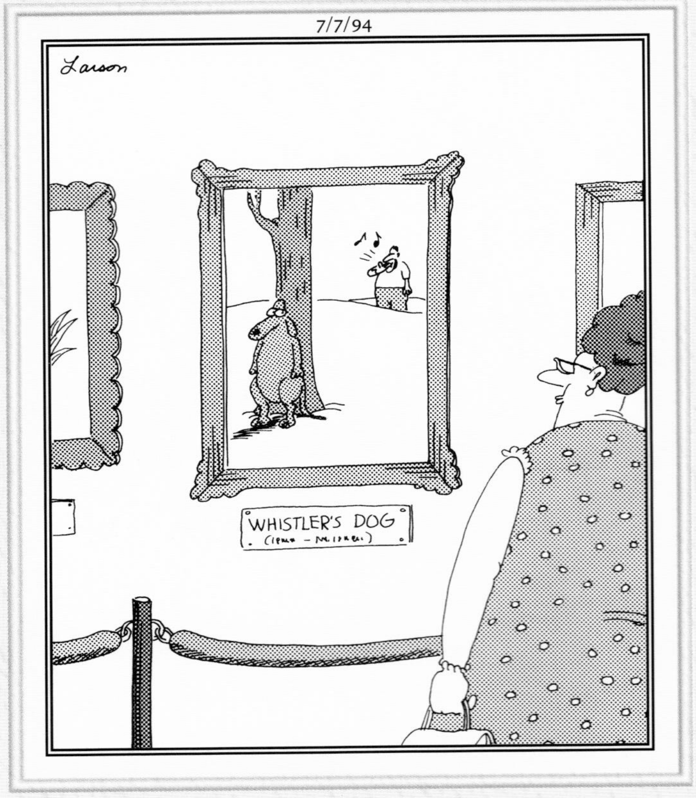
7/7/94
Larson
WHISTLER'S DOG

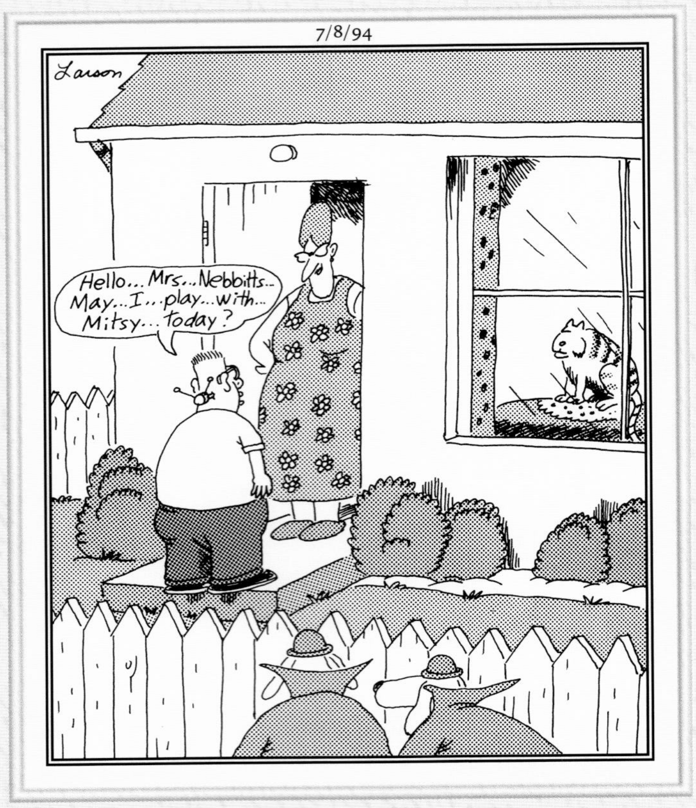
7/8/94
Larson
Hello... Mrs... Nebbitts... May... I... play... with... Mitsy... today?

Scene from *Dog Invaders from Mars*

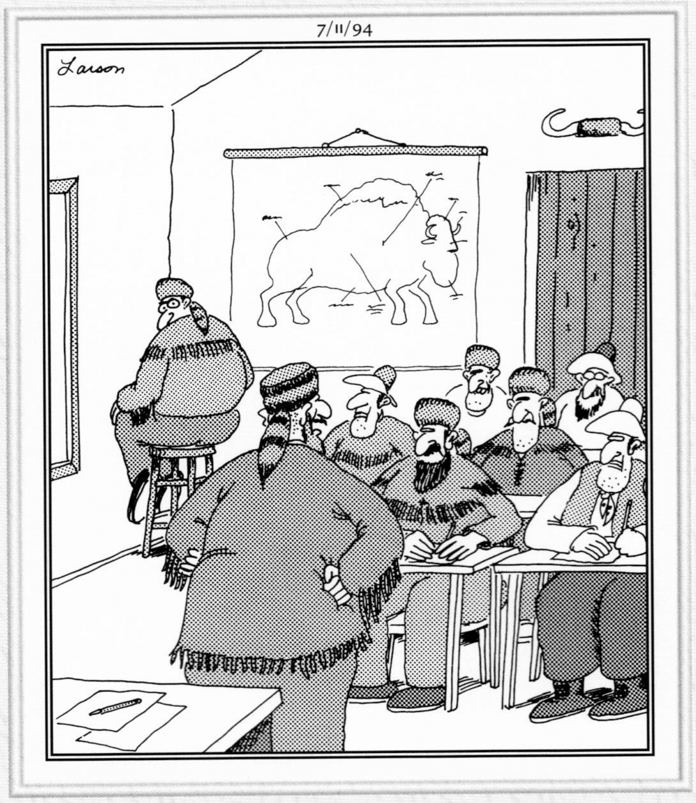
7/11/94
Larson

"Anybody else? ... This here's a school for *buffalo* hunters—and anyone who so much as utters the word 'bison' can join Morgenstern in the corner!"

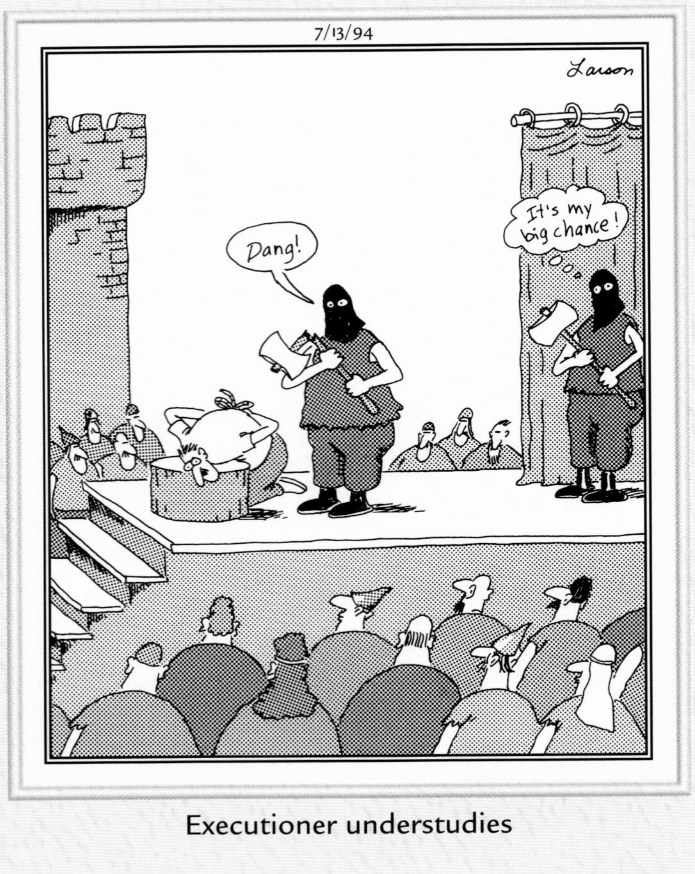
7/13/94
Larson
Dang!
It's my big chance!

Executioner understudies

7/15/94

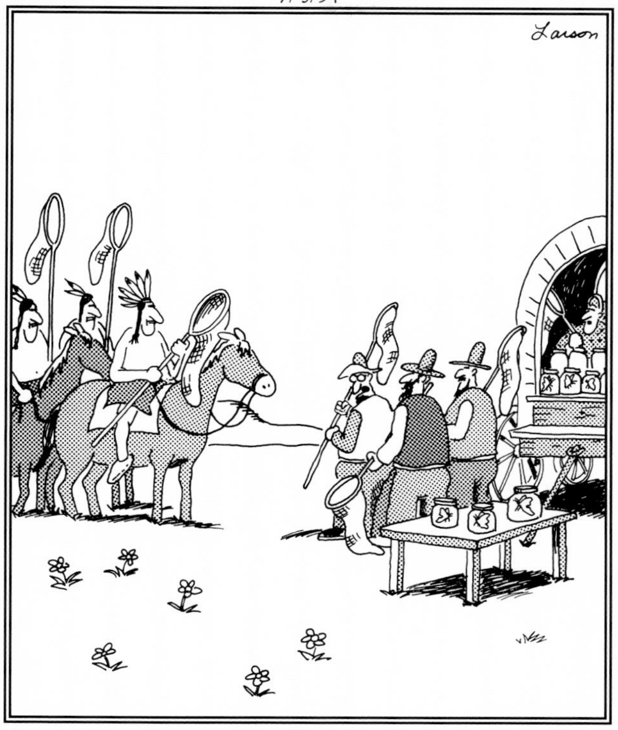
Larson

"Everyone just keep your nets real still. ...
They'll just wanna look over our jars, and
we best not try to stop 'em."

7/18/94

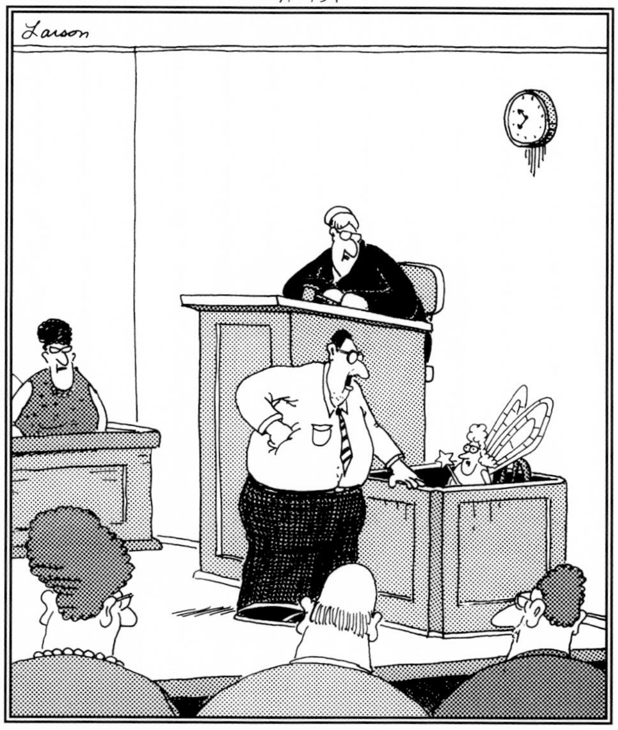
Larson

"Well, first you say you saw the defendant at the scene and now you say you *think* you saw him! ... Let's cut to the chase, Ms. Sunbeam—is it possible your entire testimony is nothing more than a mere fairy tale?"

7/19/94

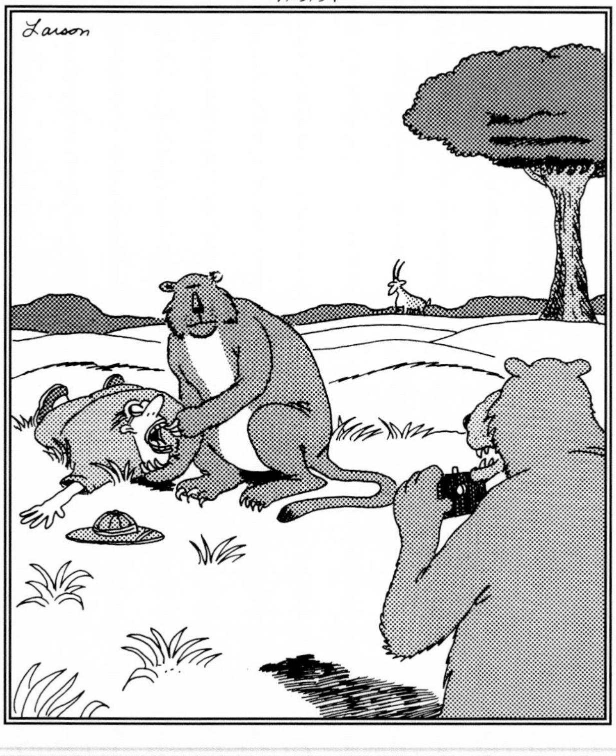
Larson

"That's just not impressive, Doris. ...
The brain! Hold up the big brain!"

7/21/94

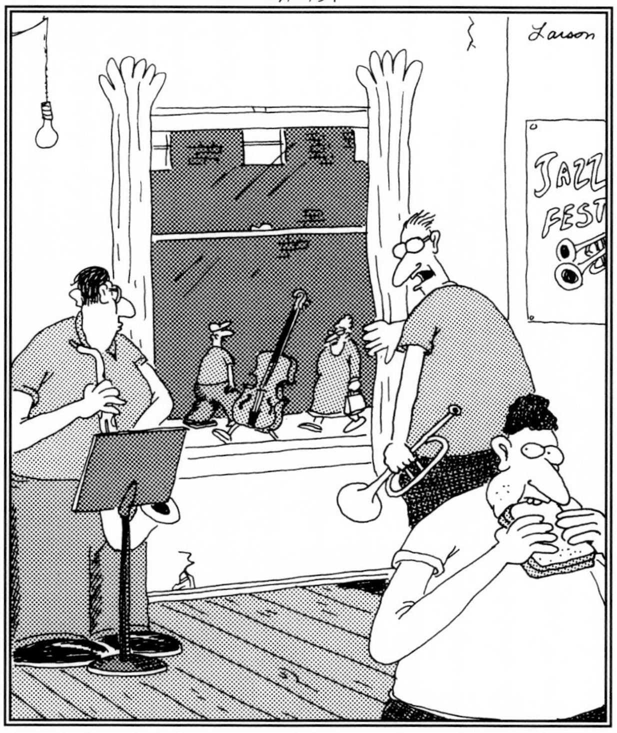
Larson

"Hey, Leon! Your bass sure is walking *now!*"

7/22/94

Larson
And just to make it interesting...
BIRDS
INSECTS
MED. SKINNED PEOPLE
LIGHT-SKINNED PEOPLE
DARK-SKINNED PEOPLE
PLANTS
JERKS
REPTILES
Amphibians
TREES

7/27/94

Larson

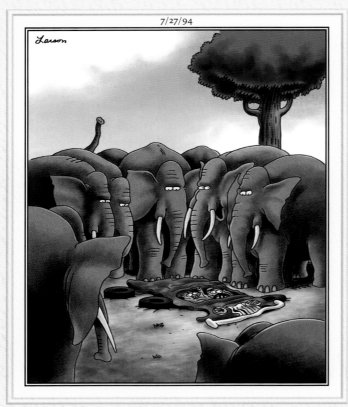

"You know, sometimes I sort of enjoy this herd mentality."

7/28/94

Larson

"It's worse than I first suspected, Mr. Binkley—you don't even *have* a funny bone."

7/25/94

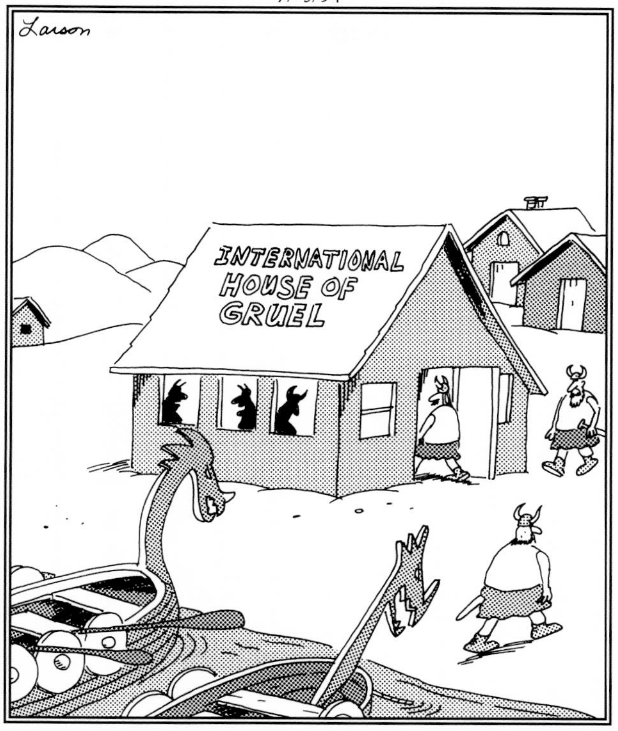
INTERNATIONAL
HOUSE OF
GRUEL

7/29/94

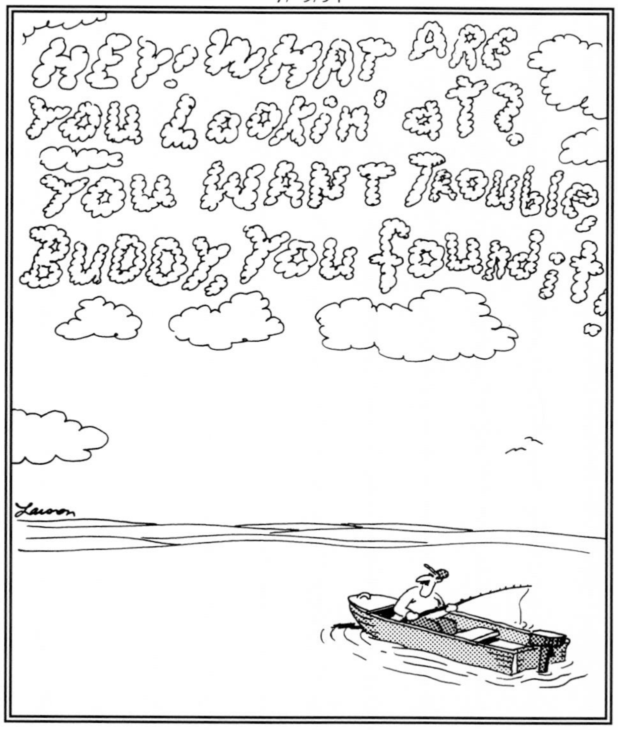
HEY! WHAT ARE
YOU LOOKIN' AT?
YOU WANT TROUBLE,
BUDDY, YOU FOUND IT!

Understanding only German, Fritz was unaware that the clouds were becoming threatening.

7/26/94

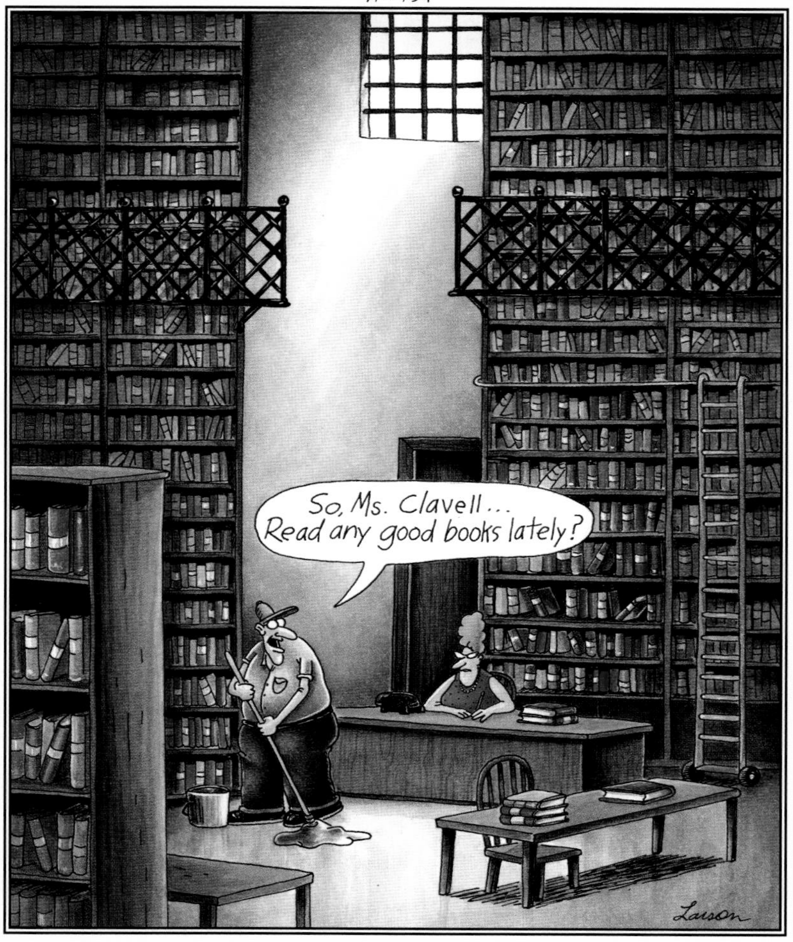
So, Ms. Clavell...
Read any good books lately?

After years of harboring his secret desires, Ned finally hits on the senior librarian.

8/2/94

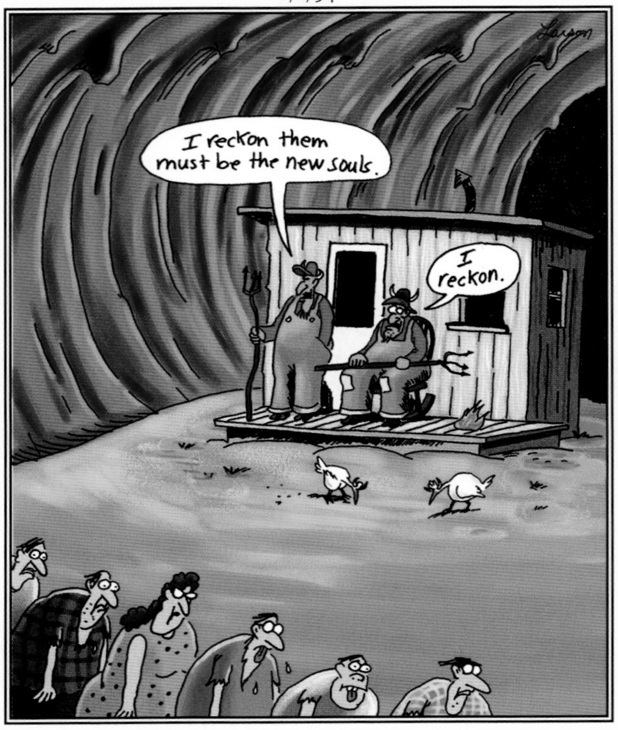
I reckon them must be the new souls.
I reckon.

Hellbillies

8/3/94

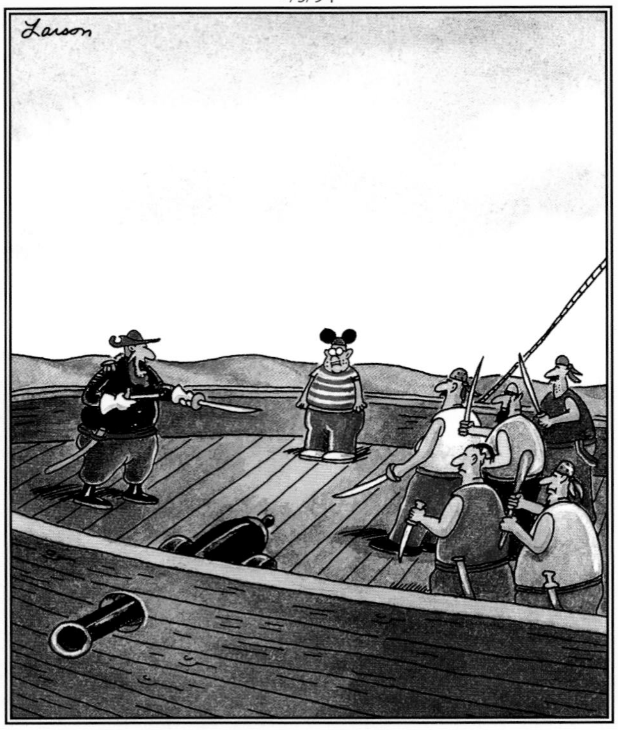

"And *you!* What's *your* story? ... If you ain't a mutineer, then what the hell are you?"

8/1/94

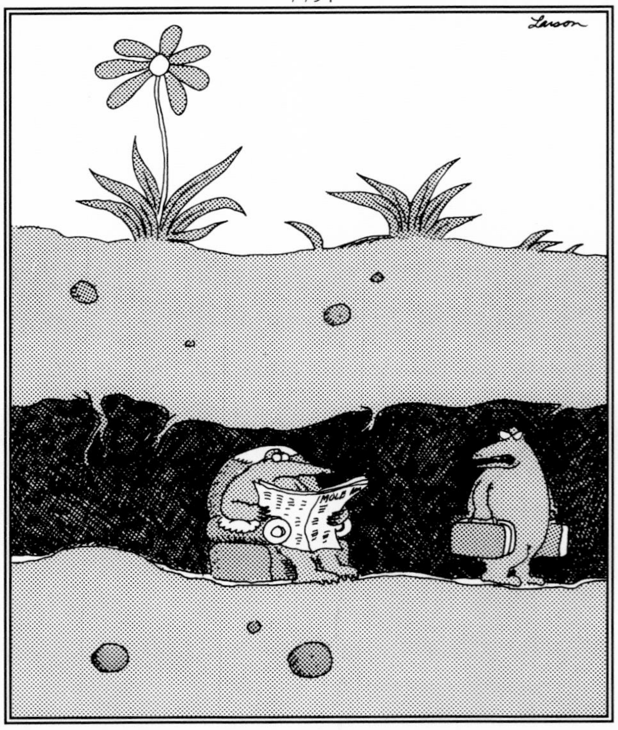

"I'm leaving you, Mitchell. You've never had tunnel vision and you never will."

8/4/94

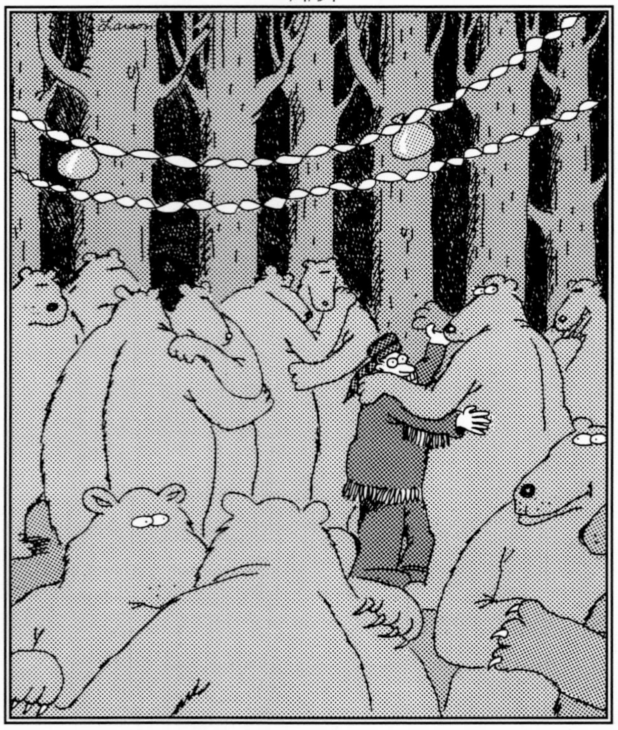

At the Grizzly Ball, only Alice, with her kind heart, would not refuse to dance with Adams.

8/8/94

Larson

"I'm afraid you misunderstood. ... I said I'd like a mango."

8/9/94

Larson

"Well, Griselda's back from the plastic surgeon's. ... Whoa! Look at the size of that wart!"

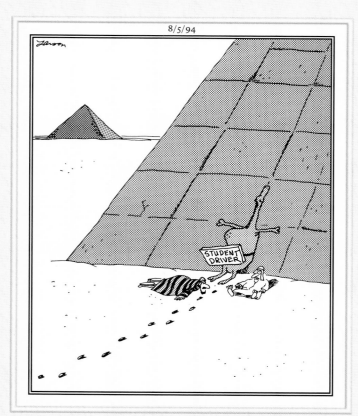

8/5/94

Larson
STUDENT DRIVER

Abdul flunks

8/10/94

Larson

"No way was it me, Mom—you must've heard a peep out of Eddie."

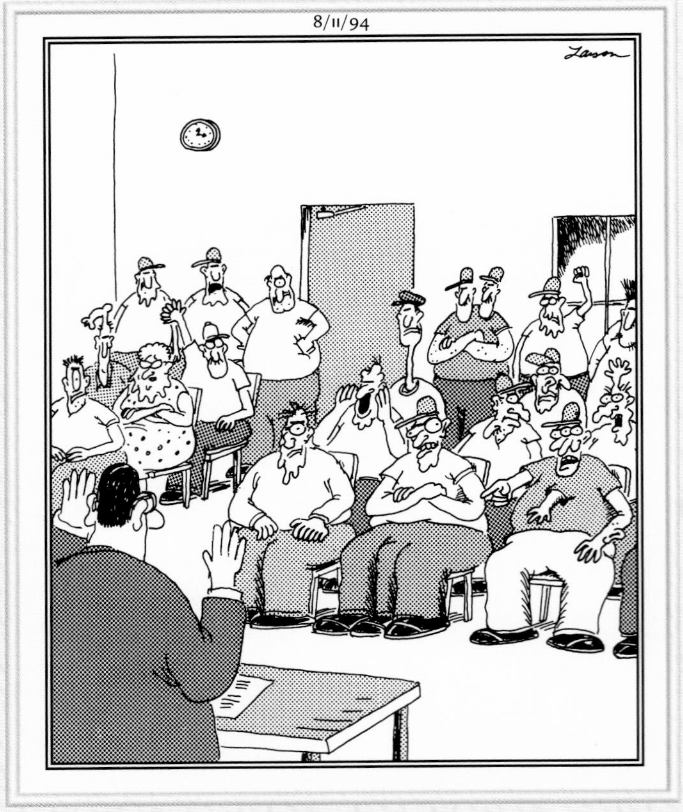
8/11/94
Larson
Once again, a meeting between management and the Plutonium Truckers' Union grows tense.

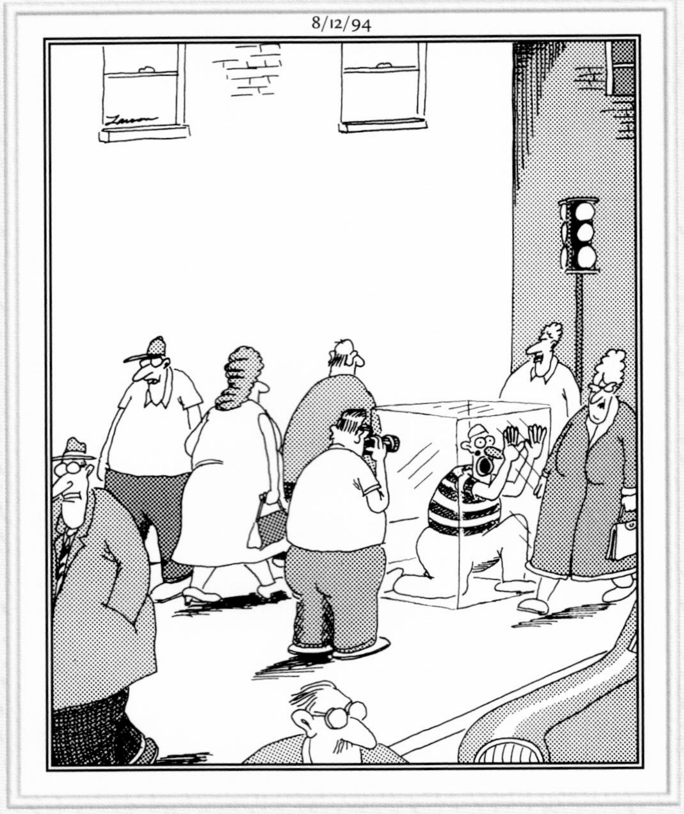
8/12/94
Larson
In its more horrific method of retribution, the mob will sometimes dress victims as mimes, place them in glass boxes, and let them perish slowly in full view of the public.

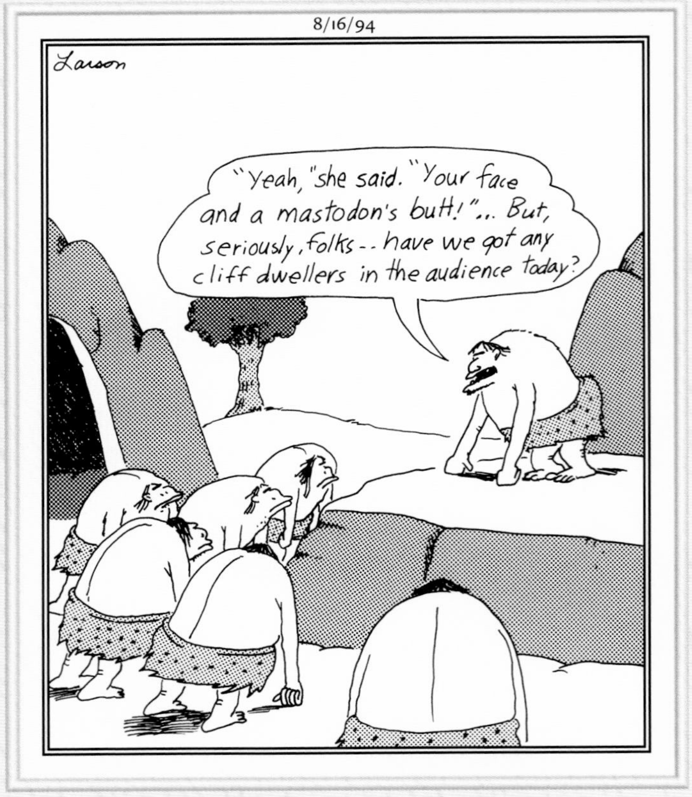
8/16/94
Larson
"Yeah," she said. "Your face and a mastodon's butt!"... But, seriously, folks -- have we got any cliff dwellers in the audience today?
Stand-semi-erect comedy

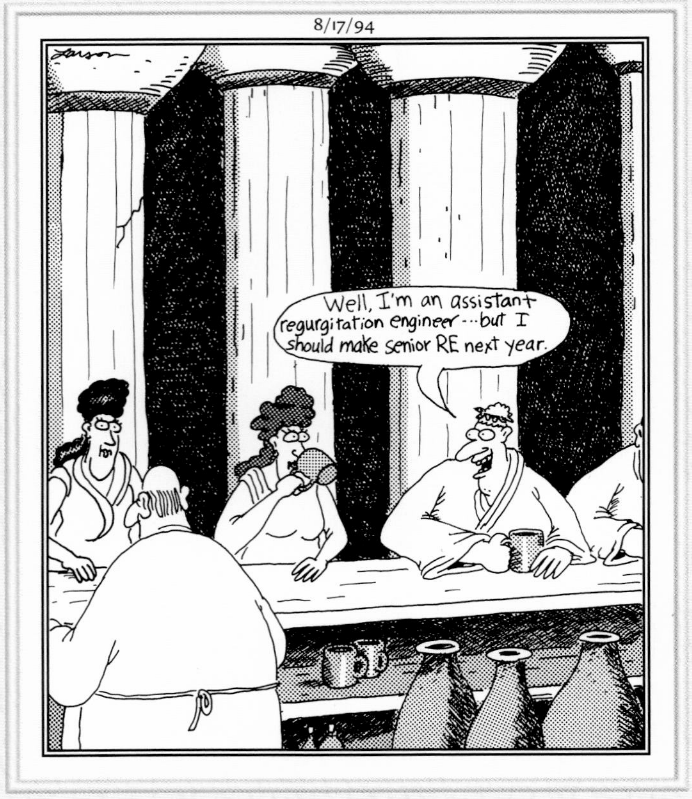
8/17/94
Larson
Well, I'm an assistant regurgitation engineer ··· but I should make senior RE next year.
In ancient Rome, it was tough for the guys who worked in the vomitoriums to get dates.

8/18/94

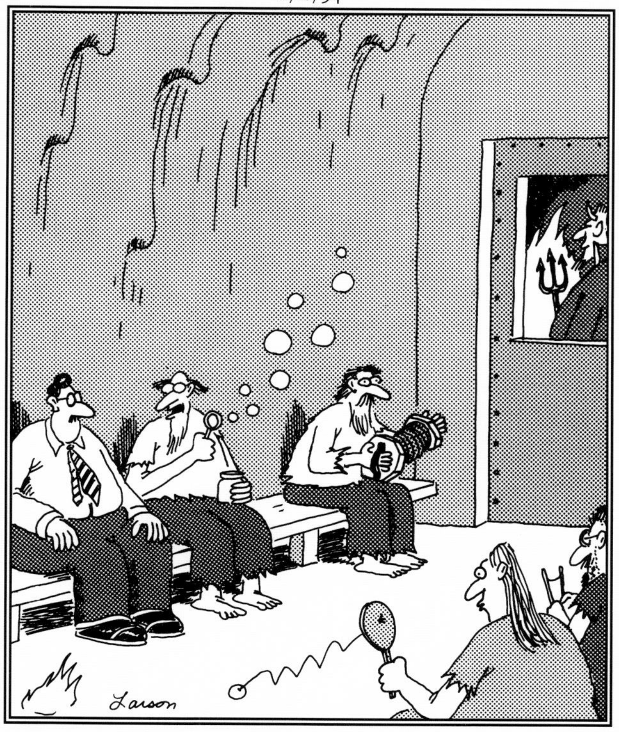

"Oh, they'll find something for you real soon. ... Me? I'm forever blowing bubbles."

8/22/94

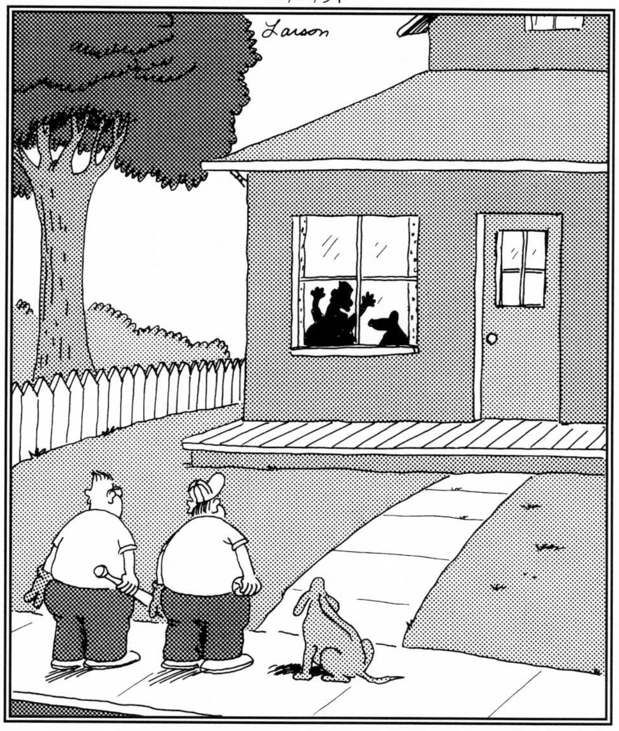

Every Saturday morning, while his playmates patiently waited, little Normy Bates would always take a few extra minutes to yell at his "dog."

8/23/94

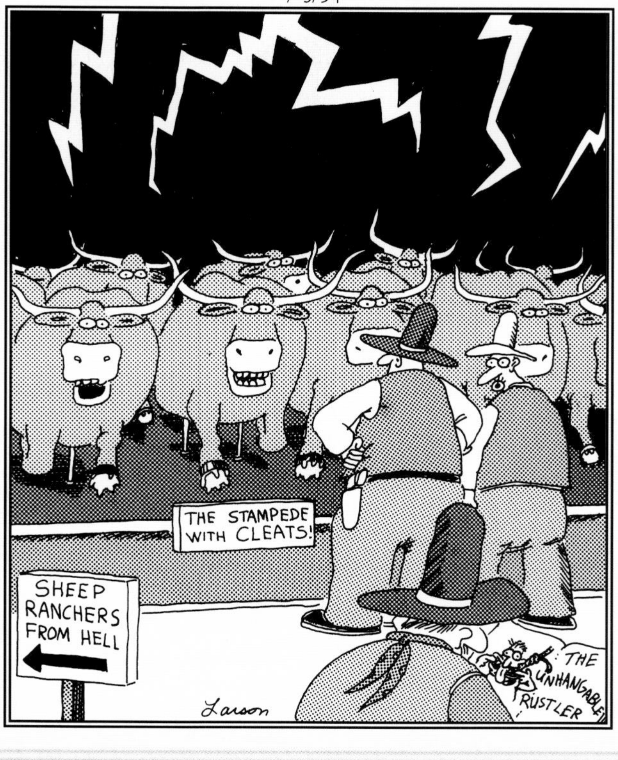
THE STAMPEDE WITH CLEATS!
SHEEP RANCHERS FROM HELL
THE UNHANGABLE RUSTLER

At the Cowboy Wax Museum

8/24/94

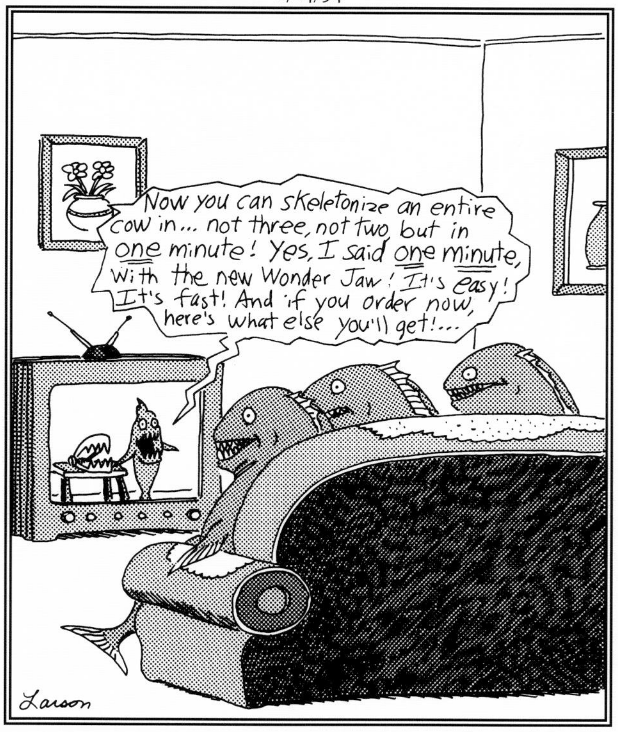
Now you can skeletonize an entire cow in... not three, not two, but in one minute! Yes, I said one minute, with the new Wonder Jaw! It's easy! It's fast! And if you order now, here's what else you'll get!...

8/15/94

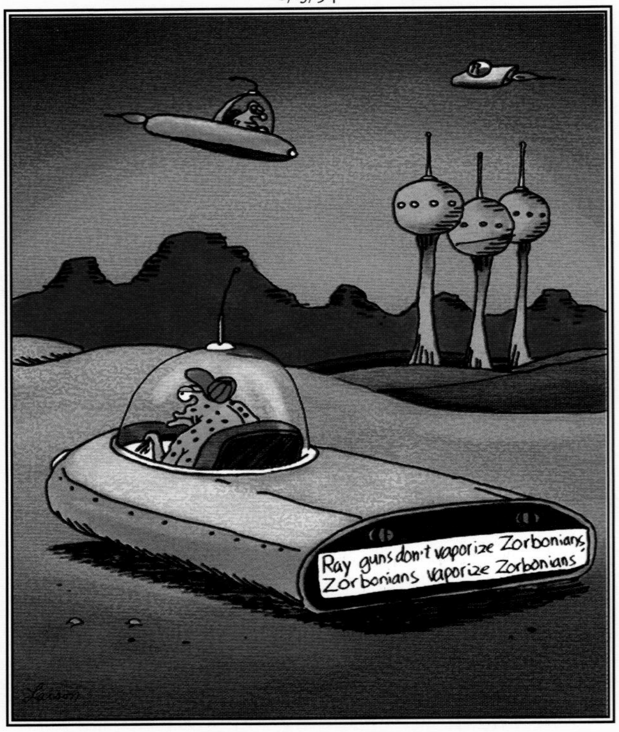
Ray guns don't vaporize Zorbonians,
Zorbonians vaporize Zorbonians

8/19/94

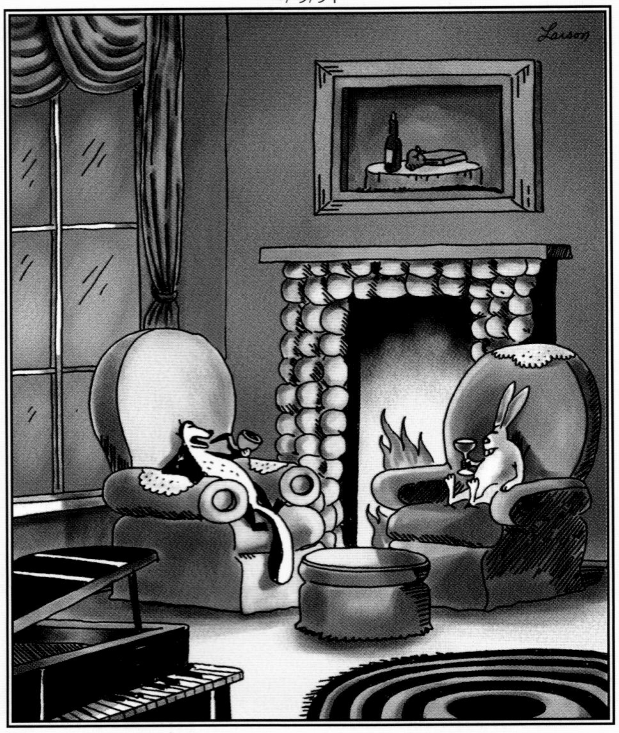

"I make no claims about all my success, Bernard. I never went to school, I never worked hard, and I'm not particularly bright. ... I'm just a lucky skunk, Bernard."

8/25/94

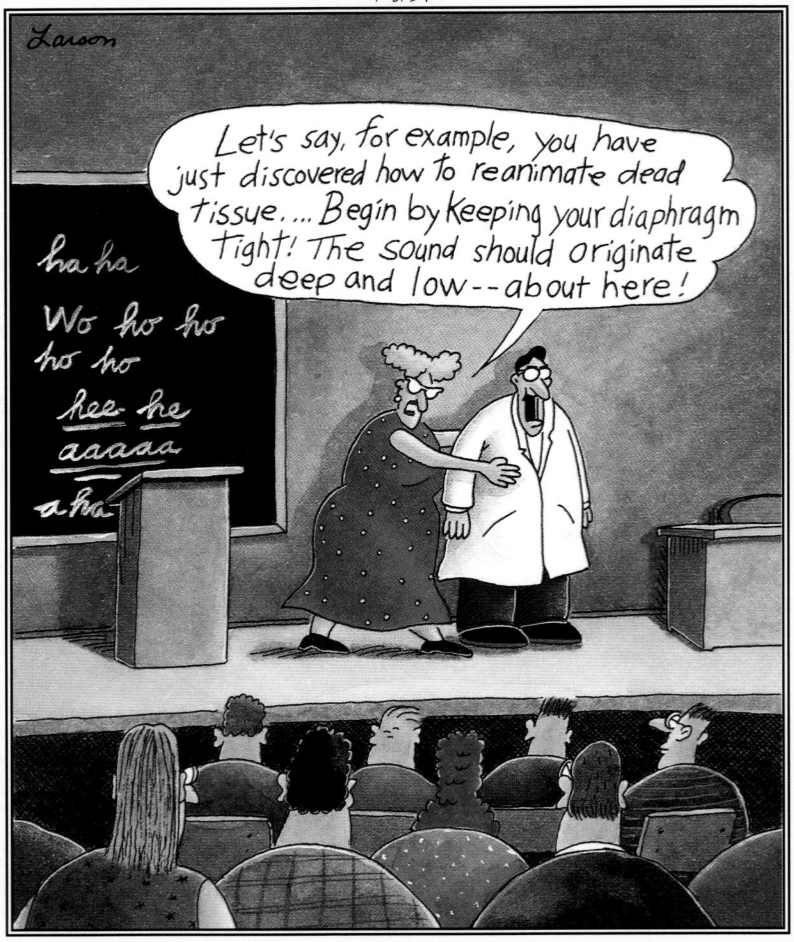
Let's say, for example, you have just discovered how to reanimate dead tissue.... Begin by keeping your diaphragm tight! The sound should originate deep and low--about here!
ha ha
Wo ho ho
ho ho
hee he
aaaaa
a-ha

In their final year, all research science students are required to take one semester of Maniacal Laughter.

8/26/94

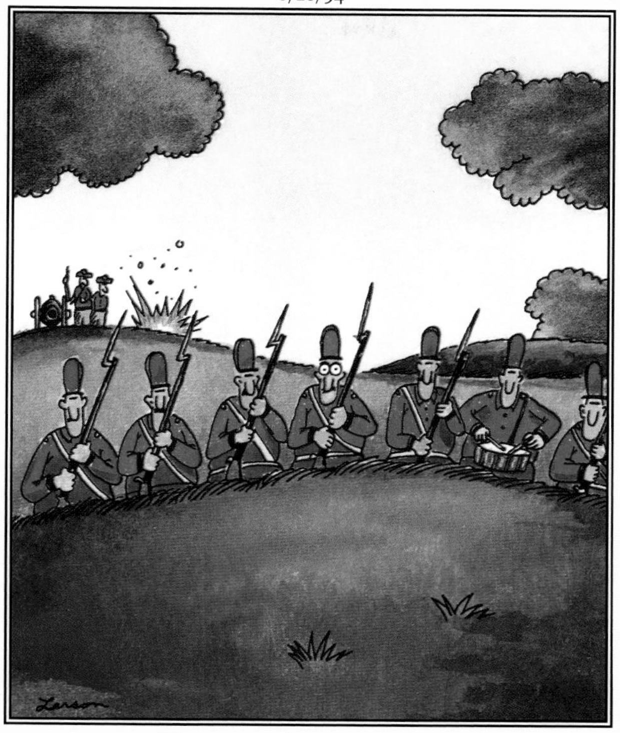
Larson

Bunker Hill, June 17, 1775: An unfortunate twist of fate for one young redcoat, Charles "Bugeyed" Bingham, was not knowing that the opposing American general had just uttered the historic command, "Don't fire until you see the whites of their eyes."

8/31/94

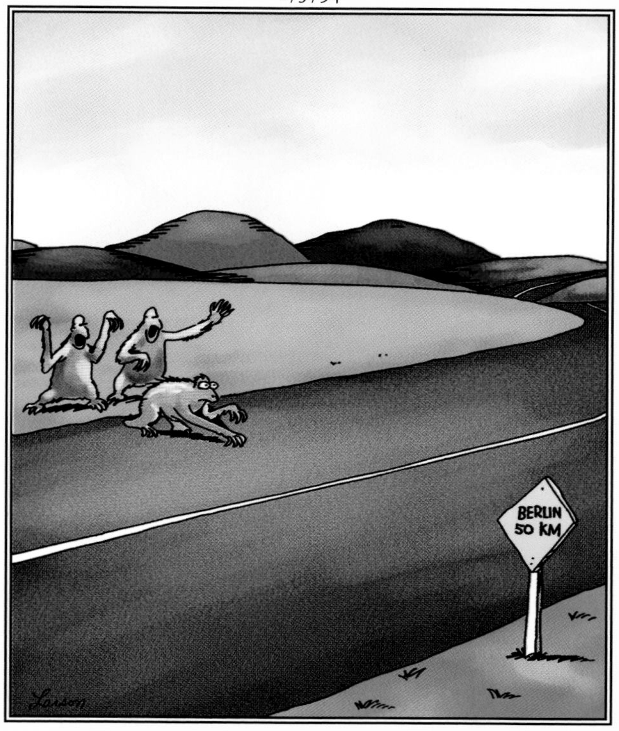
BERLIN
50 KM
Larson

In the longest hour of his life, Morty takes the dare of his sloth buddies and crosses the Autobahn.

8/30/94

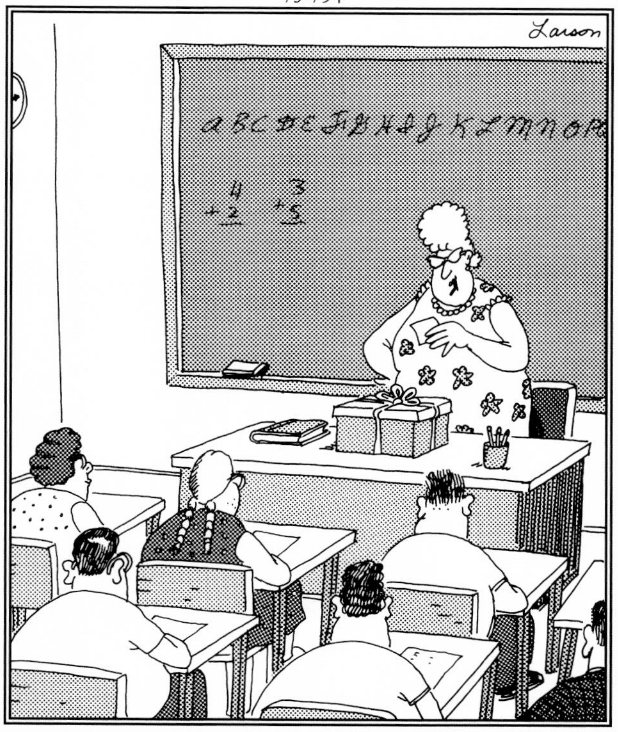
Larson

"And the note says: 'Dear classmates and Ms. Kilgore: Now that my family has moved away, I feel bad that I whined so much about being mistreated. Hope the contents of this box will set things right. Love, Pandora.'... How sweet."

8/29/94

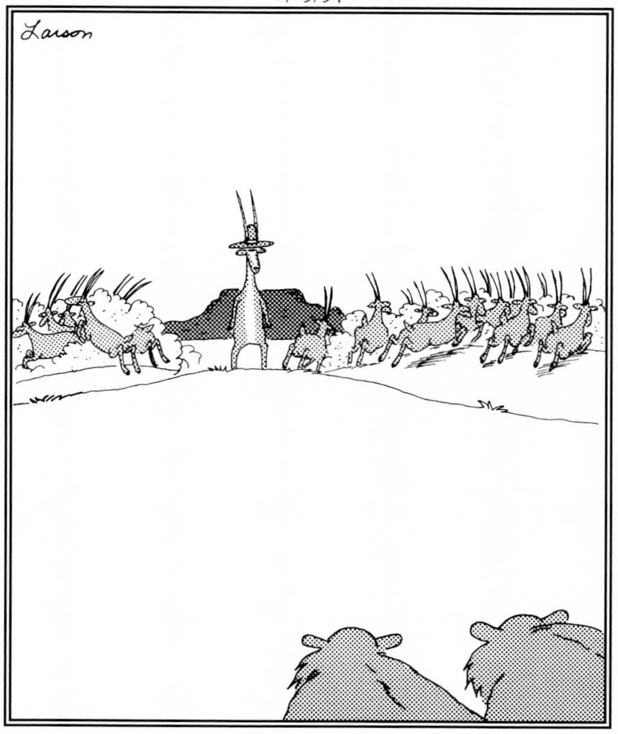
Larson

When the dust had settled, a lone figure was revealed standing on the small knoll. Yes, he, too, was a herd animal—but he was *through* running.

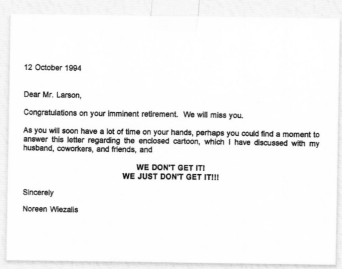

9/1/94

12 October 1994

Dear Mr. Larson,

Congratulations on your imminent retirement. We will miss you.

As you will soon have a lot of time on your hands, perhaps you could find a moment to answer this letter regarding the enclosed cartoon, which I have discussed with my husband, coworkers, and friends, and

**WE DON'T GET IT!
WE JUST DON'T GET IT!!!**

Sincerely

Noreen Wiezalis

Editor's note: The aliens here have their own religious symbol, and they've attached it to the rear of their flying saucer.

9/2/94

The often romanticized image of
cowboys and aliens

9/5/94

"We're *not* going to the mountains, so shut up
and let's go! ... Most kids would count their
lucky stars that every vacation their folks took
'em to the beach!"

9/12/94

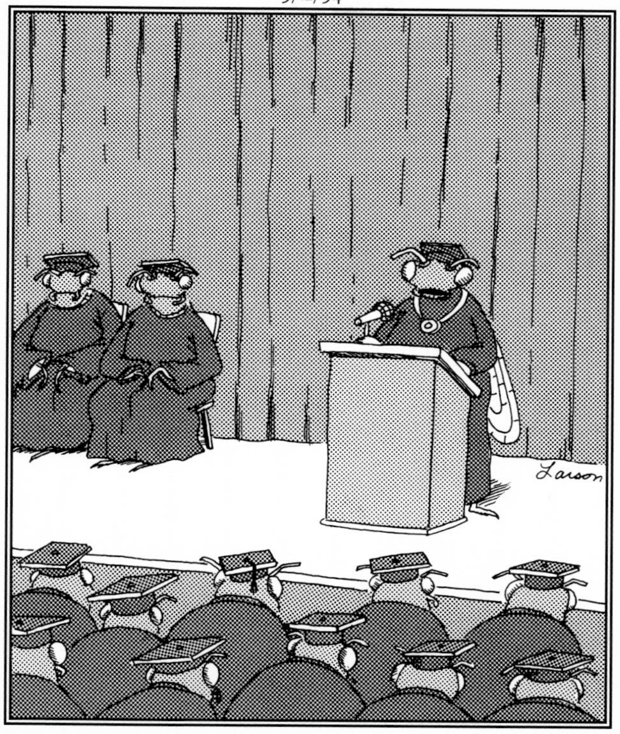

"And so, as you enter the adult phase of your life, you will thank God that these past 17 years of being stuck in the ground and unable to move are finally over. ... Congratulations, cicadas of '94!"

9/15/94

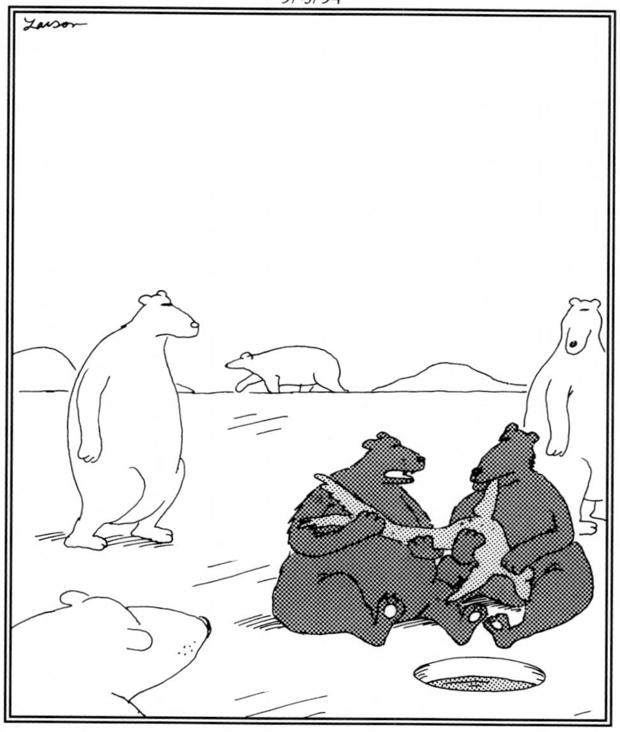

"Don't eat the flippers, Zeke, or they'll know we're tourists."

9/6/94

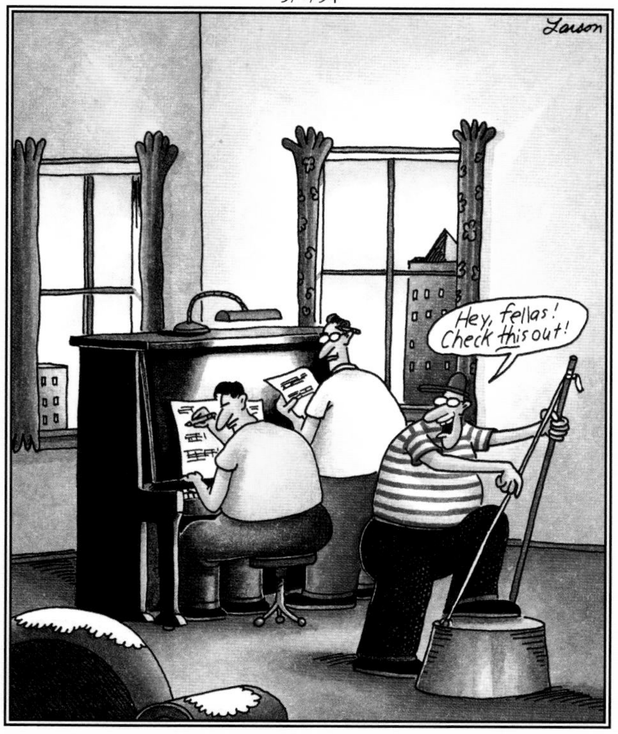
Hey, fellas! Check this out!

Throughout their songwriting careers, the Gershwins rarely discussed their younger brother, Nathan, who played gutbucket.

9/7/94

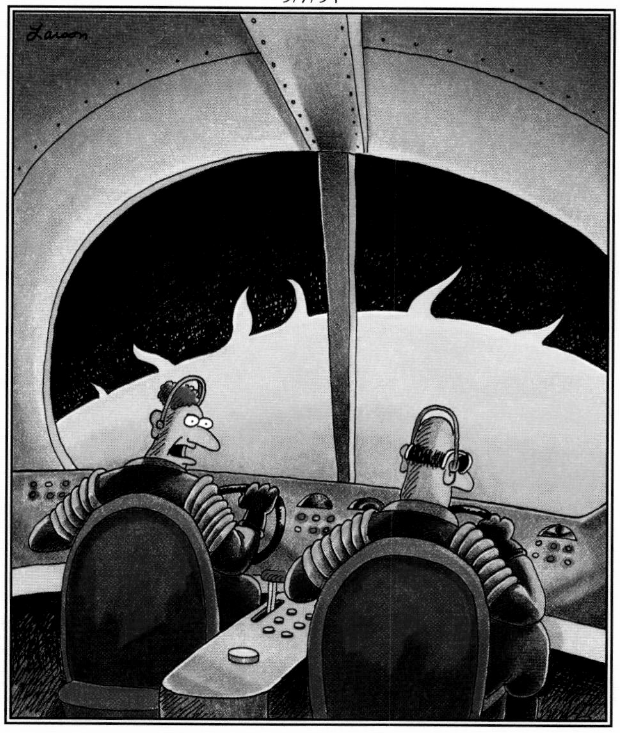

"It's no good, Dawson! We're being sucked in by the sun's gravitational field and there's nothing we can do! ... And, let me add, those are my sunglasses you're wearing!"

9/8/94

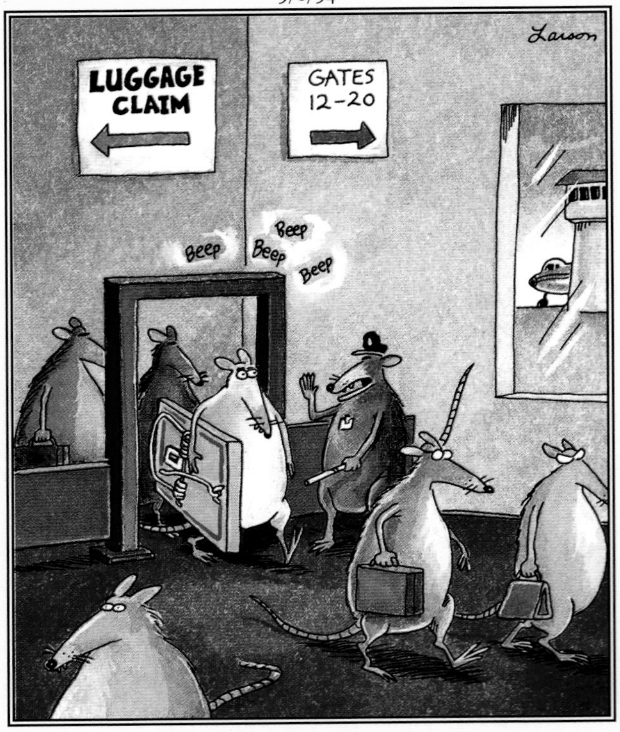
LUGGAGE CLAIM
GATES 12–20
Beep
Beep
Beep
Beep
Larson

"Whoa whoa whoa! ... You'll have to go back and walk through again."

9/9/94

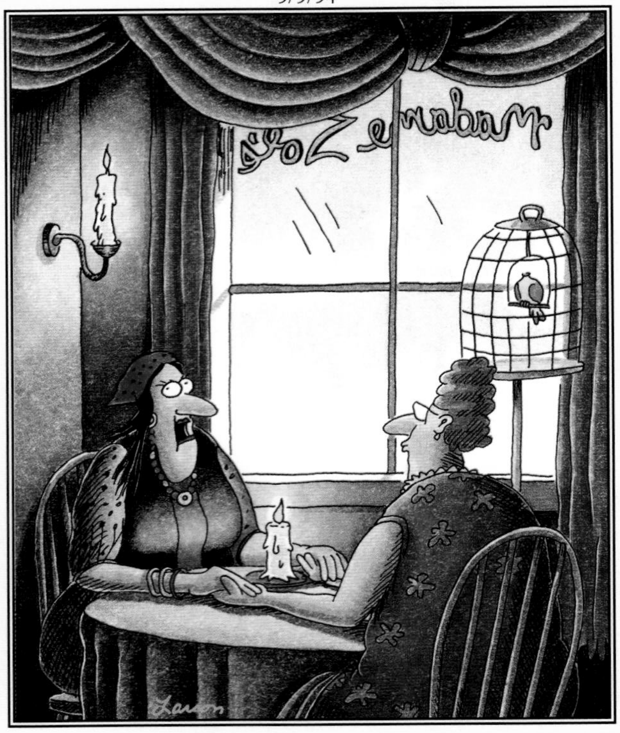
Larson

"Bootsy! ... Boooooooootsy! ... We are calling you from the world of the living! ... Meowwww! ... Are you there, Bootsy? ... Give us a sign!"

9/14/94

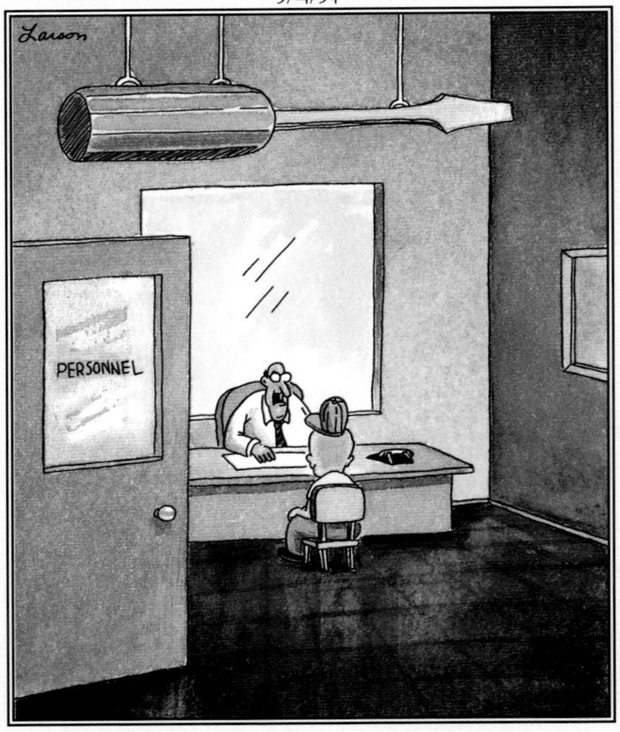
Larson
PERSONNEL

"The problem, Mr. Fudd, is that you've been having a subliminal effect on everyone in the factory. We're proud of our product, Mr. Fudd, and there's no company in the world that builds a finer skwoo dwivuh. ... Dang! Now you got *me* doing it!"

9/13/94

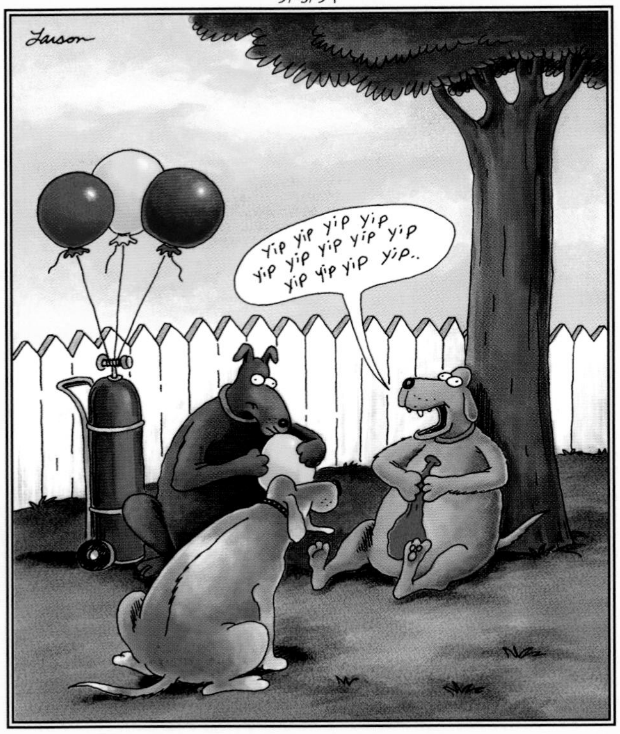
Larson
Yip yip yip yip
yip yip yip yip yip
yip yip yip yip yip..

Big dogs having fun with helium

9/16/94

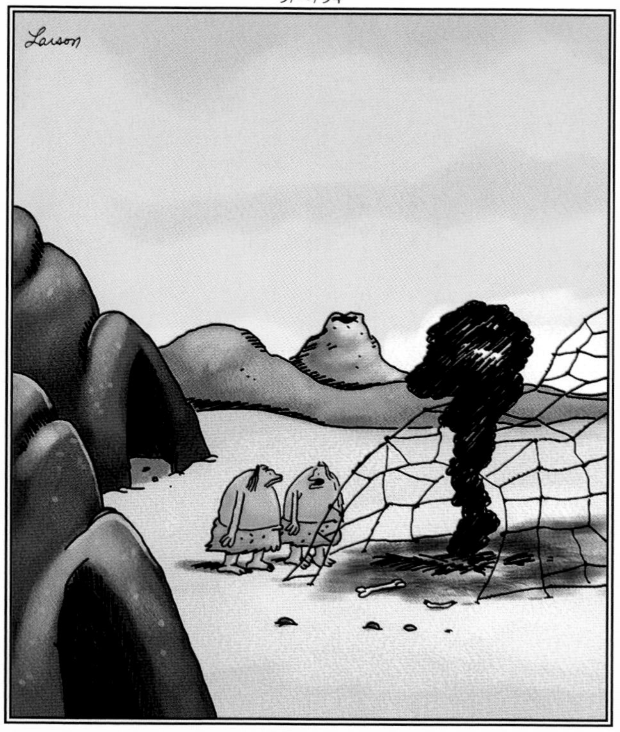
Larson

"Boy, you wiped out, Kumba. ...
Nothing left but rebar."

9/19/94

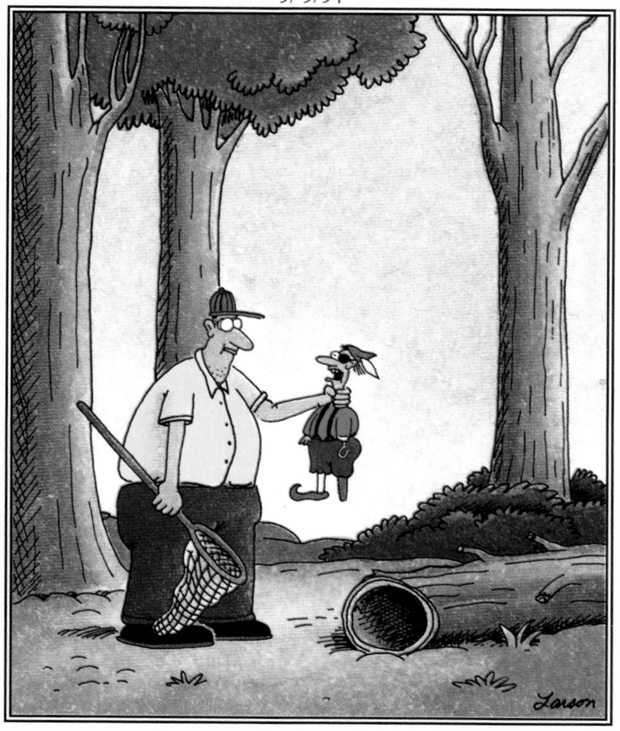
Larson

"Well, lad, you caught me fair and square. ...
But truthfully, as far as leprechauns go, I've
never been considered all that lucky."

9/20/94

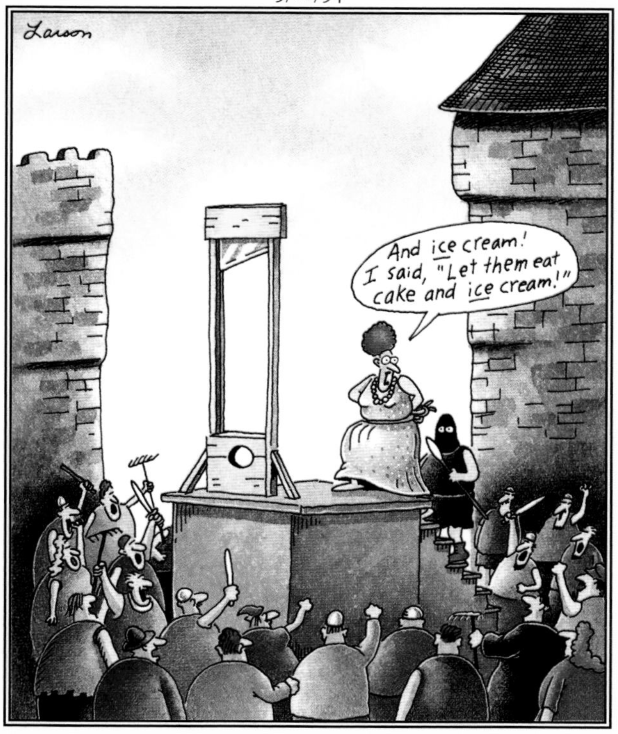
Larson
And ice cream! I said, "Let them eat cake and ice cream!"

Marie Antoinette's last-ditch effort
to save her head.

9/21/94

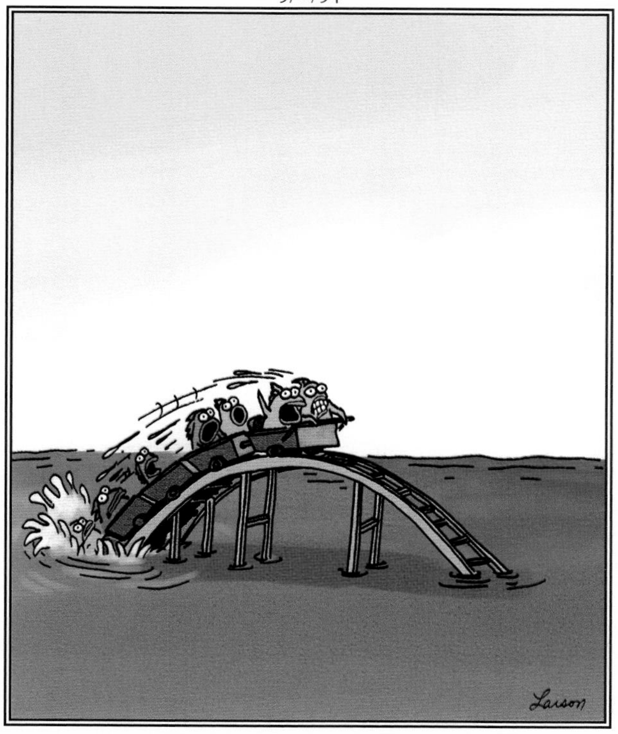
Larson

Fish thrill rides

9/22/94

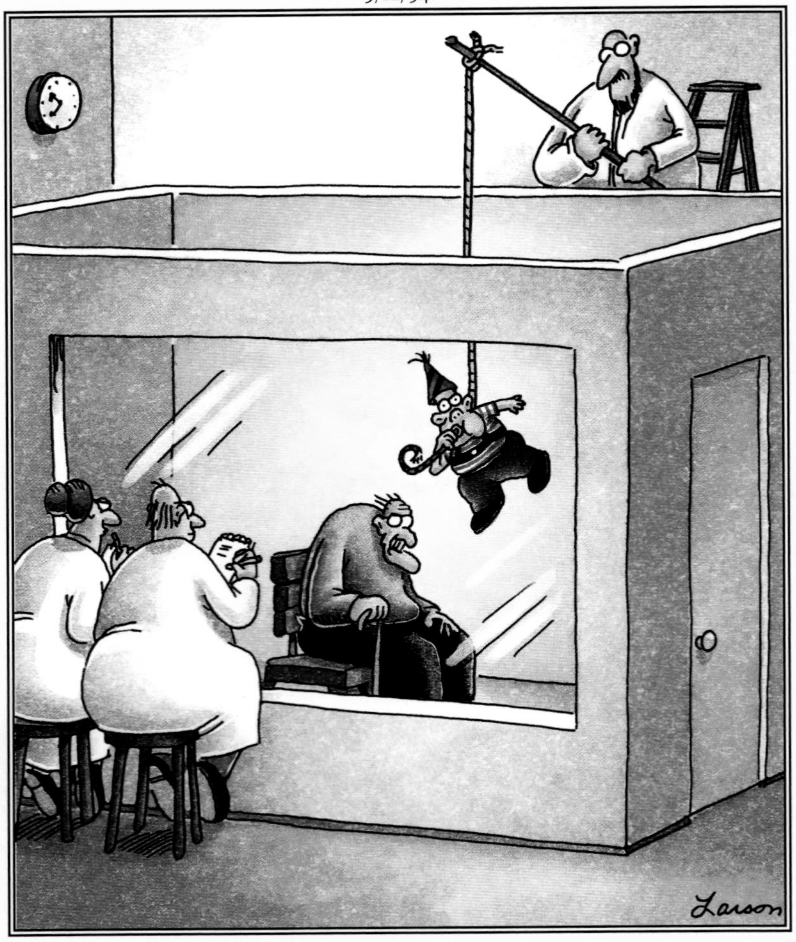
Larson

At the Crabbiness Research Institute

9/23/94

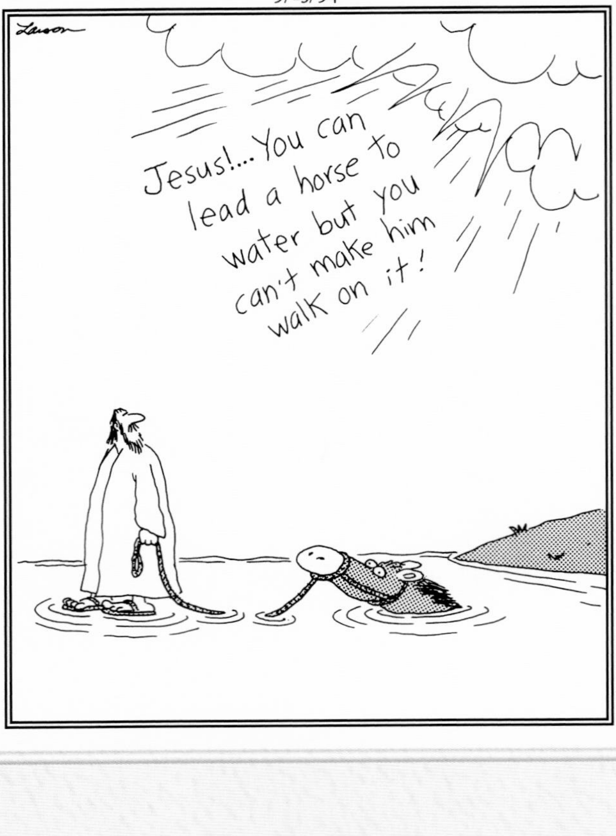
Larson
Jesus!... You can lead a horse to water but you can't make him walk on it!

9/28/94

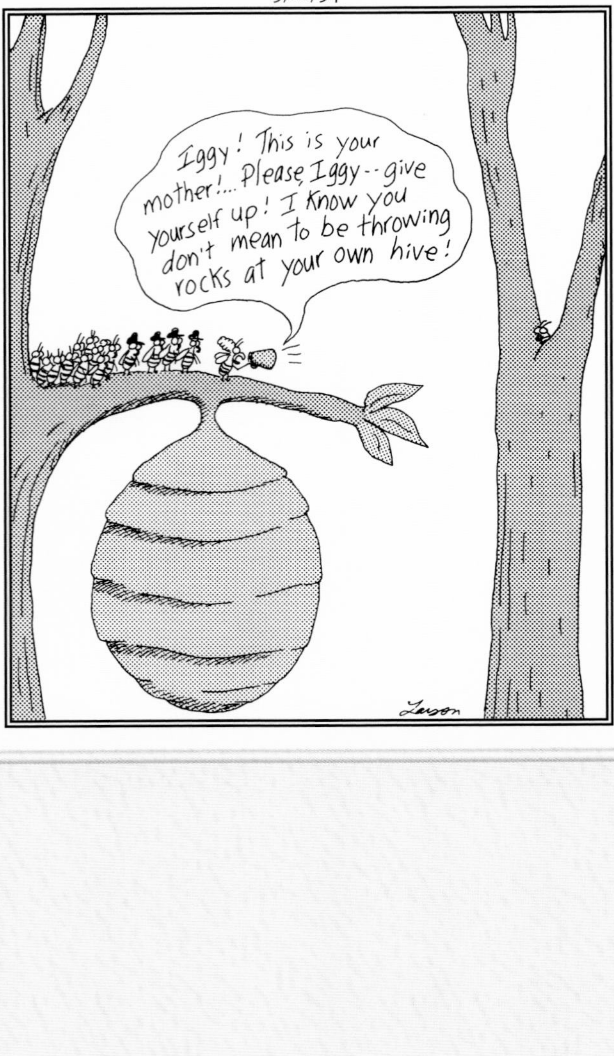
Iggy! This is your mother!... Please, Iggy--give yourself up! I know you don't mean to be throwing rocks at your own hive!
Larson

9/29/94

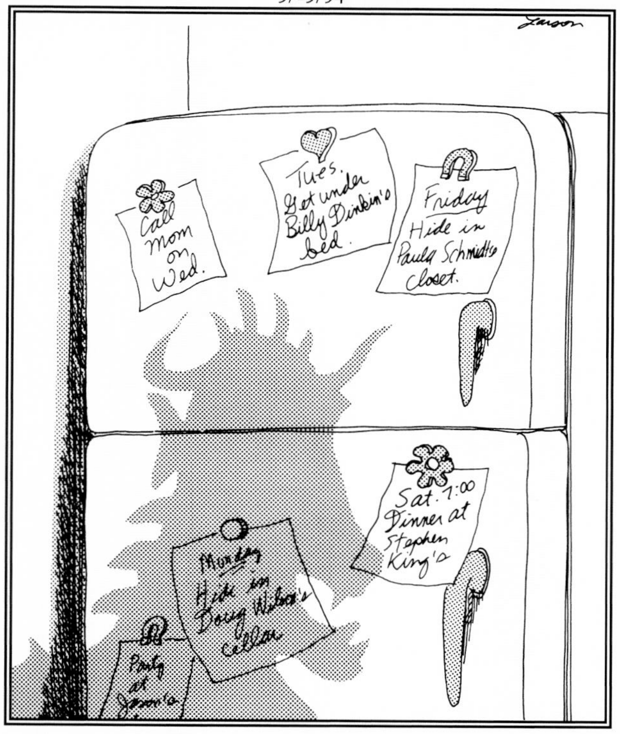
Larson
Call mom on Wed.
Tue's. Get under Billy Dinkin's bed.
Friday Hide in Paula Schmidt's closet.
Sat. 7:00 Dinner at Stephen King's
Monday Hide in Doug Wilson's cellar

On monster refrigerators

9/30/94

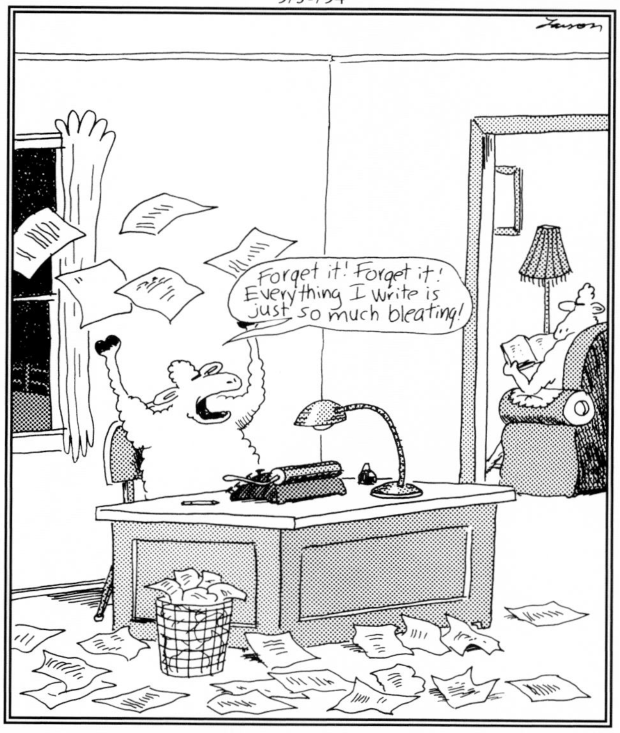
Larson
Forget it! Forget it! Everything I write is just so much bleating!

Sheep authors

9/26/94

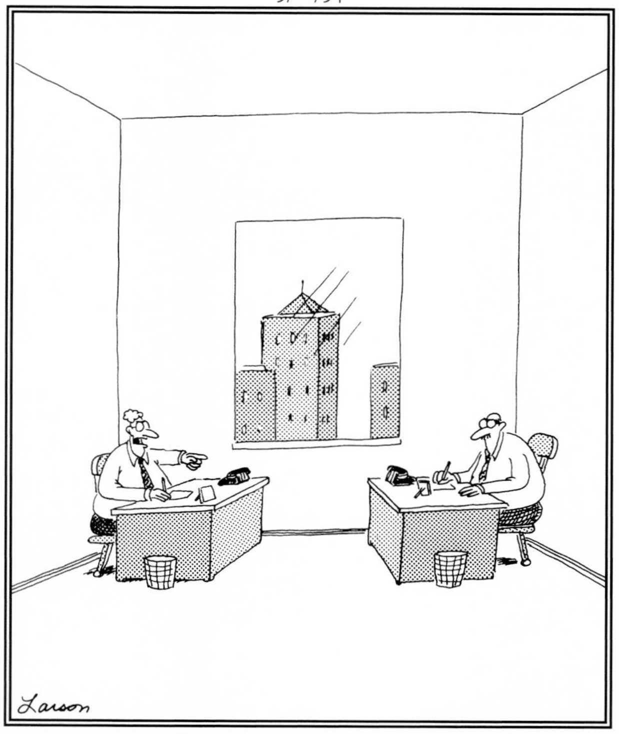
Larson

"One day, Wilson, *I'll* be sitting at that desk."

9/27/94

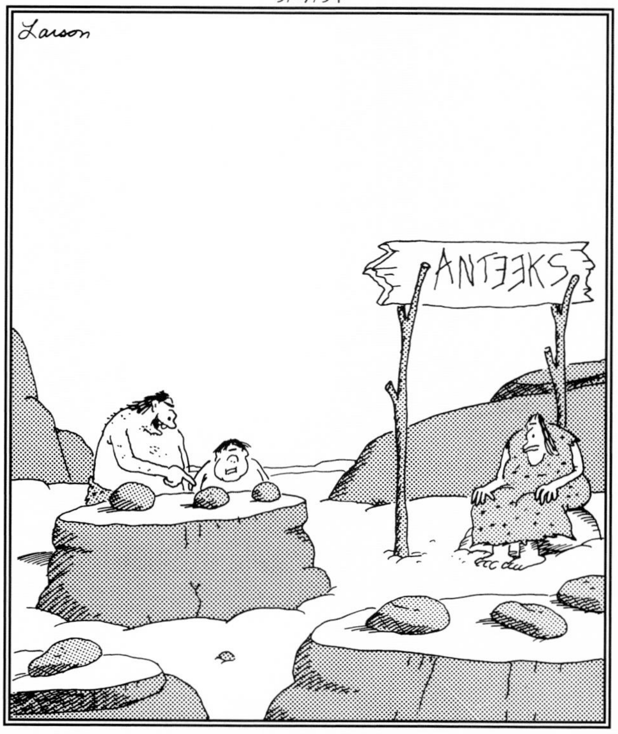
Larson
ANTƎƎKS

"Oh my gosh! You know what that is, Mooky? ...
My dad had one when I was a kid!"

10/3/94

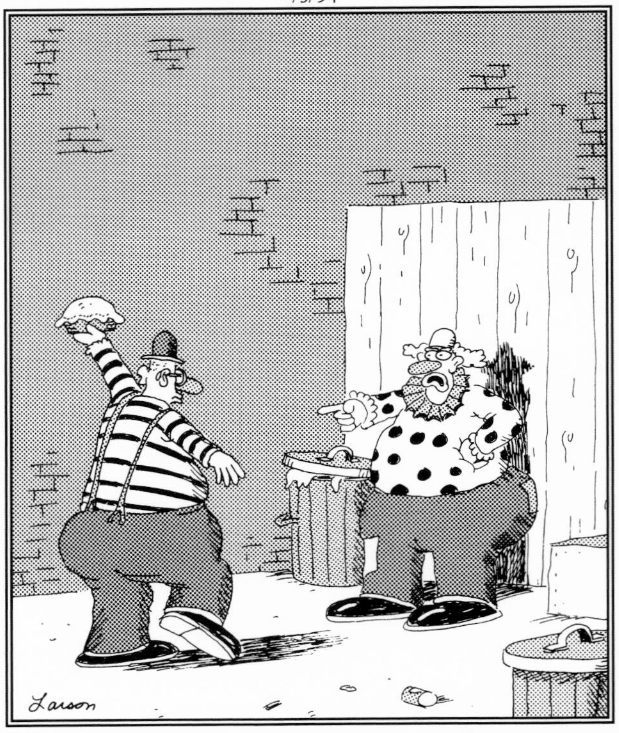

"I wouldn't do that, Spunky—I have friends in pie places."

Cartoonist's note: Above is my own nominee for the worst cartoon I ever drew. (I still cringe.)
—Gary Larson

10/6/94

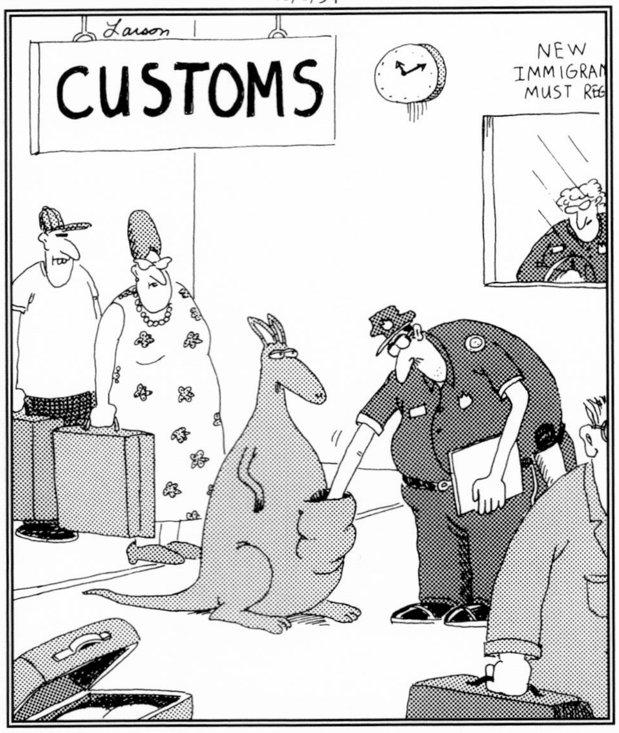
CUSTOMS
NEW
IMMIGRAN
MUST REG

Marv remained calm. No matter how thoroughly they searched, the agents never discovered his "secret" pocket.

10/4/94

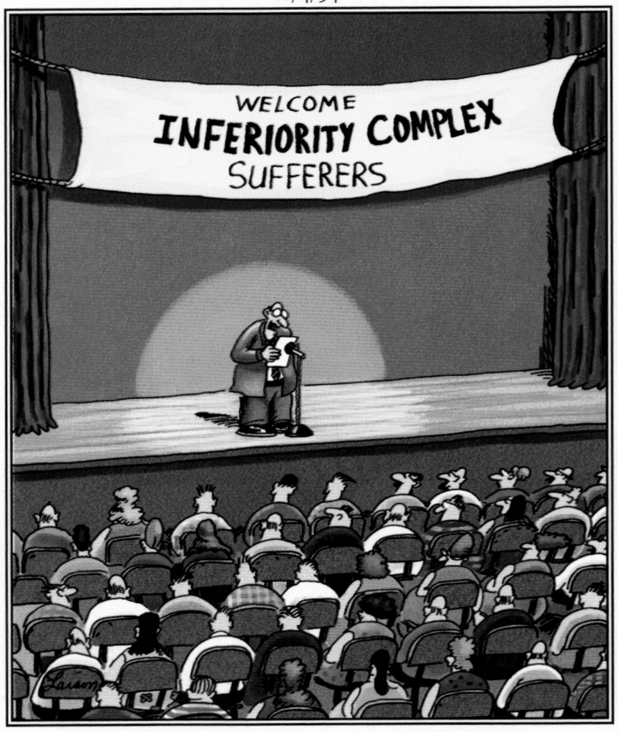
WELCOME
INFERIORITY COMPLEX
SUFFERERS

"But before we begin, this announcement: Mr. Johnson! Mr. Frank Johnson! ... If you're out there, the conference organizers would like you to know that you were never actually invited."

10/5/94

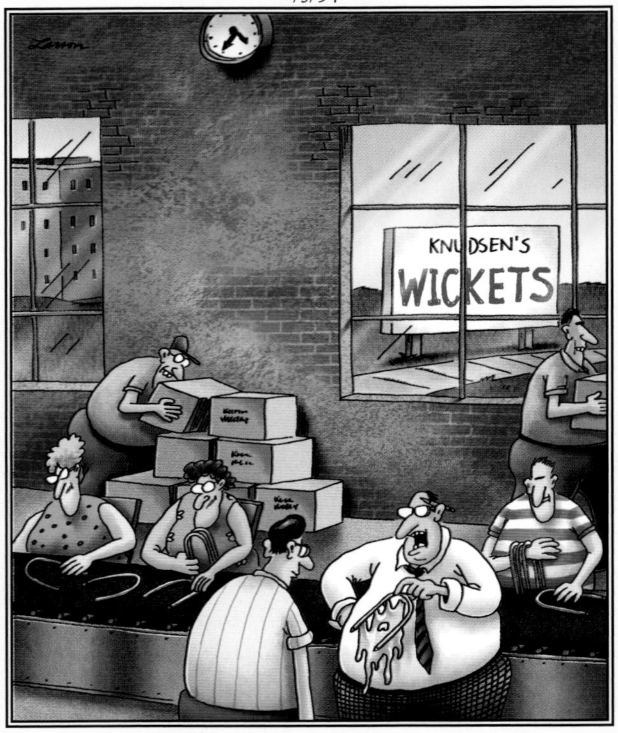
KNUDSEN'S
WICKETS

"Well, it came from your division, Sanders, and as you can see, it's covered with honey and molasses! ... You know what that makes this, Sanders?"

10/7/94

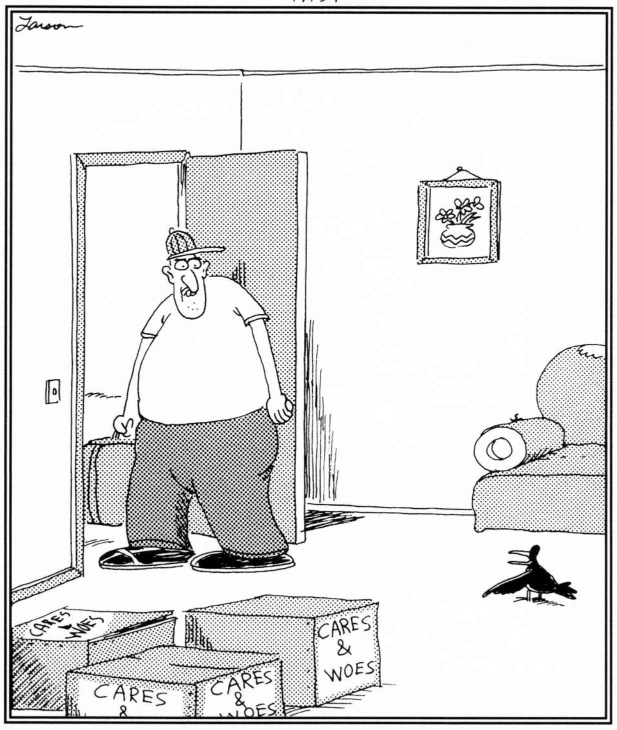
Larson
CARES & WOES
CARES & WOES
CARES
CARES & WOES
CARES & WOES

"Hey hey hey! ... Before you go, pack up this depressing garbage of yours and get it out of here!"

10/14/94

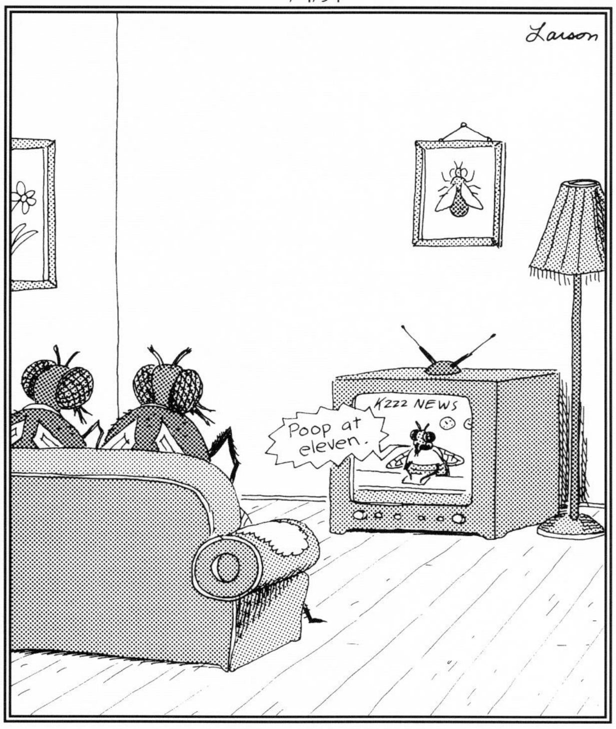
Larson
KZZZ NEWS
Poop at eleven.

10/10/94

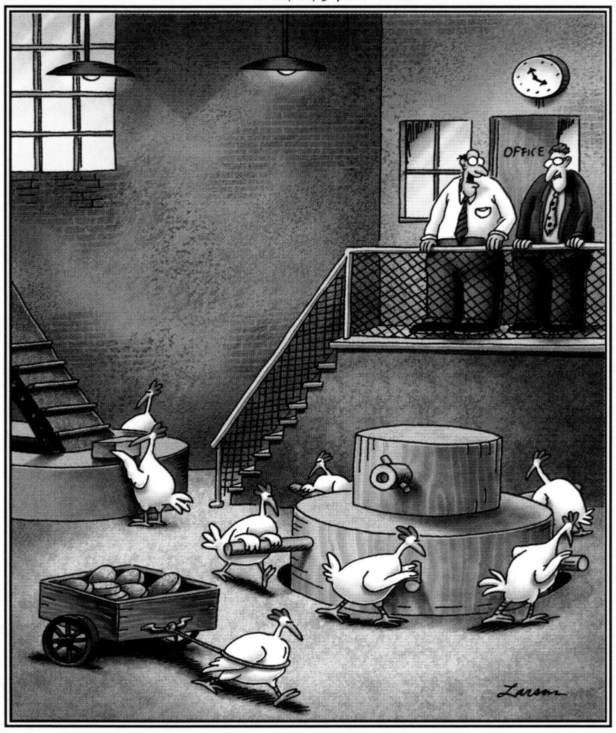
OFFICE
Larson

"Oh, yeah! They work real hard, all day long, seven days a week! ... And here's the best part—*for chicken feed!*"

10/13/94

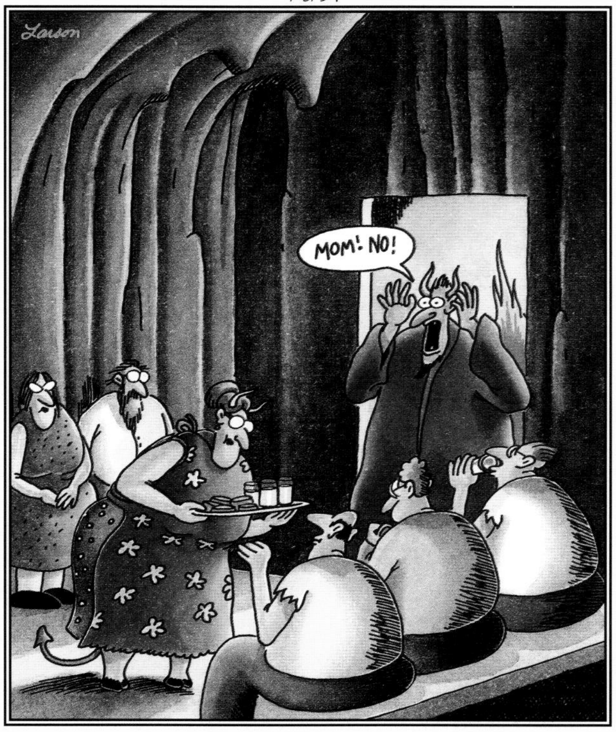
Larson
MOM! NO!

Despite his repeated efforts to explain things to her, Satan could never dissuade his mother from offering cookies and milk to the accursed.

10/11/94

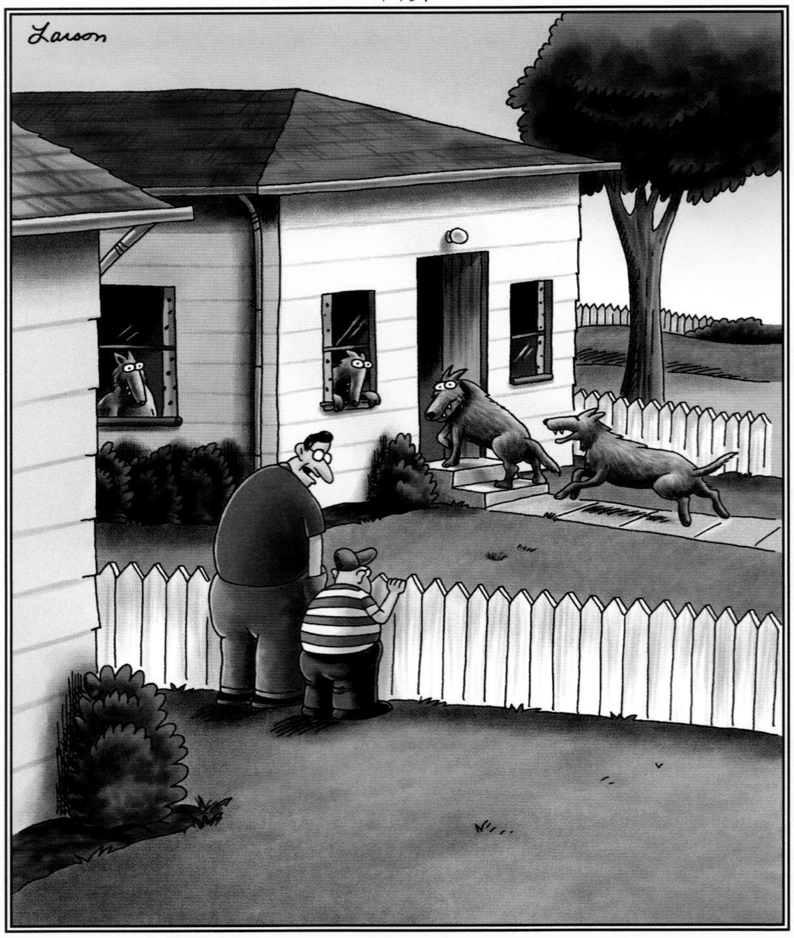

"I know you miss the Wainwrights, Bobby, but they were weak and stupid people—and that's why we have wolves and other large predators."

10/19/94

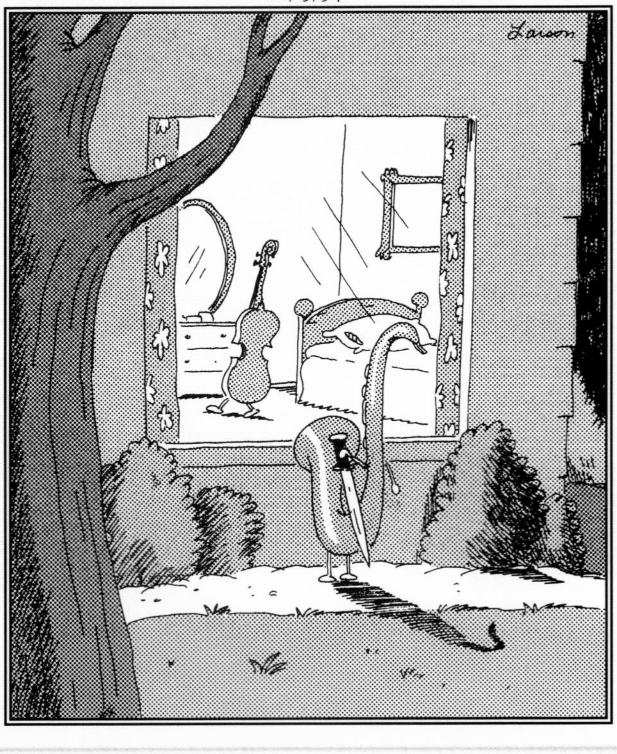

Scene from *Fiddle Attraction*

10/21/94

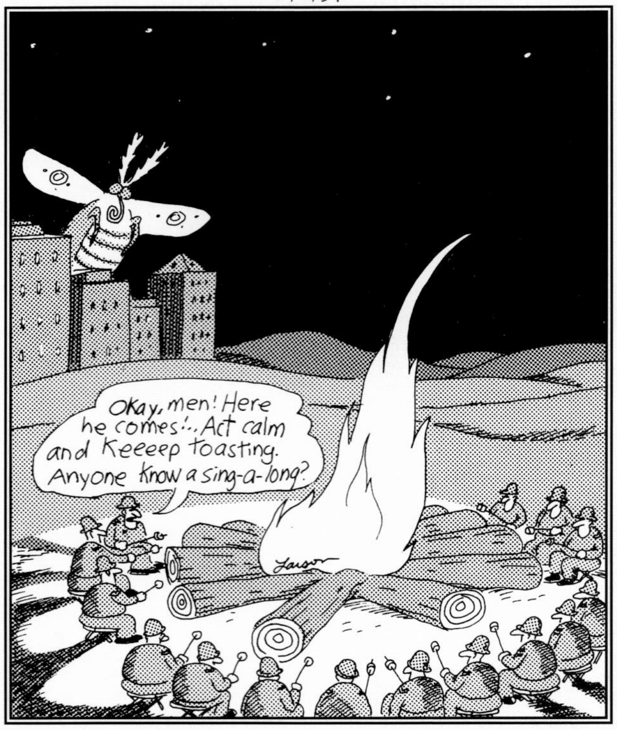
Okay, men! Here he comes!...Act calm and Keeeep toasting. Anyone know a sing-a-long?

The Army's last-ditch effort to destroy Mothra

10/12/94

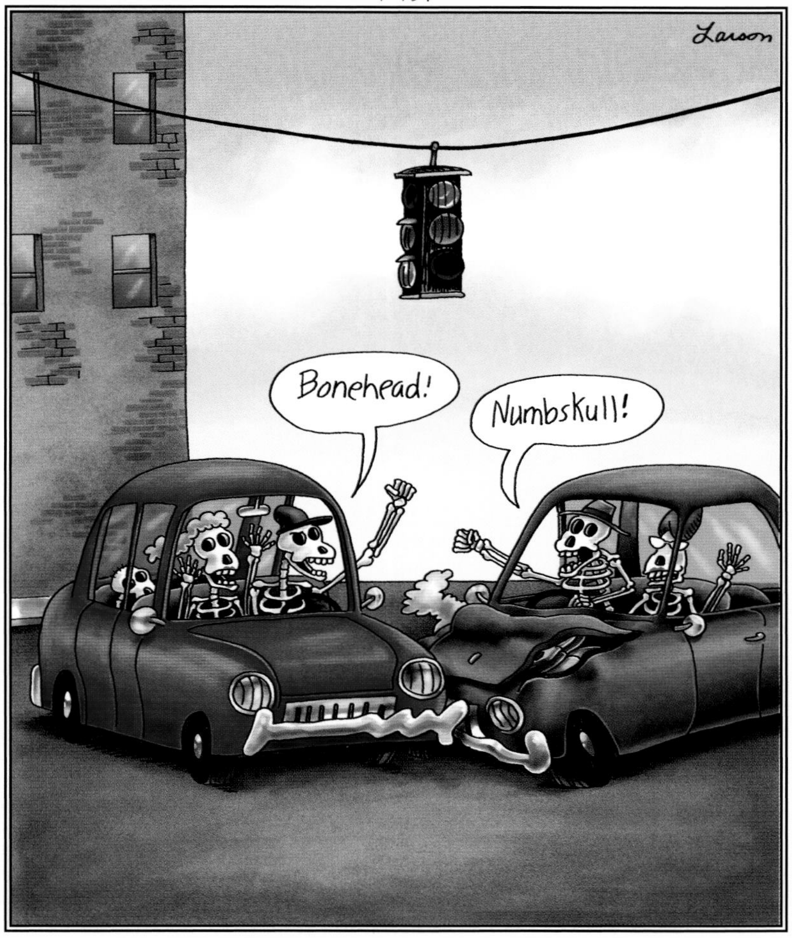
Bonehead!
Numbskull!

10/28/94

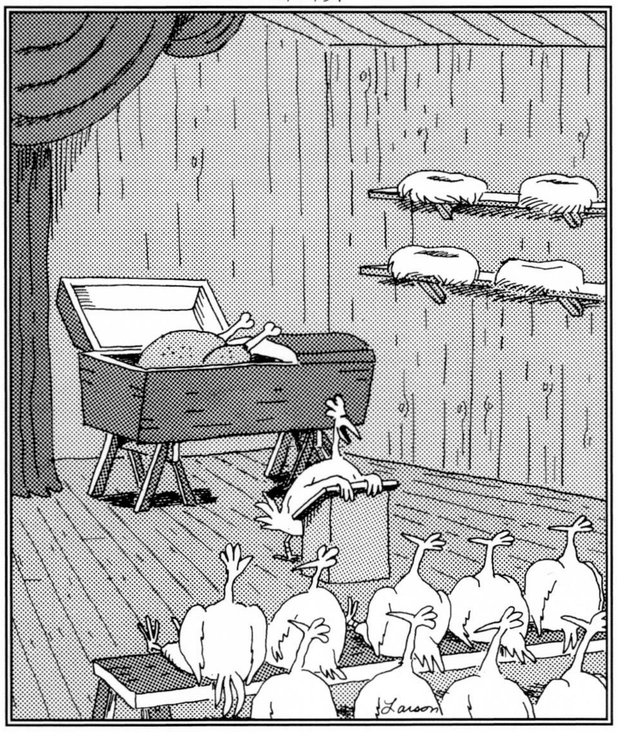

"And yes, Norman *was* beheaded, cleaned, and plucked. ... But we all know Norman's wacky sense of humor, and we can take comfort knowing he would've gotten a kick out of this."

10/31/94

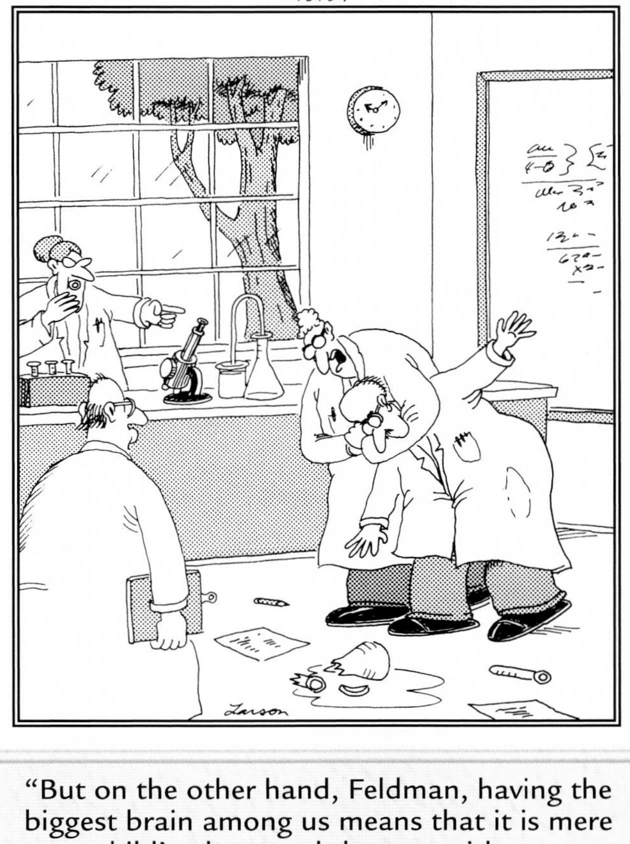

"But on the other hand, Feldman, having the biggest brain among us means that it is mere child's play to subdue you with an ordinary headlock!"

10/18/94

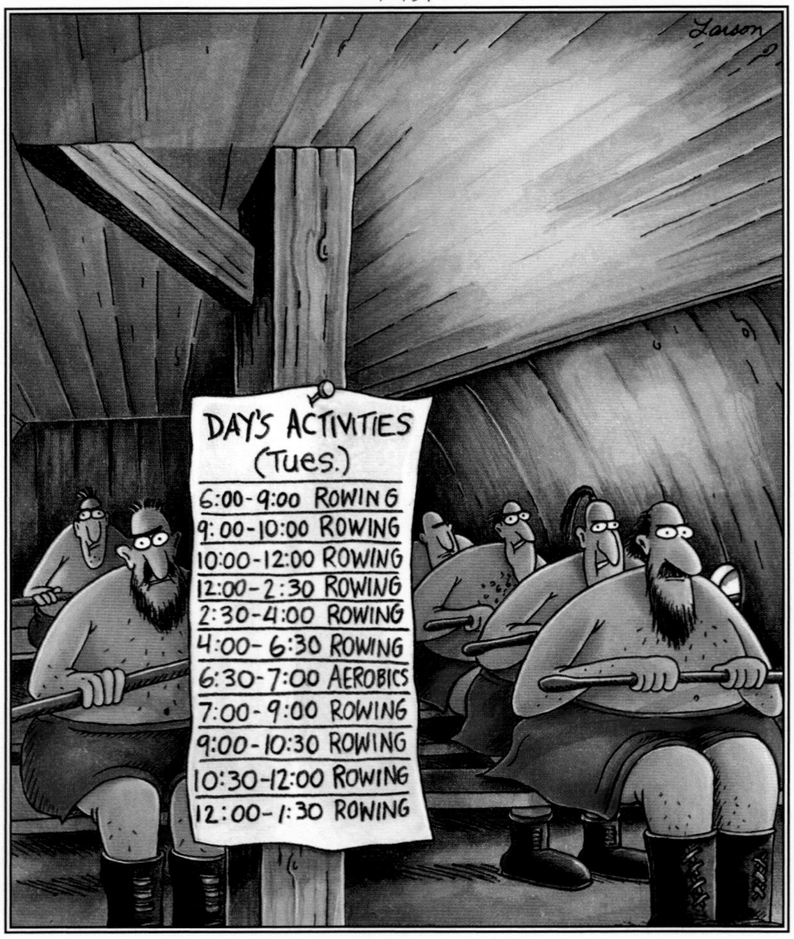
Larson
DAY'S ACTIVITIES
(Tues.)
6:00-9:00 ROWING
9:00-10:00 ROWING
10:00-12:00 ROWING
12:00-2:30 ROWING
2:30-4:00 ROWING
4:00-6:30 ROWING
6:30-7:00 AEROBICS
7:00-9:00 ROWING
9:00-10:30 ROWING
10:30-12:00 ROWING
12:00-1:30 ROWING

Slave-ship daily schedules

10/17/94

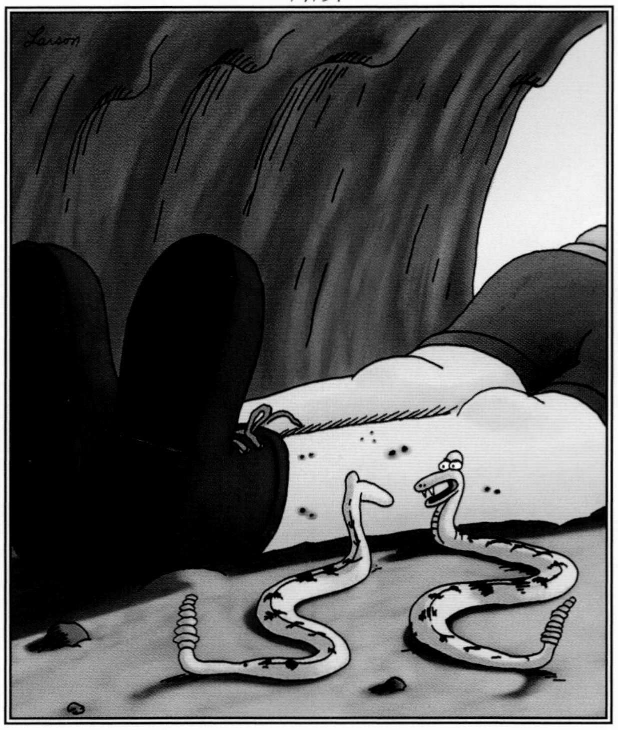
Larson

"Excuse me? *Excuse* me? ... I believe the biggest set of fang marks belongs to *me,* my friend!"

10/20/94

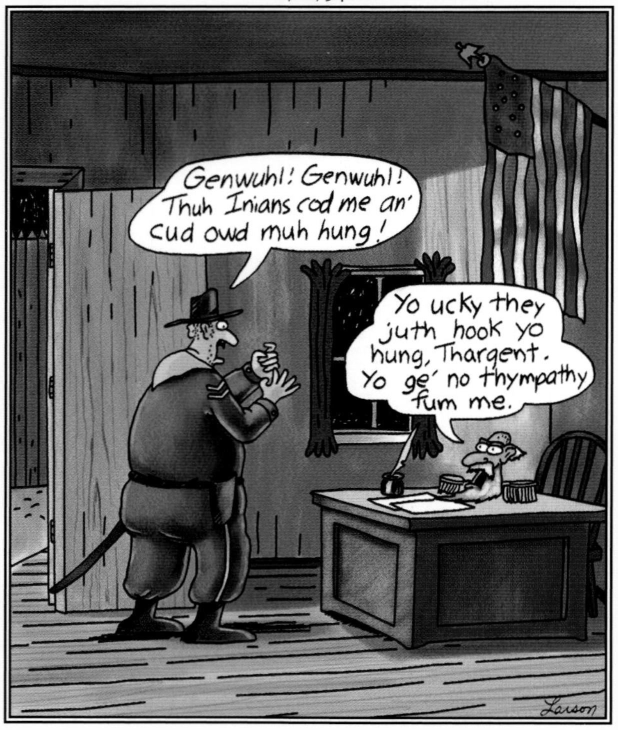
Genwuhl! Genwuhl! Thuh Inians cod me an' cud owd muh hung!
Yo ucky they juth hook yo hung, Thargent. Yo ge' no thympathy fum me.
Larson

Life in the Old Weth

10/24/94

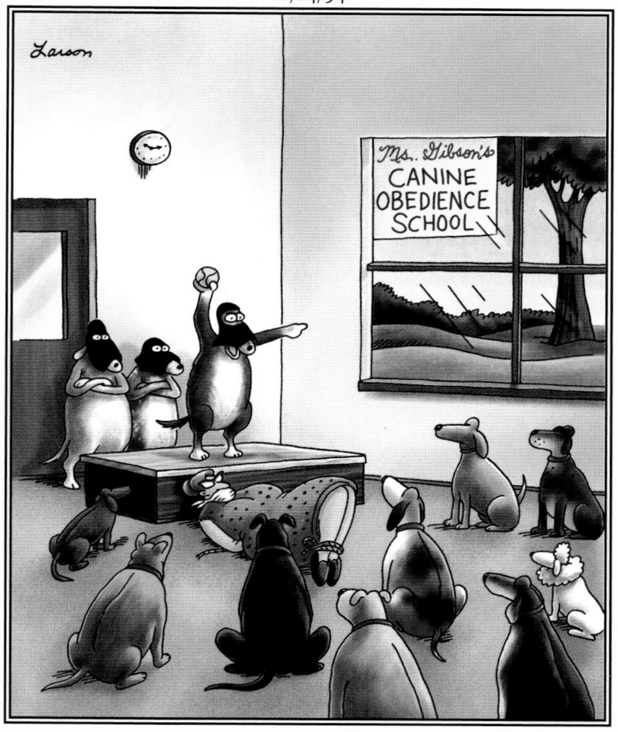
Larson
Ms. Gibson's
CANINE
OBEDIENCE
SCHOOL

"And I say we go outside and we *play with this ball!*"

10/25/94

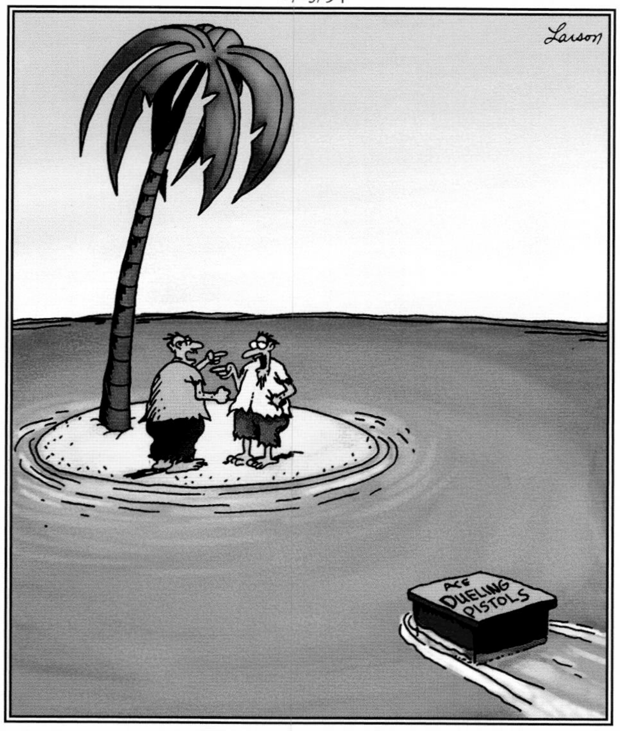
Larson
ACE
DUELING
PISTOLS

The gods play with Ted and Jerry

10/26/94

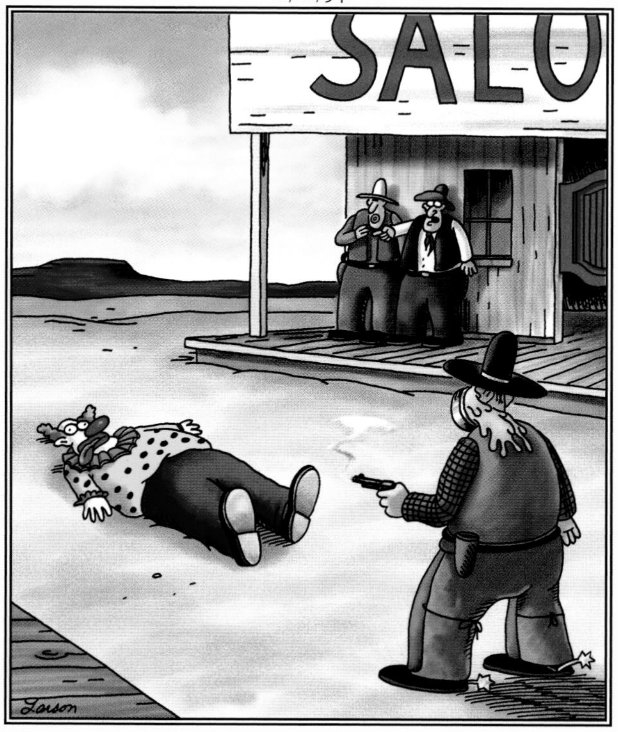
SALO
Larson

It was over. But the way the townsfolk called it, neither man was a clear winner.

10/27/94

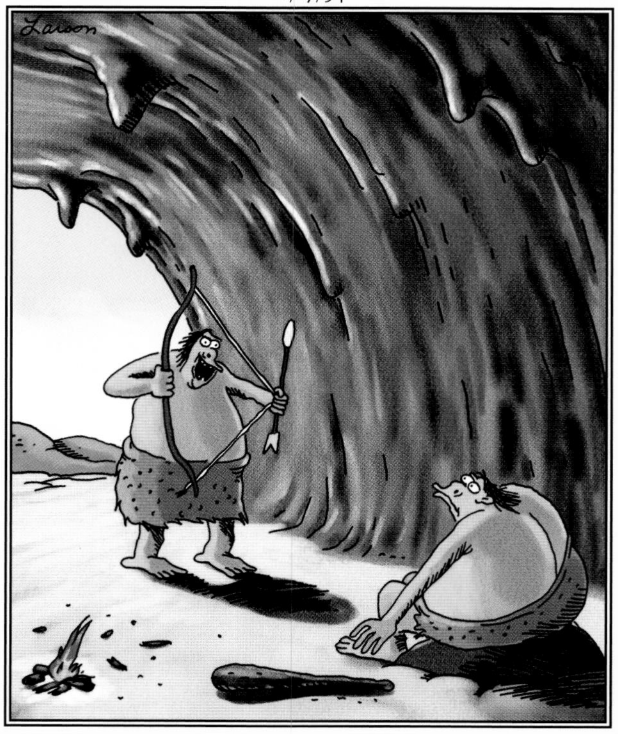
Larson

"Uh, uh, uh—I wouldn't do that, Thorg. I know how to use this thing."

11/1/94

Mrs. Gibson's
PRESERVES
La Brea
Tar Pits

11/2/94

That does it...
I'm gonna steer.

11/3/94

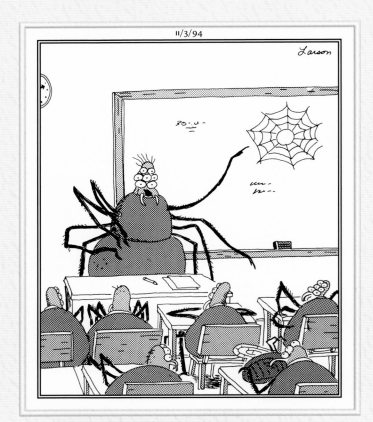

"Now what theorem applies to this ... Douglas! Is that a fly you're sucking on? Well, I hope you brought enough for everyone!"

11/7/94

STORE

"Whoa! Here we go again! ...'Pony Express Rider Walks into Workplace, Starts Shooting Every Horse in Sight.'"

11/4/94

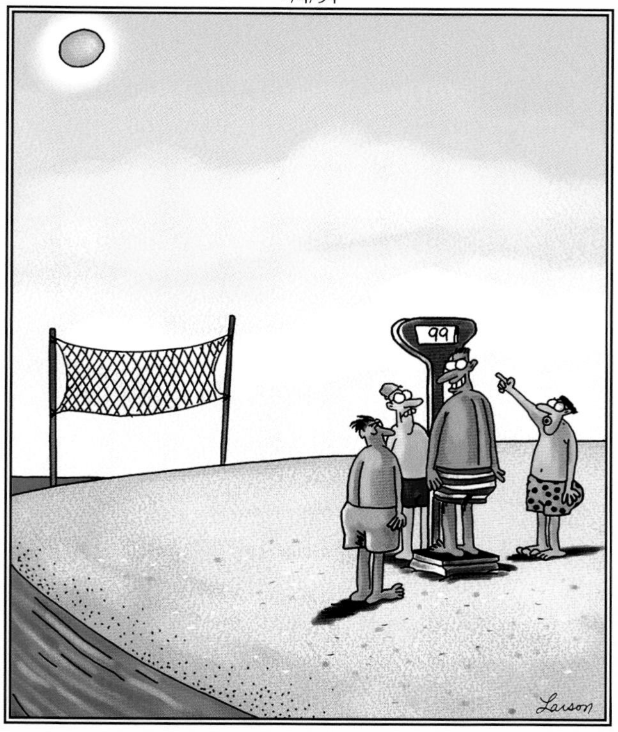
99
Larson

By secretly working out for many months, Irwin became the envy of all the 98-pound weaklings.

11/8/94

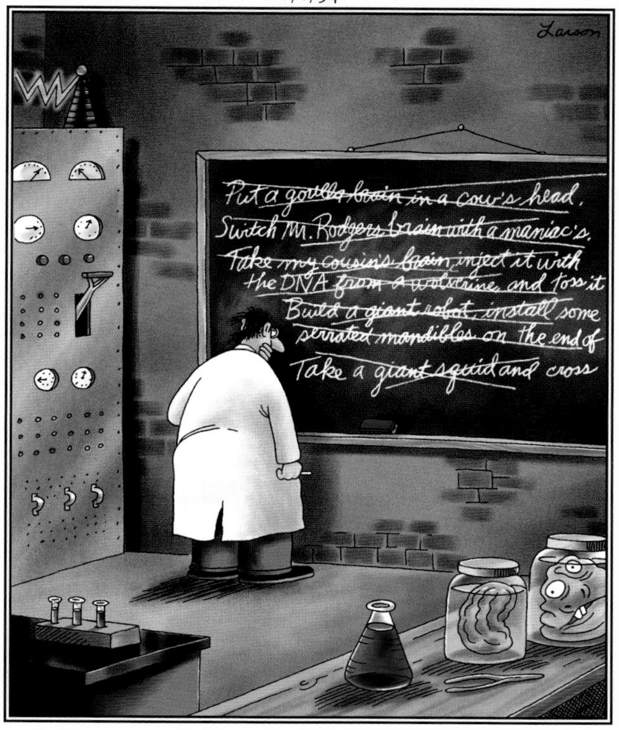
Larson
Put a gorilla brain in a cow's head.
Switch Mr. Rodgers brain with a maniac's.
Take my cousin's brain, inject it with the DNA from a wolverine, and toss it
Build a giant robot, install some serrated mandibles on the end of
Take a giant squid and cross

The curse of mad scientist's block

11/9/94

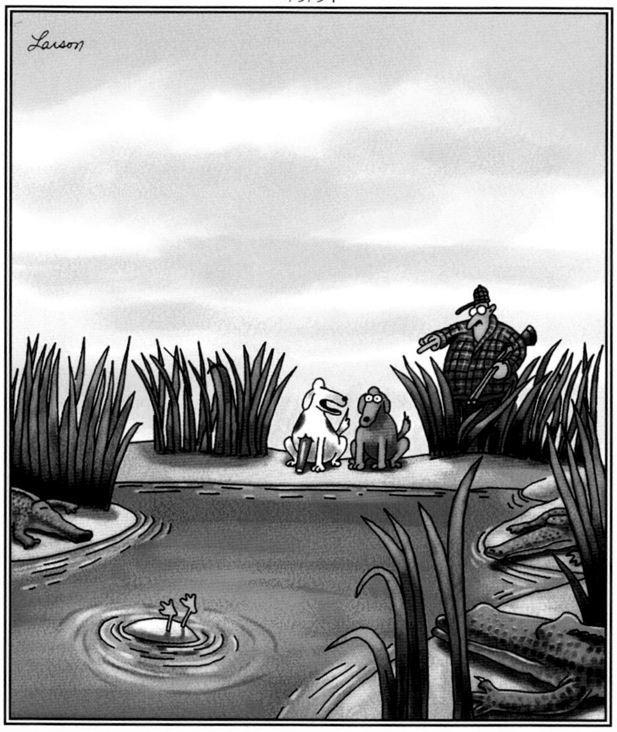
Larson

"You're up, Red."

11/10/94

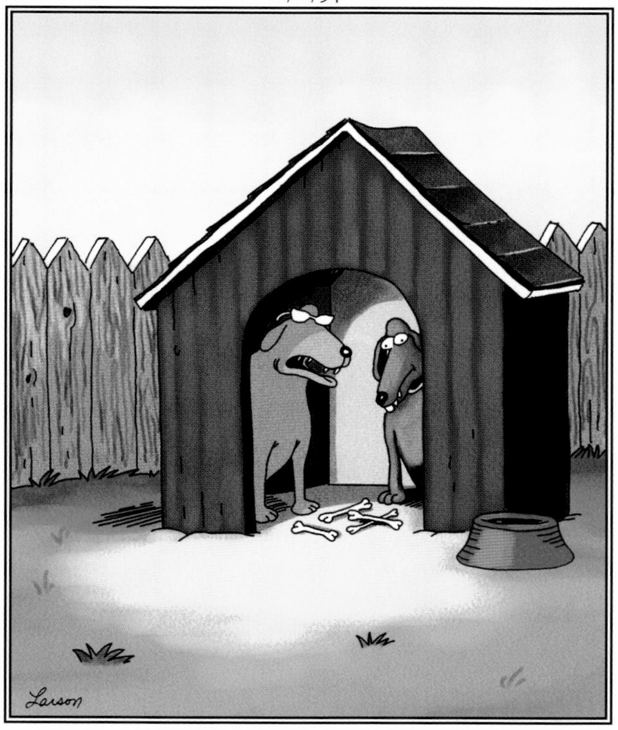
Larson

"Look. You *had* five bones, right? Your friend Zooky comes over, stays awhile, then leaves. *Now* you have *four* bones, right? ... You don't have to be a 'Lassie' to figure this one out."

11/11/94

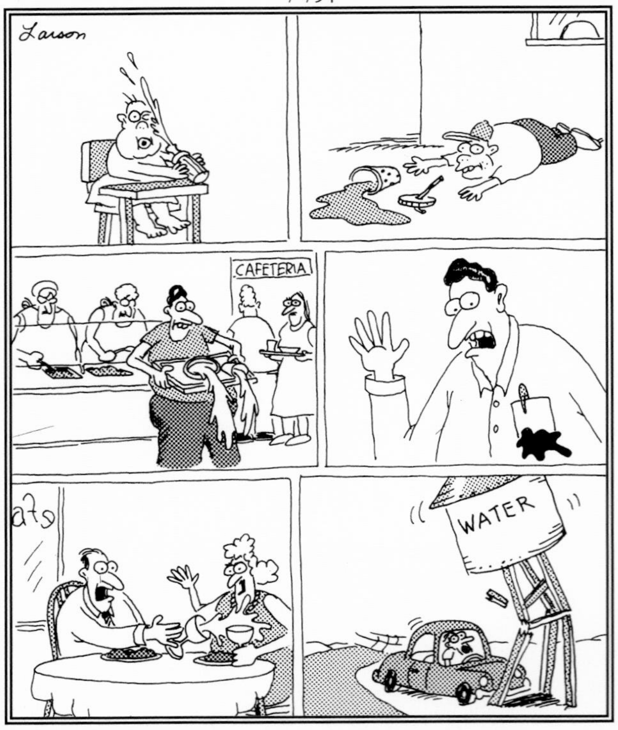
Larson
CAFETERIA
WATER

The life and times of Captain Hazelwood

11/14/94

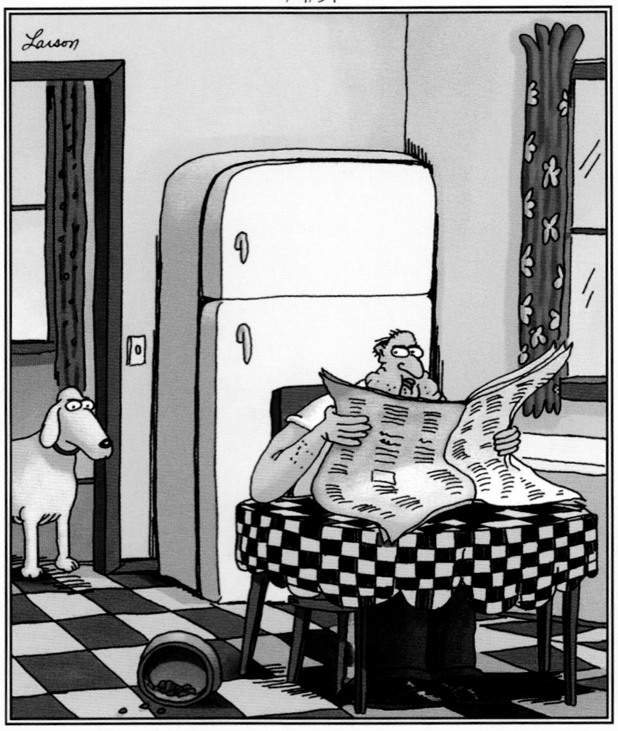
Larson

An unnatural silence hung in the kitchen, and Spunky sensed that his arrival was unexpected.

11/17/94

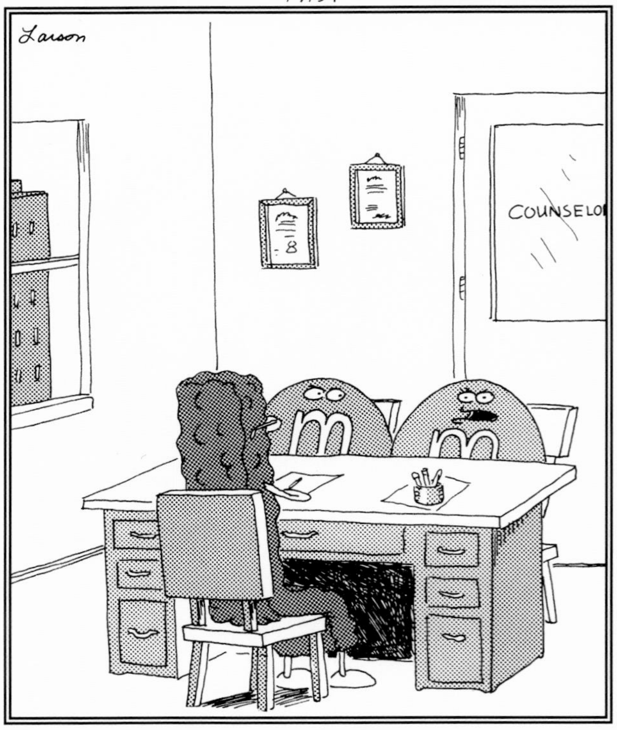
Larson
COUNSELO

"Look, marriage is okay—but I also want my own identity. ... I mean, how would *you* like it if everyone referred to *you* as 'Chocolate Bar and Chocolate Bar'?"

11/15/94

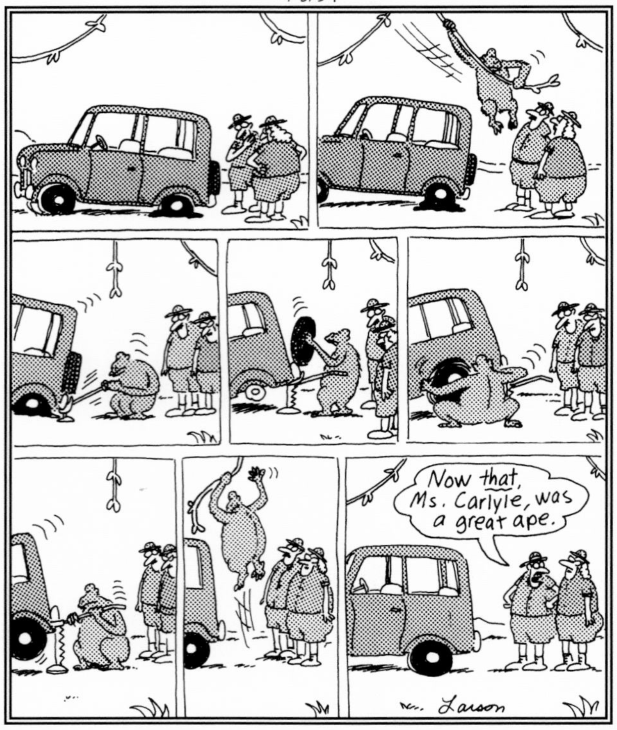
Now that, Ms. Carlyle, was a great ape.
Larson

11/21/94

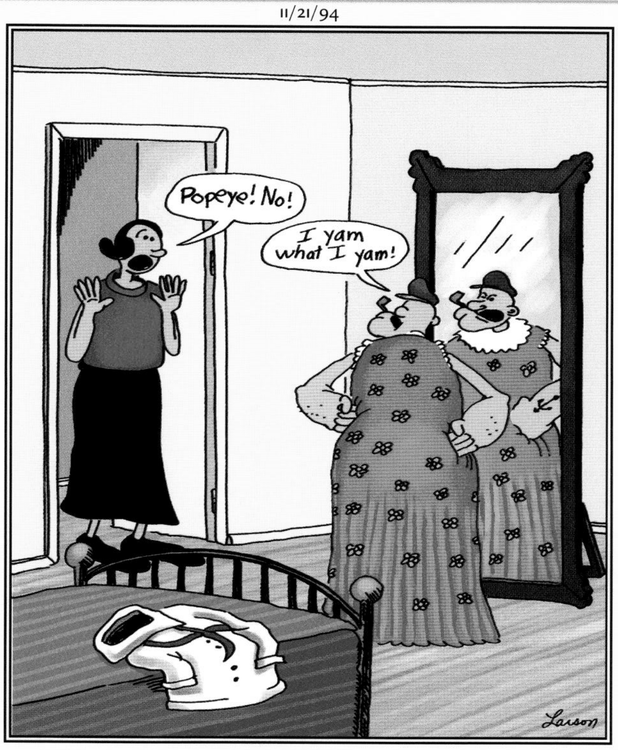
Popeye! No!
I yam what I yam!
Larson

11/22/94

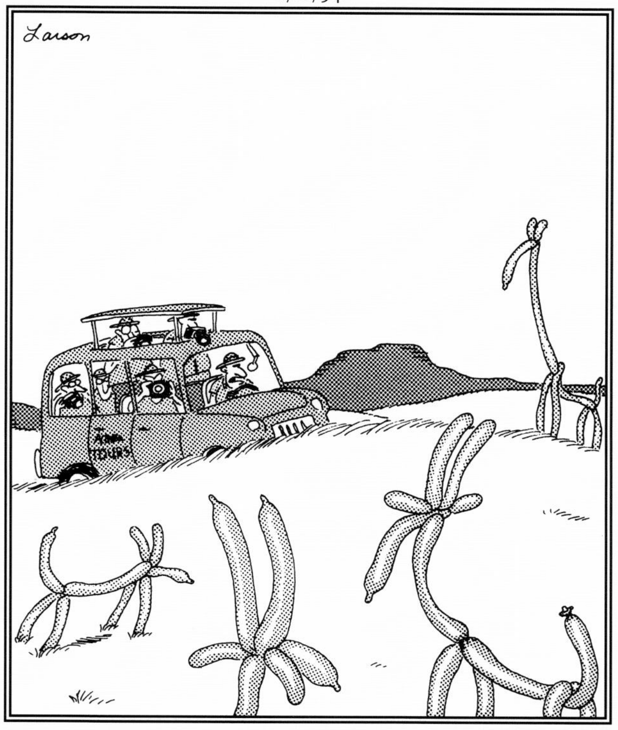
Larson

"There're some, folks! These rare and lovely creations have no natural enemies, but balloon animals never last too long in this harsh land."

11/23/94

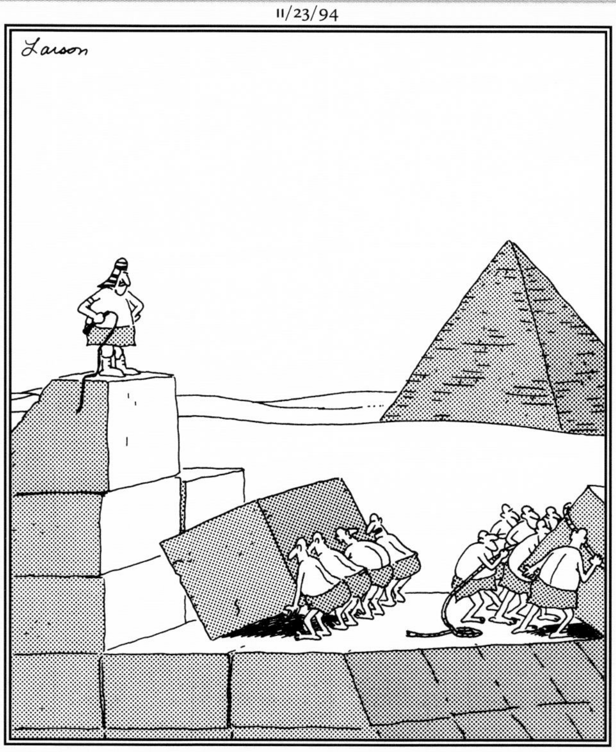
Larson

"Remo! Lift with your knees, not your back!"

11/25/94

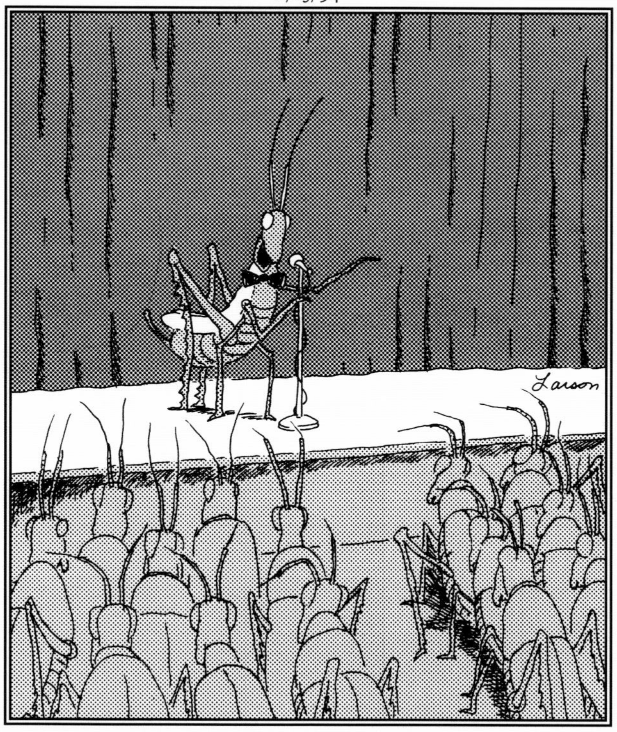
Larson

"Okay, that's pretty good! ... Now! I want everyone on this side of the aisle to come in rubbing their legs together when I signal! ... And let's show the other side how it's done!"

11/16/94

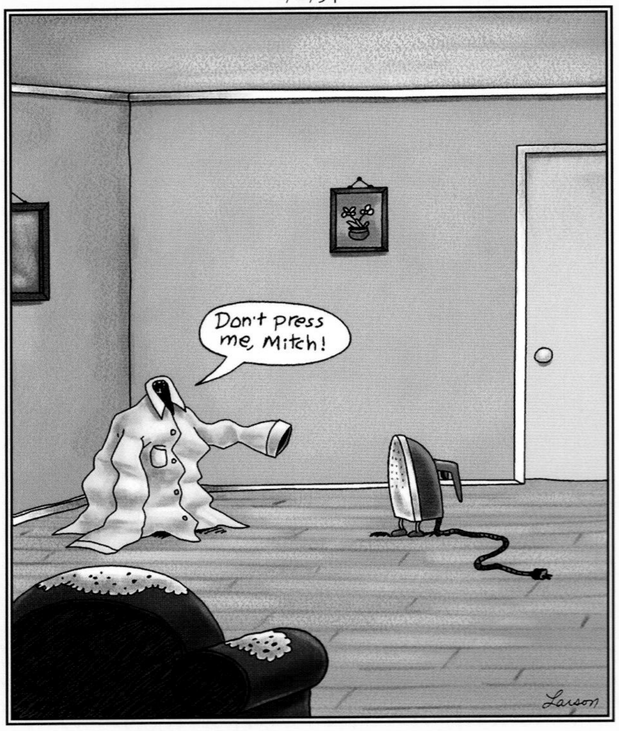
Don't press me, Mitch!
Larson

11/18/94

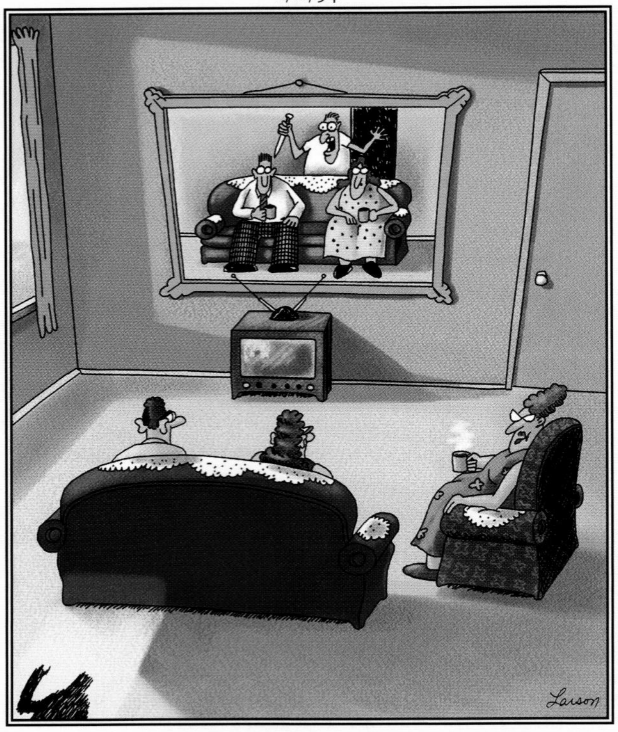
Larson

"Leonard painted that and hung it up just this afternoon. ... He calls it, *It's My Couch! My Couch! Don't They Understand?*"

11/28/94

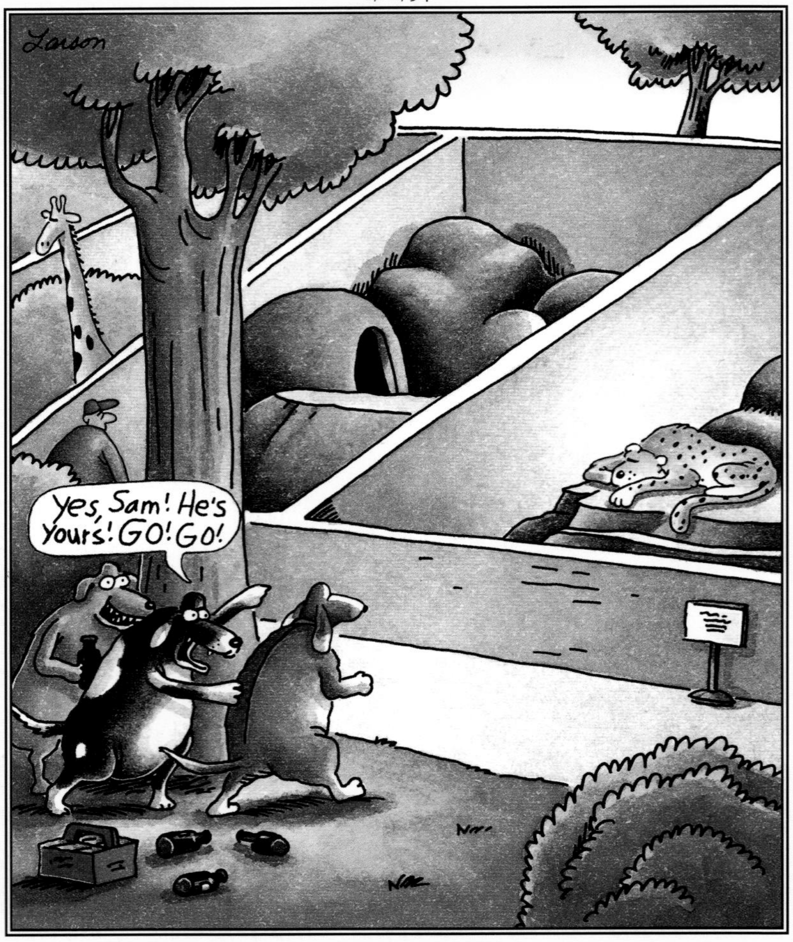
Larson
Yes, Sam! He's Yours! GO! GO!

Dogs and alcohol: the tragic untold story.

11/24/94

See that little Kid out there, Ricky?... He wouldn't stop crying either.
Larson

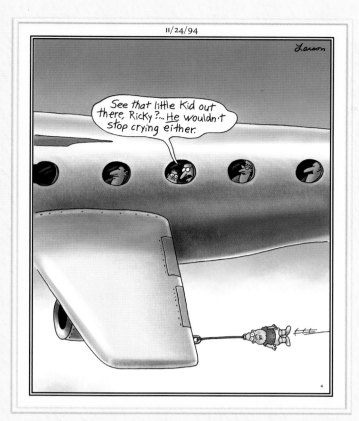

By simply attaching the new ACME Wingbaby, airlines can significantly improve their passengers' overall comfort.

11/30/94

HAPPY TABBY SCRATCHING POST
Larson

"Okay, you two! Problem solved!"

11/29/94

Larson

"Hell, Ben, you catch a few bullets through your hat during *every* holdup, and I'm finally gonna say I ain't ever been much impressed."

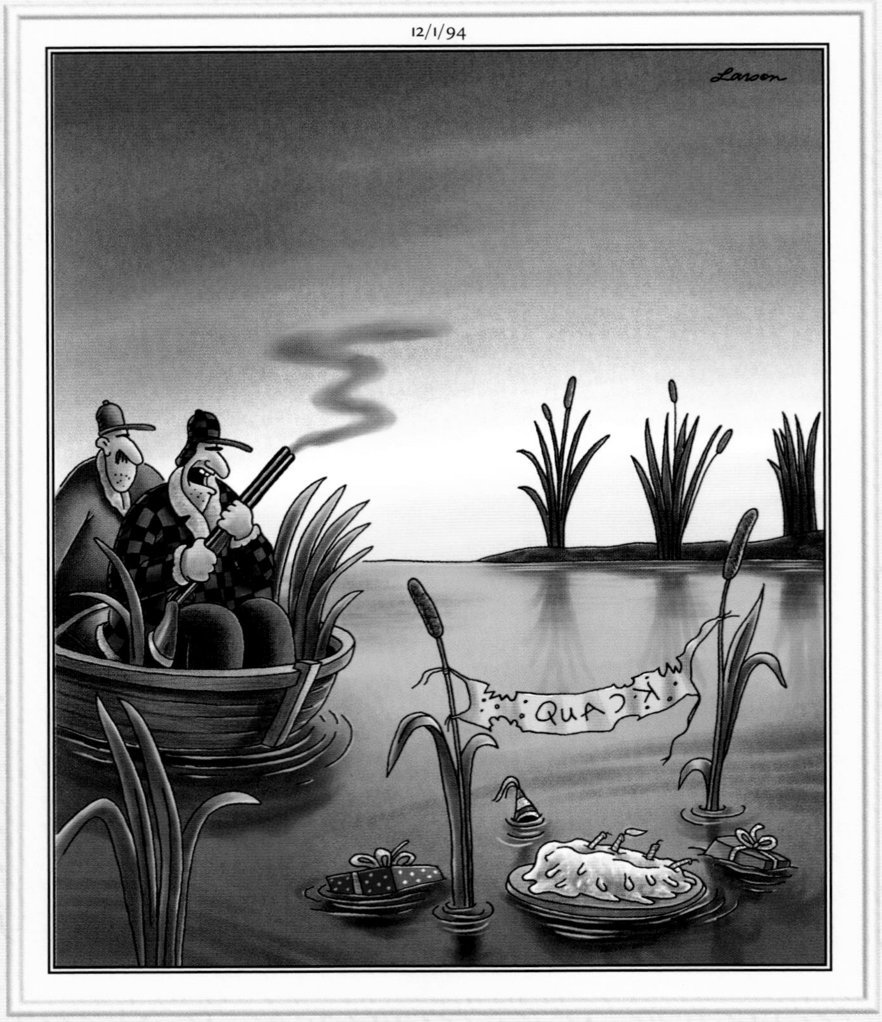
12/1/94
Larson

"I might have missed, Lou, but I take some satisfaction in knowing I busted up their little party."

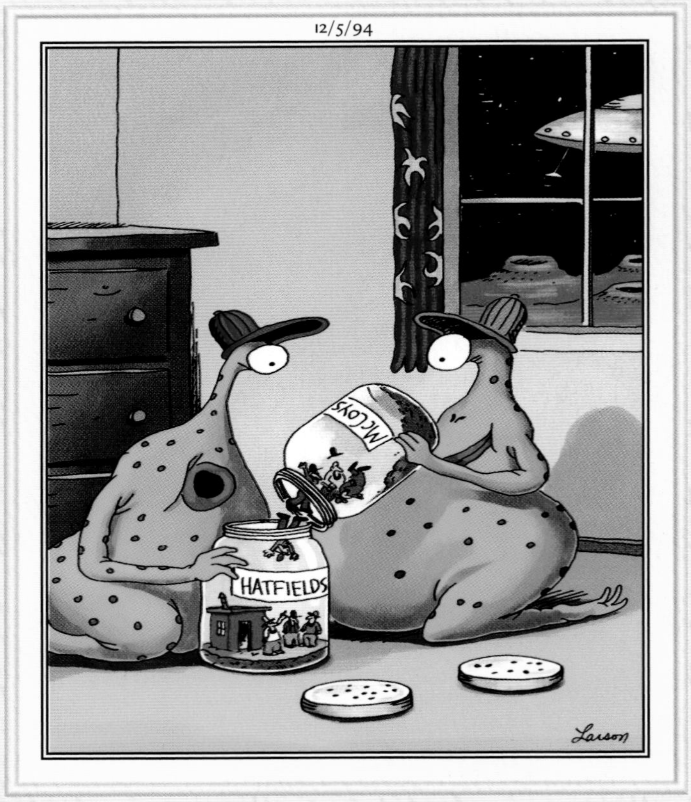
12/5/94
McCOYS
HATFIELDS
Larson

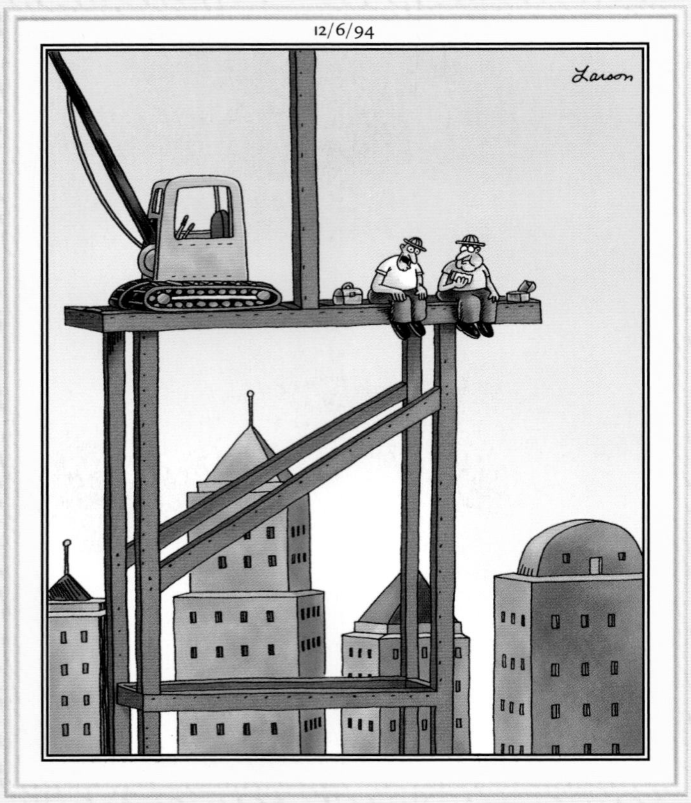
12/6/94
Larson

"You ever get that urge, Frank? It begins with looking down from 50 stories up, thinking about the meaninglessness of life, listening to dark voices deep inside you, and you think, 'Should I? ... Should I? ... Should I push someone off?'"

12/13/94

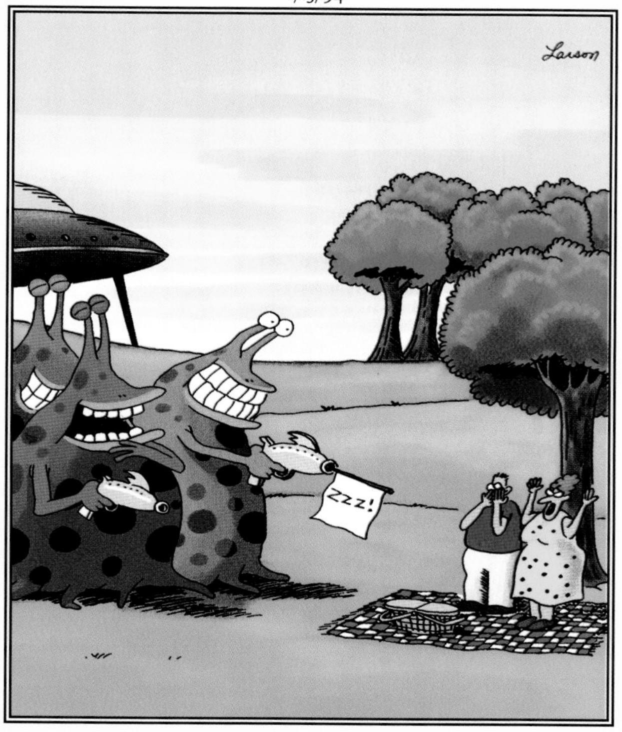
Larson
ZZZ!

12/14/94

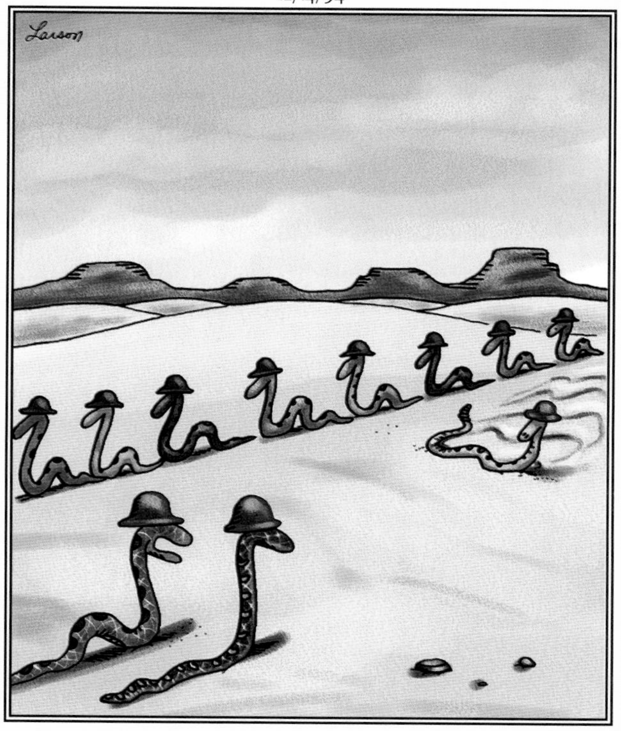
Larson

"JOHNSON! BACK IN FORMATION! ...
Dang, I hate sidewinders."

12/2/94

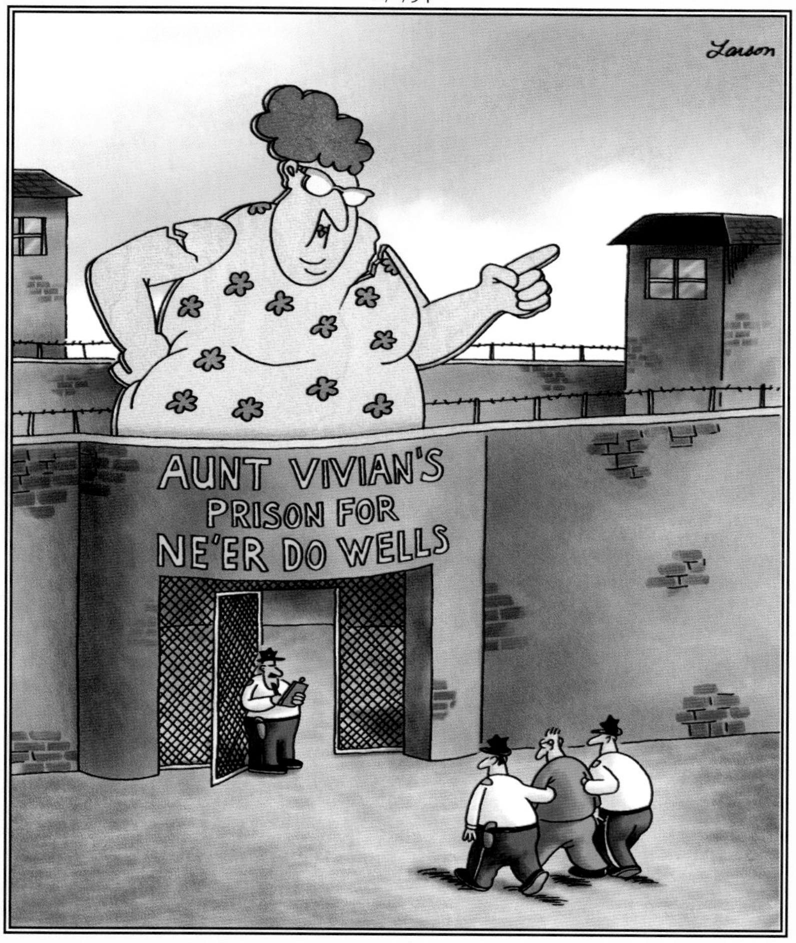
Larson
AUNT VIVIAN'S
PRISON FOR
NE'ER DO WELLS

12/7/94

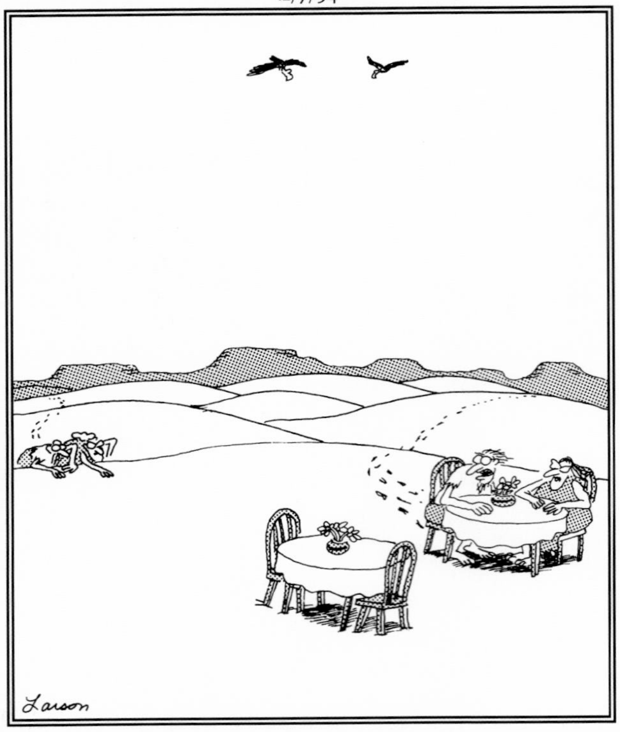

"Well, it *was* a private table."

12/8/94

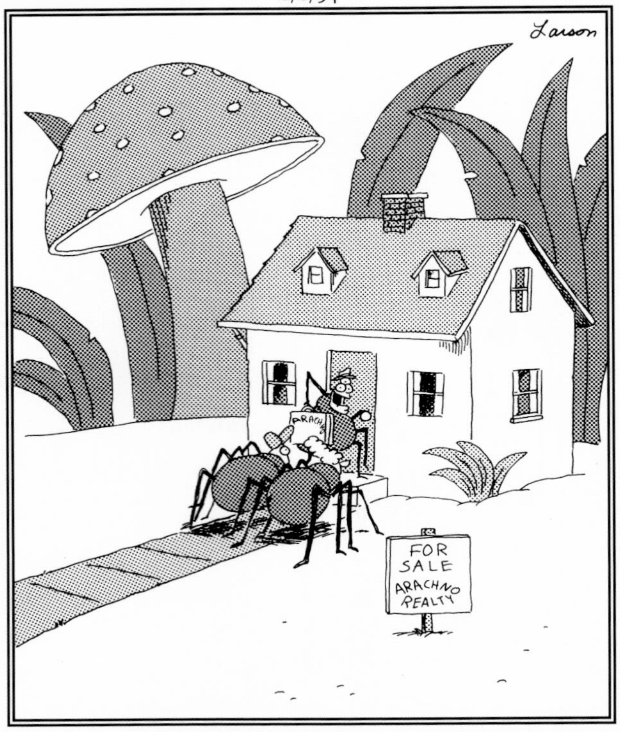
FOR
SALE
ARACHNO
REALTY

"You folks like flies? Well, wait till you see the parlor!"

12/15/94

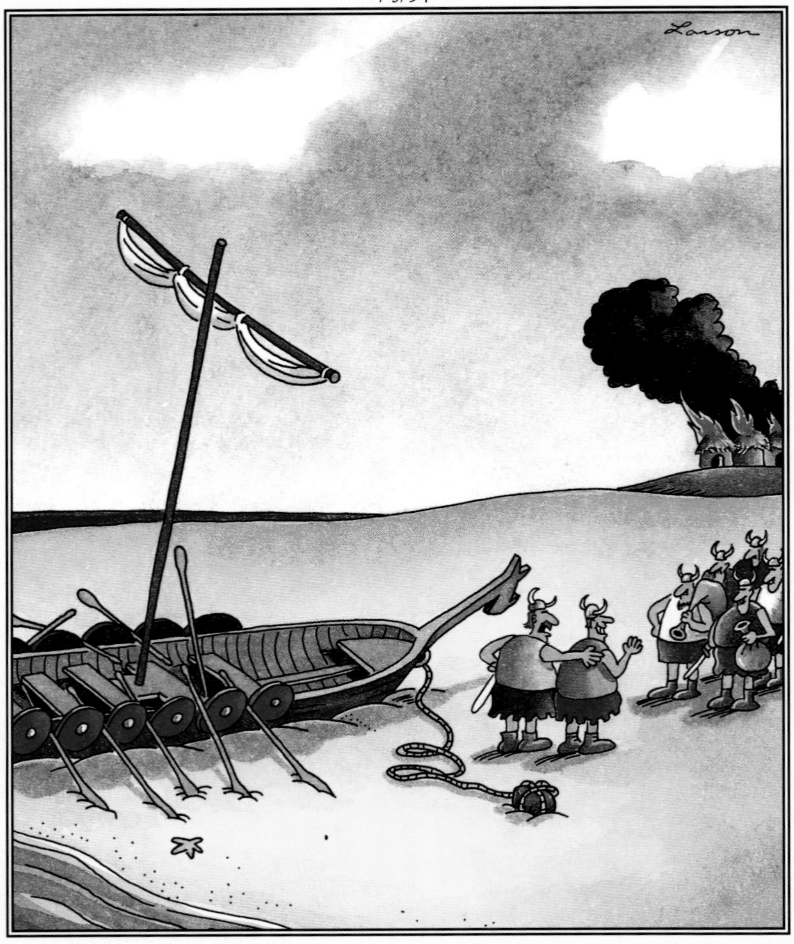

"Everyone can just put down their loot and plunder, and Sven here—yes, old Sven, who was in charge of reading the tide chart—has something to say to us all."

12/9/94
This is quite peculiar, sir.... By the looks of these holes, rocks were thrown from inside the hive!
Larson

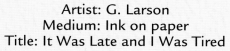

Artist: G. Larson
Medium: Ink on paper
Title: It Was Late and I Was Tired

12/12/94
Larson
WELCOME TO LETTERMAN FALLS

12/19/94
Larson

12/16/94

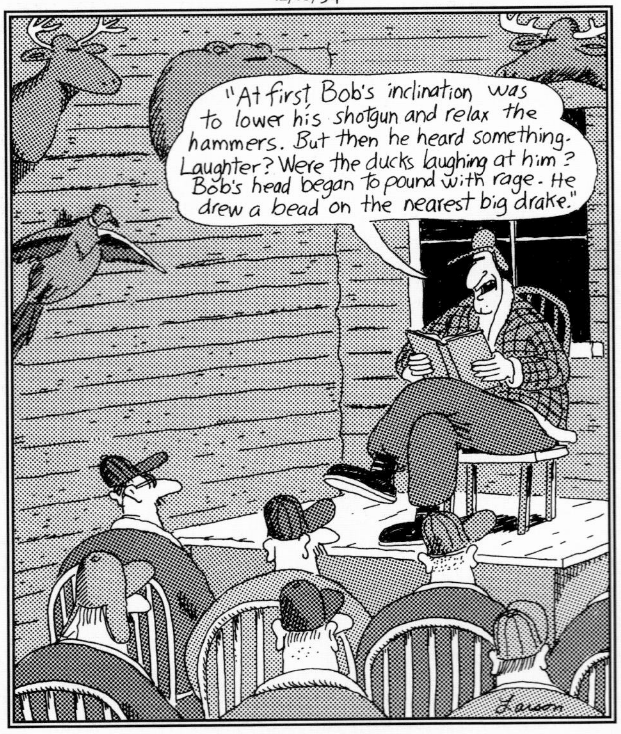
"At first Bob's inclination was to lower his shotgun and relax the hammers. But then he heard something. Laughter? Were the ducks laughing at him? Bob's head began to pound with rage. He drew a bead on the nearest big drake."
Larson

Hunting lodge readings

12/22/94

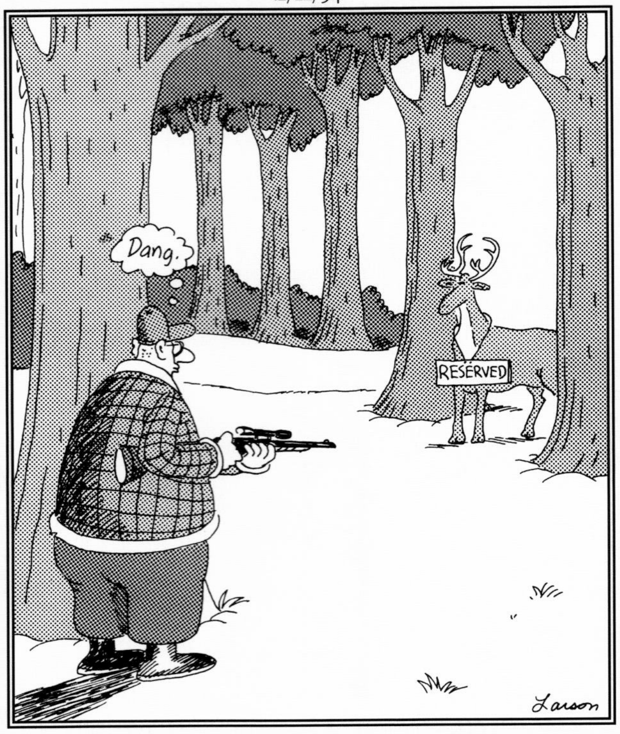
Dang.
RESERVED
Larson

12/21/94

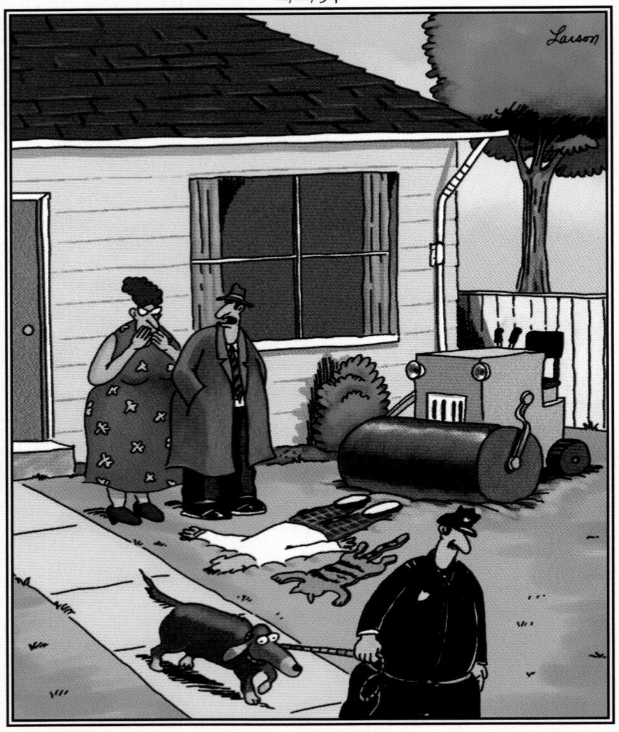
Larson

"Your dog had both motive and opportunity, ma'am: He hated the cat and he's had training in operating heavy machinery. ... Your husband, we feel, was just in the wrong place at the wrong time."

12/27/94

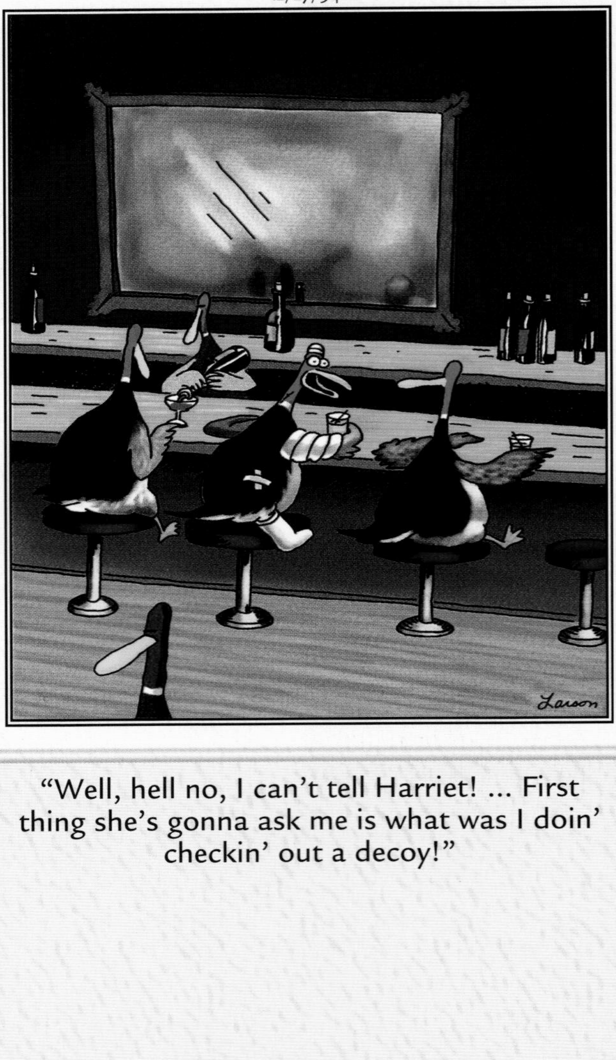
Larson

"Well, hell no, I can't tell Harriet! ... First thing she's gonna ask me is what was I doin' checkin' out a decoy!"

12/20/94

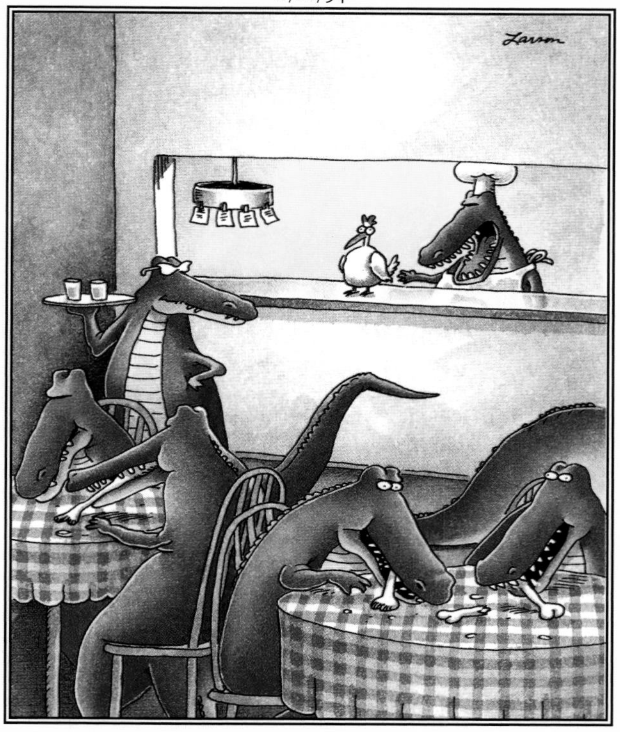
Larson

"CHICKEN UP!"

12/23/94

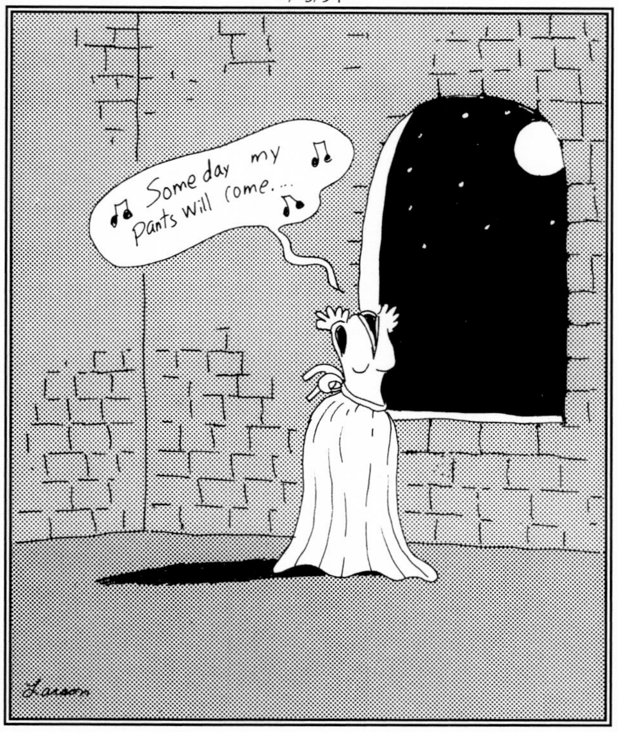
Some day my Pants will come....
Larson

12/26/94

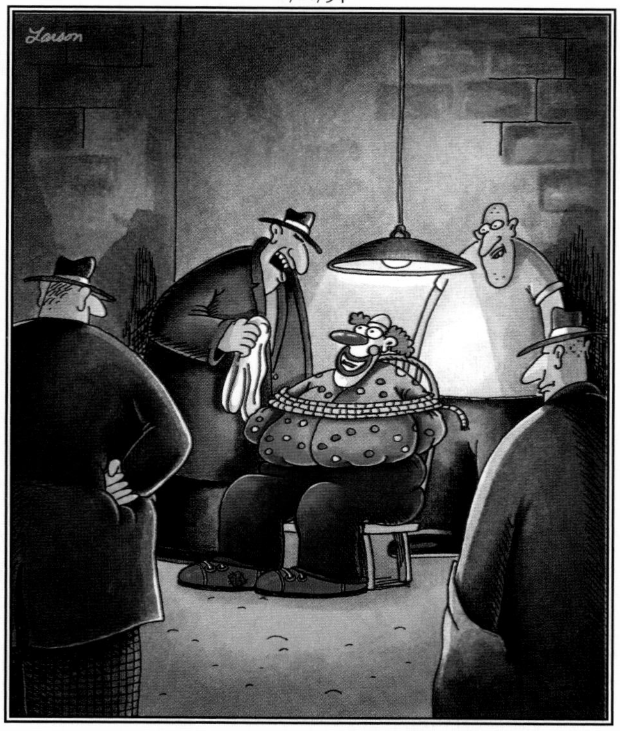
Larson

"The *first* thing I'm gonna do is wipe that smile off your face!"

12/28/94

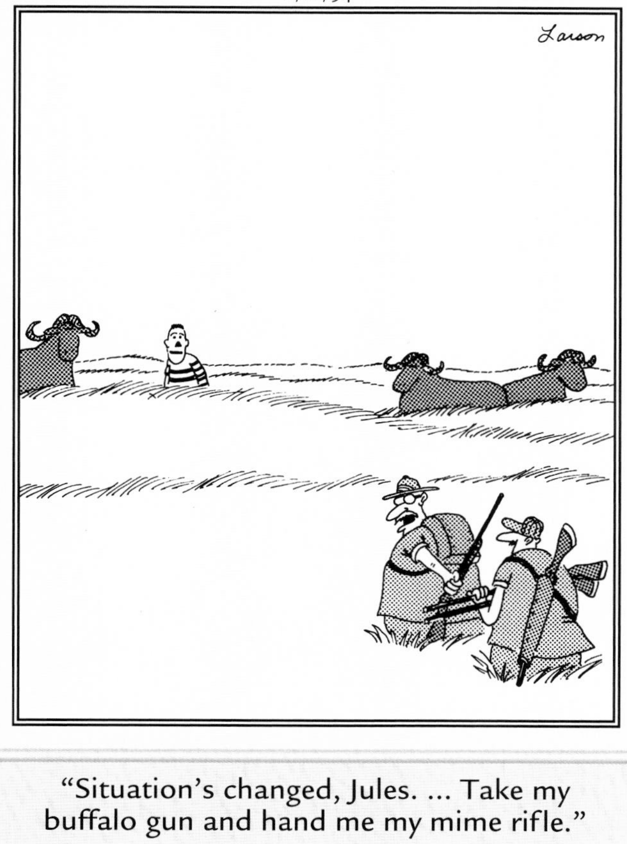
Larson

"Situation's changed, Jules. ... Take my buffalo gun and hand me my mime rifle."

12/29/94

"He's making his nest now. ... There! See it!? That son-of-a- ... he's got himself a futon!"

12/30/94

That's it. Come and try your luck.... Heh heh heh..

Until God warned him to knock it off, Noah would often try to get a little poker game going with some of the dumb animals.

The final syndicated Far Side cartoon to appear in newspapers

1/1/95

Why, Gary, you've always had the power to go home! Just close your eyes, quack three times, and think to yourself, "There's no place like home, there's no place like home..."
And Aunt Zelda all the women looked like you and Uncle Bob all the cows looked like you and Ernie there were cavemen that looked like you and there were all these nerdy little kids like you Billy and there were monsters and stupid-looking things and animals could talk and some of it was confusing and... and... and... Oh, wow! There's no place like home!

Appendix

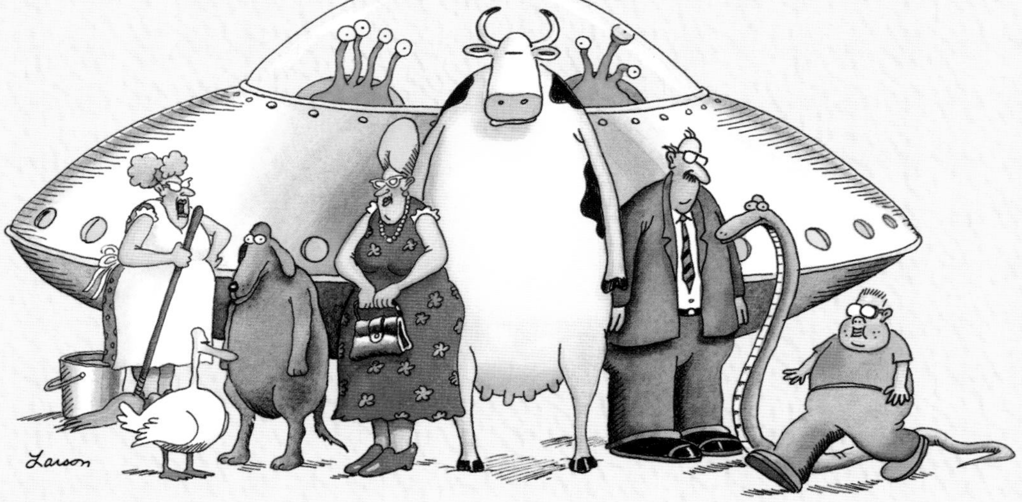
Larson

The following thirteen cartoons were created for Last Chapter and Worse, published in 1996, and were not syndicated in newspapers.

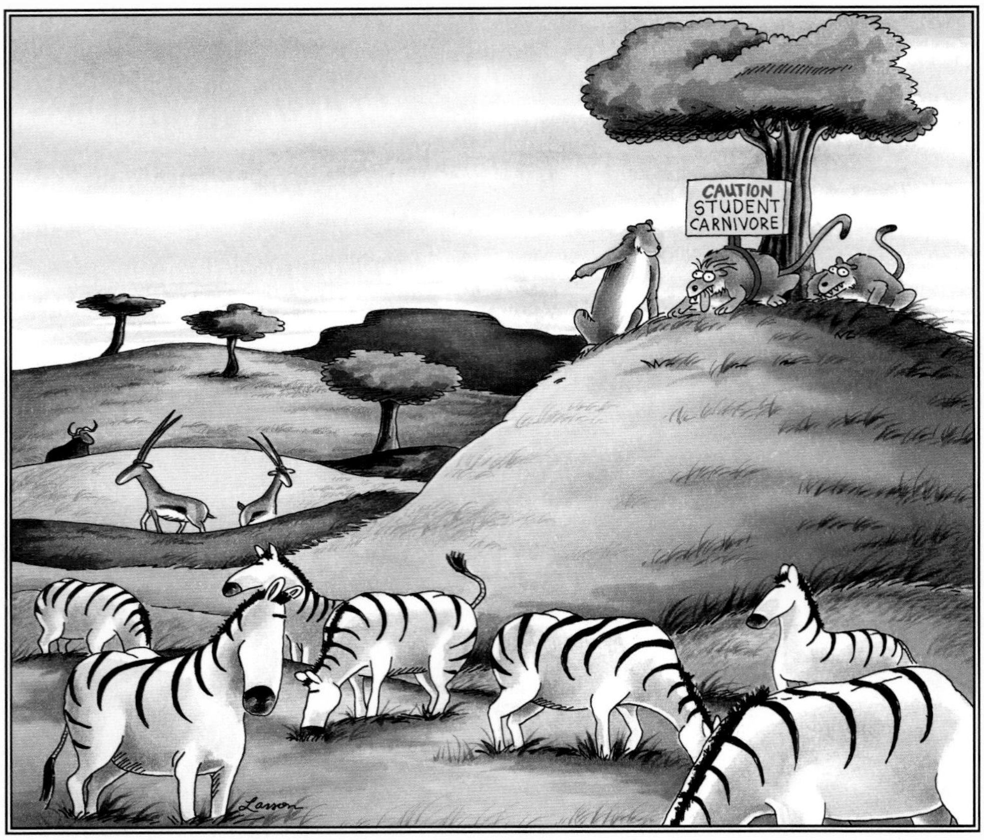
CAUTION
STUDENT
CARNIVORE
Larson

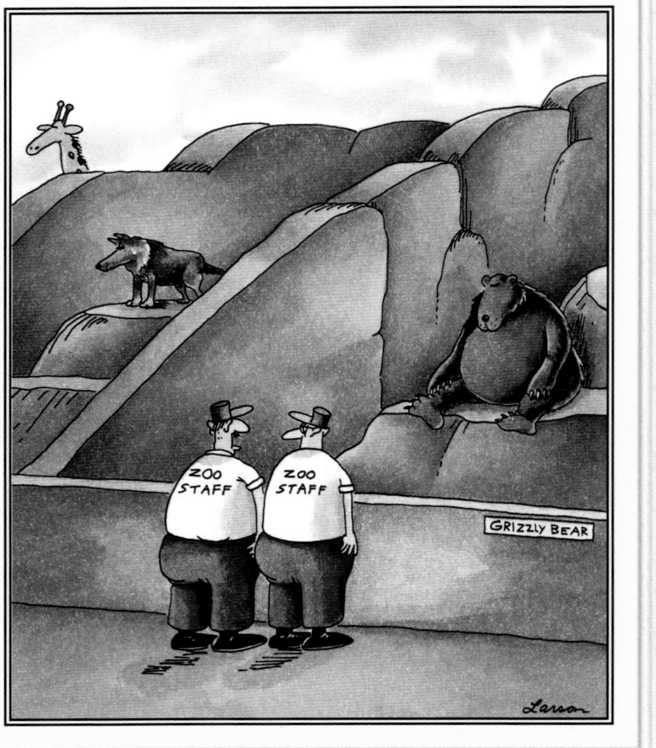
ZOO STAFF
ZOO STAFF
GRIZZLY BEAR
Larson

"You know, Ned, you're my best friend, and I just gotta tell someone. It's time I come out of the closet and stop living this lie. ... I hate animals."

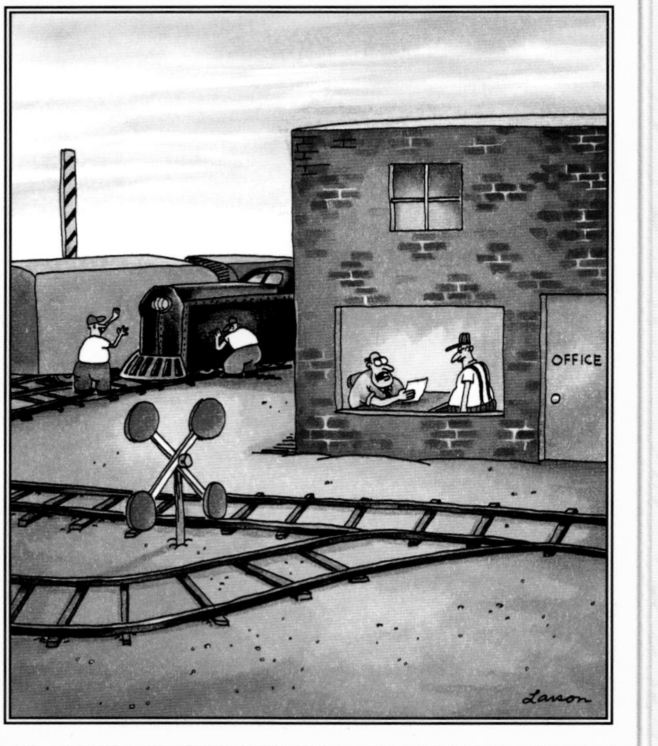
OFFICE
Larson

"I've been looking at your time sheets, Webster ... leaving early, coming in late, etc., etc. ... Working for the railroad, Webster, means working *all* the livelong day."

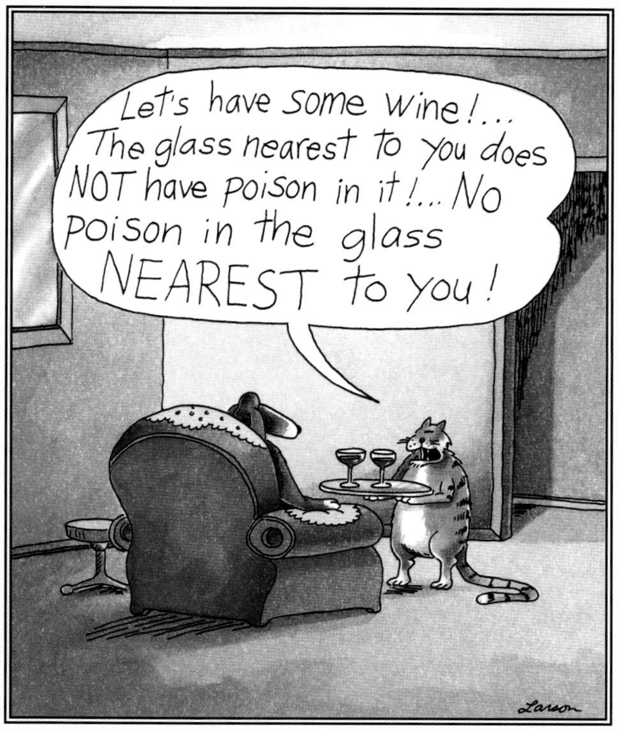
Let's have some wine!...
The glass nearest to you does NOT have poison in it!... No poison in the glass NEAREST to you!
Larson

When dumb animals attempt murder

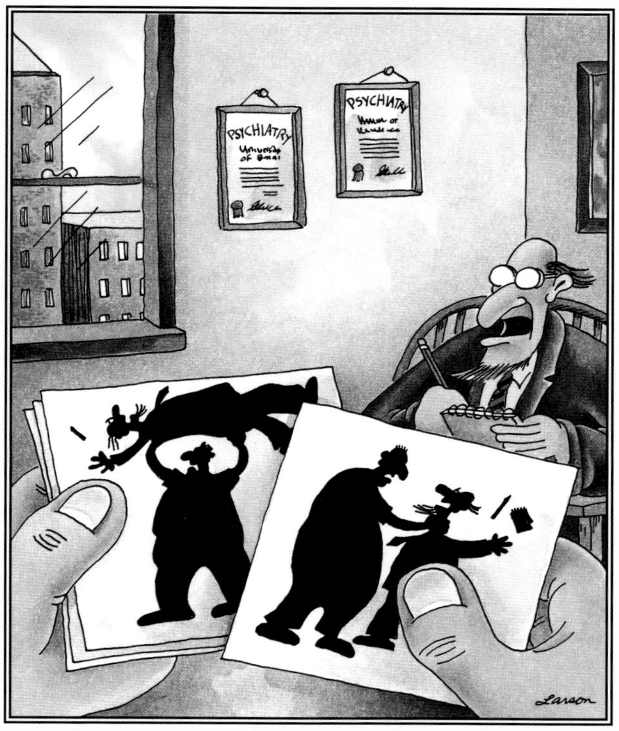
PSYCHIATRY
PSYCHIATRY
Larson

"It's just a simple Rorschach inkblot test, Mr. Bromwell, so just calm down and tell me what each one suggests to you."

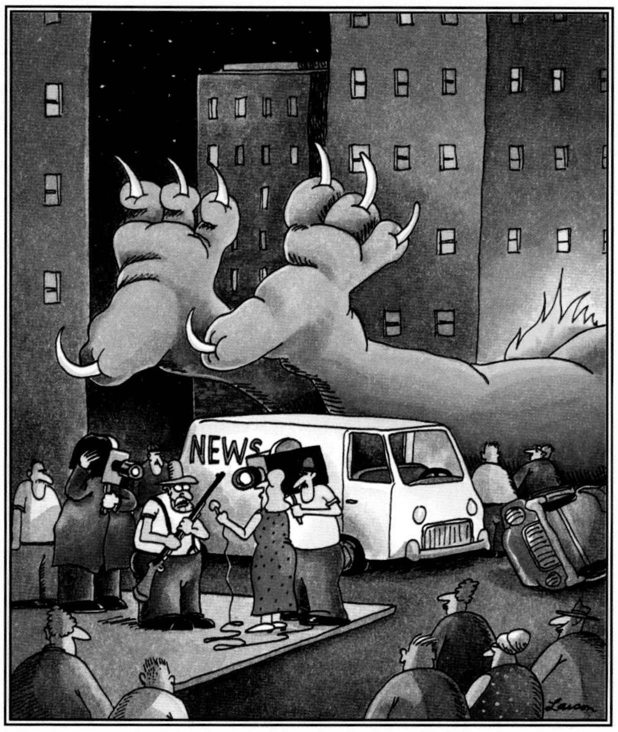
NEWS
Larson

"Well, I seen all the commotion, with that there monster destroyin' half the city and whatnot, and I says to myself, 'Hell! Why don't someone just shoot the varmint?'"

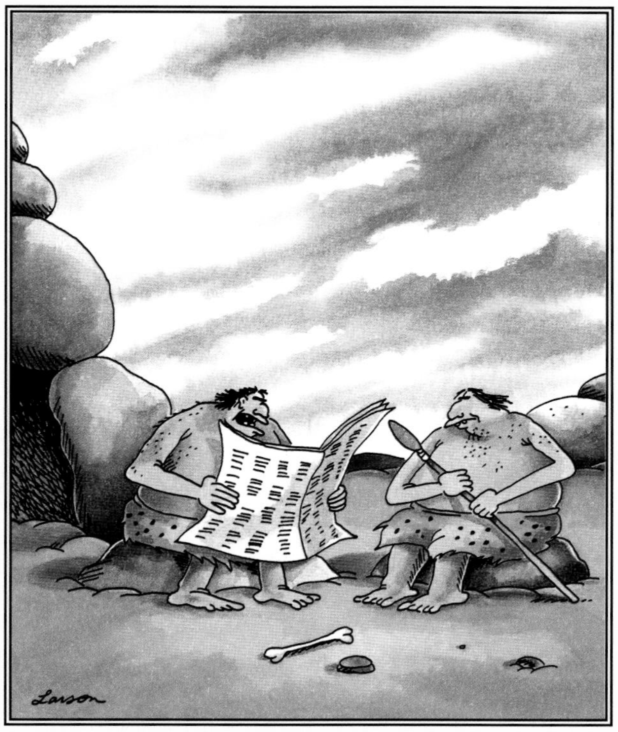
Larson

"Well, I suppose it'll be a few thousand more years before we get an 'Arts and Leisure' section."

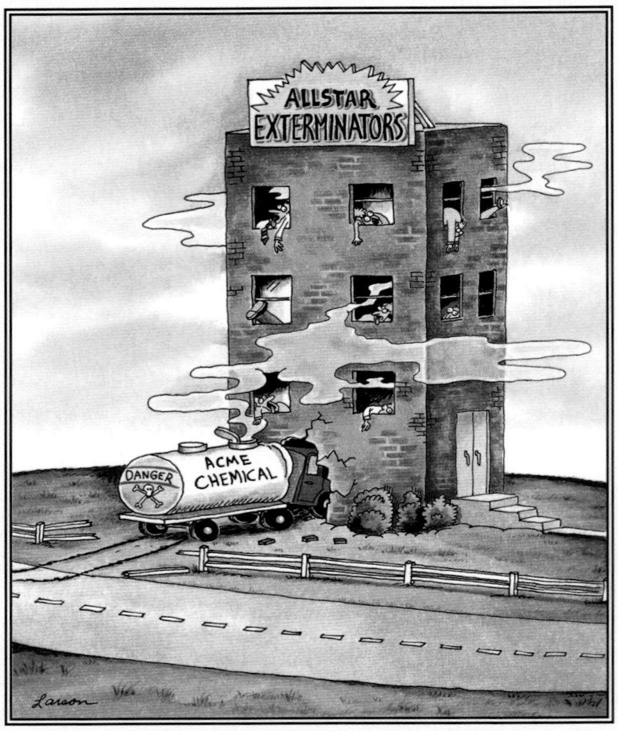
ALLSTAR
EXTERMINATORS
DANGER
ACME
CHEMICAL
Larson

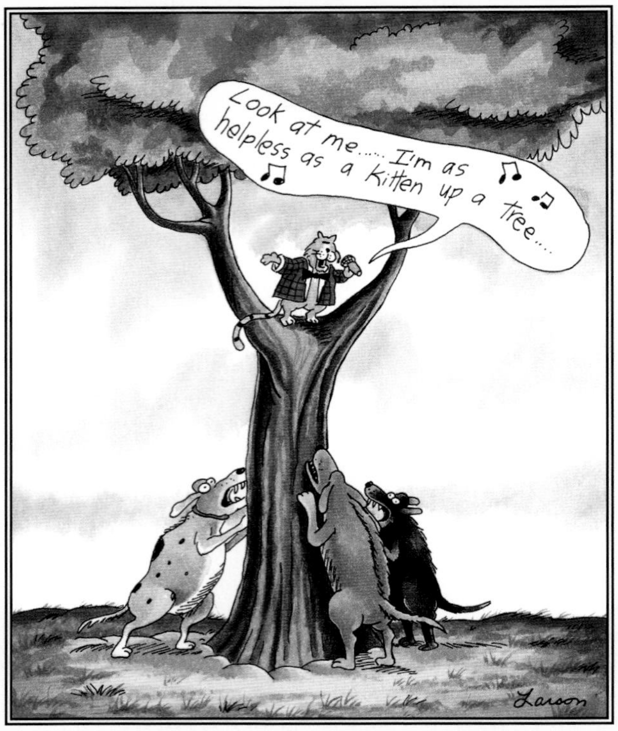
Look at me...... I'm as helpless as a kitten up a tree...
Larson

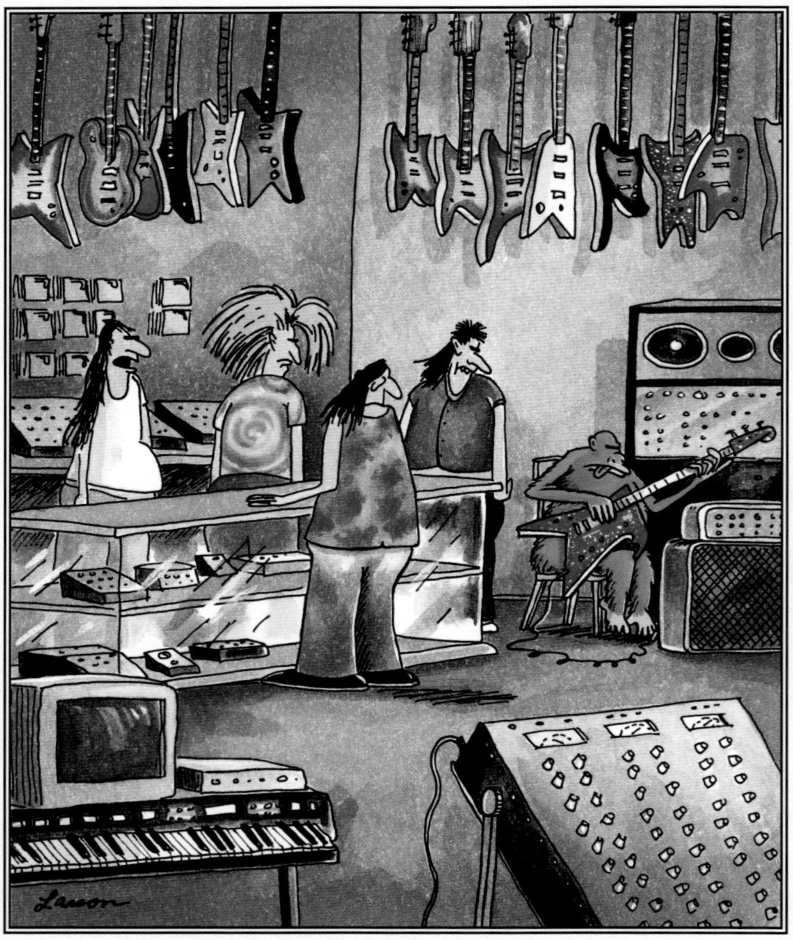
Larson

"Yeah, he comes in here a lot—never buys anything, climbs all over the store, has to try out every guitar ... and if you try taking it away from him, he starts screaming his head off."

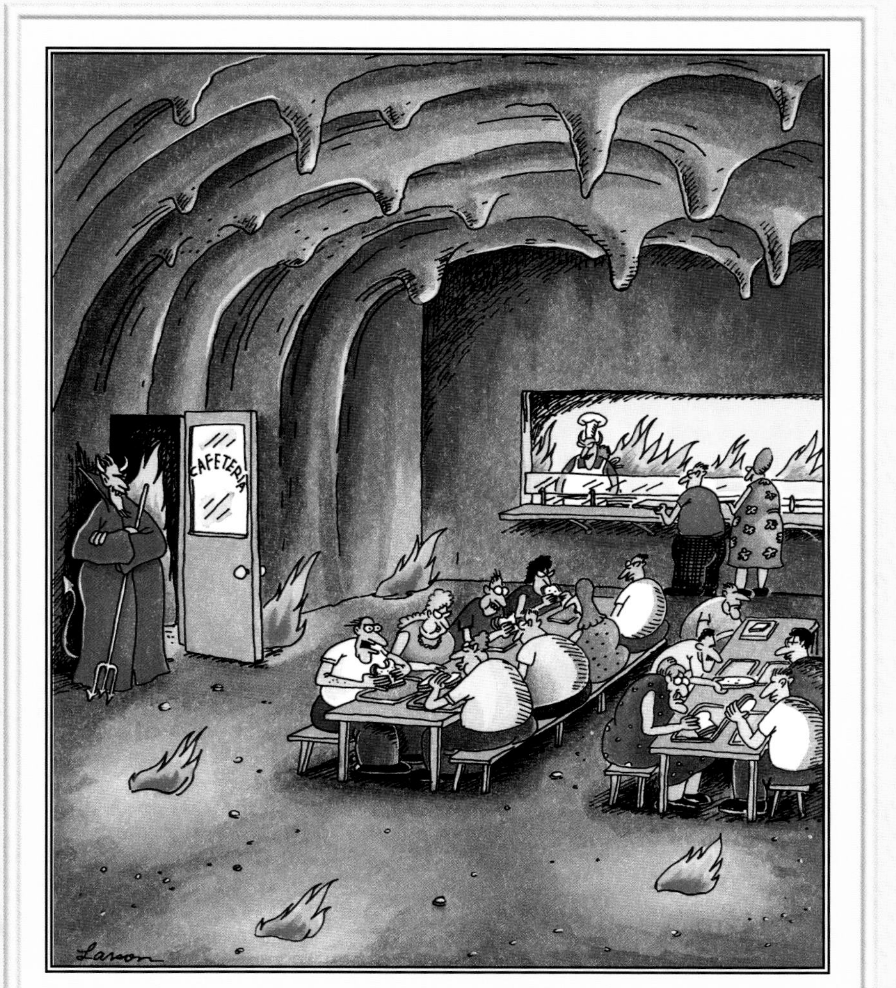
CAFETERIA
Larson

"You're new here, ain'tcha, kid? Well, on some days the sandwiches contain a dead scorpion. ... Not *every* day, but *some* days—that's why it's hell, kid."

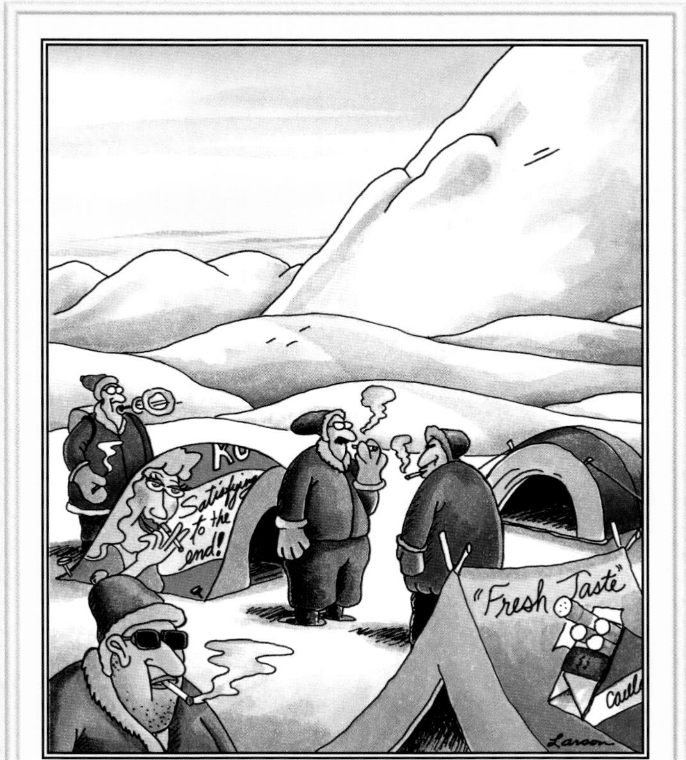
Satisfying to the end!
"Fresh Taste"
Larson

Despite being well-financed by the tobacco industry, the newly formed Smokers' Mountaineering Club met its doom just a few moments after leaving base camp.

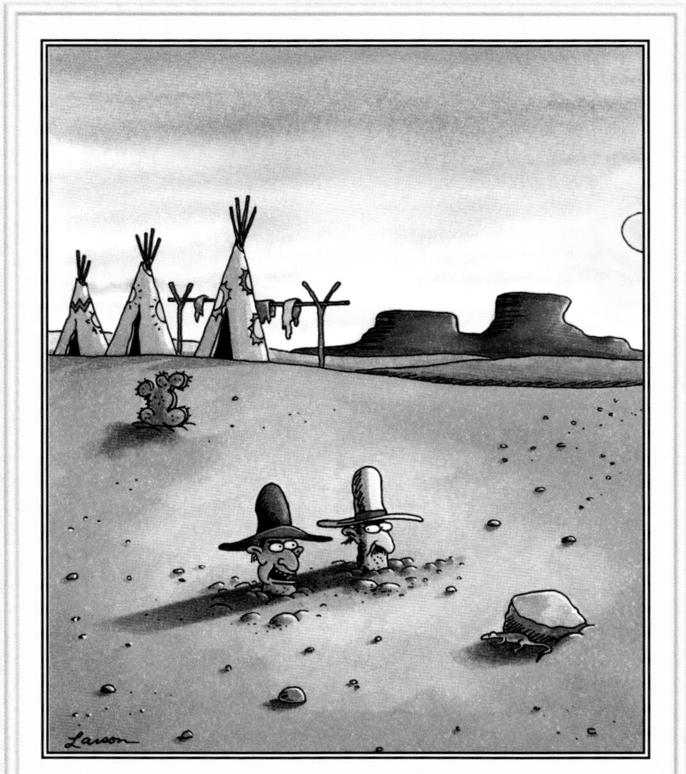
Larson

"Hey, Frank ... nice and cool here in the shade ... yesiree ... niiiiiiice and cool."

The following six cartoons were created as a special feature of the Science Times section of The New York Times called "The Far Side of Science."

10/13/98

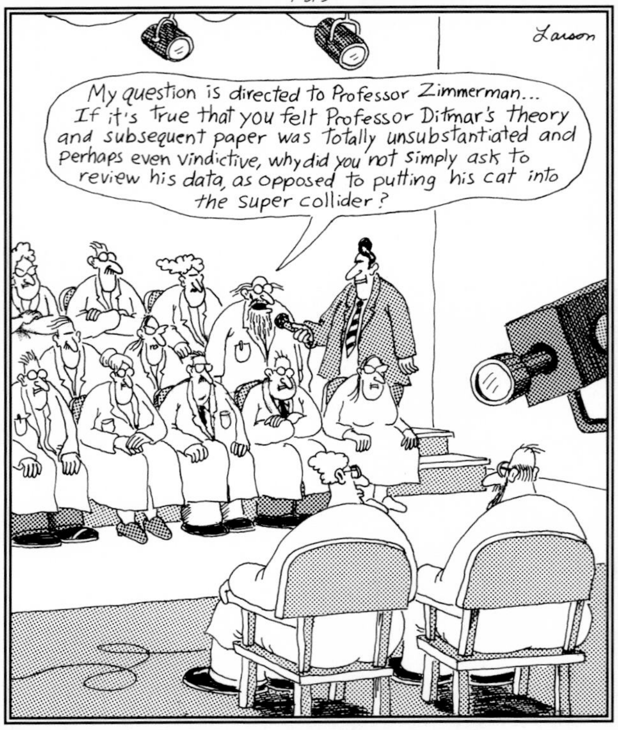
Larson
My question is directed to Professor Zimmerman... If it's true that you felt Professor Ditmar's theory and subsequent paper was totally unsubstantiated and perhaps even vindictive, why did you not simply ask to review his data, as opposed to putting his cat into the super collider?

Science meets tabloid TV

11/24/98

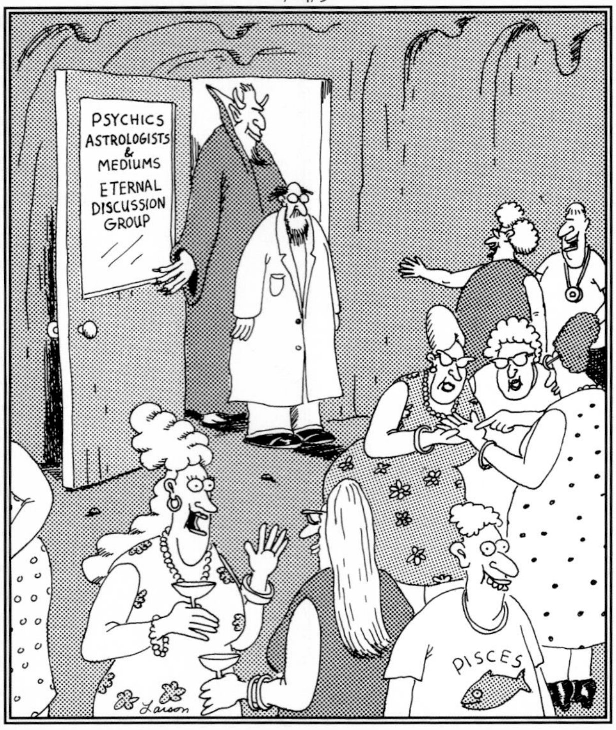
PSYCHICS
ASTROLOGISTS
&
MEDIUMS
ETERNAL
DISCUSSION
GROUP
PISCES
Larson

Scientist hell

1/19/99

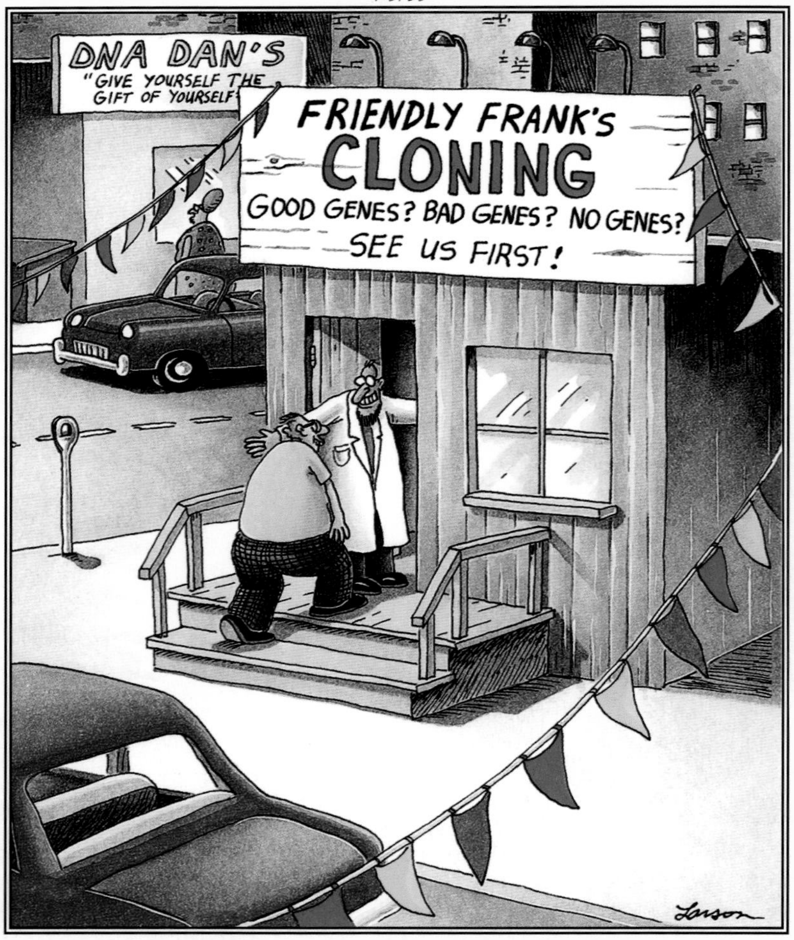
DNA DAN'S
"GIVE YOURSELF THE GIFT OF YOURSELF"
FRIENDLY FRANK'S
CLONING
GOOD GENES? BAD GENES? NO GENES?
SEE US FIRST!
Larson

9/14/99

"So, in the general relativistic sense, we find that the
dynamic friction of the tensor light cone is actually
negative, creating a local convergence of photons, which
causes the stars at night to be big and bright ...
especially here, deep in the heart of Texas."

12/22/98

"Don't threaten *me*, Thagerson! My cousin is an
anthropologist, and she can make your life *hell!*"

6/8/99

"Yes, we'll all miss him, but we must not forget:
Louis was shot while slaughtering chickens,
so we can take solace in knowing that he died
doing what he loved."

The End

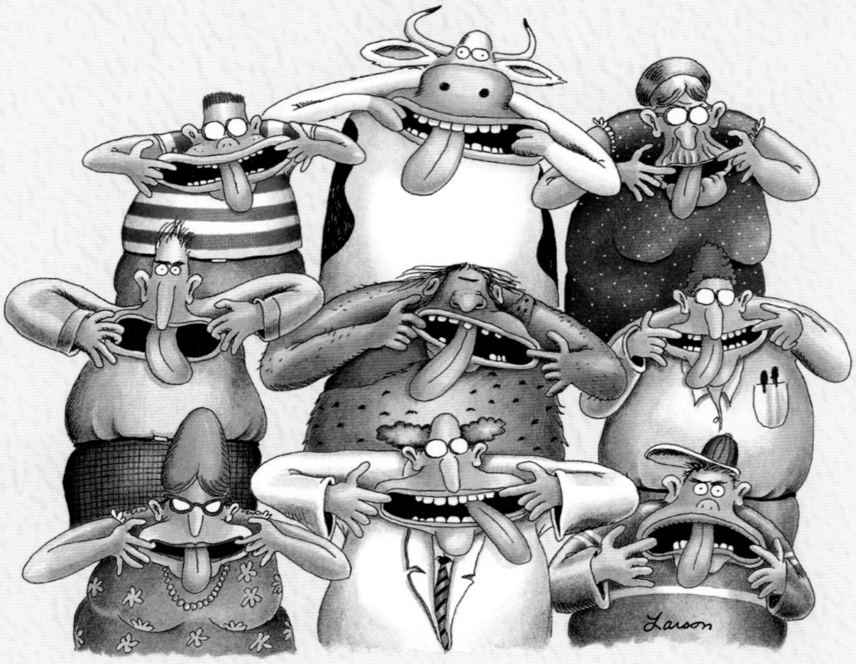
Larson

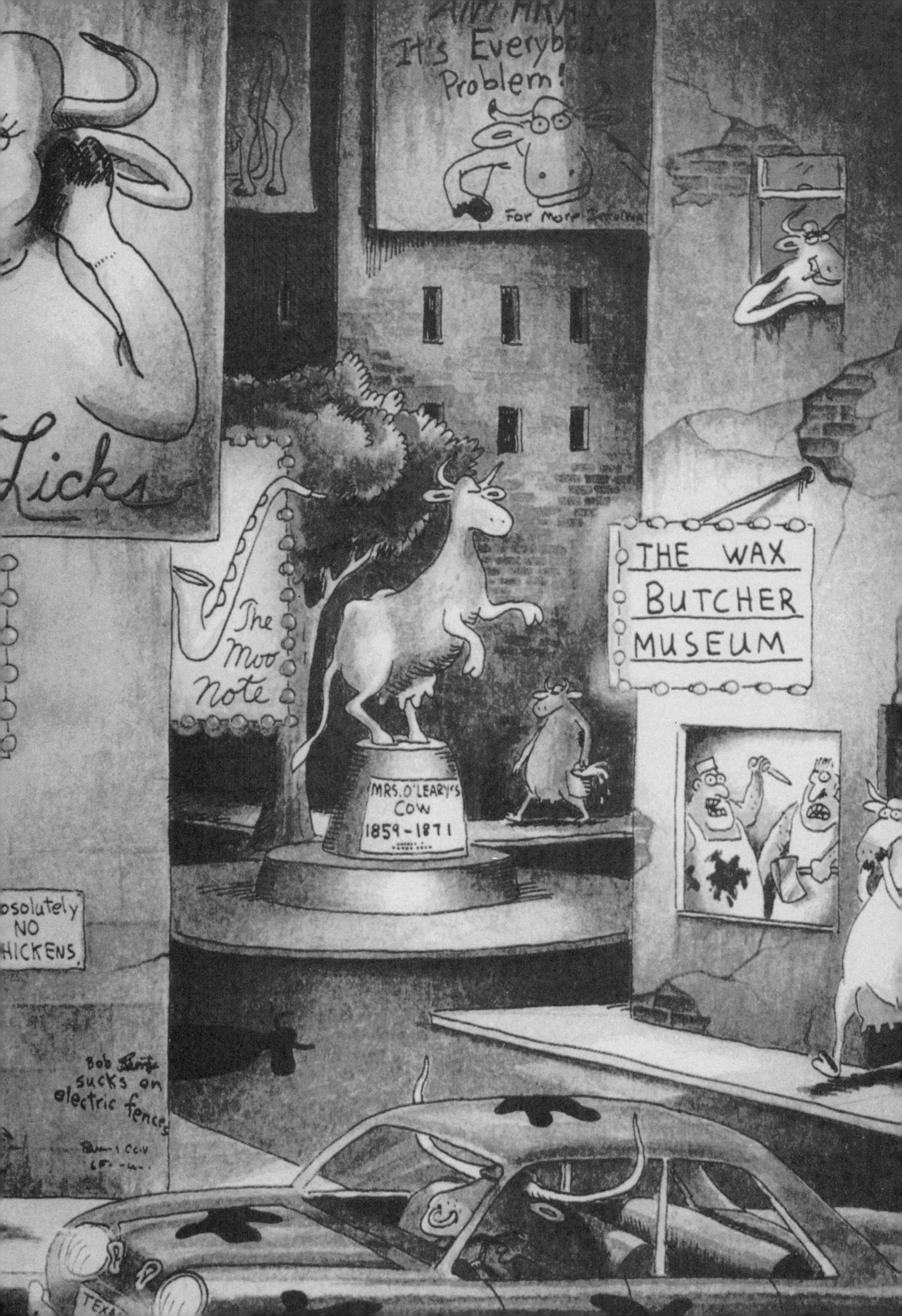

It's Everyb
Problem!
For more Informa
Licks
The Moo Note
MRS. O'LEARY'S COW 1859-1871
THE WAX BUTCHER MUSEUM
osolutely NO HICKENS
Bob
sucks on electric fences

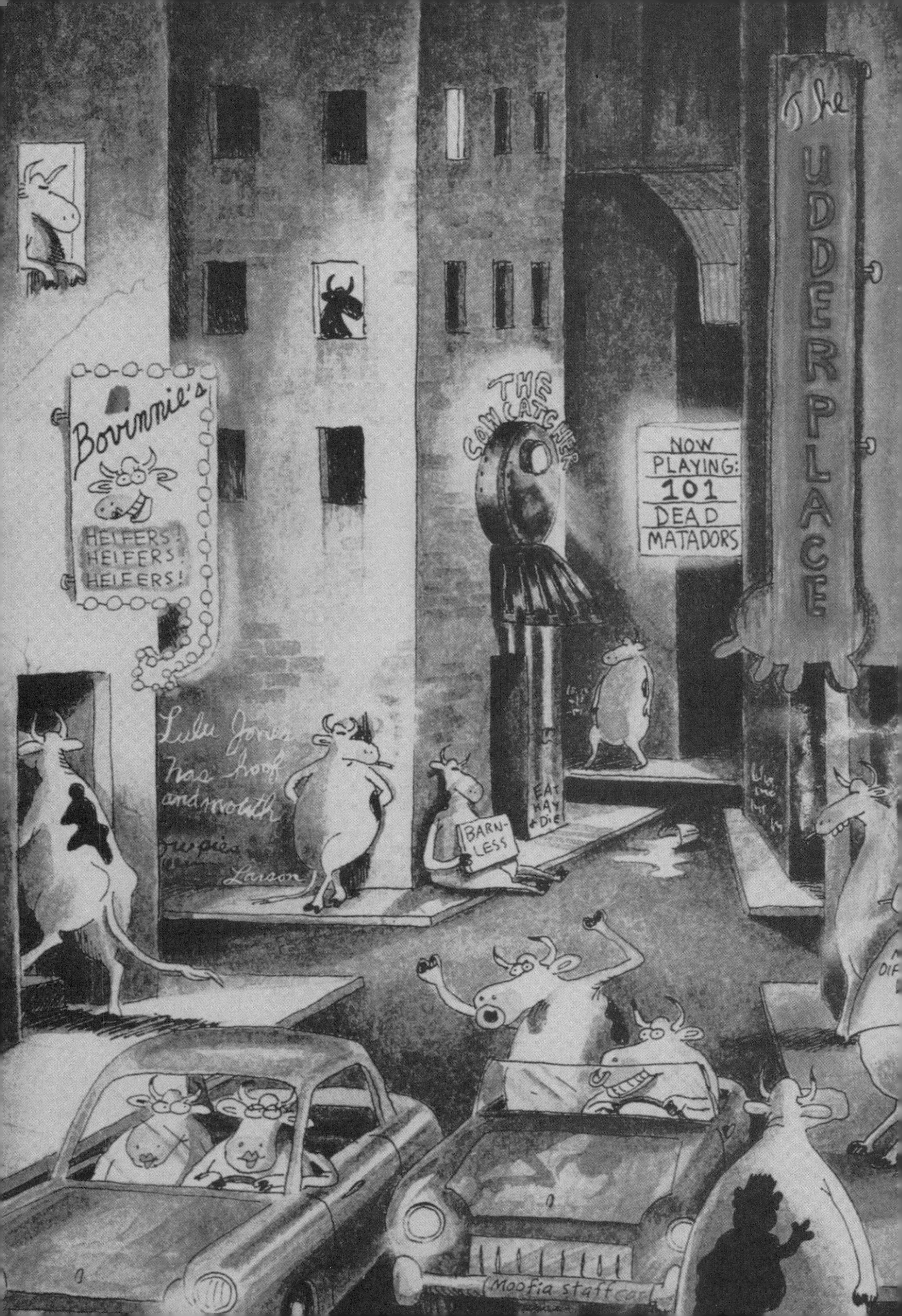
Bovinnie's
HEIFERS! HEIFERS! HEIFERS!
THE COW CATCHER
NOW PLAYING: 101 DEAD MATADORS
The UDDERPLACE
Lulu Jones has hoof and mouth
Larson
BARN-LESS
EAT HAY & DIE
Moofia staff car